Published by
Clyde P. Davis
10 Tatomuck Circle
Pound Ridge, New York 10576

ISBN: 978–0–615–54375–8

Printed in China

Library of Congress Catalog Card Number: 2011918343

Contents

9 Preface
14 Alice Henson
15 Richard Mendes
17 About the Author and His Family

Davis/Gooch Family

20 Why A Book
21 The "Roots Trips"
24 Clyde Otis Davis b. June 3, 1907
38 Clyde Otis Davis Timeline
48 Mary M. Savage Davis b. November 27, 1917
62 David Otis "Butchie" Davis b. December 26, 1945
72 June Mary "Tootsie" Davis Rogers b. May 4, 1940
78 Clyde Patrick "Duke" Davis b. January 23, 1937
- 78 Early Years
- 86 Marriage and College
- 90 Career
- 102 Giving Back
- 106 Other Interests

114 Clyde Patrick Davis Family Weddings
118 Sisters
128 Cole Davis b. November 1, 1963
142 Roots Trip II (Longwood, Missouri and Bill Claycomb)
153 An Update
154 Nathaniel Davis b. ca. 1700
170 Richard Davis b. April 1, 1734
174 Nathaniel Davis b. ca. 1750–1760
176 Solomon Davis b. ca. 1760–1770
198 Josiah Collins b. November 7, 1778
200 Richard Davis b. 1799
204 Amelia "Milly" Davis b. ca. 1831
204 Mary Jane Davis b. ca. 1832
204 Arthusa Davis b. ca. 1834
206 Josiah Davis b. February 1830
208 Albert "Bert" Davis b. ca. 1837
214 Clifton Davis b. ca. 1839
216 James Davis b. December 11, 1841
220 Jefferson C. Davis b. March 29, 1861
236 Eula Davis House Family Tree
238 John Morgan Davis b. March 16, 1863
246 Charles Davis b. Feb. 16, 1865

282 **Joseph S. Davis** b. March 11, 1867
290 **William "Will" Davis** b. June 11, 1871
302 **James Davis** b. March 4, 1875
304 **Lula "Lu" Davis Sanders** b. April 26, 1877
314 **Ollie Davis** b. January 27, 1882
318 **Edmund "Ed" Davis** b. February 13, 1868
320 **Woodson Masters Davis** b. March 7, 1899
324 **Edward Davis** b. October 14, 1923
328 **The Village of Fairmount, Illinois**
336 **Galen White** b. August 25, 1759
336 **Daniel Maupin** b. ca. 1754
346 **Thomas Gooch** d. 1803
358 **Cornelius Gooch** b. ca. 1780
360 **Eliza B. White Gooch Hill** b. ca. 1788
362 **Chiswell D. Gooch** b. ca. 1809
388 **Thomas E. Gooch** b. January 25, 1836
410 **Thomas Emanuel "Moody" Gooch** b. April 20, 1877

Savage/Benkó Family

440 **Roots Trip Hungary** June 1998
443 **Lajos (Benkó) Bolyki** b. August 8, 1926
447 **Szávics Family, Tolna County, Hungary**
456 **Szávics Family, Tolna County, Hungary,** Birth, Marriage and Death Registers
462 **Szávics Family, Tolna County, Hungary,** Data Supplement
464 **Szávics Family Tree — Hungary**
466 **Dezsó "Andrew" Szávics/Savage** b. June 2, 1874
476 **Mária "Mary" Benkó Szávics Savage** b. May 4, 1883
486 **Dezso David Andrew Szávics Savage** b. August 26, 1904
491 **Father Figures**
492 **June Julia Savage Lucas** b. August 7, 1911
501 **Michael David Szávics Savage** b. February 27, 1914
504 **John Raymond Savage** b. August 8, 1919
510 **János "John" Benkó** b. May 27, 1889
552 **Benkó/Bolyki Family Trees**
558 **Benkó/Bolyki Family Documents**
568 **Krisztina Bolyki** b. April 9, 1877
574 **Lajos Bolyki** b. 1897

Douthart/Maloney Family

588 Henry "Harry" Douthart b. September 8, 1867
598 Richard C. Douthart b. May 21, 1908
610 Ann May Bauer Douthart b. March 14, 1914
614 Richard James Douthart b. June 11, 1935
622 Robert Henry Douthart b. July 26, 1938
626 Catherine Ann Douthart Davis b. January 2, 1940

Bauer/Lauff Family

638 John William Bauer b. March 12, 1887
646 Anna Marie/Mary Lauff Bauer b. November 23, 1884
650 The Bauer Sisters

Future Fathers

660 Future Fathers
676 Epilogue
680 Acknowledgments
684 Index

Family Tree Addendum

A 60–page soft covered supplement contained in the slipcase, to be updated when future findings and revisions of the Davis Family Tree are warranted.

To Kay, without whom there would be no family

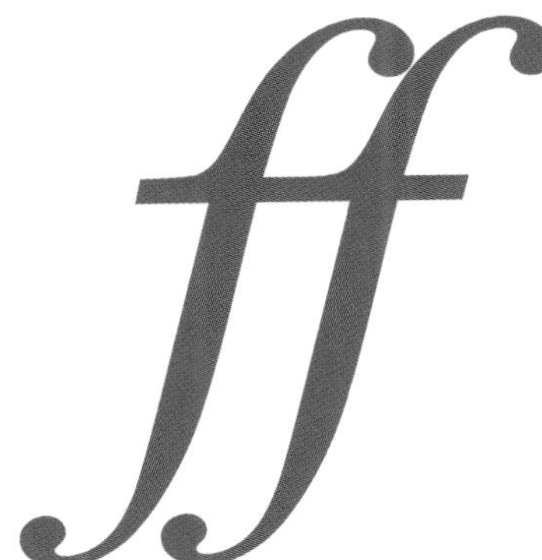

Preface

When I began this project, in earnest in 1997, little did I realize how dependent I would become on the goodwill of so many others. Their

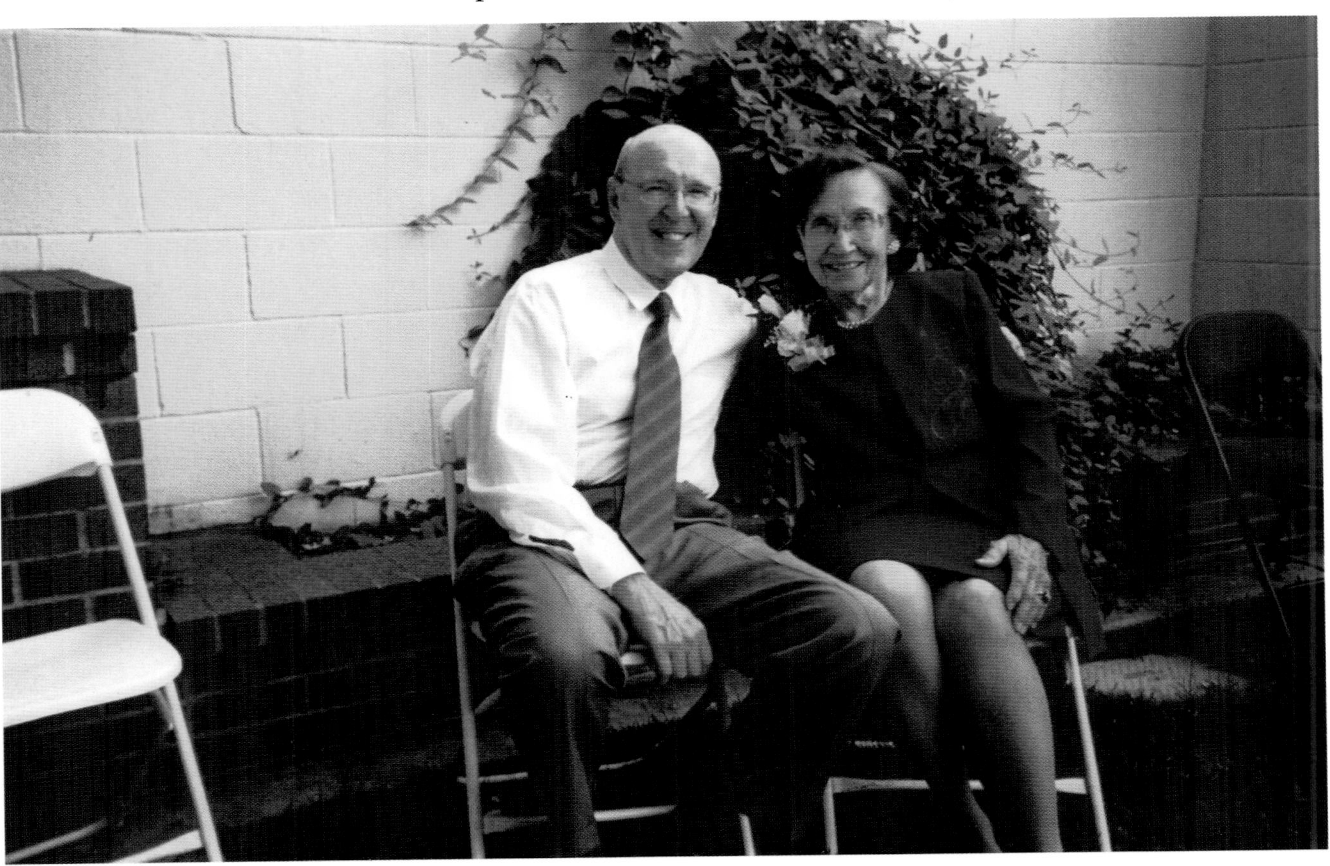

Clyde Davis with LaVerne Purkey on the occasion of LaVerne's daughter Patricia Ann's wedding to Michael Brian Entwistle Sr. on September 1, 2002.

contributions have enriched this book with information and images that have allowed me to build a family around the father I hardly knew.

My intention from the start, whenever contacting family members, was to request that they share with me photographs, letters, and other family memorabilia. As an artist it was important for me to create a genealogical publication that would be rich in visual material unlike more scholarly works before me. These "data and photo dumps" from trusting folks of goodwill became the "springtime foliage" that brought my family tree to full bloom. I spent a small fortune on FedEx charges to exchange the material both ways, but it was, I hope, well worth the cost. In addition, it often took some skill in convincing people to participate to this degree in my project. These were essentially "cold calls" on my part to names I had turned up in my early research.

Many of these folks, like Bernetta Stump of Tucson, Arizona, I have never met. Bernetta, in July of 1998, sent me nearly forty vintage photographs, a five-page family tree, and various memorial cards regarding the Jefferson C. Davis family of Missouri. I never had the opportunity to meet Lois Davis Murphy of Chilhowee, Missouri, who provided so much about the Davis, Murphy, and Sanders families.

At times, I was politely rebuffed with words to the effect that "… I really don't have the time, but my sister-in-law…" or "… Grandma would know more about that than me." Even these responses would lead to referrals of value. I was referred in August 2007 to Cindy Eilber of Pinckney, Michigan. Her brother, Richard Davis, who expressed some concern about possible identity theft in sharing information with me, thought his sister would be more helpful. This distant Detroit branch of the Davis family came to life in the hands of Cindy. She contributed many photographs of family members, carefully labeling each with names, dates, and relationships. She went on to fulfill additional requests from me for missing information. Yet she, too, had never previously been in contact with me. I hope one day to thank her in person for her aid and trust.

Everett Davis (who buried my father) met with us in the spring of 1986, starting us on our journey. His wife Vondell and daughter Darlene Ann Davis Pool were so important to our search, as was the exquisite memory of my sister June Davis Mora.

My wife Kay and I have met many on our roots road trips, such as Mr. Jack R. Greer of Longwood, Missouri, on September 21, 1997, who provided a colorful accounting of the lives of Morgan and Joe Davis, great uncles, brothers to my grandfather Charles Davis, neither ever known to me previously.

I will never forget stumbling upon Bill Claycomb of Sedalia, Missouri, an "amateur historian," who availed himself to two greenhorns from back east. Both my wife and I remember fondly our "cemetery crawls" and his mother's cherry cobbler. Bill was so instrumental in pulling the Davises of Missouri together.

Pen Bogert, a reference specialist at the Filson Historical Society Library in Louisville, Kentucky, was also another serendipitous discovery. The *Ohio Valley History* magazine published in the spring of 2002 an article by Mr. Bogert, "Sold for My Account: The Early Slave Trade Between Kentucky and the Lower Mississippi Valley," that profiled the exploits of early Davis ancestors. They were engaged in the transporting of slaves from Maryland westward, paying the ultimate price — their lives — for doing so. Mr. Bogert and I were to meet accidentally at the Kentucky State Archives in Frankfort — a very exciting moment for me.

Mary Louise Carlson and Clare Martin were to shed light on the Douthart and Bauer branches of my wife Kay's family.

Several of those who helped me this past decade while I was busily developing my story have passed, leaving me with the feeling, sadly, that I should have done more, sooner, or at the very least, shared my findings as I progressed — Mildred Gooch, Gary Gooch, Anna Benko, Edith Alan Kirby, Lois Davis Murphy, who sent me a packet of the most wonderful pictures appearing in my book of the Jefferson C. Davis and Rosa Tatum family, and John and Dorothy Savage. A special thanks to Michael Savage Jr. whose recollection of Savage family history and stories so profoundly enriched this book. Elizabeth Purkey, my father's sister, who kept intact so many family records that were to eventually find their way to me, was another valuable resource. Many of these folks are profiled in the pages to follow.

Another, discovered on the Internet by Gwen Salsig, was a cousin of ours, Lester Davis, and his lovely wife Ann. Upon our meeting at the Reisterstown, Maryland, Public Library on July 12, 2004, our wives were to remark how much we looked like one another. My great-great-great grandfather, Richard Davis, was a brother to Lester's great-great-great grandfather, Nathaniel Davis. Lester not only had a wonderful web site, but was also very helpful sharing his voluminous findings and research with us. He was far more knowledgeable than I and had been at it longer. Thank you, cousin, for sharing. My thanks to Dr. Jack Shelby Sanders, Glennice Ligon, Claude Davis, Eugene Davis and Maxine Davis, Ann Foster, all of Missouri, and Violet Davis of Lake Station and later, Hobart,

Indiana. And Fred Cornell Davis, who met with us on March 25, 1998, for a few beers and reminiscences in Topeka, Kansas, and later supplied the wonderful photo on pages 240–241 of the John Morgan Davis family. My list of contributors would be incomplete if not for Lajos Bolyki who received us so warmly during our visit to Eger and his home in Felsötárkány, Hungary, and confirmed my family ties to the Benkós and Savages.

Maxine Ball Dark of Hardy, Arizona, and Archie Holmes of Princeton, New Jersey, freely shared their extensive research on the Gooch family with me.

My Genealogical Soul Mate

A special note of appreciation must be extended to LaVerne Purkey, now residing in Virginia City, Nevada. LaVerne, now a widow, was married to my cousin Glenn, the son of Elizabeth Davis Purkey, my father's sister. It was LaVerne, on January 28, 1998, who sent me the first cache of family photographs, including a ten-minute movie film made of a "minor family reunion" in about 1952. The film begins at the home of Charles and Rebecca Davis, showing them on their front porch, and ends at the house of Everett and Elizabeth Purkey, which he built himself, in Merriville, Indiana. How exciting it was for me to see my aunts, uncles, cousins, father, and grandparents. For more than a decade, LaVerne has consistently dug deeper and deeper into family records passed on to her by her mother-in-law Elizabeth and to Elizabeth from her mother. LaVerne has been a major contributor to this book and one most eligible to vouch for its veracity. From her homilies and testimonials, her stoic ways, her generosity of spirit, frontier hardy, this lover of animals has become a dear friend from whom I've learned much.

The Genealogists

There have been so many others who have assisted me as I have added branch after branch to my family tree. Early on in Kentucky there were Anne Crabbe and Peggy Galloway, the first of several genealogists I was to engage. In the state of Virginia, it was Virginia Steele. But none was more critical than the Frankfort, Kentucky, genealogist Lynn C. McCarthy who, employed by me through Alice

Henson, was to force upon us a course correction when I strayed so far afield, claiming a family not of my own. Lynn was unforgiving, ordering me to begin all over proving my heritage, beginning with my father. It was a hard lesson learned that would, from that point on, keep me from getting ahead of myself and the facts.

On our European trips to Hungary and Slovakia we were in the able hands of genealogists Józseph Seress (who wrote a beautiful book on his ancestors) and Gyula "Julius" Fülep both of Eger, Hungary, who also served as our guide and translator. Our Hungarian archivists in Szekszárd, Gréczy Tamásné, Éva Ruzsa, and Gábor Aradi, turned up breakthrough after breakthrough regarding the Benkó and Szávicz (Savage) family histories, while navigating through the Greek Orthodox, Latin, Serbian, and Hungarian languages. Their professionalism and the presentation of their findings were impressive. In New York, Zoltan Zorandy served as my American Hungarian translator.

In Slovakia, Richard Tichánek of Dolni Brezany, Czech Republic, was our "go to person" regarding the Bauer and Lauff families.

There were several individuals with whom Alice Henson had corresponded over the Internet on my behalf, such as Carol Treybal, Drusilla Sheldon, Diana Igo, Judith Raven, Karen L. Zucal, and Mary Fern Souder, among others.

I've reached out to hundreds of folks for help over these past twenty-five years. I'm sure to have omitted someone deserving of credit. For that I sincerely apologize. And, of course, as with all nonfiction authors, it is customary for me to claim any and all remaining errors as mine.

To all, thank you.

Alice Henson

Alice Henson's interest in genealogy began as a hobby in the 1970s. During the 1980s she taught high school science and pursued her hobby in the summers. In 1990 she quit teaching and decided to pursue genealogy full time. She started researching for clients, became certified by the Board for Certification of Genealogists in 1992, and in 1993 started working for the Missouri State Archives on weekends. Her knowledge and accessibility to the Archives' holdings became invaluable to her clients. During the early '90s she co-authored several family history books for her own families and for clients.

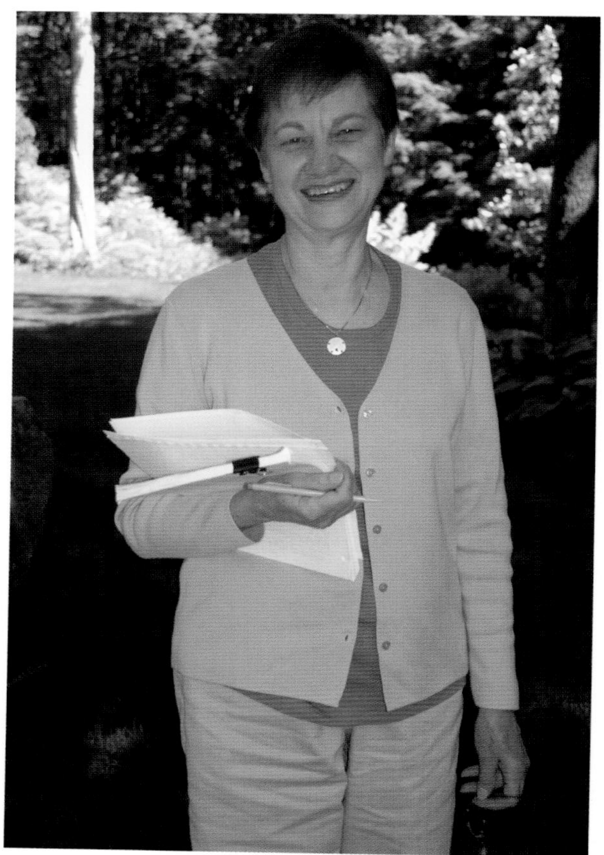

Alice Henson at Davis residence in Pound Ridge, New York, June 20, 2007

In 1998 she met me and Kay when we came to Missouri on one of our "Roots Trips." This chance meeting began a friendship and a ten-year pursuit of the Davis and Gooch families. I sent her to Frankfort, Kentucky, and Annapolis, Maryland, to do research and invited her to our New York home to help polish the book.

Many of the individual biographies, particularly the early American ancestors, were written by Alice. I have indicated these by ending those biographies with her initials, "*A.H.*"

In 2007 she decided to slow down and did not renew her credentials, but she still works for me and takes an occasional client. She lives in Jefferson City, Missouri, and spends summers in Minnesota with her husband of forty-five years, Don.

Richard Mendes

Richard Mendes spent more than thirty years in the corporate world. He has been a programmer, systems analyst, project manager, and has managed software development, technical support, and quality assurance groups. Since 1991, he has done freelance work and has built up his own consulting business. He has also supported his wife, Ruth, with her home-based desktop publishing and graphics business, during the course of which he acquired a whole new set of skills in computer-based design and graphics.

He is also a writer. He wrote an unpublished children's fantasy for his daughter, Rica, and he edited an anthology of short stories, *Prose & Cons*, which includes three of his own stories, along with those of five other writers. The anthology, which was published in 1991, has sold in places as far away as Canada and Ireland.

Richard had been helping me with my computers and home network for almost eight years. When I was ready to work on this book, I wanted to be able to work from my home in Pound Ridge where all my papers and photographs were and where my wife Kay was able to help. I wanted to work with someone local who could devote the kind of time I needed and who had knowledge of layout and graphics — preferably a desktop artist who could assist me in my usual role as an art director and former creative director. I chose Richard for this work. Our effort has evolved from me simply giving him directions to a far more collaborative effort. Which is why, if there are any problems with this book, I blame him.

When not traveling, and at home in Pound Ridge, Richard and I often worked from 10AM to 6PM daily, Monday through Friday. Actually, we have spent more time together in Pound Ridge than I have spent with anyone else besides Kay. Richard and Kay are the only ones allowed in my study; the rest of my family stops at the door.

If Alice Henson was my genealogical "soul mate," Richard was my "cell mate."

Clyde Patrick Davis
Trumbull Park Homes housing project,
10629 S. Yates Avenue, Chicago, Illinois

First Communion

About the Author and His Family

This is a story of one man's past — a quest to find out about himself and what makes him tick. It is also a deep desire to provide a family history for his children and grandchildren. All of us are shaped by our pasts. Not only do we inherit genetic material from our ancestors, but we also copy patterns of living, both good and bad. The story begins with his father, or lack thereof. Growing up in a fatherless home had to be difficult, financially and emotionally, for Clyde Davis, his mother, brother, and sister. But, perhaps, it was this void that made Clyde seek a better life and pursue his dreams. Perhaps it is this same void that compels him to fill in the blanks of his past, building the family that he never knew he had.

Although the search for Clyde Otis "Cotton" Davis (Clyde's father) was painful and left many unanswered questions, Clyde knew his father worked for the railroad and that he had owned a tavern in Lafayette, Indiana, but did not know that his father was imprisoned in Michigan for seven years, that he worked for Bell & Howell in Chicago for a time, and had died in Kokomo, Indiana, in 1974. Unfortunately, his father's death went unnoticed by his children, as they had no knowledge of their father's whereabouts. Only a surviving sister of Clyde's father was mentioned in his obituary.

The search for his grandparents Charles Davis and Rebecca Gooch was a little easier because he had visited them as a child in Rockfield, Indiana. Living relatives in Illinois told him to look in Johnson County, Missouri, for his great-grandparents. He found an old newspaper article that told of a family reunion in Missouri that his grandparents had attended. This led to his great-grandfather James's obituary and a family tree, a paper prepared by a descendant in Missouri, which stated that her father had been born in Madison County, Kentucky. Everywhere he went, Clyde asked for pictures. A cousin provided a picture of "brother Albert, grandfather's brother," whose picture had been taken in Moberly, Missouri. This name led to the generation that had come out of Kentucky.

Finding the right Davis family in Madison County, Kentucky,

was not easy. First of all, there were two Davis families in that county with sons named James, both nearly the same age. Clyde tried to make one family fit, but all evidence was pointing to a great-great-grandfather named Richard Davis who had sons Albert and James living with him in 1850. It was very puzzling, yet revealing, that the name Richard had not been carried down into the part of the family that went to Missouri.

Finding Richard's father was quite an ordeal. Even in 1800 there were several Davis families in Madison County. Thankfully, we found the answer in court records. Richard Davis and his siblings had sued their mother in 1819. This single case gave us the entire family and the name of his father — Solomon Davis. Court records would be an important source in bringing this family to life and adding "real meat" to the bare bones of genealogy.

The other families that intermarried with the Davis families will also be included in this book. They, too, are significant in the story. The Gooch, Oldham, Maupin, White, Collins, Blackwell, Savage, Benkó, Douthart, and Bauer families have all contributed to the heritage of these descendants. Our story will be as accurate as we can make it, not glossing over the facts, but exposing them to as much light as we can. If we understand where we've been, perhaps we can see where we are going.

So now, we begin with our tale of "finding fathers."

Alice S. Henson, C.G.R.S., 1992–2007

Davis Gooch

Looking back, I try to understand why I wished to write a book of this sort. I turn to the most obvious — *I can.* That is, I am able to produce a book. Financially, it's viable; I have the money. Technically, I have the skills as a graphic artist to visualize, lay out, and art direct a book. Writing, however, is an entirely different matter, and I fully expect the help of others. My task will be one of compilation, the "gatherer" of statistics, data, records, photographs, experts, relatives, and the not so relative.

My plan was to tap into the resources of my business — its desktop center and production department. To a considerable extent I was able to utilize these resources for nearly one-and-a-half years after my career ended.

Over my lifetime, I have come to realize that much of my behavior has centered around "leaving footprints," some tangible evidence of my being. All of my life and to this very moment, I've recorded in some manner my impressions of the world about me — from my earliest days in grammar school through high school, through my diaries that began as a means to contain cost escalations during the construction of my home in 1975.

The need to document was evidenced by one of the first gifts from Kay, my then steady high school girlfriend. I received a two-drawer gray metal filing cabinet. What teenager wants a filing cabinet for his birthday? This was a foreshadowing of my proclivity for documents, reference, and record keeping. Majoring in commercial art, I kept a "swipe" file of professional artists' work at the time.

Recording details gradually became a habit that daily permeated my professional life in advertising and even included personal voluminous expressions of my feelings about those with whom I interacted. I have taken thousands of photographic images, contained in shoe boxes and innumerable albums, along with hundreds of hours of videotape. This effort now seems to be about the record. That I "fit-in." That in a family of my creation, I have a place in the scheme of things. That my life is not merely contiguous only with those around me, but part of a greater, provable continuum. I can now hook-up my immediate family "box car" to this train of life having found the proper track on which to switch.

More importantly though, I wanted to leave a legacy for those who followed me. Having established myself, being surrounded by loved ones, with a successful career behind me, and now being a "free man" (we don't use the "R" word), I am able to take the time for such an undertaking.

It is January 24, 2003, and as I sit here reviewing my family tree chart I realize that the moment has arrived for me to begin in earnest the physical production of my book. Nearly seventeen years have passed since that first "Roots Trip" took place with our drive down to Fairmount, Illinois, with June and Mom to visit with Mildred Gooch, Paul, and his brother Gary Gooch. The dwindling amount of data as we reach further into the past, coupled with the increasing fear of overstaying my guest privileges at CDM, Inc., allowing me to utilize the facilities and other resources associated with the production of my book, have suddenly prompted me to *get-to-work.*

Tracing my family roots was always centered on a father I never really knew, but one I instinctively believed was part of a rich, if not noble heritage. To keep my search relatively simple, I decided to follow the DAVIS / GOOCH "blood" lines. Due often to the intermarrying of relatives, I sometimes refer to my being two-thirds Gooch and one-third Davis. Alice Henson, a genealogist working with me for some time, recently (November 19, 2002) reminded me "… that the two families (Davis and Gooch) kept in touch with each other." She goes on to say, "After all, Nannie Gooch Davis was Thomas Gooch's sister. Two of her sons married Gooch cousins. Charles Davis [my grandfather] married Rebecca Gooch and Will Davis [his brother] married (and divorced) Eliza Gooch."

These families were early Americans. The first governor of Virginia, who died "without issue," was a Gooch (there is today a

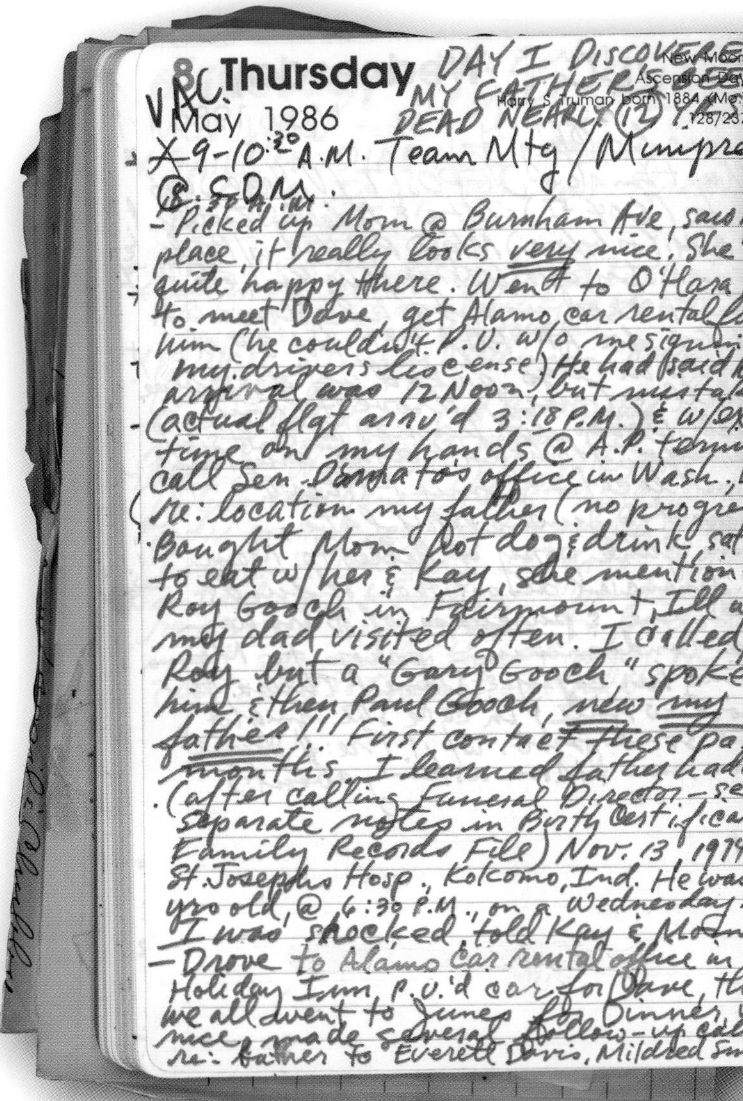

Gooch County, Virginia), and the Davises lived but a stone's throw from Fort Boonesboro in Kentucky at the time of Daniel Boone. It pleases me that they were pioneers when this country was being formed. Learning about them has led me to become better acquainted with our country's history, geography, and culture.

We started this search May 7, 1986, at my sister's kitchen table in Lansing, Illinois, and have reached back in time to the year 1700, tracing ties from Illinois and Indiana back through Virginia, Kentucky, Missouri, and have now found ourselves at the coastal state of Maryland — where we believed Davises first arrived.

On May 8, 1986, I, along with my mother and wife Kay, were at Chicago O'Hare International Airport awaiting the arrival of my brother Dave from Los Angeles. We were simply passing time discussing the whereabouts of my father. I mentioned a letter I'd written to New York Senator, Gus D'Amato, of the U.S. Congress, requesting assistance in locating my father, and given the airport waiting time, I placed a call at 2:10 P.M. to Senator D'Amato's office. I spoke with a Ms. Ivco, his assistant, who informed me that they had written to the Social Security Administration and were still awaiting their reply. Mom was getting hungry, so we got her a hot dog with the works, and it was after a bit of nourishment that she rallied forth with the suggestion we call my father's cousin, Roy Gooch, who lived in Fairmount, Illinois. She had visited with my father's friends and family in Fairmount. By 2:45 P.M., I was on the phone asking information for a Roy Gooch (not knowing Roy had died August 15, 1984, nearly two years earlier). I took the only listing, Gary Gooch, and placed the call. I remember identifying myself as Clyde Davis, and the response was one of disbelief. Paul, who answered the phone, claimed he knew Clyde Davis, and I was not that person. Upon explaining I was named after my father and was his son, Clyde Jr., there was a moment of awkward silence, and then Paul said, "I don't know how to tell you this, but your father is dead." So there I was, in the middle of an air terminal, learning quite abruptly, from a complete, even faceless stranger,

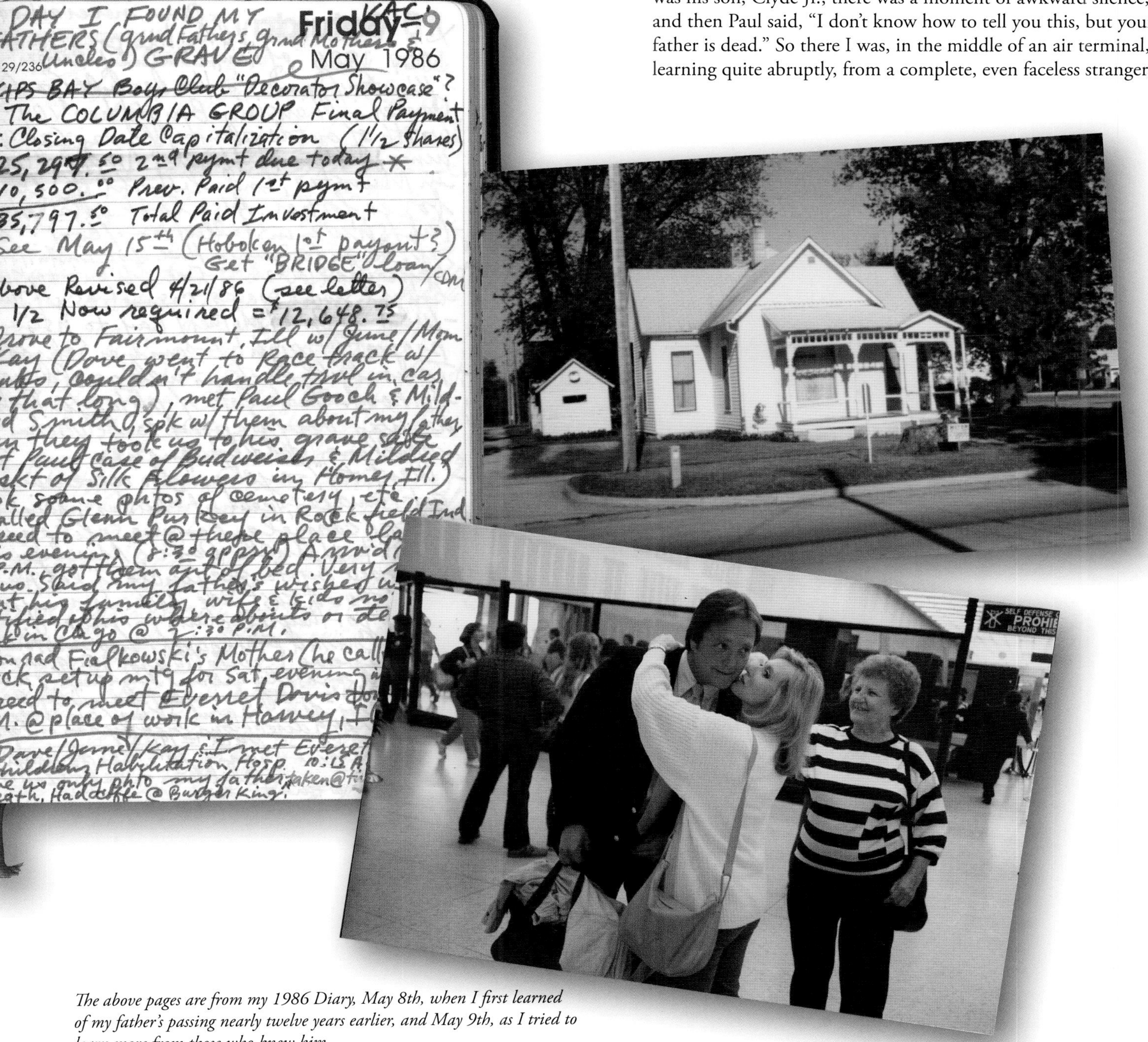

The above pages are from my 1986 Diary, May 8th, when I first learned of my father's passing nearly twelve years earlier, and May 9th, as I tried to learn more from those who knew him.

Above right, Mildred Gooch Smith's home at 305 South Main Street in Fairmount, Illinois. Also Kay Davis (my wife) and Mary Davis (my mother) greeting my brother, David "Butchie" Davis, at O'Hare Airport in Chicago, May 8, 1986.

living in a town I never knew existed, that my father had died. Paul went on to explain that Roy Gooch was his and Gary's father, and that Roy had a brother "Hoopie" Gooch. Paul continued with "you got to talk to the funeral director, Charles Kaiser, and you should talk to Mildred (Gooch) Smith…she knows more." Turns out that Paul knew my father fairly well and spoke of my father being a teller or cashier in a big restaurant in Chicago. He remarked that "… your father was a big man, weighed over 300 pounds when he died…. I was a pallbearer and helped carry the casket. He ate all the wrong foods, liked pepper, drank a lot, played cards — euchre — when he'd come down to Fairmount. Everyone liked him…knew him as 'Cotton.'" Years later, in a phone call on July 18, 2000 with Paul, who died on August 23, 2007, he confirmed that my father, "Cotton... robbed a private poker game in Michigan with guns." Two other men were with him, Kittle Burris and "Uncle Roy." It's not clear if the Roy in question was Paul's uncle, Roy Dean Gooch, or my uncle, Roy "Jack Dog" Davis, though the reference to "Uncle Roy" suggests it was Paul's uncle. My father and his brother Roy were raised by Viola and Emmanuel Gooch, who came from Missouri according to Paul. It isn't clear why Charles and Rebecca Davis would have ceded raising their sons to Rebecca's brother and sister-in-law.

I thanked Paul, somewhat overwhelmed with this flood of information, and its impact, especially in contrast to there being so little prior to my call.

I then called Charles Kaiser Funeral Home in Fairmount. Still at the airport, my brother's flight not yet in, I spoke with Mrs. Kaiser. She was nice enough to pull the records regarding my father's burial arrangement. I learned he had died at 6:30 P.M., on a Wednesday, November 13, 1974, at St. Joseph's Hospital in Kokomo, Indiana. He was sixty-seven years old. The death certificate indicated that the immediate cause of death was "aspiration of vomitus" due to, or as a cause of "congestive heart failure." A significant contributing condition was "diabetic acidosis." He was buried in the Greenview Cemetery, in Fairmount, Illinois.

Mrs. Kaiser mentioned that the person who paid for the funeral was Everett Davis. The cost was $866.50. She also said, "His obituary appeared in the *Commercial News* of Danville, Illinois." More about that later.

My brother's arrival was a bit anticlimactic.

That evening at my sister's kitchen table, we discussed who to call first for we all wanted more information. And we now had a few names. My sister June confirmed that Everett Davis lived and worked near Lansing in Woodridge, Illinois, (at 6124 Alan Drive). We contacted Everett and arranged to meet him on May 9th, 9:30 A.M., at a nearby Burger King, in Harvey, Illinois.

Everett worked at the Children's Habilitation Center (formerly Children's Haven, Inc.), 121 West 154th Street, Harvey, Illinois. The evening before our meeting, I had spoken with Vondell, Everett's wife. She said, "Your father played poker with Eddie at the Legion hall…he was a heavy drinker…a gentleman all the way…had diabetes, quit booze…but loved his beer." He was fond of saying, "When I go, I'm going happy." It seems that my father was in transition between residences at the time of his death. Everett said new carpet had been installed in his place a week before he died, but he never saw it. "When Glenn [Purkey, his nephew] came to move him to Kokomo, he couldn't sit up." Was this the night he died?

At our Burger King meeting with Everett, he confirmed much of what I had learned from my several "airport calls."

Photograph by June Mora

David "Butchie" Davis, Mary Davis, Clyde "Duke" Davis, and Everett Davis meeting at Burger King in Harvey, Illinois, May 9, 1986

My father had appointed Everett as the executor of his estate. Vondell's family were morticians and have an active practice to this day. We reminisced some — Everett spoke of how they'd drive down to Rockfield, Indiana, visiting and how they'd always bring a bottle of whiskey each for Grandma and Grandpa, and how Grandpa always drank his right away, and Grandma had to hide hers from him — and after a few tacky questions about the disposition of a ring and watch my father may have had at the time of his death, we parted. Everett did correspond with me afterwards, sharing photographs of my father and other family members, but he died from Parkinson's August 3, 2002.

I'll never forget that first trip by car to Fairmount, Illinois. I recall asking my brother if he wished to accompany us. But his response was a simple no.

After being informed upon his arrival in Chicago two days earlier that our father was deceased, he seemed to no longer care to learn more about him, preferring to cling, or shall we say, embrace the romantic notion of a father who was fun-loving, funny, sociable, often with a woman by his side, who liked a drink now and then, a man about the town, who was free of many of the normal responsibilities of adulthood.

On May 10, 1986, Mom, June, Kay, and I piled into a big, white Cadillac rental and drove first to Delphi, Illinois, where my grandparents Charles and Rebecca Davis once lived, and my sister and I often spent summers as youngsters. We never did locate their home. Perhaps it had long since been demolished. An address would have helped. But then this trip was spontaneous and not planned, with all the prior preparations that are now a usual part of similar trips.

We then drove on to Fairmount, Illinois, and hooked up with Paul Gooch, who was kind enough to share a six-pack we'd picked up, along with his recollections of his uncle Clyde and to introduce us to his grandmother Mildred (Gooch) Smith, then eighty-one years old. This, at first suspicious, soon forthcoming woman, shared with us her recollections of our father. There we were — from my sister's kitchen table to Mildred's kitchen table — poring over photographs of assorted distant relatives, some known, many of our father (among them, the cover photograph of this book). I couldn't help wondering what my mother must be feeling, hearing tales of a man she hadn't heard from in more than thirty-five years. Mom never had a camera, took no photographs, so we had none of our father except these placed before us. Mildred would part with none of them, still suspicious that we were there for something else other than family history. Mildred knew everyone and everything about the family, mostly Gooches, and was at the time, relatively well off financially, living alone in a modest, two-story, white clapboard house at 305 South Main Street in Fairmount.

Mildred agreed to accompany us to the burial site of my father, and, new to us, my grandparents Charles and Rebecca, my Uncle Roy "Jack Dog" Davis, and several Gooches, among others. Surprisingly the Greenview Cemetery was within the town of Fairmount, quite near Mildred's home. There we were, at the foot of our father's grave, smack upside the Wabash railroad tracks, surrounded by fields of corn, alfalfa, and beans as far as the eye could see. A quiet, cool evening settling over a cemetery with a big white Cadillac driven into its midst, and people scattered among headstones, eagerly trying to link these epitaphs to one another, to reveal a family not yet known.

I was deeply moved. This was the nearest I was to come to the man, my father, last seen alive by me in 1956. Somehow I felt "connected," thinking he must know I'm here. We said a prayer and departed.

Mildred's husband, Cornice Hobert Smith, had died in 1983. We returned to Fairmount many times after this visit with Mildred, but never to meet with her again, for she passed away December 19, 1992. Unfortunately, according to her court appointed guardian, Glona Howe, all her personal effects were auctioned off on the lawn of her home, including, sadly, bureaus and dressers filled with photographs that no one then wanted or cared enough about to retain.

Fairmount is a small town of approximately eight hundred people, 140 miles south of Chicago, lying directly east of Champaign-Urbana, where, off and on, I attended the University of Illinois from 1956 to 1962. During this period, my father gathered with his friends and other family in Fairmount. Neither of us was apparently aware of how close we really were.

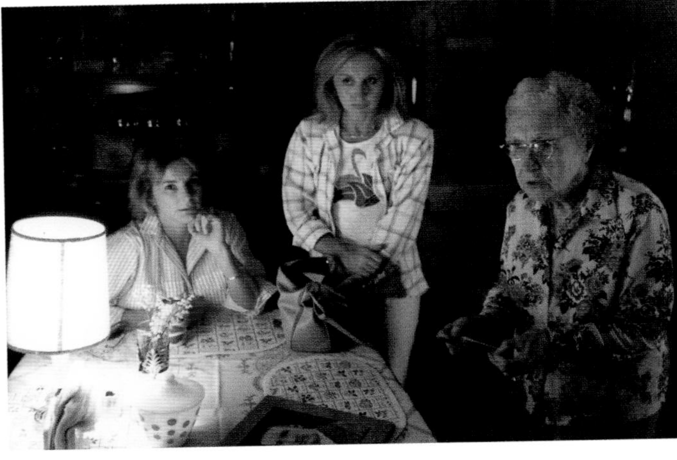

June Davis Mora and Kay Davis at Mildred Smith's kitchen table with family photos. Fairmount, Illinois, May 10, 1986.

We continued on to Rockfield, Indiana, after visiting with Paul and Mildred to meet with my cousin Glenn and his wife LaVerne Purkey. Glenn was the younger son of Elizabeth "Lizzie" and Hugh Purkey. We'd called them earlier, explaining, though the hour was quite late, perhaps 11:00 P.M. or so, that we'd driven down from Chicago, were in the area, and wished to see them. They were most gracious, although we had awakened them. There was Glenn in his blue denim work shirt and LaVerne in her nightgown and robe eagerly greeting their nocturnal guests. We found ourselves gathered, yet again, around a large dining room table, passing photographs, some framed and off the wall, chatting about relatives seen earlier in the day, the discoveries we'd made, and my mother reminiscing about her and Glenn. He was extremely goodlooking, even handsome, and a favorite of my mother. A former Troop Transport pilot and career officer of the U.S. Air Force, serving extensively during WWII in Africa and Europe. LaVerne, a former LPN nurse, was with my father when he died in a diabetic coma. Both Glenn and LaVerne were then retired, tending to their farm. LaVerne would, years later, become one of my genealogical soul mates, after Glenn died August 21, 1986. We didn't stay long with a three-hour drive back to Chicago ahead of us.

Glenn Purkey with Mom during "nocturnal visit," Rockfield, Indiana

After returning to New York, I received a written reply from Alfonse D'Amato, U.S. Senator, to my letter of April 25, 1986. He informed me that the Commissioner of Social Security had confirmed my father's passing. Now it was official, I suppose.

All of this must have been a lot to digest, or perhaps it simply allowed us to return to the everyday affairs of life. After all, hadn't I "found" my father?

We didn't take another Roots Trip until almost twelve years later.

My Father

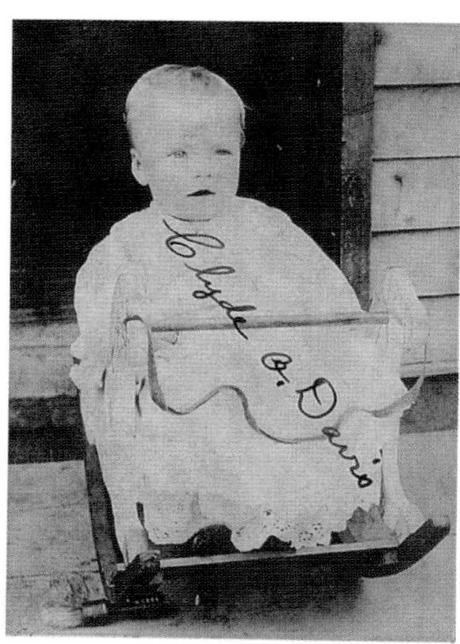

Clyde Otis Davis

Born June 3, 1907

Note shaving cream brush to steady rocker on bottom left

Interest in family history for me began with the search for my father, Clyde Otis Davis. Genealogy was to become a label covering a much broader scope of work that evolved after my initial quest was concluded.

In thinking of my father it soon became apparent that this man I hardly knew was being summed up in a few awkward paragraphs by one of his children without the benefit of all those he'd known otherwise.

We are all many things. To some, a villain, to others, a saint. To one heartless, to someone else, a person with a big heart. It became increasingly apparent that I was not fairly depicting the man, my father. Obviously he was many things to many people, and I was providing a biased, simplistic, and narrow notion of this person. All from the perspective of an abandoned son.

The photographs appearing throughout this book will certainly tell a story of Clyde Davis Sr. At least we'll have a glimpse or two of the man, where he was, perhaps when and with whom. How prominently these pictures will be displayed and their frequency as subject matter throughout this book should serve as some indication of the level of respect this son had for his father.

From 1956 through 1985, nearly thirty years, I pursued a college education (with checkered results), married, went back to school, and raised a family. I had no money, but I had an all-consuming desire to improve my life. I had dreams. I persevered.

In 1985, about a year after I'd started my own business with my two partners, Morgan Cline and Fredric Mann, I was moved to seek out my father. This was a good year for me. Our advertising agency start-up was beginning to throw off income, and we began paying ourselves salaries comparable to those earned prior to our new venture. I even bought myself a Mercedes at Morgan's insistence (he bought one too). Cynthia, my middle child, was married successfully, despite her apprehension. My daughter Christine, in her second year of marriage, was well on her way to a new life and career in Seattle, Washington, where Scott, her husband, was based as a submariner. My son Cole was under the care of the U.S. Navy in his third year of service in San Diego, California. My wife Kay was about to close-out a ten-year career as a Human Resources Director of a rapidly growing engineering firm now that we were doing so well. I was finally managing to achieve some control over my financial destiny. It seemed appropriate to now turn my attention to a fractured family of the past to try and pull everyone together, not withstanding my pride of accomplishment and the barely hidden desire to share it all with one's parents.

As Paul Gooch described my father: "He ate all the wrong foods, liked pepper, drank a lot...."

My father was a big man, easily six-foot or better, 250 pounds, 300 in his casket according to Paul Gooch, a pallbearer. My father was called "Cotton" by others. His hair was the reason, so I'm told. He loved to eat. He liked things "hot," spicy that is, peppers, chili sauce.... He drank — *always* — mostly beer, buttermilk for hang-overs, never hard liquor, slept naked, liked women, and they seemed to like him, was sociable, and, as I recall, he drove a green 1949 Buick convertible. As Paul Gooch said, "It was always a party when Clyde came to town." He worked on the railroad as a switchman when I was born. He also worked as a bartender, tavern owner, and cashier. "He read all the time, paperbacks mostly, and newspapers."

My father was also drunk a lot, broke the law, was imprisoned, abused my mother, was unfaithful, and fought with others. He seemed to care little for his offspring, seldom offering expressions of affection or love, and ultimately, like his brother Roy, walked away from his family.

I saw my father in June 1956. I was about to graduate from high school, and he had gotten wind of it. Word got to me that he would like to give me a little something for graduation. I was given an address and a time he would be available. So Kay, my high school sweetheart, later to be the centerpiece of my life, and I got a series of buses from the far South Side of Chicago to 1827 W. Cermack Road to see my father. Appearing at the door to his "flat," a woman in a nightgown greeted us. I was to learn later that this was probably Peggy Phillips, who apparently was still living with him August 23, 1967.[1] She seemed pleasant enough and directed us with, "Your father is in bed," and motioned to a nearby door. He greeted us. I can only remember his asking me to get his pants from a nearby chair and to hand them to him, from which he pulled a twenty-dollar bill and gave it to me. I don't remember anything else he said. I know that I was uncomfortable with his half naked body projecting from the covers. He was a big man, and it was a lot of flesh (he never wore underwear — oddly, a habit my son would pick up in his early adult life). Kay remained outside the dimly lit bedroom. My father worked nights tending bar and slept during the day. While I was there, he never got out of bed. Within five minutes, not longer than ten, the exchange was over. I thanked him and we said goodbye. I don't remember embracing or kissing him — perhaps we shook hands.

We left and that was the last time I would ever see or hear from my father again. This was the father I remember.

Notes

1. Letter in the author's possession to Mr. and Mrs. Hobart Smith, Fairmount, Illinois, from Peggy Phillips, 1827 W. Cermack Rd., Chicago, IL 60608, postmarked "Chicago P.M. 23 Aug 1964."

Clyde Otis Davis b. June 3, 1907

Clyde Davis Has Had Enough Of "Just Listening"

Clyde Davis, operator of a tavern at 501 Columbia street, may have his faults. Clyde will admit this. But he's a man who'll speak his mind—that is, on certain topics, and one of these is running his tavern. His advertisement in this week's Leader runs this way:

"CLYDE'S TAVERN. THREE way permit. Good yearly gross. A bargain if taken at once. Reason for selling, sick and tired of it. 501 Columbia. Phone 2-9465."

What's Clyde Davis sick and tired of? Hearing, of course, day by day, the old ones. Clyde is sick and tired of hearing other people's troubles from other people parked on stools. Of last night's round with the Lady of The House. Of hearing how the government ought to be run. Of hearing how much somebody won on the last race. He's tired of so much bragging from fellows who never got to first base. Of hearing somebody tell of all the hellum they raised about the year the Wabash started downstream.

"Yep," said Clyde, "I'm sick and tired of it. The first gent that comes in with enough to take me to Miami Beach for a few days can start listening to what I've been hearing and luck to him."

Photos courtesy of LaVerne Purkey

"Clyde's Tavern" was located at 501 Columbia Street at the corner of Columbia and 5th in the Historic District of downtown Lafayette, Indiana. Clyde is seen behind the bar in the long apron serving the very patrons that he would grow "sick and tired of hearing" from day after day. The piano player added a bit of class to the place while possibly drowning out the troubles passed across the bar by others.

In his own words...

Being a personable chap Clyde Otis Davis worked most of his life with people. After several years of employment, 1945 through 1950, at the Lafayette Country Club "… where he was liked by everybody," he established "Clyde's Tavern" at 501 Columbia Street, Lafayette, Indiana. The tavern was a going concern in the years 1950–54. By January 1954, it had become "Charlie's Tavern." The building exists today and a restaurant now occupies the former tavern's corner space.

In November 1974 Clyde's obituary mentions he was employed by the Bell & Howell Company, Chicago, Illinois. Clyde's Social Security records indicate his withholding taxes were deducted by the Canteen Corporation, Royal Way, Kansas City, his employer during the years 1970 through 1973. Since there is no record of Clyde living in Missouri, it is believed that the Canteen Corporation provided cafeteria services to Bell & Howell during this period where Clyde worked as a cashier. In February 2001 Bell & Howell was acquired by the Kodak Company.

Clyde Davis, Cashier

Despite Ailment, He Fosters Cheer

"If I didn't like to be around people, I don't think I'd be on this job. If people here at Bell & Howell feel about me like I feel about them, everything is 100 per cent."

To anyone who knows Clyde Davis, cashier in the Building 1 cafeteria, those words, alone, will identify the one who said them. A more cheerful, happy and friendly fellow would, indeed, be hard to find anywhere.

Yet, Clyde could—if it were not for his love of life and people—be a very lonely and grouchy person, for life has not always been good to him. Clyde was injured in an accident more than five years ago and despite several serious operations, he has not been able to recover the full use of his legs. He still has to walk with supports.

But the pain and inconvenience can't get him down. He sits on his cashier's stool with a friendly word for everyone and takes his disappointments in stride.

"That's been my attitude as far back as I can remember," Davis says. "My father taught me that when I was a child. He also advised me that, 'If you can't say anything nice about anyone, don't say anything at all.'

"And," Clyde continues, "my father had another piece of good advice, too. He always told me, 'You only go through this life once, so you might as well make a good job of it.' "

For much of his life, Davis has been closely associated with people, spending many years in the bar and restaurant business. Among his multitude of friends he numbers many prominent sports figures. At one time, he and former heavyweight boxing champion Ezzard Charles were very close.

Now in his 60s, Davis still has hope that he will recover the full use of his legs, and his friends share in that desire. But if by some circumstance he does not walk freely again, you can bet that he'll keep on smiling.

Without question, Clyde Davis has followed his father's advice. He's made a good job of his life by trying to make others happy.

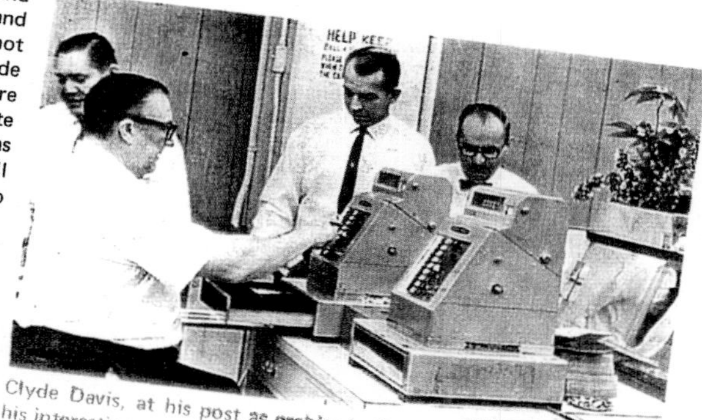

Clyde Davis, at his post as cashier in Building No. 1 cafeteria, tells his interesting story above.

Clyde Otis Davis b. June 3, 1907

Photos courtesy of **LaVerne Purkey**

Form SS-5
TREASURY DEPARTMENT
INTERNAL REVENUE SERVICE

U. S. SOCIAL SECURITY ACT
APPLICATION FOR ACCOUNT NUMBER 336-01-1635

PRINT NAME
1. Clyde (EMPLOYEE'S FIRST NAME) Otis (MIDDLE NAME) Davis (LAST NAME)
(MARRIED WOMEN: GIVE MAIDEN FIRST NAME, MAIDEN LAST NAME, AND HUSBAND'S LAST NAME)
2. 8920 Commercial Avenue (STREET AND NUMBER) 3. Chicago (POST OFFICE) Illinois (STATE)
4. Carnegie-Illinoi. Steel Corporation (BUSINESS NAME OF PRESENT EMPLOYER) 5. 3426 East 89th Street.Chicago,Illinois (BUSINESS ADDRESS OF PRESENT EMPLOYER)
6. 29 (AGE AT LAST BIRTHDAY) 7. June 3.1907 (DATE OF BIRTH: (MONTH) (DAY) (YEAR) (SUBJECT TO LATER VERIFICATION)) 8. Catlin, Vermillion Co., Illinois (PLACE OF BIRTH)
9. Charles Davis (FATHER'S FULL NAME) 10. Rebecca Gooch (MOTHER'S FULL MAIDEN NAME)
11. SEX: MALE ✓ FEMALE (CHECK (✓) WHICH) 12. COLOR: WHITE ✓ NEGRO (CHECK (✓) WHICH) OTHER (SPECIFY)
13. IF REGISTERED WITH THE U. S. EMPLOYMENT SERVICE, GIVE NUMBER OF REGISTRATION CARD
14. IF YOU HAVE PREVIOUSLY FILLED OUT A CARD LIKE THIS, STATE (PLACE) (DATE)
15. November 25,1936 (DATE SIGNED) 16. Clyde O Davis (EMPLOYEE'S SIGNATURE, AS USUALLY WRITTEN)

DETACH ALONG THIS LINE

This pictorial spread of images of Clyde Otis Davis from early childhood as a student, through young adulthood seem to show a happy and gregarious person. His application for a U.S. Social Security number, at age 29, on November 25, 1936, appears on the opposite page. He was imprisoned in 1927 at age 20 and released November 19, 1934, at 27 years of age. It has yet to be determined, as of publication of this book, whether or not any of these pictures of him as an adult, were taken after his release.

CLYDE OTIS DAVIS b. June 3, 1907

Clyde + Mary Davis + LaVerne + Glenn Purkey
This was taken right after Glenn returned home from overseas in World War II in 1945.

Photos courtesy of **LaVerne Purkey**

This was my father's drink recipe book, given to me by my cousin Debbie Davis Lane in May 2009. Debbie is the daughter of Joe "Larry" and Violet Davis. Joe "Larry" was the son of Roy Davis, my father's only brother. My father had left the book with Violet, and had told Debbie that she wanted me to have it. Debbie contacted me after her mother died August 8, 2008. This appears to be the 1944 revised edition of the Recipes guide. It contained union-sanctioned recipes for drinks from the absinthe frappe to the zombie (western and eastern styles), with tips on service and bar etiquette.

My father Clyde Otis Davis, pictured above with a bow tie, was believed to have been a bartender at Eitel's Old Heidelberg Rathskeller (restaurant), 16 West Randolph, Chicago, Illinois, which was located just off State Street, next to the Oriental Theatre in the heart of the loop. The restaurant was built in 1934 and specialized in Czechoslovakian and German food. It has not been confirmed at the time of publication of this book that he indeed was employed there. The restaurant has since been renovated and turned into a three-theater complex, named the Nobel Fool Theater, for live performances.

The two black-and-white photographs above depict my sister June, or "Tootsie," barefoot as usual when we stayed in the country. My grandfather Charlie, grandmother Rebecca, my father, and me on the front porch of the Rockfield, Indiana, house. Tootsie's short-cropped hair was probably a remedy to combat head lice, which were so rampant among children in the housing project where we lived most of the year.

June's Dad

My sister June remembers more of him, had more contact with him over the years, and made a determined effort to have some kind of meaningful relationship.

I decided after probing the shallows of my memory of limited experiences to contact and interview my sister. June, at sixty-three years, is one of those people blessed with a memory that can recall details of an event that occurred at age three. It's scary. On March 20, 2002, I called her, and though suffering with a cold and upset stomach, she agreed to talk with me about our father. I proceeded recording our conversation.

"Well, I don't know where to begin," I said. "You know this has been a long journey for me, more than five years of tracing our family roots." I mentioned the help of Alice Henson and other professional genealogists, and how I marveled at their contributions, while noting my failure until now to write a single reminiscence of our father.

There were a few documented commentaries of our father that I was able to secure. The following Lafayette, Indiana, newspaper article written about him upon his decision to sell his Tavern at 501 Columbia Street in that town was the earliest.

In a telephone conversation with LaVerne Purkey,[1] I learned that my father, who worked at the Lafayette Country Club as a bartender was liked by everyone. "He had a fantastic personality — when he wasn't drinking — always happy."

LaVerne said that he thought those people who liked him at the country club would follow him as customers if he had his own tavern. Well, they did come, but it was in the wrong part of town; "They'd drop in, take a look around, and never return."

Clyde Davis Has Had Enough of "Just Listening"

What's Clyde Davis sick and tired of? Hearing, of course, day by day, the old ones. Clyde is sick and tired of hearing other people's troubles from other people parked on stools.... He's tired of so much bragging from fellows who never got to first base. Of hearing somebody tell of all the hellum they raised about the year the Wabash started downstream.... "Yep," said Clyde, "I'm sick and tired of it. The first gent that comes in with enough to take me to Miami Beach for a few days can start listening to what I've been hearing and luck to him."

Later, perhaps when he was in his late 60s, what appears to be an internally generated Bell & Howell / Kodak? newsletter, described his outlook at the time, despite certain physical maladies:

Clyde Davis, Cashier — Despite Ailment, He Fosters Cheer

"If I didn't like to be around people, I don't think I'd be on this job. If people here at Bell & Howell feel about me like I feel about them, everything is 100 per cent."

To anyone who knows Clyde Davis, cashier in Building 1 cafeteria, those words, alone, will identify the one who said them. A more cheerful, happy and friendly fellow would, indeed, be hard to find anywhere.

My father was injured while working at Carnegie Steel in a railroad switching accident. He lost all his toes on one foot, involving extensive skin grafts from his other leg. It was at this time they discovered he was diabetic.

And, of course, we have his obituary from the *Commercial News* of Danville, Illinois:

Clyde Davis, Former Fairmount Resident Dies

Clyde "Cotton" Davis, 67, former resident died Nov. 13 in a hospital in Kokomo, Ind., after an illness.

Services were held Nov. 16 at Fairmount with Rev. Berton Heline officiating and burial was in Greenview Cemetery.

Born June 3, 1907, he was a son of Charles and Rebecca Gooch Davis. He was formerly employed with Bell & Howell Company in Chicago.

Mr. Davis is survived by a sister of Lafayette, Ind.

I had asked LaVerne, Everett, and Paul Gooch all the same question, "Why didn't my father or those around him ever include in his obituary any of his offspring, children or grandchildren?" Paul said that was what "your father wanted...told me one day when we went for 'a walk in the shade,' if you know what I mean."

Returning to my interview with June, I spoke of some videotape and personal recollections of people in Fairmount, Illinois, whom he frequently spent time with, as well as the recollections of Everett Davis, Everett's wife Vondell and of course, LaVerne Purkey, who knew him well and was with him at the time he fell gravely ill. "I could piece together a few things," I said, "but I really don't know the man. I mean, I *know* people like Morgan Cline (my business partner and long-time friend), and I know my contractor (at the time of this interview, rebuilding my house) *better* than my own father."

June responded, confirming that she, too, knew of his drinking, but she was also quick to say, "He never drank hard liquor."

"He had books and books," she said, "He read all the time. He listened to the radio when he came home...in his room. And he'd pick up a paperback and read it. As for being a loner...he always surrounded himself with people. He had a ruby pinky ring. I don't know if it was real or not. He always wore a watch, never wore jewelry, never wore underwear. Everything had to be cotton. Even wore cotton pants in the winter. And he had a hard time finding cotton pants in winter. But they were always thin, I remember, you know, cotton. He could never wear anything wool."

Hearing June say this strikes a personal note. I, too, am "allergic" to wool. I am never able to wear a wool suit, of which I've had many, without having the trousers completely lined, at considerable expense, I might add. Wool sweaters, cashmere — even some synthetics, such as rayon, are all unacceptable. I recall one of my earliest experiences when my mother sent me off to school dressed with a hand-me-down green wool sweater (see photo on page 78) and all I could do to bear the discomfort was to stand as still as possible with my arms extended and elevated at my sides, as if I were about to take flight.

June continued, "He always wore a sport coat, never wore a casual jacket (windbreaker). He wore a hat, but never wore a baseball cap. Everybody liked him. He didn't show too much respect for women, but it seemed he always had one at his side. Either they were living with him, or he was involved with one. Kinda like he never wanted to be alone."

I asked June if she had any idea when he lived with our Aunt Lizzie and worked at the Lafayette (Indiana) Country Club. "I think I was older then. I might have been in my teens." After some thought, she continued, "Oh, I can tell you when. I was in grammar school because I remember I'd be walking home from Orville T. Bright School, and he always parked the car across the street (from the housing project in which we lived) on Bensely Avenue. He always parked it there. I would see his car and get all excited. I don't ever remember any [signs of affection], hugging, kissing, or anything. When I did see him, I'd run up to him and I would just kiss him on the cheek. He'd just kind of like extend his face. But, a couple times I went and sat on his lap [in the car]."

Attempting to fix a more definitive period, I asked June, "Grammar school, like in Kindergarten, or grammar school, like eighth grade?"

She replied, "About seventh grade because I would say, 'This is my father's car,' when someone would be walking by. Do you remember the whisk boom?"

"No," I answered, yet almost simultaneously, I recalled the assigned chore by my mother of brushing her dark blue mohair armchair and sofa free of its unending lint. "It was a small stiff hand brush." And obviously prized by each of us in order to do more efficiently the work we did, whether elective or otherwise.

June continued, "I couldn't take the vacuum out to the car, so I would take the whisk broom with a bucket of water. I would sweep the floor interior and clean everything in sight. Kids would be walking by, and I'd say 'This is my father's car.' And they'd go, 'Yeah, sure.' I'd say, 'No, really, it is.' In those days, they had a state I.D. account number. It had your name, address, and everything [as to who owned the vehicle]."

"I do remember that, now that you mention it. In a small plastic sleeve…."

1949 Buick Convertible.

"Exactly. A little square plastic sleeve. It was on the right side of the [steering column]."

So this must have been a way of confirming for anyone with a passing interest that this was indeed her father's car and thereby assuring herself the proper respect by association she so coveted.

"He was a ragtop [convertible] man. I don't ever remember him having a hardtop."

As I spoke with my sister, I realized how many more firsthand experiences she had with my father than I did, or that I recall. Why this deficiency of memory? Where was I when all she describes occurred?

When my sister was ten years old, that would be approximately 1950, she would frequently accompany my father. He also made periodic visits to our home in which he did not permanently reside. He either lived elsewhere in Chicago, or at times in Lafayette, Indiana. During his stay on one occasion, she'd "go see three movies at a time" with him. She said, "I don't remember him ever getting popcorn. I would get candy, but I don't remember him eating candy. I don't remember him ever eating sweets. But, he loved the movies. And we would start at 12:00 at the Southtown [movie theater]. I guess it's a Sony now. Before we would go there we would get the car washed, and then we'd park in this area just before the show. We'd walk to the show, and we would see the three movies. We'd sit there all afternoon."

My sister continues to be an avid movie-goer, often seeing two to three movies in a day. She loves keeping up with the "stars" and other celebrities through her subscriptions to the *Star* and *National Enquirer*.

I recall my father giving my sister and me money for the movies and car fare (street cars), so he and my mother could have their time together. We used to go to Gayety's movie theater at 92nd and Commercial. We also went to the Commercial theater. "But, mostly," June recalled, "we went to Gayety's because *Superman* played there and the Westerns with Bob Steele."

Photo of the Gayety Theater and Ice Cream and Candy Store courtesy of the Southeast Historical Society, Chicago, Illinois. As the population shifted, the Gayety featured Spanish language films. James Papageorge, a Greek immigrant who came to the United States in 1904, originally owned Gayety's Candies and Ice Cream. It continues as a family-owned business on Ridge Road in Lansing, Illinois. We regularly visit the ice cream parlor with my mother for her favorite chocolate ice cream soda with their own heavy whipped cream topping and indulged as recently as August 2009.

I responded. "And Hopalong Cassidy and Lash LaRue."

"Every week *Superman* was continued, and Flash Gordon," she said.

"Before we'd go to the show, we'd stop and see Uncle Roy. Now I don't remember that street and probably if I did a déjà vu I would remember. But he was with Marie, that woman. She looked like a Kewpie doll."

"This was Roy?" I wanted to verify she meant Roy Davis and not Roy Gooch.

"Yeah, his brother."

"He was living with a woman named Marie?"

"He was with her. She had been married to a very nice man, middleclass, and I believe he died. I think she drank. But you know you could see that she had been pretty when she was young, and probably in her day upper middle class and had been around nice people. But I think her lifestyle just brought her down. She hooked up with Roy and they lived together for a long time. We'd go see them. Marie had dyed black hair, ruby red lips with the cheeks, always dressed up with make-up and everything, and they were very hospitable. Roy would cook dinner all the time. There was a place on the corner. It wasn't a White Castle, but it was similar to that. Do you remember when we used to go to the University of Chicago, Bob Roberts Hospital with Mom?"

"Yes," I said. I had spent a good deal of time at these hospital clinics. Actually my sister, brother, and I were all born at the Lying-In Hospital at the University of Chicago. We were receiving Federal Aid to Dependent Children (ADC). We could not afford private physicians or dentists.

The large building pictured above at the southwest corner of 106th Street and Torrence Avenue was Neil Duffy's Tavern. Duffy's was a local establishment that my father, Clyde Otis Davis, frequented when visiting his family in the Trumbull Park Homes housing project during the separation between him and my mother. The street car stopped at 106th at a small brick shelter, which reeked of urine, directly across from the tavern on the east side of Torrence Avenue. Even though the Wisconsin Steel Mill, which surrounded it, has long since been shut down, the shelter still stands today. Photo courtesy of the Southeast Historical Society, Chicago, Illinois.

During my father's weekend visits, he also managed to include dropping in on a neighborhood tavern or two. I do not think my mother ever accompanied him.

June asked if I remembered "the tavern on the corner"? It was called Duffy's saloon [Tavern], at the corner of East 106th Street on Torrence Avenue. I think it was on the Southwest corner.

"I think it was… I want to say '47. It can't be '45 because I think that's when we moved in to the projects. I remember I started Kindergarten, and I had this one dress when we moved there. It was in the winter, but when I started Kindergarten it was summer, and Mom would wash my one dress. I would go to school in the morning, and when I came home, she'd wash my dress and do my shoes and my shoelaces, and then I'd take a nap. I always took a nap."

June continued, "Dad was fooling around with a neighbor next door."

"When was this?" I asked.

"I want to say '46, '47," June replied. "It was when Mom had the nervous breakdown and was in Dyer, Indiana. Do you have that information?"

"No."

"He was fooling around with the neighbor next door. You, I, and Butchie were sitting in the kitchen having breakfast, and the metal garbage can came flying through the window."

"I remember, how could you forget that?"

"See Duke, you're doing good." June said, commenting on the return of my memory.

"Well, that was pretty traumatic," I replied.

"Butchie was sitting in the wooden high chair," recalled June, "and it was in front of the table and it came crashing through, and at that time Mom was very fragile. She cried all the time. She was lonely. I don't think she had any friends. The woman's name, I believe, was Margaret, and they used to call her Maggie. She was thin, dark hair, her mother was heavy set, she had two brothers, and they were all in on this. Just tormenting Mom every time she went out. I don't know how he hooked up with Maggie. She might've been at Ducky Sloan's. He was coming home then, that was on Bensley, where we eventually moved.

"So Mom had to leave him just before that to get into the projects. We lived at 10629 South Yates Avenue."

"But before we moved to the projects," said June, "we came from Indiana and went to stay at Grandma's house on 8023 Marquette Avenue. Mom had a complete breakdown and Uncle Dave stepped in. Grandma came to take care of us, and they took her to that Dyer Hospital."

This was the home of my grandmother, Mary Savage, at 8023 Marquette Avenue, Chicago, Illinois.

"What was so special about Dyer?" I asked.

"I think they had the psychiatric hospital there. There were a lot of wealthy people, mostly school teachers, who had post-partum depression, and they couldn't feed their babies. They were there for shock treatment. That's where I think Mom had her first session of shock treatment. Grandma, we called her 'Beejana,' came and stayed with us. It seemed like a long time. I remember going to visit Mom, but I don't know who with. It might have been with Uncle Dave. I remember young girls walking around with their arms in straightjackets."

Left Alone in the Car, Dad's in the Bar

Another tavern my father frequented was near the Inland Steel employees' gate, near my grandmother's house in "The Bush," as the area was called.

June said, "It was a black neighborhood then. And it was mostly black people in the tavern. I would sit outside all day long. It was summer, and he would buy me hot dogs. I'd sit there with the little black kids, and we'd play. I'd sit in the car and I'd wait for him as he bought drinks for everyone all day long.

"How old were you?" I asked.

"Probably nine or ten."

I, too, recall one late summer afternoon when I was left sitting alone in his car, parked outside this very tavern. While he caroused with his friends inside, I amused myself by going through the car's glove box. That's when I discovered a deck of pictured playing cards. I was unprepared, as a pubescent twelve year old might be, for the compendium of naked female bodies that spilled in my lap. I got quite an unexpected education that evening, the night sky occasionally being dramatically lit up from the steel mills slag dumping. Luckily, I didn't totally drain the battery by leaving the car dome light on in order to digest fully this bewildering graphic display of private parts and sexual contortion. He never knew of my discovery. I never forgot it.

"It seems like from nine or ten, you have a lot of recollection of being around him, and him visiting," I said.

June continued, "He would come home really late, maybe it'd be 1:00 or 2:00 in the morning, and Mom had cleaned all day Saturday. You remember. The clothes would go out on a line, and she'd put newspapers on the floor after she had scrubbed. He would come home with pork chops, and he would fry them at 2:00 in the morning. The grease would be all over the stove. She never yelled at him, or screamed at him. I don't know if she was afraid of him or what. She would be upstairs, just thinking that he was cooking and there was grease everywhere, and she had just cleaned.... But, she wouldn't say anything. He would leave everything out, and then he would go to bed. He'd sleep most of the day.

I believe it was in the early '40s when my father lost all the toes on one foot in an accident while working as a railroad switchman. Later, this caused difficulty in walking. This worsened following a car accident in the '60s. He walked with a brace at the time of these pictures with an unidentified friend.

June's husband Alfonse Mora in front of their home in Lansing, Illinois, standing alongside my son's Ford Ranger F150 in the spring of 1981.

"On Sunday, he would get up and read his newspaper. She would get the newspaper. He'd have his buttermilk. He'd make a pot roast, potatoes, and gravy because he knew how to make gravy," June said. "Mom wasn't a good gravy maker. I don't think she ever tried making gravy. There was black cherry pop, and ice cream cake roll."

I wanted to know if he would leave then, after satisfying himself.

"No," she said, "Mom would do the dishes, and we would sit and watch TV."

My father had bought a Muntz black and white console TV. These first went on sale in 1947 and continued to be sold into the early '50s. We were counting the number of drop-in visitors, because we were the only family in Trumball Park with such a device. June surmised that we could determine the year this all occurred "because Gorgeous George wrestling was on. And that was on channel 9, and I believe it was Friday evenings, because the Hungarian lady loved Gorgeous George. [He, like Liberace, was Hungarian, and my mother's side of our family were all Hungarians. I believe her name was Anna Kovacs.] She would come over, and we would all watch Gorgeous George; Anna loved Gorgeous George." Gorgeous George's first TV wrestling appearance was in November 1947.

"Do you remember when he took you for your graduation suit?" June asked me.

"No." Obviously there were other occasions of bar hopping with a child in tow, and June was about to jog my memory.

June recalled that it must have been for my grammar school graduation, probably around 1952. Our father drove a Buick convertible — a green car with a beige top. The day was cold, but he left me waiting in the car while he stopped at one of the taverns. June thought it might have been one on Commercial Street, as she recalled it was the one near the Commercial Theatre, but on the opposite side of the street and up a little. My father didn't leave the car running, so I just about froze to death. During

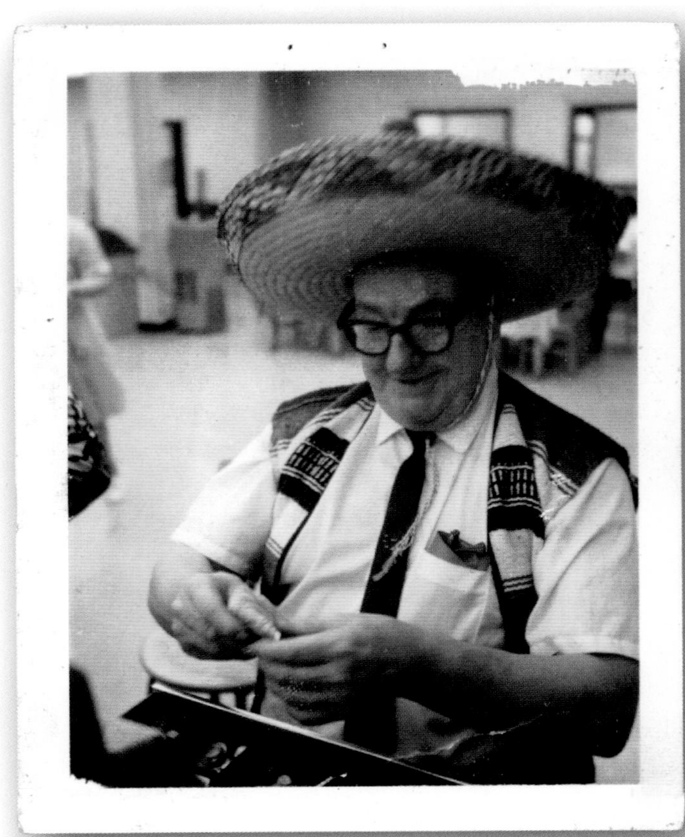

As Paul Gooch further described my father: "He drank a lot, played cards — euchre — when he'd come down to Fairmount. Everyone liked him and knew him as 'Cotton.'"

the several hours he was in there, he never came out to check on me. I didn't get my suit that day, and June said I didn't say too much when we got home. Uncle Dave ended up getting me the suit.

"How long did Dad stay?" I asked.

"He would go back Sunday night."

"How long did this go on? Months, years?"

"I think until Mom hooked up with Mervin," June answered.

"When do you think that happened?"

June paused, then said, "I started going with Al when I was fifteen. I was working at the telephone company, and that's when Al saw me. He didn't know I was fifteen, and I didn't know he was twenty-seven. Because I'd be dressed in heels, coming from work at the Hyde Park telephone company."

Apparently, 1955–1956 was something of a defining period for both my mother and sister. Mom was becoming entangled in what would be a four-year affair with a railroad man, and June would ultimately marry and divorce ten years later the father of her four children.

June was working, and Mom was busy with Mervin. So Dad sort of got pushed out of the picture, I surmised. I asked June when she recalled last seeing our father. She said she thought it was in the middle to late 1960s. "It was at a wake in Danville, Illinois, although I can't remember who the wake was for. My daughter Erin remembers meeting him, and she was born in 1959.

"But earlier than that, Dad came to see me after I had Erin, when I was living with Al, my first husband, and his mom. Dad was drunk, and he was living with some woman in Chicago at the time. He brought me receiving blankets. The visit wasn't very pleasant. I remember saying, 'If you can't come and visit sober, then you shouldn't come at all.' Then I didn't hear from him for a long time.

"When I was seeing Lee, Dad called to tell me he heard I was going with a Mafia guy, and that I should be careful. Dad was drunk then, too, and we got into a heated discussion. I hung up on him. He called back about a month later, saying he was working for Kodak or Bell & Howell."

I knew Kodak had bought Bell & Howell, so this was probably why my sister couldn't remember which company.

June continued, "He wanted my Social Security number, saying something about he needed it because he had about $3,000, and he wanted to make sure if something happened to him, I'd get it. But I didn't give him the information. I told him I didn't want his money, that he's never bothered to see his grandchildren. He said, 'Well, I've never been invited to Thanksgiving or Christmas. What kind of daughter are you?' I said, 'It comes down to this, Dad, if it's a choice between you and Mom, I have to take Mom, and her wishes are that she doesn't want you here.' And that was the end of it. That was the last time I spoke to him."

"Wasn't there a time when you asked him for some money?"

June thought. "That was for our brother Butchie. He and his wife Ginger stayed with Mom for a while, then they came and stayed with me. They weren't getting along. I told Butchie they should go back to California and try to work things out. So I called Dad and said that Butchie was here and he's having a hard time. They needed to go back to California and could he give him $200. He claimed he didn't have $200. I got mad and said,

Clyde Otis Davis in his last known photo, summer 1974, Dietz Lake Beach Club, Inc., Center Point, Indiana

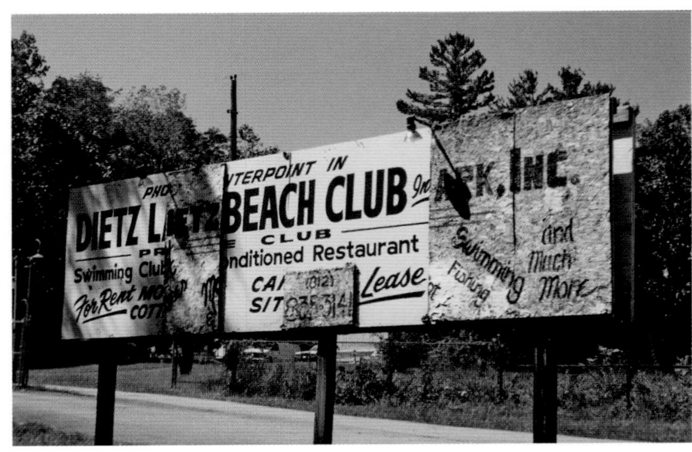

Clyde Davis, Former Fairmount Resident, Dies

Clyde "Cotton" Davis, 67, former Fairmount resident, died Nov. 13 in a hospital in Kokomo, Ind., after an illness.

Services were held Nov. 16 at Fairmount with Rev. Berton Heleine officiating and burial was in Greenview Cemetery.

Born June 3, 1907, he was a son of Charles and Rebecca Gooch Davis. He was formerly employed with Bell & Howell Company in Chicago.

Mr. Davis is survived by a sister of Lafayette, Ind.

'You've never supported him. You've never given him anything in your life, and you can't give him $200?' I don't remember what he said, but I told him to forget it, and I hung up. I scraped up some money and gave it to Butchie, and they went back to California."

I spoke with Violet Davis of Hobart, Indiana, in 2003. Violet, the wife of Joseph "Larry Joe" Davis, who is the son of my father's brother Roy, recalled my father walking with a cane. He'd had an automobile accident in the 1960s. He was driving his convertible and had been drinking. It was night time, and as he drove over a hill, he was on the wrong side of the road. He struck an oncoming vehicle. No one died, but the driver of the other car lost an eye.

Kay recalls a family gathering that she attended. She was in a car with June and our father, who was using a cane because of the accident to his foot. Some of our children were along, and perhaps Erin. "We went to a country house and ate stuffed cabbage with a group of about twenty people. In the backyard were rabbits and one of the children had an incident with them."

Michelle Schmal's letter to me (see page 272) is an example of how we knew whom we were visiting and when. As Michelle wrote, "Remembering those days, I always knew what the meal of the day would probably be by which relative we would be visiting."

Notes

1. Phone call to LaVerne Purkey, Reno, Nevada, February 19, 2003.

Clyde Davis, Former Fairmount Resident, Dies

Clyde "Cotton" Davis, 67, former Fairmount resident, died November 13, 1974, at 6:30 pm, at St. Joseph's Hospital in Kokomo, Ind., after an illness. Mr. Davis suffered from diabetes and a heart condition. Mr. Davis was living in Lafayette, Ind., prior to his hospitalization.

Born June 3, 1907, he was a son of Charles and Rebecca Gooch Davis. He was formerly employed with Bell & Howell Company in Chicago, and at one time, was the proprietor of Clyde's Tavern in Lafayette, Ind.

Mr. Davis was married on January 23, 1937 to Mary M. Savage in Danville, Ill. They were the parents of three children. He is survived by his estranged wife Mary; his two sons Clyde Patrick Davis of Pound Ridge, N. Y., and David O. Davis of West Covina, Calif.; his daughter Mrs. June Mora of Lansing, Ill.; a sister, Elizabeth Purkey, of Lafayette, Ind.; and nine grandchildren, Christine, Cynthia, and Cole Davis of Pound Ridge, N. Y.; Erin, April, Alfonse, and David Mora of Lansing, Ill.; Scott Ryan Davis of Washington State; and Shelley Davis of California. He is also survived by several nieces and nephews.

Mr. Davis was preceded in death by his parents and a brother, Roy.

Services were held November 16 at Fairmount with Rev. Berton Holeine officiating, and burial was in Greenview Cemetery.

The two obituaries above are an accounting of my father's life. The version on the left is his actual obituary, his life as he wished it to be known. The version on the right is an obituary I prepared, a facsimile of the life I wish my father had lived, acknowledging all those who could have been a part of that life.

Clyde Otis Davis Timeline

November 12, 1929

Located in the 1930 U.S. Census — a prisoner in the Jackson Prison, Wayne County, Michigan. **Clyde Davis, Serial # 25666. Crime:** Assault to rob being armed. **Sentenced:** 11–12–29. **Term:** 7½ – 15 years. **Received:** 11-12-29 from Wayne. (When arrested he was 20 years old, weighed 150 pounds, ht. 5' 9½", eyes blue, hair blond, build medium). **Occupation:** Machine operator. **Residence:** Dearborn, Mich. **Remarks:** Paroled to Thorton, Ill., 11–19–34. **Discharged for parole:** 11–25–35.

June 3, 1907

Born Catlin, Vermilion County, Illinois.

May 13, 1910

U.S. Census, State of Illinois, Vermilion County, Pilot township, Clyde Davis was enumerated as a son, age 3, b. Illinois of Charles and Rebecca Davis (ED 18, Sheet 12B, Line 48).

January 14, 1920

U.S. Census, State of Illinois, Vermilion County, Vance township, Fairmount Village, "Clide" Clyde Davis appears, age 12, with his father Charles and mother Rebecca. (ED 208, Sheet 9, Line 58).

November 25, 1936

Application for Social Security Account Number: 336–01–1635 Residence: 8920 Commercial Avenue, Chicago, Illinois, and was employed by Carnegie Illinois Steel Corp., at 3426 East 89th Street, Chicago, Illinois.

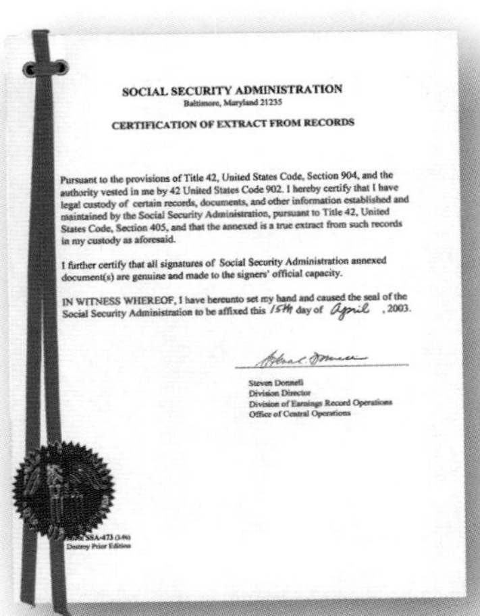

SOCIAL SECURITY ADMINISTRATION
Baltimore, Maryland 21235

CERTIFICATION OF EXTRACT FROM RECORDS

Pursuant to the provisions of Title 42, United States Code, Section 904, and the authority vested in me by 42 United States Code 902. I hereby certify that I have legal custody of certain records, documents, and other information established and maintained by the Social Security Administration, pursuant to Title 42, United States Code, Section 405, and that the annexed is a true extract from such records in my custody as aforesaid.

I further certify that all signatures of Social Security Administration annexed document(s) are genuine and made to the signers' official capacity.

IN WITNESS WHEREOF, I have hereunto set my hand and caused the seal of the Social Security Administration to be affixed this 15th day of April, 2003.

Steven Donnell
Division Director
Division of Earnings Record Operations
Office of Central Operations

SSA-473 (3-96)
Destroy Prior Edition

January 23, 1937

Married, age 29, Mary Savage, age 20, Danville Illinois. Place of residence: Chicago, Illinois.

March 17, 1938

Birth, Clyde Patrick Davis, son. Residence 8545 Mackinaw, Chicago, Illinois. Age: 30, Trade/Profession: "switchman," last Carnegie, Ill. Steel Co. — 1 year ow (out-of-work) June '37.

May 4, 1940

Birth, June Mary Davis, daughter. Residence 8227 Saginaw, Chicago, Illinois. Occupation: railroad flagman, Carnegie, Illinois.

1943

Telephone directory for Chicago, Illinois, lists Clyde O. Davis 6629 Drexal HYD Pk-6912 (Source: South Suburban Genealogical & Historical Society, Hazel Crest, Illinois, August 13, 2010).

December 26, 1945

Birth, David Otis Davis, son. Residence 10629 S. Yates Ave., Chicago, Illinois.

(continued on next page)

Clyde Otis Davis Timeline

1948

Polk's *Lafayette City Directory, Tippecanoe County, Indiana, Including West Lafayette, Buyer's Guide and a Complete Classified Directory*, Tippecanoe County Historical Assoc., 10th & South Streets, Lafayette, Indiana, page 151, — Clyde O Bartndr Laf Country Club r2412 Butler.

1950

Polk's *Lafayette City Directory, Tippecanoe County, Indiana, Including West Lafayette, Buyer's Guide and a Complete Classified Directory*, Tippecanoe County Historical Assoc., 10th & South Streets, Lafayette, Indiana, page 140, — Clyde O tavern 501 Columbia r2412 Butler.

1950s

Residence Maryland Hotel, 67th and Stony Island Blvd, Chicago, Illinois.

January, 1951

Telephone directory for Lafayette, Indiana, Associated Telephone Corporation, Tippecanoe County Public Library, 627 South Street, Lafayette, Indiana, "Yellow Pages," Taverns, page 136, CLYDE'S TAVERN, 501 Columbia... 8028 [phone].

1953

Polk's *Lafayette City Directory, Tippecanoe County, Indiana, Including West Lafayette, Buyer's Guide and a Complete Classified Directory*, Tippecanoe County Historical Assoc., 10th & South Streets, Lafayette, Indiana, page 132, — Clyde O tavern 501 Columbia r1708 N 17th.

January, 1954

Telephone directory for Lafayette, General Telephone Company of Indiana, Inc. Tippecanoe County Public Library, 627 South Street, Lafayette, Indiana, "Yellow Pages," Taverns, page 139, CLYDE'S TAVERN 501 Columbia... 2-9465 [phone].

1955

Polk's *Lafayette City Directory, Tippecanoe County, Indiana, Including West Lafayette, Buyer's Guide and a Complete Classified Directory*, Tippecanoe County Historical Assoc., 10th & South Streets, Lafayette, Indiana, page 91, COLUMBIA - Contd, 501 Charlie's Tavern. Apparently Clyde Otis Davis sold his tavern. By 1957, 501 Columbia was occupied by Swartz TV Home Improvement.

December 21, 1959

Per Violet Davis in conversation on Feb. 18, 2003, and her letter to me of Dec. 19, 2005: Violet confirmed that "On the 21st (Dec. 1959), my youngest son Rick was born. The doctor told me I could go home on Christmas day if I didn't do anything but take care of him. So Larry came and got me. He and your Dad (Clyde) fixed Christmas dinner." She added that they had duck with stuffing. He helped clean up the dishes as well. He often stopped by when in the area. She would make fried green tomatoes for him and her husband. "Your dad, Clyde, worked in hotel bars — a happy person, kids liked him. He drank at the house barbeque."

August 23, 1967

Residence of Peggy Phillips, 1827 W. Cermak, Chicago, Illinois 60608. Per letter to Mr. & Mrs. Hobart Smith, Fairmount, Illinois[1], may have lived with Clyde. See page 400 for additional information.

November 13, 1974

Died age 68. St. Joseph Hospital, Kokomo, Howard County, Indiana. Place of residence per death certificate: 3585 Greenbush St., Lafayette, Indiana, Tippecanoe County: Buried: Greenview Cemetery, Fairmount, Illinois.

1970s

Residence Damon? and 25th or 26th Street, Chicago, Illinois. Per Vondell Davis. Lived in back of building, 2nd floor when her husband picked him up for card games at Legion Hall.

1974

Family Season Membership Card. No. 1988B 1974, Dietz Lake Beach Club, Inc., R.R. 2, Center Point, Indiana 47840, 812–835–3141. Member's Address: Chicago, Illinois

1. Letter to Mr. and Mrs. Hobart Smith, Fairmount, Illinois, from Peggy Phillips, 1827 W. Cermack, Chicago, Illinois 60608, postmarked "Chicago p.m. 23 Aug 1964."

THE COMMISSIONER OF SOCIAL SECURITY
BALTIMORE, MARYLAND 21235

MAY 1 3 1986

Refer to:
SEP62
336-01-1635

Honorable Alfonse M. D'Amato
United States Senate
Washington, D.C. 20510

Dear Senator D'Amato:

This is in response to your inquiry of April 29, 1986 concerning the whereabouts of Mr. Clyde O. Davis. Mr. Clyde Davis had written to you about his father.

We regret to inform you that our records show that Mr. Davis died in November 1974.

Sincerely,

Martha A. McSteen
Acting Commissioner

INDIANA STATE BOARD OF HEALTH
MEDICAL CERTIFICATE OF DEATH

Local No. 74-593 — State No. 74-040550

PERMANENT INK SEE HANDBOOK FOR INSTRUCTIONS

DECEASED
1. Deceased—Name: First Clyde; Middle O.; Last Davis
2. Sex: M
3. Date of death (month, day, year): 11/13/74
4. Race: White
5a. Age—last birthday (years): 67
5b. Under 1 year: Mos. Days
5c. Under 1 day: Hours Min.
6. Date of birth (month, day, year): 6/13/1907
7a. County of death: Howard
7b. City, town, or location of death: St. Joseph Hospital Kokomo, Ind.
7c. Inside city limits (specify yes or no): Yes
7d. Hospital or other institution—name (if not in either, give street and number): St. Joseph Hospital
8. State of birth (if not in U.S.A., name country): Illinois
9. Citizen of what country: U.S.A.
10. Married ☐ Never married ☐ Widowed ☐ Divorced ☒
11. Surviving spouse (if wife, give maiden name):
12. Social security number: —
13a. Usual occupation (give kind of work done during most of working life, even if retired): Bartender Retired
13b. Kind of business or industry: —

USUAL RESIDENCE WHERE DECEASED LIVED. IF DEATH OCCURRED IN INSTITUTION, GIVE RESIDENCE BEFORE ADMISSION.
14a. Residence—State: Ind.
14b. County: Tippecanoe
14c. City, town or location: Lafayette, Ind
14d. Inside city limits (specify yes or no): yes
14e. Township: —
14f. Street and number: 3585 Greenbush St.
14g. Was deceased ever in U.S. armed forces? (Yes, no, or unknown) (If yes, give war or dates of service): No
14h. Is residence on a farm? Yes ☐ No ☒

PARENTS
15. Father—Name: First Charles; Middle —; Last Davis
16. Mother—Maiden name: First Rebecca; Middle; Last Gooch
17a. Informant—Name: Glenn Purkey
17b. Relationship: Nephew
17c. Mailing address (street or R.F.D. no., city or town, state, zip): 1101 Witherspoon Dr. Kokomo, In.

CAUSE
18. Part I. Death was caused by: (Enter only one cause per line for (a), (b), and (c)) — Approximate interval between onset and death
Immediate cause (a) aspiration of vomitus
Conditions, if any, which gave rise to immediate cause (a), stating the underlying cause last:
Due to, or as a consequence of: (b) Congestive heart failure
Due to, or as a consequence of: (c)
Part II. Other significant conditions (conditions contributing to death but not related to cause given in Part I (a)): Diabetic acidosis
19a. Autopsy: Yes ☐ No ☒
19b. If yes were findings considered in determining cause of death: Yes ☐ No ☐

M. D. OR D. O.
11-13-1974 6:30 P.M. — 11-13-1974
20. Date & time of death: Month 11; Day 13; Year 1974; Hour 6:30 a.m.
21a. Date signed: Month 11; Day 13; Year 74
22a. Physician's name (type or print) last in attendance: Dr. Don J. Wagoner
22b. Signature of physician: [signature] M.D.
Phy. code no.
23. Mailing address—physician (street or R.F.D. no, city or town, state, zip): 2016 W. Sycamore St. Kokomo, Indiana 46901

DISPOSITION
24a. Burial, cremation, removal (specify): Burial
24b. Cemetery, crematory, funeral home: Greenview Cem.
24c. Location (city or town, state): Fairmount, Illinois
24d. Date (month, day, year): 11/16/74
25a. Funeral home—name and address (street or R.F.D. no., city or town, state, zip): Carrington Funeral Home-Fairmount, Ill
25b.
26a. Health officer signature: [signature] M.D.
26b. Date received by local health officer: NOV 1 4 1974

113-3

ALFONSE M. D'AMATO
NEW YORK

United States Senate
WASHINGTON, DC 20510

May 22, 1986

Mr. Clyde P. Davis
Tatomuck Road
Pound Ridge, New York 10576

Dear Mr. Davis:

I regret to inform you that the Social Security Administration records show your father passed away in November of 1974. I am sorry that the results of my efforts could not have been more pleasant.

Sincerely,

Alfonse D'Amato
United States Senator

AD:li
Enclosure

Clyde Davis, Former Fairmount Resident, Dies

Clyde "Cotton" Davis, 67, former Fairmount resident, died Nov. 13 in a hospital in Kokomo, Ind., after an illness.

Services were held Nov. 16 at Fairmount with Rev. Barton Heleine officiating and burial was in Greenview Cemetery.

Born June 3, 1907, he was a son of Charles and Rebecca Gooch Davis. He was formerly employed with Bell & Howell Company in Chicago.

Mr. Davis is survived by a sister of Lafayette, Ind.

PS Form 3800, June 1985 ★ U.S.G.P.O. 1985-480-794

P 409 356 913

RECEIPT FOR CERTIFIED MAIL
NO INSURANCE COVERAGE PROVIDED
NOT FOR INTERNATIONAL MAIL
(See Reverse)

Sent to
Street and No.
P.O., State and ZIP Code
Postage
Certified Fee
Special Delivery Fee
Restricted Delivery Fee
Return Receipt showing to whom and Date Delivered
Return Receipt showing to whom, Date, and Address of Delivery
TOTAL Postage and Fees
Postmark or Date

DAVIS
CLYDE O. JUNE 3,1907 NOV. 13, 1974
ROY L. MAR.20,1890 JUNE 6, 1971

Headstone of brothers Clyde O., b. June 3, 1907, d. November 13, 1974, and Roy L. Davis, b. March 20, 1890, d. June 6, 1971, Greenview Cemetery, Fairmount, Illinois

Clyde Otis Davis Family

THIS IS MARY
AND HER
LITTLE
GIRL

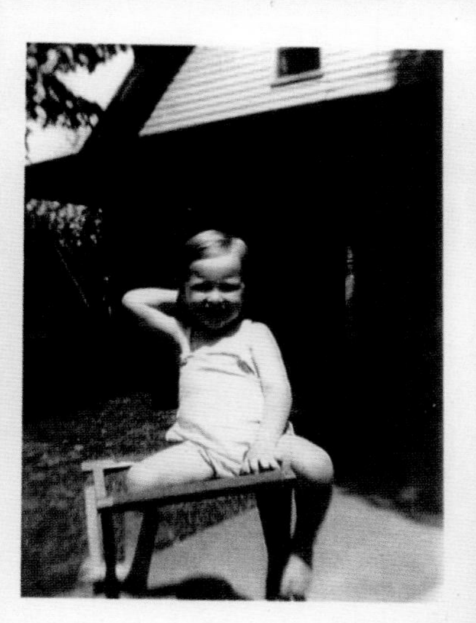

"Duke" in the above pictures at age 2–3 years?

Dukey & June
when they stayed
with mom.

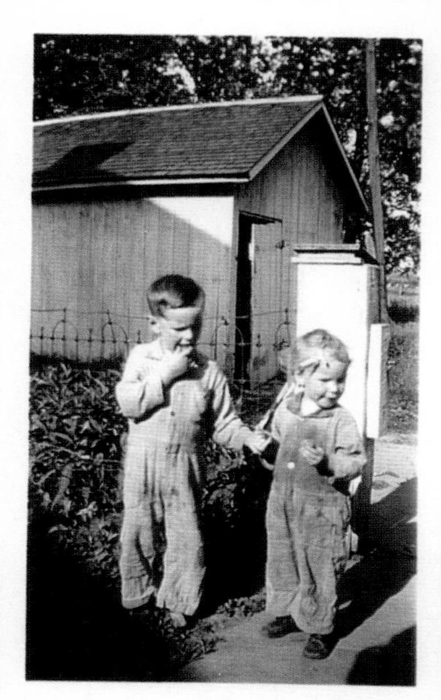

The photograph of me sitting in my father's lap and my sister June in my mother's lap is one of only two photographs in my possession, or known to me, of my father and mother with their children together at one time.
To my knowledge, neither my father nor my mother ever in their lifetime owned a camera.

Mom with June and me on the day of their first Communion (St. Kevin's Roman Catholic Church, 105th and Torrance Avenue). This photograph was taken at the rear of our home at 10629 South Yates Avenue, Chicago, Illinois.

This one is very cute. Duckie & June at Moms house

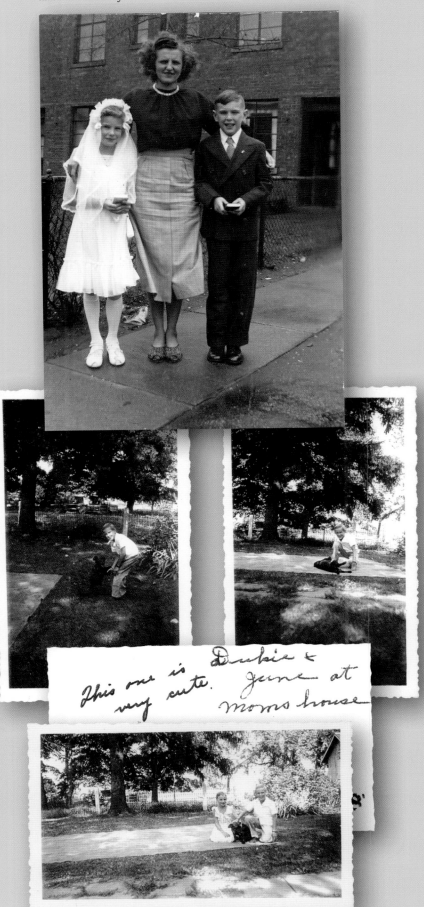

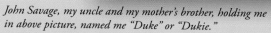

John Savage, my uncle and my mother's brother, holding me in above picture, named me "Duke" or "Dukie."

A visit to my former home at 10629 South Yates Avenue (Trumbull Park Homes Project), Chicago, Illinois. Rear of building depicted in above photos, May 26, 1986. To my right in top picture is the kitchen window and rear door, and above them, left to right, the bathroom and rear bedroom windows.

Bottom photo shows me pointing to my name painted on the side of the building as a youngster, surprisingly still intact some fifty years later. At what age I'm not sure, but I do recall the paint came from my painting a small kitchen corner shelf, which held a radio and was made by my mother's boyfriend. Mom's favorite color (and mine) is yellow. The "D" was for "Duke." The wooden enclosure with graffiti was not there at the time of my handiwork.

The three pictures on the left page were taken at Lake Michigan beach. In the bottom pictures, I am with my cousin Michael and sister June "Tootsie." In the picture at bottom left, we are with Michael's mother, Aunt Ella Savage, and at bottom right we are with Aunt June (Julia) Savage Lucas, my mother's sister.

My Mother

Mary M. Savage Davis

Born November 27, 1917

"Spare Ribs," My Mother

It's 10:49 A.M. on February 21, 2003. We've just returned from our morning run, and there's a message on the answering machine. It's Maria, my mom's caregiver. "Hi Clyde, this is Maria. I'm calling because your mom, she has high fever." (Maria's a Polish immigrant and hasn't quite mastered English grammar.) "It's 108 degrees, and I'm calling 911, and they going to take her to hospital. I don't know which one. I'm calling you later. Have a nice day, bye."

This is Mom's seventh or eighth hospitalization in the past twelve months, from a simple urinary tract infection to pneumonia. She's also had a minor heart attack requiring angioplasty and a stent to prevent future narrowing or blockage of one of her coronary arteries. Yet she has managed to survive these episodes, being more upbeat and up for anything after each event. She still wants to come down and be with us in Florida. She still talks of going to Hawaii, and has been enjoying her new townhome in Orland Park, Illinois.

As I wait for the details of today's hospitalization, hoping everything will, once again, turn out well, I'm filled with thoughts about her. It's not easy to think of my mother without first confronting the "life she's lived."

Mary Savage Davis was born November 27, 1917. Her mother, also Mary, was a seamstress and housekeeper. Her father, a steelworker, suffered from depression. Both emigrated from Hungary to the United States in 1907. Mom was not the youngest of her four brothers and one sister, yet she seems to have been the most fragile among them. A highly sensitive woman, slight of figure most of her life, so much so she was called "Spare Ribs" by other family members. Only a younger brother is alive today. This fragility has been a paramount aspect of her entire adult life. Mom was strong enough physically, but has suffered from a pertinacious, unyielding depression, probably since the birth of my younger brother David in 1946. She has been under psychiatric care almost continuously since then. She has been institutionalized, been prescribed every psychotropic medication contrived, and endured numerous sessions of electroshock treatment (ECT) when her condition worsened beyond the reach of other remedies. This condition permeated her family. As mentioned, her father was depressed. Her brother Michael was treated for depression, and both he and his son received electroshock treatment. Her sister June committed suicide.

The combination of difficult social circumstances, a number of disturbing events and changes in her life, combined with biological causes associated with manic-depressive illness, overwhelmed her time and again.

My father was paroled from Jackson Prison, Wayne County, Michigan, on November 25, 1935, after serving seven years for "assault with intent to rob." My father first applied for a Social Security card on November 25, 1936. He was twenty-nine years of age at the time and living at 8920 Commercial Avenue in South Chicago. As my mother confirmed in February 2008, this was their first home after their marriage, a one-room apartment with a two-burner stove. Obviously, my father resided at this address prior to their marriage, and my mother was to join him there as his spouse.

My mother and father had married January 23, 1937. They had met at a fish fry at The Greenbay Street Tavern directly behind my mom's home at 8227 Saginaw in Chicago. Mom was working there, and workers from the steel mill would stop in the tavern before going home after their work shift. Fourteen months later I came along.

Due to my limited memory, I cannot contribute much about the early years of my mother's life, and today she is reluctant to talk about it much. I don't recall moments of mother-son bonding, probably because my sister and I were often left with other relatives during our adolescent years, often for extended periods of time. Much of the affection, closeness, and intimacy normally accorded a maternal relationship eluded us.

This book is about finding fathers, and I don't want to skew its intent by overly dwelling on the difficulties of my mother's life.

But, I'm obligated to acknowledge for all who bother to delve into this life retrospection, that she cared for her children, that she provided for them in her way, despite the hopelessness and sense of reduced emotional well-being that consumed her life.

This woman, used and then abandoned by the man she married, will tell you stories of how she'd stolen bottles of milk left at her neighbors' apartment door steps when she had none, nor the money to buy milk. This woman stood in lines with me (this I remember) waiting for government handouts of brick butter, cheese, and a sack of potatoes. This woman sought and secured federal housing and financial aid for her children.

This woman took unending bus rides with her children from her beloved Trumball Park Homes to the University of Chicago Hospital Clinics. This woman kept her children healthy, in school, and free of the social stigma surrounding a family on welfare without a father, while confronting and coping with her own emotional needs.

Mom with Tootsie and me

Ultimately, my mother broke off her failing relationship with my father during the early '50s and entered into a relationship with a married man. This was not, in hindsight, very surprising given the life she's lived. As my sister June tells it, my mother was seeing this man "a couple of years" before June graduated from grammar school in January 1954 at age thirteen. According to June, it was during this period that Mom made the break with our father "because I think she knew something was going on; he was fooling around. He always had a woman. So when she went down there [Lafayette?], it kind of reinforced her opinion of him, thinking he's a loser, he's never going to change, and I've got this guy and maybe he's going to marry me."

During my last couple of years in high school and at least two years in college, my mother continued to carry on with this other man in her life. But I wasn't home much over those years. I met Kay in 1954, and between our falling in love and being inseparable, high school swim team

(continued on page 54)

MARY M. SAVAGE DAVIS b. November 27, 1917

Mary Davis with June "Tootsie." Written on back: "This is Mary and her little girl."

CERTIFICATE OF BIRTH

STATE OF ILLINOIS
DWIGHT H. GREEN, Governor
Department of Public Health—
Division of Vital Statistics
ORIGINAL

1. PLACE OF BIRTH
County of Cook
Chicago
Registration Dist. No. 3104 — 62556
Primary Dist. No. 3104
Street and Number 8553 Mackinaw Ave CHICAGO ILL.

FULL NAME AT BIRTH Mary Savage

Sex Male · 4. Twin, Triplet, or other? · 5. Number or order of birth 5-th · 6. Legitimate? YES · 7. Date of birth Nov 27 1917 (Month) (Day) (Year)

FATHER
Full Name Andrew Savage
Residence at time of this birth 8553 Mackinaw Chicago Ill
Color White · 11. Age at time of this birth 35 yrs.
Birthplace (City or Place) (Name State, if in U. S.) (Name Country, if Foreign) Hungary
Occupation (Nature of Industry) Machinist

MOTHER
14. Full Maiden Name Mary Benko
15. Residence at time of this birth 8553 Mackinaw Chicago Ill.
16. Color White · 17. Age at time of this birth 33 yrs.
18. Birthplace (City or Place) (Name State, if in U. S.) (Name Country, if Foreign) Hungary
19. Occupation (Nature of Industry) Housewife

(a) Number of children born to this mother at the time of and including this birth 5
(b) Number of children living at the time of and including this birth 5

I HEREBY CERTIFY that I was the Attendant at this Birth.
Signed Mrs Lorkman · This space only for signature of Dead Physician Midwife
Address Deceased · Date (Month) (Day) (Year)

IF SIGNATURE OF BIRTH ATTENDANT IS OBTAINABLE, AN AFFIDAVIT IS NOT REQUIRED.

State of ILLINOIS } ss.
County of Cook

I HEREBY CERTIFY that I have knowledge of the facts as stated in this RECORD OF BIRTH and believe them to be true; that I am related to this person as Mother
Signature Mary Savage
Present Address 8553 Mackinaw Ave
Subscribed to, and sworn before me this 2ND day of August 1943
[illegible] Notary Public
SEAL
My commission expires Feb. 17 1947
Filed AUG 4 [illegible] Registrar
Post Office Address

Mary Savage Davis. Back of photograph reads: "Momie. April 1953. Place: at home."

CERTIFICATION OF VITAL RECORD

VERMILION COUNTY, ILLINOIS

Marriage License

No. 47400

The People of the State of Illinois, Vermilion County

To any person Legally authorized to solemnize marriage—Greeting:

Marriage May Be Celebrated

Between Mr. Clyde Davis of Chicago in the County of Cook and State of Illinois of the age of 29 years, and Mary Savage of Chicago in the County of Cook and State of Illinois of the age of 20 years, the of the said having given assent to said marriage.

Witness, V. M. JONES, County Clerk, and the Seal of said County at his office in Danville, in said County, This 23 day of January A. D. 1937

V. M. Jones County Clerk

By Catherine J. Wratzke Deputy

STATE OF ILLINOIS, Vermilion County, } ss. I, Henry P. Brown Justice of the Peace hereby certify that Mr. Clyde Davis and M Miss Mary Savage were united in marriage by me at Danville in the County of Vermilion and State of Illinois, on the 23 day of January A. D. 1937

Henry P. Brown

Justice of the Peace

NOTE: Names in this certificate must be the same as names in License above. Also refer to note on reverse side.

It is the duty of the person celebrating the Marriage to fill out and sign the above Certificate, and to return the same, together with the License, to the County Clerk within THIRTY DAYS AFTER THE MARRIAGE IS SOLEMNIZED. ONE HUNDRED DOLLARS PENALTY FOR FAILING TO DO SO.

CERTIFIED COPY OF VITAL RECORDS

STATE OF ILLINOIS
COUNTY OF VERMILION } ss

DATE ISSUED July 16, 1997

This is to certify that this is a true and correct abstract from the official record filed with the County Clerk of Vermilion County, Illinois. Not valid without the embossed seal of Vermilion County, Illinois.

Lynn Foster
LYNN FOSTER
VERMILION COUNTY CLERK

This copy not valid unless prepared on border displaying seal and signature of County Clerk.

ANY ALTERATION OR ERASURE VOIDS THIS CERTIFICATE

47400

MARRIAGE LICENSE

Mr. Clyde Davis

With

M Mary Savage

Issued Jan 23 1937

FILED

FEB 1 1937

NOTE

This license can only be used in Vermilion County, Illinois.

Must be returned to the County Clerk, Danville, Illinois, within 30 days after ceremony is performed.

If not used, return immediately.

Marriage Register 11 Page 146

This Return is to be carefully filled out and returned with the Marriage License. This return does not take the place of the certificate which must be attached to the license, but is IN ADDITION THERETO.

Illinois State Board of Health

RETURN OF A MARRIAGE TO COUNTY CLERK

1. Full Name of Groom Clyde Davis
2. Place of Residence Chicago Ill
3. Occupation Labor
4. Age next Birthday 30 years. Color or race W
5. Place of Birth Eaton Ga
6. Father's Name Clyde Davis
7. Mother's Maiden Name Elvira Gooch
8. Number of Groom's Marriage First
9. Full Name of Bride Mary Savage
   Maiden Name if Widow
10. Place of Residence Chicago Ill
11. Age next Birthday 21 years. Color or race W
12. Place of Birth Chicago Ill
13. Father's Name Andrew Savage
14. Mother's Maiden Name Ag Buck
15. Number of Bride's Marriage First
16. Married at Danville
    County of Vermilion, and State of Illinois, the 23- day of January 1937
17. Witnesses to Marriage Mrs Ethel Shipps
    Mr C. W. Shipps

N. B.—At Nos. 8 and 15 state whether 1st, 2nd, 3rd, etc., marriage of each. At 17 give names of subscribing witnesses to the Marriage Certificate. If no subscribing witnesses, give names of two persons who witnessed the ceremony.

We hereby Certify that the information above given is correct to the best of our knowledge and belief.

Clyde Davis Groom
Mary Savage Bride

I hereby Certify that the above is a correct return of a marriage solemnized by me

Henry P. Brown
Justice of the Peace

Dated at Danville Ill 1937
this 23 day of January

PLEASE DO NOT WRITE BEYOND THIS LINE.

This Certifies

that

Clyde Davis and Mary Savage

of Chicago of Chicago

State of Ill State of Ill

were united in

Holy Matrimony

At Danville
Vermilion County, Illinois

According to the ORDINANCE OF GOD and the Laws of the State of Illinois, on the 23d day of January in the Year of OUR LORD, One Thousand Nine Hundred and Thirty Seven

WITNESSES

Mrs Ethel Shipps
Mr C. W. Shipps

Henry P. Brown
Justice of the Peace

MARY M. SAVAGE DAVIS b. November 27, 1917

MARY DAVIS

A UNITED LETTER

December 1, 1943.

Dear Sis.

I suppose you will be suprise to hear from me. I dont know what Clyde told you when he took the children down to your place. Well here is the story. My mother is very sick she has Sugar Diebeatis. Her blood pressure is two hundred the doctor. said she could get a stroke anytime. She has to have it very quiet. So the Social worker dideced instead of putting them in a nursery we thought it would be better to send them out there tempearly.

I have been trying to get in a Government Home you get three rooms gas and light heat for sixteen dollars a month. The Social worke from this place is going to write to you. Because she thinks Clyde is paying you or me. I told her he wasn't paying me or you. I'll maybe get this place by the first of the year. Then I will

STATIONERY FURNISHED BY UNITED SPECIALTIES COMPANY TO ENCOURAGE WRITING OF LETTERS TO OUR EMPLOYEES IN THE ARMED FORCES

come and get them when I get this place. I don't think Clyde will ever get out of debt. He gets into every day deeper. But you know I could be dirty and make him pay for them. But when they come back he'll have to pay for them. I don't care if he owes a million.

I'll send June's old Snow suit and some of her under wear. I'll get them some shoes when I come down for Christmas. maybe earlier I'm not feeling well I lost a lot of weight. Tell Dukie and June to be good kids. I'm sending her some gum she's crazy about it. I sure miss them.

Well I will close please answer when you get my letter.

Mary

Write the letter to
Miss Betty De Young
11406 Forest
Chgo Ill

Mary Davis 11406 Forest Ave,
Chgo Ill

SPECIALTIES COMPANY
COTTAGE GROVE AVENUE
CHICAGO, ILLINOIS

CHICAGO DEC 21 8 PM 1943 ILL.

US POSTAGE 1c

INDUSTRY AGRICULTURE FOR DEFENSE

BUY WAR SAVINGS BONDS AND STAMPS

Mrs E. Purkey
2412 Butler St.
Lafayette Ind.

"Duke,

This letter is from your mother to your Aunt Lizzie when you were just 5 years old. She and your Dad did not find raising children an easy job. They didn't know what to do with you and didn't know what to do without you. Ha! You & June spent quite a lot of time in Indiana. You were both such little cuties."

— LaVerne Purkey

Mom confirmed (February 16, 2008) that she attended J.N. Thorpe Elementary School at 89th and Superior Avenue. She "hated" school, but as one can see, she certainly had beautiful penmanship.

Often I'm asked if I've ever come across anyone in the family who had artistic talent. I have not, as I usually respond; however, my mother's handwriting may be, until now, an indication of a talent that went largely unrealized, yet passed on to me.

Elizabeth "Lizzie" Davis Purkey

practice, and going off to the University of Illinois down state, I was hardly home. Summers I spent with my grandmother and worked for my Uncle Vic's company, Universal Music.

I knew Mom's paramour more by the things he did for her than through personal contact. Before him, I was the man of the house. I'd cut the lawn, groom the flowerbeds, vacuum the furniture, and wax the tile floors throughout the house. Now it was he who built the kitchen corner shelf that she placed her radio on, and it was he who also built an outdoor bench for the back terrace. June remembered "he did things with her that caused her to think that she died and went to heaven. He baked, he cooked, he cleaned…they held hands. He was very romantic. All those things she never really had."

Mervin was a handsome man. And big. June agreed, "It was like Sean Connery came into her life." He looked like Randolph Scott when Randolph Scott was young.

This affair, lasting nearly six years (1952-1958) was to end tragically. Her lover returned to his wife and family, and my mother was once again alone and on her own. She continued to

Mary Savage Davis in front of her residence at 10624 South Bensly Avenue, Chicago, Illinois, watering lawn in a photo stamped "Sept 1982" on the back

live in the housing project. My sister was married and about to have her first child, Erin. My brother David was still at home and would soon quit high school and join the Marine Corps at age seventeen. I was to see my mother infrequently after my marriage. I didn't own my first car until I was twenty-four, and trips to Chicago from school were costly. Later, from New York, they were beyond affordability. I earned $75 a week in 1963 and rent was $135 a month, plus commutation costs, and three young children. Mom certainly was in no position to take up the slack.

Sometime before 1974, we managed to fund a trip for my mother to our home on Trinity Pass in Pound Ridge, New York. Kay used our rent money to take Mom shopping, buying her a new coat, slacks, blouses — for she had nothing. Her stay was aborted though at a summer's evening meal. With the sun streaming in the dining room window and my family gathered around the table, I casually mentioned her getting a job, now that all her children were gone. After all, my mom had only worked for a short period at Swifton Company in Chicago. Other than employment as a housekeeper, she never held another full-time job. Gradually over the years, Mom had become dependent on the system. Living on state and federal aid had become a way of life, a security blanket that she continues to wrap herself in to this day. A husband may abandon her, lovers may come and go, children may grow distant, but there will always be the certainty of financial government aid.

Mom's response to my suggestion was one of anger. She left, bolting from the table, saying she wished to leave for Chicago immediately and retired to her room. She departed New York the next day. Kay remembers looking for the clothes she had purchased for my mother, wondering if in her anger, she had left them behind, half thinking she could return the garments and get our rent money back, but Mom had taken them. I didn't see, speak, nor hear from my mother for nearly seven years, from 1975–1982.

So Why Haven't You Called?

One evening, in 1982, the phone rang. Ironically, it was again, during a dinner with our friends, George and Celia Euringer at our home. It was my mother, speaking as if we had just spoken earlier in the day, and she had forgotten to mention something. "So why haven't you called?" she asked. Astonished, and of course, not prepared with an appropriate response, I said, "How have you been?" "Clyde, I've got to get out of here," she responded, referring to her home of some thirty-eight years.

In March of 1938 construction had begun on the Trumball Park Housing Project by the Federal Housing Division on approximately twenty-one acres of land in South Deering (often referred to also as "Irondale"), the second largest community in an area out of Chicago's seventy-seven communities.[1] The project extended south from Trumball Park at 105th Street to 109th Street, from Oglesby on its west perimeter to Bensley on the east. There were 460 living units in two-story group houses, flats, and four-story apartments. We had lived in the low-rise units. Our home consisted of two bedrooms and a bath upstairs, and a living room, kitchen, and utility room on the lower level. There was a small, rear yard with an obligatory tree and my mother's beloved flower garden, and an even smaller yard in the front. The housing units were grouped or encircled by large landscaped rectangles,

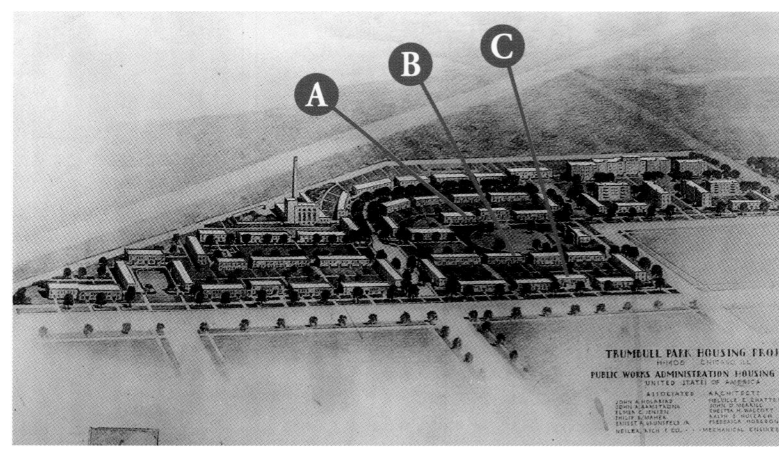

Architectural rendering of the Trumbull Park Homes, a housing project by the Public Works Administration (PWA), Housing Division. This type of low-rise public housing proved much more successful than the high-rise projects of the 1950s and '60s, many of which are being torn down. As of 2009, the Trumbull Park Homes had been restored and refurbished. From approximately 1943 through 1982, my mother had three residences within the project: A) 10646 South Yates Avenue; B) 10649 South Yates Avenue; and C) 10624 South Bensley (which only she occupied). Image above courtesy of the Southeast Historical Society, Chicago, Illinois.

LIFE

Night Watch CONTINUED

NIGHT SHIFT of Chicago policemen musters for roll call and gets its assignments on grounds of the housing project.

ANGRY WOMEN greet new Negro families. Woman at right carries stone and stick. Woman with camera was a riot leader.

CLUSTER OF COPS stands night guard before the Eugene Gully home. The Gullys have a year-old child, another on the way.

CONTINUED ON NEXT PAGE

FROM THE WINDOW OF THEIR APARTMENT MR. AND MRS. EDWARD JOHNSON LOOK DOWN AT NIGHT SHIFT OF A CONTINUOUS POLICE WATCH OVER THEM

NIGHT WATCH

It guards Negroes in a Chicago housing project against violence

Gathered around a campfire to keep warm in the autumn chill, Chicago police are on a 24-hour watch against a vicious eruption of racial hatred in a public housing project. The violence, which started last summer when the first Negro family moved into the 15-year-old Trumbull Park Homes, flamed up again when three more Negro families moved in under police convoy. Neighborhood women hurled stones and tomatoes. A gray-haired 65-year-old woman prostrated herself in front of a car carrying Negroes and had to be dragged away screaming. Police jailed her and three others for a night to show they meant business, threw in 936 men in three shifts to guard the Negro families. Still the cops could not keep the whites from spitting at a Negro woman out taking a walk, and the Negroes were keeping their youngsters indoors. "I hope it'll be all right to let them out to play next week," said one mother.

20 CENTS

NOVEMBER 9, 1953

In its November 9, 1953, issue, Life Magazine *described the protests and rioting in Chicago when Negro families moved into a public housing project which had previously been all white. Cover and text: Copyright 1953. The Picture Collection, Inc. Reprinted with permission. All rights reserved.*
Color photo "Night Watch," black and white photos "Night Shift" and "Cluster of Cops" reprinted with permission: Art Shay/TIME & LIFE Images/Getty Images. "Angry Women" photo courtesy of Corbis Images.

numerous shrubs, trees, and tenant flower gardens. The building exterior was of brick with steel doors and window casements and cement stairs. Spartan, to say the least, and strictly utilitarian, but the interiors were comfortable. There was a common laundry area nearby. The units were painted every four years and a janitor was assigned to deal with mechanical issues. This was important to a woman with three young children and no man about the house.

Over the years, my mother occupied three different units within the project: 10647 South Yates in the early years, and 10629 South Yates during our high school years. After all her children left home, she was reassigned to a one-bedroom unit at 10624 South Bensley on the second floor. For the last half dozen years of her living alone in the project, my mother tended her gardens, remained neighborly, and was mostly impervious to the ethnic change and economic and environmental decline that occurred around her until her call to me in 1982.

On August 5, 1953, a black family named the Donald Howards had entered the Trumball Park Homes.[2] As I recall, this family was moved into their dwelling under the cover of darkness and directly behind our home. That was too close, as we were to learn, when police discovered a mistakenly placed, undetonated bomb next to our rear entry. "A series of riots, confrontation and bombings [were to last] approximately ten years." A project by the Museology Class[3] of the Chicago Teachers Center, Northeastern Illinois University, National Endowment for the Humanities, summarized the situation:

> *These attacks were blamed on the South Deering Improvement Agency (SDIA) and Chicago Police Department (CPD) by the citizens, for not warning them of their incoming neighbors. This only stirred more chaos around the situation and soon the nations' eyes fell upon Trumbull Park.*
>
> *Another unsuccessful attempt to enter a small community named Merrionette Manor was made by a black family. This and other attempts fueled the anger of the community more*

and more. The majority of those who contested the migration of the incoming residents lived within a 12 mile radius of the Trumbull Park and the communities surrounding it. Also, Torrence Avenue, in the mid to late 1950's, became a tumultuous area as many of the all-white residents attacked the incoming black families. They felt these new incoming families into their neighborhood were a threat to their community. As more and more black families began to enter and settle in and around the Trumbull Park community, the riots became a constant threat. The riots began to spread as far as Rainbow Beach and Calumet Park. On July 28, 1957 an "uproar" occurred at Rainbow Beach and spread all the way back to Trumbull Park. The summer seemed to fuel chaos as well, as many of the confrontations stemmed out of territorial claims to beaches and parks.

Although these attacks slowed down the migration of minorities to their community, they did not inflict long-term effects. What was once a 99% white community has now become a minority dominated area.[4]

A once peaceful and friendly neighborhood, which was dominated by whites, had become a community of ethnic diversity — 75 percent black, 25 percent Hispanic.[5]

During my adolescent years in the mid- to late 1950s, it was common to live among hundreds of police encamped in the park and project. In the winter, behind barriers, they huddled around fires in oil drum cans like itinerant homeless in uniforms. Ultimately a permanent police headquarters was established in one of the project's vacant units. Our park was to have its shrubs removed throughout so as not to provide cover for rioters. Racism was rampant.

"By the early '80s, the racism had declined. Residents had begun to accept their fellow neighbors as neighbors."[6] But sadly, jobs for my mother's neighbors became increasingly scarce with the closing of the Wisconsin Steel Mill and four other businesses. Unemployment, by July 1983 "had climbed to nearly 25%."[7]

It was against this backdrop of increasing unemployment, poverty, and rising crime that Trumbull Park Homes began to take on a new look. My mother's gardens disappeared along with the trees; lawns became packed dirt on which nothing would grow. Families fell apart, children vandalized their park and its equipment, and many homes were abandoned for non-payment of rent, remained vacant, and were gutted or boarded up. Trash was everywhere, and drug abuse and gang violence were growing.

I flew to Chicago shortly after her call in 1982, having contacted my sister first, and the two of us embarked on the task of finding a suitable new home with Mom in tow. Proximity to June and her family in Lansing, Illinois, made the most sense. It wasn't too long before we found and purchased a new condo, less than a mile from my sister's home, and some seventy-six blocks further south of Trumbull Park Homes. Mom has lived in Lansing, Illinois, for twenty years.

Actually, the '80s saw a wholesale migration of white residents from communities like South Deering, Trumbull Park Homes, Jeffrey Manor, Merrionette Manor, The Bush, and the East Side to towns outside Chicago, to towns further south, east and west. Where their customers moved, so did the commercial establishments. The Southmoor Bank, DeYoung's Furniture, Gayety's Ice Cream, bakeries, food stores, car dealerships — all former South Chicago enterprises relocated in Lansing, Calumet City, Orland Park, and Tinley Park, Illinois, spilling over even into nearby towns in Indiana such as Munster and Merriville. And

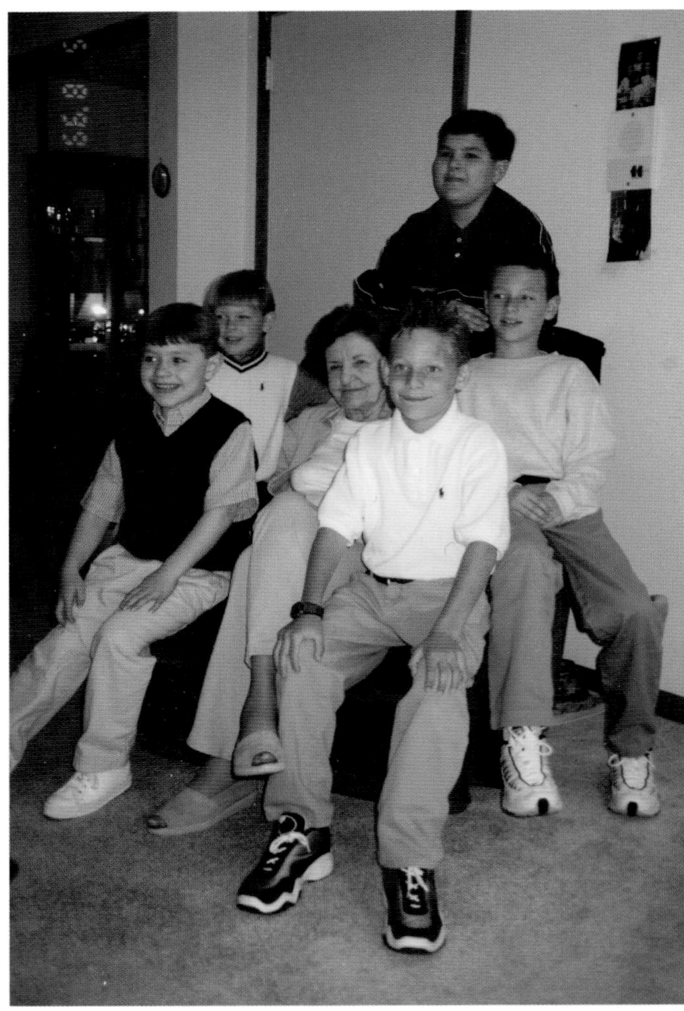

Mary Davis on Mother's Day, May 8, 1999, with her five great-grandsons, from left to right: Dylan Malara, Beau Davis, Taylor Davis (front), Ross Malara (rear), and Codie Davis

of course, black and Hispanic families eager to improve their lot in life were quick to follow.

Coincidentally, a dozen years after I moved my mother out of Trumbull Park Homes, the process was repeating itself according to Virginia Owens, a resident of the project for fifty-one years, in an interview, October 17, 2001, with Janet Green.[8] Ms. Owens also said, "After living in Trumbull Park for twenty years, in 1977, I moved my mother out. With the constant drive-bys and gang fights, I feared she was not safe any longer. It had gotten too hard for her to come outside. The police were constantly called. Although my mother did not want to move because it took her so long to get into Trumbull Park [like my own mother in 1943], I had to make her realize that Trumbull Park was not the same quiet community that she had moved into." She added, "When her front window had accidentally gotten shot out by a stray bullet, I did not hesitate moving my mother." History of the human condition repeats itself, cycling inexorably through one ethnic group after another.

During the past twenty years my mother never gave up her state aid, even insisted on food stamps, which she was entitled to despite our offers to help her financially. We were therefore required to have her pay us rent as a condition of her continuing on aid. Further testimony to her dependence on aid is her inability to accept financial windfalls. Several years ago she was injured while stepping off a curb, hit by a passing pick-up truck.

The driver's insurance company offered a $15,000 settlement, and we immediately realized upon our attorney's advice that she could not keep her status as a welfare recipient if she kept the award. Arrangements were made after confirming with the government what her obligation in this matter would be. Mom was allowed to retain $2,000, and the balance, less attorney fees, was distributed to the government.

Maria Rakoczy, May 10, 2002

On May 7, 1996, David Savage, my mother's oldest brother, died. He never married and left a modest estate, designating in his will that his only living sister, Mary, receive $50,000. By now, we knew the drill. Mom refused the inheritance, and the sum was distributed by my uncle's trustee and long-time companion, equally among Mom's children (June and David; I waived my portion) and her four grandchildren. Alas, the government missed out and Mom remained on aid. She no longer receives food stamps, but relies heavily on her medical benefits. She has excellent care. Her psychiatrist and internist are associated with a major teaching hospital in Chicago. The system does work, and for my mother, especially well.

I share this all with the reader to make the single point that Mary Davis never had anyone she could rely on completely. There was no one in her life who afforded her the security she so craved. Not her husband who faded from the responsibilities of partner and provider. Not the philandering stud who baked pies while cheating on his wife. Not the children she raised — a son, who hadn't spoken with her in seven years, another who left for military service and hadn't seen her in a decade, nor an estranged daughter, who, though just around the corner, would be more comfortable miles away.

All of this has caused me to realize that my mother's most cherished state is one of independence. She's alert, smart, determined to stay out of an assisted care facility or nursing home. She doggedly clings to the concept of remaining in her own home — the home that we make available to her.

My wife and I agreed that we could, in addition, provide her with assisted care at home, at first on a three-day-a-week basis, and then gradually requiring twenty-four-hour in-home care to ensure her independence. Though we have employed six or eight caregivers over the past several years, none really remained long. Mom was difficult; her depressive mood swings and often-abusive behavior got the best of them all. Until Maria.

Maria, Maria...

Three years ago, we were at our wits end. We had just lost yet another caregiver and the placement service was now complaining about how difficult it was to fulfill the needs of my mother while dealing with increasing reports of her idiosyncrasy. Then we were blessed with the arrival of Maria Rackoszy. A relatively young forty-five-year-old divorced Polish-speaking woman who had her own car, was slight of figure, with an elegant, but not haughty way about her, and actually wanted the job.

Maria met the most immediate demands of my mother. She was clean. She spoke English. She was sensitive and caring. She was engaging, polite, and mannerly. She was attractive. Men flirted with Maria, and Mom liked the attention, even if only vicariously. She had a bright red Jeep and took my mother everywhere. (My mother had never learned to drive.) If Mary was able, they were out and about. No longer would Mom ask, "How would you like to stare at these four walls all day?" Maria even introduced my mother to members of her own family, and they have become an important part of the social fabric of my mother's life today. As Mom puts it, "Maria's children visit me, and they hug and kiss me." Maria's brother, wife, and family priest — Mom happily knows them all.

This is the first person my mother has unabashedly accepted into her life who has provided for her daily care. They are more than client and agent. They have become close friends, each seemingly drawing from the other sustenance to fill the emptiness they must feel at one time or another.

Mom and Me

As my mom often reminded me, "You only have *one mother*, Clyde. I raised you."

True, yet I've never sensed that intimacy with my mother that undoubtedly both my sister and brother enjoyed. Dave was the baby and so cute. June and my mom were more girlfriends than mother and daughter. I always respected her matriarchal role and felt responsible to her, often serving as the surrogate father in our household, responding to her requests of "speak to your sister" when June would stay out too late at too young an age. I was frequently called upon to discipline my brother and sister. I was relied upon to do most of the chores around the house as a youngster, but one must keep in mind that I was cared for by others and away from home for significant periods of time. I don't recall much affection, hugs, kisses, or smiles of encouragement. Life, of what I recall, was bleak; mostly we did without. I was painfully shy as a child to the point that my behavior often drew the comment, "He's so quiet." Of course, the more I heard this, the more quiet I became, affording myself in a regressive way, a distinguishing characteristic and thereby setting myself apart from everyone else. I'm still soft spoken.

I must admit that my relationship with my mother has always been victimized by the effect and consequent behavior of her life-long depressive illness. Each time one would draw closer, get comfortable, give of oneself to her, she was as likely to explode in meanness or rejection as she was to embrace you. Her mood

Mom at Cole's and Tammi's house, May 10, 2002, San Diego

swings were unpredictable. She could be exceedingly critical. She employed the foulest of language in withering outbursts of temper and could drive off the most persevering loved one.

Any expression of heart-felt affection or love toward her has long ago been coupled with the caution inbred over time among all of us by this whip-saw experience of her emotional behavior.

Of course with Maria as an important member of our family, Mom's condition has improved greatly. I'm comforted by my mother's newfound joy with her constant companion, and heartened that the future will offer a continued brightening of my mother's spirit.

On October 3, 2003, while enjoying a weekend at the Sagamore Inn in Bolton Landing, Lake George, New York, a forty-fourth wedding anniversary gift given to us by our children, I received a distressing phone call. My mother had expelled from her home her caregiver, her constant companion, Maria. Fired her. Mom was home alone without care. The support system so carefully built over the past two years was now being painfully torn asunder, unraveling with each minute that passed on the phone, listening to my mother's tirade.

Obviously, my mother could no longer tolerate Maria. Maria, a sweet, gentle, kind woman, who had long suffered the indignities of a depressive, arrogant, offensive, and even abusive person, was now being cast aside.

Intrinsically an unhappy person nearly all her life, my mother slipped easily into contempt for her companion. If familiarity is known to breed contempt, this was its defining moment. My mother, controlling, physically aggressive, dominated her caregiver and then no long respecting Maria, discarded her.

Mom found her new townhome, well furnished in a mixed community, with every amenity, something of a prison. Asocial herself, Mom found the place "dead." "There's no one around. They all go to work. You never see anyone outside," she proclaimed. This, coupled with her abject refusal to participate in, take advantage of, a fine Senior Citizen Community Church, contributed to her estrangement and isolation. Her only outlet was to be driven around endlessly in Maria's car. My mother claimed she wanted to be with her family, but, of course, they all work too, only occasionally available for socializing, and were often subjected to the same unexpected mood changes and abusive behavior, so not inclined to simply hang out with Mom.

Under a ruse of accepting Maria's dismissal, for nearly a month, while utilizing the services of an interim, full-time caregiver who only spoke Polish, we managed to convince my mom that Maria could be coaxed into returning. Mom realized, ultimately, that she had lost a fair amount of freedom, that Maria wasn't that bad. After all, she was very clean, knew my mother's likes and dislikes, and spoke fairly good English.

Mom opening her gift on Mother's Day, May 12, 2002, as great-grandson "Beau Boy" looks on at Cole's and Tammi's house in Encinitas, California.

My "boots on the ground," April Mora in a photo taken on December 19, 2010

Maria's return to employment gave us renewed hope that perhaps Mom had learned a life lesson: that you often realize how valuable something is only when you lose it. This was not to be.

Home Alone

It's 2 A.M., we're asleep at home in New York, and the phone rings. This can't be good, I think, answering the Orland Park Police officer calling us from inside Mom's home. She had called 911, claiming her caregiver had abandoned her. It quickly became apparent that, indeed, Maria had gone missing. At first I feared my mother had acted out one of her threats and had done something to Maria. Maria's purse and wallet were in her bedroom. Her car was in the driveway. The police searched the basement and entire house. No Maria. Later that same morning, Maria returned. She claimed she went for a walk, to check the mail. Maria said that my mother, in a rage, had thrown a box of donuts at her and made Maria sleep on the floor next to her bed because my mother objected to a bright red bedspread Maria had bought for her bed. Maria was fatigued and mentally exhausted from my mother's abuse, and this was to be the reason for her finally ending the employ of my mother. No amount of coaxing or money this time, and we tried mightily, would change Maria's resolve. I may never know the truth of the night, and what really occurred or did not. Maria was no longer in my mother's employ, having turned over the house keys to April on October 9th, 2004.

My mother would later claim that Maria's leaving her alone was not a matter of maltreatment. Coincidentally, about this time, Maria was to meet a man who lived directly across the street from my mother's home. They had been seeing one another. Maria now lives with him and his children.

With Maria's departure we realized that we could no longer sacrifice another caregiver (there have been many in fifteen years) due to the vagaries of my mother, her mood swings, abusiveness. On November 4, I flew alone to Chicago for the first time without Kay. Mom was admitted to St. Luke's Presbyterian Hospital for "psychotic depression" on November 5, her deteriorating mental and emotional being in total collapse.

During this time period, the family struggled with "what to do next." My goal was to screen, select, and secure alternative support for my mother in a local assisted care facility. Mom had unwittingly forfeited a home of her own, unlimited freedom, and exclusive, individual care. April and I spent several days, including the weekend, visiting assisted care facilities throughout the southeast and southwest suburbs of Chicago. Following the advice of nurses, doctors, and social workers, Mom could no longer live alone. We tried to avoid their alternative recommendation of a nursing home dreaded by the family.

By November 6, we had selected Sunrise of Palos Park, Illinois, an assisted care residence. Contrasted with the bleakness of other similar facilities, Sunrise offered a welcoming, warm, home environment.

Sunrise, a pioneer in assisted living, was our collective choice as the next step to my mother's care. Their approach seemed to provide the ideal solution for my mother, who needed some help with daily activities such as bathing, dressing, toilet needs, and medication reminders. Residents appeared comfortable among new and pleasantly appointed living spaces. Sunrise offered personalized assistance and care, yet allowed Mom to maintain a life of independence among other seniors. All of this and within a half hour's drive of her family.

Of importance was that my mother would be able to retain some of her own furniture in her own apartment, scaled appropriately to her diminishing physical abilities. I particularly responded to the chocolate brown dog, "Brownie," who roamed the residence freely.

Overcoming the recommendation of her doctors and the Social Services staff at Rush Presbyterian Hospital that she be placed in a nursing home was only one hurdle to be cleared. We also had to ensure that my mother would medically and psychologically meet the qualifications for acceptance at Sunrise. Mom's medical history contained references of suicidal tendencies. Not least of all, we had to convince my mother that returning to her former living arrangement was no longer possible and that the best next step for her was becoming a resident of the Sunrise community.

We sold her townhome on December 23, 2004, after two years of residence, distributed and disposed of most of her furnishings, and moved her into Sunrise. It has been three years plus now of Mom living in an assisted care residence. She is "unhappy," dissatisfied with her care, can't stand the food, doesn't want to live among "sick people," mocks and denigrates them, fails to participate in group activities, and finds the care managers mostly incompetent. She remains asocial. She doesn't even like "Brownie."

I call her a couple times a week. She never fails to answer my greeting with "I'm very sick" or "The food is terrible," followed by, "You've got to get me out of here." We have managed to visit her three to six times a year, spending several days with her on each occasion. She does enjoy our time together. Yet she has been hospitalized two to three times a year for acute depression, usually immediately following our visits. Go figure.

April continues to serve her grandmother. She sees her every week to ten days or so depending on her work schedule and religiously gets Mom to her monthly doctor (internist and psychiatrist) appointments. April suffers my mother's abuse with a simple, stoic response, "That's Grandma."

Maria occasionally drops by Sunrise and takes Mom for a drive or to get something to eat. But most surprising of all, my sister June has found the means to draw closer to her mother. I don't know if it's Mom's quasi-confinement or the routines of community living or the social setting and proximity of so many others that affords June the comfort and cover of knowing that any visit gone awry can be quickly terminated with a simple "I've got to go now, Ma, it's time for your dinner," or "It's time for your meds and bed." A quick in, and an even quicker out, a getaway with none of the heated, protracted exchanges of the past. Anger when you're trapped in a car delivering your mother home, as June has, is something to be avoided. Visits punctuated, or book-ended, by care managers, schedules, and routines are more easily managed if timed adroitly. Whatever the underlying motivation, it is definitely a good thing for both daughter and mother.

Sunrise of Palos Park, 12828 South LaGrange Road, Palos Park, Illinois

June does Mom's laundry, picks up her dry cleaning, even ordered the *Chicago Tribune* to be delivered to her at Sunrise. June cleans Mom's apartment and often accompanies April when visiting — there's strength in numbers. As Mom has become more frail, June has ventured to draw ever closer. Mom seems to cherish the contact. I'm sure it's good for June.

Kay's Got Charisma

It's January 26th, 2007, and I'm in flight on my way from New York to Chicago. It's cold, 9 degrees upon awakening, and Kay is in Florida. This is only my second trip to Chicago without Kay accompanying me. I try to see my mom at least every two months. I mention this because there is little Mom can do for herself these days. Being with my mom for several days brings immediately to mind how I will cope with applying her make-up, selecting and laying out her clothes for the next day's activity, and assisting her in the bathroom. Kay has been, over the years, a Godsend when the personal attention of a woman is so essential to the care of another.

I have enlisted the aid of April, a long-time, loving grandchild of my mother's, who, since the age of fifteen, has tended to her grandmother. On this trip April will be riding shotgun with me.

The practical aspect of this trip resolved, I pondered the reaction of my mom when she learns that only I will be visiting with her. "Where is Kay?" she'll ask, and I will sense her disappointment. I've never really shared her interests, nor, probably, have I been very interesting to my mother. I've not lived the colorful life of my sister and brother, lives more similar in pattern and behavior to my mother's. As Mom has often said,

"There's one thing I can say about Clyde, he never caused me any trouble." I know she depends on me for economic support. But for entertainment value, I'm something of a drag to her. Kay's not. She's got charisma. More like my mom, who still, at age 89, relates, recalls. and is always ready to rekindle the life or at least the memories of a younger woman. Mom covets the occasional compliment — "How smooth your skin is Mary," or "What nice legs you have Mary." Of course, Kay is as always, with anyone, an uplifting, engaging, fun person to be in the company of, with social skills only eclipsed by her warm, generous, and loving nature. Quite an asset for a guy like me to be without. Somehow I'll have to manage.

During my three-day visit, my hope was to continue discussing my book with her. (I had, on the prior visit, shown her several pages that she enjoyed reviewing). I hoped to talk of events in her life that might open some unknown door or that she might be entertained by my ruminating through the details I had uncovered of her life. She quickly laid my interest to rest with a sharp, dismissive wave of her hand exclaiming, "I don't want to listen to that bullshit." Mostly, we cruised the malls, shopping for Chicago Bears NFL Championship sweatshirts for the family, eating at Lumes's, and dropping by Gayety's for her chocolate soda. On Sunday, April had us to her home for a dinner gathering of assorted family. The meal was cooked and delivered by June — breaded pork chops, fried potatoes, creamed corn, and salad. There was chocolate cake and cherry pie (Mom's choice). The Bears' sweatshirts were passed out to everyone in time for next week's Super Bowl. Stories were swapped amid idle banter and laughter, while Mom took it all in from her corner resting spot on

Mom with Kay and "Brownie" at Sunrise of Palos Park on one of her better days during one of our bi-monthly visits

April's overstuffed armchair and ottoman, wanting to be included, participating not, hopefully happy to be among her family. But more likely, she was simply taking our measure, each of us, held to some sinister standard of behavior, the degree of deference we showed her almost always falling short. She wants so desperately to be the center of attention. Did that one kiss me? Or fail to kiss me? On the cheek, not the lips? Did he spend too much time socializing with others, leaving his mother unattended? Did they arrive too late and leave too early?

Despite the time we have together I'm no closer to my mother than before, unendingly destined to not know her any more than I knew my father, who predeceased her by nearly thirty

Mom, seated, at her 90th birthday celebration November 27, 2007, at the Peninsula Hotel, Chicago, Illinois. Standing left to right: April Mora, Clyde Davis, his sister June Davis Rogers, Kay Davis, and Officer Alfonse Mora. April and Alfonse are June's children and Mom's grandchildren.

some years. I yearn to reach into this woman's world to learn of the life she's led.

Driving from April's home in Munster, Indiana, to Palos Park, Illinois, I couldn't help reflecting on the frail, elderly, silent woman sitting next to me, wondering what to say to her. "Mom, how come you never ask me about me, what I do, how I might feel, where have I been, my accomplishments, my hopes, desires, fears, what feelings do I have for you?" But, I knew it would be a futile attempt — too late in the day, if not in our lifetime.

Mom, I love you, there could be more for us. Perhaps the disappointment I have regarding my mother stems, in part, from knowing the mother my children have. A world of difference exists between the two — one I'll never span.

As it is so often said, you can't pick your parents. But, as Mom says, "You only have one mother, Clyde." I do, maybe. That much is true.

The Magic Pill

If you know Kay, you will not be surprised to learn that she has toiled mightly to help my mother, to please and comfort her. But what Kay does can be surprisingly simple and clever.

As Kay tells it, "Everyone who knows Mary will tell you, Mary always complains about not feeling well, saying 'I'm very sick.' No matter what you say to her or what topic you bring up she says, 'I'm very sick.'

"Some time ago I started giving her a 'magic pill.' This was a pill that only I had. And it was a secret pill that would always make her feel better. So no matter what she said was hurting her, I merely had to pull out my 'magic pill' and give it to her, then all would be better. Clyde would always feign concern, saying, 'You know, Kay, her doctor wouldn't want you to be doing this.' And, of course, Mary enjoyed getting her illicit drug even more.

"Of course, there is no magic pill. I only give her an extra-strength Excedrin — my pill of choice whenever anything is ailing me. But, nonetheless, it works. She quiets down and for a while does not complain about any aches or pains.

"Now when I arrive in town to visit her or actually, whenever I see her, she always says, 'Gimmie my pill.' It is quite annoying because I have created a monster. Denying her usual request on a recent visit I instead said, 'Mary, I'd like a hello, how are you, Kay?' Done, Mary got her pill and I reclaimed the high

Maria and Mom ready for her Mother's Day brunch with the family, on May 10, 2009. Maria recently returned to care for my mother.

ground. Oh well, whatever works!"

Over the years, Mom has been hospitalized at least once every year, and sometimes twice, when she fails physically or declines emotionally. Usually it's her psychic well-being that suffers the most and causes the most difficulty for her caregivers. On March 1, 2010, suffering from dementia and depression, Mom was admitted to the J.R. Bowman Center, at Rush Presbyterian Hospital in Chicago. Her usual stay is from two to three weeks, while her doctors restore her health, pass her through a battery of exams, and recalibrate her medications.

Mom returned to her residence at Sunrise after being released; however, by April 5, she was back in the hospital. After a week or so, I was told that she was not improving, and that she had lost the will to live. She refused to eat and would not take her medications. Her doctors recommended that she be placed in hospice care. I flew to Chicago to confirm my mother's condition, and thought it best to take the advice of those who had treated her for nearly twenty years. Unfortunately, my mother would not be allowed to return to Sunrise without one-on-one, twenty-four-hour care — this in addition to the normal staff of nearly sixty.

While my mother was in hospice care, I refused to allow them to administer any form of morphine. I was told this was part of the typical comfort care package. My mother was not in pain, and I felt that they wanted to use the drug to manage her behavior. I returned to Chicago and began canvassing every nearby nursing home and facility for the care I believed would be required. I also spent time sitting with her and holding her hand. Our usual outings, morning-to-night excursions about Chicagoland, had come to an end.

Upon her return to Sunrise, with added care, she began to thrive. Her appetite improved, her attitude brightened, and she began to accept her meds. Within two months, I was informed that, under Medicare, she no longer qualified for hospice care. She had graduated, as one nursing director told me. At ninety-two, she's thriving yet, frail, and in decline.

"Mary You're Back!"

I've been told again and again that my mother is a fighter. Every time we count her out, she seems to rally once again. She can behave when it's necessary to get what she wants, but she prefers being ornery, rather than submissive or placating. She certainly suffers from the vagaries of a long life.

Mom returned to her regular psychiatrist and internist at Rush Medical Center. Everyone there was astonished to see her again. This physical exam required April Mora to bring along one of the newly hired caregivers to assist her. As Grandma was meeting with her psychiatrist, she turned to her new caregiver and exclaimed, "I can't stand him." "Grandma," April said, "that's not nice!" But then, he is a psychiatrist, and I'm sure he's heard worse. I have. Especially from my mom.

She's Gone

Mom died May 26, 2011 after a sudden, but mercifully brief illiness. I was not beside her when she passed, although my sister, June, April and other Chicago family members were. During the flurry of hospital ICU activity I was able to speak to her in those final moments — I love you, Mom — and I'm sure she took those words with her to a better place. May she, finally, know everlasting rest and peace.

Notes

1. "South Deering Residential Architecture," (South Deering, Ill.: Trumball Park CHA Homes), a project by the Museology class of Washington High School, <http://www.neiu.edu/~reseller/sdtrmblcha.html>.
2. "South Deering Residential Architecture"
3. "South Deering Residential Architecture"
4. "South Deering Residential Architecture"
5. *Local Fact Book* (Chicago: Chicago Metropolitan Area, 1980), 134-136.
6. Janet Green, "An Ongoing Struggle in Trumbull Park," a paper delivered at Olive-Harvey College, English and Speech Department, December 2001.
7. *Local Fact Book*, 134.
8. Green, "An Ongoing Struggle"

D

David Otis Davis, U.S.M.C.

avid *(butchie)*

The Little Brother I Know Little About

Reflecting on my brotherly relationship and, as a person of images, I note that I have very few of my brother Dave. That is, for every hundred photographs of my sister, I may have two of my brother. This is not a mere accident. It is a reflection of contact (or lack of it), circumstances, and the difference of age between siblings.

My brother is seven years younger than I. We essentially grew up as children in different eras. My brother and I each went our separate ways. I went off to college, he joined the Marines. I married and went east to make my fortune. He went west to fight for our country. I remained on the East Coast, he remained west. We are very different people. He is bigger than me, better looking and, like my sister, always up for a laugh. I don't recall spending much time with him. I usually spent summers and holidays with aunts and uncles, grandparents, or in children's camps. I was often in the care of these same relatives during my mother's nervous breakdowns and medical treatment for depression, away at school, or married. He was in boot camp with the Marine Corps, overseas, or living on the opposite coast.

He had visited Kay and me in 1959 to attend a football game shortly after our marriage, when we lived in Urbana, and I had returned to continue as a student at the University of Illinois. The visit was most memorable because we had no money to entertain him and, having only a box of spaghetti in the house, we resorted to stealing a can of tomato paste and a can of mushrooms at the local Piggly Wiggly for that night's dinner.

One day in 1967, I received a phone call from my brother's wife Ginger. Dave, still in the Marine Corps, needed my help. He had been in a serious automobile accident. I traveled from New York to Downey, California, and it was a costly trip to make. These were financially hard times for my wife and me, with three young children. I used whatever funds we had available at the time to pay for my travel and to cover any unknown expenses that might occur during my visit. While I was in Downey, I had to return $140 of those funds to Kay so she could pay the rent (see the Western Union Telegraph Company receipt for $140, dated April 24, 1967, on page 65).

I have always been pulled closer to my family — brother, sister, mother — by their urgent economic need.

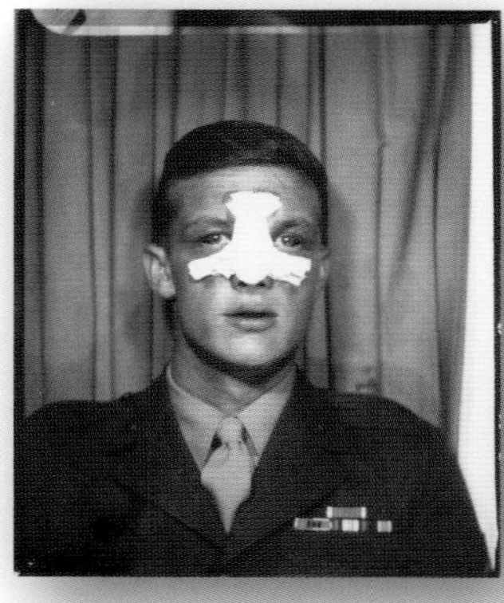

My brother as he appeared to me when I first saw him as a Marine in uniform in Downey, California in 1967. The photo is of a type produced by a classic coin-operated photo booth. Once the coin was dropped, four photos were taken automatically and then dispensed as prints in a strip.

My father was an exception to this redundancy. He never asked anything of me at any time.

Before this trip to California in 1967, I hadn't seen my brother for nearly eight years. In my first eye-to-eye contact with him, he had two black eyes and his nose was heavily bandaged (see photo above). My brother had served in Vietnam, as I recall, and was among the first Marines to land at Da Nang. He told me that he was wounded in Vietnam. I'm not sure of the date, but I do remember his tale. He said, that he was involved in a helicopter "skim jump," and as he was leaving the helicopter, still hovering over the ground, a mortar round exploded in front of him, throwing him up against the helicopter. He fell to the ground, seriously wounded, was flown back to the States and hospitalized. Dave said his nose was "blown off,"and that his physicians presented him with a display of different nose profiles and asked him to pick one. He claimed he got a much nicer nose than the one left behind. Dave also mentioned that during his hospitalization, the Marine Corps asked him to "re-up" for a second tour of duty. Dave declined.

At the time of the automobile accident that brought me to California Dave was probably on medical leave from the Marine Corps. I learned that when he was departing a commercial establishment in the early morning hours, Dave got into his car curbside, pulled out, sideswiped another parked car whose owner witnessed the damage, and who took after Dave in hot pursuit. Dave, attempting to avoid the wrath of his pursuer, sped through a red light at an intersection and struck, broadside, the vehicle of a waitress on her way home from work. The woman was hospitalized with severe head injuries and was in a coma.

On behalf of my brother, I contacted the husband of the hospitalized accident victim, conveying our heartfelt condolences. There was little else I could do other than offer moral support to all during the crisis. I returned to New York, my family, and job. After the birth of their daughter, Shelley, in 1967, Dave and Ginger's marriage continued for another three years, ending in divorce in 1970.

No longer in the Marine Corps or married, my brother remained on the West Coast, living in various beach communities in California. Kay and I remember visiting him in Redondo Beach and having lunch with him in Marina del Rey. During this time Dave also had a dog, an Irish red setter, I believe, that he named "Otis." Using the same middle name given himself and our father, Otis held a special place in Dave's heart — so much so that when Otis needed medical attention, Dave would often prefer taking the dog to a hospital emergency room rather than a veterinary clinic.

Dave, easy to greet and meet, personable, even charming, was employed in these early years as a bedding and furniture salesman.

My brother and I hooked up again in 1970 when he had remarried and wanted to start a new life on the East Coast, with his wife Barbara. We welcomed them to our home in Pound Ridge, where they remained for a few months while each looked for work and they searched for a place of their own. They settled briefly in an apartment in Stamford, Connecticut, but eventually returned to California. Taking advantage of his G.I. loan and Barbara's employment in the police department, they finally managed to buy a house in Hermosa Beach, California. It must have been a financial stretch for them. However, he had managed to buy his own home before I began construction on my first home in 1975.

Dave with Mom, in front our home at 10629 South Yates Avenue, Chicago, Illinois. The ill-itting pea coat and hat were probably hand-me-downs of mine. Note the sleeve length on my brother who, at an early age, was already destined to be much bigger than me.

Dave's second marriage to Barbara Mehl failed, lasting little more than a year, but happily produced a son, Scott Ryan. By November 1972, my brother had passed through two marriages and was on his own, living alone and getting control of his life. I didn't see him again, I believe, until the weddings of my niece Erin and my daughter Cynthia in 1984. Like me, my brother also lost contact with our mother for an extended period of time. At age thirty-nine, he had not

Left: Mary Lou Savage, June "Tootsie" Davis, and David "Butchie" Davis on the occasion of June's first Communion. Center: "Butchie" in robe, and Mom, upon graduation from Orville T. Bright grammar school and standing in our living room at 10629 South Yates Avenue. This photograph is the only existing image of the interior of that home. Right: Butchie, Duke, June Lucas, and Mary Davis.

seen her in more than fourteen years. They were to meet again at Cynthia's wedding in July of 1984.

Before that time, my brother and I corresponded little. When he did write to me, he occasionally grew sentimental. Over the years it's been difficult for me to monitor the pulse of my brother, and obviously I failed to maintain a personal link with him. On one occasion, he wrote, "I don't want your head to get big, but you're the only person in the world that I would take advice from, and, besides Scotty, the only person I really care anything about."

Another time he wrote, "It seems like just yesterday you bought me my baseball glove and ball, working at Olympia Fields golf course. You may not remember, but I shall never forget it as long as I live, it's like a tattoo on my mind." He went on to say, "Maybe someday I can do something for you. It would have such a profound effect on you like knocking you on your ass or something, Ha, Ha."

He was good at baseball, yet I have no recollection of ever seeing him play. I do recall his playing baseball with my daughter Cynthia on our lawn in Pound Ridge when he and Barbara were staying with us. They had a large wiffleball and a bat. Cynthia pitched the ball to Dave and he hit a line drive straight at her, striking her in the chin. She immediately burst into tears, so, we know he could hit the ball.Dave enjoys spectator sports, sports bars and sport gambling and he is especially fond of horse racing and betting on horses.

Brotherly Feud

In 1988 Dave was about to build a house in Cardiff by the Sea, California with his companion Beverly Philips, whom he had been with, off and on, for several years. He enlisted my aid, seeking a financial "bridge loan" of sorts. I insisted on paying his expenses, architectural and permit fees, etc., directly to the appropriate vendor or municipal department. After several thousand dollars, he continued to ask for more funding. Others, on his behalf, also contacted me for funds. I could not comfortably continue making payments for the construction of his house while inadvertantly supporting his personal lifestyle. Getting no further financial support from me, he appealed to my wife Kay. On February 14, 1988, while at our condo in Key West, Florida, I received a late evening call from Kay who was still in New York. She had just spoken with Dave.

It angered me that he had used my wife to get to me, and had not asked me directly. Kay believed that he was "trying so hard" to do the right thing. My son had requested $14,000 just the day before as a gift to bid on a house in Lakeside, California. When I asked her to make a choice between $14,000 to Cole or $10,000 to Dave, she responded, "Give it to Dave." Kay even suggested that I simply give $20,000 to Dave, because "that's the way he'd want it." At the same time my banker was calling my office in New York to say I was overdrawn in my personal checking account. The next day I called my brother and told him that I can't pay everyone's way. I'm just not prone to simply give. Let me enjoy my life; I've been working at it for fifty years. Why put me on a "guilt trip?" Dave's reply was, "What are you going to do, look me up out of curiosity twenty years from now and find I'm six feet under and kick dirt on my grave?" Then he said, "I'll never ask you again for anything," and hung up. So we have the genesis of this family feud.

We met again at my uncle John and aunt Dorothy's 50th Wedding Anniversary in Las Vegas, June 9, 1990. Kay and I, my sister, my brother, and Beverly were all guests of my uncle at the Riviera Hotel. June, Kay, and I had arrived the day before, spent some time shopping, outfitting June, gambling, and sight seeing. Dave called to say he was in town, but we didn't see him and Beverly until the Anniversary dinner. Arriving late at 8 P.M., we missed cocktails because, as I recall, we were busy acquiring a mantel clock as a gift for my uncle and aunt. Dave was seated at our table alone with Beverly as we approached them. I shook hands with Dave and kissed Beverly, chatted a bit, then got up from the table with Kay to get food from the buffet. Shortly thereafter Dave excused himself to escort Beverly to the ladies room. They never returned. We've not spoken since, despite my many attempts to contact him over the ensuing years. And yet, it's the year 2011, and we still are not speaking to one another, nor does he communicate any longer with our mother. That's twenty-two years since my brother and I last spoke to one another.

For quite a while he didn't speak to anyone in the family, including my sister June. She felt, and rightfully so, that she could break through to him. I recall one instance when June, Kay and I

Dave and Ginger on their wedding day in 1965. They would ultimately have one child, Shelley René b. January 11, 1967, and then divorce in February 1970.

WU 4178 (R 9-54)
THE WESTERN UNION TELEGRAPH COMPANY
RECEIPT DOWNEY, CALIF. 4-24 1967
OFFICE DATE
RECEIVED FROM Clyde C Davis 862-85-88
ADDRESS 9228 Stewart & Gray Downey Calif $ 140.00
One Hundred Forty Dollars
19
☐ Account for the month of
☐ Telegraphic Money Order
☐ Telegram or Cable
☐ Deposit on Collect Telegram Returnable after 24 hours
☐ Account No. for Remittance
TO Catherine A Davis
Address Tappan Ave [illegible]
Place Briarcliff Manor New York
MONEY ORDER CHARGES PAID
Chgs $ 2.55
Tolls $ 2.16
Tax $
TOTAL $ 4.71
THE WESTERN UNION TELEGRAPH COMPANY
BY Bernice Craig

Barbara Jean Mehl Davis, second wife of David Davis and mother of Scott Davis

were all on the West Coast visiting with my son in Encinitas and we drove the short distance from there to Cardiff by the Sea. My sister rang the doorbell at his home expecting to be invited inside. Dave was home, but Beverly answered the door. We were never invited inside. After informing Dave that we were at the door we were told by Beverly that he was not prepared to receive us, perhaps, another time. My sister could not believe that she was being turned away after traveling over 3,000 miles for this moment of possible kinship. As the years passed, June kept trying and eventually broke through to Dave. They have not actually seen one another for six years, but speak occasionally by phone, mostly reminiscing about the past.

Dave has also managed to connect with and maintain a relationship with June's two sons "Chubby" (Alfonse) and "Bubs" (David) Mora.

Quick with a Quip

My sister tells me that my brother is always cracking jokes when they speak. Over the years, my brother became something of a jokester. I even think he seriously entertained the notion of becoming a standup comic. Quick with a quip, no conversation or contact escapes his one-liners.

My wife and I were invited to his son's wedding, which took place on August 6, 2005, in Dinuba, California. After much discussion between my sister and brother and my sister and me, we agreed that at Dave's request, I wouldn't approach him personally during the affair. He agreed to attend. He arrived late and left early. We were in the same church, in the same banquet room, even posed for photographs (not together though). But we didn't shake hands, and we never spoke to one another. My sister sat at his table, Kay and I at another. Kay approached him and Beverly, offering her congratulations, but was coolly rebuffed. I respected his wishes.

I bear no grudge, remain open to reconciliation, and I love Dave. I harbor no ill will toward a brother who has missed — no, squandered — the opportunity to secure, over these past years a loving, intimate relationship, one absent "the root of all evil."

My wealth has, in so many ways, been a blessing, allowing me to help so many less fortunate than me. Often, it has become a wedge between myself and those whom I genuinely love. My brother and I are estranged because of money. My sister and I have tested our relationship over the issues presented when need runs afoul of reason. I am fearful, and have often expressed to my sister, that despite all my wife and I have given others in economic support, we will eventually be faulted for our excess of riches rather than embraced for our past good will. For those who see more rhyme than reason to life, I've always been a disappointment.

Competing Philosophies

There exists between me and living relatives an issue regarding money, essentially a conflict of counter-cultures. A philosophy of those who have little, who would expressly give "the shirt off their back," no-questions-asked versus the person who

David and Clyde Davis at the wedding of Clyde's daughter Christine to Sean Ledingham, July 24, 1982

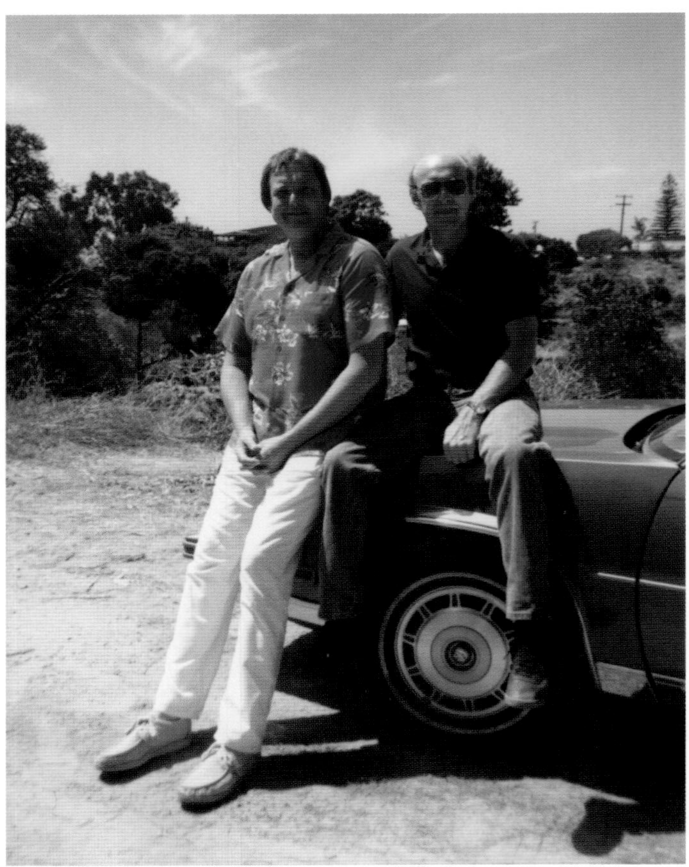

David and Clyde Davis at Dave's property at Cardif-by-the-Sea, California, in a picture taken between September 5 and October 14, 1986

David Davis and Beverly Philips residence at 411 Bristol Avenue, Cardiff-by-the-Sea, California, c. 1998

supposedly has it all. When approached, I'm the one who wants to know of the causative factors that precipitated the need, I'm the one who asks if alternative resources have been thoroughly explored. Or does one have the ability to repay and when? By insisting on documenting the terms of financial agreement and then retaining a record of the transaction, I'm the one who is undoubtedly thought to lack compassion. The why, where, when, who, and how of financial due diligence has not served me well in family financial affairs. I'm the person giving, but seldom considered a giving person. I often wonder what my relationship would be with my sister and brother if this chasm of riches were not between us?

Dave and Beverly did manage to build their dream house in Cardiff-by-the-Sea without further help from us. They sold the house in June 2004 for $1,100,000 and bought a new home in Boulder City, Nevada, not surprisingly, a quick twenty minutes from Dave's beloved Las Vegas.

In Scott's Own Words

On November 15, 2007, I had a telephone conversation with Scott Davis, the son of my brother David Davis. The purpose of my call was to try and get a better understanding of Scott's relationship with his father, since for some time now I had detected some distance between them.

In placing my call to Scott I had to be certain that he understood the purpose of the call and my motives for doing so. I mentioned to him that I had talked to his mother the other night and Scott responded, "So you heard the good news?"

"I did. I was very happy for you and pleased. Hope everything goes well. You're at the early stage I guess?"

"Exactly. Just the nausea and all that."

Jokingly, I replied "Uhh, huh. You're having nausea, are you?"

"No, no I'm not."

"Well," I continued, "it's very exciting and I'm proud to know you're going to have a child. It's important for me. In many ways, just being happy for you, first of all, and secondly, because I'm doing this book on the family. I don't know if you're aware of that, but I have been at it for quite some time."

I went on to say that I started working on it a long time ago, searching for my own father in the early eighties in an attempt to rekindle a father-son relationship that had barely existed. By then, I was already forty-five years of age, and I went looking for him and found out that he had passed away. I never had a chance to sit down and talk to him as an older adult.

I told Scott, "I was eighteen when I saw him for the last time, and I never saw him again."

I also told Scott, "I am working on the book and the last page or two in the book is about "Future Fathers." I have five grandchildren, five grandsons, and my brother has one son — and that's you. So there are six Davises going forward — my three grandsons in California are Davises and yourself, and I have two Malara boys, my daughter Cynthia's children. So I talk about these future fathers, and you're one of them."

"Awesome," Scott remarked.

"I picture you on this spread 'Future Fathers.' So, from time to time I sit down, writing a few sections or pages, captions for photographs and things of that sort, and I was looking at the last page in the book where I saw the heading 'Future Fathers,' and you're pictured there with the other boys. I started to think about you, what I knew about you, and how often I've seen you, or how little I've seen you. I started thinking about your dad, and as I thought more and more about it, I've wondered what kind of

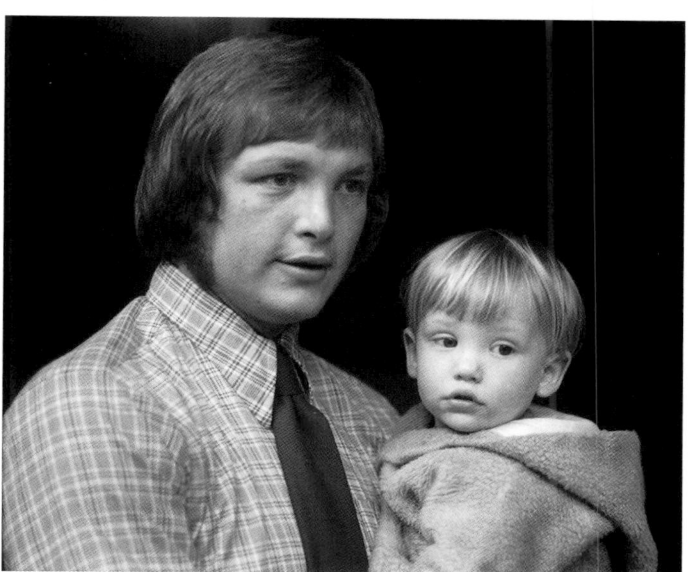

My brother with his son Scott at about 1 or 2 years of age in a photo taken by me in about 1974 or 1975.

relationship you were having with your father in comparison to the kind of relationship I had or didn't have with my father."

Continuing, I explained that I had also written about my sister and her life and of course, I had written a fair amount about my brother, Scott's father, and I think I had been reasonably balanced in my approach.

Scott recalled me telling him that his father had been in a bad automobile accident in the fall of 2007. Scott had made an attempt to contact his father by calling and leaving messages on the phone, but he got no answer. "We sent him a birthday card, a Christmas card, and we never heard anything back." Scott then returned to the accident, "So I was surprised when you told me he had been in that accident. I was surprised that we hadn't heard anything from him about that, that Beverly [his father Dave's companion] could have called to say, 'Your Dad has been in an accident.' So, that was kind of sad [that] you wouldn't get in touch with someone when you've been in a life-threatening accident. How do we know you're still around? So unless we hear about it from somebody else who would know about it, we would be totally in the dark."

As I spoke with Scott, I sensed his remorse, yet detected no bitterness in his voice as he said, "We just tried to keep the door

Scott Davis in 1979, at about age 7

open and hopefully, he knows that we care about him and want him to be part of our family if he wants to do that, but we haven't had any contact with him since the wedding. And you remember he didn't stay very long when he was there. But I'm glad that he showed up, and I think he would've regretted not coming."

"Well," I replied, "it was a pleasant experience for us even though my brother and I did not talk to one another. And for a while there I thought I was going to be the reason he might not show up."

I went on to say, "But, I was damned if I was going to stay away out of fear that he wouldn't come. I was invited and I respected your invitation and I wanted to be there for your mother and for my sister. Quite frankly, I paid for my sister's attendance [at the wedding], I flew her out, I put her up. I did whatever I could do to get her out there, so I wasn't going to stay away. But he did show and that was a great thing. I was very happy about that."

Sensing I was beginning to stray from the purpose of my call to Scott, I reiterated the concept of my book, which was finding fathers. I reminded Scott that I had lost mine along the way and then rediscovered him too late. I didn't know much about the family that was behind him — his parents, my grandparents, their parents, and so on. I told Scott I had done a great deal of work these past few years, that I had researched back to almost the late 1600s in this country on the Davis side. There weren't any bankers, or lawyers, or doctors (however, there is Dr. Sanders in Jefferson City, Missouri, a cardiologist and Harvard graduate) or Indian chiefs, presidents, or anything like that. They were mostly dirt farmers, average folks, but they did survive, and they did carry their bloodline along into the late 1900s and now the twenty-first century.

Scott Ryan Davis as a Senior, in 1990 at Columbia Christian High School, Portland, Oregon

I wanted Scott to know that if one's bloodline is going to continue, and if the message that fatherhood is something important and that message is going to get out, then we have to acknowledge past shortcomings.

"It's not just about blood, it's about doing the things that fathers do, and I think it's safe to say that your father hasn't been the ideal father; mine certainly wasn't, and there is some kind of thing missing in these men, and I'm trying to put my finger on it."

I added, "I'm not quite sure what it is, you know, and I'm not quite sure why it is. But I'm working toward it, and I'm getting a feeling about it."

Acknowledging Scott's relationship with his mother and his grandmother and what an excellent job they had done raising him, I posed the question, "But how do you feel about your father?"

Scott replied, "Even when we were together as a family for that short time, there was a kind of distance. I don't think in his mind he really knew what a father was, or that he had a clear picture in his head of the 'provider' mentality, and there was never a lack of affection or that kind of thing. I always felt like Dad kind of lived like a single person lives even when he was a father."

Scott went on to mention his recent marriage, "Now I have someone to take care of and provide for in the future, a kid, so you move into that father role. I don't think he ever moved into any role. He stayed where he was, and he was the same person before he got married and after he got married."

Scott related how he respected his father for his role, "He was my dad. We weren't buddies; I was the son. There wasn't any common interest. There wasn't a lot of curiosity there, like what's going on at school, what's going on in your life, what's bothering you, what are some of the things you're looking forward to, and things like that. I think he wanted in his heart to get to know me and had a love for me, but he didn't know how to do that. He didn't know how to express it. There was always a feeling of being loved, but at arms length. It was a strange relationship, and at any point in time it was strained."

Scott's marriage to Michelle seemed to have presented the breaking point between him and his father. Dave was against the marriage and made his feelings known to Scott. Scott went ahead and married Michelle, and they have since had a daugher Belle Marie.

Dave's feeling was, in Scott's words, "Okay, you know, you didn't do what I wanted you to do, in the way that I wanted you to do it, so I'm not going to have any kind of relationship with you at all, any more."

This behavior was all too familiar to me. I remarked, "I hope he's not going to do with you what he did with me. If I didn't perform the way he expected me to perform then he was just going to drop me. I was no longer of any use to him."

"Exactly."

"Because I wasn't playing the game the way he had expected me to, or wanted me to, I think that's probably an inability on his part to be accommodating and to be flexible and to compromise. That's what interpersonal relationships are all about. You have to give some ground to get some ground. You have to work your wonder to have your way. It isn't always just demanding and not getting, and then walking away. You end up knowing fewer and fewer people that way."

Though Scott agreed with what I had to say, I wanted

Dave with his son Scott upon Scott's graduation in May 1995 from Asbury College, a Christian liberal arts institution located in Willmore, Kentucky. Scott received a BS degree in Biology/Secondary Education.

found Ginger, his stepsister Shelley's, mother, through Classmates.com. Shelley Davis Bontemps had attended Warren High School and Columbus High School in Downey, California, graduating in 1985. They eventually exchanged e-mails with Shelley and learned that she was living in the Phoenix area, was married, and had children. Scott went on to say, "I think her husband was, and still is, a football coach for some college or university in Arizona." Of course, I asked for Shelley's e-mail address, wanting to include her as a member of our family in my book. I'm not sure Dave would like it, but this is a book about family and a family that continues. Scott had misplaced Shelley's e-mail address, but promised to ask his mother to forward it to me. I had Shelley's birth certificate

Wedding reception for Scott Ryan Davis and Michelle Dingnan on August 6, 2005, in Dinuba, California. Seated from left to right: June Rogers, Dave's companion Beverly Philips, Dave, Scott, and Michelle.

him to know that my relationship with my father was somewhat different. I never felt distanced because I had little contact with my father. He never said anything like, "Don't marry that girl," or "Don't go to that school," or "Give me money," and if I didn't give him money he blew me off. It wasn't anything like that. I just didn't have contact with him, but the thing that is so sobering and so mystifying at the same time is that my father didn't feel that need to be a father, didn't feel the need to have contact with his children. I have been told, though, that my mother did not want him around his children.

My father and my brother abandoned their families, yet my father was not raised that way. His parents remained together as husband and wife into their nineties. They were a close-knit family, as evidenced by the many photographs in this book. My father is frequently shown with his parents, often among his siblings, cousins, and various in-laws. From what LaVerne Purkey tells me, Charlie and Rebecca were a very close, loving couple who remained in touch with their children until their passing. I'm trying to find the common thread here, I said to Scott.

I changed the subject to Scott's stepsister. I was shocked when Scott responded that he was not only aware that he had a stepsister, but that they had been in contact with one another. Scott's mom had

Scott and Michelle Davis at Barrow, Alaska, September 2006

and had planned to reproduce it in the book, though I have since learned that it would be illegal to do so under California law. I didn't have her married name, and I was afraid no one would know where she went or what became of her. As it turned out, I succeeded ultimately in making contact with her.

"I'm glad that you were in touch with her," I said.

In finishing our conversation I mentioned to Scott that it was he, his stepsister Shelley, even his child to be, and others who would carry the torch forward.

"You know, you'll get to be around my age, and you'll begin thinking about these things, and you might say, I wish I'd done this and I wish I'd kept that contact up, I wish I'd done more with my father, and on and on. You'll have all these 'I wish I's.'"

I urged Scott to enrich his life by meeting these people and seeing what they do, hearing their stories, and how he might relate to them. In what way did he come in contact with them and in what way were they bound to one another?

Searching for Shelley

On March 1, 2008, I received the e-mail address for Shelley René Davis from Barbara Blackburn, Scott's mother. I dashed off an e-mail to Shelley in the long-held hope of making contact. I identified myself,

Scott Davis with his wife Michelle in a photo taken April 10, 2011. Scott is holding their daughter Belle Marie b. June 4, 2008, and Michelle is holding their son Grant Ryan b. April 28, 2010.

stating that I was the brother of her father David Davis. In the e-mail, I informed her that for nearly fifteen years, I have been engaged in the pastime of developing a family tree, and that my plan was to publish the results in a book, more than six hundred pages, which I would distribute to all interested family members at no cost to them. I continued, "Shelley, I have a copy of your certificate of birth, but know very little else about you. Besides getting to know one another better, it would be nice to have you and your family represented in my book."

Sending off the e-mail with a suggestion that she contact me at her convenience, I signed off: "Look forward to hearing from you, warm regards, Clyde."

No response from Shelley. Several weeks passed, and I was somewhat discouraged that perhaps I either had the wrong e-mail address, it had been changed, or the lack of a response indicated a lack of interest on her part. Not easily dissuaded, I picked up on Scott's mentioning that Shelley's husband was a football coach on an Arizona team. I wasn't sure whether it was a high school or college team, though. Scott's mom had also given me Shelley's married name as "Bontemps." Through the Internet I was able to quickly locate Arna Bontemps, assistant head football coach at Phoenix College. Included on the school's web site was a photograph of Coach Bontemps and the site also mentioned that

Scott Ryan Davis upon receiving his Masster of Education in Curriculum and Instruction from Portland State University, on June 12, 2011

he was "married and has four children." I hesitated to contact Mr. Bontemps by phone. I wanted to speak with his wife Shelley, but I was reluctant to insert myself in their lives if not welcome. When I finally managed to get up enough courage and place the call to Mr. Bontemps, I learned he was no longer at the college and was in transition to a coaching position at another school. At least now I had a reason for their not responding to my e-mail. Perhaps their change in residence was the answer, an answer that never came.

As a note of interest, in my search for Arna Bontemps

Left: Photo received March 3, 1967 of Ginger Lee Cleveland Davis (now Hart), who my brother David married in 1965. Right: Shelley Davis Bontemps b. January 11, 1967, with Ginger on March 18, 2009.

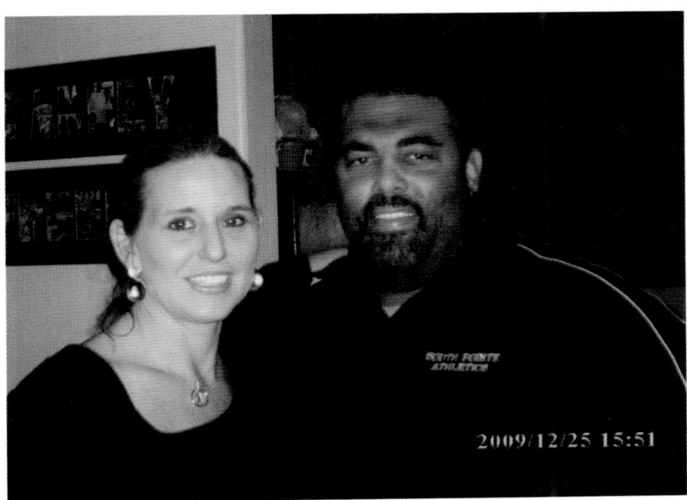

Shelley Davis Bontemps and her husband Arna Bontemps in a photo taken December 25, 2009

Shelley Davis Bontemps with her sons Tyler, age 15, on the left and Zachery, age 17, on the right

the football coach, I came across the web site for another Arna Bontemps, a noted African-American poet, author, anthologist, and librarian born in Alexandria, Louisiana, on October 13, 1902. There is an Arna Bontemps African-American Museum in Alexandria, Louisiana. As a novice researcher of family history, I'm particularly interested in the familial link between the two men.

More than two years passed before I tried one last time to locate Shelley. Again, following the football coach, I was able to make contact with a friend of his by phone. Mr. Bontemps must have passed on to Shelley that I was once again trying to reach her. On January 13, 2010, I received a call at 10:54 A.M. from Ginger Davis Hart, Shelley's mother. Shelley had asked Ginger to contact me. Shelley had heard that I was trying to reach her and acknowledged receiving my previous e-mails. I had met Ginger only once before, and as we recalled the circumstances of that occasion, she went on to say that Shelley had been reluctant to become involved in my book, since she last saw her father Dave at age sixteen. She had not been in contact with him since. Shelley's feeling was that she doesn't know her father, and "doesn't know all those people [in his family]."

Ginger was quite sympathetic to my cause of bringing families together, at least within the pages of my book, and reviewed briefly her daughter's life — that Shelley was married, was blessed with a wonderful husband, had five beautiful children, did daycare work currently out of her home, and was going to school online. Ginger promised me that she would make an effort on my behalf to convince Shelley that she should contact me; however, Ginger understood Shelley's reluctance to be involved. Shelley had my phone number and e-mail address and would contact me should she decide to participate in the book.

Later that afternoon, I received a call from Shelley Bontemps. We had the most wonderful conversation. She was forthcoming, sharing, warm, and friendly. She provided all marriage and birth dates, as well as her address and phone number. She also agreed, at my request, to forward photographs of her family, husband, and children for inclusion in my book.

I couldn't be happier, for now I have managed to embrace another person in our family and have drawn her closer to those with whom she shares so much.

Perhaps, one day my efforts to define our family will serve as a catalyst to spur my brother to reconnect with people who may wish for his presence in their lives. My brother has more grandchildren than either my sister (with five granddaughters) or myself (with five grandsons). He has seven grandchildren, five boys and two girls. As I complete this book, he has neither seen nor spoken to any of them.

Dave, we miss you and we love you.

Left to right: Zebadiah Alexander Bontemps, age 2, Arna Alexander Bontemps, age 7, and Pasia Dawn Bontemps, age 5

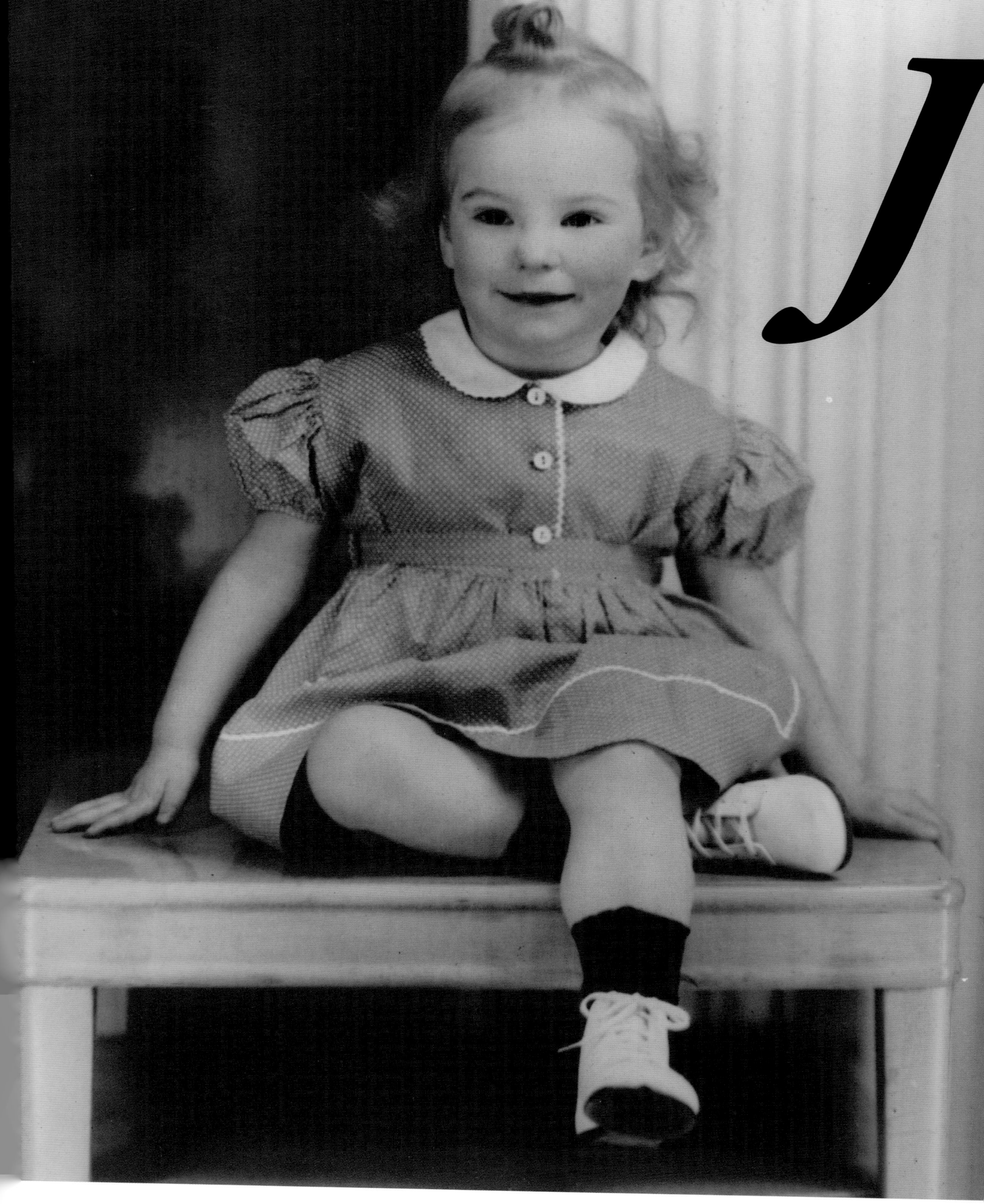
J

une *(tootsie)*

My Favorite Sister and Only Sister

…is someone whose story I would sincerely love to tell. But, unfortunately her story will have to be told another time by another person for purposes other than this family history. It's not that I didn't make the attempt. I did. Late one evening, I sat in my home with my then visiting sister and began to interview her, voice recorder in hand, with my wife Kay seated nearby. I commenced with June's approval hoping to slowly and comfortably open the floodgates to the most varied life she had led.

As she began speaking, I could see by her body posture, arms and legs crossed, deeply ensconced on the sofa in our family room, her face nearly a scowl, that she had something to say, indeed. I was unprepared for her remarks though, despite her demeanor. She seized upon the occasion to remind me of something I'd unwittingly done that betrayed a long held secret of hers of a significant, personal nature.

While employed, and during the holiday season, I often received the best wishes of those with whom I had the pleasure of doing business over prior years. On one occasion, I had received a greeting card from my personal and corporate attorney, Jacques Debrot. This particular year he had made a donation in my honor to a Catholic nun who was the director of a charitable organization and school that served the interests of troubled, often delinquent, and dependent young girls. I was especially pleased having some personal knowledge of the good they accomplished to write to my sister of my insight, his generosity, and the goodness of the cause at hand. I shared this information with my sister who had benefited from this worthy cause through my personal secretary.

And that was where I misstepped. I inadvertently exposed to others my sister's deeply held secret. Much to my sister's embarrassment, for as she so pointedly noted, from that moment on, every time she would contact or be contacted by my secretary, she would acutely suffer the exposure of that tightly held information. Obviously, few know what I know and even fewer are ever meant to know.

I'm proud of my sister. I love her dearly. I feel she has accomplished much good in her life. She is generous to a fault. Hard working, loving, and the most sensitive of people.

June is a study in contrasts. Her early life was filled with adventure and misadventure. She's bright and witty yet never finished high school. She began married life at age eighteen with a man eleven years her senior, and her last relationship was with a man she never married, but whose name she carries today.

June is fun loving, funny, and fun to be with. June's a woman with stars in her eyes. Fixated on the glamorous and the notorious, an avid reader of the *Enquirer*, *Star*, *Examiner*, and the *Globe*, she's in the supermarket line every Friday for fresh publications, not fresh fruit, and is a movie fan who views films two per evening, bringing her own soda in cans sequestered in her purse to avoid paying premium prices at the concession counter. June's a romantic. She believes, "You can't help whom you love," and though a party-girl especially early in her life (she says in those days it was called clubbing), yearns for the ideal: A home surrounded by a white picket fence and flowers to which her man would return at the end of a hard day's work. The men in June's life were more likely to be found evenings at a card table or in a casino gambling through the night or in a tavern throwing a few drinks down with the boys. And though she worked hard as a sort of June Cleaver to make a nice home, her choices in partnering as June Mora or June Rogers offered little chance that her dream would ever be fully realized. June was a beauty as a young woman … blonde, blue eyed, ample lips with fine features, tall with skin like porcelain and a figure that just wouldn't quit. A bit shy upon first meeting, with a slight lisp that contributed to the innocence of those early years.

June is now nearing the end of a career at the McCormick Place Convention Center in downtown Chicago. Starting at age thirty-two, she's worked there for nearly thirty-eight years, off and on, as need and her social calendar would permit. The decades of service have taken their toll. Rising at 3 A.M., driving from the far South Side of Chicago, in all kinds of weather, working fourteen hours straight, then facing the drive

June in photo dated July 23, 1953

May 6, 1952

January 1, 1991

September, 1984

November 2, 1986

May 8, 1986

November 2, 1986

June 27, 2003

home, can be an exhausting routine. But it was the type of work done during those years that took its physical toll, work that would wear anyone down. Carrying oversized trays piled high with sixteen dinners at a time as one of the convention center's banquet wait staff, would ultimately lead to chronic neck, shoulder, and back pain. She served as an à la carte wait staff on the President's Walk; she was a hostess but mostly, she was a convention booth server. Pushing carts (actually flat-bed hand trucks), overloaded with twenty-five cases of soda, twenty-five pounds of ice, fifty pounds of dry ice, five gallon coffee urns, and twenty trays of food, endless miles across a convention floor was hard enough. When the floor was carpeted it became even harder. On-the-job accidents combined with advancing years contributed to June's general physical decline. In December 1996, she slipped and hurt her left leg, but continued working for some time afterwards, believing it to be a minor injury. Later, it was determined that she had fractured her femur, and on August 24, 1999, an eighteen-inch titanium rod was implanted within the bone. After eight months of rehabilitation therapy, June returned to work in September 2000. This injury, a scoped left knee and broken metatarsal in her foot, along with the lasting effects of shoulder, neck, and back pain have slowed her down a bit.

JUNE ROGERS

From Beds of Flowers to Days in Bed

Ultimately, days of exhausting work coupled with an underlying depression would lead June to seek refuge, divorced from all social contact, an escape into what she terms her "sanctuary" for days at a time, coping in the only way she knew, with chronic bouts of depression, exhaustion, and physical pain. One is likely to find June tending her flower beds on her days off or at times in bed on her "off" days.

On the off days she simply "drops out," holing up in her bedroom until her mood brightens or her pain is alleviated. She is comforted by Cokes (no ice), Fannie May walnut clusters, TV, heating pad for her back, movie star tabloids, and longer than usual periods of sleep. She rebuffs all who attempt to contact her during these periods of recovery.

Equally known for her prowess about the interiors of others' as well as those of her children's homes, June freely gives of herself and her time. She's given much of her furniture away, while advising all on how to establish a comfortable and aesthetically pleasing home. Reorganizing someone's bathroom or kitchen cabinets, dresser drawers, or garage has an inordinate appeal to June. She's not averse to simply pitching in by painting a wall or two or more. She can be found equally at large in their gardens and upon their lawns. Today, when not working at McCormick Place, she's apt to be walking her children's dogs, picking up or dropping off a grandchild, watering their house plants, or dropping a son's police uniform off at the cleaners. Her car is constantly being cycled among her teenage granddaughters as well as their parents when need often arises.

But, none of this is really about June's story nor is it meant to define the person she's become.

No Shame, No Fame

Life is filled with both. My family is no exception. It is important to keep in mind that this book is basically mostly about the past, with reference to the present only as a means to jump starting a family history that, until now, lay silently dormant. It

Family gathering on June 29, 2005, Davises and Moras, at 8126 Beech Avenue, Munster, Indiana. Pictured left to right: Cynthia Davis Malara, Christine Davis Parrino, Kay Davis, Clyde Davis, June Mora Rogers, Erin Mora Quenzler, Alfonse Mora, Karen Mora, Cole Davis, David Davis Mora, Julie Mora and April Mora.

is my book. I take full and sole responsibility for its content. If I've offended anyone along the way I sincerely apologize. That was certainly not my intention. However, I am interested in the facts as nearly as I can understand them and to submit an honest portrayal of those linked, one to the other as seen and experienced through this work of social history. I have, undoubtedly, made mistakes. Errors of fact will surely occur. Judgment in error can't be far behind. This book was never meant to read like a greeting card. Nor was its purpose to only flatter those profiled in it, quite the contrary. As the reader will note, an entire chapter is devoted to critically analyzing the recurring themes of familial asocial behavior of ancestors, of those past as well as the living.

I want to share the real story of my sister, but I will respect her wishes, in hopes that this will afford her the comfort and peace she seeks. However, I still believe that had she allowed the telling of her story in an historical context, partly as a reflection of the times and circumstances in which we lived, she would understand that we are all human and a product of our environment. Not so unique, just simply humans wanting a better life. To paraphrase Katherine Scott Sturdevant in *Bringing Your Family History to Life Through Social History*, one person's "deep, dark secret" in one era may be commonplace to another.

One thing that I am at liberty to speak of is the relationship that my sister June has had with my wife Kay over the years. From the time I started dating Kay, they have been more like sisters than sisters-in-law. And because June has such an outrageous sense of humor, and Kay is always up for a good time, we have had numerous, funny and happy times together. The three of us have often found ourselves together in each other's homes, vacationing or on the road. We've taken June on trips to Las Vegas, Paris, California, Arizona, and to our homes in New York and Florida.

"Auntie Kay"

Over the years, June has referred to Kay affectionately as "Auntie Kay." Of course, Kay is not June's aunt, but she has been unstintingly available to all June's children and other family members whenever they have expressed a need for help — usually, involving counseling or advice. June would often say to one or another of her children, "Talk to Auntie Kay, she can help you." The phrase was used with such frequency that it became part of our family's colloquial language. It remains so to this day, and it is not uncommon in an exchange between the two that they each refer to the other as Auntie Kay or Auntie June. I even become confused when calling out to my sister as to whether she's June, Tootsie, or Auntie June.

There have been lots of laughs over the years. I recall on one such occasion, June was planning to visit us in New York and prefaced her visit with the statement that "all she wanted was to relax and stay at home," no Broadway, no New York City, just stay at home. When we met June at LaGuardia Airport in the baggage claim area, Kay appeared in her bathrobe and slippers and was

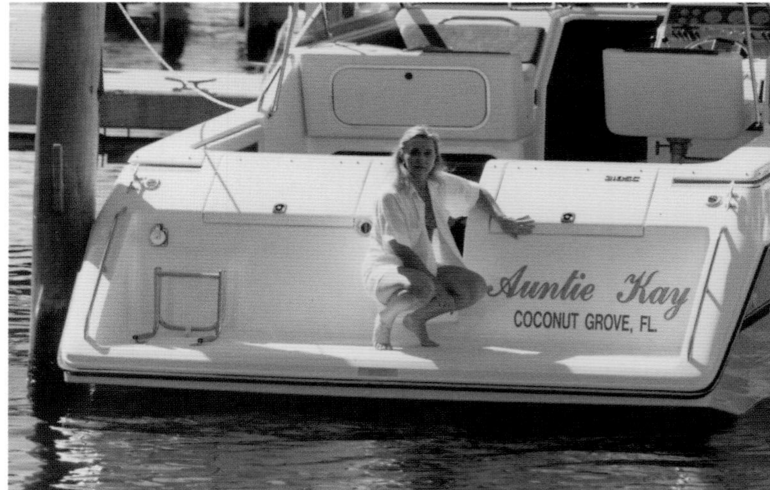

I became so accustomed to hearing my wife being called "Auntie Kay" that I placed the name on my two powerboats. June's Auntie Kay on board the Auntie Kay, *Grove Isle, Florida, November 10, 1988.*

carrying a robe for June! Needless to say they created quite a stir among arriving passengers amidst all the confusion.

Another time, while staying with us in Pound Ridge, June accompanied Kay to the New Canaan, Connecticut, train station to pick me up one evening on my return home from work in New York City. June had been regaled by numerous stories of Kay's odyssey to the train station to meet a particular incoming train only to find that I was not on it as anticipated. Sometimes, she told June, she would return two or three times to the station before I finally arrived. The drive to the station took half an hour each way, and this occurred before cell phones were in use. Kay told June, "We will have to wait for the next one," explaining that by the time they returned home and back again, the next train would have arrived. Hearing all this June decided that it was good for a laugh and that I should be taught a lesson regarding timely arrivals. Kay was quick to agree.

June and Lee Rogers in October 1978

Disembarking from the train with hundreds of other weary commuters, among bumper to bumper cars awaiting their pickups, I heard a shouting, crazy woman, my sister, leaning out the car window calling out to me, "What's wrong with you? We've been here for an hour and a half, waiting for you — where have you been? Get into the car you jerk." Embarrassment is not the word for what I felt. They, on the other hand, were having a hilarious time of it.

In Las Vegas, getting off a hotel elevator and looking down a seemingly endless corridor of white walls and ceiling, with a myriad number of white doors to hotel rooms, June exclaimed, "It's a mirage!" to which I responded, "Of course it is, we're at the Mirage!" We laughed so hard, instantly realizing that the visual effect had some how caught up with the name of our Las Vegas hotel. That moment and the next day, hurtling through the desert at one hundred miles an hour in a big ass Cadillac Deville singing at the top of our lungs, with taped songs of the '50s, are fond memories of time with my sister, Tootsie, always ready to be happy.

Upon returning to work in September 2000, and qualifying as a handicapped worker, she no longer does the heavy labor of carrying loaded trays for sit-down dinners or delivering food and beverages on hand trucks to various venues within McCormick Place. At age seventy, she continues to work. The work is less strenuous as a booth server or attending buffets. She continues to love the interaction with her fellow employees and the occasional celebrity.

These are the golden years for June, and her goal is simply to "chill." Going to the movies with her Heath candy bar (not always available at the movie theater) and a can of Coca-Cola hidden in her purse remains one of her favorite pastimes. She tends her yard and flower gardens (and, occasionally, unsolicited, those of her neighbors), and enjoys the company of her twenty-two-year-old granddaughter, Brittany, who currently works as a hostess and waitress at a well-known, downtown Chicago restaurant. June, of course, has experience to share with her granddaughter regarding the most comfortable shoes to wear while serving customers or how to properly set a table, as well as what constitutes a good tip, and whether or not, and to what extent, those tips must be shared with other co-workers. June still walks her children's dogs, advises them on how to keep their gardens and decorate their homes.

Once Brittany finds an apartment in downtown Chicago and leaves, June plans to put the house on the market for sale, probably this fall of 2010.

When it comes to discussing her troubled past with her children, or with me and Kay, June has drawn a line separating her from her younger self, and will refer to that younger self as "Oh, that was that other woman," or "...that other June."

Nearly every Wednesday, my sister takes a ten-minute drive from her home in Lansing, Illinois, to the Holy Cross Catholic Cemetery, in Calumet City, Illinois, to tend the gravesite of her companion and love of thirty years, Adrian Lee Rogers. She had promised his mother that she would look after her son's burial site. June Windexes Lee's headstone and that of a friend buried nearby, does a little trimming around the stones, and surely spends a moment reflecting on times past, before leaving her usual flower, expressing her love and devotion.

June "Tootsie" Davis Mora Rogers pictured above with Adrian "Lee" Rogers, her off and on again companion of some thirty years. He was born March 22, 1929, a father of three children with his former wife Sylvia, whom he divorced. He died July 12, 1997. Lee was a member and "shop steward" of the Structural Iron Workers Union, Local No.1, Chicago. Though June and Lee never married, she assumed his name as if they were. Their thirty-year relationship undoubtedly qualified them as being in a common law marriage. I do know for certain that my sister was carried on Lee's health insurance policy and that she filed the federal and state tax returns as husband and wife.

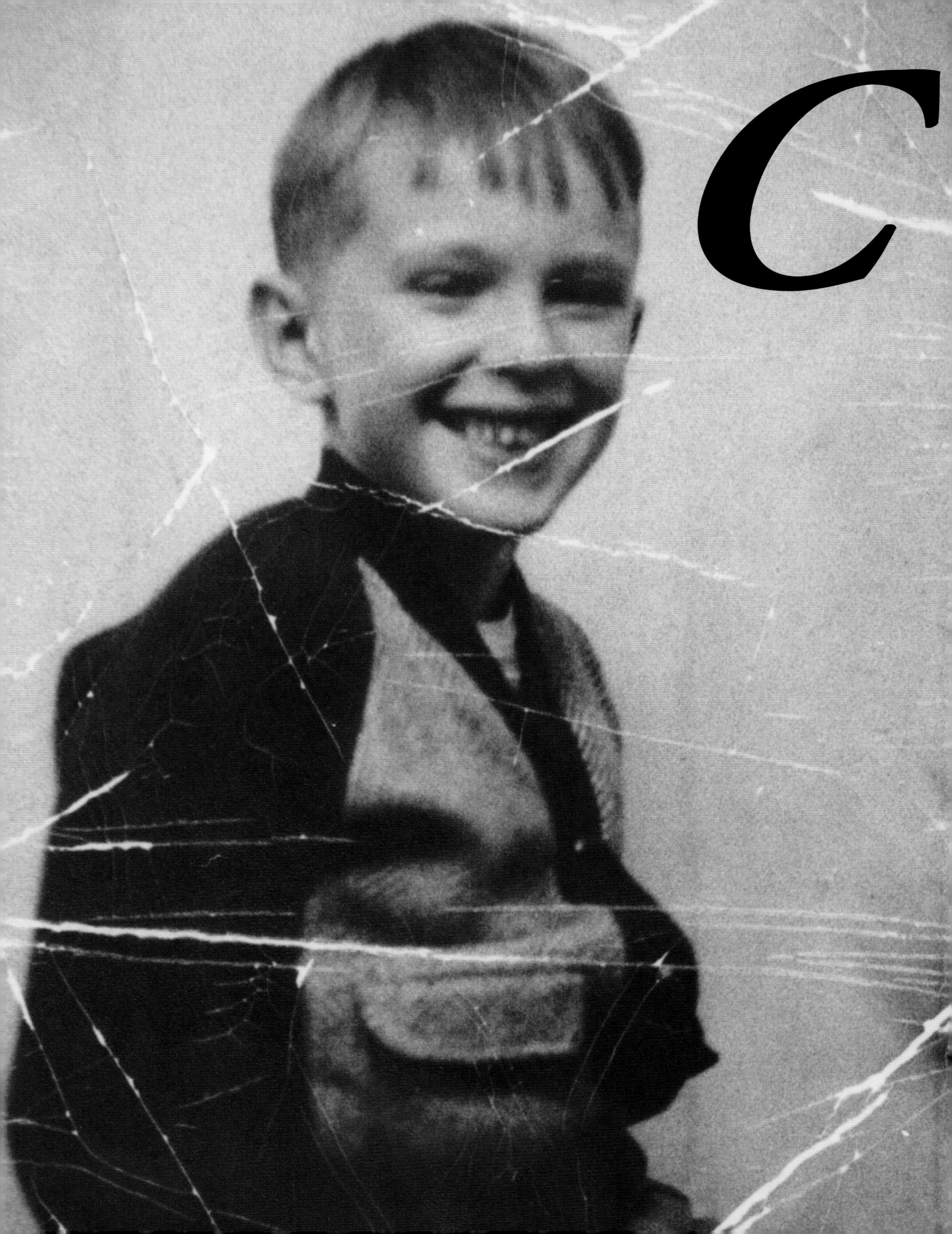
C

lyde *(duke)*

My Story

At first I thought someone else should write "My Story." Unfortunately, any professional colleague, neighbor, college friend, or family member could only offer a quasi one-dimensional view.

I've attempted to reveal the true nature or character of those around me, as well as my ancestors, to the extent I'm able. Really, no one knows my story better than I, though my wife Kay and former business partner Morgan Cline could give anyone interested a fair accounting of what I'm really about.

My wife was there with me when I was seventeen years of age. We grew up together and some fifty-five years later we're still growing, together, married fifty-one of those years.

My partner Morgan Cline and I met in 1968 at Klemptner Advertising, Inc., in New York City. My wife and I spent the past several days with him in Centerville, Iowa, for the annual "Pancake Day" festivities (September 29, 2006) and to get an updated tour of all the good works and improvements he's contributed to his beloved home town. These two relationships, each a partnership for life, are certainly the longest lasting and most significant I've formed.

I'm from a broken family. I never really knew my father, have been at odds with my mother, don't speak to my brother. All have lived a life remarkably different from mine. "My earliest memories" center around being in the company of others, that is, those other than my parents.

Compared to my sister, brother, wife, and others I know, my long-term memory is quite lacking. This is not a recent phenomenon. It seems I have always had difficulty recalling the past. It's hard for me to explain why, but I've a strong suspicion it's because I've spent, relatively speaking, little time socializing with family over the years, refreshing past common experiences, recalling, retelling, exchanging information, and thus reaffirming the sequence of events shared.

As you may recall from this book's preface, I grew up mostly without the presence of a father. We children were moved from home to home often without the company of "Dad." Often in the early years, we lived with my maternal grandmother, aunts, and uncles. Then later, I spent summers with my grandma and grandpa Davis in Indiana.

Art

I do recall a particular winter, at least I believe it was winter, perhaps early spring, when I was visiting Charlie and Rebecca Davis in their two-story farmhouse. One day I discovered that young chicks were being raised upstairs in my grandparents' house. Newspapers were spread across the floor to catch their droppings within a pen of chicken-coop wire constructed to contain them.

Just inside the door off the living room was a set of stairs leading up to the chicken coop on the second floor. And, most importantly, at the bottom of those stairs where the steps grew larger and radiated as they turned away from the door and upwards, was usually a stack of old newspapers — probably a supply from which to recover the floor above housing the chicks. There I would sit on the larger steps comfortably reading the newspaper comics, sometimes copying the cartoons when paper was available, or turning instead to a small blackboard and chalk that was surprisingly there at the bottom of the steps as well. The earliest recollection of my artistic nature was on those steps.

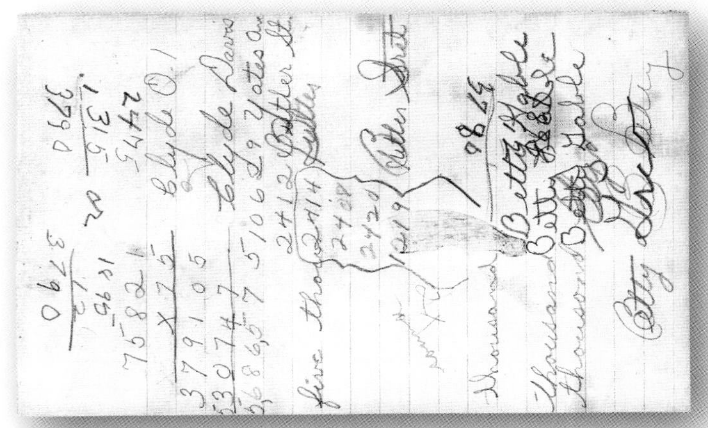

This is my earliest surviving artwork. The drawing to the right was probably copied on the reverse side of my scrap paper used for arithmetic and handwriting practice. The writing seems to be in more than one hand. I was probably 7 or 8 at the time, and just learning script.

Clyde Davis in a 1945 picture of his first grade class at the Bright School, Chicago, Illinois. Clyde is in bib overalls on the far left in the second row, next to the teacher.

Later I was to realize that in similar solitary moments I would instinctively turn to this artistic inclination in lieu of the presence of others. As a youngster, I was often sent to bed early on summer evenings so my mother could have free time for herself. Not being able to sleep I would stand at the bedroom window where I could see and hear other kids joyfully playing kick-the-can, a form of hide and seek, in the square below as dusk fell. I would draw at that window, using the deep windowsill as my drawing board, copying illustrated Civil War battles

1/24/'52
Congratulations
and Wishes
Best to a
Coming Artist!
A. Banks.

Mrs. A. Banks, my 8th grade art teacher, in a photo that appeared in the Chicago Daily Calumet, Chicago, Illinois, April 1, 1958, and a page from my autograph book signed by her upon my graduation from Orville T. Bright grammar school, which served the South Deering neighborhood.

from a library textbook. When I was hospitalized with jaundice (infectious hepatitis) at Bob Roberts Hospital, I would carve comic book characters from bars of Ivory Soap. My aunt June who frequently visited me at the hospital was particularly taken with a three-dimensional head of Donald Duck and kept it for years at her kitchen window. Later as a high school art major, I sat at the kitchen table fulfilling my weekly sketch book assignment, drawing a glass ash tray, attempting to capture its myriad reflections, late into the night.

There was no money for art supplies, good drawing paper being the hardest to come by. I would visit the local food store next to the housing project where I lived and, after a particular sale for produce or meat was over, request the used window posters, coveting the pure, snow white back of each. Another better source for drawing paper was the Calumet Bakery at 106th Street between Bensley and Oglesby avenues. The bakery had great Long Johns, Bismarks, and Cream Puffs. Donuts and such ended up in a sack or bag to the customer, but it was the Cream Puffs and other more delicate pastries that required a pressed paper plate in which to be wrapped with squares of white paper and then tied with string hanging from above. I'd ask for extra paper to draw on. After they became familiar with my artistic interest and without money for a purchase, I would still stop by and ask for "extra" paper.

In grammar school I recall painting Santa Claus and various Christmas decorations on the classroom door windows or decorating the bulletin boards for my teachers. This was done during class in lieu of my learning English or math, at my teachers' request. Knowing how to diagram a sentence or manage my multiplication tables were tasks that I happily spurned to practice my craft. At the Orville T. Bright Grammar School, probably in the eighth grade, I was formally introduced to art. My teacher, Mrs. A.J. Banks, was the first to professionally channel my talent. It was she who first taught me to draw from life. My first sketch class took place on the east stairwell landing, half way between the lower and upper floors of our school. We were

The photo below shows me at age 18 working on a poster on the theme "Employ the Physically Handicapped." I won first place and was awarded a $150 savings bond in an art contest sponsored by the Illinois department of the Disabled American Veterans in cooperation with the Governor's Committee on Employment of the Physically Handicapped. The award was presented by Mayor Richard J. Daley.

seated at a large window overlooking an alleyway in an adjoining neighborhood across from the school playground. It was this amalgam of garages, trees, telephone poles, and fences that was to be my initiation into the world of perspective, the art of conveying distance and the sense of depth.

Later, when I graduated, Mrs. Banks signed my autograph book with "To a coming artist."

Chicago Vocational High School

On the far South Side of Chicago, three high school choices existed: Bowen Public High School, Mt. Carmel Catholic High School, and the Chicago Vocational High School. Bowen was known for kids who went on to college. Mt. Carmel was for children whose parents could pay extra, and Vocational was for, let's say, those who "worked with their hands." Being from South Deering or Irondale, as it was often called, and living in a public housing project I was obviously destined for the Vocational High School.

Merrill Lyon

I had wood shop, machine shop, drafting shop, and finally commercial art shop. All "Smith Hughes" courses sprung from "The National Vocational Education (Smith-Hughes) Act, (Public Law No. 347, Sixty-fourth Congress-S. 703)," approved February 23, 1917, and still in effect thirty-nine years later when I was to graduate from Chicago Vocational High School (CVS). Smith-Hughes schools provided education in agriculture, trades, home economics, and industrial subjects to prepare students for employment, with "at least half of the time of such instruction to be given to practical work on a useful or productive basis...."

Commencing with junior year each student chose a "major." Mine was Commercial Art Shop. There I encountered Miss Merrill Lyon, a vocational teacher who, for two solid years, would wring from me every ounce of artistic growth and production that was legally permissible.

Miss Lyon inspired me from practically my first day in her class. She'd worked in New York City, discussed advertising, explained what an art director was, and regaled us with stories of how hard they worked and how they would fly from New York to Miami on weekend R & R trips. She was *the first* to peak my interest in a life beyond South Chicago.

Miss Lyon and I had a strained relationship. She found me to be challenging, distracted by things outside her classroom. She would address the other art students by their first names, but I was always called "Davis," as in "Conrad hand in your work," "Davis where's your sketch pad?" She coveted my talent. I resented her authority and brusque manner.

Over the two-year span we often butted heads. I was talented but troubled. I'd get into racial conflicts. A good friend, Chauncey Moore, was black and a fellow art student. High school whites didn't appreciate that relationship. In response to the unkindly treatment of Chauncey I made an inadvertent, disparaging remark about Mexicans, not understanding why one was accepted and the other not. That also wasn't appreciated and created a fair amount of personal turmoil for me. Being quiet, shy, skinny, and artistic I was intimidated by others. In grammar school I was picked on, chased daily, and when caught, beaten up. These frequent run-ins with students, or more appropriately

Above is an oil painting with heavy use of a spatula in evidence, a technique more like applying plaster to a surface or buttering bread than painting. The piece was executed by me in high school. It is now in the possession of my grandson, Ross, who upon seeing it stored in a closet of his great-grandmother Mary Davis, admired the painting and asked if he could have it. Below is a self portrait, body only, a charcoal drawing on Stratmore paper approximately 22" H. x 13½" W. This drawing was done in grammar school, I believe, and was on display in my mother's home until I married. Today it hangs in my son Cole's and daughter-in-law Tammi's home in Encinitas, California. Good art always finds a home.

Swimming Team Tops–Best Ever

The swimming team thus far this season has a record of eight wins and four losses and as far as Coach Peters sees they shouldn't lose any of the coming meets. Coach Peters said "This is the BEST TEAM I've had at CVS in five years".

The teams which fell in the Mermans wake are Tilden Tech, Hyde Park twice, Harper, Morgan Park, Calumet, South Shore and Parker.

The team still has meets left with Parker, Calumet, Lindbloom, and two with Tilden.

On April 16, the team will go to Roosevelt High School for the twenty-five yard pool championship meet.

The fellows on the team are given a certain number of points for the position in which they finish in a race. If a swimmer comes in first he receives five points, if he comes in second four points, and third three points. The fellow with the highest number of points is Clyde Davis with fifty-five points, right behind him in order of most points is Wally Bronkhorst with forty-nine points, Stephen Davis with forty-two points, Louie Freeland with thirty-eight points, Gary Serletic with thirty-five points, Ken Reynolds with thirty-four points, John Hill with twenty-two points, Bob Erickson with thirteen points, and with six points apiece Dave Davis, and Jack Delapena.

A swimming meet consists of nine individual races, four in the Junior Division and five in the Senior Division.

Reynolds, R. Heritage and C. Davis prepare for the next meeting.

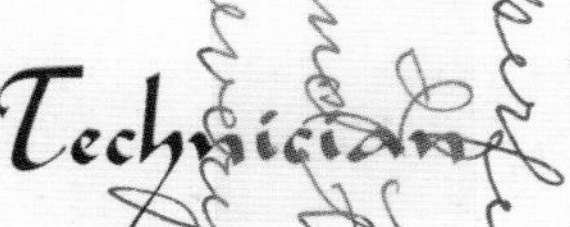

Technician

A high school yearbook always brings back wonderful memories, and we on the *Technician* Staff have endeavored to make the 1956-57 yearbook the best ever. Although many hours of hard work have been put into this book, we feel that it has been well worth while. As the end of our task draws near, we sincerely hope that we have succeeded in showing you why Chicago Vocational High School is in the spotlight. In the years to come, as you reminisce over these pages of pictures and words, we know that this graphic record of your happy days, your friends and teachers, will bring many a chuckle from you and your families.

To our administrators, to our faculty, and to the whole student body, the *Technician* Staff gives a wholehearted and sincere "thanks" for all of the help, patience, and co-operation you have given us — without which this publication would be impossible.

We leave you with this reminder:

We know there is an error or two —
It's we who are to blame;
And if we have omitted you
We hang our heads in shame!

The *Technician* Staff

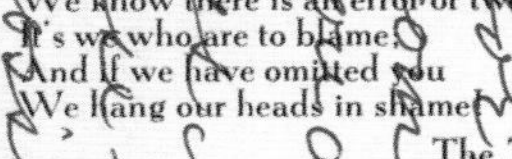

TECHNICIAN STAFF
Annette Crawley, Carol Engle, Arlene Smith, Sandra Fuller, Nancy Batista, Diane Malmberg, Shirley Andrysiak, Clyde Davis, Beverly Williams, Sylvia Kormos, Joan Abram, Barbara Sobol, Bonnie Gillette, Carol Smith, Shirley Witry, Sandra Kabelis, Margie Dahl.

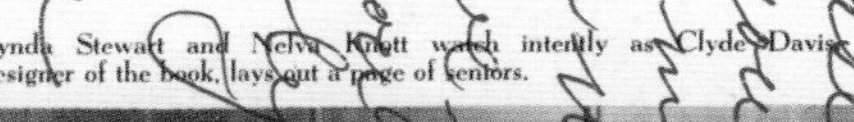

Lynda Stewart and Nelva Knott watch intently as Clyde Davis, designer of the book, lays out a page of seniors.

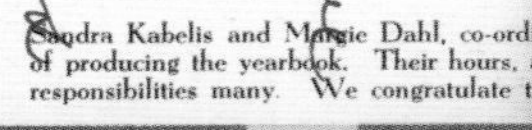

Sandra Kabelis and Margie Dahl, co-ordi[nators] of producing the yearbook. Their hours, a[...] responsibilities many. We congratulate th[...]

Page above and picture to right are from the Chicago Vocational High School yearbook, the Technician 1956–57. *I was the graphic designer for the yearbook.*

Chicago VOCATIONAL

"run-a-ways," continued into high school. It wasn't until I joined the CVS swim team, worked out, and practiced and developed physically, that my student standing improved.

Along with the social issues of fitting in, there was little sympathy and support from home. Money, or the lack of it, made continuing in school a challenge. I can remember one morning awakening my mother, asking if I could have a quarter for bus fare to school, and her response from the bed, denying me, with "Ask me where I'm going to get it, Clyde." I walked the twenty blocks to CVS that morning. Sadly, I must admit, I took to stealing from downtown Chicago art supply stores, discontinuing the practice when I was chased down the street and nearly caught by a security guard. But that didn't prevent me from clumsily attempting to steal a pair of leather gloves with rabbit fur lining at the local Sears. My mistake was in circling the glove counter one too many times. You see I would steal one glove and then return for the other. When I was apprehended, I was so scared I actually peed in my pants. After returning the one glove, I was released. Sympathy no doubt played a part in the decision, and so ended my career of crime.

My intimidation, social conflict, lack of money, shyness, all became part of the challenge that Miss Lyon faced as she cajoled and guided me along my path to artistic destiny.

My Early Work History

Looking back on my days as a youngster, I'm reminded that I began working for pay as soon as legally allowed. At age fifteen, in 1953, I was setting pins at Crest Recreation's Bowling Alley, a job my uncle Dave had secured for me. It was located at 5724 Stony Island, near the Rumpus Room tavern uncle Dave owned. My tax return for that year showed that I made a total of $56.40.

In 1955 I served as a caddy at Olympia Fields Country Club, which ultimately led to a position as bar boy, stocking and otherwise servicing the fine bars at this exclusive club. It was while working at the country club that I got my first real taste of the privileged life, seeing members with their families, especially children my age, enjoying club amenities. The summer of 1955 left its mark on me. This was the life: working the club poolside bar and serving theme parties, like Hawaiian Night, where hundreds of live orchids and floral leis were used as decoration, and everyone dressed in costume and danced to island music. I made $353.95 that summer.

Still in high school in 1956 and seeking income yearly, I worked as an usher at the Oriental movie theater on Randolph Street in downtown Chicago, making $158.20 doing that. After graduating from high school in June (185 in a class of 600), I managed to be hired by Vogue Wright Studios, falsely promising my employer that I was not planning to go on to college in the fall.

From 1957 through 1961, I struggled unsuccessfully to remain a full-time student at the University of Illinois. During that period as an on-again/off-again student, I had more than a dozen different employers, according to my federal tax returns.

In 1957–58 I worked for Newman Food Service (dorm kitchen dishwasher/server) and Universal Music Corp (summer truck delivery of juke boxes). After going on probation and being kicked out for poor grades, I had to sit out a semester in 1958 before being accepted again as a student. I got a job at Whitaker Guernsey Studio in downtown Chicago. It was a premier art studio of its time, servicing all the big Chicago ad agencies. Working in the studio mounting and matting department — all the artwork created by the illustrators and designers passed through my hands — I was exposed to the best professional art being produced by a variety of artists. So, in effect, I was serving an "externship," now often required by the better universities to introduce students, often in their junior year, to experience the real world of their chosen discipline. I earned $1,090.80.

And Then Came Kay

In my junior year I met Kay Douthart, also a student at CVS. Kay became the single stabilizing force in my life. We fell in love and have been in love for fifty-four years, fifty as a married couple. With Kay came a more focused application of my talent. Not surprisingly we met over a school assignment of hers that required art expertise. She fed me, she bought me birthday gifts, she'd return to school after having been let out earlier to meet me after swim team practice so we could simply walk the ten blocks to her home, together. Later she would ride the Chicago Transit Authority (CTA) elevated train to be with me, from the South Side to downtown Chicago, where I worked and then, alone, she'd return home. She sent me her tip money as a carhop at Richard's Drive-in Carfeteria, when I was broke in my freshman year of college. I won poster contests, scholastic achievement contests, a Minneapolis School of Art Instruction Course, and even a four-year scholarship to the Art Institute of Chicago, after a city-wide, one-day creative "shoot-out" of high school senior art students. And, despite a scholarship in hand, I gained entry as an applicant with my art portfolio submission to the School of Fine and Applied Arts at the University of Illinois at Champaign-Urbana.

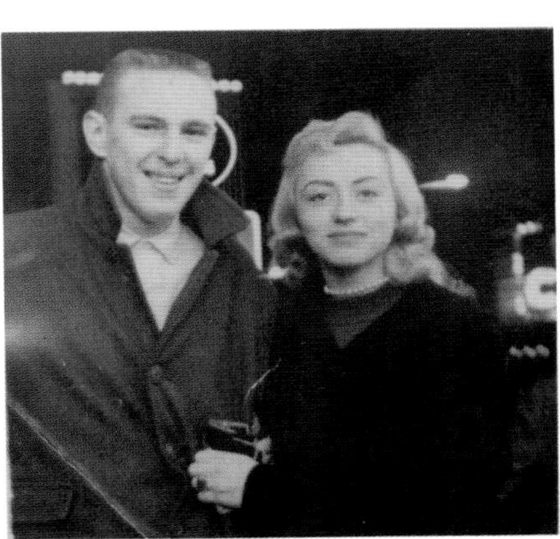

Clyde and Kay Davis on State Street, Chicago in street photographer's photo

My CVS high school portfolio qualified me for a position with Vogue Wright Studios as a commercial artist in the summer of 1956 after high school graduation while I awaited acceptance of my application to the U of I.

At Illinois I quickly realized my proficiency as an artist. When I'd be surrounded by fellow art students in figure drawing class, with one asking, "What pencil is that you're using, a 1B or is it a 2B?" I knew Miss Lyon had trained me well.

It was Miss Lyon who taught me the skills and techniques of silk screening, lettering, figure drawing — along with oil painting, watercolor, wood block, and jewelry making. She also required weekly sketch book drawings. Bless her soul for saving a young man from an otherwise uncertain future, for inspiring in him the desire to better oneself through a God-given talent.

Grades vs. Earnings

Kay graduated high school June 1957 in the top ten of a class of 485, a full year after me. She could not immediately afford to go on to college. Instead, she went to work, earned enough to enter the U of I in January 1958, the same school term that I,

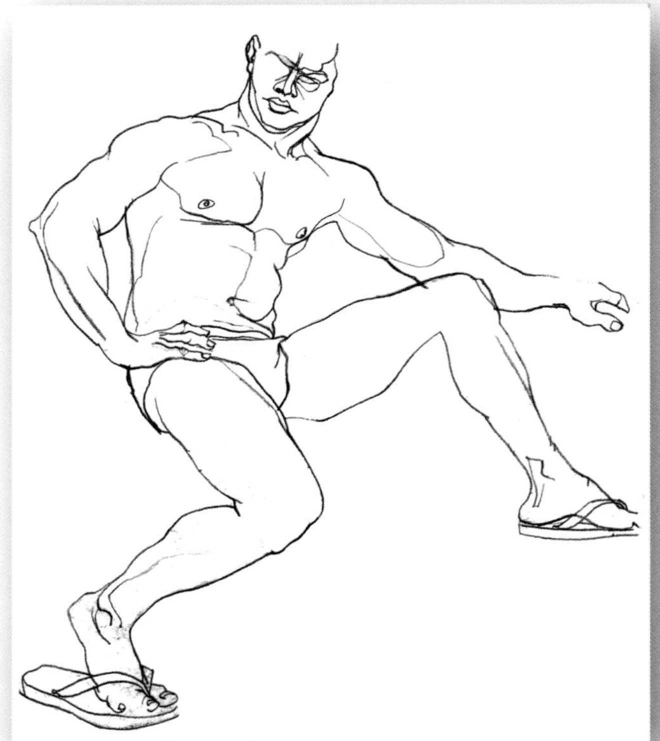

Kay Douthart in uniform at age 15 during the summer of 1955 while employed at Richard's Drive-In Carfeteria waiting for the "Mystery Customer," who was hired by the company to secretly check on the appearance and service of his carhops. If all went well, a very large tip was awarded. Though Kay was not the Mystery Customer's server, the manager received a telephone call from the Mystery Customer asking, "Who was the blonde?" and would she agree to be in a newspaper advertisement stating, "The prettiest girls in town work at Richard's." Further, he wanted Kay to be interviewed the following week at the Conrad Hilton Hotel in downtown Chicago where a radio program was aired live from the Boulevard Room. Kay agreed to do so and was indeed interviewed on this program.

having once again failed the university academic standards, was not able to return to campus after having been readmitted for a second time. We did manage to actually be on campus at the U of I for one entire semester from September to January 1958. In 1959 Kay worked for the Chicago Federation of Musicians, not following up on her two consecutive semesters at the U of I.

By May of 1959, still struggling with grades and broke, I tossed in the towel and accepted my fate: school was not for me. I was working for the University Press as a graphic designer that last semester as well as at the Agricultural Extension Service. I also waited tables at the Big Ten Restaurant on Green Street, but no way could I keep up with the expense of school. The more I worked, the more my grades suffered; without good grades I could not get a scholarship. Due to my high school art education and my quasi-professional work experience, I excelled at my art courses, getting A++ on assignments while hardly ever attending class, and consequently raising the envy and ire of my fellow students. My work was hung alongside theirs for jury grading. The time not spent in the classroom was instead time I could use to work gardening at $1.25 an hour. But the trade-off, class vs.

I loved to draw and being uncomfortable with the use of color, usually worked in black and white in a variety of media. The two line drawings above are in graphite pencil. At top on the opposite page is a lithograph printed from etched stone. The drawing at the bottom is done in grease pencil on cardboard with a rubber cement shellac overwash. I often emulated the style of a favorite Chicago artist of mine in the '50s, Franklin McMahon.

All the images on this spread were produced as a student while attending the University of Illinois.

job, was not as workable when it came to my electives, such as literature, geography, or astronomy. I did poorly by not attending class.

So I departed Chicago on a Greyhound bus early that summer with a bag full of fried chicken my grandma made, seeking my fortune in New York. I'll never forget the bus pulling into the 34th Street terminal as I sat in disbelief looking at the size of the sidewalks — nearly as wide as the street they paralleled. Walking out of the bus terminal on 34th Street I was surprised once more by the sheer volume of pedestrians hurriedly passing by me.

A few blocks east at 9th Avenue and 34th was the YMCA Sloan House, where I had gotten a room barely wide enough to fit a small bed, chair, and cabinet — very spartan. The Y had a cafeteria and community bathrooms. Not the best of accommodations. My room faced into an inner courtyard. To sense the weather, I opened my window at least once, thinking it was raining, only to realize someone above my room had chosen to urinate from his window, rather than walk to the facilities on his floor.

The USO dances were free entertainment. I watched, not being a dancer. Directly across 34th Street from the Y was a deli where I discovered my first chocolate egg cream. I remember at the subway entrance on 34th Street late one night being asked by a male pedestrian, if I had a match. "No," I replied, "I don't smoke," to which he responded, "What do you do, suck ---k?"

I'd spend the soft summer evenings sitting alongside the Seagram's Building reflecting pool, just opposite the Four Seasons restaurant, after peering through its darkened windows and shimmering chain mail curtains at the elegant clientele inside. Thirty-six years later, my partners, Kay, and I would be celebrating the sale of our ad agency with the acquirers in one of the Four Seasons' private rooms.

In the evening I would often simply walk from the Y over to 7th Avenue and then along 7th Avenue, stopping for a watermelon slice at one of the open air fruit stands on my way up to Times Square. There I'd hang out on the sidewalk outside the Metropole, a popular Dixieland Jazz Club with topless dancers. Gene Krupa regularly appeared there along with Henry Red Allen, a member of the house band. I listened to the music through the always-open entrance, people constantly flowing in and out of the place, but I was more interested in getting a glimpse of the dancers. You could, if you properly positioned yourself on the sidewalk (I wasn't the only guy attempting this), see the girls doing their thing up on a raised catwalk-like stage behind the bar.

Almost immediately upon my arrival that summer of 1959, I secured a job at the Ted Bates Ad Agency, working in the mounting and matting room. I earned $593 that summer.

On the weekends, my loneliest time, I would walk about the city. One Saturday I hopped a subway train to Far Rockaway, its last stop, Rockaway Beach in Queens. I spent a shirtless day walking along the beach among thousands of bathers. Later that evening and the following Sunday I suffered from horrific sunburn.

Usually my Sundays were spent at Central Park watching softball games between celebrities and actors. Sitting among their families and friends in the stands I became voyeuristically part of the Actors Guild. Martin Balsam was one such actor and at the time performing frequently on stage and screen. Sometimes I would walk about the Upper West Side in the late afternoon and

Form 3300C

QUICK SERVICE | **WESTERN UNION** | LOW RATES

MONEY ORDER MESSAGE

Money Sent by Telegraph and Cable to All the World

W. P. MARSHALL, PRESIDENT

MK 348 WEST 34th ST. NY — AUG 19 1959

No. NBP003

To CLYDE DAVIS
WM SLOANE HOUSE

The Money Order paid you herewith is from CATHERINE DUTHART

at CHICAGO ILL and included the following message:

HURRY UP.

...NION TELEGRAPH COMPANY

Kay and I cutting our wedding cake at the home of Kay's parents shortly after our more formal gathering at Phil Smidt's restaurant (see photograph on next page).

evening hours hearing the laughter of young children at play in the gangways or overhearing a family sitting down to dinner. Kay and I could rent one of these apartments, I thought.

This was pretty much my New York in the summer of 1959. Enthralled by a city, looming so large, spread so wide with so many, and yet I was never so lonely.

Kay was working at the Musicians Union in Chicago. School was behind me, so I believed, and my career was off to a less than spectacular start.

Marriage

Here I was, alone among eight million inhabitants in New York City, with no friends, and little family, just my great uncle John Benko and his wife Anna. I wanted to get married and have a family living in New York City. I even looked at cold-water flats in upper Manhattan, asking Kay to join me. She was non-compliant, offering an alternative: "Return home, go back to school, and I'll marry you." An offer I couldn't refuse, especially when she wired me the $69 air fare.

On September 19, 1959, we were married in Chicago. Tom Spasoff, a former roommate at the University of Illinois, was my best man and Jeanette Rock was Kay's maid of honor. My father did not attend the event, nor am I sure he was aware of its occurrence. That same day Kay and I returned to the University of Illinois at Champaign-Urbana. Two and a half years later, with two children in tow, we departed the campus for New York City, four hours short of fulfilling my requirements for graduation. Miss Lyon had planted deeply the seed that I was determined would bear fruit.

Brief digression. In 1997, Kay came up with the idea of getting the University of Illinois to grant my degree, based on my life experience. This was to be a surprise birthday present, since Kay knew how much it bothered me that I had never actually received my degree. She contacted the University and initiated the process. During our second Roots Trip, I mentioned to Kay that I thought it would be a good idea to contact the University to get my degree. Kay then told me whom I had to contact. So much for her surprise birthday present.

I was told that I would have to provide a portfolio of my work for review. Four hours of academic work versus more than thirty-five years of a highly successful career in my chosen field, and I'm being told that I have to present samples of my work to demonstrate that I deserve a degree! Nevertheless, I presented

Mary Savage, my grandmother, me, and my mother Mary Davis on September 19, 1959, our wedding day

Ann May Bauer Douthart, Catherine "Kay" Douthart Davis, and Richard Douthart on September 19, 1959

myself and my portfolio and was interviewed at length on a rainy day, while Kay sat outside in our car. They were highly impressed with what I had achieved, and on January 15, 1998, the University of Illinois bestowed on me a Bachelor of Fine Arts degree in Advertising.

The Wedding Suit

After one semester at the University of Illinois, Kay returned home to earn money to again attend the U of I. She took a job at the Musicians' Union in downtown Chicago.

While working there she decided to splurge and buy herself a really nice suit for Easter Sunday. She went to Saks Fifth Avenue on Michigan Avenue. Saks at that time was so exclusive that Kay was not able to shop for her suit by perusing the various racks of clothing available for purchase. Instead, she entered the store, was greeted by a salesperson, and asked to enter a private viewing room. Kay explained what she thought she would like to see and several items were brought to the room for consideration.

Kay loved a beige, three-piece suit, and purchased it. However, it was so expensive that several weeks of earnings were required for the purchase. The big mistake came when she left the suit hanging in full view (with all the sales tags still in place) on a closet door in her bedroom at home. When Kay's mother saw the cost of the suit she exploded, saying, "That suit is so expensive, you're going to get married in it!" Well, she did.

Our First Year of Marriage: Struggling

We were married in St. Peter and Paul's Roman Catholic Church in South Chicago. Though it was a religious ceremony, we were married "outside the altar." During my early years in college, despite living on campus in a Catholic men's dormitory, Newman Hall, with priests I might add and with an adjoining Catholic church, I fell away from Catholicism. I had been baptized a Catholic, made my Holy Communion, and had been confirmed as a Catholic. Among my early studies at the University of Illinois were courses in world religion and family life. I also recall many student conversations in our residence hall late into the night regarding the existence of an "all knowing" God vs. "free will." I recall having my roommates on an early Sunday morning pouring cold water on me because I chose to lie in bed rather than accompany them to Sunday mass.

During conversations with the priest who was to marry us, I revealed that I had fallen away from the Church. After several meetings, he required me to sign a document that committed us to raise our children as Catholic. I had no problem with this, and of course, Kay, being religious, was happy to have me comply. Many months, perhaps years, after our marriage, she would continue to attend Sunday mass alone. Another important reason for my proceeding with a Catholic ceremony was for the benefit of my beloved grandmother Mary Savage, who was very religious as were many other members of my family. My grandmother was to pass away eleven months later.

On the evening of our wedding day, we departed for the University of Illinois and our new life together in Champaign-Urbana. On the train ride down, while washing my hands on board, I had removed my wedding band and forgot to retrieve it, only discovering too late that it was missing. It was never found.

Back on campus, Kay and I secured employment. I had missed an opportunity to register for the fall semester 1959, and found part-time employment as an elevator operator transporting the handicapped in Altgeld Hall. Kay worked full-time as a clerk typist and personal assistant to professors in the organic and inorganic chemistry departments. We lived off campus at 502 Oregon Street, Urbana, as renters in a private home.

Within weeks of our marriage, we were to learn of Kay's pregnancy. It wasn't too long before we began to fall on hard times. Our daughter Christine was born nine months and one day after our marriage! Kay had worked right up to two weeks before her expected date of delivery. Her last day of work was a Friday and the following Monday her water broke, and she went into delivery.

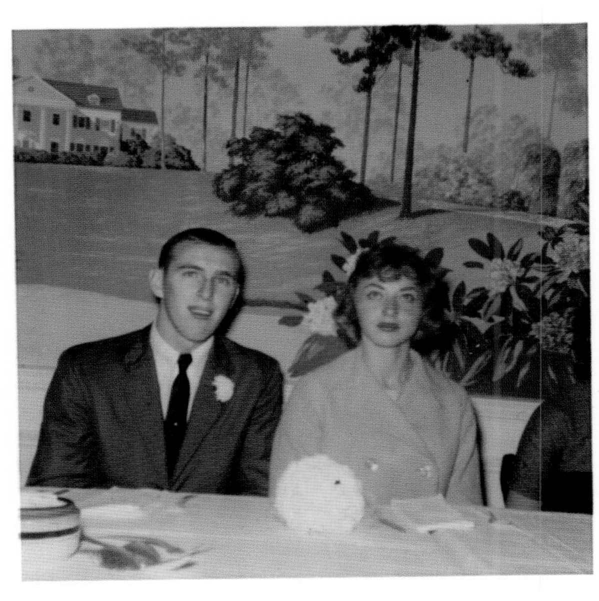

Clyde and Kay at reception held at Phil Smidt's restaurant at 1205 Calumet Avenue, Hammond, Indiana. Phil Smidt's, a long-time South Chicago popular establishment, closed on October 20, 2007, after 97 years. It was a favorite of my family's, who frequented it for many years until its closing.

Clyde at Jones Beach in May 1960 to introduce Kay (busy taking the photo) to New York City prior to our move there in 1962.

I continued working various odd jobs off and on campus after my enrollment the preceding spring semester. Within fifteen months of Christine's birth we had our second child, Cynthia. I continued juggling my time between my studies and support of my family.

With two young children and growing financial debt, it quickly became apparent that remaining on campus to complete the needed four credit hours for graduation was not to be a viable option. In early 1962 we crossed the Tappan Zee Bridge in our 1956 Pontiac Chief two-door hardtop to begin life anew as residents of New York State. That evening we were met by our good friend, George Euringer. To this day we all jokingly recall

Kay Davis holding daughter Cynthia with husband Clyde with Christine at Croton Falls, New York, in October 1962. This was our first family photo in New York State using George Euringer's camera.

RR crash

'I landed upside down'

By PHYLLIS COBBS

POUND RIDGE — "There was this tremendous sound. . .and then I cleared six rows of seats and landed upside down." This was the experience of Clyde Davis of Trinity Pass Road, a passenger on the New Haven train which collided with another at Springdale, near Darien, Conn., Wednesday, killing five persons and injuring many others.

A New Haven spokesman said Thursday morning that it was the worst wreck in his 30 years' experience with the railroad.

Mr. Davis was in the second car of a northbound three-car train on the New Canaan spur of the Ne... mostly homebound commuters — many men like Mr. Davis who had missed their regular train and were tired and ready for a drink and dinner. The accident occured at 8:20 p.m.

THE FIRST CAR of the train was kept empty, Mr. Davis said, and the lights in the car were off. This was probably fortunate because the front car of the train crumpled when it hit the empty southbound train which it was supposed to have avoided by switching to a siding. The engineer of the northbound train was killed and the engineer of the southbound train, Edward May of Watertown, N.Y., was

"Everybody was terrific and everybody helped," he said. Mr. Davis found himself attempting to aid a New Canaan resident, Hood McChord, who appeared to be badly hurt. Ambulances arrived "within five minutes," and Mr. Davis was taken off with Mr. McCord in the first ambulance which went to St. Joseph's hospital in Stamford. Mr. Davis called Mr. McChord's wife Thursday and found he was recovering nicely.

From St. Joseph's Mr. Davis rode to the Stamford Hospital with a woman who was hu... for her husband. At S... he was treated for hi... cuts and bruises...

Being greeted by Kay after a hard day at the office and a long commute home. I commuted by train over a period of forty years between New York City and my home in northern Westchester. And nearly died twice on the damn thing.

the moment. At the tollbooth rest stop, I pulled over and rolled down the window. Approaching the car, he waved, and then stuck his head in to greet us, nearly passing out from the urine fumes that permeated the interior of a car that had carried a family of four nearly 1,200 miles. We had been drying the diapers of our two girls on the car heater, and it was too cold to travel with the windows open. Our finances wouldn't allow a stopover in a motel. George recovered, good naturedly saying, "Follow me." And we did, to our newly rented apartment in Westchester County's Briarcliff Manor, New York.

We lived in a newly renovated carriage house on a former estate, including thirteen other apartments, called Tappan Arms. The estate's mansion had been turned into a very expensive French restraurant, Maison Lafitte, which was about 100 feet from our

KAY LOVES CLYDE

Dear Clyde,

Forty years later and you are still the love of my life.

These pages reflect just a few moments of our time together.

During those years we grew up, we grew older, and we grew closer.

How lucky we were...How lucky we are.

Happy anniversary
with all my love,
Kay

Kay, too, did a book: Kay Loves Clyde. *It was a surprise 40th wedding anniversary gift. The title affectionately speaks for itself. The beautifully bound, handmade book pictorially depicted our marriage by the decade — 1960s, '70s, '80s and '90s. Along with these there were sections devoted to "Grandma & Duke," Duke's favorite subject, and "Biking." Kay selected all the photographs and consulted with Ralph Skorge, Cline, Davis & Mann, Inc. Creative Director and art director extraordinaire. Ralph then produced the book with the assistance of the CDM art and production departments.*

How this project was completed without my knowledge and was ever paid for is still a mystery to me, who took pride in running a tight ship fiscally and creatively.

After completing the book, Ralph jokingly mentioned to me that at times, having seen and heard so many of the intimate details about the family, he'd felt that he'd have to enter the government's witness protection program.

Gathered for our 50th wedding anniversary celebration in Encinitas, California, are, left to right: Beau, son of Cole and Tammi Davis, and the youngest of our five grandsons; Dylan and his brother Ross, children of Cynthia and Phil Malara; Cole and Tammi's son, Taylor; John Parrino; Cynthia Malara and Christine Parrino, our two daughters; Kay and me; my son Cole with Tammi and their son Codie next to Phil Malara.

We created it ...

ADWEEK

Vol. XXV No. 3 EASTERN EDITION January 16, 1984 • $1.25

3 Klemtner Executives Take a Healthy Risk

By Christy Marshall

NEW YORK—Seized with the disease of many agency people, three executives at Klemtner Advertising—Compton's healthcare subsidiary—have come to the conclusion that they can do better on their own. Morgan E. Cline, president, and Frederic I. (Continued on page 5)

Cline Davis & Mann: A Healthy Risk

(Continued from page 1)

Mann and Clyde O. Davis, executive vice president/creative directors, popped the champagne cork on Friday to celebrate their last day at Klemtner, before going off to open their own healthcare communications agency, Cline Davis & Mann, Inc.

The agency has three unnamed clients and estimated billings of $6 million, according to Cline, president of Cline Davis & Mann. Both Mann and Davis will be executive vice president/executive creative directors of the new agency. In terms of the corporation, Cline will also be president of the board with Davis as treasurer, Mann as secretary.

Contradicting reports that Cline was taking a chunk of the Pfizer business with him, Albert Molinaro, Klemtner chairman/ceo, said: "They are not taking any Pfizer business from Klemtner. They are not taking any accounts from Klemtner."

More specifically, Morgan Cline said, "None of the [Cline Davis & Mann] business is Klemtner's business," leaving the distinct impression that both agencies will have some of the same client names in common. Cline headed up Klemtner's account team handling the Pfizer account, including such pieces of business as Vibramycin, Terramycin, Vistaril and various products in its Diagnostic Division and its Medical Systems.

The new agency has not yet found its Midtown Manhattan office space, nor even determined how much it will need. While Cline confessed opening his "own agency is the lifetime ambition of almost every advertising person," Mann added that after contemplating it for more than a decade, he hadn't thought about it much in the last year or so. "Then circumstances arose that started us thinking about it again," Mann said. Declining to specify, he added that those circumstances focused on "opportunities out there that dictated it."

All three entrepreneurs have been longtime Klemtner employees. Cline, 51, has been with the agency 16 years; Davis, 45, has been there 15 and Mann, 53, for 11 years.

Back at Klemtner, Molinaro will assume Cline's presidential duties, while the creative responsibilities formerly held by Mann and Davis will be assigned to other creatives currently on staff, according to Molinaro.

For the year, Klemtner, a Compton Advertising subsidiary since 1979 and an agency that specializes in healthcare communications, will end up with billings of $42 million, a 10-percent increase over 1982, according to Molinaro. In 1984, he expects the agency to bill $45 million. □

Reproduced with permission of Prometheus Global Media, from Ad Week, January 16, 1984; permission conveyed through Copyright Clearance Center, Inc.

We built it ...

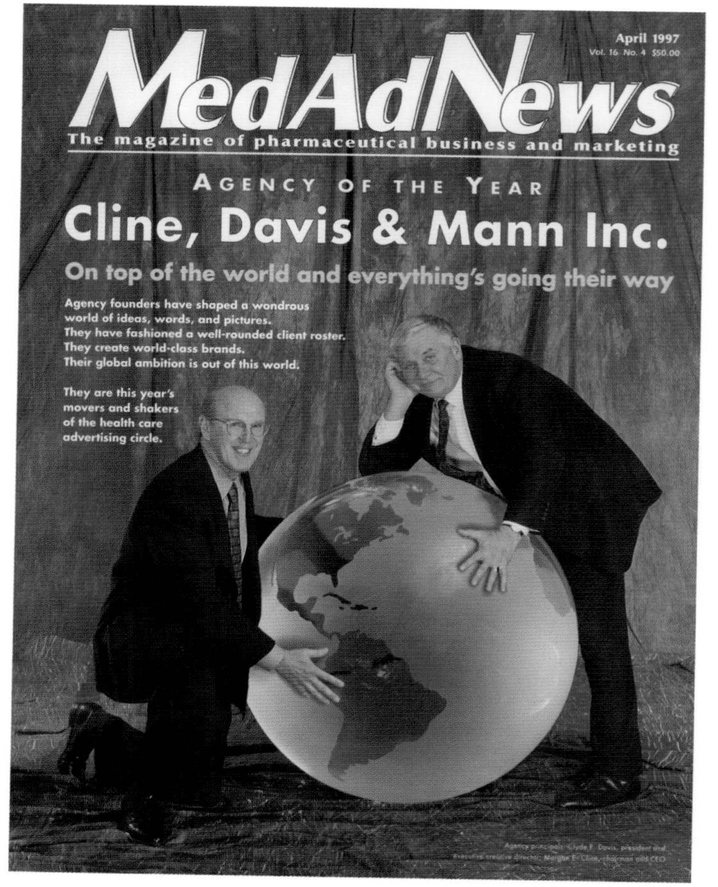

apartment. All of this on top of a wooded hill, with a view of the Hudson River and its accompanying evening sunsets. This was an ideal home from which to finally begin our life in New York.

Employment

Between the years of 1962 and 2002 I was gainfully employed in New York City. It's been difficult enough writing about myself, so from this point on, I plan to fall back on the efforts of others who have at various times attempted to define my career and contributions. My first job was as a designer with a small art studio, Designers 3 at 555 Fifth Avenue. They liked my portfolio; I liked their quarters, newly furnished with Herman Miller and Knoll desks, chairs, and workstations. I was impressed. The starting salary: $75 a week. I, with a wife and two children, an apartment in Briarcliff Manor, New York, and a monthly commutation ticket, was surely set on a path to financial disaster.

I didn't remain at the elegantly appointed Designers 3 for long. As my creditors closed in, I jumped ship for a position at William Douglas McAdams, an ethical [prescription. in contrast to proprietary, or over-the-counter] pharmaceutical advertising agency, the first of four that I would work for in my career.

In 1963 McAdams was an unusual place for me to find employment. Getting off the elevator in this office building at the corner of 59th and Lexington, I was greeted by a stone Asian statue: fake, purely decorative, I thought. Later I was to learn that Dr. Arthur Sackler was a collector of Chinese art, accumulating over the years not simply pieces, but whole movements. He would later house his collection at the Metropolitan Museum of Art under some criticism (see *NY Magazine*, November 13, 1978, issue, "Can the Met Escape King Tut's Curse?" by John L. Hess, page 83), probably allayed by his considerable gifting, especially the construction of the Temple of Den Dur and the contents within. But I'm straying far afield. The office hallways were of cinder block, lined with framed graphic design awards for the agency's creative output. McAdams meant a big jump in salary to

We sold it.

DECEMBER 23, 1996 · ADVERTISING AGE 3

Omnicom to lead health field with Cline, Davis deal

Agreement to acquire med agency is close after a year of discussions

By Mark Gleason and Pat Sloan

Omnicom Group is negotiating to acquire Cline, Davis & Mann, an independent healthcare agency in New York with $145 million in billings and $19 million in revenue.

The deal would make Omnicom the world's leading seller of health advertising services, pushing its Targis Healthcare division ahead of WPP Group's CommonHealth network in worldwide revenue.

In 1995, CommonHealth had $675 million in billings worldwide with $101 million in revenue; with Cline, Targis had billings of $752 million and $110 million in revenue.

AGREEMENT IS CLOSE

Executives familiar with the talks said they have lasted a year or more, but that an agreement is close.

The market for medical agencies has been a healthy one this year, reflecting the strong prospects for the niche, one of the fastest growing ad categories in the U.S.

In the spring, Omnicom rival Interpublic Group of Cos. acquired two health agencies roughly the same size as Cline: William Douglas McAdams, which was merged into Lowe Group; and Torre Renta Lazur Healthcare Group, merged into McCann-Erickson Worldwide.

Omnicom's Targis division includes a number of sizable medical agencies, including Corbett HealthConnect, Chicago; and New York-based Harrison, Star, Wiener & Beitler; Lyons Lavey Nickel Swift; and Kallir, Philips, Ross.

PFIZER IS BIGGEST CLIENT

While Omnicom could become the largest holder of medical agencies by revenue, CommonHealth USA will remain the largest single

Healthcare is one of the fastest-growing ad categories in the U.S.

agency, with revenue of about $7 million and billings above $40 million, according to *Med Ad Neu*

Cline was formed in 1984. I clients include Merck & C Parke-Davis Pharmaceuticals a Pratt Pharmaceuticals. Pfizer is far the biggest client, representi close to three-quarters of agency's revenue, said an execut familiar with the agency.

Two founders still run agency: Morgan Cline, chairm and Clyde Davis, president-crea director. Mr. Davis and Omni both declined to comment. □

THE NEW YORK TIMES, THURSDAY, MARCH 6, 1997

THE MEDIA BUSINESS

Advertising | Stuart Elliott

Omnicom again expands its health care advertising by buying Cline, Davis & Mann.

A GIANT agency company is again expanding in health care advertising by buying a shop that specializes in campaigns aimed at medical professionals and consumers for prescription and over-the-counter drugs, potions, lotions and pills.

Omnicom Group, the world's No. 2 agency company, with billings estimated at $20.2 billion, is acquiring **Cline, Davis & Mann**, a New York shop with nearly 170 employees and billings estimated at $170 million from pharmaceutical marketers like **Pfizer** Inc. and the Parke-Davis division of the **Warner-Lambert** Company. Terms of the deal, which had been discussed for a year and a half, were not disclosed.

The deal marks the third time in four years that Omnicom, which also owns international agencies like BBDO Worldwide and DDB Needham Worldwide, has bought a large New York shop devoted to drug and health care advertising. Omnicom and its principal competitors like the **Interpublic** Group of Companies have been eagerly expanding their health care agency holdings. Indeed, McCann-Erickson Worldwide, a unit of Interpublic, announced yesterday that its McCann-Erickson Healthcare Worldwide division would acquire a majority stake in **MCS** G.m.b.H., an independent health care agency in Munich, Germany, for undisclosed terms.

"There seems to be a feeding frenzy for health care agencies," Clyde P. Davis, president and executive creative director at Cline, Davis, said yesterday. Omnicom is acquiring Cline, Davis by buying 100 percent of its shares from the sole stockholders: Mr. Davis and Morgan E. Cline, chairman and chief executive.

The rush to snap up health care shops, Mr. Davis said, is intended to capitalize on two trends. One is the growing popularity of "direct to consumer marketing," by which sales pitches for prescription drugs are aimed at the buyers and users of those products rather than at the health care professionals who must prescribe them. Mr. Davis provided figures showing that direct-to-consumer marketing accounted for an estimated $640 million in ad spending last year, compared with $364 million in 1995 — and could increase to as much as $1 billion this year.

•

The other trend fueling the buyout boom is the panoply of what are known as Rx-to-O.T.C. switches — that is, over-the-counter drugs based on products that had only been available by prescription. Examples include Pepcid AC and Zantac 75 antacids, the baldness treatment Rogaine and the Nicoderm CQ and Nicotrol nicotine patches.

Cline, Davis was founded in 1984 by Mr. Cline, Mr. Davis and a third partner, Frederick Mann, who is now a consultant to the agency. The three had worked together at Klemtner Advertising, an agency acquired by Compton Advertising, which subsequently sold itself to what is now **Cordiant** P.L.C.

The three executives left to start Cline, Davis because "we wanted more control over our destinies," Mr. Davis said, "and create a more open, first-name-basis agency."

Why then sell out to a behemoth like Omnicom? One reason was generational, replied Mr. Davis, who is 58; Mr. Cline is 64.

The other was to bolster the agency, Mr. Davis said, as "Omnicom's market research, direct response and Internet expertise can only enhance our capabilities." He added, "And we'll be able to tap into international capabilities that we haven't had."

•

Both Mr. Cline and Mr. Davis will remain in their positions, as will other top managers of Cline, Davis.

"Everything's the same," Mr. Davis said. "John likes us just the way we are."

His reference was to John Wren, president and chief executive at Omnicom in New York. Cline, Davis will report directly to Mr. Wren rather than to an Omnicom division, Diversified Agency Services, which supervises Omnicom's interests in fields like health care and direct marketing. The other New York health care agencies acquired by Omnicom since 1993 — Harrison, Star, Wiener & Beitler, now known as Harrison & Star, and Dorritie Lyons & Nickel, which was merged with Lavey/Wolff/Swift to form Lyons/Lavey/Nickel/Swift — are part of Diversified Agency Services.

"We wanted to be autonomous, to do our own thing," Mr. Davis said, adding that he hoped to "follow in the footsteps" of Goodby, Silverstein & Partners, the hot general-advertising shop in San Francisco that also reports directly to Mr. Wren.

Products and drugs handled by Cline, Davis include Ben-Gay, Plax and Unisom, all sold by Pfizer; Neumega, a platelet-cell generator from the Genetics Institute Inc. unit of the **American Home Products** Corporation, and Lipitor, a cholesterol-reducing agent developed by Parke-Davis that is being jointly marketed with Pfizer.

$135 weekly and pharmaceutical ads and promotion were coveted assignments. Creativity abounded. These were heady times, and I wanted my share. It was before the Kefauver-Harris amendment to the Food, Drug and Cosmetic Act that created the graphically burdensome formation of FDA packaging regulations. Full product disclosures and "brief" summaries in ads along with "fair balance" — the citing of benefits of a branded pharmaceutical along with its side effects and limitations — hadn't yet impacted the creative product.

I remained at McAdams approximately eighteen months, nearly being fired for encroaching on the system of dribble-down allocation of work assignments. I wanted to do the ads for Librium and Valium as an assistant designer, while my supervisor and group art director, if left up to me, would have been relegated to designing the BRC's (Business Reply Cards). He pointedly offered the unreality of this ever happening as the reason he was firing me. My aggressiveness had not been seen as ambition, but rather as threatening. I, of course, talked my way out of it by convincing his superior, the Executive Art Director, that I deserved a second chance. Three months' probation allowed me to turn my attitude around. Within a month, the group A.D. called me in. "Clyde, I can't tell you how much you've changed for the better. You're no longer on probation, you're doing a great job." Later that same month I slipped down the fire escape stairs, portfolio in hand, to interview at Sudler & Hennessey, another award-winning studio/ad agency in the very building with the great Herb Lubalin in residence. S & H was turning itself into a pharmaceutical agency from what had been a shop that designed the NBC Peacock logo, had clients like CBS and V8, but was realizing greater growth and financial return from clients such as Warner-Lambert and Bristol Labs.

They liked my work, and I was hired at another jump in salary. Great shop, but too much talent for me to shine. Gone in nine months. Joined L.W. Frohlich, Intercon International as a Group Art Director. At L.W. Frohlich I settled down after yet another jump in salary. I was now earning nearly $11,000 a year.

My friends and family were beginning to fault me for not being able to hold a job. I had had three jobs within a period of two and a half years. Frohlich gave me my first opportunity to manage other artists — there were three to start. Four years later, having earned more than $16,000 in 1967 and after being denied a larger salary increase than one granted at an annual review, I promptly resigned.

I was thirty years old with no job, mounting debt, three children, who had recently purchased a three-acre lot in Pound Ridge, New York, with the accompanying mortgage. Things looked dire.

In March 1968 I joined Klemtner Advertising Inc., realizing my goal to earn $20,000 per year (equivalent to approximately $122,000 in 2009 dollars) by age thirty. My career simply took off. That single moment in one's work life, where all the stars are in perfect alignment, the right person at the right time, in the right place. My first assignment was a visual aid for Vibramycin, an antibiotic being introduced by Pfizer, a client I would serve for the next thirty-three years. The account executive on Pfizer was Morgan Cline, who would become a colleague, friend, and partner for life. With Pfizer as a client, ambitious marketing and creative assignments would lead me to alliances with Philco-Ford in San Francisco (Image tone enhancement — a procedure for whole human body X-ray [see "Tissue is an Issue" ad on page 94]), and Arthur D. Little in Boston (sliced rats, [see "New experiments," Vibramycin ad on opposite page]). Then there were two around-the-world photography adventures for the antibiotic Terramycin. I also had the privilege of working with an esteemed U.S. senator and presidential candidate who would serve as the spokesperson to redefine male impotence as erectile dysfunction in pre-launch TV commercials for the blockbuster Viagra.

What Goes Around Comes Around

Many times over the past years, I have been asked, "What prompted you to start your own ad agency?" My reply was usually a generic response: "We wanted to do our own thing," or "We wanted more control over our destinies," as quoted in the *New York Times* article on page 91.

Promotional ad celebrating the completion of our first year, acknowledging the contributions of clients, colleagues, family, and friends.

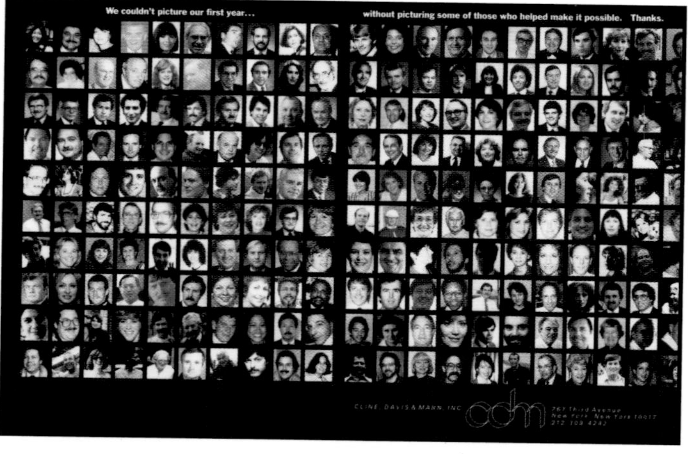

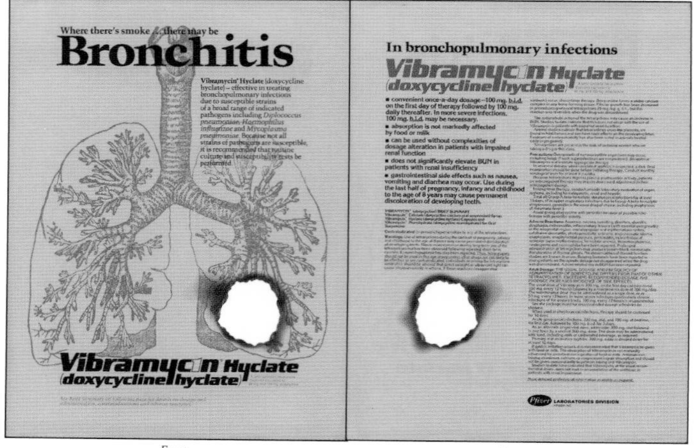

Front *Reverse*

By 1984, the year we founded Cline, Davis & Mann, Inc., I had already experienced decades of watching my friends build their careers and businesses in consumer advertising.

From the beginning of my career in advertising, I was aggressive and driven to succeed. Much of that drive was fueled by my dire financial circumstances. But long after the needs of my family and I were satisfied, I continued to be impressed by the success, some of it seemingly instant, of others. My friends worked on the consumer side of advertising, while I attempted to build a career in pharmaceuticals. Over time I learned that my friends' budgets were bigger, and they worked with the best photographers, artists, television directors, and producers. They traveled extensively to big location shoots, here and abroad. They had big expense accounts and worked with celebrities and movie stars. Their work had more exposure, since broadcast television and radio were media outlets not available to pharmaceutical

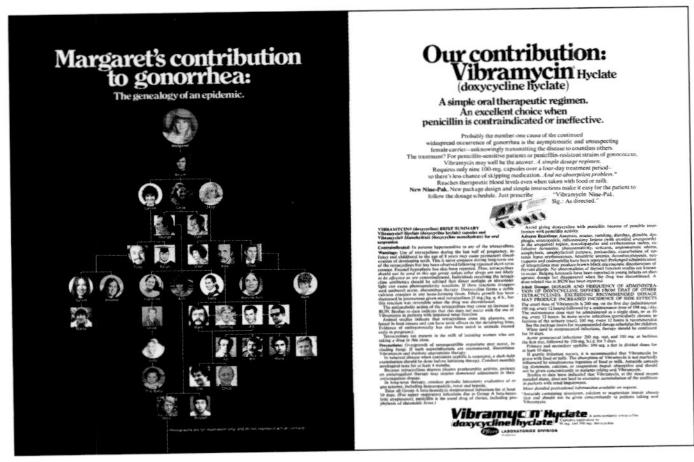

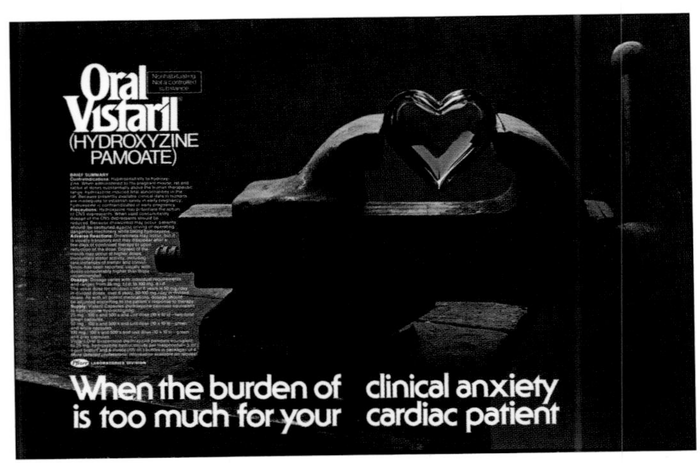

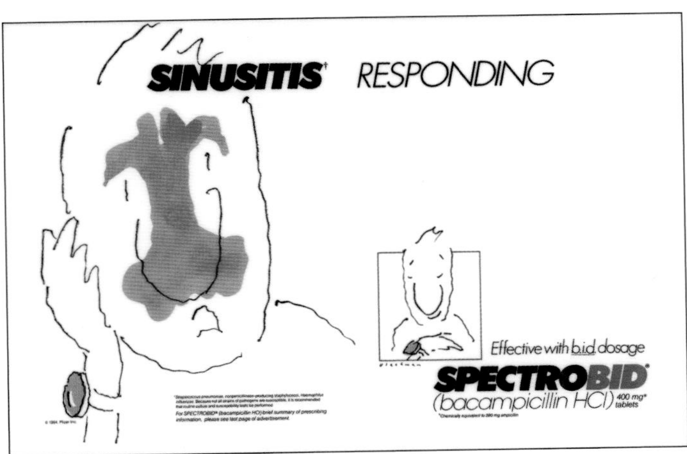

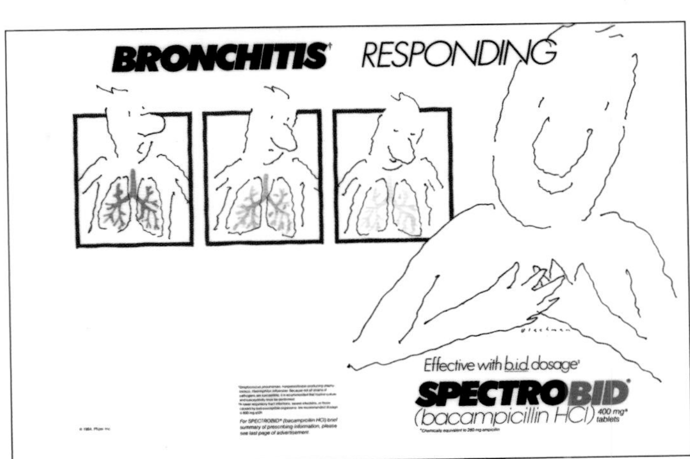

Senator Bob Dole on location at the 1999 filming of the groundbreaking first Viagra television commercial for erectile dysfunction. Senator Dole is presenting me with an autographed copy of his book Great Political Wit.

advertising agencies at the time.

In the '50s and '60s pharmaceutical design was winning the major creative industry awards. By the '70s and well into the '80s that all changed. New consumer ad agencies were being founded on creative flair and ideas. The glory, fame, and bucks went to these newcomers on Madison Avenue like Doyle Dane Bernbach, Ally & Gargano, and others. My college friend, George Euringer, worked at these agencies. Among agency startups was Backer & Spielvogal. Another college friend, Bob Lenz, was a founding partner in this agency, at the time the fastest growing advertising agency in history. Inspired by and learning from these wonderful friends, it was not surprising that I would want the same for myself. I had, at the University of Illinois, influenced their coming from the Midwest to New York to work in advertising. Now the tables were turned and it was payback time, and they didn't disappoint.

I was excited. I was proud of my friends and envious of their success, but I didn't have the qualifications to work in their business as an art director. I was in the backwaters of pharmaceutical advertising, often referred to as "trade advertising." However, I paid attention and followed their careers, met their colleagues, their partners, vendors, the artists and writers they worked and played with. It was no coincidence that when I started my own advertising agency, it was Bob Lenz's attorney who became the attorney who would successfully represent us in a non-compete lawsuit brought by our former employer to prevent our startup. This same law firm referred us to the bankers who would grant our first business loan, funding our fledgling business. George Euringer's accountant became our accountant (and is, to this day, my personal accountant, as well as that of my partners, Morgan and Fred). And, it was George who conducted lunchtime seminars at our agency, tutoring Rx art directors and copywriters on how to do a television storyboard when we had a shot at our first piece of consumer business.

Ambitious, stimulated by the business flux of acquisitions in the industry, I continued to learn.

In 1978 the agency I had been working at for nearly ten years was suddenly acquired by a large consumer ad agency, Compton Advertising. As a small-share stockholder in the acquired agency, I began to see how things worked. Ownership was important. Within a year or two, Compton was acquired by an English ad agency, Saatchi & Saatchi. As a shareholder in Compton, I was to benefit a second time and was, for the first time, put under a four-year contract. I had arrived.

There was no stopping me. My friends were doing it, my employers were doing it, and clients and colleagues were asking me to do it. "When are you going to start your own agency?"

Against this background I approached my colleague and friend of long-standing, Morgan Cline, and asked if he would like to start our own agency when our contracts expired. At the time Morgan was caught up in the politics of corporate accession and was looking forward to being named president of the Klemptner agency. It was important to him, but I was impatient and wanted an answer. I felt that management was stringing him along because this promise of the presidency seemed to be too open-ended. There was a younger, more favored candidate for the position within the agency; however, Morgan was the head of the largest account in the agency — thus, the dilemma and delay. I urged him to make up his mind, because if he didn't I was going to do it on my own, with others.

So determined was I to convince him that he should press on for the title — so we could get the hell out of there — that I took to having forty-inch-high letters, each in a different color, cut out and mounted on foam board by the studio, spelling the word P R E S I D E N T. Early each morning, over a two-week period, I would slip a letter, starting with the "P," under his door for his arrival at the agency. He got the message. Being pressured by me, he in turn pressed management and received his coveted title. Within five months we resigned when our contracts expired. Later, Morgan would claim owner to be the best title of all.

I always wanted my name on the door. I dreamed of a company that would survive me and grow and, hopefully, become one of the giants in our industry. Similar to shops like Sudler & Hennessy, a pharmaceutical agency, or Doyle Dane Bernbach, both established in the early '60s, which continue long after the founders have passed from the scene.

Cline, Davis & Mann now lays claim to being "The world's leading healthcare advertising agency" with more than 1,100 employees. Since I retired, Cline, Davis has expanded into international markets. In addition to locations in New York City, Princeton, New Jersey, and Los Angeles, Cline, Davis has

Medical Tribune
Section II • Advertisement • September 25, 1969

in infection, most often
TISSUE IS AN ISSUE.

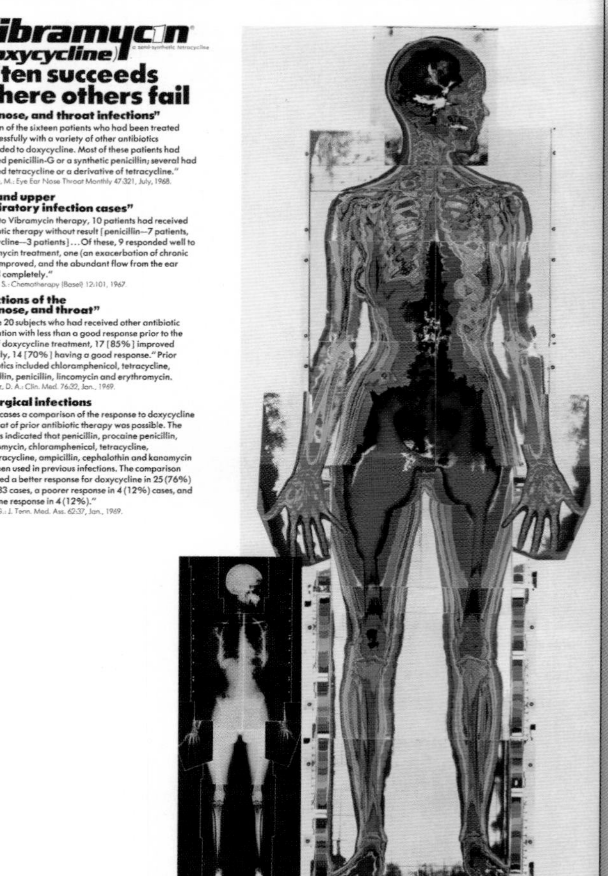

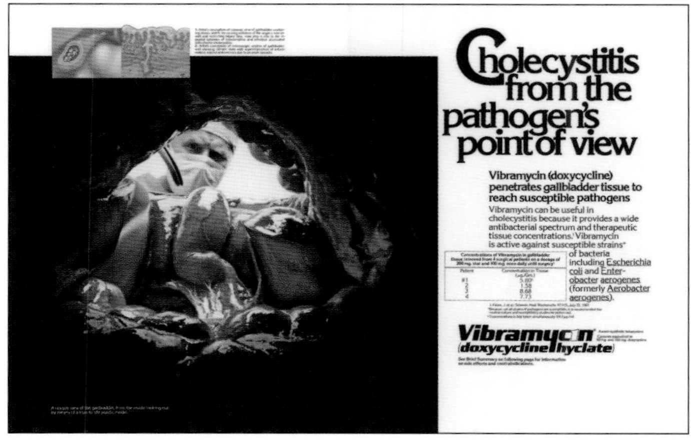

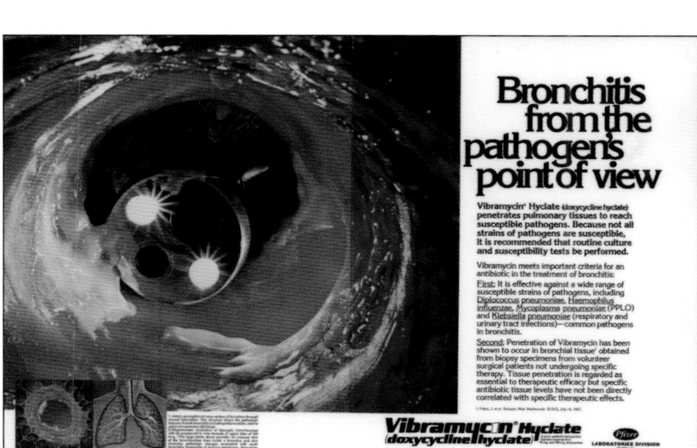

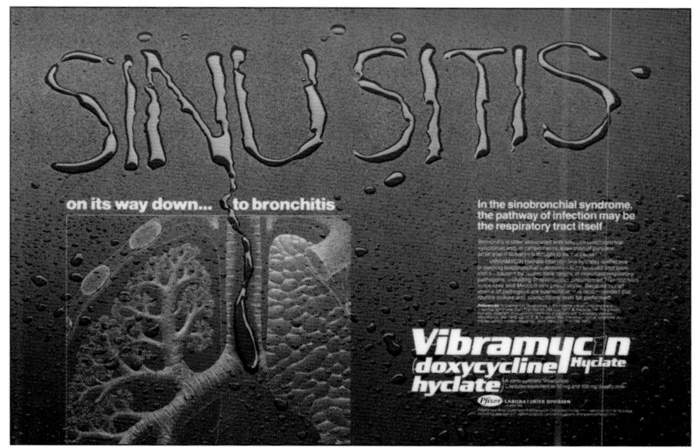

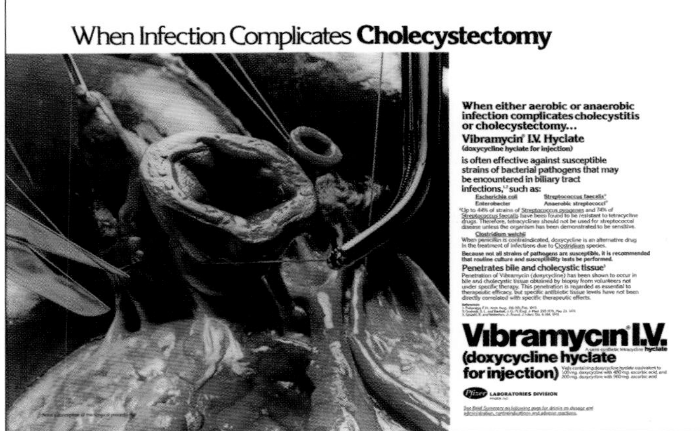

become CDM World Agency, with offices in London, Munich, Barcelona, Madrid, São Paulo, and Montreal. As it says on the current web site, "The agency has been transformed from an advertising agency into an idea agency." Yet management "is extremely protective of the environment that has made CDM a great place for the most talented people in the business to thrive and grow." For me, this is part of my legacy to my children and grandchildren: an institution bearing my name, which is admired and respected, thanks to those who took it to the next level.

The single-page Glucotrol ad insert to the right is noteworthy on two counts: First, it was a unique reproduction method, affixing glitter to the photograph of spilled sugar. This is often done on greeting cards (think: Snow), but until then, never done in a medical journal. Second, it was the last ad I was to create professionally.

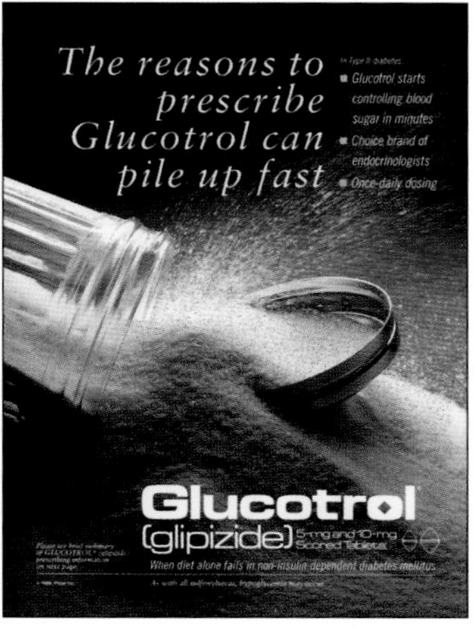

HALL OF FAME 2005

Clyde Davis

"He had a very adept sense of human nature. He challenged everybody to do better, and he usually succeeded."

Clyde Davis is renowned in the industry for the fierce drive and visionary creative mind that helped him overcome weighty obstacles and make Cline Davis & Mann (CDM) an advertising powerhouse. But Davis has also been a versatile manager, an intuitive mentor and a connoisseur of rare beauty whose exacting standards brought out the best in his agency, its people and its product. His story reads like a Horatio Alger novel. It's a tale of up-by-your-bootstraps pluck and talent that saw a shy young man from a Chicago housing project scale the heights of the New York advertising world.

Davis is soft-spoken but straightforward, in the classic Upper Midwestern vernacular. He grew up in Trumbull Park Homes, wedged between the Wisconsin Steel Works, the Ford Motor plant and the Nickel Plate Railroad tracks in the Irondale neighborhood of Chicago's Southeast side. His father absent and his mother absorbed with making ends meet on a thin dime, Davis, known then as "Duke" (his sister June was "Toots" and brother David went by "Butch"), threw himself into his schooling, and his obvious talent won him encouragement from his tutors. Mrs. Banks, his grammar school teacher, pushed him to study commercial art. He did so at a vocational high school, where his shop teacher, Mrs. Lyons, filled his head with fantastic visions of New York and its bustling advertising industry. It was there that he met his lifelong partner, Kay. When Davis passed on an scholarship to the Art Institute of Chicago, choosing instead to follow his buddies downstate to the University of Illinois at Urbana-Champaign, she helped him through school, paying his tuition with tips from her job as a car hop until her parents found out. "Kay was Clyde's right arm, his Boswell, throughout his life," says Morgan Cline, co-founder of CDM and a longtime colleague.

Davis worked full-time through school, to the detriment of his grade point average, but still couldn't make ends meet. In the meantime, he and Kay married and had two children. In 1962, with a third child on the way and just three classroom hours to go on his bachelor's degree — but broke — Davis dropped out of school and moved his young family to New York, where he found work with Designers Three. He was ambitious, and his creative vision soon established him as a hot commodity. After moving to McAdams, where he got his first acquaintance with medical advertising through work on Valium and Librium, Davis blazed through stints at Sudler & Hennessey and LW Frohlich before Bob Buechert brought him on at Klemtner, grooming him to lead creative at the firm's New York offices.

There, Davis brought on fellow Hall of Famers Lester Barnett and Sal deRouin and began his long relationship with Pfizer through epochal work on brands like Pfizer's flagship antibiotic Terramycin, for which he convinced product manager Jack Fisher to send him to the far corners of the world with a National Geographic photographer, documenting the drug's use among the Tuaregs of Niger and in the Amazonian backwaters of Mata Grosso, Brazil. "We could have gotten stock photos of these places and

CAREER CHRONOLOGY

1962 Designers Three, a NY design shop; McAdams, working on Valium and Librium

1963 Sudler & Hennessey, working on Polycin

1964 LW Frolich, works way up to art director

1969 Klemtner, worked on Pfizer's Vibramycin and Terramycin, alongside Fred Mann and Morgan Cline

1984 Davis and company leave to launch Cline Davis & Mann

1997 CDM sold to Omnicom

2003 Leaves CDM. Establishes Clyde Davis Art & Design Scholarship, University of Illinois

From real life...
A Woman satisfied with her oral contraceptive
Zorane 1/50
Progestin Estrogen content balanced for the majority

To demonstrate fully the concept of Pfizer's Terramycin, Davis persuaded product manager Jack Fisher to send him to the far corners of the world with a National Geographic photographer. He used a similar approach for Lederle's Zorane, travelling across the U.S. and stopping "anywhere we could find a patient willing to go on camera."

run them with the same tagline, but we wanted to demonstrate the concept," says Davis. The ads ran for several years.

Davis had employed a similar concept for Lederle Labs' Zorane contraceptive, a brand with poor visibility and a pauperly ad budget. To help it break out of the pack, Davis commissioned Bill Owens, a prominent photographer whose books "Our Kind of People" and "Suburbia" chronicled Main Street subcultures, to travel the country with him photographing and interviewing Zorane patients with their families. "We were in Texas, Tennessee, Virginia — anywhere we could find a patient willing to go on camera," says Davis. Getting people to provide testimonials for the pill wasn't so easy in those days. "We had a feed in through our sales reps, who contacted the doctors, who asked patients if they might be interested," says Davis, whose ads always gave the viewer a different perspective on things. For Pfizer's Vibramycin, for instance, Davis commissioned massive models of the human sinus and gallbladder, designed to be photographed from the vantage point of E. Coli or the influenza bug and looking out at the doctor peering in. The art ran with the tagline: "From the pathogen's point of view."

"Working with Clyde is different from working with other art directors," says CDM president and chief executive Ed Wise. "It's more than just pen and paper and T-Square. Clyde would make it a three-dimensional experience. It would be arts and crafts. He built ads, so that it became an experiment in creativity until something came out of it." Wise, who was hired on as CDM's first copywriter after Fred Mann, recalls working with Davis on another legendary ad, for Glucotrol, in which Davis developed a unique technique for embedding glitter in an insert.

After 15 years at Klemtner, Davis, together with Cline and Mann, struck out on his own. "Morgan said to me, 'Clyde, you're in charge of pretty,'" says Davis. He was also in charge of the company's finances, managing it from launch to the purchase of its old headquarters at 45th and Lexington to its sale to Omnicom in 1997. "I like to say I did some of my most creative work in finance," says Davis. "I was equally comfortable with bankers, realtors and accountants as with creative people. I didn't mention clients, you'll notice — I happen to be a painfully shy person, but I have had two partners who were very good at holding the attention of others."

Davis may be a behind-the-scenes guy, but he could hold his own in a pitch. "He had this brilliant presentation technique that I'm convinced was deliberate, although he denies it," says Cline. "He'd start off softly, and as he got to the meaty stuff, his voice would drop down, and you'd see them lean in and push their chairs forward so that they could hear him. He had them hanging on every word!"

And Davis was certainly no shrinking violet within the company. Taking his cue from the teachers to whom he is quick to credit his successes, Davis shaped his staff and imposed his standards of creative excellence on the organization with tools both blunt and fine. "He had a very adept sense of human nature, and he knew exactly which buttons to push to get you to do what was in the best interests of the agency," says CDM chairman Jack Slonaker. "He challenged everybody around him to do better, and he usually succeeded."

Davis would mentor staff, cajoling them to excellence. "He always had one pet," says Cline. "They changed after every few months. Once he felt they were up to snuff, he was on to the next one."

Torre Lazur McCann's Mike Lazur was one of those at Klemtner that Davis took under his wing. "As hard a taskmaster as he was, I have to say, it was really good for me," says Lazur. "He got really excited about seeing good people grow under his tutelage." Wise worked with Davis at Klemtner, which he joined as a junior copywriter when Davis was creative director. "Clyde was blind to titles and age," says Wise. "He was only interested in talent. That made me feel very energized about the business, because it seemed like there were no barriers. It was all about the idea."

Davis left CDM in 2003 (he doesn't like to use the "R-word"), and between traveling with Kay, collecting art and visiting with his kids and grandkids, he is writing a book about his family history. He has also established the Clyde P. Davis Art and Design Scholarship for Study Abroad at the University of Illinois-Chicago, enabling low-income Chicago students to broaden their horizons through travel. ■

—Matthew Arnold

Making a Contribution ...

1. *A DVD of the film produced by Cline, Davis & Mann, Inc.* A Portrait of the Artist ... *shown at the presentation and induction of electees February 8, 2005.*

2. *The Cline, Davis & Mann, Inc. corporate logo as displayed in its office lobby reception area. Designed by Clyde Davis.*

3. *Founding partners Clyde Davis, Morgan Cline, and Fredric Mann.*

4. *In 1991 we moved from our original, outgrown quarters at 731 Third Avenue into a sleek new, modern building at 450 Lexington occupying the 31st and 32nd floors. We had sixty-seven employees at the time.*

"Designed by architect David M. Childs of Skidmore Owings & Merrill, this 40-story office tower occupies the northwest corner of the Grand Central Post Office at 45th Street and Lexington Avenue. Childs's design incorporates classic motifs from the original Post Office and other outstanding buildings in the Grand Central neighborhood." Image reproduced with permission.

We would remain there until our retirement in 2003.

5. *An electee profile of Clyde P. Davis for the 2005 Medical Advertising Hall of Fame induction award ceremonies in the journal for the event. Reprinted with permission.*

1.

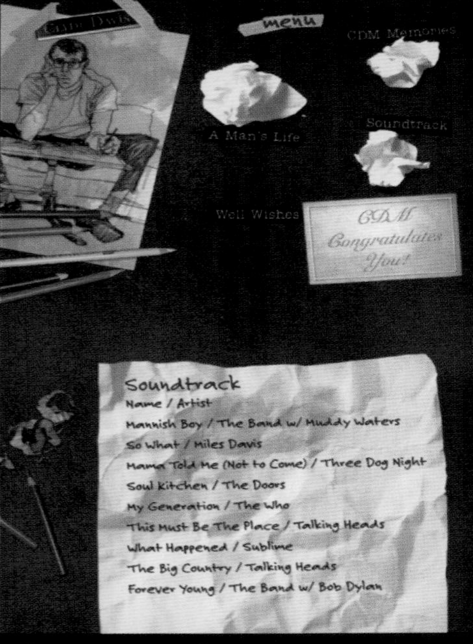

2.

3.

4.

5.

Leaders in medical advertising are always multitalented individuals. You cannot head up organizations of the scope of ad agencies and not have some capacity for all the ingredients of the job – creativity, marketing, research, organization, finance, recruitment, and the intangible of leadership. Members of the Medical Advertising Hall of Fame have been outstanding in certain of the disciplines of our business – copy, design, entrepreneurial judgment, etc. - but they have always possessed instincts for the other pieces of the equation that produce a successful medical advertising organization. Even given this generalization, the mix of proficiencies evident in Clyde P. Davis's career puts him in a special place among MAHF members. Davis is a fascinating combination of what appear to be diverse talents.

Davis got his start when a teacher recognized his ability and pushed him out of his South Side Chicago environment into an art program at the University of Illinois. He had to work his way through college doing everything from washing dishes to painting houses. Once in the commercial world, he entered pharmaceutical advertising through the training grounds of McAdams, Sudler & Hennessey, and L.W. Frohlich before moving to Klemtner Advertising. There and at Cline Davis & Mann he worked on Pfizer products, winning recognition for his work within the industry and at creativity competitions - a Clio for the first Rx ad ever honored. Outstanding campaigns were for Terramycin ("Experienced Traveler" photo series on patients around the world), Spectrobid (peaking antibiotic blood levels illustrated by silver-plated railroad spikes that representatives dropped off with MDs), Vistaril (cardiovascular advantage demonstrated by a glass heart in the grip of a vice), Vibramycin (full body x-rays on the "tissue is the issue" theme) and Glucotrol (visualizing "spilled sugar" in journal inserts and promotion). This work established Davis as a creator with a strong feel for graphic imagery and also a flare for striking sales force materials.

CLYDE P. DAVIS

Against this art director competence, is the interesting fact that Davis has acted as CDM's *financial executive* – an unlikely role for someone from the creative side of the business. Says Morgan Cline, his long-term partner, "At CDM, he quickly assumed the role of chief financial officer. That was one of his major, major interests. Finance was a secret, long held love of his and he jumped to the helm of the financial effort of the agency and ran it wonderfully." Jack Slonaker, chairman and COO at CDM, tells of Davis's financial skill in finalizing a commitment to new office space. "He would not sign. He was waiting, waiting. And while he was waiting they were throwing more things in to sweeten the pot…He was a great negotiator and always made things happen on his terms." Carol DiSanto, a CDM partner and director of client services, remarks on the apparent paradox, "How can such an unbelievable creative person, be so in tune with the bottom line in finance, stocks, and investments? The guy's a master."

Davis displayed traits common to agency leaders. He expected excellence. "His standards are high," says Cline, "and he had a short attention span for people who did not come forward quickly with what he liked. He would demand a lot [but] Clyde was never willing to ask anything of anyone that he wouldn't do himself." On Davis' expectations, Ralph Skorge, a CDM partner and creative director for art, adds, "A tough guy to work for. But it makes you better…I learned a lot…He wasn't generous with praise. But when you got it, you were hooked. It was an addicting drug to have him say 'That's good.'…This guy recognized great work and when you did it. He praised you, and you knew it."

Davis also showed leadership in advocated new technology for CDM and in being aggressive in competing with consumer agencies for DTC business. Ed Wise, the agency's president and CEO, describes him as, "something of a visionary. His creativity was expressed in a lot of ways, but one of them was in expanding the business in new directions in terms of DTC, the computer, advancing computer abilities, in film and video. He was always looking for trends and trying to put the agency on the cutting edge." Cline seconds this view of Davis: "He wanted us to assume new abilities, new roles…We bought all the equipment to edit our own films when we started doing DTC. He was the one who made this enormous investment in computers when people were just still dabbling in them."

His colleagues describe Davis as an extremely soft spoken. Frank Hughes, an MAHF member who worked with him at Klemtner, says he speaks, "pianissimo and so you are leaning in to hear him." People have trouble remembering when he raised his voice. In fact, Cline's opinion is that Davis would *lower* his voice to attract attention and make his points more emphatic which proved effective in high decibel meetings.

Davis is a complex meld of a drive for success, creativity, business acumen, low key reserve with an underlying aggressiveness, demanding standards, and a commitment to new technology that has all come together. What has made it work? Ed Wise explains: "Clyde was very much driven by the idea of creating something beautiful, creating something that other people would admire, creating something that was great. I think whatever he attacked in his life aggressively and in a disciplined manner [was] something that people would be attracted to and stand back an say that was a *contribution*…He saw the agency as one of his creative canvasses as much as it was one of his ads."

Making a Contribution ...

As an honoree, I was particularly proud to have my family and friends at the Medical Advertising Hall of Fame 2005 awards dinner at the Plaza Hotel, New York, New York. Seated left to right are grandsons Codie Davis, Ross Malara, and Taylor Davis; my son, Cole Davis; grandsons Beau Davis and Dylan Malara; my daughter Cynthia Malara and her husband Philip Malara and Cole's wife, Tammi Davis.

Introduction to Our First Web Site by Ed Wise

Following are excerpts from my favorite rendition of Cline, Davis & Mann's history, sense of purpose and operating philosophy.

Morgan and Clyde are partners. As it was in the beginning, so it is in this bio. Together.

Let's discuss the bio concept for a minute. Face it, you don't really need to know how many southside Chicago thugs Clyde had to beat up, or more likely run away from, to survive and graduate grade school. And you probably don't need to know the number of 4-H trophies Morgan brought home to roost at the farm in Centerville, Iowa, now do you? Or do you?

I, dear web surfer, have worked with these gentlemen for seventeen years, including all their years as principals of Cline, Davis & Mann, Inc. And if you hear a sucking sound, that's just me making sure I have a job tomorrow.

Let's forget bio. And think history. Let's think oral history. Loose, forgetful, short on facts, full of lore.

"There are things about running an advertising agency that you'll never know...." These were the uplifting words of encouragement that were bestowed upon Clyde, Morgan and Fred Mann when they departed Klemtner Advertising. They were all at the top of their careers. And they jumped. No net.

You know those "when-I-was-a-kid-I-walked-50-miles-to-school-barefoot-in-the-snow-and-I-liked-it" stories? Well Morgan, in particular, has similar stories relating to his devotion to his clients. The amazing thing is, they're true (according to my best, but undermotivated, research). So it was this kind of "when-I-was-in-your-position-I-worked-till-2-in-the-morning-and-seventeen-weekends-in-a-row-one-summer-and-I-liked-it" attitude that assured CDM was going to be a success. Let's not forget the 4-H values here. Waking up at dawn to milk the cows, feed the chickens. Back breaking work from dawn to dusk. Complete dedication to the task at hand. The dedication of a farmer, and the brains of a pharmacist (which I forgot to mention until that alliteration presented itself [Morgan is a graduate of Drake University School of Pharmacy]). Anyway, this aggressive pursuit of the task at hand is an attitude that gets more than the prize pig to grow. It apparently does wonders for client relationships.

Now Clyde, meanwhile, had some other things on his mind. Clyde, four hours short of his degree in fine arts when he departed the University of Illinois and came to New York, also got an informal education in finance by supporting himself while he pursued his degree (more on this later). Some of his classmate buddies include some great names in consumer advertising like Bob Lenz of McCann Erickson, Backer Speilvogel, and Bates Worldwide, and George Euringer of DDB and Ally & Gargano fame.

Clyde was drawn to the work that was being done in pharmaceutical advertising in the late '60s. It was work that was winning awards and was establishing pharmaceutical design as a hot spot. It is a vision Clyde maintains and has mercilessly beaten into our heads. Thank you, sir, may I have another? Clyde wanted to apply great creativity to the pharmaceutical business. This vision was as clear as a bell and twice as loud.

Together with their third partner, Fred Mann, the writer of the team, they borrowed a temporarily vacant apartment, bought two typewriters and a T-square (ancient art equipment) and said one January day in 1984 that they had an agency.

It was frightening and it was fun. They always made payroll, although not always to themselves. The agency started out mostly scrapping for projects. The question "Is the idea big enough?" was asked so many times I eventually came to realize size does matter. These grand projects became our trademark. And soon, based on the project work we produced, we were assigned real rent-paying pieces of advertising business.

Clyde, meanwhile, who had worked his own way through college and painfully knew the value of a dollar, especially the one you don't have, found himself becoming more involved with the financial vision of the agency. The same fastidiousness that went into every art layout soon found its way on to every spreadsheet. Clyde also brought his standards to play on the design of the office space, first at 767 Third Avenue, and then on our present space at 450 Lexington Avenue.

Business grew. Heads didn't. The philosophy and the vision never allowed it. For the most part, we worked hard, liked each other, and went home happy and tired. *[I quoted this in my acceptance speech at the Medical Advertising Hall of Fame on the following page.]*

It isn't the whole story. But in a way it is. Because the agency remains what it started out to be, about people, hard work, and growing lasting relationships

They like us. They really like us. Clyde still wants us to win more consumer awards. He still thinks this web site should be better. And Morgan wants us to spend more time with the client.

Heads stay small and noses stay well positioned against the grindstone.

[In 1997 Med Ad News named CDM Agency of the Year. In 1998 CDM was awarded Most Admired Agency honors, as well as receiving the Best Web Site award.]

Longtime University of Illinois schoolmates and family friends at the Medical Advertising Hall of Fame awards dinner at the Plaza Hotel, New York, New York, on February 8, 2005. From the left: Celia Euringer, Clyde and Kay Davis, Robert Lenz and his wife Carol, and Celia's husband George Euringer.

Thank you.

Thank you Cline, Davis & Mann for such a flattering film tribute.

And a special thank you to the Medical Advertising Hall of Fame Executive Committee and Council of Judges for bestowing this considerable honor upon me.

In 1984 we began Cline, Davis & Mann with three agency disciplines well represented. There was Morgan Cline as Account Executive, Fred Mann, Copywriter, and myself as Art Director.

Last year at this same ceremony my partner Morgan said that ours was a special relationship ... and indeed it was.

Having known both Morgan and Fred for nearly twenty years before our agency startup, I realized that turning out a great creative product was going to be the least of our challenges. For Morgan, a superb account executive, was also a fine writer and no slouch when it came to big ideas. Fred, a "writer's writer" was also an outstanding art director, who often brought headlines and concepts to the table with his own blockbuster visuals.

Ron Pantello, co-founder of the Medical Advertising Hall of Fame, presenting award to me as electee to the MAHF. Photo courtesy of Dan D'Errico.

So we were in effect three creative directors starting an agency.

With all this creative clout about, it wasn't too long before I began to focus on other matters of importance.

Finance was an interest of mine right from the start. And, quite frankly, I do believe some of my most creative work was done as treasurer and CFO of Cline, Davis & Mann. Compensating employees generously was always a part of our corporate culture. But as generous as we were, it quickly became evident that to create a company of lasting values, much more would be required of its founders.

There was an unstated code of conduct that permeated our agency in those early days. Ours was a congenial work environment. The tone was set by my partners Morgan and Fred. Gentlemen. Compassionate. Principled. Loyal. My intention was to preserve these ideals against the erosion of time, against destinies unrealized, ambition unfettered ... impatient youth.

It wasn't until some seventeen years later that I truly understood the significance of the vision I had come to embrace along with my partners. Early on we had identified a select group of managers. We gave them the freedom to flourish, yet held their feet to the fire, keeping them accountable to the highest standards of performance — insisting they support one another, each as an equal. As with any organically grown group, some rebelled, some floundered at times. One left, only to return, another we lost along the way ... but all continued to t-h-r-i-v-e.

As Ed Wise wrote about those early years of Cline, Davis & Mann "While the business grew, heads didn't. The philosophy and vision never allowed it. For the most part, we worked hard, liked each other, and went home happy and tired." They're called Managing Partners now and their goal has been to build upon their unique legacy.

When Morgan and I retired in 2001 this group of key employees, or KEs, as we called them, reintroduced the agency to its employees. With four simple words — Substance. Style. Conviction. And Grace — they were able to distill what we as founders had spent nearly two decades passing on to them.

So, whether a creative shepherd, financial guru, or simply a young man who came from one big city to another in pursuit of a better life, I could not accept this evening's honor without acknowledging those same KEs and their help along the way.

As much as any creative idea, ad campaign, or the landing of any piece of new business, this group of colleagues, has to be among my most enduring contributions to medical advertising.

I'm proud of all we accomplished together.

They have succeeded me and my partners in the truest sense.

Thank you

Newsletter of the U of I Foundation and Private Giving

University of Illinois

FALL 2001 ISSUE 36

UIF

Investing in

ILLINOIS

Inside this Issue

Husband Honors Wife Who Battled Discrimination . . . . . PG. 5
Couple Helps UIC Business Students . . PG. 14
Trailblazer Supports UIS . . . . . PG. 15
New Presidents Council Members . . . . PG. 18
Altgeld Carillon Project Gets Boost . . PG. 24

Alum's Scholarship Brings Talented Students to Art and Design at UIUC

New York Exec Clyde Davis Creates Largest, Single Award to School

CLYDE DAVIS knows something about perseverance. And talent. And sharing.

The president and executive creative director of Cline, Davis & Mann, Inc., an internationally recognized New York-based healthcare advertising agency, attended the University of Illinois as a student in Fine and Applied Arts in the late 1950s and early 1960s.

Almost 40 years later, he received a bachelor's degree in art and graphic design.

A year later, Davis decided to thank his alma mater by establishing the Clyde Davis Scholarship. His $200,000 gift created the largest, single award given to undergraduates in the School of Art and Design. To be eligible to receive it, a student must be from a high school in the greater Chicago metropolitan area and show a talent for art and graphic design.

Davis funded the scholarship to attract the most talented students from the Chicago area to the design field. The scholarship targets students who, without major financial assistance, might not otherwise be able to pursue a university education. Further, the scholarship's purpose is to develop good artists and good citizens.

"I don't want to see someone impeded for lack of resources, or even grades, especially if they have talent," Davis said.

Clyde Davis

1

Pure talent, he said, must be recognized, encouraged, and supported to flourish. Clyde Davis knows from his own experience.

A Chicago native, South Side to be exact, he was raised in a one-parent family that relied on public housing and assistance. He attended Chicago Vocational High School, where he honed his skills in drawing, designing and painting.

He won a full scholarship to the Art Institute of Chicago, but decided to attend the University of Illinois at Urbana-Champaign because he was also a competitive swimmer.

The U of I in 1956, he said, was a different world from his own. "People there wore white bucks. We wore engineering boots. They opened doors for you and said, 'Excuse me.'"

Lacking money, he waited tables, worked at the University of Illinois Press, painted houses, and juggled other jobs. His grades at the U of I suffered.

One professor at the University, though, tried especially hard to keep Davis focused on his education. Prof. Austin Briggs, who taught anatomy, which was then a requirement in art and design, was a great motivator and mentor who imparted common sense. "He told me that I didn't work hard enough with the talent that I had," said Davis. "I liked him a lot. He was more like a football coach than a professor of art."

Clyde and Kay Davis

Still, Davis left school and took at job at an advertising agency in New York. His college sweetheart, though, had other plans, rebuffing Davis's marriage offer unless he returned home and graduated.

Nine months after his return, Clyde and Kay's first child was born. A second child arrived a year or so after that. Three hours short of his degree and with four mouths to feed, Clyde Davis left school in 1962 to pursue a career. He and his family moved to the Big Apple.

He moved through the ranks of Madison Avenue advertising agencies, winding up at

2

Like so many who attended the University of Illinois, I, too, have realized the benefit of a higher education. Rather than attribute this merely to overt book learning, however, I was to also learn firsthand through personal contact just how prepared so many other students were for campus life. Most had the financial wherewithal, social upbringing, and scholastic qualifications to attend such a fine university. Unlike my peers, at the time I was to achieve these qualifications *during* my intermittent tenure at the University of Illinois. I worked to support myself financially while a student. I was something of a social misfit from the South Side of Chicago and a broken home. I learned to fit in on campus. I learned as well that I could not simply rely on my artistic skill only, but that I had to crack a book now and then and learn from the world of the humanities and science.

December 8, 2006, Chancellor Richard Harmon, gave an address, "The University of Illinois and the American Dream," at the University Club in Chicago. Among his remarks, he said, "I am fortunate because in my lifetime, I have been given the

Klemtner Advertising, where he remained for 18 years. While at Klemtner, his interest in pharmaceutical advertising took root. It became, as noted on Cline, Davis & Mann Inc.'s humor-laced, award-winning web site, "a vision Clyde maintains and has mercilessly beaten into our heads. ... This vision was as clear as a bell and twice as loud."

IN 1984, Davis linked with fellow Klemtner partners Morgan Cline and Frederic Mann, "borrowed a temporarily vacant apartment, bought two typewriters and a T-square (ancient art equipment) and said ... they had an agency," according to the Cline, Davis & Mann Inc. web site.

The agency began humbly, but snared business by addressing the question, "is the idea big enough."

Davis, while always keeping a hand in the creative work of the agency, became more involved in the financial aspects as well. Cline, Davis & Mann moved into bigger and better office space. While business also grew, the company writes, "heads didn't. The philosophy and vision never allowed it. For the most part, we worked hard, liked each other, and went home happy and tired."

Today, Morgan Cline is chairman of the board and CEO of the agency. Frederic Mann, the writer of the original team, has retired but remains in touch with his former partners. And Clyde Davis is executive creative director and president.

"I don't want to see someone impeded for lack of resources, or even grades, especially if they have talent."
Clyde Davis

Cline, Davis & Mann consistently reaps the rewards and awards of its hard work. It was named the most admired agency in the pharmaceutical category in 2000, 1999 and 1998 by *Med Ad News*, was named a finalist and world medalist by New York Festivals International Television and Cinema Advertising Competition for its work on the memorable Viagra ad with former U.S. Senator Bob Dole, and has garnered many other notable awards for its creativity in print, electronic and multimedia.

3

The company has grown into a 340-employee, $350 million agency. CDM is the ninth largest healthcare advertising agency in the United States, with four independent divisions in Manhattan and Princeton, N.J.

Davis is justifiably proud of the success of and the work produced by his company.

Still, he felt something was missing. He wanted his degree from the U of I. "I decided it was important," he said.

And the march of time seemed to add a sense of urgency. "Maybe turning 60 was the bee in my bonnet to get it done," he said.

"What do I say to the person who changed my life completely?"
Davis Scholarship recipient

As it turned out, Kay Davis had contacted administrators at the U of I to determine what Clyde needed to do to earn his degree. About the same time, and unaware of his wife's efforts, Clyde did the same thing through the College of Fine and Applied Arts. In 1998, the U of I granted him a Bachelor of Fine Arts in Advertising Design.

While the degree brought satisfaction, the scholarship he created in 1999 at his alma mater has also been rewarding.

Davis said he received a heartfelt letter from one of the recipients. The student, he said, conveyed the importance of the scholarship. "What do I say to the person who changed my life completely?," Davis read, adding that the scholarship has helped make this student's "dream come true."

The letter, Davis said, "inspired me. It made me feel wonderful and has prompted me to think of additional means of support."

The second and most recent recipient of the Clyde Davis Scholarship, Anne Lindberg, a freshman from Oakbrook Terrace, said she settled on the U of I after discussing the school's art and design program with recent grads and high school advisors. While enrolled in the School, "I really want to explore it all, find a niche."

The scholarship, she said, is vitally important, like icing on the cake.

And that is sweet to both Lindberg and Clyde Davis.

4

opportunity to achieve my dreams." However unorthodox my university education, I, too, was given that opportunity.

Chancellor Harmon also noted in his remarks that, "the rising cost of tuition nationwide is making college unaffordable to an alarming number of talented students. A report by a congressional advisory committee found that each year, 400,000 students do not attend four-year universities because of financial barriers. That's nearly half of all low and moderate-income high school graduates who are qualified to enter college. Sadly, each year, 170,000 of these bright young people do not attend any college at all."

In the process of realizing my dream, I came to understand that I wished to give something back in return for my success. I am happy to provide for the students of the next generation "the gift of opportunity" to pursue their dreams without the financial burden I had to shoulder.

Reproduced from the Newsletter of the U of I Foundation and Private Giving, *Fall 2001, Issue 36, "Investing in Illinois."*

Giving back …

A MAN WITH SOLUTIONS FOR STUDENTS

by Shelli Stine

CLYDE DAVIS

A famous artist has said, "All children are artists. The problem is how to remain an artist once he grows up." The quandary presented is something many high school graduates across the country face as they envision their future. Some realize that a dream of pursuing the arts in college may remain just that, a dream. Students everywhere face the pertinent question: "How am I going to pay for college?" And many students' answers lie in the simple truth: they can't. Because of this, talent is often denied an opportunity to develop and students are often denied the opportunity to see their dreams become a reality. Why shouldn't every talented artist be able to pursue their dreams of being an artist, especially if that is what they truly want to be when they grow up? Pablo Picasso posed the question and Clyde Davis had the answer.

University of Illinois alum, Clyde Davis first arrived at the University in the late 1950s to pursue study at the College of Fine and Applied Arts. At age 60 Davis received his degree in graphic design in 1998. Although it took forty years for Davis to earn his degree, it took only one year for him to share the joy of a graduation with others like himself.

Davis, who struggled in college to pay the cost of tuition and room and board to pursue his passion for the arts, knows the hardship of lacking the resources to develop a talent. Raised in a one-parent family on the South Side of Chicago, Davis was no stranger to public housing and assistance. He pursued his skills in drawing, designing and painting at Chicago Vocational High School and went on to win a full scholarship to the Art Institute of Chicago. Because he also wanted to pursue his love for competitive swimming, Davis declined the scholarship, which would have helped him out immensely, and chose to attend the University of Illinois. He found himself waiting tables, painting houses, and working at the University of Illinois Press to finance the cost of being in school. Davis soon found out, however, that working along with following a strict regimen of swimming practice and class attendance was all but impossible.

No longer able to afford it, Davis left school and took a job at an advertising agency in New York. He returned to the University soon after, but again had to drop out because of financial constraints, falling just three credits short of graduating. He returned to New York and continued to work for advertising agencies, moving up through the ranks and eventually found himself at Klemtner Advertising, where he remained for 18 years. In 1984, after years of experience in pharmaceutical advertising, , Davis, and fellow Klemtner partners Morgan Cline and Frederic Mann, co-founded the now internationally renowned New York-based full service pharmaceutical advertising agency, Cline, Davis, and Mann. He and his partners' successes have been recognized frequently, and on February 8, 2005, Davis was honored by being elected into the Medical Advertising Hall of Fame in New York City. Cline, Davis, and Mann was also named the most admired agency in the pharmaceutical category in 1999 and 2000 by *Med Ad News*, when their notable campaigns were recognized, including the Viagra campaign featuring Bob Dole.

Davis and scholarship recipient, art student Anne Lindberg

In 1999, finally graduated from the U of I, Davis looked back on the forty years between his arrival at the U of I, and his graduation, and remembered one thing: the struggles he faced to pursue arts due to circumstances out of his control. What he could have an impact on, he realized, was the future of students who faced similar circumstances. He sought to use his success to grant the possibility for success to a deserving student who otherwise would not have the opportunity to attend school at the University of Illinois. Davis remarked, "I don't want to see someone impeded for lack of resources, or even grades, especially if they have talent," Davis said.

That year, Davis granted the largest single award for undergraduates in the School of Art and Design at his alma mater, the University of Illinois. The Clyde Davis Scholarship, awarded to an incoming freshman preferably from the Chicago area, who expresses an interest in pursuing a degree in graphic design, provides $15,000 a year for four years, provided the student remains in the College of FAA. As of 2006, Davis has established a second fund in the School of Art and Design. The Clyde P. Davis Art and Design Scholarship for Study Abroad in Britain, provides scholarships to undergraduate students who are participating in the Study Abroad in Art and Design in Britain Program. The scholarships will be made on the basis of academic merit and/or financial need and will be in the amount of $5,000 each.

A letter written to Davis from one of the recipients reads, "What do I say to the person who changed my life completely? […you've made my] dream come true."

Anne Lindberg (BFA '05), the second and most recent recipient, remarked, "It was his drive and generosity that allowed me to fight for my own drive to continue on in the arts. I can't begin to express how grateful I am for that."

Every child is born an artist, but how to remain one in a world where it takes more than just talent to pursue a dream is the most challenging question. There are solutions. And for Anne, and students at the U of I and other colleges across the country, it takes people like Clyde Davis and their extreme devotion to their own passions, as well as their generosity, to make these talented children's dreams become reality.

You, too, can provide solutions for deserving students, dedicated faculty, and nationally-ranked programs in the College of Fine and Applied Arts. Private support of the College's alumni and friends is crucial to fulfilling our mission and maintaining our standard of excellence.

To learn more about making a significant impact on the arts at Illinois please contact:

Shelli Drummond Stine, Associate Director of Development for Communications and External Relations at sdstine@uiuc.edu or 217-333-1661.

18

COLLEGE OF FINE & APPLIED ARTS

UNIVERSITY OF ILLINOIS AT URBANA-CHAMPAIGN

2005/2006

Above cover and page 16 of the FAA 2005/2006 newsletter, *the University of Illinois Alumni Association newsletter. The cover art was created by Niki Bjorklund-Wolny, who graduated from the U of I Graphic Design program in 2002.*

Clyde Davis and Katrina Kruszewski, 2000–2004, with Robin Douglas, Associate Director, School of Art and Design — Coordinator of Graduate and Undergraduate Program at the University of Illinois College of Fine and Applied Arts School of Art + Design. Katrina's degree was a Bachelor of Arts in photography, and she was the first graduating recipient of the Clyde Davis scholarship.

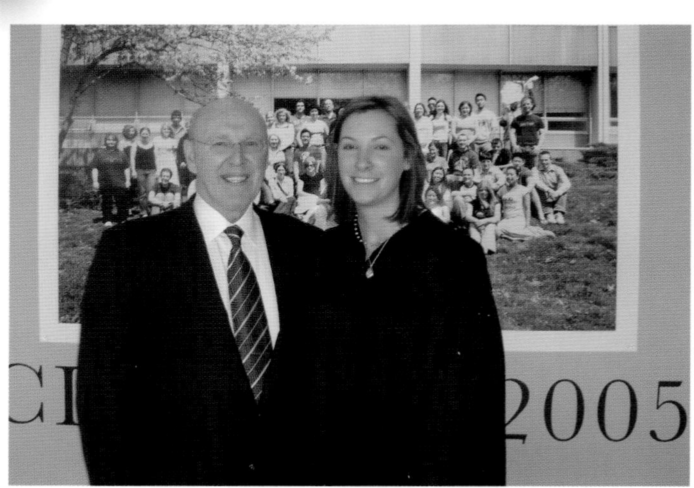

Anne Lindberg, 2001–2005, BFA in Painting

Katelyn Kappel, 2002–2006, BFA in Graphic Design

Brittany Bindrim, 2003–2007, BFA in Graphic Design

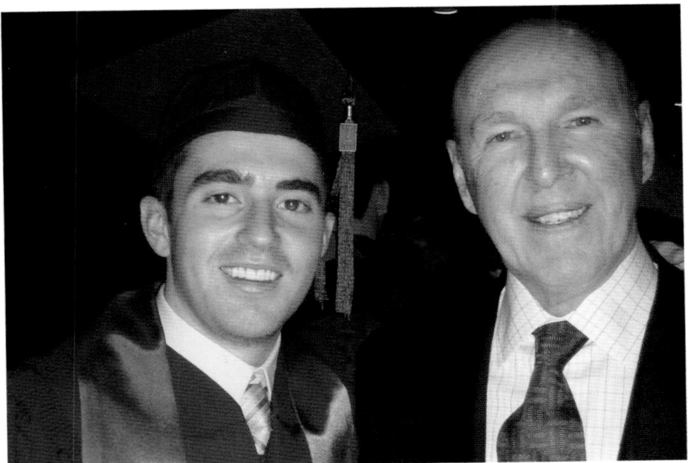

John Langan, 2004–2008, BFA in Industrial Design

Paul C. Gamo, 2005–2009, BFA in Painting

My intention as donor was to focus primarily on an individual applicant's talent as long as the minimum academic standards of the School of Art and Design were met. The review and selection process allows me to participate in determining a finalist once the field of applicants has been narrowed to five.

"An applicant for a scholarship must be a graduate of any public, private or parochial high school in the city of Chicago, Illinois or the greater Chicago metropolitan area. Among potential scholarship recipients financial need may be, but is not required to be, considered as a factor in their selection. An applicant shall be awarded a scholarship without regard to his or her grades or the result of any test. The scholarship shall be awarded solely on the basis of a talent as judged from the student's portfolio."

The scholarship is awarded in the field of graphic design; however, upon the completion of his or her sophomore year, a student may change focus (from graphic design to another focus) within the College of Fine and Applied Arts during or after his or her junior year and the student will not lose the scholarship. Graduating scholars have received their degrees in the fields of photography, graphic design, painting, industrial design, and new media.

As of December 2010, forty-three recipients of the ***Clyde Davis Scholarship in the School of Art and Design Study Abroad Program*** *have received supplementary financial stipends. Their studies have taken them to various universities in Scotland, England, Italy, and Australia.*

I am most proud of each of these scholars and especially grateful to the University staff, administrators, and faculty. Without the help of Robin Douglas, Alan Mette, Nan Coggin, Roger Laramee, and others, these programs would not be as successful as they have become.

My fervent hope is to continue funding these programs for as long as I am financially able.

William Fulara, 2005–2011, BFA in New Media and Olivia Ortega, 2006–2011, BFA in Painting

Current Recipients of the Clyde Davis Scholarship in the School of Art and Design:

Alexis Kodonsky, 2008–2012

Maria Ludeke, 2009–2013

Evan Jarzynski, 2010–2014

Melanie Leikham, 2011–2015

... and other interests

The previous pages of "my story" are filled with accomplishments of one sort or another. It is not my intention to diminish the result of pursuing one's goals, but I am more than a provider, a partner, a businessman, or a lender of last resort. I do, along with my lovely wife Kay, participate in a variety of recreational interests. Among these are gardening, jogging, biking, photography, genealogy, boating, travel, and art collecting.

Not surprisingly, a lifetime of art has led me to find joy in other areas of artistic expression that have sparked my interest. Among these are home construction, architecture, interior and industrial design, as well as collecting fine art.

Our Home

Living in Briarcliff Manor, New York, and renting with a growing family, we began thinking of a home of our own. We always wanted to build a contemporary home, of course, but first we had to find a building lot. Scanning the *New York Times* real estate section, I came upon an ad offering land for sale in Pound Ridge, New York. We learned from others in my business that well-known artists and advertising art directors like Dick Loew, Bob Gage, and Gene Federico lived in the town. Dick and Gene would become friends of ours in later years. That Sunday we drove to Pound Ridge for our appointment with Lawrence Malawista, and met with him at his home on Upper Shad Road, just off High Ridge Road, outdoors on the lawn where he was reading his Sunday paper. Kay was carrying Cole, just six months old, so the year had to be 1964.

"The Rock": Our house began with The Rock, shown with Kay standing in front of it for scale. The Rock was so predominant, we had to marry the house to it to form an aesthetic union. Over the years, Kay has served as my ruler in more ways than one, as shown by many photos in the book. The photograph below shows how we overlapped a portion of the rock with the house upper story. The house and rock thus became visually one, coexisting comfortably together.

Top left: House nearing completion in 1975. Interior is lit and appliances installed in kitchen. Top right: Foundation for the extension to our home on February 19, 1989. Middle: Foundation and commencement of framing for the first addition to our original house on July 23, 1989. The garage is in front and the driveway is to the left. Bottom: House completed with its completed second addition on March 24, 2001. The original house can be seen at the top rear of the photograph.

Mr. Malawista showed us several lots and properties he owned in town. One, a bypassed, partially cleared lot with a bulldozed driveway, appealed to us the most. On a hill, at the end of a cul-de-sac, with a small stream running between the two, there sat a huge rock. The rock, too big to ever move, seemingly occupied a future dwelling site. Obviously anyone wanting to build a house on the site would have to accommodate its presence. Most potential buyers didn't want to deal with this looming piece of granite. We paid $9,500 for the property and held it nearly eight years before beginning construction. Seven of those years we lived in Pound Ridge, renting an old school house at the intersection of Fancher Road, Barnegat Road, and Trinity Pass. Years later my daughter Christine and her husband John would also live on Barnegat Road. The idea was to raise our children in a town where we would spend the rest of our lives.

It was always our dream to own our own home. It would be designed to our specifications, would be contemporary in style, and built on property of our choosing. In 1973 we commenced construction on such a dwelling, designed by Wallace J. Toscano, that would prove to be the start of a long, arduous love affair with architectural design and home construction.

I mentioned Dick Loew earlier, a well-known advertising film director, who, I learned, was involved in building his own custom-designed home in Pound Ridge. His contractor, Vito Fosella, was a gifted man, who knew better than anyone how to site a house. He was a master, working with wood, steel, glass, and fieldstone walls. His landscaping skills were outstanding. Obviously, Vito Fosella was to become the builder of our home, then a deck, and finally an addition to that home larger than the original dwelling. Later he was chosen to build our friends, Bob and Carol Lenz's, home in South Kent, Connecticut.

With my drawing and sketching abilities, understanding of spatial relationships and form, coupled with my high school vocational training in wood shop, machine shop, and architectural drafting, I was better prepared than most homeowners to participate in the process. I thoroughly enjoyed the problem solving, aesthetics, design, and layout of space and selection of materials and hardware. My participation seemed to be well received by the vendors we engaged, but then I was the client and paying the bills.

Our economic situation improved over the years. With the increasing financial wherewithal, our attention turned to interior decoration, landscaping, and ultimately adding to its size. In addition to a wooden deck, built in 1983 and a Secret Garden created in 1994, there were basically two build-outs or extensions to the house. In 1989 we added a gallery, great room, a third

bath, a second kitchen, hot tub/spa, a garage, and a basement, along with several exterior terraces and major landscaping. In 1999, shortly before my retirement, we expanded the house, one final time. The result was a larger living room, master bedroom, bathroom for Kay, an office for me with adjoining bath, and a second basement. We also added a new cobblestone driveway with granite slab courtyard, terrace, and a newly located front entry, also of granite stairs and platforms. The main entry doors, designed by Woody Rainey, are quite beautiful, and I *never* fail to notice when passing through them how exceptional they are. The house has grown from its original size of 2,700 square feet to 11,000 square feet. Well into our seventies now, we hope to never have to downsize, believing the house will serve as a gathering place for our growing family.

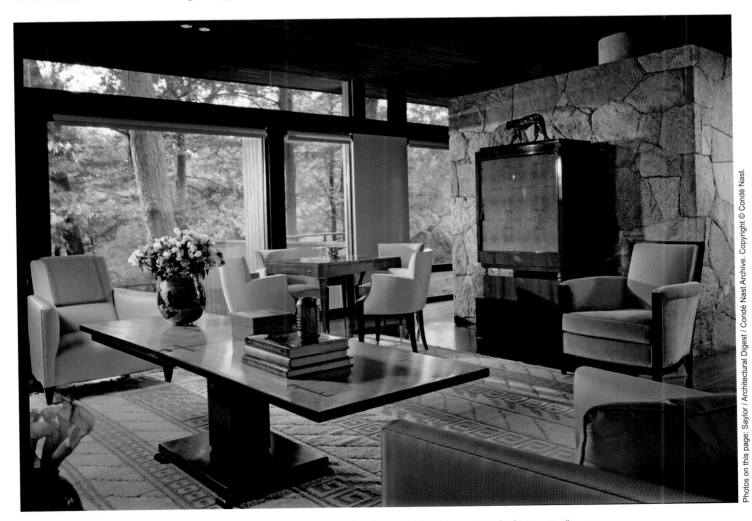

Photograph above of living area appeared in the article, "The Art and Craft of Integration" on pages 136–137 of the March 2007 issue of Architectural Digest: The International Magazine of Design. *The photograph at top right is of the dining area from page.*

Aerial view of the complete home, including both additions, on December 27, 2001. This includes a new front entry, granite courtyard, and cobblestone driveway. The dashed outline shows the original house structure, as pictured on the previous page.

Being involved so intimately in the design, construction, furnishing, and toiling on the grounds and in the gardens of our home has brought us immense joy.

We have had other homes over the years, but they have been in Florida where we spend our winters. Key West was our first (1982–1997), then Coconut Grove (1985–1996) and Aventura, Florida (1997 to the present). They have all been condominiums, and it wasn't until the Aventura project that I was able to fully indulge my penchant for modern architecture. We engaged Woody Rainey once again and turned him loose to create a most wonderful destination for our winter sojurns. Done in Maple Anigra Woods, Kay refers to Aventura as her blonde and Pound Ridge as her brunette homes. Nevertheless, I continue to enjoy the constant requirement for repairs and upkeep of our northern residence.

My 1991 Acura NSX, pictured in my driveway, which I still own and which more often can be found in my garage, mostly unused. I love the car, but seldom seem to have the time to drive it. The car has about 12,000 plus miles on the odometer and it is currently November 2009. I've never been a car guy, but this is one elegant toy.

My Office

I also became deeply involved in the recruiting and ultimate selection of a commercial interior design firm for the corporate headquarters of our advertising agency, Cline, Davis & Mann, Inc. Despite my partner Morgan Cline's wish that the agency quarters be styled similarly to those of a white shoe law firm, Fred Mann and I prevailed and realized the contemporary setting so appropriate for an advertising agency known for its creativity.

Nearly one and a half years after we had occupied these quarters, I took on the project of my own executive office with the help of the architect and my good friend, Woody Rainey. One of the fondest memories in business that I can recall was driving in my red and black 1991 Acura NSX from my home in New York, on May 10, 1994, to the architectural woodworking firm in Massachusetts, which was crafting my desk and cabinetry (see photos below), to review their progress.

I received a proposal from Gatehouse Furniture Studios, Gatehouse Road, Holyoke, Massachusetts, for a custom desk and side cabinet, credenzas, hanging cabinets, and wood-paneled wall. They are pictured above, partially completed and assembled for my first look. WOW! I particularly loved the pencil drawer (top right). All pieces were designed by Woody Rainey. Consider me a fan of his and forever grateful for allowing me, through his considerable talents, to exercise my love of design, form, and fabrication. My office at Cline, Davis & Mann, Inc., was installed August 2, 1993, approximately one year and six months after we had taken occupancy of our new quarters at 450 Lexington Avenue, New York City. During this period I happily worked in the art department and studio area from a smaller, more modest office — and loved it.

Becoming Collectors

Between 1975 and 1990, Kay and I relied mostly on my creative judgment in selecting the furnishings for our home in Pound Ridge, New York. After sensing that we were going astray, we engaged the services of an interior design firm that I had interviewed for my ad agency, when it was considering doing its first quarters in 1985. We were pleased with the results of their efforts on our behalf; however, we bristled somewhat at the cost of designing and fabricating elegant custom furniture.

Coincidentally, my financial advisor was reviewing our insurance needs and asked if I owned any expensive antiques. In responding, I came to realize that I didn't own any expensive antiques, but we did own some very expensive custom furniture — furniture, that if it were to appear for sale, would render, as beautiful as it was, only a minor percentage of the cost incurred in its design and fabrication, unlike antique furniture, which retains its value and often appreciates. This observation caused us to turn from making our home furnishings to collecting those made for others.

Our preference for Modern Art brought us to the world of French Art Deco furniture and *objets d'art*. It meant becoming familiar with the Paris gallery owners, auction houses, museums, flea markets, and those who were experts in the field. It meant learning about the trends, pricing, and politics of Art Deco collecting. All of this was in turn to require many trips abroad over the past two decades, leading us to become Francophiles of the first order.

We were to meet a wonderful young man, Alain Zlotogora, in 1992, through a fortunate series of circumstances, and he has continued to guide us through the vagaries of collecting and the market for Art Deco. In time we coupled our interest in Art Deco with other fine art, acquiring varied complementary photography, paintings, and sculpture of the twentieth century.

Over the years, we have managed to accumulate a gathering of fine objects, paintings, and sculptures. I hesitate to refer to these items as a "collection," believing it's for the judgment of others more expert than I to evaluate the worthiness of the materials we have gathered. I suppose one day it'll all be put up for auction, and at that time we'll know its importance and value. However, we have managed to acquire pieces by E. Jacques Ruhlmann, Eugene Printz, Raymond Subes, Alfred Porteneuve, Gilbert Poillerat, Georges Jouve, Ferdinand Lalique, Jean-Claude Mayodan, Jean Luce, René Buthaud, and François-Emile Décorchemont, among others. Fine art includes sculpture by Paul Manship, Boris Lovett-Lorski, Rembrandt Bugatti, Fernando Botero, and Bryan Hunt; photography by Loretta Lux and Tracy Moffatt in addition to a variety of prints by artists Joan Miro, Howard Hodgkins, David Hockney, Ellsworth Kelly, Roy Lichtenstein, Pablo Picasso, and Joseph Albers.

The appearance of two of our Emile-Jacques Ruhlmann pieces, a 1925 Sèvres Ceramic Cup and Saucer and a Daybed, ca.1928, in the New York Metropolitan Museum of Art's Special Exhibition: Ruhlmann: Genius of Art Deco, June 8, 2004 – September 5, 2004, was, for us, an affirmation of our collecting abilities. The exhibition was organized and circulated by the Montreal Museum of Fine Arts in collaboration with The Metropolitan Museum of Art and Le Musée des Années 30, Boulogne-Billlancourt.

In 2001 we engaged the well-known interior designer Juan Montoya, along with Woody Rainey, to collaborate in the renovation of our home in Pound Ridge, New York. This project culminated in March 2007 with the publication of an article in *Architectural Digest, The International Magazine of Design*, which featured our home, among others.

Our home was never intended to be a warehouse or museum. *Architectural Digest* got it right when they wrote, "As conceived, and even reconceived by the architect, it [the house] had integrity and increased logic; it was a welcoming house for the clients alone or in the company of their children and grandchildren." They went on to describe our home in the following terms: "The house [that] Rainey remade for the Davises was ranchlike in its low profile and spreading floor plan, Modernist in its use of glass and its openness to its lush setting and Arts and Crafts — like in its use of warm, earthy materials." Juan Montoya and Woody Rainey were to combine our interest in art collecting and our home into "a single, elegant, welcoming gem."

On the steps of the New York Metropolitan Museum of Art, August 14, 2004, after attending the Rhulmann Genius of Art Deco exhibition with (back row, left to right) me, grandsons Codie, Taylor, and son Cole, (front row) grandsons Beau and Dylan (seated), Kay, and Cole's wife Tammi.

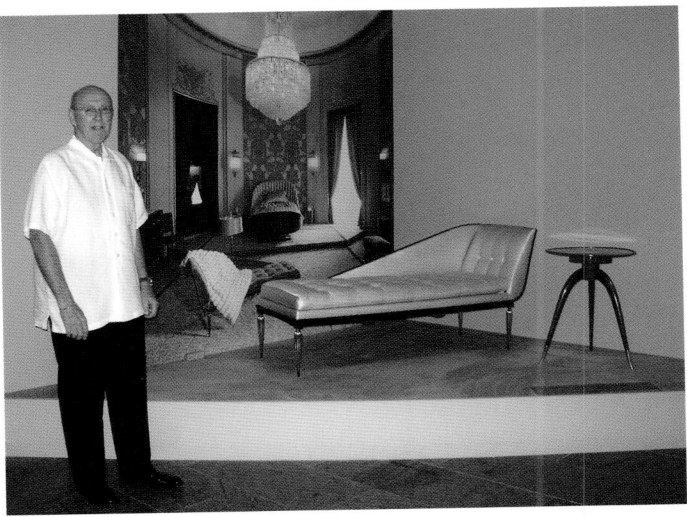

Our Ruhlmann "daybed" exhibited with a side table (not ours), also by Ruhlmann and a photograph, enlarged, depicting the piece in its original setting.

Now that our home is fully furnished we are less active as collectors and far more discrminating in our selections for purchase, though almost anything "Ruhlmann" will catch our eye at auction. We continue to participate in art fairs such as the Armory show in New York, the Frieze in London, the Biennalle in Paris, and of course Art Basel Miami Beach. We're looking forward to our first visit to The European Fine Art Fair in Maastricht, Netherlands.

Biking

Kay, who has always been athletic and active, had become quite interested in tennis in the '70s and '80s. She played on the Pound Ridge women's "A" tennis team. In the summer of 1994, in anticipation of a doubles match, Kay's partner informed her that she would like to get the event over quickly. Kay's partner had to rush home and pack for an upcoming vacation, biking abroad. Curious, Kay wanted to know more and, after quickly dispatching their opponents, her partner brought Kay to her home and gave her a promotional brochure produced by the firm Butterfield and Robinson, who specialized in hosting upscale active vacations, mostly abroad, with deluxe bike tours.

Though the destinations are often well-known to most travelers, a Butterfield and Robinson biking or walking trip is a worry-free trip. Their guides deal with luggage transportation, reservations at top-tier hotels, and the best known and best reviewed restaurants, and all travel connections. They also provide privileged access to places that are often not seen by the traveling public.

This was the beginning of a long, often arduous, physically challenging way for us to travel the world.

Biking has become a passion we've passed on to our family. Commencing with a trip to Provence, France, in 1995, we have scheduled a trip cycling in the company of others nearly every year since. At first Kay and I went alone, then our kids joined us, and in recent years, we have joined with others outside our family as well. So far our biking, or biking and walking trips include

- Provence Getaway biking May 2 – May 6, 1995
- Tuscany biking May 15 – May 22, 1996
- Morocco biking April 22 – April 30, 1997
- Corsica and Sardinia biking June 16 – June 23, 1998
- MS Bike Tour, starting and ending at the World Trade Center – September 27, 1998
- MS Bike Tour, starting and ending at the World Trade Center – September 12, 1999
- Dordogne Valley biking September 19 – September 26, 1999
- Veneto biking and walking trip June 16 – June 22, 2000
- Umbria biking May 23 – May 30, 2001
- Prague to Vienna biking July 28 – August 3, 2002
- Bike New York 2003 – May 4, 2003
- Puglia biking May 23 – May 29, 2003
- Catalonia biking September 19 – September 24, 2004
- Brazil biking September 19 – September 29, 2005
- Sicily biking April 19 – April 27, 2006
- Conques and Lot Valley biking and walking October 9 – 14, 2007
- Vietnam biking December 25, 2007 – January 6, 2008
- Burgundy, France, biking September 13 – September 19, 2008
- Italian lakes walking trip June 28 – July 4, 2010

Our daughters Cynthia and Christine and their husbands, as well as our son Cole and his wife Tammi, accompanied us on the Puglia, Italy, trip which included Sienna, Florence, and the Tuscany countryside by car. Recently, over the Christmas and New Year holidays (December 25, 2007 – January 6, 2008), we included all thirteen of our family — children, spouses, and grandchildren — on a biking trip to Vietnam. In September 2008, Kay and I went on a bike tour in Burgundy, France.

As the years passed, I began to sense that our fellow bikers were appearing younger and younger, and that perhaps I wouldn't be able to meet physically the challenges presented by the twenty-five to forty mile daily treks. At one *(continued on page 112)*

Cynthia, approximately age 10, and Cole, approximately age 8, with me and Kay, eating donuts after our bike ride to Norwalk, Connecticut, from Pound Ridge in a photo taken by Christine.

Below left: Cole at the end of the New York to Washington bike trip May 1978, and below right: Dad and the bike used for trip New York to Boston. The New York to Boston ride was featured in the August 1976 issue of Omega Connection, *the company newsletter of Omega Engineering in Stamford, Connecticut:*

> ***The Long Distance Cyclists***
>
> *Kay Davis's husband, Clyde and twelve-year old son Cole recently took a very ambitious bicycle trip. Clyde, using his old, 3-speed stand-by and Cole sporting a flashy Fuji 10-speed, departed from Pound Ridge, N.Y. at 2 P.M. on Saturday, August 28th. By that evening they had reached New Haven and at Cole's suggestion opt for a convenient Holiday Inn instead of "roughing" it. The next morning, refreshed, the pair were off for Providence, R.I. and by Tuesday evening had reached their destination, Cambridge, Mass. This gave them a full day to bike tour through Cambridge and Boston.*
>
> *While Cole may have been ready to attempt the return trip, Clyde, a bit saddle-sore, decided that a one-way trip was enough. Kay came to the rescue and picked up cyclists and bikes Wednesday evening for a more mundane but certainly quicker and more comfortable return trip by car.*
>
> *Aside from family day tours on bike, this was the first lengthy, over-night trip for both Clyde and Cole. Judging from the success of this one, Kay is sure that it is just the first of others in the future.*

October 28, 2000, Cole with boys unloading bikes for a Sunday afternoon tour around Mission Bay Park on San Diego Bay.

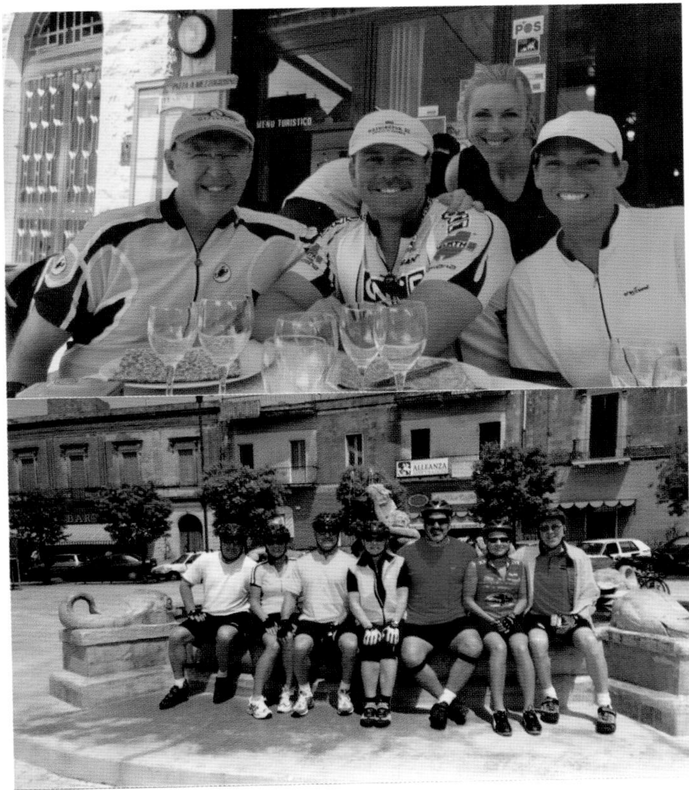

Clyde, Cole, Christine, and Tammi in the small town of Ostuni, during the Puglia, Italy, trip May 23 to May 29, 2003.

On December 27, 2007, our family, including the grandchildren this time, rendezvoused in Ho Chi Min City, Vietnam. The above family photo was taken December 28, 2007, at Xuan Huong Park in Dalat in the central highlands of Vietnam. Dalat is considered to be the city of Eternal Spring. During our trip, the Annual Flower Festival was in full bloom.

August 14, 2005, on yet another Sunday afternoon in downtown San Diego

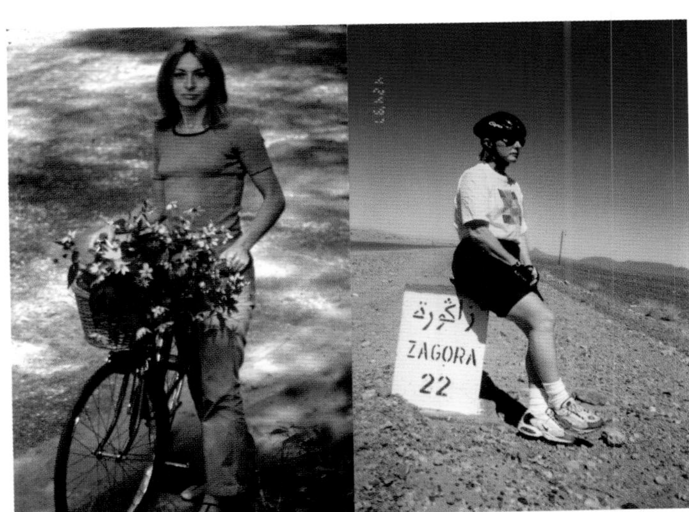

Left: Kay at the intersection of Barnegat Road, Trinity Pass, and Fancher roads in Pound Ridge, New York, in a photo dated September 1970. Right: Kay seated on roadside marker 22 kilometers from Zagora, Morocco, on April 24, 1997.

Left to right: Taylor Davis, Christine Parrino, John Parrino (seated), Ross Malara, his mother Cynthia, Dylan Malara (on bike), Phil Malara, Beau Davis (with red helmet), Codie Davis, Kay Davis, Tammi and Cole Davis at the summit of Mt. Haleakala, Maui, Hawaii, ready for the bike ride down to the base on December 30, 2006. Clyde passed on the trip because, "I had been there, done that."

point I told Kay that when I turn out to be the oldest in a group of bikers on any future trip, I would cease my biking career. However, I am happy to report that our biking trip to Brazil serendipitously hooked us up with a group of fellow bikers who were mostly all in their late sixties, including spouses, each extremely physically fit and active for their age. For this reason I rescinded my edict and we have, with our newfound friends, since completed trips, to Sicily and the Conques-Lot Valley, as mentioned on page 110, and were even planning a trip biking in Japan in the future.

At age seventy-three, I am looking forward with Kay to our next biking trip in 2012, Vienna to Budapest (we never actually bike the entire distance between the two cities). It will be a rare opportunity for us not only to revisit "mysterious Hungary," but to combine the vacation with the personal distribution of my completed book to family and friends.

Like the trip above, rated Easygoing, we're increasingly inclined to seek out the less challenging rides. A Holland biking trip in the spring, gliding through fields of tulips — think flat — may precede the Hungary trip.

Now approaching age seventy-four, I recall reading somewhere that of all athletic activities, biking, along with swimming, ranks among those the elderly can continue to perform well into their eighties.

Here's hoping.

The two of us biking in Burgundy, France, on September 14, 2008.

From the age of two, Cole has been fascinated by anything with wheels. From sitting in my lap as a youngster and steering my car as I worked the gas and brake, to the pedal car pictured on page 129, Cole has been running vehicles wherever they will take him. Only he knows for sure what thrills he associates with being on the move. From his banana seat bike to his Harleys, he has sought the thrill of the ride.

He sold his blue Harley Fat Boy when he needed cash for his newly formed construction company. Knowing how much he liked bikes, and had always wanted a black one, I purchased a Harley Fat Boy, keeping it in Pound Ridge, New York. This was supposed to draw Cole back east more frequently, but, with a growing family and a burgeoning business, Cole didn't respond to the simple draw of a motorcycle. When we did see him back east, it was usually in the winter and in Florida or traveling abroad.

Kay never allowed me to learn to ride the bike, afraid I would hurt myself. For years, I kept it in my garage and spoke of it as part of my art collection. On July 2, 2008, I shipped my black Harley to Cole, who often goes for long coastal rides with Tammi on the back. A little less speed and a more leisurely ride, I'm sure. Cole has managed to create a tapestry of scenic splendor only his eyes and heart can know.

Below: May 18, 1994, Cole on his blue Harley Fat Boy in full leathers

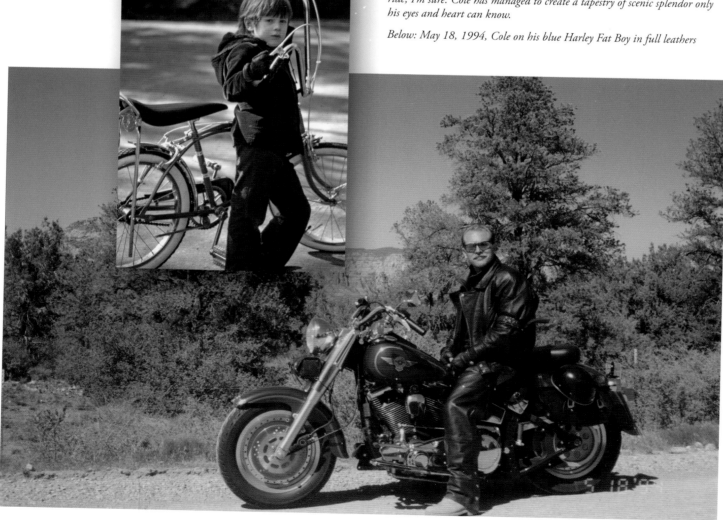

Dapper

On Christmas 1975, we gave our children a dog. We had purchased a Hungarian Vizsla puppy by the name of Dapper — meaning "courageous," according to his New Jersey Dutch breeders. He was a family dog, until as is common, the children left home for college, the military, or marriage, and gradually he became my dog. We've had many cats, Fatso and Turbo among the most unforgettable, but only one dog.

Dapper was a Hungarian hunting dog, descended from the Transylvanian hound and the Turkish yellow dog. He was often mistaken as a German Shorthaired Pointer or Weimaraner. He was a beautiful dog, powerfully muscular, with a rusty-gold coat, and no other markings or colors. His coat was short, dense, and smooth. A third of his tail was docked. His eyes were surprisingly brown, matching his coat.

Dapper loved to run, full-tilt. His stride was graceful, and boy, was he fast! We'd take him down to the Pound Ridge Park to the baseball field. While Kay held him, I would take off running with a head start. When I was about halfway across the field, she would release him. Before I could get completely to the other side, he was passing me. He loved to run, and I loved to run with him.

Driving around in my son's Ford pick-up truck with Dapper sitting beside me, erect, he would often decide to stick his head out the open window, his nose pointed straight ahead, allowing the wind to catch the lips of his soft muzzle, causing them to flutter as vigorously as his long hanging ears would flap.

Dapper was, of course, part of our family, so it was only fitting he accompany us on our motor home trip across country. This photo was taken in the midst of Petrified Forest National Park, Arizona, at Blue Mesa on September 4, 1977. The temperature probably was in the high 90s. Upon returning home three weeks later, Dapper collapsed. The vet said he was suffering from exhaustion and prescribed a regimen of rest.

Dapper in my favorite photo of him taken November 4, 1984

George Euringer drew the above picture because Dapper had completely destroyed our white sofas. I had terrorized the children for years to keep the sofas intact and pristine. While everyone else in the family shuddered in fear, Dapper chewed the sofas to pieces, yet I was petting the dog following the destruction.

Clyde Patrick Davis Family

I gaze upon the photograph below and think of fresh beginnings, a time of relative innocence, our lives before us, the future hopeful and bright. Certainly that July summer day depicted here in 1982 held great promise — some of it was to be realized, some not. The wedding pictures on these four pages span a period of eighteen years. Over that time, Christine and Scott would remain married for only five years. Christine was to marry John Parrino eighteen years later.

Alfonse Andre Mora · *David Otis Davis* · *Clyde Patrick Davis* · *June Mary Mora* · *Scott Ryan Davis* · *Richard Douthart* · *Catherine Ann Davis* · *Christine Rene Ledingham* · *Sean "Scott" Ledingham* · *Cynthia Leigh Davis* · *Cole Matthew Davis* · *April Lynn Mora* · *Alfonse Mora* · *Erin Mora* · *David Andrew Mora*

Christine and Scott Ledingham Wedding, Pound Ridge Community Church, Pound Ridge, New York, July 24, 1982

Each of these events is a celebration of love and commitment. A coming together of family — a gathering of loved ones at a moment in time, to share their joy over one more person being added to the fold.

As a father I can recall on each occasion how proud I was of my offspring, of the person being passed into the welcoming arms of another. These were happy occasions, but also occasions tinged with sadness, for these youngsters of mine

Cynthia and Philip Malara Reception, Marriott Hotel, White Plains, New York, July 14, 1984

were leaving our home for another, our family for one of their own making, our support and security being exchanged for their independence and new horizons. Little did we imagine on these occassions of wedded bliss how often they would find themselves returning to their parents for that same support and security, over and over again. Children are a joy. They can also bring you heartache and pain, but it's the love that endures long after troubling times.

With our love for one another, as young parents, physically strong and mentally persevering, we set this thing called "family" in

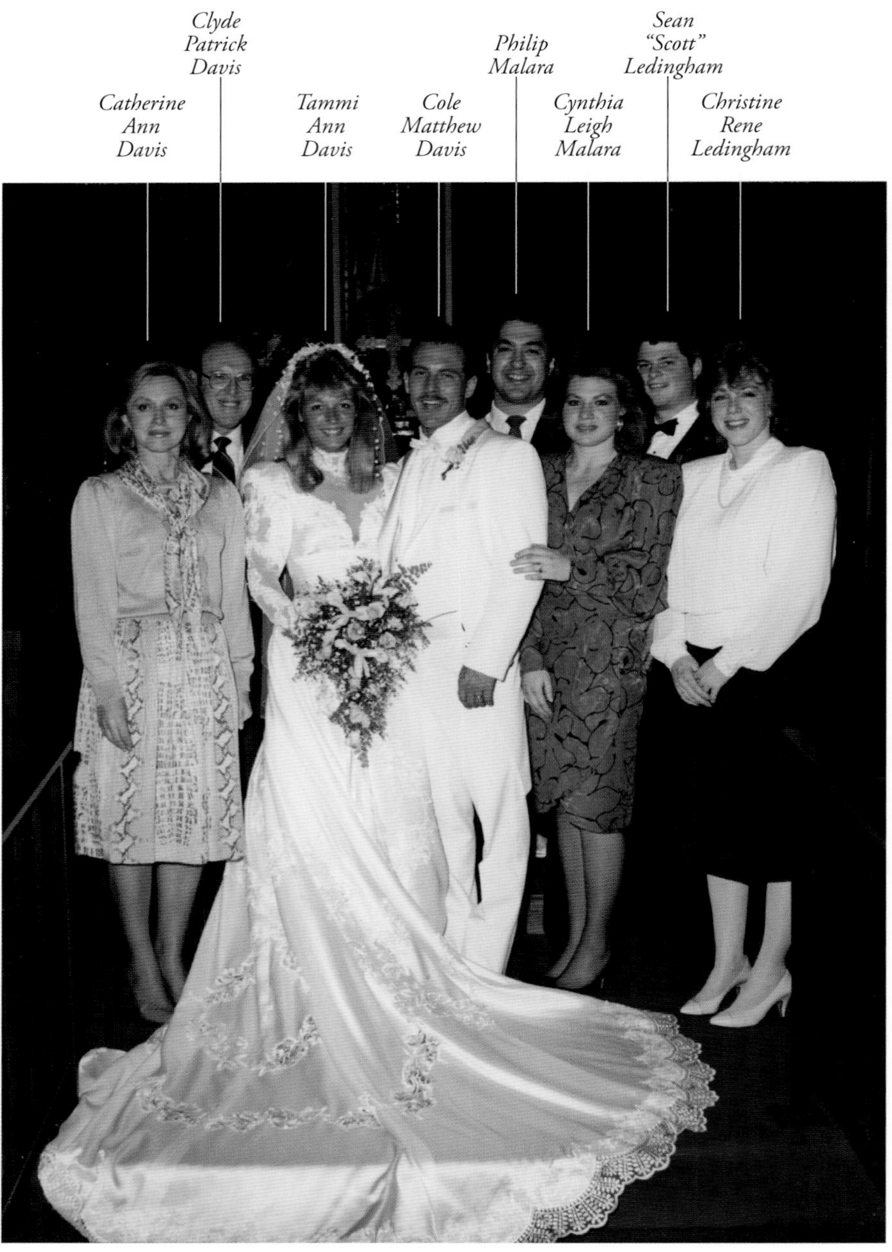

Cole and Tammi Ann Taylor Davis Wedding at St. Andrews Episcopal Church, Ben Lomond, California, February 7, 1987

motion. Children, yes, and they would surely have a better life than we. No bar would be set higher than that which we had to clear, because, after all, they would be standing on the shoulders of their parents as their lives went forward.

That was our dream. They didn't disappoint, but they sure did give us a run for our money. And I mean that, quite literally. We've undoubtedly spoiled them but, hopefully, they will forgive us our indiscretions and recover from any harm we may have done them along the way.

Christine and John Parrino Wedding, reception at Le Château Restaurant, South Salem, New York, February 6, 2000

Photo of Chris (left) and Cyn (right), October 1963

isters

My Girls

As much as I may have bristled at the imposition of changing the premise of this book — finding fathers — I've now resolved to equally greet with enthusiasm and embrace the task of exploring my personal relationship with my two daughters. Most importantly I will attempt to define their character, particular charm and grace, as I've found it to be expressed over these past nearly five decades. It's a tall order, and challenging for me, a male, preoccupied with this project of finding fathers, tracing the male bloodline of my kin and kin to be, and then having to focus on my two female offspring.

Christine (left) and Cynthia (right)

This book is about finding fathers, and I believe that the father of these two chidren will be found between the lines of this story about them, rather than directly from the words I've written. It's always best to start at the beginning, but chronically short on memory, I'll start with my girls as they are today. Grown, vibrant, assertive, complex, vivacious, striving women. There, I've done it! Well, not hardly. Let's explore "assertive" as a common trait. They are both demanding taskmasters of their households, each clearly in charge of family affairs, and captains of their respective domestic ships of state: Cynthia, vis-à-vis her "honey-do" lists and a confetti-like maelstrom of yellow stickies — Christine, through her quick wit, biting tongue, and sarcastic candor and manner. They are each hardworking, striving for the best in home, lifestyle, career path, and marriage.

They can be equally charming. Attractive women, they enjoy the hereditary enduring good looks of their mother, have infectious smiles, are quick to laugh, and are outgoing and gregarious.

Not too surprisingly, they are physically strong women, athletic with regular exercise as an important part of their lives. In 1972, when Cynthia was in the fifth grade, she was the first recipient of the Pound Ridge Elementary School Association's Mike Cotton memorial award for athletic excellence. At an early age, Christine was on top of a 1,000-pound animal while taking horseback-riding lessons. Both were on the Pound Ridge Park Swim Team for several years; both were lifeguards during summer vacations. Christine, to this day, is an avid runner and can be found jogging six miles at 5 A.M. before going off to work each morning. Cynthia still swims regularly.

I've never favored one child over another. I'll admit to wanting a son, especially after the arrival of two consecutive daughters. After my son's birth, we were done. It's not uncommon for parents to see reflected in the nature of their offspring character traits of one's own, often clearly physical, sometimes behavioral, even spiritual. I and their mother have often discussed where our influences lie with each child, as we have been reminded by others over the years that she "takes after Clyde," or he bears neither parent, or she's "Kay's daughter."

Most surprising, as the years pass, I'm increasingly aware that the best of what their parents had to offer has been adopted as a lifestyle — embraced and applied despite their independence.

As a father of three young children, I wanted the best for them. I thought that growing up in an affluent community in Westchester like Briarcliff Manor or Pound Ridge, they would attend the best schools and associate with the children of well-to-do families of doctors, lawyers, and bankers. By all my calculations, I thought it something of a certainty that they would eventually marry into these families. Falling in love with the offspring of the privileged class did not happen. Each, like their parents, married for love, never once doubting the economic consequences of their choices. We are not bred to be elitists. We are genetically, ergonomically aspirational without the underpinning of upper class, socially connected bloodlines. Dropping ourselves in the midst of the upper class was not, at least for our offspring, entry into this rarified world. We had to earn it, the old-fashioned way, generation after generation. I was the first in my family to ultimately graduate, from college. Christine was the first female in our family to earn a university degree. Each of my children at the time of this book's publication will be earning a substantial living. None will be a person, as the private bankers state, of "high net worth." We will have to look forward to the next generation with hope that one, if not all, our grandchildren will break through this economic barrier. As my daughter Christine said, "None of us kids will ever make as much as Mom and Dad, except, perhaps Cole, who has his own business."

I'll accept the fate of my children as long as they are happy, healthy, doing meaningful work of their choosing, and are in loving relationships challenged by a future bright with promise. Kay and I are truly blessed.

In the preceding pages of this book I have painstakingly acknowledged my shortness of memory. Reflecting on the childhood of my daughters yields little in detail. There is, of course, my global view of each that I continue to carry to this day.

Never was I so moved, so proud, and so happy as the evening after completing my speech to the Medical Advertising Hall of Fame, amidst applause, alighting from the podium into the standing embrace and congratulations of my daughters. Their unbridled love, delight, and pride in their father's achievement was for me, in the presence of so many, the greatest of all tributes. These were "my girls."

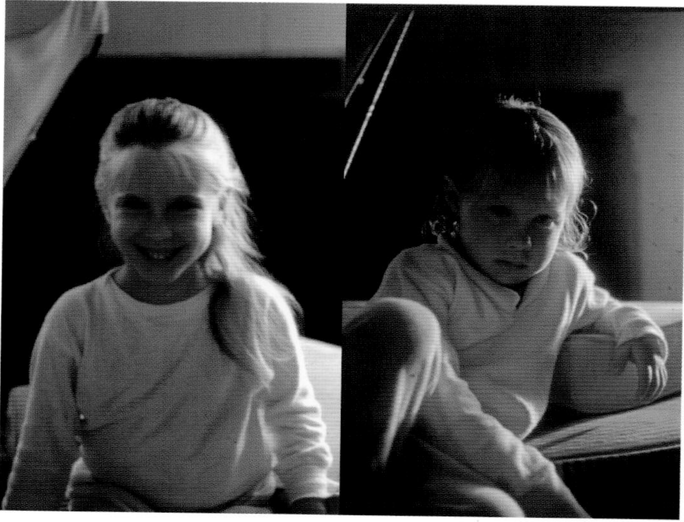

Christine (left) and Cynthia (right) in their "jammies" after a sun-filled day at Westhampton Beach. They are seated in front of a fireplace in the architecturally famous "Box Kite House" designed by Andrew Michael Geller in 1959.

Back in the "Hood" — Sisterhood

Christine has in recent years come to spend the most "face time" with her parents. The past seventeen years she has lived no more than a half hour away by car. Cynthia coaxed her return home from the West Coast after Christine's being away for ten years with "You're really missing out on a lot of 'slop-over' not being close to Mom and Dad." In order to jumpstart a faltering love life once back in New York, we encouraged Christine to date. She ruled out dating fellow employees and clients despite plenty of opportunities and, coupled with riding instructions after a long commute home evenings, there was little other time to meet men. Knowing full well her sister's disposition toward men, particularly how unyielding she could be of her standards, Cynthia was aghast one evening when her husband Phil suggested he introduce his best friend and childhood schoolmate to Christine, suggesting they go on a "blind date," even double date. "Are you crazy, Phil? You want to do what? Do you know how fussy my sister is? Why

Two peas in a pod: Pound Ridge Elementary School portraits of Chris (left) and Cyn (right), probably around fourth or fifth grade?

would you want to subject us to that, or for that matter your best friend?" Eventually, after some further family consultation, Cynthia, despite her reservation — fear is a more appropriate word — acquiesced to the outing. The rest is history. Christine fell hard for Phil's best friend, John. By evening's end they were in each other's arms. Sisterhood, and some nudging from Phil, claimed the credit for coupling the two of them.

In August 1993, Christine took up residence in Vista, New York, a town within twenty minutes drive of our home. After her marriage to John they lived in one, then another, residence in a large community, Heritage Hills, in Somers, New York, but still doable for family get-togethers.

Kay with her daughters Christine at left and Cynthia on her lap at Tappan Arms, Briarcliff Manor, New York. This photo was probably taken in the spring of 1963.

Cyn (left) and Chris (right) in a field in July 1974

Happily, after a most arduous search in a trying economic period, in December 2007, we, as parents, prevailed in finding and convincing them to purchase a home in our own town of Pound Ridge.

The premise of this book revolves around fathers. It attempts to define the role of men after having sired offspring and to determine the myriad meanings of fatherhood.

As a father of two vivacious, spirited, adult daughters, I could risk asking them, "What kind of father am I?" Surely, I would receive a litany of flattering compliments, interlaced with withering criticisms. But I'll forget that possibility in the interest of being true to my book's premise. All through my life I've related best to women. That is to say, I get along better with women than men. I cannot say why for sure; I'm just more comfortable in the company of women. As a father, I've respected my daughters' femininity. I've not attempted to turn them into baseball players or truck drivers.

My goal, for all my children, was to provide them food, shelter, a good education, a loving home environment, and a sense of respect for others — to ensure they become caring, sensitive, giving, and forgiving individuals, anchored in fortitude and principle. Mostly, I wanted our marriage to be an example for them. I failed to raise them as Christians, though each was baptized Roman Catholic. Mostly, I have always wanted to provide a stable, sustainable environment for each of them to grow comfortably, always secure in the knowledge that their father was there for them. I wanted them to experience what I never had. Simple enough. Harder to achieve. So many fathers — mine included — succumb to the vagaries of life, of poor choices, personal weakness, bad luck, bad health, temptations of the flesh, and along the way losing the sense of commitment they incurred upon bringing youngsters into this world.

I wanted to earn their respect. Once established, I wanted them each to value that standard of behavior, of fidelity, love, hard work, and bettering one's self, and the constancy of effort regarding these tenets. As I reflect on my daughters as they are today, I see these things in them. More and more, day-by-day, they honor, through their personal behavior, those same standards their father established for them. Hopefully, as their father, I'll continue to serve their interests by being that safety net should they falter, by living the remainder of my life with integrity and sensitivity, by being a loving parent, husband, and grandfather.

Looking Back

It's September 18, 2009, and we're flying cross-country from New York City to San Diego, and I've found a moment to write. Somehow, being airborne causes me to be more reflective than usual. Confined to my seat for five and one-half hours also allows for some quiet time without interruption.

Kay and I are to celebrate our 50th Wedding Anniversary at the home of our son Cole and his wife Tammi. They and our daughters have been planning this event for some time. Our five grandsons and their parents and our daughter Christine and her husband John will all be there. We're excited.

So, with our 50th a day away, I'm in a reflective frame of mind, but one mixed with nostalgia, musings of marriage, fifty years past and all it has produced.

Two of a Kind

It's certainly, at least for me, a lot easier to relate the memories of two daughters as youngsters, or even young adults, than it is to capture in words the women they are today. Approaching the fifty-year mark themselves, a father has lots to draw upon — the good, the not so good, and the vast in-between.

Each daughter is the embodiment of a spirit and dynamism that I, so introverted, am continually amazed by — these women are not demure, wallflower types. Each is outspoken, freely giving her opinion to anyone within earshot. And if you do find yourself in the same room with them, you'll have no problem hearing what they have to say. They can be loud, even raucous at times. Their laughter can be heard in the next county. They can also be quite funny. Like their mother, they are great storytellers. You do not want to be the object of their punch line.

Both daughters are workaholics, obsessed with accomplishment, whether in their respective professions or simply doing chores around the home. As one might imagine, they're equally demanding of others, those not normally inclined to strive so mightily for (thankfully) such levels of (read children and spouses here) accomplishment and perfection. Somehow, my grandsons Ross and Dylan have managed to escape their mothers' zeal for work.

Each daughter takes pride in a comfortable, well-appointed home. They love flowering gardens and find the time to put their hands in the soil. Aesthetics and appearance are important to them. Beauty is a part of their lives. Because they have remained fit and trim, each can wear the other's suit, gown, or coat, sometimes even swapping a garment or two not only between themselves, but also with their mother. I often overhear them talking, asking who among them has a particular jacket or dress. This activity cuts down on expenses, but not as much as one might think. Kay has been known to compete with her daughters to prove to them that she is still "in the game," especially Cynthia,

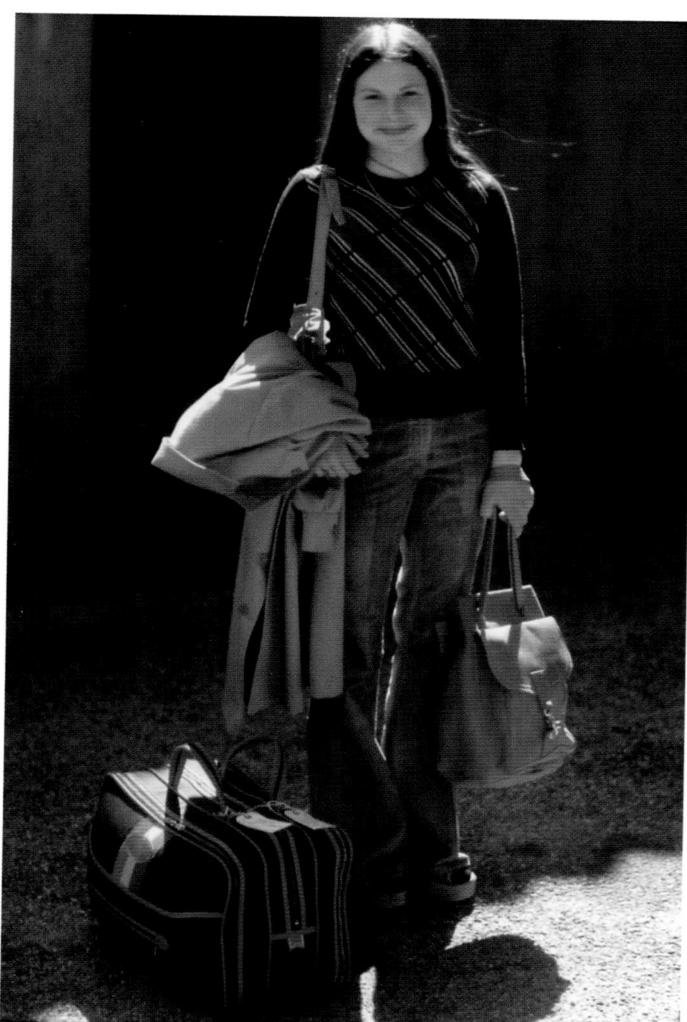

Cynthia, with her bags packed about to depart from Fox Lane Middle School to Paris on a trip for selected eighth grade students studying French. Four years later, she would spend a semester abroad, living with a French family. In a letter to her grandfather dated December 9, 1978, she wrote: "I had brought boxes of jello from the States which I made. Jello doesn't exist in France. Most of the people were amazed by it and half of them swore it was alive by the way it moved."

who has spent a lifetime career in fashion. Her mother shops deliberately for the latest this or that trend, wearing a "flared" sleeve, jacquard print high sheen blouse (for example), and catching Cynthia's eye or hearing a comment like. "Well, aren't you the one," or being asked, "Where did you get that?" It would be followed by, "Who makes it? Let me see the label." This particularly delights Kay.

Each daughter loves animals — cats, dogs, horses. Cynthia has almost always, as a child through today, had cats as pets. Today, she has two dogs, Max, a lumbering, sweet aging Lab, and Shokey, another Lab, though I'm convinced a little pitbull resides in him. Two recently acquired cats, Baby and Bella, are sometime residents, taking off for days at a time, returning spent and hungry. Cynthia has stopped posting notices and tooling about the neighborhood frantically searching for them now that their disappearances are routine.

Another two cats, Dewey and Nemo, reside indoors — only with Christine and her husband John. Chris and John have erected a bedlike window perch for "the boys," as they are affectionately called, with a bird feeder continuously replenished, at considerable cost I imagine, located within tantalizing view and a never-ending source of entertainment through all seasons. "A horse is a horse, of course, of course," but to Christine, a horse is near-human.

I could go on endlessly about the similarities of my girls without fully defining the true character of these sisters. Much of what I have discussed, obviously, springs from parents, much of it good, some not so good, and a lot in between.

"Vive la Différence"

It's the "in between" I'd like to address now. How these sisters, so much alike, sharing the same home-grown values could be so different. I have never quite felt that I shared as much with them as their mother. After all, I'm not a woman. And I was never the kind of father who wanted my daughters to play sports, so I could indulge my athletic field fantasies through them. They are quite athletic though, having been teammates on the Pound Ridge swim team. Cynthia was designated most athletic in 8th grade, and Christine is an avid biker, horse rider, and jogger.

Neither have I chosen to spend endless mall crawls with them, as has their mother, or to assist them in decorating their homes, or to teach them how to cook (I can barely fry an egg).

Over time a father does come to know his daughters, not so much by hanging out with them, but rather through years of observing the formation of their unique characters, as they moved through adolescence into womanhood. Both, approaching fifty years of age, are now fairly defined as individuals, as women, as my wonderful girls.

During the past two decades I have been called upon to assist each of them when they faltered professionally in their careers, surprisingly, each at the peak of her success.

Fast Starter

Today I enjoy their company and our exchanges regarding their careers, Cyn's boys and Chris's "boys" — her two cats Nemo and Dewey adopted from a local pound. We vacation together in Florida and abroad. We see one another regularly, but it is Christine's career in advertising that I'm most familiar with. She rekindles in me a bygone era, yet however nostalgically drawn upon, I continue to advise and counsel her in a business common to us both.

Yet it was Cynthia's career that blossomed early. Cynthia literally "exploded out of the box." Immediately upon leaving Syracuse University, she worked in a series of positions with some of the biggest names in retailing. In ten short years she worked for Orbach, Abraham & Straus (A&S), and Caldor, The Limited, as well as a number of specialty women's wear companies, such as Charming Shops, August Max, and Weathervane. By age twenty-five, at Weathervane, she was earning a high six-figure salary, working twelve-hour days and traveling extensively abroad on business to Bangladesh, Hong Kong, Bangkok, Paris, and London. Her somewhat meteoric rise in the world of garment-

Christine's and John's "boys," Dewey and Nemo

wear, though exciting, rewarding monetarily, and intellectually stimulating, was eventually to take its toll. Her family values began to kick in and became the cause of conflict. She was struggling with the working woman's dilemma: How to balance family with a career. She would ultimately crash and burn from sheer exhaustion, physical and mental, accompanied by a widening disconnect from her children, who were placed in the care of a half dozen nannies. Cynthia, with much pain and counseling (I did my share), was to opt out of her career after unsuccessfully proposing a part-time, at-home work arrangement, without any reduction in salary, with her then employer, August Max, owned by Retail Brand Alliance, Inc. Cynthia was always the prime wage earner in her family and could not afford a loss of earnings. Rebuffed, burnt out, and demoralized, she, with our help financially (a full, after-tax reimbursement of her salary), was to take a year off. A year turned

PLEASE DO NOT STRAIGHTEN UP THE MESS IN THIS ROOM. IT WILL TOTALLY CONFUSE ME AND SCREW UP MY WHOLE WORLD.

DO NOT DISTURB

This star still hangs in my bedroom dressing closet, a bright reflecting reminder of Cynthia's talent and the "star" she became.

into eighteen months before she was able to secure a position more compatible with her newfound lifestyle and to be there for her husband and two boys Ross and Dylan. It was time to recharge her batteries and reorient her thinking about how she'd like to spend the rest of her life. During this period of change — 2002–03 — I grew to know my daughter as an adult woman, about in the world yet very much the child who needed her daddy. We committed to see one another at least once a month, just the two of us, usually for dinner, sometimes lunch in Glastonbury, Connecticut, New York City, or in Pound Ridge to discuss the choices that lay ahead.

Many tears were shed. These were sober moments as we

If I have passed on my artistic genes to anyone, it's been Cynthia. She is undoubtedly the most creative of my three children. Her creativity and artistic taste was expressed early on as a child. Not only in her ceramic ashtrays, figurines, or in the rock tumbler gemstones she created, but also in sewing her own clothes and keeping a bulletin board as a teenager, which I so admired and even coveted at times.

sorted through past mistakes, working her way toward a more spiritually enriched life. Much mentoring on my part and some fine dining eventually led to a change of lifestyle that was to assuage the inner guilt of not being there for her family over so many years devoted to earning a buck.

We were proud of her accomplishments, had much empathy for her dilemma, and her newly embraced goal.

Cynthia eventually found employment in the trunk show end of retailing with a position at Carlisle, achieving her ambition to work out of the home as an independent contractor that allowed continued family presence. Recently she moved from Carlisle to Doncaster, a competitor of her former employer, with increasing income and responsibility. Sadly, she seems to have slipped back into her former work habits, with long hours, more stress coupled with less time for the family. Her boys are grown now, seventeen and twenty-one years of age. She managed to capture a few of those years.

I managed to afford her some modicum of relief; however, I never changed or altered in any significant way the behavior of this daughter I love so much. We are parents and can only be as happy as our least happy child, who for the moment is still trying to find her bliss.

Mad Ave. Maverick

Christine, my elder daughter, an avid, lifelong reader of books, was a communications major in college. She spent much of her adult life after graduating from Boston University, magna cum laude, away from her parents, living on the West Coast. This is typical Christine: out there, alone, finding her way, independent, and self-sufficient.

Christine was always, as a child, in a world of her own — lover of horses and loving to read. A perfectionist at heart. Neat, orderly, controlled. If caught misbehaving (rarely did this occur, due to her shrewdness) and being told to "Go to your room; you're grounded," she would go gladly, happy to finish that novel she was deep into. Her fastidiousness among the children got her the household chore of doing all the toilets.

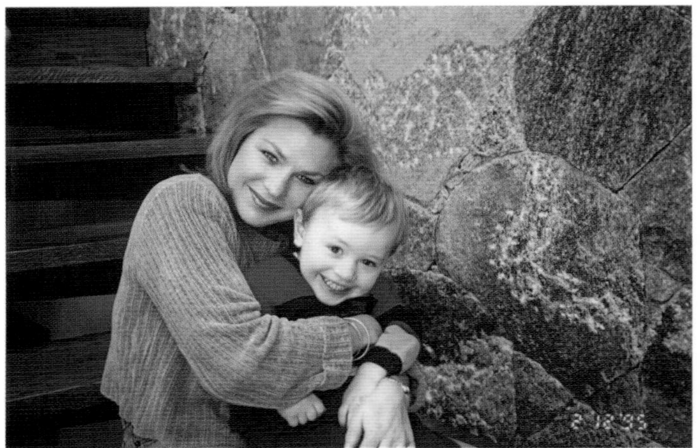

Cynthia and Dylan at our home in Pound Ridge on February 12, 1995

It wasn't until Christine returned to New York, and to the advertising business, and her marriage to John, that I truly grew to know my daughter in ways I had not previously experienced.

Like Cyn, Chris, too, had an abrupt career crisis. Like Cyn, she, too, was a top six-figure wage earner, achieving the position of Executive VP, Account Supervisor at Grey Advertising in New York City when, after eight-and-a-half years with the firm, she lost her job.

A combination of Grey Advertising being sold to WPP, Inc., a change in agency and client management, along with Christine's headstrong and outspoken nature, inflexible manner, and "kick-

Philip and Cynthia on March 14, 1992

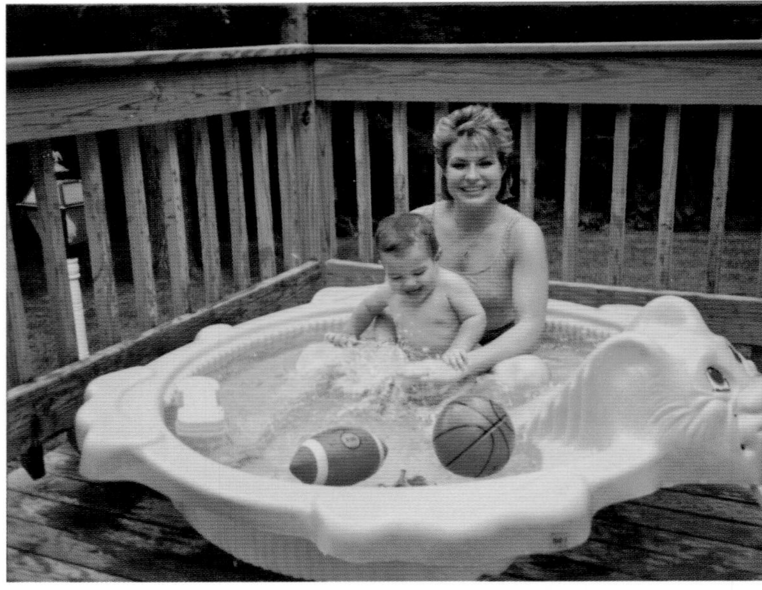

Cynthia with Ross in kiddie pool, probably in 1988. Note the football and basketball, foretelling a future sporting life his father was already shaping.

ass attitude," all contributed to her undoing at the beginning of the 2008 economic downturn.

"On the beach," humbled by the suddenness of her termination, blindsided, Christine did not wallow in her plight. She aggressively pursued employment by organizing her efforts as keenly as any marketing project for a client. She also took advantage of days not working as a professional and turned to home improvement projects such as painting, planting, planning, and constructing an outdoor terrace. Electrical, plumbing, kitchen, and bathroom upgrades were additions to a course in landscaping that resulted in a project for pay.

After Christine's considerable severance pay ran out without being re-employed, she approached her parents, seeking, like her sister, financial support. She and her husband John had rebudgeted for their aborted lifestyle. They addressed the financial shortfall of only one wage earner, projected the period over which they could sustain themselves, and after expending their savings, would only then turn to us for help.

As usual, we agreed to bridge the financial gap, allowing them to keep their house. When Christine said our assistance should be considered a loan, I declined, reminding her that no one else in the family ever repaid their "loans" — she being the exception — and that she should consider the money a gift.

1. Chris after winning her first ribbon on a school horse — Little, who wasn't very — at Primrose Farms, Katonah, New York

2. Chris on Misty in field at intersection of Barnegat Road and Trinity Pass, Pound Ridge, New York

3. Chris at Primrose Farms, Katonah, New York, in 1972

4. Chris with schoolhorse from Barnabee Farm, Bainbridge Island, Washington

5. Chris performing dressage on Dartagnan "Dart" at the USDF Regional Finals at Darien, Connecticut, 1995

6. Cooling down Dartagnan "Dart" after performance at Ox Ridge Hunt Club, Darien, Connecticut, August 24, 1996

7. Christine with Don Paolo "out to pasture" at Back Barn Farm, Bedford, New York, on June 4, 2004

1.
2.
3.
4.
5.
6.
7.
©P. Towne, 1995

John and Chris at John's gratuation from Empire State College, SUNY, on May 21, 2006

After nearly ten months of seeking employment, her mother, sister, and others ramped up the pressure for me to call upon former colleagues at Cline, Davis & Mann, Inc., the pharmaceutical advertising agency that I had founded with my partners and from which I retired in 2002.

To Christine's credit she never asked me to contact the agency. Her mother, though, let it be known that something had to be done and besides, hadn't I helped enrich those now at the helm of my former business? Despite my reservations and discomfort about approaching them, I had no choice, that is, if I wanted to continue to eat and sleep with and enjoy the company of this otherwise, lovely woman.

In my letter of introduction for Christine to the agency's chairman, I reminded him of his first job as a young copywriter hired by my partner. "Christine has no pharmaceutical experience and therefore...you might ask, 'Why is Clyde referring her to me?'" Continuing, I wrote, "I was reminded, as you recalled in your dedication speech, that you joined Cline, Davis & Mann during another economic downturn, and that as a young copywriter you had little in the way of qualifications that would suggest a career in a strictly pharmaceutical ad agency.... Christine is imbued with the Davis work ethic; she's smart and excellent on her feet. She loves to present (unlike her father) and has a high regard for the creative process as you might well imagine. I've attached her resume for your review."

CHRISTINE PARRINO
SENIOR VICE PRESIDENT
DIGITAL STRATEGIST
CLINE DAVIS & MANN
220 EAST 42ND STREET
NEW YORK, NY 10017
212.907.8404
cparrino@cdmworldagency.com
www.cdmworldagency.com
cdm
Clyde Davis
Founder
220 East 42nd Street
New York, New York 10017
212.907.4340
212.557.7193 (fax)
clyded@clinedavis.com
cdm

Four months later in an ever-increasing gloomy economic climate Christine got a break. She was hired on a two-month temporary basis. She loved the company, its culture, and the people, and basked in the glow of her father's legacy. The latter, of course, was to become something of a political issue, and she was advised by her parents and within the company to minimize the fact that her father was one of the company's founders.

Given the opportunity to become part of a new digital department being formed at the agency, she reinvented herself by building on cursory experience at her former employer and creating a foothold as the "Digital Diva," as she was called by her co-workers. Thrown into several new business pitches after becoming a permanent employee, she continues to shine as a Digital Strategist in the account service group.

Chris and Cyn on May 8, 2005, Mother's Day

For a parent, it was good to have her on someone else's payroll. For Christine, her newfound employment restored her self-esteem and confidence. The experience of a job lost has perhaps presented Christine with some insight of her character and the need for change. Showing her softer side coupled with her spirit and enthusiasm, her work ethic, will surely reap immeasurable rewards.

Time will tell.

Secret Ingredient?

I couldn't complete this summary of two sisters without mentioning how easily they can please me. Cynthia has been making me peanut butter cookies for decades now. The BEST peanut butter cookies I've ever had. Crisp, unbelievably light (cloud-like), large and sweet and buttery. And I don't even like peanut butter! Each cookie stamped on top with a fork, crosswise, forming that signature laticework that symbolizes a delight to come. Many others would like to learn this way to my heart. And though Cynthia has freely passed around the recipe, the cookies are never quite as good. Some believe she has left out a "secret" ingredient. Wouldn't you?

Christine, I've come to appreciate lately, makes the BEST frozen margaritas. She has freely shared her recipe with Kay, Cynthia, Tammi, and others. Kay, following Christine's instructions, bought the special "Back to Basics Smoothie Blender" from Target for all three of them. Each machine cost a hefty $19.99. As I turn more and more to drink, I plan to be relying on her proximity, now that she lives in Pound Ridge. I never cooked, and I don't know how to mix my own drinks.

The Kids Call Every Weekend

Mine are gone now — but as with all children
When they were first born, they were like dreams
And they had their entire lives to fulfill my dreams.

Never again are their futures unlimited.
Everything is possible when they are young.
There is everything to look forward to.

At first you may have thought as I did.
My children will have it all!
They will be bright, well-educated, play instruments,
Be athletic, indeed, team players.
They will travel — **Be Leaders!**
And of course, all will be perfect physical specimens.

Then life unfolds — with all of its realities.
As days and then years go by, those dreams change.
In many instances, limitations set in.

She's too tall — she's too fat, he isn't growing at all!
She hates sports — he's not a team player.
Indeed he hates team sports —
doesn't even like tennis —
My favorite sport. My God,
he loves hunting and fishing.
I hate guns and I can't swim.
But these are my children and my dreams.
I'm not ready to give those dreams up yet.

Other realities are more palatable.
And though not part of the stereotype for
Davis children #'s 1 thru 3
These realities are more easily received because they fit
in the scheme of things.
No matter that I didn't think of them first.

She loves horses — we will all learn about them.
They become the most precious memories of her youth.
She loves language — is fluent in French.
An International Exchange Student —
He draws people like a magnet — they adore him.
Somehow, he is very special.

But what of the plan — time is passing.
There is still so much to be done.
These are privileged children with
predetermined destinies —
No failures here — **Unacceptable.**

After all, they were to have all that we didn't.
Do all that we couldn't.
And go further than even we could dream.

But the pace was set fast.
The expectations extraordinary.
The examples tough to beat.

What room did we leave for them at the top?
What compromise did we allow for a
difference of opinion?
What margin did we give for individuality?
What freedom was there in that family,
which lived in the freest nation
in the entire world?

We sounded diplomatic all right.
But the pressure was on.
Our words were logical and understanding.
But our silent standards were there.

Somewhere along the way — they were
strong enough to breathe
And we were smart enough to let them.

Love them for all that they are.
Love them for all that they try to be.
But be sure you love them for all that they aren't.
For therein lies your true measure as a parent.
And something far more special than your dreams —
their dreams.

The kids call every weekend —
Collect.
Thank God they do.

Kay Davis, May 3, 1983

This speech was given by Kay Davis on May 3, 1983, at the Stamford, Connecticut, branch of Toastmaster's Club of America as a required "impromptu speech." She belonged to this club to gain better onstage presence for her position in Human Resources at Omega Engineering, Inc. The assignment that evening was to write an impromptu speech of no more than six minutes that would be presented to those in attendance. It won First Place and was then entered into a regional competition where it received an award as "TMI D53 Area 13 Serious Speech Runner-Up 1983." The speech took about ten minutes to write.

C

ole

My Son

Cole loved his "Dinkeys." For those of you not in the know, these are a series of toy vehicles made by the Matchbox Company and are highly collectible today. They are diminutive, die-cast (1/35) scale models of trucks and cars approximately two inches in length with rubber wheels. Late in 1967 the die-cast toy market was strongly influenced by the first Mattel Hot Wheels. When we lived at Trinity Pass and Barnegat roads in Pound Ridge, Cole would spend hours outside, traversing a stone retaining wall in the dirt above, running his Dinkeys along endless roadways he had created, his head barely clearing the top of the wall. From the kitchen window his mother could keep an eye on him as she prepared dinner for the family.

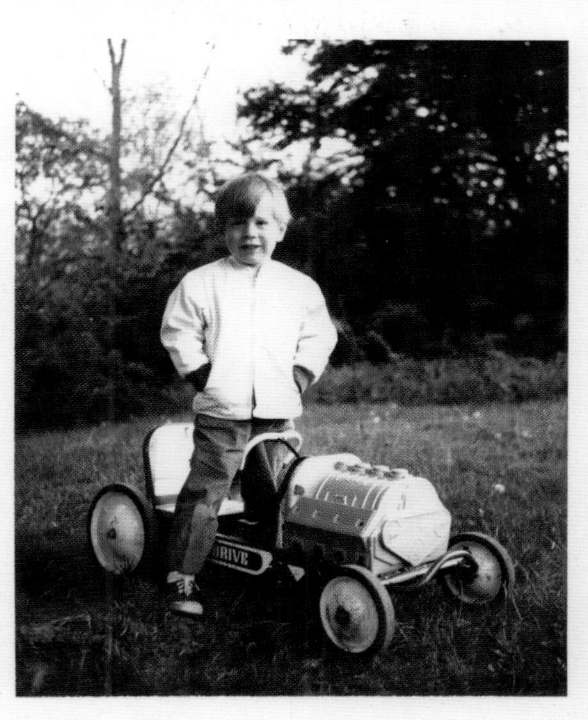

Importantly, this activity of Cole's was to be a harbinger of his growing interest in anything that had wheels, went fast, and carried him along through an early life of thrills and spills.

Cole went from his Dinkeys to his tricycle, pedal car, KTM, dirt bike (at age twelve) to the lap of his father driving the family car (actually only steering), to trucks and motorcycles.

The Headless Car

Not to digress, but there was the time when Cole was visiting a boy (we were not yet calling them "playdates"), whose father was a psychologist who lived in Bedford. His older sister and her friends were at home, while the father and mother went to play tennis.

While there, the boy invited Cole to spend the night (Cole was about eleven years old). Cole was told he could not spend the night, so the girls taunted him, calling him a baby who had to go home. Cole convinced the boy to take the keys to their family car, and the two boys (Cole driving — of course, hadn't he been behind the wheel of his father's car?) went onto Highway 684 to the first rest stop traveling north. The boys placed a call to the sister and her friends from the rest stop. The girls, panicked, called us saying, "Cole took my parents' car with my brother in it." Kay asked the color of the car; she was told it was "orange."

Kay decided to go out to look for the boys. On the way to 684, she saw more orange cars than you could ever believe existed, until she saw, while passing the strip mall in Bedford, an orange car approaching her from the opposite direction "with no heads in it." She knew this had to be the boys and turned around to follow them. Cole reached the boy's house and had already parked in their driveway. When Kay arrived she confronted him. Cole was smiling like a Cheshire cat, proud that he drove the car, even through a tollbooth with police. She then scolded his passenger for being so stupid to get in the car with Cole in the first place and endangering his life. Kay was so upset with Cole she couldn't speak to him for several weeks.

Then there was the time a few years later that he took our car. Sent to bed one evening with our dog Dapper, Cole managed to unhinge his narrow bedroom window, crawl out with dog in tow, nary a sound made between them. With black masking tape, he covered the taillights of our Oldsmobile (so his awake parents would not see the brake lights). He rolled the car down our hill and driveway (it's quite steep) and out into the road below — parents unaware of the departed duo. At age fourteen, he drove to a nearby town, hung out with his friends all night, and returned through the same window, dog and all. It was years later that I learned all the details of this escapade.

Cole would later have an avid interest in introducing his three boys to vehicular sports: bicycles, quads, trail bikes, motorized scooters, and motorcycles, spending endless hours tutoring them, developing their skills, and joining them in their pleasure. Today, at the age of forty-two, Cole drives a Ford truck and has so for nearly twenty-eight consecutive years.

Cole never liked school "right out the door." He never wanted to work indoors in an office. Today, he and his mother believe he may have had ADD (Attention Deficit Disorder). Kay has reminded me that when he was first eligible to attend school, we were advised to hold him back for a year. A combination of having ADD and starting when he did could have contributed to his difficulties in school. Two of Cole's three sons were medically treated for ADD.

Cole loves the outdoors. He learned to ice skate; he was taught by his mother on our own frozen pond. He learned to ski on Town School Trips to Mt. Stowe, Butternut, Sugar Loaf, and Killington. He became an excellent swimmer (his father was on a high school swim team), coaxed by his parents to follow his sisters on the Town of Pound Ridge Park Swim Team — winning medals and trophies as they did in 1976. He was a fast runner, winning the 1975 Pound Ridge Field Day 5 km Cross Country Race at age twelve. In 1977 at fourteen he won the Annual Pound Ridge Hamlet Fair 2 mile road race, placing first in his age group. He still has the trophies. When he was an adult he confided in us that his evening practice runs were never completed. He would sit at the end of our road and play with the family dog, Dapper, faulting my contention that his hard work paid off. Cole also became an avid weightlifter and was a Certified Scuba Diver.

Though Cole competed, his nature is not to be competitive. Though Cole was athletic he never took to any sport that had a ball as its focus. He chased butterflies in the outfield when on the park Babe Ruth baseball team, never played tennis but attended

Cole drew this picture of me weightlifting in our bedroom when he was approximately five to six years old. Note his mother's feet projecting into the picture from the left edge. The brass bed in lower right remains to this day with his sister Cynthia.

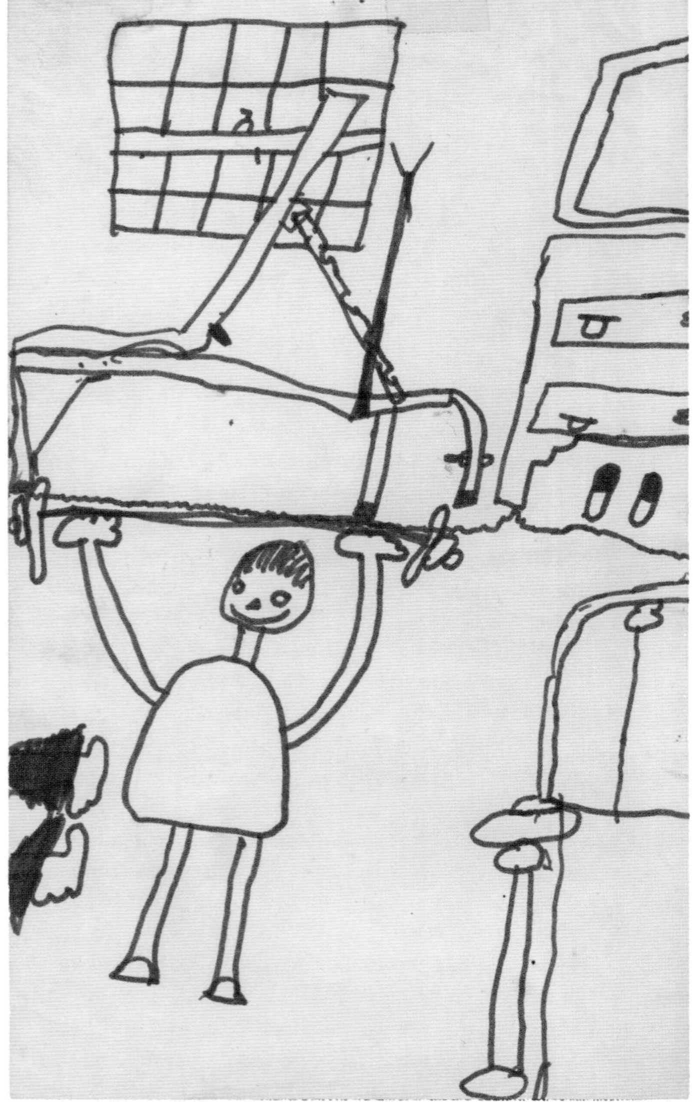

Cole at age 13 with his mom in October 1975, after a day of dirt bike riding in Pound Ridge

the P.R.T.C. Tennis Camp in the summer of 1977, a busy one for sports activity (his mother was an avid tennis player), and received the "Words Can't Describe Him" award printed on a small paper disk attached to a string for wearing around the neck. He went out for the Fox Lane High School football team, but that ended along with his continuing high school education. From his friend Peter Solomon and Peter's father, and another friend Russell Fisher, Cole learned to hunt, and became interested in firearms, the woods, lakes, and streams of the northeast.

About the time Cole turned thirteen, he was falling under the growing influence of his peers to the detriment of his parents' best efforts. Though struggling economically, we mistakenly believed that our loving, close, wholesome family life, coupled with a modicum of discipline, was the formula for raising children properly. After all, we had managed to raise concurrently two beautiful, well-behaved daughters.

I always wanted a boy, and had we not had Cole, our family would undoubtedly have numbered four, five, six, or more children until, eventually, a son was born. Somehow, long before I was to embrace this project of finding fathers, I needed to extend the bloodline. Cole wouldn't be the last of the *Cs* in the Davis line — Clyde Sr., Clyde Jr., Catherine his mother, Christine and Cynthia his sisters, and then finally Cole's first born son, Codie.

From the first moment Kay and I knew we were to be

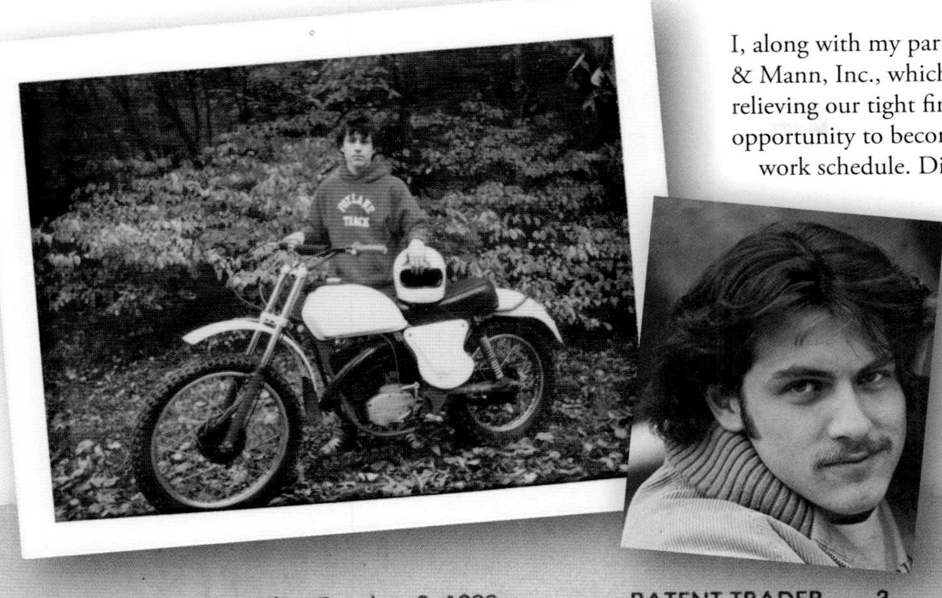

Thursday October 2, 1980 PATENT TRADER — 3

Motorcyclist, 16, seized after 80 MPH pursuit

By PATRICIA A. GORMLEY

MOUNT KISCO — An 16-year-old Pound Ridge boy was arrest in a joint effort of Town of Bedford and Mount Kisco police early Wednesday evening after the youth lead police on a chase reaching speeds of up to 80 miles an hour, police said.

The boy, name withheld due to possible youthful offender status, faces eight separate vehicle and traffic summons in village court due to the half hour chase. He was released in the custody of his mother.

The chase began when Mount Kisco police received residents' telephone calls complaining of a youth speeding on a dirt bike. It is illegal to ride a dirt bike on the street.

Mount Kisco Officer Robert Martini began the chase when he found the biker driving near the Diplomat Towers apartment complex. The pursuit moved to Kisco Avenue where officer Frank McCann picked up chase following the biker on Kisco Avenue onto the northbound lane of the Saw Mill Parkway.

Mount Kisco notified Bedford Town Police of the pursuit and then the biker turned off the parkway at the Harris Road exit. One Bedford patrol car joined the pursuit then.

The biker turned onto Beaver Dam Road only to find a Bedford patrol car waiting for him. The biker was apprehended when he attempted to swerve around the Bedford car but instead fell off the bike.

Some of the charges were two speeding summons, driving an unlicensed vehicle, driving an unregistered bike, driving without a license, failure to comply, and driving left of center.

Cole's first motorcycle, a used KTM dirt bike. He had taken it apart to repaint the frame red. I recall after he reassembled it, there was an assortment of nuts, bolts, clips, and other parts that came off the bike remaining in a shoe box. Yet the damn thing ran, and fast, as evidenced by the press clipping above.

blessed with a son, through the joy of his birth, into the early years of adolescence, we were, happily, one fine family.

Kay sought employment when Cole was twelve years old — when he changed from elementary to middle school.

In 1975 Kay went to work as a secretary, commencing a ten-year career at Omega Engineering, Inc., a newly formed manufacturing company of temperature measuring devices with seventy-five employees. She would leave Omega in 1985 as director of Human Resources, having assisted the company's growth to more than five hundred employees in several states. I, along with my partners, in 1984, had founded Cline, Davis & Mann, Inc., which within a year was doing quite nicely, relieving our tight financial circumstances and allowing Kay the opportunity to become a Realtor and to achieve a more flexible work schedule. Distracted by burgeoning careers and on a path of betterment for our beloved children, we knew little of what was ahead.

During this period, our son, so healthy, so beautiful, so well liked, loved, even adored, was to succumb to peer pressure and slip gradually into a cycle of drug abuse. We blindly trusted that we knew how to raise children, not realizing, as we were to painfully learn later, "there is no 'right' in bringing up children," and that kids who turn to drugs can come from "broken homes" as well as from "loving homes."[1]

First, it was diet pills, then beer, spirits, marijuana, and finally cocaine. Cole became a "poly-abuser," kids eighteen years old and under "using pot and alcohol and pills," and cascading into an "emotional addiction to getting high."

As Carolyn Sandberg, site supervisor of Renaissance's storefront self-help program, which Cole participated in, stated, "Not every drug is physically addicting, but every drug has the ability to be emotionally addicting."

We, too, were no match for the scourge of drugs so plentiful in our affluent community, which posted, in vain, roadside signs proclaiming, "Welcome, This is a neighborhood watch community." We responded with misplaced faith, unconditional love, denial, confrontation — teachers conferences, tutors, doctors, psychologists, recriminations, accusations, self-help programs, alternative schools, private school (more drugs than in public school), no school, and, finally, tough love.

Our marriage was in jeopardy. There was daily strife, conflict between husband and wife. We suffered as parents, as a family. Our daughters tried to cope with this affliction in our midst. Hopelessly, we invested in trust, communication, discipline, and love, love, love. All to no avail.

Cole, at a psychologist's urging, was allowed to drop out of school and to take a job installing hot tubs and wood burning stoves, complemented with a new Ford pick-up we purchased for him to secure the work. This truck only extended his reach of aberrant behavior. He incurred innumerable traffic violations and used the truck to pick up cocaine in the Bronx, which must have been cheaper than locally.

We failed miserably in keeping our son drug free. Despite our undying love and willingness to never quit on him, it became painfully clear that his behavior was in rapid decline. Good

Cole's first truck, at age 16, used in his job installing wood burning stoves and hot tubs.

APRIL 20, 1982

Tim,

So how are ya buddy? I hope your'e better than I am. Your'e probably really made at me because I haven't sent you the money I owe you yet. But so much has happened to me in the last couple of moanths its unbeleivable. #1. I moved into my own appartment with a friend named Tim #2 I got fired from my job which in turn, sent me to a life of crime. Steeling sterios (car-sterios) Selling drugs (coke-refer-downs) and the icing on the cake was I wrote about 7 get it Seven thousand dollars worth of bad checks. which of course caught up to me in the end. Which was about a month ago from the date on this letter.

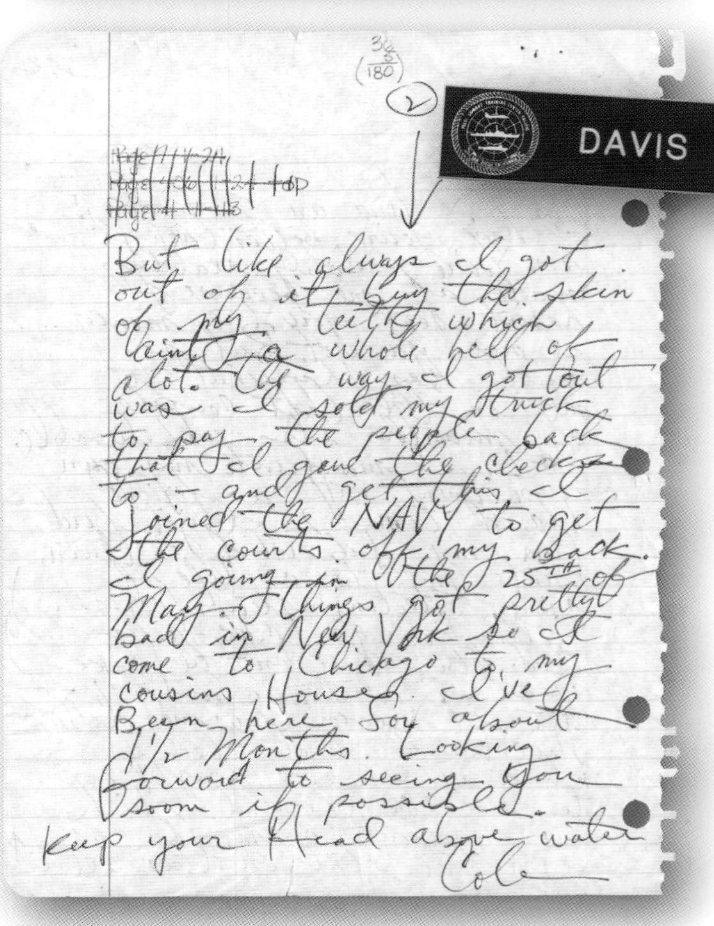

(2)

But like always I got out of it by the skin of my teeth which ain't a whole hell of alot. The way I got out was I sold my truck to pay the people back that I gave the checks to — and get this, I joined the NAVY to get the courts off my back. I going in the 25th of May. Things got pretty bad in New York so I come to Chicago to my cousins House. I've Been here for about 1/2 Months. Looking forword to seeing you soon if possible.

Keep your Head above water

Cole

parents have children that do bad. To this day I do not know where we went wrong. I do know, though, when we went right.

Enough!

In 1982 our marriage was at the breaking point, and our daughters were turning on their brother. We believed our son was planning to flee the state, so we were forced to take the final step that abruptly brought closure to this chapter of our lives. We had him arrested by the New York State Police for unlawful possession of a vehicle, since we had retained title to his truck. He was apprehended as we watched from a distance, then brought before a justice of the peace, arraigned and released in our custody (see black and white photograph on page 131). This young man, seventeen years of age was unknown to me. It was as if someone had taken my son and had substituted someone else in his place. That first night was a most tenuous one. We could not embrace Cole. He would not sleep in his room. He spent the night sleeping in front of the living room fireplace. We slept not at all, fearing he would slip out of the house.

We hired a local attorney to defend him. At his hearing in the Pound Ridge Town Court, Cole accepted a pre-arranged offer between us, his attorney, and the court to enlist in the Navy in lieu of being prosecuted. He joined the Navy, March 1983 at age eighteen.

After his enlistment, he was promptly rushed out of New York to avoid the repercussions of so abrupt a change in his exposure to the drug culture he had become an integral part of. A web of police, attorneys, dealers, other druggies that were owed money, traffic warrants, fines to be paid, and stolen merchandise to be returned — all rapidly closing in upon him. My sister June, a single mom, with four children of her own, graciously accepted Cole into her home in Lansing, Illinois, until he reported for active duty May 25, 1982, at the Naval Training Center, Great Lakes, Illinois. He was honorably discharged June 4, 1986.

The reader might feel this brought an end to his abusive behavior. Not until almost his final year in the Navy, on the verge of being dishonorably discharged, did he turn things around.

Cole served on the USS *Dubuque* (LPD-8), the second in a series of modified LPD-4 Class Amphibious Transport Docks, a combination of three older types of amphibious ships: the LSD (Landing Ship Dock), the APA (Attack Transport) and the AKA (Attack Cargo Ship). The features these ships passed along to the LPD are as follows: a flight deck capable of landing all helicopters in the Navy inventory and a well deck, from which all types of landing craft and amphibious vehicles may be launched from the LSD. Additionally, *Dubuque* is configured to provide berthing and support for a Marine Amphibious Unit of more than eight hundred Marines and their combat equipment, jeeps, trucks, tanks, and amphibious vehicles.

Just prior to and during his years of military service our letters reflected the hope, relief, and love of parents grateful for a son saved.

Cole with his grandfather, Richard Douthart, home on leave for his sister Christine's wedding July 24, 1982. In a letter dated April 18, 1983, Cole wrote to his grandfather: "It seems that the ship I'm on the USS DUBUQUE LPD-8, is also the same ship that my uncle Dave went to Vietnam in. Is that something or what."

From Kay, November 1, 1981:

Dear Cole,

It seems your eighteenth birthday has taken a very long time to arrive. I know you feel relieved because many of your activities are now legitimate.

As someone who loves you, I hope that you will pause for a moment to consider the responsibility of those feelings of freedom and legitimacy; and more seriously consider the consequences of those activities which can cause you personal harm.

In many ways you have already faced adulthood long before you "legally" arrived — and I compliment you for handling it quite well. In other ways, you are taking a long and rocky road to achieving maturity.

I will always be proud of you if you treat your life and your relationships with honesty and a sense of respect.

I send you my love as you become a man — And want you to know you will always be my special son.

Love, Mom

And again, from Kay, May 11, 1982:

Dear Cole,

I can't tell you how good it was to see you when Grandpa and I came to Chicago. You looked wonderful. I felt so good about you and the changes that are taking place.

* * *

Dad and I were very glad to have your letter — I will keep it as a reminder of your positive growth.

I think you know how very much we both love you and want for you to be happy. But, beyond that we strongly feel that a healthy mind and body are your best instruments to achieve happiness — I am so pleased with your progress. Take care my precious son — I love you more than you know.

And from me, April 20, 1982 (excerpted):

Dear Cole,

Mom and I have been very busy with work on the house. There's lots to do. She cleaned out your room Sunday for Grandpa. She was behaving very strangely all day and then I figured out why — she got high. So many marijuana seeds went through the vacuum that the air was heavier than at a Rolling Stones rock concert.

Love, Dad

And on Monday, August 16, 1982, I wrote:

Dear Cole,

... it felt good to be outdoors (building a garden retaining wall) and doing something physical. I think about you, Cole, when I'm out there, alone and working. Especially like thinking about the trip out west in the motor home. Every time an Elvis song comes on

Cole (left) with his friend Bob Workman at the Playboy Club in Manila, the Philippines.

Veggies from Tammi's garden proudly being displayed at Cole's and Tammi's home on Lemon Avenue one afternoon after work as an E3-Non-designated seaman in La Mesa, California. She was pregnant with their first child, Codie, who was born at the Naval Hospital, Balboa Park, California."

* * *

the radio I'm reminded of the trip and how much fun we all had.

Think a lot about our bike trips, too (NY to Boston and NYC to Washington, DC).

You know Cole, you and I have a great deal in common and we are very much alike in our tastes (that, too), life style and general outlook.

The past two years or so we seem to be going in opposite directions. You're going to find as you grow older that we will once again grow closer.

Love, Dad

Our persevering support as loving parents certainly contributed to Cole's salvation. And, of course, the Navy instilled in him a sense of responsibility, built on the consequences for wrongful behavior and reward for accomplishment, each when warranted.

After graduating from boot camp (see photo on page 133), Cole was sent to the Fleet Combat Training Center, Operations Systems School in Virginia Beach, Virginia. He became an Operations Specialist with the ranking of OS3, working behind the bridge of the ship in the Operations Center, essentially the brains of the ship, monitoring all air and sea traffic, weapons guidance, charting, radar work, ships' location, and communications: ship to ship, ship to air, etc.

He spent two years on the USS *Dubuque LPD8*, including a six-month deployment, visiting Hawaii, Okinawa, Australia, Fiji, Hong Kong, the Philippines, South Korea, Sasbo, and Tokyo, Japan. Another three months deployment included San Francisco, Seal Beach, Portland, Seattle, and then war games in the Pacific Ocean.

Cole saw a good part of the world as the Navy promises. Surely, he loved the adventure, the sea, the military shore leave, and his fellow enlistees. Thankfully he never saw combat.

His mother pressed him to continue his education, asking him to promise to get his GED before leaving the service. He managed to meet his commitment to her, none too soon, having accomplished the task May 1, 1986, while still aboard ship.

Prior to Cole's ship leaving for its permanent station in Sasbo, Japan, Cole began having considerable pain in his left wrist. The ship left without Cole, who remained on base in San Diego.

Before enlistment Cole suffered chronic wrist pain. While in the military this was diagnosed as a result of "Kienbock's Disease," caused by poor blood supply to the lunate bone in the wrist. We had consulted a specialist in bone disorders at Columbia Presbyterian Medical Center in New York City who recommended corrective surgery. However, the Navy was unwilling to allow Cole to take leave for such an operation or cover any cost to have surgery preformed outside the Navy. The only option Cole could have exercised was to travel home on a "medical discharge." Cost was not an issue, but Cole was loath to accept this alternative. He was intent on completing his full term in the Navy and departing with an Honorable Discharge.

In looking back, I often reflect on this decision as one of the first tangible signs of maturity and commitment. He opted to have the procedure performed in October 1985 by Dr. G.R. Mack at the Balboa Naval Hospital in San Diego, who coincidently was a prominent world authority on the disease.

The surgery was performed successfully, but complications of infection to the pelvis occurred when bone marrow was transplanted to the wrist. Cole recovered after a protracted stay in the hospital.

Cole had taken a few hits physically over the years prior to 1985. Added to the above he had broken a leg at age two, had a motorcycle collision at age sixteen, leaving him with a badly scarred shoulder (thankfully he was wearing a helmet), and he was clobbered with a baseball bat while in the Navy and beaten to within an inch of his life by an angered Marine whose girlfriend Cole had befriended. The last incident left him with a droopy left eye (see photo on page 133).

Stationed in San Diego, California, his last several months of service, Cole met a number of beautiful young women, each of whom I found to be more lovely than the previous. One of these young women, Tine Delong, was with Cole and Chris Wickam in 1985, driving between Ensenada and Tijuana, Mexico, in a Honda Civic in the days before seat belts and airbags. They had not been drinking. They had a head-on collision with an old pickup truck, which had pulled into their lane to pass another vehicle. The three men in the pickup truck left the truck and ran from the scene. Chris bit part of his tongue off, knocked out a number of teeth on the steering wheel, and ripped both kneecaps off against the dashboard. Cole hit the windshield and dashboard, and broke his left collar bone, the top three ribs on his left side, ripped ligaments in his left shoulder (which remains numb to this day), tore his left nostril, had cuts under his chin and on his throat, suffered lacerations over both eyes, and suffered a punctured lung. Both Chris and Cole were unconscious for a couple of days.

Cole and Chris Wickam were airlifted by military life flight helicopter to the Naval hospital at Balboa, and Tine Delong, who had received cuts and bruises, had to return on her own.

Cole was one banged-up "puppy."

Sense of Family and the Influences of a Generation Before

Cole is a mama's boy. This is not to imply some effete characteristic to him. Like all those athletic young men we see

You can remove the girl from the farm, but you can't remove the farm from the girl! In this case, Tammi Davis. Some twenty years later she's still hauling in the bounty of her gardens in Encinitas, California. All that 4-H training as a youth, devoted to head, heart, hands, and health seems to have contributed greatly to the general happiness and well-being of her family.

on TV, football players especially, given a moment on camera, having just done well on the field of their dreams, they shout out "Hi, Mom…." It's never "Dad." Cole and his mother have always enjoyed a close and loving relationship. His mother never gave up on him, rather, she always gave him the benefit of the doubt. Unconditional love. However, with each passing year he became more my son, adapting more and more to the masculine traits of his father. Cole is quick to note that, yes, he is a lot like me, but different because he has a lot of his mother in him. Implying, rightfully so, that this made him a better person. Each generation is shaped by the one before it.

Ensign Tammi

The other woman in Cole's life appeared during his final months of duty in San Diego. They were to meet in 1985 in Operation Systems Training School, fall in love, and marry February 7, 1987.

They were both invited to a mutual friend's birthday party, and when Tammi mentioned she didn't have a ride home, Cole offered, having driven to the party in his then girlfriend Tine's car. During the ride, as Cole so deftly put it, "Tammi mauled me." According to her, "The mauling was mutual." In the days that followed, they kicked their boyfriend or girlfriend out with whom they'd been living, and Cole moved into Tammi's apartment.

Then Cole and Tammi moved into an apartment with Navy friends Roger and Scott. Tim Fritsch would become Cole's best man at Cole and Tammi's wedding. Ultimately the group grew to three women and three men, and they rented a house in La Mesa.

Somehow this young man, our son, had made the most right decision of his life. He chose a woman who has become as important to the direction of his life as a rudder is to a sailboat in turbulent seas.

Tammi is a beautiful, green-eyed, blonde, California girl right out of a Beach Boy's song. A 4H-er (Head, Heart, Hands, Health) girl from Santa Cruz, who loves her garden and flowers and animals, is equally comfortable in her leathers on the back of Cole's Honda V65 Magna motorcycle. She gave him, in quick succession, three sons: Codie, Taylor, and Beau. Tammi remained in the Navy an additional nine months after Cole's discharge, because she was pregnant with their first child and the Navy was the sole means of their financial support.

Years of Strife and Growth

After discharge from the Navy, Cole and Tammi settled into married life, a succession of jobs, living in San Diego, La Mesa, a home in Lakeside, and finally another in Encinitas, California, where they reside today.

These years from 1986 to 1996 were not without turmoil. On May 27, 1988, we purchased a new home for Tammi and Cole. An agreement was drawn up that allowed them an equity stake in this house high on a mountain overlooking the valley below. This enterprise, so hopefully conceived, but never viably realized financially, like so many other family loans over the years, did provide shelter, a hearth, pool — a home within which the young Davises could coalesce as a family, find refuge, lick their wounds, and grow as a cohesive unit. Cole was twenty-five years old when he moved into his first home. At the same age, I bought my first car — a 1956 Pontiac. We had engaged Dave Paré, an attorney in San Diego, to prepare the documents; Mr. Paré was something of a sage, attempting to counsel us on the wisdom (or

Cole and Tammi at Encinatas, California, September 2003

the lack of it), at one time commenting, "There's nothing like starting at the top and going up from there."

Cole had not totally given up all his previous habits or indulgences that contributed to destructive behavior. There was the altercation with a woman in a sports car driving home from a bachelor party for a fellow worker. He was jailed for using his vehicle, after smoking a little weed, as a dangerous weapon and trying to prevent her passing him on a narrow road. We bailed him out of jail once again, hiring a defense attorney, the best in San Diego, and avoiding a coviction. There were a couple of faulty business startups. Partnerships went sour and one,

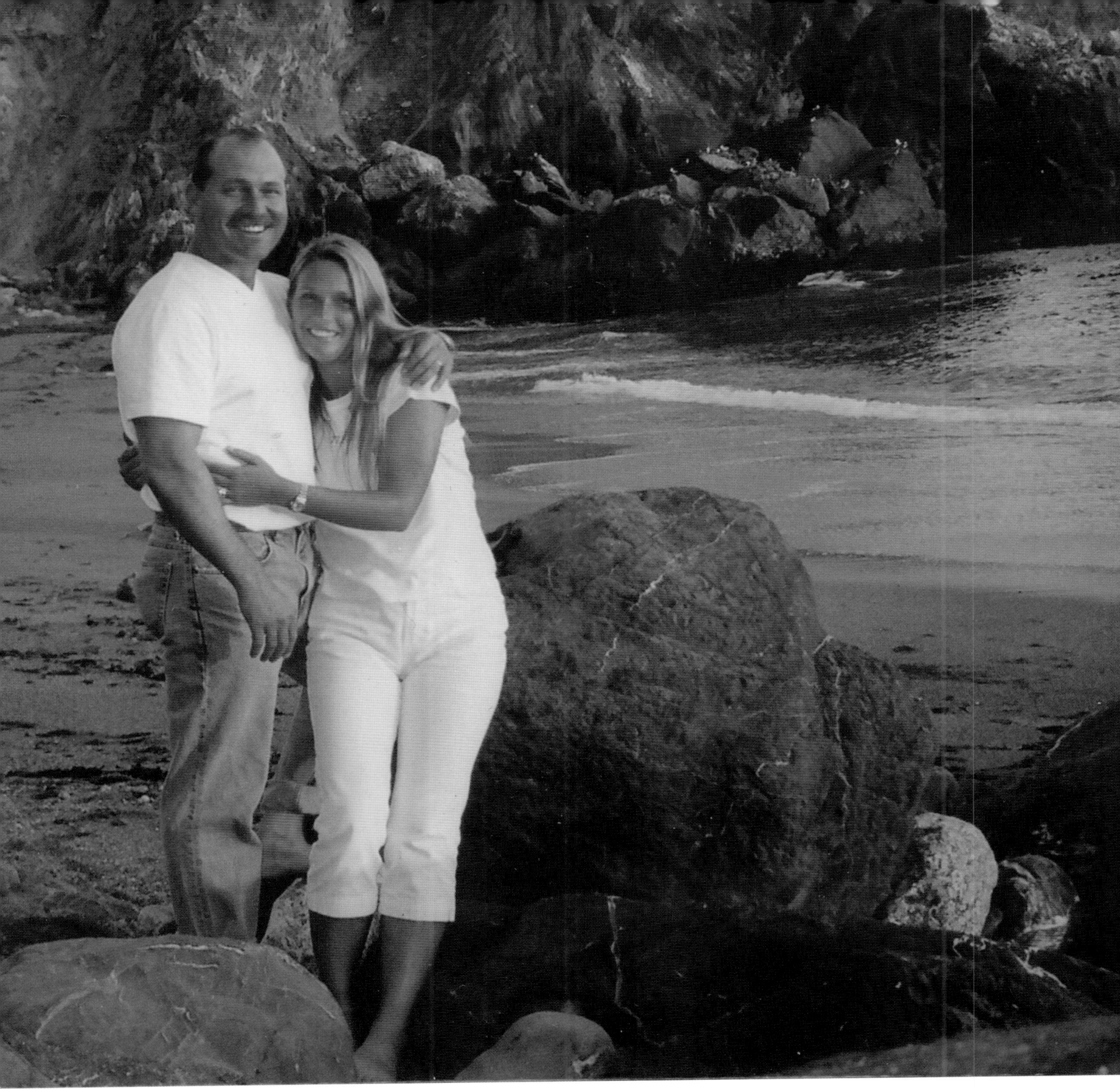

Davis Enterprises, Inc., turned downright, devastatingly bitter, ending only after considerable cost to him and us to dissolve the partnership, reimburse its clients, and settle the considerable IRS debt that Cole had incurred.

At this point I would be remiss if I didn't mention the financial cost that we incurred supporting the evolution of our son's life.

Wealth has its rewards. As my mom was fond of saying, "Money isn't everything, Clyde, but it sure drives a lot of misery away." This, for my son, could not be more true.

This early inclination to self-destruct was ameliorated repeatedly by our wealth. Many parents sacrifice much for the benefit of their children. Too often these sacrifices go unrewarded, affecting not the negative outcomes from circumstances not of their choosing, but rather choices of their children. We, however, spent freely, gave unhesitatingly of our time, and with some luck were able to change the course of events gone badly. Every ounce of energy, every effort undertaken, every tear shed, all the disappointment felt, the heartache shared was worth the son we have with us today. During each crisis, the financial cost appeared squandered, seemingly for naught. Yet with hope, love, often mindless faith, we were to endure to see our boy become the man he is today.

My Son — Husband, Father, and Builder

There is, I found in the Davises, a strain of recklessness, a spirit of adventure, always willing to test the limits of social mores. My sister, brother, mother, and father, including myself, as outlined in previous passages of this book, embody those traits. My son as well. But, happily the Davis work ethic kicks in and spares us all. That is if we survive the early years.

The addictive personality that runs like a meandering stream through the lives of so many Davises of past generations could have been a warning, if we had knowledge of the trait earlier. Perhaps we will now better prepare ourselves to ward off a repeat in future generations.

Exactly when and how Cole managed to quit drugs is not known to me. I suspect it was a gradual process over the years, influencing factors of family, marriage, coupled with the looming responsibilities of fatherhood. He was older, had been a few places, seen the other side, was growing to realize the value to life, the good life.

We've never broached the subject, my son and I; we don't speak of substance abuse, of why, or when, or even if it will ever, once again, rear its ugly head amidst our beloved family. I've mulled over the possibility of asking Cole just what was it that turned him around. Why did he go sober on drugs, but believing that might stir within him dark thoughts or cause psychic pain, I've cautiously avoided the subject. As a physician of mine once said, "Life is like a garden, and throughout this garden there are a few rocks, turning them over may result in finding things you don't want to see." Good advice?

Tammi was certainly an influence. A smoker, pregnant with their first child, she quit. She started smoking again three months after Codie's birth, but then quit for good when she became pregnant with her second child, Taylor. Cole promised to quit with her at each pregnancy, but did not.

I mention the smoking and Cole's struggle to stop as a way of determining how one finds the resolve to end habitual destructive behavior. Perhaps it was finally a request by his mother that he stop smoking by an upcoming birthday of his. Which one I have no idea. How long ago is uncertain. But the motivation to quit was engendered undoubtedly by his mom. After all, hadn't he earned his GED at her request, meeting his commitment to her just before he exited the Navy?

Cole and Tammi's home, Wildflower Estates, Encinitas, California

His mother always believed Cole had "tremendous will power." On mentioning this to Tammi in April of 2007, she was quick to respond, "He has horrible will power." So much for that theory. Accordingly, quitting became a long, drawn out affair for Cole, over a period of four to five years. First he tried nicotine gum, then tablets, and ultimately the patch through a series of steps, each purportedly with diminishing levels of nicotine. And after following the proscribed eight- to ten-week quit smoking system, Cole was free from nicotine and cigarettes.

Gum, tablets, patch, and even half a patch, were merely nicotine delivery systems for Cole to exploit during his course of treatment, which spanned nearly five years. Eventually he was able to tell his mom he had quit smoking. At the time I wrote this in 2007, Cole had been free of nicotine and cigarettes for nearly four years. His mom never waivered, will power took a back seat to her resolve on behalf of her son.

On the Move

Over a long Memorial Day weekend, Kay and I, with Cole and Tammi, were to take possession on May 27, 1988, of their new home in Lakeside, California. The following day was spent packing and moving from La Mesa to Lakeside with our rented twenty-four-foot U-Haul truck. I wrote in my diary that day, "It was so satisfying to be working with my son. If only I could be around him more." The next several days were spent making trips to Home Depot (for a new outdoor grill), the grocery store, and of course, the local bank ATM.

First house, Delmar, California

A Team

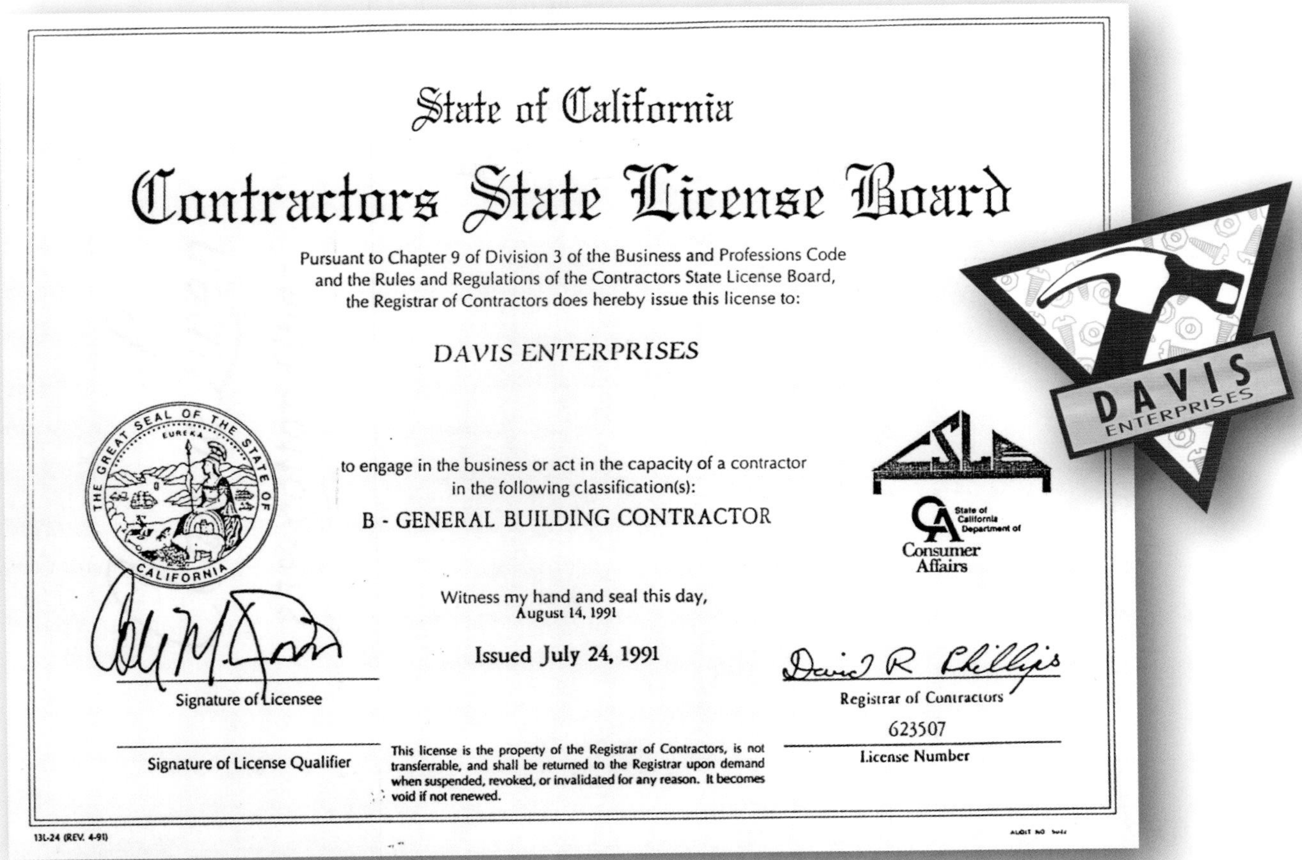

State of California

Contractors State License Board

Pursuant to Chapter 9 of Division 3 of the Business and Professions Code and the Rules and Regulations of the Contractors State License Board, the Registrar of Contractors does hereby issue this license to:

DAVIS ENTERPRISES

to engage in the business or act in the capacity of a contractor in the following classification(s):

B - GENERAL BUILDING CONTRACTOR

Witness my hand and seal this day, August 14, 1991

Issued July 24, 1991

Signature of Licensee

Signature of License Qualifier

This license is the property of the Registrar of Contractors, is not transferrable, and shall be returned to the Registrar upon demand when suspended, revoked, or invalidated for any reason. It becomes void if not renewed.

Registrar of Contractors

623507

License Number

13L-24 (REV. 4-91)

On Tuesday we sat down with the kids after dinner and reviewed 'til 11 P.M. the Equity Agreement and Straight Note regarding the house purchase along with our collective responsibilities going forward. Again, from the pages of my diary, May 31, 1988, "Cole told me how grateful he was for all our help, that it, the support, allowed him to be all he wanted to be. Really appreciative. My son is so much of what his father always wished for — he's a man, hardworking, sensitive and loving. I love him so, if only I could express it more easily and freely."

After ten years of residence in Lakeside, Cole and his family, now numbering five, were ready for another move, and we were there to help make it possible. He had changed jobs, started a business, closed down a business, and was looking forward to new beginnings.

Tammi and Cole, with the help of a local Realtor and another highly qualified real estate expert at finding homes for deserving children — his mother — began the search. Their home in Lakeside sold before they had a chance to find another, which led to a house rental in Encinitas, which they had been drawn to as a most desirable community, one they would like to live in if only the perfect home could be found. High on the list of requirements would be a place that was "critter friendly," accommodating the growing Davis menagerie of dogs, cats, birds, chickens, and rabbits. Oh, and it would be nice if horses were allowed. We found such a place in February 1999. House tours, negotiations, along with much family angst between Kay and me, eventually led to our making offers on several newly constructed homes in an upscale development in Encinitas named Wildflower.

Isn't it great!

Gotta show Mom

Another foundation

One's living environment or locale does make a difference. The mantra "location, location, location" so often heard regarding real estate may also be applied to quality of life, the proximity of living benefits. For Cole and Tammi, neither having attended college, the move was an instant immersion into a lifestyle of better schools for their children, employment opportunities for Cole, and social contacts. A beautiful 7,000 square foot house with all the amenities including pool and expansive gardens was the perfect setting from which to launch this new phase of their lives together. And so they did, at first tentatively with forays into the school system. For Cole, a stint at serving on the Association Board of their gated community's architectural review board. For

COLE DAVIS CONSTRUCTION
3369 JASMINE CREST
ENCINITAS, CA 92024
CDC
RESIDENTIAL • COMMERCIAL

Tammi, a new ladies' jogging group. All contributing to stepping out and up on a scale not previously experienced by them.

In 1990 Cole, once again at the urging of his mom, studied for and passed the State of California Contractors License Board exam and received his general building contractor's license July 24, 1991.

Cole continued working in the insurance restoration field, though with a different company, serving the north coastal San Diego area. After a year or two he was to meet an architect on one of his projects, and they would eventually create a long-time working relationship.

His career in construction began with installing hot tubs, wood burning stoves, and decks as a teenager in Pound Ridge, New York. Then, after a completed tour in the Navy, he began working as a framer on large scale, new home developments in the hills overlooking Laguna Beach. From there he honed his skills in the insurance restoration field, rebuilding kitchens and baths, garages and an occasional roof until finally reconstruction of a full house in Rancho Santa Fe upon the fire charred ruins of the previous owner's home. Cole, as an independent contractor, went from restoring fire and flood damaged homes and businesses to his first house addition in Rancho Bernardo in 1999. He was to next build a modest "spec" house in Del Mar. It wasn't too long after that project was completed that Cole's relationship with the architect really kicked into high gear. Coupled with an architect who was in considerable demand, Cole received offers to bid on one project after another, winning bids, constructing quality homes, while prospective clients were doing "drive-bys" of his growing number of job sites.

CDC Construction was formed July 20, 1999, and was incorporated on January 27, 2003, in the State of California. At the time I wrote this in April of 2007, CDC had built over twenty residences with another five under construction in various stages of completion. Cole has built homes in many of the most affluent and prestigious communities in the north coastal San Diego area. Nearly all of these homes are within gated communities in Rancho Santa Fe (Cielo Estates, Santa Luz and the Covenant), Del Mar (The Meadows/The Grand), La Costa (Rancho Bernardo), and Encinitas (Olivenhein). These homes vary in size from 6,000 square feet to 14,000 square feet and are valued between $1.5 and $5 million.

As Cole's business grew, so did his three sons. In 2007, Codie, the eldest was finishing his first year at Cal Berkeley. Taylor, the middle child was driving, and Beau was soon to be in high school. Tammi, the perfect mom, not unlike June Cleaver, of whom it has been said, "She's the quintessential TV mom — really, really swell. Being there for her family and keeping her home neat and orderly…." ("Leave it to Beaver," <http://www.tvland.com>). With a bit more free time June, I mean Tammi, migrated into the home office of CDC, Inc. Assisting Cole, she became a trustworthy, able partner. She adroitly manages the flow of documents, estimates, and quotes; all of this amid ringing phones, chugging copiers, humming scanners, whirring printers, and a voracious fax, which serve as the critical back office support to the man in the field, her husband.

In the past, especially in the early years of Cole's business being formed, I was frequently called upon for advice and the occasional financial loan. Surprisingly, but not minded by me, Cole has gradually ceased to share his day-to-day business issues

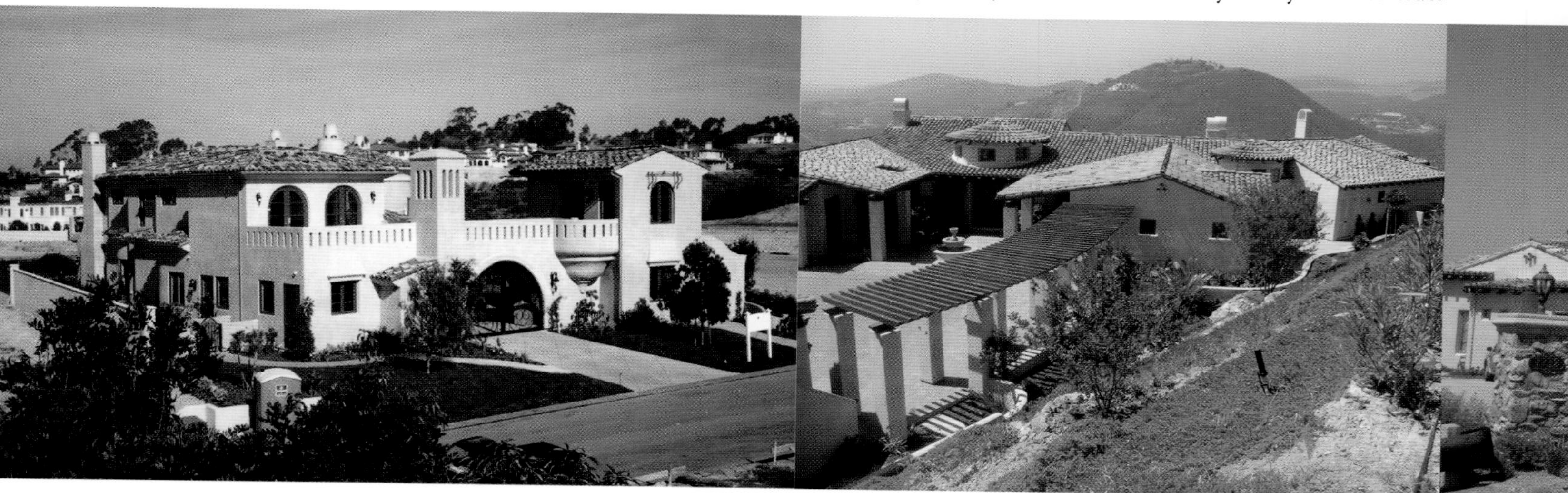

White is mighty nice…

Hacienda Heaven

Kay, Tammi, and Cole with Turk their Great Dane (and me behind the camera), Encinitas, California, January 1, 2000, on one of our twice daily dog walks, morning and evening.

with me. Though I thought a time would come when we might actually form a business together, perhaps building "spec homes" with me as the investor. I now realize that if Cole is to partner with anyone, it will undoubtedly be with one or all of his sons. After all, now in 2010, Codie is in his final year as an engineering student at Cal Berkeley. Davis & Sons has a nice ring to it.

It is interesting to note the synergies resulting from the confluence of environment, luck, and simple hard work. A charming, good looking, mannerly, non-confrontational young man — my son — armed with a cell phone, pickup truck, and the back-office support of a life partner, hasn't done too badly among the elite of San Diego County.

Family is Everything

Throughout the years of Cole's growth in California, his mother and I have made every effort to keep him, his wife, and children connected to the family on the East Coast despite distance and the busy lives we all live. Often we've come together with family trips abroad, Puglia, Italy, and Vietnam biking, Paris in the spring, Disney World over the Millenium, Maui over Christmas and New Year holidays, Macy's New York City Thanksgiving Day Parade, numerous cruises on the "Auntie-Kay" to the Bahamas, Nassau, and Eleuthera, from our homes in Florida, in addition to our regular trips west, with other family members in tow, to simply hang with Cole and his family. Added to these trips are Cole's 40th birthday surprise in Las Vegas, Kay's 68th, at the Mohegan Sun in Connecticut (there's a theme here), along with the graduations of our grandsons.

Recently, September 19, 2009, our children, their spouses, and the grandchildren planned and paid for a most wondrous 50th Wedding Anniversary celebration for Kay and me at Cole and Tammi's home in Encinitas, California (see photo on page 138).

Dire Economic Times

Unfortunately, Cole, like my two daughters and millions of other Americans have been swept up in the economic downturn of 2008 and beyond. Home values and the building boom in Southern California have plummeted. My son, who previously might have had five or six homes a year in the planning stages and/or under construction, has now seen his business evaporate to the point of being left with the completion of a single home and an addition to another. No one knows when the housing market and new construction will return to the North County of San Diego. Cole has prospects and remains hopeful, but eventually, he may have to address a lifestyle change, like so many others in his industry. He has been reluctant to discuss his finances and certainly doesn't want to be a burden for his parents.The solution, near term, may be more transparency and conversation with his parents about assets, debts, and risk going forward. After many years of success, I'm sure, he never anticipated this downturn. It's got to be demoralizing, a blow to one's ego and sense of self-esteem; however, I am so proud of the way he's handled himself during this period of unanticipated adversity.

Many married couples, faced with household income and assets that are not what they used to be, and are not living in the style they've grown accustomed to, could easily find their marriage in jeopardy. This prospect is not a serious concern of mine, for if anyone can survive this economic downturn and be the stronger for it, it will be Cole and Tammi. Their relationship is not based on lifestyle alone.

Notes

1. Carolyn Sandberg interview by Patricia Ploss, "The Drug Scene: Renaissance, a life-saving project," *Patent Trader*, August 28, 1980, Mt. Kisco, New York.

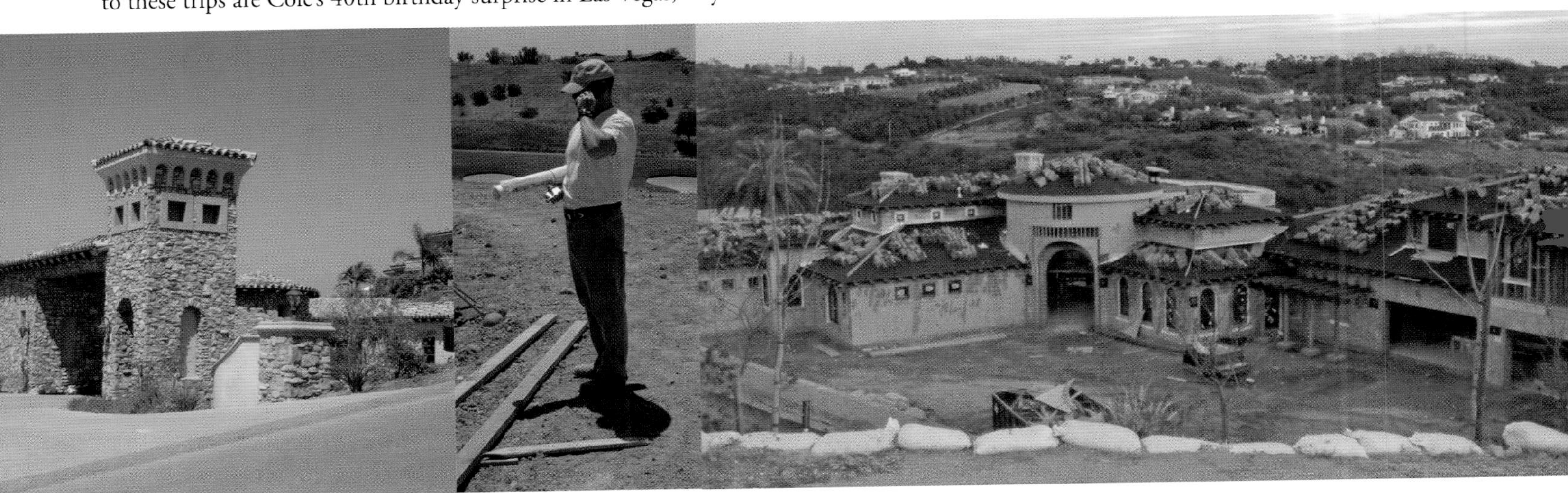

A man's castle…

On site

Improving the neighborhood — his!

In 1996 we acquired a dark cherry red, Chevrolet Suburban 250 for about $35,000. We then had it tricked-out with a sound system, which parking attendants still marvel at, a video monitor, upgraded the leather seats, and added walnut trim throughout. On the outside, we darkened the brightwork, removed excess chrome trim and manufacturer's labeling, replaced the running boards, substituted factory wheels with custom aluminum alloy wheels from California, mounted a four-capacity bike rack on the rear, and we were ready for the road at twice the cost of our original purchase.

It wasn't until the fall of 1997 that we were able to disembark on our second, but actually first fully mounted, planned trip with a pre-determined set of destinations, time frame, and goals to be accomplished.

There was a special feeling about hitting the road in a new vehicle loaded with luggage, clothes on hangers, two or three plastic crates filled with maps, motel guides, notebooks, CDs, videos, two bicycles (for off the road and neighborhood sightseeing), and plenty of snacks. We took much pleasure in believing that we were blending into this cadre of highway hipsters armed with their Allstate Trip Planners (we had ours), concerned simply with what the road offered in the way of sights, where the next rest stop might be, and having a reservation for the night. We had managed to shed most of the trappings of a New York advertising executive and affluent suburban couple. No one need know the size of our bank account. Driving in our "comfys," we were looking forward to two weeks of casual dress.

We were just folks, stopping overnight at a Hampton Inn (our preference, breakfast included), Fairfield Inn, or Marriott, handling our own luggage, eating at the Applebee's, Cracker Barrel Old Country Store, Pizza Hut, or Outback Steakhouse. Dairy Queens were a frequent stopping off spot for frozen pineapple blizzards.

As our trip progressed, we found some diversity from the familiar and learned of local eateries nearby an archival center, courthouse, or historical society we were visiting. Within the Virginia State Library, at the "A la Cart Cafe" (804-692-3808) one could order a Veggie Burger or try their Turkey and Havarti Cheese on Sourdough Sandwich with Basil Parmagiana Sauce (instead of mayonnaise), or simply try one of their wonderful hearty soups such as Tomato Parmagiana or Asian Chicken. In Frankfort, Kentucky, just up the railroad tracks from the Kentucky History Center, was a small, but popular place for lunch called Gibby's at 212 W. Broadway. Owner Michael Gibson's Italian specialties have claimed awards from the Frankfort Chamber of Commerce. In 2001, Gibby's had Frankfort's Best Reuben Sandwich and was chosen best restaurant in 2002. Soon to be expanded, Gibby's is moving just down the street to new quarters.

In Annapolis, Maryland, you'd walk out of the Maryland State Archives, through a couple of parking lots, across Taylor Avenue, to Graul's shopping center, and there buried in a line of store fronts find Bagels and... to Go, at 609A Taylor Avenue (410-263-1344). Kay would order the Reuben on a bagel, sometimes switching to Nova and Lox with cream cheese, on a bagel of course, along with a cup of Matzo Ball Soup. Then we would retreat to the Archives parking lot as previously advised and eat in our SUV as did many of the other visiting genealogists who ate in their vehicles.

In Jefferson City, it was Madison's Café, at 216 Madison (573-634-2988). It was one of the few excellent family owned restaurants we happened upon and a relief from the menu of America's family of fast food restaurants.

Not to overburden the reader with our gastronomic grubbing, but you should know that despite our desire to be just plain folks, we would find ourselves at luxury resorts and hotels like Keswick Hall, 701 Country Club Drive, Keswick, Virginia, and The Drake Hotel in Chicago, Illinois. These establishments offered some of the finest dining in the country.

Generally, after our immediate needs like gas, shelter, and food had been addressed, we found ourselves mostly visiting with people, visiting county courthouses, state archival centers, cemeteries, and libraries, as well as a variety of historical societies.

We've learned that genealogical research is an indulgence of those with time on their hands. We do not expect to see a youngster seated across from us at our table in the Pettis County Missouri Courthouse, avidly pouring through marriage records for the year 1921. No, this is a pastime for the retired, the elderly, and predominantly women. Occasionally you'll find a husband and wife tag-team, such as ourselves.

Since Alex Haley's book, *Roots,* was published in 1976, and the extremely popular television mini-series based on the book, America's interest in family history "has become one of the most popular hobbies in the nation. Sixty percent of Americans say they are interested in genealogy, a number that's increased by 33 percent in the five years since the last study was conducted," cites Nancy Shute in the *Smithsonian.*[1] She goes on to say that the "proliferation of Internet genealogy sites, and the realization by baby boomers that the World War II generation of their parents is fast disappearing" is motivating baby boomers in their 40s and 50s to pursue genealogy. "They have the time and the money and they want to prove their family history."[2]

Among those novices researching their family histories, you meet professional genealogists working for clients all over the country, but always prospecting for new contacts and future business. I, for one, have succumbed to their expertise, engaging several of them in various states.

The Search Continues

As we drove from Keswick Hall, we were increasingly excited about a planned stopover to visit the Goochland Historical Society, 2875 River Road West, Goochland, Virginia (804-556-3966). This was, of course, a no-brainer, since how many of one's ancestors have towns named after them? I had corresponded previously with Cathleen Cabell regarding any record of my Gooch ancestors in Goochland County. She had responded that, though the very first governor was a Gooch, he left no issue.

In fact, William Gooch's title was Royal Lieutenant Governor from 1727–1749, but since the actual governors remained in England, he was effectively in charge. Goochland County was formed from the original shire of Henrico in May 1728 and named after Lieutenant Governor Gooch. It was a brother of Lieutenenat Governor Gooch who had issue; however, none seem connected to my family. Nevertheless, we were ever hopeful that a site visit to the Goochland Historical Society would produce some bit of useful information. This was not to be; however, we did enjoy our visit. Perhaps this was my first realization that tucked away in contemporary towns and communities are these centers of historical societies that are staffed by volunteers and supported mostly by donations. In my own community, I have over the years received inducements to participate in the historical underpinnings of Pound Ridge and Bedford, New York. Now after years of utilizing these like repositories of information far from Pound Ridge, I have realized their significance and look forward to getting more involved with, and becoming a supporter of our local historical society.

On September 16, 1997, we passed through Roanoke, Virginia, on our way to Kentucky. We had been advised that there was a fine library in Roanoke with a knowledgeable staff in family history. It was here at the Roanoke City Library under the direction of librarians Carol Tukwilles and Brenda (Ann) Finely that we laid eyes on an 1880 census index card (see below) that clearly indicated the existence of my father's mother, Rebecca Gooch. This was undeniable proof that in 1880, she lived in Madison County, Kentucky. I believe this was also the moment that I was lured into this world of genealogical adventure. We departed Roanoke the next day, believing that we were now in possession of the key that would unlock the heretofore mysteries of my family's history. Little did I know then, that a six-year

G200

KENTUCKY

Gooch, Thomas (HEAD OF FAMILY) VOL. 20 E. D. 75 SHEET 21 LINE 34

W (COLOR) M (SEX) 44 (AGE) Ky (BIRTHPLACE)

Madison (COUNTY) Dist #5 Yates (M. C. D.)

(CITY) (STREET) (HOUSE NO.)

OTHER MEMBERS OF FAMILY

NAME	RELATION-SHIP	AGE	BIRTHPLACE
Gooch, Muldred	W	42	Ky
" Edney	D	18	Ky
" Robert	S	15	Ky
" Rebecca	D	13	Ky
" William	S	11	Ky

1880 CENSUS–INDEX #1 see #2
DEPARTMENT OF COMMERCE
BUREAU OF THE CENSUS

HALLCO PRINTING CO., NEW YORK A-1a

odyssey lay before me with more revelations to come, as well as so many unanswered questions.

Being in the vicinity of Thomas Jefferson's Monticello, we thought a side tour was in order and quite appropriate considering our mission.

Eventually we arrived at the Marriott's Griffin Gate Resort in Lexington, Kentucky, around 10:30 P.M. on September 17, 1997. We would remain at the Marriott for several days, using it as a centralized base from which we would explore the many surrounding cities and towns, like Berea and Richmond, counties, and the state capital, Frankfort.

Street scene in downtown Richmond, Kentucky, September 20, 1997, the day of our first courthouse visit

Our First Courthouse Visit

From my notes it seems that September 20th was something of a busy day for us. We'd driven down from Lexington to Richmond, Kentucky, arriving on US 25 South, which quickly turned into the main street of downtown. All over America, similar towns were filling with the cacophony of noisy rush hour traffic. We mistakenly parked across from city hall, thinking at first, this must be the courthouse. But, having realized our error, we advanced up the street on foot, on a bright, last day of summer, sunny morning infused with the eagerness that only a neophyte genealogist could feel.

Richmond, the seat of Madison County, was settled in 1785 by John Miller — the first court was held in his barn — and the town was established in 1795 as the new county seat,

STATE Kentucky

Gooch, Thomas (HEAD OF FAMILY) VOL. E. D. SHEET LINE

CONTINUATION

(COLOR) (AGE) (BIRTHPLACE) (CITIZENSHIP)

(COUNTY)

(CITY) (STREET) (HOUSE NO.)

OTHER MEMBERS OF FAMILY

NAME	RELATION-SHIP	AGE	BIRTHPLACE	CITIZEN-SHIP
Gooch, Alexander	S	9	Ky	
Eliza	D	6	Ky	
Thomas	S	2	Ky	

CENSUS–INDEX #2 see #
DEPARTMENT OF COMMERCE
BUREAU OF THE CENSUS
1880

U. S. GOVERNMENT PRINTING OFFICE A-1a 11—11871

replacing Milford, four and a half miles away. It was named for the town in Virginia. The population in 1990 was 21,155.[3] In 2000, the Madison County population was 70,872.

As we proceeded to the courthouse, I video-taped buildings of note, aligned and abutting one another in the bright sunshine: each assigned a name and date of construction. "How helpful was this?" I thought as I recorded the inscriptions on the Collins Building, constructed in 1891, the Stouffer building, 1900, and the D.M. Bright building of 1884, remarking to my wife along the way that "these were some of the same buildings that my ancestors must have lived among." I felt closer to them.

With over one hundred buildings on the National Register of Historic Places, downtown Richmond is considered one of the state's finest restored nineteenth-century commercial districts.

Always the consummate window shopper, Kay was the first to notice the Old Tyme Toys antique shop. There on display in its window were two shiny, newly restored toy pedal cars on shelves, one atop the other along with an array of other smaller items. These bright red- and cream-colored cars with their white balloon tires and shiny chrome hubcaps, were dazzling enough, but to find them here in Richmond, rather than in a shop in New York was equally surprising. Needless to say, we had to enter this world of old time toys. The storefront consisted of a display window and a door which, together, were no more than twelve-feet wide as I recall. Once within the shop, you realized that it was really an aisle, front to back, with walls of shelving to each side, filled with an array of thousands of antique collectible toys displayed and organized quite artfully floor to ceiling.

We immediately engaged its owner in conversation. This was not our usual way upon entering stores. Usually we tried our best to avoid contact and the prospect of being sold something we never knew we wanted but somehow ended up possessing.

Hunkered down in a niche carved out of this mélange of toys was the owner tinkering away. We learned he had had the shop for about four years, and I remarked, "You have wonderful things, great taste," to which he responded dryly, "I just collected what I liked. Wife suggested I get them out of the house." Kay, the avid shopper, wanted to know, "What's the most valuable thing in your shop?" Of course it turned out to be the two pedal cars in his storefront window. He acknowledged one was priced at $6,500, but the other was not for sale, which I immediately thought was an antique dealer's usual jargon for saying "make me an offer." I must have taken too much time to allow the thought to pass through my mind, for he continued with, "I already turned down $12,000."

As was my way, all I wanted was a simple memento of our visit, something I could take home, look at, and recall the association of this wonderful unexpected highlight of our visit to Richmond, Kentucky.

I purchased a toy 1930s rusting cast metal (probably tin) car slightly longer than the palm of my hand with degraded rubber wheels. No shiny hubcaps here. Just four nail head ends on two wire axles, or so it seemed to me. The shop owner said it was fashioned after Chrysler's Airflow 1934–1937, similar to one of the pedal cars in the window, a sort of take-off on the race cars of the period, because my antique car had a unique fin over its trunk. The fin undoubtedly contributed to its costliness. I paid $280. Probably $250 more than I really believed it was worth, but I was comfortable writing off the $250 difference as an entry fee to viewing this wonderful world of artifacts. Kay, a bit shocked at the price, jokingly exclaimed, "It probably needs a wheel alignment for another $280." Though she finally agreed, "It's a nice piece."

Comfortable in the knowledge we would leave Richmond with something of value, albeit inflated, we continued up Main Street to the county courthouse.

Madison County is located on the southeastern edge of the Bluegrass region of Kentucky, where the Knobs mark the boundary between the rolling bluegrass and the hillier Cumberland Plateau. Many settlers passed through Madison County. Several ferries once operated in the county, beginning with one at Boonesborough in 1779.

The Madison County Courthouse is located at 101 West Main Street in Richmond, Kentucky 40475 (859-624-4700), between N. 1st and N. 2nd Streets on US 25 South. Erected in 1849–1859, the courthouse is one of the finest examples of Greek revival-style architecture in Kentucky.[4] It was designed by Col. Thomas Lewinski and built by John McMurtry at a cost of $40,000 between 1848–1852. It was altered extensively in the mid-1890s at an additional cost of about $15,000. The courthouse is at the end of Main Street, anchoring several blocks of fine Victorian homes, churches, antique shops, restaurants, and other commercial buildings we had just walked by.

Donut Delight

Before entering the Madison County courthouse, while reading the commemorative plaque about the formation of the county, Kay detected the smell of fresh doughnuts in the air and quickly noted the location of Nicholas Donuts & Pastries directly across the street (see photo) from the courthouse. We simply had to again disrupt our quest for family ancestors and indulge in this culinary delight. Of course, over the years, this has become a ritual of ours as we returned again and again to the Madison County Courthouse.

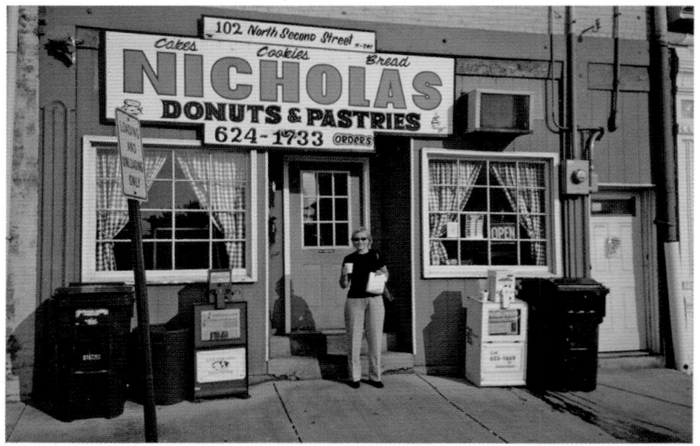

Nicholas Donuts & Pastries shop in Richmond, Kentucky, directly across the street from the Madison County Courthouse. A stop at Nicholas's became a ritual whenever we visited the courthouse.

Within the courthouse lobby are many glass display cases filled with old photographs of historical significance — groups of unsmiling school children, appearing always hardened by their rugged lifestyle, unkempt, soiled, and seemingly overdressed for whatever season they were depicted in; entire military units of soldiers strung out in succession looking all alike, one practically indiscernible from the other; vehicles; civic buildings; and even actual farm implements, tools, weapons, and other accoutrements of war.

I couldn't resist the temptation to look for Gooches or Davises among the myriad of photographic images and their various captions. From courthouse to courthouse, I continue to indulge my predilection to no avail for I have yet to find a single ancestor or someone even named Davis or Gooch. With time in the field and as the years unfolded, I came to realize that my family was not to be found among dignitaries or as participants in organizations of note. Nor were they holders of great wealth whose homes or businesses would be recorded photographically. No, these were mostly common folk, not mainstream but rather found in the eddies of the river of life, like most people caught

Kay Davis awash in a sea of ledgers while looking for Gooch and Davis records in the Madison County Courthouse, during our first visit to a courthouse for genealogical research on September 20, 1997.

up in the spiraling currents of an existence fraught with need and often ensnared by the rigors of survival in a harsh world.

Gooches, Davises, and Slaves

We were directed by a clerk in the office of the Recorder of Deeds to a large room with ceiling fans, well-lighted rows of chest-high viewing counters surrounded by racks and stacks of heavy leather-bound books. These books contained all kinds of records — births, marriages, deaths, deeds, court cases, etc.. As we entered the room, several other researchers were busily at work. They appeared to be legal professionals, checking property deeds for real estate closures. Kay avidly plunged into tome after tome, seeking marriage licenses for those on our predetermined "hit list" of ancestors. Quickly we were to realize that there were many Gooches and Davises unknown to us. We also discovered that there were many same or similar names, same period, same sex, which always produced the same question — is that *our* James Davis mentioned in the marriage license before us?

We copied everything. I must have spent a fortune in quarters in that room on that first day of research. But it felt so satisfying to leave at closing time with our sheaf of documents, looking forward to returning to our hotel room to organize this bundle of ancestry, and most importantly to determine if we indeed had much of real pertinent value.

We have returned several times to Madison County and its courthouse. We still consider it to be the wellspring of our family search. Once a part of Virginia, it welcomed the Gooches of Louisa County and Goochland. It was a gathering place for Oldhams, Maupins, Davises. Madison County, where we find Gooches in abundance, lies geographically almost midway between the coast of Virginia and the heartland of Missouri. And it is ultimately in Kentucky that we find the Davises during the period 1791–1874. James Davis sold his land in Madison County. By 1880 both he and his brother Albert had moved to Randolph County, Missouri.

It was not so odd to learn that my family, my Gooch and Davis ancestors, were involved in ownership of slaves, even traded slaves as commerce like so many others of the "period between 1650 and 1810 which saw a massive explosion of slavery in all major European empires in the Americas."[5] Slavery was a part of Southern life, especially in the colonies of Virginia and Maryland, where tobacco production was so prevalent.

> The period from 1810 to 1880 represented the final era of Slavery in the Americas. Although a number of countries abolished their transatlantic slave trades (Britain in 1807 and United States in 1810, for example), American slavery continued to expand. The plantations of Brazil, and of the Spanish and French colonies in the Caribbean imported nearly two million slaves between 1810 and 1860. In Cuba the slave population nearly doubled in these years, while in the same period the slave population of the southern United States, mainly engaged in cotton production [and indigo] increased by natural means from 0.9 to 3.7 million.
>
> The abolition of the institution of slavery, as opposed to that of the slave trade, was a long process which extended from the 1820s up to the 1880s [in various countries].[6]

Of course in the United States, slavery was ended in 1865 by the victory of the Union states over the Confederate states in the American Civil War. And although my ancestors, prior to the war's outcome, resided primarily in the "border" states of Delaware, Maryland, Kentucky, and Missouri, which allowed slavery legally, some did fight for the Confederacy (see Camp Douglas, Chicago, pages 206–207).

> The Civil War was fought at the cost of enormous loss of life, but it had the ultimate effect of preserving the United States of America as one Nation by settling the dispute over the division of power between the federal government and individual states in favor of the former. It also effectively ended the institution of slavery, although it did little to resolve the problem of race relations, which reached a climax a century later.[7]

Race and my relation to it began as a youngster in the mid-1950s with riots over the "influx of Negroes" into the Chicago federal housing project where I lived, at the Lake Michigan beaches and parks I frequented, and on the city buses I rode as a teenager. This issue was brought to a new land by my forebears. Along with the rest of America, I was caught up in the "emotional debate about what exactly it means to be American."[8]

This issue of slavery, as much an integral part of life for Thomas Jefferson as it was for my ancestors, would be ended by a great civil war, but its burden of smoldering race relations would come to rest squarely on the shoulders of all Americans like me who would come out of the 1960s as young adults.

Thomas Jefferson (born April 13, 1743, Albemarle County, Virginia, died July 4, 1826) — political philosopher, architect, musician, book collector, scientist, horticulturist, diplomat, inventor, and third President of the United States, with strong beliefs in the rights of man and a government derived from the people, in freedom of religion and the separation between church and state and in education available to all — had slaves as property.

Solomon Davis, my great-great-great-grandfather (died about 1801) — also a slave owner — was killed by slaves he was transporting to market.

It was here in the courthouse of Madison County that we first came face to face with the documentation of property, including slaves. They were inventoried, bartered, sold, and bequeathed as any other commodity of the day, and ultimately became the subject of legal disputes and finally armed conflict.

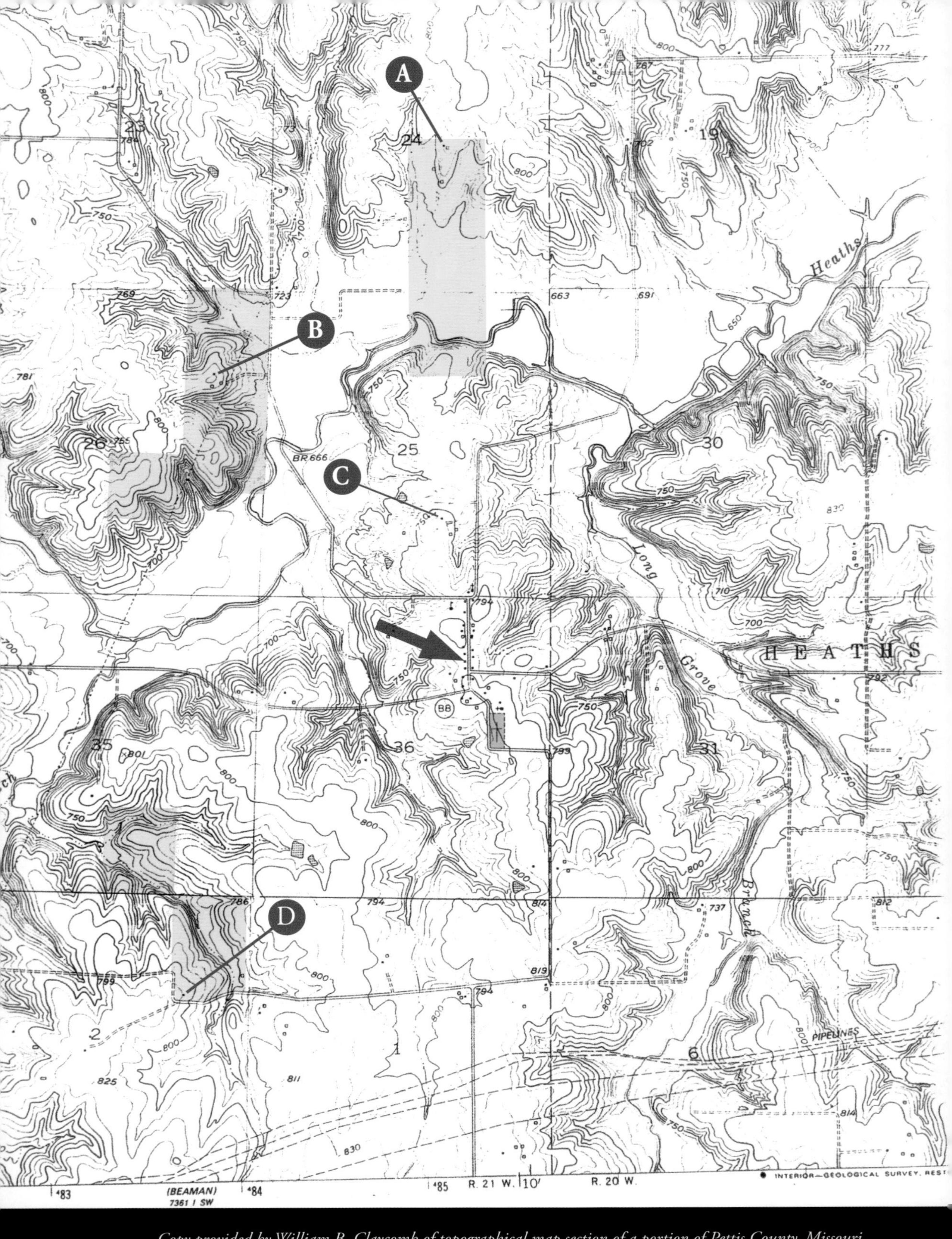

Copy provided by William B. Claycomb of topographical map section of a portion of Pettis County, Missouri, with hamlet/town of Longwood in center (see red arrow). The outlying homesteads above are approximate areas as indicated in yellow. A) Morgan and Mattie Davis, 120 acres; B) Carl Davis, 150 acres; C) The old brick house mentioned in Mr. Claycomb's book A History of Northeast Pettis County, Missouri *(see page 148); D) House Mr. Claycomb built and lived in from 1976 – 1981, 96 acres. Morgan "Morg" Davis owned a small general store in Longwood and, along with several other Davises, is buried in the cemetery next to the Longwood Presbyterian Church. A new building was dedicated on September 21, 1987.*

Pen Bogert, a reference specialist at the Filson Historical Society Library in Louisville, Kentucky, wrote of Solomon's death and that of his brother, Nathaniel Davis, in the article "Sold for my Account."[9] The circumstances of their demise in May 1801 at the hands of their captured slaves is thought to be "the first known case in the Ohio Valley in which enslaved African Americans rose up against their slave traders who were taking them down the river."[10]

Both Davis brothers perpetuated a way of life that has to this day not been completely rooted out of our thinking — that there are those of us more equal than others. The question of non-whites vs. whites continues to be the focus of some. The election of President Barack Obama in 2008 suggests we have made some genuine progress in dealing with the issue of racism. "Ethnic minorities are now encouraged by some to maintain their separate identities, although other factions have fought this idea, believing that it could undermine the cohesion of the American nation.11 Since the riots of South Chicago that I experienced and was swept up in as a young teenager, much progress has been achieved in civil rights. Our country has been forced over and over to confront successfully the issue of racial inequality.

Longwood, Missouri

The first several packets of family-related news clippings, letters, photos, and documents sent to me by LaVerne Purkey had opened the floodgate. I now knew that the Gooches had a presence in Kentucky as well as Illinois and Indiana.

At my request, I had received a certified copy of a marriage license between my paternal grandfather Charles Davis and my grandmother "Becca" Gooch from the Vermilion County clerk's office in Danville, Illinois. The marriage took place January 23, 1889, in Catlin, Illinois, at the house of W.O. Smith, a minister of the gospel and of the C.P. Church.

On the back side of the marriage license was a Return of a Marriage to County Clerk "to be carefully filled out [see certificate on page 250] and returned with the marriage license." This requirement was made by the Illinois State Board of Health and became for me a wonderful fount of information. There were eighteen questions. Among the written responses, I learned that my grandfather was a farmer, twenty-four years of age, that his place of birth was Kentucky, as was my grandmother's (they probably knew one another in Madison County), and that her mother's maiden name was Mildred E. Oldham. But most importantly, I learned where they lived at the time of their marriage. Surprisingly it was not the same place. Grandma resided with her father and mother in Fairmount, Illinois. Charles Davis, however, listed his place of residence in Longwood, Missouri. I had picked up another state to investigate.

Working with this new piece of information, I asked my assistant Marie Feldman to determine where the town of Longwood was in the state of Missouri, or if it still even existed. Marie ultimately contacted the Pettis County clerk's office (816-826-5395) and was able to determine "that there still is a tiny town called Longwood, Missouri, in Pettis County. It is not incorporated and there is no post office. There is a church there that may have kept records." The clerk, Maureen, said she knew some old timers and that she would talk to them. Marie, after giving Maureen my grandfather's name, promised to call back the next day. Maureen, who was especially helpful when we next contacted her, offered that "there was a local historian that might be of additional help in your search, a gentleman who wrote a book about the northeast part of Pettis County." This was our introduction to Bill Claycomb.

William B. Claycomb

By July 28th, after having reached Bill Claycomb by phone, I enlisted his aid for his research regarding my relatives from and around Longwood, Missouri.

William B. Claycomb, now a Sedalia amateur historian, as he described himself, was formerly a banker working for the state of Missouri as an examiner, as well as a sometime real estate entrepreneur. Bill mentioned, once after we met personally, that his father died at an early age, sixty-four, I believe. Bill decided that although he liked his job as a bank examiner, he was going to do what he really had a hankering to do — to write about local history. After all, perhaps he too was subject to a similar genetic timeline as his father that's been inexorably ticking away within him.

Bill lived just down the road south of Longwood, off Highway 65 on Claycomb Road in Hughesville, with his mother Dorothy. His brother and family lived on the adjoining farm where Bill occasionally pitched in to bring in the crops and rustle up stray cattle.

We received his book, *A History of Northeast Pettis County Missouri*,[12] and found that it quite nicely established, in a historical perspective, the town of Longwood.

Along with an exchange of letters, the book, and phone calls between us, coupled with Bill's intimate working knowledge of the area, we made quick progress toward confirming the presence of my family in and around Longwood, a surprisingly vital place in the late 1800s and early 1900s.

However, with the commencement of the Civil War, Missouri became a conflicted "border" state, its constituents siding with the Union or the Confederacy.

> Among those whose parents were early settlers of Pettis County was John Greer, three years old in 1803 who later became a blacksmith and woodworker. After a brief absence during the war he returned home and joined up with another blacksmith, Daniel M. Gray, a native of Canada, to form a business manufacturing fine wagons.[13]

We would, upon our first of many visits to Longwood, meet a fine elderly gentleman who is probably a descendant of John Greer, the wagonmaker. He was Jack Greer, and in his description of one of my ancestors, he recalled that "he generally drove a wagon and team…not too good a team and not too good a wagon, but he made his rounds."

> Situated in the northwestern part of the township is the pleasant little village of Longwood, with 125 inhabitants. It has several stores, shops, church buildings and a good school. Mail is received daily from Sedalia. The town has no railroad, but had it one giving rapid communication with its neighboring towns, it would be one of the most pleasant little places in which to make a home, that it has been the writer's privilege to visit. It is just at the edge of a splendid stretch of timber, and on high, rolling ground, and everything in the way of pleasant scenery around it to make it attractive.[14]

We arrived fairly late in the afternoon of September 21, 1997, in the town of Longwood, Missouri. I want to say the

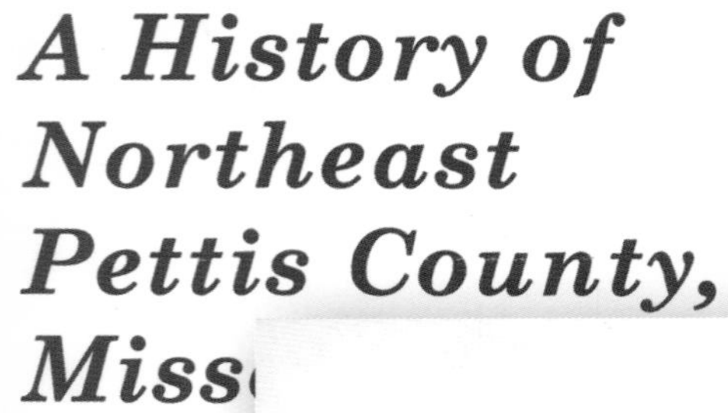

Pettis County, Missouri, circa 1916

"former" town center of Longwood, since it consisted mainly of a dozen or so occupied homes strung along a curbless half-mile-long road, with intermittent tumbled down structures, overgrown with vines, saplings, and weeds. An occasional barn could be seen out through the trees in the rolling fields from atop the hill that Longwood lay so sleepily.

We had turned off highway I-70 West onto state highway 65 South toward Sedalia for approximately four miles. We then drove east on another four miles of undulating road through fields defined by woods and thickets with nary a building or person in sight, almost turning back, thinking we were lost.

"This is a Glorious Day — Thanks Be to God!"

There was a fork in the road as we entered the town proper. A sign greeted us: "Historic site, Longwood, Est. Prior to 1825, Earliest Settlement County, Designated by Pettis County Historical Society." To our right, bathed in the setting sun, was the Longwood Presbyterian Church. Parishioners were leaving the parking area in their cars, stirring up the warm dusty soil, tires crunching on gravel as engines of pick-ups and cars revved and passed us by. Drawn by the commotion we pulled up to the church. This was a glorious day — Thanks Be To God! So proclaimed the religious brochure we were ultimately given to commemorate the church building dedication, a ceremony that had just ended.

The Longwood Presbyterian Church building dedication had started earlier with the usual Sunday morning worship led by Rev. Lou Wollenberg at 11 A.M. This led to a "carry-in" (rather than "take-out") basket dinner at noon, a photo session at 1:30 and concluded with the Longwood Building Dedication Service itself at 2 P.M.

A special thank you was extended to supporters of the building project: "We wish to thank everyone who brought their support to our needs. From the children who picked up our messes during the project, to the organizers of the project, from the talents of the contractors' special hands to the talents of our financial contributors, from the ice cream makers to the ice cream eaters, all who support our special projects, and our Lord's Acre Sales, we thank you all so much."

They'd built a fine white clapboard one-story building with a quite appropriate portico at the entry and with one rather small stained glass window to each side of the double doors. It had a steeple with cross of a scale suited to the size of the building. To the south side of the church, was the Longwood Cemetery containing many of my ancestors.

We arrived too late to participate in the services but, happily not too late to corral a lingering parishioner engaging in the fellowship that followed.

We had managed to gain the attention of a tall, elegant, elderly man in the midst of his goodbyes to fellow parishioners, who was kind enough to allow our intrusion. It wasn't until later that we realized the degree of our good fortune to have singled out, unwittingly, the one person who had lived in Longwood most of his life, and who was also old enough to recall the presence of my forebears in Longwood.

Morgan Davis, born in 1863 in Madison County, Kentucky, married Mattie Melvina Toombs at age twenty-four, in 1887 in Huntsville, Randolph County, Missouri. She was twenty-one years old.

Jack Greer claimed in 1997 that "The only Davises I knew was Mat [Mattie Melvina Toombs, born October 7, 1866] and Morgan [born March 16, 1863]…. Let's see, Mrs. Davis was a Toombs, wasn't she?" confirming for himself that he got it right the first time.

Jack R. Greer (video image)

I'd known that Jefferson C. "Jeffrey" Davis, or "JC" as some called him, Morgan's older brother (born 1861), and Ollie L. Davis (born 1882), Morgan's youngest brother, were merchants.There were several general merchandise stores in Longwood during the 1860s. These stores changed hands after the war. Among the successive owners must have been my grandfather's brother, Morgan Davis. But Jack Greer didn't seem to know Jefferson or Ollie Davis. He was familiar with the Toombs. "Went to school with the Toombs kids…Freddy and Finis I guess, right?" [Fred "Freddy," "Dick," Morgan Davis and Finis "Boss" Arnold Davis]. When I asked if they were farmers, Jack replied, "No, the Toombses were merchants. They operated the store in town here [Longwood]. He [Morgan] bought a store over in Longwood. At that time I expect he paid twenty dollars for it. He got a store, and started to put Mr. Toombs out of business. He had a long hard road, and he never did do it." "Is that right?" I asked, thinking this is not such an auspicious way to start a business. "No, he never put Mr. Toombs out of business. That man…he was a smooth operator. An intelligent business man, and Morg Davis didn't rank in his crowd at all." "No, he didn't?" I laughed, questioning Jack's recollection. "Well, I'm telling it like it is now," he said.

I wanted to know exactly where in Longwood Morg Davis's store was located. Jack said he knew, claiming he could "take us within a foot of it." It wasn't still standing. The Toombs's store was gone too, and in its place was the local fire station, building, and fire engine. Seems like the Toombs's store was in a "big two-story house" occupying the street level. "That was Bill Prowell's grandfather used to run that, several different people run it." According to Jack Greer, "But that was Toombs's store first." I never did get the exact location of the Davis store. Bill Claycomb did offer a caption that seemingly places the store.

We were to later learn of Jefferson Davis's store in Valley City, Johnson County, Missouri, which was unknown to Jack Greer and thankfully so, considering family pride, a bit more successful than Morg's store according to Jefferson's obituary.

And Ollie Davis was to also make his way as a notable merchant. I'm not sure I believe everything Jack Greer had to say about Morgan Davis's "competitive zeal" to put his brother-in-law out of business. As Bill Claycomb, in his letter to me August 17, 1997, tells it, Morg Davis "ran a general merchandise store in Longwood with his brother-in-law, Toombs" and notes that "local punks took advantage of Morg's poor eyesight to steal from him." Perhaps the two brothers-in-law had a falling out and parted company to become competitors at some later date? The Davises appeared in Missouri around the 1880s as near we can tell.

The Claycomb Cemetery Crawl

After being led to Bill Claycomb via the county clerk's office, I developed a working dialogue between us. By July 28, 1997, after a pleasant and lengthy phone conversation with Bill, I quickly forwarded him a check to cover expenses regarding his search of Longwood, Missouri, records and my grandfather Charles Davis's presence in Longwood at the time of his marriage to my grandmother, Rebecca.

By July 29, 1997, I received my first two-page, typewritten response from Bill. Though he had not yet received my check, he was to add at the bottom of his letter as a P.S.: "When we spoke I said it is helpful to have 'resources' when searching one's family. I meant local documentary resources, not financial resources. Please pardon my choice of words." This was to be the first instance of typical Bill Claycomb decorum.

Bill had jumped right in researching my family history with, as he said, "mixed results." He was quick to connect my grandfather Charles Davis with John Morgan Davis, known as "Morg" Davis, who ran a store in Longwood with his brother-in-law a Mr. Toombs. "Morg" died at the home of his son at Green Ridge and was buried in the Longwood Cemetery, Bill determined from an obituary that he had come upon. He then made a visit to the Longwood Cemetery confirming the burial of Morgan Davis along with several other Davises. This would be the first of many cemeteries that Bill Claycomb would visit or "crawl" on my behalf. During this initial search, Bill even called four Longwood natives, all in their eighties, "to ask if they knew who Morg's father was. They all remembered him and his boys, but not his father, who I guess was long gone before their time."

Having a local historian such as Bill was a distinct advantage for someone located as far away as New York and totally unfamiliar with the area. On this first pass, Bill had

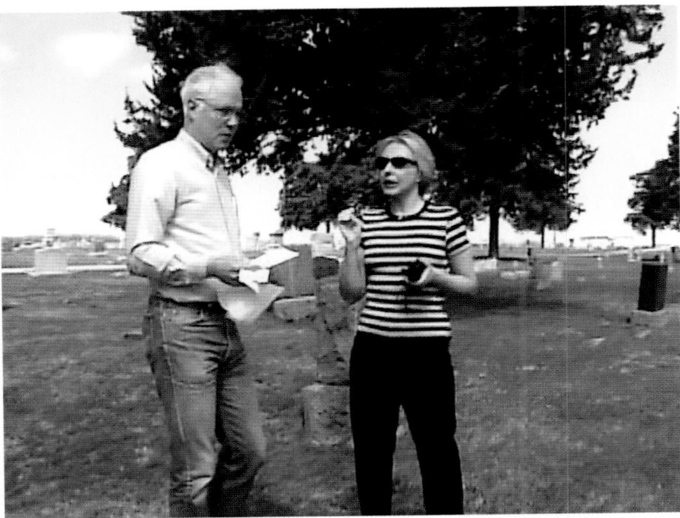

Bill Claycomb and Kay Davis in the Knob Noster Cemetery in Knob Noster, Missouri, in March 1998 during our "cemetery crawl." We visited the gravesites of Jefferson C. Davis and Rosa Tatum; Margie Davis Turner; Bessie Davis and Joe Marvin Honey; Everett and Earlene Davis; Eula Davis House; and Ethel Davis and James Elmo Triplett. (Video image.)

checked deed records, 1880 U.S. Census (the 1890 U.S. Census records were largely destroyed by fire), probate records, marriage records, as well as newspaper obituaries at the Sedalia Public Library, and was to request the death certificate of John Morgan "Morg" Davis.

Several days later Bill wrote, "What I am pretty sure of your Davises were members of the Bethlehem Christian Church (J. Morgan was; his nephew Carl W. was), but there is a cemetery there and I happen to be one of its trustees." This was probably the second cemetery that Bill would visit trying to locate my relatives. A theme was beginning to develop.

We had at this point in time not determined the burial sites of my great-grandparents, James Davis and Nancy Gooch Davis. However, by August 17, 1997, Bill had identified most of the Davis family that had settled in Missouri. I especially appreciated his canvassing of the local populace as to any memory of my relatives. In respect to Joseph S. Davis, born March 11, 1867, in Richmond, Kentucky, Bill offered that "Dump" Davis lived in the hills northeast of Longwood across the line in Saline County. Reported to have been somewhat of a shiftless recluse, he was dead prior to 1946. One of my eighty-five-year-old informants told me Joseph was "Dump." However, two elderly cousins who lived in the Davis neighborhood said "Dump" was a brother to Joe and Morg. None of my informants knew of Ali and Lou.

As previously stated, on our Roots Trip II, we stopped in Sedalia, Missouri, and on September 22, 1997, we met Bill Claycomb in the public library. At first glance, Bill appeared a

Bill Claycomb pulling his gloves on and plunging headlong into roadside brambles, barbed wire fencing, and other unknown obstacles, searching for long forgotten, overrun Davis family burial sites in March 1998. People were often buried in "pocket" cemeteries on farmers' lands.

bit stiff and proper, a middle-aged man, trim with graying hair, wearing glasses, seated at a table in his light blue, long-sleeved, starched shirt. He may be proper, but he was friendly, and we have come to know him with great affection.

After our departure, Bill went on several more field trips and cemetery crawls. In Saline County in October he located

J.C. Davis Country Store, Trickum (near Longwood), Missouri. Caption on back of photo reads "Dad — Everett — Ethel — Uncle Will — Uncle Jim — Mr. Brummit [sp.] Trickum Ethel & Everett [Davis] — born here"

an old Davis Cemetery he had heard about, a remote site where most of the stones were on the ground, and where some had disappeared beneath dirt, leaves, and brush. He also visited Smith Chapel where other Davises were buried. Bill provided a map locating these sites.

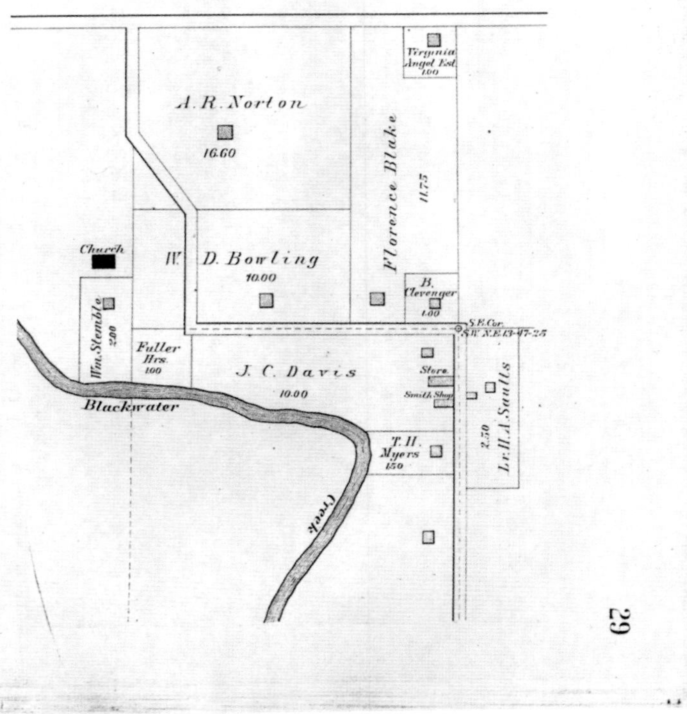

The J.C. Davis Store next to Smith Shop near Blackwater Creek, Valley City, Missouri. Drawing from "Plat Book of Johnson County, Missouri. Compiled and Published by A.R. Stinson, 1914" Copyright 1914 by A.R. Stinson; Engraved by Albert Volk, 714 Sansom St., Phila., PA.

By January of 1998, Bill had located and crawled the Lone Jack Cemetery. We had heard that Nancy Davis, the wife of James, was buried there. There were Davises there, but none were mine. Bill said in his report to me, "If Nancy is there, she lies in an unmarked grave, I believe, although a handful of stones were illegible. They were older stones, however, than I would expect Nancy's to be." This was the first of Bill's visits to the Lone Jack Cemetery. On a February trip to Warrensburg, Missouri, he had another breakthrough in finding 1918 newspaper articles in the *Star Journal* and *The Weekly Standard-Herald*, both of Warrensburg, noting that J.C. Davis, "who is very sick," was visited by his brothers Ollie Davis of Burtville, Joe Davis of Longwood, and his sister Lu Sanders, and their spouses. A second notice, an obituary for J.C. Davis, dated April 30, 1918, provided additional information naming family members Everett and Glenn Davis, Mrs. Joseph Honey, Mrs. Elmo Triplett, Julia and Margaret Davis. J.C. Davis died at his family home in Valley City, Missouri. The funeral was held at Knob Noster. Bill found more family buried at the Knob Noster Cemetery: Rosa Tatum Davis, Earlene Davis, Bessie Davis Honey, Eula Davis House, Margie Davis Turner, and Ethel Davis Triplett.

In four short months, Bill Claycomb had confirmed that my family in the late 1800s and early 1900s had established a significant presence in the heart of Missouri.

Coincidentally, I was receiving information from LaVerne Purkey, the wife of my cousin Glenn Purkey. She forwarded me a copy of a letter dated March 19, 1937, from Will Davis of Nelson, Missouri (at the time, unknown to be the brother of my grandfather Charles Davis). I sent this letter promptly to Bill Claycomb, which, of course, resulted in another cemetery crawl. Coupled with his findings at the Salt Fork Cemetery, two miles south of Nelson and his visit to Marshall, Missouri, he was to contribute four more names to my growing family: Mattie Odell Davis, Joe Marshall Davis, William Davis, and his wife Viola Ann Davis. There was also a funeral notice for Will Davis, who lived at 562 South Salt Pond Street, in Marshall, an account of the murder of Joe Davis, Will Davis's son, from the August 12, 1932, *Daily Democrat-News* (Marshall, Missouri), and an obituary for Viola Davis, naming all her children.

We made another Roots Trip in March of 1998, hooking up again with Bill Claycomb to visit the places where he had found Davises. He returned with us to Longwood, showing us where John Morgan "Morg" Davis had his store. He drove us by the farm Joe Davis lived on. On at least one occasion, armed with his rawhide gloves and loppers, with vigor, he charged through a field-side thicket, across barbed wire, and into yet another pocket cemetery. We also experienced the hospitality of Bill and his mother Dorothy in their home. Her cherry cobbler and ice cream were a delight to sample. Sadly, Bill's mother, Dorothy, passed away April 3, 2002, at age ninety-one.

I wrote on April 21, 1998, to Bill that I had been in contact with Ethel Davis Triplett, who was the daughter of Jefferson C. Davis. Ethel put me in touch with Bernetta Stump. We had earlier confirmed the death of James Davis, but had been unable to determine where he was buried. Bernetta not only knew where James Davis was buried, at the Zion Hill Cemetery, northwest of Valley City, but had a photograph of his headstone. Our hope was always that if we were to locate the burial site of James Davis, we would find buried with him Nancy "Nannie" Gooch Davis.

Bill had previously visited The Mount Zion Christian Church and Cemetery, one of several in the area, with no success. With new information, he located the Zion Hill Church and Cemetery and the gravesites of James Davis, my great-grandfather, born December 11, 1841, died April 15, 1903, S. Gertrude Murphy Davis, Earl Davis, and Maude Davis. There was no headstone for Nancy "Nannie" Gooch Davis.

One evening in early June of 1998, I received a call from Claude Davis, saying, "This is your distant cousin." Claude Davis was the son of Glenvel "Glenn" Davis, the son of Jefferson C. Davis and Rosa Tatum Davis. Claude had been in touch with Lois Murphy, with whom I had been corresponding and who had sent me an abundance of wonderful graphic material regarding the Jefferson C. Davis family. Lois had mentioned to Claude that I was searching for the gravesite of Nancy Davis. Claude wanted me to know that he recalled that Nancy, the wife of James Davis, "got sick and died on a trip. They buried her in a town called Lone Tree or Loan Elm, south of Harrisonville." After passing this information on to Bill, he located Lone Tree on some old maps in Cass County, Missouri. He did a cemetery crawl of the Pleasant Ridge Cemetery without much success. Noticing a plaque by the front gate with names and lots, he found no Davis. He then went back to Lone Tree to ask if there were any more cemeteries in the neighborhood, but was told no. He returned to Harrisonville and visited their library. Asking for their cemetery indexes, he soon found the one for Pleasant Ridge Cemetery, in the form of a history. There in Lot 46 was listed "Op," "Mary Ann Russell 1825 – 1888" and "Mrs. Davis." No further identification or information.

Bill returned to the cemetery armed with this new information and "located Lot 46 on the far edge of the cemetery, rather alone. There was Mary and lost souls Stone, a small but modern stone, certainly not an 1888 stone. And nothing else. No Opp, no Davis." He added, "But if she was buried at lone tree, this must be Nancy Davis. She is the only Davis mentioned in the cemetery history. Bad luck for us there is no more information, but good luck she is mentioned at all."

We were to visit Jefferson City, Missouri, in the fall of 1998. We managed a visit with Claude Davis in Holden, Missouri, one quiet Sunday afternoon when all the archives and libraries were closed. Claude lived alone in the house his mom and dad left him. He was a real farmer with Remington sculptures throughout his living room and more heifers pictured in his family album than folks. It was Claude who tipped us o ff to the whereabouts of another distant cousin, Eugene Davis, the living son of Ollie and Mabel Davis. Eugene lived alone, having never married, in Peculiar, Missouri.

Eugene said he had a photo of James Davis that was an exact copy of one I sent him earlier, believing that it was his mother and father. It was not as Eugene attested, but, as we've concluded, was probably a picture depicting our great-grandfather with a woman I thought to be Nancy "Nannie" Gooch Davis at the time. Instead it turned out to be James Davis with his second wife (?) "Grandma Sprinkles." Another surprising bit of information from Eugene was that "the family always stopped in Lone Jack [Missouri] on their way to Kansas City, to visit Nancy Davis's grave site."

With this new information, Bill Claycomb performed yet another cemetery crawl in search of Nancy Davis. Lone Jack was just twenty-eight miles due west of Valley City where husband James had died at home. Bill felt that had she died in Lone Jack, they would have made the effort to get her home. Both Bill Claycomb and I searched, unsuccessfully, the Lone Jack Cemetery for the burial site of a Nancy Davis.

Having exhausted most of our leads regarding the Davis family in Missouri, we moved on to other states and Bill continued writing books. Bill's short book on railroading was sponsored by the Mercantile Bank to benefit the Chamber of Commerce and the restoration of the old depot and was published by the Sedalia Heritage Foundation. Another book, *Pettis County, Missouri: A Pictorial History*, several magazine articles, and some of his poetry were also published. We've exchanged letters from 1999 through 2000. Surprisingly, for all the family research and details Bill had dug up regarding my family of mostly dirt farmers and shopkeepers, I was to learn that he was not oriented to providing literary "material from the perspective of the little man." As he remarked in a letter to me in December of 1998, "My approach to history has never been through this so-called little man. In fact I am of the school that history is mostly the biographies of so-called great men. I suppose that viewpoint is unfashionable and politically incorrect now, but if so tough."

Bill, from our first meeting, impressed us with his interest in fine art and culture. When we first met Bill at the library in Sedalia he mentioned how often he scanned copies of *Architectural Digest*, looking for homes of interest. For this reason, when our own home in Pound Ridge, New York, was featured along with others in *Architectural Digest,* we thought to send a copy to Bill, not to ruin his moment of discovery, but we weren't certain his habits remained the same or that he still had the time or interest for such things. Bill has an aversion to flying and despite our many invitations to visit, he probably will not make the trip to New York.

Bill at age sixty-six (in 2010) still lives on the Claycomb family farm in Longwood, Missouri.

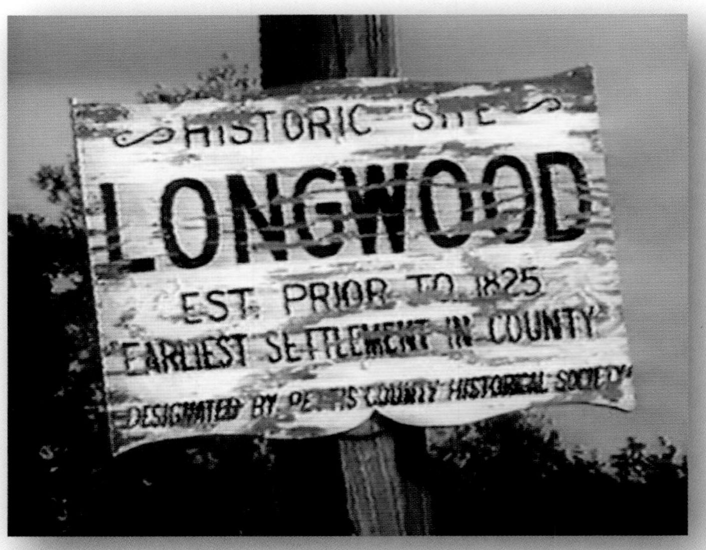

Sign identifying Longwood, Missouri, as an historic site. Longwood was the earliest settlement in Pettis County, established prior to 1825.

Notes

1. Nancy Shute, "New Routes to Old Roots," Smithsonian (March 2002): 76.
2. Barbara Walker, founding member, Afro-American Historical and Genealogical Society, as quoted in Shute, "New Routes to Old Routes."
3. *Kentucky Atlas & Gazetteer* <http://www.uky.edu/KentuckyAtlas/ky-richmond.html>.
4. Richmond Tourism and Visitor Center, 345 Lancaster Ave., Richmond, KY 40475 (859-626-8474; 1-800-866-3705), <http://www.richmond-ky.com>.
5. Patrick K. O'Brien, ed., *Philip's Atlas of World History* (London: George Philip Ltd., 2001), 126.
6. O'Brien, *Philip's Atlas of World History*, 127.
7. Ibid.
8. Ibid.
9. Pen Bogert, "Sold for My Account: The Early Slave Trade Between Kentucky and the Lower Mississippi Valley," *Ohio Valley History: Journal of the Cincinnati Historical Society* 2, no. 1 (2002): 3–16.
10. Ibid.
11. O'Brien, *Philip's Atlas of World History,* 126.
12. William B. Claycomb, *A History of Northeast Pettis County, Missouri* (Dayton, Ohio: Morningside Press, 1996).
13. Mark A. McGruder, *History of Pettis County, Missouri* (Topeka, Kan.: Historical Pub. Co., 1919), 303.
14. Correspondence between William B. Claycomb and Clyde Davis, February 19, 1998; Longwood street scenes, 1900–1910.

An Update

April 15, 2004
10 Tatomuck Circle
Pound Ridge, New York 10576

Dear Folks,

It's been some time since many of you have heard from me. You were all so helpful in the past in assisting me in my quest to define our Family Tree. You deserve to know how I'm doing.

Unfortunately, I grew to over-invest in the idea of enlisting the support of my former company's considerable electronic desktop publishing capability. After becoming a free man (we don't use the "R" word) and hanging around the office for nearly a year and a half preparing for that event, I suddenly learned that essentially I was on my own. So dear friends and family the burden of publishing my family history has fallen squarely and exclusively on my shoulders. I was also forced to give up my able personal assistant this past August and despite my wife's well meaning effort to serve as her replacement it has put our 45 year marriage to the ultimate test. Hopefully, we'll survive.

It's been nearly 18 years since the first inclination toward family history arose in me and I began this project. There have been many surprises along the way as my interest grew and this project became an obsession. I have been faulted for incorporating the incorrect branch of another Davis Family Tree. I've learned that many of my early ancestors, both Davis and Gooch, were significant slaveholders and traders, and some even murdered by slaves. Refer to Pen Bogert's excellent article "Sold for my Account", The Early Slave Trade Between Kentucky and the Lower Mississippi Valley in the Ohio Valley History Journal of the Cincinnati Historical Society. Volume 2, Number 1, Spring 2002.

I've been informed that my writing of the book has taken on an autobiographical slant and is not confined merely to the biographies of ancestors or facts of history. I've had gnawing disappointments such as never determining the date of death of Nancy Gooch Davis nor ever confirming her burial site despite much input.

I've been told that perhaps after "hitting the wall" I may have to settle for never knowing from which state or country the Davises originated. I've had, on the road, discoveries at the Johnson County Missouri Historical Society, Kentucky State Archives, The Maryland State Archives and the John Fox Library at Duncan's Tavern in Bourbon County, Kentucky.

Most importantly, I've managed to retain the professional support of Alice Henson, Certified Genealogist and Family History soul mate, keeping me on track, always the skeptic of loosely documented information and conjecture.

And, as always, I continue to meet the most pleasant, helpful and cordial people. Many are cousins I didn't even know I had such as Lester Davis at www.brookecountywvgenealogy.org, and Gwen Selig of Oregon who have done considerable work which will undoubtedly complement and add to my own findings

We have reached the "water's edge" by tracing the Davises back to Maryland. My progenitor of earliest descent seems to be Nathaniel Davis of Maryland born about 1700, wife Mary, children: Ziporah, Susannah, Richard, Margaret, Robert, Thomas and Nathaniel. All this has to be proven, of course.

So, with a recommitment to getting this done on my own, I remain respectfully yours, aware of my duty not to disappoint all who have so generously given of their time and trust. Feel free to write or e-mail me at www.cpdcdm@aol.com.

Sincerely, your kin,

Clyde P. Davis

Nathaniel Davis b. ca. 1700

Nathaniel Davis of Baltimore County, Maryland

Our earliest ancestor was Nathaniel Davis. We do not know who his parents were or where he came from. We will call him Nathaniel Davis Sr. to distinguish him from his son and grandsons who carried the same name. He was born about 1700, according to a deposition he made in a court case, when he stated that he was "aged Sixty-four Years, or thereabouts" and recalled a survey of a tract of land called "Green Spring Punch."[1] The date of the deposition was 13 March 1765. He also said that he lived with Richard Lewis on the tract of land some forty years ago and upwards.[2] So, we know that Nathaniel Davis, who signed his deposition with an "N," was living in the northern part of Baltimore County as early as 1725. We also learn that Nathaniel had carried the chain for the original survey of the "Spring Garden" tract of land, owned by the Reister family. Nathaniel Davis, age seventy-six in 1776, testified about the original boundaries of that piece of land.[3]

The area of Baltimore County where this Davis family lived was later called the Fourth District. The *Baltimore County Atlas of 1877* called this area the "largest and richest in the county." It was a healthy area with good water and pure air, with an elevation of some 1,700 feet above sea level. The soil produced abundant crops.[4]

Nathaniel Davis married a woman named Mary and some of their children were found in the baptismal records of St. Paul's Episcopal Church in Baltimore City:[5]

Susannah Davis born 6 October 1732
Richard Davis born 1 April 1734
Margaret Davis born 6 May 1736
Robert Davis born 7 June 1738

We can also add these children to the family list:

Ziporah born 11 June 1729[6]
Thomas born about 1740
Nathaniel Jr. born about 1742

The family grew and flourished. They would have traveled several miles by wagon to baptize the children in Baltimore City. When a church was built in Reisterstown, St. Thomas, or Garrison Forest Protestant Episcopal Church, the family surely would have joined. However, the old church records, including burials, do not exist.

Toward the end of his life, Nathaniel Davis Sr. deeded about sixty-two acres each to his two youngest sons, Thomas Davis and Nathaniel Davis Jr. in May of 1783.[7] At that time Nathaniel had another wife, Hannah, and he reserved a life interest for Hannah and him in the land that he deeded to Nathaniel Davis Jr. He also deeded land to Robert Davis.[8] By 19 January 1785 Nathaniel deeded more land to Thomas Davis.[9] This is the last transaction that we have found. His wife Hannah did not release her rights of dower, so we can assume that she is deceased by then. By deeding away his land during his lifetime, Nathaniel would have avoided probate — a crafty way of avoiding taxes. In 1785 he would have been about eighty-five years old, living a much longer than average life for his times.

This is what we know about the children of Nathaniel Davis and Mary:

Ziporah married William Seabrook as his second wife. They moved to Lancaster County, Pennsylvania, about 1767.[10]

One of the daughters, Susannah or Margaret, must have married a Mr. Boring/Boren, as evidenced by the rejected pension application of John Boren, born 1755, in Baltimore County.[11]

Richard Davis (our line) married Margaret Stocksdale and went to Kentucky after the American Revolution.

Robert Davis stayed in Baltimore County and married a woman named Margaret. He died in 1829 in Baltimore County, as his will was probated there 19 September 1829.[12] Children mentioned in the will were Sarah Davis, Mary Gooden?, and sons John and Isaac.

Thomas Davis — no further information.

Nathaniel Davis Jr. sold his property to John Stocksdale in 1785 and moved to West Virginia.[13]

Though the Nathaniel Davis family had been in Baltimore County more than sixty years, most of the children left and went to other states.

A.H.

Notes

1. Deposition of Nathaniel Davis, Provincial Court Ejectment Papers, 1636–1777, Samuel Owings vs. William Kelly, Baltimore Co., Maryland State Archives, Annapolis, Md.
2. Ibid.
3. Lillian Bayly Marks, *Reister's Desire* (Baltimore: Garamond/ Pridemark Press, Inc., 1975), 210.
4. G.M. Hopkins, *Atlas of Baltimore County, Maryland* (Philadelphia: 1877), 5.
5. Katherine L. Barnett, comp., *St. Paul's Register* (Baltimore: the author, 1971).
6. Richard S. Wheeler, "Seabrooks of Maryland and Pennsylvania," *Maryland Genealogical Bulletin* 34, no. 2 (Spring 1993): 138–45.
7. Baltimore Co., Maryland, Deed Book N:64, 73, FHL #13344.
8. Baltimore Co., Maryland, Deed Book N:67, FHL #13344.
9. Baltimore Co., Maryland, Deed Book U:742, FHL #13347.
10. Wheeler, "Seabrooks of Maryland and Pennsylvania," 138–45.
11. Rejected Pension Application of John Boren, R1030, National Archives, Washington, D.C.

12. Baltimore Co., Maryland, Will Book 13:280, Reel CR 72, 246-1, Maryland State Archives, Annapolis, Md.
13. Information from Lester Davis, Fairhaven C-134, 7200 Third Ave., Sykesville, MD 21784.

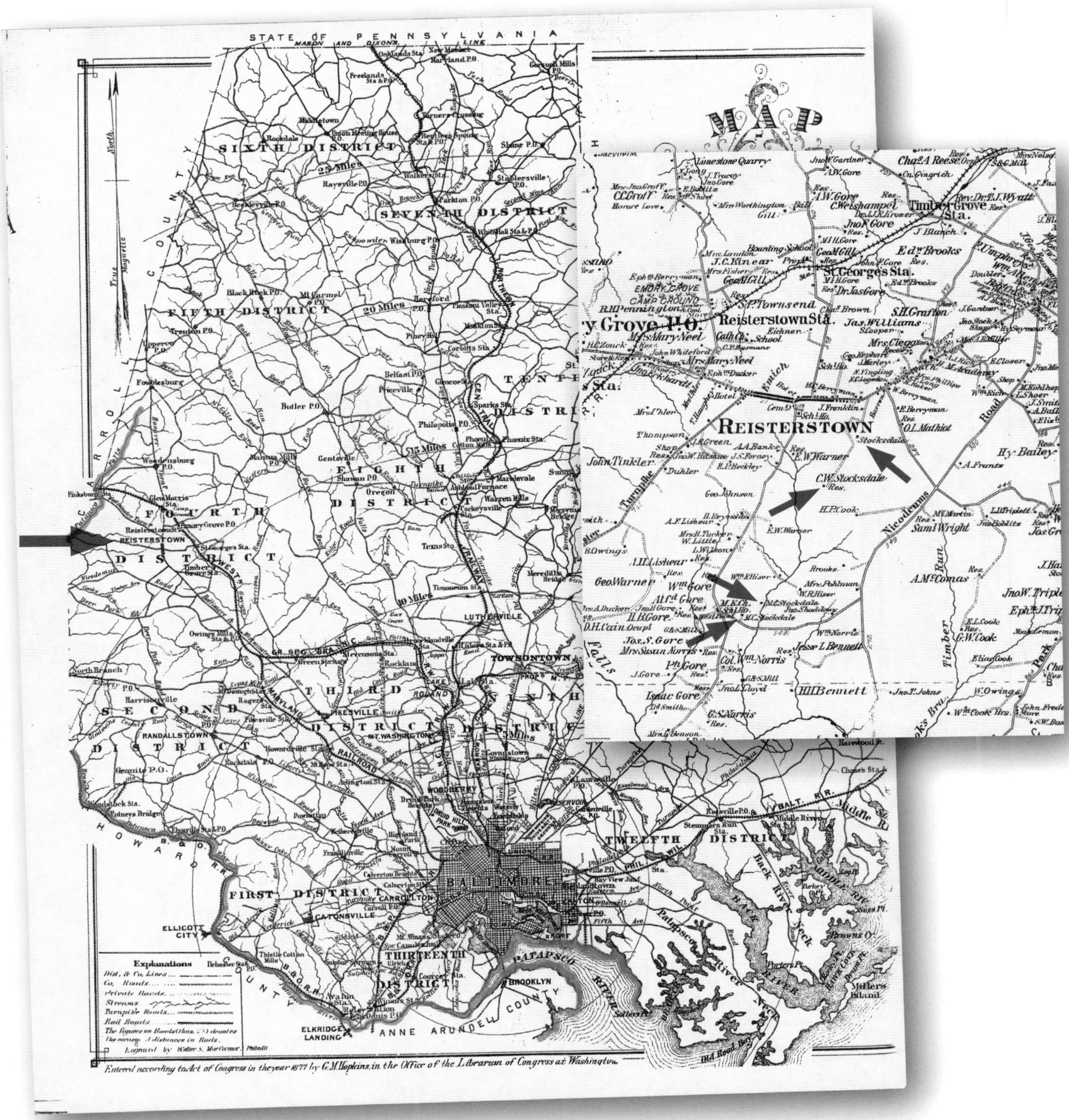

"Map of Baltimore County Maryland 1877. Entered according to Act of Congress in the year 1877 by Hopkins in the Office of the Librarian of Congress at Washington." Note the Patapsco River, highlighted in blue, especially near the Fourth District, Reisterstown area. Richard Davis, b. April 1, 1734, married Margaret Stocksdale, b. October 6, 1734, daughter of Edward and Catherine Stocksdale, whose family lived in this area (see map inset). "The Fourth District is one of the largest and richest in the County. In this District is the very flourishing town called Reisterstown, which occupies in length two miles of the Baltimore and Reisterstown Turnpike, and is 16 miles from Baltimore City."

NATHANIEL DAVIS b. ca. 1700

Maryland Sct
Balt County

By Virtue of a warrt granted unto Doctr George Buchhanon of Baltimore County out of His Lordships Land Office bearing date by Renewmt July ye 26: 1727 for one hundred and fifty acres of Land: fifty acres part of which said warrt was one the 17: day of Octobr 1727 Assignd unto Nathaniell Davis of Balt County As Appears &c

These are therefore to Certifie that I Philip Jones Junr Depty Survr under Charles Colvert Esqr Survr generll of the western Shore of this province have laid out for him the said Nathan Davis A parcell of Land Calld: Davises Purchase In this County: Begining at a bounded White oake Standing on ye North Run which Decends Into Joneses falls and Runing thence North Seaventy two Degrs West Eighty pr then North twenty two Degrs West one hundred and thirty prs then South Seaventy two Degrs East Eighty pr then by A direct line to the first bounded tree Cont and Now laid out for fifty acres of Land more or Less to be holden of the Manner of Baltimore

Survd Octob ye 20: 1727 ℔ me

Philip Jones Junr

N22W130 — N72W80 — S72E80 — A

W: A: is Davises Purchase Cont 50 Acres ℔ Scale 100 pr In An Inch

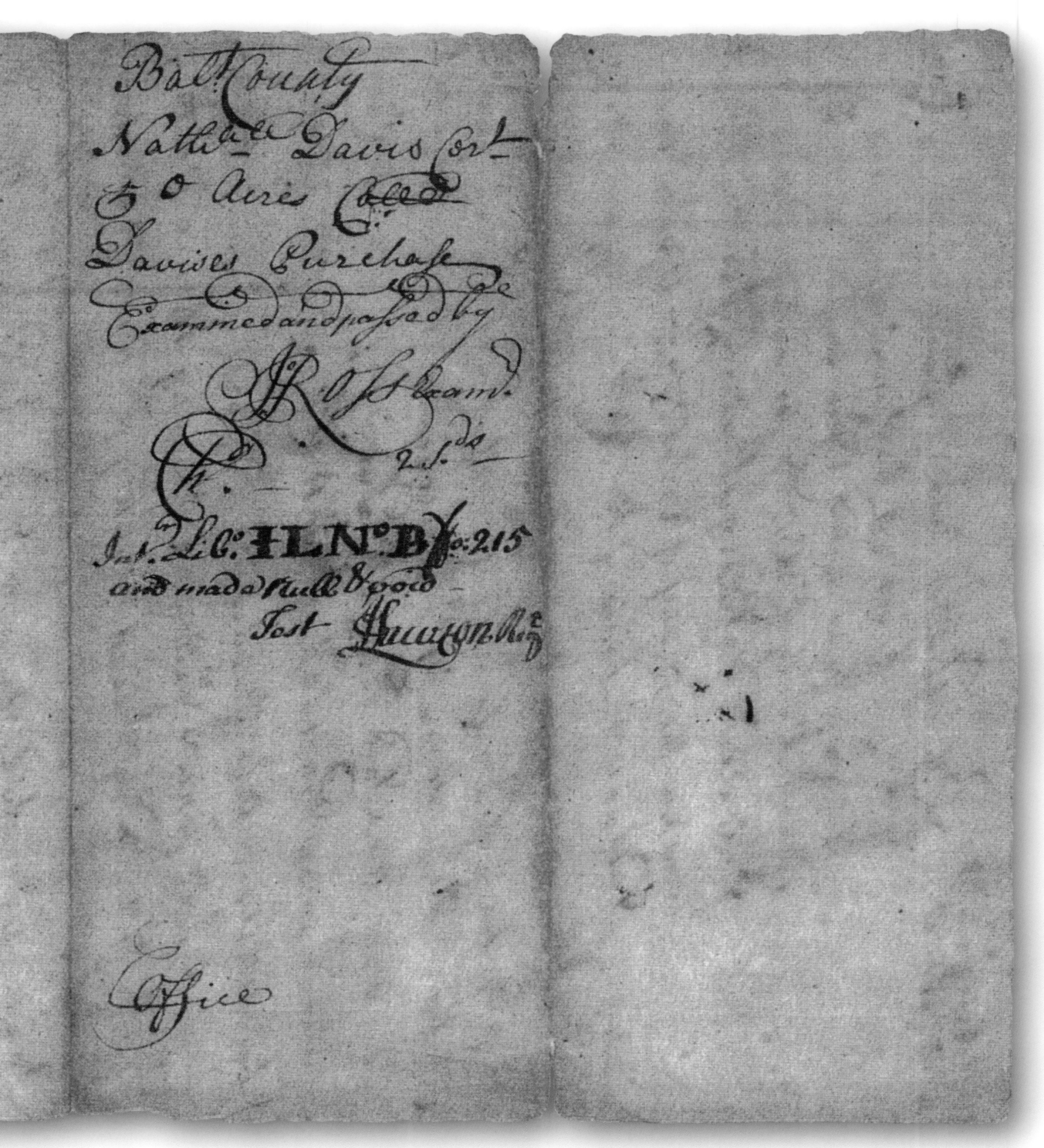
Balt. County
Nathl. Davis Cert.
50 Acres Called
Davises Purchase
Examined and passed by
J Ross Exam.
Ch. 2 s.
Int. Lib. IL No. B fo: 215
and made full & good
Test
Office

Nathaniel Davis's Land Patent 1727, Baltimore County, Maryland, Maryland State Archives, Annapolis, Maryland. Earliest land patent — Davis's purchase

Nathaniel Davis b. ca. 1700

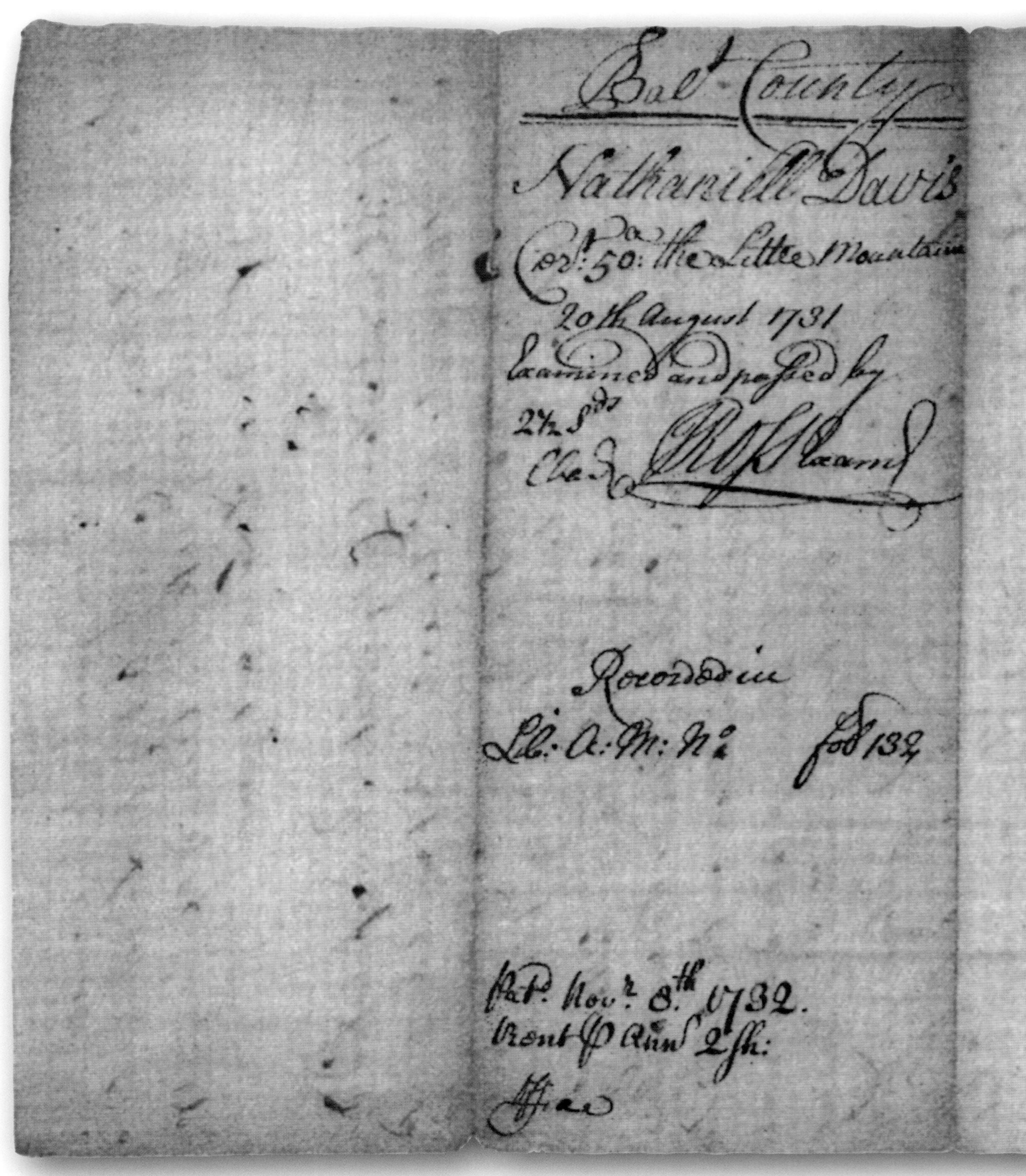

Balt County

Nathaniell Davis

Cert. 50 a. the Little Mountain

20th August 1731

Examined and passed by

2½ Sd

Clear'd

Recorded in

Lib: A:M: No. [?] fol 132 [?]

Pat. Nov. 8th 1732.

Rent ℘ Ann [?] 2 sh:

Maryland State Archives, Annapolis, Maryland Land Office (Certificate of Survey, Patented, BA) 1732, #2903 "Little Mountain" (MSA S 1190, 1-25-2-25)

Maryland } By Vertue of a Warr.t granted to Nathaniell Davis
Balt.o Co. ss } of the said County Out of his Lordships land
office baring date the 6.th day of Aprill 1731 for
fifty acres of Land as appears

These are therefore to Certifie that I Philip Jones Jun.r Dep.ty Surv.r of the County afs.d have laid Out for him the s.d Nath.ll Davis a parcell of Land in the County afs.d Called the little Mountaine beginning at two bounded White Oakes standing close by a Spring in a bottom by a steep poynt the two said trees stands the one on the one side the said Spring and the other on the other side Which said Spring desends into a branch called the great branch Desending into patapsco falls and running Thence South Sixty seaven deg.s East Eighteen p.s then North fifty deg.s East One hundred p.s then North thirty deg.s West forty p.s then North fifty seaven deg.s West Sixty p.s then South Sixty deg.s West forty two p.s then by a Direct line to the first bounded tree Cont.g and now laid Out for fifty acres of Land more or less to be holden of the manner of Baltimore Surveyed Aprill the 8: 1731 p. me

Philip Jones Jun.r
Dep.ty Surv.r

N57W60
N30E40
S60W42
2
N50E100
S67E18

No. 2 is the Little mountaine
Cont.g 50 a. Scale 100 p. in an Inch

5190-2903

159

Nathaniel Davis b. ca. 1700

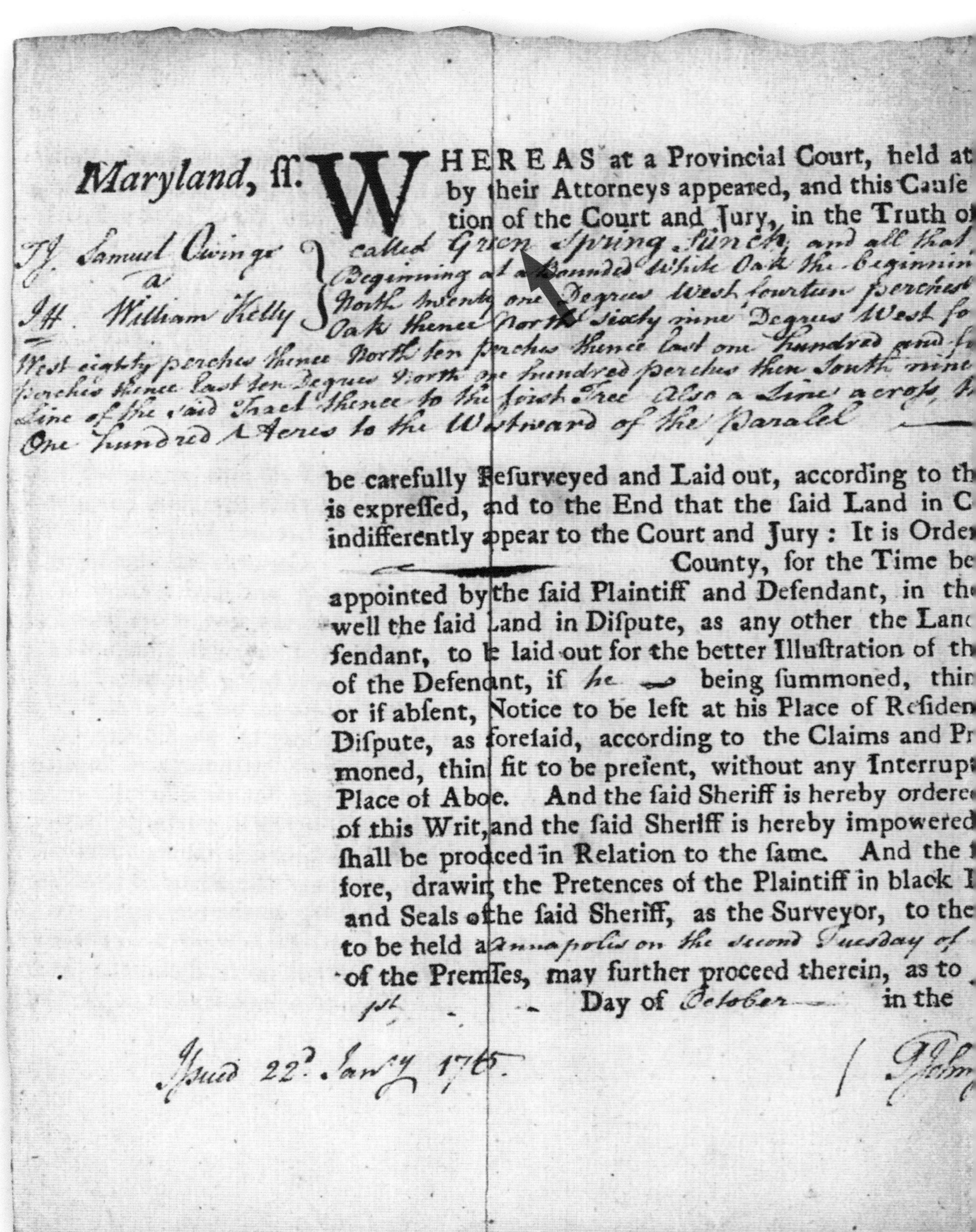

Maryland, ſſ. WHEREAS at a Provincial Court, held at
by their Attorneys appeared, and this Cauſe
tion of the Court and Jury, in the Truth o

Samuel Owings a William Kelly

called Green Spring Punch, and all that
Beginning at a Bounded White Oak the Beginnin
North twenty one Degrees West fourteen perches
Oak thence North sixty nine Degrees West fo
West eighty perches thence North ten perches thence East one hundred and f
perches thence East ten Degrees North one hundred perches then South nine
Line of the said Tract thence to the first Tree Also a Line across th
One hundred Acres to the Westward of the Paralel

be carefully Reſurveyed and Laid out, according to th
is expreſſed, and to the End that the ſaid Land in C
indifferently appear to the Court and Jury: It is Order
County, for the Time be
appointed by the ſaid Plaintiff and Defendant, in th
well the ſaid Land in Diſpute, as any other the Lan
fendant, to be laid out for the better Illuſtration of th
of the Defendant, if he being ſummoned, thin
or if abſent, Notice to be left at his Place of Reſiden
Diſpute, as foreſaid, according to the Claims and Pr
moned, think fit to be preſent, without any Interrupt
Place of Abode. And the ſaid Sheriff is hereby ordere
of this Writ, and the ſaid Sheriff is hereby impowered
ſhall be produced in Relation to the ſame. And the
fore, drawing the Pretences of the Plaintiff in black I
and Seals of the ſaid Sheriff, as the Surveyor, to the
to be held at Annapolis on the second Tuesday of
of the Premiſes, may further proceed therein, as to
1st Day of October in the

Issued 22d. Jany 1765.

Baltimore County Provincial Court. Court-Ordered Survey of "Green Spring Punch"
Samuel Owings v. William Kelly, 1st Day of October 1764

olis, the *second Tuesday of September last* the Plaintiff and Defendant,
g for Tryal, and for that it is absolutely necessary for the better Informa-
emisses, That *All that Tract of Land lying in Baltimore County*
... of which is included within the following Lines and Boundaries to wit
of the afsd Tract of Land called Green Spring Punch and running thence
North thirty two Degrees West sixty four perches to a bounded white
perches thence North thirty two Degrees West thirty perches thence
perches to a bound poplar thence North fifteen Degrees East twenty six
East across the said Tract of Land until it intersects the given
and parallel to the South nine Degrees East Line so as to leave

at Metes and Bounds thereof, as in the original Certificate of Survey thereof
rsy, and the Claims and Pretensions of both Parties, may more plainly and
he said Court, that his Lordship's Surveyor of *Baltimore*
any other discreet and skilful Person in his Absence, to be nominated and
ce of the Sheriff of the said County, carefully Resurvey and Lay Out, as
nt thereto, which shall be thought necessary by the said Plaintiff or De-
r, according to the Claims and Pretensions of the Plaintiff, in the Presence
be present, and without any Interruption of *him* the said Defendant,
last Place of Abode; and likewise Survey and lay out the same Land in
s of the Defendant, in the Presence of the Plaintiff, if *he* being sum-
he Plaintiff, or if absent, Notice to be left at his Place of Residence, or last
e both the said Parties thirty Days Notice, before the Day of the Execution
nine upon Oath any Witness or Witnesses, that by either of the said Parties
rveyor is hereby commanded, to return five fair Certificates and Plats there-
nd the Pretences of the Defendant in prick'd Lines, as well under the Hands
s of *our Provincial Court*
...next that the said Justices and Jury being rightly informed of the Truth
ppertains. Witness *Wm Brice Esqr Chief Justice* of our said Court, the
Year of his Lordship's Dominion, &c. Annoque Domini, 17*64*

Reverdy Ghiselin

"Green Spring Punch" — a tract of land or plantation in northern Baltimore County where Nathaniel Davis lived in 1725

Nathaniel Davis b. ca. 1700

The Deposition of Nathaniel Davis aged ~~forty~~ Sixty four Years or there
about being Sworn on the Holy Evangelists of Almighty God
Deposeth and Saith that the Residue of Mr. Samuel Owings's
Plantation from the End of the North Fifty two Degrees East
Forty perches Line that the Surveyor had Laid Down agreeable
to the Directions of Said Samuel Owings (the Surveyed Courses
from thence Laid Down by the Surveyor Excepted) to where
Mr. Saml. Owings begun to Lay of a part of the Plantation
was fenced or Inclosd about Forty Years ago. as well as he
the Said Davis Can Remember. The Said Davis Further
Saith that he Lived on Said Plantation being part of a Tract
of Land called Green Spring Punch about that time

14th March 1765

Sworn to before
Robt. [illegible] Balt Coty

his
Nathl. X Davis
mark

Baltimore County Provincial Court Ejectment Papers, Samuel Owings v. William Kelly, 6 October 1762

"Green Spring Punch" … Nathaniel Davis age 65 in 1765 swore that he lived 40 years ago on land of Richard Lewis.

> *… William broke & entered and the grass of him (the said Samuel) destroyed 1000 oaks of 200 £ value; 100 poplars of 20 £ value; 100 Hickorys of 10 £ value; 50 walnuts 15 £ & cut down took & carried away and the earth & soil of Samuel … 20 acres … with hoes & plows dugg and turned Issued subpoena to Sheriff of Baltimore Co 21 Mar 1763*

William did the damage between 1 April 1760 and 20 March 1763.

The Deposition of Nathaniel Davis of Baltimore County aged forty four Years or thereabouts being Summond & Sworn as an Evidence on the Execution of a Warrant of Resurvey on a Tract of Land called Green Spring Punch, deposeth & saith that about forty Years ago & upwards this Deponant lived with Richard Lewis on the aforesaid Tract of Land called Green Spring Punch & that the plantation as it was then settled lay nearly according to the Courses the Surveyor has now run & further sayth not ———

Sworn to 13th day of March 1765
Before Rob. Adair Jr. Balt Cty

his
Nathl. V Davis
mark

The Deposition of Cornelius Howard of Baltimore County aged Fifty Seven Years or thereabouts being Summond & Sworn as an Evidence on the Execution of a Warrant of Resurvey on a Tract of Land called Green Spring Punch, Deposeth & Saith that about forty years ago & upwards he remembers the Plantation as it was then settled to lay nearly agreeable to the Courses now run by the Surveyor, & further sayth not. ———

Cornelius Howard

Sworn to the 13th of March 1765
Before Rob. Adair Jr. Balt Cty

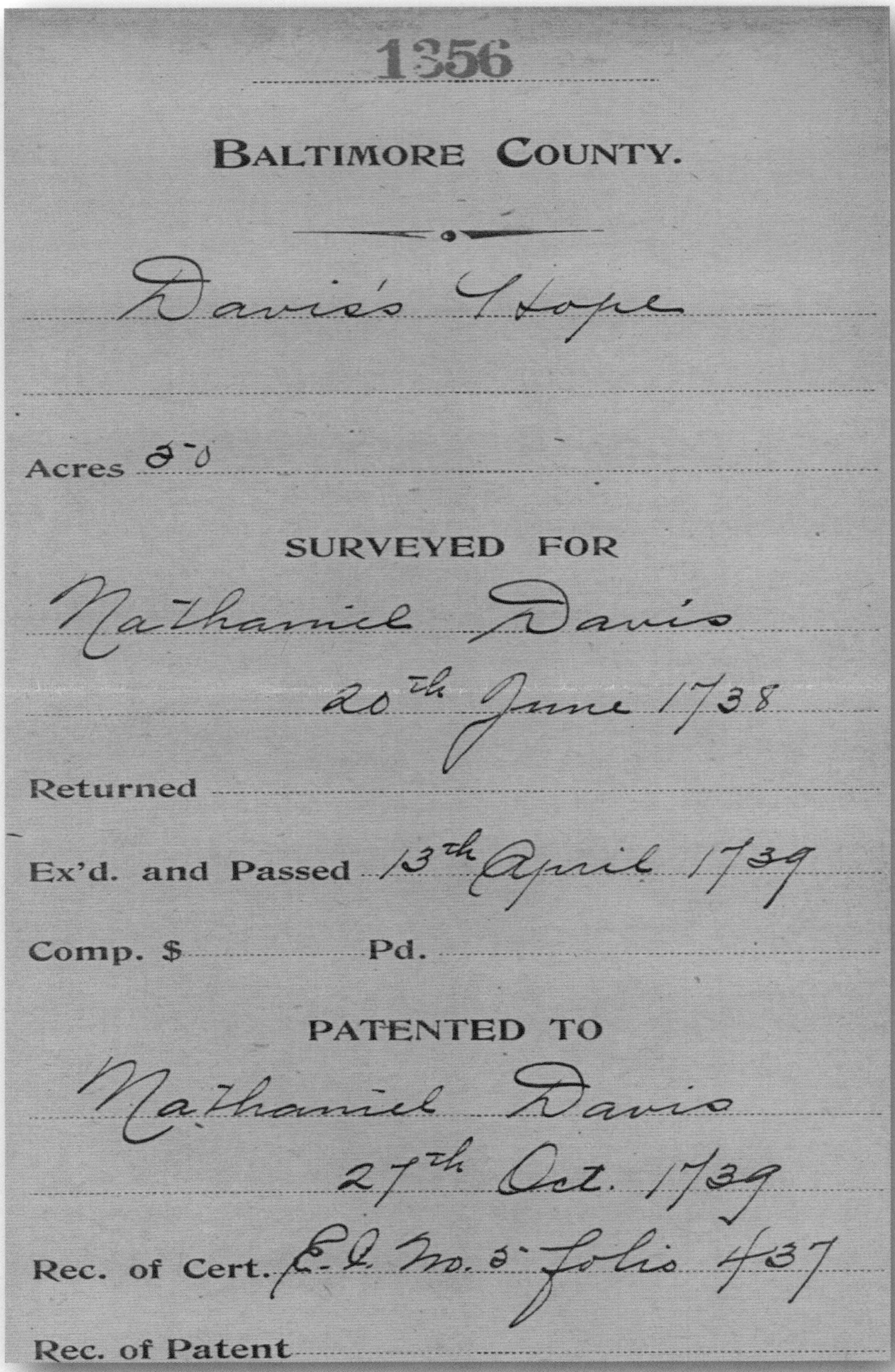

NATHANIEL DAVIS b. ca. 1700

1356

BALTIMORE COUNTY.

Davis's Hope

Acres 50

SURVEYED FOR

Nathaniel Davis
20th June 1738

Returned

Ex'd. and Passed 13th April 1739

Comp. $ Pd.

PATENTED TO

Nathaniel Davis
27th Oct. 1739

Rec. of Cert. E.I. No. 5 Folio 437

Rec. of Patent

Maryland State Archives, Annapolis, Maryland, Baltimore County
Nathaniel Davis Plat and Certificate of Davis's Hope, 50 acres. Date of Survey April 13, 1739.

Back

I Do Hereby assing and trensffer unto —
Nathaniell Davis fifty acers of Land Warrant
being part of a Warrant Granted unto me out
of his Lordships Land office bearing Datte the
thirtieth Day of December Anno Dom 1737
for one Hundred and fifty Acers of Land which
said fifty acers of Land Warrant I Do hereby
assine over unto the said Nathaniell Davis
his heirs and assines for Ever as Wittness my
hand this fourteenth Day of January
Anno dom 1737
Test
Tho: Franklin
Benj. Hammond

5190-1356

Front

Fifty acres granted to Nathaniel Davis, January 14, 1737

Nathaniel Davis b. ca. 1700

Baltimore County

Nath.l Davis plot & Cert of Davis's hope 50 a

Exam.d

2½ Sides ...

Recorded In Lib E I No 5 fol 47

April 13, 1739,

Exam.d & pass.d

Patt: 27: Octob: 1739

Rent ℔ Ann 5/

Cha.d to the rent roll

Front

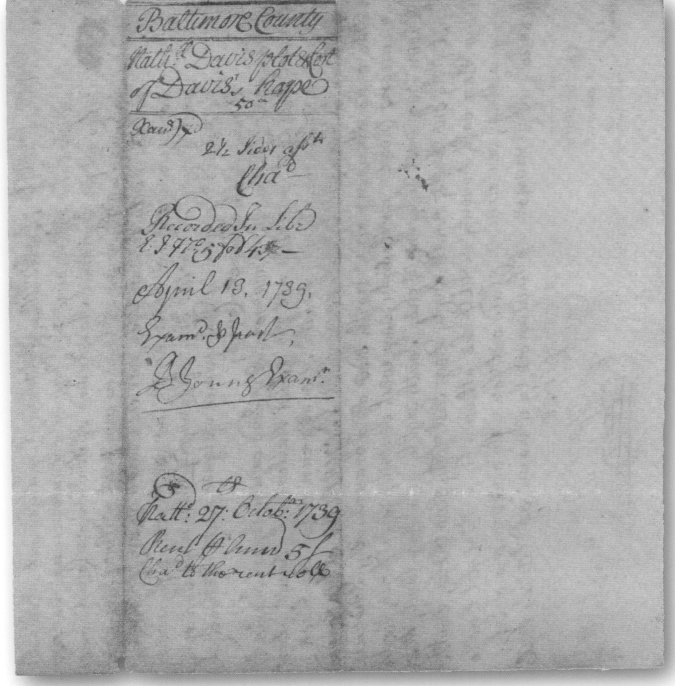

Maryland State Archives, Annapolis, Maryland, Baltimore County
Nathaniel Davis Plat and Certificate of Davis's Hope, 50 acres, Date of Survey April 13, 1739.
Land Office (Certificates, Patented, BA) MSA S1190, #1356, Davis's Hope, Dates: 1704–1965.
Description: 1351–1425, Accession No.: 40,004–1351/1425, MSA No.: S 1190–19, Location: 1/25/2/5.

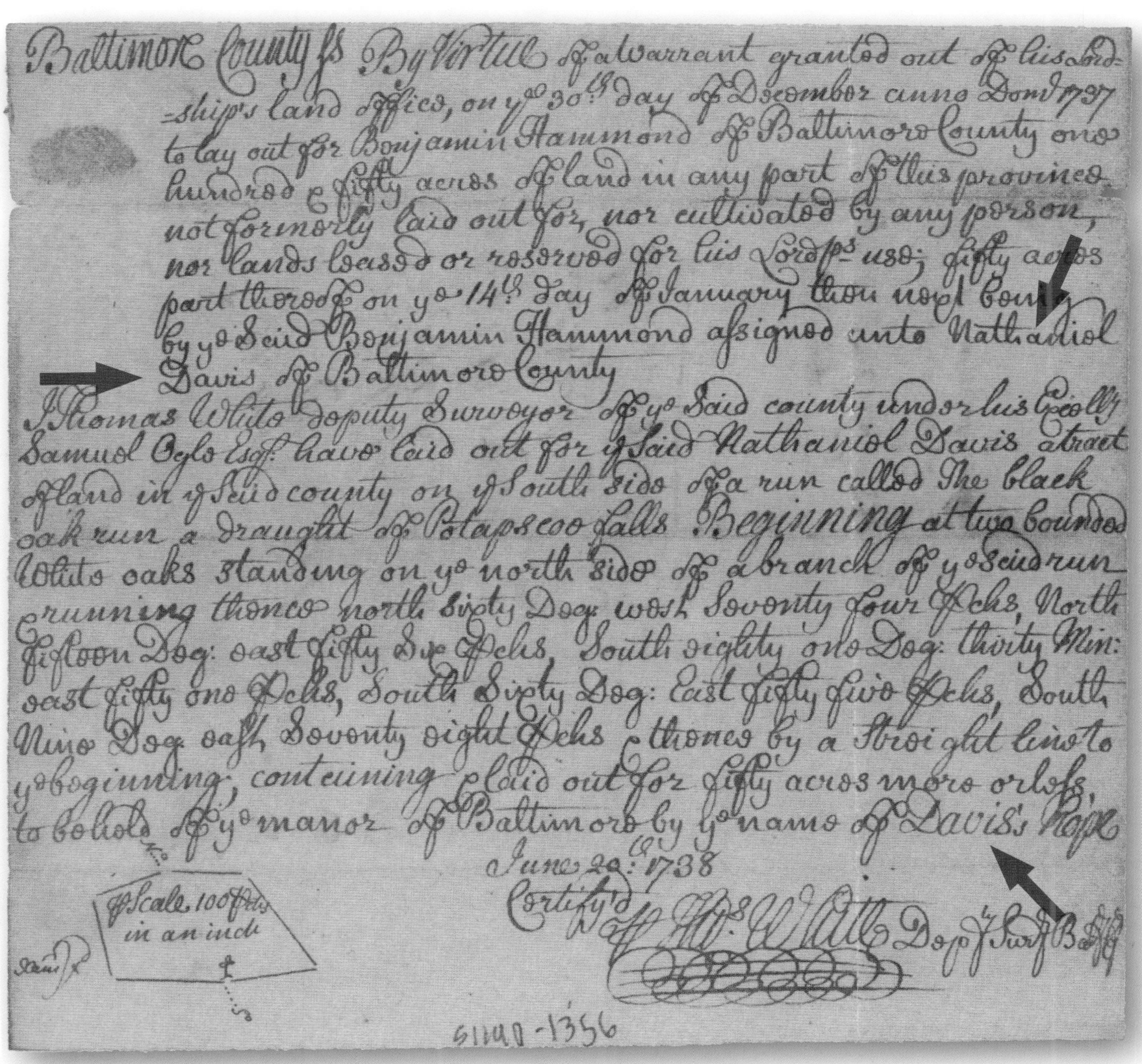
Baltimore County ss By Virtue of a warrant granted out of his Lordships land office, on ye 30th day of December anno Dom 1737 to lay out for Benjamin Hammond of Baltimore County one hundred & fifty acres of land in any part of this province not formerly laid out for, nor cultivated by any person, nor lands leased or reserved for his Lordsps use; fifty acres part thereof on ye 14th day of January then next Coming by ye Said Benjamin Hammond assigned unto Nathaniel Davis of Baltimore County

I Thomas White deputy Surveyor of ye Said county under his Excelly Samuel Ogle Esqr have laid out for ye Said Nathaniel Davis a tract of land in ye Said county on ye South side of a run called The black oak run a draught of Patapsco falls Beginning at two bounded white oaks standing on ye north side of a branch of ye said run running thence north Sixty Deg: west Seventy four Pchs, North fifteen Deg: east fifty Six Pchs, South eighty one Deg: thirty Min: east fifty one Pchs, South Sixty Deg: East fifty five Pchs, South Nine Deg: east Seventy eight Pchs thence by a Streight line to ye beginning, containing & laid out for fifty acres more or less, to be held of ye manor of Baltimore by ye name of Davis's Hope

June 20th 1738

Certifyd p Thos White Dep. Surv. B. Coty

Scale 100 Pchs in an inch

51140-1356

Back

Nathaniel Davis b. ca. 1700

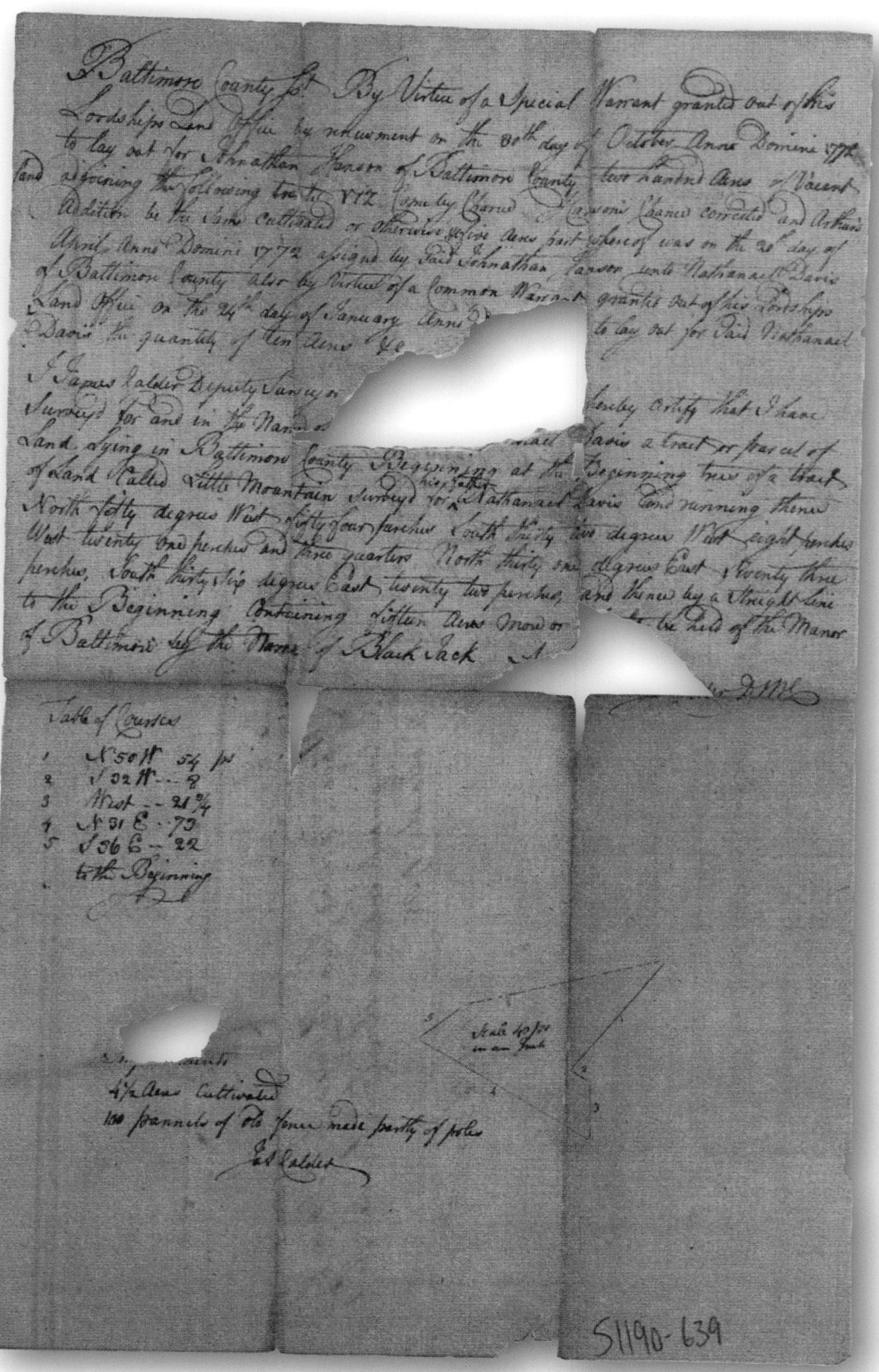

Baltimore County Sct. By Virtue of a Special Warrant granted out of his Lordships Land Office by renewment on the 30th day of October Anno Domini 1772 to lay out for Jonathan Hanson of Baltimore County two hundred Acres of Vacant land adjoining the following tracts [illegible] Addition be the same Cultivated or otherwise [illegible] Acres part whereof was on the 20th day of April Anno Domini 1772 assigned by said Jonathan Hanson unto Nathanael Davis of Baltimore County also by Virtue of a Common Warrant granted out of his Lordships Land Office on the 24th day of January Anno [illegible] to lay out for said Nathanael Davis the quantity of ten Acres &c.

I James Calder Deputy Surveyor [illegible] hereby Certify that I have Surveyed for and in the Nam[illegible] [illegible] Davis a tract or parcel of Land lying in Baltimore County Beginning at the Beginning tree of a tract of Land called Little Mountain surveyed for his father Nathanael Davis and running thence North fifty degrees West fifty four perches South thirty two degrees West eight perches West twenty one perches and three quarters North thirty one degrees East seventy three perches, South thirty six degrees East twenty two perches, and thence by a straight line to the Beginning Containing fifteen Acres more or [illegible] be held of the Manor of Baltimore by the Name of Black Jack

Table of Courses

1 N 50 W 54 p
2 S 32 W -- 8
3 West -- 21 3/4
4 N 31 E -- 73
5 S 36 E -- 22
to the Beginning

Scale 40 per. in an Inch

[illegible] Improvements
4½ Acres Cultivated
100 pannels of old fence made partly of poles
Jas Calder

S1190-639

A special warrant granted out of His Lordship's Land Office on the 30th day of October 1772, Baltimore County. This tract of land was granted to Nathaniel Davis, son of Nathaniel Davis, and adjoining a tract of land of his father's called "Little Mountain." Maryland State Archives, Annapolis, Maryland, Land Office (Certificate of Survey, Patented, BA), 1732, #2903 (MSA S 1190, 1-25-2-25).

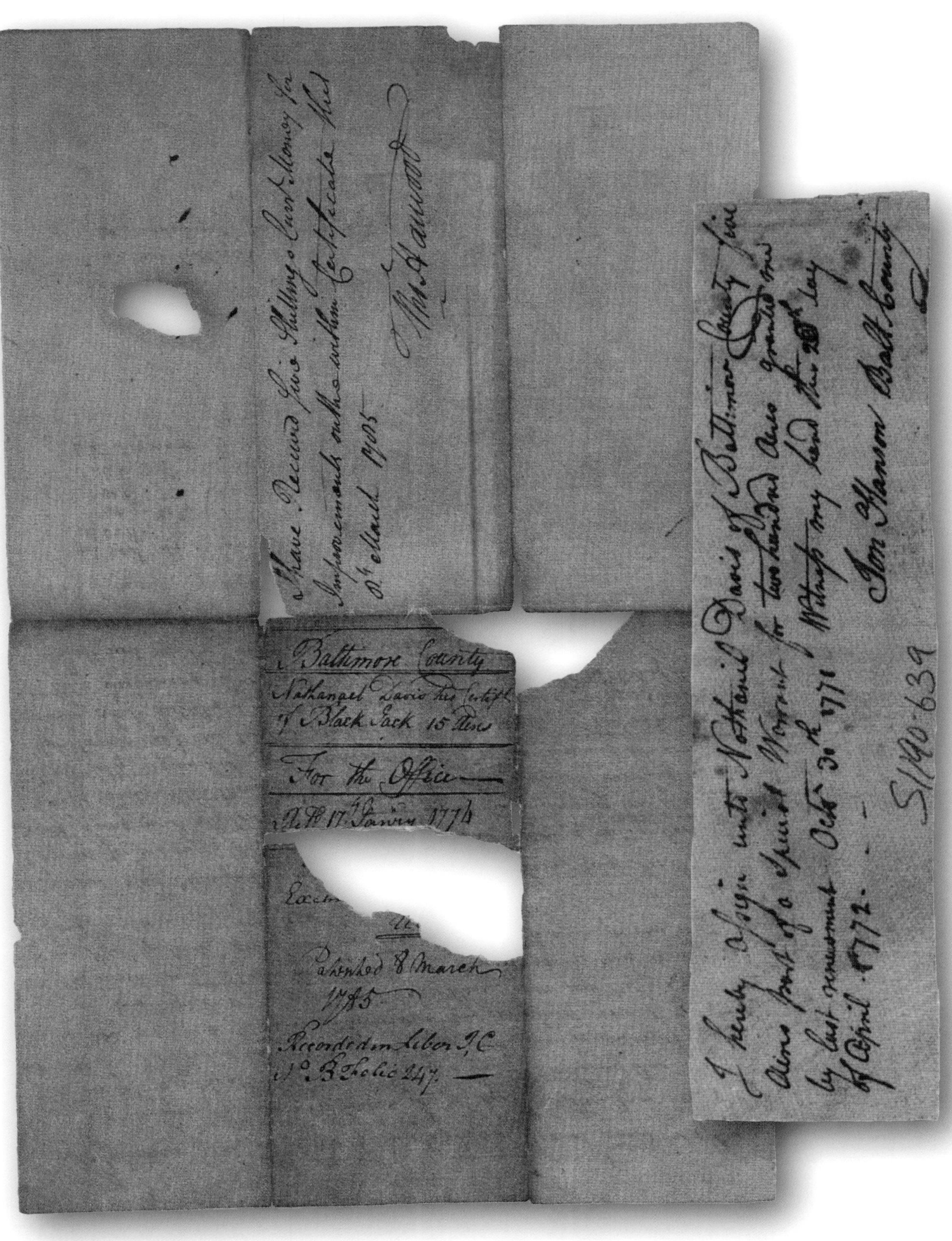

I have Received five Shillings Curt Money for Improvements on the within Certificate this 8th March 1785

Thos Harwood

Baltimore County
Nathaniel Davis his Certif of Black Jack 15 Acres
For the Office
E.H. 17th Janry 1774

Exam...

Patented 8 March 1785
Recorded in Liber I.C. No. B folio 247.

I hereby assign unto Nathaniel Davis of Baltimore County five Acres part of a Special Warrant for two hundred Acres granted me by last renewment Octr 30th 1771 Witness my hand this 20th day of April 1772.

Thos Hanson Balt County

S1190-639

Maryland State Archives, Annapolis, Maryland
Land Office (Certificates, Patented, BA) MSA S1190 #639 Black Jack, Dates: 1704–1965, Description: 601–675, Accession No.: 40,004–601/675, MSA No.: S 1190–9, Location: 1/25/1/91

Richard Davis b. April 1, 1734

Richard Davis of Baltimore County, Maryland, and Fayette County, Kentucky

Finding the father of Solomon Davis who died in 1801 in Kentucky was a monumental task. We knew that Solomon had a brother, Nathaniel Davis, who was killed in the same incident by slaves they were transporting. After gathering all the information we could about these two brothers, we knew that each man named a son, Richard Davis. So that was one clue that we could not overlook. Was Richard Davis their father's name?

Most people came to Kentucky from either Maryland or Virginia. There were several men named Richard Davis in both Maryland and Virginia. There was an indication that the slaves that Solomon and Nathaniel were carrying down the river were from Baltimore, Maryland. So thinking that Nathaniel and Solomon had returned "home" to buy slaves for trading in Kentucky, we began to look for records in that state first. We came upon a man, Richard Davis, who was born in 1734 in Baltimore, apparently married a Margaret Stocksdale, but how did we know this was the correct person? We searched as many Baltimore County records as possible, contacted Stocksdale family researchers, but did not find any probate records for this Richard Davis in Maryland. That was because we subsequently found that our Richard Davis had gone to Kentucky, probably with some or all of his sons.

Quite by accident, Clyde came upon some transcribed "burned records" at a local library in Paris, Kentucky, that indicated that a Richard Davis had died and a Margaret Davis was allotted her dower in Fayette County, Kentucky, 1799.[1] Fayette County was one of the original five counties that would become the state of Kentucky, but unfortunately, their probate records suffered a courthouse fire. Luckily, a DAR chapter located some of these books and had transcribed them.

Then Clyde found a court case in Fayette County that answered all of our questions. This case not only named Solomon Davis as a son of Richard, but named three other brothers, Nathaniel, Aaron, and Edward, with Edward as administrator of Richard Davis's estate. Several men gave depositions in the case, including Aaron Davis, Robert Tevis, and William Igo.[2] Then, in the Madison County records we found where Edward Davis had also acted as administrator for his mother Margaret in 1807.[3]

There are records that document Richard Davis's birth and death, but little information exists in between. He was listed in the baptismal records of St. Paul's Episcopal Church in Baltimore as having been born April 1, 1734.[4] His parents were listed as Nathaniel and Mary Davis.

Although a marriage record was not found, we know that he married Margaret Stocksdale because of the will and probate records of her father, Edward Stocksdale.[5] Two of their sons, Edward and Aaron Davis, were named in their grandfather Stocksdale's will, but Richard Davis was not. However, in the settling of the will, we find that "one Negro Woman named Kate and one Shilling Sterling [was] left by the deceased to Richard Davis."[6] It was customary that a son-in-law receive inherited property, rather than a daughter, because women did not have many legal rights in those days.

Richard and Margaret Davis's children were probably born during the 1750s and 1760s. The local church was named St. Thomas, but its early records do not exist. The only documented birth for the children that we have is the son Edward Davis, whose tombstone recorded that he was born March 12, 1759.[7] The other known sons were Aaron, Solomon, and Nathaniel. Edward may have been the oldest son, as he was not only mentioned first in his grandfather Stockdale's will, but he also served as administrator of his father's and mother's estates.

Much of the information that we have learned about Richard Davis has come after study of the area where he lived. He lived near what is now called Reisterstown, Maryland, in Baltimore County. In 1762 Richard Davis was appointed overseer of a road from "Josephus Murray's to St. Thomas Church, and from there to Worthington's Mill and Pipe Creek Road from the Great Falls of the Patapsco [River] where it crosses by Thomas Mathew's to the Conowangoe Wagon Road."[8] In 1763 Richard's name was on a list of taxable inhabitants in "Soldier's Delight Hundred," along with other familiar names, Stocksdale and Igo.[9] A "hundred" was a group of about one hundred families, the amount deemed necessary to form a militia to protect themselves from the Indians. Later, it became a civil division for taxation and such.

In 1768 Richard Davis patented a tract of land in Baltimore County called "Parrishes Folly."[10] By 1769 he sold the forty-acre tract to Nathan Chapman.[11] How he made his living between this time and the point when he went to Kentucky is not known. But he stayed in Maryland long enough to participate in the American Revolution. He was listed as 2nd Lieutenant Richard Davis in Company 7, of Soldiers Delight, Garrison Forest, Baltimore County, Mary 13, 1776.[12]

Another tidbit of information confirming his military service comes from a rejected pension application of John Boren, R1030.[13] Boren claimed to have served as a substitute for his uncles, Richard and Robert Davis. Boren's claim was not allowed because he failed to furnish proof of the alleged service as required by the pension laws.

At some point after the American Revolution, Richard Davis left his home in Maryland for Kentucky, most likely with his sons. There are tax lists for Fayette County, Kentucky, from 1787, and the name of Richard Davis appeared on these lists, but this man had no white males over sixteen years old. But in 1791, the names of Nathaniel, Edward, and Richard Davis appeared. This is the first year that we can definitely say that he was in Kentucky. There is also a Richard Davis in these records who owned land on Hickman Creek. He was listed as Richard Davis Junior. This man could be another son of Richard Davis, born 1734, but in those days the junior and senior designations did not necessarily mean father and son. It could mean uncle and nephew or just "younger" and "older." The last time that Richard Davis Senior appeared on a tax list, with one white male, four horses, and no land, was 1797.[14] Because he last appeared on this list of 1797 and one burned probate record in 1799, we can assume that he died in that time frame.

Why did he leave family in Maryland and go to Kentucky? There are many reasons our ancestors left civilized areas and went to the wilderness. One was that families had too many children to divide up the estate into acreages that would support a family. Another was that the cash crop of tobacco took out so many nutrients from the soil, that it became virtually sterile after a few years. Another was that land was fairly cheap in the wilderness areas. A man could sell a farm in an established state and buy a larger amount of property in the new state. Nathaniel Davis, father of Richard Davis, had remarried to a woman named Hannah. She held a life interest in the lands that Nathaniel Sr. had deeded to Nathaniel Jr. in 1783.[15] Nathaniel Davis Sr. had also deeded most of his property to sons Thomas Davis, Robert Davis, and Nathaniel Davis Jr. He did not deed any property to Richard Davis. For one or many of these reasons, Richard Davis left his home and relatives in Maryland and went to the wilderness of Kentucky.

A.H.

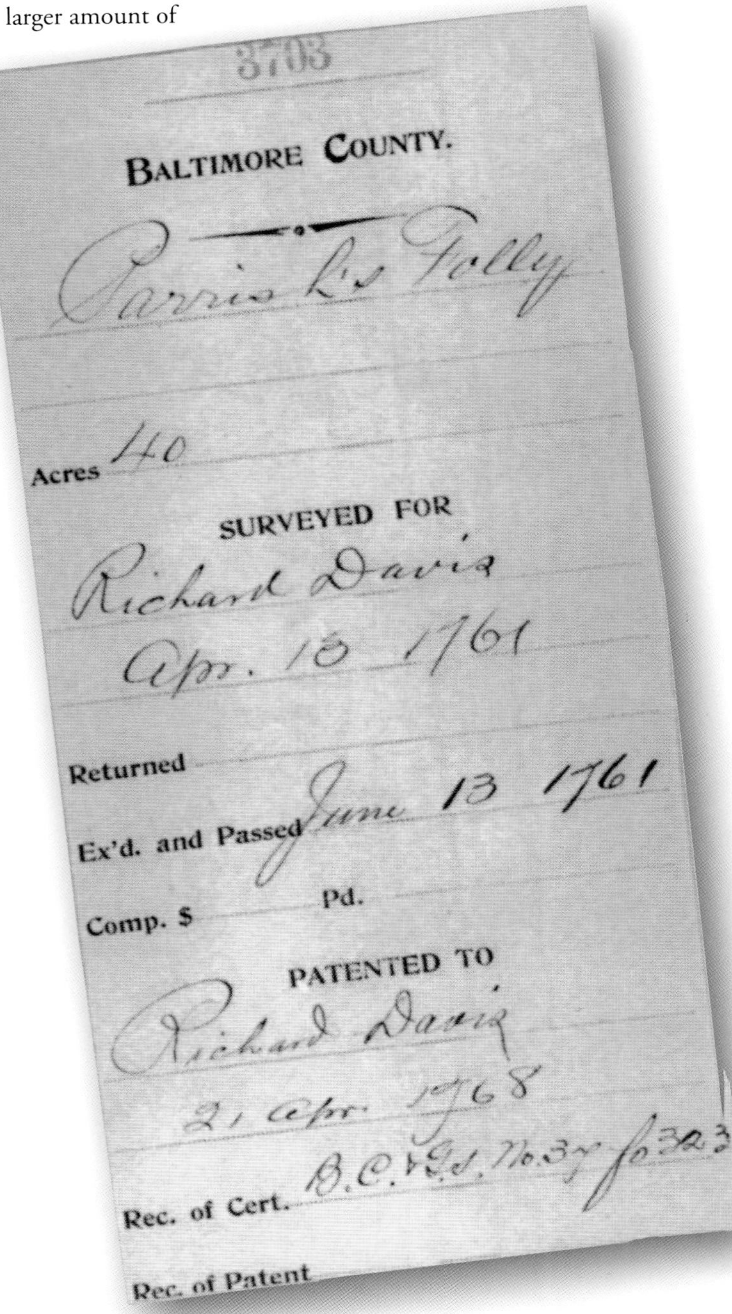
3703

BALTIMORE COUNTY.

Parrish's Folly

Acres 40

SURVEYED FOR

Richard Davis

Apr. 13 1761

Returned

Ex'd. and Passed June 13 1761

Comp. $ Pd.

PATENTED TO

Richard Davis

21 Apr. 1768

Rec. of Cert. B.C.&G.S. No. 37 fo 323

Rec. of Patent

Document dated April 21, 1768, for Parrish's Folly, a forty-acre tract in Baltimore County, Maryland, patented to Richard Davis, and sold to Nathan Chapman in 1769.

Notes

1. Kentucky Genealogical Records, Part 1, *Burnt Records of Fayette Co., Kentucky*, p. 201, compiled in 1967–1968 by the Bryan Station Chapter of the DAR of Fayette County, Kentucky, John Fox Jr. Memorial Library, Duncan Tavern, Paris, Kentucky.
2. Fayette Co., Kentucky, Circuit Court Case, James and Sarah Suddith vs. Edward Davis, administrator of Richard Davis, Book II, 1812–1819, Roll #987603, Box 247, Kentucky State Archives, Frankfort, Ky.
3. Madison Co., Kentucky, Probate Order Book C:455, FHL #183266.
4. Katherine L. Barnett, comp., *St. Paul's Register* (Baltimore: the author, 1971), 18.
5. Baltimore Co., Maryland, Will Book 3:376–77, Will of Edward Stocksdale, Maryland State Archives, Annapolis, Md.
6. Baltimore Co., Maryland, Accounts Book 11:278, Maryland State Archives, Annapolis, Md.
7. Kathy Vockery, *Cemetery Records of Madison County, Kentucky, Southern Section, Volume 2,* (Richmond, Kentucky: self-published, 1999), 24.
8. Henry C. Peden Jr., *Baltimore County Overseers of Roads, 1693–1793* (Westminster, Md.: Family Line Publications, 1992), 13.
9. Henry C. Peden Jr. *Inhabitants of Baltimore County, 1763–1774* (Westminster, Md.: Family Line Publications, 1989), 1.
10. Certificate, Liber BC & GS 37: folio 323; Patent, Liber BC & GS 33: folio 493, Maryland State Archives, Annapolis, Md.
11. Baltimore Co., Maryland, Deed Book A:484, FHL #13572.
12. Henry C. Peden Jr., *Revolutionary Patriots of Baltimore Town and Baltimore County, Maryland, 1775–1783* (Westminster, Md.: Family Line Publications, 1988), 67.
13. Rejected Pension Application of John Boren, R1030, National Archives, Washington, D.C.
14. Fayette Co., Kentucky, Tax Lists, FHL #7957.
15. Baltimore Co., Maryland, Deed Book N:64, FHL #13344.

RICHARD DAVIS b. April 1, 1734

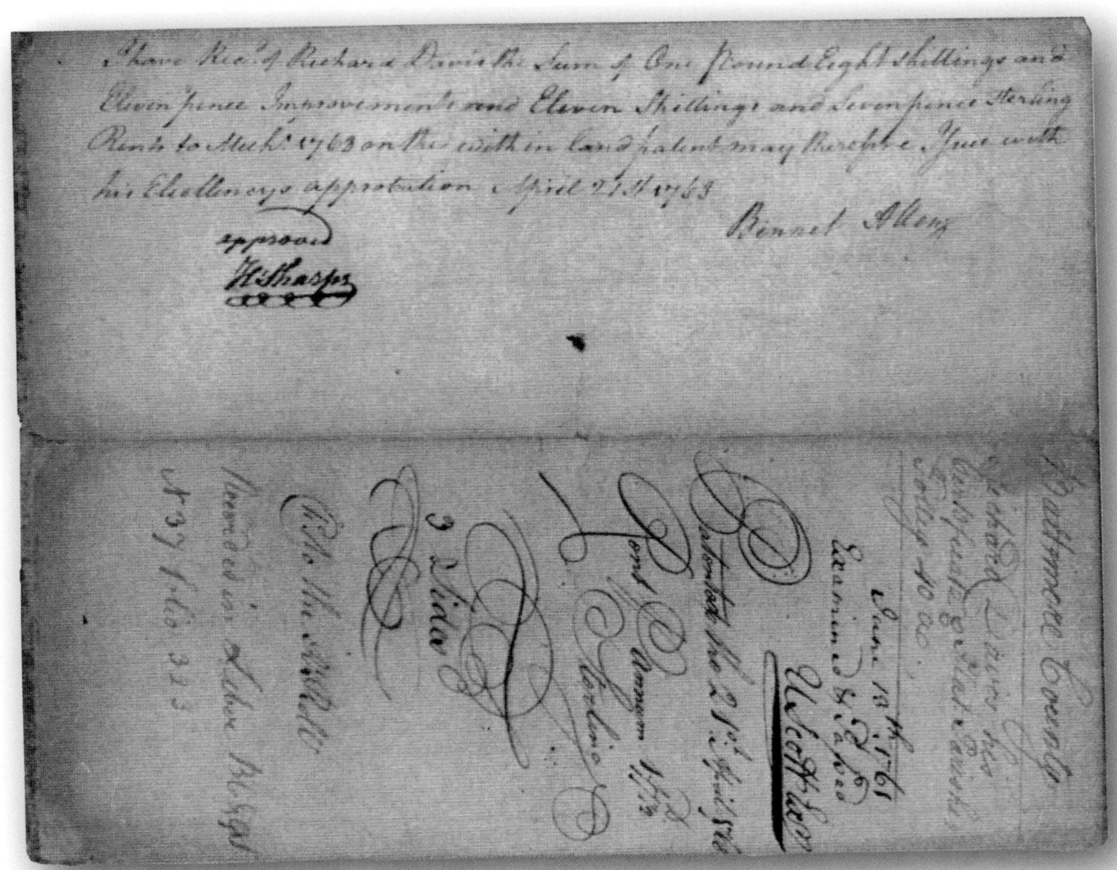

I have Rec.d of Richard Davis the Sum of One pound Eight shillings and Eleven pence Improvements and Eleven Shillings and Sevenpence Sterling Rents to Mich.s 1763 on the within land patent may therefore Issue with his Excellency's approbation April 21st 1763

Bennet Allen

approved
H. Sharpe

Land Patent of Richard Davis, Baltimore County, for Parrish's Folly, #3703, Maryland State Archives, Annapolis, Maryland

Baltimore County ss By Virtue of a Special Warrant Granted out of his Lordships land office bearing date ~~April the 13 1761~~ Feby 24th to lay out for Richard Davis of said county 40 acres of land lying and being in said county be the same cultivated or otherwise &c

I William Smith Deputy Surveyor of Baltimore County have Surveyed and Laid out for and in the Name of him the said Richard Davis a tract or parcel of land lying in the county aforesaid Beginning at the end of a hundred and twenty perches on the South sixty five degrees West one hundred and fifty perch line of a tract of land called White Oak Bottom and running thence South eighty five degrees West thirty perches North sixty seven degrees West forty four perches South twenty Nine degrees and thirty minutes West one hundred and four perches South forty one degrees East thirteen perches North Sixty degrees East thirty four perches South forty degrees East thirty perches and then with a straight line to the Beginning containing and laid out for forty acres more or less to be held of the manor of Baltimore [illegible]

April the 13th 1761

Parishes Folley

S 85 D W .. 30 ps
N 67 D W .. 44 ps
S 29 D & 30 M W 104 ps
S 41 D E .. 13 ps
N 60 D E .. 34 ps
S 40 D E .. 30 ps

40 ac

Scale 100 p in a [illegible]

Improvement &c

about 5 acres of Cleard Ground with 250 Pannils of Fence thereon and a Log House 12 foot by 10.

Wm Smith D S B C

422 *Journal and Correspondence*

C. S. C. Regulars or Militia in the Lower Counties to be thence transmitted to Philadelphia or else where they may be ordered by the Honorable Continental Congress. The Expence you will charge to the Province and render the Account to the Convention or Council of Safety as may be most convenient May 9th 1776

[Baltimore Committee to Council.]

In Committee Baltimore 13 May 1776.

Gentlemen. We recommend the companies as below, to be formed into a Battalion, and request your Honl Body to appoint Field officers for them :

1st Ad	John Cockey Owings 1st Lieutenant Richard Colegate 2d Lieutenant Joshua Cockey (of Edwd) Ensign	contg Privates.
2d Add	Samuel Owings (of Saml) Captain Alexander Wells 1st Lieutenant Thomas Owings 2d Lieutenant David Sutherland Ensign	containing 75 Privates
3d	Richard Owings (of Saml) Captain Joshua Porter 1st Lieutenant Benjamin Lawrence 2d Lieutenant James Barnes Ensign	containing 58 Privates
4th	Thomas Philips Captain Joshua Dorsey 1st Lieutenant John Chapman 2d Lieutenant Richard Shipley Ensign	containing 77 Privates
5th	Charles Carnan Captain William Hudson 1st Lieutenant Richard Marsh 2d Lieutenant Thomas Doyle Ensign	containing 79 Privates
6th	Nathaniel Stinchcomb Captain Joseph Gist 1st Lieutenant John Worthington Dorsey 2d Lieutenant Joshua Owings (of John) Ensign	containing 76 Privates
7th	Mordecai Hammond Captain Aquila Hooker 1st Lieutenant Richard Davis 2d Lieutenant Edward Parish (of Edwd) Ensign	containing 55 Privates
8th	Isaac Hammond Captain Christopher Owings 1st Lieutenant Saml Merryman Junr 2d Lieutn William Chinoweth Ensign	containing 75 Privates

We also requested you to grant commissions to the within mentd Gentlemen, except to Capt Benj. Nicholsons company,

The page shown from the Journal of Correspondence is from the Archives of Maryland, Volume 11, p. 422, Archives of Maryland Online, <http://www.msa.md.gov>. The underlined names are neighbors of Richard Davis in Reisterstown, Maryland.

NATHANIEL DAVIS b. ca. 1750–1760

An Early Kentucky Slave Trader

Nathaniel Davis was the son of Richard Davis and Margaret Stocksdale Davis. That Nathaniel Davis was a brother to Solomon Davis is proven by a court case in Fayette County, Kentucky, involving their father's estate. Robert Tevis testified that Edward Davis, their father's administrator, had sold some iron, which had belonged to his brother, Nate.[1]

Nathaniel was born probably 1750–60 in Baltimore County, Maryland, as that was where his parents lived during that time. His marriage was recorded in Baltimore County, Maryland, when he married Margaret Hutson on February 16, 1785.[2] By about 1791 he was listed in the tax lists of Fayette County, Kentucky, where he migrated with his father Richard, his mother Margaret, and several brothers. He finally settled in Montgomery County, Kentucky, and raised a family.

Nathaniel, along with his brother Solomon, was killed in May of 1801, near Smithville, Kentucky, while taking slaves down the Ohio River (see page 176). They had purchased the slaves in Baltimore and were taking them to New Orleans to sell for high prices. Nathaniel's death left his wife Margaret pregnant, with several under-age children. His inventory, filed in Montgomery County, Kentucky on September 7, 1801, listed six slaves and their valuation, several owned jointly by Nathaniel:[3]

One Negro Woman named Fillis	$80.00
One half a negro Girl named Vilett	$30.00
One negro Woman named Raney	$70.00
One half a negro woman named Fillis	$40.00
One Negro Girl named Sopha	$35.00
One Negro Girl named Becky	$25.00

The estate was not settled until 1815–1816, when the Montgomery County court assigned three commissioners to take an inventory and to allot the property to Margaret and the children. In the intervening years the slaves had grown in number and value. By 1815 there were now ten slaves worth $2,775.[4]

On March 1, 1816, the commissioners allotted Margaret Davis her dower and a portion of the property and slaves to legatees Richard Davis, Betsy McClain, Solomon Davis, Nathaniel Davis, Daniel Davis, Levi Davis, Peggy Davis, and Polly Igo.[5] Polly Igo married probably in 1809, as there was a reference in the probate settlement of Nathaniel Davis that Thomas Igo had already received a Negro girl in that year.[6]

In the final division of her husband's estate in 1816, Margaret Davis received the Negroes Fillis, Ann, and Scott, worth $950. In 1820 there was a court case in Bourbon County that listed all of the heirs of Nathaniel Davis in a case involving slaves.

> To the Sheriff of Bourbon County Greeting:
> We command you to Take William Knox if he be found within your Bailiwick and him safely keep… to answer unto Richard Davis, Thomas Igo and Polly his wife (late Polly Davis), Daniel Davis, Thomas McClain and Elizabeth, his wife (late Elizabeth Davis), Nathaniel Davis, Solomon Davis, Levi Davis, Fielding Lucas and Peggy his wife (late Peggy Davis), Heirs and representatives of Nathaniel Davis, deceased, of a plea of Detinue for the detention of a negro woman Slave named Phillis age 45 years… of value of $500 dollars, one Negro boy Slave named David,…and one Negro girl slave named Phillis… Two thousand dollars [total]…22 Dec 1820….[7]

Detinue is a legal term, which means that someone's property has been improperly detained. The case was sent by change of venue to Harrison County, but no further records were found.

Nathaniel and Margaret Davis's children were

1. Richard Davis, who moved to Gibson County, Indiana, by 1820; died in Sevier County, Arkansas, August 3, 1840.[8]
2. Mary "Polly" Davis, born about 1788; married Thomas Igo by 1809; died in Bath County, Kentucky, after 1860.[9] Their children were Daniel, Nathaniel, Jack, Polly, William, Levi, and Thomas, born between 1810 and 1825.
3. Daniel Davis.
4. Elizabeth "Betsy" Davis married Thomas McClain prior to 1816; died in Platte County, Missouri, after 1860. Their children were Rachel, Lucinda, John Thompson, Levi D., Elizabeth, Louisa "Eliza," and Malinda, born between 1816 and 1832.[10] Thomas and Betsy migrated first to Boone County, Missouri, then to Platte County, Missouri, by 1837.[11] Betsy died after 1860, and Thomas McClain died in 1871 in Missouri. Some of their descendants migrated to Kansas, Wyoming, and Washington.
5. Nathaniel Davis, born about 1796.
6. Solomon Davis, born ca. 1760–1770.
7. Levi Davis, b. 1798–1800; died before May 1838 in Red River County, Texas. Levi died while looking for some runaway slaves.[12] He was believed to have been murdered by a man named Page and two others. The accused were hanged from the "hanging tree" by locals.[13] Levi's wife was Catharine Hopkins, who

Tuesday This 13th day of October 1801 (83)

At a court called and held for the Trial of three slaves vizt yallow John Bob and Black John the property of the Heirs of Nathaniel Davis & Solomon Davis Deceased who were charged with the murder of the said Nathaniel and solomon davis

Present David Caldwell, William Prince & William Dobbins } Gentlemen Justices

Ordered that court adjourn till tomorrow morning ten oclock David Caldwell

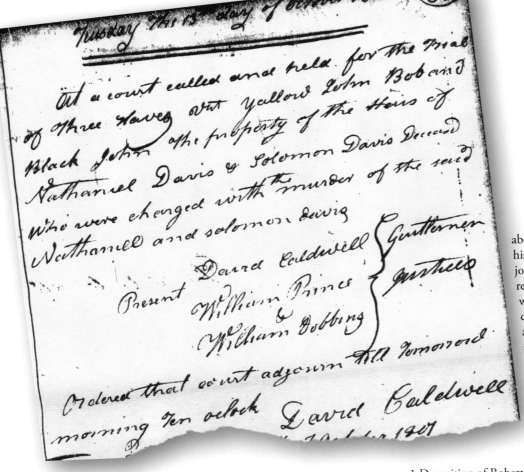

Livingston County Court of Quarter Sessions Order Book 83–93, 13 October 1801. This is the first document referring to the murder of Nathaniel and Solomon Davis by three slaves. This and related documents appear on pages 166 and 167 in Solomon Davis's biography.

married twice more. Levi and Catharine Davis's children were James Nathaniel, Margaret A., Richard H., and Elizabeth A., born between 1831 and 1837.[14]

8. Margaret "Peggy" Davis, born about 1801; died 1854 in Gibson County, Indiana. She married Fielding Lucas, a veteran of the War of 1812, in 1819 in Gibson County.[15] They had the following children: Minerva Lucas, Levi Lucas, Francis Lucas, Frances Lucas, America Lucas, Louisa Lucas, Romelia Baker Lucas, and Thomas Lucas, born between 1822 and 1839.[16]

In the 1820 federal census of Gibson County, there was a Richard Davis, head of the household, with four other males, all engaged in agriculture.[17] "Fieldan Lukes" is on the same page. It is possible that Richard Davis, son of Nathaniel, had all of his brothers in his house: Daniel, Nathaniel, Solomon, and Levi. At some point in time, Richard, Solomon, and Levi moved to Sevier County, Arkansas, by 1830, as Levi Davis had six males living with him.[18] In the 1840 federal census Richard Davis had two males 50–60 and one male 40–50 living in his house, plus thirteen slaves.[19]

One might wonder why the Davis family left Indiana for Arkansas. History tells us about the Missouri Compromise, a federal law passed that made all of the states in the Louisiana Territory free from slavery, with the exception of Missouri and Arkansas. Indiana, once a haven for slavery, became opposed to the practice about 1826.[20]

Nathaniel Davis, the father of the above eight children, met the same fate as his brother Solomon. At some point in their journey down the Ohio River, several slaves rebelled, killing their masters. The slaves were tried and some were hung for the crime of murder. Some of the slaves testified against the defendants. The slave trade was a dangerous one, and the untimely deaths of these two Davis brothers proved it. The bad luck was passed on to the next generation when Levi Davis was killed while searching for runaway slaves in Texas. *A.H.*

Notes

1. Deposition of Robert Tevis, 12 Aug. 1805, Fayette County, Kentucky, Circuit Court Case, James and Sarah Suddith vs. Edward Davis, administrator of Richard Davis, Book II, 1812–1819, Roll #987603, Box 247, Kentucky State Archives, Frankfort, Ky.
2. Robert Barnes, comp., *Maryland Marriages, 1778–1800* (Baltimore: Genealogical Publishing Co., 1978).
3. Montgomery Co., Kentucky, Will Book A:78–81, Kentucky State Archives, Frankfort, Ky.
4. Montgomery Co., Kentucky, Will Book B:131, Kentucky State Archives, Frankfort, Ky.
5. Montgomery Co., Kentucky, Will Book B:134–37, Kentucky State Archives, Frankfort, Ky.
6. Ibid.
7. Bourbon Co., Kentucky, Court Case #11314, Nathaniel Davis's heirs vs. William Knox, Kentucky State Archives, Frankfort, Ky.
8. Information compiled by Fran McLain and Judith Raven.
9. 1860 federal census, Kentucky, Bath Co., p. 147.
10. Information compiled by Fran McLain.
11. W.M. Paxton, *Annals of Platte County, Missouri* (Kansas City, Mo.: Hudson & Kimberly, 1897), 514–15.
12. Eugene W. Bowers, *Red River Dust: True Tales of an American Yesterday* (Waco, Tex.: Word Books, 1968), 137–39.
13. Ibid.
14. Information compiled by Gwen Salsig, Dallas, Oregon.
15. Indiana Marriages to 1850, Ancestry.com.
16. Names of Lucas children from Drusilla Cochran Sheldon, Corpus Christi, Tex.
17. 1820 federal census, Indiana, Gibson Co., p. 246.
18. 1830 federal census, Arkansas, Sevier Co., p. 165.
19. 1840 federal census, Arkansas, Sevier Co., p. 161.
20. "History of Slavery in Indiana," <http://en.wikipedia.org/wiki/History_of_slavery_in_Indiana>.

Solomon Davis b. ca. 1760–1770

Death by Occupation

Solomon Davis was a man of the frontier, venturing into Kentucky well before statehood. At that time Kentucky was primitive, inhabited by Indians, yet the white settlers were beginning to leave their relatively safe eastern homes and arrive in Kentucky in droves. The population of Kentucky in 1790 was 61,133 whites and 12,430 slaves.[1] Land was cheap. A man could sell a Virginia or Maryland farm for quite a profit and buy a larger portion of land in Kentucky. Solomon saw a need for slaves to clear trees and to do hard labor on these new farms, so he began a business with his brother Nathaniel Davis as slave traders, bringing slaves to areas that needed them.[2]

> In May 1801, Solomon and Nathaniel Davis of Clark County, Kentucky, purchased slaves in Baltimore, marched them overland through Maryland and the southwest corner of Pennsylvania and then took them down the Ohio River on flatboats to sell in Spanish Louisiana. Near Smithland, Kentucky, some of the slaves revolted, killed both Davises, and escaped. Within two months, local residents had captured the slaves and put six on trial in Eddyville, Kentucky, for the murders. The court found three guilty and executed them. This extraordinary event is the first known case in the Ohio Valley in which enslaved African Americans rose up against slave traders who were taking them down the river.[3]

Solomon was born probably 1760–1770 and came to Kentucky by at least 1790. He married Sarah Blackwell in Madison County, Kentucky, around Christmas of 1791.[4] She was the daughter of William Blackwell, who died and left a will in 1775 in Albemarle County, Virginia.[5] The children of Solomon Davis and Sarah Blackwell Davis were Peggy, Polly, John, Spicy, and Richard, all born between 1792 and 1801.[6]

In late December of 1793 Solomon found a stray horse in Madison County on Otter Creek.[7] This is where his descendants would live for the next eighty years. In 1794 Solomon Davis was listed as a private in Price's Battalion of the Kentucky Mounted Volunteers.[8] These units were called out to protect settlers and make raids of retribution on Indian villages.

After the murders of Solomon and Nathaniel, the slaves were executed after a trial in the court at Lexington.[9] As slaves were considered to be valuable personal property, Sarah and friends must have petitioned the governor for loss of the executed slaves as the Kentucky legislature enacted a law in December 1802 for the relief of "the heirs of Solomon Davis." They were granted $300, which would equate to $4,000 in today's money.[10]

Sarah Davis was appointed guardian of Peggy, John, Polly, Spicy, and Richard Davis in Clark County, Kentucky.[11] These children sued Sarah and her husband James Suddith in 1819 in Madison County court. By this time Polly had married Robert Brooks, Spicy married Thomas Lanter, and Peggy Davis, who by now was deceased, had married Henry Brooks and had a child Levisa who was under age twenty-one. Sarah and James Suddith had moved from Clark County to Henry County, Kentucky. The children contended that by Kentucky law, slaves could be inherited from the male owner only, not the female. Thus, they were asking for a portion of their father's slaves and also a portion of their grandfather's (William Blackwell) slaves. The inventory of Solomon Davis in this court case included a watch, a looking glass, three knives and three forks, one brown mare, and the following slaves: Stephen a boy, Bob, John Merrick, John Brown, and Jack. The latter three were half-owned by Nathaniel Davis. The court decided in 1825 to give one girl named Harriott to the children of Solomon Davis and the defendants, James and Sarah Suddith, were legally entitled to three slaves: Simon, Phillis, and Stephen.[12]

Nathaniel Davis's probate papers were filed in Montgomery County, Kentucky. His wife was Margaret and his children were Richard, Polly, Daniel, Elizabeth, Solomon, Levi, and Peggy. There was a marriage in Baltimore for a Nathaniel Davis and Margaret Hutson February 17, 1785. Later, some of this family moved to Gibson County, Indiana, as Peggy was married there in 1819.

Solomon Davis chose to try his hand at a risky business, the slave trade. Instead of choosing to *(continued on page 178)*

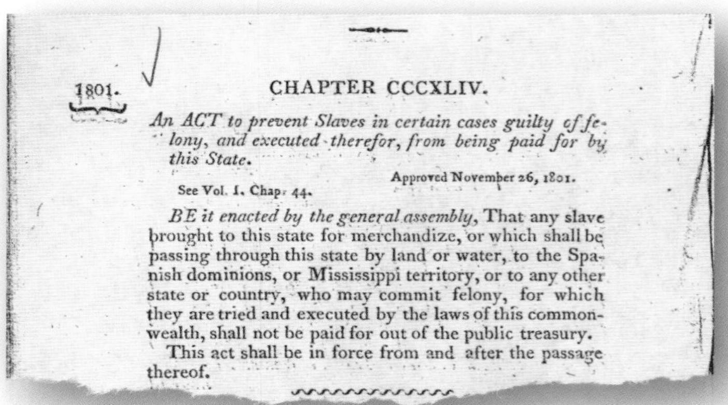

1801.

CHAPTER CCCXLIV.

An ACT to prevent Slaves in certain cases guilty of felony, and executed therefor, from being paid for by this State.

Approved November 26, 1801.

See Vol. I. Chap. 44.

BE it enacted by the general assembly, That any slave brought to this state for merchandize, or which shall be passing through this state by land or water, to the Spanish dominions, or Mississippi territory, or to any other state or country, who may commit felony, for which they are tried and executed by the laws of this commonwealth, shall not be paid for out of the public treasury.

This act shall be in force from and after the passage thereof.

An Act to prevent Slaves in certain cases guilty of felony, and executed therefor, from being paid for by this State, *approved November 26, 1801. Provided by The Filson Club, Louisville, Kentucky, from* The Statute Law of Kentucky; with Notes, Prælection, and Observations of the Public Acts, *pp. 428–429, by William Littell, Esq., 1811.*

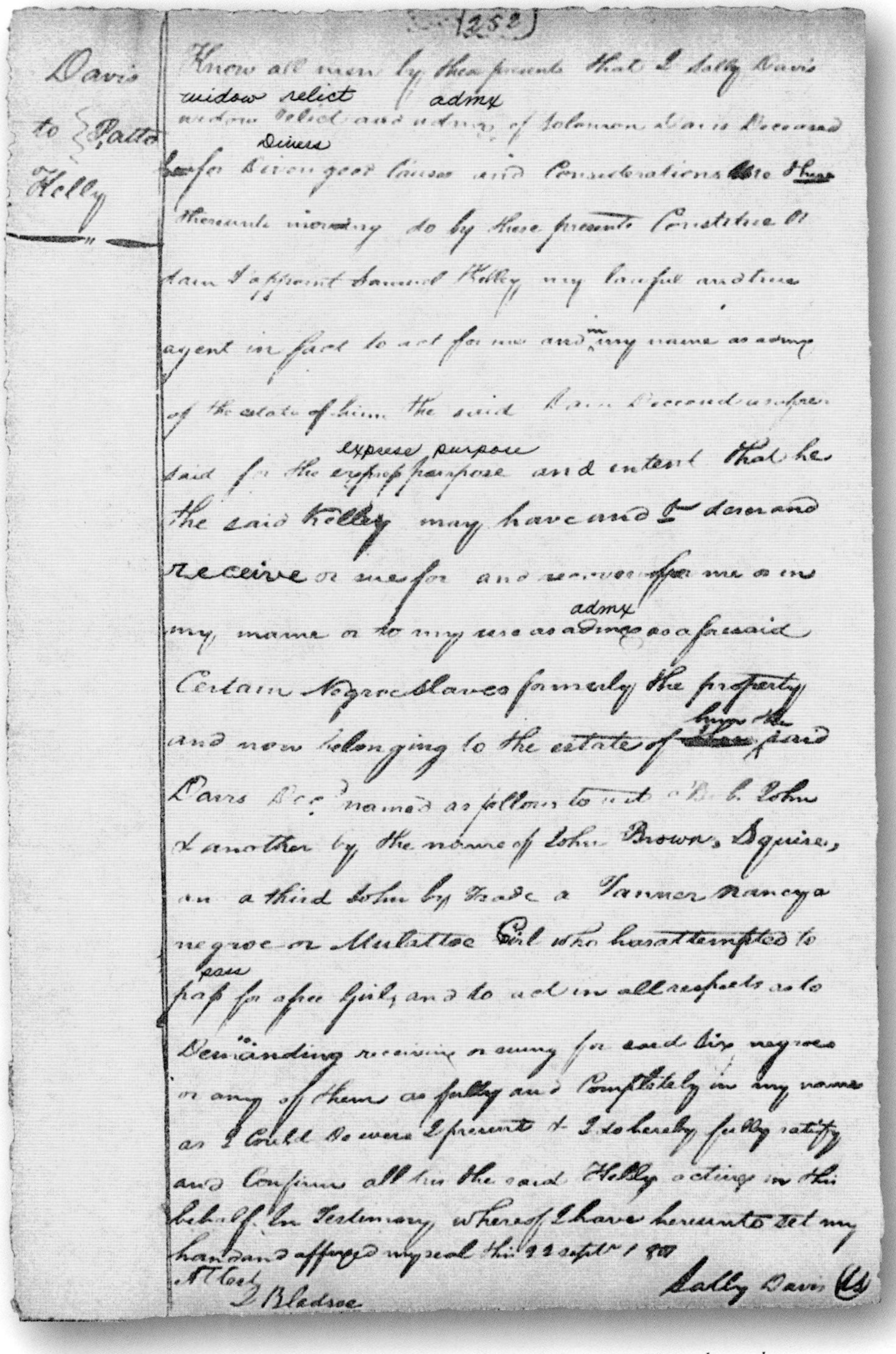

Page 252 Clark County, Kentucky. This probably came from Clark County, Kentucky, probate or will book. It is a power of attorney.

Know all men by these presents that I Sally Davis widow relict and admx [administratrix] of Solomon Davis Deceased for Divers good Causes and Considerations to these thereunto moving do by these presents Constitute ordain & appoint Samuel Kelley my lawful and true agent in fact to act for me in my name as admx of the estate of him, the said Davis Deceased aforesaid for the express purpose and interest that he the said Kelley may have and demand receive or sue for and recover for me or in my name or to my use as admx as aforesaid Certain Negroe slaves formerly the property and now belonging to the estate of him the said Davis Decd named as follows to wit: Bob, John & another by the name of John Brown, Squire, and a third John by Trade a Tanner Nancy a negroe or Mulattoe Girl who has attempted to pass for a free Girl, and to act in all respects as to Demanding recovering or suing for said six negroes or any of them as fully and Completely in my name as I could Do were I present & I so hereby fully ratify and Confirm all his the said Kelly actings in this behalf. In Testimony whereof I have hereunto set my hand and affix my seal this 22 Septr 1801.

Attest: I [or J] Bledsoe Sally Davis [seal]

Solomon Davis b. ca. 1760–1770

Livingston County Court of Quarter Sessions Order Book 83–93, 13 October 1801. The three documents on this page and the first document on the next page are court records in October 1801 for the charges and sentences relating to the murders of Nathaniel and Solomon Davis. The Negro slave Bob was sentenced to receive fifteen lashes for false testimony; one of the three accused slaves was sentenced to be "hung by the neck till he be dead, dead, dead"; and charges were dropped against Nancy Lewis for murder or accessory to murder.

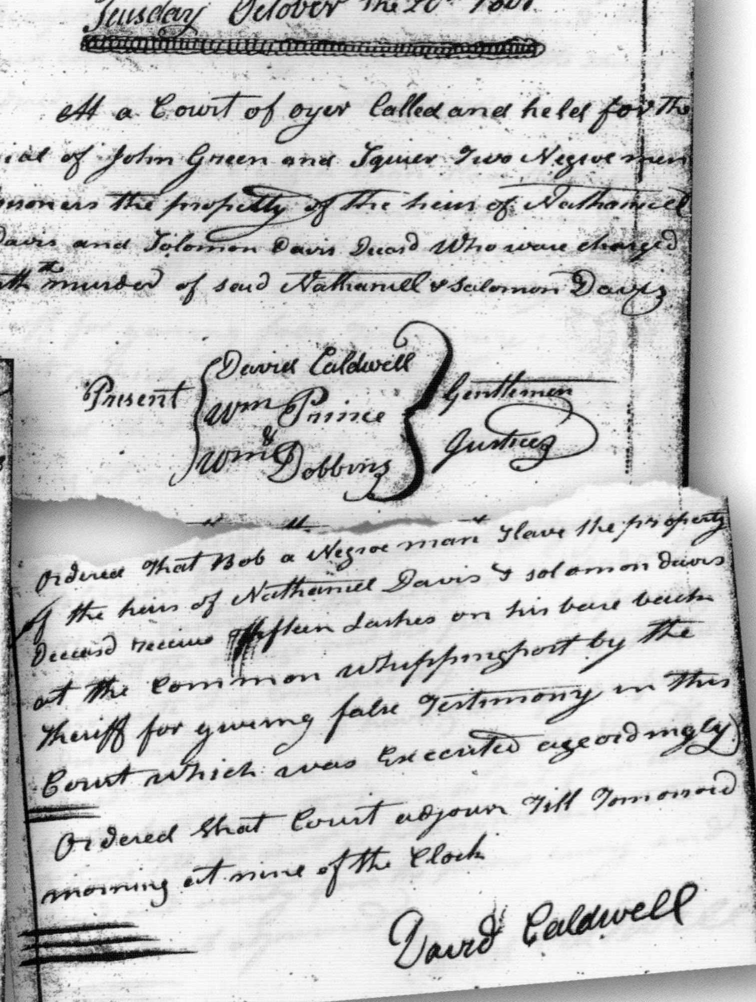

Tuesday October the 20th 1801

At a Court of oyer called and held for the Trial of John Green and Squier Two Negroe men Prisoners the property of the heirs of Nathaniel Davis and Solomon Davis Decd Who were charged with the murder of said Nathaniel & Solomon Davis

Present David Caldwell, Wm Prince & Wm Dobbins Gentlemen Justices

Ordered that Bob a Negroe man Slave the property of the heirs of Nathaniel Davis & Solomon Davis Deceased receive fifteen lashes on his bare back at the Common whipping post by the Sheriff for giving false Testimony in this Court which was executed accordingly.

Ordered that Court adjourn till tomorrow morning at nine of the Clock

David Caldwell

Tuesday the 13th day of October 1801 (83)

At a court called and held for the Trial of three slaves viz yallow John Bob and Black John the property of the Heirs of Nathaniel Davis & Solomon Davis Deceased Who were charged with the murder of the said Nathaniel and solomon davis

Present David Caldwell, William Prince & William Dobbins Gentlemen Justices

Ordered that court adjourn till tomorrow morning Ten oclock

David Caldwell

buy land and eke out an existence on the Kentucky frontier, he decided to make a profitable living. So, the short life of Solomon Davis ended in the cold waters of the Ohio River one spring day. His business, though lucrative, had finished him. *A.H.*

Notes

1. Lewis Collins, *History of Kentucky* (Covington, Ky.: Collins & Co., 1878) 1:22.
2. Pen Bogert, "Sold for My Account: The Early Slave Trade Between Kentucky and the Lower Mississippi Valley," *Ohio Valley History: Journal of the Cincinnati Historical Society* 2, no. 1 (2002): 3–16.
3. Ibid.
4. Bill and Kathy Vockery, *Madison County Marriages, 1786–1822* (Richmond, Ky.: self-published, 1993), 21.
5. Madison Co., Kentucky, Court Case #10955, Solomon Davis's heirs vs. Solomon Davis's Administrators, Kentucky State Archives, Frankfort, Ky.
6. Ibid.
7. Karen Mauer Green, *The Kentucky Gazette, 1787–1800* (Baltimore: Gateway Press, 1983), 92.
8. Virgil D. White, *Index to Volunteer Soldiers, 1784–1811* (Waynesboro, Tenn.: National Historical Pub., 1987).
9. Kentucky Legislature Session Laws, 1802, fiche 18:49–50, "An Act for the benefit of the heirs of Solomon Davis, deceased," 13 Dec. 1802, Kentucky State Archives, Frankfort, Ky.
10. Ibid.
11. Clark Co., Kentucky, Order Book 2:507–08, film #988284, Kentucky State Archives, Frankfort, Ky.
12. Madison Co., Kentucky, Court Case #10955, Solomon Davis's heirs vs. Solomon Davis's Administrators, Kentucky State Archives, Frankfort, Ky.

Wednesday October 21st 1801

Whereupon it is considered by the court that he be taken back to the Goal from whence he was brought there to be kept till the 21st day of November next and from thence taken by the Sheriff to the place of Execution and between the hours of Ten in the morning and four in the Evening he be hung by the neck till he be dead dead dead—

And the court valued said slave to two hundred and seventyfive Dollars and the court adjourned

David Caldwell

At a court of Enquiry called and held for the Examination of Nancy Lewis a black woman who claimed her freedom by suit, and who was charged with murder or being accessary to the murder of Nathaniel & Solomon Davis; [illegible] Barr in custody of the sheriff and plead not Guilty to the charge and no person appearing to prosecute it is considered by the court that she be discharged; And having sued for her freedom ordered that she be hired out by the Sheriff for the best price that can be had from time to time till the suit is determined and take bond and security from the persons hiring and the court adjourned

David Caldwell

Monday October the 19th 1801 (88)

The Court met agreeable to the adjournment of Saturday last.

Present { David Caldwell, William Prince, William Dobbins } Gentlemen Justices

This day came the attorney for the Commonwealth and Black John one of the prisoners who was charged with murder being led to the bar in custody of the sheriff and his charge being read to him it was demanded of him whether he was guilty or not Guilty he said he was in no wise thereof guilty and would be tried by God and his country Therefore Let a jury Come who neither

On Monday, October 19, 1801, the court of the Commonwealth of Kentucky demanded the plea of Black John, one of the slaves accused of murdering Nathaniel and Solomon Davis. "… he said he was in no wise thereof guilty and would be tried by God and his country."

LOUISVILLE,

DECEMBER 7, 1801.

Extract of a letter to the Editor, dated,

"EDDYVILLE, (Ky) Nov. 20th, 1801.

"To-morrow three negroes are to be hung here, for kill-[ing their] Masters on the Ohio."

From The Farmer's Library, *December 7, 1801. The last line of the item reads "[kill]ing their Masters on the Ohio." Courtesy of Pen Bogert, Reference Specialist, Filson Historical Society Library, Louisville, Kentucky.*

CHAP. IX.

AN ACT for the benefit of the heirs of Solomon Davis, deceased.

Approved December 13, 1802.

Preamble.

WHEREAS ſeveral ſlaves, the property of Nathaniel and Solomon Davis, were convicted of murder, before the court of quarter ſeſſions of Levingſton county, at the fall term held in the year 1801; and whereas it appears that all the ſaid ſlaves were executed according to the judgment of ſaid court, except one by the name of Yellow John, the property of Solomon Davis, whoſe execution was ſuſpended by the governor, in conſequence of a petition preſented to him for a reprieve of ſaid Yellow John, but the governor refuſing finally to pardon the ſaid ſlave, he was executed after the paſſage of a law at the laſt ſeſſion of the aſſembly, entitled 'an act to prevent ſlaves in certain caſes guilty of felony and executed therefor from being paid for by this ſtate;' in con-

[50]

ſequence of which law the auditor refuſes to to iſſue a warrant on the treaſury for payment of the ſaid ſlave: For remedy whereof,

Auditor to iſſue a warrant.

§ 1. *Be it enacted by the general aſſembly,* that the auditor is hereby empowered and required to iſſue a warrant on the treaſury for the ſum of three hundred dollars, the valuation of ſaid ſlave by the court; and the treaſurer ſhall pay the ſame accordingly.

This act ſhall be in force from its paſſage.

Middle and bottom: Kentucky Legislature Session Laws 1802, Kentucky State Archives, pages 49–50, Fiche 18. According to The Statute Law of Kentucky; with Notes, Prælection, and Observations of the Public Acts, *pp. 94–95, by William Littell, Esq., 1811: "This act authorized them [the heirs of Solomon Davis] to receive the price of a slave sentenced to death before the passage of the act of 1801,* (Vide *Vol. II, chapter 344,* ante) *but executed afterwards."*

SOLOMON DAVIS b. ca. 1760–1770

Governor General Executive Journal, 10 November 1801, Kentucky Department for Libraries and Archives.

Novr. 10 It having been suggested that a certain person of colour named Yellow John who had been convicted as a slave for being concerned in murdering a person who was conveying him from Maryland to the Spanish dominions, was in reality a free man, the governor in order to afford time for ascertaining the truth of this assertion, ...

NOTICE,

THAT ſome time laſt winter, a Gentleman who did not make his name known to me, left in my poſſeſſion a negro Boy about ſixteen years old, named Simon. The gentleman informed me that the Boy was to be uſed as a witneſs againſt the negroes who murdered the Daviſes, upon the the Miſſiſſippi laſt year, and would be called for in the courſe of a ſhort time. No application having been made for the Boy, I am induced to believe that the lawful owner don't know where to find him. The Boy ſays that he was purchaſed in Baltimore by the ſaid Daviſes; and he may be had by the legal owner on application to me, about five or ſix miles from Louiſville, Jefferſon County, Kentucky.

JOHN EDWARDS.

April 14th 1802. [66—tf

The Farmer's, Library 6 May 1802, Louisville, Kentucky.

Kentucky State Archives, Frankfort, Kentucky, Fayette County Circuit Court, Book II 1812 –1819, James & Sarah Sudduth v. Edward Davis, Administrator of Richard Davis, Roll # 987603 Box #247

Sudduth & ux
to } Bill
Davis &c 247

filed 7th April 1804
Copied and Spas Issued
one to Fayette & Madison
June contd July rule for
answ. Aug Bill for conf
& set for hearg Septr contd
1805 Feby & Mar contd
June leave to take
depos Septr refered to
McKinnie 1806 Mar
contd June Contd
Septr order refering [illegible]
[illegible]

June contd Septr contd
1808 Jany March June &
Sept contd - 1809 March
June & Sept contd & contd
on rules in 1810 Jany contd
March, June & Septr contd
1811 March & June contd

SOLOMON DAVIS b. ca. 1760–1770

Kentucky State Archives, Frankfort, Kentucky, Fayette County Circuit Court, Book II 1812–1819, Davis, Solomon & Edward vs. Sudduth, James & Wife Roll # 987603 Box #247

Filed April 7th, 1804

To the Honble the Judges of Circuit Court of Fayette County sitting in Chancery

Humbly complaining then unto your honors your Orator and Oratix James Sudduth and Sally his wife administrators of Solomon Davis deceased.

That the said Solomon as one of the distributees of his fathers estate was entitled to the Sum of £25.10 [25 pounds, 10 shillings] *besides Int. no part of which has ever been received by him or your orator or oratrix:*

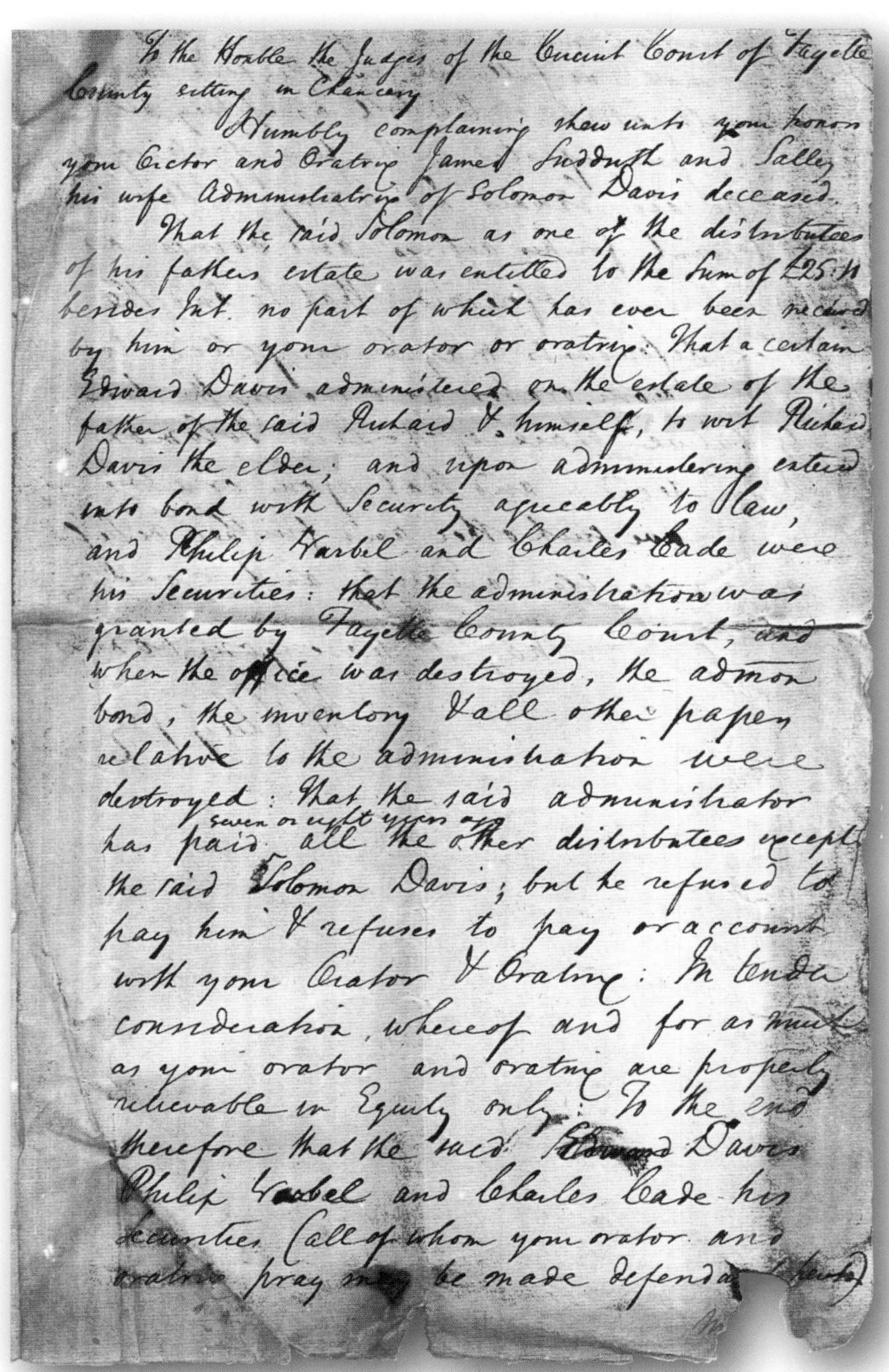

To the Honble the Judges of the Circuit Court of Fayette County sitting in Chancery

Humbly complaining shew unto your honors your Orator and Oratrix James Sudduth and Sally his wife Administratrix of Solomon Davis deceased.

That the said Solomon as one of the distributees of his fathers estate was entitled to the Sum of £25.10 besides Int. no part of which has ever been received by him or your orator or oratrix. That a certain Edward Davis administered on the estate of the father of the said Richard & himself, to wit Richard Davis the elder; and upon administering entered into bond with Security agreeably to law, and Philip Warbel and Charles Cade were his Securities: that the administration was granted by Fayette County Court, and when the office was destroyed, the admon bond, the inventory & all other papers relative to the administration were destroyed: That the said administrator has paid seven or eight years ago all the other distributees except the said Solomon Davis; but he refused to pay him & refuses to pay or account with your Orator & Oratrix: In tender consideration whereof and for as much as your orator and oratrix are properly relievable in Equity only: To the end therefore that the said Edward Davis Philip Warbel and Charles Cade his securities (all of whom your orator and oratrix pray may be made defendants hereto)

That a certain Edward Davis administered on the estate of the father of said Richard & himself, to wit Richard Davis the elder; and upon administering entered into bond with Security agreeably to law, and Philip Varbel and Charles Cade were his Securities: that the administration was granted by Fayette County Court, and when the office was destroyed, the admon bond, the inventory & all other papers relative to the administration were destroyed: That the said administrator has paid seven or eight years ago, all the other distributees except the said Solomon Davis; but he refused to pay him & refuses to pay or account with your Orator & Oratrix: In tender consideration whereof and for as much as your orator and oratrix are properly receivable in Equity only: To the end therefore that the said Edward Davis, Philip Varbel and Charles Cade his Securities (all of whom your orator and oratrix pray may be made defendant hereto) may upon their several and respective corporal oaths make as full true and perfect answer to the allegations of this bill as if they were herein again repeated in the form of interrogatory. That the said Edward Davis may be decreed to account for his actings and doings as administrator aforesaid: that he and the other defendants may be compelled to pay to your orator and oratrix the distributive share of the said Solomon Davis deced: and that your orator may have such other and further relief as is agreeable to Equity and good conscience.

May it please your honors &c.

H. Clay

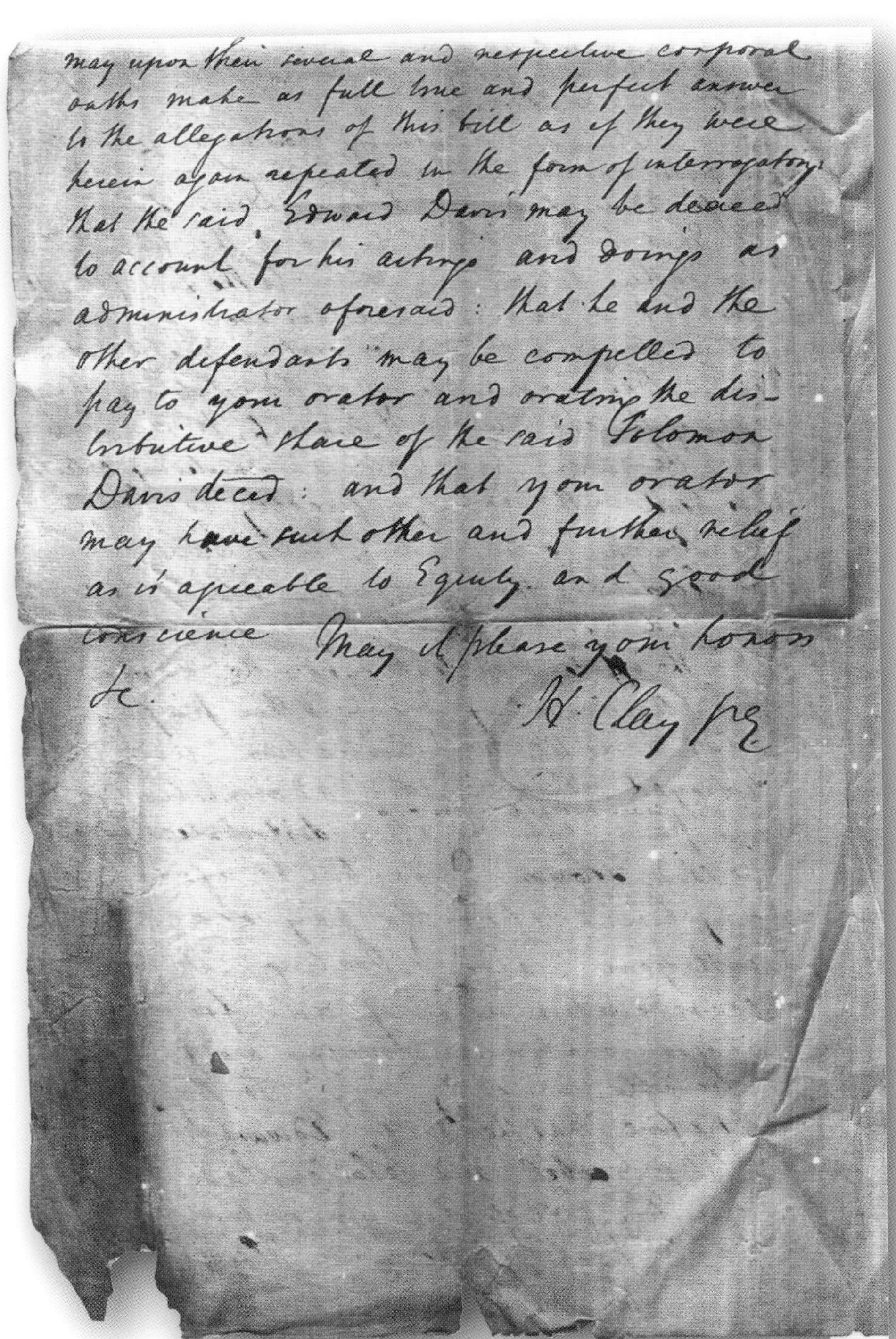

may upon their several and respective corporal
oaths make as full true and perfect answer
to the allegations of this bill as if they were
herein again repeated in the form of interrogatory:
that the said Edward Davis may be decreed
to account for his actings and doings as
administrator aforesaid: that he and the
other defendants may be compelled to
pay to your orator and oratrix the distributive share of the said Solomon
Davis deced: and that your orator
may have such other and further relief
as is agreeable to Equity and good
conscience May it please your honors
&c.
H. Clay pq

Solomon Davis b. ca. 1760–1770

Filed June 22nd 1804

The answer of Edward Davis administrator of the estate of Richard Davis deceased to a bill of complaint exhibited against him in the Fayette Circuit Court by James Suddith & Sally his wife administratrix of Solomon Davis deceased this defendant saying &c for answer saith that it is true he administered on the estate of his father Richard Davis deceased, but denies that Solomon Davis was entitled to the sum of £25–10 [25 pounds, 10 shillings] as is falsely alleged in the said bill — this defendant admits that the said Solomon was entitled to a distributive share of the said estate of Richard Davis, but he is not able to state the precise sum. He is well

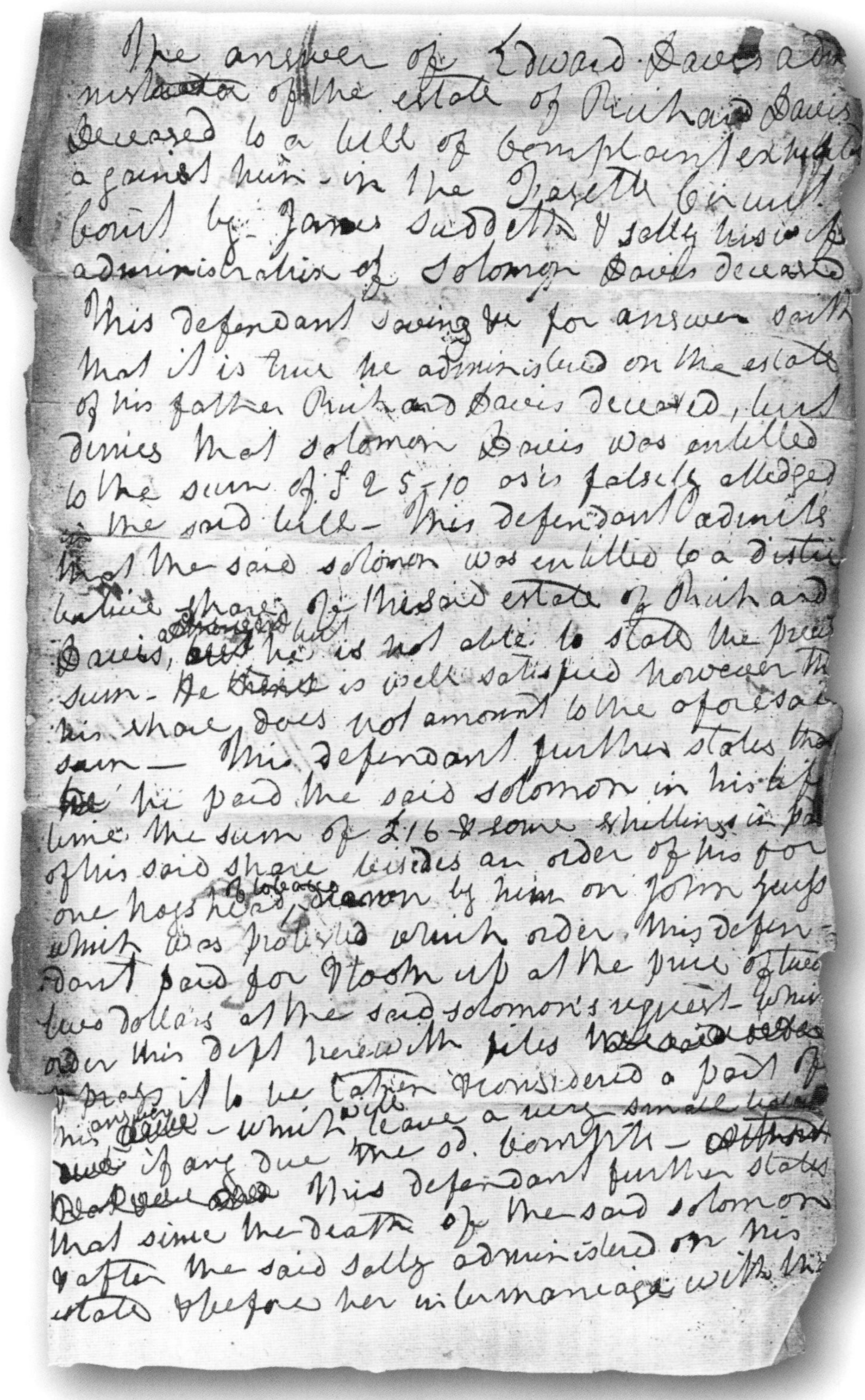

The answer of Edward Davis administrator of the estate of Richard Davis deceased to a bill of complaint exhibited against him in the Fayette Circuit Court by James Suddeth & Sally his wife administratrix of Solomon Davis deceased this defendant saying &c for answer saith that it is true he administered on the estate of his father Richard Davis deceased, but denies that Solomon Davis was entitled to the sum of £25–10 as is falsely alleged in the said bill — this defendant admits that the said Solomon was entitled to a distributive share of the said estate of Richard Davis, but he is not able to state the precise sum — He is well satisfied however that his share does not amount to the aforesaid sum — this defendant further states that he paid the said Solomon in his life time the sum of £16 & some shillings in part of his said share besides an order of his for one hogshead tobacco drawn by him on John Jeuss which was protested which order this defendant paid for & took up at the price of twenty two dollars at the said Solomon's request — which order this deft herewith files & prays it to be taken & considered a part of his answer — which will leave a very small balance if any due the sd. complt — this defendant further states that since the death of the said Solomon & after the said Sally administered on his estate & before her intermarriage with the

satisfied however that his share does not amount to the aforesaid sum — this defendant further states that he paid the said Solomon in his lifetime the sum of £16 & some shillings in part of his said share besides an order of his for one hogs head of tobacco ____ by him on John Gess which was [provided?] which order this defendant paid for & took up at the price of twenty(?) two dollars at the said Solomon's request — which order this defendant herewith files and prays it to taken & considered a part of this answer - which will leave a very small balance if any due the said comp[lainan]t. This defendant further states that since the death of the said Solomon & after the said Sally administered on this estate & before her intermarriage with the said James he this deft [defendant] offered to pay her the balance of the said Solomon's distributive share of said estate after deducting the af[oresaid] payment that she declined receiving at that time and the said deft expressly answers that he has been always ready & willing … to pay such balance after deducting the af[oresaid] payment without that &c and this defendant prays whence dismissed with costs in his behalf most wrongfully expended &c.

Edward Davis

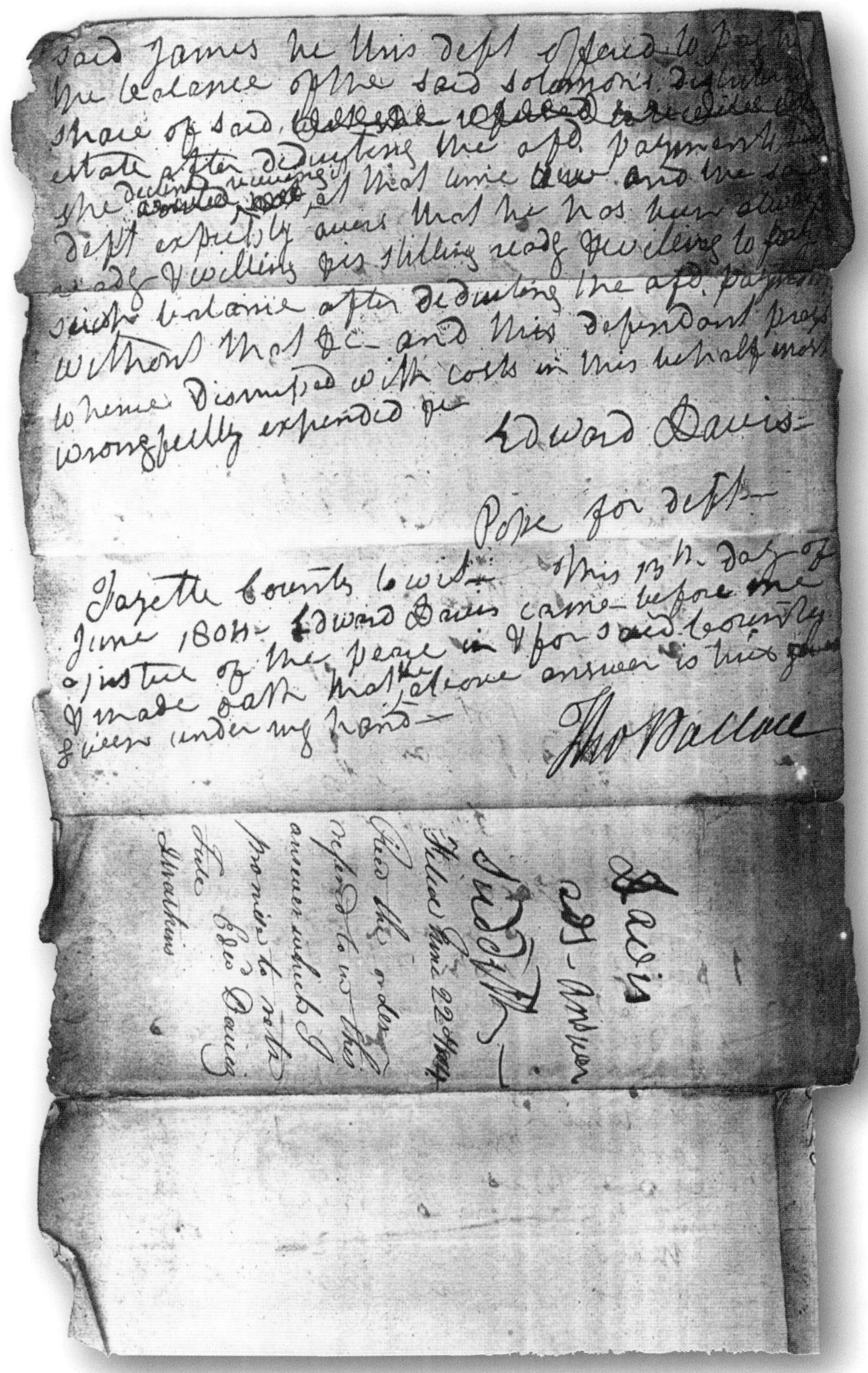

said James he this deft offered to pay her
the balance of the said Solomon's distributive
share of said estate
estate after deducting the afd. payment that
she declined receiving at that time and the said
deft expressly avers that he has been always
ready & willing ready & willing to pay
such balance after deducting the afd. payment
without that &c — and this defendant prays
to hence dismissed with costs in this behalf most
wrongfully expended &c

Edward Davis

Pope for deft

Fayette County to wit — this 13th day of
June 1804 — Edward Davis came before me
a justice of the peace in & for said County
& made oath that the above answer is true
given under my hand —

Tho Wallace

Solomon Davis b. ca. 1760–1770

Filed March 27th, 1805

The deposition of Aron Davis taken at the house of Jeremiah Davis in Mountsterling, Montgomery County this 19th day of March 1805 to be read in evidence in a Suit in Chancery in the Fayette Circuit Court wherein James Suddeth is Complainant and Edw.d Davis Administrator of the Estate of Rich.d Davis Deceased is Defendant and this Deponant being of Lawfull age and first sworn Deposeth and Saieth that in the year of 1800 in the month of Sep.r or Oct.r he was at the house of Solomon Davis and this Deponant and Solomon Davis fell in conversation Respecting what was yet due to Said Solomon Davis from Edw.d Davis as administrator of the Estate of Rich.d Davis Deceased and Solomon Davis told this Deponant that if Edw.d Davis settled forty Shillings with him this Deposant on account of the said Sollomon [sic] *Davis, then there would be about seventeen pounds Coming to him the Said Solomon Davis.*

Ques.n *by James Suddeth — did you not apply to Edw.d Davis for the bal[anc]e due you from Rich.d Davis Deceased's Estate and that he refused to pay you and Said he had not Collected the money.*

The deposition of Aron Davis taken at the house
of Jeremiah Davis in Mountsterling montgomery
County this 19th day of March 1805 to be read
in evidence in a suit in Chancery in the Fayette
Circuit Court wherein James Suddeth is Complainant and Edw.d Davis Administrator of
the Estate of Rich.d Davis Deceased is Defen.t
and this Deponant being of Lawfull age and
first sworn Deposeth and saieth
that in the year of 1800 in the month of Sep.r or Oct.r
he was at the house of Solomon Davis and this
Deponant and Solmon Davis fell in Conversa-
tion Respecting what was yet due to Said Solomon
Davis from Edw.d Davis as Administrator of the
Estate of Rich.d Davis Deceased and Solomon
Davis told this Deponant, that if Edw.d
Davis setled forty shillings with him this
Deponant on account of the said Sollomon
Davis, then there would be about seventeen
pounds Comming to him the said Soloman Davis
Ques.n by James Suddeth did you not apply to Edw.d
Davis for the bal.e ~~of the~~ due you from Rich.d
Davis Deceased's Estate and that he refused
to pay you and said he had not Collected
the money
Ans.r yes I applyd twice and he refused and said
he had not yet Collected the money

Ans.r Yes, I applied twice and he refused and said he had not yet Collected the money.

Ques.n by same — did you not always Consider Solomon Davis a man of Punctuallity?

Ans.r yes I did

Ques.n by same — did you hear Nathaniel Davis say that Edw.d Davis had observed to him that he would not pay Solomon Davis his money at that time as one Dollar would be as good to him Sollomon [sic] *Davis at that time as two would when he Returned back as he was going to Start with a drove of horses, as there was a misunderstanding between Edw.d Davis and Sollomon Davis* [sic].

Ans.r —yes I did

Ques.n by same — do you beleave that it was in the Power of Edw.d Davis to pay Solomon Davis after that time

Ans.r I do not think it was for I beleave they never saw each other afterwards and this Deponant further saieth not.

Sworn too [sic] *and Signed before me at the time and Place above mentioned.*

Jere.h Davis

his
Aaron X Davis
mark

Solomon Davis b. ca. 1760–1770

Edward/Solomon Law Suit — Several notes in the file:

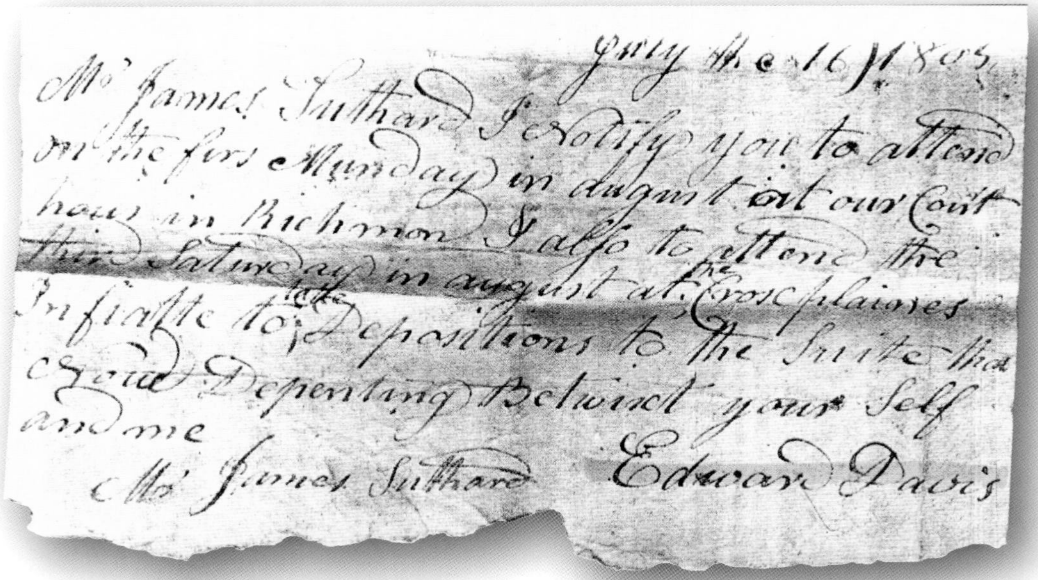

July the 16, 1805

Mr. James Suthard I Notify you to attend on the firs[t] Munday in August at our Court hous[e] in Richmond & also to attend the third Saturday in august at the Croseplaines In fiatte to take Depositions to the Suite that now Depending Betwixt your Self and me

Mr. James Suthard   Edward Davis

I do certify that I do Authorize James Suddith to Take the deposition of Aaron Davis in Montgomery County at any time he pleases to be read in evidence in a Suit in Chancery depending in Fayette Circuit Court in which S.^{d} [Said] Suddith is Complainant and my self as Excr. of Richd Davis Deft in Chancery Given under my hand 14 March 1805

Teste [witness]
[signature]

his
Edward X Davis
mark

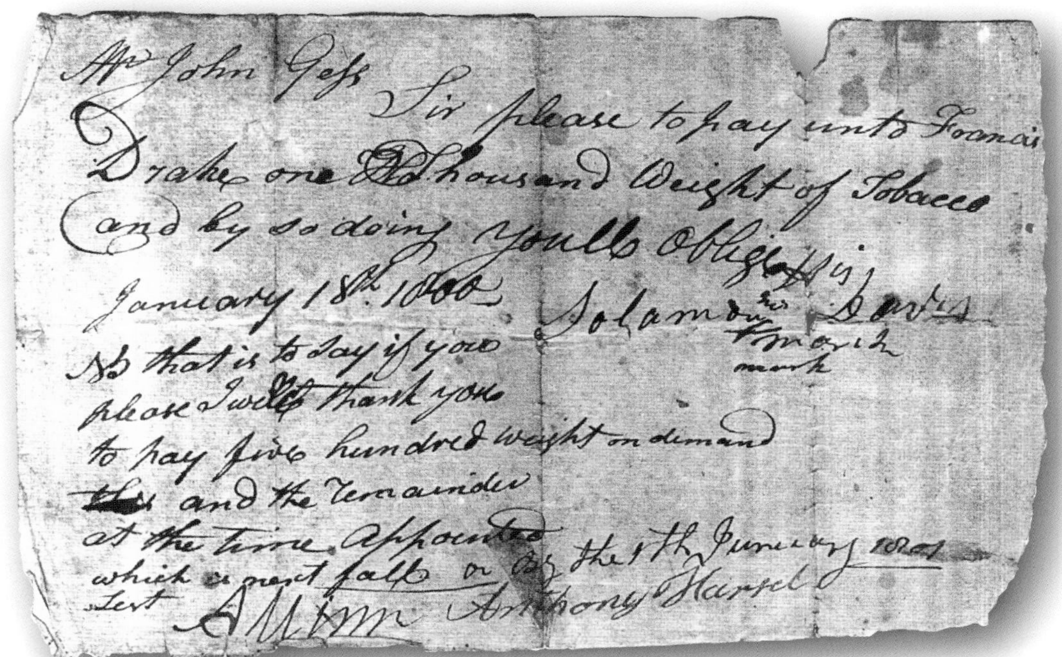

Att: John Gess

Sir please to pay unto Francis Drake One Thousand Weight of Tobacco and by so doing youll oblige.

his
Solomon X Davis
mark

January 18th 1800

NB? that is to say if you please I will thank you to pay five hundred weight on demand and the remainder at the time appointed which is next fall or by the 11th January 1801.

Anthony Harsel

Solomon Davis b. ca. 1760–1770

Filed August 12th 1805

The Deposition of Robert Tevis, Esq.r taken at Madison Courthouse on the 5th August 1805 in a suit Defending in Fayette Circuit Court between Ja.s Sudduth et al Complts [Complainants] & Edward Davis et al who being first Sworn deposeth & Saith he was called on between Edw.d & Solomon Davis to settle what was due from Edward to Solomon respecting their Fathers heirs Estate on a Settlement it was agreed that Solomon had rec.d £16.3.10. towards his part of his Fathers Estate sometime after Solomons Death, his widow & Edw.d met at this Depo.s house & there appeared an order for a 1000 [lbs.] of Tob.o [Tobacco] drawn by Solomon when Edw.d agreed to pay the balance due if he could be allowed for the amt of the said Tobacco & she refused & nothing was done.

Question by Ja.s Sudduth do you believe there was a good understanding between the Brothers at the time of the said settlement. Answer No — there was a dispute about a Negro at the time as well as I can recollect — a few days after the Settlement Solomon

The Deposition of Robert Tevis Esq.r taken at
Madison Courthouse on the 5th Aug.t 1805
in a Suit Depending in Fayette Circuit Court
between Ja.s Sudduth & als. Compts & Edward
Davis & oths who being first Sworn depos
eth & Saith he was called on between Edw.d
& Solomon Davis to settle what was due
from Edward to Solomon respecting their Fa
thers Estate on a Settlement it was agreed
that Soloman had rec.d £16..3..10. towards
his part of ~~his~~ Fathers Estate sometime
after Solomons Death, his widow & Edw.d
meet at this Depo.s house & there appeared
an order for a 1000 lbs of Tob.o drawn by So
lomon when Edw.d agreed to pay the bal
lance due if he could be allowed for
the amt of the said Tobacco & she refused &
nothing was done.
Question by Ja.s Sudduth do you believe there
was a good understanding between the Brothers
at the time of the said settlem.t Answer No —
there was a dispute about a Negro at
the time as well as I can recollect —
a few days after the Settlem.t Solomon
Davis sed he had forgot in the settle ab.t 20
or 30 lbs of Iron the first time I saw Edw.d
after told him of it & Edward sed he
had got Iron from Brooks but it was
his Brother Nates Iron & he had paid him

Davis sed he had forgot in the settle ab.[t] 20 or 30 [lbs] of Iron the first time and I saw Edw.[d] after told him of it & Edward sed he had got Iron from Brooks but it was his Brother Nate iron & he had paid him & further this Depo [deponent] Saith the Settlement took place he supposes was in the fall of 1800 or 1801 & further saith not.

Robert Tevis

Also the deposition of W[m] Igo who being first sworn Deposeth & saith that on the day after the sale of Edward & Solomon Davis Fathers Estate Edward offered to Sollomon his proportion of the amount of their Fathers Estate in bonds on Good Men & Solomon refused to take them. Question by Ja.[s] Sudduth was it by the decision of Solomon Davis that Edward paid the order to Frances Drake for 1000 [lbs] of Tobacco. Answer I cant tell. But I heard Solomon say he never told Edward to pay his debts & sed he would never pay the order up to Edward in Money because Edw.[d] had paid Drake in Bacon & further saith not.

William Igo

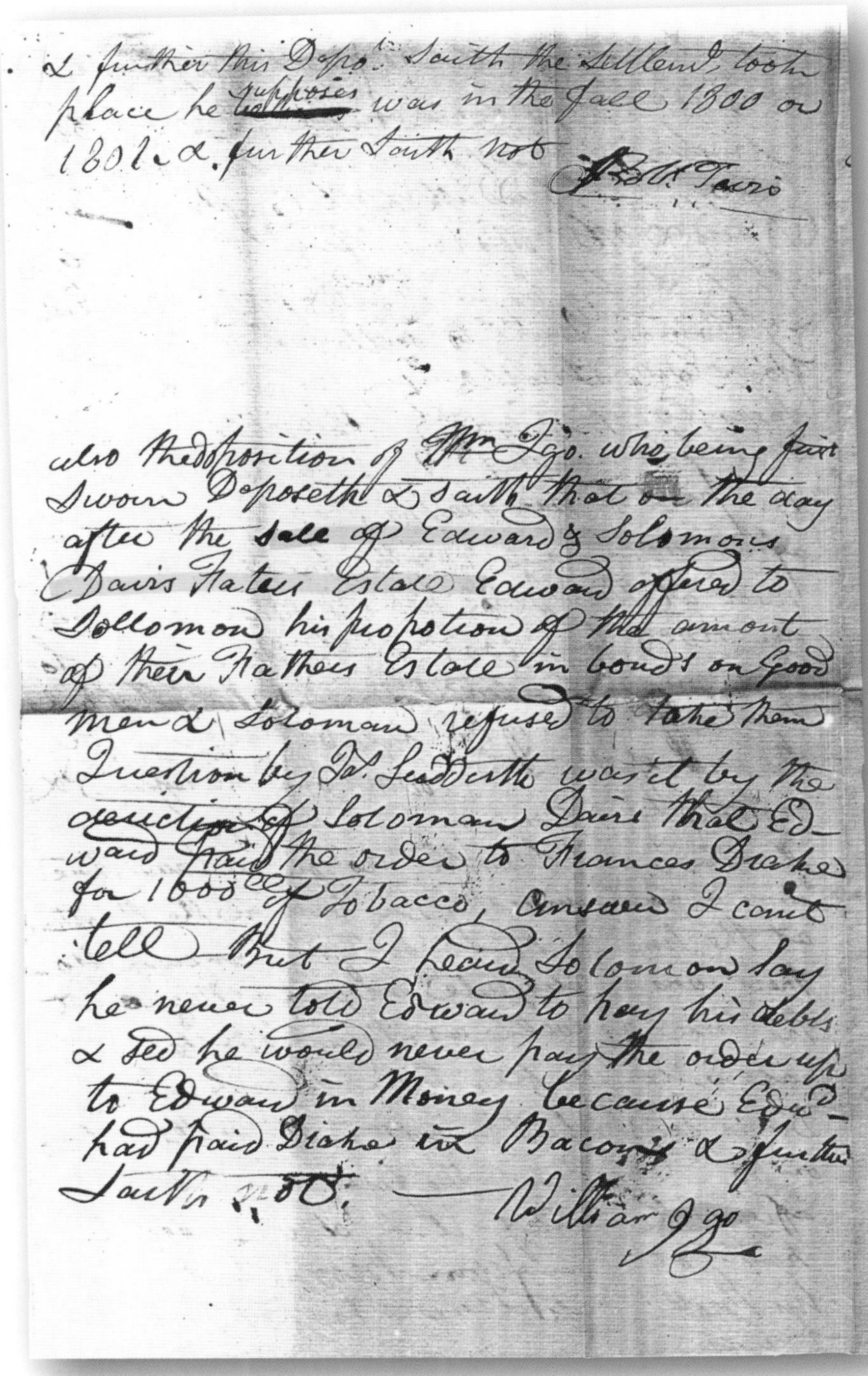

& further this Depo.t Saith the Settlem.t took place he supposes was in the fall 1800 or 1801 & further Saith not

Rob.t Tevis

also the deposition of Wm Igo who being first Sworn Deposeth & saith that on the day after the sale of Edward & Solomons Davis Fathers Estate Edward offered to Sollomon his proportion of the amount of their Fathers Estate in bonds on Good Men & Soloman refused to take them Question by Ja.s Sudduth was it by the direction of Soloman Davis that Edward paid the order to Frances Drake for 1000 lb of Tobacco, answer I cant tell But I heard Soloman say he never told Edward to pay his debts & sed he would never pay the order up to Edward in Money because Edw.d had paid Drake in Bacon & further Saith not.

William Igo

Solomon Davis b. ca. 1760–1770

The foregoing Depositions were taken & subscribed before me one of the acting Justices of the Peace in & for the County of Madison on the day & at the place first above written by consent of the parties

Green Clay

Cost one Justice attending 1 day 6/(?)

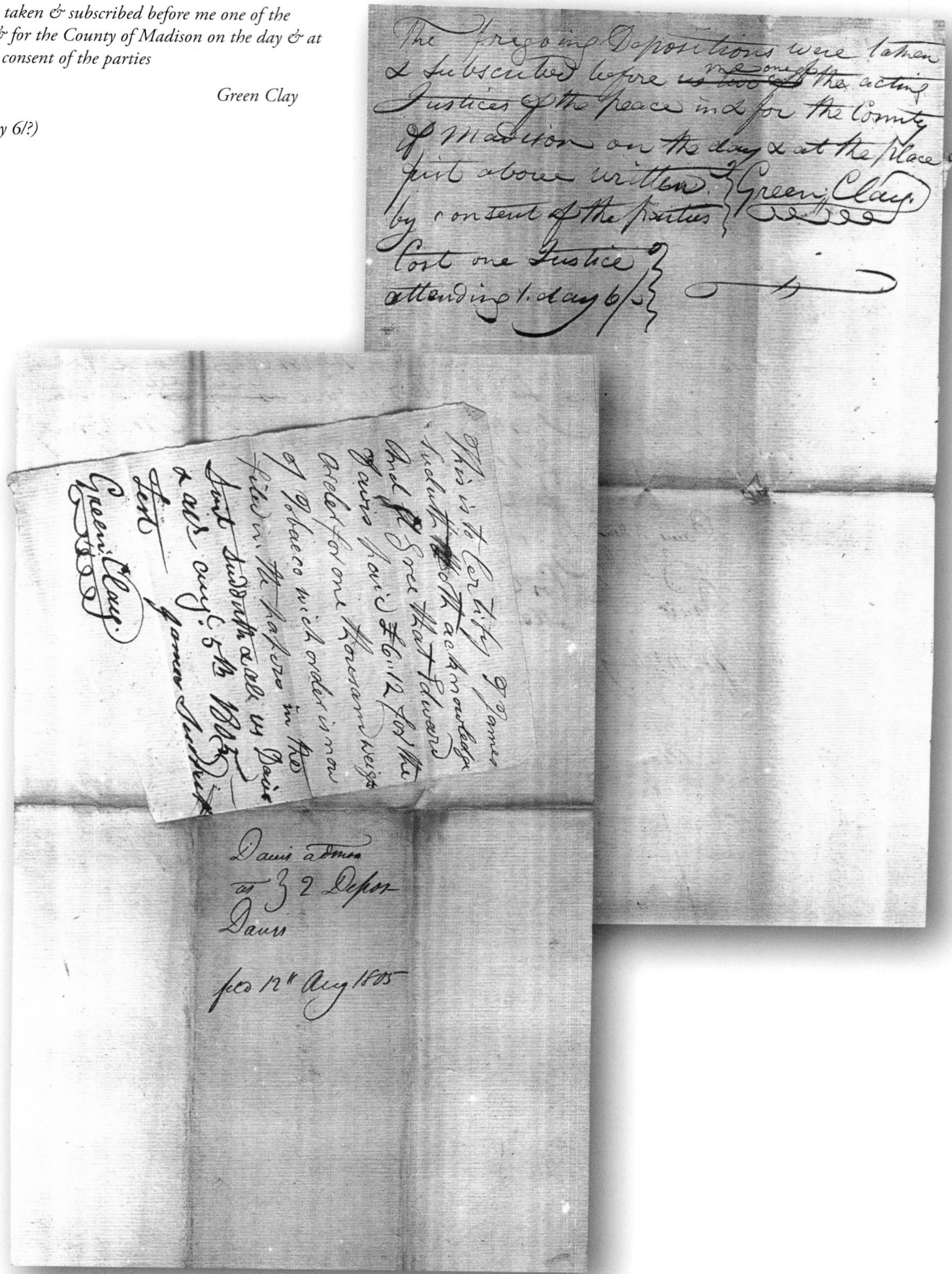

This is to certify I James Sudduth hath acknowledge and agree that Edward Davis paid £6.12 for the order for one thousand weight of Tobacco which order is now filed in papers in the Suit Sudduth et al vs Davis et al Aug.t 5 1805.

Test
Green Clay

James Sudduth

We find that by Examining the Estate of Richard Davis Deceased Exclusive of the Widows Dower to amount £123 18 4 & the part of each Legatee to Amount To twenty four pounds fifteen Shillings & eight pence £24 15 8

Test
John Turner
Wm Scott
Charles Cade

August 5th 1805 This is to Certify that I James Sudduth doth acknowledge and agree that the above account as it stands stated is Just & true. I believe that £24-15-8 is what belongs to Each legatee.

Jas Sudduth

Test
Robt Tevis
William Igo

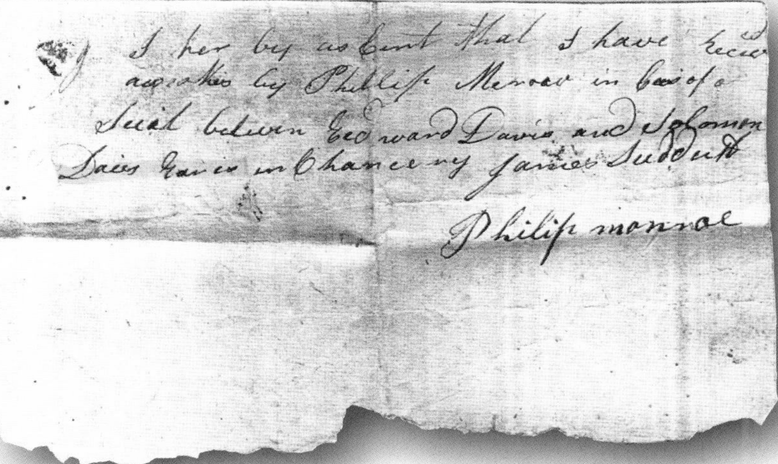

I her by as Cent that I have received apraisals? by Phillip Monroe in Cause? Case? of a Suit between Edward Davis and Solomon Davis Given in Chancery James Sudduth

Phillip Monroe

Solomon Davis b. ca. 1760–1770

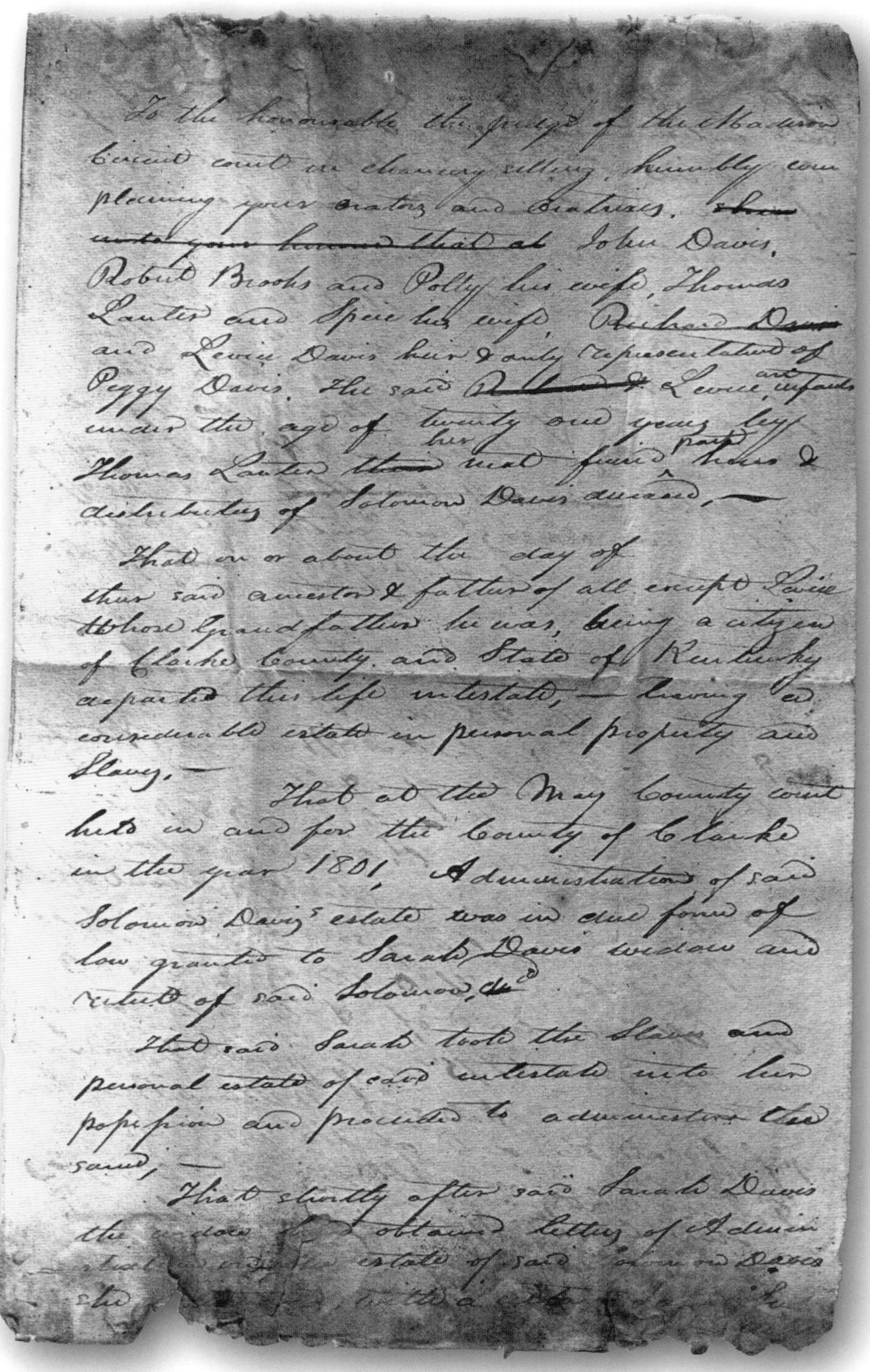

To the honourable the judge of the Madison
Circuit court in chancery sitting, humbly com
plaining your orators and oratrixes, ~~shew~~
~~unto your honour that at~~ John Davis,
Robert Brooks and Polly his wife, Thomas
Lanter and Spice his wife, ~~Richard Davis~~
and Levice Davis heir & only representative of
Peggy Davis. The said ~~Richard~~ & Levice are infants
under the age of twenty one years by
Thomas Lanter ~~their~~ her next friend [illegible] heirs &
distributees of Solomon Davis deceased, —

That on or about the day of
their said ancestor & father of all except Levice
whose Grandfather he was, being a citizen
of Clarke County and State of Kentucky
departed this life intestate, — leaving a
considerable estate in personal property and
Slaves, —

That at the May County court
held in and for the County of Clarke
in the year 1801, Administration of said
Solomon Davis's estate was in due form of
law granted to Sarah Davis widow and
relict of said Solomon, dec^d

That said Sarah took the Slaves and
personal estate of said intestate into her
possession and proceeded to administer the
same, —

That shortly after said Sarah Davis
the widow [illegible] obtained letters of Admini
[illegible] estate of said Solomon Davis
[illegible]

List of heirs of Solomon Davis: "John Davis, Robert Brooks and Polly his wife, Thomas Lanter and Spice his wife, Richard Davis and Levice Davis heir & only representative of Peggy Davis." Solomon Davis Heirs v. James & Sarah Sudduth, Madison County, Kentucky Court Case, Box 110, Bundle 279, folder #10955 Kentucky State Archives, Frankfort, Kentucky.

your [illegible] by said [illegible] wife
defts to this Bill, — That by virtue of
said intermarriage said Suddarth and wife
became in law the joint representatives
of said intestate, — and have proceeded to
administer his estate accordingly —

Your Orators charge that said Suddarth
and wife have never come to a settlement
of said Administration, and to a distri
-bution among your Orators altho requested
so to do repeatedly — Notwithstanding
said defts ~~are satisfied that~~ well know
that your Orators are each entitled to a con
-siderable amount of property ~~and~~ of said
intestates estate, —

They further shew unto your honour
that about the 23d day of November
1774 their Grandfather William Black
-well of the county of Albemarle and
State of Virginia duly made & published
his last will and testament in writing
and afterwards departed this life about the
day of leaving said Will in full
and legal force That the same was at
the March court of Albemarle county
in the year 1775 duly proved & admitted
to record, — That said William Blackwell
possessed at the date of said will and at
his death a considerable number of negroes
& other estate, —
That by said Will ~~a copy of which is~~
~~herewith filed as a part of this~~ said
William Blackwell bequeathed [illegible]

Solomon Davis b. ca. 1760–1770

estate to his wife Sarah during her widow-
hood, then to be equally divided among
his (the Testators) children — They shew
that said Sarah the compts Grandmother &
widow of the Testator took the negroes
& other estate
devised to her by said will into possession
and retained them during her life, she
having departed this life the day of
without ever having married after the
Testators death,—

That after the death of the Testator
William Blackwell, Solomon Davis the
Father of part of the compts, & Grandfather
of the balance, intermarried with the
deft Sarah Sudduth, the Mother of
the compts, and daughter of said
William Blackwell the Testator.

That said Solomon Davis the intestate
and the deft Sarah were living together
as man and wife on the 8th day of Febry 1798
sect 34 the 2d Litt page 121
when the act of assembly of Kentucky
passed vesting all the right, property
and Interest of a Feme covert in slaves
in her husband absolutely, as his own
property, and continued to reside together
as man and wife as aforesaid until
the day of when said Solomon
Davis departed this life intestate as
aforesaid, That ~~said So~~ after the death
of the widow Blackwell and of said Solomon the children ~~then~~ of William
Blackwell the Testator, & the defts
Sudduth & wife as Administrators of
[illegible] provided [illegible]

the estate of the testator William Blackwell and that on said division negro woman of the name of Leer was allotted to the defts as Administrators of said Solomon Davis decd — That Leer has seven children living Gallatin, Molly Richmond Benjamin Ralph Harrison, and a young child name not known, all which negro slaves are in the possession of the defts except, Gal-latin, who is in the possession of a certain Henry Brooks of Madison County on a loan not being disposed of so as to change the property in him. They make said Brooks a deft hereto, —

They charge that the defts Sarah Sudduths interest in the slaves bequeathed by the Will of William Blackwell decd became on her intermarriage and by vir-tue of the Statute of Kentucky aforesaid vested in the intestate Solomon Davis decease, That said Solomon, & the said Sarah Sudduth, and also Sarah Blackwell the widow of William Blackwell the Testator and also the Slaves which the said Sarah had a life estate in all being were all in the State of Kentucky at the passage of said act of assembly so that said Statute had & has full opera-tion thereon, —

[illegible] they also charge that [illegible]

Josiah Collins b. November 7, 1778

The Pioneer Preacher

Sometimes in the search for one's family, the researcher runs across a character so compelling that he deserves to be written about. Josiah Collins is one of these persons. He is a complete contrast to some of the scoundrels and shady characters. He was a minister!

Josiah Collins was born in Halifax County, Virginia, November 7, 1778, according to his own testimony.[1]

> I was born in Halifax County, Virginia in the year 1778, November the 7th day. My father immigrated to Kentucky in that hard winter 1779, When so many people and stock froze to death in the wilderness coming through....

Josiah told how the "savages" along the Sciota and Miami rivers killed and carried off the white settlers. His father was drafted into the militia, leaving his mother alone with the children. The children would search for young nettles and other wild herbs that they would boil with turnip tops. That, along with the milk from a stray cow, which wandered up from the woods, kept them from starving to death while the men were gone.[2]

After settling in the Lexington, Kentucky, area with Josiah's parents, Stephen and Catherine McHendree Collins, they lived on buffalo meat.[3] He tells how his mother helped save a man from a wildcat. The man had gone from the school house to the creek to wash his face, and the wildcat attacked him on his way back. The cat would have clawed the man to death, if not for his leather breeches.[4]

Josiah recalled another hair-raising event when the fort built by settlers near Lexington was attacked by six hundred Indians, and thirty-two wives became widows that day in 1782. Luckily, his mother was not one of them.

In 1785 Stephen Collins patented 1,200 acres on the Red River, in what would become Clarke County, Kentucky.[5] In addition to his land, he made his living by forging bar iron and shipping nails on the Kentucky River.[6] In 1789 Stephen Collins opened a hotel in Lexington. He died August 6, 1825, and was buried in Historical Cemetery, Boone County, Kentucky.[7]

Josiah Collins married Amelia "Milly" Oldham in Madison County, Kentucky, on November 25, 1802.[8] Milly was the daughter of Richard Oldham and Ann Pepper Oldham.[9] Josiah and Milly had nine children: Joel Collins born 1803; Albert G. Collins b. 1804; Paulina Collins born circa 1808, who married Richard Davis in 1826; William C. Collins; Louisa Collins; Jeremiah V. Collins born 1814; Elizabeth "Betsy" Collins born October 1, 1817; Ann Collins born 1821; and Millie Collins born 1829.[10]

Josiah Collins was a minister in the newly formed denomination that grew out of the independent pioneer spirit, the Christian Church (Disciples of Christ). This denomination had its roots in the Presbyterian Church and other protestant denominations of the American frontier. Instead of having bishops who could remove a minister, each congregation had autonomy, and could hire or fire its minister. Josiah Collins was the first pastor of the Hays Fork Baptist Church, which began in 1819.[11] James Caldwell said this about Rev. Josiah Collins:

> I have always thought he was a man of more power and influence over an audience than any man I ever saw. He was a fluent, ready, and rapid speaker and with a voice of great melody and a good singer, he could lead the masses captive at his will.[12]

The Hays Fork Baptist Church as pictured on <http://www.haysfork baptist.com> in an early incarnation. The original church burned down and was rebuilt nearby in June 1819. Josiah Collins was chosen as its first pastor. The history on the web site was compiled by Fountain Rice, 1885; Rev. Morgan Hahn, 1962; Margaret W. Tilsley, 1987, 1994, 2004; Rev. Vincent Carman, 2008; and Dedicated Church Clerks 1813–2008. Reproduced with permission.

Josiah "Si" Collins was a minister all of his adult life. He joined the Baptist church in 1811, was ordained in 1814, but at some point switched his allegiance to the Christian church. On November 2, 1869, when he was ninety-two, he attended a 50th wedding anniversary for a couple he had married — Paulina Clay, the daughter of General Green Clay, to Col. William Rodes.[13]

Perhaps Josiah Collins was worried about the future of his daughter, Paulina Davis and his Davis grandchildren, when he became trustee over the land and property of Richard Davis in 1833.[14] We can only surmise that Rev. Collins may have been disappointed in the intemperate lifestyle of his son-in-law Richard Davis, or perhaps he was worried about the health of his daughter, who died in 1846, and he wanted to protect his grandchildren's

106
Collins and Davis

Whereas the undersigned Richard Davis did on the February 1833 make a deed of trust to the undersigned Josiah Collins which is of record in the Madison Coun court Now we do agree to and do hereby disannul, do away an vacate said deed of trust and agree that all of Davis rig are reinstated and to stand as if that deed had not h been entered into. Given under our hands this day of August 1852

Josiah Collins
Richard Davis

Commonwealth of Kentucky }
Madison County } Sct.

I Thomas H. Barnes clerk of the county court f said county do certify that this agreement between Josiah Collins and Richard Davis was produced to m in my office on the 4 day of September 1852 and acknow edged before me by the said Josiah Collins and Richar Davis Whereupon said article of agreement with this c tificate has been duly recorded in my office

att Tho. H. Barn

Exam'd & Deliv'd

Prewitt — This Indenture made this 23 day of September 1852

Deed of trust between Josiah Collins and Richard Davis in February 1833, apparently entered in order to protect the interests of his daughter and grandchildren.

interests. In those days if a wife died, all property went to her husband and none was set in reserve for her children. Richard Davis was surely a poor man when he married Paulina Collins. Friends and neighbors testified during the probate settlement of Richard Davis that most of Richard's land and slaves had come from Paulina's father.[15]

Josiah Collins died just a few years before his son-in-law Richard Davis, and the Davis children were supposed to get a legacy from their grandfather's estate, as mentioned in Richard Davis's probate papers. There is some indication that the legacy went to Richard and that the Davis children never saw any money.[16]

Josiah Collins's wife Milly died in Madison County, Kentucky, March 21, 1864, and Josiah died April 18, 1871.[17] Their large home was located on Boxankle Road, northeast of Richmond, Madison County, Kentucky.[18]

A.H.

Notes

1. French Tipton Papers, Book Z:137–38, Special Collections, Eastern Kentucky University Library, Richmond, Ky.
2. Ibid.
3. Richard A. Prewitt, *The Collins Book* (Des Moines, Ia.: privately printed, 1996), 56.
4. Ibid.
5. Ibid., 57.
6. Hallie Tipton Johnstone, *History of Estill County, Kentucky* (privately printed, 1974), 38.
7. *Kentucky Pioneer Genealogy and Records: A Genealogical Journal Devoted to Kentucky* 7 (1986): 98–100.
8. Prewitt, *The Collins Book*, 60.
9. Ibid.
10. Ibid.
11. French Tipton Papers, Book Z:137–38.
12. French Tipton Papers, Book Z:159.
13. Lewis Collins, *The History of Kentucky* (Covington, Ky.: Collins & Co., 1878), 198.
14. Madison Co., Kentucky, Deed Book V:3.
15. Deposition of Robert Jordan, Madison County Court Cases, Richard Davis heirs vs. Richard Davis administrators, Box 142, #284, Kentucky State Archives, Frankfort, Ky.
16. Ibid., Deposition of James G. Walker.
17. Prewitt, *The Collins Book*, 60.
18. Ibid., 61.

Richard Davis b. 1799

Lawsuits and Liquor

Richard Davis was a man whose life seemed to be controlled by legal problems and alcohol. Involved in several court cases during his lifetime, these lawsuits provide insight into the man, his habits, and his lifestyle. He was born probably in Madison County, Kentucky, or just across the Kentucky River in Clark County in 1799 to Solomon Davis and Sarah Blackwell Davis. His father died in 1801, and his mother married again to James Suddith by July of 1802.[1] In 1819, just after he had turned twenty-one, Richard, along with his siblings, sued his mother and stepfather for their allotment of the slaves belonging to his father and also those passed down from his maternal grandfather.[2]

On March 16, 1826, Richard Davis was married to Paulina Collins, the daughter of Rev. Josiah Collins.[3] She was the mother of the following children: Josiah born 1830; Amelia/Milly; Mary Jane; Arthusa; Albert; Clifton; and James born 1841. Another child may have been Sally, who was married in 1848 to Dudley Dunbar, but was deceased by 1850, as Richard Davis was listed as father of the bride on that marriage bond.[4] Paulina Collins Davis died in 1846.[5]

Richard Davis made his first land purchase in 1828 when he purchased land on Muddy Creek, in Madison County, Kentucky, bounded on the east by the lands of Josiah Collins, known as the Jo. Bennett farm.[6] Richard was probably in financial trouble by 1833 when he "for the love and affection he has for his wife Paulina and his children born and which he may hereafter have" mortgaged "all the lands, slaves and personalty of every kind" to Josiah Collins, his father-in-law, for $1,200.[7] The deed states that this property was put in trust to pay the debts of Richard Davis and, secondly, to provide for Davis, his wife, and their children.

It was this deed of trust that would be mentioned several times in various Madison County court cases in later years. In August of 1852, just as his son Josiah Davis was going through a nasty divorce, Richard and Josiah Collins revoked this deed of trust.[8] In the suit, Sophia, the wife of Josiah, claimed that the trust had been nullified to prevent her from getting a portion of Josiah's interest in his father's property.[9] Josiah Collins also filed a lawsuit to end the trust, as he was informed that the revocation in the deed records was not sufficient to end the trust. In his deposition, he stated that he (Collins) was only the nominal trustee of the estate and that Richard was the actual manager — that besides raising a large family in comfortable circumstances, Richard had doubled the wealth of the estate.[10]

Richard Davis was sued by his son-in-law John Brooks in 1852, and also by his own son, Clifton, in 1863. In the first case, Richard had borrowed $600 from Brooks. Richard stated that he had re-paid Brooks, but that he had not destroyed the original note, putting it in a bureau drawer. He claimed that "someone" had taken the note out of his bureau and that it had gotten into Brooks's possession. There was also a considerable amount of money in that drawer that was missing. In this case, Richard stated in his own words that his drinking had gotten out of hand. He said that some four or five days before the trial in 1852, he became considerably intoxicated in town, so much so that he was unable to and did not go home that night.[11] He said that John Brooks was boasting around town that he was going to make Richard Davis pay him twice!

In the second case, Clifton Davis sued his father Richard over a slave in March of 1864. Clifton stated that in July of 1863 he "sold and delivered … to Richard Davis a Negro man slave named Silas about 17 years old, yellow complexion, at the price of Five Hundred Dollars." Richard paid $50 to Clifton at the time of the sale and was supposed to pay the balance in the fall of 1863. Previous to the sale, Richard had hired the slave at $50 per year. Clifton was hoping to collect not only the purchase price, but also the slave's wages for several months.[12]

The probate proceedings of Richard Davis in 1874 would paint a picture of a somewhat petulant man. From depositions in his probate file, it appears that when his children were younger (prior to the Civil War and before slavery was abolished), he had given one slave to each of them. Several neighbors testified that they were under that impression. Horace Parke, the administrator of Richard's estate, was trying to prove that Richard's children by his first wife had all received a good inheritance and were not entitled to much at Richard's death. However, most of the children testified that Richard himself had retained ownership of

Richard Davis married Paulina Collins in 1826. Above copy from Madison County, Kentucky, Record of Marriages, Vol. 1, 1792–1843.

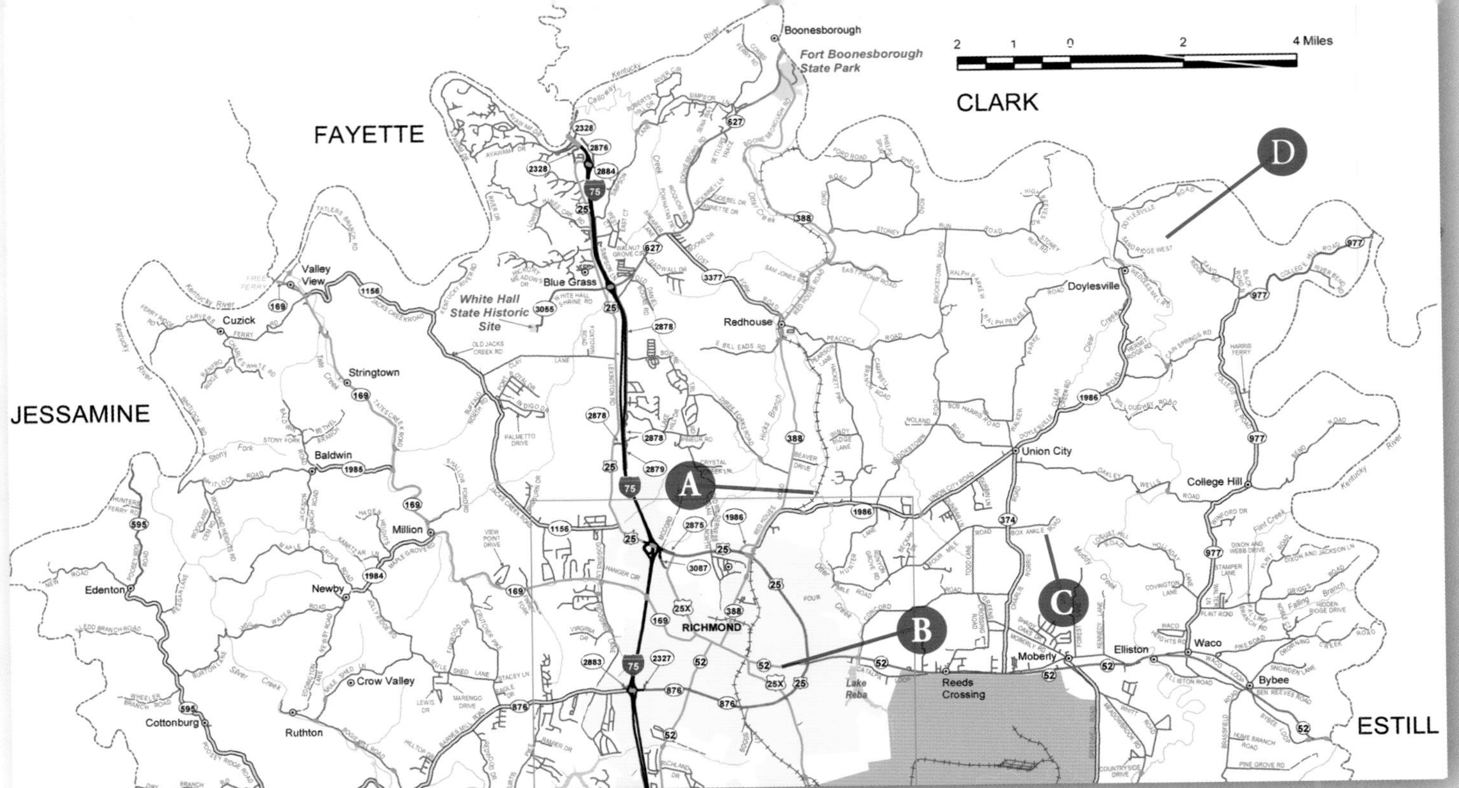

Map of Madison County, Kentucky showing: ***A****) Area where Richard Davis, b. 1799, lived — Otter Creek;* ***B****) Fourmile Road, mentioned in Richard Davis's deed description;* ***C****) Boxankle Road where Josiah Collins's house was located; and* ***D****) Doylesville where Remus Gooch and other family members lived. Map courtesy of Kentucky Transportation Cabinet.*

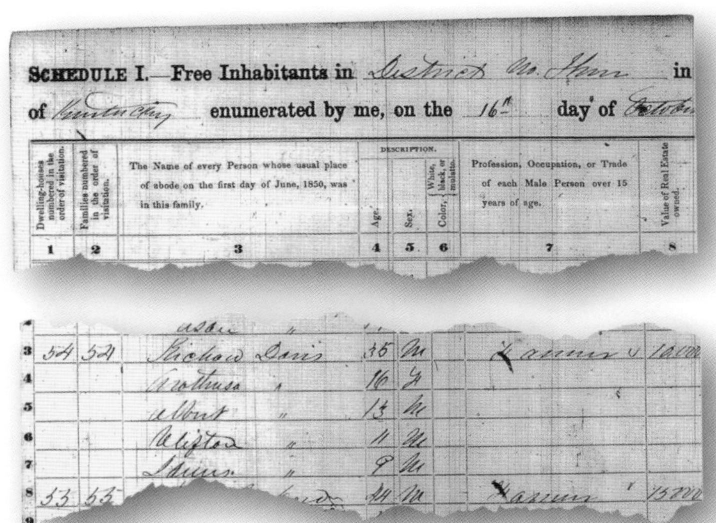

SCHEDULE I.—Free Inhabitants in District No. ... **in** ... **of** ... **enumerated by me, on the** 16th **day of** October

Dwelling-houses numbered in the order of visitation.	Families numbered in the order of visitation.	The Name of every Person whose usual place of abode on the first day of June, 1850, was in this family.	Age.	Sex.	Color, { White, black, or mulatto.	Profession, Occupation, or Trade of each Male Person over 15 years of age.	Value of Real Estate owned.
1	2	3	4	5	6	7	8
54	52	Richard Davis	35	M		Farmer	10000
		Arthusa "	16	F			
		Albert "	13	M			
		Clifton "	11	M			
		James "	9	M			
53	53	...	44	M		Farmer	15000

Page 295 of 1850 federal census, Madison County, Kentucky. Enumerated on October 16 indicating dwelling number 54, Richard Davis, age 35, with daughter Arthusa, 16 years of age, and sons Albert, 13, Clifton, 11, and James, 9.

the slaves, and had taken them back or even sold them. Thus, his children felt that they had not really received any inheritance prior to Richard's death.

Richard Davis was fairly wealthy for his time. In addition to owning real estate and slaves, he was also in the distillery business with Robert Jordan from the fall of 1859 to 1864 or 1865.[13] Eli Cornelison testified that he had built a meat house for Richard on the Brookstown farm.[14] When Richard died, his inventory included cattle, thirty head of hogs, several horses, farming equipment, and household furnishings.[15] By law, his widow and second wife, Elizabeth Baxter Davis, took one-third of the real property.[16] She had married Richard in 1859 and they had one son Edmund, born in February 1868.[17]

Richard Davis died sometime between May 10, 1874, the last time he was seen by his physician, and May 28th, when letters of administration were filed. At Richard's death he owned a mortgaged farm near Brookstown on Otter Creek in Madison County. During the probate proceedings, several neighbors and Richard's personal physician testified that Richard would "take sprees" of drinking and was not able to carry on his business.[18] Dr. French said that Richard was a "good trader when sober and you could not fool him much when he was drunk."[19]

When the commissioners of Madison County finally settled the estate, the farm was sold to Edmund Baxter, the father of Elizabeth Baxter Davis, for $6,162.50.[20] By law the widow would get one-third of that amount, and after the debts were paid, as expected, six-year-old Edmund Davis, the son of Richard and Elizabeth Baxter Davis, received about $900, while the adult children from the first family received a much smaller portion in October of 1876.[21]

A kinder side to Richard Davis surfaced in his probate papers when a bill for the schooling of two of his grandchildren, Pattie and Sallie Brooks, was found.[22] He was about seventy-five when he died, a ripe old age for a man of his times. *A.H.*

Notes

1. Clark Co., Kentucky, Order Book 2:507–08, Film #988284, Kentucky State Archives, Frankfort, Ky.
2. Madison Co., Kentucky, Court Cases, Solomon Davis heirs vs. Solomon Davis administrators, #109551, Kentucky State Archives, Frankfort, Ky.
3. Madison Co., Kentucky, Record of Marriages, 1792–1843, 1:162, Film #183302, Kentucky State Archives, Frankfort, Ky.
4. William L. and Kathy Vockery, *Madison County, Kentucky, Marriages, 1823-1851* (Richmond, Ky.: the authors, 1993–), II:22.

Richard Davis b. 1799

Davis to Collins

This Indenture Made and entered into this 12th day February 1833. by and between Richard Davis of the one part and Josiah Collins of the other part. Witnesseth that said Davis doth for and inconsideration of the love and affection he has for his niece Paulina and his children born and which he May hereafter have and of the covenants herein after entered into by the said Collins on his part doth sell and convey to said Collins all the lands slaves and personality of every kind and discription owned by him the said Davis

Madison County County Clerk, Richmond, Kentucky, Deed Book V, Page 3, State Records Retention Schedule Series Number L1317, 1833–1835

5. Deposition of Milton P. Collins, Madison Co., Kentucky Court Cases, Josiah Collins vs. Richard Davis, #21243, Kentucky State Archives, Frankfort, Ky.
6. Madison Co., Kentucky, Deed Book R:535, Film #7012661, Kentucky State Archives, Frankfort, Ky.
7. Madison Co., Kentucky, Deed Book U:271, Film #7012661, Kentucky State Archives, Frankfort, Ky.
8. Madison Co., Kentucky, Deed Book 7:106, Film #7012664, Kentucky State Archives, Frankfort, Ky.
9. Madison Co., Kentucky, Court Cases, Sophia Davis vs. Josiah Davis, #21227, Kentucky State Archives, Frankfort, Ky.
10. Ibid.
11. Madison Co., Kentucky, Court Cases, John Brooks vs. Richard Davis, #20031, Kentucky State Archives, Frankfort, Ky.
12. Madison Co., Kentucky, Court Cases, Clifton Davis vs. Richard Davis, #23821, Kentucky State Archives, Frankfort, Ky.
13. Madison Co., Kentucky, Court Cases, Richard Davis heirs vs. Richard Davis administrators, Box 142, #284, Kentucky State Archives, Frankfort, Ky.
14. Ibid.
15. Madison Co., Kentucky, Will Book V:290, FHL #1943392.
16. Madison Co., Kentucky, Will Book V:291, FHL #1943392.
17. Edmund Davis, tombstone, Richmond Cemetery, Richmond, Ky.
18. Madison Co., Kentucky, Court Cases, Richard Davis heirs vs. Richard Davis administrators, Box 142, #284, Kentucky State Archives, Frankfort, Ky.
19. Ibid.
20. Madison Co., Kentucky, Deed Book 22:541–42.
21. Madison Co., Kentucky, Court Cases, Richard Davis heirs vs. Richard Davis administrators, Box 142, #284, Kentucky State Archives, Frankfort, Ky.
22. Ibid.

3. To have and to hold to the said Collins his heirs & assigns forever in trust for the following purposes towit first for the purposes of selling and disposing of as much thereof as will pay and discharge the debts at present owing by the said Richard, and secondly to hold and dispose of the residue in trust and for the support of the said Davis & wife during their joint lives and afterwards for the support of the survivor of them during his or her life, and after the death of both the said Davis & wife then in trust for the benefit and use of the heirs of said Davis forever. And the said Collins doth bind himself to hold and dispose of the aforesaid property and faithfully to execute the trust aforesaid according to the true intent and meaning of this Indenture

In Witness whereof we have set our hands & seals the day and year aforesaid

Interlined before signed
attest Joseph Collins
Wm. S. Collins

Richard Davis (Seal)
Josiah Collins (S.)

Kentucky Madison County Sct.

I David Irvine clerk of the Court for the County aforesaid do hereby certify that this Deed of Trust was produced to me in my office on the 14 day of February 1833. and proven to be the act and deed of Richard Davis & Josiah Collins by the oath of Joseph Collins a witness thereto. and on another time towit on the 16 day of February 1833 it was also proven by William S. Collins the other witness thereto, and the same has been duly recorded in my office

Att. David Irvine Clerk

Examined

Delivd

Amelia "Milly" Davis b. ca. 1831
Mary Jane Davis b. ca. 1832
Arthusa Davis b. ca. 1834

Richard's Daughters

Richard Davis and Paulina Collins Davis had at least three daughters who lived to adulthood. There is a possibility that a fourth daughter was Sally, who was married to Dudley Dunbar in Madison County, January 27, 1848, with Richard Davis listed as father of the bride on the marriage bond.[1] Sarah/Sally was the name of Richard's mother, Sarah Blackwell, so it does not seem too far-fetched that Sally was also Richard's daughter. Dudley Dunbar lived alone by 1850, so Sally probably died. Dudley Dunbar was the man who was the person of interest in the divorce proceedings for Josiah Davis, brother to Sally Davis. Dudley apparently had a liason with his brother-in-law's wife, Sophia. This case is reviewed in Josiah Davis's biography (see page 206).

Amelia (Milly) Davis, named after Paulina's mother, Amelia Oldham Collins, was born about 1831. She married George Johnston/Johnson. We did not find a recorded marriage (although she named him as her husband in the deposition below), but George Johnston was a witness to the marriage of Milly's brother, Clifton Davis, to Pamelia Elliott in 1859.[2] Milly gave a deposition in the court case to settle her father's probate, in which she said that her father had given her a Negro girl named Eliza.

> He told me to take that Negro girl and keep her till he called for her. My Father afterwards sent for her and took her back to his House & I went over & told him I could not do without her and he told me he would let me have her back & did let me have her back upon condition that I would let him have her whenever he sent for — & he called James Davis' wife to witness it. She was the same Negro that George Johnson afterwards sold. My Father was very mad when she was sold & said he intended to have her back & would pay anybody a good price to bring her back. My Father came to my House [to get back the slave]. We lived in Clarke County, Kentucky. My [father] said that he gave none of his children any Negroes, that he loaned the Negroes to them till he called for them. My husband George Johnson sold her. I got no part of the money — he bought me nothing with the money. I do not know what became of the money. I was living with Geo Johnson at that time as his wife, & did so live with him till within three or four months of the time he was sentenced to the penitentiary.[3]

When cross-examined, Milly said that she lived with George Johnson for two or three years while he was indicted for burglary and grand larceny. She was divorced by 1874.[4] We did not find her in the census of 1870. We do not know if she had any children.

Mary Jane Davis was born about 1832 in Madison County, Kentucky. She married John Brooks in Madison County, May 7, 1849.[5] Elisha Roberts was listed as guardian of the groom, and Richard Davis was listed as father of the bride.[6] Their son, Archibald Brooks, testified at his grandfather's probate hearing that they had moved to Missouri "just before the war and came back to Kentucky just afterwards." The relationship between Mary Jane's husband, John Brooks, and his father-in-law, Richard Davis, must have caused Mary Jane some discomfort. Richard Davis sued John Brooks, and John Brooks countersued his father-in-law in the Madison County Court over a $600 note that Richard owed to John Brooks. One of the people who testified on Richard's behalf was Arthusa Davis, who said that she had seen her father pay to Brooks "five or six piles of money." But Richard Davis testified that John had bragged that he was going to make his father-in-law pay *twice!*[7]

According to the federal censuses of 1860 for Cass County, Missouri, 1870 for Madison County, Kentucky, and 1880 for Boone County, Missouri, and *Boone County Marriages 1871–1899* by K.E. Weant, compiler, John Brooks and Mary Jane had the following children:

1. Archibald Brooks born March 1850 in Madison County, Kentucky; living in 1900 in Boone County, Missouri; died 1912 in Boone County, Missouri, after falling from a wagon.[8]
2. Pauline Brooks born about 1852; married to Baxter Wells; lived in Boone County, Missouri, in 1880, and Madison County, Kentucky, in 1910; died 1930, Lexington, Kentucky.
3. Mary/Mollie Brooks born about 1857 in Kentucky or Missouri; married E.S. Elkin; lived Randolph County, Missouri, in 1910 and 1920. She signed Arch Brooks's death certificate as his sister.
4. Pattie Brooks born about 1862 in Missouri; married November 3, 1881, to Lewis A. Varnon in Boone County, Missouri.
5. Sallie Brooks born about 1866 in Missouri; married February 24, 1891, to George McCarty in Boone County, Missouri.
6. Lucy Brooks born about 1869. No further record.
7. Mattie Brooks born about 1872 in Kentucky; married December 24, 1890, to Emmett Turner in Boone County, Missouri.

At Richard Davis's probate hearing, Mary Jane Brooks testified that she lived with her father during his last illness and that she and her daughter did "all of the work for the household."[9] She was a widow in 1880, living in Boone County, Missouri.[10] We did not find her in the 1900 census of either Kentucky or Missouri, so her date of death and burial place are unknown.

The youngest daughter of Richard and Paulina Davis was Arthusa Davis, born about 1834, married Noah Tevis May 1, 1854. Richard Davis was listed as the father of the bride.[11] Arthusa, at age twelve, was probably the surrogate mother for her three younger brothers, Albert, Clifton, and James, who would have been nine, seven, and five when their mother died in 1846. Her older sisters were out of the house and married by 1850.

Arthusa and Noah Tevis lived only a short distance from Richard's farm during the 1860s and, according to Noah's testimony during Richard's probate hearings, Tevis helped Richard with his business dealings. Noah explained how each of Richard's children by his first wife Paulina had been given a slave, a horse, cow and calf, sow, pigs, and bed. The slaves were young when Richard gave them, worth approximately $500, and the other items were worth a total of $140. Tevis explained that although Richard had *given* slaves to his children, he would take them back on a whim.[12]

Noah said that he had handled Richard's business for several years before Richard's death. He said he had taken slaves to Lexington to sell, that he had supervised the sale of Richard's distillery in 1860, and that he had done other business and "writings" for Richard. Tevis asked for $600 from Richard's estate, but the court granted his wife only $102.39.

According to the 1860, 1870, and 1880 federal censuses of Madison, Kentucky, and *Vital Statistics of Madison County, Kentucky, Vol. 1, Births, Deaths, Marriages, 1852–1859, 1874–1878*, by Bill and Kathy Vockery, Arthusa and Noah Tevis had the following children:

1. Mary M. Tevis born about 1855; not in 1870 census; may have died young.
2. Ann Eliza Tevis born October 9, 1856; not in 1870 census; may have died young.
3. Robert Evan Tevis born December 29, 1858.
4. William Tevis born about 1862.
5. Ida Tevis born about 1864.
6. Cleopatra Tevis born about 1866.
7. Clifton Tevis born about 1869.
8. Marion Tevis born about 1871.
9. Tilton Tevis born about 1873.
10. Richard Davis Tevis born about 1877.

While we did not find where Noah and Arthusa Davis Tevis were buried, we did find an obituary for their youngest son. It was found at Eastern Kentucky University, the date of death was penciled in as 3/16/1974:

> Richard Davis Tevis, 96, Central Court, died at 5 p.m. Tuesday at his home following a long illness. He was a native of Madison County, a retired farmer and member of the Flatwood Christian Church. He is survived by four daughters, Mrs. A.T. (Bernice) Douglas and Mrs. W.C. (Minnie) Howell, both of Lexington; Mrs. Morbin (Hallie) Hayse, Tempe, Ariz., and Mrs. S.J. (Bertha) McAugham, Houston, Tex.; six sons, William Edward Tevis and Charles R. Tevis, both of Richmond; John R. Tevis, Paint Lick; Neal E. Tevis, Ben F. Tevis, both of Lexington, and J.C. Tevis, Brockton, Mass.; 23 grandchildren, 16 great-grandchildren, and several nieces and nephews. Funeral services will be conducted at 11 a.m. Friday at Turpin Funeral Home with Rev. Charles Blakemore officiating. Burial will follow in Richmond Cemetery. Pallbearers: Charles Wagers, Andrew Wilson, Harold Moberly, John Adams, Roy Agee, Coleman Edwards.[13]

Among the four daughters, perhaps only two or three had descendants. Sarah/Sally Davis Dunbar apparently had no surviving children, as none were mentioned in Richard Davis's probate estate file. Amelia/Milly Davis Johnston's descendants, if any, are unknown. But Mary Jane Davis Brooks and Arthusa Davis Tevis had large families with many descendants, who established homes in Kentucky and Missouri. *A.H.*

Notes

1. Madison Co., Kentucky, Marriage Bonds 3:155.
2. Madison Co., Kentucky, Marriage Bonds 6:59, Film #183317, Kentucky State Archives, Frankfort, Ky.
3. Deposition of Milly Johnson, Madison Co., Kentucky, Court Cases, Richard Davis heirs vs. Richard Davis administrators, Box 142, #284, Kentucky State Archives, Frankfort, Ky.
4. Ibid.
5. William L. and Kathy Vockery, *Madison County, Kentucky, Marriages, 1823–1851* (Richmond, Ky.: the authors, 1993–), II: 70.
6. Ibid.
7. Madison Co., Kentucky, Court Cases, John Brooks vs. Richard Davis, #20031, Kentucky State Archives, Frankfort, Ky.
8. Arch Brooks, Missouri death certificate, 1912, #320026.
9. Deposition of Mary Jane Brooks, Madison Co., Kentucky, Court Cases, Richard Davis heirs vs. Richard Davis administrators, Box 142, #284, Kentucky State Archives, Frankfort, Ky.
10. 1880 federal census, Missouri, Boone Co., Rocky Ford Twp., p. 244.
11. Madison Co., Kentucky, Marriage Bonds 3:15.
12. Deposition of Noah H. Tevis, Madison Co., Kentucky, Court Cases, Richard Davis heirs vs. Richard Davis administrators, Box 142, #284, Kentucky State Archives, Frankfort, Ky.
13. Obituary of Richard Davis Tevis, Madison Co., Kentucky, Newspaper Death Notices and Obituaries, 1/17 to 6/78, Special Collections, Eastern Kentucky University Library, Richmond, Kentucky.

Marriage document for "Mr. Noah H. Davis and Arthusa D. Davis at the house of Richard Davis." Above copied from Madison County, Kentucky, Marriage Records, Volume 2, Page 75, Madison County Courthouse.

This is to certify that on the 2nd day of May 1854 the Rites of marriage were legally solemnized by me between Mr Noah H Davis And Arthusa D Davis at the house of Richard Davis in the County of Madison Ky in the presence of Jeremiah Collins And Absolem Shearer

Josiah Collins

JOSIAH DAVIS b. February 1830

A Man of Dissipated Habits

The oldest son of Richard Davis and Paulina Collins Davis was born, according to his own affidavit, in February of 1830.[1] He was most likely named after Paulina's father, Josiah Collins, who was an early minister in the Christian Church (Disciples of Christ). Although named after a religious leader, his life would be more like one in a trashy romance novel.

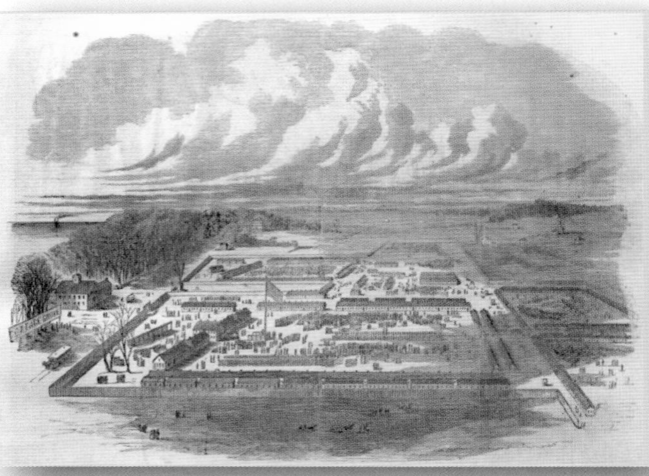

"Camp Douglas," Harper's Weekly, *5 April 1862, <http://www.sonofthesouth.net>, see images linked through Google.*

When he was only nineteen, he married Sophia Pully on November 12, 1849, in Madison County, Kentucky.[2] They lived together two or three years when he sued her for adultery and abandonment.[3] In those days there was no such thing as a no-fault divorce. Imagine a neighborhood choosing sides and the residents taking a wagon to Richmond to testify for the young husband or the young wife. Several neighbors swore that they had seen Dudley Dunbar being "entertained" by Mrs. Davis; and when she moved out, it was Dudley who drove the wagon, loaded with her belongings. Others came to court and stated that Josiah Davis was a drunkard and a loafer who would not do a day's work and that he was renting a farm from Dudley Dunbar. Sophia testified that she married Josiah only to spite his grandfather, Rev. Collins. She accused Josiah of trying to hide his assets from her. She said that he was "habitual drunken and neglected to provide." Margaret Reeves, a servant in the household of Richard Davis, testified that one day when she came to visit Sophia Davis, she peeked through a chink in the chimney and saw Sophia and Dudley Dunbar in bed together. Sometime after the 1850 census was taken, Sophia had a baby. To add insult to injury, she named the baby, Dudley.[4]

In Sophia's cross-suit, John Dunbar testified that Josiah "was a man of dissipated habits," drinking and "floating about in bad houses."[5] The divorce case ended in a semi-stalemate. Sophia was granted a small amount of maintenance ($25 per year), but Josiah swore that he would never pay it.[6] Eventually, her suit was dismissed, and Josiah was granted a divorce on the grounds of abandonment. The judge stated that neither was "well-qualified to take charge of the infant child," but that perhaps Sophia was best qualified of the two.[7] Neither Sophia Davis nor little Dudley appeared in later censuses of Madison County.

According to testimony in the settlement of his father's estate, Josiah lived with his father "several years before the War and several years after the War" until Richard's death. However, in 1860 Josiah Davis was living with his sister Arthusa Tevis and family.[8] In 1862 Josiah enlisted in Company B, 11th Regiment Cavalry, CSA, and was captured during the battle of Cheshire, Ohio.[9] While imprisoned at Camp Douglas, Illinois, Richard Davis sent Josiah money, a fact that was brought out during the court case that settled Richard Davis's estate.[10] In 1870 Josiah was back in his father's household, who by now had a new wife and infant son.[11] The last known record for Josiah Davis listed him as a

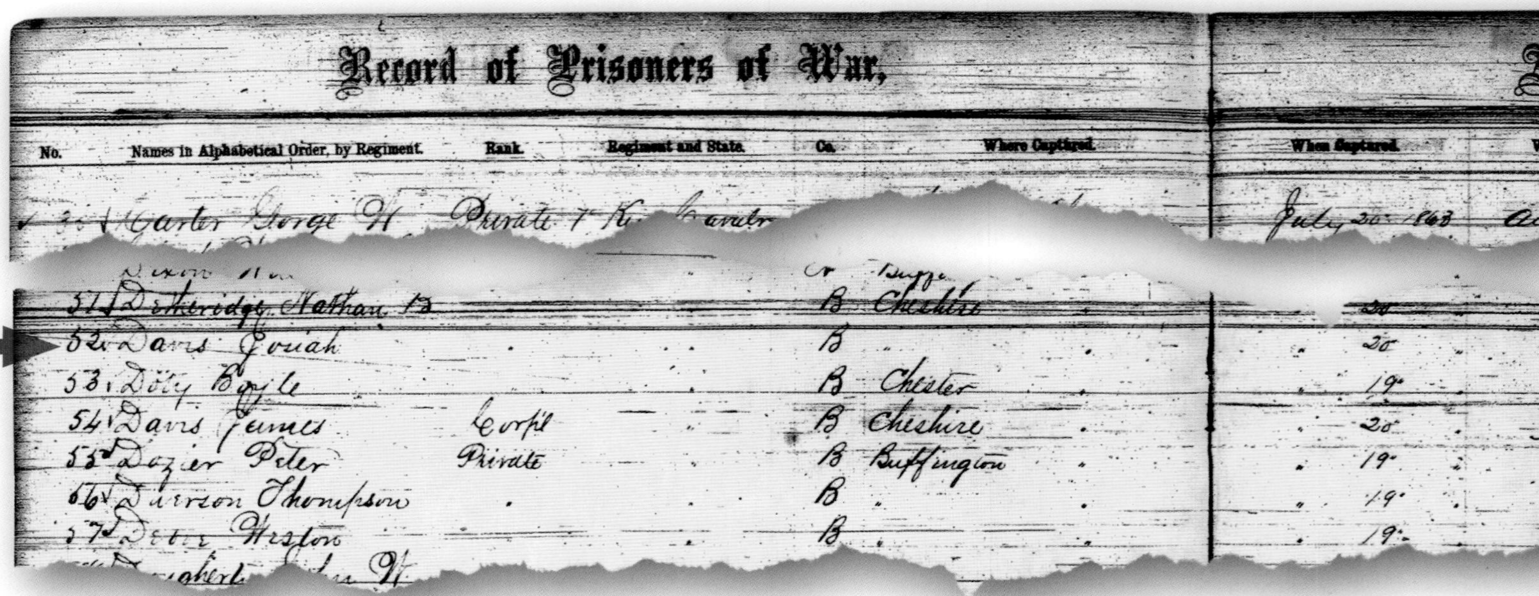

Record of Prisoners of War,

No.	Names in Alphabetical Order, by Regiment.	Rank.	Regiment and State.	Co.	Where Captured.	When Captured.
	Carter George W	Private		K		July 20 1863
51	Detheridge Nathan B			B	Cheshire	20
52	Davis Josiah			B		20
53	Doty Boyle			B	Chester	19
54	Davis James	Corp'l		B	Cheshire	20
55	Dozier Peter	Private		B	Buffington	19
56	Dirrson Thompson			B		19
57	Deter Weston			B		19

General Register of Prisoners, August 1864 – December 1864, Selected Records of the War Department Relating to Confederate Prisoners of War, 1861–1865, NARA M598 (Washington: National Archives), Roll 53

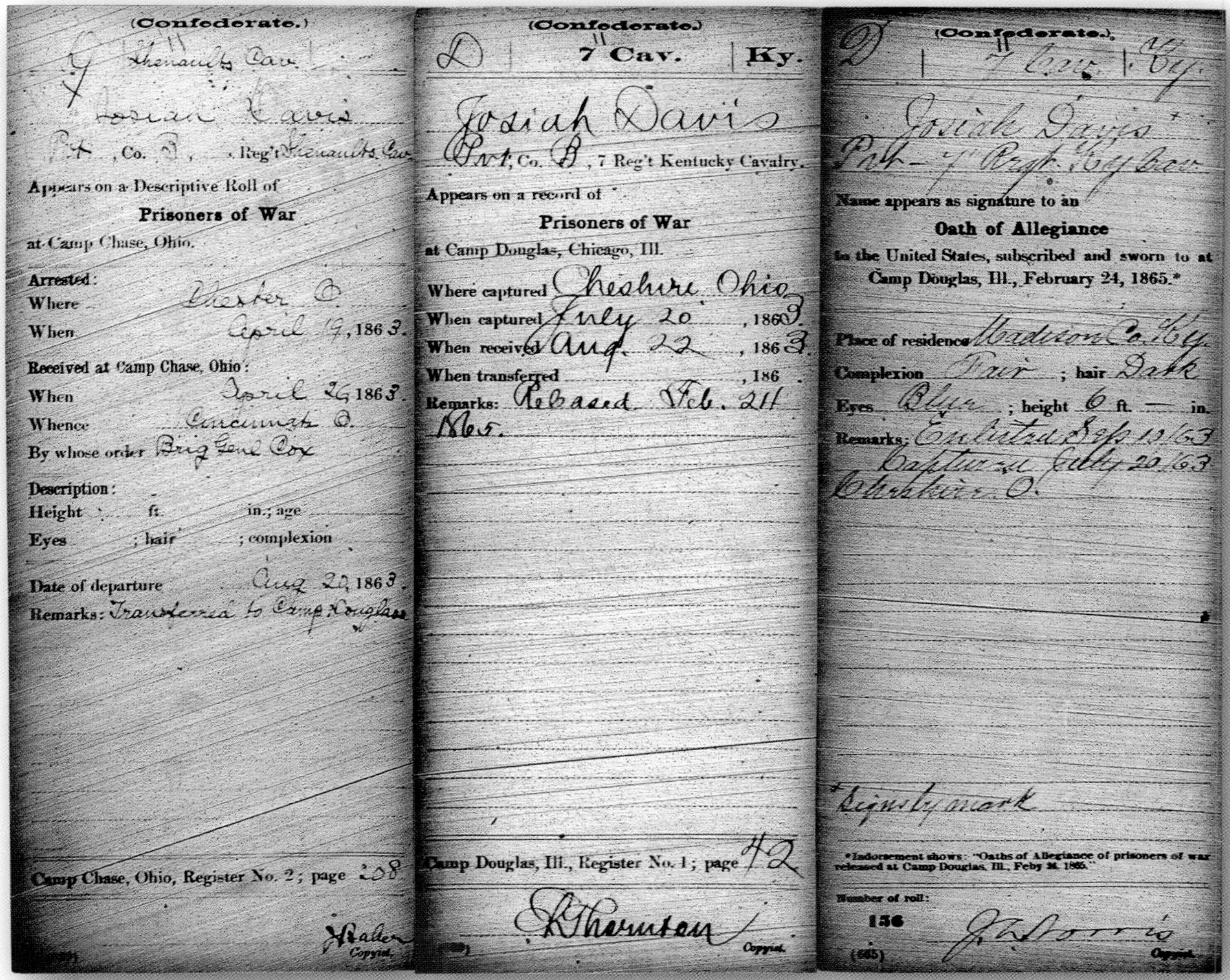
(Confederate.)
G [?] Shenault's Cav.
Josiah Davis
Pvt, Co. B, Reg't Shenault's Cav.
Appears on a Descriptive Roll of
Prisoners of War
at Camp Chase, Ohio.
Arrested:
Where Chester O.
When April 19, 1863.
Received at Camp Chase, Ohio:
When April 26 1863.
Whence Cincinnati O.
By whose order Brig Genl Cox
Description:
Height ft. in.; age
Eyes ; hair ; complexion
Date of departure Aug 20, 1863.
Remarks: Transferred to Camp Douglass
Camp Chase, Ohio, Register No. 2; page 208
Copyist.

(Confederate.)
D | 7 Cav. | Ky.
Josiah Davis
Pvt, Co. B, 7 Reg't Kentucky Cavalry.
Appears on a record of
Prisoners of War
at Camp Douglas, Chicago, Ill.
Where captured Cheshire Ohio
When captured July 20, 1863
When received Aug. 22, 1863
When transferred , 186
Remarks: Released Feb. 24 1865.
Camp Douglas, Ill., Register No. 1; page 42
Thornton
Copyist.

(Confederate.)
D | 7 Cav. | Ky.
Josiah Davis
Pvt 7 Regt Ky Cav
Name appears as signature to an
Oath of Allegiance
to the United States, subscribed and sworn to at Camp Douglas, Ill., February 24, 1865.*
Place of residence Madison Co. Ky.
Complexion Fair; hair Dark
Eyes Blue; height 6 ft. — in.
Remarks: Enlisted Sept 1 1863 Captured July 20 1863 Cheshire O.
Signs by mark
*Indorsement shows: "Oaths of Allegiance of prisoners of war released at Camp Douglas, Ill., Feby 24 1865."
Number of roll:
156
Copyist.

Josiah Davis (private, Company B, 11th Kentucky Cavalry). Compiled Service Records of Confederate Soldiers Who Served in Organizations From the State of Kentucky, NARA M319 (Washington: National Archives), Roll 60.

boarder, living in 1880, with the Jerry Collins family in Madison County, Kentucky.[12] As with almost all of the early Davis family, we have never been able to find a record of his burial. Josiah lived life "hard," drinking in the same pattern as his father. *A.H.*

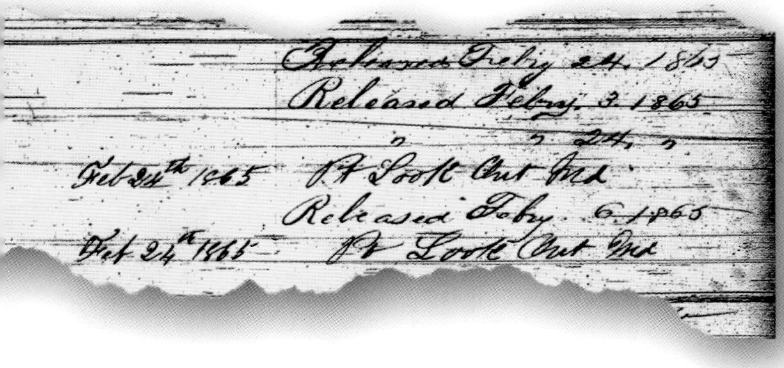
...mp Douglas, Chicago, Ills. 42
When Transferred. REMARKS.
Released Feby 24. 1865
Released Feby 3. 1865
" " 24 "
Feb 24th 1865 Pt Look Out Md
Released Feby 6. 1865
Feb 24th 1865 Pt Look Out Md

Notes

1. Madison Co., Kentucky, Court Cases, Richard Davis heirs vs. Richard Davis administrators, Box 142, #284, Kentucky State Archives, Frankfort, Ky.
2. William L. and Kathy Vockery, *Madison County, Kentucky, Marriages, 1823-1851* (Richmond, Ky.: the authors, 1993–), II:19.
3. Madison Co., Kentucky, Court Cases, Josiah Davis vs. Sophia Davis, #21227, Kentucky State Archives, Frankfort, Ky.
4. Ibid.
5. Madison Co., Kentucky, Court Cases, Sophia Davis vs. Josiah Davis, #21298, Kentucky State Archives, Frankfort, Ky.
6. Ibid.
7. Ibid.
8. 1860 federal census, Kentucky, Madison Co., 1st dist., p. 282.
9. Record of Prisoners of War, Camp Douglas, Chicago, Ill., Publication. No. M598, Roll 145, Vol. 426, Library of Congress, National Archives, Washington, D.C.
10. Madison Co., Kentucky, Court Cases, Richard Davis heirs vs. Richard Davis administrators, Box 142, #284, Kentucky State Archives, Frankfort, Ky.
11. 1870 federal census, Kentucky, Madison Co., Union pct., p. 283.
12. 1880 federal census, Kentucky, Madison Co., Elliston pct., p. 7.

ALBERT "BERT" DAVIS b. ca. 1837

Albert "Bert" Davis, son of Richard Davis and Pauline Collins, and brother to James Davis, the author's great-grandfather. It is not known who wrote the inscription on the back of the photograph.

Brother Albert

Sometimes in genealogical research an obscure clue becomes the key to unlocking the family history. This was the case with an old picture, labeled "Brother Albert, grandfather's brother." The picture was taken by a Moberly, Missouri, photographer and was in the hands of descendants of James Davis of Johnson County, Missouri. Even though Johnson County, Missouri, and Randolph County are many miles apart, we knew that "brother Albert" had a link to our James Davis. After we found Albert in the later censuses of Randolph County, Missouri, we knew that he would be a help in finding the father of our Davis family in Kentucky. Instead of looking at every Davis family in Madison County, Kentucky, we had only to look for one with both an Albert and a James.

At the time our research began in the late 1990s, we knew little about Albert Davis. We tried to find him in the censuses and in some obituary listings in Randolph County, hoping to get a death certificate that would name his father. We found him in the 1880 census of Randolph County, Missouri, with a wife Margaret and one child, Richard, age twenty-one.[1] Also living in the same township in Randolph County were James Davis and his family.[2] We believed that the two brothers had traveled together from Kentucky to Missouri.

Since we could not find Albert in the 1900 census, we assumed that he had died prior to 1900. But it is dangerous to assume anything in genealogy — as we found him in the 1910 census, living with his son, John Richard Davis and his wife Dora.[3] Since Missouri began keeping death certificates in 1910, we checked the Missouri Archives web site and found that his death certificate had been recently posted on their new online database in 2006.[4]

His death certificate revealed the "proof" for which we had been looking at the beginning of our search eight years prior — the name of the father of James and Albert — Richard Davis. His mother was given as Pauline Collins and his birthplace as Madison County, Kentucky. The informant was Mrs. Dora Davis, wife of John Richard Davis (son of Albert). The certificate gave Albert's birth date as March 6, 1836, and stated that he died in Huntsville, Missouri, on April 26, 1912, and was buried in the Huntsville Cemetery.

What a confirmation of items that we had already pieced together! We had looked for a Davis family in Kentucky with both an Albert and a James. There were several children named James Davis in Madison County, Kentucky, in 1850, but only one family with both an Albert and a James. It was Richard Davis and Paulina Collins, and that story has been told in the Richard Davis biography.

Albert Davis was about ten years old when his mother died in 1846. His father Richard hired a neighbor girl to watch the younger children. Her name was Margaret Reeves, and Albert married her prior to 1860. She was about five years older than Albert. By the 1860 census, they had one child, John R., age ten months in June of 1860.[5] By 1870 they added a daughter to their family, Mellisa, born about 1862.[6] We have no further record of this daughter, as she does not appear with the family on the 1880 census in Missouri.

John Richard Davis was born August 23, 1859, in Madison County, Kentucky.[7] About 1884 he was married to Dora Hogue in Randolph County, Missouri. By 1900 they had two children, Albert and Opal, and John Richard was a farmer. At some point John Richard Davis must have gone to work for the railroad, because he was listed as a "helper" for the railroad, and the family was living in the city of Moberly in 1910.[8] Dora stated that she had three children, but only two were living. Albert L. Davis, age 23, lived with them and was also working for the railroad as a brakeman.

Albert gave the information for his World War I Draft Card that he was single in 1917, that he was the sole support for his mother, and that he was a brakeman for the Wabash Railroad.[9] He married a woman named Bertha between 1920 and 1930, and his mother lived with them in 1930.[10] In his later years he became a conductor for the Wabash Railroad and was still working at age sixty-nine at the time of his death. He died in 1956, and his obituary and a funeral notice appeared in a Moberly newspaper.[11]

Mrs. Dora Davis lived to the age of ninety-four. The only clue we have to the death of John Richard Davis, her husband, was in her obituary.[12] It stated that John R. Davis died "about 10 years ago," but we could not find his death certificate in the online database of the Missouri State Archives. In 1930 Dora lived with her son Albert, and in 1920 she lived with her daughter, Mrs. Opal Kimbrough. According to her obituary, Dora Hogue Davis was an active member of Central Christian Church. She enjoyed quilt-piecing and visiting with friends and neighbors. Burial was in Oakland Cemetery. Her death certificate listed her parents as John Hogue and Sarah Coulter.[13]

To our knowledge, neither Albert Lloyd Davis nor Opal Davis Kimbrough had any children. Opal Davis Kimbrough's obituary stated that "she was the last of her family." This notice said that her father, J.R. Davis died in 1935. Opal was a graduate of Moberly High School and Sheldon Business School in St. Louis. She was active in the Red Cross during World War I. Active in Republican politics, she was "the first woman to be appointed chief clerk of a state department at the capitol in Jefferson City."[14] She died June 3, 1968, with one cousin, Mrs. Mary Phillips of

Kansas City, surviving. There was no mention of her husband, Roscoe, whom she had married in 1906.

Though the descendants of "brother Albert" had dwindled away by 1968, his story is told here because he was the key to our finding the correct Davis family in Kentucky. James and Albert Davis were about five years apart in age. When their mother died, they were watched by a neighbor girl, who would become Albert's wife. In 1870 they lived side-by-side, and together they moved away from Madison County, Kentucky, to Randolph County, Missouri. They surely had a special relationship. *A.H.*

Notes

1. 1880 federal census, Missouri, Randolph Co., Salt Spring Twp., p. 172A.
2. 1880 federal census, Missouri, Randolph Co., Salt Spring Twp., pp. 182B and 183A.
3. 1910 federal census, Missouri, Randolph Co., Sugar Creek Twp., town of Moberly, p. 231A.
4. Albert Davis, Missouri death certificate, Randolph Co., 1912, #14633.
5. 1860 federal census, Kentucky, Madison Co., p. 285.
6. 1870 federal census, Kentucky, Madison Co., p. 282A.
7. William L. and Kathy Vockery, *Vital Statistics of Madison County, Kentucky* (Richmond, Ky.: the authors, 2000), 1:24. John R. Davis born 23 Aug. 1859 to Albert Davis and Margaret Reeves.
8. 1910 federal census, Missouri, Randolph Co., Sugar Creek Twp., town of Moberly, p. 231A.
9. World I Draft Registration, Albert L. Davis, Randolph Co., Missouri, Ancestry.com.
10. 1930 federal census, Missouri, Randolph Co., Moberly City, p. 197B.
11. Albert Davis death notice and funeral notice, *Moberly* (Missouri) *Monitor Index and Democrat*, 9 May 1956.
12. Dora Hogue Davis obituary, *Moberly* (Missouri) *Monitor Index and Democrat*, 30 Nov. 1954.
13. Dora Hogue Davis, Missouri death certificate, 1954, #38383.
14. Opal Davis Kimbrough obituary, *Moberly* (Missouri) *Monitor Index and Democrat*, 4 June 1968.

N. B.—Every item of information should be carefully supplied. AGE should be stated EXACTLY. PHYSICIANS should state CAUSE OF DEATH in plain terms, so that it may be properly classified. Exact statement of OCCUPATION is very important.

PLACE OF DEATH
County Randolph
Township ___ or Village ___ or City Huntsville (No. ___ St. ___ Ward) [If death occurred in a hospital or institution, give its NAME instead of street and number]

MISSOURI STATE BOARD OF HEALTH
BUREAU OF VITAL STATISTICS
CERTIFICATE OF DEATH

Registration District No. 733 File No. 14633
Primary Registration District No. 4458 Registered No. 72

FULL NAME Albert Davis

PERSONAL AND STATISTICAL PARTICULARS

SEX Male COLOR OR RACE White SINGLE, MARRIED, WIDOWED OR DIVORCED (Write the word) Widower

DATE OF BIRTH Mar 6, 1836 (Month) (Day) (Year)

AGE 76 yrs. 1 mos. 20 ds. If LESS than 1 day, ___ hrs. or ___ min.?

OCCUPATION (a) Trade, profession, or particular kind of work None Formerly Farmer
(b) General nature of industry, business, or establishment in which employed (or employer) [illegible]

BIRTHPLACE (City or town, State or foreign country) Madison Co Ky

PARENTS
NAME OF FATHER Richard Davis
BIRTHPLACE OF FATHER (City or town, State or foreign country) Don't Know
MAIDEN NAME OF MOTHER Pauline Collins
BIRTHPLACE OF MOTHER (City or town, State or foreign country) Don't Know

THE ABOVE IS TRUE TO THE BEST OF MY KNOWLEDGE
(Informant) Mrs Dora Davis
(Address) Moberly Mo

Filed April 26th 1912 G. G. Bragg REGISTRAR

MEDICAL CERTIFICATE OF DEATH

DATE OF DEATH April 26, 1912 (Month) (Day) (Year)

I HEREBY CERTIFY, that I attended deceased from Nov ___, 1911, to April 26, 1912, that I last saw h__ alive on April 26, 1912, and that death occurred, on the date stated above, at 11:30 __m.

The CAUSE OF DEATH* was as follows:
Chronic Cystitis
(Duration) 3 yrs. ___ mos. ___ ds.
Contributory (Secondary) Senility & Prostatic Enlargement ___ mos. ___ ds.
(Signed) D A Bamback [illegible] M. D.
4-26, 1912 (Address) Huntsville

*State the Disease Causing Death, or, in deaths from Violent Causes, state (1) Means of Injury; and (2) whether Accidental, Suicidal, or Homicidal.

LENGTH OF RESIDENCE (For Hospitals, Institutions, Transients, or Recent Residents)
At place of death ___ yrs. 8 mos. ___ ds. In the State 35 yrs. ___ mos. 1 ds. County Infirmary
Where was disease contracted if not at place of death? Randolph Co
Former or usual residence Jacksonville Mo

PLACE OF BURIAL OR REMOVAL [illegible] DATE OF BURIAL 4-27, 1912
UNDERTAKER [illegible] ADDRESS Huntsville

Certificate of Death for Albert Davis b. March 6, 1836, d. April 26, 1912, father of John Richard and Melissa Davis

Albert "Bert" Davis Family

Dora May Hogue Davis b. October 31, 1860, Missouri, John Richard Davis (son of Albert) b. August 23, 1859, and their children, Opal b. July 21, 1885, and Albert Lloyd b. February 17, 1887

Albert "Bert" Davis Family

TWELFTH CENSUS OF THE UNITED STAT

SCHEDULE No. 1.—POPULATION.

State Missouri
County Randolph
Township or other division of county Jackson Township
Name of incorporated city, town, or village, within the above-named division, x
Enumerated by me on the 7th day of June, 1900, Richard H. Hinton

Line	Dwelling	Family	Name	Relation	Color	Sex	Month	Year	Age	Conjugal	Years married	Mother of how many children	Children living	Place of birth of this person	Place of birth of Father	Place of birth of Mother
1	63	63	Stigall, Algie	Head										Missouri	Missouri	Missouri
			Harry	Son	W	M	Jun	1884	16	S				Missouri	Missouri	Missouri
31			Hade	Son	W	M	Aug	1892	7	S				Missouri	Missouri	Missouri
32	70	70	Davis, John R.	Head	W	M	Aug	1859	40	M	16			Kentucky	Kentucky	Kentucky
33			Dora	Wife	W	F	May	1860	40	M	16	3	2	Missouri	Kentucky	Kentucky
34			Opal	Daughter	W	F	July	1887	12	S				Missouri	Kentucky	Missouri
35			Albert	Son	W	M	Jan	1891	9	S				Missouri	Kentucky	Missouri
36			Durham, Harvey	Servant	W	M	Dec	1880	19	S				Missouri	Missouri	Missouri
37	71	71	Hoze, George	Head	W	M	Oct	1826	74	M	16			Virginia	Virginia	Virginia

Twelfth Census of the United States of 1900 for Jackson Township, Randolph County, Missouri, enumerating John R. Davis b. August 23, 1859 (the son of Albert "Bert" Davis); his wife Dora; his daughter, Opal; and his son, Albert. This copy was filed in the Missouri State Archives, Randolph County, 1900 census, ED131, Page 42A, Reel F302.

42 A

...ervisor's District No. 143 — Sheet No. 4

...umeration District No. 131

Ward of city, X

Enumerator. 3/3/9

...CUPATION, TRADE, OR PROFESSION (...ach person TEN YEARS of age and over.)		EDUCATION.				OWNERSHIP OF HOME.			
Occupation.	Months not employed.	Attended school (in months).	Can read.	Can write.	Can speak English.	Owned or rented.	Owned free or mortgaged.	Farm or house.	Number of farm schedule.
19	20	21	22	23	24	25	26	27	28
...armer	0		yes	yes	yes	O	M	F	54
			yes	yes	yes				
...at School	16		yes	yes	yes				
...armer	0		yes	yes	yes	O	M	F	61
			yes	yes	yes				
at School	6		yes	yes	yes				
...y laborer	4		yes	yes	yes				
...armer	0		yes	yes	yes	O	F	F	62

Albert L. Davis, Rail-Conductor, Dies Here at 69

Albert L. Davis, 69, Wabash Railroad passenger conductor, died at 7 o'clock Sunday morning in Wabash Hospital. The Davis home is at 422½ South Williams street.

Mr. Davis was born in Jacksonville, but lived here for the past 50 years. A Wabash employe 47 years, he was conductor on passenger trains Nos. 11 and 14 at the time of his death.

He was a member of Central Christian church, having served as deacon for a number of years, and belonged to the Order of Railroad Conductors and various Masonic orders, including the Blue Lodge, Royal Arch Masons and Knights Templar.

Surviving are his wife; and a sister, Mrs. Opal Davis Kimbrough, Moberly.

The body will remain at Cater Funeral home until services at 2 o'clock Tuesday afternoon in Central Christian church by the Rev. A. E. Landolt, pastor. Burial will be in Oakland cemetery.

Albert L. Davis death notice, Moberly Monitor Index and Democrat *(Missouri), May 9, 1956. Albert "Bert" Davis was the grandfather of Albert L. Davis.*

Moberly Monitor Index and Democrat — Page 5 — Wed., May 9, 1956

Many Attend Funeral Of Albert L. Davis

Many friends in Moberly and from Jacksonville attended the funeral services yesterday for Albert L. Davis, Wabash Railroad passenger conductor, in Central Christian Church yesterday afternoon.

Among the out-of-town friends were: Mr. and Mrs. J. B. Davenport and Mrs. Harry LaRue, Columbia; Mr. and Mrs. Arthur Howard, Clifton Hill; Mr. and Mrs. Forrest Parcells, Kirksville; and Chester Johnson, Chillicothe.

Mr. Davis attended Moberly High School and Pritchett College, conducted by U.S. Hall at Glasgow. He was a descendant of the Coulter and Houge families, pioneers in the northern part of Randolph county.

Mr. Davis' mother, Mrs. Dora Hogue Davis, died in 1954. Mr. Davis and his sister, Mrs. Opal Davis Kimbrough, 531 Fisk avenue, are relatives of Mrs. Mary Elkins Phillips of Kansas City, a former Moberly resident.

Albert L. Davis funeral notice, Moberly Monitor Index and Democrat *(Missouri), May 9, 1956. Albert "Bert" Davis was the grandfather of Albert L. Davis.*

Dora Hogue Davis, Moberly Monitor Index and Democrat *(Missouri), November 30, 1954*

Mrs. Dora Davis, 94, Dies; Funeral to Be Held Tomorrow

Mrs. Dora Hogue Davis, 94, died at 7:40 o'clock last night in Whitaker Hospital, where she became a patient for bed rest last Aug. 1.

She is survived by a daughter, Mrs. Opal Davis Kimbrough, Overfelt Apartments, 509 South Clark street; a son, A. L. Davis, 721 West Rollins street; and a half-sister, Mrs. Annie Parcells, San Diego, Calif. Cousins are Mrs. Mellie Scrutchfield, Jacksonville, and Frank Carlisle, Des Plaines, Ill.

Mrs. Davis, widow of J. R. Davis, who died about 10 years ago, made her home with the son and his wife. She was born and reared near Jacksonville, where she lived until coming to Moberly 35 years ago. She observed her 94th birthday on Oct. 31 in Whitaker Hospital. Mrs. Davis was a member of the pioneer Hogue and Coulter families of Macon and Randolph Counties. She was always interested in local and state civic and religious affairs. She organized the Farm and Home Club at Jacksonville long before these clubs became extension service projects. She was an active member of Central Christian Church and a member of its Women's Bible Class.

Until a few months ago Mrs. Davis took a short daily walk with assistance. She enjoyed sewing and quilt piecing and visits with friends and neighbors.

A few years ago Mrs. Davis was honored on the "Orchid for You" program of Station KNCM, which gave at that time biographies of outstanding citizens.

The body is in the Snow Funeral Home and services will be held at 2 o'clock tomorrow afternoon in its chapel by the Rev. C. W. Cornn, at one time her pastor. Burial will be in Oakland cemetery.

Opal Davis Kimbrough, Moberly Monitor Index and Democrat *(Missouri), June 4, 1968*

Mrs. Kimbrough, Active in Clubs And Politics, Dies

Mrs. Opal Davis Kimbrough, 79, died at 12:15 p.m. Monday at Community Hospital after a long illness. She had been living at the U-Rest Boarding Home, 824 South Morley.

Mrs. Kimbrough was the last of her family. Her mother, Mrs. Dora Hague Davis, died in 1954; her only brother, A. T. (Al) Davis, died in 1956, and her father, J. R. Davis, died in 1935. Mrs. Kimbrough was born July 21, 1888, at Jacksonville and sepnt her entire life in Randolph County. She was a member of the Christian Church. Mrs. Kimbrough was a graduate of Moberly High School and the Sheldon Business School of St. Louis. She was a former member of Sorosis and Shakespeare Club of Moberly. She was an active member of Home Service Station of the Red Cross during World War One, receiving a special citation from Herbert Hoover for her service in the Red Cross.

Before World War One, Mrs. Kimbrough organized the civics and Health League in Moberly that developed the first sanitary measures for all food makers and dairies. She had long been active in civic and political affairs in Moberly and Missouri. The Chamber of Commerce, during Mr. Lams-n's term of office, appointed Mrs. Kimbrough on a committee of business and professional people to seek the approval of the late Governor Hyde to locate the State Industrial Home for Girls in Moberly.

Mrs. Kimbrough did much work in organizing the Rebublican Women of Missouri. She gave the address of welcome in the House of Representatives at Jefferson City at the first meeting in the state of Republican women. She was also the first woman in the state to be appointed as chief clerk (Means Office Manager) of a state department at the capitol in Jefferson City.

While in Kansas City, Mrs. Kimbrough was active in Dr. Burris Jenkins Church and the Athenaeum Club and Fine Arts Committee of Nelson Art Gallery. Mrs. Kimbrough thought of herself as a crusader in spirit, endeavoring to develop public sentiment against crime and hypocrisy. She was a descendant of several of the pioneer families of northern Randolph County including the Hogues, Coulters and McCarvers, who built the first churches and schools in that section of the country.

Surviving is a cousin, Mrs. Mary Phillips, Kansas City.

The body is at the Cater Funeral Home. Funeral services will be at 2 o'clock tomorrow afternoon in the funeral chapel. The Rev. C. W. Cornn, Chrisitan minister, will be in charge. Burial will be in Oakland Cemetery. Visitation began this afternoon.

Clifton Davis b. ca. 1839

Merchant and Cattle Trader

Clifton Davis, the son of Richard Davis and Paulina Collins Davis, was born about 1839 in Madison County, Kentucky, and appeared as eleven years old on the 1850 census in his father's household.[1] Clifton was married to Pamelia Elliott, daughter of Thomas Elliott, on April 4, 1859, in Madison County, with Albert Davis as witness and Richard Davis, father of Clifton. George Johnson (brother-in-law) and Clifton Davis posted bond.[2] The newlyweds moved to Johnson County, Missouri, where they appeared on the 1860 census with a baby Clayton, six months old.[3]

Several of the Davis siblings moved back and forth to and from Missouri, and Clifton was to follow the same pattern. Clifton's sister, Mary Jane Davis Brooks, had spent time in Missouri both "before the War and after the War," according to testimony by her son Archibald.[4]

Clifton's stay in Missouri must have been short, because in 1863 Clifton was back in Kentucky, helping his father on the farm. Robert Jordan testified that sometimes Clifton would help his father in his business dealings with "writings."[5] In 1863 Jordan and Clifton took a bunch of hogs to Cincinnati to sell, a distance of more than one hundred miles.[6] Jordan accompanied Clifton on the trip at Richard Davis's request, "because Richard said that 'he (Clifton) was young and wild and they all wanted to get all of him they could.'"[7]

Richard's statement suggested that his children wanted to take advantage of him. It is debatable about who took advantage of whom, for Clifton sued his father in 1863 in Madison County Court. He stated that he "sold and delivered to Richard Davis a Negro man slave named Silas about 17 years old, yellow complexion at the price of Five Hundred Dollars." At the time of sale, Richard gave Clifton $50 for a down payment. Clifton sued his father for the balance of the purchase price and also for several months' hire, because Richard had been using the slave on his farm.[8] In 1865 Clifton purchased from John P. Collins and Martha his wife a small tract of land in Doylesville, on the waters of Clear Creek.[9]

By 1870 Clifton and "Permelia" Davis were living in Estill County, Kentucky, with an infant born in May named Webber.[10] Clifton's occupation was listed as "Ret. Merchant," and he had $1,200 worth of real estate and $2,500 worth of personal property. Does "Ret. Merchant" mean "retail merchant?" The answer to this question is unknown, but Clifton was a merchant of some kind. He must have been living in a village, as there were a gunsmith, cabinetmaker, and stone mason nearby. Neither of the two infant males born to Clifton and Pamelia Davis lived very long lives, as they did not appear on the next census.

In October of 1874 Clifton loaned Noah Tevis, his brother-in-law, $617.54 at 10 percent interest. Noah Tevis put up several horses and cattle as collateral along with "all of the right, title and interest which he [Noah] had made to a claim for services against the estate of Richard Davis, deceased" in the amount of about $700.[11] (Noah's claim against the estate of Richard Davis was denied by the court.)[12]

By October of 1874, an attorney told the court that Clifton Davis and John Brooks (Mary Jane's husband) were non-residents (of Kentucky). Clifton received $254.24 from Richard Davis's estate in September of 1876, and Mary Jane employed Baxter Wells in Madison County to get her part, as she and her family were living in Randolph County, Missouri.[13] She may have been the first of the siblings to travel to Randolph County, Missouri, but two of her brothers, James and Albert, would follow.

By 1880 Clifton and Permelia Davis were living in Vernon County, Missouri, and Clifton's occupation was listed as "cattle trader."[14] They had a nine-year-old daughter named Hattie. This is the last information we have on this family. *A.H.*

Notes

1. 1850 federal census, Kentucky, Madison Co., p. 295.
2. Madison Co., Kentucky, Marriages 6:59.
3. 1860 federal census, Missouri, Johnson Co., p. 1001.
4. Deposition of Arch Brooks, Madison Co., Kentucky, Court Cases, Richard Davis heirs vs. Richard Davis administrators, Box 142, #284, Kentucky State Archives, Frankfort, Ky.
5. Deposition of Robert Jordan, Madison Co., Kentucky, Court Cases, Richard Davis heirs vs. Richard Davis administrators, Box 142, #284, Kentucky State Archives, Frankfort, Ky.
6. Ibid.
7. Ibid.
8. Madison Co., Kentucky, Court Cases, Clifton Davis vs. Richard Davis, #23821, Kentucky State Archives, Frankfort, Ky.
9. Madison Co., Kentucky, Deed Book 14:136–37.
10. 1870 federal census, Kentucky, Estill Co., Crooked Creek pct., Irvine P.O., p. 22.
11. Madison Co., Kentucky, Deed Book 21:30, Film #992372, Kentucky State Archives, Frankfort, Ky.
12. Madison Co., Kentucky, Court Cases, Richard Davis heirs vs. Richard Davis administrators, Box 142, #284, Kentucky State Archives, Frankfort, Ky.
13. Ibid.
14. 1880 federal census, Missouri, Vernon Co., Centre Twp., Nevada, p. 558B.

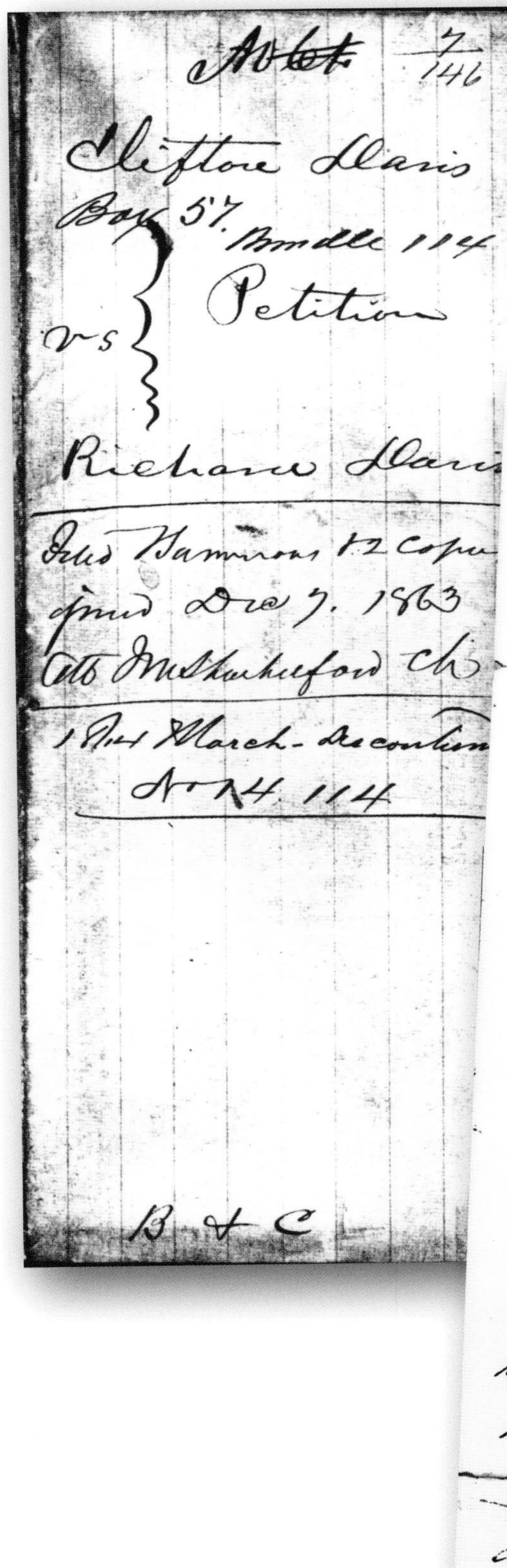

Abt [struck through] 7/146

Clifton Davis
Box 57. Bundle 114
vs } Petition
Richard Davis

Filed Summons + 2 copies
issued Dec 7. 1863
Att M Shackelford Ch

1st ... March - discontinued
No 24. 114

B & C

Petition of Clifton Davis in his lawsuit against his father, Richard Davis, for nonpayment for the sale and use of a slave in 1863

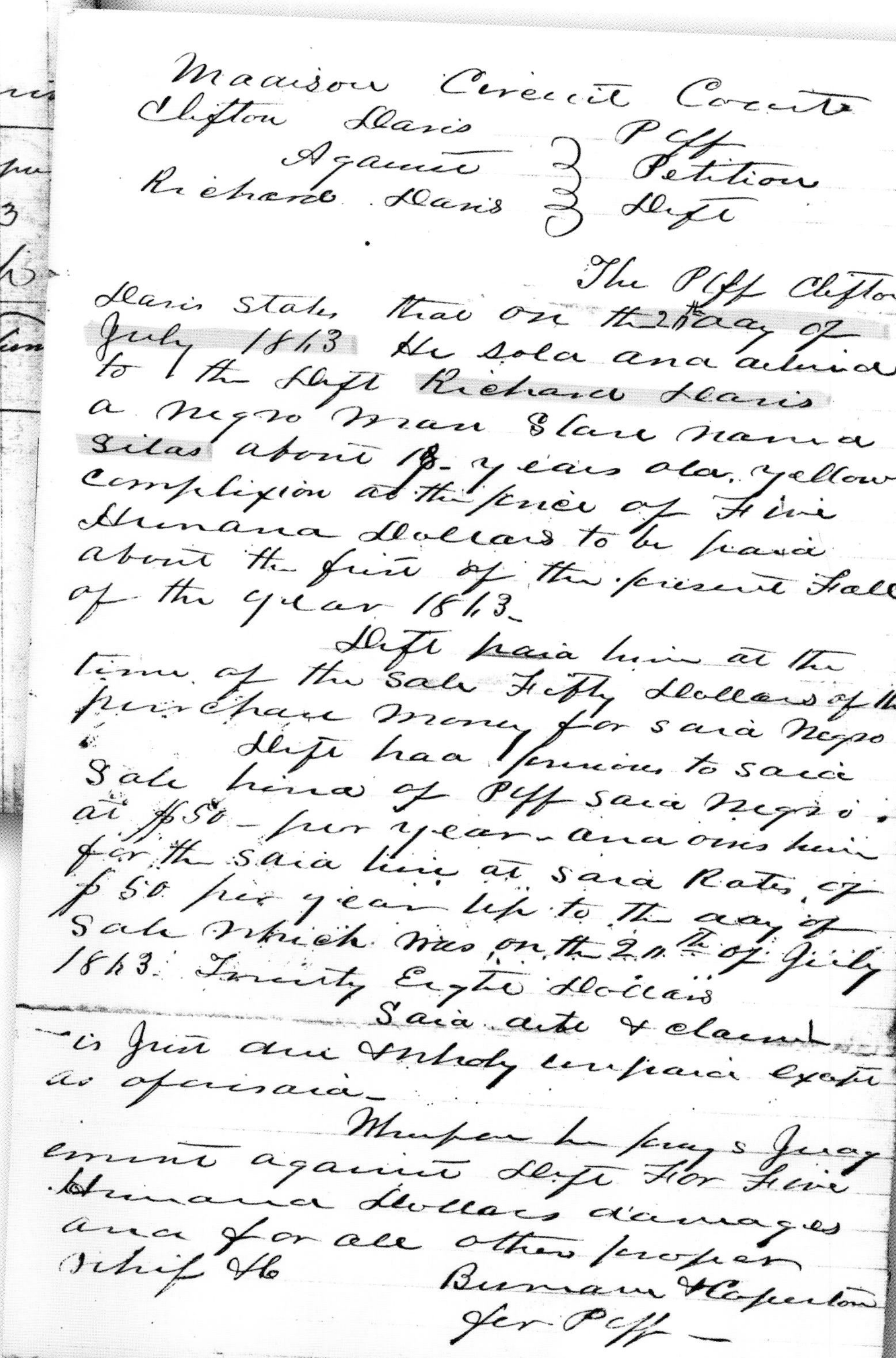

Madison Circuit Court
Clifton Davis Pltff
Against } Petition
Richard Davis Deft

The Pltff Clifton Davis states that on the 21 day of July 1863 He sold and delivered to the Deft Richard Davis a Negro man Slave named Silas about 18 years old, yellow complexion at the price of Five Hundred Dollars to be paid about the first of the present Fall of the year 1863.

Deft paid him at the time of the sale Fifty Dollars of the purchase money for said Negro

Deft had previous to said sale hired of Pltff said Negro at $50 per year and owes him for the said hire at said Rate of $50 per year up to the day of sale which was on the 21st of July 1863. Twenty Eight Dollars

Said debt & claim is just due & wholly unpaid except as aforesaid.

Wherefore he prays Judgment against Deft for Five Hundred Dollars damages and for all other proper relief &c

Burnam & Caperton
for Pltff

JAMES DAVIS b. December 11, 1841

James Davis with unidentified woman thought to be Miriam "Mimi" Dodd Marquess, his second wife, whom he married in 1890

James Davis — From Kentucky to Missouri

James Davis, youngest son of Richard Davis and Paulina Collins Davis, was born December 11, 1841, according to his tombstone.[1] His mother died when he was about five years old, and he was most likely raised by his older sisters and hired help. In about 1859 he married Nancy "Nannie" Gooch, daughter of Chiswell and Eliza Maupin Gooch, when he was about nineteen years old. The 1860 census of Madison County, Kentucky, showed the young couple living with his father, Richard, and the census indicated that that they had been married within the year, though no record of marriage was found in Madison County.[2] By 1870 the couple had four sons: Jeffrey (Jefferson), Morgan, Charles, and Joseph, and the family lived next door to his brother Albert Davis and family.[3]

It would seem that the sons of a wealthy land and slave-owner would probably stay in Kentucky, but the Civil War intervened. There were two men by the name of James Davis who enlisted in Company B, 11th Kentucky Cavalry, CSA. One of the James Davises was captured at Cheshire, Ohio, and held in prison at Camp Douglas in Chicago, Illinois. He was a corporal and was released in February of 1865. The other James Davis was a private. Which of these men was our James Davis we do not know, but James's oldest brother, Josiah, was also in this unit, and was held at Camp Douglas. James probably named his first son Jefferson C. Davis for the president of the Confederacy, and his second son John Morgan Davis for a Confederate General. For several reasons, it is unlikely that either of these was our James Davis. There is no gap in the ages of the children to indicate James's absence in a POW camp; a descendant of another James Davis believes that he is the one who was interned in the camp; and no one from our James's family had ever joined the Sons of Confederate Veterans.[4]

When Richard Davis died in 1874, most of his estate went to his young widow, Elizabeth, and her son, Edmund Davis. The seven surviving children of Richard's first family could only squabble over the "leavings." At the estate sale of Richard Davis in 1874, James Davis purchased a cow and calf, a shovel plow, a looking glass, and a bed and furniture.[5] James Davis received his share of his father's estate in 1876, a total of $106.24.[6]

James and Nancy Davis sold their thirty-seven-acre property in Madison County, Kentucky, in 1875 to William A. Lanter for $212.50. The land was located on Rock Lick branch (of Otter Creek) and bounded by lands of John Lanter, Reavis Shearer, and others.[7]

By 1880 both the Albert and James Davis families had moved to Randolph County, Missouri. Why they decided to move there, we do not know, but perhaps some of their siblings were living in the area. Their sister, Mary Jane Brooks, was living with her family in the northern part of Boone County, Missouri, close to the Randolph County line. A brother, Clifton Davis, had lived in Johnson County, Missouri, in 1860, later returning to Kentucky.

The 1880 census showed that James and Nannie had added three more children to their family: William, James, and Lula.[8] All of the children were born in Madison County, Kentucky, except the last child, Ollie Lester, who was born January 27, 1882, in Missouri.

Nannie Gooch Davis apparently died shortly after the birth of Ollie, and the family left Randolph County, moving to the Pettis, Johnson, and Saline county areas. Although we searched available cemetery records in Randolph, Pettis, and Johnson counties, we could not find a burial record. Clyde walked through several cemeteries where we thought she might have been buried. Because the 1890 census was destroyed in a fire in Washington, D.C., we do not know where the family was living in 1890. After her death, James was left with a large family and no daughters old enough to keep house. Perhaps he left Randolph County to be closer to his sons, who had located in Pettis and Johnson counties.

James Davis married again on November 19, 1890, to a widow, Miriam Dodd Marquess, at Marshall, in Saline County, Missouri.[9] The record stated that both were of Longwood, Missouri, which is in the northern part of Pettis County, close to the Saline County line. Miriam was the widow of L.W. Marquess, whom she had married in 1888.[10]

The 1900 census showed James and Mimi living in Valley City, Johnson County, Missouri. James was fifty-eight years old and she was thirty-nine.[11] Apparently she brought no children into her second marriage, and she and James Davis did not have any children.

James Davis died suddenly April 15, 1902, in Valley City, Missouri, where he had been a resident for seven years. His obituary in the *Warrensburg Daily Star* indicated that six of his eight children attended the funeral, except Charles and Will of Illinois.[12] Another obituary in the *Knob Noster Gem* said that James was an "exemplary and consistent follower of the Savior," a member of the Christian Church.[13] (This was the Christian church of his grandfather, Josiah Collins.)

We could not find any record of any probate in Johnson County for James Davis. He did not own any real estate there; he was probably helping in his son's (Jefferson C.) business.

After his death, Mimi married a third time to Jacob S. Sprinkle on June 28, 1903.[14] She and Jacob Sprinkle moved to Las Animas, Colorado, where she died January 15, 1924.[15] Mimi probably did most of the upbringing of the last child, Ollie Davis, because some of his family recalled visiting a "Grandma Sprinkle."

JAMES DAVIS b. December 11, 1841

It took us quite a while to figure out this puzzle of who was Grandma Sprinkle.

The children of James Davis and Nancy Gooch Davis were

1. Jefferson C. Davis born March 29, 1861; married Rosa Nannie Tatum in Clarke County, Kentucky, in 1889; he died in Johnson County, Missouri, April 24, 1918.
2. John Morgan Davis born March 16, 1863; married Mattie Melvina Toombs in Randolph County, Missouri; he died June 11, 1951.
3. Charles Davis born February 16, 1865; married Rebecca Gooch in Vermilion County, Illinois, in 1889; he died May 4, 1957.
4. Joseph S. Davis born March 11, 1867; married Alice Toombs; he died December 1, 1946.
5. William Davis born 11 June 1871; married (1) Lena Garrison; (2) Eliza Gooch (his first cousin) in 1899 in Morgan County, Illinois; and (3) Viola Bowman in 1907 in Saline County, Missouri. Will died September 22, 1941, in Pettis County, Missouri.
6. James Davis born March 4, 1875; married Sarah Gertrude Murphy. They had two children: Earl born about 1901, and Maud R. born about 1903. Both died of tuberculosis in 1918 and 1923, respectively. We have been unable to locate James Davis in the census after 1900.
7. Lula Davis born April 26, 1877; married Thomas Luther Sanders in 1897 in Johnson County, Missouri; she died September 13, 1952, in Nevada, Vernon County, Missouri.
8. Ollie Lester Davis born January 27, 1882; married Myrtle; he died September 25, 1963 in Kansas City, Jackson County, Missouri.

Because times were hard, James Davis moved his family from Kentucky to Missouri, hoping for a better life. In a few years he would bury his wife, the mother of eight children. The couple's Davis and Gooch ancestors had been some of the first families in Madison County, Kentucky, living there for more than eighty years, but they had chosen to leave their home place to follow some of James's siblings to the "greener pastures" of Missouri. James helped his sons in their merchandizing businesses at Longwood and in Valley City; he married again and died in Missouri. Both James and Nannie were laid to rest in Missouri soil.

A.H.

Notes

1. James Davis, tombstone, Zion Hill Cemetery, Lafayette Co., Mo.
2. 1860 federal census, Kentucky, Madison Co., p. 275.
3. 1870 federal census, Kentucky, Madison Co., p. 282.
4. E-mail from Alice Henson to Clyde Davis, July 23, 2010.
5. Madison Co., Kentucky, Will Book V:292–94, FHL #1943392.
6. Madison Co., Kentucky, Circuit Court Order Book 22:70.
7. Madison Co., Kentucky, Deed Book 22:6.
8. 1880 federal census, Missouri, Randolph Co., E.D. 114, p. 34.
9. Saline Co., Missouri, Marriage Records 4:56.
10. Saline Co., Missouri, Marriage Records 3:215.
11. 1900 federal census, Missouri, Johnson Co., p. 12.
12. James Davis, obituary, *Warrensburg* (Missouri) *Daily Star*, 24 Apr. 1902.
13. James Davis, obituary, *Knob Noster Gem* (Missouri), 18 Apr. 1902.
14. Johnson Co., Missouri, Marriage Records O:182, Missouri State Archives, Jefferson City, Mo.
15. Miriam Sprinkle, burial record, Las Animas Cemetery, Las Animas, Colo.

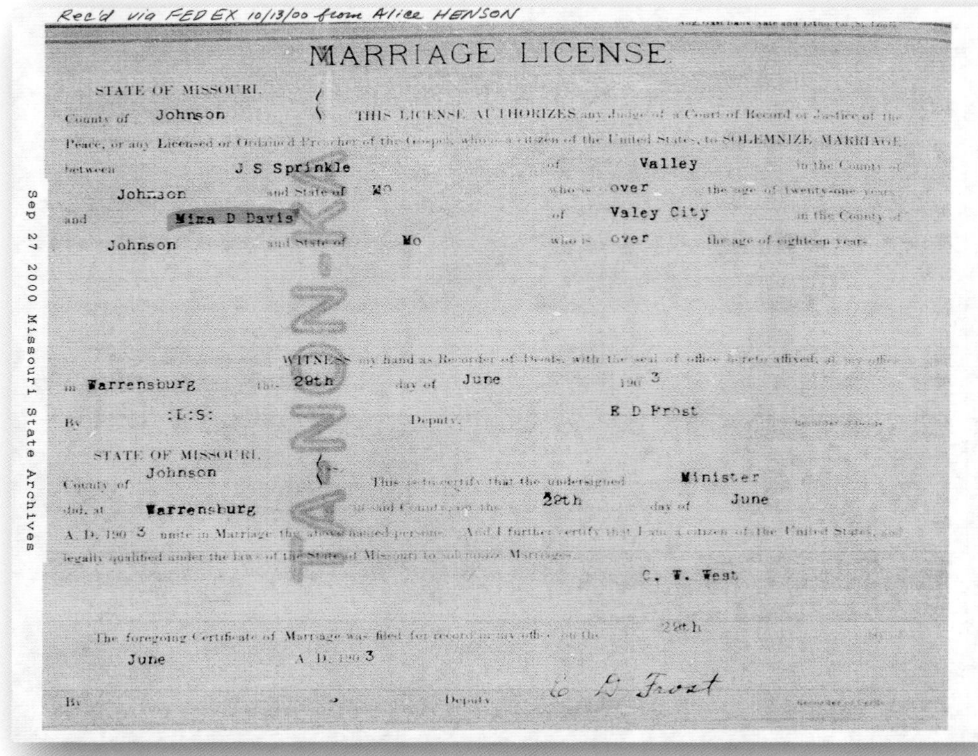

Rec'd via FEDEX 10/13/00 from Alice HENSON

MARRIAGE LICENSE

STATE OF MISSOURI,
County of Johnson

THIS LICENSE AUTHORIZES any Judge of a Court of Record or Justice of the Peace, or any Licensed or Ordained Preacher of the Gospel, who is a citizen of the United States, to SOLEMNIZE MARRIAGE between J S Sprinkle of Valley in the County of Johnson and State of Mo who is over the age of twenty-one years and Mima D Davis of Valey City in the County of Johnson and State of Mo who is over the age of eighteen years.

WITNESS my hand as Recorder of Deeds, with the seal of office hereto affixed, at my office in Warrensburg the 29th day of June 1903

:L:S: E D Frost

By Deputy.

STATE OF MISSOURI,
County of Johnson

This is to certify that the undersigned Minister did, at Warrensburg in said County, on the 28th day of June A. D. 1903 unite in Marriage the above named persons. And I further certify that I am a citizen of the United States, and legally qualified under the laws of the State of Missouri to solemnize Marriages.

C. W. West

The foregoing Certificate of Marriage was filed for record in my office on the 29th day of June A. D. 1903

E D Frost

By Deputy

Sep 27 2000 Missouri State Archives

State of Missouri Marriage License, copy from the Missouri State Archives, Johnson County. Record: Marriage Vol. 0, Page 182, Reel C3496, J.S. Sprinkle and Mima D. Davis (b. October 15, 1856, d. January 15, 1924) married June 28, 1903. Per Alice Henson: "I think this is the second marriage of Mimi Davis to Jacob S. Sprinkle both of Valley City."

VALLEY CITY.
(Too late for last week.)

Mr. Davis of Valley City, who has been very sick, is reported some better.

Died at Valley City.

James Davis, aged 60 years past died suddenly at Valley City Tuesday evening. He had been troubled for some time with heart disease but was around as usual until a late hour Tuesday afternoon when he was suddenly stricken and died. He was the father of J. C. Davis the Valley City merchant. He was a member of the Christian church and is said to have been a very exemplary and consistent follower of the Saviour. He leaves a widow to mourn his loss. The funeral sermon was preached by Elder West at Valley City yesterday and the body was interred there.

VALLEY CITY.

Quite a large crowd attended the funeral of Mr. Davis at Valley City Thursday.

CERTIFICATION OF VITAL RECORD

STATE OF COLORADO

STATE OF COLORADO
Bureau of Vital Statistics
Certificate of Death

1. PLACE OF DEATH County Bent 65 File No. Town Registration District No. 12 Registered No. 1 or City Las Animas No. St. Ward (If death occurred in a hospital or institution, give its name instead of street and number)

2. FULL NAME Mima Sprinkles

(a) Residence. No. 9th St. St. Ward. (Usual place of abode) (If nonresident give city or town and State) Length of residence in city or town where death occurred yrs. mos. ds. How long in U. S. if of foreign birth? yrs. mos. ds.

PERSONAL AND STATISTICAL PARTICULARS

3 SEX Female · 4 COLOR OR RACE White · 5 Single, Married, Widowed, or Divorced (write the word) Married

5a If married, widowed or divorced HUSBAND of (or) WIFE of J. S. Sprinkle

6 DATE OF BIRTH (month, day, and year) 10/15 1856

7 AGE Years 67 Months 3 Days · IF LESS than 1 day, hrs. or min.

8 OCCUPATION OF DECEASED (a) Trade, profession, or particular kind of work Housewife (b) General nature of industry, business, or establishment in which employed (or employer) Housewife (c) Name of employer

9 BIRTHPLACE (city or town) Howard Co, (State or country) Mo,

PARENTS: 10 NAME OF FATHER James Dodd · 11 BIRTHPLACE OF FATHER (city or town) (State or country) W. V. A. · 12 MAIDEN NAME OF MOTHER Unknown · 13 BIRTHPLACE OF MOTHER (city or town) (State or country) Unknown

14 Informant (Address) J. W. Cook Las Animas, Col.

15 Filed Jan 16, 1924 J. W. Hardy Registrar

MEDICAL CERTIFICATE OF DEATH

16 DATE OF DEATH (month, day and year) Jan 15, 1924

17 I HEREBY CERTIFY, That I attended deceased from Jan 1922, to Jan 15, 1924, that I last saw her alive on Jan 14, 1924 and that death occurred, on the date stated above, at 1.15 P.m. The CAUSE OF DEATH* was as follows: Carcinoma - Rectum 4/7 (duration) yrs. mos. ds. CONTRIBUTORY (Secondary) (duration) yrs. mos. ds.

18 Where was disease contracted if not at place of death? Did an operation precede death? Date of Was there an autopsy? What test confirmed diagnosis? (Signed) J. R. Garner, M. D. (Address) Las Animas

*State the Disease Causing Death, or in deaths from Violent Causes, state (1) Means and Nature of Injury, and (2) whether Accidental, Suicidal, or Homicidal. (See reverse side for additional space.)

19 PLACE OF BURIAL, CREMATION, OR REMOVAL Las Animas, Colo. DATE OF BURIAL 1/16 1924

20 UNDERTAKER Geo. Powell ADDRESS Las Animas, Colo.

Doctors and Undertakers Will Please See Last Note on Other Side.

THIS IS TO CERTIFY THAT THIS IS A TRUE AND CORRECT COPY OF THE OFFICIAL RECORD WHICH IS IN MY CUSTODY.

DATE ISSUED DEC 07 2000

CAROL J. GARRETT, PH.D.
STATE REGISTRAR

Do not accept unless prepared on security paper with engraved border displaying the Colorado state seal and signature of the Registrar. PENALTY BY LAW, Section 25-2-118, Colorado Revised Statutes, 1982, if any person alters, uses, attempts to use or furnishes to another for deceptive use any vital statistics record. NOT VALID IF PHOTOCOPIED.

SL H303037

ANY ALTERATION OR ERASURE VOIDS THIS CERTIFICATE

Rec'd from Alice HENSON 1/16/01

State of Colorado Bureau of Vital Statistics — Certificate of Death.
A certified copy, December 7, 2000, of the original document.
Mima Sprinkles b. October 15, 1856, d. January 15, 1924. Second wife of James Davis (b. December 11, 1841), whose first wife was Nancy.

James Davis, Dec. 11, 1841 — Apr. 15, 1902
Zion Hill Cemetery, Lafayette County, Missouri

Above, top left: Kay Davis on March 28, 1998, with Mary Rainey, research librarian at the Johnson County Historical Society located in the Mary Miller Smiser Heritage Library in Warrensburg, Missouri. Kay is holding the death notice for James Davis, shown in closeup at top right. The three clippings below that note James Davis's illness, his death notice from the April 18, 1902, issue of the Knob Noster Gem *(Missouri), and a follow-up on attendance at his funeral. I videotaped my approach to the library, and as I neared the door, I said, "…I discovered the long lost James Davis. A little newspaper clipping inside this historical society, the Johnson County Historical Society building. Kay's in there, she's with some of the women who have helped me in my search. It's so exciting, I can hardly stand it!" I was so delighted with our "find" of James Davis that I made a $500 donation to the Johnson County Historical Society in his name.*

JEFFERSON C. DAVIS b. March 29, 1861

Grandmother Rosa Tatum Davis
holding Eula (Davis) House - Bessie
(Davis) Honey - Grandfater
Jefferson C Davis & (Bud)
Standing Ethel (Davis) Triplett
Twins Everett Davis

Photos courtesy of **Bernetta Stump**

First Born

Jefferson C. Davis was born March 29, 1861, in Madison County, Kentucky, the oldest child of James Davis and Nancy Gooch Davis. Born at the beginning of the Civil War, he surely was named after the president of the Confederacy. He returned to Kentucky for a bride, because he was married September 6, 1889, in Clarke County, Kentucky, to Rosa Nannie Tatum.[1]

She was born October 6, 1868, in Berea, Kentucky, the daughter of John Thomas Tatum and Mary Ann Vaughn. The 1900 census gave her birth year as 1869, however.[2] Rosa died July 24, 1956, in Warrensburg, Johnson County, Missouri.[3]

Jefferson C. Davis lived in Pettis County, Missouri, when his twins were born in 1891. But by 1900 he was in Valley City, Johnson County, Missouri, where he had a general store. His father, James Davis, also helped in the store until his death in 1902.

The children of Jefferson C. Davis and Rosa Nannie Tatum Davis were

1. Ethel Davis born April 22, 1891, near Longwood, Missouri; married James Elmo Triplett August 6, 1913, at Valley City, Missouri. James Triplett was born October 1, 1891, and died February 20, 1954. Their children were Bernetta Fae Triplett and Elmo Dean Triplett.[4]
2. Everett Davis twin of Ethel, married Frances Earlene Oglesby June 3, 1914, at Valley City. They had one daughter, Lois Frances Davis born 1917. She married Robert Murphy. Everett Davis died March 13, 1964, in Warrensburg, Missouri. He was buried at Knob Noster, Missouri.[5]
3. Bessie Davis born February 4, 1893, near Longwood, Missouri; married to Joe Marvin Honey November 12, 1913, in Warrensburg, Missouri. They had one son, Emory Dale Honey. Bessie Davis Honey died March 10, 1958, in Warrensburg, Missouri. She was buried at Knob Noster.[6]
4. Eula Davis was born August 12, 1895, in Valley City, Missouri; married Fred Byron House. He was a member of the Missouri House of Representatives, Sixty-Ninth General Assembly, representing Johnson County. They were married March 18, 1920, in Valley City, Missouri. Apparently, they had no children.
5. Glennvel Lewis Davis was born September 28, 1899, in Valley City; married Minnie Irene Arnold October 17, 1919, in Warrensburg, Missouri. They had two children: Glennice Irene Davis, who married Harold E. Ligon, and Claude Beverly Davis.
6. Margie Davis born August 17, 1905, in Valley City; married Earl Clifton Turner April 3, 1927, in Warrensburg, Missouri. This couple had four children: Donald C. Turner, who lived only about twelve days; Margie Ann Turner, who married Melvin B. Foster; James Edward Turner; and Gary Earl Turner.[7]

Jefferson C. Davis died April 24, 1918, in Johnson County, Missouri, at the age of fifty-seven. His death certificate was signed by "Evert" Davis of Valley City, Missouri. Jefferson's occupation was listed as farmer. He was buried in the Knob Noster Cemetery.[8]

Born in Kentucky, named for the president of the Confederacy, Jeff went back to Kentucky to get a bride, but he spent most of his adult life in Missouri, raising children, operating a store, and farming. *A.H.*

Notes

1. Eula Davis House, *Family Tree of My Father, Jefferson C. Davis* (privately printed, 1955), 1.
2. 1900 federal census, Missouri, Johnson Co., p. 195A.
3. Rosa Nannie Tatum Davis, Missouri death certificate, 1956, #24237.
4. House, *Family Tree of My Father*, 2.
5. Ibid., 3.
6. Ibid., 4.
7. Ibid., 7, 8.
8. Jefferson C. Davis, Missouri death certificate, 1918, #13701

Jefferson C. Davis and Rosa Tatum Davis with Eula (Davis) House and Bessie (Davis) Honey in front and twins Ethel (Davis) Triplett and Everett Davis in back. Jefferson C. Davis had several nicknames, according to the backs of various photos. In this photo, he is referred to as "Bud." Elsewhere, he was referred to as "J.C." or "Jeffrey."

Photographs courtesy of **Bernetta Stump**

Jefferson Davis Family

No. 2. (S)
Front - Earlene Davis - Bess D. Honey - son
Emory Dale Honey - Ethel D. Triplett
Eula D. House
Back
Everett Davis, Dave ~~Epple~~ Mollie
(Tatum) Epple, J. C. Davis - Rosa Tatum
Davis, Joe Honey, Margie Davis,
Glenn Davis - Elmo Triplett

Photos courtesy of **Bernetta Stump**

No. 2

Front: Earlene Davis, Bess D. Honey, son Emory Dale Honey, Ethel D. Triplett, Eula D. House

Back: Everett Davis, Dave Epple, Mollie (Tatum) Epple, J.C. Davis, Rosa Tatum Davis, Joe Honey, Margie Davis, Glenn Davis, Elmo Triplett

Eula Davis House
daughter of Jefferson
C Davis & Rosa
Tatum Davis

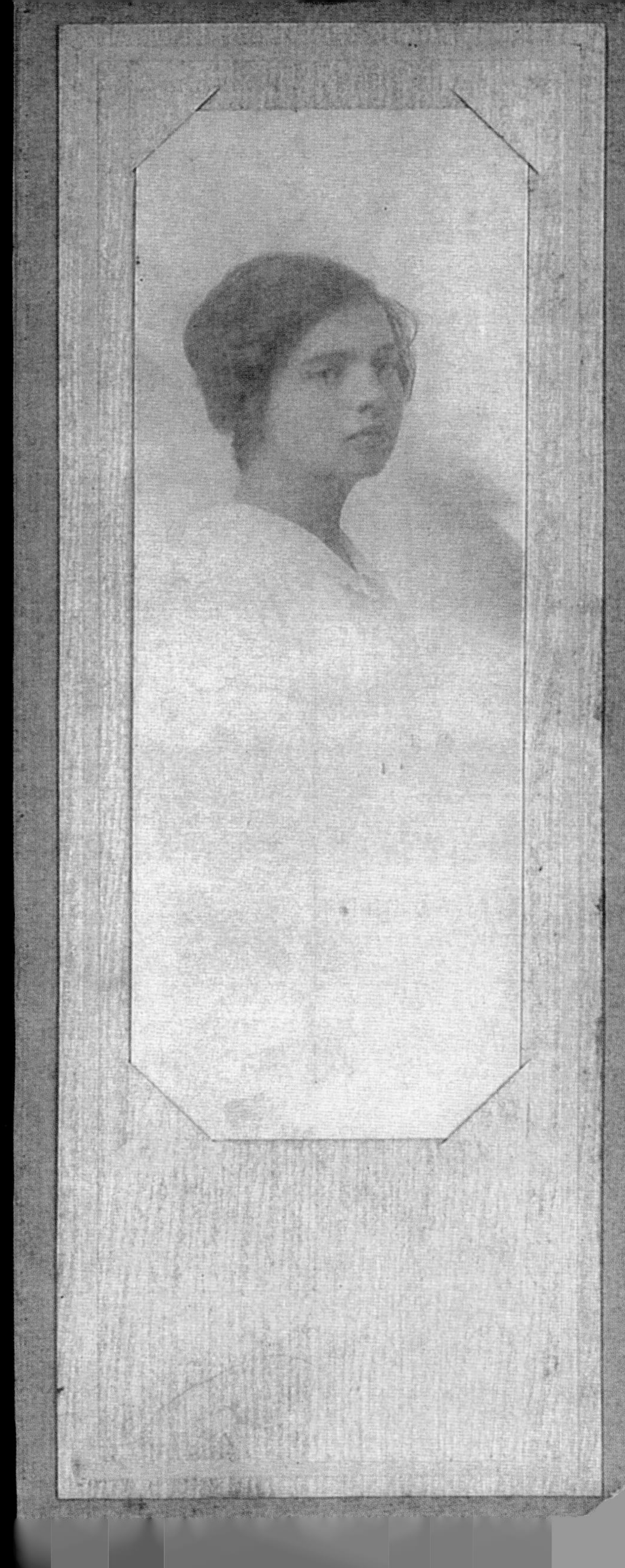

Everett- Ethel Davis
Twin Children of Jefferson C
Davis & Rosa Tatum Davis

Everett on left
Ethel on right

Photos courtesy of **Bernetta Stump**

Everett and Ethel Davis, 12 years of age. On the following two pages is an enlargement of the image above. I so admired the moment, captured photographically, that I just had to give it greater emphasis visually.

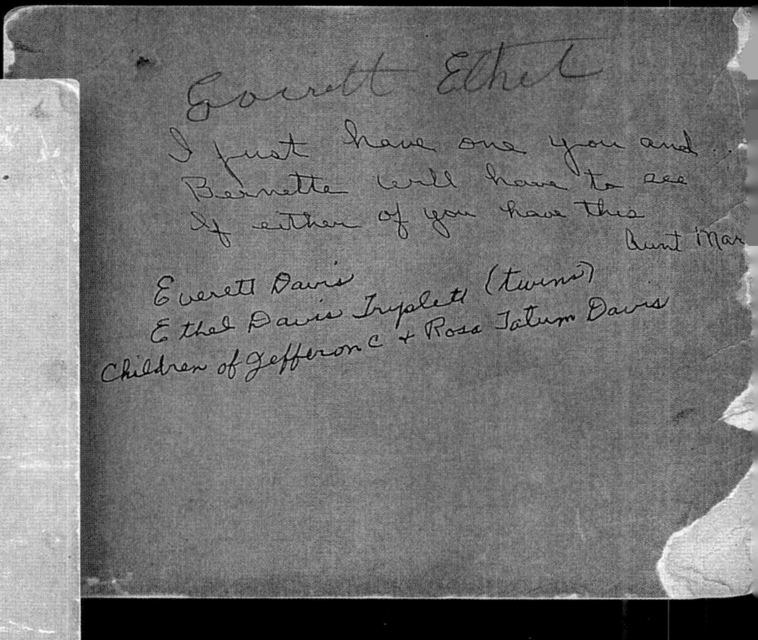

Everett Ethel

"The Twins"

Ethel Davis

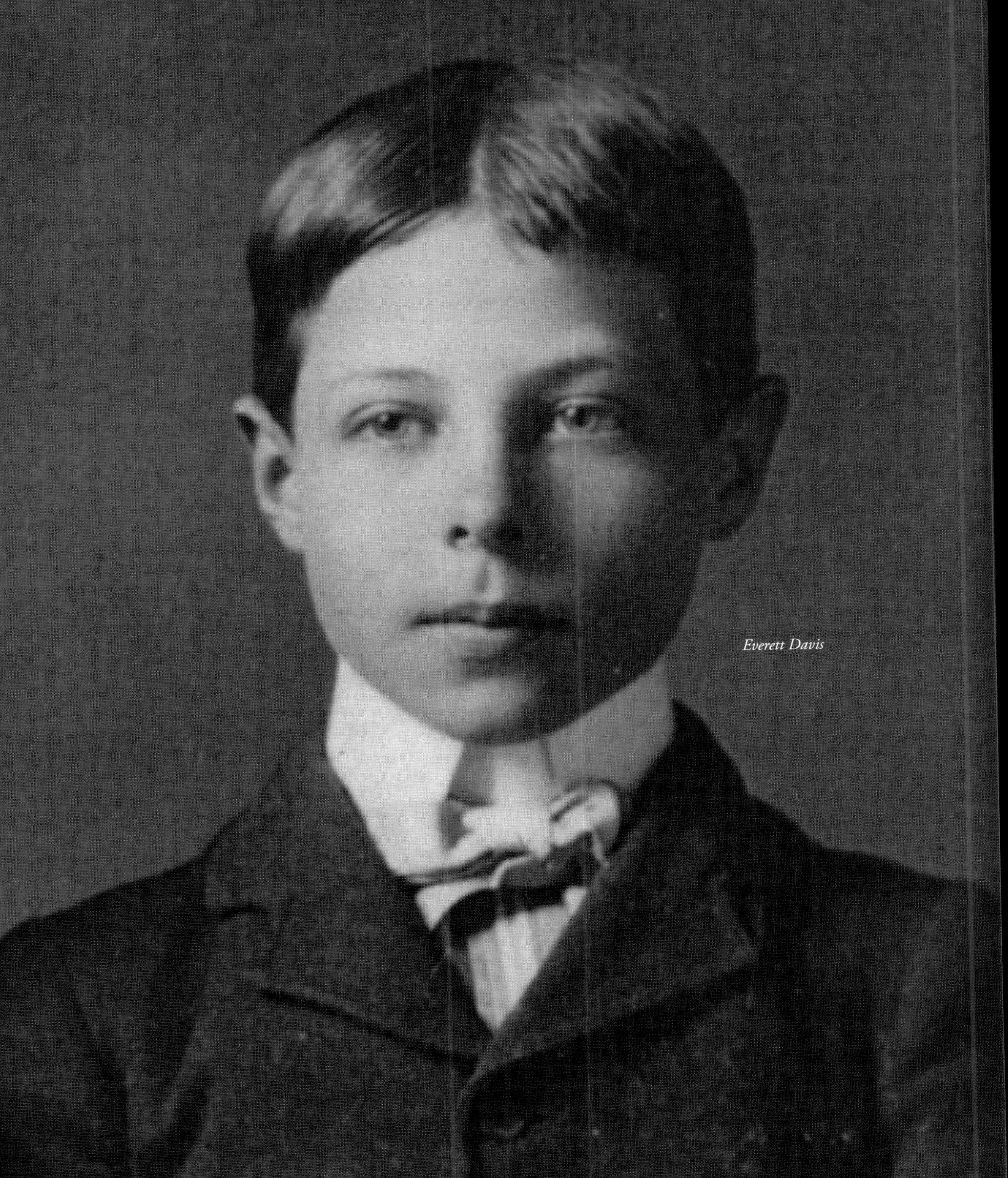

Everett Davis

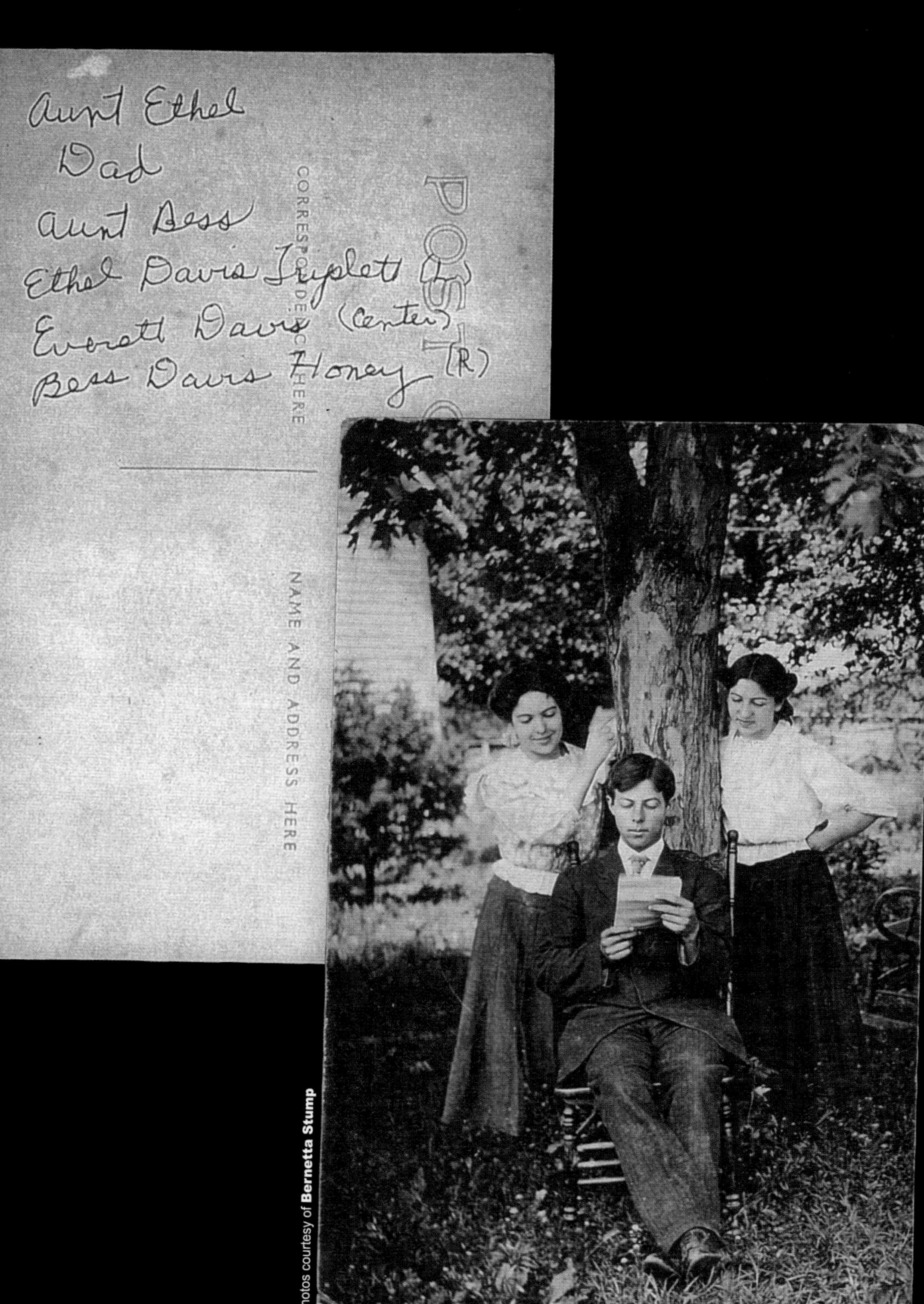

Photos courtesy of **Bernetta Stump**

Aunt Ethel, Dad, Aunt Bess,

Everett Davis
taken 1909

Everett & Earlene Davis
in 1960

Davis Twins
Everett Davis
Ethel (Davis) Triplett
Birthday

Photos courtesy of **Bernetta Stump**

Lois Davis Murphy, daughter of Everett & Earlene Oglesby Davis, granddaughter of Jefferson C. Davis (photo at right)

AT REST
DAVIS
JEFFERSON C.
1861 — 1918
HIS WIFE
ROSA TATUM
1868 — 1956

Jefferson C. Davis headstone in Knob Noster, Johnson County, Missouri, Cemetery. Date of burial April 26, 1918.

...OCUMENT.
...n cannot be felt.)

THE ... 3.245, 193.255, and 193.315 RSMo 1994)

STATE OF MISSOURI } ss
CITY OF JEFFERSON }

I HEREBY CERTIFY that this is an exact reproduction of the certificate for the person named therein as it now appears in the permanent records of the Bureau of Vital Statistics of the Missouri Department of Health. Witness my hand as State Registrar of Vital Statistics and the Seal of the Missouri Department of Health this date of

SEP 22 2000

Garland H Land
Garland H. Land
State Registrar of Vital Statistics

MISSOURI STATE BOARD OF HEALTH
BUREAU OF VITAL STATISTICS
CERTIFICATE OF DEATH

1 PLACE OF DEATH
County Johnson
Township or Village or City Grover ... (NO. ... St.; ... Ward)
Registration District No. 112 — File No. 13701
Primary Registration District No. 4586 — Registered No. 4
[If death occurred in a hospital or institution, give its NAME instead of street and number.]

2 FULL NAME Jefferson C. Davis

PERSONAL AND STATISTICAL PARTICULARS

3 SEX: male
4 COLOR OR RACE: white
5 SINGLE, MARRIED, WIDOWED OR DIVORCED (Write the word): married
6 DATE OF BIRTH: Mch (Month) 29 (Day), 1861 (Year)
7 AGE: 57 yrs. ... mos. 26 ds. If LESS than 1 day, ... hrs. or ... min.?
8 OCCUPATION (a) Trade, profession, or particular kind of work: Farmer
(b) General nature of industry business, or establishment in which employed (or employer): X
9 BIRTHPLACE (City or town, State or foreign country): Kentucky

PARENTS
10 NAME OF FATHER: James Davis
11 BIRTHPLACE OF FATHER (City or town, State or foreign country): Ky
12 MAIDEN NAME OF MOTHER: K Gooch
13 BIRTHPLACE OF MOTHER (City or town, State or foreign country): Ky

14 THE ABOVE IS TRUE TO THE BEST OF MY KNOWLEDGE
(Informant) Evert Davis
(Address) Valley City Mo

15 Filed apr 28, 1918 Florence S[illegible] Registrar

MEDICAL CERTIFICATE OF DEATH

16 DATE OF DEATH: apr (Month) 24 (Day), 1918 (Year)

17 I HEREBY CERTIFY, that I attended deceased from Feby 1, 1918, to apr 24, 1918, that I last saw h[im] alive on apr 24, 1918, and that death occurred, on the date stated above, at 5 P.m.
The CAUSE OF DEATH* was as follows:
Carcinoma Liver
46E 40
(Duration) ... yrs. 6 mos. ... ds.
CONTRIBUTORY (Secondary) ...
(Duration) ... yrs. ... mos. ... ds.
(Signed) H. A. Saults M. D.
apr 24, 1918 (Address) Knob Noster

*State the Disease Causing Death, or, in deaths from Violent Causes, state (1) Means of Injury; and (2) whether Accidental, Suicidal or Homicidal.

18 LENGTH OF RESIDENCE (For Hospitals, Institutions, Transients, or Recent Residents)
At place of death ... yrs. ... mos. ... ds. In the State ... yrs. ... mos. ... ds.
Where was disease contracted if not at place of death? ...
Former or usual residence ...

19 PLACE OF BURIAL OR REMOVAL: Knob Noster — DATE OF BURIAL: Apr. 26, 1918
20 UNDERTAKER: C. L. Saults — ADDRESS: K. N. Mo

State of Missouri Division of Health — Standard Certificate of Death. A certified copy, September 22, 2000, of the original document, Jefferson C. Davis b. March 29, 1861, d. April 24, 1918.

Irene Arnold Davis Kansas City Times, *January 6, 1978 (notation at top is incorrect).*

June 6, 1978

HOLDEN—Mrs. Irene Arnold Davis, 76, Holden, died Wednesday at the home. She was born near Knob Noster, Mo., and had lived in Holden 30 years. She was a member of the Holden First Christian Church. She leaves her husband, Glenn L. Davis, and a son, Claude B. Davis, both of the home; a daughter, Mrs. Glennice Ligon, 5411 Oliver, Kansas City, Kansas; a sister, Mrs. Pansy Moser, Holden; a granddaughter and two great-grandchildren. Services will be at 2 p.m. today at the Cast Chapel, Holden; burial in Medf

Mrs. Irene Arnold Davis

Funeral services for Mrs. Irene Davis, who died Jan. 4, were held at 2 p.m. today at the Ben Cast & Son Funeral Home in Holden. Rev. Robert Hoffman officiated. Burial was in Medford Cemetery.

Pallbearers were Whitman Hanes, Lloyd Strate, Reeves Geary, Ewing Geary, Donald Buckstead and Harold Chaney. Burial was in the Medford Cemetery.

Mrs. Davis was born April 6, 1901, near Knob Noster the daughter of Charles E. and Lacy Frances Geary Arnold. She was married Oct. 17, 1919, to Glenn L. Davis and they were parents of two children.

Mrs. Davis joined the Valley City Christian Church at an early age and was church pianist for many years. She was a member of the First Christian Church in Holden and has been a resident of Holden since 1945. She died Jan. 4 at her home in Holden, after a long illness.

Mrs. Davis was preceded in death by a grandson, Hal Ligon II, in 1974.

She is survived by her husband, Glenn of the home; a son Claude B. Davis, Holden, a daughter, Mrs. Glennice Ligon, Kansas City, Kans.; a sister, Mrs. Pansy Moser, Holden, a granddaughter, Mrs. Beverly Witt, Tuscon, Ariz.; and two great grandchildren, Jennifer Ann DeWitt and Hal Ligon III.

Irene Arnold Davis
Holden Progress *(Missouri), January 12, 197*

Mrs. Earlene Davis

Mrs. Earlene Davis, 87, Chilhowee, died Thursday at Johnson County Memorial Hospital. She was born Feb. 11, 1894 in Knob Noster, the daughter of Joseph M. and Sarah Sappington Oglesby.

She married Everett Davis on June 3, 1914 in Knob Noster. He died March 13, 1964.

Mrs. Davis was a resident of Warrensburg for more than 50 years before moving to the home of her daughter near Chilhowee.

She attended the Normal School and taught in rural schools in Pettis and Johnson County. In Warrensburg, she was a member of the First Christian Church, the Loyal Daughters Sunday School Class, the Rebekah Lodge, and the Cecelia Garden Club.

Survivors include one daughter, Mrs. Robert (Lois) Murphy, Route 1, Chilhowee; two grandsons; and one great grandson.

Funeral services will be held at 3 p.m. Sunday at the First Christian Church in Warrensburg. Dr. Richard N. Johnson will officiate and burial will be in the Knob Noster Cemetery under the direction of Ward Funeral Home, Chilhowee.

Friends may call from 9 a.m. to 9 p.m. Saturday at Ward Funeral Home in Chilhowee or at the Robert Murphy home.

The family suggests memorials to the American Cancer Society. These may be left at the Ward Funeral Home.

Earlene Davis death notice
Warrensburg Star-Journal *(Missouri), May 1, 1981*

Mrs. Earlene Davis

Funeral services for Mrs. Earlene Davis, 87, formerly of Warrensburg, who died April 30 at Johnson County Memorial Hospital, were held at 3 p.m. Sunday at the First Christian Church in Warrensburg. Dr. Richard N. Johnson officiated and burial was in the Knob Noster Cemetery under the direction of Ward Funeral Home, Chilhowee.

Pallbearers were Jim Turner, Harold Ligon, John Eppright, Gary Turner, George Stump, and Melvin Foster.

Earlene Davis funeral notice
Warrensburg Star-Journal *(Missouri), May 4, 1981*

Deaths/Funerals

Eula House

Eula House, 89, 302 E. Market St., died on Tuesday, Feb. 19, at Warrensburg Manor Care Center. She was born in Valley City on Aug. 12, 1895, the daughter of J.C. and Rosa (Tatum) Davis.

She married Fred House on March 18, 1920, in Valley City. He preceded his wife in death on Oct. 22, 1973.

Mrs. House was a member of the Christian church.

She is survived by one brother, Glenn Davis, Holden; two sisters, Mrs. Margie Turner, Knob Noster and Mrs. Ethel Triplett, Warrensburg; and several nieces and nephews.

Private funeral services will take place at Holdren Funeral Home. The Rev. Jan Weston will officiate.

Burial will be in Knob Noster Cemetery under the direction of Holdren Funeral Home.

Eula House
February 19, 1985

LOIS FRANCES MURPHY

Lois Frances Murphy, 81, Chilhowee, MO, died Tuesday, May 25, 1999, at Research Medical Center, Kansas City. Funeral services will be 10 a.m. Friday, May 28, at Consalus Funeral Home, Chilhowee; burial in Chilhowee Cemetery. The family will receive friends 7-8 p.m. Thursday at the funeral home. The family suggests memorial gifts to the Chilhowee Cemetery Association in care of the funeral home.

Mrs. Murphy was born September 30, 1917, in Valley City, north of Knob Noster, MO, to Everett and Earlene Oglesby Davis. In 1931, her family moved to Warrensburg, where she resided until her marriage to Robert M. Murphy on October 27, 1946. She then moved to her husband's farm near Chilhowee, where she lived for the rest of her life. Mrs. Murphy graduated from Training High School in Warrensburg and Central Missouri State Teachers College. She began her teaching career in 1937 in a one-room rural school northeast of Warrensburg. She then taught business for three years in Trenton before returning to Warrensburg, where she was employed by People's National Bank. She returned to teaching in 1961 and taught business at Chilhowee High School for 21 years, retiring in 1982. Mrs. Murphy was a member of Chilhowee Baptist Church, the Missouri State Teachers Association, Retired Teachers of Missouri, and Retired Teachers of Johnson County. She was a longtime member of the Chilhowee Progressive Extension Club, the V.I.C. Club, and Western Missouri Medical Center Auxiliary. She served on the auxiliary's board for four years. Mrs. Murphy was preceded in death by her husband on April 28, 1983. She is survived by two sons, Robert Davis Murphy and his wife, Vivian, Jefferson City, MO, and John Clinton Murphy and his wife, Karon, Chilhowee, MO, and two grandsons, John Joseph Murphy and Robert Benjamin Murphy, both of Chilhowee, MO.

Lois Frances Davis Murphy, died May 25, 1999, in Chilhowee, Missouri

Eula Davis House Family Tree

The picture and text are from the State of Missouri Official Manual for the Years 1957–1958, Published Under Direction of Walther H. Toberman, Secretary of State and Thelma P. Goodwin, Editor*:*

Fred B. House (Republican), Representative from Johnson County, was born on March 6, 1895, in Knob Noster, Missouri. Educated in the Johnson County Rural Schools, Central Missouri State College, Warrensburg, and the University of Missouri, Columbia. He has a Bachelor of Science degree in Education and the Master of Arts degree. He was married to Miss Eula Davis, in March, 1920 in Knob Noster, Missouri. Has been a teacher in the rural schools of Lafayette and Johnson counties, superintendent of Centerview schools, county superintendent of schools in Johnson County, and high school principal and superintendent of schools in Johnson County, and high school principal and superintendent of the Warrensburg Public Schools. He retired July 1, 1956. Served in World War I, and World War II, 1940–1949, in United States Navy, 1917–1918, the Missouri National Guard, 1924, where he was promoted from a private to a colonel. Is a member of the Christian Church, American Legion, and Benevolent and Protective Order of Elks. Was twice elected to office of county superintendent of schools, 1927–1931. He was elected to the House of Representatives in 1956. In the Sixty-ninth General Assembly he served as a member on the following committees: Public Schools; Universities and School of Mines; State Teachers Colleges; and Military and Veterans' Affairs. Address: 302 East Market, Warrensburg, Missouri.

FRED B. HOUSE
JOHNSON COUNTY

The family tree information below compiled by Eula Davis House is written on her husband's Missouri House of Representatives stationery, as reproduced below. Bernetta Fae Triplett Stump, daughter of Ethel Davis Triplett, provided the originals of the documents.

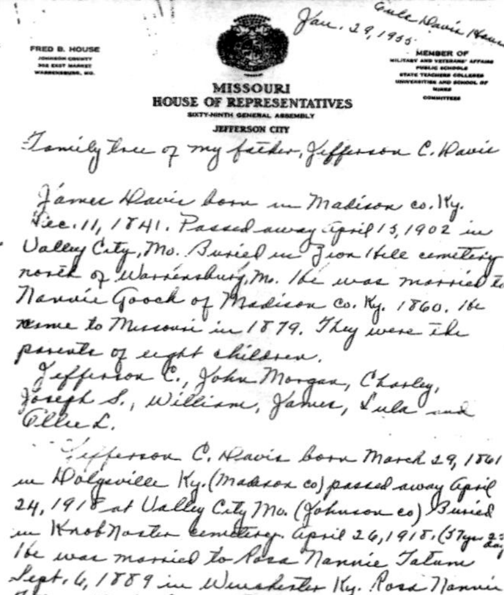
FRED B. HOUSE
JOHNSON COUNTY
302 EAST MARKET
WARRENSBURG, MO.

MEMBER OF
MILITARY AND VETERANS' AFFAIRS
PUBLIC SCHOOLS
STATE TEACHERS COLLEGES
UNIVERSITIES AND SCHOOL OF MINES
COMMITTEES

MISSOURI
HOUSE OF REPRESENTATIVES
SIXTY-NINTH GENERAL ASSEMBLY
JEFFERSON CITY

Jan. 29, 1955.
Eula Davis House

Family tree of my father, Jefferson C. Davis

James Davis born in Madison co. Ky. Dec. 11, 1841. Passed away April 15, 1902 in Valley City, Mo. Buried in Zion Hill cemetery north of Warrensburg, Mo. He was married to Nannie Gooch of Madison co. Ky. 1860. He came to Missouri in 1879. They were the parents of eight children.
Jefferson C., John Morgan, Charley, Joseph S., William, James, Lula and Ollie L.

Jefferson C. Davis born March 29, 1861 in Dolgeville Ky. (Madison co) passed away April 24, 1918 at Valley City Mo. (Johnson co) Buried in Knob Noster cemetery. April 26, 1918. (57 yrs 26 day) He was married to Rosa Nannie Tatum Sept. 6, 1889 in Winchester Ky. Rosa Nannie Tatum Davis born Oct. 6, 1868 near Berea Ky passed away July 24, 1956 in Warrensburg. Mo. Their children are —

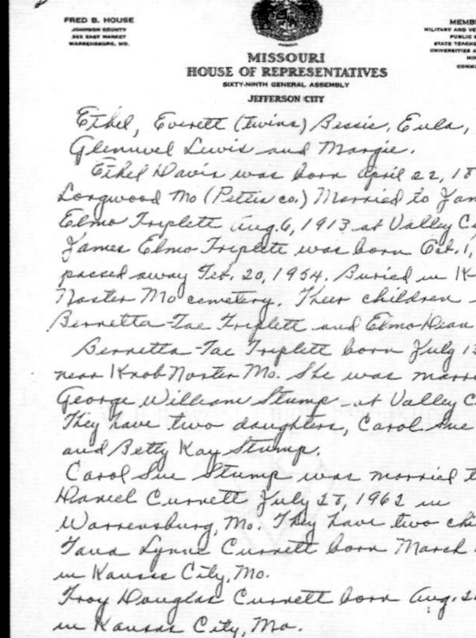
2

FRED B. HOUSE · MISSOURI HOUSE OF REPRESENTATIVES · SIXTY-NINTH GENERAL ASSEMBLY · JEFFERSON CITY

Ethel, Everett (twins) Bessie, Eula, Glennvel Lewis and Margie.
Ethel Davis was born April 22, 1891 near Longwood Mo (Pettis co.) Married to James Elmo Triplett Aug. 6, 1913 at Valley City Mo. James Elmo Triplett was born Oct. 1, 1891, passed away Feb. 20, 1954. Buried in Knob-Noster Mo cemetery. Their children are Bernetta-Fae Triplett and Elmo Dean Triplett.
Bernetta-Fae Triplett born July 13, 1919 near Knob Noster Mo. She was married to George William Stump at Valley City Mo. They have two daughters, Carol Sue Stump and Betty Kay Stump.
Carol Sue Stump was married to Daniel Currett July 28, 1962 in Warrensburg, Mo. They have two children, Tana Lynne Currett born March 17, 1963 in Kansas City, Mo.
Troy Douglas Currett born Aug. 24, 1964 in Kansas City, Mo.

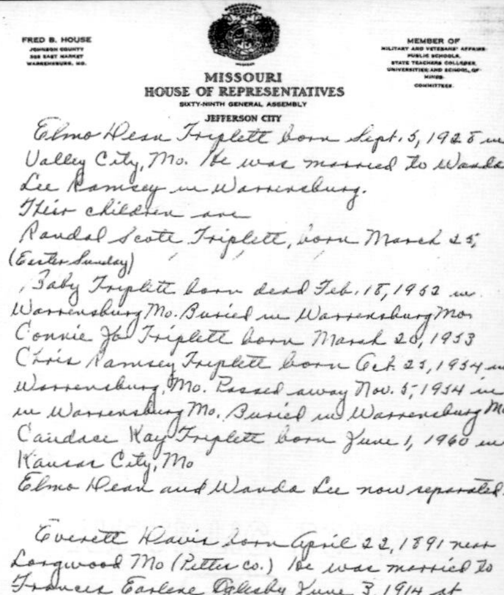
FRED B. HOUSE · MISSOURI HOUSE OF REPRESENTATIVES · SIXTY-NINTH GENERAL ASSEMBLY · JEFFERSON CITY

Elmo Dean Triplett born Sept. 5, 1928 in Valley City, Mo. He was married to Wanda Lee Ramsey in Warrensburg.
Their children are
Randal Scott Triplett, born March 25, (Easter Sunday)
Baby Triplett born dead Feb. 18, 1952 in Warrensburg Mo. Buried in Warrensburg Mo.
Connie Jo Triplett born March 20, 1953
Chris Ramsey Triplett born Oct. 25, 1954 in Warrensburg, Mo. Passed away Nov. 5, 1954 in in Warrensburg Mo. Buried in Warrensburg Mo.
Candace Kay Triplett born June 1, 1960 in Kansas City, Mo
Elmo Dean and Wanda Lee now separated.

Everett Davis born April 22, 1891 near Longwood Mo (Pettis co.) He was married to Frances Earlene Oglesby June 3, 1914 at Valley City, Mo. One daughter, Lois Frances born Sept. 30, 1917 at Valley City Mo. She was

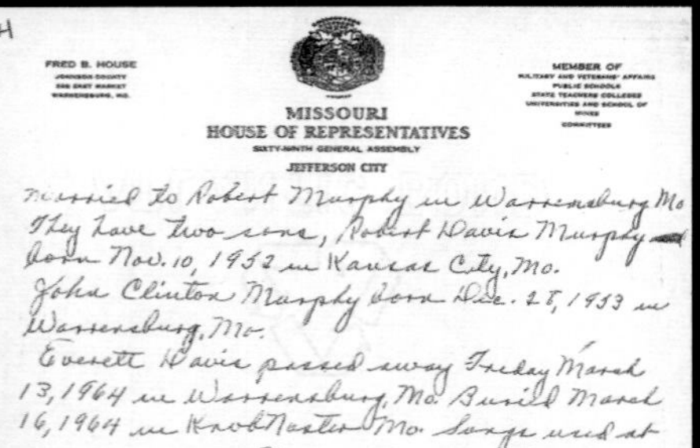
4

FRED B. HOUSE · MISSOURI HOUSE OF REPRESENTATIVES · SIXTY-NINTH GENERAL ASSEMBLY · JEFFERSON CITY

married to Robert Murphy in Warrensburg Mo They have two sons, Robert Davis Murphy born Nov. 10, 1952 in Kansas City, Mo.
John Clinton Murphy born Dec. 28, 1953 in Warrensburg, Mo.
Everett Davis passed away Friday March 13, 1964 in Warrensburg, Mo. Buried March 16, 1964 in Knob Noster Mo. Songs used at service were Abide with me and The Lord's Prayer.

Bessie Davis born Feb 4, 1893 near Longwood, Mo (Pettis co.) She was married to Joe Marvin Honey Nov. 12, 1913 in Warrensburg, Mo. They had one son, Emory Dale Honey.
Bessie Davis Honey passed away March 10, 1958 in Warrensburg Mo. Burial in Knob Noster Mo. March 12, 1958.
Joe Marvin Honey passed away Oct. 26, 1918 Buried at Knob Noster, Mo.
Emory Dale Honey was married to

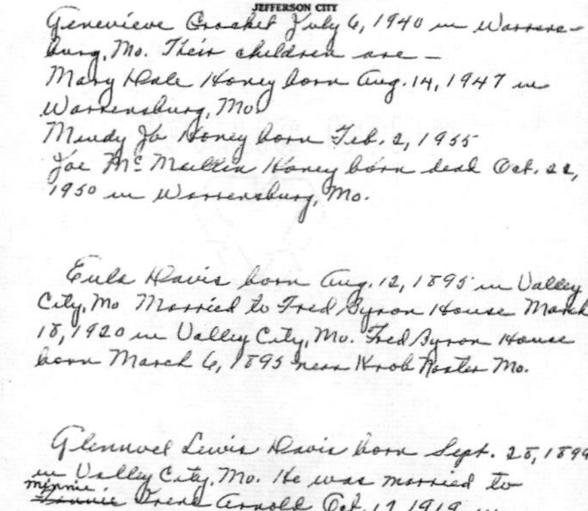
5

FRED B. HOUSE · MISSOURI HOUSE OF REPRESENTATIVES · SIXTY-NINTH GENERAL ASSEMBLY · JEFFERSON CITY

Genevieve Crocket July 6, 1940 in Warrensburg, Mo. Their children are —
Mary Dale Honey born Aug. 14, 1947 in Warrensburg, Mo
Mindy Jo Honey born Feb. 2, 1955
Joe McMullin Honey born dead Oct. 22, 1950 in Warrensburg, Mo.

Eula Davis born Aug. 12, 1895 in Valley City, Mo Married to Fred Byron House March 18, 1920 in Valley City, Mo. Fred Byron House born March 6, 1895 near Knob Noster Mo.

Glennvel Lewis Davis born Sept. 28, 1899 in Valley City, Mo. He was married to ~~Minnie~~ Minnie Irene Arnold Oct. 11, 1919 in Warrensburg, Mo. There are two children, Glennice Irene Davis born July 25, 1920 in Valley City Mo. She was married to Harold

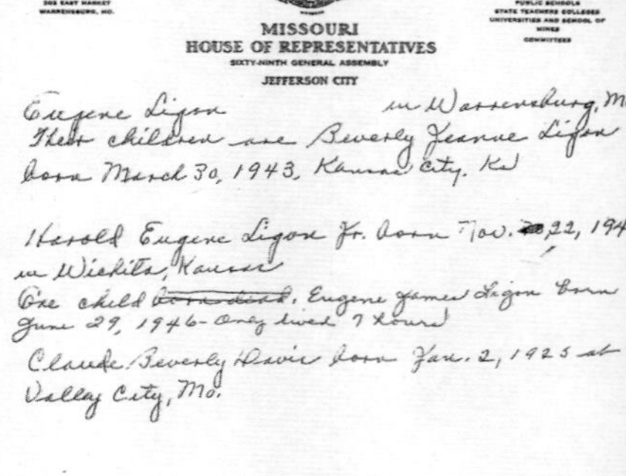
6

FRED B. HOUSE · MISSOURI HOUSE OF REPRESENTATIVES · SIXTY-NINTH GENERAL ASSEMBLY · JEFFERSON CITY

Eugene Ligon in Warrensburg, Mo. Their children are Beverly Jeanne Ligon born March 30, 1943, Kansas City, Ks

Harold Eugene Ligon Jr. born Nov. ~~20~~ 22, 194[illegible] in Wichita, Kansas
One child ~~born dead~~. Eugene James Ligon born June 29, 1946 - only lived 7 hours
Claude Beverly Davis born Jan. 2, 1925 at Valley City, Mo.

FRED B. HOUSE
JOHNSON COUNTY
302 EAST MARKET
WARRENSBURG, MO.

MISSOURI
HOUSE OF REPRESENTATIVES
SIXTY-NINTH GENERAL ASSEMBLY
JEFFERSON CITY

MEMBER OF
MILITARY AND VETERANS' AFFAIRS
PUBLIC SCHOOLS
STATE TEACHERS COLLEGES
UNIVERSITIES AND SCHOOL OF MINES
COMMITTEES

Margie Davis born Aug. 17, 1905 in Valley City Mo. She was married to Earl Clifton Turner April 3, 1927 in Warrensburg, Mo.
There were four children of this union,
Donald Clifton Turner born Dec. 27, 1928 north of Warrensburg, Mo. Passed away Jan. 9, 1929. Buried in Knob Noster Mo. cemetery.
Margie Ann Turner born Aug. 21, 1934 in Warrensburg, Mo. She was married to Melvin B. Foster Oct. 20, 1956 in Knob Noster Mo. They have two daughters —
Connie Ann Foster born April 21, 1961.
Melinda Sue Foster born Jan. 2, 1963 in Warrensburg, Mo.

James Edward Turner born Dec. 3, 1937 in Warrensburg, Mo. He was married to Sandra Kay Davis Aug. 22, 1964 in Eldon Mo. Their son Christopher Davis Turner was born Oct. 1, 1966 in Sedalia Mo.

FRED B. HOUSE
JOHNSON COUNTY
302 EAST MARKET
WARRENSBURG, MO.
MISSOURI
HOUSE OF REPRESENTATIVES
SIXTY-NINTH GENERAL ASSEMBLY
JEFFERSON CITY
MEMBER OF
MILITARY AND VETERANS' AFFAIRS
PUBLIC SCHOOLS
STATE TEACHERS COLLEGES
UNIVERSITIES AND SCHOOL OF MINES
COMMITTEES

Gary Earl Turner born July 1, 1951 in Warrensburg Mo.

John Morgan Davis
His wife Mattie Toombs
Their children — Tinie, Ora, Fred and Cecil.

Charley Davis — died May 4, 1957 at ~~[illegible]~~ Lafayette, Indiana
His wife Rebecca Gooch
Their children — Roy, Elizabeth and Clyde.
(Elizabeth's married name is Purdy)

Joseph S. Davis (Buried at Longwood Mo.)
His wife was Alice Toombs 1869–1957 — sister of Mattie Toombs.
Their children are Carl, Pearl, Clyde and Hazel.
Carl Davis born April 14, 1890 passed away Feb. 19, 1965; Buried at Longwood Mo.

FRED B. HOUSE
JOHNSON COUNTY
302 EAST MARKET
WARRENSBURG, MO.
MISSOURI
HOUSE OF REPRESENTATIVES
SIXTY-NINTH GENERAL ASSEMBLY
JEFFERSON CITY
MEMBER OF
MILITARY AND VETERANS' AFFAIRS
PUBLIC SCHOOLS
STATE TEACHERS COLLEGES
UNIVERSITIES AND SCHOOL OF MINES
COMMITTEES

Pearl Davis and Clyde Davis deceased.
Hazel Davis —

William Davis (deceased) was married to Linnie Garrison. One child — Blanch Davis
His second wife was Eliza Gooch — one child Fred Davis.
His third wife Viola —
Children of this union were Nellie, Ola, Cecile, Joe Marshall and James.

James Davis (deceased)
Married to Gertrude Murphy (born March 4, 1881 died April 27, 1905).
Three children of this union were
Earl Davis born Dec. 8, 1901 passed away May 12, 1918
Maud Davis born Jan. 10, 1903 passed away Aug. 29, 1923. Gertrude and her children buried at Zion Hill cemetery north of Warrensburg Mo. One child born dead.

FRED B. HOUSE
JOHNSON COUNTY
302 EAST MARKET
WARRENSBURG, MO.
MISSOURI
HOUSE OF REPRESENTATIVES
SIXTY-NINTH GENERAL ASSEMBLY
JEFFERSON CITY
MEMBER OF
MILITARY AND VETERANS' AFFAIRS
PUBLIC SCHOOLS
STATE TEACHERS COLLEGES
UNIVERSITIES AND SCHOOL OF MINES
COMMITTEES

Lula Davis born — passed away Sept. 13, 1962, buried at Nevada Mo.
She was married to T. Luther Sanders March 17, 1897 in Warrensburg Mo. Luther Sanders passed away Feb 27, 1951 at Nevada Mo.
Their children are S. Otis Sanders, J. Arnold Sanders and Mary May Sanders.
S. Otis Sanders was married to Rosmond Rahm. They had one son, Jack. (an M.D.)
S. Otis and Rosmond separated and Otis married again. No children by this union.
Rosmond is deceased.
Mary May Sanders was married and separated and later married Ludwell Meinecke. No children.
J. Arnold Sanders — no record

FRED B. HOUSE
JOHNSON COUNTY
302 EAST MARKET
WARRENSBURG, MO.
MISSOURI
HOUSE OF REPRESENTATIVES
SIXTY-NINTH GENERAL ASSEMBLY
JEFFERSON CITY
MEMBER OF
MILITARY AND VETERANS' AFFAIRS
PUBLIC SCHOOLS
STATE TEACHERS COLLEGES
UNIVERSITIES AND SCHOOL OF MINES
COMMITTEES

Ollie L. Davis was born in Grundy Co. Mo.
He was married to Myrtle Cox. They were the parents of Mable, Loren, LaVonne, Ethel Earlene and Mildred.
Their married names — Mable Pulley, LaVonne Bennett, Ethel Earlene Scott and Mildred Webster. Loren — deceased.
Ollie L. and Myrtle Cox Davis separated and he married Mable — . They have one son Eugene Davis.
Ollie L. Davis passed away Sept. 25, 1963.
Buried in Floral Hills cemetery, Kansas City, Mo Sept. 28, 1963

Albert Davis, (deceased) — brother of grandfather James Davis. His wife — They have one son, Richard. Richard was married to Dora —
There were two children Richard Jr. and Opal.
(all of Moberly Mo.

JOHN MORGAN DAVIS b. March 16, 1863

Uncle Morgan - Aunt Mattie
Finis - Ora
Morgan Davis brother of
Jefferson C Davis

John Morgan "Morg" "J.M." Davis and Mattie Melvina Toombs Davis with daughter Ora Mae Davis and son Finis "Boss" Arnold Davis

The Merchant of Longwood

John Morgan Davis, called "Morg," was born March 16, 1863, in Madison County, Kentucky, the son of James Davis and Nancy Gooch, although his death certificate lists his mother's name as "Gouge."[1] He married September 19, 1887, in Randolph County, Missouri, to Mattie Melvina Toombs, the daughter of Jefferson and Melvina Toombs.[2] She was born October 7, 1866, and died December 18, 1944, in Pettis County, Missouri. John Morgan Davis died June 11, 1951, in the same county. Both were buried in Longwood Cemetery, Pettis County, Missouri.[3]

Their children were

1. Finess Arnold Davis born December 17, 1894, in Pettis County, Missouri; died October 25, 1984 in Macon, Macon County, Missouri. He was married January 20, 1921, to Marie Freeman in Moberly, Randolph County, Missouri. Survivors included his wife Marie, one daughter Marie Kilgore of Macon, and one brother, Fred Davis of Harding, Kansas. He was a farmer and operated a portable grinding machine, serving area farmers some twenty-seven years. Burial was in the Woodlawn Cemetery, Macon.[4]
2. Ora M. Davis born about 1898; married Charles Kennedy. According to her father's obituary, she was living in Springfield, Missouri, in 1951, and was still there in 1976 when her brother Cecil died..[5]
3. Fred M. Davis born March 20, 1902. His father resided at Fred's residence at Green Ridge when John Morgan Davis died in 1951.[6] In 1976 when his younger brother Cecil died, he still lived in Green Ridge, but by 1984, when his brother Finess died, Fred lived at Harding, Kansas.[7] In the 1930 census, Cecil and Fred were still at home, unmarried, helping on the farm.[8]
4. Cecil Wilburn Davis born January 7, 1905, and died May 22, 1976, in Springfield, Missouri. He was a retired truck driver and his surviving spouse was Velma Thomas Davis. He lived at 1100 N. Davies. He was buried in Mt. Carmel Cemetery, Clever, Missouri.[9] He had resided in Springfield for thirty-five years and was a member of Brown Avenue Baptist Church. Besides his wife, Velma, two daughters survived: Mrs. Clara Lou Latimer and Mrs. Neldean Churchill.[10] His sister Mrs. Ora Kennedy of Springfield, and two brothers, Finnis of Macon and Fred of Green Ridge also survived him.[11]

John Morgan Davis and Mattie Melvina lived most of their adult lives in one county, Pettis County. *A.H.*

Notes

1. John Morgan Davis, Missouri death certificate, 1951, #20960.
2. Randolph Co., Missouri, Marriage Records 2:488.
3. Mrs. J.R. Carter, *Tombstone Inscriptions of Pettis County, Missouri, Volume 1, Longwood Cemetery* (Warrensburg, Mo.: West Central Missouri Genealogical Society and Library, 1997 reprint), 9.
4. Finess Davis, obituary, *Macon* (Missouri) *Chronicle-Herald*, Thurs., 25 Oct. 1984, p. 2, col. 4.
5. John Morgan Davis, obituary, *Sedalia* (Missouri) *Democrat*, Tues., 12 June 1951, p. 6.
6. Ibid.
7. Finess Davis, obituary, *Macon* (Missouri) *Chronicle-Herald*, Thurs., 25 Oct. 1984, p. 2, col. 4.
8. 1930 federal census, Missouri, Pettis Co., Longwood Twp., p. 3B.
9. Cecil Wilburn Davis, Missouri death certificate, 1976, #76 010740.
10. Cecil W. Davis, *Springfield* (Missouri) *Leader & Press*, 23 May 1976, p. A15, col. 4.
11. Ibid.

Cecil Davis, b. January 7, 1905

JOHN MORGAN DAVIS FAMILY ca. 1908

Mattie Melvina Davis

Ora Mae Davis

Cecil Wilburn Davis

Photograph and description provided by **Fred Cornell Davis**

John Morgan "Morg," "J. M." Davis
Finis "Boss" Arnold Davis
Fred "Freddie," "Dick"
Morgan Davis

Finis Davis b. December 17, 1894 (photos above and below)

Finis Davis, son of John Morgan "Morg" "J.M." Davis, at age 28, Lillie Marie, age 2, and Marie Freeman Davis, age about 25. Picture taken November 7, 1923, La Monte, Missouri.

Fred "Freddy" "Dick" Morgan Davis b. March 20, 1902, son of John Morgan "Morg" "J.M." Davis at age 32

Fred Cornell Davis in a photo taken when he was 68 years of age

Fred M. Davis, age 58, Nellie Thomas Davis, age 46, their grandson Rory Cornell Davis b. April 18, 1959, at age 1, and their son Fred Cornell Davis b. November 23, 1936, at age 23

Rory Cornell Davis, son of Fred Cornell Davis and Betty Jean Tucker Davis. Rory is age 24(?) in this picture with sister Tonya Renee Davis b. March 10, 1972, at age 11. Photo about 1983.

On March 25, 1998, we managed to contact Fred Cornell Davis by phone at his place of work. He was working for the Santa Fe Railway (B.&S.F.) Company located at 10th and Quincey Streets, in Tokepa, Kansas. After introducing myself and offering a brief explanation of my Davis family roots quest and our presence in Missouri, he agreed to meet with us after work.

The meeting, over a few beers, took place around 3 PM at Terry's Bar and Grill in Topeka. Fred was extremely helpful, spoke of his mother Nellie's health and care, and his eventual retirement. He promised to send family photographs, which appear on these immediate pages. The photo on pages 240–241 of the John Morgan Davis family came from his living room wall, and is among my favorites in the book.

Fred M. Davis and Nellie M. Thomas Davis, married August 15, 1935

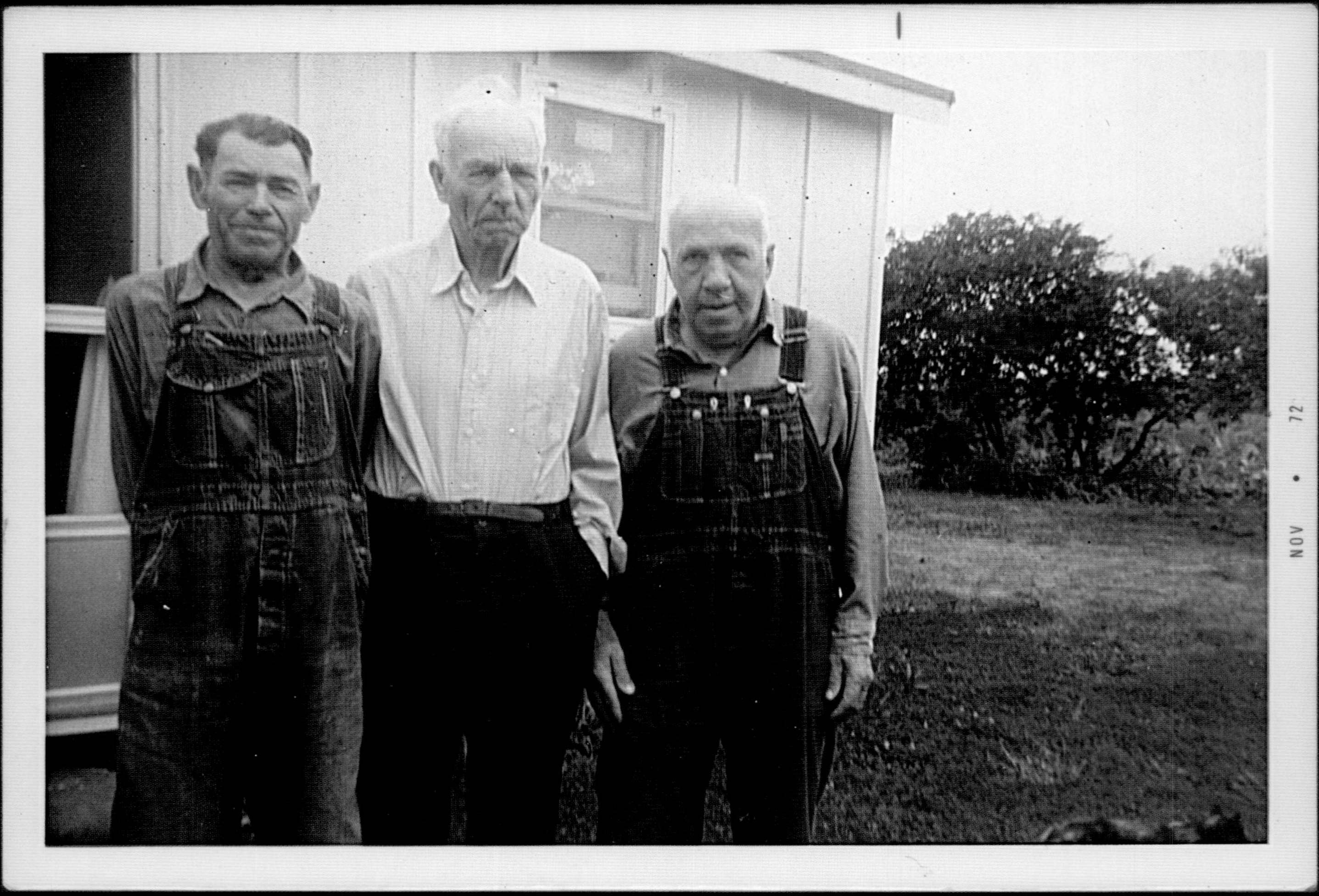

Photos courtesy of **Fred Cornell Davis.**

Back side of photo reads "July 7 1972 Freddie, Finess and Cecil Davis Bros."

John Morgan Davis

John Morgan Davis, 78, died at the home of his son, Fred Davis, of Green Ridge, at 1:50 p. m. Monday.

Mr. Davis was married at Huntsville to Mattie Tommbs. Mrs. Davis preceeded him in death December 18, 1944.

He is survived by four children, Fred Davis of Green Ridge, Finis Davis of Macon, Cecil Davis of Springfield and Mrs. Charles Kennedy of Springfield, two brothers, Ollie Davis of Kansas City and Charlie Davis of LaFayette, Ind., one sister, Mrs. Lou Sanders of Nevada. He is also survived by 8 grandchildren, and 3 great grandchildren, several nieces and nephews.

Mr. Davis was a member of the Bethlehem Christian church.

Funeral services will be held Wednesday at 2 p. m. at the Longwood Presbyterian church. The Rev. J. W. Watts, pastor of the East Broadway Christian church, will officiate.

Burial will be in the Longwood cemetery.

Henry Evon

Henry Evon, ...

The Sedalia Democrat — *Sedalia, Missouri, Tues., June 12, 1951*

CECIL W. DAVIS

Cecil W. Davis, 71, of 1100 North Davies, died about 10 a.m. Saturday in Park Central Hospital where he had been a patient for one day.

Mr. Davis was a 35-year resident of Springfield, and was a retired truck driver. He was a member of Brown Avenue Baptist Church.

Survivors include his wife, Velma; two daughters, Mrs. Clara Lou Latimer, 3001 West Harrison, and Mrs. Neldean Churchill, 216 North Burton; two brothers, Finnis, of Macon City, and Fred, of Green Ridge; a sister, Mrs. Ora Kennedy, 2101 West Scott; and three grandchildren.

Ayre-Goodwin will announce arrangements.

Cecil W. Davis, Springfield Leader & Press *(Missouri), May 23, 1976*

THIS IS A CERTIFIED COPY OF AN ORIGINAL DOCUMENT.
(Do not accept if rephotographed, or if seal impression cannot be felt.)

THE REPRODUCTION OF THIS DOCUMENT IS PROHIBITED BY LAW (sec 193.245, 193.255, and 193.315 RSMo 1994)

STATE OF MISSOURI } ss
CITY OF JEFFERSON }

I HEREBY CERTIFY that this is an exact reproduction of the certificate for the person named therein as it now appears in the permanent records of the Bureau of Vital Statistics of the Missouri Department of Health. Witness my hand as State Registrar of Vital Statistics and the Seal of the Missouri Department of Health this date of

SEP 22 2000

Garland H Land
Garland H. Land
State Registrar of Vital Statistics

FILED JUN 26 1951

THE DIVISION OF HEALTH OF MISSOURI
STANDARD CERTIFICATE OF DEATH

State File No. 20960

BIRTH NO. ___ REG. DIST. NO. 274. PRIMARY REG. DIST. NO. 5922 Registrar's No. 203

1. PLACE OF DEATH a. COUNTY: Pettis
b. CITY OR TOWN (If outside corporate limits, write RURAL and give township): Green Ridge Mo c. LENGTH OF STAY (in this place): 4 years
d. FULL NAME OF HOSPITAL OR INSTITUTION (If not in hospital or institution, give street address or location): R.F.D. #1

2. USUAL RESIDENCE (Where deceased lived. If institution: residence before admission) a. STATE: Missouri b. COUNTY: Pettis
c. CITY OR TOWN (If outside corporate limits, write RURAL and give township): Green Ridge Mo
d. STREET ADDRESS (If rural, give location): R.F.D. #1

3. NAME OF DECEASED (Type or Print) a. (First) John b. (Middle) Morgan c. (Last) Davis

4. DATE OF DEATH (Month) June (Day) 11 (Year) 1951

5. SEX: Male 6. COLOR OR RACE: White 7. MARRIED, NEVER MARRIED, WIDOWED, DIVORCED (Specify): widowed 8. DATE OF BIRTH: March 16-1863 9. AGE (In years last birthday): 88 If under 1 year: Months 2 Days 25 If under 24 hrs.: Hours Min.

10a. USUAL OCCUPATION (Give kind of work done during most of working life, even if retired): Retired 10b. KIND OF BUSINESS OR INDUSTRY: Farmer 11. BIRTHPLACE (State or foreign country): Kentucky 12. CITIZEN OF WHAT COUNTRY? U.S.A

13a. FATHER'S NAME: James Davis 13b. MOTHER'S MAIDEN NAME: Nannie Gouge 14. NAME OF HUSBAND OR WIFE: Mattie Malirna

15. WAS DECEASED EVER IN U.S. ARMED FORCES? (Yes, no, or unknown) (If yes, give war or dates of service): no 16. SOCIAL SECURITY NO.: none 17. INFORMANT'S SIGNATURE OR NAME: Fred Davis ADDRESS: Green Ridge

MEDICAL CERTIFICATION

18. CAUSE OF DEATH
Enter only one cause per line for (a), (b), and (c)
*This does not mean the mode of dying, such as heart failure, asthenia, etc. It means the disease, injury, or complication which caused death.

I. DISEASE OR CONDITION DIRECTLY LEADING TO DEATH* (a) Chronic Myocardial disease

ANTECEDENT CAUSES
Morbid conditions, if any, giving rise to the above cause (a) stating the underlying cause last.
DUE TO (b)
DUE TO (c)

II. OTHER SIGNIFICANT CONDITIONS
Conditions contributing to the death but not related to the disease or condition causing death. Arteriosclerosis, hypertension

INTERVAL BETWEEN ONSET AND DEATH

19a. DATE OF OPERATION 19b. MAJOR FINDINGS OF OPERATION 20. AUTOPSY? YES ☐ NO ☑

21a. ACCIDENT SUICIDE HOMICIDE (Specify) 21b. PLACE OF INJURY (e.g., in or about home, farm, factory, street, office bldg., etc.) 21c. (CITY, TOWN, OR TOWNSHIP) (COUNTY) (STATE)

21d. TIME OF INJURY (Month) (Day) (Year) (Hour) m. 21e. INJURY OCCURRED WHILE AT WORK ☐ NOT WHILE AT WORK ☐ 21f. HOW DID INJURY OCCUR?

22. I hereby certify that I attended the deceased from Jan 8, 1951, to June 11, 1951, that I last saw the deceased alive on June 5, 1951, and that death occurred at 1:50 P. m., from the causes and on the date stated above.

23a. SIGNATURE: H. A. Hite (Degree or title) M.D. 23b. ADDRESS: Green Ridge Mo. 23c. DATE SIGNED: 6-13-51

24a. BURIAL, CREMATION, REMOVAL (Specify): Burial 24b. DATE: 6-13-51 24c. NAME OF CEMETERY OR ~~CREMATORY~~: Longwood 24d. LOCATION (City, town, or county): Longwood (State): Mo

DATE REC'D BY LOCAL REG.: 6-13-51 REGISTRAR'S SIGNATURE: [illegible] 25. FUNERAL DIRECTOR'S SIGNATURE: McLaughlin Bros ADDRESS: Sedalia

(Licensed Embalmer's Statement on Reverse Side)

WRITE PLAINLY—USING UNFADING BLACK INK—MAKE A PERMANENT RECORD

State of Missouri Division of Health — Standard Certificate of Death. A certified copy, September 22, 2000, of the original document, John Morgan Davis b. March 16, 1863, d. June 11, 1951.

Finess Davis

Finess Davis, 89, of Macon died Oct. 25, 1984 at his home in Macon.

He was born in Pettis County, Mo., on Dec. 17, 1894, the son of John M and Mattie Toombs Davis.

Finess married Marie Freeman at Moberly on Jan. 20, 1921.

Survivors include his wife Marie, one daughter, Marie Kilgore of Macon, one brother, Fred Davis of Harding, Ks., one grandson, Larry Kilgore of Macon and four great grandchildren.

He was a farmer for several years. He operated a portable grinding machine, serving area farmers for more than 27 years.

He was a member of the Church of Christ in Macon.

Funeral services will be Saturday at 1:30 p.m. at the Carney Funeral Chapel in Macon. Burial will be in the Woodlawn Cemetery.

Visitation will be from 5-8 p.m. Friday at the funeral home.

Finess Davis Chronicle-Herald *(Missouri), October 25, 1984*

CHARLES DAVIS b. February 16, 1865

Photos courtesy of **LaVerne Purkey**

My Grandfather

Charles Davis was born February 16, 1865, in Madison County, Kentucky, to James Davis and Nancy Gooch Davis. He moved with his parents to Randolph County, Missouri, by 1880.[1] His mother died after 1882, and most likely he spent his teen years in his father's house in Randolph County and later Pettis and Johnson counties, Missouri. There must have been some interaction (letter-writing and possible visits) between the Gooch families of Vermilion County, Illinois, and the Davis families of Missouri, because two of the Davis boys, Will and Charles, married their Gooch first cousins, Eliza and Rebecca Gooch, daughters of their uncle, Thomas Gooch, who was a brother to Nancy Gooch Davis. It was not unusual for first cousins to marry prior to 1900.

Charles Davis married Rebecca Gooch January 23, 1889, in Danville, Vermilion County, Illinois. His home residence was listed as Longwood, Missouri, which is in Pettis County. He was twenty-four years old and a farmer.[2] The marriage application listed his parents as James Davis and Nancy Gooch and her parents as Thomas E. Gooch and Mildred E. Oldham.[3]

The 1900 census indicated that Charles was a coal miner. He was renting a house. His first child, Roy, was ten years old and his daughter Lizzie was eight. If the census is correct, Roy was born in Missouri in 1890, and Lizzie was born in Illinois in 1892.[4] Indeed, Roy Davis's Social Security application stated that he was born in Longwood, Missouri, in 1890,[5] so Charles Davis must have taken his new wife Rebecca back to Missouri and returned to Illinois (where her parents lived by 1900). By 1910 a third child was born, Clyde, age three.[6] Both Charles and son Roy, age eighteen, were farm laborers. Charles Davis returned to coal mining by 1920, and the family consisting of Charles, Rebecca, and Clyde, age twelve, lived in the village of Fairmount in Vermilion County.[7] Elizabeth "Lizzie" had married Hugh Purkey in 1910, and Roy Lee Davis had married Mae Renfro in 1914.

At some point in time the Charles Davis family moved to Delphi, Indiana. (See newspaper clipping from *Sedalia Democrat*, Johnson County, Missouri on page 255).

My mother told me of a visit to Rebecca and Charles's home, probably in Rockfield, Indiana. She was with my father, perhaps after their wedding ceremony in Danville, Illinois, January 23, 1937. She related me shock at her in-laws sleeping on mattresses filled with straw.

I remember that my grandmother Rebecca would place a half-dollar over my navel, taped to my belly, when I was two, maybe three years old. This was because my belly button protruded, a sight most were undoubtedly uncomfortable witnessing. Surprisingly, when my daughter Christine was born, she too suffered from the genetic defect of a herniated umbilical cord.

When I was about eight or nine and visiting my grandparents, I had a dog, at least I thought he was my dog. I don't know where he came from, but I remember his name was "Boy." "Here Boy, here Boy, good dog, good Boy." Worked for me. (See photos of me with "Boy" on page 45.)

Born at the end of the Civil War, Charles Davis certainly saw changes in his lifetime. As a child he left the relative comforts of Kentucky, where he had many relatives, to live in Missouri. After marrying in Illinois, he and his wife returned there and raised three children, where he found coal mining to be more lucrative than farm labor.

I often asked others who knew my grandparents what they were like to be around, hoping their recollections will rekindle in me a lost memory or two.

Recently, LaVerne Purkey, along with her 2007 St. Patrick's Day birthday wishes to me, responded with the following:

> You asked about your grandparents Charlie and Rebecca Davis. I wish you could have known them when you became an adult. I liked them so much. The love they had for each other was like something out of a storybook. Both of them had a keen sense of humor and did lots of teasing. Your grandfather always called your grandmother 'Johnnie.' This started when they were young and lived as neighbors to a man named John who had a crush on your grandma. This tickled Charlie and from then on she became 'Johnnie.' The last time they saw each other was when he became sick and was taken to the hospital, and as he was going out the door, he reached in his pocket and

(continued on page 252)

Charles Davis Family

Photos courtesy of **LaVerne Purkey**

Rebecca Gooch Davis

Believed to be a photograph remnant of Charles Davis

Cut this off and give to Parties married.

Marriage Certificate

STATE OF ILLINOIS

County of VERMILION

This Certifies

That Charles Davis of Longwood in the State of Missouri
and Becca Gooch of Fairmount in the State of Illinois
were at my House in said County by me joined together in

HOLY MATRIMONY

According to the Ordinance of GOD and the Laws of the State of Illinois
on the 23 day of January in the year of
OUR LORD One Thousand Eight Hundred and Eighty nine

IN PRESENCE OF
W. H. Delany
William Duncan

W. O. Smith
Minister of the Gospel

The handwriting and commentary on the photographs to the left and below, as well as many others relating to the Davis and Gooch families, is believed to be that of Elizabeth "Lizzie" Davis Purkey, daughter of Charles and Rebecca Davis.

Charles Davis Family

No. 7021

Marriage License.

ADULT.

Charles Davis

AND

Beca Gooch

Issued Jan 23 1889

Married Jan 23 1889

Returned 188

Registered 188

On Page of Marriage Register.

Filed 188

FILED FEB 9 1889

Clerk.

By W. C. Tuttle Co Clerk. Deputy.

ILLINOIS STATE BOARD OF HEALTH.

Return of a Marriage to County Clerk.

1. Full name of GROOM, Charles Davis
2. Place of residence, Longwood Missouri.
3. Occupation, Farmer
4. Age next birthday, 24 years. Color, White Race,
5. Place of birth, Kentucky
6. Father's name, James Davis
7. Mother's maiden name, Nancy Gooch
8. Number of groom's marriage, 1
9. Full name of BRIDE, Beca Gooch
   Maiden name, if a widow,
10. Place of residence, Fairmount Illinois
11. Age next birthday, 22 years. Color, White Race,
12. Place of birth, Kentucky
13. Father's name, Thomas E. Gooch
14. Mother's maiden name, Mildred Oldham
15. Number of bride's marriage, 1
16. Married at W. O. Smiths in the County of Vermilion and State of Illinois, the 23 day of January 1889
17. Witnesses to marriage, W. H. Delany, Wm Duncan

N. B.—At Nos. 8 and 15 state whether 1st, 2d, 3d, 4th, &c., marriage of each. At 17 give names of subscribing witnesses to the Marriage Certificate. If no subscribing witnesses, give names of two persons who witnessed the ceremony.

We hereby certify that the information above given is correct, to the best of our knowledge and belief. Charles Davis (Groom.) Beca Gooch (Bride.)

I hereby certify that the above is a correct return of a Marriage solemnized by me. W. O. Smith

Dated at Catlin this 23 day of Jan 1889.

This Return is to be carefully filled out and returned with the Marriage License. This return does not take the place of the Certificate which is attached to the License, but is IN ADDITION THERETO.

UNKNOWN / EDWARD OLDHAM → MILDRED OLDHAM

LIZA MAUPIN / CHISLE GOOCH → THOMAS GOOCH

MILDRED OLDHAM / THOMAS GOOCH → REBECCA GOOCH

LIZA MAUPIN / CHISLE GOOCH → NANCY GOOCH

UNKNOWN / UNKNOWN → JAMES DAVIS

NANCY GOOCH / JAMES DAVIS → CHARLES DAVIS

THOMAS GOOCH ↔ NANCY GOOCH: BROTHER AND SISTER

REBECCA GOOCH ↔ CHARLES DAVIS: 1ST COUSINS

REBECCA GOOCH / CHARLES DAVIS → ELIZABETH DAVIS (PURKEY)

THIS CHART EXPLAINS HOW CHARLES AND REBECCA WERE FIRST COUSINS.

CERTIFICATION OF VITAL RECORD

VERMILION COUNTY, ILLINOIS

MARRIAGE LICENSE

THE PEOPLE OF THE STATE OF ILLINOIS, COUNTY OF VERMILION

To any person legally authorized to solemnize Marriage Greeting.

Marriage may be celebrated

Between Mr Charles L Davis of Longwood in the County of Pettis and State of Missouri of the age of 23 years and M Beca Gooch of Fairmount in the County of Vermilion and State of Illinois of the age of 21 years

Witness Walter C. Tuttle, County Clerk, and the seal of said County, at his Office in Danville in said County this 23d day of Jany A.D. 1889

W C Tuttle County Clerk.

By Deputy County Clerk

State of Illinois, Vermilion County, ss. I W O Smith a Minister of the Gospel hereby certify that Mr Charles Davis and Miss Beca Gooch were united in Marriage by me at my house in the County of Vermilion and State of Illinois on the 23 day of Jan. A.D. 1889.

W. O. Smith a minister of the Gospel, and of the C.P. Church

CERTIFIED COPY OF VITAL RECORDS

STATE OF ILLINOIS
COUNTY OF VERMILION ss DATE ISSUED July 16, 1997

This is to certify that this is a true and correct abstract from the official record filed with the County Clerk of Vermilion County, Illinois. Not valid without the embossed seal of Vermilion County, Illinois.

Lynn Foster
LYNN FOSTER
VERMILION COUNTY CLERK

This copy not valid unless prepared on border displaying seal and signature of County Clerk.

ANY ALTERATION OR ERASURE VOIDS THIS CERTIFICATE

Charles Davis and Rebecca Gooch were married on January 23, 1889, as the above copy of the marriage license made July 16, 1997, shows. On the upper left of the page is the reverse side of the license. In the lower left is a hand-drawn chart (probably by Elizabeth Purkey, Rebecca and Charles's daughter), received from LaVerne Purkey, explaining how Rebecca and Charles were first cousins.

Charles Davis Family

took out his pocket knife and gave it to your grandma and said 'Here, Johnnie, keep this for me.' Charlie always smoked '5 Brothers' tobacco which was so strong that when he lit up his pipe it would clear the room of all the people in it. Ha! He loved playing cards and at family gatherings when the guys played poker he would always win. One day they laughed at him winning so much he was putting money in his shoe. Your grandma was a softie. One year she raised a goose to have at Thanksgiving. She named it 'Sammy' and it became quite a pet. She would go outside and call it and it would come flying to her. When Thanksgiving came and Sammy became roast goose, of course, Rebecca couldn't eat a bite and was upset the whole day. She didn't like my name and always called me 'Fern.' I didn't blame her for not liking my name 'cause *I* never liked it either.

On or about April 6, 2007, I received a letter from Violet Davis, wife of Joe "Larry" Davis, son of Roy Lee "Jack Dog" Davis. She wrote: "Speaking of Grandma & Grandpa (Becky & Charles), We used to go there and see them now and then. I'll never forget the first time I met them. Grandma was out in the yard making home made soup in a big black pot.

"Grandpa always used to meet Larry on the porch and ask him if he had something for him — Larry always took him a pt. or ½ pt. of whiskey.

"Aunt Lizzie and Uncle Hugh lived cross the street."

Vondell Davis, coincidentally, told me that she and her husband, Everett, when visiting with his grandparents, would always bring with them two bottles of whiskey. "Grandma would always hide hers because, as Vondell tells it, Grandpa no sooner finished his than he was about looking for hers." I'm sure they're sharing spirits of another kind now. His bad habits did not interfere with a long life. He died at age ninety-two, on May 4, 1957, at a hospital in Lafayette, Indiana, just across the state line from Fairmount.

Rebecca Gooch Davis and Charles Davis

Photo courtesy of **LaVerne Purkey**

His wife Rebecca survived him by only a few months. She died September 24, 1957.

When Charles died, his obituary stated that Roy Davis and Mrs. Elizabeth Purkey lived in Lafayette, Indiana, while Clyde O. Davis resided in Chicago. A brother, Ollie L. Davis of Belton, Missouri, also survived.[8]

Notes

1. 1880 federal census, Missouri, Randolph Co., p. 34.
2. Charles Davis and Rebecca Gooch, marriage license and application, Vermillion Co., Illinois, copy in possession of Clyde Davis.
3. Ibid.
4. 1900 federal census, Illinois, Vermillion Co., Catlin Twp., p. 61B.
5. Roy Lee Davis, Application for a Social Security Number, Social Security Administration, copy in possession of Clyde Davis.
6. 1910 federal census, Illinois, Vermillion Co., Pilot Twp., pp. 185A and B.
7. 1920 federal census, Illinois, Vermillion Co., Vance Twp., Fairmount Village, p. 80B.
8. Undated, uncited newspaper clipping in possession of Clyde Davis.

Charles Davis Family

CERTIFICATE No. 42070

STATE OF ILLINOIS

DEPARTMENT OF MINES AND MINERALS

State Miners' Examining Board

Certificate of Competency of Coal Miner

To Whom It May Concern:

This Is to Certify, That Chas Davis of Fairmount Vermillion County, State of Illinois, whose description is attached hereto, having made oath, and given satisfactory evidence, that he has worked in Coal Mines for not less than two years, and having answered intelligently and correctly, the questions required by law and the Rules of this Board; and being found duly qualified, is hereby granted this **Certificate of Competency**, and is entitled and authorized to seek and accept employment as a Coal Miner in the Mines of the State of Illinois.

Age 54; height 5 feet 10 inches; weight 185; color of hair Gray; color of eyes Brown nationality American; distinctive marks None; years of experience 20

DONE BY authority of the State Miners' Examining Board, this 17 day of Jan 1920, in proof of which we hereby affix our seal and attach our signatures.

W. Hall, President

Miners' Examining Board: W. H. [illegible], Jos. Collins

Jno. A. [illegible], Secretary

Photographs courtesy of LaVerne Purkey

As indicated by the above "Certificate of Competency of Coal Miner" issued by the State of Illinois, Charles Davis undoubtedly worked the coal fields of Illinois around Fairmount where his wife's family resided, and he rented a house at 226 Park Street. At age 54, coal mining was certainly hard work, and it's not surprising to find Charles in the 1930 U.S. Census, State of Ohio, Lucas County, Toledo City, enumerated on April 18th as renting a home with his wife Rebecca at 1222 Front Street. He was listed as proprietor, Lunch Counter. Perhaps the store was at the same location.

Vondell Davis, wife of Everett, related to Clyde Davis that Charlie was run out of Illinois for operating a "still," literally escaping out the back door as the "revenuers," agents of the IRS, hellbent on destroying moonshine stills came through the front door. After all, this was in the midst of Prohibition, making the manufacturing and sale of liquor illegal. Making moonshine, though risky, would have been a lot easier than coal mining or farming, especially if you liked the stuff as Charlie did. Note in photo to left, Grandpa lovingly cradling a bottle of whiskey in his arm alongside Grandma Rebecca.

A family reunion was held on Sunday at the farm home of Mr. and Mrs. Carl Davis, one mile north of Longwood, in honor of Mr. and Mrs. Charles Davis and son, Roy, of Delphi, Ind.

A basket dinner, to which all contributed, was served at noon.

Attending were: Mr. and Mrs. Charles Davis and son, Roy, of Indiana, Mr. and Mrs. Luther Sanders and daughter, Mary of Nevada, Mr. and Mrs. Ollie Davis and son, of Kansas City, Mr. and Mrs. Marge Davis of Longwood, Mr. and Mrs. Will Davis and family, Mr. and Mrs. Joe Davis, Marshall, Mrs. Rosa Davis and daughter, Bessie Honey, of Mr. and Mrs. Everett Davis and daughter, Earlena Davis, Warrensburg, Mr. and Mrs. Finis Davis and daughter, Mason, Glen Davis and daughter, Knob Noster, Mr. and Mrs. Cecil Davis and daughters, Longwood, Mr. and Mrs. Cecil Davis and son, Marshall, Mr. and Mrs. Fred Davis and son, Longwood, Mr. and Mrs. Ivan Summerville and son, Lexington, Mrs. Elizabeth Purkey and son, Glenn of Indiana.

on my Family Tree Diagram as of 1/5/98
Mrs. Joseph HONEY ?
①NEW
②NEW
③NEW
④NEW
"MORG" John Morgan DAVIS
NEW⑦
Darlene ?
⑤NEW
"JW"
⑥NEW
?? Town between Sedalia & Warrensburg A.F. Base
Part of a "Column" (No Heading) Longwood News Society
Fred Cornell DAVIS (Topeka, KA)
Sedalia DEMOCRAT ??
2/16/98

255

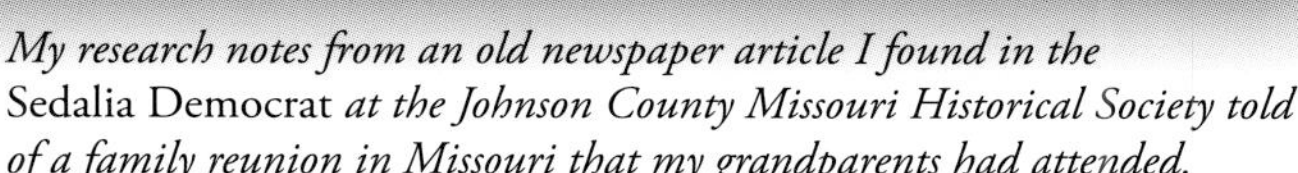
My research notes from an old newspaper article I found in the Sedalia Democrat *at the Johnson County Missouri Historical Society told of a family reunion in Missouri that my grandparents had attended.*

Charles Davis Family

As I look upon this black-and-white photograph taken in the early 1940s, I'm filled with mixed emotions. How could I not be drawn to the small boy seated on his grandmother's lap, who appears to withdraw, looking out at the camera with apprehension, while hiding behind his hands drawn to the mouth. That small, shy boy, of course, is me, sitting next to my sister, who in contrast, on my grandfather's lap, sits erect, leaning forward, eager to be immortalized at her tender young age. Prior to receiving this photograph from LaVerne Purkey I had no idea of its existence nor have I any memory of being there at the time, surrounded by a family that I would later spend so much time trying to reconstruct.

There are my father and mother standing next to each other, one of the few times they were ever photographed together. On what occasion did this event take place? Was it a birthday, summer holiday, or wedding anniversary? My grandparents married January 23, 1889, and my Aunt Lizzie and Uncle Hugh married December 28, 1910, so we weren't celebrating one of their anniversaries. Most likely, this was the wedding celebration of LaVerne and Glenn Purkey and a sendoff for Glenn, proudly displaying his newly earned staff sergeant stripes. According to the history of the 32nd Troop Carrier Squadron compiled by Donald L. van Reken, Glenn arrived at Ellington Field, Texas, in July 1942, prior to his marriage to LaVerne on Augusst 5. Whatever the reason I'm grateful for the gathering and record it produced.

Originally, I had received an enlargement of the small picture above from LaVerne Purkey, but was disappointed that the feet were cut off in the duplicate. I requested that she send the original picture shown above. I was somewhat astonished at its diminutive size, and that the feet were still cut off, if not by quite as much as in the earlier version.

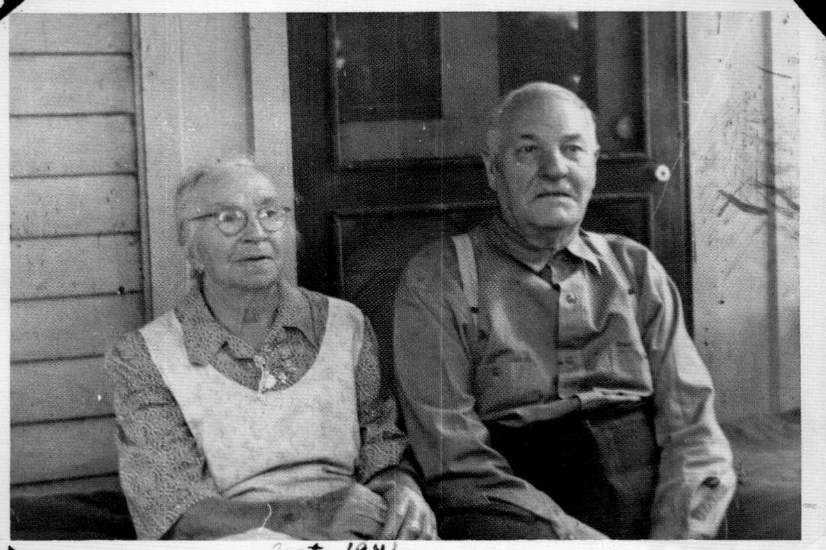

lived close to Rockfield, Ind.

See the house as it stood in May 2007 on the following pages.

With the exception of the photograph showing the rear of the house (with the windmill and car), all images depict the same gathering of family and friends at Charlie's and Rebecca's home near Rockfield, Indiana, in September 1946. As a child, I recall the front porch with the swing at right and especially Grandpa's wooden rocker pictured below, which freely moved from inside to outside along with his pipe and spittoon. Note the chickens in the front yard. The sidewalk went out to the dirt road and corn fields beyond. Grandpa would sit on the porch and whenever a cloud of dust would be seen way off in the distance, he'd say "Here comes a car across the field pickin' up dust like an automobile." Prominently shown in the photo below on the right is Charlie and Rebecca's son, Clyde Otis Davis.

After seeing copies of the photos on the opposite page, LaVerne Purkey acknowledged in her letter to me of October 24, 2007, that her husband Glenn and Bob Deel "were in the same class at school. His father owned one of the three grocery stores in Rockfield that he called 'Square Deel.' Grace (Bob's wife) was not a local girl, but when she married Bob, she fit right in the town as if she'd always lived there and kept involved with everything that was going on."

LaVerne claimed that she did not know the Garrison boys, but she was "assuming that their father was Ray, who was in my graduating class at school. He lived in the next house on the left down from where your grandparents (Rebecca and Charles Davis) lived."

The House

The spring of May 2007, on a trip to Chicago to visit Mom on Mother's Day and concurrently attend the University of Illinois, School of Art + Design Convocation Ceremony (another of my Scholarship recipients, Brittany Bindrim, was graduating), we were able to squeeze in a few additional days of "roots research." Since 1986 when I began this project (see page 20) I, with my sister, longed to locate our grandparents', Rebecca and Charlie Gooch's residence, that is, if it was still standing. We had spent many months of our early 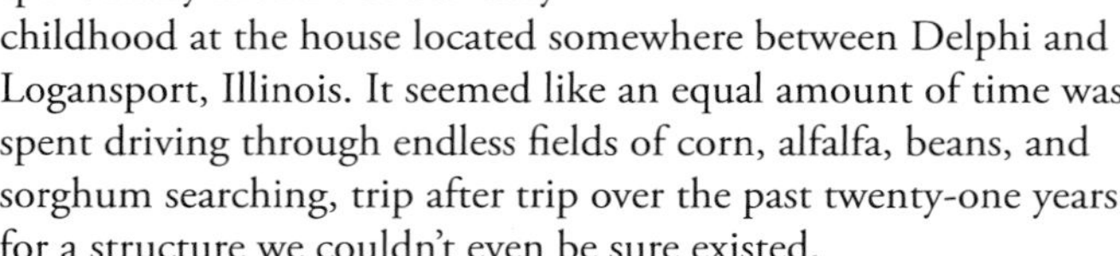 childhood at the house located somewhere between Delphi and Logansport, Illinois. It seemed like an equal amount of time was spent driving through endless fields of corn, alfalfa, beans, and sorghum searching, trip after trip over the past twenty-one years, for a structure we couldn't even be sure existed.

A review of my notes, prior to the trip revealed a comment made by Vondell Davis during lunch with her and LaVerne Purkey in Reno, Nevada. Vondell, in response to my question as to the location of Grandma and Grandpa's house said, "I know exactly where it is. It's one and a half miles out of Rockfield (near Glenn and LaVerne's farm), over Rock Creek, up a hill, first road to the right, first house on the right."

Well, we took these directions along with us to the Midwest and got to Rockfield easy enough. Not knowing in which direction out of Rockfield (east, west, north or south), we ended up at the Rockfield Post Office. The attendant on duty was too young to recall Grandma and Grandpa (we say "Gran-MAW" and "Gran-PAW"), and since we had no address, she could not help us. However, she did know someone who might. She immediately placed a call and within two to three minutes a pleasant, ebullient woman appeared. Her husband was summoned and soon arrived to join in our effort.

In backgrounding Grace and Robert Deel (see photos on opposite page), the mention of Glenn and LaVerne Purkey triggered an outpouring of information, for Grace and Robert were good friends of the Purkeys. "Bob" had gone to high school with Glenn, had flown with Glenn locally, and the Deels had visited the Purkeys after they relocated to Washington state just prior to Glenn's passing.

We were pointed in the right direction out of Rockfield and within five minutes pulled into our destination. There stood the house that I remembered so vividly. It was smaller; the front lawn had overgrown the sidewalk that went from the front porch out to the road, across which lay a field of beans. The windmill was gone, but the hand pump remained. Also to one side was a barn and field in which I recall cows were penned along with impressive, oversized salt licks scattered about, which, as a child, I had to sample with my tongue. A stand of trees was to the other side.

Walking around to the back of the house I confirmed the kitchen was where I last left it, and there was Grandpa's window where he'd sit in his rocking chair (see photo page 259) looking out, smoking his pipe, or chewing "tobacca," with a spittoon at his feet.

We knocked on the door. No one answered, but peering into the window, we determined that the house was being lived in. I began photographing the house and within ten minutes we were confronted by Andrew, and shortly after, Charles Garrison, sons of the owner, their mother. Charles lived in the house. They were, after hearing our story, extremely accommodating, even agreed to being photographed themselves.

As we drove off, I took one, probably my last ever look, at the house where I spent time in the security of grandparents, when my parents were struggling to figure out what to do with us during their hard times. I have fond, warm memories of my time in the "country," of Grandma and Grandpa, their love for one another and for me.

I experienced my first artistic moments in that house, drawing on the stairs to the floor above, but most importantly, I, to this day, am convinced that "the country" in me sprung from those halcyon days living with my grandparents in that simple frame farm house set amidst the fields of grain. I'm just a country boy.

Below: Kay with the Garrison brothers. Opposite page, bottom left: me with Grace Deel. Bottom right: Robert and Grace Deel, Kay and me standing in front of the Rockfield, Indiana, Post Office.

Grandma Rebecca on Grandpa's lap with Clyde "Cotton" Davis on the front porch of their home near Rockfield, Indiana

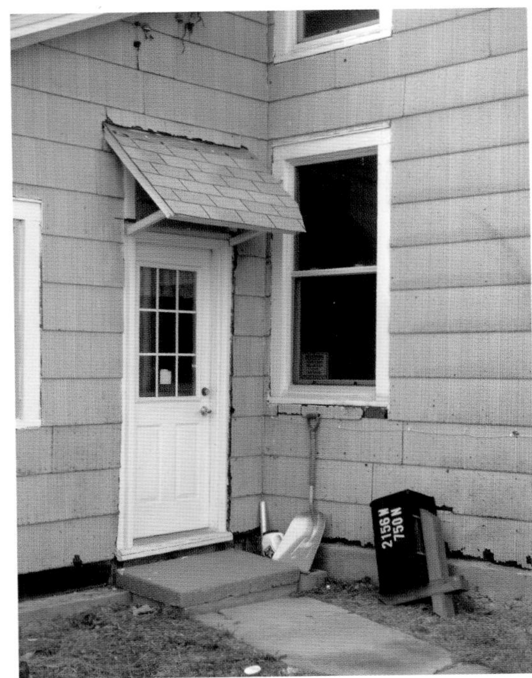

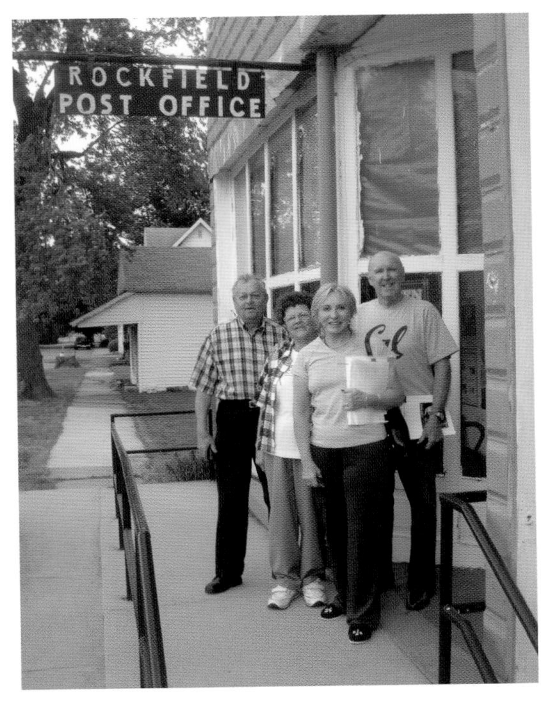

1. Front of post card: "Charley Davis
Dad had small pox…papa was sitting in a window when this was taken. The dr. had it done for he said it was the worst case he ever met with, but he was worse than this picture looks.
Love to all."
Post card addressed to Mrs. Dollie Reeves, Fairmount, Ill.
"Let them all see this. give our love and best wishes to all."

2. Charlie Davis

3. Charles Davis, Jessie Doney "Doll — Dolly" Gooch, Rebecca "Becca" Gooch, Eliza "Liza" Gooch, Clyde Otis, Davis and Thomas "Tom" Goodwin

4. Roy, Everett, Rebecca, and Darlene Davis

5. "Back yard spoof" with Clyde Otis Davis, Hugh Purkey in policeman's uniform, Roy Davis, and Charlie Davis with bottle

6. Charlie, Larry, and son Larry Joe Davis

7. Rebecca and Duke, about 3 years of age

8. "Taken Aug. 9, 1942 at Perk's grandparents' house." Everett Lee Purkey and Glenn Purkey in uniform with Rebecca Davis and Everett's daughter, Beverly and Clyde "Duke" Davis, age 4, with sister June "Tootise" Davis, age 2

9. John Woodward, Jessie Gooch, Charles and Rebecca Davis

2.

3.

POST CARD
PLACE STAMP HERE
CORRESPONDENCE HERE
NAME AND ADDRESS HERE
et them all ee this. ive our love nd best wishes all.
Mrs. Dollie Reeves. Fairmount Ill.
Charley Davis.
Dad had small pox
Love to all.
papa was sitting in a window when this was taken. The dr. had it done for he said it was the worst case he ever met with, but he was worse than this picture looks.

1.

4.

5.

7.

8.

9.

6.

Photos courtesy of **LaVerne Purkey** and **Vondell Davis**

Charles Davis Family

1. *The Charles Davis family. Standing: Roy Lee "Jack Dog," sister Elizabeth "Lizzie," and brother Clyde Otis "Cotton" Davis. Seated: parents Rebecca "Becca" and Charles "Charlie" Davis.*

2. *Clyde, Rebecca, Roy, and Lizzie. In a letter from LaVerne Purkey dated November 15, 2007, she writes, "Grandma Davis with her three kids? They all look so happy. Notice Grandma touching both her boys. She didn't always approve of their life styles, but she loved them anyway. She said 'When they are little they step on your toes and when they are big they step on your heart.'"*

3. *Vondell Davis, daughter Darlene, and husband Everett "Eddie" Davis*

4. *Rebecca Davis with sons Roy Lee and Clyde Otis Davis. Clyde's children, June "Tootsie" and Clyde "Duke" Davis in background.*

5. *Everett "Eddie" Davis with first daughter, Darlene Ann Davis b. September 23, 1946, Jacksonville, Illinois, with Rebecca "Becca" Davis and her son Roy Lee "Jack Dog" Davis.*

1.

4.

5.

2.

3.

6. Rebecca "Becca" Davis. In her November 15, 2007, letter, LaVerne Purkey observes, "She always got teased about her one-handled rolling pin and somebody — I don't know who — got a great shot of her shaking it at someone."

7. Charlie with son Clyde settin' on the front porch, Grandpa in his rocker which freely moves in and out of the house.

8. Clyde, Elizabeth, and Roy at the funeral of their mother, Rebecca "Becca" Davis, who passed away September 24, 1957.

6.

Charles Davis

FAIRMOUNT (CNS)—Services for Charles Davis, 92, who died Saturday (May 4, 1957) at St. Elizabeth Hospital at Lafayette, will be at 2 p. m. Monday at the Carrington Funeral Home. The Rev. Don C. Goodwin will officiate, with burial in Greenview Cemetery.

The body is being brought to the funeral home where friends may call after 7 p. m. today.

Mr. Davis was born in 1865 in Madison County, Ky., the son of James and Nancy Davis. He was married to Rebecca Gooch in 1889 at Fairmount.

Survivors include the wife, two sons, Roy L. Davis of Lafayette and Clyde O. Davis of Chicago; a daughter, Mrs. Elizabeth Purkey of Lafayette; a brother Ollie Davis of Belton, Mo.; 9 grandchildren, and 16 great grandchildren.

Charles Davis, died May 4, 1957

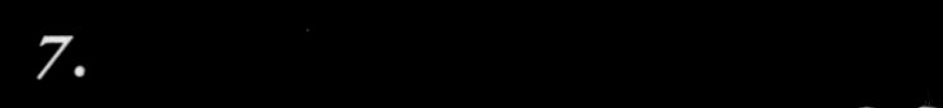

7.

8.

Photos courtesy of **LaVerne Purkey** and **Vondell Davis**

I'm not sure but this
looks like Roy
Davis

Roy Lee "Jack Dog" Davis b. March 28, 1890

Mae Renfro and Roy Lee "Jack Dog" Davis (before marriage). Note the similar backgrounds in all three photos.

Roy Lee "Jack Dog" Davis with unknown woman

MARRIAGE LICENSE

THE PEOPLE OF THE STATE OF ILLINOIS,

COUNTY OF VERMILION

To any person legally authorized to solemnize Marriage Greeting

Marriage may be celebrated

Between Mr Roy T. Davis of Danville in the County of Vermilion and State of Illinois of the age of -24- years and M May Renfro in the County of Vermilion and Sta of Oakwood Illinois of the age of -17- years the Father of the said minor having given assent to said Ma

Witness JOHN R. MOORE ~~Thomas J. Dale~~ County Clerk and th of said County at his Office in Danville, in said County this day of Dec A.D. 1914 John R. Moore County

By Deputy C

State of Illinois VERMILION COUNTY, ss. I W. J. Goodwin a Probate Judge hereby certify that Mr Roy T. Davis Miss May Renfro in the County of Vermilion, were united in Marriage by me at Danville and State of Illinois on the 28th day of Dec A

W. J. Goodwin, Probate Judge of

It is the duty of the person celebrating the Marriage to fill out and sign the above Certificate and to return the same, together with County Clerk within thirty days after the Marriage is solemnized ONE HUNDRED DOLLARS PENALTY FOR FAILING S

State of Illinois Marriage License, copy from the County Clerk of Vermilion County, State of Illinois, Filed for Record: December 28, 1914, Roy J. Davis and May Renfro,

Ethel Davis Singleton
Daughter of Roy Davis
wife of Onnus

Left to right: Ethel Davis holding sister Maxine with brother Joe "Larry" Davis and Myrtle Gooch Woodard, daughter of Rosa Lee Gooch, sister to my grandmother, Rebecca Gooch Davis

Above: Ethel "Eddie" Davis Singleton, wife of Onus and daughter of Roy Lee "Jack Dog" Davis and Mae Renfro Davis. Below: Onus Singleton with wife Ethel "Eddie" Davis Singleton and son Robert "Bobby" Singleton.

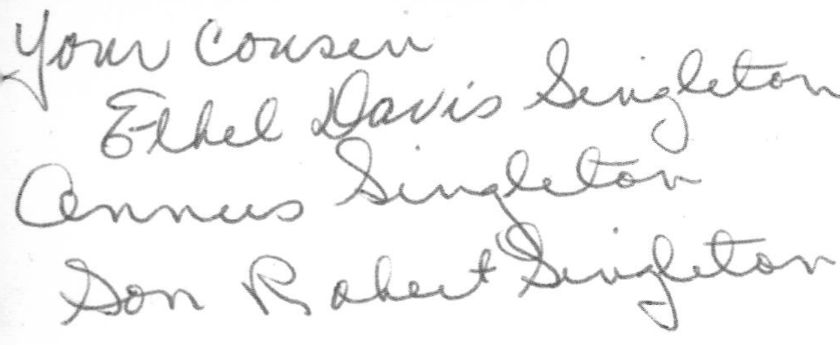

Your cousin
Ethel Davis Singleton
Onnus Singleton
Son Robert Singleton

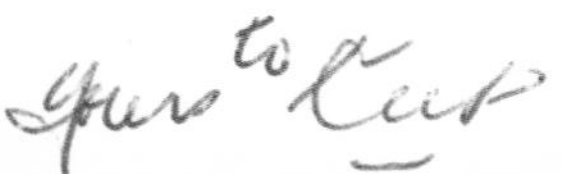

1.

3.

2.

4.

Roy Lee "Jack Dog" Davis with

1. Sister Elizabeth "Lizzie" Purkey. Back of photo reads, "Taken when we came home from Missouri."

2. Wife Mae Renfro

3. Mother Rebecca "Becca" and sister Lizzie

4. Jesse Young. Back of photo reads, "Jesse Young & Roy taken the day of Dad's funeral Chas. Davis." Charles Davis d. May 4, 1957.

Left to right: Ethel Davis b. 1916 with brother Larry b. August 23, 1918, and baby sister Maxine b. 9 September 1929, children of Roy Lee "Jack Dog" Davis and Mae Renfro Davis. All were born in Fairmount, Illinois.

Photo courtesy of **Michelle Schmal**

Larry and Violet Davis.

Cousins Coming Together

On December 11, 2008, I called Debbie Davis Lane. Debbie is the daughter of Violet Davis, with whom I had visited in Lake Station, Indiana, sometime ago. Debbie had called me around August 30, 2008, shortly after her mother passed away. Debbie recalled my previous visit with her mother and thought that I might like to have a large black-and-white, elaborately framed, photograph of James Davis, my great-grandfather and grandmother. I remembered this photograph hanging on the wall during my last visit with Violet in her home. Debbie also said that she had a bartender's recipe book, which was at one time my father's.

We arranged to meet during my next trip to the Chicagoland area in May of 2009. I usually visit with my sister June and her family in Lansing, as well as with my mother in Palos Park, Illinois. Debbie said she lives on a farm in Michigan City, Indiana, approximately forty-five minutes from Lansing. Debbie expressed interest in my book, saying that she is the "keeper of things" in their family.

We met for lunch on May 13, 2009, on the lakefront in Michigan City, Indiana, at Debbie's place of work where she was newly employed as a server. With Debbie's approval and with my wife Kay's participation, I recorded the conversation, from which excerpts follow. Debbie's father, Larry, probably learned how to cook in the Merchant Marines and had a tattoo on his arm that said "Navy." According to Debbie, "He was a chef at Jackson's Restaurant, on Route 20, in Gary, Indiana. His [specialities were] Lobster Thermidor and Shrimp Dijon." Debbie mentioned that when she had to have her tonsils removed by Dr. Bergal, it was a Lobster Thermidor dinner that covered the cost. Debbie also acknowledged that her father "had a drinking problem."

"And I don't know why my father hung out with your father," Debbie said. "You don't know why?" I asked. "Well, I think because Daddy was in the restaurant business and Uncle Clyde was a bartender. Also, my home was a good home. My mom was always welcoming to everybody and my daddy was the same way. You never knew when you woke up who was going to be on the couch. It could have been a dishwasher that he had hired, or it could have been a cousin who didn't go home. And I do that now. We were always like that, our home was his home."

At one point early in the conversation, Kay had asked, "Did you know he [my father, Clyde] had children?" Debbie replied, "No." Kay said, "Do you ever remember him talking about children?" Debbie said, "No. But you know he was always good to us. He was always very welcomed."

Both my father and my brother Dave are very similar in nature and behavior. Fun guys to be around, but both with children that they didn't acknowledge.

Debbie remembered washing Clyde's car. She mentioned
hat she would have been too young to wash it herself, but maybe t was her brother. "Everyone has good stories to tell about Clyde. My brother was three years older than me, and Larry was three ears older than him. It seems that Clyde was close to Larry Debbie's dad] and Larry ["Larry Joe," Debbie's brother] also. He s six years older than me and might remember some things."

I asked, "Where is your brother now?" She replied, "Right now, he's in Minnesota."

Larry Joe had a bizarre story. He worked for IBM and took a buyout. She didn't know what he did for IBM, though Debbie said he had no college education. She went on to say that after he got this buyout he called her up one day and said he bought *lemon*. Debbie said do you mean a *lemon* car? What kind of car did you buy? He said "No, a lemon." She said, "What kind of *emon* are you talking about?"

"You know, those that you have at a (state) fair. The ones hat make those lemon squishy things. So he went down to the Keys that summer, then they went to California. They spend time with Erica in the summer and Minnesota in the winter. Now he has two *lemons* and he does kettle corn and he loves it. It just cracks me up because Larry, who was 'rather cool,' lived in Boston and had no car. You don't need a car in Boston. I remember he came home one time and said, 'I need a pair of jeans,'" Debbie said. "'OK we will go get you some,' and he said, 'We should go to Kmart.' He added, 'They have good ones called Wrestlers.' So he has changed. He has his lemons and his kettle corn and he s happy. He is married to a good girl [Michelle], they've been married since '90, since Michael was four years old."

Debbie then mentioned Michelle "Micki," her older sister, and Rickie, her younger brother, and in so doing was quick to note that "I'm different. My brother [Larry] sends me an e-mail igned da-lemon, da-lemon — he's a trip. I love him. It's like Larry and I are the same, and Rickie and Mickie are the same. I ob-hop. I'm switching jobs all the time. If I'm not happy, I'm not going to stay there. I did my job, I raised my children. I could have worked for the phone company, but that would not have been me. I wouldn't have been happy there. My mother worked for the phone company for eleven years. Her sister, Stacy, also works there and has since 1975, for many years.

"Stacy has been a really good aunt to me and very good to my children. She bought me a dress once, and I said that is a very expensive dress ($40). Can't we take it back, and we can get four at Kmart? She said, 'No.'"

Debbie is attending Brown Mackie College. "It is part-time schedule, once a week for a month at a time duration."

She thinks she may get some more Pell Grant money now that Obama is President, but she is not sure. "I raised these two children, and I had an '87 Cadillac and it's working right now. I'm happy now. When I was twenty-one years old I had a Porsche 911. Who needs a Porsche 911 when they are twenty-one? I'm ust as happy now as I was then. Michael, my son, bought a aguar. I said, one of these days you're going to fall in love and you're going to have a wife. He said, 'I know, Mom. I'm going to have a minivan like you.' Well, I have a minivan now [referring to

her companion] — he works for a trucking company. It's a good life."

I asked where her brother Rickie worked, and Debbie said that he worked at IBM also.

I asked, "What nationality do you think your father was?" Debbie replied that she thought he was English. But that "there was also some Italian somewhere down the line because of the look of my father. My father looked like Chef Boyardee. I don't have a lot of pictures of Daddy."

I filled in Debbie on my family history research. I told Debbie about Glona Howe and the Greenview Cemetery in Fairmount, Illinois (see page 335), where Gooches and Davises were buried and my $1,500 donations each year regarding its care and upkeep. Debbie said, "Thank you," and that she worried about that. She explained that her mother is "in her bedroom," having been cremated. Her father is in Merrillville, Illinois. Her mother cancelled her life insurance policy, so they were not able to bury her anywhere yet. They were going to do it this month, but that is not going to happen, so her mother's ashes may be with her for another year. "She is in my bedroom, which would have been her bedroom had she moved in with me as we planned before her death."

Near the end of the interview, Debbie told me that her full name is Debbie Lenore Davis Lane, and that she was named after singer-actress Debbie Reynolds. Her brother Rickie Dean Davis was named after Ricky Nelson, singer and onetime actor on the radio and TV series *The Adventures of Ozzie and Harriet*.

Debra "Debbie" Davis Lane at the Harbor Grill Restaurant, Michigan City, Indiana, May 13, 2009, with me after our lunch meeting and exchange of family information, anecdotes, and memorabilia. Debbie is the daughter of Larry and Violet May Davis. Debbie's father died December 5, 1986, and her mother passed August 8, 2008. Larry was the son of my father's brother, Roy, and though Larry was eleven years younger than my father, they were close, and my father, Clyde, spent a good deal of time with his nephew.

Rebecca Davis, great-grandmother to Larry Joe and Michelle "Micki" Davis, children of Larry Davis and Violet May Gillow.

Growing up Sundays

The letter below, dated September 24, 2009, was sent to me by Michelle Schmal. Michelle is the daughter of Larry and Violet Davis, and the granddaughter of my Uncle Roy.

Clyde,

Sorry this took so long. I had the pictures laying out and just kept spacing them out. You asked for a short version of our weekends so here goes.

Growing up Sundays for our family we always used to spend time together. Many Sundays a month were spent at one of the cousins' houses. If our family was traveling that Sunday we would pack up the car and head out early. Remembering those days, I always knew what the meal of the day would probably be by which relative we would be visiting.

Aunt Ethel would always serve the best breakfasts. We would gather around her table and she would bring out heaping dishes of the greasiest eggs, bacon, and potatoes you could imagine. It was the BEST!!! We would then head to the park and put on plays for ourselves on the stage (or torment whichever cousin was on the hit list for the day).

When we went to Uncle Eddie's house the girls would have to wear dresses because sometimes we went to church with their family. We always brought play clothes because after church we would play in the yard or walk up and down their street. Aunt Vondell always served spaghetti for dinner. It must have been good or I would not have remembered it.

Aunt Max' house was always a surprise. We would arrive there and didn't care what we ate because when you saw Aunt Max and Uncle Dick's big smiles we didn't care what was going on.

Larry Joe, Roy, Debbie, Micki, and Rusty

When the family came to our house it was usually a grilling day. My dad loved to cook on the grill. If the weather was too bad for grilling I can remember all of the aunts in the kitchen making pots of whatever was on the menu for the day. When Uncle Eddie's family came we always made sure we had extra play clothes for his girls because they would always show up with dresses on and, just in case they forgot to bring play clothes, we wanted to make sure we could all go outside. After dinner the uncles would all sit around the table and play poker. The kids would just wait to see if anything was needed because if someone was thirsty or needed us to get something we would get a tip and that was great. The best was if you got to actually sit in on a hand. We learned how to play poker quite early in life.

On weekends we were always outside. Whether it would be sled riding, ice skating, visiting the Brookfield Zoo, etc.... Sunday was always a great family day.

I don't want everyone to believe that every day was perfect. We had bad days like everyone else's family. However it is good to remember the fun times in life just to make us smile for a while.

Michelle
(Micki)

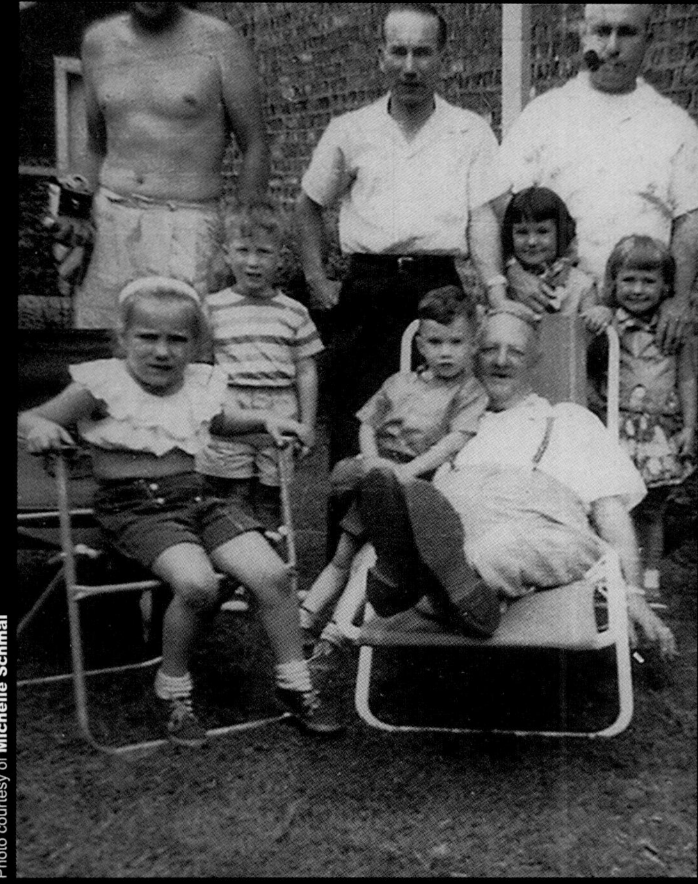

Photo courtesy of **Michelle Schmal**

Rear: Dick Anders, Everett and Larry Davis. Middle: Mike Anders, Micki and Debbie Davis. Front: Donna Davis, Bobby Singleton, Onus Singleton.

Photo courtesy of **Michelle Schmal**

Michelle, Debbie, Larry Joe, and Rick Davis

Photo courtesy of **Michelle Schmal**

Left to right: Larry Joe, Debbie, Violet, Rick, Larry , and Michelle Davis

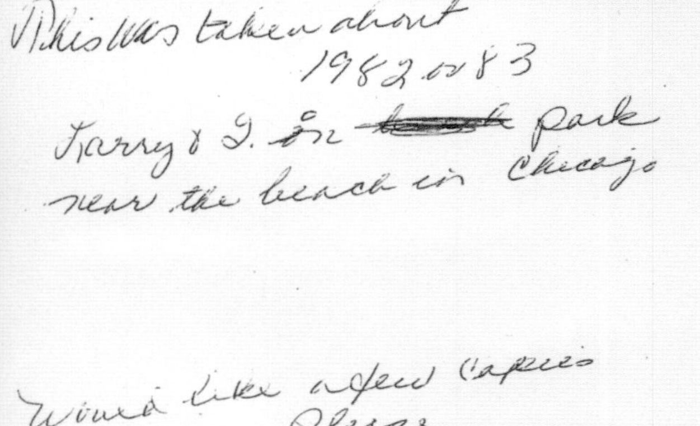

This was taken about
1982 or 83
Larry & I. in ~~[illegible]~~ park
near the beach in Chicago

Would like a few copies
please

Photo courtesy of **Violet Davis**

Violet Davis sent me this picture of her and her husband, Larry Davis. The picture was taken in 1982 or 1983. Larry and Violet had a son, Larry Joe, which has been confusing to me at times.

Photos courtesy of **LaVerne Purkey**

Elizabeth "Lizzie" Davis b. February 16, 1892, and Hugh Purkey b. June 21, 1886 (before marriage)

in Lafayette, I

Hugh and Elizabeth "Lizzie" Purkey.

later from researching
s a bartender
y Club and was listed
anoe County, Indiana,
1948, making me ten

nd when I lied about
ime stock car races with
whose parents bothered
at Aunt Lizzie's. Well,
bbed me by the arm,
ith the words, "Son, this
eded to whip me good.
afternoon and never
delible mark on me, for
to note, this "contact"
ent, for my father never

recall trekking to Missou
that bystanders would po
her pet chicken got eaten

Hugh's birth certifi
a small town nestled in th
Mountains, Hancock Co
Father: Unknown, Mothe
Cherokee Indian, accordi
from home at age eightee
his way to Fairmount, Illi
was to meet Elizabeth Da
upon seeing Hugh at the
"There is Lizzie's man!"

Hugh Purkey, at th
December 28, 1910, gave
was twenty-five years of a
However, Hugh listed his

mother's name as Nancy Green. According to LaVerne Purkey, Hugh never knew who his father was.

In a phone conversation on October 12, 1997, LaVerne Purkey said that Hugh's mother Nancy Jane and his father Sam, surname unknown, had a second child "out of wedlock," a daughter (name unknown). Nancy's parents "kicked her out of the house" with daughter and son in tow.

Nancy Jane married a Mr. Johnson, who was one-quarter or one-half Negro. According to LaVerne, Hugh had an older half-sister, daughter of Nancy Jane and Mr. Johnson, but she couldn't keep the child and found a home for her.

Nancy Jane had three additional children with Mr. Johnson, all sons. One died young, two were "raised."

In response to my request for additional family history on the Purkey family, I received the following on October 24, 2007, from LaVerne Purkey:

"As for information on Hugh Purkey's family history, he was born out of wedlock in Tennessee to Nancy Purkey and his father's last name was Hurd. The story was told that the man had two women pregnant at the same time, and he chose to marry the other woman. Nancy married a man named Johnson when Hugh was still a baby, and she had three more baby boys with that man. One was killed in an accident as a teenager. Hugh left Tennessee at age 18 and ended up in Illinois where he met your aunt Lizzie and they eventually married."

LaVerne added that on a trip to Tennessee, while Hugh's mom was still alive, they "met all the cousins by the dozens." They "also looked up some of the relatives of Hugh's real father and met several of his half siblings on that side of the family." They

Clyde O. Davis with his sister Elizabeth "Lizzie" Purkey and LaVerne Purkey, wife of Glenn Purkey, Elizabeth's son (far right).

Photos courtesy of **Michelle Schmal**

Rear row: Glenn and LaVerne Purkey and far right, my father Clyde O. Davis. Front row: Jon and Darlene Pool, Vondell Davis, Al Aszman the groom, Donna Ann the bride, Everett Davis, Violet Davis, Michelle Davis, and Debra Davis. The wedding of Donna Ann Davis took place on July 13, 1974.

Elizabeth and Hugh Purkey with their sons Everett (at left) and Glenn

learned "that the baby born to the other woman at the same time that Hugh was born was a girl and [they] met her too, and she and Hugh looked so much alike they could have been twins." It remains unclear whether Hugh had both a sister and a half-sister.

LaVerne then discussed information she had learned about the Purkey name, that the "original Purkey came from Alsace-Lorraine, back in the 1700s, to America and the spelling of the name was Perquay and somehow got changed to the spelling that it is today." She added that "Hugh's two half brothers on the Johnson side had lots of kids. George had eleven and Jess had twelve. I don't know how many kids are on the Hurd side — too many to count, I'll bet."

At this time in her review of the Purkey family history, LaVerne realized that at "some point stories start becoming hearsay."

Elizabeth and Everett Purkey

Daniel Alan Purkey, Patricia Ann Purkey, and Thomas Edward Purkey, children of LaVerne and Glenn Purkey

Tom, Patricia, and Dan Purkey in a picture enclosed with a note from LaVerne Purkey dated July 6, 2009, in which she writes "got your cousins in the same place at the same time for a picture."

Charles Davis Family

Marriage of Patricia Ann Purkey and Michael Brian Entwistle Sr., September 1, 2002, Sparks, Nevada. Family members above, left to right, include Adam and Eric; Marcie, daughter of Becky and Tom; LaVerne with her daughter, the bride, Patricia Ann; and the groom, Michael Brian. Next to "Mike" is Terrie with husband Dan and "Becky," wife of Tom Purkey, and Tom.

Photos courtesy of **LaVerne Purkey**

Pat, her brother Tom, and mom LaVerne Purkey reviewing with me the family tree I had laid out for them on the dining room table in Tom and Becky Purkey's home in Virginia City, Nevada.A special cake was served afterward, made from a family receipe.

Video capture by **Clyde Davis**

LaVerne wanted us to see her horse "Lady" during our visit.

Glenn Purkey — Airborne

From the "History of the 32nd Troop Carrier Squadron of the 314th Troop Carrier Group of the 52nd Troop Carrier Wing during the years 1942–1946," the following represents in part the military career of Glenn E. Purkey.

Glenn arrived at Ellington Field, Texas, in July 1942, and was assigned with nine other men to the 314th Troop Carrier Group. They were transferred to Troop Carrier Headquarters at Bowman Field in Louisville, Kentucky, arriving there on August 10, and were immediately sent to Stout Field, Indianapolis, Indiana, for a month of training on C-47 airplanes. In September 1942, Glenn and the other nine men, all staff sergeant pilots, were transferred to the 32nd Troop Carrier Squadron, which was based in Louisville, Kentucky.[1]

On August 5, 1942, a significant event for the 32nd Troop Carrier Squadron occurred at Ellington Field, Texas. On that date 89 Staff Sergeant Pilots graduated from flying school and, of that number, 80 pilots went to the 52nd Troop Carrier Wing. Many of these men came to the 314th T.C. Group and the following ten men came to the 32nd Troop Carrier Squadron.

(D) PLEZ T. NALL
(D) GLENN E. PURKEY
(D) MARSHALL A. ROCKETT, JR.
EDDIE R. RUSSELL
HARLEY E. SHOTLIFF Bella Vista, Ark.
MILLER R. PEARSON Purcell, OK
(D) GEORGE (NMI) RISLEY, JR. (killed in plane crash
DAVID E. ROSENGRANTS Abilene, TX
(D) EMIL R. SCHMIDT
JONATHAN C. WATSON Tallahassee, FL

When these men arrived at Troop Carrier Headquarters at Bowman Field, they were immediately (August 10, 1942) sent to Stout Field, Indianapolis, Indiana, for a month of training in [illegible]

In early November 1942, the 314th T.C. Group received orders to move its men and equipment to Alliance, Nebraska, but these orders were changed while they were en route, and they were sent instead to Sedalia Army Air Field at Warrensburg, Missouri. Some of the group traveled by train, others by car, and others, including Glenn, by military aircraft.[2]

At Sedalia, training continued. The 32nd Troop Carrier Squadron was divided into two flights, with Glenn assigned to Flight B.[3] In February 1943, a third flight group was added.[4] On January 18, 1943, the squadron's ten staff sergeant pilots, including Glenn, were discharged from their enlisted ranks and the next day, they were appointed Flight Officers.[5]

After only three months at Sedalia, the 32nd was transferred to Lawson Field at Fort Benning, Georgia, in February 1943. There they flew single and formation flights for paratrooper training jumps.[6]

In April 1943, the 32nd T.C. Squadron received its orders for North Africa, which U.S. Army forces had invaded in November 1942. On May 12, 1943, the last Axis troops in North Africa surrendered. The squadron was divided into air and ground echelons. The ground echelon went to Camp Shanks, New York, for processing on May 12, then transferred by rail and ferry to Staten Island where they boarded the USS *West Point*,[7] formerly the SS *America*. The trip was made without escort except for the beginning and end of the voyage, and the ship arrived at Casablanca, Morocco, on May 20, 1943.[8]

The air echelon, including Glenn Purkey, flew to West Palm Beach, Florida. The 32nd left Morrison Field at West Palm Beach on May 10, 1943, using a regular Air Transport route, which led them to Puerto Rico, then Trinidad, then Belem, Brazil, then Natal, Brazil, where they laid over for a day of airplane inspections. Then they flew on to Ascension Island in the South Atlantic, leaving there on May 16 and continuing to Accra, Gold Coast. The next day they flew to Dakar, French West Africa. On May 18, they left Dakar, but had to divert to Tindouf because a dust storm kept them from flying through the low altitude pass in the Atlas Mountains. They flew from Tindouf to Ouidja and the next day arrived at their final destination, Berguent, Morocco. It is worth noting that this flight, totaling 159 C-47 and C-53 airplanes, was the largest movement of tactical aircraft ever included in one set of orders.[9]

On the 29th and 30th, the squadron's planes brought the

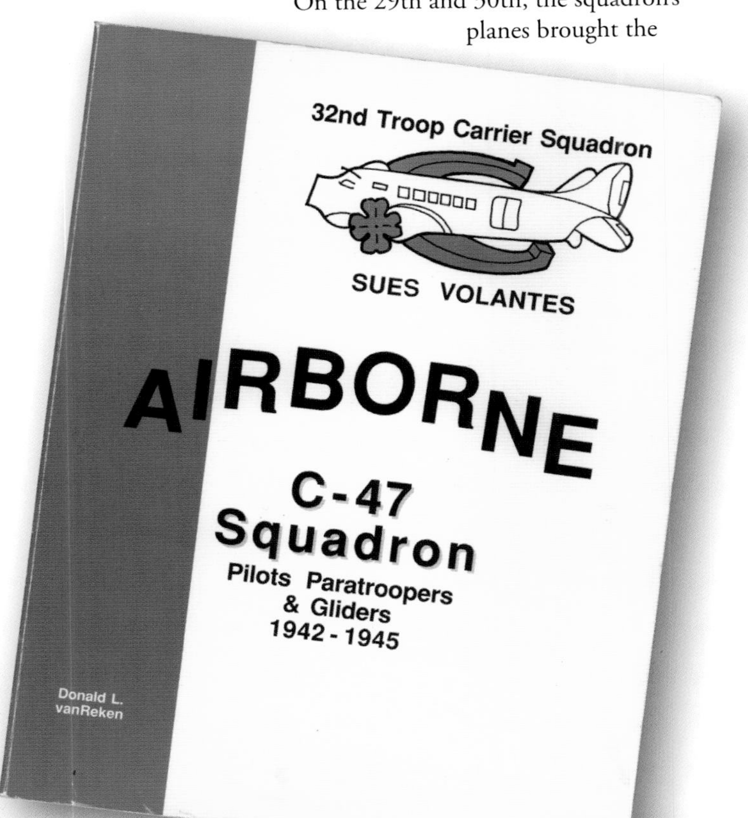

This photo of a C-47 "Skytrain" was found at <http://www.travisair museum.org/html/c-47.html>, the web site of the Travis Air Museum, which is run by the Jimmy Doolittle Air and Space Museum Foundation.

Ground Echelon from Casablanca to Berguent. On June 25, the squadron was moved from Berguent to newly engineered airstrips at Kairouan, Tunisia, in preparation for their first combat missions, the invasion of Sicily. Facilities were poor and water was in short supply. A storm of hurricane force flooded the area, loosened glider moorings, and caused a dozen gliders to become airborne. All the tents were blown down.

The 32nd's first combat mission took place on July 9, 1943, as part of the invasion of Sicily, (code named Husky). The 314th Troop Carrier Group, which included the 32nd, carried the Third Battalion of the 505th Parachute Infantry Regiment. The Troop Carrier invasion armada flew in five serials with the 314th being in the second serial. The flight plan carried them from Tunisia, east to Malta, and then northwest to Sicily, then over Lago Di Bivarre, a large lake, to their individual drop zones. The route was laid out to avoid Allied shipping lanes, though ships in the invasion fleet supporting the landings did fire on them. Strong twenty to thirty-mile west winds further complicated the 415-mile flight.

The Group C.O. of Glenn's group missed one of the checkpoints that night, but Captain Bomar and Lieutenant David Rosencrantz noted this and proceeded to the correct drop zone at Gela with two other planes, including Glenn's.

Two nights later, the 32nd Troop Carrier Squadron flew again to Gela, carrying several thousand paratroopers of the 504th Regimental Combat Team. Containers were parachuted with supplies at the Ponte Oliva airfield northeast of Gela, some from pararacks and some from containers pushed out the cargo doors by flight crew and paratroopers. On the way back, the Commanding Officer, Captain Bomar, was injured in the wrist by anti-aircraft fire. Bomar was flying as co-pilot, and Lt. Rosencrantz, flying as pilot, took control of their aircraft. Bomar was hospitalized for eighteen months, and after much surgery, was able to resume his civilian career as an airline pilot.[10]

German anti-aircraft fire was not the only problem they faced. "There is still more that can be said about that night, July 11, 1943. During the first two days in Sicily things had not gone too well for the Allied troops. The initial air drop was widely scattered. Since there weren't enough troops to hold important road junctions, General Patton asked for airborne reinforcements to land beyond the airfield at Gela which was already controlled by the Allies. This should have been an easy mission, but the German airforce, the Luftwaffe, staged four separate air raids on the Allied naval forces that day, with the final raid taking place at 10 P.M. When the Troop Carrier planes came on the scene a few hours later, the fearful men on the Allied ships, not being aware that these were American airplanes, began shooting at the planes and paratroopers. Of the 144 airplanes which had left Tunisia, 23 were shot down, and 37 others were very badly damaged. Most others had lesser damage. More than 300 paratroopers and airmen were killed or wounded."[11]

In later missions, the squadron continued to take casualties from friend and foe alike. Both Allied ground and naval forces fired on them, mistaking them for the enemy or not trusting the recognition signals.

Subsequent missions involved dropping paratroops and their supplies by parachute, ferrying men and equipment into Sicily, and bringing out wounded:

> The official Air Force history, authored by Craven and Cate, states: In the week after the 13th, lack of air service personnel to move supplies and establish dumps threatened to curtail combat operations, but Troop Carrier saved the situation by flying in fuel, ammunition, rations and other supplies. Planes of Troop Carrier added…a substantial number of sorties to the total,…flying many missions which carried supplies and personnel to Sicily and which brought out hundreds of wounded and sick soldiers.[12]

Photo courtesy of **LaVerne Purkey**

Glenn in uniform with his brother Everett and grandmother Rebecca. In front, standing left to right are Everett's daughter Beverly, me, and my sister Tootsie. Beverly is actually Rebecca's great-granddaughter.

Conditions at the Kairouan base continued to create difficulties. Another rain and wind storm on July 24 "blew the PX all over the camp" and wrecked a number of gliders, which hampered operations over the next several months.[13]

Starting July 29, the air echelon flew to Gabes, Tunisia, to train for large-scale formation flights for both paratroop drops and glider operations. The glider training was done with open radio communications in the hopes that the Italians would listen in and be appropriately frightened by the prospect of a glider invasion. "At the close of July 1943, the 32nd T.C. Squadron had 34 pilots, 15 combat crews, 26 glider crews, 24 glider mechanics, 13 airplanes and only 8 Waco CG-4A gliders."[14]

On September 1, 1943, the 314th T.C. Group relocated to Castelvetrano, Sicily. Castelvetrano had served Italian and German fighters and bombers, and there was a large bomb and munitions dump in the southeast part of the field. It was estimated that there were 50,000 bombs of various sizes weighing a total of more than fifteen tons, along with thousands of rounds of .30 caliber rifle ammunition, plus signal flares, underground storage areas of dynamite (requisitioned by the Army engineers), hand grenades, land mines, and other weaponry left behind by the Italians and Germans.

Lt. Glenn Purkey's airplane after a crash landing on December 25, 1944

At the beginning of September, the 32nd had seventy-three officers and 244 enlisted men, but by the end of October, this was down to forty-eight officers and twenty-four enlisted men. Some personnel were transferred in and out of the squadron for training or combat operations elsewhere. In September, the entire 314th T.C. had only twenty-two gliders.

Italy surrendered to the Allies on September 13, 1943.

On November 10, 1943, eight air crews and six C-47 airplanes of the 32nd Troop Carrier Squadron were placed on temporary duty with the 42nd Bomb Wing at the Cagliari-Elmas airfield on the island of Sardinia.[15] Numbering among these crews was 2nd Lt. Glenn E. Purkey.

On May 30, 1944 the former Sergeant Pilot Glenn E. Purkey was honored by the award of the Good Conduct Medal for his "faithful and exact performance of duty" as an enlisted man.

On July 33, 1944 lst Lt. Glenn E. Purkey was awarded a second Bronze Oak Leaf Cluster along with other Officers and Enlisted Men, for their actions during the Invasion of France. The ceremony took place at Saltby, England.

On December 25, 1944, another of the Squadron's C-47's was lost while at Chilbolton Airfield. First Lt. Glenn Purkey, a skilled pilot with a great amount of C-47 experience, gave a good report of this accident. Before his 9:50 a.m. takeoff he, together with his crew, had cleared the frost from the wings of the airplane. They loaded 19 paratroops with a gross weight of 5,200 pounds. Purkey was the second ship of a formation and many other airplanes were flying that day. As he took off at a speed of over 105 miles per hour, the left wing caught some prop wash and sank down. As he recovered the right wing dipped and, upon recovering from this, the left wing struck the ground and broke the wing tip. Purkey gave full power in an effort to recover flight but the loss of altitude made him decide to cut the switches as the airplane struck the ground. The airplane slid 150 feet on the frozen ground.

No one was hurt in this crash except the crew chief who had a very minor injury. Everyone left the airplane hastily. The damage to the airplane was severe for the wings, the propellers, and the fuselage were all affected. Lt. Purkey attributed the accident to the frost on the wings and a wingtip stall.

When December, 1944, ended, the 32nd was still at Saltby and still undergoing training for future missions.[16]

In the book *Air Force Combat Units of World War II*, the 32nd Troop Carrier Squadron is reported as inactivated on 30 September 1946.[17]

Notes

1. Donald L. vanReken, *32nd Troop Carrier Squadron, Sues Volantes, Airborne C-47 Squadron Pilots Paratroopers and Gliders, 1942–1945* (Holland, Mich.: the author, 1989), 3.
2. Ibid., pp. 4–5.
3. Ibid., p. 8.
4. Ibid., p. 9.
5. Ibid., p. 10.
6. Ibid., p. 11.
7. Ibid., p. 15.
8. Ibid., p. 18.
9. Ibid., pp. 18–20.
10. Ibid., pp. 28-30.
11. Ibid., p. 31.
12. Ibid., pp. 33–34.
13. Ibid., p. 34.
14. Ibid., p. 36.
15. Ibid., p. 53.
16. Ibid., pp. 145-46.
17. Ibid., p. 187.

Pictured above, left to right, Carl Davis, Alice Toombs Davis, and Joseph S. "J.S." Davis

Joe Davis, Dad's brother
wife & son

(Charles Davis' brother)

These are my only kin.
Mother Daddy and Brother
the only Brother I got and poor
me. And now it's Mother Brother
and me.

Joseph Davis of Longwood, Missouri

Joseph S. Davis was born March 11, 1867, near Richmond, Kentucky, the son of James and Nannie Gooch Davis.[1] After coming to Missouri with his father, he married Alice Toombs, who was a sister to Mattie Toombs, who married his brother, John Morgan Davis.[2] Joseph and Alice Davis had four children:

1. Carl W. Davis born April 14, 1890; married (1) Florence Brant and (2) Ethel Reed. He died February 20, 1965, and was buried at Longwood, Missouri. He and Florence had one son, Ernest Davis, born June 4, 1911. Florence Davis died of peritonitis shortly after the birth of Ernest on June 28, 1911. Joe Davis was the informant who said that her parents were Phillip Brant, born in Virginia, and Nancy Sinels, born in Missouri.[3] Ernest Davis died in Kansas City January 23, 1929, from burns caused by a cigarette that caught his bed clothing on fire. The informant was Carl Davis. Ernest's occupation was a laborer.[4]
2. Pearl Davis born January 23, 1894. She appeared on the 1900 census only. No further record.
3. Clyde Davis, born about 1901–02; first wife Carrie, second wife Agnes. Relatives say that he was killed in a vehicle accident as a young man. We have searched the states of Kansas, Missouri, and Illinois, but have not found his death certificate. In 1930 he was living alone in his parents' rooming house in Kansas City, Missouri, so it is not known if he had any children.
4. Hazel Irene Davis born January 7, 1906, married December 27, 1922, to William Edward Mullins. They separated in 1939, and Mr. Mullins raised the five children. Hazel married Albert Thomas, then James Warford, then George Kirby.[5] She died November 3, 1991, and was buried in the Longwood Cemetery, Pettis County, Missouri.[6]

Joseph Davis was a farmer most of his life. In the 1900 and 1910 censuses he lived in Johnson County, Missouri. By 1920 he lived in Saline County. Apparently, he left farming, however, because in the 1930 census he was living in Kansas City, Missouri.[7] Joseph was renting a house for $80 per month. He had three lodgers living in the home. His son Carl and daughter-in-law Ethel lived with him. His other son, Clyde Davis, lived there, also. Joseph's occupation was listed as proprietor of a rooming house.

Joseph and Alice came back to Longwood, Pettis County, Missouri, at some point in time, probably to be near his brother John Morgan Davis and Alice's sister, Mattie Toombs, wife of John Morgan, because his obituary appeared in the *Sedalia Democrat*, December 2, 1946:

> Joseph S. Davis died Sunday morning at 3:00 at his home north of Longwood. Mr. Davis was born March 11, 1867 at Richmond Ky., the son of James and Nanwnie [*sic*] Davis.
>
> Surviving are his wife, Alice Davis, a son, Carl Davis of Longwood, a daughter Mrs. Albert Thomas of Marshall; five grandchildren, J.R. Mullins, Ruby Mullins, Helen Mullins, Martha Jean Mullins, all of Marshall, and Mary Ford, of Napton; three brothers, J.M. Davis LaMonte, Charles Davis, state of Indiana, and Ollie Davis, Kansas City, and one sister, Mrs. Luther Saunders [*sic*], of Nevada. Funeral services will be held Tuesday at the Longwood Presbyterian church, with the Rev. W.L. Robb to officiate. Pallbearers will be J.W. Ezell, Sam Kearney, David Epple, Dan Schlomer, Sam Hieronymus and J.W.Greer. Music will be by the church choir. The body is at the Gillespie funeral home, where it will remain until the funeral hour.

Alice Toombs Davis died in 1957 and was also buried in the Longwood Cemetery.[8]

So ends the life story of Joseph S. Davis. His only grandson with the surname Davis died tragically, as well as his son, Clyde. His surviving grandchildren were the children of his daughter, Hazel Davis Mullins.

A.H.

Notes

1. Joseph S. Davis, Missouri death certificate, 1946, #41592.
2. Eula Davis House, *Family Tree of My Father, Jefferson C. Davis* (privately printed, 1955), 8.
3. Florence Davis, Missouri death certificate, 1911, #25013.
4. Ernest Davis, Missouri death certificate, 1929, #1759.
5. Information from Carol Treybal, a descendant of Hazel Davis Mullins.
6. Hazel Irene Kirby, Missouri death certificate, 1991, #91024635.
7. 1930 federal census, Missouri, Jackson Co., p. 5A.
8. Davis, *Family Tree of My Father*, 8.

Top photo: Carl W. Davis with his mother Alice Toombs Davis and his wife Ethel S. Reid Davis. Lower photo is with Carl and his mother with his sister Hazel Irene.

Clyde Davis 

A. HINKEL, WARRENSBURG, MO.

Clyde Davis b. 1901 to Joseph S. Davis and Alice Toombs is believed to be the "namesake" of both Clyde O. Davis, son of Charles Davis, Joseph's brother, and Clyde Patrick Davis, son of Clyde O. Davis.

Joseph and Alice's son Clyde was enumerated and living with his parents in the 1930 census in Jackson County, Missouri. He disappeared and no additional record — census, marriage, certificate of death — has since been uncovered by the author. It is believed that he died in a motor vehicle accident.

TAKEN
JUNE 26-1953
ALICE-ETHEL-CARL-DAVIS

Above photo depicts Alice Toombs Davis (far left), with son Carl Davis and wife Ethel. On the opposite page (top), we see a family gathering, from left to right, that includes Joeseph S. Davis (Uncle Joe?), with his spouse, Alice Davis, Ethel Davis, Lulu Davis Sanders (Aunt Lou), (Dad?), Carl Davis and (me?). Joeseph and Lulu are brother and sister.

The photo below, left to right, adds Nellie and Fred Davis, husband and wife, includes again Lulu Davis Sanders (Aunt Lou), and introduces us to John "Morg" Davis (Uncle Morg), also a brother to Lulu and Joseph, and Mattie Toombs Davis (Aunt Mattie), Morg's spouse. "Fred and Nellie's Boy" is Fred Cornell Davis, the smaller of the two boys.

Regarding the identity of "Dad" and "me," I can only speculate that "Dad" is Cecil W. Davis, brother to Fred and that "me" may be his son, James W. "J.W." Davis.

From left to right:
Uncle Joe, Aunt Alice,
Ethel, Aunt Lou, Dad,
Carl Davis and me.

Left to right:
Nellie Davis, Fred Davis,
Aunt Lou, Uncle Morg,
Dad, Aunt Matt,
Fred and Nellies boy
and me.

THIS IS A CERTIFIED COPY OF AN ORIGINAL DOCUMENT.
(Do not accept if rephotographed, or if seal impression cannot be felt.)

THE REPRODUCTION OF THIS DOCUMENT IS PROHIBITED BY LAW (sec. 193.315, RSMo 1994)

STATE OF MISSOURI } ss
CITY OF JEFFERSON }

I HEREBY CERTIFY that this is an exact reproduction of the certificate for the person named therein as it now appears in the permanent records of the Bureau of Vital Statistics of the Missouri Department of Health. Witness my hand as State Registrar of Vital Statistics and the Seal of the Missouri Department of Health this date of

AUG 5 1999

Garland H Land
Garland H. Land
State Registrar of Vital Statistics

DEPARTMENT OF COMMERCE
BUREAU OF THE CENSUS

THE STATE BOARD OF HEALTH OF MISSOURI
STANDARD CERTIFICATE OF DEATH

41592
State File No.

FILED DEC 17 1946

Registration District No. 274 Primary Registration District No. 5933 Registrar's No. 454

1. PLACE OF DEATH: (a) County PETTIS (b) City or town LONGWOOD RURAL (If outside city or town limits, write "RURAL" and name of township) (c) Name of hospital or institution: (If not in hospital or institution, write street number or location) (d) Length of stay: In hospital or institution ... In this community 35 YEARS (Specify whether years, months or days)

2. USUAL RESIDENCE OF DECEASED: (a) State MO (b) County PETTIS (c) City or town LONGWOOD RURAL (If outside city or town limits, write "RURAL") (d) Street No. (If rural, give location) (e) Citizen of foreign country? ... (Yes or No) If yes, name country

3. (a) PRINT FULL NAME JOSEPH S. DAVIS
3. (b) If veteran, name war 3. (c) Social Security No.
4. Sex MALE 5. Color or race WHITE 6. (a) Single, widowed, married, divorced MAR.
6. (b) Name of husband or wife ALICE 6. (c) Age of husband or wife if alive 77 years
7. Birth date of deceased 3 (Month) 11 (Day) 1867 (Year)
8. AGE: Years 79 Months 8 Days 20 If less than one day ... hr. ... min.
9. Birthplace RICHMOND (City, town, or county) KY (State or foreign country)
10. Usual occupation FARMER
11. Industry or business
FATHER 12. Name JAMES DAVIS 13. Birthplace LOUISVILLE (City, town, or county) KY (State or foreign country)
MOTHER 14. Maiden name NANNIE GOOCH 15. Birthplace (City, town, or county) (State or foreign country)
16. (a) Informant MRS. J. S. DAVIS (b) Address LONGWOOD, MO.
17. (a) BURIAL (Burial, cremation, or removal) (b) Date thereof 12-3-46 (Month) (Day) (Year) (c) Place: burial or cremation LONGWOOD, MO.
18. (a) Signature of funeral director Geo Dillard (b) Address Sedalia, Mo
19. (a) 12/2/46 (Date received local registrar) (b) Betty Yeager Deputy (Registrar's signature)

MEDICAL CERTIFICATION

20. DATE OF DEATH: Month DEC. day 1 year 1946 hour 3 minute a M.
21. I hereby certify that I attended the deceased from Apr 1946 to Dec. 1 1946 that I last saw him alive on Nov 30 1946 and that death occurred on the date and hour stated above.
Immediate cause of death Cancer of Stomach Duration 6 months
Due to
Due to
Other conditions (Include pregnancy within 3 months of death)
Major findings: Of operations / Of autopsy 46
PHYSICIAN Underline the cause to which death should be charged statistically.
22. If death was due to external causes, fill in the following: (a) Accident, suicide, or homicide (specify) (b) Date of occurrence (c) Where did injury occur? (City or town) (County) (State) (d) Did injury occur in or about home, on farm, in industrial place, in public place? (Specify type of place) While at work? (e) Means of injury
23. Signature John McNeish (M. D. or other) M.D. Address Houstonia Mo Date signed 12-2-46

251

(Licensed Embalmer's Statement on Reverse Side)

State of Missouri Division of Health — Standard Certificate of Death. A certified copy, August 5, 1999, of the original document, Joseph S. Davis b. March 11, 1867, d. December 1, 1946.

Joseph S. Davis

Joseph S. Davis died Sunday morning at 3:00 o'clock at his home north of Longwood.

Mr. Davis was born March 11, 1867, at Richmond, Ky., the son of James and Nanwnie Lavis.

Surviving are his wife, Alice Davis, a son, Carl Davis, of Longwood; a daughter, Mrs. Albert Thomas, of Marshall; five grandchildren, J. R. Mullins, Ruby Mullins, Helen Mullins, Martha Jean Mullins, all of Marshall, and Mary Ford, of Napton; three brothers, J. M. Davis, LaMonte; Charles Davis, state of Indiana, and Ollie Davis, Kansas City, and one sister, Mrs. Luther Saunders, of Nevada.

Funeral services will be held Tuesday at the Longwood Presbyterian church, with the Rev. W. L. Robb to officiate.

Pallbearers will be J. W. Ezell, Sam Kearney, David Epple, Dan Schlomer, Sam Hieronymus and J. W. Greer.

Music will be by the church choir.

The body is at the Gillespie funeral home, where it will remain until the funeral hour.

Joseph S. Davis Sedalia Democrat *(Missouri), December 2, 1946*

Rev. J.R. Mullins

Rev. J.R. Mullins, 72, of Humboldt, Tenn., formerly of Hartshorne, Okla., died Sunday, March 28, 1999, in Jackson, Tenn.

Funeral services will be held at 2 p.m. Friday, April 2, at Mills Funeral Home Chapel in Hartshorne, Okla. Rev. Mike Hibbard will officiate. Pallbearers will be Jason Mullins, David Mullins, Buddy Jones, Ronnie Davidson, Wylie Morgan and Charles Wall. Honorary pallbearer will be Rev. Simon Ellis. Visitation will be from 6:30 to 8 p.m. Thursday, April 1. Burial will be in Maxey Cemetery in Wister, Okla.

Born Nov. 30, 1926, in Nelson, he was the son of the late William Edward and Hazel Davis Mullins. He had lived in Hartshorne, Okla., for close to 30 years. On Sept. 12, 1998, in Hartshorne, he married Mary Bizzle, who survives of the home. He retired from the Rock Island Railroad and was an ordained minister for 20 years. He was a minister at the Nelson Baptist Church in Nelson and also Cambridge Baptist Church in Hartshorne.

Additional survivors include three daughters, Delores Isaacs and Marie Mick, both of Dow, Okla., and Linda Roberts of Belton; three sons, David Mullins of Topeka, Kan., Jason Mullins of Fulton and William Mullins; four sisters, Mary Ford of Rosefield, Calif., Ruby Thorton, Helen Williams and Jean Hibbard, all of Gilliam; 10 grandchildren; eight great-grandchildren and several nieces and nephews.

In addition to his parents, he was preceded in death by one son, Johnny Mullins, and one grandchild.

Obituary in the Marshall Democrat-News *(Missouri), March 31, 1999, for the Reverend Edward "J.R." Mullins b. November 30, 1926, d. March 28, 1999. He was the son of Irene Hazel Davis and William Edward D. Mullins, and the grandson of Joseph S. Davis*

WILLIAM "WILL" DAVIS b. June 11, 1871

William "Will" Davis and second spouse Eliza. Note the unusual "scalloped" trim of the photograph similar to one on opposite page. Obviously, these photos were taken in the same general time period and area, but the identities of the elderly couple seated on the stairs have not yet been determined. They are clearly older than Will and Eliza, although the photos were probably taken within a relatively short time frame. Alice Henson is of the opinion that they may be Eliza's parents, Thomas E. Gooch and Mildred Elizabeth Oldham Williams Gooch.

Three Marriages and Many Children

The link between the Gooch and Davis families shows up in the life story of William Davis. He was born June 11, 1871, in Madison County, Kentucky, the son of James Davis and Nannie Gooch Davis. He came with his parents to Randolph County, Missouri, by 1880 and then followed his father to Johnson County, Missouri. His death certificate gave his birth date as January 11, 1872, but the 1900 and 1910 censuses indicate that he was born in June of 1871. His handwritten letter (see page 293) also states that he would be sixty-seven on June 11th, 1937.

He married first to Lena Garrison, January 19, 1895, according to their divorce, which was granted in February 1900, Johnson County, Missouri Circuit Court. Lena/Linnie declared that they lived together until August 1897.[1] Blanch Davis, their daughter, was born August 15, 1897. In 1900 Lena and Blanch Davis were living in Johnson County, but William Davis was living with a new wife, Eliza Gooch, his first cousin, in Vermilion County, Illinois. They had apparently married 24 June 1899 in Morgan County, Illinois.[2] Note that his second marriage in Illinois happened prior to his divorce in Missouri.

It is not known how long William Davis and Eliza Gooch lived together. They appeared on the 1900 census of Vermilion County, Illinois, p. 317A. Living with them are two young boys, with the surname Pettis: Jessie Pettis born in September 1891, and Freddie Pettis born August 1895. Both were listed as stepsons of William Davis. They lived near the James Gooch family (brother of Eliza). William Davis was a day laborer. Apparently, Eliza had a third son, Daniel Pettis (see page 403). He was taken away from her when he was young and raised by another woman. The family story is that when he became an adult, he found his mother again.

We do not know when or where William Davis and Eliza Gooch Pettis Davis divorced, but by 1910 William Davis was back in Missouri with a third wife, Viola Bowman, whom he married July 31, 1907, in Saline County.[3] Viola Davis was fourteen and William Davis was thirty-five when they married. By 1910 they had one daughter, Nellie M., age one, and Jessie Pettis, age twenty, was living with them, and also Fred Davis, not Pettis, age fifteen. Both boys were born in Illinois.[4] Is Fred Pettis/Davis actually a son of William Davis? We think so, because Fred is mentioned as a child of William Davis and Eliza Gooch Davis in Eula House's history of the family.[5] If Fred was a child of William Davis, he was born to Eliza Gooch six months after William Davis married his first wife, Linnie Garrison.

In the 1930 census, Saline County, Blackwater Township, page 21B, there was a Jess Pettis and wife Victoria with a large family. A few pages away there was a Fred Davis, wife Anna or Anne, and two daughters.[6] One of Fred's daughters, Leoma, died in 1931. On her death certificate her parents were listed as Fred Davis, born in Illinois, and Anne Snider, born in Kentucky.[7] Eliza Gooch Goodwin, mother of Jessie and Fred, was enumerated on page 22A of the same census. The close physical proximity of Eliza Gooch Goodwin to these two sons — all living in the same neighborhood — is significant.

We did not find William and Viola Davis in the 1930 census, so we do not have good birth information for their later children. William Davis died September 22, 1941, in Pettis County.[8] His usual residence was Marshall, Missouri, where he lived on South Salt Pond Street. The informant was Mrs. Nellie Brandkamp, most likely his oldest daughter. He was buried in the Salt Fork Cemetery, at Nelson, Missouri. Viola Bowman Davis died at the hospital in Marshall, Missouri, February 10, 1955. Her parents were Charles Bowman and Minnie Chaffee.[9]

Eliza Gooch Pettis Davis was married to Thomas Goodwin, fourteen years younger than she, May 24, 1911. They appeared in the 1930 census of Saline County, Missouri, Blackwater Township, page 22A. There were no children living with them. She died February 27, 1951, in Beaman, Pettis County. Thomas C. Goodwin was the informant on her death certificate. Because we could not find Thomas Goodwin and Eliza on the 1920 census, we do not know if they had any children.

William Davis and Viola Bowman Davis had the following children:

1. Nellie M. Davis born about 1909.

2. Olalee Davis born about 1911.
3. Joe Marshall Davis born about 1913; died 1932.
4. Carl Cecil Davis born about 1916.
5. James C. Davis born about 1919.
6. Mattie Odell Davis, born about 1920; died January 6, 1933.[10]
7. Paul Davis born after 1920.
8. Kenneth Davis born after 1920.
9. Betty Davis born after 1920.
10. Opal Davis born April 3, 1925; died April 18, 2000; married (1) Farris A. Sheperd; (2) Herschel Foster.
11. Child Davis born 1936.

How many children did William Davis father? In 1937 when he wrote to his sister-in-law Rebecca Gooch Davis in Illinois, he said he had eleven children, the oldest twenty-eight years, the youngest four months. The twenty-eight year old would be Nellie. In the letter he mourned the loss of a daughter, whom he did not name, and a son. In checking for a death certificate for this daughter, we found that she was Mattie Odell Davis. According to the death certificate, she was born September 21, 1919. This information was given by her mother, Mrs. Viola Davis. However, this daughter was not on the 1920 census, although her family was enumerated on January 27, 1920, so she was born most likely in September 1920, not in September 1919. In his letter, William Davis told his cousin and sister-in-law Rebecca Gooch Davis that the girl had fallen against a stove when she was about five and, afterward, suffered epileptic seizures until her death at age twelve, which also disagrees with the death certificate, where her age was reported as thirteen.

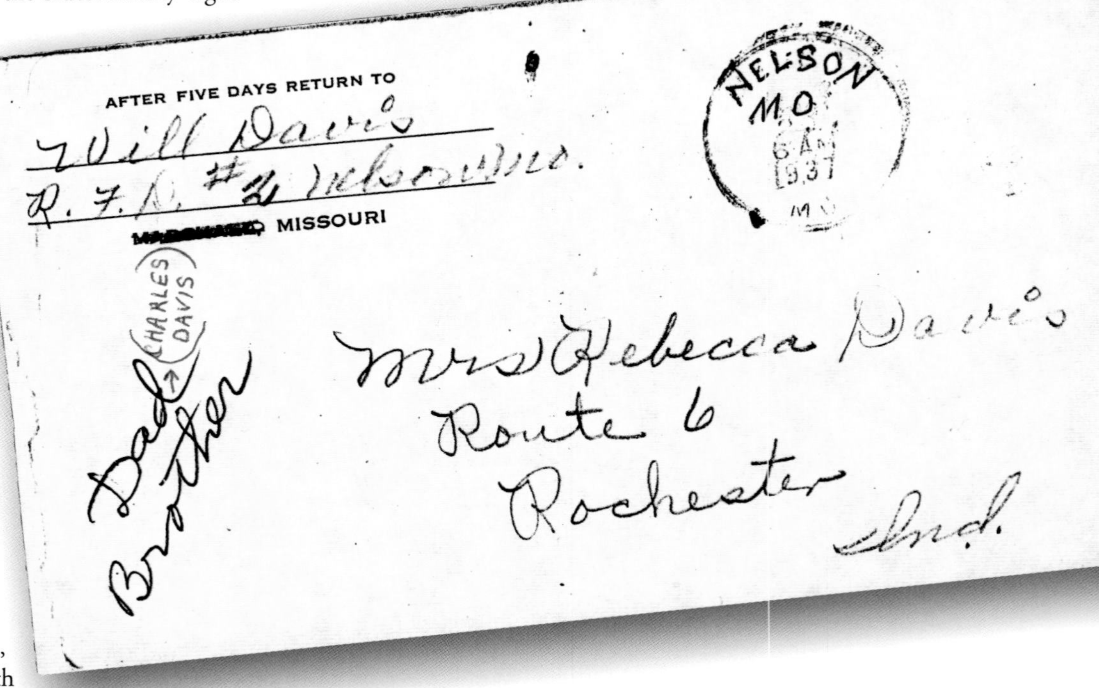

Note that in saying he had eleven children, William Davis did not include either Jesse or Fred (children of Eliza Gooch), nor Blanch Davis, daughter of his first wife.

Joe Marshall Davis died in 1932 of a gunshot wound in Saline County, Missouri. He was about nineteen years old when he took Lucille Scott, about sixteen, to a dance. Lucille's father, Henry Scott, was also at the dance and objected to Davis's taking her home. Scott put his daughter in his car, but then she discovered that she had left her purse in Davis's car. Davis got the purse and handed it to her in the car. Scott said something to Davis as he returned the purse, and Davis said, "I'll see you later about that remark." Scott then pulled his gun and shot Davis in the stomach. Joe Davis died in about twenty-four hours.[11] We did not find a death certificate for him on file in Missouri.

William Davis had three marriages, but only one lasted more than a few years. With the deep connections to the Davis and Gooch families in Illinois, William wrote to his relatives about Joe's murder and the death of young Mattie. Eliza Gooch Pettis Davis Goodwin also kept in touch with the Illinois family, sending pictures of her and third husband, Thomas Goodwin. The historic entanglement of the Gooch and Davis families makes its mark in the life story of William Davis. *A.H.*

Notes

1. Johnson Co., Missouri, Circuit Court Case, Linnie J. Davis vs. William Davis, February 1900, Warrensburg, Mo.
2. Morgan Co., Illinois, Marriage Book D:174.
3. Saline Co., Missouri, Marriage Book 8:231.
4. 1910 federal census, Missouri, Johnson Co., Simpson Twp., p. 11B.
5. Eula Davis House, *Family Tree of My Father, Jefferson C. Davis* (privately printed, 1955), 9.
6. 1930 federal census, Missouri, Saline Co., Blackwater Twp., p. 24A.
7. Leoma Davis, Missouri death certificate, 1931, #4133.
8. William Davis, Missouri death certificate, 1941, #32228.
9. Viola Bowman Davis, Missouri death certificate, 1955, #3547.
10. Mattie Odell Davis, Missouri death certificate, 1933, #4271.
11. *Marshall Citizen* (Saline Co., Missouri), 18 August 1932, p. 7, col. 8; *Marshall Citizen* (Saline Co., Missouri), 25 August 1932, p. 1, col. 2.

Nelson Mo. R. 2.
March-19-1937

Dear Brother & Sister:
Guess you all will be somewhat surprised to hear from us. But this is the first I have heard of you all for 25 years. Joe sent me the letter you wrote him. So thought we would write. Hope these few lines find you all well and enjoying your selves. Lots of things can happen in a few years can't they. I will be 67 years old the 11th June. I have 11 children the oldest 28 yrs. the youngest 4 months old. I have 2 children dead a boy 19 a girl 12. Have been almost crazy ever since my boy got killed. He was a fine boy. started going with a girl and her father got drunk at a dance one night and shot my boy Joe". Do you remember him when you was at our house the last time. he lived just about 24 hours sure was terrible. I have been in pretty bad shape for 10 years with Asthma and seems like I worry so much since Joe died 5 years ago it seems like I can't ever forget it. Oh I have been up and been down I have had plenty now back just like I started. I was pretty well fixed in 1926 and had little girl 15 years old to fall against the heating stove and

MURDER CHARGE FILED AGAINST HENRY SCOTT

Joe Davis, Whom He Shot, Died at the Hospital.

Charge of first degree murder was filed today against Henry Scott following the death of Joe Davis last night at Fitzgibbon Hospital. Scott shot Davis about midnight Wednesday.

The shooting occurred at an open air dance operated by Walter Davenport near a filling station on No. 40 highway about five miles east of Marshall Junction. Scott lives near No. 65 highway about half a mile north of the junction. Davis lived in the Blue Lick neighborhood.

Perry G. Storts, prosecutor, said he had the following information about the case:

Davis took Lucile Scott, a girl about 16 years old to the dance. Scott also was there and when he got ready to go home told the girl to accompany him. The daughter demurred and he put her in his car. As he started to drive off it was found her purse still was in the car of Davis, who got the purse and took it to her. When Davis arrived back at the car Scott said something to him and Davis said, "I'll see you later about that remark." Then Scott shot him in the stomach.

Davis was brought to Fitzgibbon Hospital and Scott was arrested Thursday morning and placed in jail under a charge of assault with intent to kill. He did not make bond.

Virginia Maupin, after a week-end visit with home folks, returned home with her cousin, Mirian Sutherland. They are e[...] six week's out[...] wika, Over[...]

The envelope and letter above was passed on to me by LaVerne Purkey. The notation on the envelope "Dad Brother" was by Elizabeth Davis Purkey, the daughter of Charles Davis, my grandfather. This letter shed a great deal of light on a great-uncle of mine totally unknown to me at the time.

The Daily Democrat-News *(Marshall)*
Friday, August 12, 1932

shock her spine. which caused her
to have some kind of spells like
Epleptic fits and we sent her +
took her to ever doctor we heard of
and had her in Kansas city Hospital
and just done ever thing possible
to save her she died when she was
12 years old I spent ever dollar
I could get to get her cured but
didnt do any good just Broke me
plum up with Doctor bills But we
never regret a penny of it. we finally
came down here in 1928 spent $500.
for 40 acres timber land and built
a log cabin on it have been living
here ever since but seems like I
never will have any thing anymore
just cant work a bit and havent
even been out of the house but about
twice this winter no good no more. the
kids and viola does all there is
to do. I have 5 children at home. nellie
is married and has 7 children thats my
oldest Daughter she is 28. the next 26 Ola
shes is married and carl cecil is 21 and
married nellie lives 12 miles from us
Ola live $\frac{3}{4}$ miles from us and cecil
lives in marshall 17½ from us I
have a boy 19 James in the c c camp
he sends us $25. per month sure
helps out. I am just all in I
cant do a thing but viola is still
as big and tough as ever hasnt got
a grey hair in her head. Guess you
all hear from Liza all the time they
dont live far from us do you ever
hear from Moze he still lives

at the same old place. Joe's boy carl lives at Longwood Stamp with his father in law Reed guess carl will be pretty well fixed when the old man dies. If living expences high out there they sure are here. Saw John Collier awhile back, said you + Becca was seperated and clyde was in the pen. But we let it go in one ear and out the other funny how people tell things. too bad about John Googe's children dosent look like going to colo. helped them much. well its raining here and I have to get this off on the mail so you all be good and take good care of your selves would give most any thing to see you all sure would be worth while cant you all ever come down and give us a long visit Sure will be glad to have you. answer soon and God be with you untill we meet again.

Love to you All.

Your Brother + Sister
Will + Viola

Will Davis
R. F. D. # 2
Nelson Mo.

SCOTT IS HELD OVER FOR TRIAL IN MURDER CASE

Preliminary Hearing Held on Joe Davis Murder Charge.

Charged with first degree murder, Henry Scott was bound over to the September term of circuit court at a preliminary hearing held Tuesday afternoon and evening before Justice of the Peace A. F. Downs. Scott was refused bond.

The preliminary hearing was held on murder charges filed against Scott, August 12, after Joe Davis, whom he had shot August 10, died in the Fitzgibbon hospital.

The hearing was conducted in the courthouse and the court room was crowded with spectators until the hearing ended late in the evening. More than twenty witnesses were called and cross-examined. The defendant was represented by William H. Meschede; the state by Prosecuting Attorney Perry G. Storts.

Shooting Was August 10

The shooting took place about midnight, Wednesday, August 10, near a filling station operated by Walter Davenport on highway No. 40 about five miles east of Marshall Junction. Scott's home is on highway No. 65 about a half mile north of the junction. Davis lived in the Blue Lick neighborhood.

It was brought out at the hearing by witnesses called that Davis took Scott's sixteen year old daughter Lucille to a dance held that evening on an open air dance pavilion near the Davenport filling station and that Scott objected to Davis taking his daughter home.

Had Started Home

When she insisted on accompanying Davis, he put her in his car and, with another daughter, Leona, started to drive away. At this point, Lucille discovered that she had left her purse in Davis's car. Davis got the purse and handed it to her in the car.

Scott said something to Davis as he returned the purse and Davis said, "I'll see you later about that remark." Scott then pulled out his gun and shot Davis through the left arm and stomach, the latter died in about 24 hours.

Self Defense Indicated

The defense indicated that the act was committed in self-defense it being brought out by several witnesses that Davis had at various times carried a pistol and that just before Scott fired he had stepped toward the car, throwing one arm forward and dropping the other toward his hip pocket as though he might be reaching for a gun. There was no evidence brought forward to show that he had a gun in his possession at this time, however.

Marshall Saline County Citizen
Thursday, August 25, 1932, pg. 1, col. 2.

471

In the Circuit Court of Saline County, Missuri, January Term, 1935, 10th day, Monday, January 28, 1935.

cause be and it is hereby continued generally to the May Term, 1935, of the Circuit Court of Saline County, Missouri, and that the said cause be and it is hereby set for trial on Thursday, May 30, 1935, said continuance being agreed to by both the State and the defendant, and the defendant is released until said time, he being on a continuing bond heretofore taken and approved by the court herein.

-o-o-o-o-o-o-o-o-o-o-o-o-o-o-o-o-o-o-o-o-o-o-o-o-

State of Missouri, Plaintiff,

vs No. 5017 Possession of a deadly and dangerous weapon while intoxicated.

Henry Scott, Defendant,

Now at this day, comes the State of Missouri, by the Prosecuting Attorney of Saline County, Missouri, and comes also the defendant in his own proper person and with his attorneys and counsel, Charles Bacon and Robert L. Hay, the defendant being in the custody of the Sheriff of Saline County, Missouri, and the State now dismissed as to the charge of carrying concealed weapon, and the defendant now in open court withdraws his plea of not guilty and now enters a plea of guilty to the charge of possession of a deadly and dangerous weapon while intoxicated, as charged in the information, and the court being advised that the said plea is voluntarily made and made upon the advice of his counsel and friends, accepts said plea and adjudged the said defendant guilty thereon and the punishment of the defendant is fixed by the court at imprisonment in the County Jail for a term of six months, and it is further ordered and adjudged by the court that the defendant be allowed the time he has served in jail prior to his trial on his sentence herein.

It is, therefore, considered, ordered and adjudged by the court that the said defendant, Henry Scott, is guilty of possession of a deadly and dangerous weapon while intoxicated, as charged in the information and as aforesaid; and that he be confined in the county jail of the County of Saline and State of Missouri, at Marshall, Missouri for a period of six months from the 28 day of January, 1935, and it is further ordered and adjudged by the court that the defendant be and he is hereby allowed the time he has been in jail prior to his trial, said time to be applied upon his sentence herein.

It is further ordered and adjudged by the court that the defendant be and he is hereby ordered to be confined in the said jail until he shall be otherwise discharged by the due course of law. It is further considered, ordered and adjudged by the court that the State of Missouri, to the use of Saline County, Missouri, have and recover of the said defendant the costs in this suit expended and that hereof execution issue therefor.

It is further ordered and adjudged by the court that the defendant be and he is required to perform labor upon the public roads of this county under the direction of the County Court of Saline County. It is further ordered and adjuged by the court that the defendant be and he is hereby remanded to the custody of the Sheriff of Saline County, Missouri, to await his commitment, which is this day issued by the Clerk of this Court and delivered to the Sheriff of Saline County, Missouri.

-o-o-o-o-o-o-o-o-o-o-o-o-o-o-o-o-o-o-o-

"In the Circuit Court of Saline County, Missouri, January Term ,1935, 106h day, Monday, January 28, 1935." Saline County, Missouri Circuit Court Record, Volume 27, p. 471, Reel # C12031, Missouri State Archives, Jefferson City, Missouri.

579

In The Circuit Court of Saline County, Missouri.

State of Missouri)
County of Saline) SS

IN THE CIRCUIT COURT OF SALINE COUNTY, MISSOURI.

Now at this day comes the Defendant, Henry Scott, as principal, and John E. Gerhard, as surety, and each acknowledge himself to owe and stand indebted to the State of Missouri, in the penal sum of One Hundred Dollars ($100.00), to be levied of his respective goods, chattels, lands and tenements, but to be void on the condition that the said Defendant, Henry Scott, shall be and personally appear before the Circuit Court of Saline County, Missouri, at its May Term, 1935, thereof, to answer his parole herein, and shall appear on the first day of each and every term of the Circuit Court of Saline County, Missouri, until he is finally discharged ~~in~~ herein his parole and shall not depart the court without due leave or until discharged by the due course of law; otherwise this recognizance shall remain in full force and effect.

Witness my hand and seal this 26th day of April, 1935.

HENRY B. SCOTT, Principal
(SEAL) John E. Gerhard Surety

Appproved this 26th April, 1935.

PERCY M. BROWN
Circuit Clerk of Saline County, Missouri,
in vacation this 26th day of April, 1935.

-o-o-o-o-o-o-o-o-o-o-o-o-o-o-o-o-o-o-o-o-o-o-o-o-o-o-o-o-o-o-o-o-o-o-

"In the Circuit Court of Saline County, Missouri." Bond and parole stipulation, approved 26th of April, 1935, Saline County, Missouri Circuit Court Record, Volume 27, p. 579, Reel # C12031, Missouri State Archives, Jefferson City, Missouri.

LaVerne Purkey forwarded me a copy of a letter dated March 19, 1937, from Will Davis of Nelson, Missouri, (see pages 293–295). At the time, I was unaware that my grandfather, Charles Davis, had a brother named William. I forwarded the letter to Bill Claycomb. Coupled with his findings at the Salt Fork Cemetery two miles south of Nelson, and his visit to Marshall, Missouri, Bill was able to contribute four more names to my growing family: William "Will" Davis; his wife Viola Ann Bowman Davis; and two of their children, Mattie Odell Davis and Joe Marshall Davis. Mattie and Joe Marshall are buried alongside their mother and father. These two children predeceased their parents, Mattie Odell at age 13 and Joe Marshall who was murdered at age 19. William and Viola had at least eleven children.

Bill Claycomb's further research found the funeral notice for Will Davis; an account of the murder of Joe Davis from the August 12, 1932, Daily Democrat – News *(Marshall, Missouri); and an obituary for Viola Davis, naming all her kids. (See "The Claycomb Cemetery Crawl," which starts on page 149.) After receiving the information from Bill Claycomb, I visited the site and took the photo of their tombstone in the Salt Fork Cemetery.*

Liza Gooch Davis Pettis Goodwin
Jesse Pettis (little boy)
Ford Davis (baby)

THIS IS A CERTIFIED COPY OF AN ORIGINAL DOCUMENT.
(Do not accept if rephotographed, or if seal impression cannot be felt.)

THE REPRODUCTION OF THIS DOCUMENT IS PROHIBITED BY LAW (sec. 193.315, RSMo 1986)

STATE OF MISSOURI }
CITY OF JEFFERSON } ss I HEREBY CERTIFY that this is an exact reproduction of the certificate for the person named therein as it now appears in the permanent records of the Bureau of Vital Records of the Missouri Department of Health. Witness my hand as State Registrar of Vital Statistics and the Seal of the Missouri Department of Health this date of

AUG 5 1999

Garland H Land
Garland H. Land
State Registrar of Vital Statistics

DEPARTMENT OF COMMERCE
FILED OCT 18 1941
MISSOURI STATE BOARD OF HEALTH
STANDARD CERTIFICATE OF DEATH
State File No. 32228

Registration District No. 610 Primary Registration District No. 5896 Registrar's No.

1. PLACE OF DEATH: (a) County Pettis Co. (b) City or town Hughesville
(d) Length of stay: In hospital or institution 1

2. USUAL RESIDENCE OF DECEASED: (a) State Mo. (b) County Saline (c) City or town Marshall (d) Street No. South Salt Pond
(e) Citizen of foreign country?

3. (a) FULL NAME William Davis

MEDICAL CERTIFICATION

20. DATE OF DEATH: Month Sept day 22 year 41 hour 6 minute A.M.

21. I hereby certify that I attended the deceased from Sept 22, 1941 to Sept 22, 1941, that I last saw h im alive on Sept 20, 1941 and that death occurred on the date and hour stated above.

4. Sex Male 5. Color or race White 6. (a) Single, widowed, married, divorced Married
6. (b) Name of husband or wife Viola Davis (c) Age of husband or wife if alive 49 years
7. Birth date of deceased January 11 1872
8. AGE: Years 69 Months 8 Days 11

Immediate cause of death: Chronic myocarditis 1 1/2 yrs.

9. Birthplace Pettis Co. Mo.
10. Usual occupation Laborer
12. Name (Father) James Davis 13. Birthplace Unknown Kentucky
14. Maiden name (Mother) Unknown 15. Birthplace Unknown Kentucky

16. (a) Informant Mrs Nellie Bradham
(b) Address Hughesville Mo R.R.
17. (a) Burial (b) Date Sept 23 1941
(c) Place: burial or cremation Salt Fork Cem.—Nelson, Mo.
18. (a) Signature of funeral director A. J. Sweeney
(b) Address Marshall Mo.
19. (a) Sept 22, 1941 (b) Flossie Ferguson

23. Signature [illegible] M.D. Address Marshall Mo. Date signed 9/22/41

(Licensed Embalmer's Statement on Reverse Side)

State of Missouri Division of Health — Standard Certificate of Death. A certified copy, September 22, 2000, of the original document William Davis b. January 11, 1872, d. September 22, 1941.

Davis Funeral To Be Wednesday

Funeral services for Will Davis, South Salt Pond, who died yesterday while visiting at Longwood, will be held at 2 o'clock tomorrow at Salt Fork Church.

Will Davis, The Daily Democrat-News, *Marshall, Missouri, September 23, 1941.*

Rites To Be Sunday For Mrs. Viola Davis

Rev. Warner L. Miles Will Conduct Services at Campbell-Lewis Chapel

Funeral services for Mrs. Viola Ann Davis, 473 South Redman, who passed away Thursday, February 10, at the Fitzgibbon hospital after a three month illness, will be at 2 o'clock Sunday afternoon, February 13, at the Campbell-Lewis chapel. The Rev. Warner L. Miles, pastor of the Assembly of God church, will officiate. Interment will be in Salt Fork cemetery at Nelson. The body will remain at the funeral home through the service.

Mrs. Davis was born September 10, 1892, in Miami, the daughter of Charles and Minnie Bowman. She was married to Will Davis in 1906. She was a member of the Christian church. Mrs. Davis entered the Ellis-Fischel hospital in Columbia December 3, and entered Fitzgibbon hospital January 7. Her daughter, Mrs. Farris A. Shepard and Mr Shepard, have been with her constantly since last Monday.

Surviving are four daughters, Mrs. Farris A. Shepard (Opal), Marshall; Mrs. Buddy Sommeville (Ola) Channelview, Texas; Mrs. Dan Sloan (Nellie) Sedalia; Mrs. Robert Laxson (Betty), Marshall; five sons, Cecil Davis, Kansas City; Paul Davis, Marshall; James, Henry and Kenneth Davis of the state of California; two brothers, James Bowman, St. Louis; Lester Bowman, of the state of California; a sister, Mattie Biles, Lexington; 18 grandchildren. Mrs. Davis was preceded in death by her husband in September, 1941, a daughter and a son.

Above: Announcement of the funeral rites for Viola Davis in The Daily Democrat-News, *Marshall, Missouri, Friday, February 11, 1955.*
Left: The family headstone in Salt Fork Cemetery, Nelson, Missouri.

MISSOURI STATE BOARD OF HEALTH
BUREAU OF VITAL STATISTICS
CERTIFICATE OF DEATH

Do not use this space. 4133

1. PLACE OF DEATH
County Saline — Registration District No. 796 — File No.
Township — Primary Registration District No. 3038 — Registered No. 6
City Marshall, Mo. — No. — St. — Ward)

2. FULL NAME Leoma Davis
(a) Residence. No. — St., — Ward. (Usual place of abode) (If nonresident, give city or town and State)
Length of residence in city or town where death occurred yrs. mos. ds. How long in U.S., if of foreign birth? yrs. mos. ds.

PERSONAL AND STATISTICAL PARTICULARS

3. SEX Female — 4. COLOR OR RACE white — 5. SINGLE, MARRIED, WIDOWED OR DIVORCED (write the word) child
5A. IF MARRIED, WIDOWED, OR DIVORCED HUSBAND OF (OR) WIFE OF unknown
6. DATE OF BIRTH (MONTH, DAY AND YEAR) 1925
7. AGE — YEARS 6 — MONTHS — DAYS — If LESS than 1 day, hrs. or min.
8. OCCUPATION OF DECEASED
(a) Trade, profession, or particular kind of work none child
(b) General nature of industry, business, or establishment in which employed (or employer)
(c) Name of employer
9. BIRTHPLACE (CITY OR TOWN) Blackwater (STATE OR COUNTRY) Mo.
PARENTS
10. NAME OF FATHER Fred Davis
11. BIRTHPLACE OF FATHER (CITY OR TOWN) (STATE OR COUNTRY) Illinois
12. MAIDEN NAME OF MOTHER Anne Snider
13. BIRTHPLACE OF MOTHER (CITY OR TOWN) (STATE OR COUNTRY) Kentucky
14. INFORMANT Tom Goodman (Address)
15. FILED 1-12, 1931 Mr John H. McGuire REGISTRAR

MEDICAL CERTIFICATE OF DEATH

16. DATE OF DEATH (MONTH, DAY AND YEAR) Jan 6 1931
17. I HEREBY CERTIFY, That I attended deceased from Jan 4, 1931, to Jan 6, 1931, that I last saw her alive on Jan 6, 1931, and that death occurred, on the date stated above, at 10 A.m.
THE CAUSE OF DEATH* WAS AS FOLLOWS:
Erysipelas
158 (duration) yrs. mos. 16 ds.
CONTRIBUTORY (SECONDARY) (duration) yrs. mos. ds.
18. WHERE WAS DISEASE CONTRACTED IF NOT AT PLACE OF DEATH?
DID AN OPERATION PRECEDE DEATH? no DATE OF
WAS THERE AN AUTOPSY? no
WHAT TEST CONFIRMED DIAGNOSIS? Clinical
(Signed) Robert Haynes M. D.
1/6, 1931. (Address) Marshall, Mo.
*State the DISEASE CAUSING DEATH, or in deaths from VIOLENT CAUSES, state (1) MEANS AND NATURE OF INJURY, and (2) Whether ACCIDENTAL, SUICIDAL, or HOMICIDAL.
19. PLACE OF BURIAL, CREMATION, OR REMOVAL Marshall Mo — DATE OF BURIAL Jan 7 1931
20. UNDERTAKER J. L. Sweeney — ADDRESS Marshall, Mo.

N. B.—Every item of information should be carefully supplied. AGE should be stated EXACTLY. PHYSICIANS should state CAUSE OF DEATH in plain terms, so that it may be properly classified. Exact statement of OCCUPATION is very important.

Missouri State Board of Health, Bureau of Vital Statistics — Certificate of Death. Leoma Davis b. 1925 — d. January 6, 1931. Her father was listed as Fred Davis and her mother as Anne Snider.

Fred Pettis/Davis was born August 1895 in Vermilion County, Illinois. According to the 1900 federal census, Illinois, Vermilion County, p. 317A, he lived with William Davis and Eliza Gooch Davis. By 1910 he was living in Missouri as Fred Davis with William Davis and his new wife Viola Bowman. In 1930 he lived close to his mother, Eliza Gooch Davis Goodwin, and his stepbrother, Jesse Pettis, in Saline County, Missouri.

We believe that since William Davis did not marry Eliza Gooch until June 1899, Fred was listed as a Pettis in 1900, but that he, Fred Davis, Leoma's father, was apparently William Davis's child because he took the name Davis.

N. B.—Every item of information should be carefully supplied. AGE should be stated EXACTLY. PHYSICIANS should state CAUSE OF DEATH in plain terms, so that it may be properly classified. Exact statement of OCCUPATION is very important.

MISSOURI STATE BOARD OF HEALTH
BUREAU OF VITAL STATISTICS
CERTIFICATE OF DEATH

Do not use this space.

1. PLACE OF DEATH
97 County Saline — Registration District No. 798 — File No. 4271
Township Blackwater — Primary Registration District No. 6042 — Registered No.
City (No. St. Ward)

2. FULL NAME Mattie Odell Davis

(a) Residence, No. St., Ward. (Usual place of abode) (If nonresident, give city or town and State)
Length of residence in city or town where death occurred yrs. mos. ds. How long in U. S., if of foreign birth? yrs. mos. ds.

PERSONAL AND STATISTICAL PARTICULARS

3. SEX Female | 4. COLOR OR RACE White | 5. SINGLE, MARRIED, WIDOWED, OR DIVORCED (write the word) single

5A. IF MARRIED, WIDOWED, OR DIVORCED HUSBAND OF (OR) WIFE OF

6. DATE OF BIRTH (MONTH, DAY, AND YEAR) Sept. 21, 1919

7. AGE — YEARS 13 — MONTHS 3 — DAYS 16 — If LESS than 1 day, hrs. or min.

OCCUPATION
8. Trade, profession, or particular kind of work done, as spinner, sawyer, bookkeeper, etc. School
9. Industry or business in which work was done, as silk mill, saw mill, bank, etc.
10. Date deceased last worked at this occupation (month and year) — 11. Total time (years) spent in this occupation

12. BIRTHPLACE (CITY OR TOWN) (STATE OR COUNTRY) Saline Co. Mo.

FATHER
13. NAME Will Davis
14. BIRTHPLACE (CITY OR TOWN) (STATE OR COUNTRY) Ky

MOTHER
15. MAIDEN NAME Viola Bowman
16. BIRTHPLACE (CITY OR TOWN) (STATE OR COUNTRY) Saline Co. Mo.

17. INFORMANT Mrs. Viola Davis (ADDRESS) Nelson, Mo.

18. BURIAL, CREMATION, OR REMOVAL PLACE [illegible] DATE Jan. 8 1933

19. UNDERTAKER Vandiver Mortuary (ADDRESS) Marshall, Mo.

20. FILED 1/15 1933 Mrs Hall Williams Registrar.

MEDICAL CERTIFICATE OF DEATH

21. DATE OF DEATH (MONTH, DAY, AND YEAR) Jan. 6, 1933

22. I HEREBY CERTIFY, That I attended deceased from , 19 , to , 19
I last saw h alive on , 19 Death is said to have occurred on the date stated above, at 7[45] A m.
The principal cause of death and related causes of importance were as follows: Date of onset

Epilepsy — 1926

35 85

Other contributory causes of importance:
Don't know

Name of operation Date of
What test confirmed diagnosis? Was there an autopsy?

23. If death was due to external causes (violence), fill in also the following:
Accident, suicide, or homicide? Date of injury , 19
Where did injury occur? (Specify city or town, county, and State)
Specify whether injury occurred in industry, in home, or in public place.
Manner of injury
Nature of injury

24. Was disease or injury in any way related to occupation of deceased? no
If so, specify
(Signed) J R Durrett , M. D.
(Address) Nelson Mo

Missouri State Board of Health, Bureau of Vital Statistics — Certificate of Death. Mattie Odell Davis b. September 21, 1920, d. January 6, 1933.

The Certificate of Death says that Mattie was born "Sept. 21 1919," but she was not on the 1920 census with her family. Her mother must have made a mistake about the year she was born. She died of epilepsy, according to her death certificate, and under "Other contributory causes of Importance" it says "Don't know." Will Davis's letter (see page 293) to Rebecca and Charles Davis dated March 19, 1937, indicated that she fell against a heating stove several years before and suffered spinal injury, which led to her epileptic spells.

JAMES DAVIS b. March 4, 1875

The Elusive James Davis

James Davis, the son of James Davis born 1841 and Nannie Gooch Davis, was born March 4, 1875.[1] However, the 1900 census listed his birth date as July 22, 1874.[2] He moved with his family from Madison County, Kentucky, to Randolph County, Missouri, by 1880. After the death of his mother, the family moved to Johnson County, where he was married to Sarah Gertrude Murphy on May 1, 1895.[3]

Though married only ten years, the couple had two children who lived beyond infancy, Earl N. and Maud R., born about 1900 and 1903 respectively. Their mother died in 1905. Eula Davis House says that another child was stillborn.[4]

By 1910 the two children were living with their Murphy grandparents in Warrensburg.[5] They were listed as grandchildren of Columbus and Fannie Murphy. Both children died of tuberculosis and were buried in the Zion Hill Cemetery where their mother and grandfather, James Davis, were buried. Maud R. Davis died August 29, 1923, in Warrensburg. She was twenty years old and single. Earl died at age seventeen on May 12, 1918.[6] In the 1920 census Maud lived with an uncle, Newt Murphy, and was working in a bakery,[7] but her death record showed her "at home."[8]

Tuberculosis was rampant in the late nineteenth and early twentieth century. It was commonly called "consumption." Sarah Murphy Davis died prior to the recording of death records, so we do not know the cause of her death, but she may have had tuberculosis and passed it on to her children. The germ can lie hidden in the body for years before erupting into a full-blown case. After a baby was weaned, some mothers partially chewed food then gave it to the infant, much like a baby bird.[9]

With such a common name as James Davis, it was hard to track him down after 1900. In the 1910 census, Johnson County, Missouri, there was a James Davis married for the second time to a Laura, who had been married three times. They had one child, J. Ernest Davis, who was one year and seven months old.[10] If this is "our" James Davis, he had left his children by Sarah Gertrude Murphy with the Murphy grandparents. We tried to find James and Laura in 1920 and 1930, but had no luck. We also looked through the available Missouri death certificates from 1910 to 1920, but did not find a death record for our James Davis. There is no tombstone for him in the Zion Hill Cemetery.

A.H.

Zion Hill Church, a Methodist church organized in 1889, and its cemetery are located in Lafayette County, Missouri, south of Aullville and five miles northwest of Valley City where James Davis Sr. lived.

In a conversation with me just prior to April 21, 1998, Bernetta Triplett Stump identified the burial place of James Davis Jr., as well as several other family members. I promptly contacted Bill Claycomb, who responded after one of his "cemetery crawls" with the following comments:

> Gertrude's stone is confusing. The tablet indicates S. Gertrude Davis, although "Murphy" is inscribed below. You can see it in the picture. There is an identical stone in front of hers that lists Beulah M. Collier with Murphy below. So I presume Gertrude was a Murphy, and that Earl and Maude and the infant were her children, but am not sure of that. There were other Murphys nearby, possibly her parents. Also some Sanders, but neither Lou nor Luther. There was no sign of James Davis Jr., and, unhappily, no stone for Nancy Davis, if she is there. Note that the dates of birth and death for Gertrude are the same as those given you for James Jr.

Notes

1. Eula Davis House, *Family Tree of My Father, Jefferson C. Davis* (privately printed, 1955), 10.
2. 1900 federal census, Missouri, Johnson Co., Simpson Twp., p. 195B.
3. Johnson Co., Missouri, Marriages L (1888–94):160, Missouri State Archives, Film #C3492.
4. House, *Family Tree of My Father*, 10.
5. 1910 federal census, Missouri, Johnson Co., Warrensburg, p. 210B.
6. Earl Davis, Missouri death certificate, 1918, #17442.
7. 1920 federal census, Missouri, Johnson Co., Warrensburg Twp., Warrensburg (city), E.D. #129, p. 4A.
8. Maud R. Davis, Missouri death certificate, 1923, #24556.

James Davis
Dec. 11, 1841 — Apr. 15, 1902

An Infant

Maude Davis
January 10, 1903 – August 29, 1923

Earl Davis
December 8, 1901 – May 12, 1918

S. Gertrude Davis
March 4, 1881 – April 27, 1905

Zion Hill Methodist Church and Cemetery, organized in 1889, Lafayette County, five miles northwest of Valley City, South of Aulville, Missouri, on State Route "YY" (a mile west of "CC")

9. Personal knowledge of Alice Henson's mother Vergie M. Spalding, who became a registered nurse in 1930, and whose mother, brother, and sister contracted or died from tuberculosis. Vergie Spalding witnessed many relatives, neighbors, and farm women who, after weaning their babies, pre-chewed food before giving it to their babies.
10. 1910 federal census, Missouri, Johnson Co., Grover Twp., p. 57B.

Death of Earl Davis.

Earl Davis, 17 years old, died at the home of his uncle, Newt Murphy, at 7:20 o'clock Sunday night from tuberculosis. He had been confined to his home for more than a year. Prior to making his home with his uncle, he lived with his grandfather in the Valley City neighborhood. When his grandfather and grandmother died, he moved to the Murphy home.

He leaves one sister, Miss Maude Murphy. The funeral services were held at 3 o'clock Monday afternoon at the Zion Hill church, conducted by Rev. West.

Earl Davis, Warrensburg Star-Journal *(Missouri), May 14, 1918*

Death of Miss Maude Davis.

Miss Maude Davis died Wednesday morning at 10 o'clock at the home of her uncle, Newt Murphy. She had been ill since February when she had the Flu which developed into tuberculosis. During the early part of her illness she was at the G. W. O'Neal home on West Gay street but was moved eight weeks ago to the home of her uncle where her death occurred. She was a member of the Baptist Church.

The body was moved to the White parlors to await the burial which will be sometime Friday in Zion Hill Cemetery.

Miss Davis was born January 10, 1903. She is the last of her family. Her parents, Mr. and Mrs. James Davis, and two brothers, who were residents of Valley City, have been dead several years. She resided for a few years in Kansas City with an aunt, Mrs. Ollie Davis. Her only relatives here are three uncles, Newt, Ollie and Albert Murphy.

Maude Davis, Warrensburg Star-Journal *(Missouri), August 30, 1923*

Lula "Lu" Davis Sanders and Thomas Luther Sanders. Imprinted on back of photo are two lot numbers: 13 4251 and 14 4251. It is stamped and labeled: "Photo-No." with a handwritten number, and "belongs to

The Only Daughter

The only daughter born to James Davis and Nannie Gooch Davis was Lula, born in Madison County, Kentucky, April 26, 1877.[1] Shortly thereafter, the family moved to Randolph County, Missouri, where they appear in the 1880 census.[2] Lula was age two. Her mother must have died shortly after the birth of her brother, Ollie, in 1882, when Lula was only four years old. In Lula's 50th Anniversary album, it says that her mother died in Lone Jack, Missouri, in 1879.[3] The date is obviously incorrect, but if Nannie Gooch Davis was buried in the Lone Jack Cemetery, she does not have a tombstone, as she was not listed in any available cemetery inventory.

Photograph of Lula "Lu" Davis Sanders courtesy of Jack Shelby Sanders (received by C. Davis July 23, 2001).

Lula was married to Thomas Luther Sanders at Warrensburg in Johnson County, Missouri, March 17, 1897.[4] Her 50th Anniversary album says that Joseph and Alice Davis were witnesses. The Sanders family lived near Aullville in Lafayette County in 1900.[5] Their first son Shelby Otis was born in February of 1899. By 1910 two more children joined the family: James Arnold in 1903 and Mary M. in 1908.[6] The family lived on this farm for many years. They attended the Baptist church at Aullville, Missouri.[7] Jack Shelby Sanders, the only grandson of Lula and Luther Sanders, remembers visiting the family farm in Lafayette County during his childhood. Being the only grandchild on either side of the family, Jack spent periods of time with the Sanderses. He recalls life on the three hundred-acre farm near Higginsville, Missouri, in Lafayette County. Lula was a good grandmother, kind, and a wonderful cook, providing a table filled with fried chicken and an abundance of garden produce. She had a temper, though, and did not hesitate to speak up when bothered. Luther was an old-fashioned farmer, refusing to enter the mechanical age — he always farmed with teams of horses. He had a good sense of humor and gave Jack small chores to do around the farm.[8]

Luther Sanders, born in October of 1869, was a Confederate sympathizer and named his first son for Colonel Joe Shelby, a famous Missouri Confederate.[9] After their farming years were over, Luther and Lula moved to Nevada, Missouri, where their daughter Mary lived. On March 16, 1947, Lula and Luther Sanders celebrated their 50th wedding anniversary in Nevada, Missouri. Many Davis relatives from Johnson County attended and signed the guest book, including Ethel Triplett, Margie Turner, Jimmie Turner, Eula Davis House, Rosa Davis, Glenn Davis, Bernetta Fae Stump, Carol Sue Stump, Earlene Davis, Everett Davis, George Wm. Stump, and Mrs. Rosamond Sanders with her son Jack.[10] Luther died September 27, 1951, and Lula died September 13, 1952, in Nevada. The *Nevada Herald* of September 13, 1952, page 6, column 8, gives this obituary for Mrs. T.L. Sanders:

Mrs. T.L. Sanders died early this morning.

Mrs. T.L. (Lula) Sanders 75 died early this morning at the home of her daughter, Mrs. Ludwell Meinecke, 2200 West Austin. She was born April 26, 1877 in Kentucky. Her husband T.L. Sanders died September 27, 1951. She was a member of the Christian Church.

Survivors are her daughter Mrs. Meinecke, with whom she made her home; and two sons, S.O. Sanders and J.A. Sanders of St. Louis. One grandson, Jack Sanders is a student at the University of Missouri. Two brothers also survive: O.L. Davis of Kansas City and Charles Davis of Lafayette, Ind.

Funeral services will be held Monday afternoon at 2:30 o'clock at the Hays Service Rooms under the direction of Rev. Pliney C. Elliott. Burial will be at Newton Cemetery.

Lula and Thomas Luther Sanders had three children:

1. Shelby Otis Sanders born February 16, 1899, married September 4, 1920, to Rosamond Rahm. He died October 26, 1976, in Jackson County, Missouri.[11] Shelby Otis Sanders worked as a supervisor for REA and as a manager for Southwestern Bell Telephone. He also became an attorney after attending night school at Benton College in St. Louis. They had one son, Jack Shelby Sanders, born January 3, 1929, at St. Louis (see his profile on page 313).
2. James Arnold Sanders born October 3, 1903, married Winifred Travernicht September 30, 1933. He was a trouble supervisor for Bell Telephone, and died May 6, 1982.[12] They had no children.

Photos courtesy of Jack Shelby Sanders

3. Mary Mae Sanders was born May 26, 1908, and was married August 3, 1935 to Ludwell Meinecke.[13] She was a credit manager and died September 28, 1995, in Nevada, Missouri.[14] They had no children.

Jack Shelby Sanders was born January 3, 1929, in St. Louis, Missouri, only child of Shelby Otis Sanders and Rosamond Rahm Sanders. His mother had come from a musical family in Lafayette County, Missouri, some of whom had been on the Chatauqua circuit. Her health was delicate, however, and she died in September of 1947 of tuberculosis. His father married again, when Jack was in college, to Glenna Auffenberg.[15]

Jack Sanders attended Washington University in St. Louis where he received an A.B. degree, then received his B.S. at the University of Missouri. He went to Harvard Medical School and received his M.D. degree in 1955. He completed residencies in Internal Medicine and Cardiology, served in the Air Force, then opened a medical practice in Jefferson City in 1961. He practiced there until 2001, when he retired. However, he remains the chief administrator for his medical group, Capital City Medical Associates, which he founded. In retirement, he is also the director of cardiac rehabilitation at Capital Region Medical Center. He has been very active in the medical community locally, but also served as president of the Missouri Heart Association and as one of the vice presidents of the American Heart Association.[16]

He was married July 14, 1952, to Patricia Smashey, who was born in St. Louis April 27, 1931, and they have three children: Linda Ellen Sanders, born April 5, 1955; Jeffrey Stewart Sanders, born June 6, 1957; and Laura Sanders, born March 29, 1960. Linda Ellen Sanders married Shawn Gary, had three children, and they live in Grand Rapids, Michigan. Jeffrey Sanders, M.D., followed in his father's footsteps and became a cardiologist who practices in the same group his father founded. He married Linda Thomure, and had two children before they divorced. Laura Sanders married Roger Arndt, and they live in Franktown, Colorado, with their two sons.[17]

On December 30, 1978, Jack was married to Jimmy Kay Trenkle, who was born December 17, 1948, in Jefferson City, Missouri.[18] Dr. Jack and Jimmy Kay Sanders make their home in Jefferson City. Dr. Jack Sanders is the only descendant of Lula Davis Sanders, who was the only daughter of James Davis and Nancy Gooch Davis. With seven grandchildren, however, Dr. Jack Sanders will leave several descendants who have inherited the Davis, Gooch, and Sanders heritage. *A.H.*

Notes

1. Lula Sanders, Missouri death certificate, 1952, #34012.
2 1880 federal census, Missouri, Randolph Co., p. 172.
3. Lula and Luther Sanders, 50th Anniversary Wedding Album, in possession of Jack S. Sanders, M.D., of Jefferson City, Missouri.
4. Johnson Co., Missouri, Marriage Records M:398.
5. 1900 federal census, Missouri, Lafayette Co., Freedom Township, E.D. 154, p. 3.
6. 1910 federal census, Missouri, Lafayette Co., Freedom Township, p. 180B.
7. Lula and Luther Sanders, 50th Anniversary Wedding Album, in possession of Jack S. Sanders, M.D. of Jefferson City, Missouri.
8. Alice Henson interview with Jack S. Sanders, M.D., July 2000.
9. Ibid.
10. Lula and Luther Sanders, 50th Anniversary Wedding Album, in possession of Jack S. Sanders, M.D. of Jefferson City, Missouri.

(continued on page 308)

this is me taken
at home Love
aunt Lou Sanders
She's dead
now
Dad only sister
(Charles Davis' sister)

Photograph of Elizabeth Davis Purkey taken at the home of Lula "Lu Lu" Davis Sanders, her aunt and only sister of Elizabeth's father, Charles Davis.

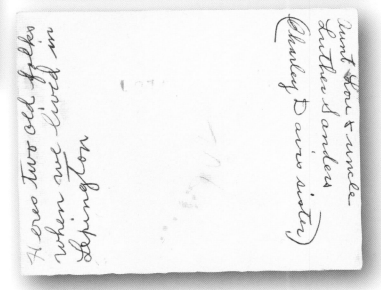

Aunt Lou & uncle
Luther Sanders
(Charley Davis sister)
Heres two old folks
when we lived in
Lexington

The automobile shown with Luther and Lula "Lu Lu" Sanders above is probably a 1929 or 1930 Packard roadster coupe. The grille insignia, St. Louis, may indicate where the car was built

A “L

Note in above photo Lulu Davis Sanders is wearing the same dress as depicted in two group family photos on page 287

Picture is probably miscaptioned on the back. Alice Henson suggests that the couple in the picture are Emeline and Andrew Jackson Sanders, the parents of Thomas Luther Sanders and Lula “Lu” Davis Sanders's in-laws.

12. Ibid.

Notes (*continued*)

11. Ibid.
12. Ibid.
13. Ibid.
14. Social Security Death Index, <http://www.rootsweb.com>.
15. Alice Henson interview with Jack S. Sanders, M.D., July 2000.
16. Ibid.
17. Alice Henson interview with Patricia Smashey Sanders, April 2002; Alice Henson interview with Linda Thomure Sanders, June 2000.
18. Alice Henson interview with Jimmy Kay Trenkle Sanders,

Wed 50 Years

Mr. and Mrs. T. L. Sanders of 2200 West Austin street are shown cutting the wedding cake at a celebration held at their home Sunday, commemorating their fiftieth wedding anniversary. An open house was held in the afternoon during which time many friends dropped in to wish the couple many more years of happiness together.

Celebrate 50 Years Together

Mr. and Mrs. T. L. Sanders, 2200 West Austin street, celebrated their fiftieth wedding anniversary Sunday in their home.

The couple was married in Warrensburg on March 17, 1897. They have been residents of Nevada since 1937. Mr. Sanders is a retired farmer. The Sanders have three children, a daughter, Mrs. Mary Meinecke of Nevada, and two sons, S. O. Sanders of Joplin and J. A. Sanders of St. Louis. J. A. Sanders was unable to be here for the celebration, but called his parents during the day to send his best wishes.

At the noon hour dinner was served to about 20 members of the family.

An open house, honoring the occasion, was enjoyed from 2:30 p. m. to 4:30 p. m. at which time about 60 friends and relatives called to wish the couple happiness. The entire house was decorated with bouquets of gold and yellow spring flowers, presented to them by their many friends.

The lace covered serving table was centered with a large three-tiered white and gold decorated wedding cake topped with a miniature bride and groom. During the receiving hours punch and cake were served to the guests. Those who assisted in serving were Mrs. Clarence Oberlin, Mrs. Betty Brown, Miss Jessie Bullock, Mrs. Jane Adams and Mrs. Meinecke.

Out-of-town guests included Mrs. Rosa Davis, Mr. and Mrs. Everett Davis, Glen Davis and his son, Mrs. Earl Turner and her son, Jimmy, Mr. and Mrs. Stump and their daughter, Carol Sue, Mrs. Bessie Honey, Mrs. Fred House and Mrs. Doc Triplett, all of Warrensburg. Other guests were Mrs. Rosmond Sanders of Higginsville, Mrs. Eva Blanche Vassar of Kansas City and S. O. Sanders of Joplin.

50th Wedding Anniversary Celebration March 16, 1947

"An invitation to a Golden Wedding Open House is extended to all of the Church Family today.

Mr. and Mrs. T.L. Sanders, parents of Mrs. Ludwell Meinecke, have reached the fifty-year milestone, a very distinctive accomplishment. All members of the Church will be welcomed at the home, 2200 West Austin, between the hours of 2:30 and 4:30 this afternoon."

Announcement: The First Baptist Church, Main and Hunder Streets, Nevada, Missouri, E. Paul Fisher, Pastor, Sunday, March 16, 1947

Luther Sanders and Lula Davis Sanders 50th Wedding Anniversary
March 17, 1897 — March 17, 1947, Nevada, Missouri

Reproduced below are several pages from a register and compendium celebrating the couple's 50th Wedding Anniversary. The register was presented to them by Marsh and Gertrude Eichinger.

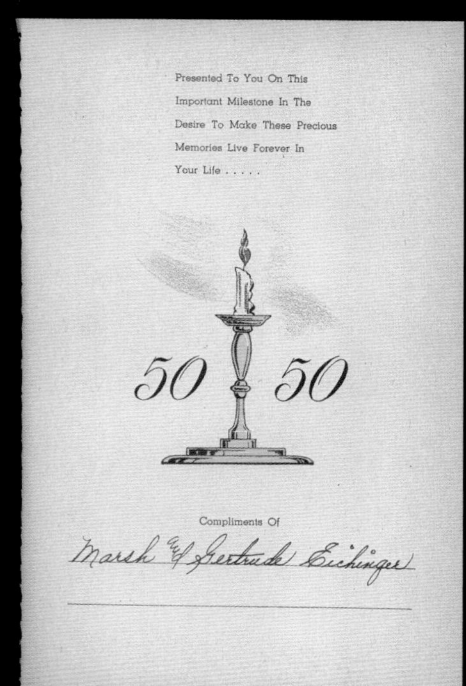

Presented To You On This
Important Milestone In The
Desire To Make These Precious
Memories Live Forever In
Your Life . . . . .

50 50

Compliments Of

Marsh & Gertrude Eichinger

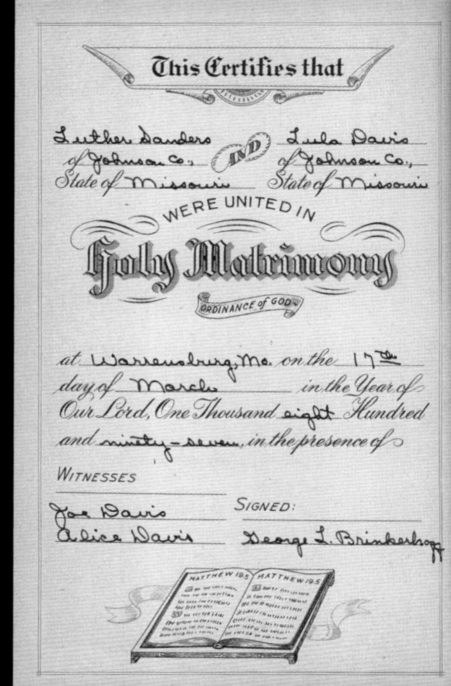

This Certifies that

Luther Sanders AND Lula Davis
of Johnson Co., of Johnson Co.,
State of Missouri State of Missouri

WERE UNITED IN

Holy Matrimony

ORDINANCE of GOD

at Warrensburg, Mo. on the 17th
day of March in the Year of
Our Lord, One Thousand eight Hundred
and ninety-seven, in the presence of

WITNESSES SIGNED:

Joe Davis
Alice Davis George L. Brinkerhoff

MATTHEW 19:5 MATTHEW 19:5

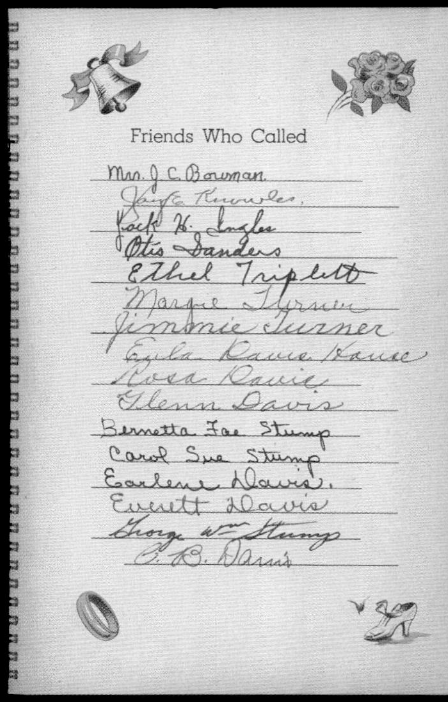

Friends Who Called

Mrs. J. C. Bowman
Jay C. Knowles
Jack H. Ingles
Otis Sanders
Ethel Triplett
Margie Turner
Jimmie Turner
Eula Davis Hause
Rosa Davis
Glenn Davis
Bernetta Fae Stump
Carol Sue Stump
Earlene Davis
Everett Davis
George Wm Stump
C. B. Davis

Friends Who Called

Velma Oberlin
Clarence Oberlin
Joe Brockman
Bessie Honey
J. R. Davis
Mrs J. R. Davis
E. Paul Fisher
Betty Brown
Mrs J. D. Higgins
Jessie Bullock
John Higgins
Mrs. Omer Lee Horton
Omer Lee Horton
Mr. J. H. Scott
Mrs. J. H. Scott
Claude Orval Kiger

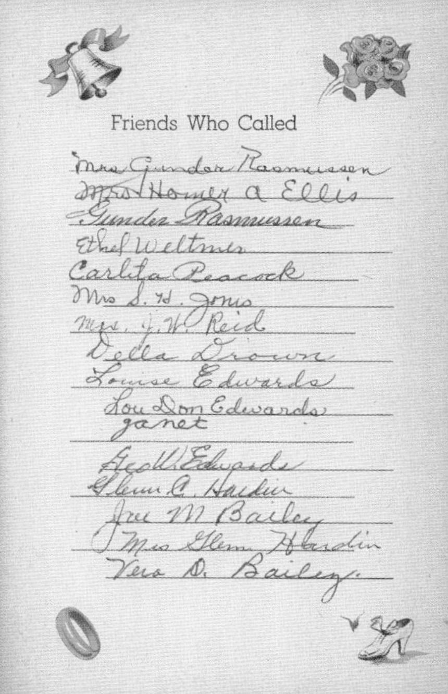

Friends Who Called

Mrs Gunder Rasmussen
Mrs Homer A. Ellis
Gunder Rasmussen
Ethel Weltmer
Carlita Peacock
Mrs S. H. Jones
Mrs. J. W. Reid
Della Brown
Louise Edwards
Lou Don Edwards
Janet
Scott Edwards
Glenn A. Hardin
Joe M Bailey
Mrs Glenn Hardin
Vera D. Bailey

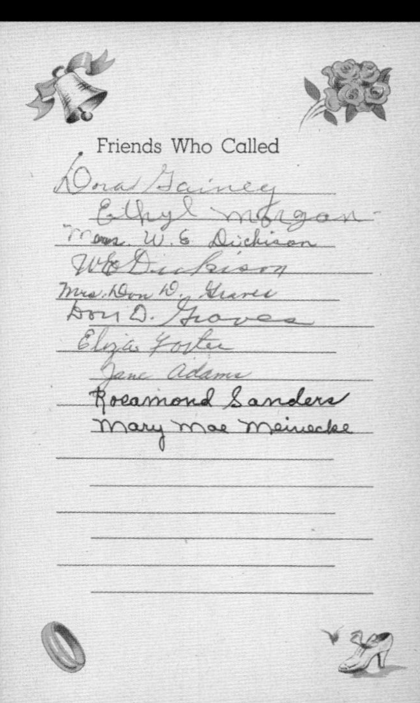

Friends Who Called

Dora Gainey
Ethyl Morgan
Mrs. W. E. Dickison
W. E. Dickison
Mrs. Don D. Graves
Don D. Graves
Eliza Foster
Jane Adams
Rosamond Sanders
Mary Mae Meinecke

Bouquets

Secret Sister, Dorcas S.S. Class,

First Baptist Church, Nevada, Mo.

Mr. + Mrs. Ludwell Meinecke,

2200 W. Austin, Nevada, Mo.

For Your Golden Wedding

Family History

Names	Religion	Converted; Confirmed		Baptized	
		When	Where	When	By Whom
Shelby Otis	Baptist		Aullville, Mo.		
James Arnold	Baptist		Aullville, Mo.		
Mary Mae	Baptist		Aullville, Mo.	1920	Rev. Payne
Thomas Luther	Baptist		Aullville, Mo		
Lula Davis	Baptist		Aullville, Mo.		

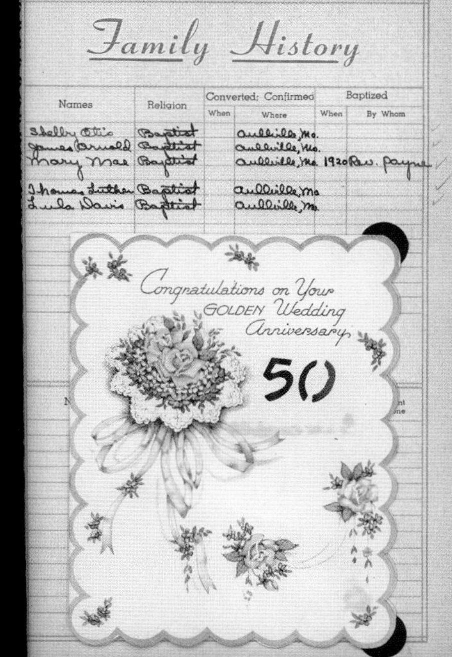
Congratulations on Your
GOLDEN Wedding
Anniversary
50

Family History

Great Grand Parents

FATHER'S GRAND PARENTS

Names	Born		Died	
	When	Where	When	Where
Grand Father's Father				
Grand Father's Mother				
Grand Mother's Father				
Grand Mother's Mother				

Mother's Grand Parents

Names	Born		Died	
	When	Where	When	Where
Grand Father's Father				
Grand Father's Mother				
Grand Mother's Father				
Grand Mother's Mother				

Grand Parents

Names	Born		Died	
	When	Where	When	Where
Father's Father: Mr. K. Sanders		Ireland	1882	N.C.
Father's Mother: Mrs. K. (Rachel) Sanders		Ireland	1883	N.C.
Mother's Father				
Mother's Mother				

3

Parents

Names	Born		Died	
	When	Where	When	Where
Mr. A. J. Sanders		Winston Salem, N.C.	1921	Concordia, Mo.
Mrs. A. J. Sanders			1915	
Mr. James Davis		Ky.	1902	Valley City, Mo.
Mrs. James Davis		Ky.	1879	Lone Jack, Mo.

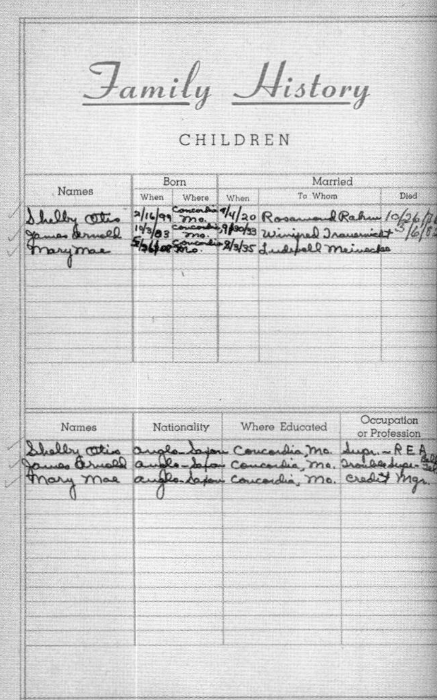

Family History

CHILDREN

Names	Born		Married		Died
	When	Where	When	To Whom	
Shelby Otis	2/16/99	Concordia Mo.	9/4/20	Rosamond Rahm	10/26/76
James Arnold	10/3/03	Concordia Mo.	9/30/33	Winifred Trauernicht	5/6/82
Mary Mae	5/26/08	Concordia Mo.	8/3/35	Ludwell Meinecke	

Names	Nationality	Where Educated	Occupation or Profession
Shelby Otis	Anglo-Saxon	Concordia, Mo.	Supr.–REA
James Arnold	Anglo-Saxon	Concordia, Mo.	Trouble Supr.–Bell Tel.
Mary Mae	Anglo-Saxon	Concordia, Mo.	Credit Mgr.

Cards

Davis Family,

Warrensburg, Mo.

Mr. + Mrs. J. A. Sanders

4963 Winona, St. Louis, 9, Mo.

Mr. + Mrs. J. R. Davis

322 W. Austin, Nevada, Mo.

Mrs. Olive Trauernicht,

4963 Winona, St. Louis 9, Mo.

S. O. Sanders

224 N. Moffitt, Joplin, Mo

Mrs. Homer A. Ellis + Employees,

Nevada, Mo.

George
Louise
and
Jill

ANNIVERSARY Greetings

Cards

Rev. + Mrs. E. Paul Fisher + Family,

525 W. Austin, Nevada, Mo.

Mrs. Rosamond Sanders + Jack

2200 W. Austin, Nevada, Mo.

Jane Adams,

1303 N. Main, Nevada, Mo.

Mr. + Mrs. Bill Carr + Bob,

422 N. Washington, Nevada, Mo.

Mr. + Mrs. Clarence Oberlin,

329 N. Clay, Nevada, Mo.

Mrs. Preston Bullock + Jessie,

512 E. Hickory, Nevada, Mo.

Mr. + Mrs. J. C. Bowman,

R#1, Nevada, Mo.

Eddie Scholer,

820 Douglas St., Fayetteville, Ark.

STATE OF MISSOURI } ss
CITY OF JEFFERSON }

I HEREBY CERTIFY that this is an exact reproduction of the certificate for the person named therein as it now appears in the permanent records of the Bureau of Vital Statistics of the Missouri Department of Health. Witness my hand as State Registrar of Vital Statistics and the Seal of the Missouri Department of Health this date of

JUL 17 2000

Garland H. Land
Garland H. Land
State Registrar of Vital Statistics

THE DIVISION OF HEALTH OF MISSOURI
STANDARD CERTIFICATE OF DEATH

34012

FILED SEP 30 1952

1. PLACE OF DEATH a. COUNTY Vernon — b. CITY OR TOWN Nevada — c. FULL NAME OF HOSPITAL OR INSTITUTION At home

2. USUAL RESIDENCE a. STATE Missouri — b. COUNTY Vernon — c. CITY OR TOWN Nevada — d. STREET ADDRESS West Austin Street

3. NAME OF DECEASED Lula Sanders — 4. DATE OF DEATH Sept. 13 1952

5. SEX Female — 6. COLOR OR RACE White — 7. MARRIED, NEVER MARRIED, WIDOWED, DIVORCED Widowed — 8. DATE OF BIRTH 4-26-1877 — 9. AGE 75

10a. USUAL OCCUPATION Homemaker — 11. BIRTHPLACE Kentucky — 12. CITIZEN OF WHAT COUNTRY? U.S.A.

13. FATHER'S NAME James Davis — 14. MOTHER'S MAIDEN NAME Anna Hooch — 15. WIFE'S OR HUSBAND'S NAME T. L. Sanders

16. WAS DECEASED EVER IN U.S. ARMED FORCES? — 17. SOCIAL SECURITY NO. None — 18. INFORMANT'S SIGNATURE OR NAME Mrs. Ludwell Meinecke — ADDRESS Nevada, Mo.

MEDICAL CERTIFICATION

19. CAUSE OF DEATH — I. DISEASE OR CONDITION DIRECTLY LEADING TO DEATH (a) Coronary thrombosis & myocardial infarction — ANTECEDENT CAUSES Arteriosclerosis — INTERVAL BETWEEN ONSET AND DEATH 3 days

II. OTHER SIGNIFICANT CONDITIONS Diabetes mellitus

22. I hereby certify that I attended the deceased from 3-10 1950 to 9-13 1952, that I last saw the deceased alive on 9-12 1952 and that death occurred at the hour stated above.

23a. SIGNATURE Braxton Davis, M.D. — 23b. ADDRESS Nevada, Mo. — 23c. DATE SIGNED 9-16-52

24a. BURIAL, CREMATION, REMOVAL Burial — 24b. DATE 9-15-52 — 24c. NAME OF CEMETERY OR CREMATORY Newton Burial Park — 24d. LOCATION Nevada, Mo.

DATE REC'D BY LOCAL REG. 9-27-52 — REGISTRAR'S SIGNATURE — FUNERAL DIRECTOR Albert V. Hays, Nevada, Mo.

(Licensed Embalmer's Statement on Reverse Side)

State of Missouri Division of Health — Standard Certificate of Death. A certified copy, July 17, 2000, of the original document. Lula Sanders b. April 26, 1877, d. September 13, 1952.

SATURDAY, SEPT. 13, 1952

Mrs. T. L. Sanders died early this morning

Mrs. T. L. (Lula) Sanders, 75, died early this morning at the home of her daughter, Mrs. Ludwell Meinecke, 2200 West Austin.

She was born April 26, 1877, in Kentucky. Her husband, T. L. Sanders, died Sept. 27, 1951. She was a member of the Christian Church.

Survivors are her daughter, Mrs. Meinecke, with whom she made her home; and two sons, S. O. Sanders and J. A. Sanders of St. Louis. One grandson, Jack Sanders, is a student at the University of Missouri. Two brothers also survive: O. L. Davis of Kansas City and Charles Davis of Lafayette, Ind.

Funeral services will be held Monday afternoon at 2:30 o'clock at the Hays Service Rooms under the direction of the Rev. Pliney H. Elliott. Burial will be at Newton cemetery.

Lula Sanders, death notice
Nevada Daily Mail *(Missouri)*, *September 13, 1952*

Hold funeral rites for Mrs. T. L. Saunders

(Monday, Sept. 15)

Funeral services for Mrs. T. L. (Lula) Sanders, who died Saturday morning at the home of her daughter, Mrs. Ludwell Meinecke, 2200 West Austin, were held at a local funeral home this afternoon with the Rev. Pliney H. Elliott officiating.

The soloist, Mrs. Harry McCarter, sang "The Old Rugged Cross" and "In the Garden". She was accompanied by Mrs. Chester Whitehead.

Pallbearers were: Dr. B. L. Rhea, John H. Scott, N. P. Limbaugh, Clarence Oberlin, Francis Woodfill and Sim Scrutchfield.

Interment was in Newton cemetery.

Lula Sanders, funeral notice
Nevada Daily Mail *(Missouri)*, *September 15, 1952*

DID YOU KNOW?

Jack Sanders:

Doctor, Student, Mountain Climber

By Vicki K. Brown
Portrait by Jennifer Kettler

Over the years, support of the health-care profession, a love of community and an insatiable curiosity have fueled the accomplishments of longtime Jefferson City cardiologist Jack Sanders. The doctor's drive and dedication have led to local gains such as the establishment of a YMCA in Jefferson City in the early 1970s, but Sanders's passions often have led him on challenges around the world as well.

The Harvard Medical School graduate moved to Jefferson City in 1961 to work for Internal Medicine Consultants, now Capital City Medical Associates. He jumped right into the community, joining the Rotary Club.

As his children reached their teens, Sanders recalled the "wonderful YMCA" he had frequented while growing up in Joplin. "I

JACK SANDERS, AT A GLANCE

PROFESSION: Cardiologist. Currently serves as chairman of Capital Region Medical Center's foundation.

JEFFERSON CITY LEGACY: First YMCA board president. Integral in founding the organization's local chapter.

HOBBIES & INTERESTS: Mountain climbing, hiking, gemology, foreign languages, culinary arts.

Jimmy Kay and Jack Sanders walking the "Haute Route" (high route) between Chamonix, France and Zermatt, Switzerland in 1990.

LEFT: Sanders takes Sir Edmund Hillary's blood pressure in 1986, during a trek in northern Nepal.

BELOW: The Sanderses on their most recent trip, walking the Pilgrim Trail to Santiago Decompostella in Spain.

had the idea in the late 1960s that we needed a place in town where kids could go," he explains.

In 1969, he teamed up with fellow doctor Kenneth Siu and lawyer Wade Baker, executive director of the Missouri Bar Association, and held a town meeting. "The people who asked questions or made comments—I put them in charge of committees," Sanders laughs.

Chartered in 1970 with Sanders as board president, the YMCA opened in a storefront on High Street. The offices were moved a couple of times, and programs were operated out of schools and other venues until the Y's first facility was built in 1974.

"The key thing to founding something like this is finding key people," he notes. Sanders remained active until resigning from the board in 2004.

The Outdoorsman

Sanders's Colorado vacations led to mountaineering and to expertise in altitude's effect on the human heart. With a study grant, a student to draw blood samples and an early heart monitor, he climbed Long's Peak. His study drew responses from around the world.

Throughout the 1960s and 1970s, Sanders climbed in the Teton Range, the Alps and the Peruvian Andes, offering free medical clinics during each trip. He made his last technical climb on the northwest frontier of Pakistan in 1978.

In December that year, he and his wife, Jimmy Kay, married. He gave up climbing for hiking—something the pair could enjoy together. The two have hiked in New Zealand and in the Alps. In 1986, they hiked in Nepal with Sir Edmund Hillary, one of the first climbers to reach the summit of Mount Everest.

The Sanderses made a 15-day hike across England several years ago. Their most recent trip took them to northern Spain to walk the Camino Santiago de Compostela, a pilgrimage route from France to the northwest Spanish coast.

"I had read about it, and I wanted to explore its history," Sanders explains. "We enjoy the outdoors, and it was a bit of a challenge."

The Eternal Student

That strong interest in history even led Sanders to write *High School on the Home Front*, a book about how World War II affected him as a high schooler.

Sanders loves to travel in France, so much so that he learned French. "I used to be fairly proficient in the language, even reading books in French," he says.

He tends to pursue whatever interests him. Attracted to gemology, he took several courses, even traveling to New York City to study. His eclectic music interests sent the 78-year-old to an Elton John concert last fall.

Though his health has slowed him down somewhat, Sanders says he plans to visit more of the United States and Canada. He remains chairman of the Capital Region Medical Center Foundation and still lectures on heart disease.

He also plans to continue following new interests—the culinary arts are high on his list. "I think there will always be something that I will want to learn," he says. "I'm just interested in what life has to offer." ■

The above article by Vicki K. Brown, which was received from Alice Henson on March 27, 2008, appeared in the Jefferson City Magazine *for January/February 2008, published by the Columbia Business Times Company, Columbia, Missouri. Jack Shelby Sanders, b. January 3, 1929, was the son of Shelby Otis Sanders and Rosamond Rahm. Jack's father, Shelby, was the son of Lula "Lu" Davis, my grandfather Charles's sister, and Thomas Luther Sanders. Coincidentally, Dr. Sanders lives with his wife, Jimmy Kay, in Jefferson City, Missouri, where my longtime genealogical consultant and advisor, Alice Henson, lives, hence the local updates regarding the Sanders, from time to time.*

OLLIE DAVIS b. January 27, 1882

Photo courtesy of **Eugene L. Davis**

Ollie L. and Mabel M. Davis — Kansas City, Missouri

Uncle Ollie
Ollie Davis youngest
brother of Jefferson C.
Davis
(wife Myrtle)

Photo courtesy of **LaVerne Purkey**

The Youngest Child

Ollie L. Davis, the youngest child of James Davis and Nannie Gooch Davis, was born in 1882. Eula Davis House said that he was born in Grundy County, Missouri. We have not been able to prove or disprove this fact. In the 1880 census, the family was in Randolph County, Missouri, and they were possibly still there when John Morgan Davis married Mattie Toombs in 1887. Ollie's death certificate says that he was born in Pettis County, Missouri. The informant was Mrs. Mabel M. Davis, his second wife. He was a retired butcher, and his parents were James Davis and Nancy Gooch.[1]

Ollie's mother died some time after his birth, because his father James married again in 1890. By then the family had moved to the Saline/Pettis County area, and later would go to the Valley City, Johnson County, Missouri, area. According to House's family history, Ollie first married Myrtle Cox. They were the parents of Mable, Loren, LaVonne, Ethel Earlene, and Mildred. Their married names were Mable Pulley, LaVonne Bennett, Ethel Earlene Scott and Mildred Webster. Loren is deceased.[2]

On his World War I Draft Registration Ollie, was in Knob Noster, Johnson County, Missouri. He stated that he was born January 27, 1882, that he was a merchant and farmer, self-employed, and that his nearest relative was Myrtle Davis.[3]

We did not find the family in 1910, but in the 1920 census, they were living in Johnson County. Ollie was listed as a farmer. Myrtle was thirty-six, Mabel sixteen, Loren twelve, Lavon nine, Ethel five, and Mildred two-and-a-half.[4] By 1930 Ollie and Myrtle divorced. I found her as "Eileen" on the census with Mabel, twenty-six, a bookkeeper; Loren, twenty-three, a truck driver; and Ethel, seventeen, a clerk in a grocery. Myrtle Eileen was not working. All were lodgers with Percival and Edith Delton.[5]

According to Eula Davis House, Ollie L. Davis and Myrtle Cox Davis divorced, and he married Mabel Garner (Mabel's maiden name was provided by her son, Eugene L. Davis).[6] When Ollie died, they lived at 5309 The Paseo in Kansas City, Missouri.[7] He and Mabel had one son, Eugene Davis. Eugene was interviewed by Clyde Davis on one of his early roots trips to Missouri.

The baby of the family, Ollie Lester Davis, was probably raised by his older brothers and sisters after the death of his mother. He stayed near the family in Johnson County before going to the big city, Kansas City, after 1920. He was the last born of the children of James and Nannie Davis and the last to die on September 25, 1963, in Kansas City, Missouri. He was buried in Floral Hills Cemetery.

A.H.

Notes

1. Ollie Lester Davis, Missouri death certificate, 1963, #63-036078.
2. Eula Davis House, *Family Tree of My Father, Jefferson C. Davis* (privately printed, 1955), 11.
3. World War I Draft Registration, Johnson Co., Missouri, FHL #1683327.
4. 1920 federal census, Missouri, Johnson Co., Warrensburg Twp., E.D. 129, p. 15B.
5. 1930 federal census, Missouri, Jackson Co., Kansas City, Ward 6, E.D. 48-94, p. 6B.
6. House, *Family Tree of My Father*, 11.
7. Ollie Lester Davis, Missouri death certificate, 1963, #63-036078.

Belton Mo
Oct 18th 1957

Dear Lizzie and Hugh
I got your letter was so glad to hear from you But was sorry to hear about your mother Oh there has Been So Much happened in Our family in such a short time it makes any one hart sick did Carl Write you about his mother dying yes she died just a few days Before We heard that your mother Was dead She was Berried at longwood Beside Your uncle Joe Davis We never new She was Sick till Carl Phoned and Said She was dead Carl Said She Lost her mind She never new any Body Poor Old Jack. its hard to say But she is

Eugene L. Davis and mother Mabel M. Davis (Ollie L. Davis's son)

2
Better off She never had any home are any thing her and Ethel never got a long and as long She could walk She dun all the work [illegible] after al[illegible] [illegible] for the Davises and more heart akes Well it makes me feel so sad to think I am the Only One left I havent got a Brother Or a Sister Or a sister-in-law its just hard to Believe That it all happend in Such Short time Well I was sorry to hear that You was feeling so Weak and Bad You had Better Take it Easy

[illegible] at You[illegible] Eugene is going to School Learning TV Sure Keeps him Busy Mabel is Still Working her Work Been Very Bad Well I guess I had Better Ring Off for now hoping this Will find all of You folks OK hoping to hear from You Soon

Love and Best Wishes to all

PS I Will Send the money for the flowers

Thanks for Ever thing

From Your Uncle
Ollie and family

Letter from Ollie Davis to his niece Elizabeth "Lizzie" (daughter of Charles and Rebecca Davis) and her husband, Hugh Purkey, dated October 18, 1957, from Belton, Missouri

OLLIE L. DAVIS

Ollie L. Davis, 81, of 5309 the Paseo, died yesterday at St. Mary's hospital. He was born in Grundy County, Missouri, and lived here 40 years. Surviving are his wife, Mrs. Mabel M. Davis of the home; two sons, Eugene L. Davis of the home, and Loren Davis, Upland, Calif.; four daughters, Mrs. Mabel Pulley, 414 West Thirty-third; Mrs. Ethel Scott, Lake Tapawingo; Mrs. Lavon Bennett and Mrs. Mildred Webster, both of Los Angeles; a stepdaughter, Mrs. Virgil Stillwagon, 11516 Sunnyside, Hickman Mills, and six grandchildren. Services will be held at 3 o'clock Saturday at the Newcomer chapel, Brush Creek and the Paseo; burial in Floral Hills cemetery.

Ollie L. Davis d. September 25, 1963

THIS IS A CERTIFIED COPY OF AN ORIGINAL DOCUMENT.
(Do not accept if rephotographed, or if seal impression cannot be felt.)

THE REPRODUCTION OF THIS DOCUMENT IS PROHIBITED BY LAW (sec 193.245, 193.255, and 193.315 RSMo 1994)

STATE OF MISSOURI } ss
CITY OF JEFFERSON }

I HEREBY CERTIFY that this is an exact reproduction of the certificate for the person named therein as it now appears in the permanent records of the Bureau of Vital Statistics of the Missouri Department of Health. Witness my hand as State Registrar of Vital Statistics and the Seal of the Missouri Department of Health this date of

SEP 22 2000

Garland H Land
Garland H. Land
State Registrar of Vital Statistics

DIVISION OF HEALTH – STANDARD CERTIFICATE OF DEATH

63-036078 STATE FILE NUMBER

Registration District No. 149 Primary Registration District No. 1002 Registrar's No. 5233

FILED OCT 9 1963

1. PLACE OF DEATH a. COUNTY: JACKSON
b. CITY OR TOWN: KANSAS CITY — Length of stay in 1b: 40 YEARS
c. FULL NAME OF HOSPITAL OR INSTITUTION: ST. MARY'S HOSPITAL — Inside Limits: Yes ☒

2. USUAL RESIDENCE a. STATE: MISSOURI b. COUNTY: JACKSON
c. CITY OR TOWN: KANSAS CITY — Inside Limits: Yes ☒
d. STREET ADDRESS: 5309 THE PASEO — Reside on Farm: No ☒

3. NAME OF DECEASED: OLLIE L DAVIS
4. DATE OF DEATH: SEPTEMBER 25 1963
5. SEX: MALE
6. COLOR OR RACE: WHITE
7. Married ☒
8. DATE OF BIRTH: 1/27/1882
9. AGE (last birthday): 81
10a. USUAL OCCUPATION: BUTCHER - RETIRED
11. BIRTHPLACE: PETTIS COUNTY, MO.
12. CITIZEN OF WHAT COUNTRY: U.S.A.
13a. FATHER'S NAME: JAMES DAVIS
13b. MOTHER'S MAIDEN NAME: NANCY GOOCH
14. NAME OF HUSBAND OR WIFE: MRS. MABEL M. DAVIS
15. WAS DECEASED EVER IN U.S. ARMED FORCES? NO
16. SOCIAL SECURITY NO.: 510-05-4693
17. INFORMANT: MRS. MABEL M. DAVIS, Address 5309 THE PASEO KANSAS CITY, MO.

18. CAUSE OF DEATH
PART I. IMMEDIATE CAUSE (a): Acute Cardiac Failure — 24 hrs
DUE TO (b): Lobar Pneumonia Bilateral — 9 days
DUE TO (c): Diabetes Mellitus — 1 yr

19. WAS AUTOPSY PERFORMED? NO ☒

21. I attended the deceased from 1-7-49 to 9-25-63 and last saw him alive on 9-25-63. Death occurred at 8:20 A.m on the date stated above, and to the best of my knowledge, from the causes stated.

22a. SIGNATURE: *James W Downey M.D.* 22b. ADDRESS: 425 E 63rd - K.C. Mo 22c. DATE SIGNED: 9-25-63

23a. BURIAL 23b. DATE: SEPT. 28, 1963 23c. NAME OF CEMETERY: FLORAL HILLS CEMETERY 23d. LOCATION: KANSAS CITY, MISSOURI

24. FUNERAL DIRECTOR: D.W. NEWCOMER'S SONS, Address 1331 BRUSH CREEK KANSAS CITY, MO.
25. DATE RECD. BY LOCAL REG.: 9-26-63
26. REGISTRAR'S SIGNATURE: *Bessie Smith*

(Licensed Embalmer's Statement on Reverse Side)

State of Missouri Division of Health — Standard Certificate of Death. A certified copy, September 22, 2000, of the original document Ollie L. Davis, b. January 27, 1882, d. September 25, 1963.

Headstone of Ollie L. Davis, b. January 27, 1882 and Mabel M. Davis, b. December 9, 1901, d. February 16, 1993 at Floral Hills Cemetery, Kansas City, Missouri. Their son, Eugene, has a gravesite to the right of theirs.

Eugene L. Davis's headstone is located next to his parents' graves. Eugene resides in Peculiar, Missouri.

Edmund "Ed" Davis b. February 13, 1868

The Second Family

Edmund Davis was the son of Richard Davis by his second wife, Elizabeth Baxter. Elizabeth was the daughter of Edmund Baxter, a wealthy farmer in the Brookstown neighborhood.[1] Edmund Davis was born February 13, 1868, according to his tombstone.[2] His father, Richard Davis, died in 1874, and, at first, his grandfather Edmund Baxter was his guardian.[3] Edmund Baxter died in July of 1884.[4] In 1885, Edmund Davis went to court and chose Hiram Jett to be his guardian.[5] On 2 December 1886 Edmund Davis married Letha A. Masters, with Hiram Jett, his bondsman.[6]

found severally due to each share, as follows: to Milly Johnson $254 24/100. to Clifton Davis $254 24/100. to M J Sparks $254 24/100. to Arthusa Davis $102 39/100. to James Davis $106 24/100. to Josiah Davis $516 24/100. to Albert Davis nothing (he being indebted by judgment to the estate over and above his share $167 72/100) and to the Guardian of Edmund Davis $594 24/100.

By 1900 the couple had five children: Lizzie, age twelve; John, age ten; Leona, age seven; Andrew, age four and Woodson, age one. Edmund owned a farm, free of mortgage.[7] By 1910 Edmund was a widower with two additional sons, Arthur, age eight, and Newland, age four, who is most likely the son who was called Everett, born 1905.[8] Their mother, Letha Masters Davis, died December 11, 1909.[9] Edmund Davis married again a Mrs. McGuire, according to his obituary, which appeared in *Madison County, Kentucky, Newspaper Death Notices.*[10]

> Mr. Ed Davis, a prominent farmer and splendid citizen, died at his home in this Brookstown neighborhood last Sunday night after an illness of Brights disease. Deceased was forty-nine years of age and had been twice married. His first wife was a Miss Masters, daughter of Woodson Masters, and died about eight years ago. His second wife was a Mrs. McGuire, who together with five sons and two daughters, survive. The bereaved family has the sympathy of many friends. Mr. Davis was an exemplary citizen and numbered his friends by his acquaintances. His death has caused much sorrow in the community in which he lived. Funeral services were held at the Brookstown Christian Church, Tuesday morning at ten-o'clock, conducted by Rev. O.J. Young, of this city, thence the burial in the Richmond Cemetery.

Edmund Davis died March 18, 1917. H.P. Dykes of Redhouse, his son-in-law, gave the information on his death certificate.[11] His property, approximately 105 acres, was sold to E.E. Davis in 1922 for $16,536.35, a princely sum then.[12]

The children of Ed and Letha Masters Davis were Elizabeth Etta Davis, who married J. Richa [*sic*] Wells in Madison County in 1908.[13] John Davis married Mary S. Jenkins in 1924.[14] He was thirty-four, and she was twenty-four. Leona Davis married H.P. Dykes. At some point, Woodson and Everett Davis moved to Detroit, Michigan. When they died, Woodson was married to Loyola Remmant,[15] and Everett Davis was married to Florentine Verkennis.[16] Both Woodson and Everett Davis and their wives chose to be buried in the Richmond Cemetery, Richmond, Kentucky, near the graves of their father and mother, Ed and Leatha Davis, their sister Elizabeth E. Wells, and brother John W. Davis.[17] Woodson Davis died April 6, 1978, in Southfield, Michigan, leaving one son Edward Davis, five grandchildren, and two great-grandchildren.[18] Everett Davis died June 18, 1983. His home address was 24327 Hopkins, Dearborn Heights, Michigan.[19] Both Everett and Woodson Davis had been employed in the automotive industry. We do not have further information on the deaths of the two brothers, Arthur and Andrew/Anderson Davis.

In 1924 Elizabeth Etta "Lizzie" Davis Wells, wife of J.R. Wells passed away at age thirty-seven from tuberculosis.[20] At that time her brothers and sisters were listed as Mrs. Lena Dyke [*sic*] of Bokelia, Florida; Woodson and Arthur Davis of Jacksonville, Florida; Everett, Anderson, and John Davis of Richmond.[21]

In 1942 Mrs. Lena Davis Dykes must have died as her siblings were sellers in a deed to H.P. Dykes in Madison County, and they are listed as John Davis and Mrs. John Davis, his wife; Andrew Davis and Ada Bicknell Davis, his wife; Woodson Davis and Layola [*sic*] Davis, his wife; Arthur Davis and Mrs. Arthur Davis, his wife; Everett Davis and Maude Davis, his wife; and then the children and husband of Lizzie Davis Wells: Mr. Richard Wells and Mrs. Richard Wells, his wife; Richard Wells Jr., and Mrs. Richard Wells Jr.; Altha Wells, a single woman; Elizabeth Wells Luth and Carl Luth, her husband.[22] The property they sold was a house and lot in Redhouse, Madison County, Kentucky.

Neither Edmund Davis nor his wife, Letha Masters Davis, lived long lives, but they left behind seven children and many grandchildren.

A.H.

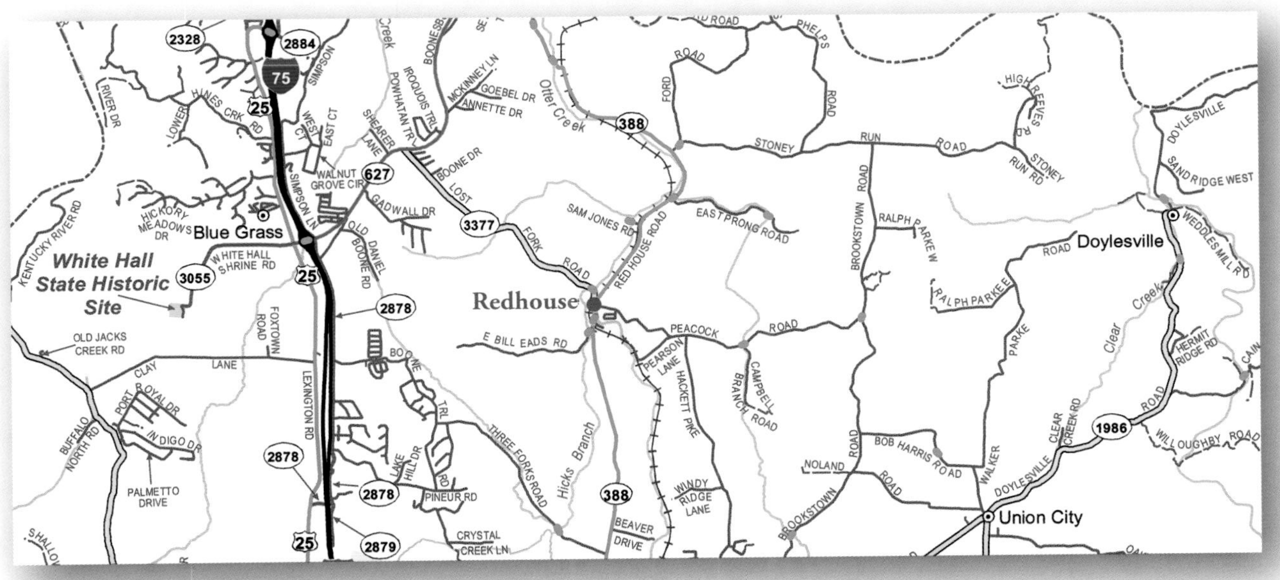

Edmund "Ed" "Edward" Davis owned 105 acres approximately on the waters of East Fork, Otter Creek near Redhouse, Madison County, Kentucky. Map courtesy of Kentucky Transportation Cabinet.

Notes:

1. Allan Sparrow Humphreys, *Some Maryland Baxters and Their Descendants* (Fayetteville, Ark.: A.S. Humphreys, 1948), 36, 37.
2. Edmund Davis, tombstone, Richmond Cemetery, Richmond, Kentucky.
3. Madison Co., Kentucky, Order Book P 1873–1876:115, FHL # 1912821.
4. Madison Co., Kentucky, Order Book T:443, FHL #1912821.
5. Bill and Kathy Vockery, *Madison County Cemetery Records* (Richmond, Ky.: K. Vockery, 1999), C56-Baxter Cemetery, p. 136.
6. Madison Co., Kentucky, Marriages Book 20:133.
7. 1900 federal census, Kentucky, Madison Co., E.D. 45, Lipton Precinct, p. 22.
8. 1910 federal census, Kentucky, Madison Co., Union City, E.D. 66, p. 5.
9. Letha Davis, tombstone, Richmond Cemetery, Richmond, Ky.
10. Madison County, Kentucky, Newspaper Death Notices, Vol. 15, p. 3402
11. Ed Davis, Kentucky death certificate, 1917, #11973.
12. Madison Co., Kentucky, Deed Book 96:19-20.
13. Madison Co., Kentucky, Marriage Bonds 32:327-28.
14. Madison Co., Kentucky, Licenses and Bonds 53:32.
15. Woodson Masters Davis, Michigan death certificate, 1978, #236662.
16. Everett Davis, Michigan death certificate, 1983, #36965.
17. Cemetery records, Richmond Cemetery, Richmond, Ky.
18. Richmond, Kentucky, Cemetery Book of Interments, January 1974-June 1978, Eastern Kentucky University, Special Collections and Archives, Richmond, Ky.
19. Everett Davis, Michigan death certificate, 1983, #36965.
20. Madison County, Kentucky, Newspaper Death Notices (pub info, 1924), Eastern Kentucky University, Special Collections and Archives, Richmond, Ky.
21. Ibid.
22. Madison Co., Kentucky, Deed Book 127:238-39.

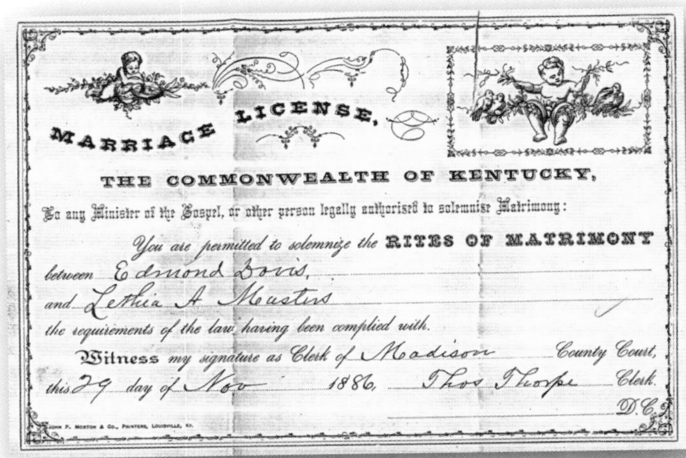

MARRIAGE LICENSE,

THE COMMONWEALTH OF KENTUCKY,

To any Minister of the Gospel, or other person legally authorised to solemnise Matrimony:

You are permitted to solemnize the RITES OF MATRIMONY between Edmond Davis, and Lethia A Masters the requirements of the law having been complied with.

Witness my signature as Clerk of Madison County Court, this 29 day of Nov 1886, Thos Thorpe Clerk. D.C.

John P. Morton & Co., Printers, Louisville, Ky.

MARRIAGE CERTIFICATE.

This is to Certify That on the 2nd day of December, 1886 the Rites of Marriage were legally solemnized by me between Edmond, Davis, and Letha, A, Masters, at Woodson, Masters in the County of Madison, Ky. in the presence of T, G, Pirkens, Edmond, Baldwin.

Note.—The Statute requires the names of at least two Witnesses to be inserted in the foregoing Certificate.

Signed. O, J, Young.

John P. Morton & Co., Printers, Louisville, Ky.

Marriage License of Edmund Davis and Eleatha "Letha" Masters dated November 29, 1886, and Marrriage Certificate dated December 2, 1886. Source: Madison County Courthouse, Richmond, Kentucky, Marriage License File (Box #26) 1884–1888.

Photos courtesy of Cynthia Eilber

Woodson Masters Davis with his wife, Loyola Davis, in 1921

Back of picture reads: "Woodson, Loyola, Edward Davis 1927"

Andrew, Woodson, Everett, and Art Davis ("1927?" on reverse side of picture)

Woodson Davis in photo taken in January 1973

Written on back of photo: "Grandma & Pa Davis, Dad, Ernst & Maxine"
Pictured left to right are Loyola Davis, Woodson Davis, Edward Davis, Maxine Barkley, and Ernest Barkley

Woodson Masters Davis Family

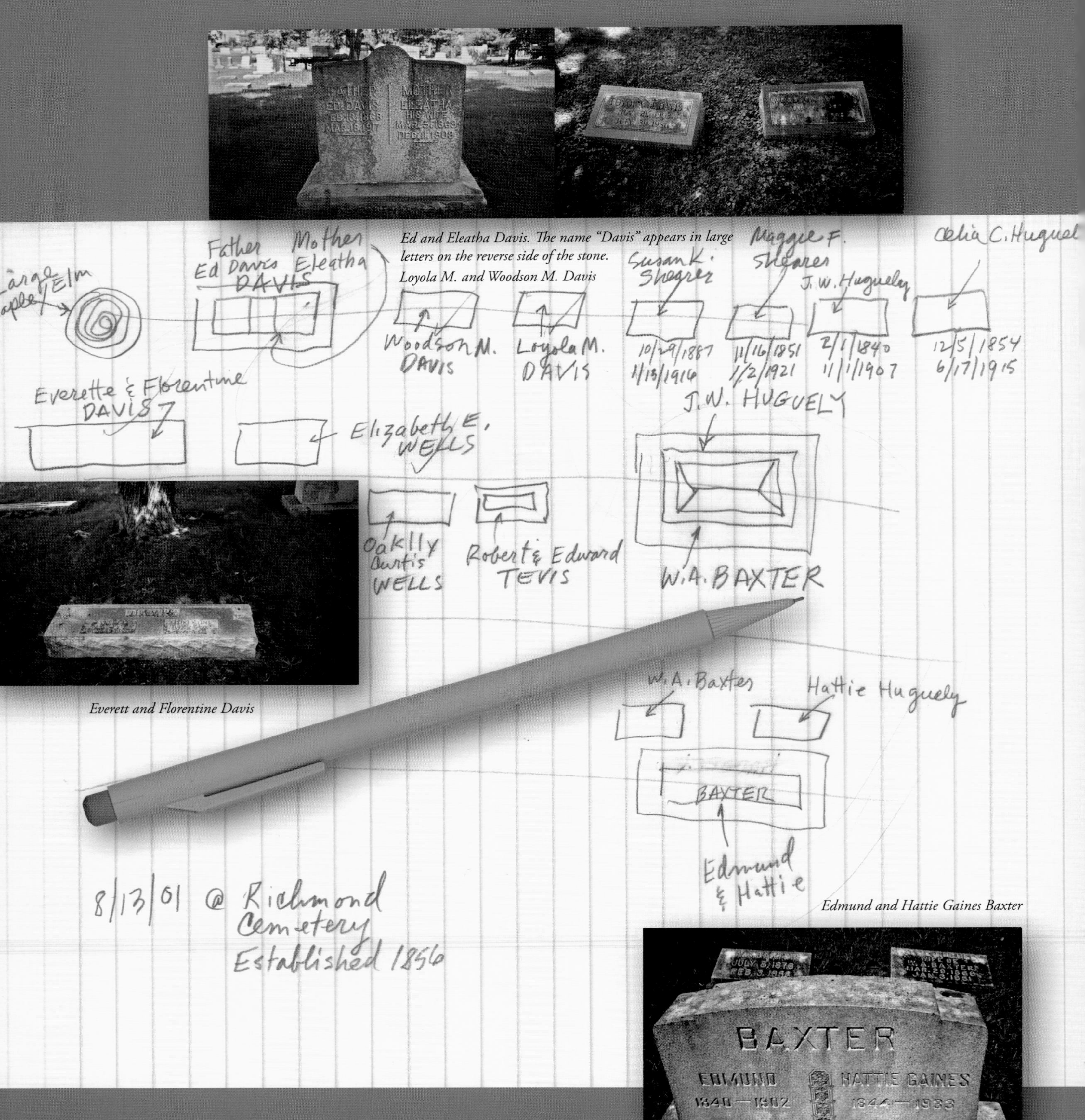

Ed and Eleatha Davis. The name "Davis" appears in large letters on the reverse side of the stone.

Loyola M. and Woodson M. Davis

Everett and Florentine Davis

Edmund and Hattie Gaines Baxter

LF 338
CF
8531

STATE OF MICHIGAN
DEPARTMENT OF PUBLIC HEALTH 0036969
STATE FILE NUMBER

CERTIFICATE OF DEATH

1. Decedent name: EVERETT DAVIS
2. Sex: MALE
3. Date of death: June 18, 1983
4. Race: White
5a. Age: 78
6. Date of birth: April 2, 1905
7a. County of death: WAYNE
7b. Location of death: WESTLAND
7c. Hospital or other institution: WAYNE COUNTY GENERAL HOSPITAL
8. State of birth: Kentucky
9. Citizen of what country: U.S.A.
10. Married
11. Surviving spouse: Florentine Verkennis
13. Social security number: 376-05-6162
14a. Usual occupation: Inspector
14b. Kind of business or industry: Automotive
15a. Current residence state: Michigan
15b. County: Wayne
15c. Locality: Dearborn Heights
15d. Street and number: 24327 Hopkins
16. Father: Ed Davis
17. Mother: Letha Masters
18a. Informant: Florentine Davis
18b. Mailing address: 24327 Hopkins Dearborn Heights, Michigan 48125
19. Part I. (a) Ventricular asystole — Minutes; (b) Atherosclerotic heart disease — Years
Part II. Other significant conditions: Cardiac arrest
20. Autopsy: NO
21. Was case referred to medical examiner: No
22a. Place of death: HOSPITAL
22b. INPATIENT
23a. Signature: M. Rozboril, M.D.
23b. Date signed: June 20, 1983
23c. Hour of death: 9:15 P.M.
25. Name and address of certifier: M. Rozboril, M.D. Wayne County General Hospital Westland, Michigan 48185
25a. Acc. suicide hom. natural: Natural
27a. Burial
27b. Cemetery: Richmond Cemetery
27c. Location: Richmond, Kentucky
27d. Date: June 23, 1983
28a. Name of facility: Querfeld Funeral Home, Inc.
28b. Address of facility: 1200 Oakwood Dearborn, MI 48124
Funeral service licensee: William A. Querfeld
Registrar: Janet A. White
Date received by registrar: June 21 1983

State of Michigan Department of Public Health — Certificate of Death.
Everett Davis b. April 2, 1905, d. June 20, 1983, 9:15 P.M.

LF 269-78
CF
57 B 354.01

STATE OF MICHIGAN
DEPARTMENT OF PUBLIC HEALTH
23662
STATE FILE NUMBER

CERTIFICATE OF DEATH

1. Decedent name: Woodson Masters Davis
2. Sex: Male
3. Date of death: April 6, 1978
4. Race: White
5a. Age: 79
6. Date of birth: March 7, 1899
7a. County of death: Oakland
7b. Location of death: Southfield
7c. Hospital: Providence Hospital
8. State of birth: Kentucky
9. Citizen of what country: USA
10. Married
11. Surviving spouse: Loyola Remmant
12. U.S. armed forces: No
13. Social security number: 372-07-7496
14a. Usual occupation: Inspector Auto Wheels, Ret.
14b. Kind of business or industry: Kelsey Hayes
15a. Current residence: Michigan
15b. County: Wayne
15c. Locality: Detroit
15d. Street and number: 9066 Artesian
16. Father: Edward Davis
17. Mother: Letha Woodson
18a. Informant: Edward W. Davis
18b. Mailing address: 39567 Greenlawn, Canton, Mich. 48187
19. Part I. (a) Cardiac arrest secondary to tachy-arrhythmia. — Sudden; (b) Chronic active cholecystitis, Cholelithiasis with rupture. — Surg. 3/19/78, 22 days; (c) Post operative nephrosclerosis with uremia. — 10 days
Part II. Common duct stone. Removed 3/19/78
20. Autopsy: no
21. Referred to medical examiner: no
22a. Place of death: Providence Hosp.
22b. Inpatient
23a. Signature: S. A. Heyner M.D.
23b. Date signed: April 6 1978
23c. Hour of death: 4.25 A.m.
23d. Name of attending physician: S.A.Heyner, M.D.
25. Name and address of certifier: S.A. Heyner, M.D. 15901 W. Nine Mile Rd. Southfield, MI. 48075
26a. none
26b. none
26c. none
26e. none
27a. Burial-Transit
27b. Cemetery: Richmond Cemetery
27c. Location: Madison Co., Kentucky
27d. Date: April 10, 1978
28a. Name of facility: Leonard A. Turowski, F.H. Inc.
28b. Address of facility: 19400 Joy Road, Det. 48228
Funeral service licensee: Leonard A. Turowski
29b. Date received by registrar: 4-7-78

State of Michigan Department of Public Health — Certificate of Death.
A certified copy, July 10, 2001, of the original document
Woodson Masters Davis b. March 7, 1899, d. April 6, 1978, 4:25 A.M.

LF 16
CF
3030

STATE OF MICHIGAN
DEPARTMENT OF PUBLIC HEALTH 0005918
STATE FILE NUMBER

CERTIFICATE OF DEATH

1. Decedent name: LOYOLA M. DAVIS
2. Sex: Female
3. Date of death: January 5, 1986
4. Race: White
5a. Age: 82
6. Date of birth: November 21, 1903
7a. County: Wayne
7b. Location of death: Garden City
7c. Hospital: Garden City Osteopathic Hospital
8. State of birth: Michigan
9. Citizen of what country: U.S.A.
10. Widowed
11. Surviving spouse: None
12. U.S. armed forces: No
13. Social security number: 384-20-3920
14a. Usual occupation: Sales
14b. Kind of business or industry: Sears
15a. Current residence: Michigan
15b. County: Wayne
15c. Locality: Detroit
15d. Street and number: 9066 Artesian
16. Father: William Remant
17. Mother: Anna McNamara
18a. Informant: Edward W. Davis
18b. Mailing address: 9066 Artesian Detroit, Michigan 48228
19. Part I. (a) Acute Myocardial Infarction — Seconds; (b) Arteriosclerotic Heart Disease — Years
20. Autopsy: Yes
21. Referred to medical examiner: No
22a. Place of death: Hospital
22b. DOA
23a. Signature: D. Dreyfuss
23b. Date signed: January 6, 1986
23c. Hour of death: 3:30 P M
25. Name and address of certifier: Donald Dreyfuss, D.O. 81 Whysall Lane, Bloomfield Hills, MI 48013
26a. Natural
27a. Burial
27b. Cemetery: Richmond Cemetery
27c. Location: Richmond, Kentucky
27d. Date: January 9, 1986
28a. Name of facility: LEONARD A. TUROWSKI & SON FUNERAL HOME, INC.
28b. Address of facility: 19400 Joy Rd. Detroit, Michigan 48228
Funeral service licensee: Leonard A. Turowski
Registrar: Donald D. Showalter
29b. Date received by registrar: Jan. 7, 1986

State of Michigan Department of Public Health — Certificate of Death.
Loyola M. Davis b. November 21, 1903, d. January 5, 1986

Registrar of Vital Statistics
Certified Copy

THE FACE OF THIS DOCUMENT HAS A COLORED BACKGROUND - NOT A WHITE BACKGROUND

Commonwealth of Kentucky
BUREAU OF VITAL STATISTICS
CERTIFICATE OF DEATH
11975

1. Place of death: County Mad Co; Vot. Pct. McCreary
2. Full name: Ed Davis

PERSONAL AND STATISTICAL PARTICULARS
Sex: M; Color or race: W; Single, married, widowed or divorced: married
Age: 49 yrs.
Occupation: Farmer
Birthplace: Mad Co
Name of father: Richard Davis
Birthplace of father: Mad Co
Maiden name of mother: Elizabeth Baxter
Birthplace of mother: Mad Co
The above is true to the best of my knowledge
(Informant) W. T. Dykes
(Address) Red House
Filed Mar 21 1917 Thos. A. Shelton, Registrar

MEDICAL CERTIFICATE OF DEATH
Date of death: 3 18 1917
The cause of death was as follows: Gall Stones
(Signed) R. M. Phelps, M.D.
Place of burial or removal: Richmond Ky; Date of burial: 3/20 1917
Undertaker: Oldham Luxon, Richmond Ky

THE BACK OF THIS DOCUMENT CONTAINS AN ARTIFICIAL WATERMARK - HOLD AT AN ANGLE TO VIEW

I, Sandra J. Davis, State Registrar of Vital Statistics, hereby certify this to be a true and correct copy of the certificate of birth, death, marriage or divorce of the person therein named, and that the original certificate is registered under the file number shown. In testimony thereof I have hereunto subscribed my name and caused the official seal of the Office of Vital Statistics to be affixed at Frankfort, Kentucky this 27th day of July 2001 KG

Sandra J. Davis, State Registrar

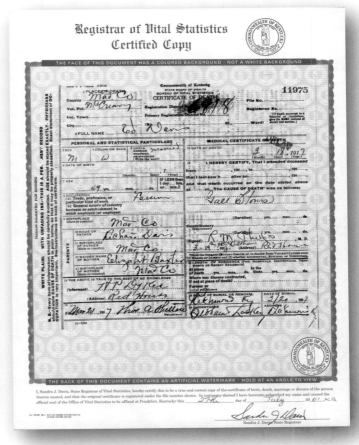

Commonwealth of Kentucky State Board of Health — Certificate of Death.
A certified copy, July 27, 2001, of the original document
Ed Davis d. March 18, 1917

Edward Davis b. October 14, 1923

Edward Davis in 1934

Edward Davis b. October 14, 1923, in a photo from 1943. Edward served in World War II in the 28th Infantry and was on the frontlines in Germany when he was wounded in November of 1944. He was buried in the Great Lakes National Cemetery in Holly, Michigan, a veterans memorial cemetery about forty-five miles northwest of Detroit, and the second national cemetery in Michigan.

Photos courtesy of **Cynthia Eilber**

Army of the United States

SEPARATION QUALIFICATION RECORD

SAVE THIS FORM. IT WILL NOT BE REPLACED IF LOST

This record of job assignments and special training received in the Army is furnished to the soldier when he leaves the service. In its preparation, information is taken from available Army records and supplemented by personal interview. The information about civilian education and work experience is based on the individual's own statements. The veteran may present this document to former employers, prospective employers, representatives of schools or colleges, or use it in any other way that may prove beneficial to him.

1. LAST NAME—FIRST NAME—MIDDLE INITIAL: DAVIS EDWARD W 36 579 631 PVT

2. ARMY SERIAL No. / 3. GRADE / 4. SOCIAL SECURITY No.: 12640 ROSELAWN DETROIT 4 WAYNE MICH 385-12-4695

5. PERMANENT MAILING ADDRESS (Street, City, County, State)

6. DATE OF ENTRY INTO ACTIVE SERVICE	7. DATE OF SEPARATION	8. DATE OF BIRTH
11 Mar 43	23 Dec 45	14 Oct 23

9. PLACE OF SEPARATION: Sep Cen Camp Atterbury, Ind.

MILITARY OCCUPATIONAL ASSIGNMENTS

10. MONTHS	11. GRADE	12. MILITARY OCCUPATIONAL SPECIALTY
4	Pvt	Basic tng (Inf) 521
24	Pfc	Rifleman 745

SUMMARY OF MILITARY OCCUPATIONS

13. TITLE—DESCRIPTION—RELATED CIVILIAN OCCUPATION

RIFLEMAN: Placed rifle fire upon designated targets of enemy lines to change position as situation demanded. Used automatic rifle. Cleaned and kept gun in firing condition. Served with 109th Infantry.

WD AGO FORM 100 1 JUL 1945 — This form supersedes WD AGO Form 100, 15 July 1944, which will not be used.

The two documents above are copies of the originals, and were provided by Cynthia Eilber, the daughter of Edward W. Davis.

EDWARD W DAVIS

To you who answered the call of your country and served in its Armed Forces to bring about the total defeat of the enemy, I extend the heartfelt thanks of a grateful Nation. As one of the Nation's finest, you undertook the most severe task one can be called upon to perform. Because you demonstrated the fortitude, resourcefulness and calm judgment necessary to carry out that task, we now look to you for leadership and example in further exalting our country in peace.

Harry Truman

THE WHITE HOUSE

Cynthia "Cindy" Eilber and Edward Davis b. October 14, 1923. As mentioned in the acknowledgments of this book, it was Cynthia who was most accommodating in helping to collect, collate, and forward all the photographs on these pages for my use. She also did additional work securing vital genealogical information that otherwise would have been unavailable to me.

Back of picture reads, "Edward Davis 2005 at his favorite Ice Cream parlour in Jackson Michigan where he grew up."

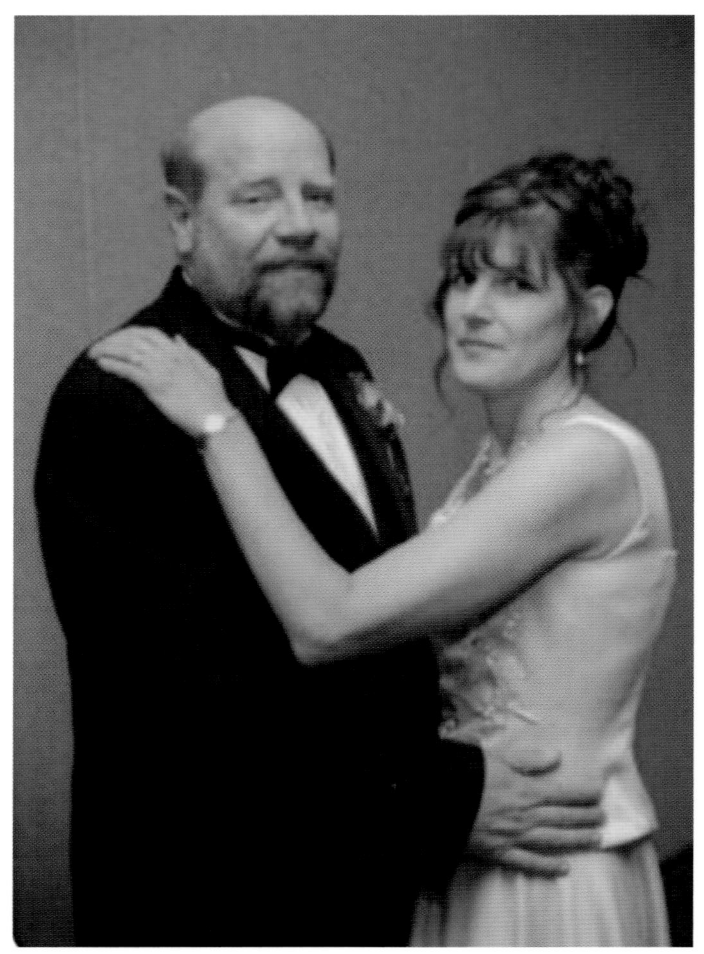

Michael Eilber and Cynthia "Cindy" Davis Eilber b. September 13, 1954, pictured in 2000

Top: Edward Davis b. August 18, 1957, pictured with wife Marelyn. Bottom: Richard William Davis b. January 27, 1964 with wife Diane.

Photos courtesy of **Cynthia Eilber**

Pictured in 2005: Edward Davis, Kathryn "Kathy" Davis Charnock b. December 8, 1956, Daniel "Dan" Davis b. December 16, 1958, Cynthia "Cindy" Davis Eilber, and Richard William Davis

Left to right: Brittany Charnock b. February 3, 1984, Kathy Davis Charnock b. December 8, 1956, her husband Brent Charnock and Justin Charnock b. July 9, 1981

Derek Mitchell Davis b. June 23, 1992, son of Richard William Davis and Norma Ruth Gardner Davis

Above left: Daniel "Dan" Davis with his wife Marie. Below: his daughter, Chantel Davis b. 1987. Above right: Shannon Eilber Armstrong b. April 1, 1973, and Michelle Eilber Pomorski b. September 4, 1977, daughters of Cynthia Davis Eilber, in a photo taken June 27, 2007.

Edward Davis, son of Edward Davis Jr., b. July 20, 1987

Amanda Davis, daughter of Edward Davis Jr., b. July 27, 1989

The Village of Fairmount, Illinois

Arriving on N 580 East Road

No family history of the Davises or Gooches could be written without mentioning the village of Fairmount, Illinois. Located in Vance Township, Vermilion County, Fairmount lies just twenty-two miles east of Champaign, Illinois, and is 166 miles south of Chicago, my home town. Being just west of Danville, it is considered a part of that town's metropolitan area.[1]

My version of the early history of Fairmount is drawn from several, often-conflicting sources. An article from *The* (Danville) *News,* January 27, 1875, was my primary reference. I also reviewed notes taken from an address given by Mr. Charles V. Tilton to the Fairmount Lions Club sometime during the 1950s, along with another version of the *Early History of Vance, Village of Fairmount*, collected by Wilfred Hickman. I concluded they were largely drawn from the first reference. However, both Mr. Tilton and Mr. Hickman supplemented their reviews of Fairmount's past with additional personal notes particular to their time. I have also drawn upon Wikipedia, the free online encyclopedia, as my most current resource.

Before there was a Fairmount, there was Vance Township. "It was named in honor of Major John Vance, one of the early settlers, first senator from this county (Vermilion) and brother of Governor Joseph Vance of Ohio." The preceding statement was excerpted from *The* (Danville) *News,* January 27, 1875. I am quoting freely from this source since I believe it to be an accurate accounting of the early days of Vance Township, the Village of Fairmount, and the surrounding area (Vance Township originally included what was then Catlin and Oakwood townships; however, the south line was extended to include Sidell). The township name was changed from Union on June 13, 1851, according to the Vermilion County, Illinois, State Archives web site.

As stated in *The* (Danville) *News,* January 27, 1875:

> The greater portion of the township consists of as fine prairie, farming and grazing land, as can be found, perhaps, in the world. Beautifully undulating, fertile, well drained and otherwise improved, nothing could be more desirable. It is a notable fact that crops are invariably good, or best in the immediate vicinity of Fairmount, the past season [1874] being the sole exception; and this cannot be counted a failure, when compared with neighboring districts.

The News goes on to mention a variety of natural features of the land and subsequent resources that prompted the area's development:

> A small portion of the township lies north of the Salt Fork [River], on either side of which is a belt of fine timbered land, the bluffs containing inexhaustible deposits of sandstone. The entire area is rich in rare and precious geological specimens.
>
> Extensive and valuable limestone seams crop out near the southern limits, while large drifts of the best sand for building purposes can be found in the Salt Fork bottoms. Several never failing springs exist, the most important is the 'Big Spring' which starts from the limestone above alluded to, about two miles south of Fairmount.... The entire area is under laid with coal seams, one of which, known as the 'blossom seam,' 18 inches thick, crops out in the bluffs, and underlies the village at a depth of 4 feet. The working vein lies at a

depth of 200 feet, but is reached in the Salt Fork bottom at a much less depth. The mining of coal which has been extending up the Salt Fork has reached this township in the extreme northeast corner, where one shaft, owned by William Moore, yields annually about 50,000 bushels."

My grandfather, Charles Davis, had already worked in the coal mines for at least two years prior to his receiving his Certificate of Competency of Coal Miner, on January 7, 1920, from the State of Illinois Department of Mines and Minerals, Examining Board (see page 254 for facsimile).

One might speculate that the mining of coal and its promise of employment, coupled with Charlie's recent marriage and bride's family living in Fairmount, was simply too strong a draw for this young man from Missouri. He returned from Missouri with his wife Rebecca and their son Roy to Fairmount approximately a year and a half after Roy's birth.

Fairmount is a quiet, sparsely populated place. According to the 2000 U.S. census, approximately 640 people were residents of the village. The village of Fairmount was founded in anticipation of the coming of the railroad around 1850. The plan was for a town to be established every seven miles approximately, probably to meet the limitations of fuel and water required to run the locomotives. The town was first named by "Joseph (or Josiah)

U.S. Post Office in Fairmount, Illinois, ZIP code 61841

Hunt, a railroad engineer who reportedly used inside information about the coming of the Great Northern Railroad to purchase 40 acres of land along the new route to found a town."[2] "He originally named the town Salina," according to Mr. Charles V. Tilton, "when the village trustees attempted to get a post office and the Postmaster General refused the name Salina because of an existing Illinois town named Saline." Mr. Tilton goes on to say that "the citizens held a meeting and changed the name to Fairmount. Francis Dougherty, an early settler is said to have selected the name Fairmount." However, contrary to the above, Mr. Hickman claims "the T. W. & W. Railway having been originally laid off by the Company on 40 acres (was) donated for the purpose by George Cornelius."

The railroad that passes through Fairmount today has gone through a variety of name changes, as the industry advanced and consolidated over these past 158 years. As of January 2006 the "Norfolk Southern Railway operates the railroad line that passes through Fairmount" on its way from Danville to Decatur [Wikipedia]. The tracks run parallel to the Greenview Cemetery,

Above: The signpost for West Clyde Street in Fairmount. Life is full of minor coincidences. My father, Clyde "Cotton" Davis, was born in Catlin, Illinois, and lived in Fairmount, with its street named after some other Clyde. His son, Clyde Patrick, married a woman who grew up and lived in a house on Clyde Avenue in Chicago. 'Round and 'round it goes!

separating the cemetery from the cornfields beyond. Standing there before my father's headstone, I have more than once been startled by the train as it roared by, its roar and rumble not only waking this small sleepy village, but also causing me to believe it was loud enough to wake even those who seemingly lie in peace beneath my feet.

The following is a list of "firsts" I've managed to compile from *The* (Danville) *News*, 1875 article:

1823 First settlement by Robert Osborne from Tennessee, who built the first frame house, soon to be followed by a second settler (name not verifiable).

1826 First entry of land made in the township by William O'Neil, also the first blacksmith.

1833 First wedding in the township, John Burns to Miss Van Duzan (by the bride's father).

? First death among the early settlers, William Sheer.

1857 First house to be built in Fairmount as a station for section hands on the north side of the railroad and east side of Main Street.

1858 First dwelling in Fairmount was built by John Allen, and he was therefore considered the founder of the village. Mr. Allen was elected first supervisor from Vance Township.
The town was incorporated in 1863 [Wikipedia]. The Village (of Fairmount) was incorporated in 1861 (Charles V. Tilton).
First newspaper was the *Fairmount Glen*, published by G.C. Adams and Wilbur Short.

1865 First schoolhouse built.

The area in and around Vermilion County was once settled by the Miami, Kickapoo, and Potawatomi tribes. Salt was of great attraction to both Indians and the white man.

"As late as 1834 the Indians exceeded the whites in numbers, especially in winter. This being their favorite hunting ground" according to *The News*.

There is a marker, one among many, a metal plaque, embedded in a boulder beside a farm driveway on 1250N (Catlin-Homer Road) 1/10 mile east of 250E, 3.6 miles east of Homer, and just outside of the village of Fairmount. The marker was erected in 1991 by Boy Scout Andy Chase as an Eagle Scout project.

(continued on page 332)

The Fairmount Drug Store
Claude E. Tilton, R. Ph.
Where every purchase must be right.
Coal Mine at Bennett Station near Fairmou
End of Fox Drive - W. H. Cattett Farm. 1-30-2
Wabash Freight Wreck - Fairmount, Il.

...an. He had, perhaps, a dozen
The last sale of leather was made
345, although he had discontinued
manufacture some years previously.
his sale sole leather brought from
7 cents per pound.
n the winter of 1833 occurred the
t wedding in the township. The
ord reads thus: "Married! John
rns to Miss Van Duzen! by the
de's father! 10 o'clock, night!"
This year Thomas Deacon arrived
l settled on the land on which he
w resides, and which he has farmed
interruptedly ever since.
As late as the year 1834 the Indians
ceeded the whites in numbers,
pecially in winter, this being their
winter hunting ground. They
especially affectionate towards
rs, yet no one was ever seri-
ested by them. They had
lible hatred of labor.
ring to roast a rabbit or
they invariably set but one
the other end of the pole
s and relieving each other

occurred the advent of
s of the Davis family, Wm
Two years later five
s and two daughters join-
Also the father, Henry
am and James are still
ownship; Vanmeter at
Like the Dougherty
not especially migra-
scendants are numerous
pecatable. Eli, son of
ezeriah, is the oldest native of the
ownship, 39 years.

The first death among the settlers did not occur until this year. William Shear, a young man, was thrown from a horse and died from the effects of his injuries, but was not buried in this township.

OTHER OLD SETTLERS.

Widow Sally Sheaphard and her son George are 36 years residents of the township. W. E. and Charles Lee and sister, 31 years. Hiram Hickman, 46 years; Jeremiah Pate, 45 years; Mrs. Hiram Hickman, 40 years; Jesse Burroughs and son, Wilson, 38 years; John Allen and D. B. Stogden, 36 years; Moses Boggess 35.

T. M. Brittenham is the oldest native
county, 41 years.
have herein endeavored to give
l review of the early history of
the best townships in the coun-
l of one that has grown to be a
y, intelligent and important
n of the community. It is not
mplete as it might be but it is
l we have been able to rescue
items of interest from that for-
ness that will in a few years
with the departure of our old
rs. It may also induce some one
o snatch from the memories of
ld pioneers, incidents and facts
ave been unable to get, to be sent
e Danville News for publication
preservation.

VILLAGE OF FAIRMOUNT.

EARLY SETTLEMENT.

The village was originally known as "Salina," but owing to difficulties encountered by the railroad authorities, on account of the existence of another place of the same name in the State, it was changed to its present name.

The place is purely a creature of the T., W. & W. Railway, having been originally laid off by the Company on 40 acres donated for the purpose by George Cornelius. Additions have since been made by R. Q. Cornelius, Joseph Reese, John Allen, and John Foulks.

THE FIRST HOUSE

was built by the Company in 1857, as a station for the use of the section hands; is yet standing on the north side of the railroad and east side of Main street; it is now used as a depot and office.

The following year John Allen built and occupied the first dwelling, and therefore has the honor of being the founder of the village.

The house was built on the west end of lot 8, block 34, old plat —High street between South and Front—is now owned and occupied by Mrs. Conner. Mr. Allen also built and occupied the first store house, jointly with James W. Booker, the second settler, and father of L. E. and George Booker. The pioneer business house is still standing, occupied by Levi Gibson, on the north-east corner Main and South streets, lot 7, block 27. Mr. Allen was elected first supervisor from Vance township, and is yet residing in the village—a much respected and very useful citizen. His son, Elijah, was the first agent of the company at this station. Mr. Booker has the honor of being the first postmaster.

Michael Dunn, although not properly the pioneer settler, was earlier on the spot than Mr. Allen, in the employ of Pat Kurn, section hand, but was soon appointed section boss, which position he maintained many years, until succeeded by his son Peter, who still holds the place, with prospects of continuing many years. Both gentlemen own comfortable homes, models of neatness and industry.

The next settlers were respectively, George Browning, —— Goodwin, A. Howden, John Harvey, and Ellis Adams.

Of the earliest settlers, T. E. and George Booker, Ellen Booker, John Cordts, Jacob Hall, John Coatney and F. K. Adams remain here.

SUBSEQUENT GROWTH.

From the beginning it was evident that the settlement was determined to repeat the mistakes, and duplicate the experiences of all towns large or small. Undue stimulus was imparted to the spirit of improvement, and unreasonable expectations were excited by the sound of the carpenters hammers, and rattling tongues of real estate dealers. The result w... that the vill...e was

During a visit to the Fairmount Jamaica Historical Society Building on Main Street in the Village of Fairmount, I found the document below, laminated on two sides. I borrowed it for inclusion in this book. After reproducing it above with the accompanying photos, I returned the original to the Historical Society and gave a duplicate framed copy to the Vance Township Library, where it currently hangs on the wall of the library. This article is frequently quoted — and misquoted — by others as well as myself as noted in the text of this story.

[illegible] ...ending rapid improvements, and the novelty of the opening of a new market attracted a temporary patronage, disguising the fact, and gradually developing the real condition of affairs. Following the reaction a large amount of property was thrown upon the market, causing it to depreciate far below its true value.

This depreciation is purely fictitious—now that churches, school houses, bridges, sidewalks, shade trees, and other improvements are secured, property is really much more valuable, than when the burden was yet in the future.

Improvements are now of a more desirable character, re-painting, repairing, ornamenting, and otherwise improving places already began; this is the great need of all towns.

The village possesses three handsome church edifices, Methodist Episcopal, Baptist and Cumberland Presbyterian; each with a large and prosperous membership. These societies are presided over respectively by Revs, C. L. Robinson, Alexander Cummings and James Ashmore, all of whom are unusually able, and remarkable; the former for his depth of thought and reasoning; the next for his oratory, and devotion to the cause of religion; and the latter for his forcible and practical common sense sermons.

The Masonic brotherhood have a large and very flourishing society, with the following officers: S. W. Cox, W. M.; B. F. Keyhoe, J. W.; W. W. Stogden, Sec.; John Baldwin, J. D.; Henry Davis, S. W.; D. Gunder, Treas.; John L. Carr, G. D.; John Reese, Tyler.

Other society meetings, of various kinds, with the cornet band of E. Robinson, serve to keep up animation, and no evening passes without some pleasant occasion.

The chief excellence of the village is its extraordinary freedom from sickness, and entire absence of saloons. The word itself is odious, and the citizens are determined to permit no such institutions to enter herein.

The great want of the village is a public hall. Societies having no rooms of their own are suppressed, concerts, exhibitions, and entertainments of all kinds are excluded, consequently persons who seek enjoyment in avenues not specially provided for, are driven to seek it elsewhere, and the public deprived of many a pleasant or profitable evening entertainment.

The village organization is as follows:

Councilmen—Hiram Catlett, President; S. W. Cox, G. W. Powell, James Thomas, James Poindexter, trustees. Police Magistrate, H. M. Robinson; Policeman, Hiram Hickman; Population, 737.

The various branches of trade are now more fully represented than at any time previously, as the directory [illegible] will show:

John H. Dougherty, Flouring Mill;

Grain Merchants—Parish & Iles, J. N. Wilcox, Jacob Hall;

Dry Goods—D. Binkley;

General Merchandise—F. K. Adams, Catlett & Booker;

Groceries and Provisions—J. S. Cox. Levi Gibson, J. D. Downey;

Stock Dealers—Stogdon & Son, G. W. Powell;

Drugs and Medicines—Elias Halliday, S. W. Cox;

Hardware, stoves, tinware, roofing, spouting, &c.—B. F. Keyhoe;

Furniture and cabinet making and repairing—John Morrison;

Agricultural implements, building material, &c.—James Thomas;

Boots and Shoes—Michael Rodgers;

Millinery and dress making—Jane Baldwin, Lizzie Love;

Bakery—Mary Love;

Dealers in poultry—Coatney & Booker; in Hides—J. S. Cox;

Pump Maker—John Coatney;

Doctors—Wilkins, Ray, Mott, and Chapin,

Shoemakers—Mont Robinson, R. Jack, —— Clinkenbeard;

Carpenter—John Cordts, L. B. Loomis, E. Hawkins;

Blacksmiths—G. A. Elgin & Son, T. E. Carey, Edwin Robertson, Wesley Denman, Isaac Simpson & Son.

Wagon Makers—Isaac Simpson, George Yates, Adam Pate;

Harness Makers—Stover & Watkins;

Barber—Charley Grey;

Restaurant—F. M. Brittenham & Son, Mary Love;

Plastering and mason work—W. E. Lee;

Butchers—Manning and Reese;

House painter and grainer—W. McCollester;

Wagon, sign and ornamental painter—Asa Denman;

Hotels, Witherspoon House—Mrs. M. Witherspoon;

Union House—Jacob M. Hall;

Station Agent—Isaiah O'Conner; Assistant—David O'Connor.

The following is the amount of railroad business for 1874:

Freights, express and dispatches forwarded	$39,220 32
Amount received	5,992 58
Tickets	3,401 10
Telegraphing	645 14
Total	$49,259 14

BUSINESS PROSPECTS.

The aggregate trade of the year just closed, is not as favorably as that of former ones; but yet satisfactory, when the causes which operates to produce the result are duly considered, viz the partial failure of crops, and the adoption of the cash system, the later being a matter of necessity as well as policy. Merchants were not able or willing to carry full stocks and at the same sime carry ten to twenty thousand dollars in outstanding accounts, necessitating an annual loss of one to three thousand dollars interest, and bad accounts. Farmers fully understand the justice of the system, and freely recognize the many advantages to be derived from it, yet, when the new order of things was actually applied to them it was not relished as it should be, and as a consequence many excellent customers were soured against the place, and their patronage diverted elsewhere. Fortunately the rule works both ways, and is now beginning to tell in the opposite direction. Excellent theory as it was it was still "only theory;" but now that all have actually experienced it, however unwillingly, the economy, justice and necessity of it is fully indorsed, and all parties are entirely reconciled to it. One result of the dispensation was that prices were necessaraly high and quality poor, giving the place a bad repute among buyers—some are yet deluded by the impression that goods are higher here than elsewhere. This can be speedily dispeled by examining goods and prices, as established under the new system.

Save the scarcity of produce in this locality, and the general depression, the current year opens out with higher prospects. A short time since seven empty rooms served to darken business prospects—now all are occupied, and more demanded. The prospect is that another year will witness the erection of brick blocks, and a more healthy action in all departments of trade.

This marker was placed to commemorate a point in the route of the "Trail of Death" of the Potawatomi Indians of which 850 were, in September 1838, rounded up and marched at gunpoint from their Indiana homeland. "Many walked the 660 mile distance, which took two months. More than 40 died, mostly children, of typhoid fever and the stress of the forced removal [<*http://www.kansasheritage.org*>]."

The Trail of Death has been declared a Regional Historic Trail through the efforts of the Trail of Death Commemorative Caravan group.

"The first school was a frame building built in 1859 at a cost of $400." Mr. Tilton claims the first schoolhouse to be built in 1865, which ultimately became Goodwin Maxfield's Garage. In 1917 a severe storm badly damaged the high school, and a new school building was approved and the cornerstone laid on May 6, 1924. At the ceremony a copper box was placed in this cornerstone to be opened sixty-three years later. Among the items contained in the box was a listing of Fairmount businesses in 1924.[3]

My father Clyde, at age twelve in the 1920 U.S. census, would have been sixteen years old and perhaps attended the new high school when construction was completed. My ancestors living in Fairmount at that time had available to them "9 stores, 4 garages, 2 banks, 2 barbers, and 2 restaurants, plus an undertaker, lumber yard, elevator and theater."

The articles in *The* (Danville) *News,* January 27, 1875, were a major source of information. The two other sources I drew upon regarding early Village of Fairmount and Vance Township history are in the Vance Township Library, 107 South Main Street, Village of Fairmount.

Something Borrowed, Something New

Two pages of the January 27, 1875 issue of *The* (Danville) *News* are reproduced on pages 330–331, along with several postcards depicting various events in and around Fairmount. These pages contain portions of the historical overviews of Vance Township and the village of Fairmount, which lies within its lines. I discovered this material at the Fairmount-Jamaica Historical Society. Two pages of the original newspaper articles had been laminated in plastic on both sides. On May 14, 2007, Kay and I visited Fairmount with the intention of returning this artifact to the Historical Society,[4] but on that day no one was available. We had hoped, at the very least to see Glona Howe, our longtime contact in Fairmount, but she, too, was away visiting family. I felt that this document, recalling the history of the village of Fairmount and borrowed by me, should upon its return be prominently displayed, perhaps in the village library and not buried in the files (or rather piles) of the historical society. I had copies made, mounted each page, side-by-side, and then had them framed. With no one to accept my offering, we went into the First National Bank of Fairmount and left it with Donna Flutz, an employee of the bank, with a note to Glona requesting she return the original to the Historical Society and accept the framed copy on behalf of the folks of Fairmount as a token of my appreciation for its use. As is our usual custom we also left an annual donation for maintenance of the Greenview Cemetery (more on that later).

In January of 1889 Charles, my grandfather, then from Longwood, Missouri, was to marry Rebecca "Becca" Gooch in Catlin, Vermilion County, Illinois, according to their marriage license. The Gooches continue to have a presence, though a diminishing one, to this day in the village of Fairmount and Vermilion County. Other Gooches are in Morris, Illinois. As stated on page 247, after a brief stint in Missouri, Charles Davis returned to Illinois. By 1892 his second child Lizzie was born and along with my father, Clyde, age three, were to appear in the 1910 U.S. census, Vance Township, Village of Fairmount.

By the 1920 census my father was still living in the village of Fairmount, age twelve, at home with his parents Charles and Rebecca. His older brother Roy and sister Elizabeth, having married, had apparently left the household. Clyde probably spent the intervening years between 1920 and 1927 in Fairmount as a teenager. A thorough search of Fairmount School records has been requested of the Vermilion County and Jamaican School district to determine if he remained in the village. No other record has been found to verify his presence in Fairmount during that period. By November 1929 at age twenty-two, he was arrested for "assault to rob being armed."

At the time of his arrest, my father's residence was given as Dearborn, Michigan. Perhaps he had drifted north seeking employment in the auto or steel industry. Times were bad economically, and Clyde was to sit out the Great Depression in a Michigan penitentiary.

The 1930 U.S. census lists many Gooches. The Davises had left Fairmount. The Gooches, being the first to arrive in Fairmount, spread their family wings throughout the village, surrounding towns, and counties, and are there today.

My wife and I have frequently visited Fairmount. Since May 10, 1986, we have returned, time and again, to refamiliarize ourselves with the family history of the Davises and Gooches. Since 1997 we have made occasional trips there, often linked to our visits at the University of Illinois in Champaign-Urbana to support my art and design student scholarship programs.

My purpose for returning is always to draw a little closer to the family I knew little of by somehow tapping into the culture and social fabric of the community in which they lived and to which they too so often returned, especially my father.

First Baptist Church at the corner of S. Main Street and W. South Street in Fairmount, Illinois

Fairmount is a quiet, small village, long since passed by, its main street intersected by ten or so cross streets. Coincidentally, one named Clyde, runs east and west over a span of four blocks. The Norfolk Southern Railroad passes through Fairmount today on its way from Danville to Decatur and beyond, bifurcating the village as it runs east and west. A small U.S. Post Office, at 106

S. Main Street, and the Vance Township Library of Fairmount, at 107 S. Street, are seemingly the only government buildings in Fairmount, though there is listed a Fairmount Village Hall at 301 S. Main Street, and as I've been told, sparingly used for town meetings. There are no longer any schools in Fairmount; those were merged into the Jamaica School District in the early 1950s.

What the Village lacks in public institutions it more than compensates for in places of worship. There are three churches on Main Street alone — First Baptist Church, New Hope Community Church, and the Faith Evangelical Methodist Church, and on S. High Street, one finds the Fairmount United Methodist Church.

Another noticeable presence on Main Street is the Jamaica and Vance Township War Veterans Memorial, which was dedicated August 24, 1997. The Fairmount memorial honors all local veterans who served in World War I, World War II, and the Korean, Vietnam, and Persian Gulf wars. More than four hundred names are included on the memorial. Among those who served are Fairmount's war hero, Carlos C. Ogden, who received the Congressional Medal of Honor for his outstanding service in World War II.

The Jamaica and Vance Township War Veterans Memorial in Fairmount, Illinois, honors those who served in war. There is a plaque at the Memorial for 1st Lt. Carlos C. Ogden, a Congressional Medal of Honor winner.

Also listed on the war memorial are five of my kinfolk, Thomas and William Delaney and Robert O. Gooch, who served in World War I, and Dale and Dean Gooch, who served in the Korean War.

The First Illinois National Bank, at 109 South Main on the east side of the street, is the sole bank in the village, and Casey's General Store and gas station, just north of the village proper, are the primary places of business we've noticed. I'm told that there is a new hair salon, The Hair Gallery, at 201½ S. Main Street, and the Fairmount Lounge, 104 S. Main (the only establishment that serves liquor in town), is doing business on a limited hourly basis; however, the Sunrise Café has gone out of business as hav George's Gun Shop, and "What Nots," which was located at 108 N. Main Street. There are other businesses about town, but not as visible to this infrequent visitor, such as Country Insurance & Financial Services, Fairmount Redi-Mix Co., Decatur Aeration & Temperature Metal Shop, and Farm Business Farm Management.

Of course, one would expect an individual like me, searching for long lost family ties to be ultimately referred to the

Vance Township building in Fairmount, Illinois

Carrington Funeral Home, just off Main Street, at 110 E. Court Street. It was here that I received much information regarding family members buried in the Greenview Cemetery.

Farming was an occupation of many early Gooches and Davises, and one only has to look across the vast plains of surrounding crops to understand the attraction for migrants going west to settle in Fairmount. Limestone quarries, coal mines, and the railroad were industries for those seeking employment.

My grandfather Charles was both, at varying times, a farmer and a coal miner. By 1930 Charles and Rebecca were in Toledo, Ohio, having departed Fairmount, perhaps needing a change of venue after their son's arrest in 1929, or merely leaving because all their children had gone elsewhere. There was even talk by some and shared with me (see page 254), that my grandfather was chased out of Illinois by the law for operating an illegal "still."

However, folks leave a place for many reasons. At the top of any list are being near loved ones and seeking employment. After what I believe to be a brief stay in Toledo, Charles and Rebecca settled in Rockfield, Indiana, in the same town where Glenn Purkey, their grandson was living with his wife LaVerne. Just down the road "a piece," along Route 25 in Lafayette, lived Elizabeth and Hugh Purkey, Glenn's mom and dad, and living with them for a while was Clyde, my father and brother of Lizzie.

As stated earlier, Mildred Gooch Smith was the last Gooch of stature and economic substance to remain in Fairmount. With her passing on December 19, 1992 (see page 11), I lost an opportunity to deepen my ties with a somewhat resolute, mistrusting woman, who could have been a major resource in my search for family. Mildred, from all I can tell, was a beacon of light, a magnet of sorts, for all in her family. She knew the family history of Davises and Gooches, she collected the photos, and it was she through whom they all corresponded, one to another from places like Sedalia, Missouri, Chicago, Illinois, and Evansville, Indiana. It is to her credit that much of the fabric of this book exists. Another woman, Glona Howe, was designated her court-appointed guardian, as Mildred grew increasingly less able in her later years. Thankfully, Glona was there after Mildred's passing to assist me in closing the gaps in my family's history in Fairmount. Mildred was on the scene, so to speak, the last credibly knowledgeable family member residing in Fairmount.

Glona Howe

Looking back I now realize that Glona Howe helped fulfill the need in me to find closure regarding my father's passing. I'm not sure the word, closure, used much too often in today's culture, is an appropriate label for the task I've undertaken in this book of "finding fathers" and for compiling my father's life experiences. Glona, in 1997, was not only employed to deliver the U.S. mail town wide, and was familiar with most living there, but she had also recently taken on the duty of Greenview Cemetery caretaker. Mildred Gooch led my mother, sister, wife, and me to the Greenview Cemetery and to the headstones of my father and grandparents, as well as many other Davises and Gooches buried there. But, it was Glona, in her new role as cemetery volunteer and recordkeeper, to whom I turned in my attempt to expand my family tree, filling in the blanks with the help of Glona's mother Edith Allen Kirby. According to Glona Howe, Allen was her father's name and Edith was her mother's. Her parents wanted to name her after both of them.

Edith Allen Kirby above, exclaiming that "I have thousands of 'em [obituaries]; it's my hobby." I had brought notebooks with me to our sit-down, filled with photos, censuses, marriage, birth, and death certificates. As we reviewed them, this firm, perky lady regaled us with her memories of family.

Edith, whose dad, Allen Goodwin, "was killed in October 1920 in the coal mine had been at station," and may have known my grandfather, Charles Davis, who also worked in the mines around Fairmount, since he had received his state miner's examining boards certificate in 1920. Edith remarked, "Emmanuel Gooch, my cousin, talked my dad into going to work in the coal mine."

Edith was quite helpful in identifying folks and establishing familial links between them, all the while sharing with us her humor and incredibly sharp memory. At one point an exchange erupted between Edith and Glona over "Aunt Bertie." Glona respectfully challenged Edith with, "You mean, Aunt Bertha?" "No," replied Edith, "Bertie was Aunt Maude's and Uncle Bill's daughter, and Bertha, Mother's half-sister, wasn't a Gooch. She was a Higgins and she married Harry Hoffman." Edith went on to say that "Bertie married Freddy Meyer."

Kay, so overwhelmed with this exchange, said, "I gotta go now, Clyde — I'm so confused...," with Glona then replying to her mom, "I got it straight now." And Kay asking, jokingly, "Glona, have you got it straight now?"

"Roy and May Davis used to live there where I used to live in the same house — ain't there now — that's how I got to know, well, of course, everybody knew everybody then anyhow, still do, but that's how I got to know all you people — Clyde and all the Davises and all of you, through May and Roy. I grew up with all of them kids, Ethel, Joe, Everett — went to school with them, me and Everett were in the same grade."

Edith added, "Ethel Davis married Onus Singleton. He run [*sic*] the shoe repair shop over in Danville."

Sadly, Edith passed away July 13, 2007. She was eighty-seven and had been a lifelong resident of Fairmount. Her obituary in *The Sidell Reporter* mentioned that she was a longtime Fairmount area housekeeper and that she had worked in several local establishments, including 38½ years at the First National Bank of Fairmount and thirty years with the Carrington Funeral Home. She was survived by three sons, two daughters, fourteen grandchildren, thirty great-grandchildren and two great-great-grandchildren. But it was her penchant for working on her scrapbooks that was of particular interest to me. She would delight in regaling who was related to whom in and around the village, because Edith Allen's passion was collecting obituaries.

We gathered around the dining table in this comfortable home, spreading out our documents and recording equipment, as the grandfather clock softly chimed and the decorative Halloween, doll-like, electrically powered "witch" stood on a table behind us, holding a lighted pumpkin, as it gyrated rhythmically in the background.

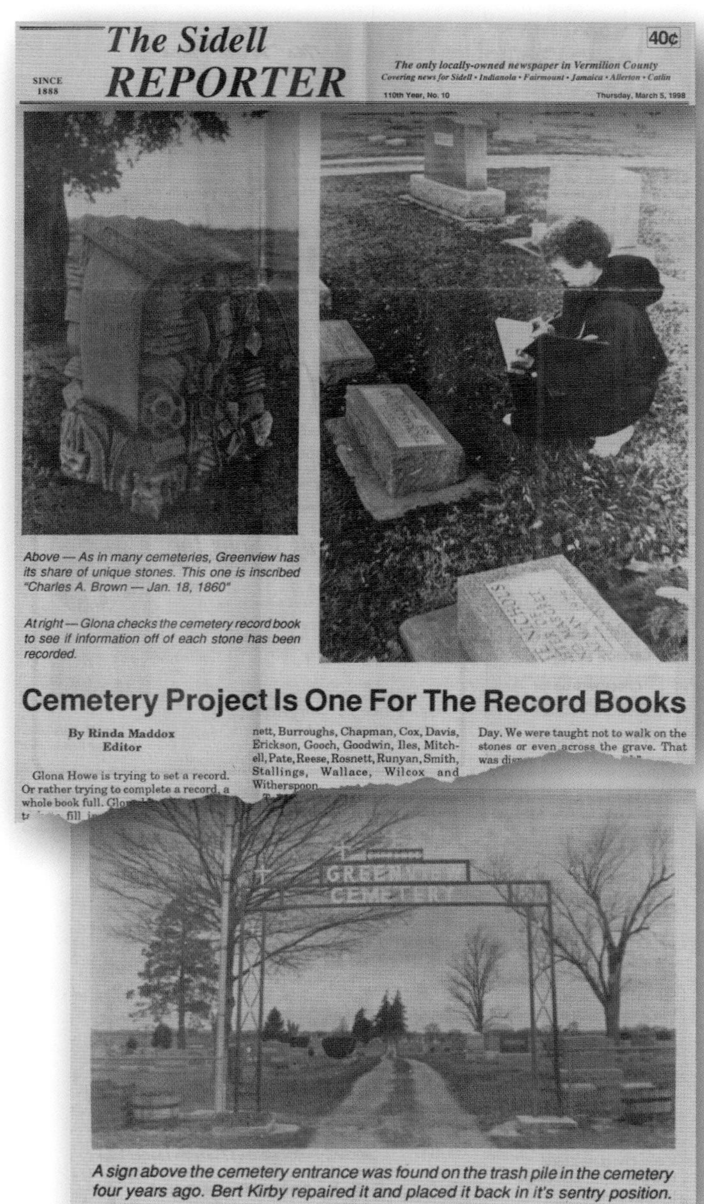

The Sidell REPORTER

SINCE 1888

40¢

The only locally-owned newspaper in Vermilion County
Covering news for Sidell • Indianola • Fairmount • Jamaica • Allerton • Catlin

110th Year, No. 10 Thursday, March 5, 1998

Above — As in many cemeteries, Greenview has its share of unique stones. This one is inscribed "Charles A. Brown — Jan. 18, 1860"

At right — Glona checks the cemetery record book to see if information off of each stone has been recorded.

Cemetery Project Is One For The Record Books

By Rinda Maddox
Editor

Glona Howe is trying to set a record. Or rather trying to complete a record, a whole book full. Glo...

...nett, Burroughs, Chapman, Cox, Davis, Erickson, Gooch, Goodwin, Iles, Mitchell, Pate, Reese, Rosnett, Runyan, Smith, Stallings, Wallace, Wilcox and Witherspoon.

Day. We were taught not to walk on the stones or even across the grave. That was di...

A sign above the cemetery entrance was found on the trash pile in the cemetery four years ago. Bert Kirby repaired it and placed it back in it's sentry position.

"Greenview Cemetery is located in the Village of Fairmount in Vance Township. The plat was filed November 29, 1864. The cemetery is two-tenths of a mile west of the intersection of North Main Street and West State Street." Source: <http://www.bumbery.com/genealogy/> web site.

Edith Allen Kirby's obituaries were a daisy chain of family links that she referred to during our meeting at Glona's home to spark her memory and to punctuate her rich stories of Fairmount's past inhabitants. Many of the obits reproduced in this book were those provided by Edith Allen and Glona. For that I remain ever grateful to them both.

Glona's husband George had been "helping the late David Glenn in the summer of 1993 mow the cemetery." Since 1994 the care, upkeep, and recordkeeping of the cemetery had become a family affair of the Howes. Even the Howe children and grandchildren volunteered their time. Mounting several mowers, they would take off from the Howe residence on East State Street in a straight shot over to the cemetery six blocks across town. They kicked in for the gas for mowers and weed wackers. In 2004 Vance Township took over the mowing and for the first time in eleven years, they and the neighbors didn't have to mow. Now, donations can be applied to projects such as repairing headstones and restoring the road within the cemetery.

Having so many relatives buried in the Greenview Cemetery, being indebted to Glona for all her help with my family history, and equally impressed by her good deeds, I began, in 1997, to make annual financial contributions toward the upkeep of the cemetery.

There are more than three hundred names represented in the Greenview Cemetery. Among Davises and Gooches are other family relations — Goodwins, Delaneys, Woodards, Reeves, Smiths, among others. Surprisingly, just outside of the village of Fairmount lays the Davis Cemetery. Larger than Greenview, it is filled with Davis headstones, not one of which has been confirmed as a relation of mine. Not that we didn't try to make a connection.

Glona Howe's work has not gone unrecognized by the community. To realize that Glona and her commitment to the resting place of so many of its citizens is greatly appreciated, one only has to refer to the newspaper article "Cemetery Project Is One For The Record Books," which appeared on March 5, 1998, in *The Sidell Reporter.*

Down Home

Each of my visits to Fairmount and the surrounding area is always filled with hope and the expectation of turning up one more clue to the life of my father. His life is for me an unfinished puzzle with many missing pieces. Material clues remain increasingly elusive. So for now, I'm more mollified than content. Between visits to Fairmount, I frequently recall this serene sense of place. A village set upon a landscape of fields, homes, churches, and some businesses under a vast sky split by a horizon line, which is barely disrupted by the occasional farmhouse, granary, or village water tower. A place my father and his family called home for more than forty years.

Fairmount, like other towns I've visited, such as Longwood, Missouri, and Richmond, Kentucky, was a hub of hospitality for the Davises and Gooches. The colloquial "down home" was probably more than a simple phrase if ever used by my father. Because of his numerous trips from Chicago to Fairmount during his lifetime, the 166 mile drive "down" Interstate 57 or Routes 41 and 63 in Indiana, meant going "home." "Going home" to the comforting embrace of family and friends, where he lies today.

Notes

1. "Fairmount, Illinois," <http://www.wikipedia.com>. See links to USGS detail on Fairmont; Katherine Stapp and W.I. Bowman, *History Under Our Feet: The Story of Vermilion County, Illinois* (Danville, Ill.: Interstate Printers and Publishers, 1968), 34–35; U.S. Gazetteer files: 2000 and 1990; U.S. Census Bureau (2005–05–03); American FactFinder, U.S. Census Bureau; Illinois Railroad Map, Illinois Department of Transportation (January 2006).
2. Ibid.
3. Ibid.
4. Ibid.

Galen White b. August 25, 1759

Daniel Maupin b. ca. 1754

Two Patriots

Two Revolutionary War veterans, both serving from Virginia, and both participating in the last conclusive battle of the war, were ancestors of Thomas Gooch. On his mother's side was his grandfather, Daniel Maupin, and on his father's side of the family was his great-grandfather, Galen White.

Daniel Maupin was born about 1754, according to the deposition of Matthew Mullins in Daniel's Revolutionary War pension file.[1] Daniel was called into the service for two tours of duty, beginning in 1780. Residing in Albemarle County, Virginia, when he was drafted, he served a total of about one year. Maupin was a sergeant during the first and second tours of his service and an orderly sergeant during the last six months of his service.[2] Daniel saw action at Jamestown and marched some prisoners of war back to Richmond, Virginia. He served under the Marquis de Lafayette at one point; his unit destroyed bridges over the Chickahominy River, which is a tributary of the James River. In 1781 he was involved in the siege of Yorktown and remained there until the surrender of Cornwallis.[3]

Most Maupin researchers agree that Daniel was married probably three times: the first wife unknown; the second was Betsy Gentry, daughter of Martin Gentry, of Albemarle County, Virginia.[4] His third wife was Margaret (Peggy) McWilliams, whom he married in Madison County, Kentucky, in 1805.[5] She received $89 for Daniel Maupin's pension. In 1853 she applied for a pension as a widow of a Revolutionary War veteran, and in 1855 she applied for bounty land.[6]

Daniel Maupin died August 29, 1832, according to George W. Maupin, a son.[7] Daniel's will was filed in Book E, page 308, in Madison County, Kentucky:

> 3 April 1829 I, Daniel Maupin of Madison County, KY…my desire is that my…wife Peggy Maupin…. In case I made any advancement to any of my children by my last wife before my death…, I have already advanced to my son Washington Maupin $1200.00 and to my daughter Cynthia who married Thomas Gates $600.00…. The children which I had by my first wife Betsy Maupin, I have done for them what I consider as much as I? Have? Able? It is my wish…that they have no further share…. I hereby revoke all former wills and do declare this my only last will and testament, and I do hereby constitute and appoint my son, Washington Maupin and son Leland Maupin when they are age 21, and my friend Archibald Woods Jr. Executors. Recorded 15 Oct 1832.[8]

Though Eliza Ann Maupin was not named in her father's will, a deed in Madison County, Kentucky, dated February 9, 1838, speaks for itself:

> Chiswell Gooch and Eliza his wife, formerly Eliza Maupin of the County of Rockcastle…sell for $460.00 to L.D. Maupin all their right, title, and interest that they acquired by the last will and testament of Daniel Maupin, Deceased, father of said Eliza….[9]

The author of a recent Maupin genealogy, Mrs. Dorothy Shaffett, says that Daniel Maupin's grave, and that of his father, lies in a neglected graveyard "on the Big Hill Road, 3 or 4 miles out of Richmond, Kentucky."[10] She also says that Daniel was a courier for General George Washington, but there was no evidence in the pension file to attest to that fact, except that Daniel's rank was that of an orderly sergeant, an officer who carries messages.[11]

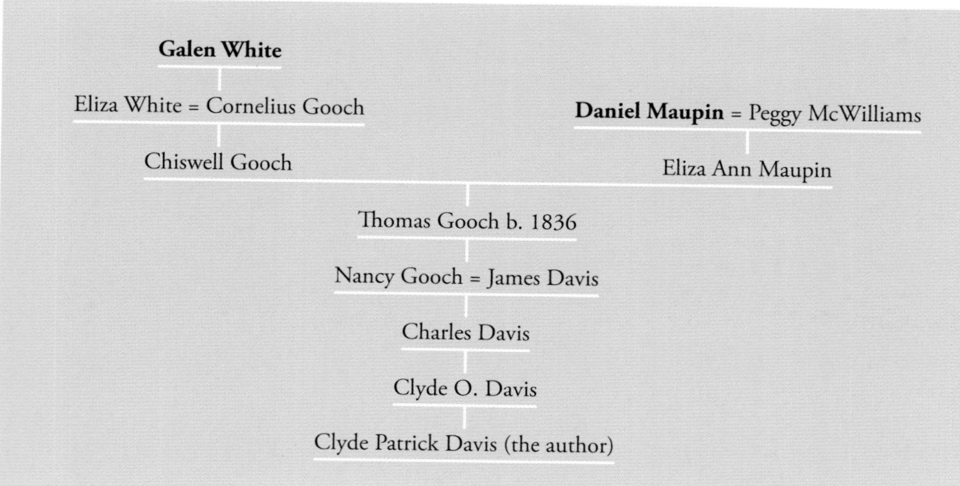

Mrs. Shaffett and other Maupin genealogists estimate that Daniel Maupin may have had twenty-three children by his three wives.[12] He lived a long life for those times, leaving his home in Albemarle County, Virginia, and taking the risk of coming to the wilderness of Kentucky at an early day, prior to 1805.

Thomas Gooch's paternal great-grandfather was Galen White. He was a private in the company commanded by Captain Pollard and Colonel Parker in Virginia from 1776–1778. On August 1832, at age seventy-three, he appeared in open court in Madison County, Kentucky, and declared that he had enlisted in the Marine Services in June of 1776 in Orange County, Virginia, had served eighteen months, and

Know all men by these presents that we Daniel Maupin & John McWilliams are held and firmly bound unto Christopher Greenup Esquire Governor of the Commonwealth of Kentucky in the Just and full sum of fifty pounds current money to which payment well and truly to be made to the said Governor or his Successors we bind ourselves our heirs Exrs and admrs firmly by these presents Sealed with our seals and dated this 10th day of June 1805

The Condition of the above Obligation is such that whereas there is a Marriage Shortly intended to be had and Solemnized between the above Daniel Maupin & Peggy McWilliams both of Madison County if there be no lawfull cause to obstruct the same then the above obligation to be void otherwise to remain in full force and virtue

Daniel Maupin (Seal)

Signed Sealed & Delivered In presence of — John McWilliams (Seal)

Madison County, Kentucky, Bond for Daniel Maupin and Peggy McWilliams to marry June 10, 1805

46 I do hereby certify that I joined together in the holy state of matrimony the man named persons by virtue of license and in the order of their several states ...

Daniel Maupin and Peggy McWilliams this 16th day June 1805

was honorably discharged in December 1777 at Williamsburg, Virginia. In the spring of 1778 he again enlisted under Commander Ambrose Madison and exchanged service with his brother, Ambrose White, and went into the 1st Virginia Regiment under Captain Alexander Parker and Colonel Richard Parker. He was honorably discharged in August of 1780 at Charleston, South Carolina, by General C. Scott.[13]

He also served as a substitute for his father Henry White, who was drafted in the summer of 1781. He served until the surrender of Cornwallis and was discharged at Yorktown. He was involved in the sieges of Savannah, Georgia, and Charleston, South Carolina and was at Camden, South Carolina when General Gates was defeated. He was also involved in a siege of Yorktown.[14]

Galen White drew a pension of $80 per year until his death November 2, 1833. His grave has fared better than Daniel Maupin's, as Galen White's has been marked by the DAR in Madison County, Kentucky in the Galen White Cemetery. "Galen White born in Orange County Virginia Aug 25 1759 – 4 Nov 1833."[15] His wife Mildred (28 May 1762? – 10 Dec 1819) and probably several of their children were buried there, as was the second husband of their daughter Eliza White Gooch Hill (John Hill 1778 – 15 Feb 1831).[16] *A.H.*

Notes

1. Deposition of Matthew Mullins, Daniel Maupin, Revolutionary War Pension File W-556, Roll #1655, NARA, Washington, D.C.
2. Ibid.
3. Ibid.
4. Dorothy Shaffett, *The Story of Gabriel and Marie Maupin* (Baltimore: Gateway Press, 1993), 250.
5. Shaffett, *The Story of Gabriel and Marie Maupin,* 248.
6. Daniel Maupin, Revolutionary War Pension File W-556, Roll #1655, NARA, Washington, D.C.
7. Ibid.
8. Madison Co., Kentucky, Will Book E:308-09, FHL #183268.
9. Madison Co., Kentucky, Deed Book W:272, FHL #183294.
10. Shaffett, *The Story of Gabriel and Marie Maupin*, 247.
11. Shaffett, *The Story of Gabriel and Marie Maupin*, 248.
12. E-mail from William Albertson to Alice Henson, 2 April 2002.
13. Galen White, Revolutionary War Pension File S331476, Roll #2553, NARA, Washington, D.C.
14. Ibid.
15. Kathy Vockery, *Madison County Cemetery Records* (Richmond, Ky.: K. Vockery, 1999), II: 14.
16. Ibid.

Galen White b. August 25, 1759

Daniel Maupin b. ca. 1754

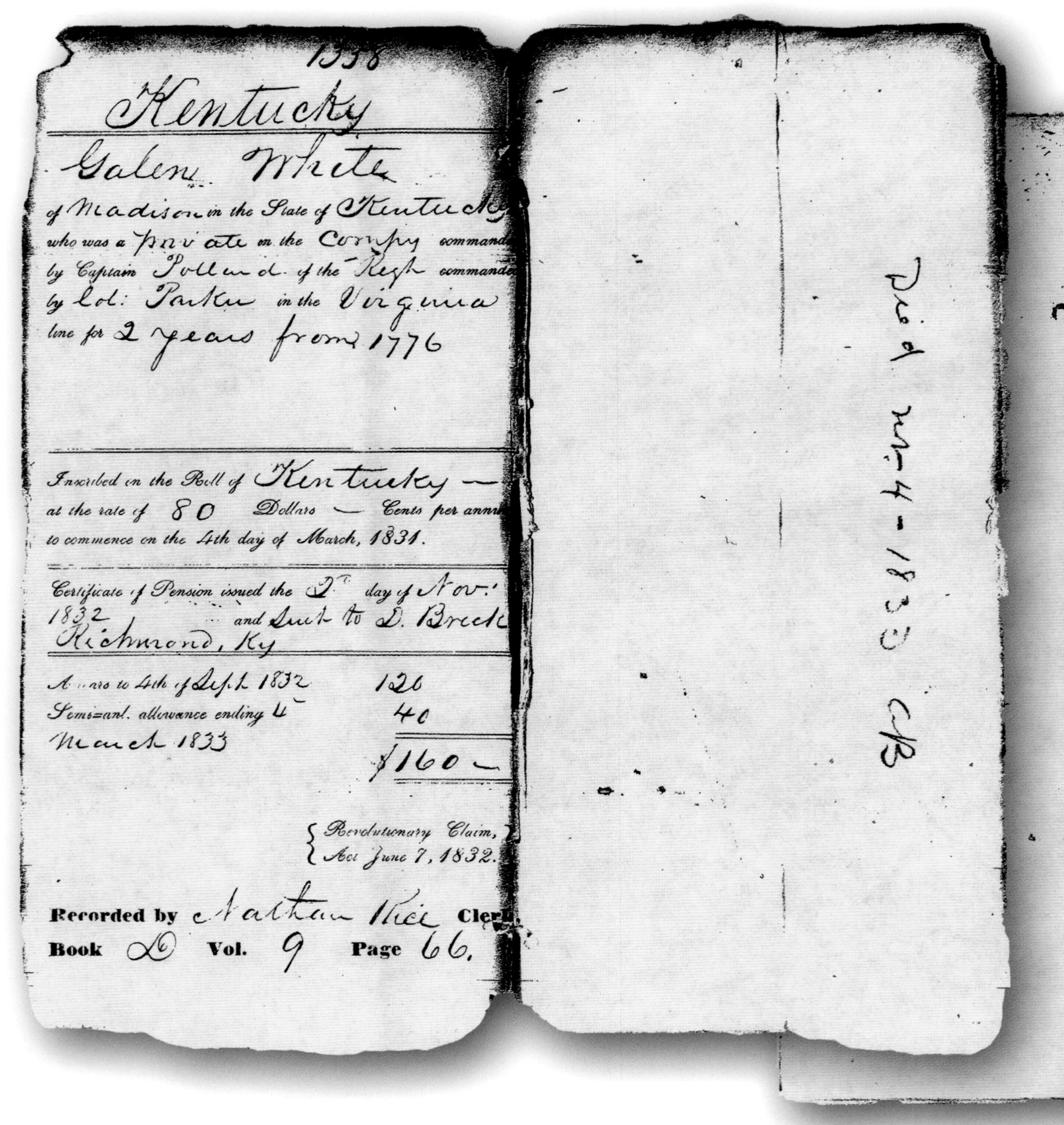

1338

Kentucky

Galen White

of Madison in the State of Kentuck

who was a private in the Compy commande

by Captain Pollard of the Regt commande

by Col: Parker in the Virginia

line for 2 years from 1776

Inscribed on the Roll of Kentucky —

at the rate of 80 Dollars — Cents per ann

to commence on the 4th day of March, 1831.

Certificate of Pension issued the 2d day of Nov.

1832 and Sent to D. Breck

Richmond, Ky

Arrears to 4th of Sept 1832	120
Semi-anl. allowance ending 4th March 1833	40
	$160 —

Revolutionary Claim, Act June 7, 1832.

Recorded by Nathan Rice Cler

Book D Vol. 9 Page 66.

Died Nov 4 - 1833 CB

Galen White, Revolutionary War Pension and Bounty Land Files, 1800 – 1900; micropublication M804 (National Archives), Roll 56

(8—1776)

SERVICE Va. White, Galen NUMBER S. 31476

CONTENTS

5713

White, Galen

Virginia.

(Revolutionary War.)

Private | Private

CARD NUMBERS.

39172567

№ 2993

Galen White,

Declaration

£O Sep 16

from 1777

private 2 years

$80

on Roll

W | Va.

Galen White

Sol Inf.

Appears in a

Book *

under the following heading:

"A List of Soldiers of the Virginia Line on Continental Establishment who have received Certificates for the balance of there full pay Agreeable to an Act of Assembly passed November Session 1781."

(Revolutionary War.)

By whom Received himself

Day when Sept 16, 1784.

Sum £19-4-10

Remarks:

*This book bears the following certificate: "This Register contains a true abstract of all the certificates issued at the Auditor's Office to Officers & Soldiers of the Virginia line on Continental establishment. J. Pendleton, Auditor.

Aud[rs] Office, 1 Aug[t] 1792.
Teste: J. Carter."

Vol. 176; page 331

RWLarson

(547) Copyist.

At right: Galen White, compiled military record (private, Virginia), compiled service records of soldiers who served in the American Army during the Revolutionary War, micropublication M881 (National Archives), Roll 1096

GALEN WHITE b. August 25, 1759

DANIEL MAUPIN b. ca. 1754

R

3—525.

DEPARTMENT OF THE INTERIOR,

BUREAU OF PENSIONS.

S.F. 31476

Washington, D. C., ..., 19...

In reply to your request of ...., received .... for a statement of the military history of Galen White a soldier of the REVOLUTIONARY WAR, you will find below the desired information as contained in his (or his widow's) application for pension on file in this Bureau.

DATES OF ENLISTMENT OR APPOINTMENT.	LENGTH OF SERVICE.	RANK.	OFFICERS UNDER WHOM SERVICE WAS RENDERED.		STATE.
			CAPTAIN.	COLONEL.	
June 1776	18 mos.	Pvt.	Benjamin Pollard	"	Va.
			Davis	"	
Spring 1778	Aug. 1780		Ambrose Madison		
⁘			Alexander Parker	Richard Parker	
* Summer 1781	Tr. of Commissar		Hawkins	Edmunds	
* Substituted	for his father Henry White				

Battles engaged in, Savannah, Charleston, Camden, Siege of York

Residence of soldier at enlistment, enlisted in Orange Co. Va.

Date of application for pension, Aug. 13, 1832. His cl. was al.

Residence at date of application, Madison Co. Ky.

Age at date of application, 73 yrs.

Remarks: "

⁘ Substituted for his brother Ambrose when he entered Capt. Alexander Parkers co.

Very respectfully,

6—2856

Commissioner.

Bureau of Pensions response to a request for Galen White's military record during the Revolutionary War. The application for pension was dated August 13, 1832, at which time he was 73 years old, according to this document.

SERVICE

Va.

Maupin, Daniel
Margaret

NUMBER

W. 556

B.L. Wt. 26486-160-55

CONTENTS

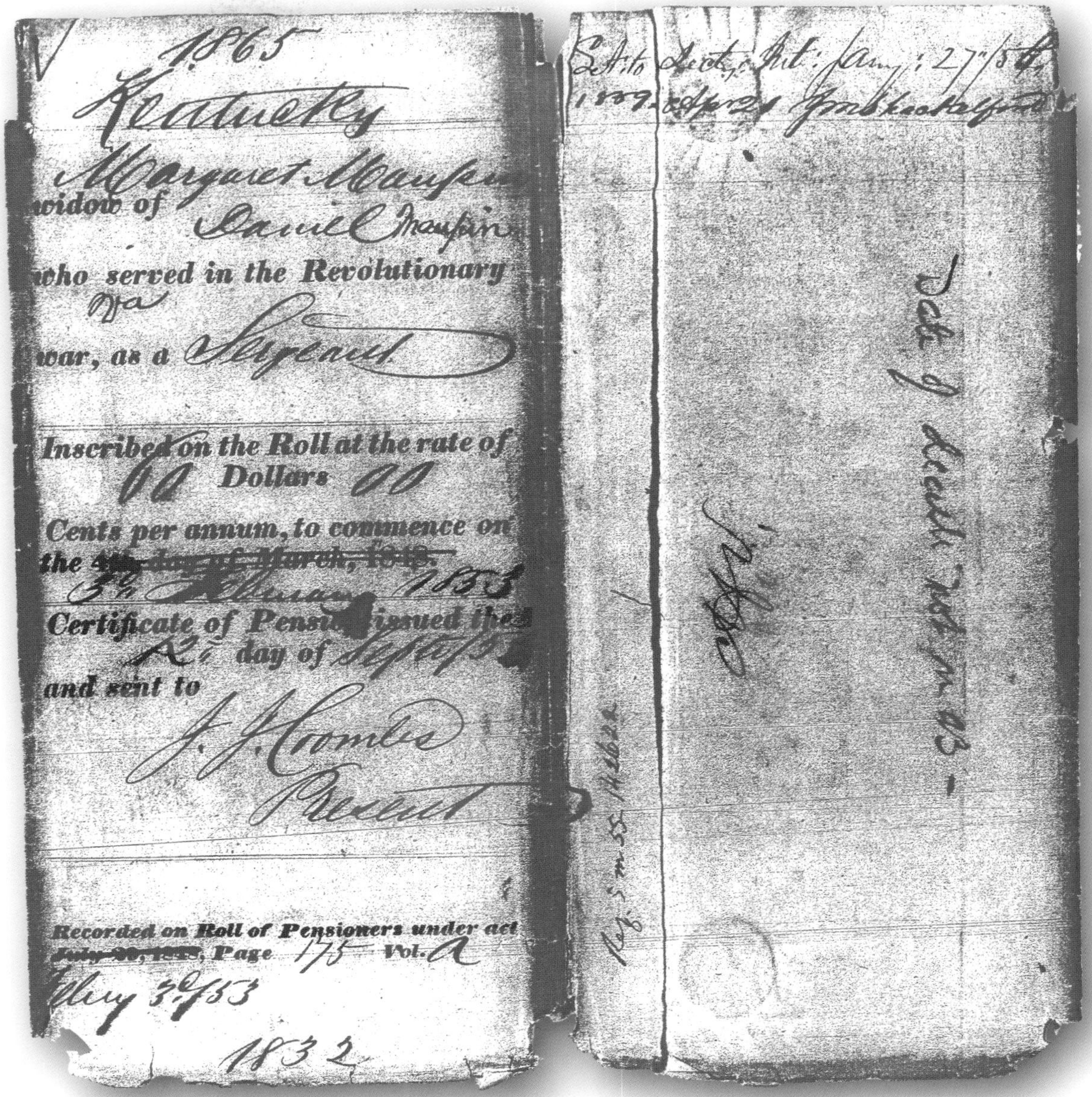

1865

Kentucky

Margaret Maupin

widow of Daniel Maupin

who served in the Revolutionary

Va

war, as a Sergeant

Inscribed on the Roll at the rate of

60 Dollars 00

Cents per annum, to commence on

the ~~4th day of March, 1848.~~

3rd February 1853

Certificate of Pension issued the

22 day of Sept 53

and sent to

J. J. Coombs

Present

Recorded on Roll of Pensioners under act

~~July 29, 1848~~, Page 175 Vol. A

1832

Date of death not on G3 -

Record of enrollment of Daniel Maupin's widow, Margaret Maupin, to receive $60 per year in pension.

Galen White b. August 25, 1759

Daniel Maupin b. ca. 1754

SERVICE

Va.

Maupin, Daniel
Margaret

NUMBER

W. 556

B.L.Wt. 26486-160-55

he died Aug. 29, 1832.
CONTENTS

State of Kentucky } sct.
Madison county, }

On this 3rd day of December, 1832, personally appeared in open Court, before the Worshipful, the County court of Madison, now sitting Matthew Mullins, a resident of Madison county, State of Kentucky, aged 68 years, who being first duly sworn according to law, doth, on his oath make the following declaration, for the benefit of Margaret Maupin, widow of Daniel Maupin, deceased, in order to obtain for said Margaret Maupin, the benefit of the act of Congress, passed June 7, 1832. He, the said Mullins states that the said Daniel Maupin, now deceased, entered the service of the United States under the following named officers and served as herein stated. He was drafted into the militia service in the year 1780, (the time he does not recollect,) under Capt. John Harris, Lieut. James Jones he thinks, Maj. McElhoney, Col. Holt Richardson, and Gen. Stevens. He rendezvoused at Sneed's below Charlottsville, marched from thence to Rich

Testimony of Matthew Mullins on December 3, 1832, in support of Margaret Maupin's petition for benefits under the act of Congress of June 7, 1832. Mullins testified regarding Daniel Maupin's service during the American Revolution.

mond, from thence to the Maupin Mills, from thence to Jamestown, where he was attacked by the British; from there he went to Williamsburgh, and thence to Little York, and back to the Half way House, and thence to Richmond, Va. with some prisoners of War, where he Maupin was discharged, and received a discharge signed by Col. Holt Richardson. He cannot say the precise time Maupin was discharged. But in a very short time after his discharge he was again drafted into the service under Capt. John Hunt, Maj. Dabney, Col. James Ennis, and Maj. Gen. Lafayette, the commander. He again rendezvoused at Sneed's below Charlottesville, marched to Richmond, from thence on a scouting expedition and tore up and destroyed the Bridges over Chickahominy river; during this there were some little fighting or skirmishing with the British; from thence he returned to Albermarle county to intercept the British troops and keep them from taking the goods belonging to the Americans stationed at the Point-Fork of James River, near Albermarle old court house; from thence he was marched to Louisa county, Va. where the Marquis Lafayette commanded, and received a discharge signed by Col. Ennis, which deponent thinks was in the winter 1780 and 1781. He was again drafted into the service in April or May 1781, for six months, under Capt. John Miller, Col. Reuben Lindsay and again rendezvoused at Sneed's below Charlottsville, marched from thence to Richmond, Virginia, from thence to Williamsburgh, where all the Virginia Militia rendezvoused under Governor Nelson, and from thence to the Siege of York, and there remained in the service until after the Capture of Cornwallis, and was discharged and received a discharge signed by Col. Reuben Lindsay. Maupin resided in Albermarle county, Virginia, when he entered the service at each of his tours. Gen Wayne of the continental line was with the troops on his second tour. he joined him at West Ham on James River. Col. Dick and Maj. Boice was with us, part of the time. He believes Maupin has lost all his discharges, and has no documentary evidence; This deponent knows Maupin was nine or ten years older than himself. He has known the said Maupin intimately for the last sixty years. They were born and raised in the same neighborhood, and have always resided within a few miles of each other. This deponent further states that himself and Maupin belonged to the same company on

each of the above tours of duty, and messed in the same mess with him during their whole service, and he knows said Maupin served in all twelve months. Maupin was a Sergeant during the first and second tours of his service, and an Orderly Sergeant during the last six months of his service. Maupin is known in his late neighborhood to the Rev. Thomas Ballew and James Still.
Sworn to, and subscribed, the day and year aforesaid.

Mathew Mullins (seal)

GALEN WHITE b. August 25, 1759

DANIEL MAUPIN b. ca. 1754

Know all men by these presents, that we, Daniel Maupin and John McWilliams are held & firmly bound unto Christopher Greenup Esquire, Governor of the Commonwealth of Kentucky in the just & full sum of fifty Pounds, Current Money, to which payment well and truly to be made to the said Governor or his successors, we bind ourselves our heirs Exe^rs, and adm^rs firmly by these presents. Sealed with our seal and dated this 10th day of June 1805

The Condition of the above obligation is such, that whereas, there is a Marriage shortly ~~to be had~~ intended to be had and solemnized between the above bound Daniel Maupin and Peggy McWilliams both of Madison County. If there be no lawful Cause to obstruct the same, then the above obligation to be void, Otherwise to remain in full force and virtue.

Signed, Sealed and delivered in presence of. Daniel Maupin (Seal)
John McWilliams (Seal)

I do hereby certify that I joined together in the holy state of Matrimony the under named persons by virtue of license and in the order of the several dates, viz: Daniel Maupin and Peggy Williams, this 16th day of June Eighteen hundred and five

Marriage record of Daniel Maupin and Peggy McWilliams as copied by the clerk at the Office of Pensions in Madison County, Kentucky, as proof of their marriage.

further ... in fact of ...

She further States that She was married to the said Daniel Maupin in Madison County and State of Kentucky on the 16th day of July A.D. 1806 by one Mr Clarke a minister of the gospel, and that her name before her said Marriage was Margaret McWilliams, That her said husband died in Madison County and State of Kentucky on the 29th day of August A.D. 1832, and that She is now a widow

The above document in part states that Peggy McWilliams Maupin "... was married to the said Daniel Maupin in Madison County and State of Kentucky on the 16th day of July A.D. 1806 by one Mr. Clarke a Minister of the gospel and that her name before her said Marriage was Margaret McWilliams, that her said husband died in Madison County and State of Kentucky on the 29th day of August A.D. 1832 and that she is now a widow...."

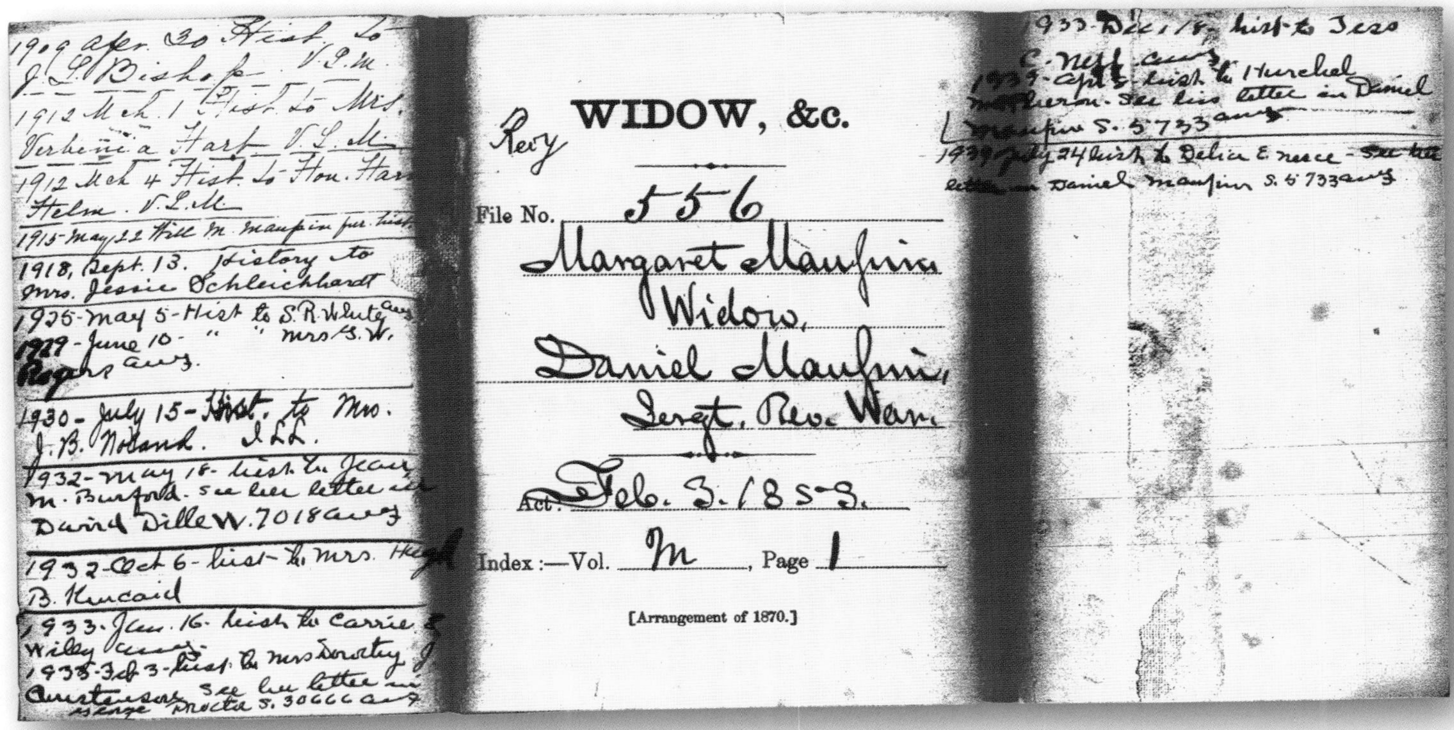

1909 Apr. 30 Hist to J. L. Bishop V.S.M.
1912 Mch. 1 Hist to Mrs. Verhenia Hart V.L.M.
1912 Mch 4 Hist to Hon. Harr Helm. V.L.M.
1915 May 22 Hill M. Maupin fee. hist
1918, Sept. 13. History to Mrs. Jessie Schleichhardt
1925 May 5 Hist to S. R. White aws
1929 June 10 " " Mrs. S. W. Rogers aws.
1930 July 15 Hist. to Mrs. J. B. Noland. I.L.L.
1932 May 18 hist to Jean M. Burford. See her letter in David Dille W. 7018 aws
1932 Oct 6 hist to Mrs. Hugh B. Kincaid
1933 Jan. 16 hist to Carrie E. Wiley aws
1938 3d 3 Hist to Mrs Dorothy J. Austensar See her letter in George Procter S. 30666 aws

Rev

WIDOW, &c.

File No. 556

Margaret Maupin
Widow.

Daniel Maupin,
Sergt. Rev. War

Act Feb. 3. 1853.

Index:—Vol. M, Page 1

[Arrangement of 1870.]

1933 Dec 18 hist to Jess C. Neff aws
1939 Apr 5 hist to Herschel McPherson. See his letter in Daniel Maupin S. 5733 aws
1939 July 24 hist to Delia E. Neace See her letter in Daniel Maupin S. 5733 aws

Declaration of Margaret "Peggy" McWilliams Maupin to procure a Revolutionary War widow's pension.

Thomas Gooch d. 1803

A Fortune Divided Eight Ways

The Gooch family name appeared in Virginia well before the American Revolution. A William Gooch was a colonial governor of Virginia from 1727–1749, an astounding twenty-two years. There was another William Gooch who died as early as 1655 in York County, Virginia. Whether our Thomas Gooch was a member of one of these early families in Virginia, we have not been able to determine.

We know more about the death of Thomas Gooch of Louisa County, Virginia, than we do about his life. His estate papers and records show that he died a wealthy man. The inventory of his property filed January 13, 1806 included twenty-two Negroes, a desk and book case, walnut table, candlesticks, 4,000 pounds of tobacco, 2,000 nails, 4,000 bricks, a still, cattle, sheep, and oxen.[1] This kind of personal property indicates that Thomas was well-to-do. In 1807 his estate totaled 1,220 pounds, six shillings and eleven pence. This amount converts to about $174,000 today.[2]

Thomas Gooch owned about 350 acres of land. To settle his estate, the heirs, including Lucy, his widow, sued the administrator, Gideon Gooch.[3] The chancery court of Louisa County, Virginia, appointed three commissioners: Garland Anderson, William Thomson, and Henry Bibb to partition the land among Gideon Gooch, James Gooch, Polly Gooch, Cornelius Gooch, William Gooch, Thomas Washington Gooch, and Overton Gooch. The latter two were under age when their father died, so Gideon Gooch was appointed their guardian.[4] William became twenty-one by September of 1804.[5]

The chancery court case stated that Thomas Gooch died sometime in the fall of 1803. A plat was drawn by John Edwards in 1804 to parcel the land to each heir. The land cornered on McGehee, Henry Edwards, and Richard Thomson. An older daughter, Elizabeth, who had married John Draper, had previously received her share of land, so she was not included in the partition. Lucy, the widow, received one-third of the property, or about ninety-nine acres. She also received two Negroes, Tom and Jack.[6] As a widow, she was entitled to one-third of Thomas's property by virtue of her dower rights, which derived from English common law, and which was followed in the American colonies and continued in most U.S. states well into the nineteenth century.

Thomas Gooch had purchased this land from Thomas Thomson and his wife Ann on November 10, 1777.[7] We could speculate on Thomas Gooch's origins, but it would only be guessing. Some say that he was the overseer for Cornelius Dabney from 1773–1777 in Louisa County, Virginia.[8] Some say he may be related to a James Gooch of King William County, Virginia, who purchased land adjacent to Thomas Gooch in Louisa County in 1778, but did not move there.[9] The "Douglas Register," a book of records by the Reverend Douglas, lists the birth date and baptism of a Gideon Gooch, who could be the one in our family:[10] "Gideon Gooch born 20 June 1773 and baptized 15 August 1773 to Thomas Gouge and Lucy Higgins."

Whether this Gideon is the son of our Thomas and Lucy Gooch has not really been proven. Whether the wife of our Thomas Gooch was Lucy Higgins, we do not know. Many Gooch family researchers claim this Gideon as their own.

Piecing together the children of Thomas and Lucy Gooch, we have

1. Gideon Gooch born possibly 1773; married November 3, 1794 to Sally Maddison, daughter of John Maddison. Surety [bondsman for the marriage] Benjamin Hollins.[11] Gideon bought the parcels of land inherited by some of his brothers and sisters: James, Polly, William, Thomas W., and Cornelius. Then in 1815 he sold some of this land to Hugh Goodwin.[12] The deed stated that he and wife Sally lived in Orange County. We think that Gideon was a sibling to the others because he received an equal share in the estate of £117.[13]
2. Elizabeth Gooch married John Draper December 8, 1795, Surety, Thomas Gooch.[14]
3. James Gooch married Elizabeth Anthony October 11, 1803.[15] He sold his parcel of land inherited from his father to Gideon Gooch in 1804.[16]
4. Cornelius Gooch born possibly between 1775–1782, as he was twenty-one or older when his father died. He sold his land to Gideon Gooch in 1805 and left Louisa County about 1807, going to Madison County, Kentucky, where he married Eliza White, daughter of Galen White. (See his biography, page 358)
5. Thomas Washington Gooch died June 26, 1856.[17] He was twenty-one or over when his father died, and he sold his portion of land to Gideon Gooch in 1804.[18]
6. William Gooch born about 1783; became of age in September 1804, married Elizabeth Terry October 29, 1802. Surety, Gideon Gooch.[19] He sold his portion of his father's land in 1804 to Gideon Gooch.[20] He may be the William Gooch in the 1850 census of Louisa, Virginia, with a younger wife, Catharine. If so, his age is seventy.[21]
7. Mary "Polly" Gooch married James McAllister March 10, 1809. Surety, Overton Gooch. Witnesses: Susan Gooch and Polly C. Cole.[22] Polly Gooch sold her portion of her father's land to Gideon Gooch in 1804.[23]
8. Overton Gooch youngest child, born about 1790–1800; married Polley C. Cole June 24, 1809.[24] In the 1820 census of Louisa County, Overton and James Gooch were listed on the same page.[25] In 1830 Overton was listed as age 30–40, with two males and three females, and five slaves.[26]

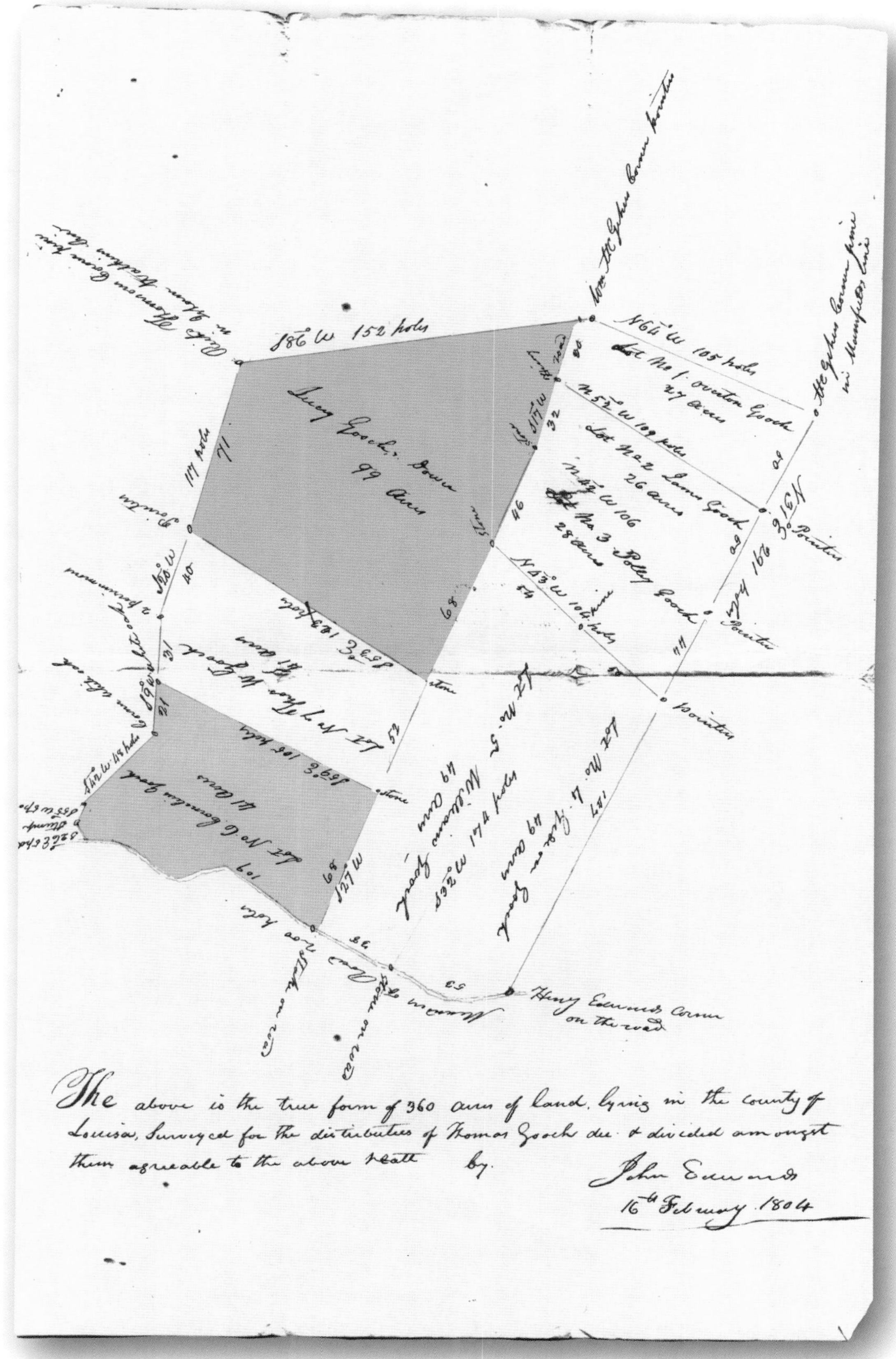

"The above is the true form of 360 acres of land lying in the county of Louisa, Surveyed for the distributees of Thomas Gooch dec & divided amongst them agreeable to the above platt by John Edwards, 16th February 1804." Highlighted sections are Lot No. 6 Cornelius Gooch, 41 acres, and Lucy Gooch, 99 acres.

Thomas Gooch died intestate in the fall of 1803. In February 1804, the Chancery Court awarded Lucy Gooch one third of the land and two slaves and ordered the sale of the remaining slaves. The land was divided as follows: Overton Gooch — 26 acres; James Gooch — 28 acres; Polly Gooch — 49 acres; William Gooch — 49 acres; Cornelius Gooch — 40 acres; Thomas W. Gooch — 41 acres; and Lucy Gooch — 99 acres. John Draper had already received a tract of land. Each heir received 117 pounds and 2 shillings.

THOMAS GOOCH d. 1803

After the death of Thomas, Lucy Gooch was listed on the 1810 Louisa County, Virginia, tax list.[27] The last deed that we could find for her was the epitome of creative financing. She used two Negroes, York and Charles, as collateral for a debt of her son Cornelius. The deed stated that if Cornelius did not pay $225 to Young Clayton and others by December 25, 1807, then James Gooch would sell the Negroes to pay the charges. This deed was a family affair, as it was signed by Cornelius Gooch, James Gooch, and witnessed by John Draper, Mary Gooch, and Thomas W. Gooch.[28]

We checked later deed and probate records to see if there was a record of the disposition of Lucy Gooch's property, but we did not find anything. She apparently was still living in 1815 when Gideon sold a large portion of the estate, as the deed stated that the land was bordering on his mother's dower.[29]

Though Thomas Gooch was a wealthy man when he died in 1803, his estate was divided according to Virginia law with one-third going to his widow and two-thirds to be divided among seven children, Elizabeth Gooch Draper having already received her part. Each child received only 117 pounds — a stake, perhaps, but not really an inheritance. Some of the children stayed in Virginia, but several possibly sought greener pastures in the west. Maybe that is why our Cornelius Gooch took off for Kentucky. He could not make much of a living on his forty-one acres and, perhaps, he wanted to begin a new life and make his own fortune. Unfortunately for him, the frontier of Kentucky was cruel and he died in 1810. *A.H.*

Notes

1. Louisa Co., Virginia, Will Book 5 (1801-1817):213, FHL #32194.
2. Lawrence H. Officer, "Purchasing Power of British Pounds from 1264–2006," <http://www.measuringworth.com>.
3. Louisa Co., Virginia, Chancery Court Cases, Lucy Gooch, et al., vs. Administrator of Thomas Gooch, 1809, #025, Library of Virginia, Richmond, Va.
4. Louisa Co., Virginia, Guardian Bonds and Accounts, 1767–1819, p. 355, Library of Virginia, Richmond, Va.
5. Ibid.
6. Louisa Co., Virginia, Chancery Court Cases, Lucy Gooch, et al., vs. Administrator of Thomas Gooch, 1809, #025, Library of Virginia, Richmond, Va.
7. Louisa Co., Virginia, Deed Book E:200–01, FHL #32203.
8. Daniel Mahar website, <http://www.geocities.com/Heartland/Farm4162/goochtom.html?200723>.
9. Maxine Ball Dark note to Clyde P. Davis, 1999; Daniel Mahar website.
10. William Douglas, *The Douglas Register: being a detailed record of births, marriages and deaths together with other interesting notes, as kept by the Rev. William Douglas, from 1750 to 1797: an index of Goochland wills, notes on the French-Huguenot refugees who lived in Manakin-town* (Richmond, Va.: J.W. Fergusson & Sons, 1928), 201.
11. Kathleen Booth Williams, comp., *Marriages of Louisa County, Virginia, 1766–1815* (Alexandria, Va.: K.B. Williams, 1959), 41.
12. Louisa Co., Virginia, Deed Book M:592, FHL #32207.
13. Louisa Co., Virginia, Chancery Court Cases, Lucy Gooch, et al., vs. Administrator of Thomas Gooch, 1809, #025, Library of Virginia, Richmond, Va.
14. Williams, *Marriages of Louisa County, Virginia*, 29.
15. Ibid., 41.
16. Louisa Co., Virginia, Deed Book J:748, FHL #32205.
17. Daniel Mahar website.
18. Louisa Co., Virginia, Deed Book J:749, FHL #32205.
19. Williams, *Marriages of Louisa County, Virginia*, 42.
20. Louisa Co., Virginia, Deed Book J:759, FHL #32205.
21. 1850 federal census, Virginia, Louisa Co., p. 413B.
22. Williams, *Marriages of Louisa County, Virginia*, 66.
23. Louisa Co., Virginia, Deed Book J:750, FHL #32205.
24. Williams, *Marriages of Louisa County, Virginia*, 41.
25. 1820 federal census, Virginia, Louisa Co., p. 131.
26. 1830 federal census, Virginia, Louisa Co., p. 17A & B.
27. Netti Schreiner-Yantis, trans. and ed., *A Supplement to the 1810 Census of Virginia: Tax lists of the counties for which the census is missing* (Springfield, Va.: Genealogical Books in Print, 1971), A-3.
28. Louisa Co., Virginia, Deed Book L:43, FHL #32206.
29. Louisa Co., Virginia, Deed Book M:592, FHL #32207.

To the worshipfull the justices of the County Court of Louisa sitting in chancery. humbly complaining shew to your worships your orators & oratrixes Lucy Gooch widow and relict of Thomas Gooch decd. John Draper and Elizabeth his wife formerly Gooch, James Gooch. Polly Gooch, Cornelius Gooch Thos. Washington Gooch & Wm. Gooch that the said Thos. Gooch departed this life some time in the fall of the year 1803 without first having made any will but died wholly intestate leaving a considerable estate consisting of both real & personal property. That a certain Gideon Gooch hath taken upon himself the administration of said estate whom together with Overton Gooch an infant child of sd. Thos. Gooch decd your orators & oratrixes pray may be made defendants to this their bill of complaint. That the said defts. together with your orators & oratrixes, James, Polly, Cornelius. Thos. Washington Gooch & Wm. Gooch are the only children of the said Thos. Gooch decd. That your orators & oratrixes are desirous to have their several & respective portions of said estate allotted to them to which they are entitled But that they are advised. it cannot be effected without the interposition of this worshipfull Court in as much as they are infants interested in the distribution of the same your orators & oratrixes therefore pray that your worships will appoint commissioners to audit state & settle the accounts of the administration of the said Gideon Gooch and also for the purpose of laying off and allotting to the compt. Lucy Gooch her dower in the real and personal estate of said decedant, and for dividing the remainder of said estate among the several distributees of sd. Thos. Gooch decd according to law upon their executing to said admr to refund their proportion of whatever debts may be hereafter found to be due and unpaid from said estate To the end therefore that the said defendants may be compelled to answer the several allegations in said bill contained may it

Above: Part of the record in the suit to settle the estate of Thomas Gooch, who died intestate in 1803. Gideon Gooch had appointed himself adminsitrator of the estate, and other heirs sued for their shares. The document continues on the next two pages.

please your worships to grant your orators and oratrixes the commonwealths writ of subpoena &c directed &c

The answer of Gideon Gooch admr of Thos Gooch decd & of Overton Gooch an infant by Gideon Gooch guardian & next friend by the Court appointed to defend him to a bill of complaint exhibited against them in the County Court of Louisa by Lucy Gooch widow & relict of Thos Gooch decd and by John Draper & Elizabeth his wife formerly Elizabeth Gooch, James Gooch, Polly Gooch, Cornelius Gooch & Thos Washington Gooch. These defts now and at all times hereafter saving and reserving to themselves all exceptions to the errors &c contained in said bill of complaint say that they do admit the truth of the allegations therein contained and are willing that this worshipfull Court should make a decree agreeable to the prayer thereof appointing proper commissioners carry said decree into effect hoping that the Court will pay due regard to their interest as infants incapable of acting for themselves. these defendants deny all fraud and combination & pray to be hence dismissed with their reasonable costs in this behalf expended

Gooch &c
against } Chancery
Gooch's admr &c

Gideon Gooch is appointed to answer for the infant defts whereupon this cause coming on tobe heard by consent of the parties on the bill answer and exhibits & the arguments of council. It is ordered & decreed by the Court that Garland Anderson William Thompson Henry Bibb

Continuation of the records in the suit over Thomas Gooch's estate. The document on the bottom of the next page addresses the sale of Thomas Gooch's slaves so that the proceeds can be divided among the heirs.

Charles Wright, Wm White or any three of them do audit state & settle the accts of the administration of the deft Gideon Gooch on the estate of Thos Gooch decd and that they lay off & allott to the compt Lucy Gooch as her dower one third part of the said decedants estate both real & personal & that they divide the ballance equally amongst the several distributees children of sd decedant according to law upon their executing to the admr bonds to refund their several proportions of whatever debts may hereafter be found to be due & unpaid from the said estate & make report to Court in order to a final decree, and in the division such of the distributees as may have received any real or personal estate from the sd decedant in his lifetime, by way of advancement shall bring the same into hotchpot before they can be entitled to any part of the real estate of said decedant. ~~and such of the distributees as may have received any personal estate from the said decedant in his lifetime by way of advancement shall also bring the same into hotchpot before they can be entitled to any part of the personal estate of said decd~~

A Copy John Poindexter Cll

Gooch &c
vs } In Chey
Gooches admr

The parties ~~compts~~ &c as a suppliment to ~~their bill~~ the foregoing decree pray that this worshipful court will order & decree that the balance of the slaves belonging to the decedants estate, except the widows dower, be sold by the admr on twelve months credit [illegible] of the purchaser or purchasers bonds with approved security to be by him sd admr & divided amongst the several distributees agreeable to the former decree in this cause

Thomas Gooch d. 1803

Pursuant to a decree of Louisa Court we have
proceeded to lay off and allott to Lucy Gooch the
widow of Thomas Gooch deceased as her dower one
third part of the land and Negros Tom and
Jack; and find it impracticable to divide the
balance of the Negros equally amongst the several distributees
children of the said decedant, and are of opinion
that it would be best to sell them. We have
also laid off and allotted the balance of the land in
the following manner viz. the lot number one
as in the annexed platt containing twenty seven acres
to Overton Gooch. Lot No. 2 containing twenty six acres
to James Gooch. Lot No. 3 containing twenty eight acres
to Polly Gooch. Lot No. 4 containing forty nine acres
to Gideon Gooch. Lot No. 5 containing forty nine
acres to William Gooch. Lot No. 6 containing forty
one acres to Cornelius Gooch. Lot No. 7 containing forty
one acres to Thomas W. Gooch. John Draper having
received from the sd decedant in his lifetime a Tract
of land by way of advancement and refusing to bring the same into hotchpot
is excluded from any part of the above land. Given
under our hands this 16th February 1804

Garld. Anderson
Wm. Thomas
Henry Bibb
Wm. White
Charles Wright

"Pursaunt to a decree of Louisa court…," the court-appointed commissioners divided Thomas Gooch's estate among his heirs, including the sale of several of Thomas Gooch's slaves.

The answer of Gideon Gooch admr of Thos Gooch decd & of ~~William~~ & Overton Gooch an Infant by Gideon Gooch their guardian and next friend by the court appointed to defend them to a Bill of complaint exhibited against them in the county court of Louisa by Lucy Gooch widow & relict of Thos Gooch decd and by John Draper & Elizabeth his wife formerly Elizabeth Gooch James Gooch Polly Gooch Cornelius Gooch & Thos Washington Gooch These Defts now and at times hereafter saving and reserving to themselves all exceptions to the errors &c contained in said Bill of complaint, say that they do admit the truth of the allegations therein contained and are willing that this worshipfull Court should make a decree agreable to the prayer thereof appointing Commissioners to carry said Decree in to proper effect hoping that the Court will pay due regard to their interests as infants incapable of acting for themselves. These Defts deny all fraud and Combination and pray to be hence dismissed with their reasonable Costs in this behalf expended.

Gooch &c
vs } In Chy.
Goochs admr &c

Gideon Gooch is appointed to answer for the Infant Defts. whereupon this cause coming on to be heard by consent of the parties, on the bill ans. & exhibits & the arguments of counsel. It is ordered & decreed by the court that Garland Anderson William Thompson Henry Bibb. Charles Wright Wm White & ~~Benjn Hollins~~ or any three of them do audit state & settle the acct. of the administration of the sd Deft. Gideon Gooch on the estate of Thos Gooch decd & that they lay off & allott to the Compt Lucy Gooch for her dower, one third part of the sd decedents estate both real & personal, & that they divide the balance equally amongst the several distributees of sd decedent according to law, upon their receiving to the sd admor bonds to refund their several proportions of whatever debts may hereafter be found to be due & unpaid from the said estate [illegible] court in order to a final decree & in that division such of the distributees as may have received any real or personal estate from the sd decedent in his life time, by way of advancement shall bring the same into hotchpot before they can be intitled to any part of the real or personal estate of said decedent — ~~and such of the distributees as may have received any personal estate from the said decedent in his life time by way of advancement shall also bring the same into hotchpot before they can be intitled to any part of the personal estate of said decd~~

Top: Request to the court to appoint commissioners to carry out the court's decree.
Bottom: Appointment of five commssioners, any three of whom can administer the estate.

THOMAS GOOCH d. 1803

354

To the worshipfull the Justices of the County Court of Louisa sitting in chancery Humbly Complaining sheweth to your worships your Orators and Oratrixes Lucy Gooch widow and relict of Thos. Gooch decd. John Draper and Elizabeth his wife formerly Elizabeth Gooch James Gooch. Polly Gooch. Cornelius Gooch & Thos. Washington Gooch & William Gooch — That the said Thos. Gooch departed [illegible] sometime in the [illegible] without first having made any will, but died wholly intestate. leaving a considerable estate consisting of both real and personal property. That a certain Gideon Gooch hath taken upon himself the administration of said estate, whom together with ~~William Gooch~~ & Overton Gooch infant children of said Thos. Gooch decd. your Orators & Oratrixes pray may be made Defendants to this their Bill of complaint. That the said Defts together with your Orators & Oratrixes James Polly [illegible] Washington Gooch & William Gooch are the only [illegible] [illegible] Orators & Oratrixes are desirous to have their several and respective portions of said estate alotted to them to which they are entitled. But that they are advised it cannot be effected without the interposition of this worshipfull Court. in as much as they are infants interested in the distribution of the same. your Orators & Oratrixes therefore pray that your worships will appoint Commissioners to audit. State and settle the accounts of the administration of the said Gideon Gooch. And also for the purpose of laying off an [illegible] to the Compl[t]. Lucy Gooch her dower in both real and personal estate of said decedent. And for dividing the remainder of said Estate among the several distributees of said Thos. Gooch decd. according to Law. upon their executing to said Admr. Bonds to refund their proportion of whatever debts may be hereafter found to be due and unpaid from said Estate. To the End therefore that the said Defts may be compelled, to give

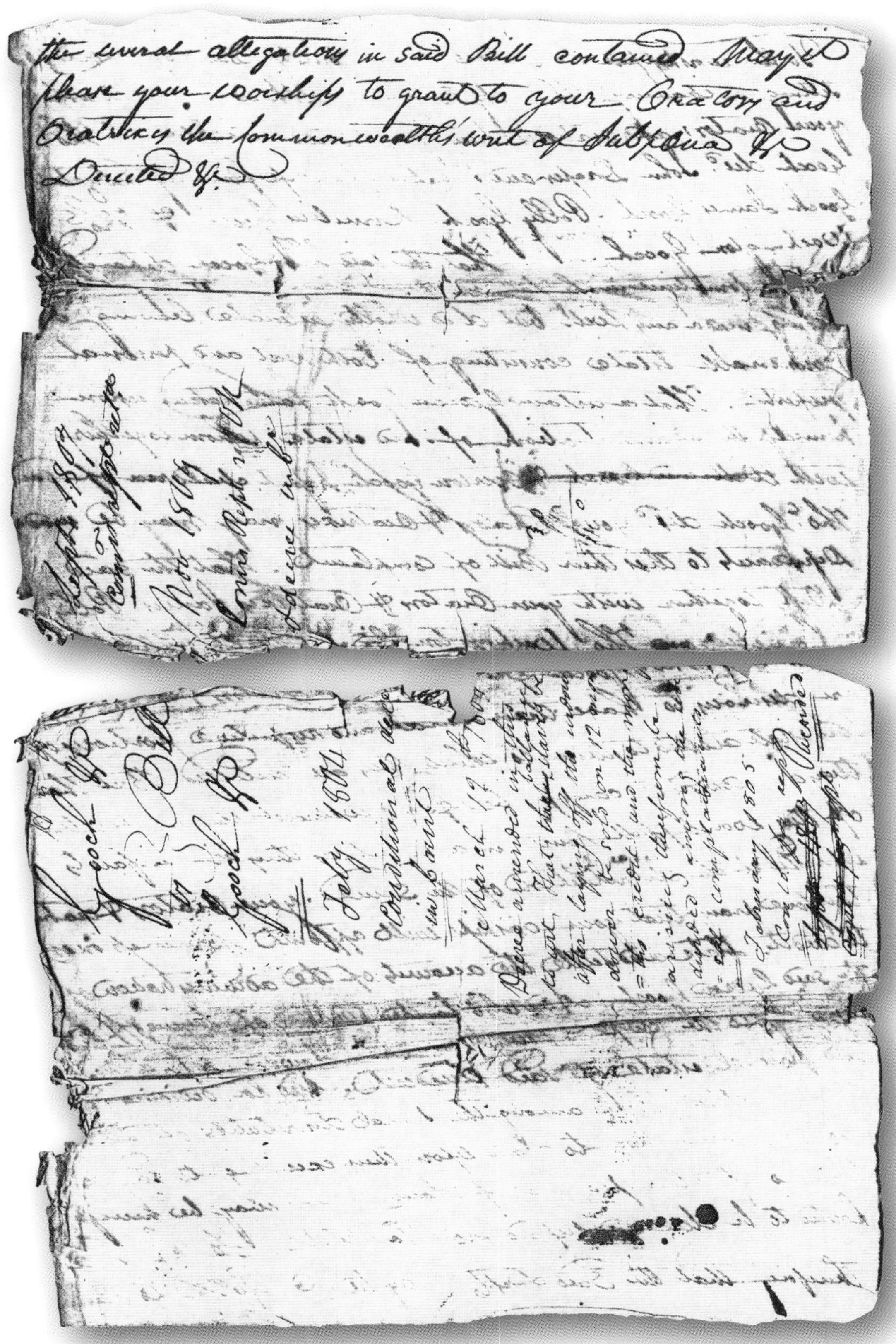

The wording on the document on the preceding page and above is virtually identical to the document on page 349. The name of William Gooch is crossed out in several places and inserted elsewhere on this copy. Perhaps one was a court document, and the other given to an attorney. This copy is in considerably worse condition than the one on page 349.

Thomas Gooch d. 1803

Dr The estate of Thomas Gooch deceased in acc

1804			
To this sum paid different persons for which vouchers were produced	112	7	1½
" This sum paid James Young & Co.	36	6	-
" This sum paid Young Clayton & Co.	37	10	5
" This sum paid John Draper being his proportion of the decedents estate	117	-	2
do — Thomas W. Gooch	117	-	2
William Gooch	117	-	2
Cornelius Gooch	117	-	2
James Gooch	117	-	2
Gideon Gooch	117	-	2
Overton Gooch	117	-	2
Mary Gooch	117	-	2
Lucy Gooch being the amt. of her dower exclusive of the Negros she having received her proportion of the Negros Viz Tom & Jack	115	9	-
	1237	13	10½
2½ per Centum allowed the Administrator	30	18	10
	1268	12	8½
	1220	6	11
Balance in favor of the Administrator	48	5	9½

acc.o with Gideon Gooch administrator Cr

	£	s	d
By amt. of Sales	1094	19	10¼
By Cash left by the decedent	8	2	—
By 2 Hhds Tobo: sold Arthur Clayton	60	7	6
By 2 do do	50	3	—
By Thomas & Henry Bibbs Notes	5	11	1
By a parcel Tob.o	1	3	5¾
£	1220	6	11

Pursuant to the annexed order of Louisa Court we have proceeded to state and settle the accounts of the Administration of Gideon Gooch on the Estate of Thomas Gooch deceased, and to allot to the several distributees their proportions of the decedents Estate, and have found a Balance in favor of the Administrator of forty eight pounds five shillings 09 p. Given under our hands this 7th February 1807

Gar'd Anderson
Charles Wright
Wm. White

Accounting for the settlement of the estate of Thomas Gooch 7th February 1807. It ends: "… and have found a balance in favor of the Administrator of forty eight pounds five shillings 09 ps. [pence]*…"*

Cornelius Gooch b. ca. 1780

A Brief Life

The earliest appearance of Cornelius Gooch in Madison County, Kentucky, was on November 4, 1807, when he married Eliza White, the daughter of Galen White.[1] Cornelius "Gouge" appeared on the 1808 tax list of Madison County with one slave and one horse, but no land. Giddeon Gouge appeared on the same list with seventy-seven acres on Paint Lick Creek. In 1809 "Cornelison" Gooch had one slave over age sixteen; a total of two slaves and five horses.

Cornelius Gooch died in Madison County, Kentucky, in 1810, when he was probably about thirty years old. An inventory of his estate was filed December 10, 1810, in the Madison County Court.[2] He did not own any land, so he left his young wife Eliza White Gooch with little money and an infant son, Chiswell D. Gooch, about a year old. We did not find any additional probate records for Cornelius Gooch in Madison County.

Finding his origins was equally as frustrating. A major clue was the name Giddeon Gouge or Gooch on the same page with Cornelius on the early tax lists of Madison County, Kentucky. But Gideon Gooch was a popular name in many Gooch families in both Virginia and North Carolina. The name Cornelius, however, was unusual in the various Gooch families. We finally found a Cornelius in the Thomas Gooch family of Louisa County, Virginia. Circumstantial evidence points to this man being the Cornelius Gooch who went to Madison County, Kentucky.

Cornelius Gooch of Louisa County, Virginia, was of legal age when his father died in 1803, so we believe that he was born probably between 1775 and 1781. Some Gooch researchers suppose that he was the son of Thomas Gooch and Lucy Higgs or Higgins of Louisa County.[3] His brother Gideon was administrator of the estate of Thomas Gooch. Whether this Gideon was the same man who owned seventy-seven acres on Paint Lick in Madison County, Kentucky, is not known.

In the chancery case that settled Thomas Gooch's estate, Cornelius Gooch was allotted forty-one acres, which bordered his brothers, Thomas W. Gooch and William Gooch.[4] Gideon Gooch was appointed guardian of his underage brothers, William and Overton Gooch, in 1804.[5] There was a "friendly" lawsuit to divide Thomas Gooch's property, and each heir, including Cornelius, received approximately 117 pounds and a parcel of land.[6]

Ready cash was hard to come by in the early 1800s. There were no banks in the rural areas. If one needed money, he would go to a wealthy neighbor and make a promissory note. These notes were often sold to others — similar to banks of today selling mortgages. Cornelius Gooch was involved in two court cases regarding money owed and notes. Both of them included the sale or swap of a horse.

One of the suits was *Thomas Bibb v. Cornelius & James Gooch.*[7] In this case Colby (or "Coleby") Cowherd declared that he sold a stud horse to Misters Thomas Bibb and Cornelius Gooch for $600. (This is a tremendous price for a horse in 1804.) They made a partial payment, and Gooch made a deed of trust to Cowherd and owed a balance of about $75 due from August 30, 1806. Thomas Bibb stated that he owed $45 to Cornelius Gooch and had paid it down to about $18. Gooch was also indebted to Nathan Smith for $25 and used the bond of Bibb as security for his note to Smith. Bibb found out that Gooch was leaving the state, and he feared that he would have to pay Gooch's debt to Smith for $25. In July 1806 James Gooch testified that Cornelius Gooch had transferred the bond of Thomas Bibb to him (James); that James had spoken with Bibb several times and told him that he now held the bond. Bibb wanted to pay the debt in whiskey, which did not suit James Gooch. On November 24, 1806, Colby Cowherd said that he had received full satisfaction for all claims he had against Cornelius Gooch. Gideon Gooch testified that he had a deed of trust on two Negroes, York and Charles, the property of Cornelius Gooch. Eventually, the suit was dismissed in April 1807.

In another suit Joshua Morris sued Cornelius Gooch, saying that Gooch owed him about $16 from swapping a horse. Cornelius's brothers James, Thomas Washington, and Gideon testified on his behalf, but a jury decided in Morris's favor.[8]

Cornelius Gooch sold his property on October 30, 1805, which he had inherited from his father, to Gideon Gooch of Orange County for 100 pounds, land on Duckinghole Creek, containing forty-one acres, Lot 7, containing a part of the tract of Thomas Gooch, deceased, adjoining therein Thomas W. Gooch and William Gooch, "aeiers" of Thomas Gooch, deceased, it being a part of the land of Thomas Gooch, deceased.[9]

The last record we have for Cornelius Gooch was a deed contracted on February 3, 1807. He and James Gooch received a payment from Lucy Gooch for "a Negro man York and a boy Charles…with Lucy Gooch paying $1.00…that if Cornelius Gooch shall on or before the 25th day of December pay to Young Clayton & others the sum of 225 pounds which the said Lucy Gooch is bound with him for otherwise the aforesaid James Gooch shall as soon as conveniently he can after 25 December set the said Negroes up and sell them for ready money & pay the said Lucy Gooch the said sum of 225 pounds and charges."[10] This was apparently done as a form of collateral to ensure that Cornelius paid his debt; if he failed to do so, Lucy could sell the two slaves.

Did Cornelius leave Louisa County, Virginia, for Madison County, Kentucky, in the spring of 1807? We believe so, as he was married in November of that year in Madison County, and

Louisa County, Virginia Deed Book I (1793–1800) pg. 714, Reel #6. Record of the sale of 41 acres by Cornelius Gooch to Gideon Gooch.

we found no evidence of a Cornelius Gooch in the later deed records or the 1810 census of Louisa County, Virginia.

A short life means that a man leaves behind only a few records. Cornelius Gooch fathered only one son, but he might have been surprised to learn that he was the progenitor of fourteen grandchildren in Madison County, Kentucky. *A.H.*

Notes

1. Bill and Kathy Vockery, comp., *Madison County, Kentucky, Marriage Records, 1786–1822* (Richmond, Ky.: the authors, 1993–), I:33.
2. Madison Co., Kentucky, Wills and Probate, 1787–1813:561, FHL #183266.
3. Daniel Mahar website, <http://www.geocities.com/Heartland/Farm4162/goochtom.html?200723>.
4. Louisa Co., Virginia, Order Book 1808–1810:457–58, Library of Virginia, Richmond, Va.
5. Louisa Co., Virginia, Guardian's Bonds and Accounts, 1767–1819, p. 355, Library of Virginia, Richmond, Va.
6. Louisa Co., Virginia, Chancery Court Cases, Lucy Gooch, et al., vs. Administrator of Thomas Gooch, 1809, #025, Library of Virginia, Richmond, Va.
7. Louisa Co., Virginia, Chancery Court Cases, Thomas Bibb vs. Cornelius & James Gooch, 1807, #008, Library of Virginia, Richmond, Va.
8. Louisa Co., Virginia, Chancery Court Cases, Joshua Morris vs. Cornelius Gooch, 1806, #011, Library of Virginia, Richmond, Va.
9. Louisa Co., Virginia, Deed Book K:201–02, FHL #32206.
10. Louisa Co., Virginia, Deed Book L:43, FHL #32206.

ELIZA B. WHITE GOOCH HILL B. CA. 1788

A Remarkable Woman

Women in the 1800s did not usually make a mark on the local history. They led quiet, ordinary lives from cradle to the grave, learning in between the crafts of being good homemakers, wives, and mothers. The laws of the times prohibited a woman from owning property in her own name unless she was single or widowed, or unless she was given it and there was a prenuptial agreement saying it was hers, or she had her husband's permission to own it. A woman could not inherit property from her own father if she was married and her husband was still living; the inheritance went to the husband.

Most women gave birth about every two years, that being the amount of time given to nurse the previous baby. Medically speaking, it is more difficult, though not impossible, to become pregnant while nursing. Because women had so many babies, sapping them of their health, many died young.

But Eliza B. White, the daughter of a Revolutionary War veteran, Galen White, was a remarkable woman for her time. She out-lived two husbands and two of her children, so it seems that she knew very well the kind of tribulations that women had to face and endure.

Eliza married Cornelius Gooch in November of 1807 in Madison County, Kentucky. Her father was an early settler there, and Cornelius had recently arrived from Virginia. Their son Chiswell D. Gooch was born in 1809 and by December of 1810, Cornelius had died. Life on the frontier was not easy. Even young people were subject to injuries, as well as diseases, such as cholera. Cornelius was listed on the 1809 tax list of Madison County as having two slaves and one horse. After the death of a spouse, it was common to marry again soon afterwards. Men married in order to find a caretaker for the children and house; women married quickly to have a breadwinner. So Eliza married John Hill in 1811. By him she had three more children: Jane, Jefferson A., and Henry L. Hill. John Hill died in 1831, and was buried in the Galen White Cemetery, Madison County, Kentucky.

Jane married Edmond Oldham in 1838 in Madison County. Jane and Edmond Oldham had one daughter Mildred, who married first, Nathan Williams, divorced him, and married, second, Thomas Gooch, son of Mildred's half-uncle, Chiswell. Thus, Mildred's uncle Chiswell also became her father-in-law. But Jane Hill Oldham died before 1850. Therefore, her daughter Mildred was the sole heir to her mother's portion of Eliza B. Hill's estate. Jefferson Hill pre-deceased his mother and left a widow and some young children. Henry L. Hill, who was a widower in the 1850 census, married his brother's widow, Emily Noland Hill, and became guardian of his brother's children. Therefore, Henry Hill had control over two portions of Eliza B. Hill's estate.

One would think that all of this intermarriage between the Hill and Gooch families might help strengthen family ties, but that was not the case. Perhaps Eliza knew that there might be trouble between her heirs, because she wrote a will on November 21, 1859, which was recorded on December 21, 1859, at a time in history when women did not usually write them. She also signed the will, which means that she had some education. [Alice Henson notes that "In about thirty years of 'doing genealogy,' I have seen few wills written exclusively by women in the 1850s. In fact, the only other one that I can recall was written in the 1920s in Illinois in which a woman willed her Hoover vacuum cleaner and her automobile to a descendant."] In the will she stated that she did not want her son-in-law, Edmond Oldham, to have any say over her granddaughter Mildred's inheritance, nor did she want Nathan Williams (Mildred's husband) to have any control. Eliza appointed her two living sons, Chiswell D. Gooch and Henry L. Hill as co-executors.[1]

Even though Eliza wrote a will and made her two sons co-executors, they still squabbled over her estate. Eventually, the

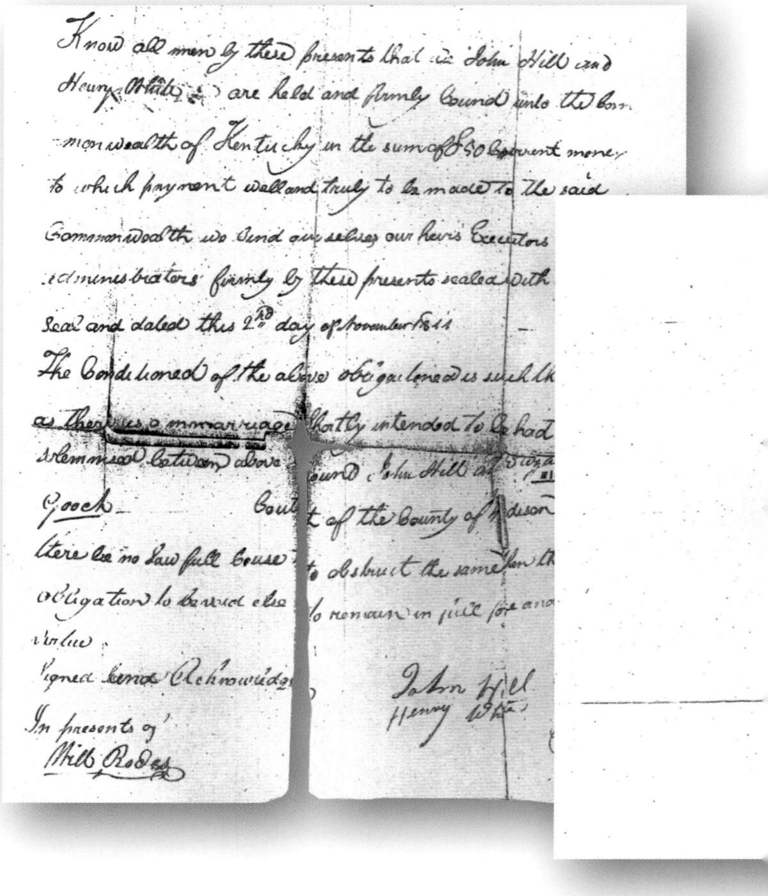

Know all men by these presents that we John Hill and Henry White are held and firmly bound unto the Com-
-monwealth of Kentucky in the sum of $50 current money
to which payment well and truly to be made to the said
Commonwealth we bind our selves our heirs Executors
administrators firmly by these presents sealed with
seal and dated this 2nd day of November 1811
The Condition of the above obligation is such that
as there is a marriage shortly intended to be had
solemnized between above bound John Hill and Eliza
Gooch ... Court of the County of Madison
there be no lawfull cause to obstruct the same then the
obligation to be void else to remain in full force and
virtue
Signed sealed acknowledged
In presents of
Will Rodes
John Hill
Henry White

…Eliza B Hill left Chiswell D Gooch and Henry L Hill her two surviving children. She left Mildred Gooch wife of Thomas Gooch her grand daughter being the only child of [illegible] Oldham decd the daughter of Eliza Hill. & She left Amanda. Pleasant. Eliza B Jr & Cyntha Hill children of her decd son Jefferson Hill. In the fall of 1855 or 185[illegible] she

Eliza B. White married 1) Cornelius Gooch — only son was Chiswell D. Gooch, and 2) John Hill — had Jane, Henry, and Jefferson D. Hill. Jane died after Mildred's birth, and Jefferson was deceased by the time of Eliza Hill's will.

Mildred Oldham Williams was the daughter of Jane Hill and Edmond Oldham. Father's name per Mildred's death certificate. She married 1) Nathan Williams and 2)Thomas Gooch, son of Chiswell. Thomas Gooch and Mildred Oldham Williams were first cousins, both grandchildren of Eliza B. Hill, but they had different grandfathers.

court of Madison County appointed a neighbor, Jesse Cobb, who was also a witness to the will, as administrator of the estate. Chiswell D. Gooch sued the administrator in 1862, as the estate had not been settled.[2] The case stated that Henry Hill had married the widow of Jefferson Hill (Emily), and that the estate was valued at $4,243.16 plus the value of six slaves: Kitty, Schuyler, Jack, Capius, Eliza and Ibsan, worth $5,400. The slaves were divided between the four heirs. Chiswell Gooch received Ibsan. Kitty and Schuyler went to Henry Hill. Jefferson Hill's heirs received Capius and Eliza, and Mildred took Jack.[3]

Chiswell Gooch testified that he owed two notes to his mother, and that he had paid them, but that the notes had not been credited. He said that Henry Hill "utterly refuses" to settle matters. Samuel Williams, son-in-law of Chiswell Gooch, testified that Eliza Hill had told him that C.D. Gooch had given her two notes he held on Thomas Ody/Oder to be credited toward the notes she held on Gooch.[4]

Probate estate files and lawsuits to settle estates help to give us a picture of life in rural Madison County, Kentucky. Eliza Hill was visited every day by Dr. Rains between October 26 and December 13, 1859. He charged $2 per visit. Another doctor. C.J. Walker, billed the estate for $36 for five visits of eleven miles travel, with consultation to Dr. Rains, and prescriptions.[5]

Eliza must have lived an active life until the fall of 1859. When she died, Eliza owed a bill to Mr. Shearer, who ran a store, for black cambric (a fabric) and clean flax seed. Also, she owed a woman named Nancy Kennedy for weaving three blankets.[6]

Eliza was exceptional in that she lived a long life in a time when women died young. She wrote a will at a time when women did not usually do so, trying to protect her granddaughter, Mildred, from any male control by Mildred's father or her husband to Mildred's inheritance. She also tried to protect her deceased son's children by willing them an equal portion of her estate. Although wealthy when she died, her estate dwindled during the Civil War, while her family squabbled over their inheritance.

A.H.

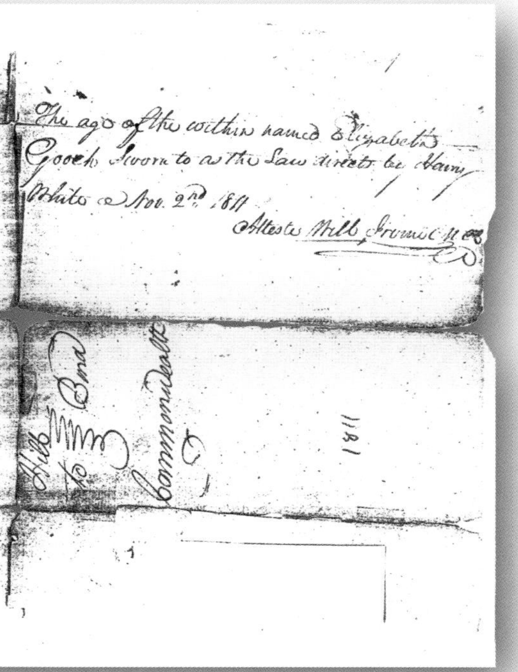
The age of the within named Elizabeth Gooch Sworn to as the Law directs by Henry White Nov. 2nd 1811

Attest Will. Irvine C.M.C.

Hill Bond to Commonwealth

1811

Madison County Courthouse, Richmond, Kentucky, Bond for Elizabeth Gooch and John Hill to marry November 2, 1811. These bonds were on small slips of paper, high on the right as you walk into the vault.

Notes

1. Madison Co., Kentucky, Will Book N:526-27.
2. Madison Co., Kentucky, Court Cases, C.D. Gooch vs. Jesse Cobb, Administrator, 1862, #23869, 23870, 23847.
3. Ibid.
4. Ibid.
5. Ibid.
6. Ibid.

Chiswell D. Gooch b. ca. 1809

Rags to Riches and Back Again

Chiswell D. Gooch was born about 1809 in Madison County, Kentucky, the only son of Cornelius Gooch and Eliza White Gooch.[1] His father died in 1810 and his mother married again to John Hill, November 2, 1811.[2] Chiswell grew up with his half-brothers and half-sister: Jefferson A. Hill, Henry L. Hill, and Jane Hill. On February 18, 1830, Chiswell married Eliza Ann Maupin, the daughter of Daniel Maupin and Margaret/Peggy McWilliams Maupin in Madison County, Kentucky.[3] They had fourteen children with twelve living to maturity, but only eight were living when their mother Eliza died July 24, 1892.[4] The children were

1. Cornelius Gooch born about 1831; married September 18, 1855, to Mahala Golden. In the 1860, 1870, and 1880 censuses, he was living with his parents. He was alive in 1892 to receive a share of his mother's estate.
2. Arzelia Gooch born about 1835; married October 3, 1855, to Samuel Williams. She was not on the 1870 census. She had two children by 1860: Thomas and Lucy. But her daughter Lucy, who married Isaac Shoop, was her only heir. Lucy Shoop was alive in 1892 and inherited her mother's share from grandmother Eliza Gooch's estate.
3. Thomas Gooch born January 25, 1836; married December 13, 1860, to Mrs. Mildred Oldham Williams, his first cousin. They had the same grandmother, Eliza White Gooch Hill, but they had different grandfathers. Cornelius Gooch was Thomas's paternal grandfather and John Hill was Mildred's maternal grandfather. It was common for first or second cousins to marry in the 1800s, as most people married within their neighborhood (about a five- to six-mile radius). A man could travel by horseback about that far to court a neighbor girl and still get home by dark. Thomas and Mildred Gooch's daughter, Rebecca, married her first cousin, Charles Davis, a son of the next couple. Thomas Gooch died in Fairmount, Illinois, in 1918.
4. Nancy "Nannie" Gooch born about 1838; married about 1859 to James Davis. No record of the marriage has been found, but the couple was listed as "being married within the year" on the 1860 census of Madison County, living with Richard Davis. Nannie died in Missouri after 1882. The place of her burial is unknown.
5. Remus Gooch born 1840–42; married September 28, 1867, to Cynthia Ann Hill; he was murdered in July of 1872. They had two children in 1870, Mary and Charley, who lived in Missouri in 1892.
6. Mary Gooch born 1841–44; married James Turner; died before 1860. Seven Turner children inherited their mother's part of Eliza Gooch's estate: Joseph, Robert, Maggie, Mollie, Della, Neal, and Ida.
7. Henry Gooch born September 1846; married October 3, 1876, to Martha Woolery. The family lived in Madison County, Kentucky, in 1900, E.D. 49. Children were Sallie, Any, Lillie, Bettie, Viney, and Mary.
8. S.B. Gooch born about 1848. He was administrator of his mother's estate in 1892. His first name on the census looks like Sarshel or Sashel.
9. Jo Ann Gooch born between about 1850; married March 1, 1875 to Daniel Maupin. They had two daughters by 1880: Lola and Elizabeth.
10. Laura Gooch born between 1852–56; married Mr. Young. She lived in Fairmount, Vermilion County, Illinois, in 1892.
11. George Gooch born about 1853; died of pneumonia, April 20, 1854, Madison County, Kentucky.[5]
12. John Gooch born about 1856; died young.
13. James Gooch born November 1858; married Mary Addie Graves. They lived in Vermilion County, Illinois, in 1900. Children: Ann, Byler, Jesper, Verlea.
14. Lucy Gooch born about 1859; married Milton Graves. They lived in Pennington, Illinois, in 1892.

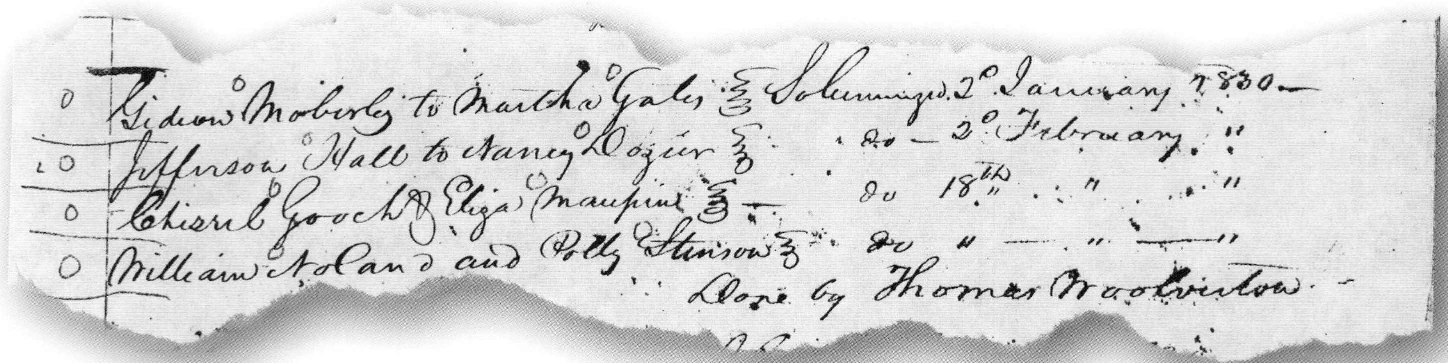

Gideon Moberly to Martha Gates } Solemnized 2d January 1830
Jefferson Hall to Nancy Dozier } do 2d February
Chisel Gooch & Eliza Maupin } do 18th
William Noland and Polly Stinson } do
Done by Thomas Woolverton

Document recording marriage of Chiswell Gooch and Eliza Maupin on February 18, 1830

When Chiswell's mother died in 1859, she willed that her land be divided into four equal parts, and Chiswell was one of the four heirs to 225 acres of land that sold for $25 per acre = $5,625. So each of the heirs was to receive $1,406.25, which would be worth about $29,000 in today's money. However, Chiswell's half-brother, Henry Hill, bought the land and failed to give security for the land by December of 1860. So the other heirs, Chiswell, Mildred Oldham Williams (who would become Chiswell's daughter-in-law), and the children of Jefferson Hill, deceased, sued in Madison County, Kentucky, Court to ask for a resale of the land.[6] The case was not settled until 1864, and the land had gone down in value so that each heir received only $964.[7] Cornelius Gooch, son of Chiswell, bought the land.[8]

After his marriage in 1830, Chiswell was listed on the tax list of Madison County as having a valuation of $80, without any land.[9] To compare, Josiah Collins was worth $5,500, and Richard Davis was worth $2,935. By 1840 Chiswell owned two slaves.[10] In 1849 Chiswell Gooch had a tavern license, no horses, and no cattle.[11] By the 1850 census he was not listed as a slave owner, nor did he own any land.[12] By 1860, however, he was listed on the census as having land worth $4,450 and personal estate of $5,400, which usually means a number of slaves.[13] This is most likely a reflection of his inheritance from his mother. By 1870 his land was only worth $1,000, and his personal property only $300. With the Civil War in this interval, it is understandable why hard times had set in.

Chiswell was involved in several court cases in Madison County, Kentucky, which helped to illuminate his character and his lifestyle. In 1853 and 1854 he sued Daniel Bates. The first case had to do with a runaway slave named Jane. Bates had advertised that he would pay $100 for her reward. Chiswell caught her, was paid $50, but was owed the remainder, so Gooch sued Bates for the balance.[14] In 1854 Chiswell also sued Bates for $50, the amount of a lien on a slave, Bob.[15]

Another case was a dispute over a slave. Chiswell sued John H. Glover in 1863, saying that Glover enticed a Negro man away from him, also taking a horse and saddle. Glover gave the Negro a pass. Gooch lost the service of the Negro man for a long time and was "put to great expense in capturing and returning him."[16]

Between 1854 and 1858, Chiswell rented out his farm for $300 per year and moved to Jackson County, Kentucky. In 1859 he moved back, as Kiah Crooke, a surveyor in Madison County, declared that Gooch was "hard run for money; and Crooke did not know if he wanted to rent him land — if he was good for it — as he had been living in the Big Hill in Jackson County."[17]

Chiswell probably did a bit of land speculation and borrowing money. In those days, when people needed money, they did not usually go to a bank. They simply borrowed from wealthier neighbors and gave security in some kind of property: a horse, a plot of ground \ Sometimes, the notes would be sold to others, without the borrower's knowledge. Such was the court case he was involved in with Milo Baxter as the plaintiff.[18] In January of 1860 C.D. Gooch purchased 64½ acres of land from John Denney for $1,190.32. This land was then sold to his daughter-in-law Mildred Gooch. (It is rather unusual for a woman to purchase land, but she was a granddaughter of Eliza B. Hill and had received an inheritance.) Milo Baxter held a note on a previous owner of this parcel of land, and he petitioned the court to have the land sold to pay off the note. This case went all the way to the Kentucky Court of Appeals, which decided in June of 1866 that the present owners of the land, Thomas and Mildred Gooch, had bought the land in good faith, not knowing that there was a lien on the property. The court said that if there was money owing on a tract

INHUMAN MURDER.

One of the most dreadful and brutal murders ever recorded was perpetrated on Rock Lick, near Doylesville, in this county, on Sunday night last. Remus Gooch, son of Chisel D. Gooch, was the victim. He was at home with his wife and two small children. He retired at his usual bed-time, and about twelve or one o'clock was awakened by the barking of his dogs in the yard. He paid little attention to the noise at first, but the barking grew louder and fiercer and fearing that something was wrong he got up, went to the door, and, opening it to look out, was shot down by a volley of shots poured into his body from a party of men some twenty yards away. He dropped back upon the bed of his little boy, standing just by the door, and expired instantly. The fiends who committed the inhuman deed then approached the house, and with loud curses and oaths, ordered the wife of the murdered man to drag his body outside the door, threatening to burn the house unless she instantly obeyed. They said they had come there to kill Gooch and intended to be satisfied that he was dead before leaving. Fearing for her own life the frightened woman dragged the bleeding and mutilated body of her dead husband as near the door as her strength would permit, when one of the assassins reached in his hand, took Gooch by the leg, hauled him out upon the ground, and with a malice more than fiendish two of them inhumanly stamped and kicked the lifeless body of their victim, determined to see that no spark of vitality remained. After this they mounted their horses and rode away.

Upon examining the body the following morning it was found that twenty eight buck-shot had pierced the face, and over one hundred were lodged in the neck and breast, besides seventy or eighty that were counted in the door and door-facings. The murderers went prepared to do their work well, and the riddled corpse shows how they executed their purpose.

On Monday the Coroner, Mr. T. J. Cornelison, was sent for and he went immediately into an examination of the case. He summoned a jury and examined a number of witnesses but has not yet concluded the investigation. The wife of the murdered man identified several of the party, twenty in number she said, and upon her testimony the Coroner felt justified in issuing warrants for the arrest of Dr. C. F. Butler and his brother Henry Butler—both of whom have fled the country. Further developments, as the case is continued, will bring to light others who took part in this savage butchery, as the Coroner is determined to sift the matter to the bottom. We hear that several previous difficulties had occurred between the Butlers and the deceased, the nature of which we have not learned, and that bad feeling had prevailed on both sides for months past. But no sort of bad feeling or previous wrong, could palliate the heinousness of so cold-blooded a murder; and the reputation of the neighborhood and the county in which it was done demand that the whole set implicated should be sought out and brought to punishment.

Madison County, Kentucky, Newspaper Obituaries *Vol. 1, p. 171*
Eastern Kentucky University Library, July 26, 1872

Chiswell D. Gooch b. ca. 1809

of land, that it had to be "expressly written in the deed," and in this case, it was not mentioned in any of the deeds involved.

In case #21315 in Madison County, Chiswell Gooch sued James McWilliams. Chiswell was security on a note from James McWilliams to William Williams for $100. "James has left the state and has resided in Missouri for four months and has no property to pay the note except two jackasses in possession of John C. McWilliams, his father." In this case, the security for the loan was two donkeys. The McWilliams were probably relatives of his wife, Eliza Maupin, as her mother was Peggy McWilliams.

In 1864 Robert Jordan and William Lanter sued Chiswell D. Gooch and his son-in-law James Davis. The plaintiff said that they owned a field of growing corn on Clear Creek and Muddy Creek, about eighteen acres. The defendants allowed their stock of horses and cattle to eat up the grain. Allegedly, the defendants drove off the plaintiff's cattle and then put a fence around the field.[19]

In 1865 there is an intriguing case involving Chiswell. He sued William J. Golden and Mahala J. Gooch. Chiswell stated that in 1858 he was living in Jackson County, Kentucky. The defendants charged him with "feloniously giving counsel to one Neill S. Gooch to shoot and kill one Mahala Jane Gooch, and the said Neill S. Gooch aided and abetted by C.D. Gooch did shoot Mahala Jane on 20 September 1858 in Jackson County with malice and intent to kill her. She suffered a mortal wound in the left side of her body, but did not die."[20] Chiswell was arrested and imprisoned in Rockcastle County. He was "put to great trouble, vexation and expense" to defend himself. He was acquitted of the offense, but after the verdict, the defendants continued to carry on a smear campaign against him. He sued for $10,000 in damages, but the suit was dropped.

Cornelius "Neill" Gooch, the first born son of Chiswell, married Mahala Jane Golden in Madison County, Kentucky, September 17, 1855.[21] The marriage lasted only three years when Cornelius shot and wounded his wife, Mahala, in 1858. We also found a suit in Madison County, Kentucky, in which Cornelius Gooch was sued by the state for carrying a concealed weapon, a Bowie knife, on the same day he shot his wife, September 20, 1858. This suit was also dropped because the witnesses against Cornelius left the state for "parts unknown."[22]

Chiswell D. Gooch was born on the frontier and was left in extreme poverty when his father died. He and his wife raised a huge family in Madison County. One of his sons was murdered, and Chiswell was accused of aiding and abetting the murder of his daughter-in-law. Chiswell Gooch died of pneumonia in Madison County on May 27, 1877, age sixty-eight.[23] His wife survived him until 1892, when her farm was sold for $420 or about $4 per acre. Chiswell and his wife did not leave much of anything behind for their many descendants. None of the heirs inherited more than a few dollars.

A.H.

Notes

1. Madison Co., Kentucky, Will Book N:526–27.
2. Bill and Kathy Vockery, comp., *Madison County, Kentucky, Marriage Records, 1786–1822* (Richmond, Ky.: the authors, 1993–), I:40.
3. Madison Co., Kentucky, Marriages 1:175, Film #183302, Kentucky State Archives, Frankfort, Ky.
4. Madison Co., Kentucky, Court Cases, S.B. Gooch, Administrator of Eliza Gooch vs. Eliza Gooch's Heirs, Box 287, #574, Kentucky State Archives, Frankfort, Ky.
5. Bill and Kathy Vockery, *Vital Statistics of Madison County, Kentucky* (Richmond, Ky.: B. Vockery, 2000–2001), 102.
6. Madison Co., Kentucky, Court Cases, Petition of Eliza B. Hill's Heirs vs. Commissioner's Report of Sale, Eliza B. Hill's Heirs vs. Eliza B. Hill's Heirs, Box 48, #17390, Kentucky State Archives, Frankfort, Ky.
7. Madison Co., Kentucky, Court Cases, Eliza B. Hill's Heirs vs. Eliza B. Hill's Heirs, Box 48, #17390, Kentucky State Archives, Frankfort, Ky.
8. Madison Co., Kentucky, Court Cases, Eliza B. Hill's Administrator v. C.D. Gooch, Box 48, #23847, Kentucky State Archives, Frankfort, Ky.
9. 1830 Madison Co., Kentucky, Tax List, Box 259, Allen County Public Library, Fort Wayne, Ind.
10. 1840 federal census, Kentucky, Madison Co., p. 256.
11. 1849 Madison Co., Kentucky, Tax List, Film #249, Allen County Public Library, Fort Wayne, Ind.
12. 1850 Madison Co., Kentucky, Tax List, Film #8129, Kentucky State Archives, Frankfort, Ky.
13. 1860 federal census, Kentucky, Madison Co., First Division, Richmond, p. 281.

Madison County, Kentucky, 1854 Tax List, which includes the property of Richard Davis. Note the value of slaves!

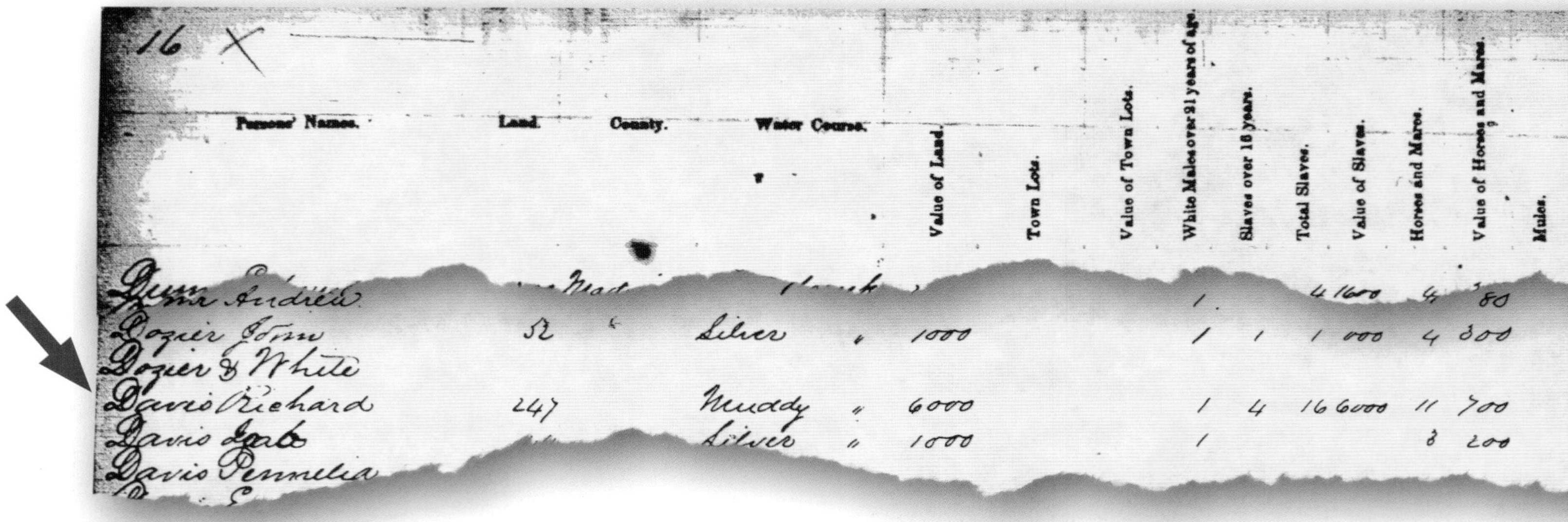

16 X

Persons' Names.	Land.	County.	Water Course.		Value of Land.	Town Lots.	Value of Town Lots.	White Males over 21 years of age.	Slaves over 16 years.	Total Slaves.	Value of Slaves.	Horses and Mares.	Value of Horses and Mares.	Mules.
[illegible] Andrew		Mad	[illegible]					1.		4	1600	4	80	
Dozier John	52	"	Silver	"	1000			1	1	1	000	4	300	
Dozier & White														
Davis Richard	247		Muddy	"	6000			1	4	16	6000	11	700	
Davis Jacob			Silver	"	1000			1				3	200	
Davis Pennelia														

14. Madison Co., Kentucky, Court Cases, Chiswell D. Gooch vs. Daniel Bates, #21017, 1853, Kentucky State Archives, Frankfort, Ky.
15. Ibid.
16. Madison Co., Kentucky, Court Cases, Chiswell D. Gooch vs. John H. Glover, #23434, 1863, Kentucky State Archives, Frankfort, Ky.
17. Madison Co., Kentucky, Court Cases, C.D. Gooch vs. Eliza B. Hill's Administrators, #A02-1104, Kentucky State Archives, Frankfort, Ky.
18. Madison Co., Kentucky, Court Cases, Milo Baxter vs. C.D. Gooch, et al., #311, Summer term 1866, Kentucky State Archives, Frankfort, Ky.
19. Madison Co., Kentucky, Court Cases, Robert Jordan & William Lanter vs. Chiswell D. Good and James Davis, #24047, 1864, Kentucky State Archives, Frankfort, Ky.
20. Madison Co., Kentucky, Court Cases, Chiswell D. Gooch vs. William J. Golden and Mahala J. Gooch, #24033, Kentucky State Archives, Frankfort, Ky.
21. Bill and Kathy Vockery, comp., *Madison County, Kentucky, Marriage Records, 1852–1876* (Richmond, Ky.: the authors, 1993–), III:26.
22. Madison Co., Kentucky, Court Cases, Commonwealth of Kentucky vs. Cornelius Gooch, #20699, Kentucky State Archives, Frankfort, Ky.
23. Vockery and Vockery, *Vital Statistics of Madison County, Kentucky*, 102.

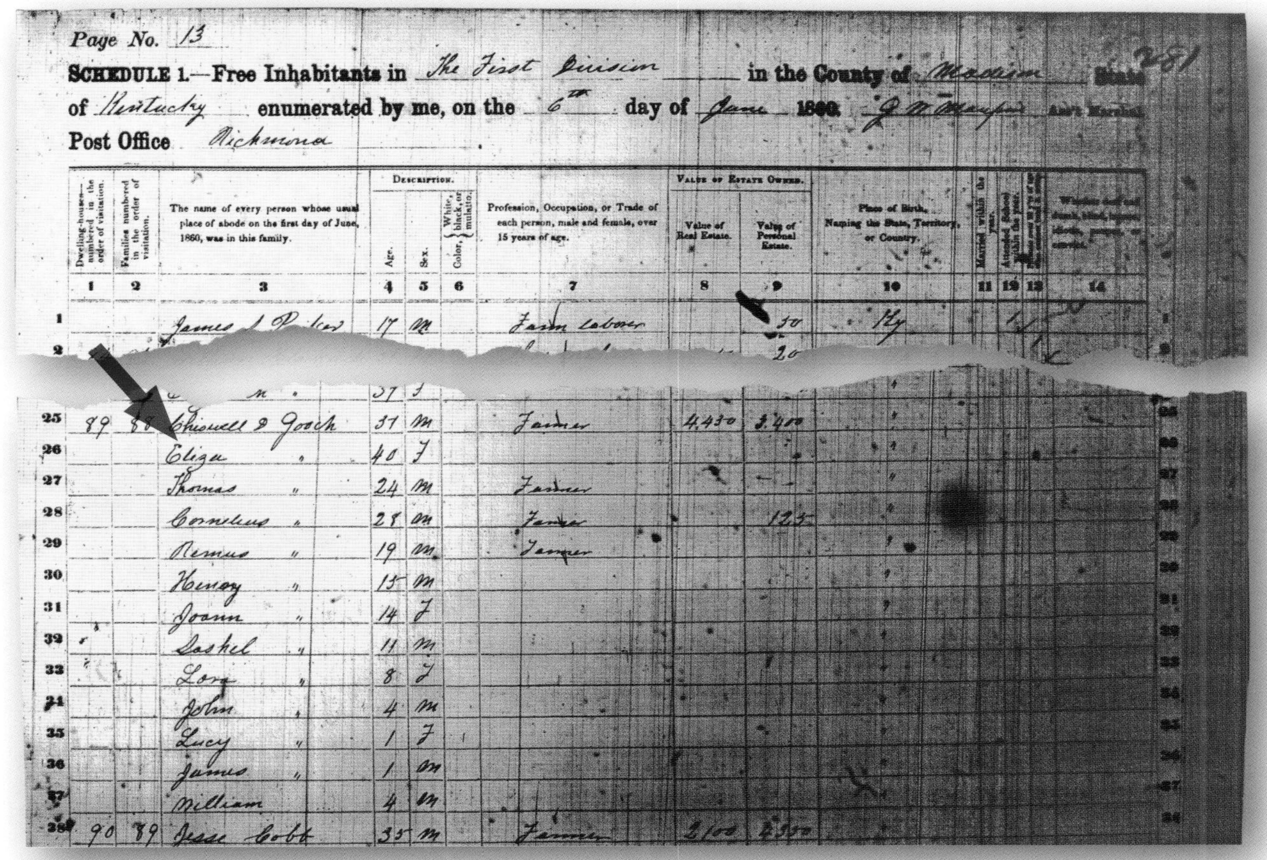

Page No. 13 281

SCHEDULE 1.—Free Inhabitants in The First Division in the County of Madison State of Kentucky enumerated by me, on the 6th day of June 1860.

Post Office Richmond

Line	Dwelling	Family	Name	Age	Sex	Color	Occupation	Real Estate	Personal Estate	Place of Birth
1			James ...	17	M		Farm laborer		50	Ky
25	89	88	Chiswell D Gooch	51	M		Farmer	4,430	3,400	
26			Eliza "	40	F					
27			Thomas "	24	M		Farmer			
28			Cornelius "	28	M		Farmer		125	
29			Remus "	19	M		Farmer			
30			Henry "	15	M					
31			Joann "	14	F					
32			Lashel "	11	M					
33			Lora "	8	F					
34			John "	4	M					
35			Lucy "	1	F					
36			James "	1	M					
37			William "	4	M					
38	90	89	Jesse Cobb	35	M		Farmer	2100	4350	

Above: Madison County, Kentucky, 1860 Federal Census, page 281, Roll M653–384. Chiswell D. Gooch and his family are enumerated. William, the last name in the list, is the son of Cornelius, Chiswell's oldest son.

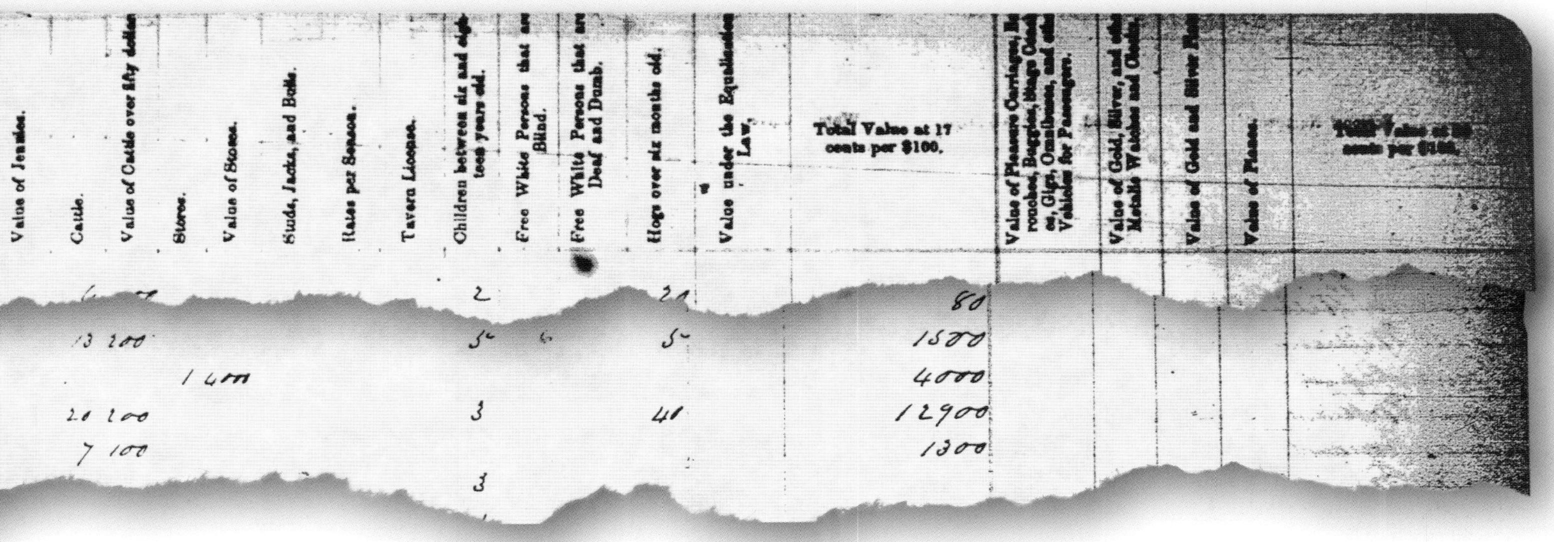

Chiswell D. Gooch b. ca. 1809

366

Gooch to Maupin

This Indenture made and entered into between L.D. Maupin of Madison County Ky of the one part and C.D. Gooch and Eliza his wife formerly Eliza Maupin of the County of Rockcastle Ky of the other part Witnesseth. That for and in consideration of the sum of four hundred and sixty dollars to them in hand paid the said C.D. Gooch and Eliza his wife hath this day bargained sold aliened and confirmed unto the said L.D. Maupin all the right title and interest which they acquired by the last Will and Testament of Daniel Maupin Decd. father of said Eliza in and to the tract of land upon which said Daniel Maupin lived at the time of his death. Also all the interest of every kind which they have or may acquire in any of the estate of said decedent, whether personal real or mixed, and by these presents do alien release bargain sell and confirm unto the said L.D. Maupin his heirs and assigns forever the interest above mentioned including all the interest conferred upon them by the Last Will & Testament of Daniel Maupin Decd. To have and to hold the landed real and personal estate before described to the said L.D. Maupin his heirs and assigns forever. And the said C.D. Gooch and Eliza his wife for themselves their heirs &c. do hereby covenant to and with said L.D. Maupin his heirs and assigns that they will warrant and forever defend the before described interest in land &c. against the claim or claims of all and every person whatever.

In Testimony whereof the said C.D. Gooch and Eliza his wife have hereunto set their hands and affixed their seals this the 9th day of February 1838.

C.D. Gooch (seal)
Eliza Gooch (seal)

State of Kentucky Madison County Sct.

I David Irvine clerk of the Court for the County aforesaid certify that this Deed from Chiswell D. Gooch and Eliza his wife to L.D. Maupin was on the 9 day of February 1838 produced to me in my office by the said grantors and acknowledged by Chiswell D. Gooch to be his act and deed. And the said Eliza being examined by me privily and apart from her husband declared that she did freely and willingly seal and deliver said writing and wishes not to retract it, and acknowledged said writing again shown & explained to her to be her act and deed, and consented that the same might be recorded and the same has been duly recorded in my office.

Examd & Del.

Att. David Irvine Clerk

The above land personalty represents proof of Chiswell D. Gooch's marriage to Eliza Maupin, and that her father was Daniel Maupin. Kentucky State Archives, Frankfort, Kentucky, Gooch To Maupin Deed Book X, page 272, Land Personalty, February 9, 1838.

Transcription

This indenture made and entered into between L.D. Maupin of Madison County, Ky of the one part and C.D. Gooch and Eliza his wife formerly Eliza Maupin of the County of Rockcastle Ky of the other part. Witnesseth that for and in consideration of the sum of four hundred and sixty dollars to them in hand paid the said C.D. Gooch and Eliza his wife hath this day bargained, sold aliened and confirmed unto the said L.D. Maupin all the right, title and interest which they acquired by the last Will and Testament of Daniel Maupin, Decd, father of said Eliza in and to the tract of land upon which said Daniel Maupin lived at the time of his death. Also all the interest of every kind which they have or may acquire in any of the estate of said decedent, whether personal, real or mixed, and by these presents do alien, release, bargain, sell and confirm unto the said L.D. Maupin, his heirs and assigns forever the interest above mentioned including all the interest conferred upon them by the Last Will & testament of Daniel Maupin, Decd to have and to hold the landed real and personal estate before described to the said L.D. Maupin, his heirs and assigns forever.— And the said C.D. Gooch and Eliza his wife for themselves, their heirs, &c. do hereby covenant to and with said L.D. Maupin, his heirs and assigns that they will warrant and forever defend the before described interest in land, &c. against the claim or claims of all and every person whatever.

In testimony whereof the said C.D. Gooch and Eliza his wife have hereunto set their hands and affixed their seals this the 9th day of February 1838.

C.D. Gooch
Eliza Gooch

State of Kentucky, Madison County

I, David Irvine, clerk of the Court for the County aforesaid, certify that this deed from Chiswell D. Gooch and Eliza his wife to L.D. Maupin was done the 9 day of February 1838 produced to me in my office by the said grantors and acknowledged by Chiswell D. Gooch to be his act and deed. And the said Eliza being examined by me privily and apart from her husband declared that she did freely and willingly seal and deliver said writing and wishes not to retract it and acknowledged said writing again shown explained to her act and deed and consented that the same might be recorded and the same has been duly recorded in my office.

David Irvine, MCC

Researched this date 9/5/96
Peggy Galloway
808 Vinson Rd
Danville Ky 40422

Commonwealth of Kentucky Marriage Bond for Remus Gooch, son of Chiswell D. Gooch and Eliza Ann Maupin, and Nancy Hill to marry, dated September 28, 1867

305

Marriage Bond.

THE COMMONWEALTH OF KENTUCKY.

Be it Known, that we, Remus Gooch
as principal, and W J Walker
as surety, are jointly and severally bound to the Commonwealth of Kentucky, in the sum of One Hundred Dollars.

The Condition of this Bond is as follows:

That, whereas Marriage is intended to be solemnized between the above bound Remus Gooch
and Mrs Nancy Hill
Now, if there is no lawful cause to obstruct said marriage, this bond shall be void, otherwise it shall remain in full force and effect.

Dated at Richmond Madison County, this 28th day of September 1867.

Remus Gooch
Will J Walker

Attest:
J R Williams D Clerk
County Court.

This is to certify that on the 16 day of December 1855 the rites of marriage were legally solemnized by me between Samuel Williams and Arzelia Gooch at Chisel Gooch in the County of Madison in the presence of Solomon Abrams and James Maupin.
James Asbill

The above document certifies "that on the 16 day of December 1855 the rites of marriage were legally solemnized by me between Samuel Williams and Arzelia Gooch at Chisel Gooch in the County of Madison in the presence of Solomon Abrams and James Maupin."

CERTIFICATION OF VITAL RECORD

VERMILION COUNTY ILLINOIS

STATE OF ILLINOIS

MARRIAGE LICENSE

THE PEOPLE OF THE STATE OF ILLINOIS COUNTY OF Vermilion

To any person legally authorized to solemnize Marriage Greeting

Marriage may be celebrated

between Mr James Gooch of Catlin Tp in the County of Vermilion and State of Illinois of the age of 22 years and Miss Mary A Graves of Catlin Tp in the County of Vermilion and State of Illinois of the age of 19 years

Witness John W Dale County Clerk and the seal of said County at his Office in Danville in said County this 21st day of November A.D. 1881

John W Dale County Clerk

STATE OF ILLINOIS COUNTY s.s. I W O Smith a Minister of the Gospel hereby certify that Mr James Gooch and Mary A Graves were united in Marriage by me at Robert C Smith's in the County of Vermilion and State of Illinois on the 22 day of November A.D. 1881

W O Smith Minister of the Gospel

It is the duty of the person celebrating the Marriage to fill out and sign the above Certificate and to return the same, together with the License, to the County Clerk within thirty days after the Marriage is solemnized. ONE HUNDRED DOLLARS PENALTY FOR FAILING SO TO DO.

Cut this off and give to Parties married.

MARRIAGE REPORT TO COUNTY CLERK. No. 3144

CERTIFIED CO...

STATE OF ILLINOIS
COUNTY OF VERMILION) SS

This is to certify that this is a true and correct abstra... official record filed with the Illinois Department of Pu... Not valid without the embossed seal of Vermilion Co...

This copy not valid unless prepared o...

ANY ALTERATION OR I...

ILLINOIS STATE BOARD OF HEALTH.

Return of a Marriage to County Clerk.

1. Full Name of Groom, James Gooch
2. Place of Residence, Vermilion Co Illinois
3. Occupation, Farmer
4. Age next Birthday 23 years. Color White Race,
5. Place of Birth, Madison Co Ky
6. Father's Name Chisel Gooch
7. Mother's Maiden Name, Eliza Maupin
8. Number of Groom's Marriage, 1
9. Full Name of Bride, Mary Addie Graves
   Maiden Name, if a Widow,
10. Place of Residence, Vermilion Co Ill
11. Age next Birthday 20 years. Color White Race, American
12. Place of Birth, Madison co Ky
13. Father's Name, Milton Graves
14. Mother's Maiden Name, Mary Hill
15. Number of Bride's Marriage, 1
16. Married at Robt C. Smiths in the County of Vermilion Co and State of Illinois, the 22 day of Nov 1881
17. Witnesses to Marriage, Columbus Montgomery A. F. Wood

N. B.—At Nos. 8 and 15 state whether 1st, 2d, 3d, &c., Marriage of each. At 17 give names of subscribing witnesses to the Marriage Certificate. If no subscribing witnesses, give names of two persons who witnessed the ceremony.

Nov 22 1881

We Hereby Certify that the information above given is correct, to the best of our knowledge and belief.

Jas Gooch [Groom.]
Mary A Graves [Bride.]

I Hereby Certify that the above is a correct return of a Marriage solemnized by me.

W O Smith

Dated at Catlin this 22 day of Nov 1881

This Return is to be carefully filled out and attached to and returned with the Marriage License. This Return does not take the place of the Certificate which comes attached to the License, but is IN ADDITION THERETO.

Illinois State Board of Health.

RETURN OF A MARRIAGE TO COUNTY CLERK.

1. Full Name of GROOM. James Gooch
2. Place of Residence, Vermilion County Illinois
3. Occupation, Farmer
4. Age next Birthday, 23 years. Color, White Race, American
5. Place of Birth, Madison County Kentucky
6. Father's Name, Chisel Gooch
7. Mother's Maiden Name, Eliza Maupin
8. Number of Groom's Marriage, 1
9. Full Name of BRIDE, Mary Addie Graves
   Maiden Name, if a Widow,
10. Place of Residence, Vermilion County Illinois
11. Age next Birthday, 20 years. Color, White Race, American
12. Place of Birth, Madison County Kentucky
13. Father's Name, Milton Graves
14. Mother's Maiden Name, Mary Hill
15. No. of Bride's Marriage, 1
16. Married at Robert H. Smiths in the County of Vermilion and State of Illinois, the 22 day of November 1881
17. Witnesses to Marriage, A F Woods, Columbus Montgomery

N. B.—At Nos. 8 and 15 state whether 1st, 2d, 3d, 4th, &c., Marriage of each. At 17 give names of subscribing witnesses to the Marriage Certificate. If no subscribing witnesses, give names of two persons who witnessed the ceremony.

We Hereby Certify that the information above given is correct, to the best of our knowledge and belief.

James Gooch [Groom.]
Mary A Graves [Bride.]

I Hereby Certify that the above is a correct return of a Marriage solemnized by me.

Dated at ______ this ____ day of ______ 18__

Marriage license of James Gooch, son of Chiswell D. Gooch and Eliza Ann Maupin, and Mary Addie Graves, November 21, 1881

VERMILION COUNTY, ILLINOIS

STANDARD CERTIFICATE OF DEATH

State of Illinois Standard Certificate of Death. Certified copy from the State of Illinois, Vermilion County, William Gooch b. February 9, 1849, d. March 9, 1929. We believe this is the same man as S.B. Gooch. Perhaps he did not like his name, or changed it for some ulterior motive? He was married to a Lucy in 1880 and appeared in the 1900 Madison County, Kentucky, census, where he was listed as William B. Gooch.

VERMILION COUNTY, ILLINOIS

CERTIFICATE OF DEATH

State of Illinois Certificate of Death. Certified copy from the State of Illinois, Vermilion County, Lucia Gooch d. January 14, 1937

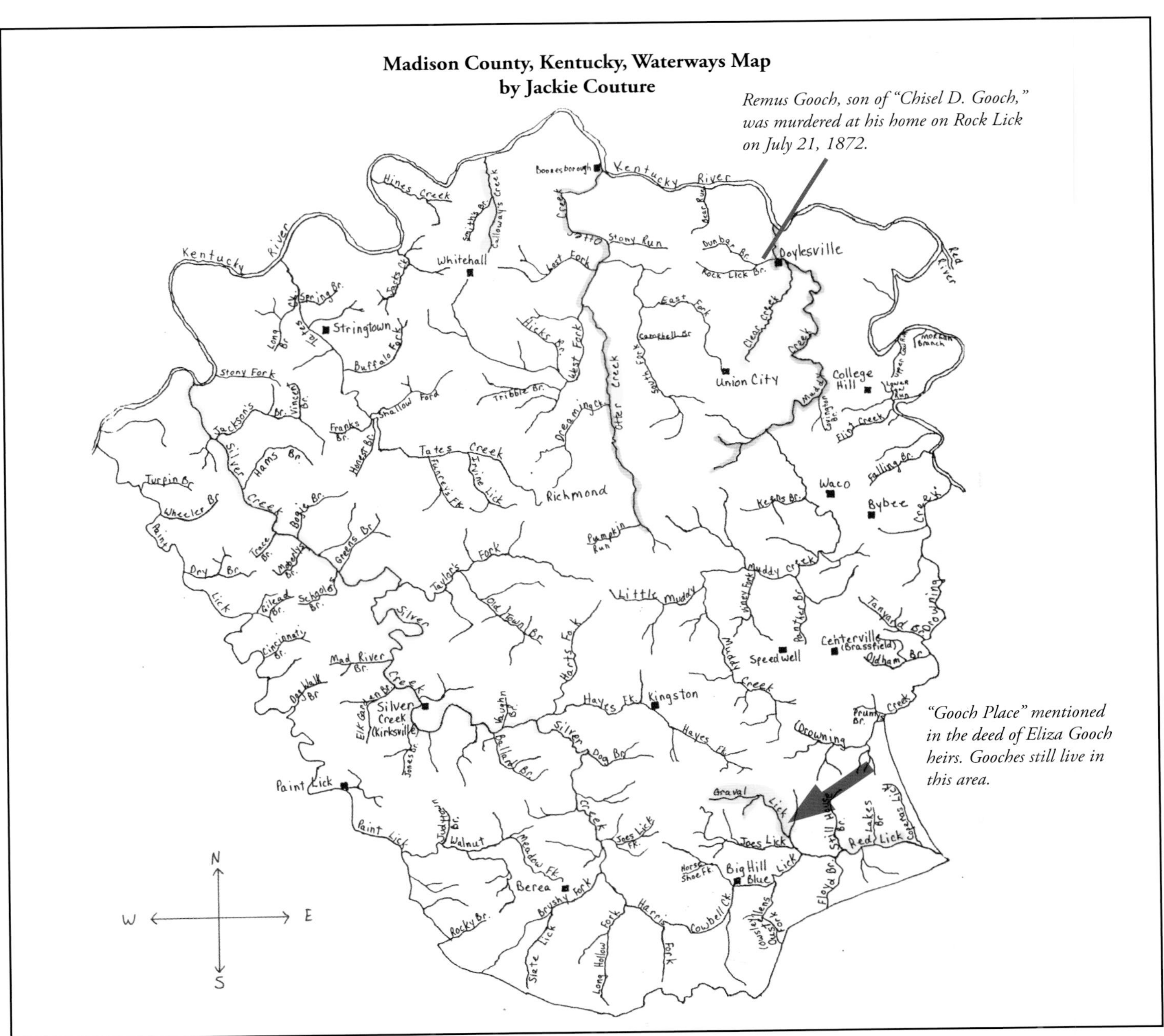

Index to Waterways

Ballard Branch-SW
Bear Run-NE
Blue Lick-SE
Bogie Branch-NW
Brushy Fork-SW
Buffalo Fork-NW
Calloways Creek-NW
Campbell Branch-NE
Cincinnati Branch-SW
Clear Creek-NE
Coperas Lick-SE
Covington Branch-NE
Cow Run, Upper and Lower-NE
Cowbell Creek-SE
Dog Walk Branch-SW
Dog Branch-SE
Dreaming Creek-NE
Drowning Creek-NE, SE
Dry Branch-SW
Dunbar Branch-NE
Elk Garden Branch-SW
Falling Branch-NE
Flint Creek-NE
Floyd Branch-SE
Franks Branch-NW
Funreys Fork (Finneys Fork)-NW
Gilead Branch-SW
Graval Lick-SE
Greens Branch-NW
Hams Branch-NW
Harris Fork-SE
Harts Fork-SW
Hayes Fork-SE, SW
Hicks Branch-NW
Hines Creek-NW
Honest Branch-NW
Horse Shoe Fork (Horse Cove Branch)-SE
Irvine Lick-NW
Jacks Creek-NW
Jacksons Branch-NW
Joes Lick-SE
Joes Lick Fork-SE
Jones Branch-SW
Judytown Branch-SW
Keens Branch-NE
Lakes Branch-SE
Little Muddy Creek-SE
Long Branch-NW
Long Hollow Fork-SE
Lost Fork-NE, NW
Madison River Branch-SW
Moberlys Branch-NW, SW
Muddy Creek-NE, SE
Old Town Branch-SW
Oldham Branch-SE
Otter Creek-NE, NW
Owsley Fork-SE
Paint Lick-NW, SW
Panther Branch (Hickory Lick)-SE
Pruntys Branch-SE
Pumpkin Run-NE
Red Lick-SE
Rock Lick Branch-NE
Rocky Branch-SW
Schoolers Branch-SW
Shallow Ford-NW
Silver Creek-NW, SW, SE
Slate Lick-SW
Smiths Branch-NW
Spring Branch-NW
Still House Branch-SE
Stony Fork-NW
Stony Run-NE
Tanyard Branch-SE
Tates Creek-NW
Taylors Fork-SW
Trace Branch-NW
Tribble Branch-NW
Turpin Branch (Sled Branch)-NW
Vaughn Branch-SW
Vincent Branch-NW
Viney Fork-SE
Walnut Meadow Fork-SW
Wheeler Branch-NW

COMMISSIONER'S

SALE

ELIZA GOOCH'S ADMR., Plaintiff,
against
ELIZA GOOCH'S HEIRS, Defts.
} Notice of Sale—In Equity.

By virtue of a judgment and Order of Sale of the Madison Circuit Court rendered at the December Term, thereof, 1893, in the above styled cause the undersigned will,

ON MONDAY, FEBRUARY 5TH, 1894,

about the hour of 12 o'clock M., at the court house door in Richmond, Madison County, Ky., (being County Court day), proceed to expose to public sale to the highest bidder the following described property, viz:

ABOUT 105 ACRES OF LAND

on Gravel Lick Fork of Red Lick known as the Gooch farm and described as follows: Beginning at a stake on a line of Bruce Kidwell near a gate on the north side of the farm, thence S 19½ W, 98 poles to a stake in Gravel
Lick below the sinh… …th the meanders thereof S
54° E, 16 poles, S 1…
E, 8 poles, S 60 E. …
creek, S 7 E, 17 po…
to some mulberry …
oak sapling in a dr…
water-fall; thence …
with his line S 60 …
line; thence with …
ner to Geo. Morton…
bush on north bank…
bushes; thence N …
poles to a stake; th…
S 67 E, 19 poles; t…
S 67 E, 19 poles, th…
thence N 65 W, at …
to a stake in a bran…
this land is a good …
with some good bo…

TERMS.—Sale will be made on a credit of six months. The purchaser will be required to give bond with approved security for the payment of the purchase money, to have the force and effect of a judgment, bearing legal interest from the day of sale, with a Lien reserved upon said property until all the purchase money is paid.

J. R. BURNAM,
Commissioner of Madison Circuit Court.

THE CLIMAX, … RICHMOND, KY.

Book 45 Page 418

Eliza Goochs
Heirs By Comr
To
T. J. Coyle

Whereas, in the action of Eliza Gooches Administrator Plaintiff against Eliza Gooches Heirs Defendents pending in the Madison Cir Court, an order was entered at the December Term 1893 directing the Master Commissioner of said Court to expose for sale at Public auction, to the highest and best bidder, the property hereinafter described; and Whereas said property was sold in accordance with said order on the fifth day of February 1894, for the Sum of Two Hundred and forty ($240) Dollars and cents Where-

Above left: Commissioner's Sale notice for the sale of 105 acres of land to settle the estate of Eliza Gooch. The proceeds of the sale, scheduled for February 5, 1894, were to be divided among her heirs.

Above right and following pages: Kentucky State Archives, Frankfort, Kentucky, Eliza Gooch's Heirs by Commissioners to T.J. Coyle, Madison County, Kentucky, Deed Book 45:418–419 and 420, December 1893

T. Y. Coyle became the purchaser thereof; and Whereas
the report of said sale was confirmed by said Court
at the April Term 1894, and at the April Term 1894
an order was entered directing said Master Commissioner
to execute a deed of Conveyance of said property
to said T. Y. Coyle, but for greater certainty the record
and proceedings in said Case are referred to;
Now therefore this indenture made and entered into
this 12th day of Dec 1894. between Cornelius Gooch,
Lucy Shoop, Isaac Shoop, Thos Gooch, Jeff Davis,
John Davis, Charley Davis, Joe Davis, William Davis,
James Davis. Lula Davis, Charley Gooch, Mary E Gooch
Joe Turner, Bob. Turner, Maggie Turner, Mollie Turner
Della Smith, Wm Smith. Neal E. Turner, Ida Turner
Jo Ann Maupin, Daniel Maupin, Laura Young,
James Gooch, Lucy Graves, Milton Graves, Henry
Gooch, and S. B. Gooch, by J R Burnam Master
Commissioner of the said Court, of the first part
and T. Y. Coyle of the Second part, Witnesseth, that
for and in Consideration of the premises, and for
the further consideration of the full payment of
the purchase price aforesaid, the receipt whereof
is hereby acknowledged the parties of the first
part by J R Burnam Master Commissioner aforesaid
hath sold and by this writing do convey to said
party of the second part and his heirs and
assigns forever the following described property
to wit, A Certain tract of land lying on Gravel
Lick Fork of Red Lick Creek in Madison County
known as the Gooch place and described
as follows towit; Beginning at a Stake on a
line of Bruce Kidwell near a gate on north side
of the farm, thence S. 19½° W 98 poles to a Stake
in Gravel Lick below the sinks, thence down
the Creek with the meanders thereof S. 54° E 10
p. S12° E 10 po. S75° E 10 po S.58° E 10 p. S21° E 8 p.
S16° E 20 po to a stake in the branch, thence leav
ing the creek S. 7° E. 17 p to a Sycamore in a drain
thence S64° E 9½ po to some Mulberry Sprouts
on a point, thence S5½° E 18 p to a Spotted oak
Sapling in a drain; thence up said drain S. 61° W
6 p. to a Stake on a water fall; thence S42° W 20 p.
to a Stake in Wm Witts line, thence with his line

Book 45 Page 419

Sale of 105 acres to settle Eliza Gooch's estate. Property was sold in February 1894 for $240 to T.Y. Coyle. Eliza's heirs were Cornelius Gooch, Lucy Shoop, Isaac Shoop, Thos. Gooch, Jeff Davis, John Davis, Charley Davis, Joe Davis, William Davis, James Davis, Lula Davis, Charley Gooch, Mary E. Gooch, Joe Turner, Bob Turner, Maggie Turner, Mollie Turner, Della Smith, Wm. Smith, Neal E. Turner, Ida Turner, Jo Ann Maupin, Daniel Maupin, Laura Young, James Gooch, Lucy Graves, Milton Graves, Henry Gooch, and S.B. Gooch.

Book 45 Page 420

S 60° E 44 p. to three pin oak on a hill side in Stones old line, thence with his line N 25° E 21 p to a Stake on Gravel Lick a Corner to George Morton Alias Worford; thence with his line N 15 W 17 p to a black oak on north bank of the Creek, thence N 52 W 6 p to some Sycamore bushes. thence N 13 E 22 p to an elm tree thence up a branch N 56¼° E 10 p to a Stake; thence N 73 W 72 p. thence N 37 E 40 p; thence S 67° E 19 p. thence N 23 E 78 p. to a White oak near a hollow, thence N 65' W at 44 p. Wm Heirs White oak Corner in all 98 p. to a Stake in a branch; thence S 72° W 34 p. to the begining Containing 105 acres more or less by survey of B.F. Crooke made in 1874

To have and to hold said property with its appurtenances unto the said grantee his heirs and assigns,

The said Commissioner conveys all the right title and interest legal and equitable of the said Comelius, Thomas, Charley, Mary E. James, Henry, and B B Gooch. Lucy & Isaac Sharp. Jeff. John. Charley. Joe Wm. James & Lulu Davis, Joe, Bob. Maggie & Mollie Turner, Dellie & Wm Smith, Neal E. & Ida Turner Jo Ann & Daniel McIlpin. Laura Young & Milton Graves Jr. in and to said property, and warrants the title thereto, so far as he is, authorized by the Judgment orders and proceedings in said cause and no further but he does not bind himself personally by anything Contained herein in any event Whatever;

In Testimony Whereof, said J R Burnam Master Commissioner aforesaid, has hereunto subscribed his name this 12th day of December 1894.

J R Burnam Commissioner M.C.C.

Acknowledged by the Commissioner Examined and approved in open Court. this day of 12 Dec 1894

T. J Scott Judge, M.C.C.

State of Kentucky
Madison Circuit Court } Sct

I S.H. Thorpe Jr Clerk of the Madison circuit Court do hereby certify that this deed from Eliza Gooch Heirs by J R Burnam Master Commr

[illegible]

by J R Burnam Commissioner, and was
duly acknowledged to be his act and deed, and
the said Deed having been examined by the Court
was approved and confirmed and so endorsed by
the Judge, and ordered to be transmitted, duly
certified to the Clerk of the Madison County
Court for record, which is now done accordingly
Given under my hand, this 9 day of Janry
1895.

Attest S H Thorpe Clerk

State of Kentucky }
County of Madison } Sct

I John F White Clerk of the Madison County
Court do hereby certify that the foregoing Deed
from Eliza Gooches Heirs by J R Burnam
Master Commissioner of the Madison Circuit Court to
Thos J Hoyle was produced to me in my office
on the 9 day of January 1895, certified as
above for record. Whereupon the same and the
foregoing, and this Certificate have been
recorded in my office

Given under my hand, this 27 day of Sept
1897

Attest John F White Clerk
By Thos Thorpe D.C.

Delivered

Book 45 Page 421

Description of the 105 acres sold to settle Eliza Gooch's estate and terms of sale

Kentucky State Archives, Frankfort, Kentucky, Madison County Circuit Court Case File Box 287 #574.
Gooch court case listing all heirs of Eliza Gooch, wife of Chiswell.

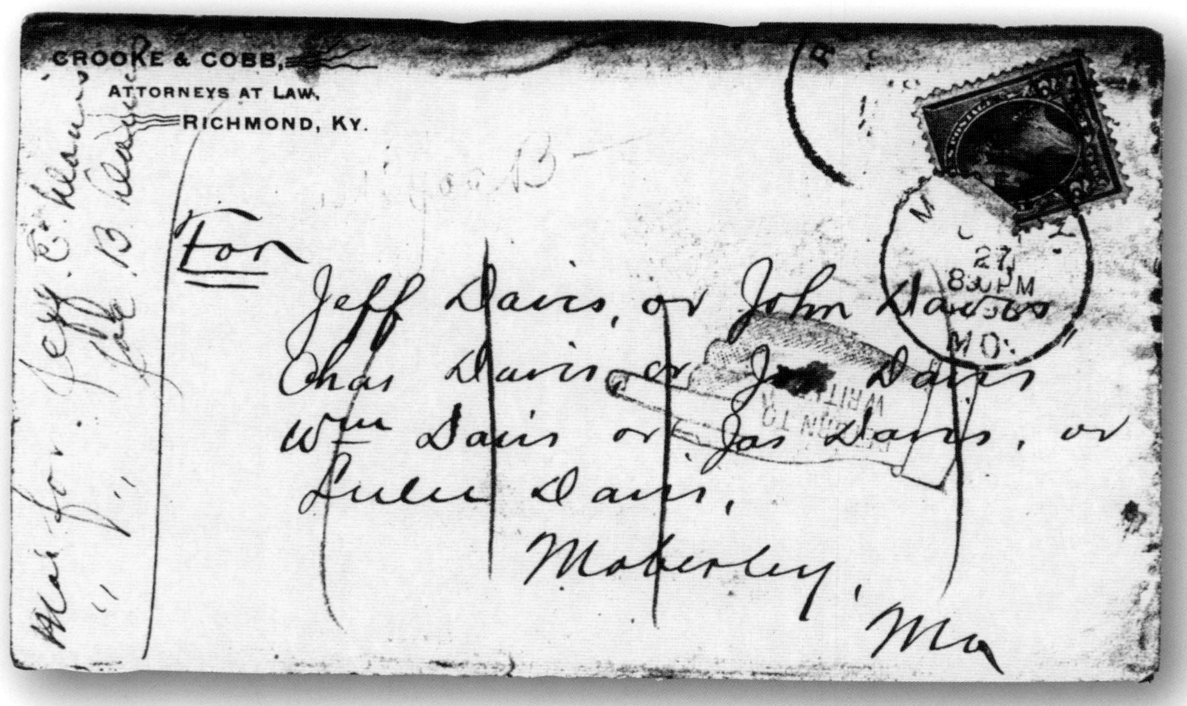

"Eliza Gooch departed this life intestate this 24th day of July 1892 and at the time of her death she was seized and possessed of about 105 acres of land situated in Madison County Ky. on Gravel Lick fork of Red Lick Creek...."

This letter was returned. There is some question as to whether the Davis heirs ever received their small portion of the estate.

Madison Circuit Court

12 S.B. Gooch, Admr of Eliza Gooch dec. Jeff.

vs

		Name		Residence	
✓	1	Cornelius Gooch ✓		Madison.	
✓	2	Lucy Sharp ✓		Madison.	
✓		Isaac Sharp ✓		Madison.	Petition
✓ c	3	Thomas Gooch ✓		Catlin Ill.	in
✓ c		Jeff Davis	1 ✓	Moberly Mo	Equity.
c		John Davis	2 ✓	" "	
c		Charley Davis	3 ✓	" "	
c	4	Joe Davis	4 ✓	" "	
c		William Davis	5 ✓	" "	
c		James Davis	6 ✓	Dfts "	
c		Lulu Davis	7 ✓	" "	
c		Charley Gooch	1 ✓	Missouri	
c	5	Mary E. Gooch	2 ✓	"	
✓	✓	Joe Turner	1 ✓	Washington Co. Ky.	
a		Bob Turner	2	Madison.	
c		Maggie Turner	3 ✓	Ill.	
c	6	Mollie Turner	4 ✓	Ill.	
a		Della ~~Smith~~	5	Clark Co. Ky.	
a		Wm. Smith		" " "	
c		Mal E. Turner	6 ✓	Unknown	
c		Ida Turner	7 ✓	"	
✓		Jo Ann Maupin	✓	Madison	
✓	7	Daniel Maupin	✓	"	
c	8	Laura Young	✓	Fairmount Ill.	
c	9	James Gooch	✓	" "	
c		Lucy Graves	✓	Penington P.O. Ill.	
c	10	Milton Graves Jr.	✓	Ill. Penington P.O.	
✓	11	Henry Gooch (Madison)			

Plaintiff say that Eliza Gooch departed this life intestate on the 24 day of ~~July~~ 1892 and at the time of her death she was seized and possessed

My grandfather, Charley Davis. was designated as an heir of Eliza Gooch, deceased, along with his brothers Jeff Davis, John Davis, Joe Davis, William Davis, James Davis, and his sister, Lulu Davis (Sanders). Note that my grandfather's brother, Ollie Davis, b. January 27, 1882, does not appear in the above list.

of about 105 acres of land situated in Madison County Ky. on Gravel Lick fork of Red Lick Creek and bounded by the lands of Thomas Hill, Geo. Morton, R.T. Young and J.M. Carmack, the same having been conveyed to the said Eliza Gooch dec. by deed from Wm. and Lydia Cope, said deed being of record in the Madison County Clerks Office and is referred to for metes and bounds and made part hereof.

Plaintiff further states that he is the duly qualified Administrator of the said Eliza Gooch dec. and that he and the defendants in this action are the only and all the heirs at law of the said Eliza Gooch dec.; that there are 12 whole shares in said estate and that plaintiff and defendants are children and grandchildren of the said Eliza Gooch dec. and that each of said shares are worth less than $100.00 and that it will be to the best interests of all concerned for the court to decree a sale of said land and to divide the proceeds of same among said heirs according to their respective interests in said land.

Plaintiff says that Cornelius Gooch, Thomas Gooch, Henry Gooch, Jo Ann Maupin, S.B. Gooch, Laura Young, James Gooch and Lucy Graves are all children of deceased Eliza Gooch and are each entitled to one twelfth of the whole estate (1/12); that Daniel Maupin is the husband of Jo Ann Maupin and Milton Graves Jr is the husband of Lucy Graves; that Lucy Sharp is the daughter and only child of A → Angela Williams dec. who was a daughter of Eliza Gooch dec. said Lucy Sharp is entitled to 1/12 of said estate and Isaac Sharp is the husband of Lucy Sharp; that Jeff Davis, John Davis, Charley Davis, Joe Davis, William Davis, James Davis and Rubin Davis are the

Lucy Gooch Graves, spouse of Milton Graves Jr.

only children of Nannie Davis dec. she being a daughter of Eliza Gooch dec. said Jeff, John, Charley, Joe, William, James and Lulu Davis being each entitled to 1/84 of the whole estate and they all live at Moberly Missouri; that William, James and Lulu Davis are under the age of 21 years and they have no statutory guardian in this state known to the plaintiff; that Charley Gooch and Mary Gooch are the only children of Remus Gooch dec. who was a son of Eliza Gooch dec. and they are each entitled to 1/24 of the whole estate and they live in Missouri their post office being unknown to plaintiff; that Joe Turner, Bob Turner, Maggie Turner, Mollie Turner, Della Smith, Neal Everett Turner and Ida Turner are the only children of Mary Turner dec. who was a daughter of Eliza Gooch dec. and they are each entitled to 1/84 of the whole estate; that Wm Smith is the husband of Della Smith and they Wm Smith and Della Smith live in Clark County Ky. Joe Turner lives in Washington County Ky and that Maggie Turner, Mollie Turner, Neal E. Turner and Ida Turner's residence is unknown but supposed to be living in the State of Illinois; that Laura Young lives in Fairmount Illinois, James Gooch in Fairmount Ill. Lucy Graves and her husband Milton Graves live in Pennington Ill. ~~their Post Office not known~~. x

x and Thomas Gooch lives in Catlin State of Illinois

Plaintiff says that Eliza Gooch dec. in her life time became the surety of James Gooch to A. J. Reed atty for the sum of fifteen dollars and that the said Reed now has an unliquidated judgment in the Richmond Police Court against the said Eliza Gooch dec for said $15.00 with legal interest and cost and the administrator will be

379

Lucy Gooch Graves, b. ca. 1859, the 14th child of Chiswell D. Gooch and Eliza Ann Maupin Gooch, lived in Pennington, Illinois, at the time of her mother's passing. Lucy was to receive 1/12 of the value ($420) of the land owned and left by Eliza in the Yates District on Gravel Lick fork of Red Lick Creek, Madison County, Kentucky. This document is continued on the following page.

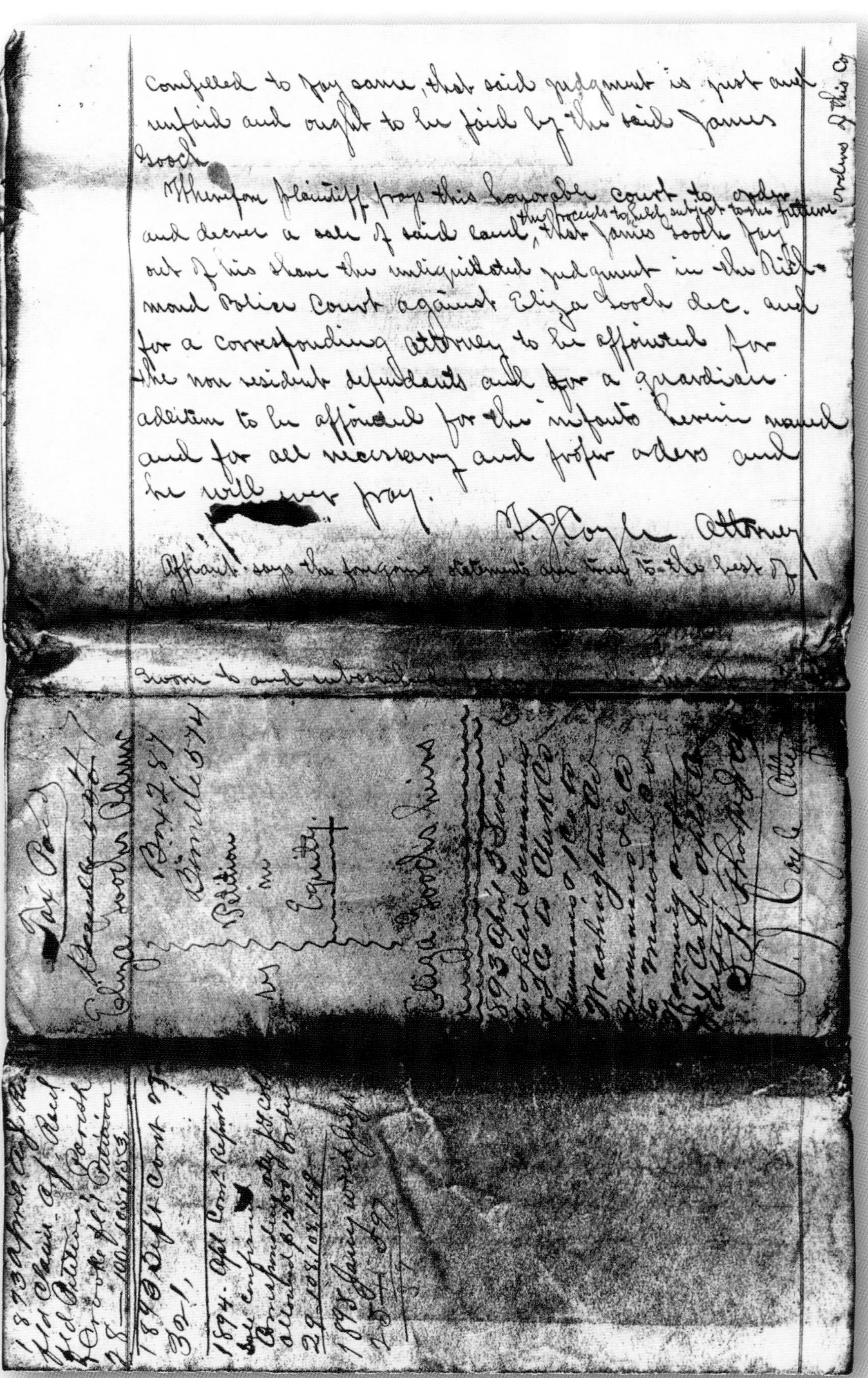

compelled to pay same, that said judgment is just and unpaid and ought to be paid by the said James Gooch.

Wherefore plaintiff prays this honorable court to order and decree a sale of said land, the proceeds to be held subject to the future ... that James Gooch pay out of his share the unliquidated judgment in the Richmond Police Court against Eliza Gooch dec. and for a corresponding attorney to be appointed for the non resident defendants and for a guardian ad litem to be appointed for the infants herein named and for all necessary and proper orders and he will ever pray.

T. J. Coyle Attorney

Affiant says the foregoing statements are true to the best of

Madison Circuit Court

Eliza Gooch's Admr.
vs
Eliza Gooch's Hrs.

Report of Corresponding Attorney.

Your corresponding attorney would most respectfully say that the non resident defendants herein are numerous – that they reside in many different places in the United States.

He states that he has addressed letters to them at the Post Offices designated in Petition herein as their place of residence & instituted other means of inquiry, to find out if there is any reason of contradicting statements of petition herein.

He concludes that there is no reason apparent to him why the prayer of petitioner should not be granted, & praying the protection of this honorable Court to the nonresident defendants & for a reasonable allowance herein, he most respectfully submits this report

J Tevis Cobb, Cor. Atty.

Above: Corresponding attorney's report to the Madison Circuit Court in the case of Eliza Gooch's administrator vs. her heirs, describing the attempts made to contact Eliza Gooch's heirs in "many different places in the United States" to find out if there were any "contradictory statements of petition herein." He goes on to ask the court to grant the petition and to grant the court's protection against the nonresident defendants.

For and in consideration of the sum of twenty dollars in hand paid the receipt whereof is hereby acknowledged, in one cow at $25, I to pay F. J. Coyle $5.00 back, I have this day sold to F. J. Coyle my undivided one twelfth interest in 100 acres of land on Gravel Lick Creek in Madison County, owned by my mother Eliza Gooch at the time of her death, and I authorize the Master Commissioner of the Madison Circuit Court to pay over to said F. J. Coyle the full amount of my distributable share in said land when sold and allow F. J. Coyle to receipt for same.

My interest is one undivided twelfth and is unencumbered and free from debt, there are no debts against said Gooch estate except $15.00 and interest to A. J. Reed and $5.00 to J. W. Boles, this is guaranteed.

Witness my hand Dec. 16th 1893.

Attest

Ruben Gabbard

S. B. his X mark Gooch

For and in consideration of the sum of twenty dollars paid in two bull calves, the receipt whereof is hereby acknowledged, I have this day sold to T. J. Coyle my undivided interest in the 105 acres of land, on Gravel Lick Creek Mad. Co owned by my mother Eliza Gooch at the time of her death and I hereby authorize the Master Commissioner of the Madison Circuit Court to pay over to T. J. Coyle the full amount of my distributable share in said land when sold and allow T. J. Coyle to receipt for same.

My interest is an undivided one twelfth and is unencumbered in any way and free from debt, there are no debts against the Gooch estate except the amount of $15 and interest going to A. J. Reed and $5.00 to J. W. Boles this is guaranteed.

Witness my hand Dec. 16" 1893.

Attest
Ruben Gabbard

Henry his X mark Gooch

Document on left is a receipt of payment by S.B. Gooch for his 1/12 interest in 105 acres of land on Gravel Lick Creek in Madison County, Kentucky, owned by his mother, Eliza Gooch, at the time of her death. S.B. Gooch received a cow worth $25 and agreed to pay R.J. Coyle $5, making the value of his share of the land $20.

Below is the receipt of payment by Henry Gooch, S.B. Gooch's brother, for his 1/12 interest in the 100 acres of land on Gravel Lick Creek. He also received $20 in the form of two bull calves.

State of Kentucky }
Madison County } SS.

Personally appeared before me Wm C. Garrett, who states on oath as follows towit:

I am acquainted with the 105 acres of land owned by Eliza Gooch dec. at time of her death. Said land is in the Yates District in Madison County on waters of Gravel Lick fork of Red Lick Creek. Said land is worth about $420 or $4 per acre. I do not believe the land can be divided into twelve shares without greatly injuring the value of same. I think it would be impossible to divide the land into twelve shares of equal value.

I believe it would be to the best interest of all concerned to sell the land and divide the proceeds. I am 32 years of age and am not of kin to any of the parties in interest nor in any way concerned in this suit.

W C Garrett

Sworn to and subscribed before me by W. C. Garrett Dec. 2nd 1893.

[Seal: ... NOTARY PUBLIC MADISON COUNTY]

J. P. Coyle Notary Public

Crooke and Cobb,
ATTORNEYS AT LAW.
OFFICE: COLLINS BUILDING.

R. H. CROOKE.
J. TEVIS COBB.

Richmond, Ky., 189

Thos. Gooch, Esq

Dear Sir:

Sometime in July 92 Eliza Gooch of this County, died leaving about 105 acres of land, to sell which there is a suit now pending in Madison Circuit Court. You are one of the heirs in it & I am appointed corresponding attorney to confer with non residents. Do you want the land sold? I am of the opinion that it would be best to sell it & divide the proceeds equally among all the heirs. Let me hear from you with regard to it at once.

Can you give me the Post office address of Neal Turner, Ida Turner, Maggie Turner & Mollie Turner?

Yrs truly

J. Tevis Cobb

Document on previous page is a sworn statement by William C. Garrett that the 105 acres on Gravel Lick Road in Madison County, Kentucky, which had belonged to Eliza Gooch, is worth about $420, and that it is his belief that it is impossible to divide the land into twelve shares of equal value "without greatly injuring the value of same."

The letter above from J. Tevis Cobb to Thomas Gooch, Esq., notified him that he was one of Eliza Gooch's heirs and recommended the sale of his share in the 105 acres of land. Tevis also asked for the post office addresses of Neal, Ida, Maggie, and Mollie Turner.

Crooke and Cobb,
ATTORNEYS AT LAW.
OFFICE: COLLINS BUILDING.

R. H. CROOKE.
J. TEVIS COBB.

Richmond, Ky. Sept 18th 189[illegible]

Dear Sirs:

There is a suit pending in the Madison Circuit Court, seeking to sell a piece of land that belonged to Eliza Gooch who died 24 July 1892 Henry Gooch is administrator & I have been appointed corresponding Attorney for non residents. There are about 105 acres in it & you will be entitled to a small interest in it when sold. There is a small judgment here that will have to be paid
Please write me at once what you wish done in the matter. I am inclined to think it best to sell the land & distribute the proceeds to the heirs. Please write [illegible] at once.

Yrs truly
J. Tevis Cobb

The letter above is from J. Tevis Cobb notifying unidentified parties to a suit regarding the sale of the 105 acres of land in Eliza Gooch's estate.

—PUBLIC SALE OF 3—
FINE MAUPIN FARMS

ON THE PREMISES

Wednesday, Sept. 30th

BEGINNING AT 10 A. M. 1931

The following personal property will first be sold: Household furniture, 4 cows, 1 mule, farm wagon, wheat drill, mowing machine, hay rake, 50 acres of corn in field, about 25 tons timothy hay in stack, and many other articles too numerous to mention.

This personal property will be sold on the following terms: All sums under $25.00, cash on day of sale; all sums over $25.00, ninety days time, with good negotiable note bearing six per cent interest.

—FARMS TO BE SOLD—

TRACT NO. 1: The old Maupin home, located on the Stagner dirt road about three-fourths mile from the Richmond-Irvine pike, consisting of 175 acres of good blue grass land. On this tract is a modern 8-room house, with cellars, cistern on porch; one large tobacco barn and one large stock barn, scales, good orchard, abundant water supply, etc.

TRACT NO. 2: Known as the T. J. McKinney farm, directly across the dirt road from Tract No. 1, consisting of 175 acres of fine blue grass land, with 6-room house, good stock barn, good orchard, well of never failing water and all necessary outbuildings.

TRACT NO. 3: Known as the Vaught farm, located on the Richmond-Irvine pike, about 3½ miles from Richmond consisting of 85 acres, on which is a nearly new 6-room house, good orchard, new stock barn, cistern, all necessary outbuildings, etc.

TERMS

Tracts No. 1 will be sold by the heirs of Mrs. Mollie Maupin and Tracts No. 2 and 3 by the State Bank & Trust Company, as the Administrator of the real estate of C. H. Maupin upon the following terms:

Ten per cent of the purchase price in cash on day of sale; Fifteen per cent cash when deed is executed and possession is given purchaser on or about January 1, 1932; Balance in six and twelve months, with six per cent interest and lien retained on land to secure payment of purchase price.

Seeding privileges in Fall of 1931 be given purchaser.

E. C. McDOUGLE, Agent of Maupin Heirs.
STATE BANK & TRUST CO., Administrator of C. H. Maupin
LONG TOM CHENAULT, Auctioneer; J. B. SHEARER, Clerk

Anne Crabb, a genealogist of Richmond, Kentucky, found this Public Sale notice in the Maupin Family F.H. #263, Eastern Kentucky University Library. In an accompanying note, she wrote:

"I found this in the Maupin Family History file and include it as some local color. Have no idea whether any of the property described would have belonged to your Maupin family of Madison County, Kentucky. (E.C. McDougal, agent for the Maupins, owned the first house we lived in when we moved to Richmond over 30 years ago.)" Daniel and Jo Ann Maupin are listed among the heirs of Eliza Gooch (see page 377). We don't know the exact relationship of these two particular Maupins.

THOMAS E. GOOCH b. January 25, 1836

Thomas E. Gooch b. January 25, 1836, and Mildred Elizabeth Oldham Gooch b. May 2, 1838

A Prolific Family

Thomas Emanuel Gooch was born January 25, 1836,[1] in Madison County, Kentucky, to Chiswell D. Gooch and Eliza Ann Maupin. He grew up in Madison County and married his cousin Mildred Elizabeth Oldham on December 13, 1860.[2] Mildred was the daughter of Ed Oldham[3] and Jane Hill. Jane was the daughter of John Hill and Eliza White Gooch Hill. Eliza was also Thomas Gooch's grandmother, although the couple had different grandfathers. As so often happened in the 1800s, relatives married relatives making for a confusing genealogy. Mildred's uncle, Chiswell Gooch, became her father-in-law when she married Thomas E. Gooch.

Mildred married at the age of fourteen to Nathan Williams on March 1, 1853.[4] Consent for Mildred was given by Joel Karr, her guardian. Nathan Williams was twenty. This marriage ended in divorce. A family story was handed down that Mildred had two children from this marriage that she had to give up. We have not been able to verify this story. In the 1860 census, Mildred Williams was living with the Joel Karr family; she was age twenty-one, her occupation was a seamstress, and she had no children living with her.[5]

After her marriage to Thomas Gooch, Mildred inherited her mother's share of Eliza Gooch Hill's estate, according to her grandmother's will.[6] One item that she inherited was a Negro slave named Jack. Thomas Gooch and Mildred sold him for $300 to Milo Baxter on October 6, 1863, during the peak of the Civil War.[7]

By the 1870 census, Thomas and Mildred had four children: Edna, Robert, Rebecca, and John, who was born in September of 1869.[8] Thomas was a common laborer. By the 1880 census, they had added four more children: William, Alexander, Eliza, and Thomas.[9] They lived next to Eliza Maupin Gooch, Thomas's mother.

Rosa M. Gooch, born October 1883, and Jessie D., born October 1888, completed the family. Sometime after Rosa's birth in 1883, the family moved to Vermilion County, Illinois, because the last daughter, Jessie D., was born there in 1888. However, some of the older children in the family may have moved to Illinois prior to their parents, as Edna Gooch married William Harry Delaney in May of 1882 in Vermilion County.[10]

In the 1900 census, the family lived in Vermilion County, and Robert T. and Thomas M. Gooch were listed as coal miners. William T. and Joel Gooch were working on farms. Mildred declared that she had nine children and nine were living. However, we believe there were at least eleven children in the family. In the 1900 census, there was a son named Joel M. Gooch, who was listed as born in September of 1871, but he was apparently missed on the 1880 census, unless he is the same person as the child named Alexander, age nine, in that census.[11]

In their declining years Thomas and Mildred lived with their daughter Edna Gooch Delaney and sonThomas "Mann" Gooch in Vermilion County, Illinois.[12] The 1910 census showed that Mildred had been married twice and that she had twelve children with nine living. Thomas was listed as "having an income."

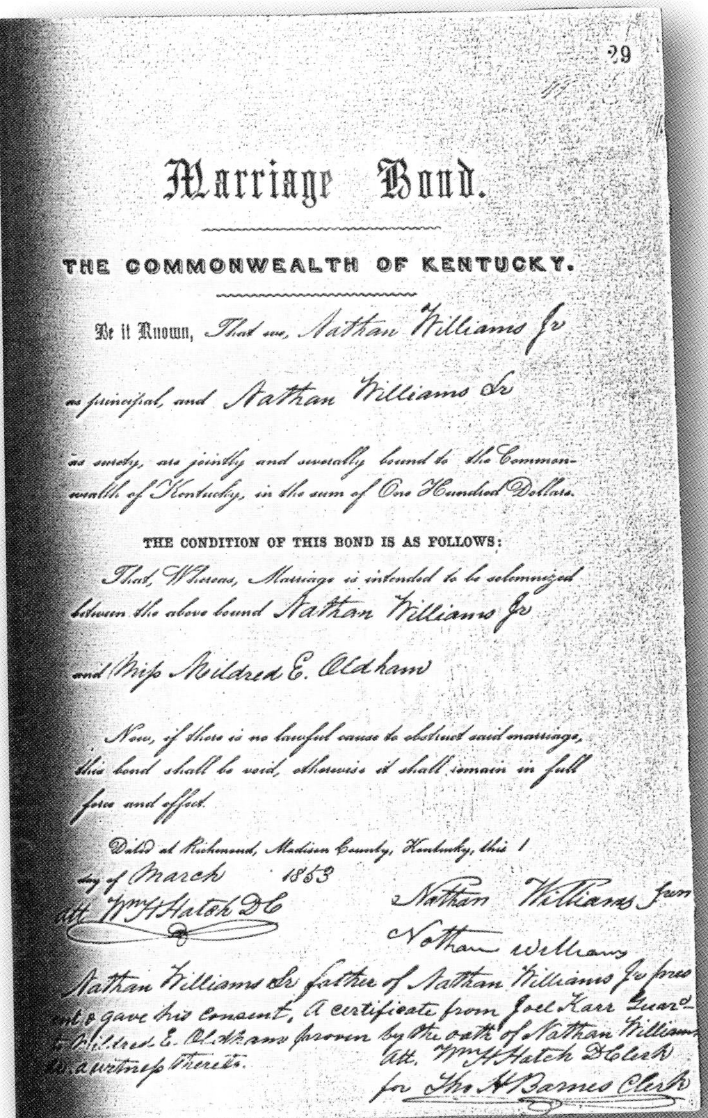

29

Marriage Bond.

THE COMMONWEALTH OF KENTUCKY.

Be it Known, That we, Nathan Williams Jr as principal, and Nathan Williams Sr as surety, are jointly and severally bound to the Commonwealth of Kentucky, in the sum of One Hundred Dollars.

THE CONDITION OF THIS BOND IS AS FOLLOWS:

That, Whereas, Marriage is intended to be solemnized between the above bound Nathan Williams Jr and Miss Mildred E. Oldham

Now, if there is no lawful cause to obstruct said marriage, this bond shall be void, otherwise it shall remain in full force and effect.

Dated at Richmond, Madison County, Kentucky, this 1 day of March 1853

att. Wm H Hatch DC

Nathan Williams Jun

Nathan Williams

Nathan Williams Sr father of Nathan Williams Jr present & gave his consent, A certificate from Joel Karr Guard to Mildred E. Oldham proven by the oath of Nathan Williams Jr a witness thereto.

Att. Wm H Hatch D Clerk for Tho H Barnes Clerk

Commonwealth of Kentucky Marriage Bond for Nathan Williams Jr. and Mildred Oldham dated March 1, 1853

THOMAS E. GOOCH b. January 25, 1836

373

Marriage Bond.

THE COMMONWEALTH OF KENTUCKY.

Be it Known, That we, Thomas E Gooch as principal, and Chiswell D Gooch as surety, are jointly and severally bound to the Commonwealth of Kentucky, in the sum of One Hundred Dollars.

THE CONDITION OF THIS BOND IS AS FOLLOWS:

That, Whereas, Marriage is intended to be solemnized between the above bound Thomas E Gooch and Mrs Mildred E Williams

Now, if there is no lawful cause to obstruct said marriage, this bond shall be void, otherwise it shall remain in full force and effect.

Dated at Richmond, Madison County, this 13 day of December 1860. Thos E Gooch

Att. Thos H Barnes Clk C D Gooch

Thomas E. Gooch, 23 years of age, born & residing in Madison Co. Ky – 1st Marriage – Mildred E. Williams, 22 years of age, born & residing in Madison County, Ky – 2nd Marriage – divorced. – Marriage intended to be solemnized on this evening at the house of C. D Gooch in this County

Att Thos H Barnes Clk

Commonwealth of Kentucky Marriage Bond for Thomas E. Gooch and Mildred E. Williams dated December 13, 1860

Mildred Gooch died November 6, 1917, and Thomas E. Gooch followed a few months later on January 26, 1918.[13] Both were buried in the Greenview Cemetery in Fairmount, Illinois. Mildred's obituary, received from LaVerne Purkey in 1998, reads as follows:

> Mrs. Mildred Gooch, a highly respected and estimable lady of Fairmount, departed this life Tuesday Nov. 6, 1917, aged 79 years and 4 days. She had been in poor health for some time and in addition to the infirmities of old age she suffered from heart trouble and dropsy. Mrs. Gooch was married to Thos. E. Gooch, Dec. 11, 1860. She was the mother of ten children, four sons and five daughters, all living except one daughter who had preceded her to the better world. Those living are: Mrs. Harry Delaney, Robert Gooch, Mrs. Rebecca Davis, John Gooch, Mrs. Eliza Goodwin, Will Gooch, Mrs. Rosa Woodard, Manuel Gooch, and Mrs. Jessie Reeves. Besides her aged husband and children she leaves to mourn her death 38 grandchildren and her life was in her children. Funeral services in her memory were held at the home of Mann Gooch, with whom they made their home for sometime, at 2 o'clock Wed. Nov. 7th conducted by Miss Corrie Rhein, after which the body was laid to rest in Greenview Cemetery. A large assembly of people attended attesting the high esteem in which she was held. There were many beautiful floral offerings.

The children of Thomas Emanuel and Mildred Gooch were

1. Edna "Edney" Gooch born April 3, 1862; married May 16, 1882, in Danville, Vermilion County, Illinois, to William Harry Delaney. She died May 3, 1918, leaving the following children: Thomas E. Delaney born August 6, 1886, or about 1887 per the 1910 census; Hallie M. Delaney born March 1889; Willie Delaney born September 1892; Dorsa J. Delaney born November 1897;[14] Dale W. Delaney born 1901; Doyle Delaney born 1904, and Mildred Delaney born 1907.[15]
2. Robert T. Gooch born May 31, 1865; married Dora Alice Hill in 1893, but was listed as a widower in the 1900 census. He was also married to Lucia Lucy Lane and Mae Lane Gooch Shuman. In the 1920 census of Vermilion County, page 68A, we find Robert age fifty-two, Mae age thirty-two, with Oakey age sixteen, Harold age six, and Robert Jr. age twenty-four. Robert Sr. was a barn boss in a quarry and Robert Jr. was a watchman. Robert Sr. died May 29, 1930.
3. Rebecca Gooch born September 7, 1867, married her cousin Charles Davis in 1889. For their children, see page 247.
4. John Gooch born September 1869. He was also listed by the family as being born on September 20, 1872 or 1873. He married Minnie Reffett December 22, 1900, and died April 23, 1957, at Hegeler, Illinois. In 1910 they had Ada, born about 1901, Addie born 1904, Rosa born about 1905, and Thomas born September 7, 1907. John was a coal miner.[16] The 1920 census showed another child, Walter, born about 1918.
5. William T. Gooch born April 27, 1870. He married Maude Ethel Higgins and died September 7, 1945, in Fairmount, Illinois. Both were buried in Greenview Cemetery, Fairmount, Illinois. Their children were Charles W. "Charley" born 1904, Elizabeth Bell born 1906, and Bertha "Bertie" born 1909.
6. Joel Gooch born September 1871. In 1900 he lived with his parents in Vermilion County, Illinois. No further information.
7. Alexander Gooch appeared only on the 1880 census at age nine. No further information.
8. Eliza Gooch born June 30, 1875, or, according to the 1880 census, in 1874. She married three times: (1) to a Mr. Pettis, (2) to her cousin, William Davis, and (3) to Thomas C. Goodwin, a relative of her sister-in-law, Viola Goodwin Gooch. For more information on Eliza Gooch Davis, see William Davis's information on page 291.

9. Thomas Emanuel "Moody" or "Mann" Gooch born April 20, 1877; married September 14, 1904, to Viola May Goodwin. Their children were Mary Mildred born about 1905; Roy Dean born about 1908; Darrel Ira "Hoopie" Gooch born about 1913; and Audrey Lee born about 1916. For more information on his family, see page 411.
10. Rosa Lee Gooch born October 13, 1880; married December 24, 1900, to John R. Woodard. She died in 1939. Their children were Eddie born 1902; Freddie born 1905; Myrtle born about 1908; Lester born about 1911, Jessie, a daughter, born about 1913; and Carl born about 1915.
11. Jessie Doney "Dollie" Gooch born October 18, 1888; married July 18, 1907, at Urbana, Illinois, to Ernest W. Reeves, and died January 13, 1969 in Fairmount, Illinois. Their children were Leoria born about 1909; Norman born about 1912; Ruby born about 1915; Ruth born about 1917; Grace born about 1919; Alice born about 1924; and Mary L. born about 1926.

Thomas and Mildred Oldham Gooch had a huge family and many descendants. She had twenty-six years of having babies — from 1862 to 1888 — and many more of childrearing. A married life that began in a more rural setting in Kentucky ended in a coal-mining town in Illinois. Most of their children lived out their lives in the same vicinity. *A.H.*

Notes

1. 1900 federal census, Illinois, Vermilion Co., Catlin Twp., 1st Precinct, E.D. 60, p. 10A. His tombstone shows a birth year of 1837.
2. Madison Co., Kentucky, Marriage Book 6:373, FHL #183317.
3. Mildred Gooch, Illinois death certificate, 1917, #42511.
4. Madison Co., Kentucky, Marriage Book 3:29, FHL #183316.
5. 1860 federal census, Kentucky, Madison Co., Western Subdivision No. 2, p. 50.
6. Madison Co., Kentucky, Will Book N:526.
7. Madison Co., Kentucky, Deed Book 13:160.
8. 1870 federal census, Kentucky, Madison Co., Union Precinct, Richmond, KY, p. 50.
9. 1880 federal census, Kentucky, Madison Co., E.D. 75, p. 21.
10. Illinois Statewide Marriage Index, Illinois State Archives, <http://www.cyberdriveillinois.com/departments/archives/marriage.html>.

(continued on page 392)

Above: Elizabeth Bell "Betty" Gooch Brown b. November 6, 1906, the daughter of William Tearle Gooch and Maude Ethel Higgins. Elizabeth married Everett E. Brown in 1927. They were living in Allerton Village, Sidell Township, Vermilion County, Illinois, according to the 1930 census.

Below, left to right: Elizabeth Bell "Betty" Gooch Brown and her husband Everett Brown; Elizabeth's mother, Maude E. Higgins Gooch, spouse of William T. Gooch; and Bertha "Bertie" Gooch, Maude and William's other daughter. Photo originally given to Rebecca "Becca" Gooch Davis by Maude, her sister-in-law.

See chart on page 438 for relationships of Thomas E. and Thomas Emanuel "Moody" Gooch family members pictured here.

Thomas E. Gooch Family

William T. "Will" Gooch b. April 27, 1870, brother of Rebecca "Becca" Gooch Davis. Married Maude E. Higgins. Died September 7, 1945, and buried at Greenview Cemetery, Fairmount, Illinois.

Top: William Tearle Gooch and Maude Ethel Higgins Gooch
Bottom: Maude Gooch with her children, Charlie, Elizabeth, and Bertha

See chart on page 438 for relationships of Thomas E. and Thomas Emanuel "Moody" Gooch family members pictured here.

Notes (*continued*)

11. 1900 federal census, Illinois, Vermilion Co., Catlin Twp., 1st Precinct, E.D. 60, p. 10.
12. 1910 federal census, Illinois, Vermilion Co., Vance Twp., E.D. 187, p. 5B.
13. Thomas E. Gooch, Illinois death certificate, 1918, #52848.
14. 1900 federal census, Illinois, Vermilion Co., Oakwood, E.D. 92, p. 8B.
15. 1910 federal census, Illinois, Vermilion Co., Vance Twp., Fairmount Village, E.D. 187, p. 5B.
16. 1910 federal census, Illinois, Vermilion Co., Vance Twp., E.D. 187, p. 23A.

aude and Bertha Gooch. Back of photo reads: ertie & Maude”

Bertha Gooch. Back of photo reads: “Bertie”

Elizabeth Gooch

Left: Back of photo reads: “Bertie & Lizzy”
Middle of page: Back of photo reads: “Lizzie & Bertie”

Thomas E. Gooch Family

Bertha "Bertie" Gooch

eft: William T. "Will" Gooch and his wife Maude E. Higgins Gooch and

William T. "Will" Gooch on left and brother Thomas Emmanuel "Moody"

Roger Gooch, son of William Tearle Gooch and Maude Ethel Higgins Gooch. Roger was killed in World War II. Back of photo reads: "To Aunt Edith from Roger"

Charles W. "Charley" Gooch b. October 18, 1904, son of William T. Gooch and nephew of Rebecca "Becca" Gooch Davis

Left: Back of photo reads: "Bill & Charlie Gooch"
Above: Roger, Melvin, Stanley and Vivian Gooch

Robert Gooch b. May 21, 1865, Madison County, Kentucky, brother of Rebecca "Becca" Gooch Davis

Robert Gooch b. May 21, 1865, Rebecca "Becca" Gooch's brother, and Everett Bulger Turner, his cousin.

On opposite page, photos of Robert Gooch in military uniform, probably during the period of conflict with Spain.

The Spanish-American War between the Kingdom of Spain and the United States took place from April to August 1898. The United States threatened Spain with war due to Spain's inability to guarantee peace and stability in Cuba. The war ended 113 days after its outbreak with the Treaty of Paris, which ended the Spanish Empire in the Caribbean and Pacific. The United States gained control over the former Spanish colonies of Puerto Rico, the Philippines, and Guam, and control over the process of independence of Cuba, which was completed in 1902.

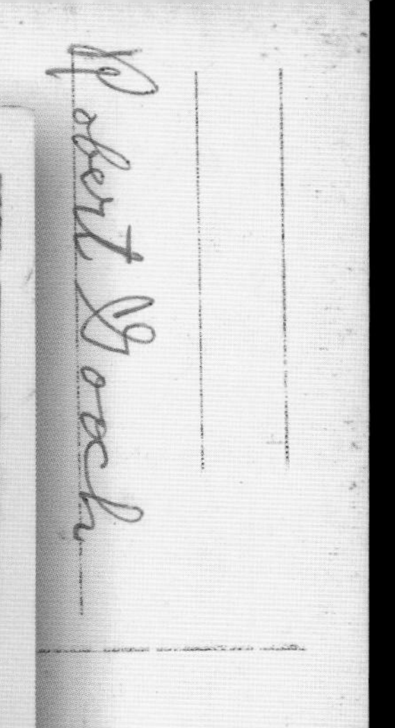

Harold Gooch b. November 8, 1913, d. March 25, 1955, son of Robert T. Gooch.

Robert Gooch. Back of photo reads "CUTLER'S Colortone Sep 24 1933 Photo Prints Danville, Ill." His death was recorded as May 29, 1930, at age 64 in Danville, Illinois. This is probably

See chart on page 138 for relationships of Thomas E. and Thomas Emanuel "Moody" Gooch family members pictured here.

Rebecca "Becca" Gooch b. September 7, 1867, Kentucky, married Charles Davis January 23, 1889, in Danville, Vermilion County, Illinois, died September 24, 1957, Kokomo, Lafayette, Indiana, and buried in Greenview Cemetery, Fairmount, Illinois.

Edney "Edna" Gooch Delaney b. 1862, d. 1918, Fairmount, Illinois, buried in Greenview Cemetery. Her two sons, Dale and Tom Delaney, and Dale's son are pictured on page 402.

Rosa Lee Gooch b. October 13, 1880, in Madison County, Kentucky, d. 1939, married John Woodward.

Above right: Jessie Doney "Doll — Dolly" Gooch b. October 18, 1888, Vance Township, Vermilion County, Illinois. This is Rebecca "Becca" Gooch's youngest sister, whom everyone called "Doll." Jessie married Ernest W. Reeves July 18, 1907, in Urbana, Illinois, died 2:00 P.M. January 13, 1969, at the Vermilion Nursing Home, Fairmount, Illinois. Right: Jessie Gooch and

Aunt Dall & her 4 girls

Rebecca's youngest sister Jessie

58

Ruby Reeves

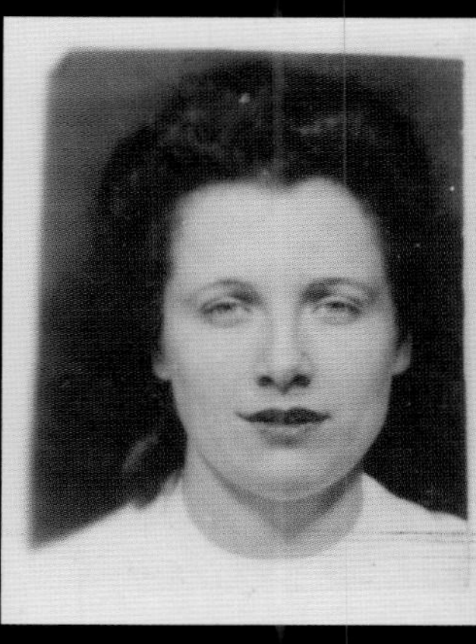

Grace Reeves

Jessie Gooch Reeves had six daughters, Leoria "Peggy," Ruby, Ruth, Grace, Alice, and Mary, and a son, Norman. She is pictured with four of her daughters at left. Above left is Ruby and above right is Grace. The two photos at the bottom are of Ruby.

See chart on page 438 for relationships of Thomas E. and Thomas Emanuel "Moody" Gooch family members pictured here.

Leoria "Peggy" Reeves, daughter of Jessie Doney "Doll" or "Dolly" Gooch and niece of Rebecca "Becca" Gooch Davis. The three pictures on this page and on the bottom left of the next page depict Leoria. On the back of the picture, on the bottom right on this page, is imprinted "Cutler's colortone Nov 13 1933 Photo Print Danville, Ill." The two pictures on the left appear to have been from the same period. The picture above appears to have been taken at a later date. Note the different spellings of her name ("Leora" and "Leoria").

Another entanglement between the Davis and Gooch families appears in the relationship between Clyde O. Davis and Leoria Reeves. She was born June 18, 1909, in Fairmount, Illinois, the daughter of Ernest W. and Jessie Doney "Doll" Gooch Reeves. The 1910 census of Vermilion County, Fairmount Village, page 262A, showed that Ernest was a coal miner and Leoria was their first child. She was listed as 3 or 4 months old. In 1920, she was still living with her parents as a 10 year old (1920 Census, Vermilion County, page 78B). She married at age 25 to Arthur Kenny on May 27, 1935, in Vermilion County. The application stated that it was her third marriage and that her maiden name was Leoria Gough, and that her mother's maiden name was Jessie Gooch. Obviously, either the clerk wrote down the misinformation, or Leoria made a false statement.

She married a second time as Leoria P. Reeves to Joseph Phillips on December 1, 1945, also in Vermilion County. Her application this time said that it was her first marriage. We did not research either divorce in Vermilion County, but sometimes women revert to their maiden names after a divorce.

We could not find Leoria in the 1930 census, but this was the woman who was living with Clyde O. Davis in 1967 in Chicago, according to her letter to Mildred Gooch Smith, daughter of Thomas E. "Moody" Gooch, her first cousin. She said in the letter that when Clyde's Social Security check came, they would be making a trip to Fairmount, Illinois, to see the Smiths. Clyde O. Davis's mother, Rebecca Gooch, was also a sister to Leoria's mother, Jessie Doney "Doll" Gooch. So Leoria and Clyde were first cousins and were living together. This is probably the woman who stood in the shadows when Clyde F. Davis visited his father when he graduated from high school (1956). Leoria Reeves Phillips died November 19, 1972, in Fairmount, Illinois, in a nursing home, two years before Clyde O. Davis died in 1974.

Pictured on the top left and right on the opposite page are Rosa Woodard and her daughter Myrtle. Pictured on the bottom right are, from left to right, "Mat" (unknown), Rosa Lee Gooch Woodard, and Rebecca "Becca" Gooch Davis.

Rosa & Myrtle
aunt cousin
Woodard
Moms sister & neice

(Rebecca Gooch Davis' sister Rosa)

Myrtle Woo

Lena Reeves

Mat Rosa Rebecca

THOMAS E. GOOCH FAMILY

Delaney b. August 6, 1886, son of Edney "Edna" Gooch, in
d War 1 "doughboy" uniform

From left to right: Elizabeth "Lizzie" Davis Purkey, her son Glenn Purkey, Eliza "Liza" Gooch Goodwin with her husband Tom Goodwin. Photo taken February 7, 1943, at Sedalia, Missouri.

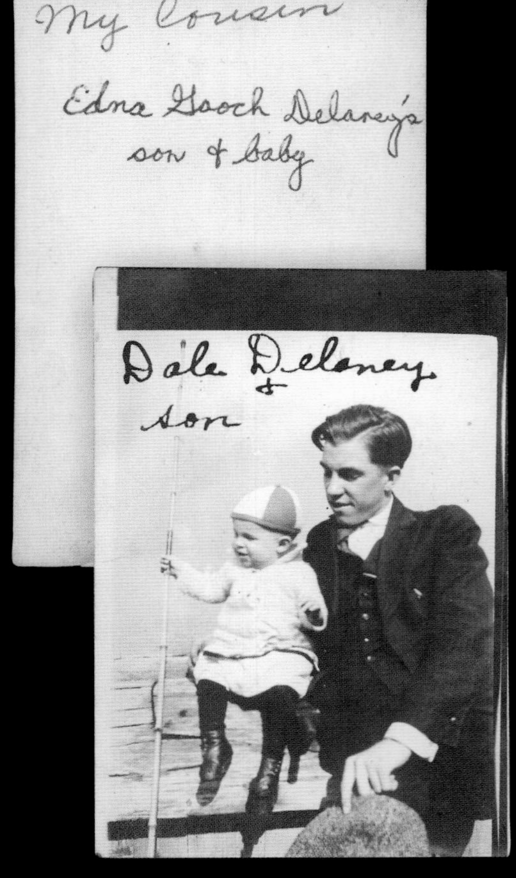

My Cousin
Edna Gooch Delaney's
son & baby
Dale Delaney
&
Son

Dale Delaney b. September 21, 1900, son of Edney

Mr. and Mrs. Tom Goodwin

Photo to the left is of Daniel Pettis. The following quotes were transcribed from the backs of this photo and two others.

"Daniel Pettis He was Aunt Lizas boy — He was stolen from her when he was a lttle baby."

"She prayed she would see him before she died & she did."

"aunt Liza & her son that was stolen from her when he was a baby. The one that stole him after many years she got converted & had to tell Eddie every thing that she was not his real mother & he was born in Illinois, when one night they moved to an other state & aunt Liza never did find him until he was a grown man Eddie advertised in Ill. papers & found his mom"

At this point in time, it is not known whether "Daniel" and "Eddie" are the same person, though it seems likely, unless more than one child was stolen.

Written on the back of the photo to the left:

"dont git skird Put this in yur garden sister and Brother Pray get rite with god I am goning to try to make heven my home We can all meat good By from Eliza goodwin
Beaman Mo R1"

Beaman, Missouri, is a small town northeast of Sedalia, Missouri. According to William B. Claycomb in his book A History of Northeast Pettis County, Missouri *(pp. 113–114), Northeast Pettis County started the new century (the 1900s) with eleven post offices. Among them were Longwood, which had five, and Beaman, which had only one. Beaman had two postal routes with a total of 42 miles and 175 families.*

THOMAS E. GOOCH FAMILY

CERTIFICATION OF VITAL RECORD

VERMILION COUNTY, ILLINOIS

STATE OF ILLINOIS.

MARRIAGE LICENSE

THE PEOPLE OF THE STATE OF ILLINOIS COUNTY OF Vermilion

To any person legally authorized to solemnize Marriage Greeting

Marriage may be celebrated

between Mr William H. Delaney of Fairmount in the County of Vermilion and State of Illinois of the age of 22 years and Miss Edna Gough of Fairmount in the County of Vermilion and State of Illinois of the age of 18 years.

Witness John W. Dale County Clerk and the seal of said County at his Office in Danville in said County, this 16th day of May A.D. 1882

John W. Dale County Clerk.

STATE OF ILLINOIS, COUNTY } s.s.

No. 343a

MARRIAGE LICENSE.

ADULT.

Mr. Wm H. Delaney with Miss Edna Gough

Issued May 16th 1882

Married May 16th 1882

Filed May 16" 1882

J. W. Dale Clerk.

Registered 18

On page of Marriage Register.

Illinois Printing Co., Printers, Danville, Ills.

This Return is to be carefully filled out and returned with the Marriage License. This Return does not take the place of the Certificate which is attached to the License, but is IN ADDITION THERETO.

Illinois State Board of Health.

RETURN OF A MARRIAGE TO COUNTY CLERK.

1. Full Name of GROOM. William H Delaney
2. Place of Residence, Fairmount
3. Occupation, Farmer
4. Age next Birthday, 23 years. Color, White Race.
5. Place of Birth, Kentucky
6. Father's Name, William Delaney.
7. Mother's Maiden Name, Lizzie Mize
8. Number of Groom's Marriage, 1st
9. Full Name of BRIDE. Edna Gough
   Maiden Name, if a Widow,
10. Place of Residence, Fairmount
11. Age next Birthday, 19 years. Color, White Race.
12. Place of Birth, Kentucky
13. Father's Name, Thomas Gough
14. Mother's Maiden Name, unknown
15. No. of Bride's Marriage, 1st
16. Married at Danville in the County of Vermilion and State of Illinois, the 16th day of May 1882
17. Witnesses to Marriage, Geo A Foxt Samuel Kirkpatrick

N. B.—At Nos. 8 and 15 state whether 1st, 2d, 3d, 4th, &c., Marriage of each. At 17 give names of subscribing witnesses to the Marriage Certificate. If no subscribing witnesses, give names of two persons who witnessed the ceremony.

18

We Hereby Certify that the information above given is correct, to the best of our knowledge and belief.

William H Delaney [Groom.]

Edna Gough [Bride.]

I Hereby Certify that the above is a correct return of a Marriage solemnized by me.

Dated at Danville this 16th day of May 1882 } John W. Parker Justice of the peace

Illinois Printing Co., Printers, Danville, Ills.

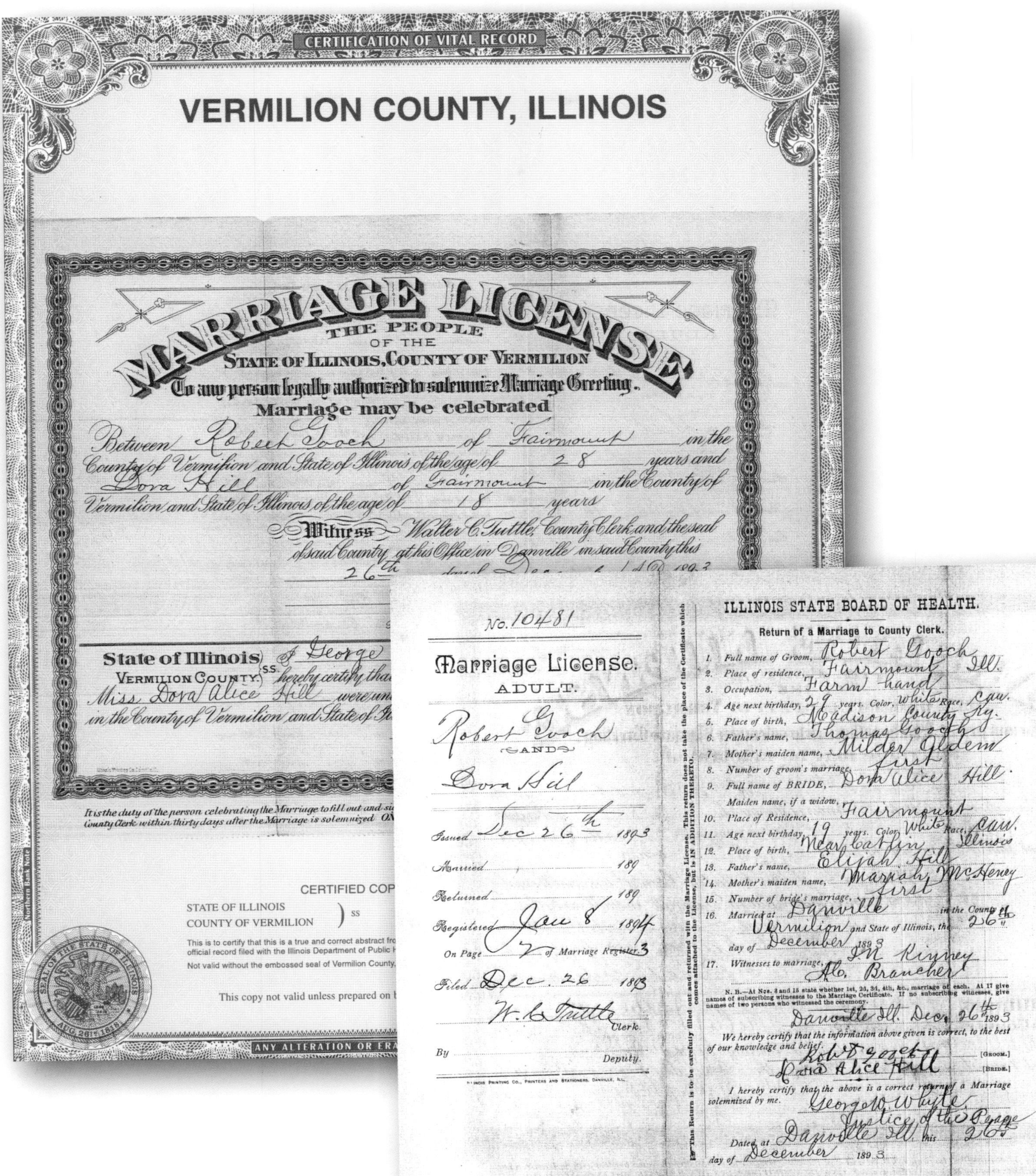

CERTIFICATION OF VITAL RECORD

VERMILION COUNTY, ILLINOIS

MARRIAGE LICENSE
THE PEOPLE
OF THE
STATE OF ILLINOIS, COUNTY OF VERMILION
To any person legally authorized to solemnize Marriage Greeting.
Marriage may be celebrated

Between Robert Gooch of Fairmount in the County of Vermilion and State of Illinois of the age of 28 years and Dora Hill of Fairmount in the County of Vermilion and State of Illinois of the age of 18 years

Witness Walter C. Tuttle, County Clerk and the seal of said County at his Office in Danville in said County this 26th ... Dec ... 1893

State of Illinois, VERMILION COUNTY. ss. I George ... hereby certify tha... Miss Dora Alice Hill were un... in the County of Vermilion and State of Il...

It is the duty of the person celebrating the Marriage to fill out and si... County Clerk within thirty days after the Marriage is solemnized. O...

CERTIFIED COP...

STATE OF ILLINOIS
COUNTY OF VERMILION) SS

This is to certify that this is a true and correct abstract fro... official record filed with the Illinois Department of Public H...
Not valid without the embossed seal of Vermilion County, ...

This copy not valid unless prepared on b...

SEAL OF THE STATE OF ILLINOIS AUG. 26th 1818

ANY ALTERATION OR ERA...

No. 10481

Marriage License.
ADULT.

Robert Gooch
AND
Dora Hill

Issued Dec 26th 1893
Married 189
Returned 189
Registered Jan 8 1894
On Page 2 of Marriage Register 3
Filed Dec. 26 1893
W. C. Tuttle Clerk.
By Deputy.

ILLINOIS PRINTING CO., PRINTERS AND STATIONERS, DANVILLE, ILL.

This Return is to be carefully filled out and returned with the Marriage License. This return does not take the place of the Certificate which comes attached to the License, but is IN ADDITION THERETO.

ILLINOIS STATE BOARD OF HEALTH.
Return of a Marriage to County Clerk.

1. Full name of Groom, Robert Gooch
2. Place of residence, Fairmount Ill.
3. Occupation, Farm hand
4. Age next birthday, 29 years. Color, White Race, Cau.
5. Place of birth, Madison County Ky.
6. Father's name, Thomas Gooch
7. Mother's maiden name, Milder Olden
8. Number of groom's marriage, first
9. Full name of BRIDE, Dora Alice Hill.
Maiden name, if a widow,
10. Place of Residence, Fairmount
11. Age next birthday, 19 years. Color White Race, Cau.
12. Place of birth, Near Catlin Illinois
13. Father's name, Elijah Hill
14. Mother's maiden name, Mariah McHenry
15. Number of bride's marriage, first
16. Married at Danville in the County of Vermilion and State of Illinois, the 26th day of December 1893
17. Witnesses to marriage, I. M. Kinney, Alo. Brancher

N. B.—At Nos. 8 and 15 state whether 1st, 2d, 3d, 4th, &c., marriage of each. At 17 give names of subscribing witnesses to the Marriage Certificate. If no subscribing witnesses, give names of two persons who witnessed the ceremony.

Danville Ill. Dec. 26th 1893

We hereby certify that the information above given is correct, to the best of our knowledge and belief.
Robt Gooch [GROOM.]
Dora Alice Hill [BRIDE.]

I hereby certify that the above is a correct return of a Marriage solemnized by me.
George W. White
Justice of the Peace

Dated at Danville Ill. this 26 day of December 1893.

Left page: State of Illinois Marriage License Certified copy from the State of Illinois, Vermilion County, William H. Delaney and Edna Gough, May 16, 1882

Right page: State of Illinois Marriage License Certified copy from the State of Illinois, Vermilion County, Robert Gooch and Dora Hill, December 26, 1893

CERTIFICATION OF VITAL RECORD

VERMILION COUNTY, ILLINOIS

ORIGINAL 36376 STATE OF ILLINOIS

CORONER'S CERTIFICATE OF DEATH — Registration District No. 92.0 — Registered Number 363

1. Place of Death: a. County: Vermilion, County, Illinois; b. Township: Danville
2. Usual Residence: a. State: Illinois; b. County: Vermilion; Township: Danville; d. City, Village, or Town: 1181 Second St, Danville Ill. (Ayler)
3. Name of Deceased: (a) First: John (b) Middle: (c) Last: Gooch
4. Date of Death: Apr. 23, 1957
5. Sex: Male
6. Race: White
7. Married, Never Married, Widowed, Divorced: Married
8. Date of Birth: Sept. 20, 1872
9. Age: 84 yrs
10a. Usual Occupation: coal miner; 10b. Kind of Business or Industry: Retired
11. Birthplace: Richmond, Kentucky
12. Citizen of what country: U.S.A.
13. Father's Full Name: Thomas E. Gooch
14. Mother's Full Maiden Name: Mildred Oldham
15. Was deceased ever in U.S. Armed Forces? No
17. Informant: Jessie Reeves; Address: Fairmount, Ill.; Relationship to Deceased: Sister
18. Medical Cause of Death: Part I. Immediate Cause (a): Chronic myocarditis
19. Autopsy? No
22. Disposition: Burial — April 25, 1957; Cemetery: Greenview; Location: Fairmount, Ill.; Funeral Director: Carrington Fun. Home, Fairmount, Ill.; License Number: F 4002
24. Received for filing on: April 23, 1957 — Clarence O'Nelan, Local Registrar

VS & R 202 — BUREAU OF STATISTICS — ILLINOIS DEPARTMENT OF PUBLIC HEALTH — SPRINGFIELD

CERTIFIED COPY OF VITAL RECORD — STATE OF ILLINOIS, COUNTY OF VERMILION — DATE ISSUED May 14, 2007

This is to certify that this is a true and correct abstract from the official record filed with the Illinois Department of Public Health. Not valid without the embossed seal of Vermilion County, Illinois.

Lynn Foster, Vermilion County Clerk

This copy not valid unless prepared on border displaying seal and signature of Registrar.

ANY ALTERATION OR ERASURE VOIDS THIS CERTIFICATE

State of Illinois Standard Certificate of Death Certified copy from the State of Illinois, Vermilion County, John Gooch b. September 20, 1872, d. April 23, 1957

CERTIFICATION OF VITAL RECORD

VERMILION COUNTY, ILLINOIS

STATE OF ILLINOIS — DEPARTMENT OF PUBLIC HEALTH — DIVISION OF VITAL STATISTICS AND RECORDS

DELAYED RECORD OF BIRTH — ORIGINAL COPY — State File No. 200708

1. Place of Birth: Township of Vance Twp., Vermilion County, Illinois
2. Full Name at Birth: ROBERT OTIS GOOCH
3. Date of Birth: May 9, 1895
4. Color or Race: White
5. Sex: Male
6. Father's Full Name: Robert Gooch
7. Father's Birthplace: Madison Co., Kentucky
8. Mother's Maiden Name: Dora Alice Hill
9. Mother's Birthplace: Catlin Twp., Illinois

AFFIDAVIT: I hereby declare upon oath that the above statements are true to the best of my knowledge and belief.

Signed: Robert Otis Gooch — Address: Stevens Point R# 4

Subscribed and sworn to before me this 21 day of July 1951, Stevens Point, Wis. — Walter Murat, Notary Public

APPLICANT! DO NOT WRITE BELOW THIS LINE

Kind of Document and Date Made	Information Given in Document as to Birth Date, Birthplace, and Parents
Document No. 1: Certificate of marriage, Vermilion County, October 22, 1921	Age or birth date: 26 yrs. old; Birthplace: Fairmount, Vance Twp., Illinois; Father: Robert Gooch; Mother: Dora Hill
Document No. 2: Affidavit of Uncle John Gooch, Fairmount, Illinois	Age or birth date: May 9, 1895; Birthplace: Vance Twp., Illinois; Father: Robert Gooch; Mother: Dora Hill
Document No. 3:	

Report of search made by Co. Clk. 3-22-51

For the Director of Public Health: Accepted and filed at Springfield by Leo A. Ozier, Deputy State Registrar, on August 24, 1951

STATE OF ILLINOIS, COUNTY OF VERMILION — DATE ISSUED May 14, 2007

This is to certify that this is a true and correct abstract from the official record filed with the Illinois Department of Public Health. Not valid without the embossed seal of Vermilion County, Illinois.

Lynn Foster, Vermilion County Clerk

This copy not valid unless prepared on border displaying seal and signature of Registrar.

ANY ALTERATION OR ERASURE VOIDS THIS CERTIFICATE

State of Illinois Delayed Record of Birth Certified copy from the State of Illinois, Vermilion County, Robert Otis Gooch b. May 9, 1895

CERTIFICATION OF VITAL RECORD

VERMILION COUNTY, ILLINOIS

5631

STATE OF ILLINOIS
DWIGHT H. GREEN, Governor
Department of Public Health—Division of Vital Statistics
COUNTY CLERK'S RECORD

CERTIFICATE OF BIRTH

1. PLACE OF BIRTH
County of Vermilion — Registration Dist. No. 1051
Catlin Township — Primary Dist. No. — Street and Number
*(Cancel the three terms not applicable—Do not enter "R. R.," "R. F. D.," or other P. O. address.)

2. FULL NAME AT BIRTH Elizabeth Bell Goach

3. Sex Female
4. Twin, Triplet, or other? (To be answered only in the event of plural births)
5. Number in order of birth
6. Legitimate? Yes
7. Date of birth Nov (Month) 6 (Day) 1906 (Year)

FATHER

8. Full Name William Tearle Goach
9. Residence at time of this birth Catlin Ill
10. Color white
11. Age at time of this birth 36 yrs.
12. Birthplace (City or Place) Madison County (Name State, if in U. S.) Kentucky (Name Country, if Foreign)
13. Occupation (Nature of Industry) miner

MOTHER

14. Full Maiden Name Maud Ethel Higgins
15. Residence at time of this birth Catlin Ill
16. Color white
17. Age at time of this birth 21 yrs.
18. Birthplace (City or Place) Martinsville (Name State, if in U. S.) Illinois (Name Country, if Foreign)
19. Occupation (Nature of Industry) Housewife

20. (a) Number of children born to this mother at the time of and including this birth 2
(b) Number of children living at the time of and including this birth 2

21. I HEREBY CERTIFY that I was the Attendant at this Birth. Physician Midwife
Signed
Address
Date (Month) (Day) (Year)

IF SIGNATURE OF BIRTH ATTENDANT IS OBTAINABLE, AFFIDAVIT IS NOT REQUIRED.

GENEALOGY ONLY

STATE OF Illinois } ss.
County of Vermilion

I HEREBY CERTIFY that I had actual knowledge of the facts as stated in this RECORD OF BIRTH at the time the birth occurred, and know them to be true; and that I am related to this person as mother

Signature Maud E. Goach
Present Address Fairmount Illinois
Subscribed to, and sworn before me this 5 day of November, 1942
Olive B. Salrin Notary Public
SEAL
My commission expires Jan 17, 1946

22. Filed 11-5, 1942 John A. Russell Registrar
Post Office Address Catlin Illinois

CERTIFIED COPY OF VITAL RECORDS
COUNTY OF VERMILION
DATE ISSUED May 14, 2007
This is to certify that this is a true and correct abstract from the official record filed with the Illinois Department of Public Health.
Not valid without the embossed seal of Vermilion County, Illinois.
Lynn Foster
LYNN FOSTER
VERMILION COUNTY CLERK

This copy not valid unless prepared on border displaying seal and signature of Registrar.

ANY ALTERATION OR ERASURE VOIDS THIS CERTIFICATE

State of Illinois Certificate of Birth Certified copy from the State of Illinois, Vermilion County, Elizabeth Bell Gooch b. November 6, 1906

CERTIFICATION OF VITAL RECORD

VERMILION COUNTY, ILLINOIS

14696

STATE OF ILLINOIS
HENRY HORNER, GOVERNOR
Department of Public Health—Division of Vital Statistics
COUNTY CLERK'S RECORD

CERTIFICATE OF DEATH

1. PLACE OF DEATH.
County of Vermilion — Registration Dist. No. 1010
Danville *Village *City *Township *Road Dist. — Primary Dist. No. 3676
*(Cancel the three terms not applicable—Do not enter "R. R.," "R. F. D.," or other P. O. address).
Registered No. 571 (Consecutive No.)
Street and Number, No. St., Ward, St. Elizabeth Hospital.
(If death occurred in a hospital or institution, give its NAME instead of street and number.)
LENGTH OF TIME AT PLACE WHERE DEATH OCCURRED? yrs. mos. 2 hrs ds.

1a. PLACE OF RESIDENCE: STATE Illinois County Township Road Dist.
(Usual place of abode) City or Village Danville Street and Number 306 Bryan Ave.

2. FULL NAME Frances Mae Gooch

PERSONAL AND STATISTICAL PARTICULARS

3. SEX Female
4. COLOR OR RACE white
5. Single, Married, Widowed, or Divorced (write the word) single
5a. If married, widowed, or divorced HUSBAND of (or) WIFE of – –
6. DATE OF BIRTH (month, day, and year) November 9, 1937
7. AGE Years – Months – Days – – IF LESS than 1 day, 2 hrs. or min.

OCCUPATION
8. Trade, profession, or particular kind of work done, as spinner, sawyer, bookkeeper, etc. None
9. Industry or business in which work was done, as silk mill, saw mill, bank, etc.
10. Date deceased last worked at this occupation (month and year)
11. Total time (years) spent in this occupation

12. BIRTHPLACE (city or town) Danville (State or country) Ill

FATHER
13. NAME Harold Gooch
14. BIRTHPLACE (city or town) Fairmount (State or country) Ill.

MOTHER
15. MAIDEN NAME Marjorie Newberry
16. BIRTHPLACE (city or town) Henning (State or country) Ill

17. INFORMANT Harold Gooch (personal signature with pen and ink)
P. O. Address Danville, Ill

18. PLACE OF BURIAL, Cremation or Removal
Cemetery Songer
19. DATE Nov. 10, 1937
Location Catlin twp (Township, Road Dist., Village or City)
County Vermilion State Ill.

20. UNDERTAKER C. S. Dickson (personal signature with pen and ink) ADDRESS Danville
Edmund & Dickson (firm name, if any) Ill

MEDICAL CERTIFICATE OF DEATH

21. DATE OF DEATH (month, day, and year) Nov. 9, 1937
22. I HEREBY CERTIFY, That I attended deceased from Nov. 9, 1937, to Nov. 9, 1937
I last saw her alive on Nov. 9, 1937 death is said to have occurred on the date stated above, at 1:30P
*The principal cause of death and related causes of importance were as follows: Date of onset
Premature infant
6 mos. gestation

Other contributory causes of importance:

23. Was an operation performed? no Date of
For what disease or injury?
Was there an autopsy? no
What test confirmed diagnosis? clinical
24. If a communicable disease; where contracted?
Was disease in any way related to occupation of deceased?
If so, specify how:
(Signed) Harlan S. Cox, M. D.
Address Danville, Ill
Date Nov. 10, 1937 Telephone 214

*N. B.—State the disease causing death. All cases of death from "violence, casualty, or any undue means" must be referred to the coroner. See Section 10 Coroner's Act.

25. Filed Nov. 10, 1937 C. M. Cook, MD Registrar.
P. O. Address Danville Ill.

Has decedent ever served in military or naval service of U. S.?

CERTIFIED COPY OF VITAL RECORDS
STATE OF ILLINOIS
COUNTY OF VERMILION) ss
DATE ISSUED May 14, 2007
This is to certify that this is a true and correct abstract from the official record filed with the Illinois Department of Public Health.
Not valid without the embossed seal of Vermilion County, Illinois.
Lynn Foster
LYNN FOSTER
VERMILION COUNTY CLERK

This copy not valid unless prepared on border displaying seal and signature of Registrar.

ANY ALTERATION OR ERASURE VOIDS THIS CERTIFICATE

State of Illinois Certificate of Death Certified copy from the State of Illinois, Vermilion County, Frances Mae Gooch b. November 9, 1937, d. November 9, 1937

CERTIFICATION OF VITAL RECORD

VERMILION COUNTY, ILLINOIS

Marriage License No. 45707

The People of the State of Illinois, Vermilion County

To any person Legally authorized to solemnize marriage—Greeting:

Marriage May Be Celebrated

Between Mr. Arthur Kenney of Danville in the County of Vermilion and State of Illinois of the age of 27 years, and Leora Reeves of Danville in the County of Vermilion and State of Illinois of the age of 25 years, the — of the said — having given assent to said marriage ... nty at his office in ... A. D. 1935 ... County Clerk ... Deputy

... A. D. 1935

... license, to the County Clerk within ... NG TO DO SO.

... FOSTER ... COUNTY CLERK

No. 45707

MARRIAGE LICENSE

Mr. Arthur Kenney

With

M. Leora Reeves

Issued May 27th 1935

FILED 1935 ... Jones CLERK

NOTE

This license can only be used in Vermilion County, Illinois.

Must be returned to the County Clerk, Danville, Illinois, within 30 days after ceremony is performed.

If not used, return immediately.

Marriage Register 11 Page 91

This Return is to be carefully filled out and returned with the Marriage License. This return does not take the place of the certificate which comes attached to the license, but is IN ADDITION THERETO.

Illinois State Board of Health

RETURN OF A MARRIAGE TO COUNTY CLERK

1. Full Name of Groom Arthur Kenney
2. Place of Residence Danville Ill.
3. Occupation Labor
4. Age next Birthday 28 years. Color or race W
5. Place of Birth Galway Ills
6. Father's Name Arthur Kenney
7. Mother's Maiden Name [illegible]
8. Number of Groom's Marriage third 3d
9. Full Name of Bride Leora Reeves
   Maiden Name if Widow [illegible]
10. Place of Residence Danville Ill.
11. Age next Birthday 26 years. Color or race W
12. Place of Birth [illegible] Ills
13. Father's Name [illegible] Reeves
14. Mother's Maiden Name [illegible]
15. Number of Bride's Marriage [illegible] 3d
16. Married at Danville Ills
    County of Vermilion, and State of Illinois, the 27th day of May 1935
17. Witnesses to Marriage

N. B.—At Nos. 8 and 15 state whether 1st, 2nd, 3rd, etc., marriage of each. At 17 give names of subscribing witnesses to the Marriage Certificate. If no subscribing witnesses, give names of two persons who witnessed the ceremony.

We hereby Certify that the information above given is correct to the best of our knowledge and belief.

Arthur Kenney Groom

Leoria Reeves Bride

I hereby Certify that the above is a correct return of a marriage solemnized by me.

Henry [illegible]

Justice of the Peace

Dated at Danville Ills

this 27 day of May, 1935

PLEASE DO NOT WRITE BEYOND THIS LINE.

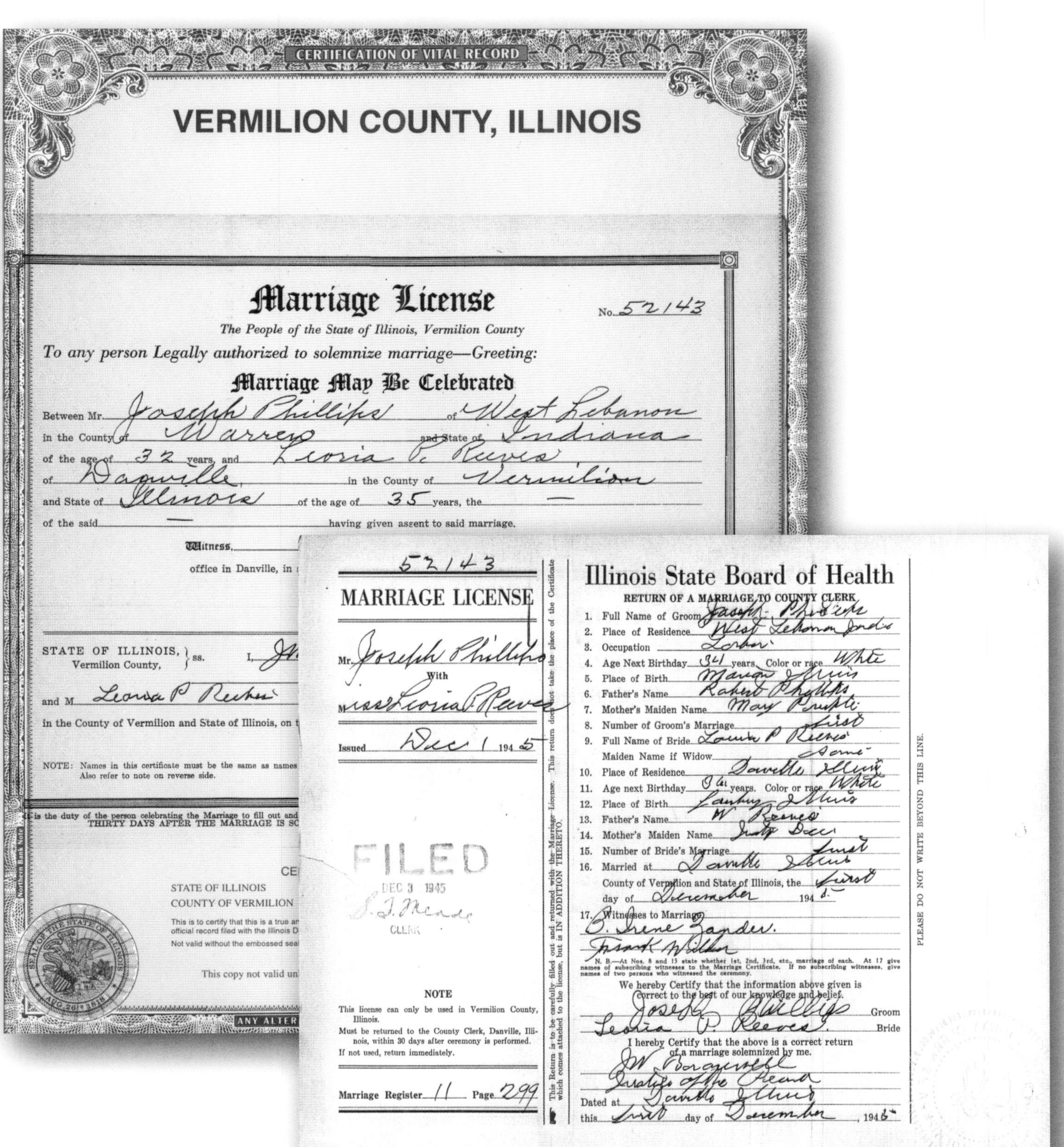

CERTIFICATION OF VITAL RECORD

VERMILION COUNTY, ILLINOIS

Marriage License No. 52143

The People of the State of Illinois, Vermilion County

To any person Legally authorized to solemnize marriage—Greeting:

Marriage May Be Celebrated

Between Mr. Joseph Phillips of West Lebanon in the County of Warren and State of Indiana of the age of 32 years, and Leoria P. Reeves of Danville in the County of Vermilion and State of Illinois of the age of 35 years, the — of the said — having given assent to said marriage.

Witness, ... office in Danville, in ...

STATE OF ILLINOIS, Vermilion County, } ss. I, ...

and M Leoria P Reeves ...

in the County of Vermilion and State of Illinois, on t...

NOTE: Names in this certificate must be the same as names ... Also refer to note on reverse side.

...is the duty of the person celebrating the Marriage to fill out and ... THIRTY DAYS AFTER THE MARRIAGE IS SO...

CE...

STATE OF ILLINOIS
COUNTY OF VERMILION

This is to certify that this is a true ar... official record filed with the Illinois D...
Not valid without the embossed seal...

This copy not valid un...

ANY ALTER...

52143

MARRIAGE LICENSE

Mr. Joseph Phillips
With
Miss Leoria P Reeves

Issued Dec 1 1945

FILED
DEC 3 1945
S. T. Meade
CLERK

NOTE
This license can only be used in Vermilion County, Illinois.
Must be returned to the County Clerk, Danville, Illinois, within 30 days after ceremony is performed.
If not used, return immediately.

Marriage Register 11 Page 299

This Return is to be carefully filled out and returned with the Marriage License. This return does not take the place of the Certificate which comes attached to the license, but is IN ADDITION THERETO.

Illinois State Board of Health

RETURN OF A MARRIAGE TO COUNTY CLERK

1. Full Name of Groom Joseph Phillips
2. Place of Residence West Lebanon Ind.
3. Occupation Labor
4. Age Next Birthday 34 years. Color or race White
5. Place of Birth Marion Illinois
6. Father's Name Robert Phillips
7. Mother's Maiden Name May Pruitt
8. Number of Groom's Marriage first
9. Full Name of Bride Leoria P Reeves
   Maiden Name if Widow same
10. Place of Residence Danville Illinois
11. Age next Birthday 36 years. Color or race White
12. Place of Birth Lanbury Illinois
13. Father's Name W Reeves
14. Mother's Maiden Name Ivy Dee
15. Number of Bride's Marriage first
16. Married at Danville Illinois
   County of Vermilion and State of Illinois, the first day of December 1945
17. Witnesses to Marriage
   B. Irene Zander.
   Frank Wilder

N. B.—At Nos. 8 and 15 state whether 1st, 2nd, 3rd, etc., marriage of each. At 17 give names of subscribing witnesses to the Marriage Certificate. If no subscribing witnesses, give names of two persons who witnessed the ceremony.

We hereby Certify that the information above given is correct to the best of our knowledge and belief.

Joseph Phillips Groom
Leoria P. Reeves Bride

I hereby Certify that the above is a correct return of a marriage solemnized by me.

J.W. Bor...
Justice of the Peace

Dated at Danville Illinois
this first day of December, 1945

PLEASE DO NOT WRITE BEYOND THIS LINE.

Left page: State of Illinois Marriage License Certified copy from the State of Illinois, Vermilion County, Arthur Kenney and Leoria Reeves married May 27, 1935

Right page: State of Illinois Marriage License Certified copy from the State of Illinois, Vermilion County, Joseph Phillips and Leoria Reeves married December 1, 1945

Maude, will Grandma Liza Mae + Fred Davis
Gooch Gooch Gooch Gooch Gooch
all them are dead now

Photogaph courtesy of LaVerne Purkey. From left to right: Maude Gooch and husband William T. Gooch. According to LaVerne, "The Grandma here was Mildred, this was her house, but I don't know where." Mildred Elizabeth Williams was the spouse of Thomas E. Gooch. The third woman from the left is Eliza "Liza" Gooch who married (second) William Davis. "Mae" Gooch is probably Viola Mae Goodwin, spouse of Thomas Emanual "Moody" Gooch. The young boy pictured above is indicated as Fred Davis, the son of Eliza "Liza" Gooch and William Davis.

See chart on page 438 for relationships of Thomas E. and Thomas Emanuel "Moody" Gooch family members pictured here.

The Third Thomas Gooch

Thomas Emanuel Gooch was born April 20, 1877, in Madison County, Kentucky.[1] He moved with his parents, Thomas and Mildred Gooch, to Vermilion County, Illinois, in the late 1880s. He married Viola Goodwin September 14, 1904, in Fairmount, Vermilion County, Illinois. She was the daughter of John Goodwin and Matilda Sanders.[2] Viola's brother was Thomas Goodwin, who married her husband's sister, Eliza Gooch, and moved to Missouri. The Davis, Gooch, and Goodwin families were definitely intertwined.

The 1900 census showed Thomas M. Gooch, age twenty-one, born April 1879, living with his parents, occupation coal miner.[3] The discrepancy in his age comes from three different sources; the discrepancy in his middle initial comes from his nickname. Some descendants say he was always called "Mann." His 1917 World War I Draft card called him "Manuel" Gooch, born April 20, 1878, that he was a coal miner for the Taylor-English Coal Company and that his wife was Viola Gooch. He was tall with a medium build, had blue eyes and black hair.[4]

Thomas E. "Moody" Gooch b. April 20, 1878, d. August 24, 1955, son of Thomas E. Gooch, in a photo dated 1921. "Moody" Gooch was the brother of my grandmother, Rebecca "Becca" Gooch Davis.

By the 1910 census, Thomas and Viola Gooch had two children: Mary M. and Roy.[5] Darrel and Audrey joined the family by 1920.[6] By 1930 Thomas was no longer a miner; his occupation was listed as straw-bailer, and they lived in Fairmount, Vance Township, Vermilion County, Illinois, where they rented a house for $8 per month.[7]

Thomas Emanuel Gooch and Viola celebrated their 50th wedding anniversary, according to this account in the newspaper:[8]

> Fairmount — The golden wedding celebration on Sunday of Mr. and Mrs. Emanuel Gooch was attended by approximately 100 friends and relatives in addition to their direct descendants. Mrs. Naomi Morris, Mrs. Roy Gooch and Mrs. Audrey Waggoner served at a table centered by a three tiered wedding cake. Music was provided by Mrs. Frances Rowlen of Danville.
>
> Among the many messages of congratulation were a telephone call from a grandson in South America, Robert E. Smith, and one from a nephew, Dale Delaney, in Savannah, Ga. Another grandson unable to attend was Pfc. Dale Gooch, U.S. Marines, who is at Camp Lejeune, South Carolina. Mr. and Mrs. Gooch were married Sept. 14, 1904, in the home of Mr. and Mrs. John Woodard, Fairmount. Their children, all of whom attended the Golden wedding [*sic* anniversary], are Roy of Lafayette, Ind., Darrel of Morris, Ill., Mrs. Mildred Smith of Winslow, Ind., and Mrs. Audrey Waggoner of Homer. Seven grandchildren and three great-grandchildren also were present. Their great-grandchildren are Patty Dean and Barbara Jean Hughes, Michael Smith and Cindy Lou Smith, all of Danville.
>
> On Tuesday, a letter of congratulations was received by Mrs. and Mrs. Gooch from Governor and Mrs. William Stratton.

Thomas E. Gooch died not quite a year later, August 24, 1955. His wife Viola died in 1964.[9]

> Mrs. Viola Gooch, 81, Fairmount, died last night (October 13, 1964) in the Vermilion Nursing Home where she had been a patient since January of 1963. She had been ill several years. Born May 16, 1883 in Hillsboro, Ky., she was the daughter of John B. and Matilda Sanders Goodwin. She was married Sept 14, 1904 to Emmanuel Gooch who preceded her in death in 1955. Surviving are two daughters, Mrs. Hobart Smith of Fairmount and Mrs. H.M. Waggoner of Homer; two sons, Roy of Danville and Darrel of Morris, Ill.; 11 grandchildren and 24 great-grandchildren; a brother, Thomas Goodwin of Sedalia, Mo., and a sister, Mrs. Guy Cook of Fairmount. She was also preceded in death by a brother and a sister. Most of her life had been spent in the Fairmount area. She was a member of the Fairmount Nazarene Church.... Services with the Rev. Don C. Goodwin officiating. Burial will be in Greenview Cemetery.

The children of Thomas Emanuel "Moody" and Viola Gooch were

1. Mary Mildred Gooch born August 21, 1905; married

Thomas E. "Moody" Gooch Family

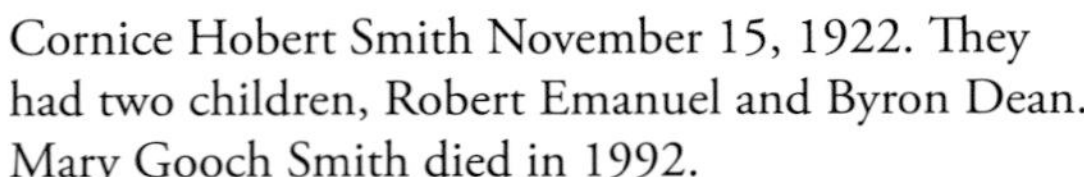

The two photographs on this page depict Thomas Emmanuel "Moody" or "Man" Gooch. He is Rebecca "Becca" Gooch Davis's brother, who married Viola May Goodwin September 4, 1904.

Emmanuel is pictured with his son-in-law Cornice Hobert Smith on the right page. Hobert married Emmanuel's daughter Mary Mildred Gooch.

See chart on page 438 for relationships of Thomas E. and Thomas Emanuel "Moody" Gooch family members pictured here.

Cornice Hobert Smith November 15, 1922. They had two children, Robert Emanuel and Byron Dean. Mary Gooch Smith died in 1992.

2. Roy Dean Gooch born August 17, 1908; married Hazel E. Lane in 1933. They had two children, Roy Dean and Mildred. Roy Dean Gooch died in 1984.
3. Darrel Ira "Hoopie" Gooch born October 27, 1913; died in 1969 in a car accident. He married Bessie Evans in 1933. They had Dale, Paul, Marlene, and Gary.
4. Audrey Lee Gooch born about 1916. In 1934 she `married Erville Jesse "Smitty" Smith in Vermilion County, Illinois. Later she married H.M. Waggoner. No further information.

Thomas Emanuel Gooch, born ca. 1877–79, was the third Thomas Gooch in a line spanning more than one hundred years, going back to the Thomas Gooch who was born in the 1700s and died in 1803 in Louisa County, Virginia.

Notes

1. Information provided by LaVerne Purkey, 1997.
2. Ibid.
3. 1900 federal census, Illinois, Vermilion Co., Catlin Township, 1st Precinct, E.D. 60, p. 10A.
4. World War I Draft Registration, Fairmount, Vermilion Co., Illinois, <http://www.ancestry.com>.
5. 1910 federal census, Illinois, Vermilion Co., Vance Twp., E.D.187, p. 14B.
6. 1920 federal census, Illinois, Vermilion Co., Vance Twp., Fairmount Village, E.D. 208, p. 2A.
7. 1930 federal census, Illinois, Vermilion Co., Vance Twp., Fairmount Village, E.D. 92–73, p. 2B.
8. News clipping, undated, not cited, in possession of Clyde Davis.
9. Ibid.

POST CARD

AZO PLACE STAMP HERE

CORRESPONDENCE

ADDRESS

Emanuel Gooch (holding gun)
Holbert Smith

Ain't Dad some man?

1924

Dad & Holbert

Thomas E. "Moody" Gooch Family

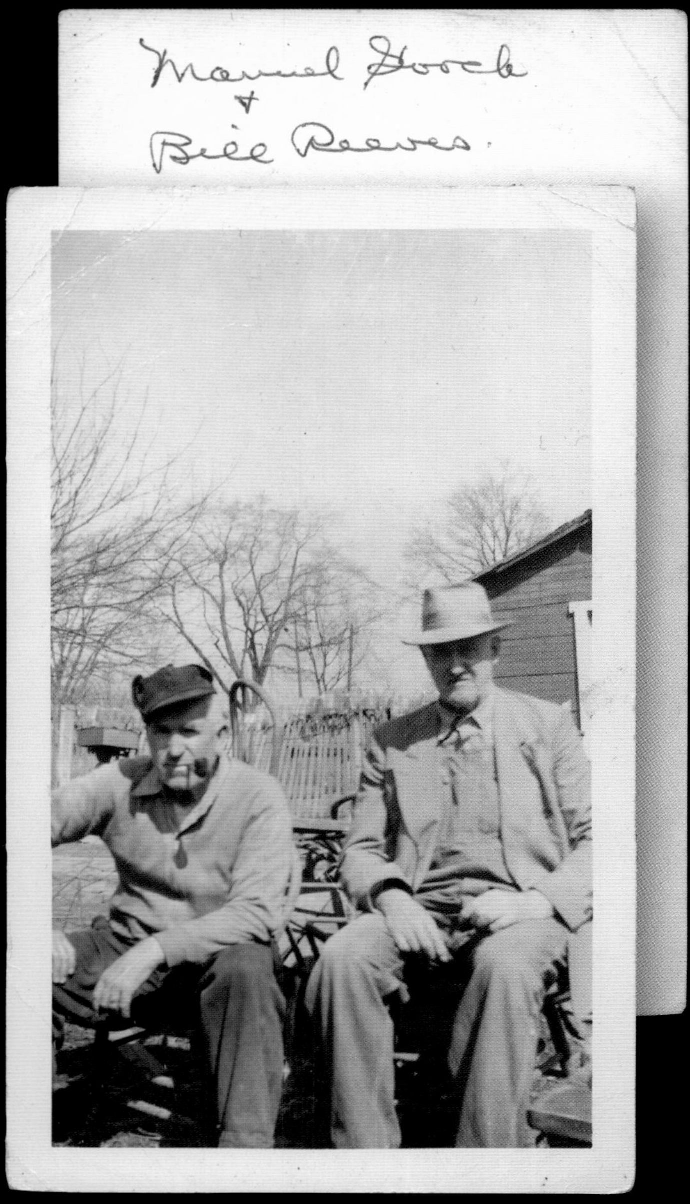

Thomas Emanuel "Moody" Gooch and Bill Reeves

Thomas E. and Viola May Gooch, Mary Mildred's parents. Mr. and Mrs. Gooch were married September 14, 1904.

Note 50th Anniversary

MR. AND MRS. EMANUEL GOOCH

FAIRMOUNT—The golden wedding celebration on Sunday of Mr. and Mrs. Emanuel Gooch was attended by approximately 100 friends and relatives in addition to their direct descendants. Mrs. Naomi Morris, Mrs. Roy Gooch and Mrs., A u d r e y Waggoner served at a table centered by a three tiered wedding cake. Music was provided by Mrs. Frances Rowlen of Danville.

Among the many messages of congratulation were a telephone call from a grandson in South America, Robert E. Smith, and one from a nephew, Dale Delaney, in Savannah, Ga. Another grandson unable to attend was Pfc. Dale Gooch, U. S. Marines, who is at Camp Lejeune, S. C.

Mr. and Mrs. Gooch were married Sept. 14, 1904, in the home of Mr. and Mrs. John Woodard, Fairmount. Their children, all of whom attended the golden wedding, are Roy of Lafayette, Ind., Darrell of Morris, Ill., Mrs. Mildred Smith of Winslow, Ind., and Mrs. Audrey Waggoner of Homer. Seven grandchildren and three g r e a t -grandchildren also were present. Their great-grandchildren are Patty Dean and Barbara Jean Hughes, Michael Smith and Cindy Lou Smith, all of Danville.

On Tuesday, a letter of congratulations was received by Mr. and Mrs. Gooch from Governor and Mrs. William Stratton.

Aunt Viola
4-14-57
Home in Fairmount
Granny

Viola May Gooch at home in Fairmount, Illinois, April 14, 1957 (?)

Mary Mildred Gooch Smith

My mother and I.
This was my Halloween outfit. Of course, I did not wear my dresses quite that short. This was taken last Nov.
M.G.S.

Above: Mary Mildred Gooch Smith, far right, and unknown others
Left: "M.G.S." Mildred Gooch Smith. "My mother and I. This was my Halloween outfit. Of course I did not wear my dresses quite that short. This was taken last Nov."

ot: Mary Mildred Gooch

In photo at bottom of right-hand page, Cornice Hobert Smith in lower left corner (seated) above handwritten indication ("X") at what appears to be a family gathering

ove: Mary Mildred Gooch ith at 1933 Chicago World's r at about age 28

ow: snapshot, unknown time l place.

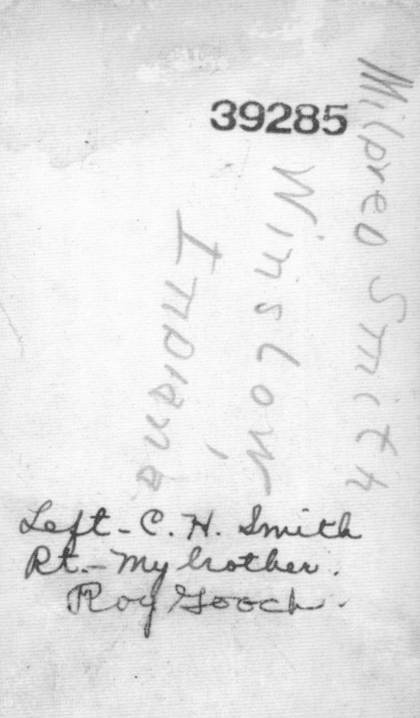

39285
Mildred Smith
Winslow,
Indiana
Left - C. H. Smith
Rt. - My brother.
Roy Gooch.

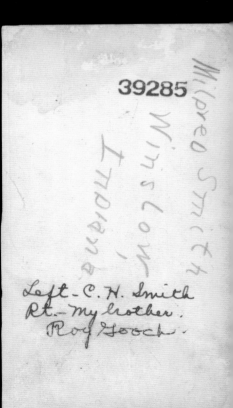

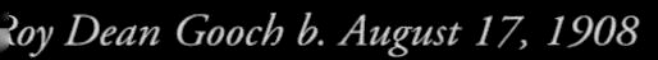

Roy Dean Gooch b. August 17, 1908

Chuck (?) with Cornice Hobert Smith

Hobert Smith
Bob Smith 5
Viola Gooch
Darrell Gooch 3
Audrey Gooch Smith
Emanuel Gooch

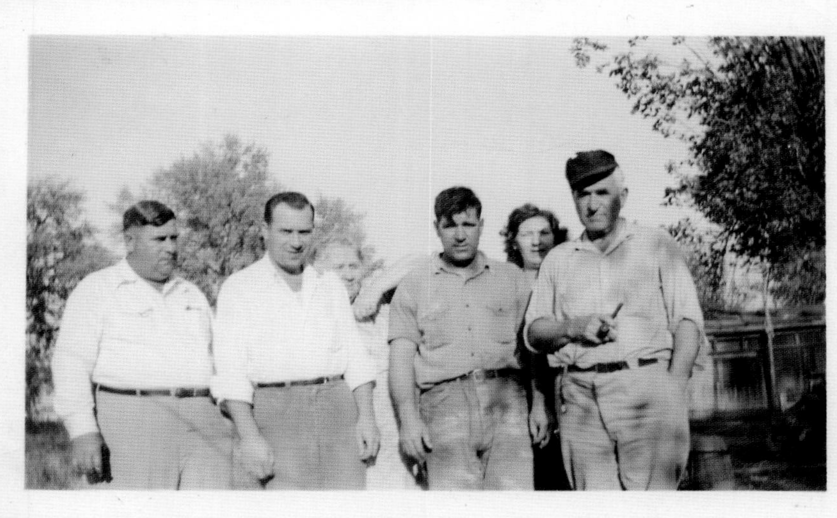

Hobert Smith in a Polaroid. The woman with him is probably his niece Marlene Gooch Smith, wife of James "Jim" Smith and daughter of Darrel Ira "Hoopie" and Bessie Gooch.

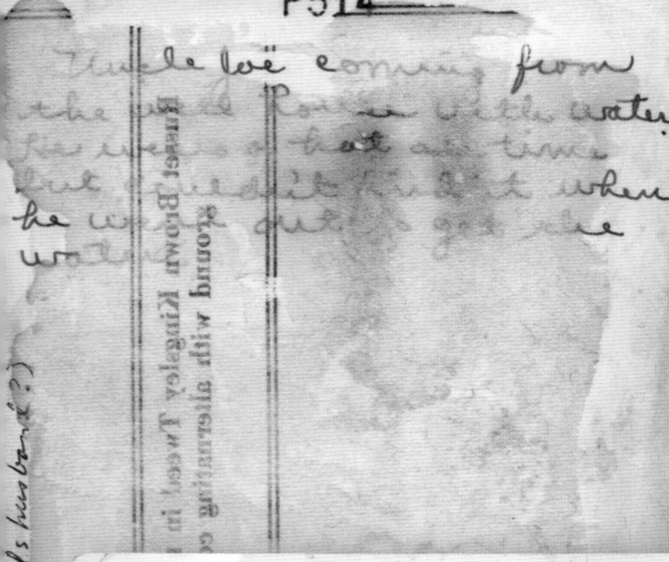

Photos courtesy of **Dale Gooch**.

Hobert Smith. Back of photo reads: "Uncle Joe coming from the well house with water;

Bobbie Smith

Robert "Bobby" Smith b. May 28, 1924, son of Mary Mildred Gooch Smith and Cornice Hobert Smith. Back of this photo spells his nickname "Bobbie," but "Bobby" is used elsewhere.

Has Hoopy grown?

Roy + Darrell (Hoopy) (He is in love, too) Bessie Evans from Homer is the lucky lady.

Pettitt Photo Service Quality Photo Finishing Chrisman

Roy Dean Gooch b. August 17, 1908, and Darrell Ira "Hoopie" Gooch b. October 27, 1913. The back of the photo reads: "Has Hoopy grown? Roy & Darrell (He is in love, too) Bessie Eveans from Homer is the lucky lady." The photo is stamped "Pettitt Photo Service Quality Photo Finishing Chrisman, Ill."

Myrtle
Lester
Mildred

Myrtle and Lester Woodard, brother and sister, with Mary Mildred Gooch.

...ly man on far left is James Robert Smith. Also ...d as appearing in the photograph are Flora, Sarah

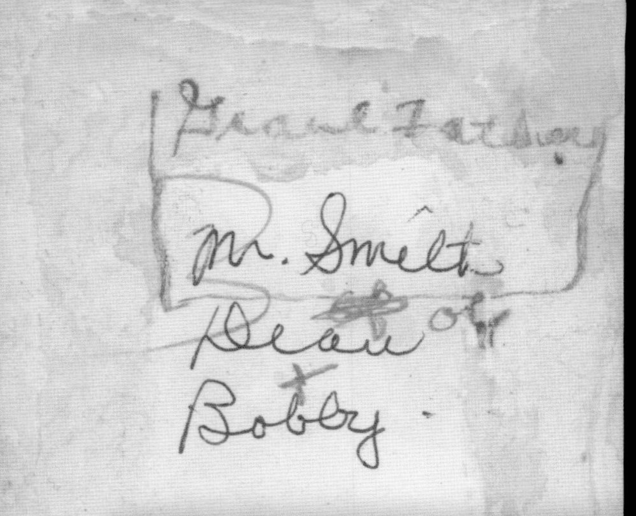

"Grandfather" Mr. Smith is probably James Robert Smith, father of Cornice Hobert Smith. "Grandfather" Smith is pictured above with grandsons Robert "Bobbie" Smith and Dean Smith.

In back of car, Bessie Evans Gooch, wife of Darrel Ira "Hoopie" Gooch; their son, Paul b. February 19, 1942; and their daughter, Marlene b. February 24, 1934. "Hoopie" is at the wheel of the car, and their son Dale b. September 2, 1936, is seated next to him.

Deanie, Dawn, and Mary Mildred Gooch Smith

Thomas E. "Moody" Gooch Family

Left to right: Roy Dean Gooch b. August 17, 1908, his brother Darrel Ira "Hoopie" Gooch b. October 27, 1913, with their older sister Mary Mildred Gooch b. August 21, 1905. All three were born in Fairmount, Illinois.

Thomas Emanuel "Moody" Gooch with daughter Audrey Lee "Bug" and wife Viola May Goodwin Gooch. Written on back of photo is "Dad, Mom & Bug."

See chart on page 438 for relationships of Thomas E. and Thomas Emanuel "Moody" Gooch family members pictured here.

Audrey Lee "Bug" Gooch Smith b. 1916, Fairmount, Illinois, daughter of Thomas Emanuel "Moody" Gooch and Viola May Goodwin, with husband Erville Jesse "Smitty" Smith

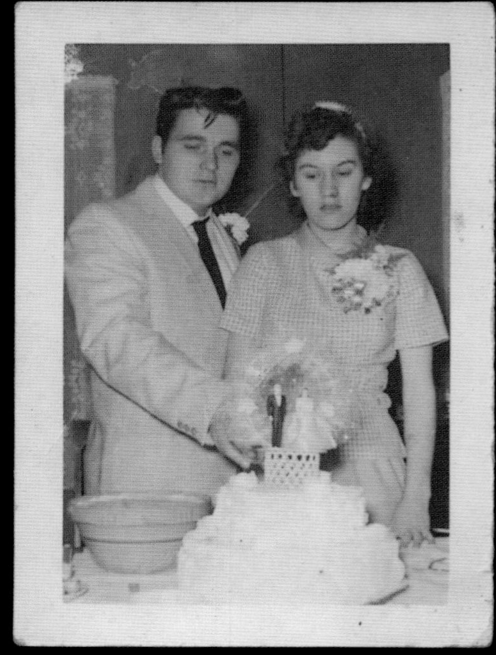

Dale and Sharon Viano Gooch, married February 3, 1958

Baby Gary, this is mom house - real cute - they Dont have the ford now though

Gary "Bone" Gooch b. July 17, 1955, son of Darrel Ira "Hoopie" Gooch, in a photo dated 1958

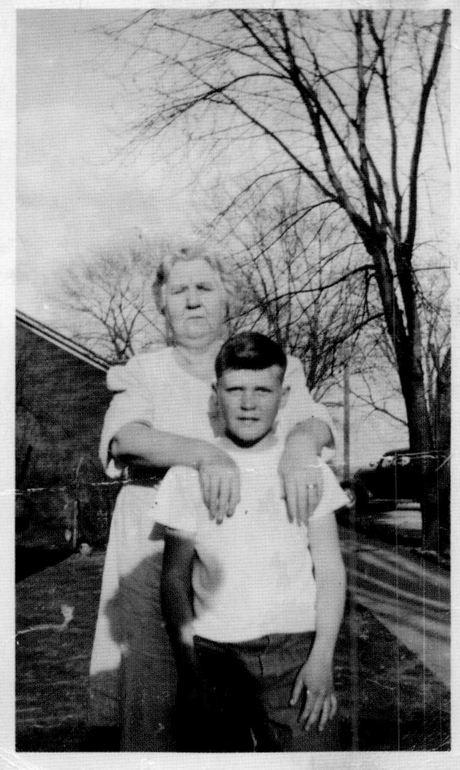

Viola May Gooch with her grandson Dale "Jessie" Gooch, son of Darrel Ira "Hoopie" Gooch b. September 2, 1936.

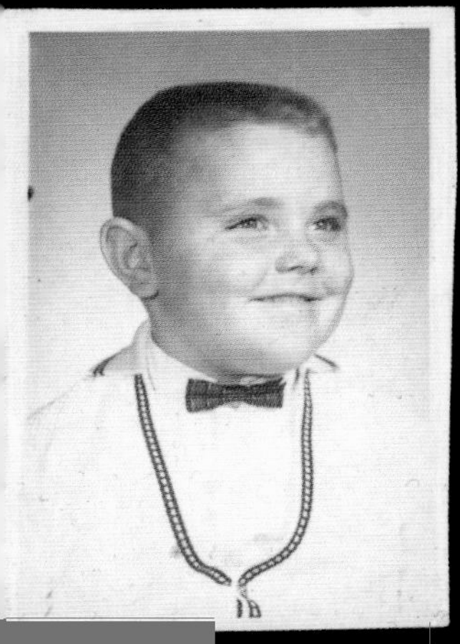

ds: "To Gammy

Judy L. Olinger Gooch, second wife of Dale Gooch

James "Jim" Smith with spouse Marlene Gooch b. February 24, 1934, oldest child of Darrel Ira "Hoopie" and Bessie Gooch. Sherry Lynn Hyde, daughter of Marlene's brother Dale, referred to Marlene as "The rock of the family."

Marlene Gooch Smith (seated) with daughters Debra "Debbie" Lynn b. July 10, 1955, in Danville, Illinois, and Tina Marie b. June 10, 1962, in Morris, Illinois

Bessie Evans Gooch b. November 15, 1914, wife of Darrel Ira "Hoopie" Gooch

Audrey Gooch and Tammy Gooch

Tammy Gooch. Father, Dean Gooch.

*Audrey Lee "Bug" Gooch Smith Waggoner.
Written on back of photo is: "Audrey
March 16, 86 Norma Jean's Mom Bug"*

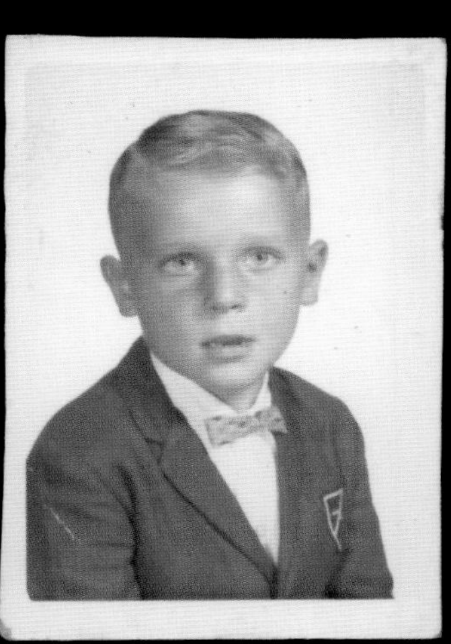

Jeffrey Gooch, 1969

Robert "Bobbie" Smith b. ca. 1924, son of Hobert and Mildred Gooch Smith

See chart on page 438 for relationships of Thomas E. and Thomas Emanuel "Moody" Gooch family members pictured here.

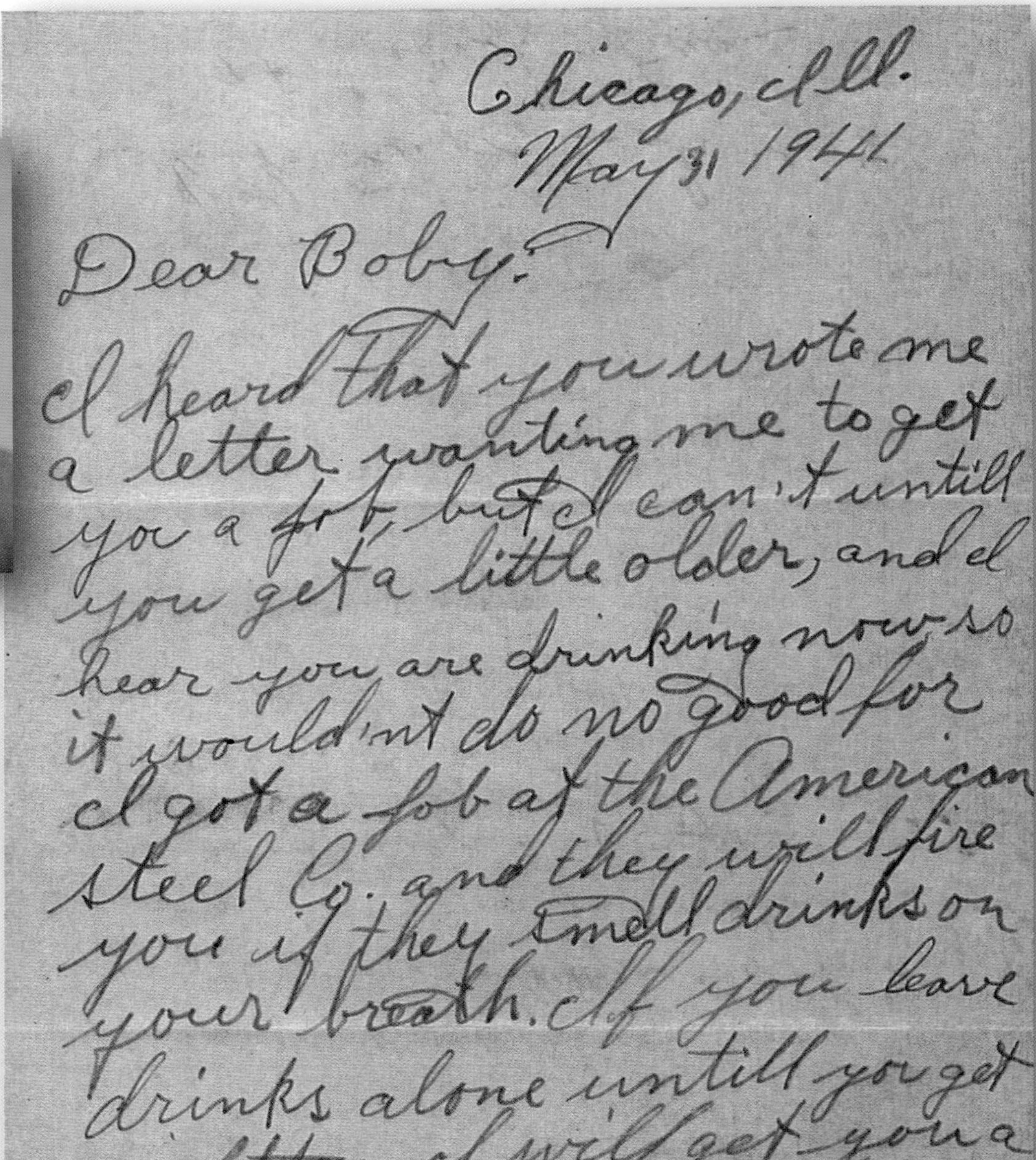

Chicago, Ill.
May 31 1941

Dear Boby:
I heard that you wrote me
a letter wanting me to get
you a job, but I can't untill
you get a little older, and I
hear you are drinking now so
it would'nt do no good for
I got a job at the American
Steel Co. and they will fire
you if they smell drinks on
your breath. If you leave
drinks alone untill you get
eighteen I will get you a
job hear with me the
least they pay is $5 80 a
day. I do not drink any
more myself. I have had
2 beers in 2 months, so

Letter from Darrel Ira "Hoopie" Gooch, 28 years of age, to Robert "Bobbie" Smith (?), probably mailed to Mildred Gooch Smith, his sister, Winslow, Indiana, dated May 31, 1941.

Boby don't drink for I
used to want to have a
name of being a bad man
and I got it by fighting and
getting drunk then after I
got it I didn't want it for
it is bad when you walk
into a place you never was
in before and the fellow says
Gooch you will have to go
for I don't want no fights
in here he says I hear you
would rather fight than
eat and you know that
is not true. Ha. Ha.

Your Uncle
Hoopie

6630. S. Ellis ave
% Chester Evans
Chicago Ill

Darrel Ira "Hoopie" Gooch, b. October 27, 1913

CHICAGO
JUN 1
930 PM
1941
22
ILL.

Mrs Mildred Smith
Winslow, Ind

Chicago, Ill.
May 31, 1941

Dear Hobart and Sis:

I hate to ask the thing I am going to ask but it is the only way out. I want to barrow $20 for I have a job at the American steel Co. I will make between $1.20 and $1.80 a month I have got $6. And a lady let me have two rooms untill payday but six dollars won't keep me untill I get on my feet. I would get along alright for Aunt Bess was keeping the kids and she went every where

Darrel Ira "Hoopie" Gooch with wife Bessie Evans Gooch. "Hoopie" and Bessie were married August 23, 1933.

Letter from Darrel Ira "Hoopie" Gooch, 28 years of age, to his sister, Mildred Gooch Smith, and Cornice Hobert Smith, Winslow, Indiana, dated May 31, 1941. The letter continues on the following pages.

talking about me and the
kids, said they didint have
no clothes, and that me and
Bessie didint want them, so
I went and got them, Mom
told me to write that you
might let me have it, this
is the first time I ever had
a chance at a good job, so
if you dont let me have it you
wont injoy your meals
very good thinking that me
and my family is not eat-
ing. in about a month I can
start paying you what I
owe you & I will pay so much
a pay untill paid so if you
let me have it send it as

See chart on page 438 for relationships of Thomas E. and Thomas Emanuel "Moody" Gooch family members pictured here.

III

soon as you can, you
can't charge unless you
have worked a month or
two. I tried to sell my
truck but I didn't have
very good luck, Sis they
have all been good to me,
but Paul got killed and
his wife is going back
home and that will leave
me in a spot, but I will
stick it out if I have to
eat out of the alleys I don't
worry about myself but it is
the kids Payday I will
draw one weeks work and
owe two weeks rent & so so

IV

if I get the money I can make it, I don't drink any more, how are all of you fine I hope. Tell every body hello.

Signed off
Hoopie

P.S. I know Roy asked but I have a way to pay back, I will either get 76¢ an hour or $1, I know I would got a $1, if Paul had of lived

Ans. Soon

I hated to ask but that is the last chance

Thomas E. "Moody" Gooch Family

Letter from Darrel Ira "Hoopie" Gooch, 28 years of age, to his sister, Mildred Gooch Smith, Cornice Hobert Smith, and kids Winslow, Indiana, dated June 8, 1941.

Cornice Hobert Smith and Mary Mildred Gooch Smith. The car appears to be about a late 1930s model, perhaps around 1937. This picture may have been taken some time around the writing of this letter.

Tell every one
Hellow for me
and family

Chicago, Ill.
June 8, 1941

Dear Sis.
Hobart and Kids.
I thot I would drop a
line or two before I go to
work I wanted to tell you
about my job, I got started
at 76c an hour. Common labor
is 72½c that isn't much but
at 72½c you got to go in a
run and at 76 you work
about 1/3 of the time, Sis you
said Algonquin was better
for the kids because it
was small but I made
45c an hour and rent was
$30 a month and you paid

my ass when there is a letter
for me. I can't figure Roy
out he had a job at 55c an
hour, he sleep in the car
and get a meal ticket untill
he got payed Sis I never
asked for no money untill I
had a job in two months I go to
80c Sis I may go down and trade
my truck to Spyers for a 1937 ford
for I drive 17 mile to work and
can't find no place closer I ride
with Chester but it costs so much
10 galon of gas 2 gal of oil every
three days and he is broke so you
see where my 20 is going besides
eats I went out to Thorton and
saw Lyle H. Judge H. Cherry, Jack dog. Don
Comer. They all have a job but
common labor they are not
smart like me, Ha Ha

See chart on page 438 for relationships of Thomas E. and Thomas Emanuel "Moody" Gooch family members pictured here.

for the gas, lights, and coal the coal was $10 a ton so that
would be $45 or $50 a month, the eats are cheaper here
than there, I worked 6 days last week $6 and 8¢ a day
only on Sat. I made $9 and 12¢ $60 for the week I
made $39 and 52¢ pretty good I think, Ha. Ha. When I
get to making more money than Hobart I will have
the big head, it will be hard for me for a month
for I will draw one weeks work and pay out $4
union $20 and 50¢ rent $1 for glasses but after that I
will be in the money, I aim to pay Moms light
bill and send her a little money now and then, but
you know I can't send much for awile for I am in
the hole pretty bad, I aim to pay every thing I owe
I want to look every body in the face, you and
Hobart saved my life when you sent that money, Sis
don't think because I don't write every day that I didn't
appreciate that money, cause I did plenty, I about break

I want you to write often as
I don't know very many
people up here, and get lonesome
Hobart the only time I have
drank since I been up here
is when I bring a bottle home
for dinner, a half gallon 29¢
Is every body allright I
hope so. We are felling fine Bob
and every thing. We pay to much
rent but we can't help it now
but I will move when I get
my first full pay, The fellers
wants to rent me rooms 3 for
$35 a month but they get drunk
every pay so I won't take
the rooms or go about them I
pay $10 and 25¢ a week here for
two rooms but they are clean
and no bugs so that is worth
something

If I was on my feet I would
help Roy but with that eye
he can't get a job where I
work Sis Hobart might think
I am trading cars to soon but I
live in the same place with
Chester and I depend on him if he
didn't work I would lose the
time to. I can trade for $125
and pay $10 a month then I can
move away from them the kids
lives is hell here the only place
they can play is on their porch I
can't bring the truck up here because
there is roads that they don't allow
trucks so I would be lost all the
time Tell Hobart to write and
tell me what he thinks about
me trading. Hope all is well
Tell the Kids Hello
Answer Soon
Hoopie

I HEREBY CERTIFY that the foregoing is a true and correct copy of the death record for the decedent name in ITEM 1 and that this record was established and filed in my office in accordance with the provisions of the Illinois statutes relating to the registration of births, fetal deaths and deaths.

DANVILLE, ILLINOIS Date 8-24-07 Signed Stephen Laker jr Seal

OFFICIAL TITLE - LOCAL REGISTRAR

STATE OF ILLINOIS

MEDICAL EXAMINER'S – CORONER'S CERTIFICATE OF DEATH

☒ PERMANENT CERTIFICATE ☐ TEMPORARY CERTIFICATE

REGISTRATION DISTRICT NO. 920 — REGISTERED NUMBER 007-0575 — STATE FILE NUMBER

DECEASED

1. DECEASED–NAME: PAUL DUANE Gooch — 2. SEX: MALE — 3. DATE OF DEATH: August 23, 2007
4. COUNTY OF DEATH: VERMILION — 5a. AGE–LAST BIRTHDAY (YRS): 65 — 5d. DATE OF BIRTH: FEBRUARY 19, 1942
6a. CITY, TOWN, TWP, OR ROAD DISTRICT NUMBER: FAIRMOUNT — 6b. HOSPITAL OR OTHER INSTITUTION: 109 EAST STATE — 6c. His Home
7. BIRTHPLACE: Chicago IL — 8a. MARRIED, NEVER MARRIED, WIDOWED, DIVORCED: NEVER MARRIED — 8b. NAME OF SURVIVING SPOUSE: — 9. WAS DECEASED EVER IN U.S. ARMED FORCES?: NO
10. SOCIAL SECURITY NUMBER: 322-32-6774 — 11a. USUAL OCCUPATION: OPERATOR — 11b. KIND OF BUSINESS OR INDUSTRY: Gravel Pit — 12. EDUCATION: 12
13a. RESIDENCE: 109 EAST STATE — 13b. CITY, TOWN, TWP, OR ROAD DISTRICT NO.: FAIRMOUNT — 13c. INSIDE CITY (YES/NO): YES — 13d. COUNTY: VERMILION
13e. STATE: Illinois — 13f. ZIP CODE: 61841 — 14a. RACE: White — 14b. OF HISPANIC ORIGIN?: ☒ NO ☐ YES SPECIFY:

PARENTS

15. FATHER–NAME: DARRELL Gooch — 16. MOTHER–NAME: BESSIE EVANS
17a. INFORMANT'S NAME: GARY Gooch — 17b. RELATIONSHIP: Brother — 17c. MAILING ADDRESS: 304 E. Chandler FAIRMOUNT IL 61841

CAUSE

18. PART I. Immediate Cause: (a) Probable Myocardial Infarction
(b) DUE TO, OR AS A CONSEQUENCE OF
(c) DUE TO, OR AS A CONSEQUENCE OF
PART II. Other significant conditions
19a. AUTOPSY (YES/NO): NO — 19b.
20a. NATURAL, ACCIDENT, HOMICIDE, SUICIDE, UNDETERMINED: Natural — 20b. DATE OF INJURY — 20c. HOUR — 20d. HOW INJURY OCCURRED
20e. INJURY AT WORK — 20f. PLACE OF INJURY — 20g. LOCATION — 20h. IF FEMALE, WAS THERE A PREGNANCY IN PAST THREE MONTHS? YES ☐ NO ☐

CERTIFIER

21a. I CERTIFY THAT IN MY OPINION BASED UPON MY INVESTIGATION AND/OR THE INQUISITION, THIS DEATH OCCURRED ON THE DATE, AT THE PLACE AND DUE TO THE CAUSE(S) STATED, AND THAT ...
21b. THE DECEDENT WAS PRONOUNCED DEAD ON: August 23, 2007 — 21c. AT: 3:07 P. M.
22a. CORONER'S–MEDICAL EXAMINER'S SIGNATURE: Peggy Johnson by [signature] Chief Deputy Coroner — 22b. DATE SIGNED: August 24, 2007
23a. CORONER'S PHYSICIAN'S NAME — 23b. DATE SIGNED

DISPOSITION

24a. BURIAL, CREMATION, REMOVAL: CREMATION — 24b. CEMETERY OR CREMATORY–NAME: Kelley Crematory — 24c. LOCATION: Champaign Illinois — 24d. DATE: 8-28-2007
25a. FUNERAL HOME: CARRINGTON 110 E. COURT FAIRMOUNT ILLINOIS 61841
25b. FUNERAL DIRECTOR'S SIGNATURE: Rodyn B. Wolf — 25c. FUNERAL DIRECTOR'S ILLINOIS LICENSE NUMBER: 031-009703
26a. LOCAL REGISTRAR'S SIGNATURE: Stephen Laker jr — 26b. DATE FILED BY LOCAL REGISTRAR: 8-24-07

VR202 (Rev. 5/89) Illinois Department of Public Health—Division of Vital Records (BASED ON 1989 U.S. STANDARD CERTIFICATE)

PRINTED BY THE AUTHORITY OF THE STATE OF ILLINOIS

State of Illinois Medical Examiner's/Coroner's Certificate of Death of Paul Duane Gooch, b. February 19, 1942, d. August 23, 2007, son of Ira Darrel "Hoopie" Gooch and Bessie Evans.

An obituary appeared for him in the Sidell Reporter, *which covers Vermilion County, Illinois, in August, 2007:*

> Paul D. Gooch, 65, of Fairmount died at 3:07 p.m. Thurs. (Aug. 23, 2007) at home. Born Feb. 19, 1942, he was the son of Darrell and Bessie (Evans) Gooch of Fairmount. He attended Fairmount schools. Paul is survived by two brothers, Dale (Judy) Gooch of Morris and Gary (Karen) Gooch of Fairmount, and several nieces and nephews. Funeral services were at 2 p.m. Tuesday at Carrington Funeral Home, 110 E. Court St., Fairmount. Pastor Mike Roberts officiated. His remains were cremated.

Mildred E. and Thomas E. Gooch

William T. and Maude E. Gooch

Thomas E. Gooch Sr.

Area Deaths

Mrs. Viola Gooch

Fairmount (CNS)—Mrs. Viola Gooch, 81, of Fairmount, died last night (Oct. 13, 1964) in the Vermilion Nursing Home where she had been a patient since January of 1963. She had been ill several years.

Born May 16, 1883, in Hillsboro, Ky., she was the daughter of John B. and Matilda Sanders Goodwin.

She was married Sept. 14, 1904, to Emmanuel Gooch who preceded her in death in 1955.

Surviving are two daughters, Mrs. Hobart Smith of Fairmount and Mrs. H. M. Waggoner of Homer; two sons, Roy of Danville and Darrell of Morris, Ill.; 11 grandchildren and 24 great-grandchildren; a brother, Thomas Goodwin of Sedalia, Mo., and a sister, Mrs. Guy Cook of Fairmount.

She also was preceded in death by a brother and a sister.

Most of her life had been spent in the Fairmount area. She was a member of the Fairmount Nazarene Church.

The body is at the Carrington Funeral Home where friends will be received Thursday afternoon and night. Services will be at 2 p. m. Friday at the funeral home with the Rev. Don C. Goodwin officiating. Burial will be in Greenview Cemetery.

Viola Gooch, October 13, 1964

Roy Gooch

Roy Gooch, 75 of Danville, died Aug. 15 at St. Elizabeth Hospital, Danville.

Mr. Gooch was born Aug. 17, 1908 at Fairmount, the son of Emmanuel and Viola Goodwin Gooch. He married Hazel E. Lane in 1932 in Danville. She preceded him in death in 1947.

Survivors include ; daughter, Mildred Hughes of Danville; one son, Dean Gooch of Maroa; 11 grandchildren; 1(great-grandchildren; and two sisters, Mildred Smith of Fairmount and Audrey Waggoner of Homer.

Mr. Gooch was a painter.

Family memorial services were held Aug. 20 at the Greenview Cemetery, Fairmount.

Roy Gooch, August 23, 1984

THOMAS E. "MOODY" GOOCH FAMILY

Charles W. Gooch

Robert E., Mildred, and Hobert Smith

Rosa Lee, Addie, and Margie Gooch

Viola M. and T. Emanuel Gooch

Charles Gooch

Charles W. Gooch, 68, of 23½ S. Gilbert, manager of)anville Tile and Sewer Co., lied at 10:45 a.m. Sunday Feb. 25, 1973) at Lake View Memorial Hospital, where he iad been a patient four veeks.

Born Oct. 18, 1904, at Catlin, he was the son of William and Maude Higgins Gooch. On March 15, 1952, he narried Parquila Collings in)anville, who survives.

A resident of Danville for he past 23 years, he had nanaged the Danville firm on N. Logan for the past 20 years. He had formerly worked at the Oakwood Coal Co.

He was a member of the Olive Branch Masonic Lodge 38 and the Scottish Rite, both of Danville. He attended the United Church of Christ at Tilton.

His hobbies were fishing and baseball.

Other survivors include two sons, Charles M. of Danville and Stanley L. of Muncie; a daughter, Mrs. Vivian Dodge of Danville; a step-son, Everett Collings of Catlin; a step-daughter, Mrs. Barbara Crabtree of Danville; two sisters, Mrs. Elizabeth Brown and Mrs. Bertie Williams, both of Danville; 10 grandchildren; three step-grandchildren; and a great-grandchild.

Services will be at 2 p.m. Wednesday at the Carrington Funeral Home in Fairmount, with the Rev. Don C. Goodwin officiating. Burial will be in Greenview Cemetery at Fairmount. Visitation will be at the funeral home from 2-4 and 7-9 p.m. Tuesday, with Masonic services by Olive Branch Lodge at 7 p.m. Tuesday.

Charles Gooch
February 25, 1973

Mildred Smith

FAIRMOUNT — Mildred Smith, 87, a Fairmount resident, died at 5:05 p.m. Saturday (Dec. 19, 1992) at USMC, Sager Campus, Danville.

She was born Aug. 21, 1905, in Fairmount, a daughter of Emmanuel and Viola Goodwin Gooch.

She was married to Hobart Smith on Nov. 16, 1922. He preceded her Sept. 16, 1983.

Survivors include: one daughter-in-law, Myrna Smith of Evansville, Ind.; three grandchildren and two great-grandchildren; and one sister, Audrey Waggoner of the Vermilion Manor Nursing Home. She also was preceded in death by two sons, Dean and Bob and two brothers.

Funeral services: 10 a.m. Tuesday, Dec. 22 at Carrington Funeral Home in Fairmount; Officiating: Rev. Don Strohl; Burial: Greenview Cemetery in Fairmount; Visitation: 6-8 p.m. Monday at the funeral home.

Mildred Smith
December 19, 1992

Hobert Smith

FAIRMOUNT, Ill. — Hobert Smith, 85, of Fairmount was dead on arrival at 10:25 a.m. Friday (Sept. 16, 1983) at Lakeview Medical Center.

The Vermilion County coroner's office attributed death to natural causes.

Smith had worked at the Fairmount Stone Quarry before moving to Winslow, Ind., in 1928, where he worked for AMAX Coal Co. Upon retiring from AMAX in April 1955, he returned to Fairmount. He was a member of Local 4343 in Oakland City, Ind.

Born Sept. 29, 1897, in Richelieu, Ky., he was a son of James Robert and Clara King Smith. He married Mildred Gooch on Nov. 15, 1922 in Danville. She survives.

Other survivors include two grandchildren, James and Linda Smith, both of Evansville, Ind., and a great-grandson, Mathew Smith.

Two sons preceded him in death, Robert in 1970 and Dean in 1974.

Services will be at 11 a.m. Monday at Carrington Funeral Home in Fairmount. The Rev. Harold Simmons will officiate, and burial will be in Greenview Cemetery in Fairmount. Visitation will be 7-9 p.m. Sunday at the funeral home.

Hobert Smith
September 16, 1983

Leoria "Peggy" Reeves Phillips *Bessie and Darrell "Hoopie" Gooch* *Greenview Cemetery, Fairmount, Illinois*

D. H. Gooch

FAIRMOUNT (CNS) — Services for Darrell "Hoopy" Gooch, 55, of Morris, a former Fairmount resident, who died at 1:30 a.m. Thursday at St. Joseph Hospital in Joliet of injuries sustained in a two car accident Sept. 30, will be at 2 p.m. Sunday at the Carrington Funeral Home in Fairmount, with the Rev. Don C. Goodwin officiating.

Burial will be in Greenview Cemetery at Fairmount. Friends may call from 2 to 4 and 7 to 9 p.m. Saturday at the funeral home.

Mr. Gooch was born Oct. 27, 1913, in Fairmount, a son of Emanuel and Viola Goodwin Gooch. He was married to Bessie Evans, who survives. They had resided at Morris for the past 16 years, moving there from Fairmount.

Also surviving are one daughter, Mrs. Marlene Smith of Morris; three sons, Dale and Paul, both of Morris, Garry at home; two sisters, Mrs. Mildred Smith of Fairmount, Mrs. Audrey Waggoner of Homer; one brother, Roy of Morris; six grandchildren; four nephews; and two nieces.

A coroner's inquest into the accident is pending. Mr. Gooch was reported to be enroute to work at the Material Service Corp. in Morris when the accident occurred.

Darrel Ira "Hoopie" Gooch
October 6, 1969

Wilford R. 'Woody' Woodard

Wilford R. 'Woody' Woodard, 71, of Danville, passed away at 7:29 a.m. Wednesday (Nov. 10, 1993) at USMC, Logan Campus.

He was born May 25, 1922, in Fairmount, the son of Richard T.

Wilford 'Woody' Woodard

and Ada Gooch Woodard. He married Daisy Kinney on March 16, 1944, in Covington, Ind. She survives. Also surviving: two sons, Gene (Barbara) Woodard of Danville and Robert (Donna) Woodard of Oakwood; two daughters, Myrna (James) Creason and Kathy (Robert) Turner, both of Danville; two sisters, Shirley (Harold) Cromwell of Homer and Marilyn (Robert) Miller of Reno, Nev.; an uncle, Walter Gooch of Grandby, Colo.; nine grandchildren, Sheri (David) Beck, Scott (Jamie) Creason, Tony Creason, Tara Jo Woodard, Jeremy McMasters Woodard, Clay and Bobby Woodard, and Chad and Farrah Turner; two special children, Mary and Jessica McMasters; and five great-grandchildren. He was preceded in death by his parents.

He was an Illinois State Trooper from 1957-82. He was a ranger at Kennekuk Cove County Park from 1988 until the time of his death. He was in his second term as Danville Township trustee. He was a U.S. Marine veteran of World War II, serving from 1944-46 in the Pacific Theater, where he received the Purple Heart.

He was a member of the Homer Masonic Lodge and Danville Olive Branch #38. He was a 32nd degree member of Scottish Rite Bodies of the Valley of Danville Consistory. He was also a Golden Eagle Scottish Rite member. He belonged to the Troopers Lodge #41, Illinois Police Association, Pollywogs Association, American Legion Post 610, and Danville Township Officials of Illinois. He was involved in numerous community activities. He attended West Side Church of the Nazarene.

Services: 10 a.m. Saturday at Sunset Funeral Home; Officiating: Kenneth Bostwick; Burial: Oakwood Cemetery; Visitation: 3-8 p.m. Friday at the funeral home, with Masonic services provided by Olive Branch Lodge #38 at 7:30 p.m.; Memorials: charity of donor's

Wilford R. "Woody" Woodard
November 10, 1993

Thomas E. and Mildred Gooch and Thomas Emanuel "Moody" and Viola Gooch Families — Chart of *only* those family members pictured on previous pages and their relationships. For a more complete representation of the Gooch family tree, refer to the Supplement volume.

- **Thomas E. Gooch** b. 1836, KY, d. 1918, IL
  & Mildred Elizabeth Oldham
  - Edney M. "Edna" Gooch b.1862, KY, d. 1918, IL
    - Thomas E. Delaney b. 1886 IL
    - Dale Wilbur Delaney b. 1900, IL, d. 1967, FL
      - Son Delaney
  - Robert T. Gooch b. 1865, KY, d. 1930, IL
    - Robert Otis Gooch b. 1895, IL
    - Harold Gooch b. 1913, IL, d. 1955
  - Rebecca "Becca" Gooch b. 1867, KY, d. 1957, IN
    - Elizabeth "Lizzie" Davis b. 1892, IL, d. 1982, IN
      - Glenn Edward Purkey b. 20 Apr 1922, d. 1986
  - William Tearle Gooch b. 1870, KY d. 1945, IL
    & Maude Ethel Higgins
    - Charles W. "Charley" Gooch b. 1904, d. 1973, IL
      - Roger Gooch d. Killed in Second World War
    - Elizabeth Bell Gooch b. 6 Nov 1906, , IL
      & Everett E. Brown
    - Bertha "Bertie" Gooch b. 1909, IL
    - Stanley Gooch
    - Melvin Gooch
      - Vivian Gooch
  - Eliza "Liza" Gooch b. 1875, KY, d. 1951, MO.
    & Thomas C. Goodwin
    - Fred Davis b, Aug 1895
  - **Thomas Emanuel "Moody" Gooch** (see below)
  - Rosa Lee Gooch b. 13 Oct 1880, KY, d. 1939
    - Myrtle Woodard b. ca 1908
  - Jessie Doney "Doll-Dollie" Gooch b. 1888, IL, d. 1969, IL
    - Leoria "Peggy" Reeves b. 1909, IL, d. 1972, IL
    - Ruby Reeves b. ca 1915
    - Grace Reeves b. ca 1919

- **Thomas Emanuel "Moody" Gooch** b. 1877, d. 1955
  & Viola May Goodwin
  - Mary Mildred Gooch b. 1905, IL, d. 19 Dec 1992, IL
    & Cornice Hobert Smith
    - Robert Emanuel "Bobby" Smith b. 1924, d. 1970
    - Byron Dean Smith b. 1929, d. 1973
  - Roy Dean Gooch b. 1908, IL, d. 1984, IL
  - Darrel Ira "Hoopie" Gooch b. 1913, IL d. 1969
    & Bessie Evans
    - Marlene Gooch b. 1934, IL, d. 1999, IL
      & James "Jim" Smith
      - Debra "Debbie" Lynn Smith b. 1955, IL
      - Tina Marie Smith b. 1962, IL
    - Paul Duayne "Frank" Gooch b. 1942, IL, d. 2007
    - Gary "Bone" Gooch b. 1955, IL
    - Dale "Jessie" Gooch b. 1936
      & Sharon Viano
      & Judy L. Olinger
  - Audrey "Bug" Lee Gooch b. 1916, IL
    & Erville Jesse "Smitty" Smith

Savage Benkó

Roots Trip Hungary June 1998

Minorite Church (templom), founded by Franciscan friars. The statue in front is the castle warriors statue — Végvári Harcosok Szobra.

A Visit to the "Old Country"

After our fourth biking trip with Butterfield and Robinson to Corsica and Sardinia, June 16–23, 1998, we flew from Milan, Italy, to Vienna, Austria. On June 23 we checked into the Hotel Bristol Sheraton on the Kaerntner Ring 1 for one night.

Our plan was to rent a car in Vienna, travel east, cross the border into Hungary and continue on to Budapest to spend the day there sightseeing. After an overnight in Budapest, our next destination would be Eger, Hungary, to visit relatives Benkó (Bolyki) and then head south from Eger to Pecs and Bonyhád returning from Pecs to Vienna. A diagram drawn on a map of this trip by car would look something like a triangle — east, southwest by northwest.

On June 24 in Budapest, we went to pick up our Avis rental car, reserved from New York, but we could not get the Mercedes requested, we were told, due to the high rate of theft in Hungary of expensive cars. Only smaller, less-expensive cars were available, and we were offered an Opal Vectra. Disappointed, we went to a nearby Hertz rental office and got a larger car. Despite learning that we were about to enter a country of rampant theft, we were undeterred from making ourselves an even bigger target.

We had reservations at the Hotel Eger Park in Eger, Hungary, for the evening of June 24. After check-in and being shown to our room and finding it disappointing — a worn, tired, communist-run facility, and lacking air conditioning — we decided to leave the hotel. There seemed to be a pattern developing around us of expectations not being realized. At the registration desk a managing clerk informed us that our deposit in full could not be refunded. He found it difficult to believe that we would leave the hotel and seek lodging elsewhere. We were

Looking north on Széchenyi Street (Utca) in Eger, Hungary

Nineteenth century St. John's and Michael's Basilica

Photos by **Julius Fülep**, Eger, Hungary, October 2009

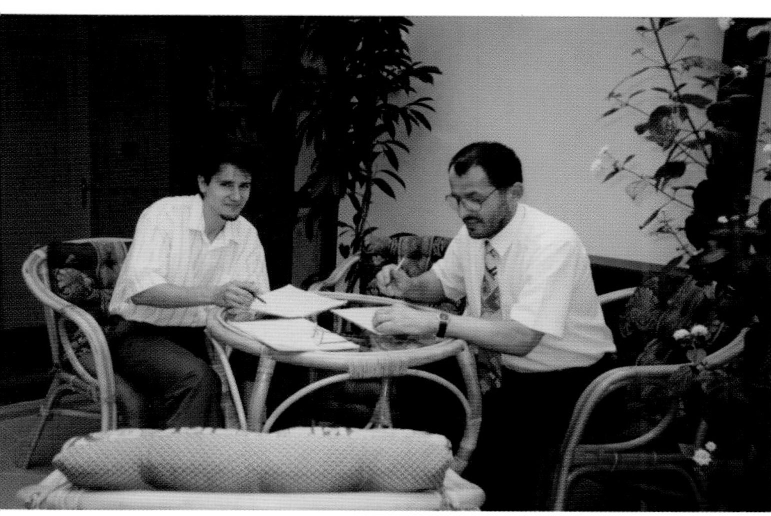

Gyula "Julius" Fülep and Józseph Seress in consultation at the Szent János Hotel in Eger, Hungary in a photo by me.

able to convince him of our intention and even asked if he could recommend another hotel more fitting of our expectations. He offered to take us to a friend's hotel, and we quickly took him up on his recommendation. As we followed him through winding roads and depressing neighborhoods, away from the main highway and past block after block of large high-rise housing — apartment buildings erected, we were later informed, by the communists — we wondered aloud if we were being set up for a car hijacking, a robbery, or kidnapping. Ultimately he led us to the Hotel Romantik, H-3300 Eger, Csiky Sándor utca 26. The Romantik was a lovely, small, boutique hotel, one that provided us acceptable lodging, a bathroom shared with other guests, and the next morning, breakfast in a solarium. Coincidentally, the referring hotel manager, Józseph Seress, after discussing our genealogical mission in Hungary, informed us that he, too, was writing a book, one that involved a history of Hungarian royalty and the genealogy of his family. I was quick to pick up on his expertise, his ability to speak English, and his willingness to help, and asked if he would assist us in our search and serve as a consultant and guide.

On June 26 we checked into another hotel in Eger that Józseph had originally intended for us to stay in, but no rooms had been available the previous night. We left the Romantik and spent the next two nights at the Hotel Szent János, 3300 Eger, Szent János u. 3. It was another boutique hotel, recently modernized, nicely furnished, and owned by the same person who was, we were informed, the Hungarian national distributor for Nike sporting-goods (a Nike shop was next to the hotel). The hotel was in the heart of the historical town center, and though small (it had only ten rooms), was fully equipped with air conditioning, bathroom shower, color television, and mini-bar. The hotel manager, who was an outgoing, robust woman, embraced us and could not do enough to please us. Inquiring about laundry facilities and being informed that they had none, she nevertheless arranged for our laundry to be done by hand. When we returned later that day, we found our laundry hanging about the breakfast room, drying.

A friend of Józseph, she learned of our quest and referred us to Gyula "Julius" Fülep, a teacher of English in a local grammar school and local tour guide. I introduced Józseph to Julius Fülep, who was to become our primary contact in Eger. Together they were the perfect team, one that we could never have hoped for prior to our departure from the States.

When we finally departed, the hotel manager presented us with a gift of a bottle of the local wine and Hungarian blood sausage. Eger, a town about 130 kilometers from Budapest that lies at the foot of the picturesque Bukk hills, is famous for its Baroque architecture and its wine, often referred to as "Bull's blood."

On the first morning at the Hotel Szent János, I arranged for a roundtable discussion with our two Hungarian consultants, Julius and Józseph. They reviewed the data that I had collected before our arrival in Hungary, and we divided responsibilities between our two advisers. Julius, our primary contact, would accompany us and serve as an interpreter in our first meeting with my family, the Bolykis. He would give us a tour of Eger and the town of Andornaktálya (known as Kistálya when my grandmother was born and lived there), where he would introduce us to the local priest and we would gain access to the church cemetery where other kinfolk were buried (see pages 558–559 for more about this visit). Józseph was to take us on a tour of the cemetery in Felsötárkány, the town where the Bolykis lived.

On June 28, we drove south along the E73 from Eger to the Hotel Palantinus in Pecs in the south of Hungary. Little did we realize as we passed through Bonyhád, our destination

Church of the Virgin Lady in Andornaktálya [Kistálya], Hungary.

Photos by **Julius Fülep**, Eger, Hungary, October 2009.

Statue in center of Tér (Square) is of Dobó István, the greatest hero of Eger, who saved northern Hungary and Austria from Ottoman invasion in 1552 and led 2,000 defenders — men, women and children — against 60,000 Turkish invaders.

for the following morning, that we were near to other villages around Bonyhád — Grábóc, Szálka, Alsónána and Bátaszék — that would figure so much more importantly in our search for my ancestors, the Szávics.

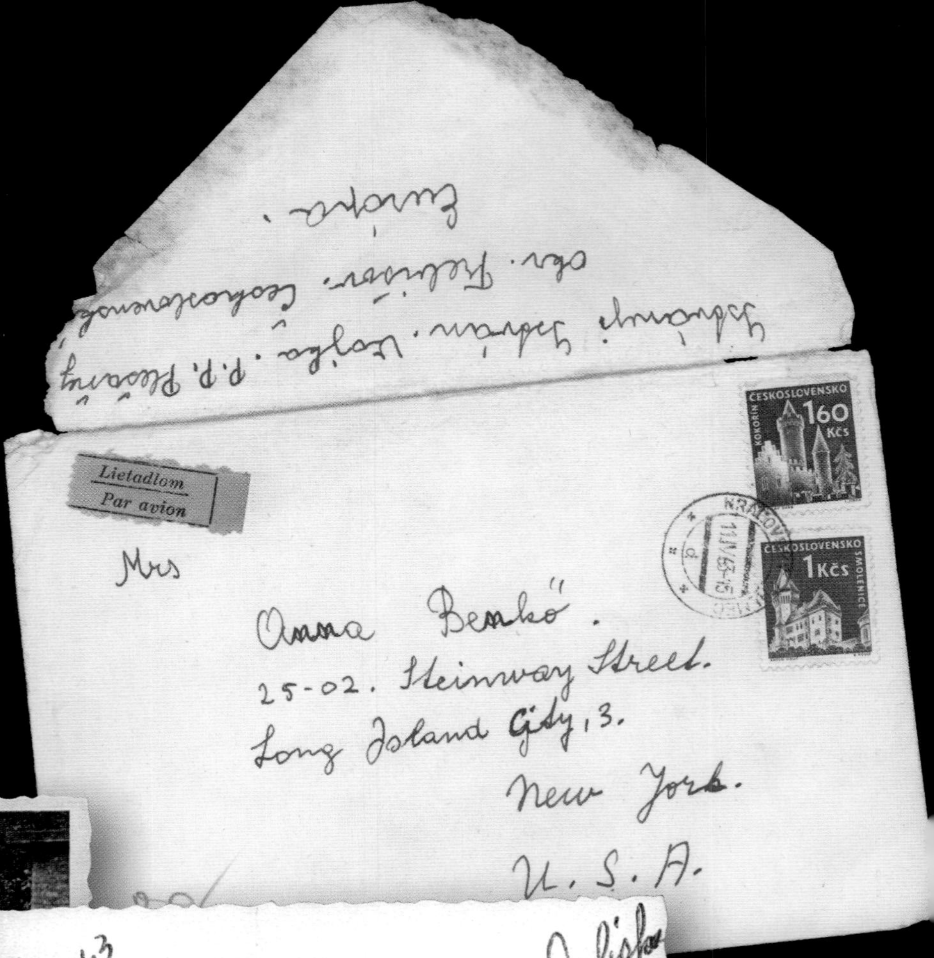

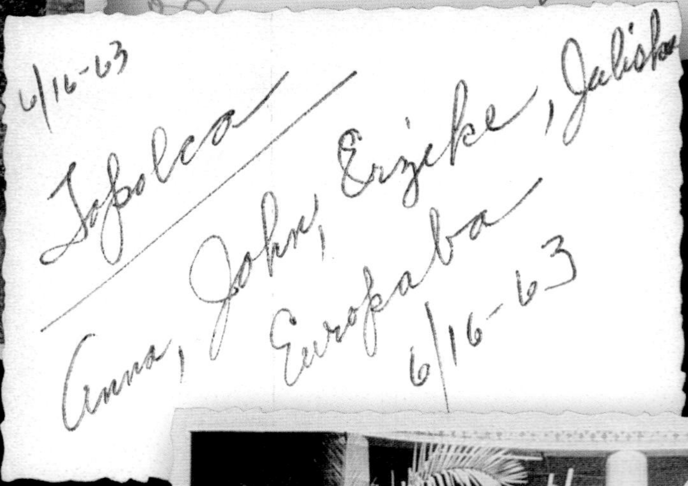

The letter, which came in the envelope pictured top right and signed by Kornelia (Istvánji) from Trebisov, Czechoslovakia, on April 11, 1963, documents the planned trip of Anna and John Benko from New York to Europe. There were two other women traveling on the same ship to Vajka (Véke) according to the "welcoming remarks" contained in the letter. The photographs on this page, which I had received from Anna Benko, and seeing duplicates of the same photographs in the possession of Lajos (Benkó) Bolyki b. August 8, 1926, during our trip to Hungary in June 1998, was evidence enough to confirm our familial relationship.

John Benko and his wife Anna are seated on the right in these two pictures. Their two traveling companions are identified only as "Juliska" (far left in the photo above and second from left in the photo at right) and "Erzike" (second from left in the photo above and far left on the photo at right).

Bound for Bonyhád

On the morning of June 29, we drove from Pecs to Bonyhád. My grandfather Dusán Szávics, also known as Dezsó David Andrew "Andy" Savage, was born in Bonyhád, incorrectly recorded as "Bonghard," Hungary, according to information on his death certificate, Cook County, Illinois (see page 474). He died June 15, 1949. Upon our arrival in Bonyhád w went looking for the local Catholic Church and its p that there would be religious records kept by the Ca of Szávics living in the area, either now or in the pas

It was a pleasant morning with church bells pe parishioners to mass. I recall filming a tall, elderly m sweater, with a limp and a cane, walking across the s the church. I followed him into the church and up t the altar with my camera as he found his seat. After we did not attend, and after the priest tended to the offerings of his parishioners being picked up by a co met with us in his office, a dark wood-paneled, diml smelling of incense, with a statue of the Virgin Mary crosses on its walls. He was surrounded by what app old record books. I recall one of the books being date still, to this day, find it remarkable that, despite the c Hungary by the Germans in World War II and more Russians and Communists, these ancient records rem

Fortunately, while waiting outside for mass to we met a former autoworker from the States who wa the area at the time, and he offered to serve as our in The priest went through ledger after ledger, page afte no avail, seeking the name Szávics. He asked whethe

Lajos (Benkó) Bolyki at the home of Imre (Benkó) Bolyki at

Imre (Benkó) Bolyki at his home at 230 FO UT Felsötárkány

nnet Bajzat and Kay Davis at the home of Imre (Benkó) Bolyki at 230 FO UT Felsötárkány, Hungary, on June 26, 1998

Left to right, Annet Bajzat, Margit Bolyki Bajzat, Margit (Sütó) Bolyki, Rozalia (Kakukk) Bolyki, Clyde Davis, Lajos (Benkó) Bolyki and Imre (Benkó) Bolyki, at the home of Imre (Benkó) Bolyki at 230 FO UT Felsötárkány, Hungary, on June 26, 1998. Note the bottle of local Eger "Bull's Blood," or Bikavér wine, and the blood sausage that Clyde Davis is holding. These were the gifts from the manager of the Hotel Szent János, which Clyde passed on to the Bolykis.

Lajos (Benkó) Bolyki and Rozalia (Kakukk) Bolyki

Catholics. My reply was yes. I recorded our meeting with the priest on my video camera, including Kay seated against the wall, with both hands up to the camera, fingers crossed wishing for luck when, perhaps, considering the setting, she should have been offering a prayer instead. There were no Szávics in the church's records and although an archival center was mentioned in Szekszárd, the county seat, he was not hopeful that we would find our ancestors in their records either, and he discouraged us from trying. We had a long drive to Vienna ahead of us, but we thought we should take a stab at the Szekszárd archival center, since it was on our way, and we had to pass through the outskirts of the town as we headed north. This was one of the most serendipitous decisions we've ever made in our roots research.

Hungarian women lining up for water to tend the flowers at their loved ones' gravesites in Felsötárkány in the late evening. This is a common sight.

Wood cross with plaque at headstone 78 of Lajos Bolyki b. 1897 d. 1975, as seen from rear with floral arrangement pulled back for viewing (See headstone below)

Above left: Closeup of the headstone of Lajos Bolyki b. 1897 d. 1975 and his wife, Margit Bakondi b. 1900 d. 1963. The headstone also lists Juliska Bakondi, whose relationship is not known, and József Bolyki b. 1920 d. 1942. József was Lajos and Margit's son who died on the Russian Front in World War II and whose body was buried in the Ukraine. Center: The full headstone of Lajos Bolkyi and Margit Bakondi and its surroundings. Right: The back of the headstone of Lajos Bolyki and Margit Bakondi and what appears to be the temporary marker for their daughter, Maria Bolyki b. September 9, 1922 d. May 15, 1998. The "76" on the marker probably refers to her age at the time of her death.

Municipality of Tolna County Archives Szekszárd, Hungary. Pictured are Gábor Aradi, Éva Ruzsa, and Kay Davis on June 29, 1998.

Record found: Janos Szávics. Gábor Aradi, Clyde Davis, and Éva Ruzsa

Serendipity in Szekszárd

Pressed for time, having spent a fruitless morning in Bonyhád, and facing a long trip to Vienna, there was some urgency to our going through the records at the Municipality of Tolna County Archives in Szekszárd. We arrived shortly before noon and after much paperwork and processing, we received our stamped research permit and were admitted into the archives to search the Roman Catholic and Greek Orthodox birth registries. As we pored through the records with little success in finding the name Szávics, with time running out and our frustration obviously beginning to show, the attending archivists Gábor Aradi and Éva Ruzsa took pity on us, and over their lunch continued to discuss our dilemma. Upon returning, Gábor greeted us with good news. At lunch he recalled that there was a small enclave of Serbian settlements in the southern part of Tolna County in the early 1800s. The first appearance of the name Szávics was in Sióagárd in 1716, as we later learned.

We left Szekszárd elated with our breakthrough. We also left Gábor and Éva with a request that they continue the search for Szávics in Tolna County and prepare a report, one we would be more than happy to pay for.

I could now rest a lot easier with this information in hand. The Szávics family history would be well documented on a par with the Davises, the Gooches, and the Benkós — taking us back in time well into the 1700s.

Later, the evening of June 29, we arrived at the Vienna Marriott Hotel, Park Ring 12-A, Austria. We spent the night and dropped off our Hertz rental car the next morning at 8:10 A.M.

By September 12, 1998 (see correspondence on following pages), we received the most thorough compilation of records, including drawings, archival photocopies, photographs of former Szávics residences, maps, and even a book on the history of Tolna County. Much of this material appears within the pages of this book.

Photo by **Julius Fülep**, Eger, Hungary, October 17, 2009.

Holy Trinity statue in Szekszárd. The photo was taken October 17, 2009, from the steps of the Roman Catholic Church.

Clyde P. Davis

Gábor Aradi
Tamásné Gréczy
Szekszárd-Hungary

12. September, 1998

Dear Clyde,

We are glad to send you the results of our researches. It took a little bit more time as we thought because we went through not only the registers of births, marriages and deaths, but also the population censuses (written in Latin) and other important documents like the list of the house numbers and the owner 's list. We could verify the residence of the Szavics family only with the help of these documents.

We went to the villages of Szálka, Grábóc and Bátaszék. It has no sense to do researches in the registers of Grábóc written before 1827, for the Szavics family lived that time neither in Szálka nor in Bátaszék. This family name appears in the documents for the first time in the year of 1843, but the register of 1841 is in Bátaszék missing, however we know from the marriage record that Joann (the child of György) was born in this year (1841) in Bátaszék. The other son of György Szavics, Pál (Pavel) was born some years before in 1837, not in Bátaszék but in Somberek (Baranya county) which means that the family lived at first in this other village and once between 1837 and 1841 they settled down in Bátaszék.

We took photos for you, but we could find the old houses of the family neither in Szálka nor in Bátaszék in their original form, because they were either rebuilt or a new house was built at their place. You can see in the photos of the cemeteries that they are in a very bad condition, the graves are unfortunately not recognizable, for 95% of the Serbian inhabitants settled back into their native land, so the deceised persons do not have any relatives in Hungary who could take care of their graves.

After translating the Serbian registers, we noticed that the name of Joann Szavics ' wife was written false, because her name is not Tonkovics but Palkovics.

The Serbian letter П = P
л = l
в = v
и = i
ч = cs

Палкович= Palkovics, Савич = Szavics

The name of the villages found in the registers: Somberek and Dunaszekcső are in Baranya County, not far away of Bátaszék, but our archives has no documents about them.

We are enclosing the following documents:

- Maps of Bátaszék, Szálka and Tolna County
- Registers of Grábóc and Bátaszék
- 1 page family history
- censuses of several villages
- book about Tolna County
- photoalbum
- Family-tree

First of all people who spoke Hungarian lived at the beginning of the 16. century in our country. But this situation changed under the Turkish rule (lasting 150 years) which begann after the defeat in Mohács (1526) and the occupying of the capital, Buda (1541). The Muslim Empire held possession of the middle of Hungary. The Tolna county belonged also to this region. The continuous wars and campaigns made the middle of the country depopulated. But after the Turks had been driven out of the country, several people (not Hungarian) were settled or wandered spontaneously there. Slavonic people: Serbian and Croatian came into the Southern part of Tolna county. That time it was characteristic of the Slavs that they wandered from region to region.

We did researches on the place of residence of the Szavics family in the oldest documents of our archives. These censuses show us the datas of the inhabitants in every village and are written in Latin, therefore at first we had to translate them. The first censuses were taken in 1696, we read each data of every village of Tolna county, but the name Szavics can not be found in these old documents.

The family name Szavics (Savage) appears for the first time after the Turkish occupation in **1716**. The village Agárd (today said: Sioagárd) was settled that time again and Stefan Szavics arrived also as a settler there. But in 1728/29 many Hungarian settlers went to Agárd to live there and so almost every Serbian left the village and wandered away. In **1752** two names were written elsewhere: Joannes Szavics in Alsonána and Ignác Szavics in Szálka. Twenty years later, in **1771** we can find only Ignác Szávics in Szálka. The census of the year **1828** contains this name no more, we know only that "strangers live" in the house number 183 in Szálka. The register of births, marriages and deaths writes that the Szavics family lived in the first half of the 19. century at this place.

The register of an other village: Bátaszék shows also this family name, Szavics (some years later), because many Serbian inhabitants lived in Bátaszék. They had an Orthodox church, but unfortunately it exists no more. The registers are in our archives in Szekszárd and we looked for the datas of the Szavics family also in the documents of Alsonána and Bátaszék.

The registers can be found from **1827** in Tolna County Archives. So we did researches from this year to **1930**. The Szavics family (György and his wife, Julianna) lived at first probably in Somberek (Baranya County), because their son Pál was born in this village and then they settled down in 1838-40 in Bátaszék.

Joann, the other son of György Szavics moved after his marriage into the house of his wife, Julianna Palkovics. This building was the house number 183 in Szálka and it belonged in 1860 to Jakov Palkovics (according to the list of the house numbers).

In 1883 Joann Szavics was the owner of the house number 187/a in Szálka, but he sold it together with his vine-yard and other gardens to Lázár Komadenovics on 17th November,1889. The list of the house numbers writes in the years of 1897-1912 that Joann lived that time in Bátaszék with her daughter, Mileva Szavics, who was the wife of József Tolnaity.

The Szavics and Szlavics families lived also in Bonyhád and Szekszárd, but only as tenants, for their name can not be found on the owner 's list.

After the First World War, 95% of the Southern Slavonic (Serbian) inhabitants settled back into the Serbian-Croatian-Kingdom (from 1929 it was named Yugoslavia), and according to the peace convention of Trianon they were allowed to take their fortune into their native land. In 1926 the Serbian school was also closed because there was no more Serbian student in the village. After this date (after 1912) the registers write nothing about the Szavics and Szlavics family, we don't have any datas, therefore it is possible that they left our country for Yugoslavia

It was so nice to meet you and your wife in Hungary and it was a very good feeling for both of us to talk with you. So we worked for you with pleasure and are also glad that we could get to know the interesting life of a nice family. If you need anything, write us please! We are happy if we can help you.

We hope that you like our work and you are content. We thought that we would like to get about dollars per person for our work and charges, if it is all right for you. If you have any question, please write us at our home address and not at the archives because we did the researches in our free time.

(I made every English translation, my name is Boglárka Gréczy, I am the daughter of Tamásné and I talked with you at phone. I hope very much that everything is easy to understand.)

If you have any question or request, please send your answer at this address:

Tamásné Gréczy
Fürt u. 2.
7100 Szekszárd
Hungary

Thank you. With kind regards, Yours sincerely,

Tamásné Gréczy Gábor Aradi

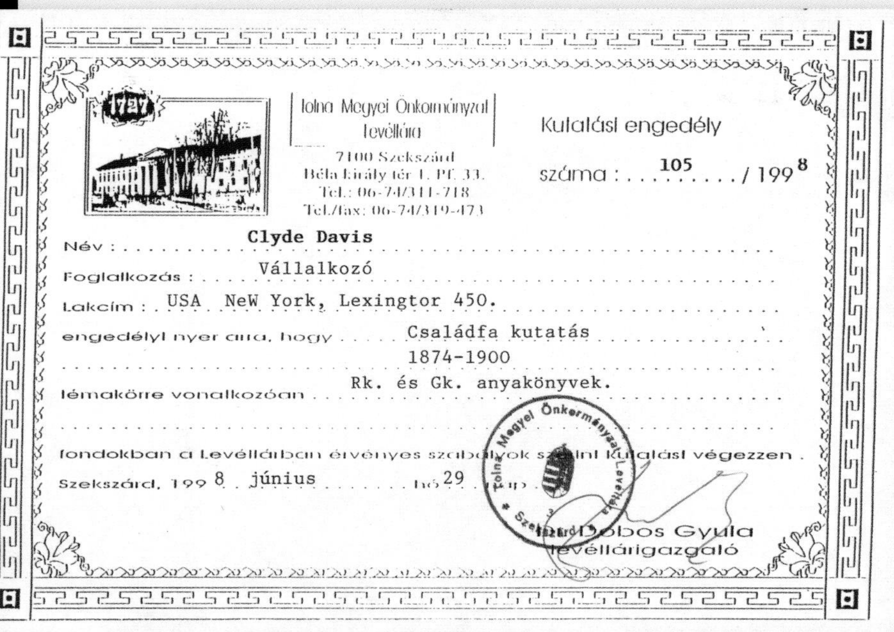

Tolna Megyei Önkormányzat Levéltára
7100 Szekszárd
Béla király tér 1. Pf. 33.
Tel.: 06-74/311-718
Tel./fax: 06-74/319-473

Kutatási engedély

száma: 105/1998

Név: Clyde Davis

Foglalkozás: Vállalkozó

Lakcím: USA NeW York, Lexingtor 450.

engedélyt nyer arra, hogy Családfa kutatás 1874-1900

Rk. és Gk. anyakönyvek.

témakörre vonatkozóan

fondokban a Levéltárban érvényes szabályok szerint kutatást végezzen.

Szekszárd, 1998 június hó 29 nap.

Dr. Dobos Gyula
levéltárigazgató

Translation of the above research permit: "Archives of Tolna County Municipality Research permit, 7100-- Szekszárd, Béla Király tér 1 P.O. Box 33 Number: 105/1998, Tel: 06-74/311-719, Tel./fax: 06/74/319-474, Name: Clyde Davis, Occupation: Entrepeneur, Address: USA New York, Lexington 450, Received permission for…Family tree research 1874–1900, Concerning subjects: Roman Catholic and Greek Othodox Birth registries, Is entitled to do research under the rules governing the Archives, Szekszárd, June 29, 1998. Stamp of Municipality of Tolna County Archives, Signed by: Dobos Gyula, Director of Archive."

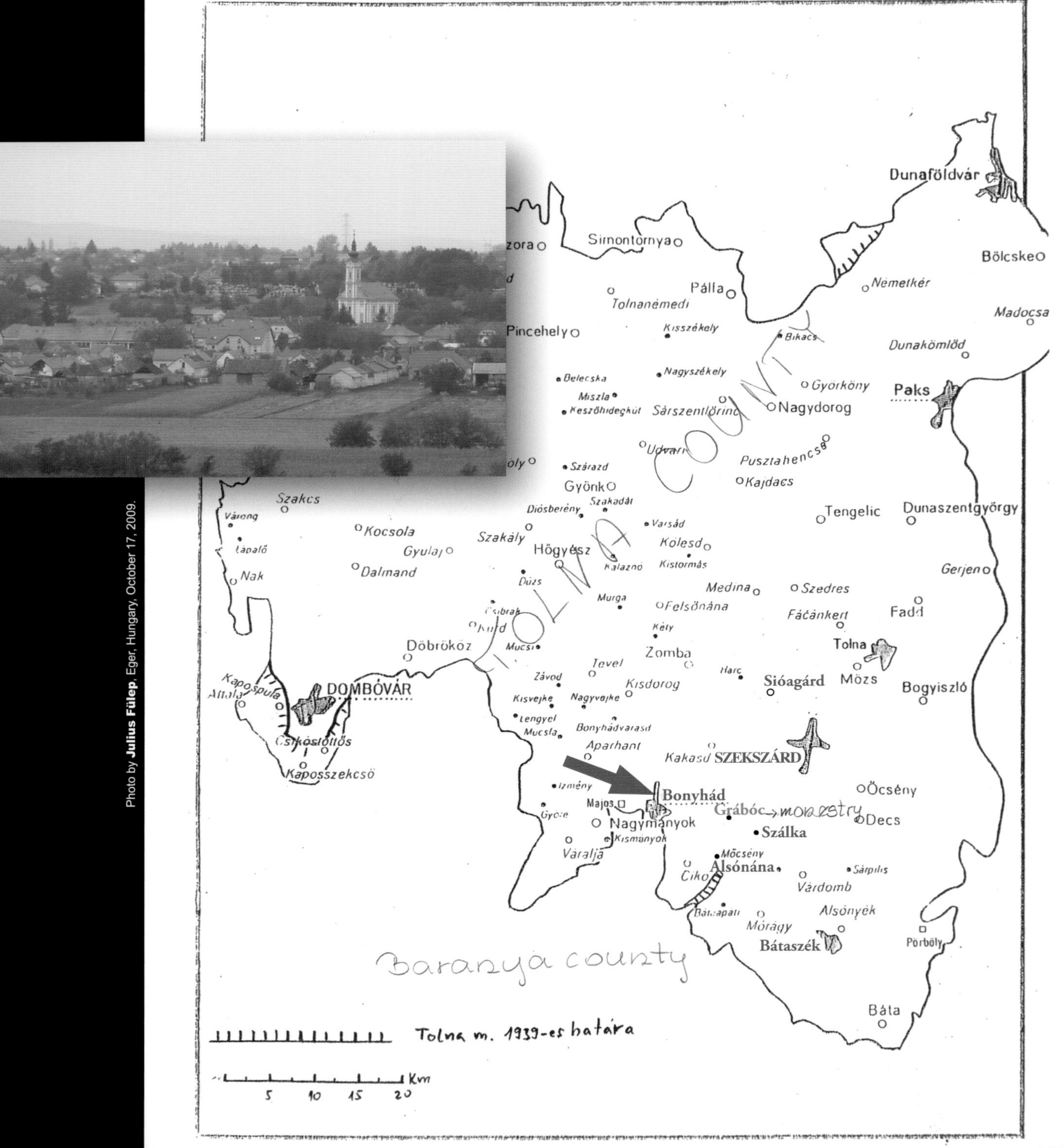

Photo by **Julius Fülep**. Eger, Hungary, October 17, 2009.

The hand-drawn map above of Tolna County in Hungary in 1939 shows the location of the villages of Sióagárd, Szálka, Alsónána, and Bátaszék where the Szávics and Szlavics family settled from 1716 to 1771. The map was provided by Tamásné Gréczy and Gábor Aradi, archivists in Szekszárd, Hungary.

Bonyhád (Bonnhard), Hungary, was the birthplace of my grandfather, Dusán (Dezsó) Andy/Andrew/David Szávics/Savich/Savage b. June 2, 1874. Photo of Bonyhád on October 17, 2009.

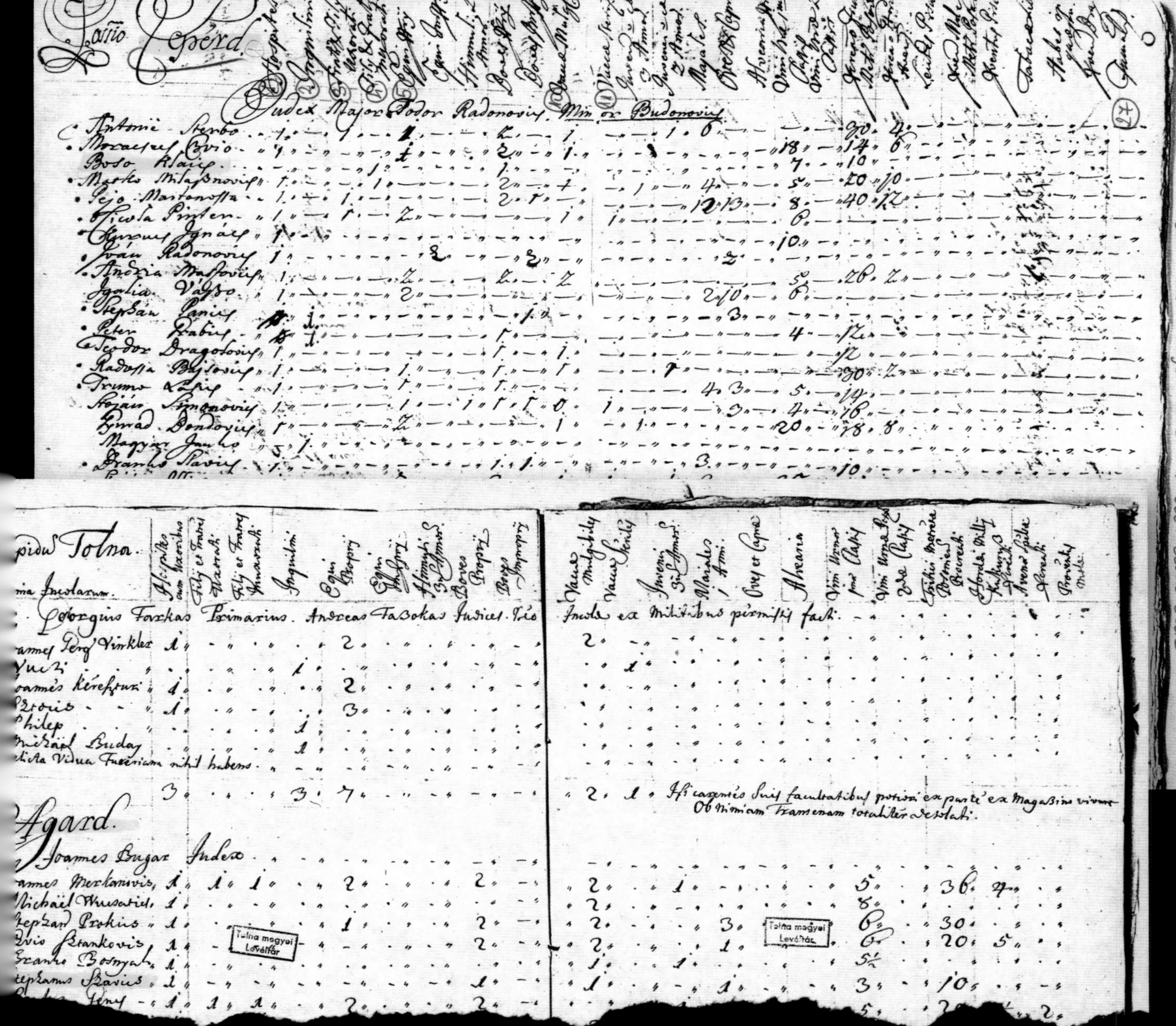

Tamásné Gréczy and Gábor Aradi, archivists in Szekszárd, Hungary, researched the population census data on this and the following pages. They have highlighted the towns and the names of members of the ***Szávics/ Szlavics*** *families.*

Population Censuses:

These data show us when (in which year) and where the ***Szávics*** *and* ***Szlavics*** *family settled.*

The Villages:	***The Years:***
• *Agárd*	*From 1716 – 1771*
• *Alsónána*	
• *Leperd — a part of Bátaszék*	
• *Szálka*	

The meaning of the lines: *(Circled numbers over columns)*

1 *Hospites = settler*
2 *Inquilini = a farmer with a house*
3 *Child and wife*
4 *Child and widower*
5 *Animals*

Lower document: "Ö: 272" 1716 records for the village of Agárd/Sióagárd

Upper document: "Ö: 285" 1725–26 records for Leperd, a part of the village of Bátaszék. The red notations are described in legend, "The meaning of the lines" described in the column to the left.

"The family name Szavics (Savage) appears for the first time after the Turkish occupation in 1716. The village Agárd (today said: Sióagárd) was settled tha time again and Stefan Szavics arrived also as a settler there."

— From the letter to Clyde Davis from Tamásné Gréczy and Gábor Aradi dated 12 September 199

Szávics Family — Hungary

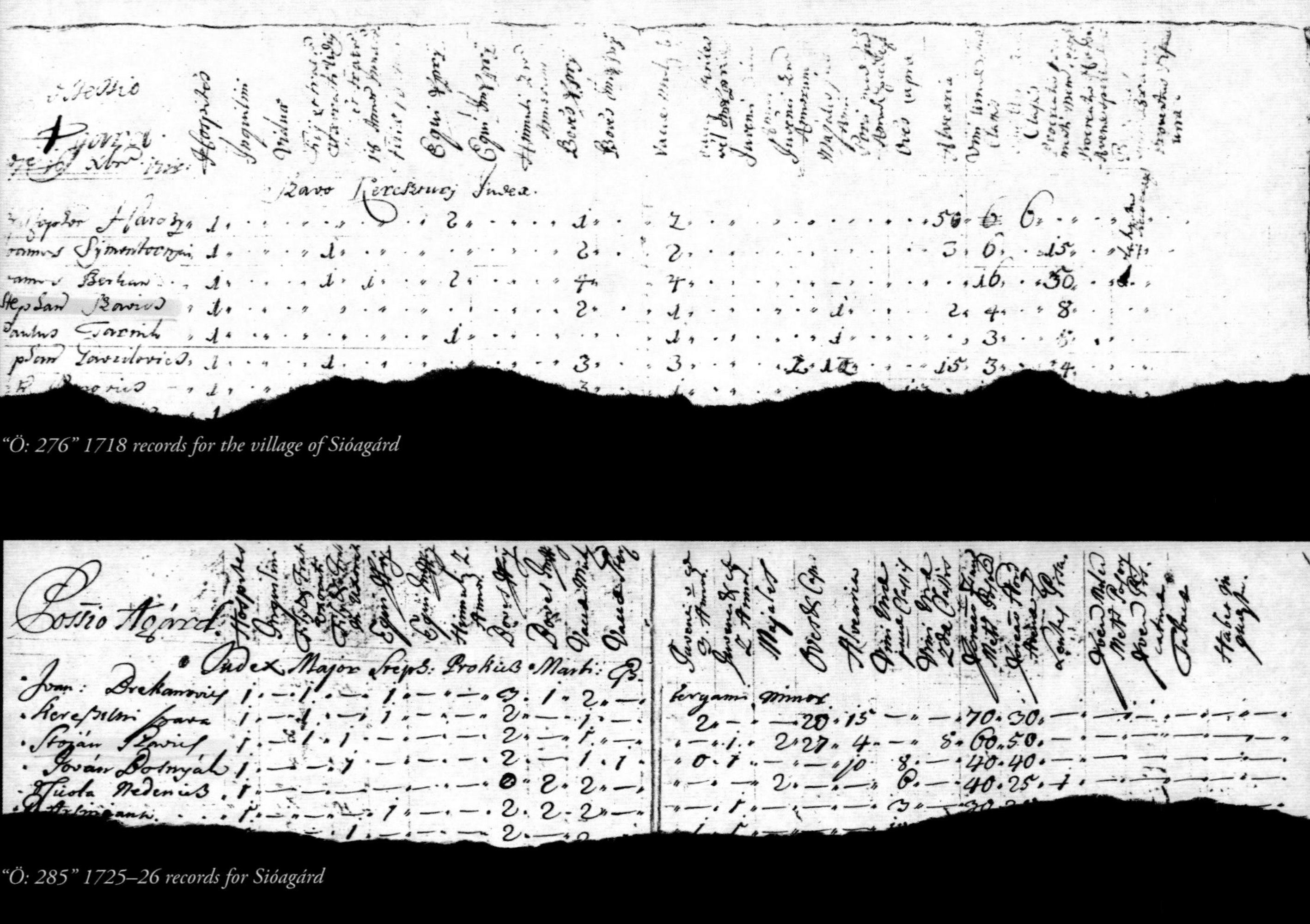

"Ö: 276" 1718 records for the village of Sióagárd

"Ö: 285" 1725–26 records for Sióagárd

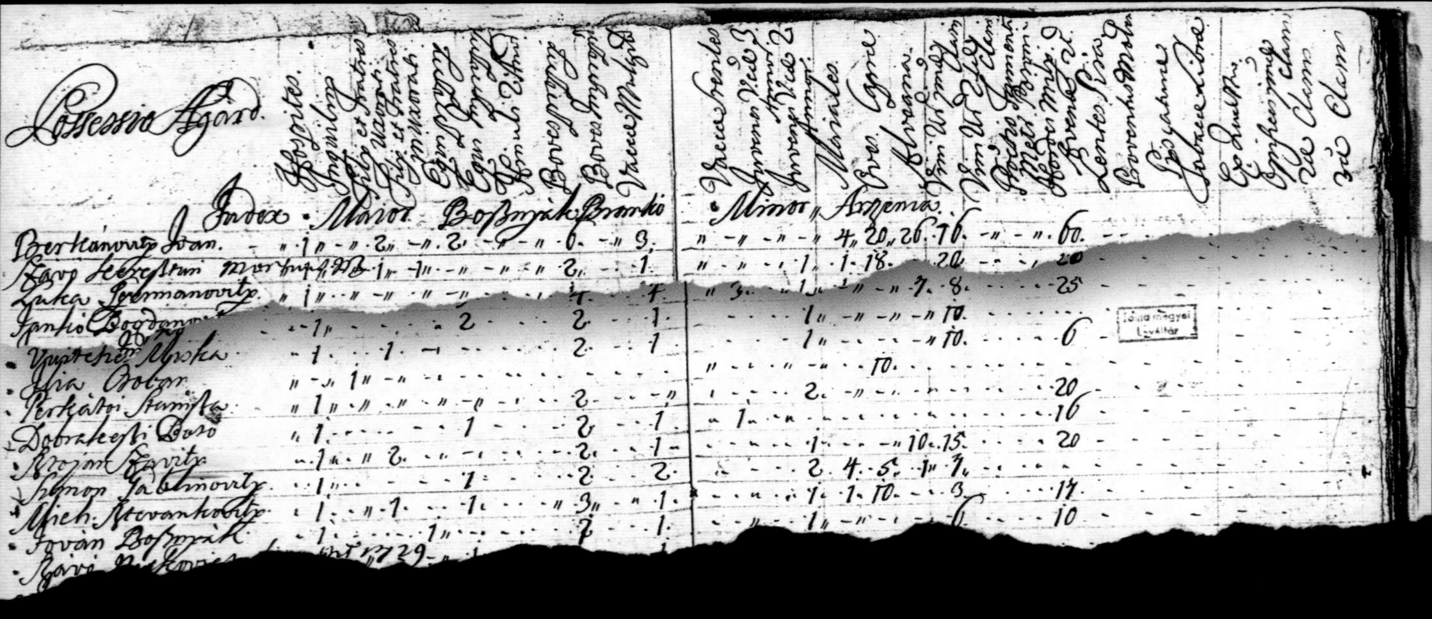

"Ö: 288" 1727 records for Sióagárd

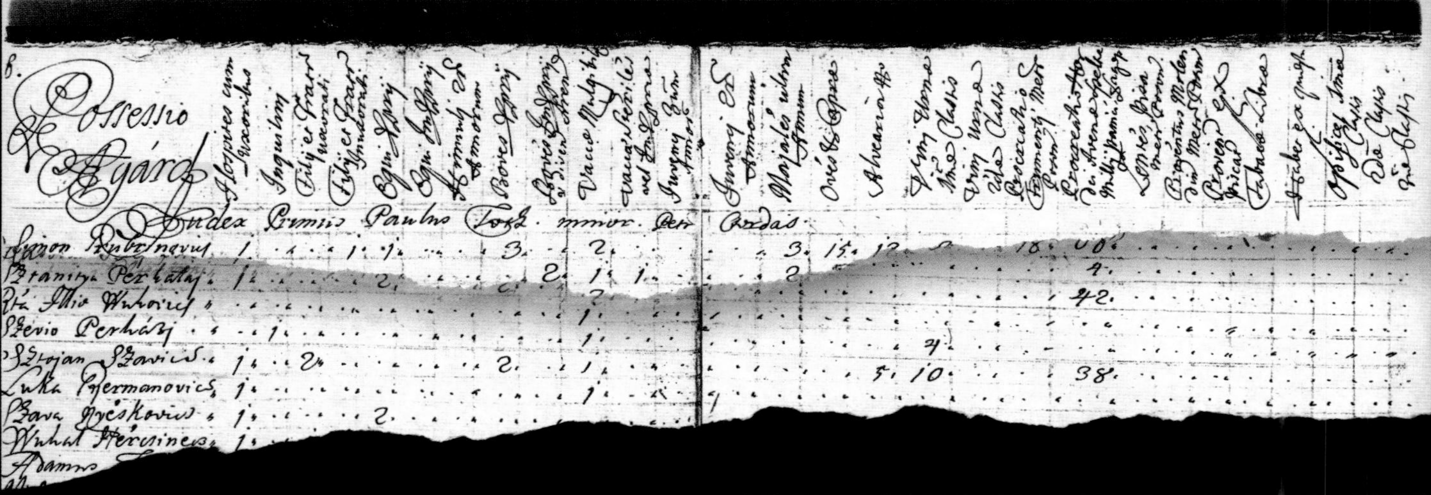

"Ö: 288" 1728 records for Sióagárd

"… in 1728/29 many Hungarian settlers went to Agárd to live there and so almost every Serbian left the village and wandered away."

— From the letter to Clyde Davis from Tamásné Gréczy and Gábor Aradi dated 12 September 1998

Traditional "cellar cottages" in Sióagárd, Hungary, across from vineyards. Old meets new as a horse-drawn wagon on automobile tires passes a parked car. These wagons are common in the Hungarian countryside.

Photos by **Julius Fülep**, Eger, Hungary, October 17, 2009.

"Ö: 305" 1752 records for Szálka

"In 1752 two names were written elsewhere: Joannes Szavics in Alsónána and Ignác Szavics in Szálka."

— From the letter to Clyde Davis from Tamásné Gréczy and Gábor Aradi dated 12 September 1998

Photo by **Julius Fülep**, Eger, Hungary, October 17, 2009.

"Welcome to Szálka" sign in Hungarian and German

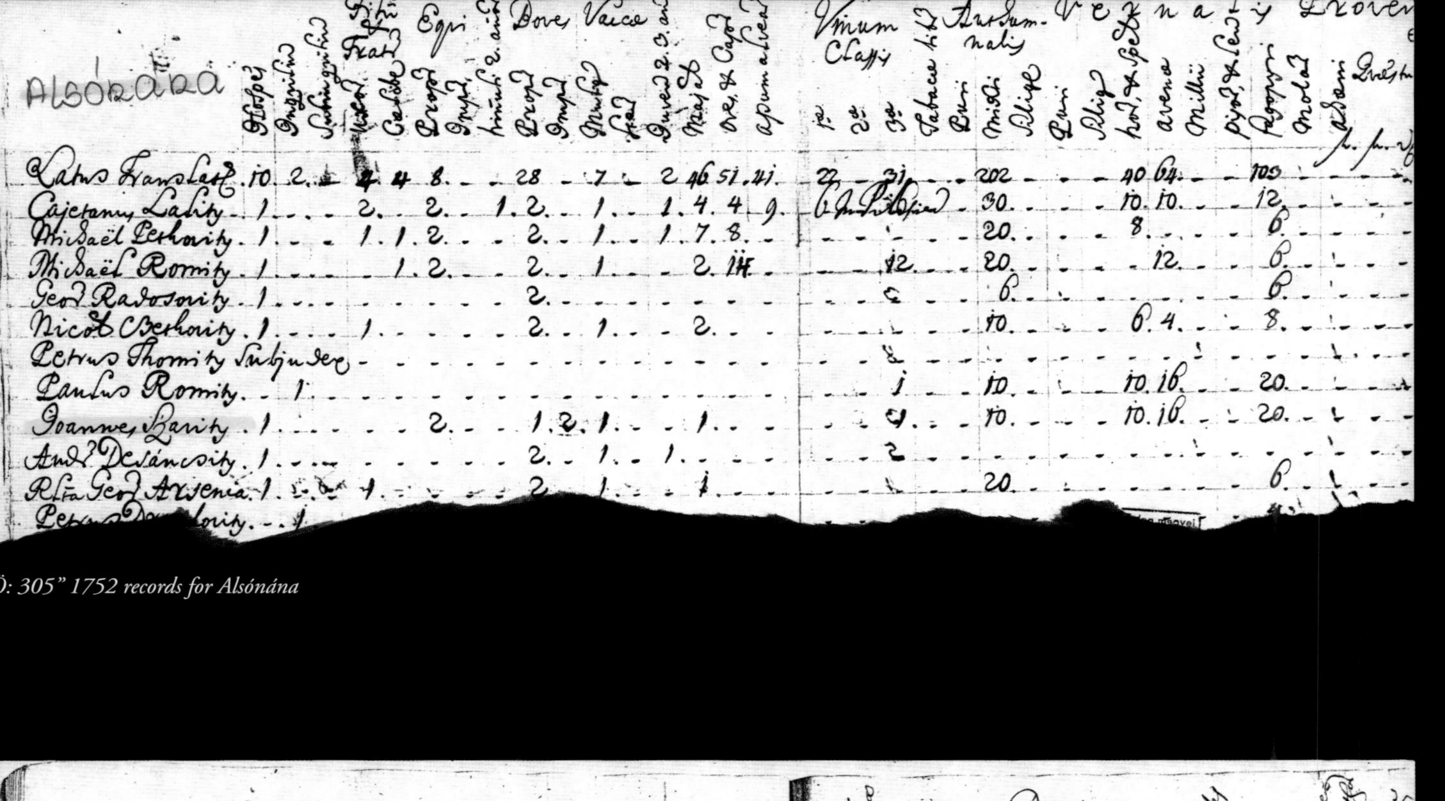

"Ö: 305" 1752 records for Alsónána

"Ö: 308" 1771 records for Szálka

"Twenty years later, in 1771 we can find only Ignácz Szavics in Szálka."

— From the letter to Clyde Davis from Tamásne Gréczy and Gábor Aradi dated 12 September 1998

№ 5. По трекратном въ Церкви ѡглашенїи, и ни единомъ препятствїи ѡбрѣтшуся, ѡбручися и вѣнчася женихъ Јаковъ, сынъ Јакова Палковичь жителя Салчковъ, съ невѣстою именемъ Матроною дщерїю Јоанна Сечуица жителя Салчковъ, мца Ноемврїа дне 12. лѣта 834 чрез мене Јеромонаха Макарїа Цвеича Пострижника С.А.О.М.Г. въ Монастырѣ Грабовцѣ. Кумъ бысть имъ Данїилъ Бошнякъ житель Грабовачкїй, иже и свидѣтелствуетъ со мною.

1834: Marriage Record

Number 5:
The marriage was announced three times in the church, but no one opposed it. **Jakov**, the son of Jakov Palkovics, who lives in Szálka, was the bridegroom and married **Matrona**, the daughter of Joann Szecsuác, who lives also in Szálka. This happened on 12th November 1823 in my presence, the monk Makavia Cveics in the monastery of Grábóc. The witness was Daniel Bosnyák.

Photo by **Julius Fülep**, Eger, Hungary, October 17, 2009.

Gráboczi Zárda

és hozá tartozandó filialisoknak, ugy mint: Szállá i Alsó-Náná Kereszt, Esküvös és hallotak anya könyvei az 1838 — 1845ik bezárolag.

1839.

1839: Baptism Record

Number 5:
On 21st August 1839 a little girl was born. Her father is Jakov Palkovics, her mother's name is Matrona, they live in Szálka. She was baptized on 24th August 1839 by me the monk Geranim Rajkovics in the monastery of Grábóc. The girl's name is **Julianna**, the godfather is Epjoan, the son of Daniel Bosnyák, who lives in Grábóc.

Serb-Orthodox Church consecrated to the honor of Archangel Gabriel,

Photo by **Julius Fülep**, Eger, Hungary, October 17, 2009.

Interior of the Serb-Orthodox Church in Grábóc, Hungary. The icon

Birth, Marriage, and Death Registers

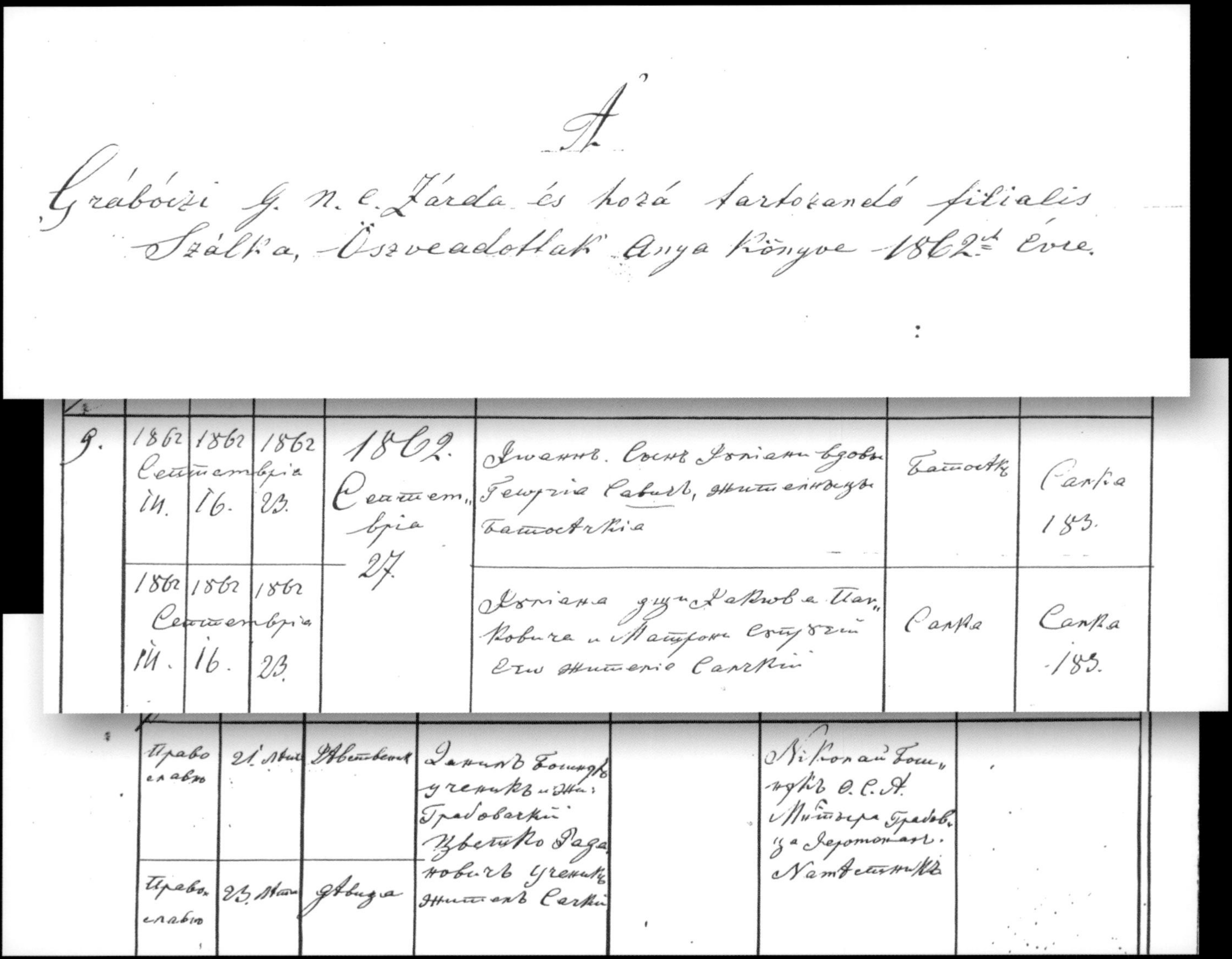

A.

Grábóczi g. n. e. Zárda és hozzá tartozandó filialis Szálka, Összeadottak Anya Könyve 1862ik Éve.

1862: Marriage Record

Number 9:

The first lines show the dates of the annoucements made three times in the church.

The day of the marriage is 27 September 1862.

The name of the bridegroom is **Joann Szávics**, the son of Julianna. She is the widow of György Szávics and lived in Bátaszék with her son. Joann is 21 years old.

The name of the bride is **Julianna**, the daughter of Jakov Palkovics and Matrona, who lives in Szálka. Julianna is 23 years old.

The bridegroom was born in Bátaszék, the bride in Szálka, they both live now in house number 183 in Szálka.

Photo by **Julius Fülep**, Bátaszék, Hungary, October 17, 2009.

Budai út (Road) in Bátaszék

Gráboczi görög keleti Zárda és hozzá tartozandó filiales Szálka Keresztelő Anya Könyve 1867. 1868. 1869. 1870. és 1871. Évekre

Völgységi járásba

Krisztus Urunk Születése Után 1868.

Hó Nap. Születés Keresztel	A Keresztelnek és Bérmálotnak Neve és Törvényessége	Az Atya és Anya		A Keresztelő Vezetékk és Kereszt Neve Életneme és lakhelye	Keresztelő és Bérmáló
		Vezetékk és Kereszt Neve Hitvalás	Életneme és lakhelye		
Julius 9 ik. Kereszt. 10 ke	György Törvényes	Szávics János és Szávics Juliana Kelet. h	Pandur Bonyhád lakos	Bosnyák Sándor Grábóci lakos föld Müves	Sebestyén Dobrics Lelkész

1868: Baptism Record of the Church in Grábóc

Number 8:
Birth date: 9 July 1868
Baptism date: 10 July 1868
Name of the baptized child: **György**
Sex of the child: male
Legal or illegal: legal
Name and occupation of the parents: father — Joann Szávics, mother — Julianna Szávics, occupation [father]: policeman
Religion: Orthodox
Place of residence: Bonyhád
Name, occupation, residence of the godparents: Sándor Bosnyák, farmer, he lives in Grábóc
Signature and name of the service leader: Dobries Sebestyén, priest of the church

Szávics Family — Tolna County, Hungary

Birth, Marriage and Death Registers

A Gráboczi gör: Kel: Zárda és hozzá tartozandó filiális Szálka. Keresztelő Anya Könyve 1874. Évre

Krisztus Urunk Születése után 1874

Hó, Nap, Születés Keresztel	A kereszteltnek és Bérmálotnak neve és Törvényessége	Atya és Anya: Vezeték- és Kereszt neve, Hittvallása	Atya és Anya: Foglalkozás, mesterség, vagy más életfoglalása, lakhelye	A keresztelő vezeték és Keresztneve, Életneme és lakhelye	Keresztelő és bérmáló
Junius 2 született 3 kereszt.	Dusán Törvényes férfi	Szavics János ~ Juliana gör: Keleti	Frajtkór Bonyhád	Bosnyák Dániel föld Müvelő Grábóc	Teodorovics Gedeon Szerzetes
Junius 11	Damjánka Törvényes	Bosnyák János	föld Müves	Venenact	Kukics

1874: Baptism Record of the Church in Grábóc

Number
Birth date: 2 June 1874
Baptism date: 3 June 1874
Name of the baptized child: **Dusán**
Sex of the child: male
Legal or illegal: legal
Name and occupation of the parents: father — Joann Szavics,
mother — Julianna Szavics,
occupation [father]: policeman
Religion: Orthodox
Place of residence: Bonyhád
Name, occupation, residence of the godparents: Daniel Bosnyák, farmer, lives in Grábóc
Signature and name of the service leader: Gedeon Teodorovics, monk

Photo by **Julius Fülep**, Eger, Hungary, October 17, 2009.

Vineyard between Bátaszék and Szekszárd. The hills are gently rolling and the weather is warmer than the national average, allowing the production of savory grapes and fiery wines.

Страна

ПРОТОКОЛЪ УМЕРШИХЪ ПРАВОСЛАВНЫЯ ВОСТОЧНЫЯ ЦЕРКВЕ, ХРАМА

Meghaltak anyakönyvi másolata Bátaszéki gör. kel. szerb egyház anyakönyvéből 1895. Jan 1től – 1895 Oktober 1-ig.

449 | 1895. Марта 2. | Јулијана Савић | жен. | Cotka | Батасек б. 280

1895: Death Record of the Orthodox Church in Bátaszék

Number: 449
Death date: 2 March 1895
Name: **Julianna Szávics**
Sex: female
Name and residence of the husband: Joann Szávics, Bátaszék
Birthplace: Szálka
Residence: Bátaszék 280
Religion: Orthodox
Age: 50 years
Illness or reason for the death: lungs — disease
Place and date of the funeral: Serbian cemetery in Bátaszék, 3 March 1895
Signature and name of the service leader: Figmilijan Krecsut, monk of the monastery in Grábóc

462

This document was also written in Slav language (Probably some part of the region was bilingual due to being close to Jugoslav territory (my comment)

TRANSLATE

Joann Szavics
Julianna Palkovics

Nikolaj Uritz
Maria Palkovics

kids

child

Joann
died 1866. VI. 24/73.

Протоколъ Венчанныхъ Церк...

Число порядку	Мѣсяц и день Оглашения I.	II.	III.	Венчания	Имя Прозвание ...
6.	1861. Декем. 26.	1861. Декем. 27.	1861 Декем. 31.	1862. Януарія 18.	Фома Ра... Грабовца ... Анна ...
7.	1862. Януарія 7.	1862. Януарія 14.	1862 Януарія 21.	1862. Януарія 25.	Тимотей ... Софіа ...
8.	1862. Янув. 30.	1862. Февр. 2.	1862. Февр. 4.	1862 Февруарія 4.	Николай ... Пелагія, ...
9.	1862. Септембрія 14.	1862. 16.	1862. 20.	1862. Септембрія 27.	Іоаннъ Сав... Іуліана ... Палковичь ...
10.	1862 Септембрія 30.	1862 Октобр. 7.	1862. Октобр. 14.	1862. Октобрія 15.	Николай ... Марія ...
11	1862 Октобр. 6.	1862 Октобр. 13.	1862. Октобр. 21.	1862. Октобрія	Данилъ Сав...

Translation of this register and comments were provided by Tamásné Gréczy and Gábor Aradi. This was among the documents sent with their letter to Clyde Davis dated September 12, 1998.

463

Мѣсто рожденія	Мѣсто пребыванія	Вѣроисповѣданіе	Лѣта возраста	Состояніе двоженства или вдовства	Свидѣтели	Примѣчаніе
Рацкозаръ	Деркое бердо	Правос.	58	вдовъ		
Медица	Деркое бердо	Правос.	57	вдовица		
Горецкъ	Салка ч. 88	Правос.	36	двоженникъ		
	Салка ч. 88	Правос.		вдовица		
Салка	Салка ч. 183	Правос.	25	двоженникъ		
Салка	Салка 101	Правос.	21	дѣвица		
Батасекъ (Bátaszék)	Салка ч. 183 (Szalka)	Правос.	21	двоженникъ		
Салка	Салка 183	Правос.	23	дѣвица		
Шомберке	Салка (Szdlka)	Правосл.	23	двоженникъ		
Салка (Szdlka)	Салка 183	Правос.	16	дѣвица		
Салка	Салка	Правосл.		вдовъ		

Palkovics Jakov ?

Palkovics/Палковић/Jakov/Јаков/

Szecsuác Joann ?

Szecsuác/Сечуач/Matrona/Матрон

marriage in 1834.IX.12. Szálka

I. child: Anna
born in 1836.V.23. Szálka

II. child: Julianna
born in 1839.VIII.21. Szálka
died in 1895.III.2. Bátaszék

I child: Petronella=Petra
born in 1863.IV.28. Szálka
⚭ 1884.V.20. Szálka
husband: Szlavics Dionizius=Dénes
born in 1861.I.3. Bátaszék ⟷ died in 1892.I.12. Szekszárd

I. child: Lázár born in 1885.III.28 Bátaszék — died in 1889.I.18. Bátaszék
II. -"- : Fülöp -"- 1886.IX.17. Szálka — died in 1888.III.24. Bátaszék
III. -"- : Joann -"- 1895.I.5. Bátaszék /illegal/

II. Mileva=Emilia
1865.V.16. Szálka
⚭ unknown, possible: Dunaszekcső ?
husband: Tolnaics József
born: Dunaszekcső
child: Károly
born: Dunaszekcső 1895 ?
died in 1903.VI.14. Bátaszék

III. Teréz
born unknown
died in 1898.XI.8. Bátaszék
⚭ unknown
husband: Szlavics Miklós

IV.
186

The hand-drawn and configured Szávics Family Tree was sent to me September 12, 1998, by Tamásné Gréczy and Gábor Aradi, archivists from Szekszárd, Hungary.

? ? ? ?

a/ Szavics/Cabur/ György /Georgius/ ? Julianna

⚭
marriage: unknown, possible: Somberek ? /Baranya county/

I. child: Pál /Pavel/
born in 1837. ? Somberek
died in ?
Job: sailor
⚭ 1862. II. 4. Bátaszék
wife: Zsizsic Ljubica ⟨ Zsizsic David ?
born: 1840. ?

II. child: Joann
born in 1841 ? Bátaszék ?
died in ? register is missing

III. child: Szofia
born in 1843. IV. 16. Bátaszék
died in ?

⚭
marriage in 1862. IX. 27. Szálka

György/
8. VII. 9. Bonyhád
died in 1874. II. 12
Bonyhád

V. Perszida
1870. XII. 22. Bonyhád
died in 1871. XII. 31.
Szálka

VI. Dusán
1874. VI. 02. Bonyhád
died in 1949. VI. 15.
⚭ ? Felsőtárkány
wife: Benkó Mária

VII. Józó /József/ Szálka
1877. ? regiszter is missing
died in 1902. III. 22.
Bátaszék

VIII. Mihály
1880. I. 17. Szálka
died in 1880. I. 26.
Szálka

My Grandparents

⚭ = marriage

Dusán Szávics and Maria Benkó are the maternal grandparents of Clyde Patrick Davis. As was true of many immigrants, Dusán Szávics's name underwent a variety of transformations, ending up as the Anglicized Andrew "Andy" Savage. His first name was variously "Dusán," "Dezsó," "David," "Andrew" and "Andy." On the List or Manifest of Alien Passengers for the U.S. Immigration Officer at Port of Arrival *dated March 8, 1907, he was listed as "Desso Szavics," occupation "Locksmith." On the* U.S. Department of Labor Naturalization Service Certificate of Arrival — For Naturalization Purposes *dated July 5, 1924, he was listed as "Dezsó, Szavics." On the* U.S. Department of Labor Naturalization Service Declaration of Intention *dated June 12, 1918, when he was declaring his intention to become a U.S. citizen, he was listed as Andy Savich and his occupation was given as "Machinist." On the* Petition for Naturalization *dated January 14, 1925, he was listed as Andrew Savich, and his occupation was "Gas line, mechanic & inspector." His Certificate of Death filed April 16, 1943, listed him as "David Savage," and his "Usual occupation" was given as "Machinist."*

On the List or Manifest of Alien Passengers for the United States Immigration Officer at Port of Arrival *dated July 30, 1909, Mária was listed as "Szavics Dersöné Maria," occupation "house-wife." In the 1920 Census, she was listed as "Mary." She was also known as "Maria" and "Mary" with a variety of versions of her last name.*

My grandfather, standing in the gangway between his home and another, at 8545 Mackinaw Avenue, in the "Bush" on the southeast side of Chicago. The building was at one time a pool hall (billiards), which explains the storefront-size window partially shown. The building was two stories with stairs at the rear for access to the second floor.

b. June 2, 1874

An Enigma Wrapped in a Riddle...

Dezsó "Andrew" Szávics/Savage was a true family enigma, at least to me. I have heard many stories about each member of the family over the years, as I came to know them, but seldom did I ever hear much about my grandfather.

My grandfather Savage died April 14, 1943 — I had just turned five years old. I have no recollection of the man or his passing. I also don't recall my mother ever speaking to me about him.

I do recall my grandmother Savage's house at 82nd and Marquette Avenue on the South Side of Chicago. Someone told me that my grandfather Savage suffered from acute depression and for that reason he was confined to a room, which served previously as a coal bin, in the basement of the house. My grandfather was an accomplished machinist in the "old country." When employed as a common laborer in the steel mills, he was unable to reconcile the loss of self-esteem, and this, according to my cousin Michael, led to our grandfather's depression. The basement was an active living space for most all of us. It was where the laundry was done, as well as where the cooking and eating took place. I played in that basement. At the time, the main floor upstairs was under renovation by my uncle, Victor Lucas.

My grandfather, David Savage

On April 14, 1943, at 1:15 A.M., my grandfather died at home, 8023 Marquette Avenue, Chicago, Illinois, where he had lived twenty years prior to his death.

According to the death certificate, Cook County, Illinois, his "full" name was given as David Savage. The immediate cause of death was given as "Chronic Myocarditis (Duration 2 years)."

"The Informant of the above" was David A. Savage Jr. David Sr. was buried in St. Mary's Cemetery, Evergreen Park, Cook County, Illinois, on April 17, 1943.

Other documents clearly indicated that during his lifetime he was known by a variety of names — Dusán, Dezsó, Andrew, Andy, David Szávics, Savage — other than the name he took to his final resting place. His age was given as sixty-eight years, ten months and twenty-eight days. He was married to my grandmother, Mary Savage, who was alive and fifty-eight years old.

Of all the information contained in the death certificate, none was more important than learning of his place of birth: "Bonghard" (Bonyhád, we later determined), Hungary. His father was John Savage of Bonghard, Hungary, and his mother was Julia Tornovich, whose place of birth in Hungary was listed as unknown. In June of 1998, armed with this other data, we would travel to Hungary, visiting the town of Bonyhád and the surrounding area, seeking more information about my ancestors.

My grandfather was an engineer in Europe before he immigrated to the United States. There is some mention of him traveling about Europe and working on municipal water systems; however, his death certificate said that his usual occupation was as a machinist in the steel mill (Carnegie Steel Corporation.)

The 1930 U.S. census, State of Illinois, City of Chicago, 7th Ward, Block No. 162, enumerated David Savich as head of household. He owned his own home at 8545 South Mackinaw Street, was fifty-five years of age, had been married at age twenty-seven, his place of birth was given as Hungary, mother tongue: Magyar. (The Hungarian name for the language is Magyar. Hungarian was spoken in areas that were once part of the Kingdom of Hungary before the treaty of Triaon in 1920. Magyar is also spoken in Romania, Slovakia, Serbia, Ukraine, Croatia, Austria, and Slovenia).[1] Both his parents were born in Hungary. He was working at the time of the census, no small feat considering the dire economic times, as a machinist in the steel mill (Carnegie Steel Corporation). Living with him were his wife Mary, forty-six years of age; David Jr., son, twenty-five years of age, single, born in Hungary, speaks Magyar. David Jr. was working as an investigator/brokerage; Michael, son, age sixteen, single, in school and born in Illinois; Mary, daughter, age fourteen, single, in school, also born in Illinois; John, son, age ten, in school, born in Illinois.

Notes

1. "Hungarian language," Wikipedia.com.

IMMIGRATION SERVICE.
Form 1500 B.

SALOON, CABIN, AND STEERAGE ALIENS MUST BE COMPLETELY MANIFESTED.
THIS SHEET IS FOR STEERAGE PASSENGERS.

LIST OR MANIFEST OF ALIEN PASSENGERS FOR THE U. S. IMMIGRATI

Required by the regulations of the Secretary of the Treasury of the United States, under Act of Congress approved March 3, 1903, to be
Officer of any vessel having such passengers on board upon arrival at a port in the Uni

S.S. Pannonia sailing from Fiume on the 16th of February 1907 Arriving at Port of

1	2	3	4	5	6	7	8	9	10	11	12	13	14	15
No. on List.	NAME IN FULL.	Age. Yrs. Mos.	Sex.	Married or Single.	Calling or Occupation.	Able to Read. Write.	Nationality. (Country of last permanent residence.)	Race or People.	Last Residence (Last permanent residence, Country and City or Town.)	Final Destination (State, City, or Town.)	Whether having a ticket to such final destination.	By whom was passage paid?	Whether in possession of $50, and if less, how much?	Whether ever before in the United States; and if so, when and where?
1	Szabó István V.L. 405/165	20	m	m	[illegible]	no no	Hungary	Magyar	T. Torda	Pottsville	yes	himself	10	no
2	[illegible]	18			7-97978-500-17/13/10								18	
25	[illegible]													
26	Borsa Ferenc	24	m	s										
27	Barsa [illegible]	11	m	m									15	
28	Balázs [illegible] VL-39/45[illegible]	13	m	s	5-77318-5/24/39-575			Magyar	Tekó	[illegible]	yes		12	
29	[illegible]	32	m	m	Locksmith								25	
30	Bali Mihály	18	m	s	[illegible]				Varta	[illegible]			7	

Augustus Kiss
Inspector

Race or People is to be determined by the stock from which they sprang and the language they speak. List of races wil

Pictured above: SS Pannonia, *launched May 9, 1902, built by John Brown Clydebank, Yard No 348. Port of Registry: Liverpool. Propulsion: Steam triple expansion, speed approximately 15 knots. Owner: Cunard Line. Scrapped in October 1922 at Hamburg, Germany. Updated by Gavin Stewart and Paul Strathdee from the original records by Stuart Cameron. Information found at: <http://www.clydesite.co.uk/clydebuilt/viewship.asp?id=2195>*
Photograph courtesy of the Peabody Essex Museum, PEM image 32162, SS Pannonia

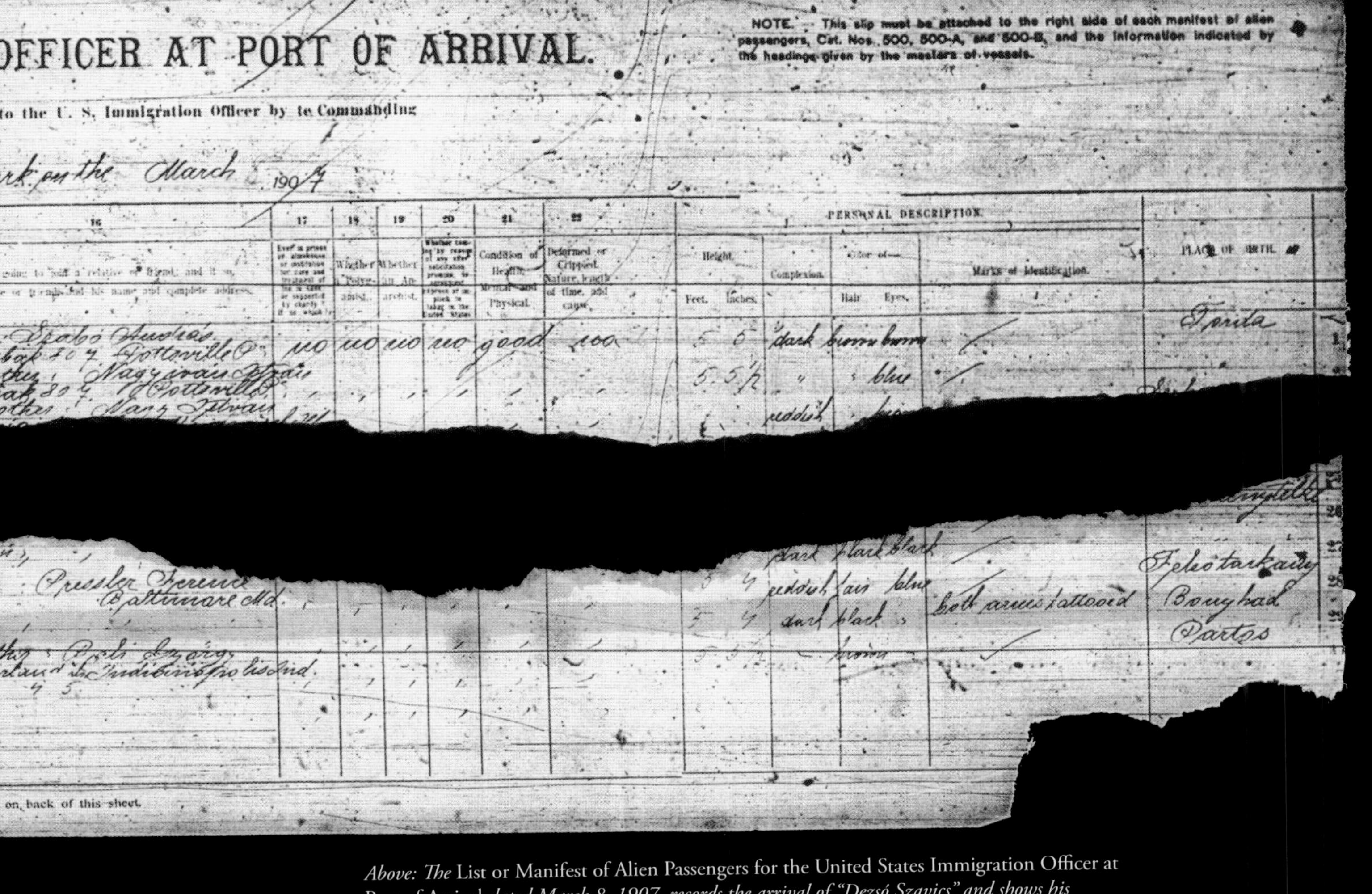

List

OFFICER AT PORT OF ARRIVAL.

NOTE. — This slip must be attached to the right side of each manifest of alien passengers, Cat. Nos. 500, 500-A, and 500-B, and the information indicated by the headings given by the masters of vessels.

d to the U. S. Immigration Officer by the Commanding

...ark on the March 1907

16 — ...er going to join a relative or friend; and if so, ...ative or friend, and his name and complete address.
17 — Ever in prison or almshouse or institution for care and treatment of the insane or supported by charity? If so, which?
18 — Whether a Polygamist.
19 — Whether an Anarchist.
20 — Whether coming by reason of any offer, solicitation, promise or agreement, express or implied, to labor in the United States.
21 — Condition of Health, Mental and Physical.
22 — Deformed or Crippled. Nature, length of time, and cause.
PERSONAL DESCRIPTION. — Height (Feet, Inches). Complexion. Color of — Hair, Eyes. Marks of Identification.
PLACE OF BIRTH.

Pressler Ferenc Baltimore Md.
both arms tattooed
Felsőtarkány
Bonyhad
Partos

d on back of this sheet.

Above: The List or Manifest of Alien Passengers for the United States Immigration Officer at Port of Arrival *dated March 8, 1907, records the arrival of "Dezsó Szavics" and shows his occupation as Locksmith. Dezsó Szávics appears on line 29 of the listing (lower portion) of the ship's passenger list above.*

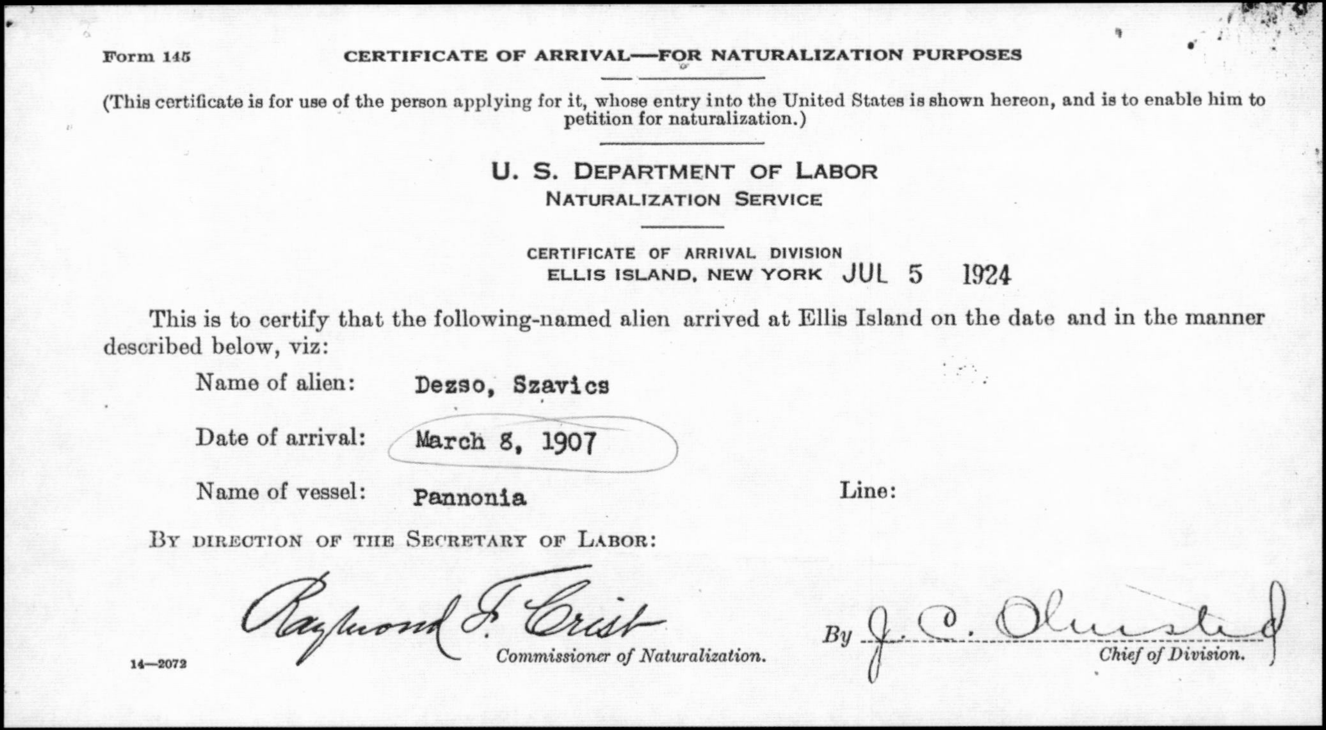

Form 145 CERTIFICATE OF ARRIVAL—FOR NATURALIZATION PURPOSES

(This certificate is for use of the person applying for it, whose entry into the United States is shown hereon, and is to enable him to petition for naturalization.)

U. S. DEPARTMENT OF LABOR
NATURALIZATION SERVICE

CERTIFICATE OF ARRIVAL DIVISION
ELLIS ISLAND, NEW YORK JUL 5 1924

This is to certify that the following-named alien arrived at Ellis Island on the date and in the manner described below, viz:

Name of alien: Dezso, Szavics

Date of arrival: March 8, 1907

Name of vessel: Pannonia Line:

By direction of the Secretary of Labor:

Raymond F. Crist
Commissioner of Naturalization.

By J. C. Olmsted
Chief of Division.

14—2072

Above: Certificate of Arrival for Naturalization Purposes dated July 5, 1924, certified that "Dezsó, Savics" arrived in the United States on March 8, 1907, aboard the Pannonia.

On the following page is the Declaration of Intention of "Andy Savich" to become a United States citizen, dated June 12, 1918, nearly ten years after his arrival. In addition to the misspelling of my grandfather's name (Szavics), the clerk completing this document also incorrectly entered the place (Bonyhád) and date (2 June 1874) of my grandfather's birth. According to the above document, the vessel he arrived on (Pannonia), *as well as the date of his arrival (March 5, 1907), are misstated as well.*

750

Form 2203
U. S. DEPARTMENT OF LABOR
NATURALIZATION SERVICE

TRIPLICATE
[To be given to the person making the Declaration]

No. 90434

UNITED STATES OF AMERICA

DECLARATION OF INTENTION

☞ **Invalid for all purposes seven years after the date hereof**

State of Illinois, } ss:
County of Cook, }

In the Circuit Court of Cook County.

I, Andy Savich, aged 42 years, occupation Machinist, do declare on oath that my personal description is: Color white, complexion Dark, height 5 feet 5 inches, weight 155 pounds, color of hair Black, color of eyes Blue, other visible distinctive marks Stub finger. I was born in Bubura Austria on the 16 day of May, anno Domini 1876; I now reside at 8553 Mackinaw Ave (Give number and street.), Chicago, Ill. I emigrated to the United States of America from Fiume, Hungary on the vessel Carolina (If the alien arrived otherwise than by vessel, the character of conveyance or name of transportation company should be given.); my last foreign residence was Austria; I am married; the name of my wife is Mary; she was born at Austria and now resides at With me. It is my bona fide intention to renounce forever all allegiance and fidelity to any foreign prince, potentate, state, or sovereignty, and particularly to Charles, Emperor of Austria and Apostolic King of Hungary, of whom I am now a subject; I arrived at the port of New York, in the State of New York, on or about the 22 day of February, anno Domini 1907; I am not an anarchist; I am not a polygamist nor a believer in the practice of polygamy; and it is my intention in good faith to become a citizen of the United States of America and to permanently reside therein: SO HELP ME GOD.

Andy Savich
(Original signature of declarant.)

Subscribed and sworn to before me in the office of the Clerk of said Court at Chicago, Ill., this 12 day of JUNE anno Domini 1918

[SEAL]

AUGUST W. MILLER,
Clerk of the Circuit Court.

By J Perry, *Deputy Clerk.*

14—736

No. ....

UNITED STATES OF AMERICA

PETITION FOR NATURALIZATION

To the Honorable the District Court of the United States, Northern District of Illinois:

The petition of ANDREW SAVICH, *hereby filed, respectfully showeth:*

First. My place of residence is 8553 Mackinaw Ave. (Give number and street.) South, *Chicago, Illinois.*

Second. My occupation is Gas line, mechanic & inspector

Third. I was born on the 16th *day of* May, *anno Domini* 1874, *at* Bonyraid, Hungary,

Fourth. I emigrated to the United States from Fiume, Hungary, *on or about the* 16th *day of* February *anno Domini* 1907, *and arrived in the United States, at the port of* New York, *on the* 8th *day of* March *anno Domini* 1907, *on the vessel* Pannonia (If the alien arrived otherwise than by vessel, the character of conveyance or name of transportation company should be given.)

Fifth. I declared my intention to become a citizen of the United States on the 12th *day of* June, *anno Domini* 1918 *at* Chicago, Illinois, *in the* Circuit *Court of* Cook County,

Sixth. I am married. *My wife's name is* Mary. *She was born in* Bonyraid, Hungary, *and now resides at* with me (Give number and street.), *Chicago, Illinois.*

I have 5 *children, and the name, date and place of birth, and place of residence of each of said children is as follows:*

Andrew born August 27th, 1904 at Teles Taikany, Heves County, Hungary,
Julia " August 7th, 1911, at South Chicago, Illinois,
Mike " February 27th, 1914, " " " "
John " August 8th, 1919, " " " "
Mary " November 27th, 1916 " " " " All residing in South Chicago, Illinois.

Seventh. I am not a disbeliever in or opposed to organized government or a member of or affiliated with any organization or body of persons teaching disbelief in or opposed to organized government. I am not a polygamist nor a believer in the practice of polygamy. I am attached to the principles of the Constitution of the United States, and it is my intention to become a citizen of the United States and to renounce absolutely and forever all allegiance and fidelity to any foreign prince, potentate, state, or sovereignty, and particularly to The Present Government of Hungary, *of whom at this time I am a subject, and it is my intention to reside permanently in the United States.*

Eighth. I am able to speak the English language.

Ninth. I have resided continuously in the United States of America for the term of five years at least immediately preceding the date of this petition, to wit, since the 8th *day of* March, *anno Domini* 1907, *and in the State of Illinois, continuously next preceding the date of this petition, since the* 10th *day of* March, *anno Domini* 1907, *being a residence within this State of at least one year next preceding the date of this petition.*

Tenth. I have not heretofore made petition for citizenship to any court. (I ~~made petition for citizenship to the~~ .... Court of .... at ...., on the .... day of ...., anno Domini 1............, and the said petition was denied by the said Court for the following reasons and causes, to wit, ... ~~and the cause of such denial has since been cured or removed.~~)

Attached hereto and made a part of this petition are my declaration of intention to become a citizen of the United States and the certificate from the Department of Labor, together with my affidavit and the affidavits of the two verifying witnesses thereto, required by law. Wherefore your petitioner prays that he may be admitted a citizen of the United States of America.

Andrew Savich
(Complete and true signature of petitioner.)

Declaration of Intention No. 90434 *and Certificate of Arrival from Department of Labor filed this* 14th *day of* January, 1925

NOTE TO CLERK OF COURT.—If petitioner arrived in the United States ON OR BEFORE JUNE 29, 1906, strike out the words reading "and Certificate of Arrival from Department of Labor."

AFFIDAVITS OF PETITIONER AND WITNESSES

UNITED STATES OF AMERICA,
Northern District of Illinois, } ss:

The aforesaid petitioner being duly sworn, deposes and says that he is the petitioner in the above-entitled proceedings; that he has read the foregoing petition and knows the contents thereof; that the said petition is signed with his full, true name; that the same is true of his own knowledge except as to matters therein stated to be alleged upon information and belief, and that as to those matters he believes it to be true.

Andrew Savich
(Complete and true signature of petitioner.)

Charles Banfe, *occupation* barber, *residing at* 2801 E. 77th Pl., *Chicago, Illinois,*
and Joseph Takacs, *occupation* mechanic, *residing at* 3018 E. 79th Pl., *Chicago, Illinois,*
each being severally, duly, and respectively sworn, deposes and says that he is a citizen of the United States of America; that he has personally known Andrew Savich, *the petitioner above mentioned, to have resided in the United States continuously immediately preceding the date of filing his petition, since the* 1st *day of* January, *anno Domini* 1919, *and in the State in which the above-entitled petition is made continuously since the* 1st *day of* January, *anno Domini* 1919; *and that he has personal knowledge that the said petitioner is a person of good moral character, attached to the principles of the Constitution of the United States, and that the petitioner is in every way qualified, in his opinion, to be admitted a citizen of the United States.*

X Charles Banfe
(Signature of witness.)

X Joseph Takacs
(Signature of witness.)

[SEAL.]

Subscribed and sworn to before me by the above-named petitioner and witnesses in the office of the Clerk of said Court at Chicago, Ill., this 14th *day of* January, *anno Domini* 1925.

Blanche L. Adman
Deputy Clerk of the United States District Court.

[OVER.] 14—450

Petition for Naturalization of "Andrew Savich" dated January 14, 1925

Filed ...., 19......

TO BE ADMITTED A CITIZEN OF THE UNITED STATES OF AMERICA.

OATH OF ALLEGIANCE

I hereby declare, on oath, that I absolutely and entirely renounce and abjure all allegiance and fidelity to any foreign prince, potentate, state, or sovereignty, and particularly to .... the .... of The Present Government of Hungary *of whom I have heretofore been a subject; that I will support and defend the Constitution and laws of the United States of America against all enemies, foreign and domestic; and that I will bear true faith and allegiance to the same.*

Andrew Savich

Subscribed and sworn to before me, in open Court, this .... day of JUN 1 5 1925, *A. D. 19......*

........................, *Clerk.*

NOTE.—In renunciation of title of nobility, add the following to the oath of allegiance before it is executed: "I further renounce the title of (give title), an order of nobility, which I have heretofore held."

ORDER OF COURT ADMITTING PETITIONER

Upon consideration of the petition of Andrew Savich *, and affidavits in support thereof, and further testimony taken in open Court, it is ordered that the said petitioner, who has taken the oath required by law, be, and hereby is, admitted to become a citizen of the United States of America, this .... day of* JUN 1 5 1925, *A. D. 19......*

(It is further ordered, upon consideration of the petition of the said ...., that his name be, and hereby is, changed to ...., under authority of the provisions of section 6 of the act approved June 29, 1906 (34 Stat. L., pt. 1, p. 596), as amended by the act approved March 4, 1913, entitled "An act to create a Department of Labor.")

By the Court:

Wilkerson J

........................, *Judge.*

ORDER OF COURT DENYING PETITION

Upon consideration of the petition of .... and the motion of .... for the United States in open Court this .... day of ...., 19......, it appearing that........................

THE SAID PETITION IS HEREBY DENIED.

MEMO

Continued from........................

to........................

Continued from........................

to........................

NAMES ...

........................, *occupati...*

........................, *occupati...*

Certificate of Naturalization, No. 2071227 *issued on the .... day of ...., A. D. 19......*

14—215

[INSERT ON FOLLOWING LINES MARRIAGES AND BIRTHS OCCURRING AFTER PETITIONING AND BEFORE NATURALIZATION.]

S 120

Family name	Given name or names
Savich	Andrew

Address: 8553 Mackinaw Av. Chg. Ill.

Certificate no. (or vol. and page)	Title and location of court
P-17756 CN 2071227	U.S.Dist. Chg.

Country of birth or allegiance	When born (or age)
Hungary	May 16,1874

Date and port of arrival in U. S.	Date of naturalization
Mar.8,1907 New York	Jun.15,1925

Names and addresses of witnesses

Charles Banfe 2801 E.77th.Place Chg.Ill.

Joseph Takacs 3018 E.79th.Pl. Chg.Ill.

U. S. Department of Labor, Immigration and Naturalization Service. Form No. 1-IP.

Above: Oath of Allegiance of Andrew Szavich dated June 15, 1925. Inset: U.S. Department of Labor, Immigration and Naturalization Service index card showing his date of naturalization, June 15, 1925.

SEP 9 - 1997

STATE OF ILLINOIS
County of Cook, } ss. DAVID D. ORR. County Clerk

I, DAVID D. ORR, County Clerk of the County of Cook, in the State aforesaid, and Keeper of the Records and Files of said County, do hereby certify that the attached is a true and correct copy of the original Record on file, all of which appears from the records and files in my office.

IN WITNESS WHEREOF, I have hereunto set my hand and affixed the Seal of the County of Cook, at my office in the City of Chicago, in said County.

David D. Orr
County Clerk

V. S. 4 FILL IN THIS FORM (except signature) WITH TYPEWRITER OR LEGIBLE PRINTING

1940 REVISION

STATE OF ILLINOIS ORIGINAL
DEPARTMENT OF PUBLIC HEALTH—DIVISION OF VITAL STATISTICS

CERTIFICATE OF DEATH

Registered No. 11503

1. PLACE OF DEATH. Registration Dist. No. 3104
County of Cook
Chicago — Primary Dist. No. 3104
Street and Number, No. 8023 Marquette Avenue, Ward 7th
LENGTH OF TIME AT PLACE WHERE DEATH OCCURRED? 20 yrs.

2. PLACE OF RESIDENCE: STATE Illinois County Cook
City or Village Chicago Street and Number 8023 Marquette Avenue

3 (a) PRINT FULL NAME DAVID SAVAGE

3 (b) If veteran, name war None
3 (c) Social Security No. None
4. Sex Male
5. Color or race White
6 (a) Single, widowed, married, divorced Married
6 (b) Name of husband or wife Mary Savage
6 (c) Age of husband or wife if alive 58 years
7. Birth date of deceased May 16th 1874
8. AGE: Years 68 Months 10 Days 28
9. Birthplace Bonghard Hungary
10. Usual occupation Machinist
11. Industry or business Carnegie Steel Corp.
12. FATHER Name John Savage
13. Birthplace Bonghard Hungary
14. MOTHER Maiden name Julia Tornovich
15. Birthplace Unknown Hungary
16. INFORMANT David G. Savage Jr.
P. O. Address 8023 Marquette Ave
17. PLACE OF BURIAL — (a) Cemetery St. Marys (b) DATE April 17th 43
Location Evergreen Park
County Cook State Illinois
18. Funeral director Thomas Shannon — ADDRESS 9814 Ave L
Henry C. Nick Funeral Home

19. LIST NO. 93 D

MEDICAL CERTIFICATE OF DEATH

20. Date of death: Month April day 14 year 1943 hour 1:15 A.M.

21. I hereby certify that I attended the deceased from April 13 1943, to April 14 1943; that I last saw him alive on April 14 1943; and that death occurred on the date and hour stated above.

Immediate cause of death: Chronic myocarditis — Duration 2 yrs

22. Was an operation performed? no
Was there an autopsy? no

23. If a communicable disease; where contracted? none

Was disease in any way related to occupation of deceased? no

24. (Signed) W. K. Harrison M.D.
Address 9135 Exchange ave.
Date April 14 1943

*N. B.—State the disease causing death. All cases of death from "violence, casualty, or any undue means" must be referred to the coroner. See Section 10 Coroner's Act.

25. Filed — Registrar
P. O. Address 1943 APR 16 PM 8 10

Copy of Death Certificate of David Savage b. June 2, 1874, d. April 14, 1949. It was the information on the death certificate about his place of birth, "Bonghard" in Hungary, which actually turned out to be "Bonyhád," that led to our later travels in Hungary (see page 440).

M. D. Savage
2920 E. 78th ST
CHGO. 49, Ill

AIRMAIL

5c U.S. POSTAGE

Mr + Mrs John Benko
c/o Istvanyi István
Vojka J. p. Plešöny
OKR. Lubršov Chěskoslovenská
Europe

Portions of a letter dated May 27, 1963, from Michael David Savage to his uncle, John Benko, in which he discusses the estate of his mother, Mary Benko Savage, and his parents' gravestone (top right).

May 27, 1963

Dear Uncle + Aunt:
I was really surprised to
hear that you have gone to
Europe...

As you know we have settle
the estate of my mother, and ther
is just the house to get rid of
I have been trying to sell
it but no luck so far. I
hope to fix it up so we can

rent it or do something with it.
We bought a grave stone for
my father and mother for $475
and it is beautiful. My brother
Dave didn't want to do it but I
insisted as my promise to my
dear mother had to be kept. I
hope you can see it some day.
My son got married and he...

and write to us if you can.
God bless you both and I
hope you have a safe return
to America.
Love, your nephew
Mike.

The Davis family at St. Mary's Cemetery, Evergreen, Illinois, on Mother's Day, May 8, 1999. Left to right, rear: Christine Davis Ledingham; Cole Davis; grandson Ross Malara; me (Clyde Patrick Davis); my daughter-in-law, Cole's wife, Tammi; Kay Davis; Cynthia Davis Malara and her husband Phillip. Front row: grandsons, Taylor and Beau Davis; Dylan Malara; and Codie Davis.

MÁRIA "MARY" BENKÓ SZÁVICS/SAVAGE

Mária "Mary" Savage, b. May 4, 1883, d. August 18, 1960, with sons Dezsó-David Andrew Szávics/Savage, b. August 26, 1904, d. May 7, 1996, and József "Joe," b. February 18, 1906.

bove, the reverse side of the photo clearly indicates it was taken prior to Mary Savage's coming to America in 1909, ince most of the label is in Hungarian with the exception of "The Progressive Portrait & Frame Co." stamped on the left side of he photo. Also, in handwriting are the addresses of June Lucas, 7134 Sacramento (Chicago, Illinois) and an address 553 "Mc Na…" (most likely "Mackinaw," Chicago, Illinois), where Mary was to reside with her family. 8553 Mackinaw s the same address given by Andrew Savich, Mary's husband, upon his entry into the U.S. on March 8, 1907. The Graf Rudolph F. hotography studio ("Fotografisches Atelier") was undoubtedly located in the town of Eger, Hungary, since that is the area

Mária "Mary" Benkó Szávics/Savage

Pictured above: Ultonia *(1898) Cunard Line. Built by Swan & Hunter, Ltd., Wallsend-on-Tyne, Newcastle, England. Tonnage: 10,402. Dimensions: 500' x 57' Twin-screw, 13 knots. Triple expansion engines. Four masts and one funnel. Maiden voyage: Liverpool–Boston, February 28, 1899. Transferred to Trieste–New York service in 1904. Torpedoed and sunk without warning by the German submarine U-53 190 miles from Fastnet, June 27, 1917, with loss of one life.*

It was the Ultonia *that brought Mária Szávics and her two sons, Deszó and József, to the shores of America in 1909 (see the ship's manifest below) from the port of Fiume, Italy.*

Photo courtesy of The Steamship Historical Society of America, www.ssha.org.

SALOON, CABIN, AND STEERAGE ALIENS MUST BE COMPLETELY MANIFESTED.

LIST OR MANIFEST OF ALIEN PASSENGERS FOR THE UNITED

Required by the regulations of the Secretary of Commerce and Labor of the United States, under Act of Congress approved February 20, 1907, to be delivered

S. S. Ultonia sailing from Fiume on the 10th of Juli 1909

No. on List	Family Name	Given Name	Age Yrs.	Sex	Calling or Occupation	Nationality	Race or People	Last Permanent Residence: Country	City or Town	Nearest relative or friend in country whence alien came	Final Destination: State	City or Town
1	Popovics	Mihályné	32	f	house-wife	Hungary	Magyar	Hungary	O. Paulis	mother: Lovan Vilaune O. Paulis	Pa	Pittsburg
2	"	Ilona	11	f	child					grand mother		
3	"	Margit	8	f								
4	"	Rezsö	6	m								
5	Csavanyak	Gyorgyne Veronka	25	f	house-wife				Csorvás	mother: Rácz Mihályné Csorvás	Ill	Aurora
6		Erzsébet	2	f	child					grandmother		
7	Kafka	Gyula	48	m	locksmith						N.Y.	New York
8		Magdolna	47	f	house-wife			Hungary	Cegléd			
9		Maria	10	f	child							
10	Lebovics	Samuel	16	m	labourer		Hebrew		M. Szlget	mother: Lebovics Hani M. Szlget		
11		Dezsö	14	m								
12	Szávics	Dezsöné Mária	26	f	house-wife				Felsö Farkany	father: Benkó Mihály Felsö Farkany	Pa	McKees Rocks
13		Dezsö	4	m	child					grandfather		
14		József	3	m								
15	Cseke	Mária	27	f		Hungary	Magyar	Hungary	Arad	father: Cseke Ferenc Arad		
16	Titko				servant		Slovak			father: Titko		Cleveland

b. May 4, 1883

The documents on the right, received from Julius Fülep on September 30, 1998, register the birth or baptism (which one is undetermined) of Mária Angyela Benkó, daughter of Julianna Tôth Benkó and Mihály Máté Benkó, May 4, 1883.

A[N]YAKÖNYVE.

Lakhely ház-szám.	A keresztatyák és anyák neve és állapotja.	A keresztelő neve és állapotja.	Jegyzetek.
Kis-Tálya	Marsanyics Julia örregy.	u. a.	

Borsod megye
Kis-Tálya
Andornak
Ostoros
községek
rom. katholikus
kereszteltjeinek
Anyakönyve
1883. dik évről.

KERESZTELTEK

Folyó szám	A születés	A keresztelés	A kereszteltnek Neve.	Neme fi.	Neme nő.	törvényes.	törvénytelen.	elsőszülött.	A szülők neve, vallása, állapotja, és származás helye.
	éve, hava, napja.								
50.	5.	6.	Mária angyela	"	nő	tör.	"	"	Benkó Mihály jászói ahaj. Tóth Julianna hs. Rk. izaro.

THIS SHEET IS FOR STEERAGE PASSENGERS.

List 50

STATES IMMIGRATION OFFICER AT PORT OF ARRIVAL. 2 PM

to the United States Immigration Officer by the Commanding Officer of any vessel having such passengers on board upon arrival at a port in the United States.

Arriving at Port of New York *on the* Jun. 30, 1909.

SUPPLEMENTAL INFORMATION REQUIRED BY NATURALIZATION ACT APPROVED JUNE 29, 1906.

13 No. on List.	14 Whether having a ticket to such final destination.	15 By whom was passage paid?	16 Whether in possession of $50, and if less, how much?	17 Whether ever before in the United States; and if so, when and where? If Yes— Year or period of years. Where?	18 Whether going to join a relative or friend; and if so, what relative or friend, and his name and complete address.	19	20 Whether a Polygamist.	21 Whether an Anarchist.	22	23 Condition of Health, Mental and Physical.	24 Deformed or Crippled. Nature, length of time, and cause.	25 Height. Feet.	Inches.	26 Complexion.	27 Color of— Hair.	Eyes.	28 Marks of Identification.	29 Place of Birth. Country.	City or Town.
1	Yes	husband	$ 70	no	husband: Popovics Mihály Park Ave 113 E Pittsburg Pa	no	no	no	no	good	no	5	2	dark	brown	blue	/	Hungary	O Tárkány
2	S	father	trav. with her mother		father							/	/	/	/	/	/		
3												/	/	/	/	/	/		
4												/	/	/	/	/	/		Ostoros
5	S	husband	$ 7	no	husband: Csavanyos György Oscre St 255 Aurora Ill.							5	3	dark	black	black	/		
6	S	father	trav. with her mother		father							[illegible]	[illegible]	[illegible]	[illegible]	[illegible]	[illegible]		[illegible]
7		Self	$ 50	yes 1907 New York	[illegible] G. Mlnar 323 E. 9th St. New York							5	4	dark	gray	brown	/		
8		husband	trav. with h. husband									5					/		
9		father		father								/	/	/	/	/	freckled		A. Szeged
10		father	$ 25	no	father: Lebovics Antal 197 [illegible] St. New York							5	1	dark	brown	brown	/		
11			trav. with his brother									4	11	"	"	"	[illegible]		Felső Tárkány
12		husband	$ 20	no	husband: Szavics Dezső Mc Kees Rocks Pa							5	3	"	fair	blue	/		
13	S	father	trav. with his mother		father [illegible] in english							/	/	/	/	/	/		
14												/	/	/	/	/	/	Hungary	[illegible]
15	Yes	uncle	$ 30		uncle: Junginger Stefan 1630 [illegible] St. Louis Mo							5	4	dark	brown	brown	/		[illegible]

STATE Illinois
COUNTY Cook
TOWNSHIP OR OTHER DIVISION OF COUNTY
NAME OF INSTITUTION

DEPARTMENT OF COMMERCE AND LABOR—BUREAU OF THE CENSUS
THIRTEENTH CENSUS OF THE UNITED STATES: 1910—POPULATION

NAME OF INCORPORATED PLACE Chicago
ENUMERATED BY ME ON THE 4 DAY OF Ap

Line	House no.	Dwelling	Family	Name	Relation	Sex	Color	Age	Marital	Yrs. married	Children born	Living	Birthplace	Father's birthplace	Mother's birthplace	Year of immigration	Naturalized	Language	Trade
51			192	Larson — Julius	Head	M	W	34	M1	12			Sweden	Sweden	Sweden	1893	Na	English	Car Rep[illegible]
52				— Ida	Wife	F	W	34	M1	12	4	3	Sweden	Sweden	Sweden	1895		English	None
53				— Lawrence	Son	M	W	8	S				Illinois	Sweden	Sweden				None
54				— Roy	Son	M	W	7	S				Illinois	Sweden	Sweden				None
55				— Harold	Son	M	W	4	S				Illinois	Sweden	Sweden				None
56				Nelson — Oscar	Roomer	M	W	34	M1	13			Sweden	Sweden	Sweden	1910	Al	Swedish	Car Repairer
57	8917	80	193	Osborg — August	Head	M	W	62	M1	30			Sweden	Sweden	Sweden	18[illegible]	Na	English	[illegible]
58				— Eliza	Wife	F	W	54	M1	30	6	5	Sweden	Sweden	Sweden	1876		English	None
59				— Edward	Son	M	W	20	S				Illinois	Sweden	Sweden			English	None
60				— Arthur	Son	M	W	16	S				Illinois	Sweden	Sweden			English	[illegible]
61			194	Nelson — Gustav	Head	M	W	40	M1	6			Sweden	Sweden	Sweden	1895	Pa	English	Machinist
62				— Frida	Wife	F	W	29	M1	6	2	2	Sweden	Sweden	Sweden	1901		English	None
63				— Donald	Son	M	W	5	S				Illinois	Sweden	Sweden				None
64				— Mildred	Daughter	F	W	4	S				Illinois	Sweden	Sweden				None
65				Anderson — Carl	Boarder	M	W	20	S				Sweden	Sweden	Sweden	1906	Pa	English	Painter
66			195	Kraus — William	Head	M	W	47	M2	3			Germany	Germany	Germany	1885	Na	English	Painter
67				— Adelaine	Wife	F	W	35	M2	3	1	1	Illinois	Germany	Germany			English	None
68				Normanson — Anthony	Step son	M	W	15	S				Illinois	Illinois	Illinois			English	None
69				Shinkey — Charles	Father-in-law	M	W	60	Wd				Germany	Germany	Germany	1875	Na	German	None
70	8915	81	196	Savich — Andrew	Head	M	W	33	M1	8			Hungary	Hungary	Hungary	1907	Pa	Hungarian	Machinist
71				— Juliet	Wife	F	W	27	M1	8	2	2	Hungary	Hungary	Hungary	1907		Hungarian	None
72				— Joseph	Son	M	W	3	S				Hungary	Hungary	Hungary	1907			None
73				— Andrew	Son	M	W	6	S				Hungary	Hungary	Hungary	1907			None
74				Deutch — Jos	Boarder	M	W	28	S				Hungary	Hungary	Hungary	1906	Pa	Hungarian	Machinist
75				Noga — Paul	Boarder	M	W	27	S				Hungary	Hungary	Hungary	1908	Pa	Hungarian	Machinist
76				Shinko — John	Boarder	M	W	34	S				Hungary	Hungary	Hungary	[illegible]		Hungarian	Machinist
77	8910	82	197	Sleight — Eugene H.	Head	M	W	49	M1	24			Illinois	New York	New York			English	Elec[illegible]
				— Annie	Wife	F	W	43	M1	24	7	7	Canada	Canada	Canada	1885		English	Janitor
				— Albert	Son	M	W	20	S				[illegible]	Illinois	Canada				[illegible]

STATE Illinois
COUNTY Cook
TOWNSHIP OR OTHER DIVISION OF COUNTY
NAME OF INSTITUTION

DEPARTMENT OF COMMERCE—BUREAU OF THE CENSUS
FOURTEENTH CENSUS OF THE UNITED STATES: 1920—POPULATION

NAME OF INCORPORATED PLACE
ENUMERATED BY ME ON THE 23rd DAY OF Ja

Line	House no.	Dwelling	Family	Surname	Given name	Relation	Owned/rented	Free/mortgaged	Sex	Color	Age	Marital	Year of immigration	Naturalized or alien	Year of naturalization	Attended school	Read	Write	Birthplace	Mother tongue	Father's birthplace	Father's mother tongue
51	8548	87	197	Zeno	Bessie	daughter			F	W	6	S							Illinois		Hungary	Magyar
52				—	Frank	son			M	W	4 6/12	S							Illinois		Hungary	Magyar
53				—	Anna	daughter			F	W	11/12	S							Illinois		Hungary	Magyar
54			198	Breba	Julius	Head	R		M	W	46	M	1910	Pa			yes	yes	Hungary	Magyar	Hungary	Magyar
55				—	Rose	wife			F	W	40	M	1910	Al			yes	yes	Hungary	Magyar	Hungary	Magyar
56	8547	88	199	Redvay	John	Head	R		M	W	27	M					yes	yes	Penna		Hungary	Magyar
57				—	Julia	wife			F	W	23	M	Un	Na			yes	yes	Hungary	Magyar	Hungary	Magyar
58				—	Julia	daughter			F	W	3 [illegible]/12	S							Illinois		Penn.	
59			200	Krisoel	Rose	Head	O	M	F	W	48	Wd	1897	Na	1904		yes	yes	Hungary	Magyar	Hungary	Magyar
60				—	John	son			M	W	28	S	1897	Na			yes	yes	Hungary	Magyar	Hungary	Magyar
61	8553	89	201	Sevach	Andrew	Head	O	F	M	W	45	M	1908	Pa			yes	yes	Austria	Slavak	Austria	Slavak
62				—	Mary	wife			F	W	35	M	1908	Al			yes	yes	Austria	Slavak	Austria	Slavak
63				—	Andrew	son			M	W	17	S	1908	Al		yes	yes	yes	Austria	Slavak	Austria	Slavak
64				—	Joseph	son			M	W	14	S	1908	Al		yes	yes	yes	Austria	Slavak	Austria	Slavak
65				—	Julia	daughter			F	W	8	S				yes	yes	yes	Illinois		Austria	Slavak
66				—	Michael	son			M	W	6	S							Illinois		Austria	Slavak
67				—	Mathie	daughter			M	W	4	S							Illinois		Austria	Slavak
68				—	John	son			M	W	4/12	S							Illinois		Austria	Slavak
69	8550	90	202	Deak	Michael	Head	R		M	W	30	M	1908	Pa			yes	yes	Hungary	Magyar	Hungary	Magyar
70				—	Irma	wife			F	W	29	M	1908	Al			yes	yes	Hungary	Magyar	Hungary	Magyar
71				—	Alex	son			M	W	[illegible]								Illinois		Hungary	Magyar
																					Austria	Slavak
																						Slavak

b. May 4, 1883

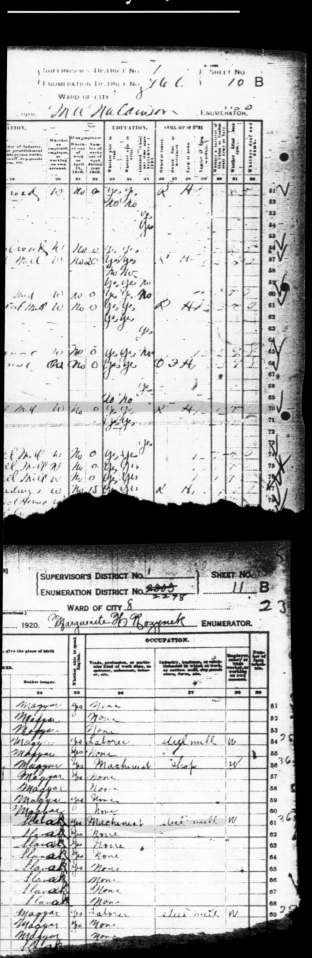

Grandma Savage and Her Homes

By March 17, 1938, my birth, my parents were living with my mother's parents at 8545 Mackinaw, in the "Bush" where they first met. This was the first of my grandmother's homes. The "Bush" was one of the first neighborhoods to emerge on the South Side of Chicago. It was bounded by U.S. Steel on the east and South Shore Drive on the west, between 83rd Street and 86th Street. It was called the "Bush" because in the early days it had nothing but a strip of sandy beach with some shrubbery. My father was "OW" ("out of work") for one year, according to my birth certificate. This may have been due to his losing all five toes in a switching accident and consequent period of recovery.

Mary Savage

According to a twenty-year payment life insurance policy with the American Sick Benefit and Life Insurance Association of Bridgeport, Connecticut, (policy number 49323) taken out by my mother, Mary Davis, on October 8, 1943, her residence was 8023 Marquette Avenue, Chicago, Illinois. This was the second of my grandmother's homes. Incidentally, the face amount of the policy was $1,000, and the monthly rate was $2.20. In her "Application for Membership" dated September 29, 1943, she gave her occupation as "lunch press hand." The beneficiaries of the policy were "Clyde and June Davis, Children, and Mary Davis, Mother."

In a letter I received in August 1997, from my cousin, Michael D. Savage, along with other information regarding Michael's father and our grandfather, he included the following about our grandmother, referring to "… the Ada S. McKinley Community Services Center, more commonly known to our family as the 'South Chicago Neighborhood House.' As you can see from the address, it is only a half a block from the old homestead at 8548 [*sic*] S. Mackinaw. When Grandma went to work as a seamstress at the South Shore Country Club in the early 30's, her children were sent there to keep them off the streets. This organization may have records, documents, or other information which might provide historical insights of the family."

The Neighborhood House is further described in *Images of America Chicago's Southeast Side* by Rod Sellers and Dominic A. Pacyga (Arcadia Publishing, 1998), page 104.

Note the discrepancy between the 1910 and 1920 United States census records. In the 1910 census (top left), Andrew Savich's wife was enumerated as "Juliet," while in the 1920 census (bottom left), his wife was listed as "Mary." Children and their ages are correctly shown.

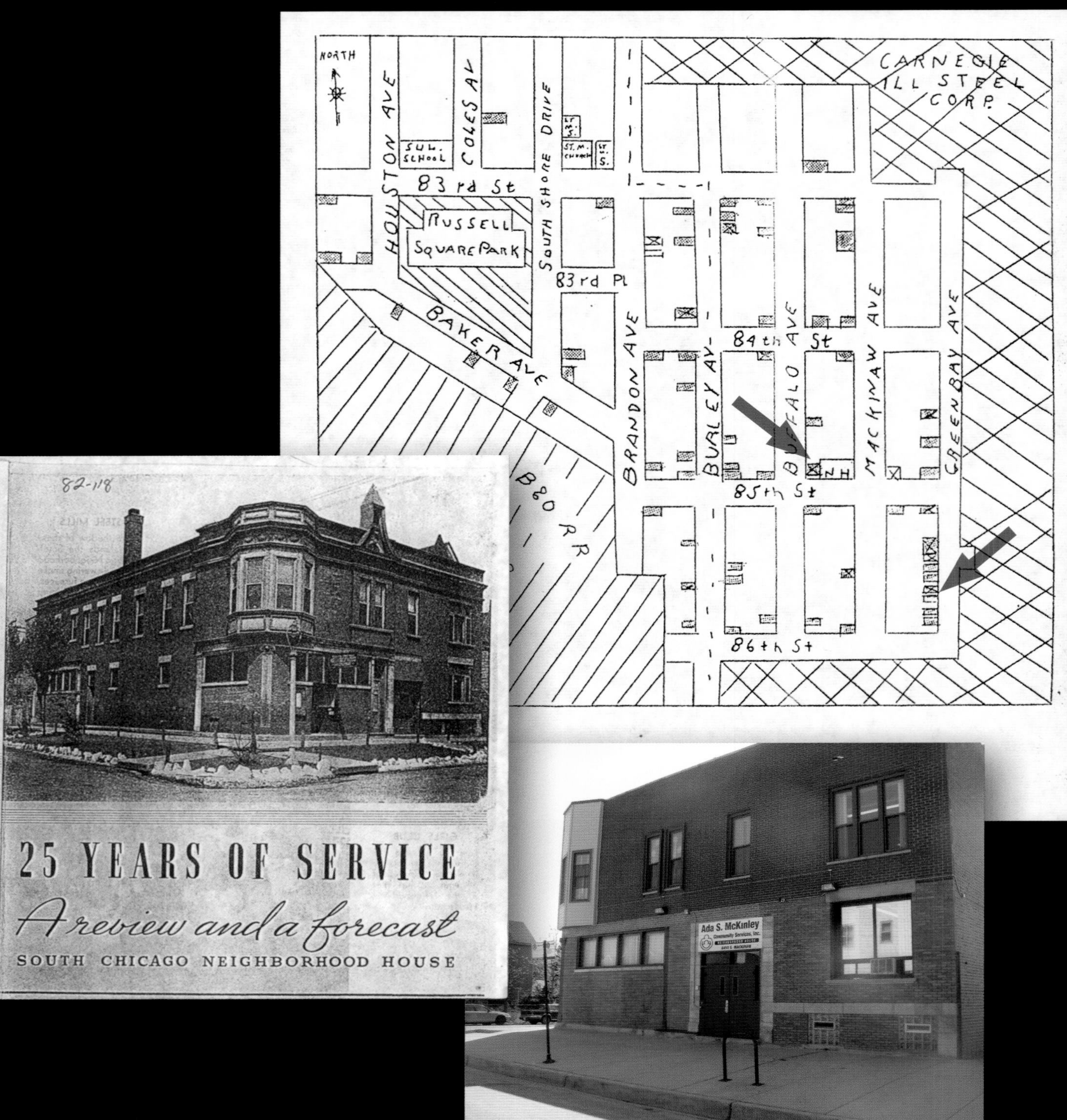

The Ada S. McKinley South Chicago Neighborhood House pictured in a report, "25 Years of Service," ca. 1939, and to the right, the Neighborhood House as it existed in May 2009, still serving the community as it exists today in the "Bush" (top arrow). The street diagram was photocopied from this 1939 report, which depicted "Tavern Locations" throughout the "Bush." At the time there were "60 taverns open and doing business in this community." Also, "Every building between 85th and 86th streets on Green Bay Avenue facing an entrance to the Steel Mill is a tavern." My mother, Mary Savage, worked at one of these taverns — Lako's, according to my mother — (bottom arrow), which was directly behind her home on Mackinaw Avenue. As mentioned earlier in the book, it was here, at a "fish fry" that she first met my father.

"The South Chicago Neighborhood House has been helping the people of the 'Bush' since 1911. The American Baptist Church originally opened the settlement house, later affiliated with the Hull House organization founded by Jane Addams. The agency provides numerous social services to neighborhood residents including counseling programs."

Grandma Savage and Me

My grandmother, Mary Savage, was born May 4, 1883, in Kistálya, Hungary. Coincidently, my sister June and my grandson Codie were also born on May 4th. Kistálya has since been renamed Andornaktálya. Her parents were Mihály Máté Benkó and Julianna Tóth, who lived in Felsötárkány, a larger adjoining town also listed as her place of birth. Very little is known about my grandmother's life in Hungary prior to her immigration to the United States or her family's economic status, except I do recall hearing, "the floor in her home was dirt." She was aboard the SS *Ultonia* in steerage with her two sons Dezsó (David), age four and József, age three, not in the ritzier saloon class or a cabin, when it set sail from Fiume on the Adriatic, July 10, 1909. Her intention was to join her husband who had preceded her to the States. She arrived at the port of New York on July 30, 1909, with $20 and a ticket to Pittsburgh, although her final destination was McKees Rocks, Pennsylvania.

By April 1910, according to the U.S. census, my grandmother and grandfather were living at 8915 Superior, Chicago, Illinois, with their children Joseph, Andrew, and three boarders.

As a youngster, I had spent a fair amount of time with my paternal grandparents, Charles and Rebecca Davis. Whether it was my young age or the fact that my time was shared between them and my maternal grandmother, it was Mary Savage who would earn a special place in my heart. As a teenager I spent a good deal of time living with my Grandma Savage.

Both my grandmothers were "old-fashioned" women. They had long, often braided hair wrapped about their heads. They always wore long flowered dresses with blocky, high heeled, laced shoes, and carried pocketbooks not purses. Seldom was either pictured in a hat; however, one rare exception was when my grandmother Savage attended my wedding (see photo on page 86). Neither adopted the dress style of changing times. Photographs of them in the 1920s, '30s, '40s, '50s, and even the '60s could easily be swapped, one decade with another, and you would detect little difference in their fashion style over the years.

Mary Savage in front of fence in the "Bush"

Mary Savage was a worker. She essentially kept the family together throughout her children's teenage years and, after her husband died in 1943, well into their adulthood. My grandfather had worked as a machinist for the Carnegie Steel Corporation, as did so many immigrants from the old country. Eventually his sons Mike and Johnny would also seek employment there as well.

According to my cousin Michael, Grandma Savage worked for the South Shore Country Club at 71st Street and South Shore Drive as a seamstress. I also recall someone mentioning that she worked as a chambermaid at the Southmoor Hotel located at 66th and Stony Island Avenue in Chicago. She spoke English, but favored her native language, Magyar, or Hungarian. All of her children were able to speak with her in Hungarian, and I remember learning a few Hungarian words, long since forgotten.

Within the family there was so much discord, plenty of feuding and fighting, and simply bad behavior, not to mention the years of pain for those making wrong choices. My mother, during most of her troubled life, relied a great deal on my grandma for help, especially with the children. Grandma, for as long as I can remember, was always a part of my growing up, but it was during my teenage years that she and I had the most contact and grew increasingly close. My grandma cared for me, provided a stress-free environment, fed me well, asked nothing of me, and allowed me a freedom that I seldom enjoyed at home.

Photographs show me at age five or six at her side and again depict her at my first communion and confirmation when I believe I was thirteen years old. I probably spent the summer of 1955 at my grandma's. I had gotten a job through my uncle Vic (Lucas), working as a helper on a truck, delivering cardboard boxes, as well as dropping off and picking up jukeboxes from various bars and restaurants throughout Chicago. I spent a lot of time in the warehouse cleaning those same jukeboxes. After work I returned to my grandma's house in the "Bush," at 8545 S. Mackinaw, ate dinner, and then went to my girlfriend's house. Grandma was a good cook, and I loved her *paprikash* (chicken, paprika, and cream sauce) with drop noodles, and her chicken soup and dumplings. Mornings, I'd find Grandma in her small kitchen, sitting at the window, brushing out her long blonde hair, separating it into strands to be braided in golden ropes, which she would wind, again and again, around her head. Breakfast for Grandma was

Grandma Mary Savage with her daughter June Savage Lucas and June Davis

Mary Savage, John Savage, Mary Davis, June "Tootsie" Davis, Mary Lou Savage, and Clyde Davis on the occasion of June's first communion

usually half a grapefruit and oatmeal topped with a poached egg. Grapefruit and oatmeal are favorites of mine to this day; however, I never cared for the poached egg part.

It was at my grandma's, on that same kitchen table, that I hand lettered the small poster cards for my uncle Vic's American Legion Post carnival in Twin Lakes, Wisconsin. He had gotten the merchant booth sponsors to pay me $20 per poster, and there were dozens and dozens that I produced.

After my first year at the University of Illinois, I had been put on probation and then, failing scholastically, I returned from Champaign-Urbana to, where else, Grandma's. I had to sit out a semester before I could reapply to the University of Illinois. During that period, I worked as an apprentice for a small art studio, Whittaker Guernsey, in downtown Chicago, in the matting and mounting department. At some point I recall sharing my grandma's home with my uncle Dave, who also lived with her. He had one of the two bedrooms, Grandma the other, so I slept on the sofa in the living room. The sofa was a short distance from Grandma's open bedroom door. Often I'd overhear her cry out softly as she said her prayers, "Oh, dear God, Jesus, Madia (Mary) and Joseph." By this time she was seventy-seven years old and was suffering a number of ailments. Besides diabetes (she died from complications associated with the disease) and problems with her heart, Grandma had a large, benign cyst on the right side of her upper back for at least ten years, and when I'd hug her, it was difficult not to notice. The cyst gradually increased in size to approximately the circumference of a saucer and was quite thick. Despite her physical maladies, Grandma continued to care for herself and those she loved. Uncle Dave worked nights, both tending bar and as a cashier. Eventually he became the bar owner. As he became acquainted with my skill as a young artist, he helped me financially. Living together in my grandma's home I can still see him getting ready for work, walking between his bedroom and the bathroom in his boxer shorts, a glass in one hand and, in the other, a double-sided, used razor blade, which he swirled back and forth inside the glass, in an apparent attempt to sharpen the blade.

While staying with my grandmother, after work I would go to South Chicago to the YMCA to swim and work out with weights. There I met my future roommate, Tom Spasoff, who was also planning to attend the University of Illinois. Tom would later become the best man at my wedding.

Grandma attended my wedding at St. Peter's and Paul Catholic Church in South Chicago on September 19, 1959. Within a year, on August 18, 1960, my grandmother died. Attending her funeral was the most dreaded occasion for me. It was traumatic, and though I went to the wake at the Donnellan Funeral Home with my wife Kay, I refused, despite much coaxing by relatives, to view my grandmother laid out in a casket. I wanted my last memory to be of her alive, the ever sweet, generous of spirit, loving and kind person I cherished. I recall uncontrollably sobbing throughout the services.

b. May 4, 1883

Mary Savage in January 1957

Above: Mary Savage in doorway of an Indian hut while on vacation. Victor Lucas is behind her in the shadows to the right. Below: Certificate of Registration acquired in May 1998, along with one for Janos F. Benko.

ELLIS ISLAND
1892–1992
TM © 1987 SL/EIF, INC.

The Statue of Liberty-Ellis Island Foundation, Inc.

proudly presents this

Official Certificate of Registration

in

THE AMERICAN IMMIGRANT WALL OF HONOR

to officially certify that

Mary Benko Savich

came to the United States of America from

Hungary

joining those courageous men and women who came to this country in search of personal freedom, economic opportunity and a future hope for their families.

Lee Iacocca

Lee A. Iacocca
The Statue of Liberty-Ellis Island Foundation, Inc.

David Savage was an avid swimmer and regularly swam long distances along the Lake Michigan shoreline, which could be seen for miles from his home high above Lake Shore Drive. He also was known to take long walks in the parks and beaches of Chicago, contributing to his excellent physical shape, as seen in the black and white photograph above with his nephew, Michael Savage Jr. (probably in Hayward, Wisconsin). Dave enjoyed a lively verbal exchange, often holding court in his living room (below).

My uncle David loved to engage in vigorous discussion. He is shown above in his apartment with his beloved dog, Smokey, at his side in animated conversation with my brother, David "Butchie" Davis. Both of them had strong opinions on many subjects and were never at a loss for words.

David Savage with unknown woman. My uncle Dave, the eldest of six children, was born in Hungary and immigrated to the United States in 1909 with his mother Mary Szavics and his brother Joseph. He never married.

My Uncle Dave

Dezsó David Andrew Savage, brother to my mother, was born August 26, 1904, in Felsötárkány, Hungary. His certificate of death lists his place of birth as Budapest, Hungary. At age four he accompanied his mother and younger brother Joseph, immigrating to the United States in 1909. He was the eldest of six children.

He grew up in a family largely devoid of a father, who suffered from depression and who could not provide the anchoring most families required, especially in a new homeland. My uncle would relate to me later in life that he grew up in a family whose "father was not there mentally." It is believed that his father suffered from acute depression, which afflicted many in the family. Not surprisingly, my uncle as a young teenager traveled a rather rocky road. He became a ward of the court as a teenager, being placed as a truant in the care of Emma Apel. My uncle credits the Apels as having saved him from a life of uncertain outcomes. The 1920 census for Illinois, January 8 and 9, 1920, Cook County, 32nd ward, listed Emma Apel as head of household, at 6842 Normal Boulevard, Chicago. She owned her own home, mortgage free. She was white, forty-five years of age, and divorced. She was born in Illinois and her father was born in New York, as was her mother. She was a doctor working for the Board of Education. Also enumerated with Emma Apel were a thirty-two-year-old son Robert, an aunt, Amanda McKay, age seventy-six, widowed, and a cousin Florence Apel, thirty-four, who was single. Most importantly, my uncle Andrew David Savage was also enumerated in this household as a "stepson," age fifteen.

Kay Davis, David Andrew Savage, Mary Savage Davis, and David Otis Davis in a photo taken on May 26, 1986, outside David Savage's apartment building at 4800 Chicago Beach Drive, Chicago, Illinois.

Although he never married there always seemed to be a woman in his life. For some time he went out with a woman named Frances Normile. Frances was divorced and had a son, Bernie Cassatta. She was a salesperson for Merle Norman Cosmetics. His last relationship was with Maralyn Judy, a cherished companion of many years. Maralyn was a former teller and bank manager at the Hyde Park Bank and Trust on the South Side of Chicago where they first met. They lived in a rather exclusive condominium, owned in common, in a high-rise building, "The Newport," just off Lake Shore Drive. The building, twenty-seven stories and built in 1963, was architecturally modern in style with an indoor pool, which was unusual for the time. From the 15th floor they had beautiful views of downtown Chicago and Lake Michigan. On a clear day you could see the shoreline of the state of Michigan.

Uncle Dave was the most entrepreneurial of all his brothers and sisters. In the 1930 U.S. census, at age twenty-five, my uncle gave his occupation as brokerage/broker. He was the only male in the family who did not seek work in the steel mill. In the 1950s he worked as a bartender and cashier (with a .38 revolver behind his back and in his belt), and he owned the "Rumpus Room," a bar located on Stony Island near 68th Street. My cousin Michael Savage recalls how he, his mother, and father used to clean the place at 4 A.M. each morning. Dave was involved in local Democratic politics and was a member of the AFL/CIO unions. In the 1960s he was a part owner in a Chicago hotel, The Cornell Arms at 53rd and Cornell in Hyde Park. My uncle's involvement in this hotel is, like so many other stories in my family, intertwined with crime. There's talk that the Chicago "Jewish Mafia" was involved in the acquisition of the hotel, and my uncle, though not an outright owner, received "points" for managing the property. The hotel was in a generally rundown condition. The owners were able to secure a FHA loan for its restoration, which my uncle oversaw. During his retirement, my uncle spoke often of a legal entanglement, unresolved, between him and his former partners in the hotel. The hotel had a busy bar, which contributed to its success. Dave had secured the services of an attractive woman who ran "26," a popular dice game in the Midwest in the 1930s through the 1950s, which would make "payoffs" in drinks. Anti-gambling legislation killed the game off eventually.

Dave saw himself as the penultimate salesman. He worked in a bar in Hayward, Wisconsin, a place frequented by loggers or lumberjacks. In order to drum up business, Dave enticed one of the local Chippewa Indians to catch a good-sized Muskie fish, which he placed live in a large fish tank on the premises. This was part of a scheme, of course. He named the fish "Julius." He then created what he termed a fishing tournament with a $5,000 prize, stating that on a certain day Julius would be released in the lake and the fisherman who caught Julius would be the winner. There was a $5 entry fee per person to participate in the contest. On the day of the contest, early that morning, Dave along with my cousin Michael, took Julius to the basement of the tavern and stuffed him with several pounds of "split-shot" fishing line lead pellets. When released in the lake, the Muskie went straight to the bottom. It was easy money, and I'm sure my uncle shared his illicit gains with my cousin, who related the story to me.

I didn't hang out with my uncle, but because he lived with my grandmother in the 1950s, I saw a fair amount of him. He was a bit brusque, fairly opinionated, and not easy to warm up to.

Dave Savage with his companion of nineteen years, Maralyn Laier Judy, in a photo taken in February 1978. They first met some time in 1977 at the Hyde Park Bank and Trust Company, where Maralyn was a long-time employee.

Because I was shy, I would go out of my way to avoid being in his company. He was, however, quite good to me and sensitive to my needs as a youngster.

My uncle never married, but managed to have at least two relatively long-term relationships. In the latter years of his life, he seemed to have found a person of considerable tolerance and loyalty.

Maralyn Laier Judy was born November 3, 1904. Maralyn first met David Savage some time during 1977, according to Jeanne Gilman, Maralyn's niece. Dave apparently was a customer of the Hyde Park Bank and Trust Company located at 1525 E. 53rd Street, Chicago, Illinois (its location in February 1967), where Maralyn had a long-time career. Jeanne recalls in her letter to me of May 19, 2009, that Maralyn had called both Jeanne and her brother to ask them "how we felt about her living with David without being married." Apparently Maralyn received their "blessing" — the relationship lasted nearly twenty years.

b. August 26, 1904

As Jeanne mentioned in her letter, Maralyn was "blessed with good health most of her life … a tough lady, who never complained about anything." Knowing my highly opinionated uncle and his penchant for arguing about almost everything and with everyone, this was an attribute that certainly contributed greatly to her life with Dave.

Maralyn loved working. She never had children, though I recall my uncle saying, "The woman's buried three husbands," and himself, as fate would have it. Her first husband, Daniel L. McCarthy, met her at the bank while both were working as tellers. Dan and Maralyn were married February 6, 1933. Dan served in the Army during World War II. A heavy smoker, he died from emphysema. The marriage had lasted twelve years. Maralyn's second marriage was to Mr. Morass, a piano player from New Orleans. He "swept her off her feet," according to Maralyn's niece, Jeanne Gilman. However, the marriage was "stormy" and lasted only a year. Her final marriage was to Robert V. Judy, August 15, 1959, in Cook County, Illinois (Marriage Index, 1930–1960). Bob was an engineer with Western Electric, Inc., who died in 1969. Maralyn's aging mother, who lived well into her nineties, lived with Maralyn through all three marriages. Her parents were Barbara Bauer and Gottlieb Laier.

Her career in banking began in late 1927 as a switchboard operator with the Hyde Park State Bank. She remained with the bank through a series of name changes, relocations, and even survived the Great Depression and a general run on banks. Although the bank was idle for several years during this period (1931–1940), Maralyn was the only bank employee retained.

During World War II Maralyn sold bonds. In 1950 she became an assistant cashier and officer of the bank, her favorite job, securing many new accounts.

Maralyn retired December 31, 1969, but returned part-time in personal banking. She belonged to the Association of Chicago Bank Women from 1950 to 1969. Maralyn loved banking. It was a career that brought her much pleasure and satisfaction, including a husband and later in life a companion of nineteen years.

Sandy.

Over the years, when visiting my mother in Lansing and Orland Park, we would, at Mom's request, visit her brother Dave and Maralyn. A woman well into her eighties when we first met, Maralyn was somewhat frail, but spry and gracious. She liked a martini now and then, especially when company came calling.

After Uncle Dave's passing, we visited Maralyn in their apartment. Maralyn was using the dining table to organize what appeared to be numerous requests for animal shelter funding. She had a generous nature and love of animals Their two dogs were strays found at the "point" on the shore of Lake Michigan, where Dave and Maralyn used to go to swim. They proved to be the solace of her being alone.

Smokey

Within two years of my uncle's passing, Maralyn, no longer able to care for herself, sold the condominium she and Dave owned at The Newport and lived out her final years in a care facility in Brookfield, Wisconsin. There she remained under the watchful eye of her niece, Jeanne Gilman, until Marayln's death September 19, 2001, at age ninety-three.

ALWAYS CARRY THIS CARD
QUARTERLY MEMBERSHIP CARD
1970
County, Municipal Employees', Supervisors, and Foremen's Union, Local 1001
Affiliated with A.F.L.–C.I.O. and Congress of Industrial Organizations
When Requested this Card Must be shown

Front

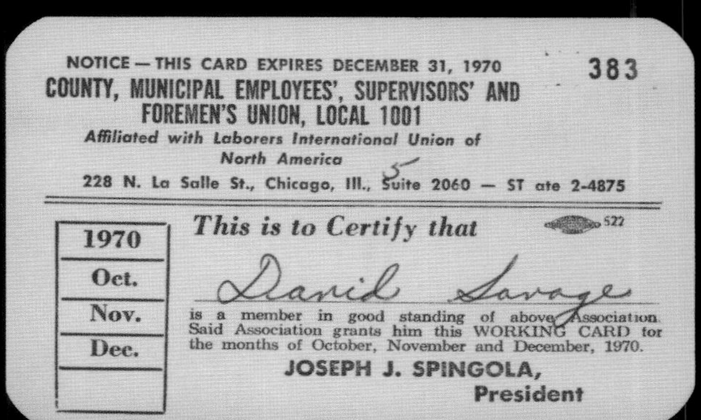

NOTICE — THIS CARD EXPIRES DECEMBER 31, 1970 383
COUNTY, MUNICIPAL EMPLOYEES', SUPERVISORS' AND FOREMEN'S UNION, LOCAL 1001
Affiliated with Laborers International Union of North America
228 N. La Salle St., Chicago, Ill., Suite 2060 — ST ate 2-4875

1970
Oct.
Nov.
Dec.

This is to Certify that
David Savage
is a member in good standing of above Association. Said Association grants him this WORKING CARD for the months of October, November and December, 1970.
JOSEPH J. SPINGOLA,
President

Back

DEZSÓ DAVID ANDREW SZÁVICS SAVAGE

SAVAGE
David A. Savage, May 7th, dear brother of Mary Davis and John (Dorothy) Savage; uncle of Clyde P. (Catherine) Davis, June Rogers, David Davis, Michael and Patricia Savage; cherished companion of Marilyn Judy. Funeral services 9:30 a.m. Friday at **Donnellan Funeral Home,** 10525 S. Western Ave. Interment St. Mary. Visitation Thursday 2 to 9 p.m. 312-238-0075

Chicago Tribune, *Thursday, May 9, 1996. When I prepared this obituary, I did not realize how Maralyn spelled her name, hence the "Marilyn" that appeared in the newspaper.*

David A. Savage d. May 7, 1966, buried at St. Mary's Cemetery, Evergreen Park, Illinois. He is buried next to his brother, Michael Savage, and his wife. His mother and father are also buried in the same cemetery. A burial site also exists for Mary Savage Davis next to her brothers, Mike and Dave.

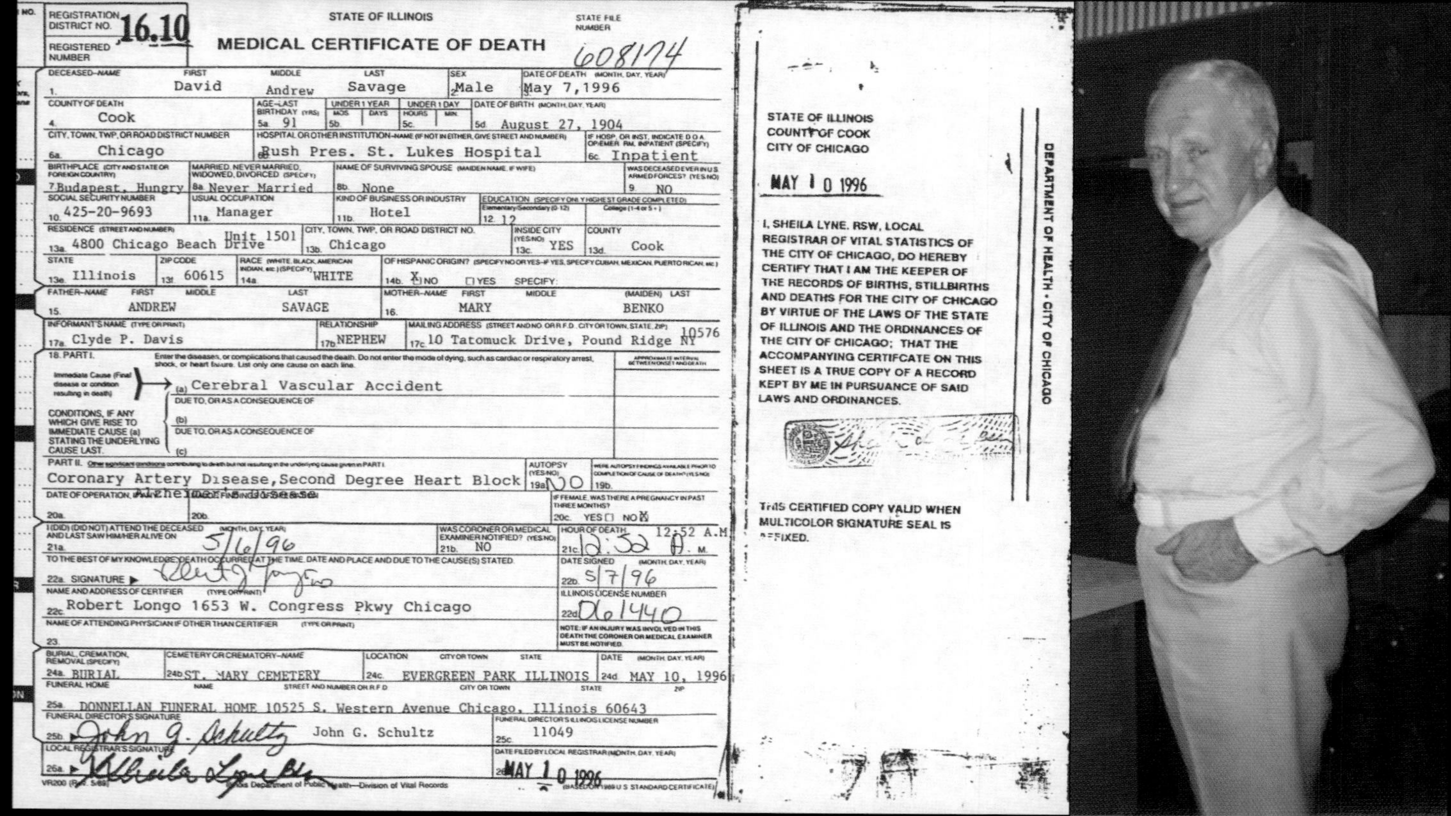

REGISTRATION DISTRICT NO. 16.10
STATE OF ILLINOIS
MEDICAL CERTIFICATE OF DEATH
STATE FILE NUMBER 608174

1. DECEASED–NAME: David Andrew Savage
2. SEX: Male
3. DATE OF DEATH: May 7,1996
4. COUNTY OF DEATH: Cook
5a. AGE–LAST BIRTHDAY (YRS): 91
5d. DATE OF BIRTH: August 27, 1904
6a. CITY, TOWN, TWP, OR ROAD DISTRICT NUMBER: Chicago
6b. HOSPITAL OR OTHER INSTITUTION–NAME: Rush Pres. St. Lukes Hospital
6c. Inpatient
7. BIRTHPLACE: Budapest, Hungry
8a. MARRIED, NEVER MARRIED, WIDOWED, DIVORCED: Never Married
8b. NAME OF SURVIVING SPOUSE: None
9. WAS DECEASED EVER IN U.S. ARMED FORCES?: NO
10. SOCIAL SECURITY NUMBER: 425-20-9693
11a. USUAL OCCUPATION: Manager
11b. KIND OF BUSINESS OR INDUSTRY: Hotel
12. EDUCATION: 12
13a. RESIDENCE: 4800 Chicago Beach Drive Unit 1501
13b. CITY: Chicago
13c. INSIDE CITY: YES
13d. COUNTY: Cook
13e. STATE: Illinois
13f. ZIP CODE: 60615
14a. RACE: WHITE
14b. OF HISPANIC ORIGIN?: X NO
15. FATHER–NAME: ANDREW SAVAGE
16. MOTHER–NAME: MARY (MAIDEN) BENKO
17a. INFORMANT'S NAME: Clyde P. Davis
17b. RELATIONSHIP: NEPHEW
17c. MAILING ADDRESS: 10 Tatomuck Drive, Pound Ridge NY 10576
18. PART I. (a) Cerebral Vascular Accident
PART II. Coronary Artery Disease, Second Degree Heart Block, Alzheimer's Disease
19a. AUTOPSY: NO
20c. IF FEMALE, WAS THERE A PREGNANCY IN PAST THREE MONTHS? NO
21a. LAST SAW HIM/HER ALIVE ON: 5/6/96
21b. WAS CORONER OR MEDICAL EXAMINER NOTIFIED?: NO
21c. HOUR OF DEATH: 12:52 A.M.
22a. SIGNATURE: [signature]
22b. DATE SIGNED: 5/7/96
22c. NAME AND ADDRESS OF CERTIFIER: Robert Longo 1653 W. Congress Pkwy Chicago
22d. ILLINOIS LICENSE NUMBER: 061440
24a. BURIAL
24b. CEMETERY: ST. MARY CEMETERY
24c. LOCATION: EVERGREEN PARK ILLINOIS
24d. DATE: MAY 10, 1996
25a. FUNERAL HOME: DONNELLAN FUNERAL HOME 10525 S. Western Avenue Chicago, Illinois 60643
25b. FUNERAL DIRECTOR'S SIGNATURE: John G. Schultz
25c. FUNERAL DIRECTOR'S ILLINOIS LICENSE NUMBER: 11049
26a. LOCAL REGISTRAR'S SIGNATURE: [signature]
26b. DATE FILED BY LOCAL REGISTRAR: MAY 10 1996
VR200 — Illinois Department of Public Health—Division of Vital Records

STATE OF ILLINOIS
COUNTY OF COOK
CITY OF CHICAGO

MAY 10 1996

I, SHEILA LYNE, RSW, LOCAL REGISTRAR OF VITAL STATISTICS OF THE CITY OF CHICAGO, DO HEREBY CERTIFY THAT I AM THE KEEPER OF THE RECORDS OF BIRTHS, STILLBIRTHS AND DEATHS FOR THE CITY OF CHICAGO BY VIRTUE OF THE LAWS OF THE STATE OF ILLINOIS AND THE ORDINANCES OF THE CITY OF CHICAGO; THAT THE ACCOMPANYING CERTIFICATE ON THIS SHEET IS A TRUE COPY OF A RECORD KEPT BY ME IN PURSUANCE OF SAID LAWS AND ORDINANCES.

THIS CERTIFIED COPY VALID WHEN MULTICOLOR SIGNATURE SEAL IS AFFIXED.

DEPARTMENT OF HEALTH - CITY OF CHICAGO

David Andrew Savage, age 91, died May 7, 1996, at Rush Presbyterian St. Lukes Hospital after elective heart surgery. I was for the first time an "informant" on a death certificate.

Providers Three

David Savage b. August 26, 1904

Interestingly enough, there are three men profiled rather extensively in this book who are not fathers. David A. Savage, an uncle and my mother's eldest brother; John Benko, my mother's great uncle and brother to my grandmother Mary Benko Savage; and Victor Lucas, another uncle, husband of June Savage, my mother's only sister. All three of these men had no known children. None has "family" that today, probably, spends much time considering the significant contribution these men made during their lifetimes to the betterment of their relatives. One, Dave, never married. Yet each man became a father figure to several of their less-fortunate family members, especially the young.

David Savage rescued my mother from the depths of depression by securing a sanitarium for her care after what was then referred to as a "nervous breakdown." He bought the suit I wore for my First Communion (see photo on page 17). David Savage gave me money to purchase art supplies when I was in high school and unable to afford the expensive red sable lettering brushes essential to creating the specific forms of Garamond Bold, or Caslon, or Franklin Gothic in India Ink black. David Savage assisted me with my University of Illinois student housing bills by driving down to Champaign-Urbana to bail me out so I could continue to reside on campus at Newman Hall. He was there for my sister, assisting her financially when she needed a new car. Being in the hotel business, he even provided me and my young family with furniture. I was finished with college, and we were in our first home in New York with only a crib and bassinet for furniture. He had my wife fly into Chicago and accompany him to a wholesale furniture distributor, where he allowed her to select our first living, dining, and bedroom furniture. We had been sleeping on my wife's fake-fur winter coat, unable to afford a bed.

Victor Lucas b. January 20, 1910

Some years before his death, David Savage discussed with Kay his intentions to bequest a sum of money to her in his will. Kay suggested he leave the money to children in the family who could use it for educational purposes, indicating that it would be a wonderful way for him to "leave a legacy" for the generations to come, especially since he had no children of his own, and because he did not wish to name other relatives in his will. He never followed Kay's advice and upon his death bequeathed a sum of money to her. She used the gift for the educational needs of my sister June's five grandaughters, youngsters who, although grateful to their aunt Kay, never will have the opportunity to thank the man who helped change their lives. The money has paid private high school tuition, SAT test preparation, tutoring, academic travel abroad, and college tuition. His gift to Kay continues to this day to help the children of a family he never had.

And the reader only has to thumb through the pages; page after page of money orders sent to desperately needy relatives in the "old country" by John Benko, as well as those he also helped in his newly adopted United States. A man who served his country in three branches of military. A hard working machinist. A man many others depended on. A man I proudly honor by telling of a noble life in pictures and words herein.

John Benko b. May 27, 1889

It was to John Benko that his nephews turned when they were glowing in the pride about success in school, or work, or how well their children were doing. All documented in letter after letter reproduced in this book. Appeals for a graduation suit, or assistance with travel, or an apartment's rental all came his way. It was John Benko who saved the home of his sister Mary Savage from foreclosure.

Victor Lucas was an adopted child of Lithuanian descent, born in the United States, who never forgot his good fortune to be raised in an affluent family. An ebullient man of considerable size, he was nevertheless always on the move, hardworking, energetic, with no time for leisure. I spent many hours at his side learning the merit of his industry. His efforts in my behalf and in others' are profiled on the pages immediately following, with his spouse, June Savage Lucas.

Sadly, upon their passing, few of these folks who benefited from these "fatherly" men were at their funerals. Few living today even know where they were buried. But my wife and I acknowledge their departure from this life as well as their good deeds and selfless acts of caring. The pages of this book record these achievements, and as long as it sits on my shelf or in the home or library of another, to be discovered by some future generation, these men will not be forgotten. None a father, but all providers.

June Julia Savage Lucas b. August 7, 1911

Victor J. Lucas b. January 20, 1910, with wife June Julia Savage Lucas. Photo possibly taken on or about their wedding on February 15, 1943.

Permanent File No. 64-AL-175
Clair J. Wilson Commercial Photographers
Aerial Surveys
UPtown 1-2883 2133 West Hopkins St.
MILWAUKEE 6, WISCONSIN

OCT 17 1964

Mary Savage seated on car top with her sister June below on trunk

June Savage Lucas with June "Tootsie" Davis. Written on back of photo is "This is June and Mary's little girl."

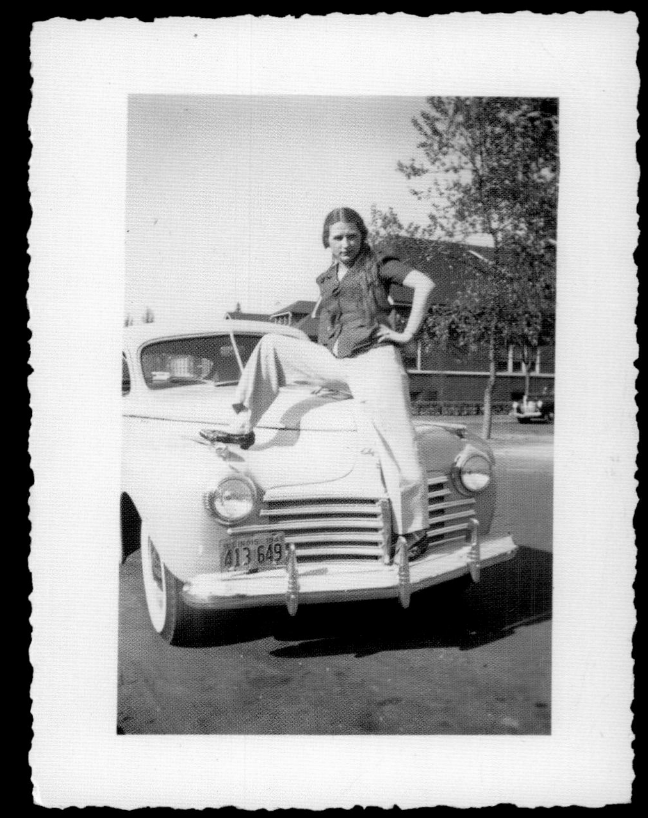

June "Aunty June" Savage Lucas

Mary Savage with daughter June Lucas on rear lawn of 8023 Marquette Avenue, Chicago, Illinois

Mary Savage with daughter June Lucas and grandsons Michael Savage on left and Clyde "Duke" Davis on rear lawn of 8023 Marquette Avenue, Chicago, Illinois

June Savage Lucas on the road

June Savage Lucas standing in front of home at 7134 Sacramento Avenue, Chicago, Illinois

JUNE JULIA SAVAGE LUCAS b. August 7, 1911

Victor Lucas loved food, loved to cook (was a cook in the Army), and loved to eat.

Victor Lucas b. January 20, 1910, on the far right in the picture below, was an adopted child. On the far left are, it is believed, his adoptive parents, Julius and Olga Janelunas. The woman sitting in the swing is probably Julius's mother, Johanna, who was living with them at the time of the 1930 census. The census listed Victor as adopted.

June Savage Lucas with her nephew Michael D. Savage

Aunt June

June Savage Lucas, my mother's only sister, loomed large in my life. According to my mother, my aunt June ran away from home at seventeen years of age. My cousin Michael confirms this and adds that the man she left with was Fred Bass, who married June and took her to San Francisco, where he abandoned her. My mother claims that June first married Sheldon Morris, and I have found supporting records (Cook County Illinois Marriage Index) that the marriage took place November 5, 1930. My mother went on to say that June's second marriage was to a Rae Lamar and that he was a taxi driver; however, I have found no information to confirm this event. Her third marriage was to Victor Lucas. They were married February 15, 1943, in Chicago, Cook County, Illinois. This was his first marriage and rather late in life.

Despite my aunt June's several marriages, she never had children of her own, so it was not unusual for her to gravitate to the children of others, specifically those of her sister and brothers. Aunt June and Uncle Vic were financially better off than most in the family, and were in a position to provide a secure and supportive environment for those youngsters of need.

June Savage Lucas with collection of Venetian glass clowns. She was also an avid collector of miniature shoes in a variety of materials — bronze, ceramic, glass, wood, etc. She had hundreds of them on display in her home.

June Savage Lucas with her nephew Clyde "Duke" Davis

June Savage Lucas with her nephew Paul Savage

It was their nephews, "boys being boys," who received the most help — namely me and my cousin Paul. I can't recall either of their nieces, my sister June (Tootsie), Mary Lou, or Pattie Sue, children of my aunt's brother John, ever in their care.

Most surmised, myself included, that my aunt married my uncle not because he was the most handsome of men or most charming, but because he was generous to a fault, kind to her when others were not, and he adored her with a deep and abiding love. She loved nice things and my uncle loved giving them to her. My aunt was an attractive woman, well figured and fun to be around, and if she did not love my uncle initially as much as he loved her, that surely changed over the years. One only has to read the letters she wrote late in her life to know how much she loved him and missed him after he was gone. In the end she loved him so much she couldn't live without him.

Aunt June worked mostly as a waitress in fairly popular restaurants, among them the Black Angus and the Tropical Hut, which was located on 43rd and Lake Shore Drive in Chicago.

She collected shoes. No, not the wearable kind, but miniature figurine shoes of all types and styles — ceramic, silver, gold, and wooden shoes. Bronzed baby shoes, shoes in the form of cups you drink from, shoes as ashtrays or worn as charms, earrings, or pendants. Whatever their form or purpose, you name it, she had them in her collection.

She also collected Venetian Glass clowns, and many were gifts from my uncle. But she was most fond of her jukebox filled with two hundred records, a veritable library of favorite songs and artists, that my uncle gave her. She loved clothes, new homes, and cars. Each year, when they lived in Wisconsin, he would buy her a new Chrysler Imperial car.

My uncle was happy to comply with her wishes and worked mightily to please her. As I recall, they began with a renovation of my grandmother's house at 8545 Marquette Avenue and upon completion of the work, they convinced my grandmother to sell the house and divide their gains appropriately. This being their grubstake, June and Victor Lucas purchased a newly constructed home at 7134 Sacramento Avenue, Chicago and my grandmother moved to 8543 Mackinaw in the "Bush." Almost immediately my uncle began to improve their new home by removing the wall between the living and dining rooms and expanding the space. Other projects soon followed, including tiling the kitchen, all under the direction of my aunt.

Having contracted infectious hepatitis, or yellow jaundice as it was called then, I was hospitalized at Bob Roberts Hospital at the University of Chicago Clinic, where my aunt visited me often. I had just started high school, but missed so much of the first semester due to my illness it was determined that I would, after being released from the hospital, stay with Aunt June and Uncle Vic until the next semester began. It was at the Sacramento Avenue home that I truly became acquainted with them and familiar with the life they led. Happily and thankfully, it included me.

Uncle Vic

Victor Lucas was born January 20, 1910. According to the 1930 U.S. census, State of Illinois, County Cook, Victor, age sixteen, was enumerated on April 10, 1930, with Julius, age forty-two, and Olga Janelunas, age thirty-two. They owned their own home at 6338 South Mozart Street, Chicago, Illinois, and had been married approximately five years. Julius and Olga were born in Lithuania as were their parents. According to the census, Julius Janelunas immigrated to the United States in 1910 and his spouse in 1903. Julius was employed as a retail auto dealer and Olga as a stenographer in auto sales. Living with them was Johanna Janelunas, age sixty-five, and mother of Julius. Victor Lucas was listed as an adopted son. His place of birth was given as Illinois.

I enjoyed being with them. My uncle took me everywhere he went, whether it was doing simple chores around the house, going to work with him on his rounds collecting coins from jukeboxes throughout the city, or accompanying them on their vacations. Uncle Vic was handy and proud of his collection of tools. During my rehabilitation from hepatitis at my aunt and uncle's, I continued working on a model car, a project I had begun before my hospitalization. I was participating in the GM Fisher Body Craftsmen's Guild competition to design and build a model of a future car. One day when my aunt and uncle were out of the house, I went down to my uncle's workshop, fired up his table saw, and proceeded to trim excess wood from a block of balsa, creating the shape of a car. I had turned the car on its top, directing it into the circular saw blade. Suddenly, the block of wood flipped, pulling my left guiding hand into the blade, catching my hand between my small finger and ring finger, nearly severing the small finger. Clutching my bloody hand, I ran next

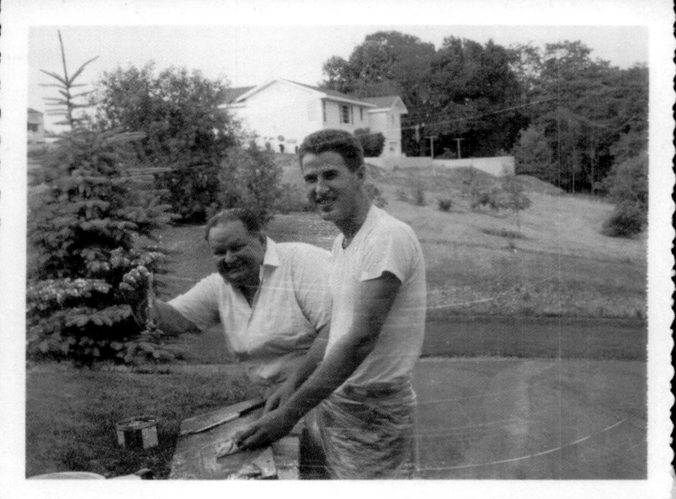

Victor Lucas and Paul Savage

door for help and was taken to a doctor's office where my finger was stitched up. I had severed the tendons in my finger and even now cannot close it fully. However, I did manage to complete my model car and won an honorable mention.

Ultimately the House on Sacramento Avenue in Chicago was sold, and they purchased a home in Twin Lakes, Wisconsin.

1973 FEB BANQUET
TWIN LAKES POST
544
VILLAGE INN

Uncle Vic helped
me alot.
Paulo 2001

This entailed a commute by train for Uncle Vic to his job in Chicago. I was frequently in their company, and I would spend weekends in Twin Lakes and commute on Monday mornings to Chicago with my uncle. He was a big man who liked to eat. We would have breakfast in his home, catch an early morning train and then have breakfast again when we arrived in Chicago at the train station. Often my uncle would spend several days in the city before returning to Twin Lakes, and I would be with him, during school vacations and holidays, going on his collections and sometimes sharing the "booty" — excess odd coins improperly put in the jukeboxes and other amusement machines.

Uncle Vic was a generous man. One winter evening a day or two before Christmas, I helped him assemble many baskets of food, candy, and toys for the less fortunate in Twin Lakes. We loaded up the car, and he drove from home to home in town, having me take a basket to each door, knock or ring the bell, and return to the car. When someone opened the door and saw the basket, he would reach out the window and wave to them, then we'd drive on to the next stop.

Uncle Vic served in the Army as a cook. He was a member of the American Legion post in Twin Lakes and was Grand Chef de Gare for 1965. The back of the picture on page 493 is stamped with the date "Oct 17 1964," yet the hat he was wearing definitely reads "Grand Chef de Gare 1965." It's possible that the photography studio's date stamp was set to the wrong year. The American Legion was the only organization that I ever knew he belonged to. Every year the American Legion sponsored, along with local merchants, an annual carnival in town. My uncle secured for me the assignment of hand lettering small posters for each of the merchant booth sponsors, who paid me $20 per poster. There were dozens that I produced, resulting in a sizable financial windfall for a teenager. After sixteen years in Twin Lakes, they sold their home and bought a place on Silverteen Way in Sarasota, Florida. I believe the motivating factor was my aunt's health and my uncle nearing retirement. Despite their love for one another, they often lived apart over many years. He, working in Chicago, staying in hotels and apartments, and she living in whatever home they owned at the time. Their final home was at 2312 Fairfield Avenue, Sarasota, Florida.

Various members of my family believe that my uncle worked for the "mob" or "outfit." When he expressed a desire to retire from his career in coin-operated phonographs and amusement games, there was a disagreement between him and his employers about him getting some sort of payment. He wanted to be paid for his jukebox route. They claimed it was their route and not his to sell. Supposedly, he countered that he knew of criminal activity, which he was prepared to share with the authorities. Two weeks after this dispute, he was shot in the thigh, going to his car in a garage on George Street in Chicago. He did not get his money. He left Chicago practically penniless. My aunt and uncle spent their last two years, finally together, in Sarasota, Florida. Those weren't the best of years, for Uncle Vic suffered a stroke a year after retiring and Aunt June (she was a heavy smoker most of her life) had vascular and colon surgery.

He died November 25, 1978. Aunt June committed suicide five months after her beloved Vic left her so alone.

June's brother, Mike Savage, settled their estate. Mike then called his son Michael Jr. for help. Michael was living in San Francisco at the time and was an attorney. They had to dispose of Vic's and June's belongings before the Sarasota house could be put up for sale. In the attic of that home were all of Vic's tools, assembled from years during various home improvement projects — tools that served him so well in happier times. Getting the table saws, belt sanders, and such out of an attic posed quite an ordeal, the only access being a spring loaded ladder from the ceiling, so they engaged a local tool rental company to remove everything. The house in Sarasota was sold, as well as an empty lot in Twin Lakes, Wisconsin, which they had owned for years. The properties were mortgaged to the hilt. There was little left to distribute to the remaining family.

June Savage Lucas in happier times in her Sarasota, Florida, home. Her death, a suicide, on April 21, 1979, took place just five months after the passing of her beloved husband, Vic. Despondent, she wrote to me of her loss December 18, 1978, "this is unreal to me at this time and I hope the Dear Lord takes me so I can be with my Darling. I can't believe he's gone, 35 years of Love...."

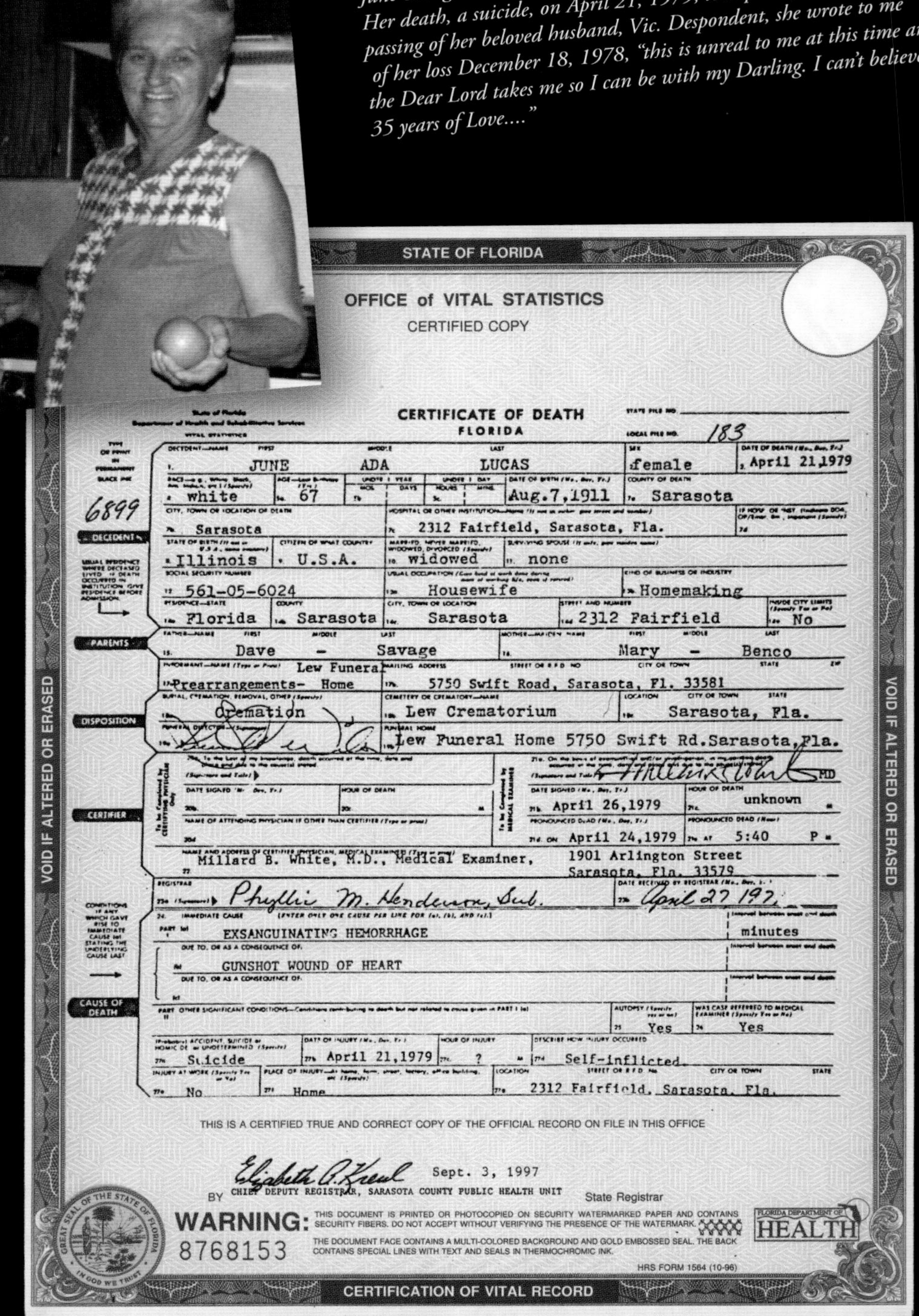

STATE OF FLORIDA

OFFICE of VITAL STATISTICS

CERTIFIED COPY

VOID IF ALTERED OR ERASED

CERTIFICATE OF DEATH
FLORIDA

LOCAL FILE NO. 183

6899

DECEDENT
1. JUNE ADA LUCAS
2. female
3. April 21,1979
4. white
5a. 67
6. Aug.7,1911
7. Sarasota
8. Sarasota
2312 Fairfield, Sarasota, Fla.
9. Illinois
U.S.A.
10. widowed
11. none
12. 561-05-6024
13a. Housewife
Homemaking
14a. Florida
14b. Sarasota
14c. Sarasota
14d. 2312 Fairfield
14e. No

PARENTS
15. Dave - Savage
16. Mary - Benco

17. Lew Funeral Prearrangements- Home
17b. 5750 Swift Road, Sarasota, Fl. 33581

DISPOSITION
18a. Cremation
18b. Lew Crematorium
18c. Sarasota, Fla.
19b. Lew Funeral Home 5750 Swift Rd.Sarasota,Fla.

CERTIFIER
MD
21b. April 26,1979
21c. unknown
21d. on April 24,1979
21e. at 5:40 P.M.
22. Millard B. White, M.D., Medical Examiner, 1901 Arlington Street Sarasota, Fla. 33579

23a. Phyllis M. Henderson, Sub.
23b. April 27 197

CAUSE OF DEATH
24. Part I (a) EXSANGUINATING HEMORRHAGE — minutes
(b) GUNSHOT WOUND OF HEART
25. Yes
26. Yes
27a. Suicide
27b. April 21,1979
27c. ?
27d. Self-inflicted
27e. No
27f. Home
27g. 2312 Fairfield, Sarasota, Fla.

THIS IS A CERTIFIED TRUE AND CORRECT COPY OF THE OFFICIAL RECORD ON FILE IN THIS OFFICE

Sept. 3, 1997

BY CHIEF DEPUTY REGISTRAR, SARASOTA COUNTY PUBLIC HEALTH UNIT State Registrar

WARNING: THIS DOCUMENT IS PRINTED OR PHOTOCOPIED ON SECURITY WATERMARKED PAPER AND CONTAINS SECURITY FIBERS. DO NOT ACCEPT WITHOUT VERIFYING THE PRESENCE OF THE WATERMARK.

8768153

THE DOCUMENT FACE CONTAINS A MULTI-COLORED BACKGROUND AND GOLD EMBOSSED SEAL. THE BACK CONTAINS SPECIAL LINES WITH TEXT AND SEALS IN THERMOCHROMIC INK.

FLORIDA DEPARTMENT OF HEALTH

GREAT SEAL OF THE STATE OF FLORIDA IN GOD WE TRUST

HRS FORM 1564 (10-96)

CERTIFICATION OF VITAL RECORD

Michael David Szávics/Savage b. February 27, 1914

Written on the back of this photo of Michael Savage Sr. with his son Michael Jr. is "Mike & his Boy, had his hair cut."

Michael David Szávics/Savage, father of Michael David Savage Jr.

Michael David Savage Jr.

Michael David Savage b. February 27, 1914

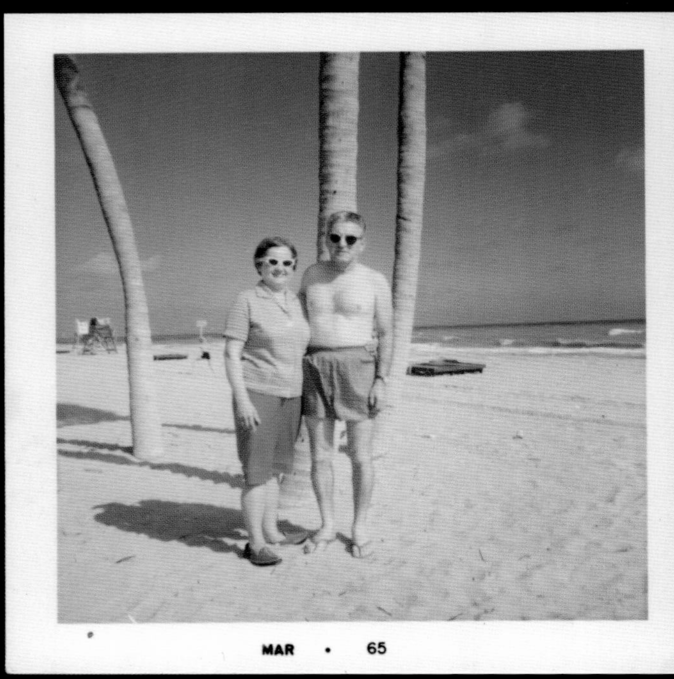

Mike and Ella Savage at the beach in photo dated March 1965. This is one of my favorite photos in the book. Its sheer starkness, half sky, half beach and a wedge of ocean barely disecting the two, with three palm trees, trunks devoid of their fronds, more like telephone poles than trees — all, including my aunt, fully dressed, contribute to the "nakedness" of my uncle, as white as the driven snow, standing in the center of this typically white frame '60s photo.

Michael Savage Jr. playing the accordion. Written on the back of the picture is "This is Michael, my son, a wonderful boy." As a young adult, he would later form the Mike Savage Quintet, playing jazz clubs such as the Birdhouse, Mr. Kelly's, and London House in Chicago.

Michael David Savage and his wife Ellen "Ella" Scrip Savage at their 50th wedding anniversary celebration. They were married August 15, 1938.

Mária "Mary" Benkó Szávics/Savage with Michael Savage Jr.

Aichael D. Savage, Class of '57
At. Carmel High School, Chicago

Of all my cousins, at least those I had contact with as a youngster, it was Michael who appeared destined for promise and prosperity. Michael, born June 22, 1939, was an only child. As such, his parents, Mike and Ella, spared no expense raising him. Both worked, intent that their son have it all.

His father was a common laborer who had an aptitude for math, and at mid-careeer had positions as an inspector of steel plate, measuring the metal with a Vernier caliper, and in quality control of steel axles for cars. Mike Sr. spent forty-two years working in various shifts at the nill and retired at age sixty-two with a pension.

Michael's mom, Ella, also secured a job in the mill. This, of ourse, meant that Mike Jr. at seven or eight years of age became "latch-key kid." His mother worked as a file clerk in "tub" files nd, later, tracked production planning over a period of fifteen ears.

Michael Jr. attended Catholic schools and graduated in 957 from Mt. Carmel, an all boys, Catholic high school, located n the Woodlawn Neighborhood on the South Side of Chicago. s a Carmelite in his sophomore year, feeling a call to the riesthood, Micheal attended the Mt. Carmel Prep Seminary in Jiagara Falls, Ontario.

Michael enjoyed competitive sports and was highly touted s a promising Frosh lightweight football player, as described in is high school yearbook: "The fullback slot was held down by Aike Savage, one of the finest Freshman prospects ever to come o Carmel. It was Mike's hard running and plunging, plus his fine efense work that made him one of the mainstays of the team." Ie also participated in intramural sports, including basketball and andball.

Michael's parents rented various apartments on the outheast side of Chicago in neighborhoods that at the time were onsidered among the best in that part of the city. They resided at 9th and Phillips, 78th and Coles, 3440 North Lake Shore Drive, nd 10601 Avenue H on the east side.

Mike Jr., to me, was, privileged, gifted musically, athletic, a evout Catholic, and well-educated.

Mike and Nancy McGiveron Savage with their dog. Photo taken by me during my visit to their home March 29, 2004, in Mequon, Wisconsin, with my mother and Kay.

Mike received a scholarship to Notre Dame, though he didn't go there. He attended Loyola University, Chicago, another Catholic institution, and then joined the Navy. He had three year of law school while in the Navy and later worked as an attorney i a variety of places, including California, Colorado, New York, an Illinois.

Mike Savage, number 44, circled in picture below of the Carmel "Lights" lightweight football team

N RAYMOND SAVAGE b. August 8, 191

John Savage with, from left to right, his sister June Lucas, wife Dorothy, and daughter Mary Lou

Dorothy, wife of John Savage, and Mary Savage holding grandson Clyde "Duke" Davis

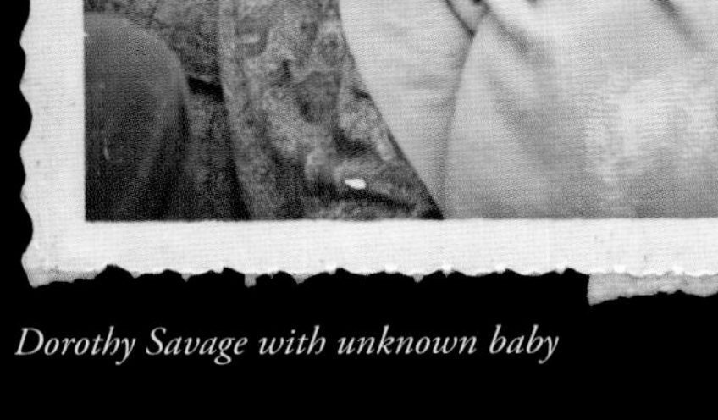

Dorothy Savage with unknown baby

Binion's HORSESHOE CLUB
DOWNTOWN LAS VEGAS

The 'Bright Spot' on the world's brightest 2 blocks, features the most unique display seen anywhere; $1,000,000.00 in cash. One hundred $10,000 bills encased in an 8 foot golden horseshoe. Long famed for 'Fast Action', the new beautiful Horseshoe Hotel and Casino is now considered the "Showplace of Casino Center." The popular new Sombrero Room features the most authentic Mexican food in Las Vegas.

273626

ADDRESS

Kodak
PLACE STAMP HERE
Paper

taken 4/5-73

nna Benko, wife of John Benko with nephew John "Johnny" avage. Johnny was the son of John Benko's sister, Mary Benko Savage.

My uncle and aunt John and Dorothy Savage with me, "Duke," in the living room of their home in Las Vegas, Nevada, around 1969

As of 2007, Paul Savage lives in San Francisco, California, with his two dogs. He is divorced and works as a "garden maker." He has a living sister, Patti Sue Savage, and a sister (actually a cousin), Wendy, adopted by her grandparents, Dorothy and John Savage, after her parents died. Wendy lives in Las Vegas, Nevada, and works as an occupational drug manager for Psychomedics, Inc. She married Emron Falahi, April 14, 1996.

Paul Savage in photo dated November 5, 1950 on back

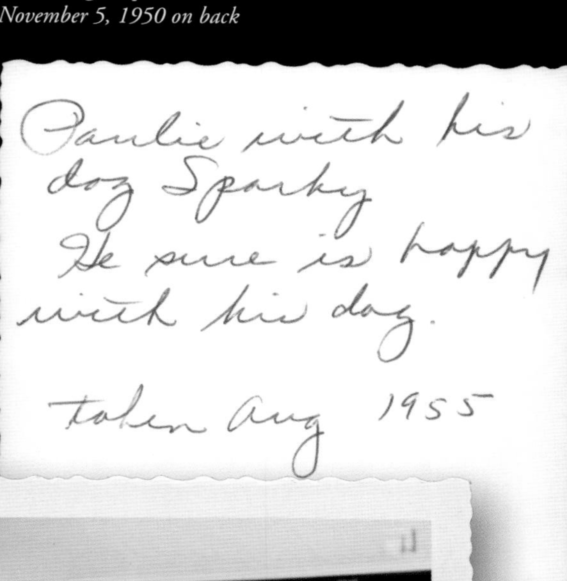

Paulie with his
dog Sparky
He sure is happy
with his dog.
taken Aug 1955

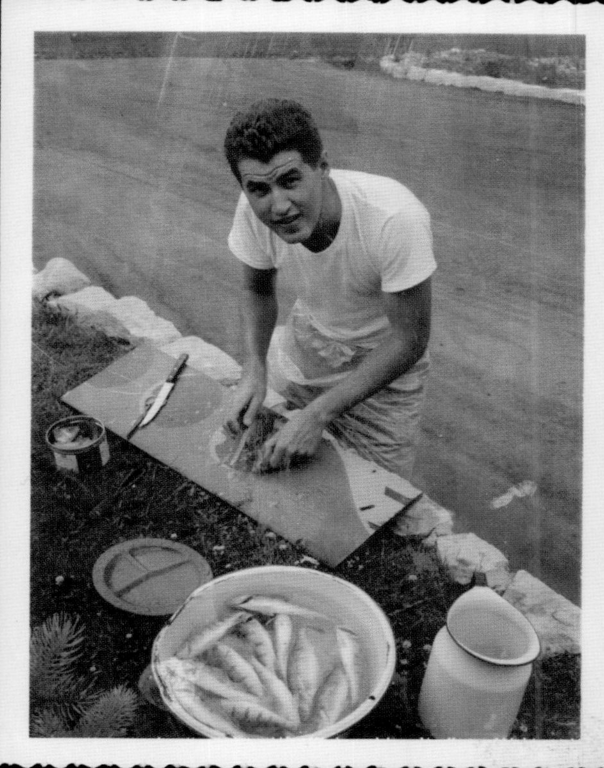

Paul Savage cleaning fish

Paul Savage and his wife Nicky. Photo taken by me at their home in San Francisco before the birth of their son, Jesse (b. 1973). Paul loved his Pembroke Welsh Corgi. In later years, he had two, "Boogie" and "Woogie."

John Raymond Savage Family

This is mother and Johnnie's little girl, she is a darling you would love her.

over

508

Chicagó 1956 = február 12

Szeretet drága jó testvérem és sógornőm az levelet meg az karácsonyi ... meg kaptam aminek ... örül-tem és meg értetem ...

jöni hogy én it vagyok és az is bán Aja az Dartit de én nem bánom én nem szólok semit mert én nem akarok trabet és az gyerekek jól vanak az Pál már második éve megy hájszkulba és az Marylu az 4 gerdba van nagyon aranyosak én nagyon szeretem őket és ő esztis ivegyli látam vóla és majd haza megy... ek marczi usba már az tavaszi hónapba de it akartam ...

telefon szám ... az Majk telefon száma ... 4-7179 Most kint voltam az kis Jhani val rajzolni meg az kis lány mutata Mind azokat az klabokat ahol gemliznek

... tek magatokat és majd megint fogok írni és halesz idöd irjál

Mary Savage
431 St 16 PX
Las Vegas Nev

LAS VEGAS FEB 15 11 AM 1956 NEV.

AIR MAIL 6¢

Ms John Benko
25-02 Steinway St
Long Island
City 3 N.Y.

*ary Lou Savage in photo dated
ovember 5, 1950, on back*

*Mary Lou Savage in photo
dated November 1955 on back*

*etter at left from Mary Savage, 431 So. 16th St. Las Vegas, Nevada, to John
enko, 25-02 Steinway St., Long Island City 3 N.Y., postmarked in Las
egas Feb. 13, 1956, and Chicago Feb. 12, 1956, reads in part as follows.
he letter's spelling, punctuation, and grammar are exactly as received in
oltan Zorandy's translation.*

y dear beloved brother and sister-n-law,
received the letter and the Christmas Card which made me very appy and I understood all the contents and I am very sorry your ere ill but thanks the good Lord that you now feel better I felt uite well for a while but yesterday I has pains again but now it is etter and miss the children a lot but I'll stay here while it is cold ome John is a very good son but his wife is very jealous she just an't accept that he loves me, you know how it is, but this does ot bother me, she'll be mother-in-law eventually, too, and get her wn share and now that I'm here she is too ashamed to act like he used to, she wants to become a rich lady, this boy works like a og and is getting nowhere but she does not care because she just eeps hugging and kissing him he thinks that this is everything, I an't help that but he'll learn when his wife gets old.... but I ask he good Lord to help him and turn his luck around they like very ery much at his job. He is a good worker works all the time,... e children are fine Paul is in second grade in high school and arylou is in 7th grade they're very sweet and I love them dearly ut she is jealous about that, I can see it, I'll go home in March at's spring already but I wanted to stay here till it gets very warm hich is very difficult, here it is very pleasant weather it's not hot o snow or rain I would love to have all the kids here.... I was out or a ride with Johnny, the little girl showed all the gambling clubs ow many crazy folks are there losing their money but that's how e world is and the children there all OK my Mariska visits home o do the cleaning and Dezsó works....
kiss you both many times
our loving sister and sister-in-law Mariska
nd may the good Lord grant you good health and I'll write again

Mary Lou Savage Receives Scholarship

AWARD WINNER

The newly established "Christian Leadership" award of the Catholic Daughters of America went to Miss Mary Lou Savage, right, on her graduation from the St. Joseph's Parochial School. Mrs. George Schwartz, grand regent of the CDA, made the presentation

To encourage education in the Catholic schools, the Catholic Daughters of America, Court Ave Maria, has inaugurated a "Christian Leadership" award, which was presented this spring for the first time. The honor of being the first recipient went to Miss Mary Lou Savage upon her graduation from the eighth grade of the St. Joseph's Parochial School. The award was presented by Mrs. George Schwartz, grand regent of the CDA, at commencement exercises held in the school patio Tuesday evening.

As the outstanding girl student from the school, Miss Savage received a certificate from the women's organization and a scholarship of $50 to be used toward tuition for enrollment next fall at the Bishop Gorman High School.

Miss Savage is the only daughter of Mr. and Mrs. John Savage, 1910 E. Charleston Blvd. She moved with her family from Chicago to Las Vegas two years ago. She has been active in student functions while a student at St. Joseph's. She organized the school talent show last fall and served as mistress of ceremonies at the CYO Talent Show. She also is an active member of St. Bridget's Catholic Church Choir. Her ambition upon completing her education is to become a teacher.

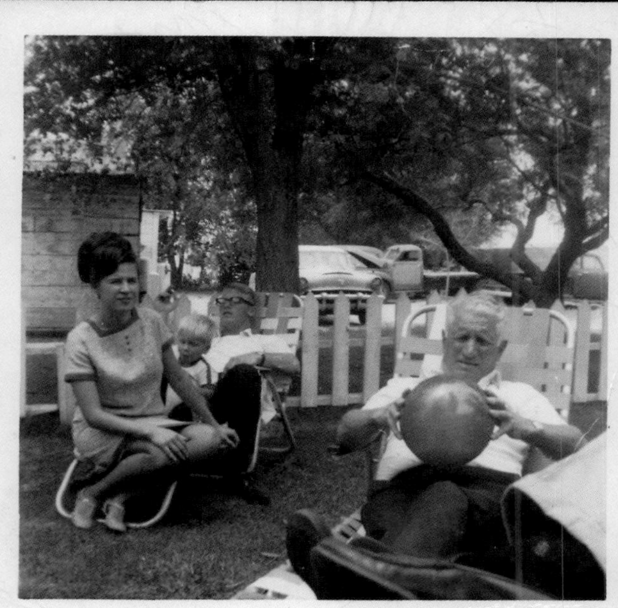

Mary Lou Savage Johnson seated on chaise with her son, James John "Jimmy John," and her husband, James Arthur Johnson. On far right is her father-in-law. On July 25, 1974, Mary Lou, her son, and husband were all tragically killed when their pick-up truck left a mountainside road. Their daughter, Wendy Louise, b. April 14, 1968, was the only

János "John" Benkó b. May 27, 1889

A Journey Taken

Those who scan the pages of this book might wonder why someone so devoted to the subject of fatherhood and finding his own father would review the life of another man, his great-uncle, John Benko. John Benko and his wife Anna Arendes never had children.

I met my great uncle John Benko on perhaps only two occasions. One time was when I was young, and he visited Chicago and my grandmother Mary Benko Savage, his sister. The only thing that I recall of our first meeting was that he brought with him a large set of kitchen knives. This impressed me as a young boy, especially when I learned that he had made them himself. My uncle was a machinist from the Naval Yard in Brooklyn, New York.

When I left the University of Illinois as a junior during the summer of 1959, having run out of money and doing poorly scholastically, I left Chicago to begin a career in advertising in New York City. Somehow, I don't recall exactly, I made contact with my great uncle John and aunt Anna. I remember them coming to New York and taking me with them to Astoria, Queens, where I met an elderly woman, still unknown to me, in her kitchen. My memory of that meeting is of one detail, that this woman had covered her kitchen floor with newspapers. My mother, after scrubbing our kitchen linoleum floor at home (on her hands and knees) would cover it, too, with newspapers. This was done, I believe, to keep the floor clean for a few days, until the newspapers were tattered and had to be removed, thereby extending the time until the next scrubbing. I have no idea if this was an American trait or a practice of immigrants and their offspring brought from the old country. Both these women were Hungarian.

Though our meeting was brief, John and Anna were warm and welcoming and more than willing to help me get settled in New York.

As the letter at the right indicates, in my rush to leave New York to get married, I needed a "gentle reminder" to repay them for shipping my belongings back to me.

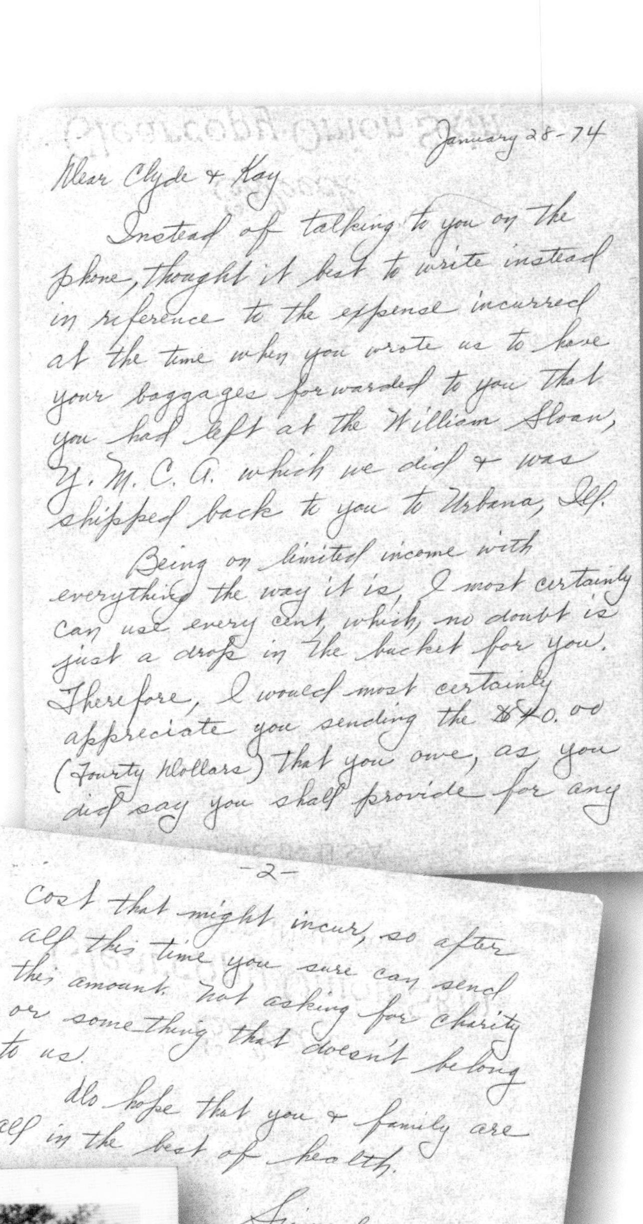

January 28-74

Dear Clyde & Kay

Instead of talking to you on the phone, thought it best to write instead in reference to the expense incurred at the time when you wrote us to have your baggages forwarded to you that you had left at the William Sloan, Y.M.C.A. which we did & was shipped back to you to Urbana, Ill.

Being on limited income with everything the way it is, I most certainly can use every cent, which, no doubt is just a drop in the bucket for you. Therefore, I would most certainly appreciate you sending the $40.00 (Fourty Dollars) that you owe, as you did say you shall provide for any

-2-

cost that might incur, so after all this time you sure can send this amount. Not asking for charity or something that doesn't belong to us.

Do hope that you & family are all in the best of health.

Sincerely

Mrs John Benko
Hayward Ave
Mt Sinai, L.I., N.Y.
11766

Caption on back of photo reads: "May 6, 1934 Anna and John Benko just before married" written in Anna Benko's hand, as is the case with most of these pictures.

János "John" Benkó b. May 27, 1889

Caption on back of photo at right reads: "Jones Beach Anna and John Benko before married"

The Stuff of Life

János "John" Benkó was born May 27, 1889, in Felsötárkány, Hungary. He was the younger brother of my grandmother, Maria Benkó Savage. He immigrated to the United States on October 28, 1907, probably following the lead of my grandfather, Andreso Dezsó Savich (Savage), who was first to come to the United States on March 8, 1907. These two men preceded my grandmother's arrival, with her two children, Dezsó (Jr.) and József on June 30, 1909.

John Benko was, as was my grandfather, a machinist by trade, a skill highly valued in their new homeland. After only two years in this country, John was hired by the Standard Steel Car Company, located in Gary, Indiana. He was particularly well paid, according to his wife Anna. By 1913 he had petitioned for naturalization, seeking U.S. citizenship, and was sending money to his father, Mihály Máté Benkó in Hungary — beginning a pattern of largesse he would continue most of his adult life.

After two years in the Navy, serving on the USS *Minnesota*, he was discharged, purchasing his release, which was allowed at the time. His freedom was cut short, however, by being inducted into the Army April 19, 1918 to serve in World War I.

On November 25, 1930, at the beginning of the Great Depression, John Benko became a U.S. citizen.

In the 1930 census he was enumerated in New York, Queens, New York City: John Benko, thirty-eight years of age, single. His year of immigration was given as 1905 from Hungary, and he was employed as a machinist/paper press. He spoke Hungarian.

In 1933 John began employment in the Brooklyn, New York, Naval Shipyard. He remained working there until his retirement in 1957, a period of twenty-two years. He was also a member of the International Association of Machinists and Aerospace Workers and was honored in 1968 for fifty years of membership.

On the 14th of July 1934, John and Anna Arendas were married at St. Stephen of Hungary Parish, a Roman Catholic church, on East 82nd Street. Anna, born in Manhattan, was Hungarian on both sides of her family. They remained parishioners of St. Stephen's all their lives.

When I first began assembling material for this book, I was impressed with the photographs, letters, and other artifacts of a life lived. Always a gatherer of sorts, a record keeper, bereft of memory, I relied heavily on the visual flotsam and jetsam of life to remind me of what I'd done, with whom, where, and why. It's not surprising then that the collection of material I have gathered regarding John Benko, my great uncle on my mother's side, and his wife, Anna Arendas Benko, would have so much meaning to me. No one in this book presented me with as much documentation of their lives — from birth to death, as these two people.

I did not know them well.

Sometime in the summer of 1996, Anna Benko left a message on our answering machine. I had not heard from her for nearly twenty-five years. A return call to Anna brought me up to date. Uncle John had died in 1971. Anna remained in their home in Mt. Sinai, New York, after her husband's passing, but as she informed me, she was getting old and said, "I have all this stuff here, and when I go it will go with me." It was midsummer, a hot day, prearranged, that we spent with Anna at her home.

Anna didn't have any food in the house. Kay and I took her to the grocery store and bought groceries for her. We also picked up some peaches at the famous Davis Peach Farm, Wading River, Long Island, New York, which was less than a dozen miles from Anna's home in Mt. Sinai. The Davis Peach Farm had more than seventy varieties of peaches. We got a small bushel basket for Anna, with the residual to be passed around to her neighbors.

Alone, frail, and eighty-seven years of age, she had spent the last twenty-five years, or at least the latter part of that period, as something of a recluse. Her sister had died twenty years previously, and a niece living in Cleveland was moving to Arizona. She was estranged from her other relatives. Anna had become a hoarder. Shown about the house, we were struck by its clutter. Anna had price tags affixed to almost every object in the house. It may have been simply her keeping an inventory of items along with their respective value. Perhaps these were the remnants of a previous tag sale or sale to be? She showed us stacks and stacks of old newspapers, brown shopping bags, opening dresser drawers, revealing hats never worn, purchased decades ago, still with the original price tags, sacks of rotting potatoes. Many of the items were stored in her master bedroom. Kay recalls being struck by the contrast of an immaculately made double bed with perfectly pressed linens surrounded by this sea of clutter. I believe she never slept in it, probably since John had died. There was a sofa bed in the living room where she may have slept. Hanging outside on a line were Zip-lock plastic food storage bags held by clothespins, obviously clean and meant for re-use. The woman kept everything. Alone, clinging to a past she had so carefully preserved, she was frugal to a fault.

During our visit she passed on the stuff mentioned in her call to us. There were few family photographs she was willing to part with, mostly early school records, immigration papers, military, and work documents. We exchanged stories of relatives from the past and were grateful for her offerings.

We saw Anna again, after she had suffered a serious fall outdoors and was hospitalized. A neighbor called us. We visited Anna in the hospital, bringing her a robe and slippers purchased on the way. Anna, now nearly ninety years old, was overtly concerned, even paranoid, about family members anticipating her eventual passing, encroaching on her assets — bank accounts, personal possessions, and even her house. We learned later that family members had gained access through a kitchen window while she was hospitalized. As we conversed and walked slowly through the corridors of the hospital, she would hush me,

John and Anna Benko as I remember them during the summer of 1959, when I was living in New York City and they were so helpful to me.

implying others overhearing us would pass information on to those less trustworthy.

On this last visit to Long Island, we were allowed by a compassionate neighbor, the same person who had summoned us to her hospital bedside, entry to Anna's house to gather any remaining family documents or memorabilia. What Anna failed to provide before, we were now able to supplement from piles of letters and photographs strewn about, apparently of no value to those who had ransacked the house before us.

John Benko was a hard-working, caring, and generous man. Nearly all his adult life, he responded to the financial needs of family in the old country, while simultaneously addressing the concerns of family in this country.

If John was the benefactor, Anna served as his gatekeeper. She saved everything, much of which led me to my family abroad. Letters, money orders, promissory notes, in many instances, carefully annotated by Anna. This was a true treasure trove of information that allowed me to define the Benkó and Savage family trees. In 1998, after a bicycling vacation in the Czech Republic, we visited Hungary and those relatives and places Anna revealed to us.

Anna Arendas Benko passed on January 30, 1999, at age ninety, nearly twenty-eight years after her beloved John. His memory is now to be passed on to others through the efforts of a grateful grandnephew.

Mr. J Banko

Photograph of John Benko and Anna Arendas on their wedding day, July 14, 1934, at St. Stephen of Hungary Parish located at 404-414 East 82nd Street, New York, New York.

szám.
Numerus

FELSŐTÁRKÁNYI plébánia
EGRI Főegyházmegye
HEVES vármegye

FEL-NÉMETHI RÓM. KAT. EGYHÁZ PECSÉT

ILLETÉK 1000 FORINT

Keresztlevél

Alulírott ezennel hivatalosan bizonyítom, hogy a római katolikus anyaegyház kereszteltek anyakönyve ______ kötet 117 lapján az 1889 azaz ezer nyolcszáznyolcvankilencedik -ik év május hó huszonhetedik napjáról a következők foglaltatnak:

Folyószám *Numerus currens*		30
Éve, hava, napja *Annus, mensis, dies*	**a születésnek** *nativitatis*	1889. május 27
	a szent keresztség fölvételének *collati s. baptismi*	1889. május 28
A kereszteltnek *Baptisati*	**neve** *nomen*	JÁNOS
	neme *sexus* **fi** *mas*	fi
	leány *foemina*	—
	törvényes *legitimus (a)*	törvényes
	törvénytelen *illegitimus (a)*	—
A szülők *Parentum*	**vezeték- és kereszt-neve, vallása, állása és születéshelye** *nomen, religio, conditio et locus nativitatis*	BENKÓ MIHÁLY Rk. kovácsmester JÁSZÓ TÓTH JULIANNA RK. — Kis-Tállya
	lakóhelye *locus domicilii*	Felsőtárkány 56 sz.
A keresztszülők neve, vallása, állása és lakása *Nomen Patrinorum, eorum religio, conditio et locus habitationis*		Karanyicz Julia özvegy nő
A keresztelő lelkész neve és hivatala *Nomen et officium baptisantis*		Less Lajos helybeli lelkész
Észrevételek *Observationes*		

Rakt. sz. I. csop. 18. — Egyházmegyei Szent János-Nyomda, Eger. 43-2

Jelen adatok hitelességét nevem aláírásával és a plébánia egyház pecsétjével hivatalosan bizonyítom.

Kelt Felsőtárkány 1947. évi november hó 28 n.

Szabó József Béla
plébános

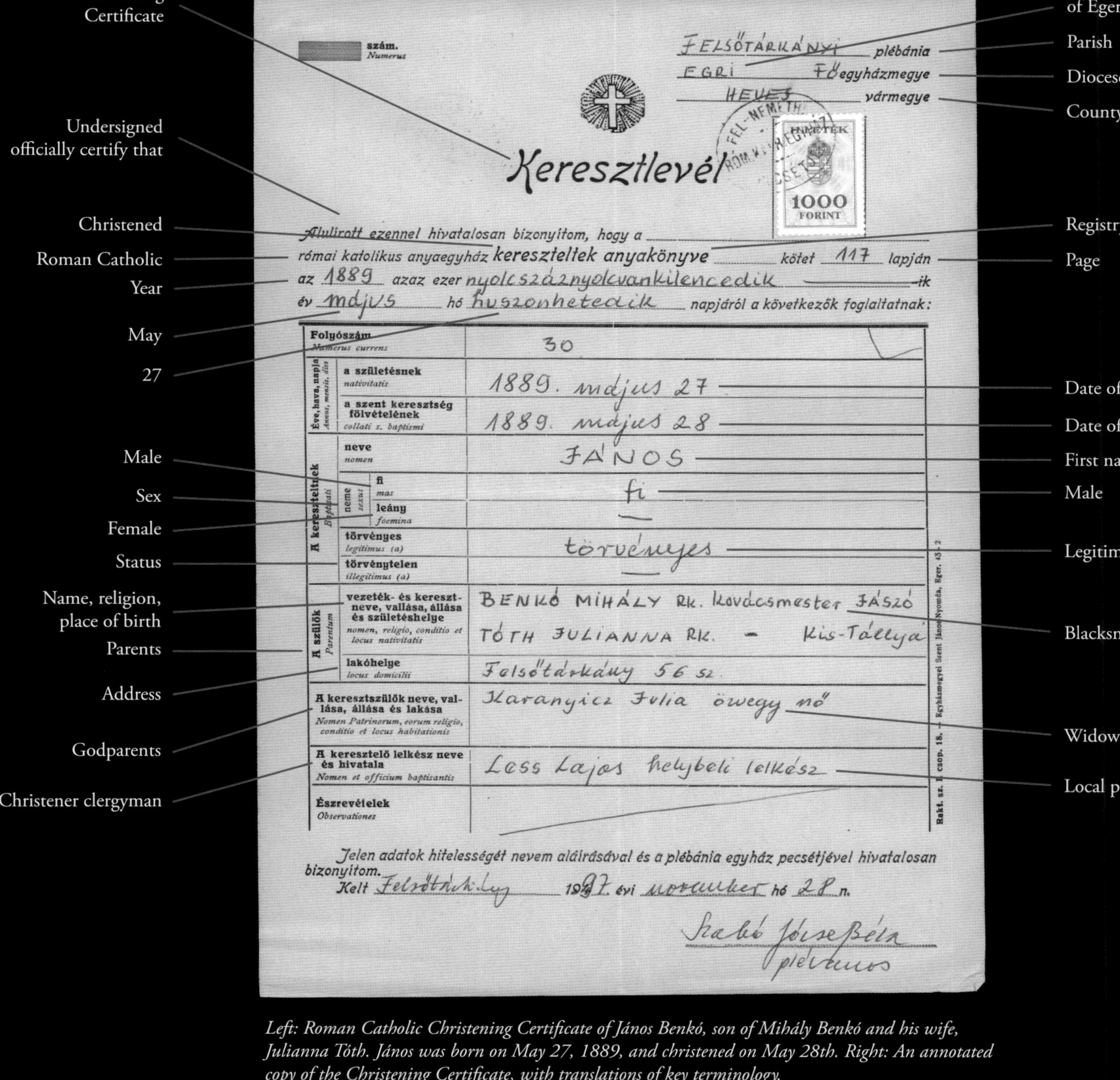

szám.
Numerus

FELSŐTÁRKÁNYI plébánia
EGRI Főegyházmegye
HEVES vármegye

Keresztlevél

Alulírott ezennel hivatalosan bizonyítom, hogy a római katolikus anyaegyház kereszteltek anyakönyve ______ kötet 117 lapján az 1889 azaz ezer nyolcszáznyolcvankilencedik ______-ik év május hó huszonhetedik napjáról a következők foglaltatnak:

Folyószám *Numerus currens*			30
Éve, hava, napja *Annus, mensis, dies*	a születésnek *nativitatis*		1889. május 27
	a szent keresztség fölvételének *collati s. baptismi*		1889. május 28
A kereszteltek *Baptisati*	neve *nomen*		JÁNOS
	neme *sexus*	fi *mas*	fi
		leány *foemina*	—
	törvényes *legitimus (a)*		törvényes
	törvénytelen *illegitimus (a)*		—
A szülők *Parentum*	vezeték- és kereszt-neve, vallása, állása és születéshelye *nomen, religio, conditio et locus nativitatis*		BENKÓ MIHÁLY RK. kovácsmester JÁSZÓ TÓTH JULIANNA RK. — Kis-Tállya
	lakóhelye *locus domicilii*		Felsőtárkány 56 sz.
A keresztszülők neve, vallása, állása és lakása *Nomen Patrinorum, eorum religio, conditio et locus habitationis*			Karanyicz Julia özvegy nő
A keresztelő lelkész neve és hivatala *Nomen et officium baptisantis*			Less Lajos helybeli lelkész
Észrevételek *Observationes*			

Rakt. sz. I. csop. 18. — Egyházmegyei Szent János Nyomda, Eger. 43-2

Jelen adatok hitelességét nevem aláírásával és a plébánia egyház pecsétjével hivatalosan bizonyítom.
Kelt Felsőtárkány 1947. évi november hó 28 n.

Szabó József Béla
plébános

Left: Roman Catholic Christening Certificate of János Benkó, son of Mihály Benkó and his wife, Julianna Tóth. János was born on May 27, 1889, and christened on May 28th. Right: An annotated copy of the Christening Certificate, with translations of key terminology.

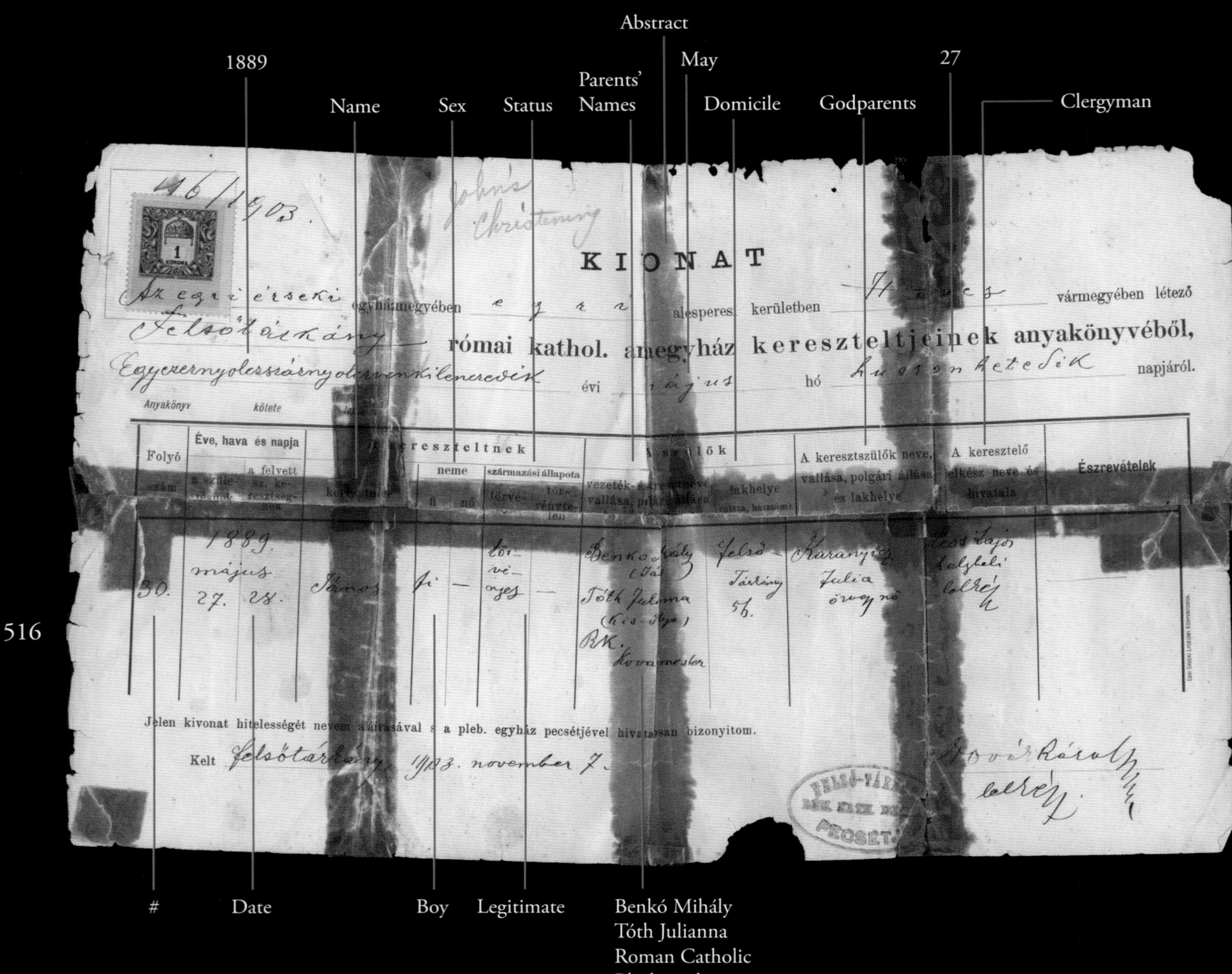

46/1903.

John's Christening

1 KORONA

KIVONAT

Az egri érseki egyházmegyében egri alesperesi kerületben Heves vármegyében létező Felsőtárkány római kathol. anyaegyház kereszteltjeinek anyakönyvéből, Egyezernyolcszáznyolcvankilencedik évi május hó huszonhetedik napjáról.

Anyakönyv kötete lap

Folyó szám	Éve, hava és napja: a születésnek	a felvett sz. keresztségnek	A kereszteltnek neve	neme: fi	neme: nő	származási állapota: törvényes	származási állapota: törvénytelen	A szülők vezeték- és keresztneve, vallása, polgári állása	lakhelye (utcza, házszám)	A keresztszülők neve, vallása, polgári állása és lakhelye	A keresztelő lelkész neve és hivatala	Észrevételek
30.	1889. május 27.	28.	János	fi	—	törvényes	—	Benkó Mihály (Ját) Tóth Julianna (Kis-Nya) RK. kovácsmester	Felső-Tárkány 56.	Karanyis Julia özvegy nő	[illegible] Lajos helybeli lelkész	

Jelen kivonat hitelességét nevem aláírásával s a pleb. egyház pecsétjével hivatalosan bizonyitom.

Kelt Felsőtárkány, 1903. november 7.

[illegible] Károly lelkész

FELSŐ-TÁRK... RÓM. KATH. ... PECSÉT...

Christening/Baptismal Certificate of János "John" Benkó b. May 27, 1899, indicating his father, Mihály Benkó and his mother, Julianna Tóth. The Certificate is dated November 7, 1903.

38. szám.

[Stamp: IPARTANODAI IGAZGATÓSÁG 1893]

John Benko learnt trade here — & this is report card

Értesitő.

Benkó János róm. Kath. vallású Kovács tanuló, született Felső-Tárkány 1889. évben május hó 27-én, az 1904/1905 tanévben az egri államilag segélyezett községi iparos-tanoncziskola B.) I-ső osztályában a következő osztályzatot nyerte:

		I. félév	II. félév
Erkölcsi magaviselete		Szab. szerü	Szab. szerü
Szorgalma		változó	Kellő
Hit- és erkölcstanban		jó	jó
Olvasás reáloktatással	földrajzban	jó	jó
	történelemben	jó	jó
	természettanban		
	vegytan- és technologiában		
	közgazdaságtanban		
Üzleti fogalmazásban és irásban		elégséges	elégséges
Iparszámvetésben		jó	jó
Könyvviteltanban			
Rajz	szabadkézi	elégséges	elégséges
	mértani	elégséges	elégséges
	szakbeli		
Általános osztályzata		elégséges	elégséges

Az I. félévben mulasztott ...... órát; ezekből kimentett ...... órát, ki nem mentett ...... órát. Az egész tanév alatt mulasztott 28 órát; ezekből kimentett 8 órát, ki nem mentett 20 órát.

Eger, 1905 év február 1-én és junius 20 n.

Horváth Lajos — oszt. főnök. Simon Imre — igazgató. Horváth Lajos — oszt. főnök.

Látta: Erdődy István mester. Látta: ...... mester.

Egri nyomda r.t. : 2166

1905 "School Report" (report card) for Trade School. "Writing skill quite bad" with a D average.

30 FILLÉR 1903

.... szám.

Előmeneteli napló szám: 56.
1901/902 tanév

Elemi népiskolai bizonyitvány.

Benkó János Felsőtárkányi születésü, *róm. kath.* vallású tanuló, született 18*89*-ik évben, a *Felsőtárkány*-i elemi népiskola *hatodik* osztályában előadott tantárgyakból általánosan *kitűnő* osztályzatot nyert.

Erkölcsi magaviselete: *dicséretes.*

Szorgalma: *ernyedetlen.*

Egyes tantárgyakban való előmenetele.

Hit- és erkölcstanban ... *kitűnő.*

Anyanyelvben:
- Beszéd- és értelemgyakorlatokban ... *o*
- Olvasásban ... *jeles.*
- Irásban ... *jeles.*
- Nyelvtanban és fogalmazásban ... *jeles.*

Számtanban és mértanban ... *kitűnő.*

Földrajzban ... *kitűnő.*

Történelemben és alkotmánytanban ... *kitűnő, kitűnő.*

Természetrajzban ... *kitűnő.*

Természettanban ... *kitűnő.*

Egészségtanban ... *o*

Éneklésben ... *kitűnő.*

Testgyakorlatban ... *jeles.*

Kertészeti gyakorlatokban ... *kitűnő.*

Rajzban ... *kitűnő.*

Irásbeli dolgozatainak külalakja ... *rendes.*

A mulasztott fél napok száma ... *kilencz.*

Ezekből igazolt ... *kilencz* fél napot.

Nem igazolt ... *o* fél napot.

Kelt *Felsőtárkányon 1903. November hó 11-én*

Novotny igazgató.

Novotny hitoktató.

Mentusz József osztálytanító.

RÓM. KATH. ... PECSÉTJE

EGRI ÉRSEKI LYCEUMI KÖNYVNYOMDA.

Kapható Szolcsányi Gyula Könyvkereskedésében Egerben.

János "John" Benkő's school report, as Anna Benko notes in pencil in the right corner. John was 14 in November 1903, and obviously an excellent student. For example, he received a grade of "jeles," meaning

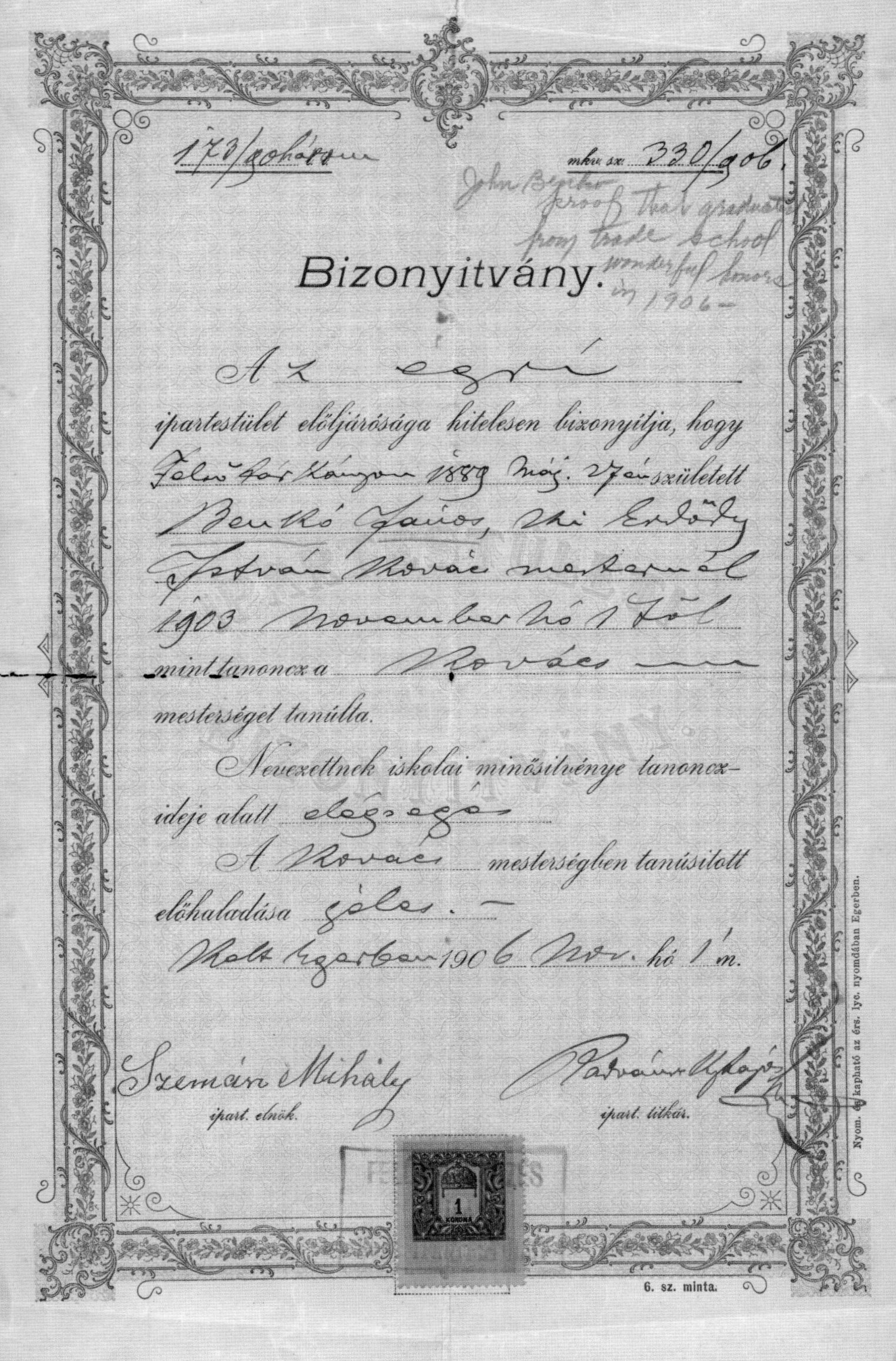

173/[illegible] mkv. sz. 330/906.

John Benko proof that graduated from trade school wonderful honors in 1906—

Bizonyitvány.

Az egri ipartestület elöljárósága hitelesen bizonyitja, hogy Felsőtárkányon 1889 máj. 27én született Benkó János, aki Erdődy István kovács mesternél 1903 november hó 1től mint tanoncz a kovács mesterséget tanúlta.

Nevezettnek iskolai minősitvénye tanoncz-ideje alatt elégséges.

A kovács mesterségben tanúsitott előhaladása jeles.

Kelt Egerben 1906 Nov. hó 1-én.

Szemán Mihály
ipart. elnök.

[illegible]
ipart. titkár.

1 Korona

Nyom. és kapható az érs. lyc. nyomdában Egerben.

6. sz. minta.

Certificate testifying that János Benkó had become a "Kovach" master toolmaker (blacksmith). Handwritten pencil notation at top reads, "John Benko proof that graduated from trade school wonderful honors in 1906."

Form 526

CERTIFICATE OF ARRIVAL—FOR NATURALIZATION PURPOSES

(For use of aliens arriving in United States after June 29, 1906. To be issued immediately prior to petitioning for naturaliz

Serial No. 749

NOTE TO CLERK OF COUR
Insert the above serial num
duplicate petition at the point
and immediately above the line
tificate "Declaration of Intentio
Serial No.............
tificate of Arrival from the Depa
Commerce and Labor, filed this...
19....."

Department of Commerce and Labor

IMMIGRATION SERVICE

PORT OF New York, Jan. 4, 1913

78436-S/749607

The immigration records at this port show the following as to the alien named below:

Name of alien: Benko, Janos

Date of arrival: Oct. 28, 1907

Name of vessel: *Ultonia

Line. Cunard

(Title) Acting Commissioner

11—4391

*Or railroad company, or any other conveyance.

6

Both my grandmother Mary Benkó Savage and her brother John Benkó came to the United States on the Ultonia, *departing from the port of Fiume, Italy. At various times Fiume was part of Austria, Hungary, and Italy, and following World War II it became part of Yugoslavia. Now it is part of Croatia and is known as Rijeka/Fiume.* *(See photo of the ship* Ultonia *on page 478.)*

There are minor discrepancies in the documents shown here. On the Certificate of Arrival above, the date of John's arrival is October 28, 1907. On the Declaration of Intention on the next page, it says he "… emigrated to the United States of America from Fiume, Hungary…" instead of Italy, and arrived "… on or about the 25th day of October, anno Domini 1907…."

No. 6275

Form 2203

TRIPLICATE
[To be given to the person making the Declaration]

UNITED STATES OF AMERICA

Department of Commerce and Labor

BUREAU OF IMMIGRATION AND NATURALIZATION

DIVISION OF NATURALIZATION

DECLARATION OF INTENTION

(Invalid for all purposes seven years after the date hereof)

United States of America }
District of Indiana } ss:

In the United States District Court of Hammond, Indiana.

I, John Benko, aged 21 years, occupation finisher, do declare on oath that my personal description is: Color white, complexion dark, height 5 feet 5 inches, weight 160 pounds, color of hair black, color of eyes brown other visible distinctive marks scar on side of left thumb; I was born in Felsotrokwoy, Hungary. on the 27th day of May, anno Domini 1889; I now reside at Fields Ave., Hammond, Indiana. I emigrated to the United States of America from Fiume, Hungary on the vessel Ultonia [If the alien arrived otherwise than by vessel, the character of conveyance or name of transportation company should be given.]; my last foreign residence was Felsotrokwoy, Hungary It is my bona fide intention to renounce forever all allegiance and fidelity to any foreign prince, potentate, state, or sovereignty, and particularly to Francis Joseph Apostolic King of Hungary, of which I am now a subject; I arrived at the port of New York, in the State of New York on or about the 25th day of October, anno Domini 1907; I am not an anarchist; I am not a polygamist nor a believer in the practice of polygamy; and it is my intention in good faith to become a citizen of the United States of America and to permanently reside therein: SO HELP ME GOD.

John Benko
(Original signature of declarant.)

Subscribed and sworn to before me this 24th day of September, anno Domini 1910.

[SEAL.]

Noble C. Butler,
Clerk of the United States District Court.

By Charles L. Surprise, Deputy Clerk.

Three years after his arrival at Ellis Island, New York, John Benko declared his intention of becoming a citizen of the United States. He was living in Hammond, Indiana, and working at the Standard Steel Car

PETITION FOR NATURALIZATION

...strict Court of The United States for the District of Indiana. hereby filed, respectfully showeth:

... Benko

496 Merrill Ave, Hammond, Indiana (Give number, street, city or town, and State.)

Machinist

May, anno Domini 1889, at Felsotarkany, Hungary

...f Fiume, Hungary, on or about the 5th day of October

from New York, on the 28th day of October

...ted States, at the port of

...ltoona (If the alien arrived otherwise than by vessel, the character of conveyance or name of transportation company should be given.)

... a citizen of the United States on the 24th day of September, anno Domini 1910

...Indiana, in the United States District Court of District of Indiana

~~She was born~~

~~...'s name is~~

..., and now resides at ... (Give number, street, city or town, and State.)

...and place of birth, and place of residence of each of said children is as follows:

...

...pposed to organized government or a member of or affiliated with any organization or body of persons teaching disbelief in or opposed ...nist nor a believer in the practice of polygamy. I am attached to the principles of the Constitution of the United States, and it is my ... States and to renounce absolutely and forever all allegiance and fidelity to any foreign prince, potentate, state, or sovereignty, and ...eror of Austria and Apostolic King of Hungary of whom at this time I am a subject, and it is my intention

... language.

...the United States of America for the term of five years at least, immediately preceding the date of this petition, to wit, since the ... anno Domini 1907 and in the State of Indiana, continuously next preceding the date of this ... July, anno Domini 1909 being a residence within this State of at least one year next preceding the date of this

...tition for citizenship to any court. ~~(I made petition for citizenship to the ... Court of~~ ..., anno Domini 1..., and the ... at ..., on the ... day of ...

~~...r the following reasons and causes, to wit, ..., and the cause of such denial has since been cured or removed.)~~

...is petition are my declaration of intention to become a citizen of the United States and the certificate from the Department of Commerce ...e affidavits of the two verifying witnesses thereto, required by law. Wherefore your petitioner prays that he may be admitted a citizen of

John Benko
(Complete and true signature of petitioner.)

Arrival No. 749607 from Department of Commerce and Labor filed this 10th day of January, 1913.

AFFIDAVITS OF PETITIONER AND WITNESSES.

...erica
...iana } ss:

...worn, deposes and says that he is the petitioner in the above-entitled proceedings; that he has read the foregoing petition and knows the ... signed with his full, true name; that the same is true of his own knowledge except as to matters therein stated to be alleged upon ...e matters he believes it to be true.

John Benko
(Complete and true signature of petitioner.)

...atz, occupation Car worker, residing at 560 Morton Ave, Hammond, Indiana

~~..., occupation ..., residing at ...~~

... citizen of the United States of America; that he has personally known ...ectively sworn, deposes and says that he is a citizen of the United States of America; that he has personally known ... Benko, the petitioner above mentioned, to have resided in the United States continuously ...s petition, since the 5th day of July, anno Domini 1909 and in the State in which the above-... ...ce the 5th day of July, anno Domini 1909 and that he has personal knowledge that ...oral character, attached to the principles of the Constitution of the United States, and that the petitioner is in every way qualified, in his ...ited States.

IN THE MATTER OF THE PETITION OF

John Benko

TO BE ADMITTED A CITIZEN OF THE UNITED STATES OF AMERICA.

Filed January 10th, 1913

OATH OF ALLEGIANCE

I hereby declare, on oath, that I absolutely and entirely renounce and abjure all allegian[ce] foreign prince, potentate, state, or sovereignty, and particularly ~~to~~ ~~of~~ **Francis Joseph, Emperor of Austria and Apostolic King of Hungary** *of whom I have heretofore bee[n] ~~I further renounce the title of~~ ~~, an order of nobility, which I~~ that I will support and defend the Constitution and laws of the United States of America foreign and domestic; and that I will bear true faith and allegiance to the same.*

[SEAL.]

John Benko

Subscribed and sworn to before me, in open Court, this 16th *day of* Ap[ril] ... 19[13]

ORDER OF COURT ADMITTING PETITIONER

Upon consideration of the petition of John Benko *, and affidavits i[n] ...er testimony taken in open Court, it is ordered that the said petitioner, who has taken the oath required by law, be, an[d] ...come a citizen of the United States of America, this* 16th *day of* April *, A. D. 19*13.

~~(It is further ordered, upon consideration of the petition of the said~~ ... hereby is, changed to ..., under authority ~~of the provisions of sectio[n]~~ ... Act to establish a Bureau of Immigration ~~and Naturalization, and to provide for a uniform rule for the naturalizatio[n]~~ ~~[U]nited States," approved June 29, 1906.)~~

By the Court:

Albert W. Anderson

ORDER OF COURT DENYING PETITION

Upon consideration of the petition of ...

... *for the United Sta[tes]*

... *day of* ..., 19..., *it appearing that* ...

[THE] SAID PETITION IS HEREBY DENIED.

MEMORANDUM OF CONTINUANCES

REASONS FOR CONTINU[ANCE]

[Con]tinued from ..., 19...

to ..., 19...

[Con]tinued from ..., 19...

to ..., 19...

NAMES OF SUBSTITUTED WITNESSES

occupation ..., *residing at* ...

The Petition for Naturalization and the Oath of Allegiance on these two pages, both of which are dated January 10, 1913, show John Benko's intent to become a naturalized citizen of the United States.

No. 287892

To be given to the person Naturalized.

THE UNITED STATES OF AMERICA

CERTIFICATE OF NATURALIZATION

Petition, Volume 8 page 28 Stub, Volume 10488 page 42

Description of holder: Age, 26 years; height, 5 feet, 6 inches; color, white; complexion, fair; color of eyes, gray; color of hair, brown; visible distinguishing marks, scar on forehead

Name, age and place of residence of wife Annie 29 794 Steinway Av. L. I. City

Names, ages and places of residence of minor children Annie 3 yrs. 794 Steinway Av. L. I. City

ORIGINAL

State of New York, County of Queens } S.S.: Charles Arendas (Signature of holder.)

Be it remembered, that at a Special term of the Supreme court of the State of New York held at Long Island City on the 15 day of November, in the year of our Lord nineteen hundred and twelve, Charles Arendas, who previous to his naturalization was a citizen subject of Hungary, at present residing at number 794 Steinway Av. L. I. City street, City Town of Borough of Queens, State Territory District of New York, having applied to be admitted a citizen of the United States of America, pursuant to law, and the court having found that the petitioner had resided continuously within the United States for at least five years and in this State Territory District for one year immediately preceding the date of the filing of his petition, and that said petitioner intends to reside permanently in the United States, had in all respects complied with the law in relation thereto, and that he was entitled to be so admitted, it was thereupon ordered by the said court that he be admitted as a citizen of the United States of America.

In testimony whereof the seal of said court is hereunto affixed on the 15 day of November in the year of our Lord nineteen hundred and twelve and of our Independence the one hundred and thirty seventh

MARTIN MAGER, Clerk,
Per James W. Winters
Assistant Deputy Clerk
(Official character of attestor.)

DEPARTMENT OF COMMERCE AND LABOR

John Benko's recordkeeping serves as a perfect example of one man's decision to come to America. He became a U.S. citizen and lived a decent and responsible life. Throughout his story, nearly every important step along the way is visually documented in these pages.

Form 2603

THE UNITED STATES OF AMERICA

No. 371322

CERTIFICATE OF  CITIZENSHIP

Application No. 2 B - 3565.

Personal description of holder as of date of issuance of this certificate: Age 41 *years; sex* Male *; color* White *; complexion* Med. Dark *; color of eyes* Brown *; color of hair* Black *; height* 5 *feet* 7 *inches; weight* 157 *pounds; visible distinctive marks* Scar on thumb of left hand. *Marital status* Single *; race* Magyar *; former nationality* Austro-Hungarian

I certify that the description above given is true, and that the photograph affixed hereto is a likeness of me.

DUPLICATE

ORIGINAL

John Benko
(Complete and true signature of holder)

John Benko

Seal

The United States of America
District of Columbia } *ss:*

Be it known, that -----JOHN BENKO-----, *residing at* 2136 - 24th Street, Long Island City, New York *having applied to the Commissioner of Naturalization for a new certificate of citizenship pursuant to Section 32(a) of the act of June 29, 1906, as amended, having proved to the satisfaction of the commissioner that the applicant is now a citizen of the United States of America* having been naturalized by the United States District Court for the District of Indiana, at Hammond, on April 16, 1913

that a certificate of citizenship was lawfully issued to the applicant, and that such certificate has been lost, mutilated or destroyed:

Now Therefore, *in pursuance of the authority contained in Section 32(a) of the act of June 29, 1906, as amended, this certificate of citizenship is issued this* 25th *day of* November *in the year of our Lord nineteen hundred and* thirty *, and of our Independence the one hundred and* fifty-fifth *, and the seal of the Department of Labor affixed pursuant to statute.*

5217

Raymond F. Crist
Commissioner of Naturalization.

DEPARTMENT OF LABOR

These pages show the process John Benko followed to become a United States citizen.

In 1907, the naturalization laws required an alien to declare his intention under oath to become a citizen of the United States and to renounce allegiance to any foreign prince or state. The declaration of intention had to be filed at least two years prior to admission. Within two to seven years of filing the declaration of intention, the applicant had to file a petition, with affidavits of two U.S. citizens, that he had resided continuously in the United States at least five years, and he intended to become a citizen and permanent resident. He had to state that he was not a disbeliever in organized government, did not believe in polygamy, and forever renounced allegiance to any foreign country.

To become a citizen, he had to take an oath of allegiance to the Constitution, and was a resident of the United States for at least five years. He had to renounce any hereditary title or order of nobility, could not be associated with any organization opposing organized government, or advocated killing any officer of organized government. He had to be able to speak English, and could not be Chinese.

This information was abstracted from the web site of the Gjenvick-Gjønvik Archives — "The Future of our Past" <http://www.gjenvick.com/Immigration/1907-SummaryOfNaturalizationLaws-US.html>.

János "John" Benkó Documents

U.S.S. MINNESOTA,
Philadelphia, Pa.,
June 9, 1915.

Discharged prior to expiration of enlistment with purchase discharged in accordance with Bureau's letter of May 8, 1915.

Lieut. Comdr., U.S.N.,
Commanding.

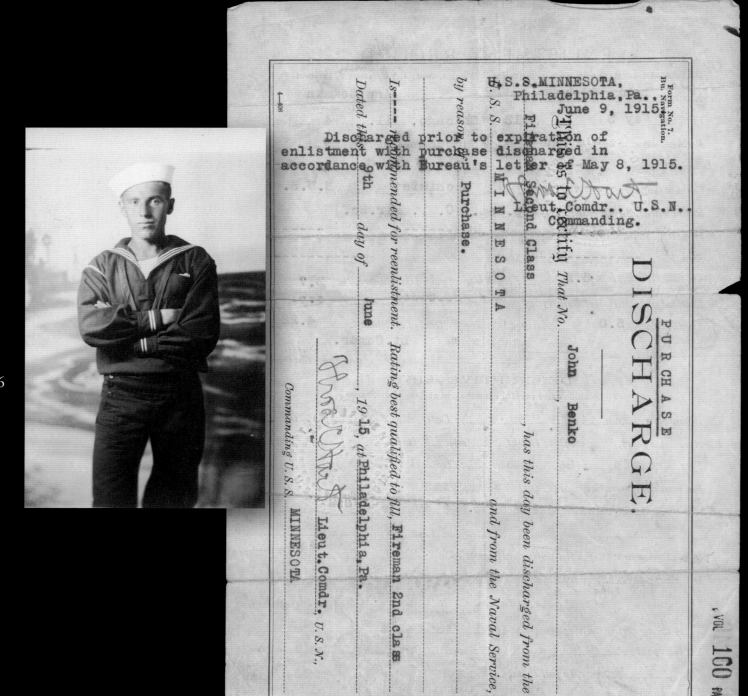

Form No. 7.
Bu. Navigation.

PURCHASE

DISCHARGE.

This is to Certify That No. ____, John Benko

Fireman Second Class, has this day been discharged from the

U. S. S. MINNESOTA and from the Naval Service,

by reason of Purchase.

Is---- recommended for reenlistment. Rating best qualified to fill, Fireman 2nd class

Dated this 9th day of June, 1915, at Philadelphia, Pa.

Lieut. Comdr., U. S. N.,
Commanding U. S. S. MINNESOTA

4—408

VOL 160 PAGE 245

Quoted from letter from Anna Benko to Clyde Davis:
"Then on May 3–1913 — John (in Chicago) enlisted in the U.S. Navy for 4 yrs., but was in for only 2 yrs, as he got out or discharged with a Purchase Discharge, which cost him $60.00, on June 9–1915, he wanted to get out. Then on April 29–1918— W. W1 — John was drafted into U.S. Army in N. York was in until May 9–1919 discharged —"

ENLISTMENT RECORD.

SCALE OF MARKS: 0, Bad; 1, Indifferent; 2, Fair; 3, Good; 4, Very Good; 5, Excellent.

Name, Benko, John ; *Rate,* App.Seaman ;
(*At enlistment.*)

Enlisted May 3 , 1913 , *at* Chicago, Ill. , *for* 4 *years;*

Previous naval service, none *years; Served apprenticeship,* No ;

Gun Captain certificate, -------- ; *Certificate graduation P. O. School,* -------- ;

Seaman Gunner, ----------- ; *Trade,* Machinist ; *Citizenship,* N.U.S. ;

Ratings held during enlistment, App.Sea., C.P., Fir.2c. ;

Proficiency in rating, 3.9 ; *Seamanship,* ------- ; *Ordnance,* -------- ;

Signaling, -------------- ; *Marksmanship, small arms,* ------------- ;

Mechanical ability, 3.5 ; *Knowledge of marine machinery,* 3.7 ;

Knowledge of electrical machinery and appliances, --------- ; *Sobriety,* 5.0 ;

Obedience, 5.0 ; *Average standing for term of enlistment,* 4.22

[signature] Lt.Comdr., *U. S. N.,*
and Executive Officer.

DESCRIPTIVE LIST.

(To be made after careful examination at date of discharge.)

Where born, Austria ; *Date,* May 27, , 1889 ;

Age, 26 *years,* 0 *months; Height,* 5 *feet,* 7 *inches; Weight,* 129 *lbs.;*

Eyes, Brown 4 ; *Hair,* Brown ; *Complexion,* Ruddy ;

Personal characteristics, marks, etc., sc l eyebrow. sc inner r palm sc l thumb. sc 2' inner lfa. m over r ilium.

Percentage of time on sick list during enlistment, 00.08%

Is ---- *physically qualified for reenlistment.*

[signature] P.A. Surgeon, *U. S. N.*
(*Signature medical officer.*)

I hereby certify that the above-named John Benko
has been paid No *dollars* *cents*
(*$*), *in full to date.*

June 9, 1915

[signature] Paymaster, *U. S. N.*
(*Signature Paymaster.*)

4—408

VOL 100 PAGE 246

Cost of Purchase, discharge $60—

Order of Induction into Military Service of the United States.

THE PRESIDENT OF THE UNITED STATES,

To John Benko
(Christian name.) (Surname.)

Order Number 1017 *Serial Number* 2250

Greeting: *Having submitted yourself to a local board composed of your neighbors for the purpose of determining the place and time in which you can best serve the United States in the present emergency, you are hereby notified that you have now been selected for immediate military service.*

You will, therefore, report to the local board named below at 328 E. 67th St. (Basement), *at* 7:30 *a.m.,*
(Place of reporting.) (Hour of reporting.)
on the 29th *day of* April *, 19*18*,*
for military duty.

From and after the day and hour just named you will be a soldier in the military service of the United States.

Fred'k Pavlicek

Member of Local Board for Div. 133

Report to Local Board for Div. 133
328 E. 67th St
N. Y.

Date April 19th 1918

FORM 1028. P.M.G.O. (See Sec. 157, S. S. R.) 3—5115

Three years after purchasing his discharge from the Navy, John was inducted into the Army on April 19, 1918. The United States had declared war on Germany on April 6, 1917.

To be inclosed with each order into military service (Form 1028) sent to a selected man.

IMPORTANT NOTICE TO ALL MEN SELECTED FOR MILITARY SERVICE AND ORDERED TO REPORT TO A LOCAL BOARD FOR MILITARY DUTY.

The day and hour specified on the Classification List of this Local Board, and on the order and notice of induction into military service which accompanies this notice for you to report to this Local Board for military duty is the time that marks your actual obligation as a soldier of the United States.

Failure to report promptly at the hour and on the day named is a grave military offense for which you may be court-martialed. Willful failure to report with an intent to evade military service constitutes desertion from the Army of the United States, which, in time of war, is a capital offense.

Upon reporting to your Local Board, you will not need, and you should not bring with you, anything except hand baggage. You will not be permitted to take trunks or boxes with you on the train. You should take only the following articles: A pair of strong comfortable shoes to relieve your feet from your new regulation marching shoes; not to exceed four extra suits of underclothing; not to exceed six extra pairs of socks; four face and two bath towels; a comb, a brush, a toothbrush, soap, tooth powder, razor, and shaving soap. It will add to your comfort to bring one woolen blanket, preferably of dark or neutral color. This blanket should be tightly rolled, the ends of the roll should be securely bound together and the loop of the blanket thus formed slung from your left shoulder to your right hip.

You should wear rough strong clothing and a flannel shirt, preferably an olive-drab shirt of the kind issued to soldiers.

NOTE.—Local Boards may have prepared, in the form of a rubber stamp, and stamp in below or on the back hereof any special instructions such as a direction to request permission to eat and spend the last night at home, as it may desire to give.

LOCAL BOARD FOR DIVISION 133,
FOR THE COUNTY OF NEW YORK, STATE OF NEW YORK.

(Stamp in designation of Local Board.) 3—5116

P. M. G. O. Form 1028A

P.S. You are hereby notified to appear at this Board on Friday evening, April 26th, at eight o'clock, and bring your final classification card with you.

JÁNOS "JOHN" BENKÓ DOCUMENTS

Assembly Dist. No.............Borough of.......................New York City

STATE OF NEW YORK

Military Census and Inventory of 1917

BY COMMAND OF THE GOVERNOR

This Certifies that the bearer whose signature appears on the line following

Name John Benko

Residence 1259-3D ave N.Y.

has been enrolled in the Census and Inventory of Military Resources of the State.

NOT TRANSFERABLE

E. P. Goodrich
New York City Director of Census

by Ida Oppenheimer
Agent

The State of New York Military Census and Inventory of 1917 was a comprehensive inventory of the state's resources in preparation for war carried out over a fifteen-day period. It also registered potential enemy aliens of German origin or from areas under German control. According to the New York Census and Military Inventory, A Report to Hon. Charles S. Whitman, Governor of the State of New York, 1917, by J.H. Sears, Director on October 20, 1917, "The task of persuading 5,600,000 men and women to answer the eighty odd questions was alone a difficult and unprecedented one." Cards of this type showed availability for military service.

WAR DEPARTMENT
LOCAL BOARD FOR
LOCAL BOARD FOR DIVISION 133,
FOR THE COUNTY OF NEW YORK,
STATE OF NEW YORK.
OFFICIAL BUSINESS

PENALTY FOR PRIVATE USE, $300

PUBLIC LIBRARY
328 EAST 67th ST.
C

John Benko
327 E 65 St
City

Local Board for LOCAL BOARD FOR DIVISION 133,
NOTICE OF CLASSIFICATION FOR THE COUNTY OF NEW YORK, STATE OF NEW YORK.

I	II	III	IV	V
A				

John Benko .... Order No. 1017 Serial No. 2250 has been classified by the ~~Local~~ District Board on appeal ~~or original claim~~ in the classes under which letters are placed on the above schedule, and on the grounds indicated by such letters, (see Form 1001-A for key to meaning of letters). This entitles him to a place in Class 1 and he has been so recorded on the Classification List of this Local Board. Appeals may be taken from classification by a Local Board, within five days from the date of this notice, by any person who filed a claim with this Local Board. Appeals may be taken from classification by a District Board within five days from the date of this notice only in certain cases specified in section 80 of Selective Service Regulations and when claimed by a person who filed a claim of classification with the District Board. To file an appeal it is only necessary to go to the office of the Local Board and write your claim of appeal in the place provided on the registrant's questionnaire.

JAN 29 1918
(Date.)

Fred Ir Pawlick
Member of Local Board.

FORM 1005—PMGO. (See Sec. 103, S. S. R.) c3—5133

JAN 29 1918

Front and back of postcard

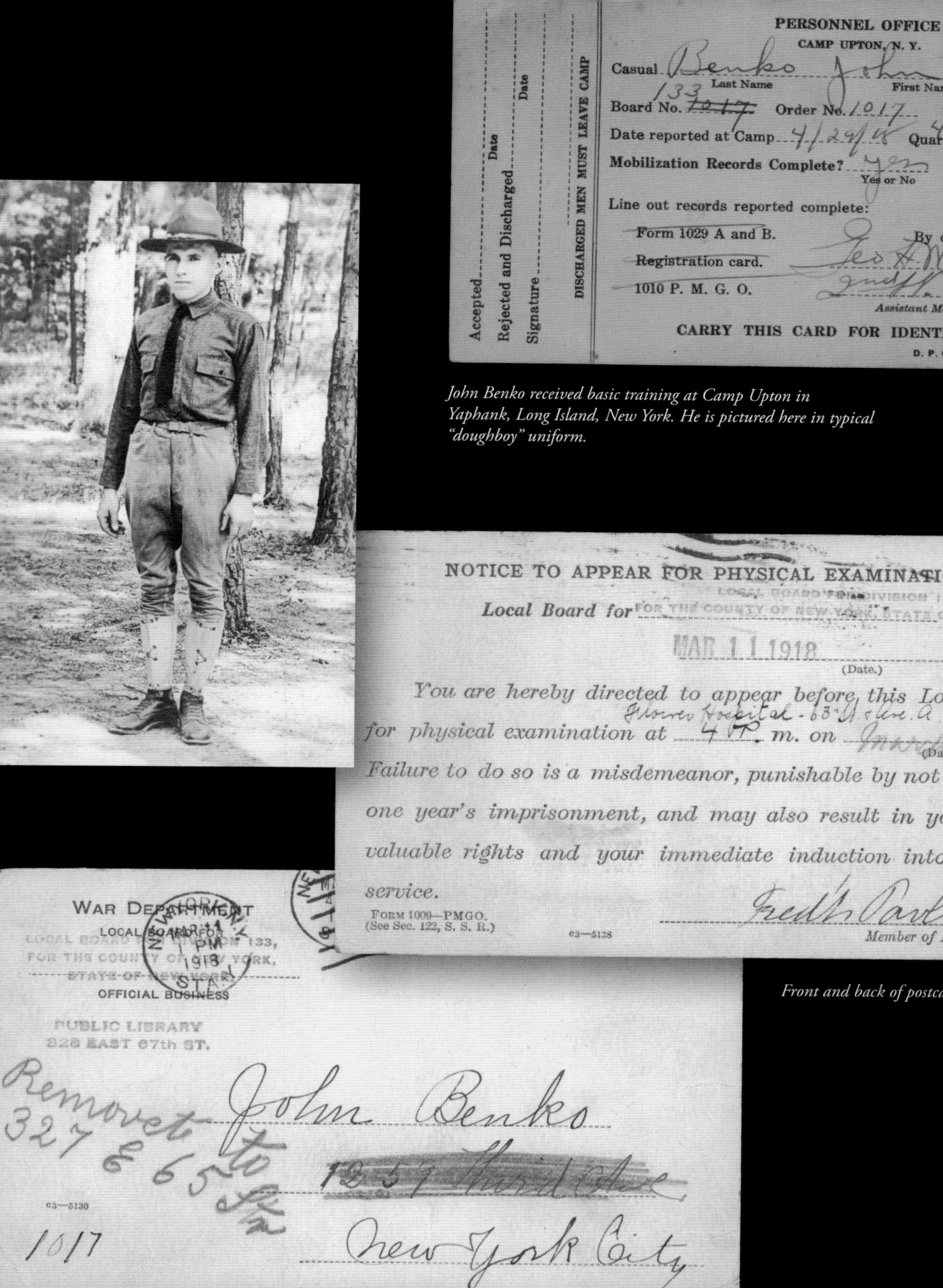

PERSONNEL OFFICE
CAMP UPTON, N. Y.

Casual Benko John
Last Name First Name Middle Name

Board No. 133 ~~1017~~ Order No. 1017 Serial No. 2250

Date reported at Camp 4/29/18 Quartered at No. 417-15-2 N

Mobilization Records Complete? Yes
Yes or No

Line out records reported complete:

~~Form 1029 A and B.~~

~~Registration card.~~

~~1010 P. M. G. O.~~

By direction:
Geo. A. McKeever
2nd Lt. Inf. R.C.
Assistant Mobilization Officer

CARRY THIS CARD FOR IDENTIFICATION

D. P. O. FORM 392—(536-10M)

Accepted .... Date ....
Rejected and Discharged .... Date ....
Signature ....

DISCHARGED MEN MUST LEAVE CAMP

John Benko received basic training at Camp Upton in Yaphank, Long Island, New York. He is pictured here in typical "doughboy" uniform.

NOTICE TO APPEAR FOR PHYSICAL EXAMINATION

Local Board for LOCAL BOARD FOR DIVISION 133, FOR THE COUNTY OF NEW YORK, STATE OF NEW YORK

MAR 11 1918
(Date.)

You are hereby directed to appear before this Local Board for physical examination at 4 P. *m. on* March 13-1918 (Date) Flower Hospital - 63rd St. & Ave. A

Failure to do so is a misdemeanor, punishable by not to exceed one year's imprisonment, and may also result in your losing valuable rights and your immediate induction into military service.

FORM 1009—PMGO.
(See Sec. 122, S. S. R.)

c3—5138

Fred'k Varlick
Member of Local Board.

WAR DEPARTMENT
LOCAL BOARD FOR
LOCAL BOARD FOR DIVISION 133,
FOR THE COUNTY OF NEW YORK,
STATE OF NEW YORK
OFFICIAL BUSINESS

PUBLIC LIBRARY
328 EAST 67th ST.

John Benko
~~1257 Third Ave~~
New York City

Removed to 327 E 65 St.

c3—5130

1017

Front and back of postcard

VOL 100 PAGE 247

Honorable Discharge from The United States Army

TO ALL WHOM IT MAY CONCERN:

This is to Certify, That* John Benko, 2793412
† Private 1st Class, Motor Transport Corps
THE UNITED STATES ARMY, as a TESTIMONIAL OF HONEST AND FAITHFUL SERVICE, is hereby HONORABLY DISCHARGED from the military service of the UNITED STATES by reason of ‡ W.D. Cir. 77, 1918; S.O. 188, Par 1, Hq. Ft. Oglethorpe, Ga.
Said John Benko was born in Felsoparkany, in the ~~State~~ Country of Hungary
When enlisted he was 29 years of age and by occupation a machinist
He had brown eyes, dark hair, black complexion, and was 5 feet 5 1/4 inches in height.

Given under my hand at Ft. Oglethorpe, Georgia this 9 day of May, one thousand nine hundred and nineteen

R. B. Powers
Major-Cavalry
Motor Transport Corps
Commanding.

Form No. 525, A. G. O.
Oct. 9-18.
3—2155

*Insert name, Christian name first; e. g., "John Doe."
†Insert Army serial number, grade, company and regiment or arm or corps or department; e. g., "1,620,302"; "Corporal, Company A, 1st Infantry"; "Sergeant, Quartermaster Corps"; "Sergeant, First Class, Medical Department."
‡If discharged prior to expiration of service, give number, date, and source of order or full description of authority therefor.

Above is John Benko's Honorable Discharge from the Army on May 9, 1919, following World War I. On the reverse side of the Discharge is his Enlistment Record, which summarized his service. The card shown below on the bottom right of page 533 is John's Selective Service Registration Certificate issued in April 1942, a few months after the start of World War II. It is worth noting that John would have been 54 at the time, and had been working at the New York Naval Shipyard as a machinist since 1933. He worked there until his retirement in 1957.

VOL 100 PAGE 248

ENLISTMENT RECORD.

Name: John Benko Grade: Pvt. 1st Class

Enlisted, or Inducted, April 29, 1918, at New York, N.Y.

Serving in first enlistment period at date of discharge.

Prior service:* none

Noncommissioned officer: none

Marksmanship, gunner qualification or rating: † none

Horsemanship: not mounted

Battles, engagements, skirmishes, expeditions: none

Knowledge of any vocation: machinist

Wounds received in service: none

Physical condition when discharged: good

Typhoid prophylaxis completed May 14, 1918

Paratyphoid prophylaxis completed

Married or single: single

Character: Excellent

Remarks: No A.W.O.L; No absence under G.O. 31-12 + 45-14

Travel pay to New York, N.Y.

Signature of soldier: John Benko

PAID IN FULL $ 108.30 INCLUDING $60 BONUS, AS PROVIDED IN SEC. 1406, REVENUE ACT OF 1918, APPROVED, FEB. 24th, 1919, FT. OGLETHORPE, GA.

MAY 9 1919

GEO. H. CHASE CAPTAIN Q. M. C. FINANCE SEC.

TRANSPORTATION ISSUED.

R B Powers

Major-Cavalry

Commanding M.T.C.

RECORDED

JAN 22 1970

@ M.

LESTER M. ALBERTSON

Clerk of Suffolk County

* Give company and regiment or corps or department, with inclusive dates of service in each enlistment.
† Give date of qualification or rating and number, date and source of order announcing same.

3—3164

REGISTRATION CERTIFICATE

This is to certify that in accordance with the Selective Service Proclamation of the President of the United States

JOHN BENKO
(First name) (Middle name) (Last name)

25-02 Steinway St. L.I.C.
(Place of residence)
(This will be identical with line 2 of the Registration Card)

has been duly registered this 27 day of April, 1942

Elizabeth Whiteacre
(Signature of registrar)

Registrar for Local Board Local Board #242 (Number) (City or county) (State)

(Registrant must sign here)

THE LAW REQUIRES YOU TO HAVE THIS CARD IN YOUR PERSONAL POSSESSION AT ALL TIMES

D. S. S. Form 2
(Revised 6/9/41)

16—21631

DESCRIPTION OF REGISTRANT

Race		Height (Approx.)		Weight (Approx.)		Complexion	
		5' 6"		185		Sallow	
White	V	Eyes		Hair		Light	
		Blue		Blonde		Ruddy	V
Negro		Gray		Red		Dark	
		Hazel	V	Brown		Freckled	
Oriental		Brown		Black	V	Light brown	
Indian		Black		Gray		Dark brown	
				Bald		Black	
Filipino							

Other obvious physical characteristics that will aid in identification

glasses

U. S. GOVERNMENT PRINTING OFFICE 16—21631

Felsötárkány, Hungary, June 26, 1998

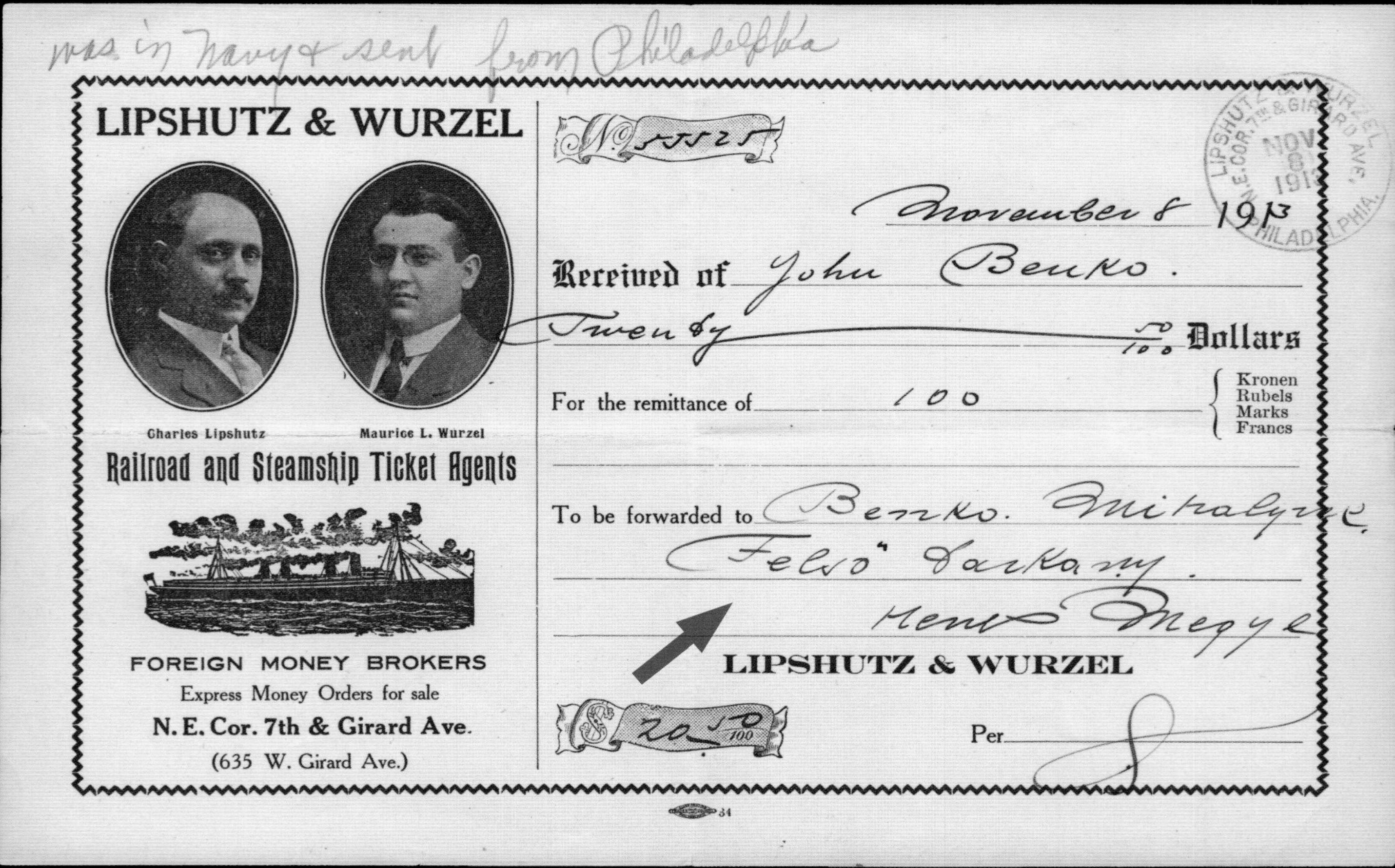

was in Navy & sent from Philadelphia

LIPSHUTZ & WURZEL

Charles Lipshutz — Maurice L. Wurzel

Railroad and Steamship Ticket Agents

FOREIGN MONEY BROKERS

Express Money Orders for sale

N. E. Cor. 7th & Girard Ave.

(635 W. Girard Ave.)

No. 55525

LIPSHUTZ & WURZEL N.E. COR. 7TH & GIRARD AVE. NOV 8 1913 PHILADELPHIA.

November 8 1913

Received of John Benko.

Twenty 50/100 **Dollars**

For the remittance of 100 Kronen / Rubels / Marks / Francs

To be forwarded to Benko. Mihalyne.
Felsö Darkany.
Heves Megye

LIPSHUTZ & WURZEL

$ 20 50/100

Per

34

Money order sent by John Benko on November 8, 1913, to his 64-year old father, Mihály Benkó, in Felsötárkány, Hungary, from Philadelphia, Pennsylvania, while he was in the Navy. One hundred dollars in 1913 would be worth about $2,175 in 2008 dollars, which shows that John Benko was a generous man even at an early age. The penciled note in the top margin was written by John's wife, Anna Arendas, whom he married in 1934.

ARTHUR HERRMAN
NOTARY PUBLIC
BRANCH AGENT
American Express Company
First Ave. Cor. 67th Str.
NEW YORK

RECEIPT FOR FOREIGN MONEY ORDER. No. 8393219

SUBJECT TO CONTRACT PRINTED ON THE BACK.

New York N.Y. State of ... March 6 1920

Received from Mr. John Benko

Address 332 E. 57 N.Y.

Forty ... $\frac{\#}{100}$ Dollars

NOT EXCEEDING FIFTY DOLLARS

For the purchase of

NOT EXCEEDING 500 KRONEN; 350 LIRE; 350 FINMARKS; 400 MARKS; 185 KRONER; 300 RUBLES; 300 FRANCS; 125 GUILDERS; 260 DRACHMAS; 250 PESETAS.

For remittance to

At

NOT NEGOTIABLE

NOT EXCEEDING $50.00

AMERICAN EXPRESS COMPANY

A. Herrman

BRANCH AGENT.

(5264 Aug., 1919.)

Receipt for money order from John Benko to his sister, Krisztina, dated March 6, 1920

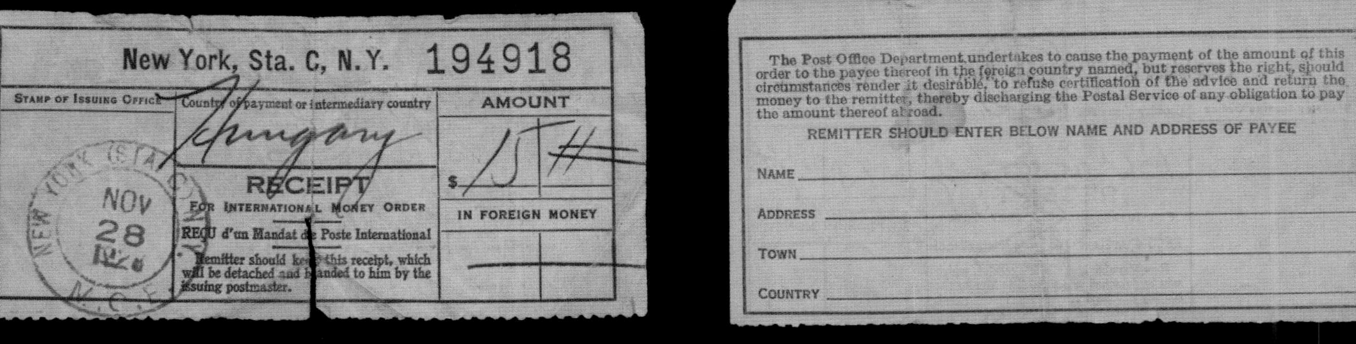

New York, Sta. C, N.Y. 194918

Stamp of Issuing Office	Country of payment or intermediary country	AMOUNT
NEW YORK (STA. C) NOV 28 N.Y.	Hungary	$ 15 #
	RECEIPT For International Money Order	IN FOREIGN MONEY
	REÇU d'un Mandat de Poste International	
	Remitter should keep this receipt, which will be detached and handed to him by the issuing postmaster.	

The Post Office Department undertakes to cause the payment of the amount of this order to the payee thereof in the foreign country named, but reserves the right, should circumstances render it desirable, to refuse certification of the advice and return the money to the remitter, thereby discharging the Postal Service of any obligation to pay the amount thereof abroad.

REMITTER SHOULD ENTER BELOW NAME AND ADDRESS OF PAYEE

NAME

ADDRESS

TOWN

COUNTRY

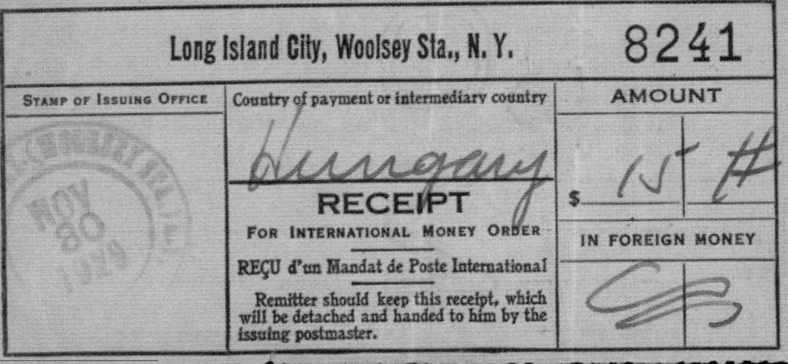

Long Island City, Woolsey Sta., N.Y. 8241

Stamp of Issuing Office	Country of payment or intermediary country	AMOUNT
NOV 30 1920	Hungary	$ 15 #
	RECEIPT For International Money Order	IN FOREIGN MONEY
	REÇU d'un Mandat de Poste International	
	Remitter should keep this receipt, which will be detached and handed to him by the issuing postmaster.	

Long Island City, Woolsey Sta., N.Y. 15983

Stamp of Issuing Office	Country of payment or intermediary country	AMOUNT
JUL 1921	Hungary	$ 10 #
	RECEIPT For International Money Order	IN FOREIGN MONEY
	REÇU d'un Mandat de Poste International	
	Remitter should keep this receipt, which will be detached and handed to him by the issuing postmaster.	

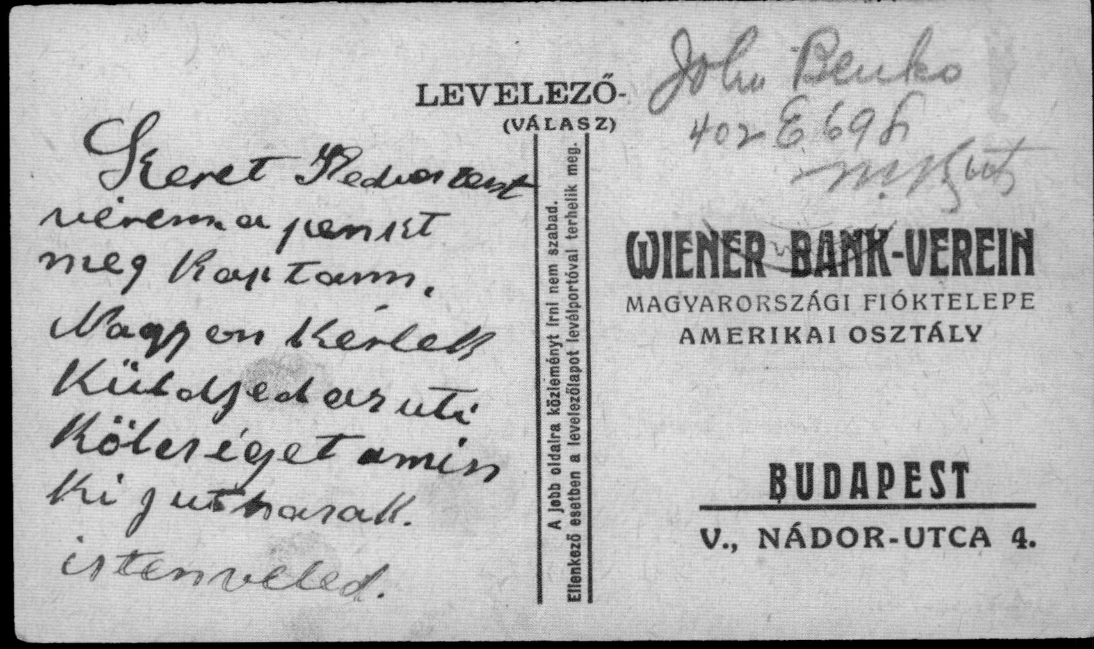

LEVELEZŐ-
(VÁLASZ)

A jobb oldalra közleményt írni nem szabad.
Ellenkező esetben a levelezőlapot levélportóval terhelik meg.

John Benko

WIENER BANK-VEREIN
MAGYARORSZÁGI FIÓKTELEPE
AMERIKAI OSZTÁLY

BUDAPEST
V., NÁDOR-UTCA 4.

istenveled.

Front and back of postcard

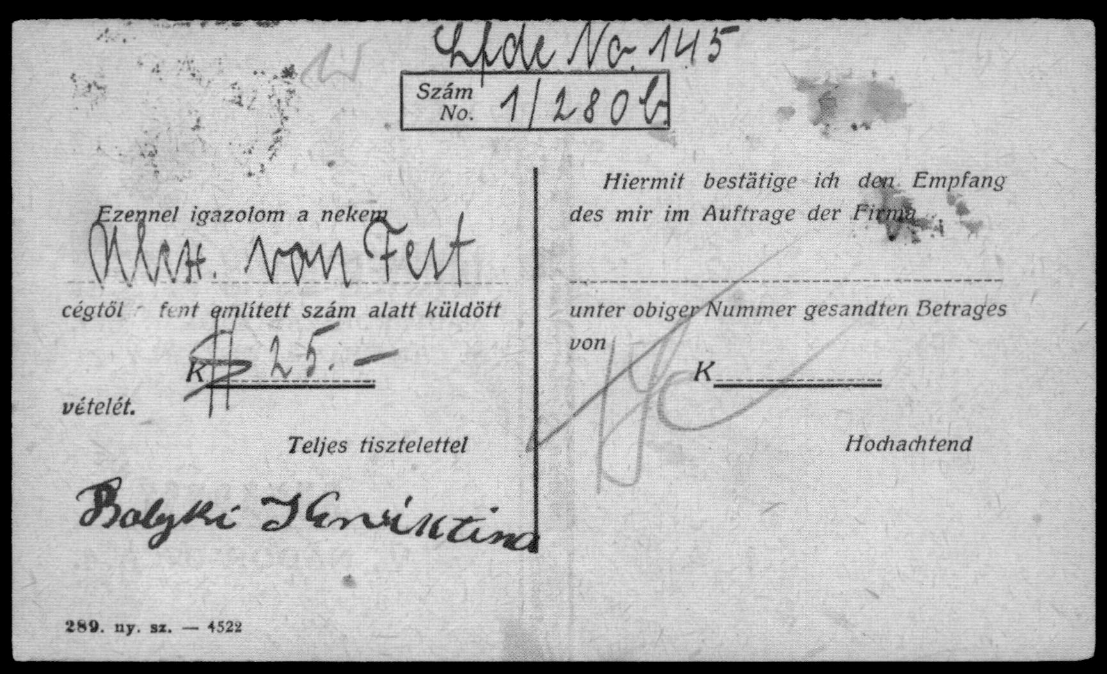

Szám No. 1/2806

Ezennel igazolom a nekem ... cégtől fent említett szám alatt küldött K $25.— vételét.

Teljes tisztelettel

Hiermit bestätige ich den Empfang des mir im Auftrage der Firma ... unter obiger Nummer gesandten Betrages von K ...

Hochachtend

289. ny. sz. — 4522

Reply post card to Weiner Bank-Verein. Note reads:
"My beloved dear sister/brother I received the money I beg you send me the traveling expenses to go out there. Goodbye."
Reverse side at bottom is a receipt for $25 signed by Krisztina Bolyki

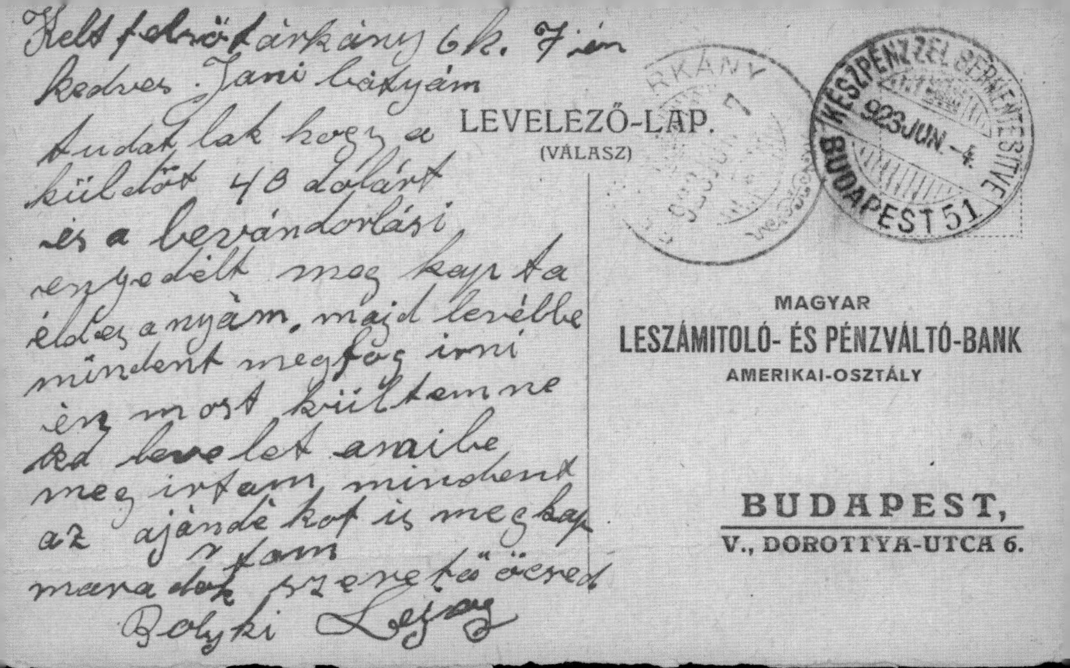

LEVELEZŐ-LAP.
(VÁLASZ)

MAGYAR
LESZÁMITOLÓ- ÉS PÉNZVÁLTÓ-BANK
AMERIKAI-OSZTÁLY

BUDAPEST,
V., DOROTTYA-UTCA 6.

Front and back of postcard

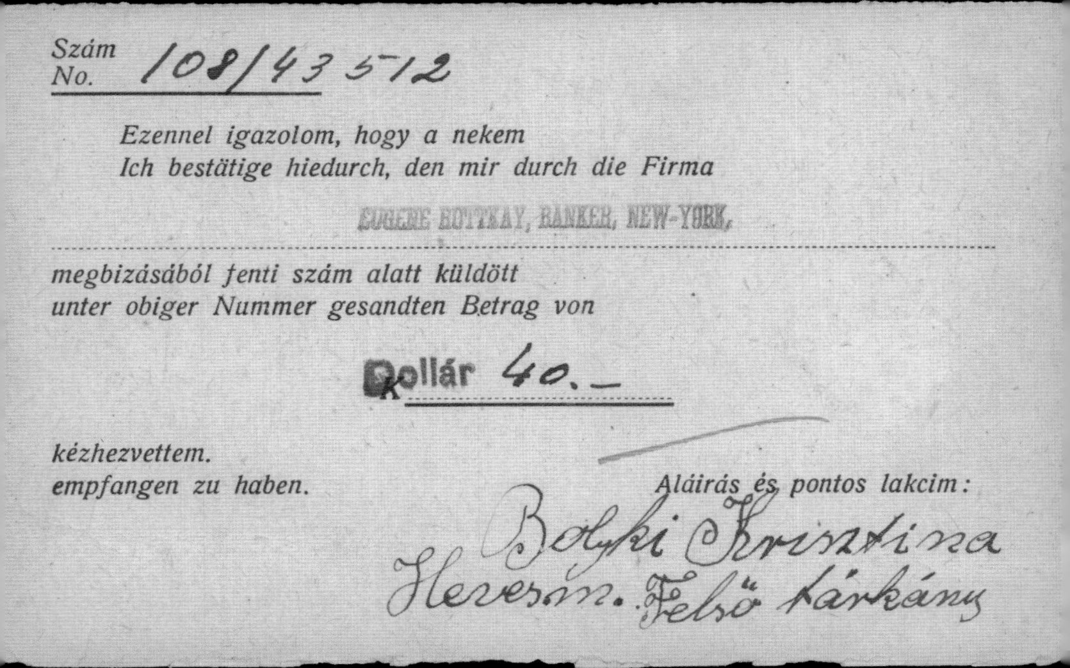

Szám
No. 108/43512

Ezennel igazolom, hogy a nekem
Ich bestätige hiedurch, den mir durch die Firma

EUGENE ROTTKAY, BANKER, NEW-YORK

megbizásából fenti szám alatt küldött
unter obiger Nummer gesandten Betrag von

Dollár 40.–

kézhezvettem.
empfangen zu haben.

Aláirás és pontos lakcim:

Bolyki Krisztina

eply post card to Magyar Leszámitoló-És Pénzváltó-Bank postmarked June 4, 1923. Note reads:
My dear brother Johnny, Mother received the $40 you sent and the emigration permit. She'll write a letter about
erything. I've just sent you a letter with all the news, I received the gift, too. I remain
our loving younger brother Lajos Bolyki"

JÁNOS "JOHN" BENKÓ CORRESPONDENCE

Kedves János!

A pénzt köszönettel megkaptam, levél megy.

Csókollak ezerszer

1923 VIII. 20. Bolyki Krisztina

LEVELEZŐ-LAP.

(VÁLASZ)

FELSŐ TÁRKÁNY 92. AUG 21

KÉSZPÉNZZEL BÉRMENTESÍTVE 923 AUG. 18. BUDAPEST

MAGYAR

LESZÁMITOLÓ- ÉS PÉNZVÁLTÓ-BANK

AMERIKAI-OSZTÁLY

BUDAPEST,

V., DOROTTYA-UTCA 6.

Front and back of postcard

Szám
No. 119/44048

Ezennel igazolom, hogy a nekem
Ich bestätige hiedurch, den mir durch die Firma

EUGENE BUTTKAY, BANKER, NEW-YORK.

megbizásából fenti szám alatt küldött
unter obiger Nummer gesandten Betrag von

Dollár 175.—

kézhezvettem.
empfangen zu haben.

Aláirás és pontos lakcim:

Bolyki Krisztina.

Felsőtárkány. (Heves m.)

Reply post card to bank. Note on top reads:
"Dear John! I received the money with thanks. Letter to follow. Thousand kisses. Krisztina Bolyki"
Reverse side at bottom is a receipt signed for $175 by Krisztina Bolyki (not her handwriting).

A felvevő hivatal bélyegzője
Timbre du bureau expéditeur

Térti vevény.
Avis de réception.

A feladó címe: A WIENER BANK-VER[EIN]
Magyarországi Fióktelepe
BUDAPEST

Rendeltetési hely — *Lieu de destination*

utca *rue* házszám *No*

Szolgálati ügy.
Service des postes.

Rendeltetési ország — *Pays de destination*

691. *sz. nyomtatvány* Térti vevény.

1924. I. megr. 3 r. = 96,000 db. 1 íven 32 db *d p.* — FRANKLIN-TÁRSULAT

Front and back of postcard

133/12498

MAGYAR POSTAIGAZGATÁS. — ADMINISTRATION DES POSTES DE HONGRIE.

American Union Bank, New-York

Térti vevény
Avis de réception

A felvevő hivatal bélyegzője

Timbre du bureau expéditeur

az alább leirt[1] 10 dollárt tartalmazó értéklevél ról.
d'un(e)

Száma: ______ súlya ______ kg ______ g; értéke 750.000 K ______ f
No ______ *poids* ______ *valeur* ______ *Cour* ______

Cime (teljes cim): Bolyki Krisztina rendeltetési helye Felsőtárkány
Adressé(e) à M.

Feladatott: Ujpest ban. 1924. évi dec. hó ______ n.
Déposé(e) à ______ 19 ______

Felsőtárkány

Alulirott kijelenti, hogy fent leirt küldemény szabályszerűen kézbesíttetett 1924. év decemb. hó 27 n.
Le soussigné déclare que l'objet décrit ci-dessus a été dûment livré le ______ *19* ______

A kézbesítő postahivatal bélyegzője

Timbre du bureau expéditeur

Aláírás[2] — *Signature*[2]

a címzett, *du destinataire* — a kézbesítő postahivatal tisztviselője, *de l'agent du bureau distributeur*

Bolyki Krisztina

[1] Ide irandó a küldemény neme. Ajánlott levél — *lettre recommandée;* értéklevél — *lettre avec valeur déclarée;* nemzetközi csomag — *colis postal;* nemzetk. közönséges cs. — *envoi de messagerie.*

[2] Ezt az értesitést a címzettnek, vagy ha a rendeltetési ország szabályai úgy rendelik, a kézbesítő hivatal tisztviselőjének kell aláirni, azután azt boríték nélkül haladéktalanul a túloldalon megjelölt feladónak kell küldeni. — *Cet avis doit être signé par le destinataire, ou si les règlements du pays de destination le comportent, par l'agent du bureau distributeur, et renvoyé ensuite par le premier courrier directement à l'adresse indiquée au recto*

Front

8545 Mackinaw Ave
Chicago, Ill.
Jan-16-1928

Dear John,
We recieved the check but we could not cash it because the bank will not take any chances with it. You had the check made to pay to you instead of Mary Savich. Just look at it John you got to write that on fromt of check.
Dear John the bank ~~the~~ cashier in Chicago said you should go to a bank in New

York and make a bank draft out to pay to Mrs Savich then send it to us and they'll cash it at any bank. ~~Or if you don't want to do that send it~~

Please send the money as soon as possible. ~~We~~ appreciate your kindness very much and will never forget it to pay you back

Your Loving brother Mike Savage

(Send back check by Special Delivery)

We got to have money by Jan. 19

In the late 1920s and early '30s, Grandpa and Grandma's home at 8545 Mackinaw, Chicago, was in imminent danger of foreclosure, and John Benko, Grandma's brother, eventually prevented this occurring. In January 1928, Michael Savage wrote to his uncle John requesting special delivery of a replacement for a check John had written, on which he had accidentally made himself the payee. In closing, Michael signs as "Your Loving brother Mike Savage." Michael had a brother, John, but he would have been about 10 years old at this time, so the reference to "Your Loving brother" is obviously a form of familiar closing on behalf of his mother. Additional correspondence on financing

C. ARTHUR CARLSON
(SUCCESSOR TO NIEL LYKKE)
INSURANCE, REAL ESTATE AND LOANS
(OFFICE OF CROWN BUILDING & LOAN ASSOCIATION)
3022 East 92nd Street

TELEPHONES REGENT 0128-0129

Chicago, Jan. 2, 1929

Mr. Andrew Savich,
8545 Mackinaw Ave.,
Chicago, Ill.

Dear Sir:

We wish to inform you that on December 24th, 1928 we wrote Mr. S. H. Greenwald with regard to your loan which we have for collection. In the letter we mentioned that unless this loan was paid off by December 28th we were going to turn the matter over to our attorney for foreclosure up to this date your loan has not been paid. We do not like to force you to pay an additional $100.00 which will be the Attorneys fee for starting foreclosure. We will therefore give you an extension of five days which means that your loan should be paid off by January 8th. Unless this is done we will not give you further notice but start foreclosure immediately.

Trusting you will take advantage of this extension, we are

Very truly yours,

CAC GW

C. Arthur Carlson

Judgment Note

$ 836.00 Chicago Ill. Sept 17 1930

One Year after date, for value received we promise to pay to the order of John Benko

Eight hundred & thirty six Dollars,

at UNION STATE BANK OF SOUTH CHICAGO with interest

at 6 per cent, per annum after date until paid.

And to secure the payment of said amount we hereby authorize, irrevocably, any attorney of any Court of Record to appear for us in such Court, in term time or vacation, at any time hereafter, and confess a judgment without process in favor of the holder of this Note for such amount as may appear to be unpaid thereon, together with costs, and just dollars attorney's fees, and to waive and release all errors which may intervene in any such proceeding, and consent to immediate execution upon such judgment, hereby ratifying and confirming all that our said attorney may do by virtue hereof.

Mary Savich

No. ________ Due ________

Form 31 Stuart-Hooper Co., Chicago

(over)

Dear John,

I am very sorry to trouble you about that money mother asked you about but send the $300 dollars immediatly. We were suppose to pay it Jan. 8 but we got a extension of time till Jan. 15 so please send the money here before that time. Because if you don't we'll have to pay a hundred dollars more.

What with hope your brother,

Michael Savage

Please send money immediately as possible

(over)

"Mike D. Savage 8a — 112 graduating class of 1929"

8545 Mackinaw Avenue
Chicago, Illinois
Feb. 19, 1930

Dear John:

I am still going to high school I have been working after school but I have been laid off and I need money to buy a suit. I have been laid off for a month and my clothes are terrible I can hardly go to school in them. I don't want to quit school because I want to finish and go to college to be a lawyer.

Will you please send me a few dollars. I am in need of them very badly I have been going too high school for 2 yrs. and I don't want to quit. Please if it is possible send me a few dollars. I know work is slow. But I assure you, you will not regret if you do this.

I am very anxious to hear from you.

Yours loving nephew
Michael Savich

Keveves testvérem és
sogornem már idehaza
vagyok és it hon miden
jólvan csak az idő rossz
haza jötem márczius 24-én
és elég jól vagyok és majd
fogok többet irni isten
veletek csokolak az
gyermekejimel együt
szerető növered es Sogor
néd Marika

CHICAGO APR 18 6 PM 1957 ILL. 5

AIR MAIL 6¢ U.S. POSTAGE

M. John Benkó
2502 Steinway St
Long Island
City 3 N.Y.

"Dear sister and sister-in-law, I'm at home and everything is well. I'll write some more later. Many regards your loving sister and sister-in-law Mary"

Mary Benko Savage in front of 8023 Marquette Avenue, Chicago, Illinois

kedves öcsem ez
az én házam ez
eleje az háznak ez
én vagyok
aki ot áll s,ok
szép virág van
ottan szeret nem
halátnad

530L

"My dear younger brother this is my house the front of the house, the one standing there is me there are lots of beautiful flowers I wish you could see it"

5519

STANDARD STEEL CAR CO.

John Benko

$ 55.50
7. 50
55.00

OCT 31 1909

2102

[ST]ANDARD STEEL CAR CO.

PASSENGER.

[J]ohn Benko

$ 47.85
Tools 1.00
46.85

JUL 31 1910

2402

[ST]ANDARD STEEL CAR CO.

PASSENGER.

[J]ohn Benko

$ 64.20

OCT 31 1910

FIRE INSURANCE

Lake County Savings & Trust Co.

BANK

3 Per Cent Interest on Deposits

Fire Insurance--Safety Deposit Boxes

OPEN EVENINGS

Cor. State and Hohman St., Hammond, Ind.

FIRE INSURANCE

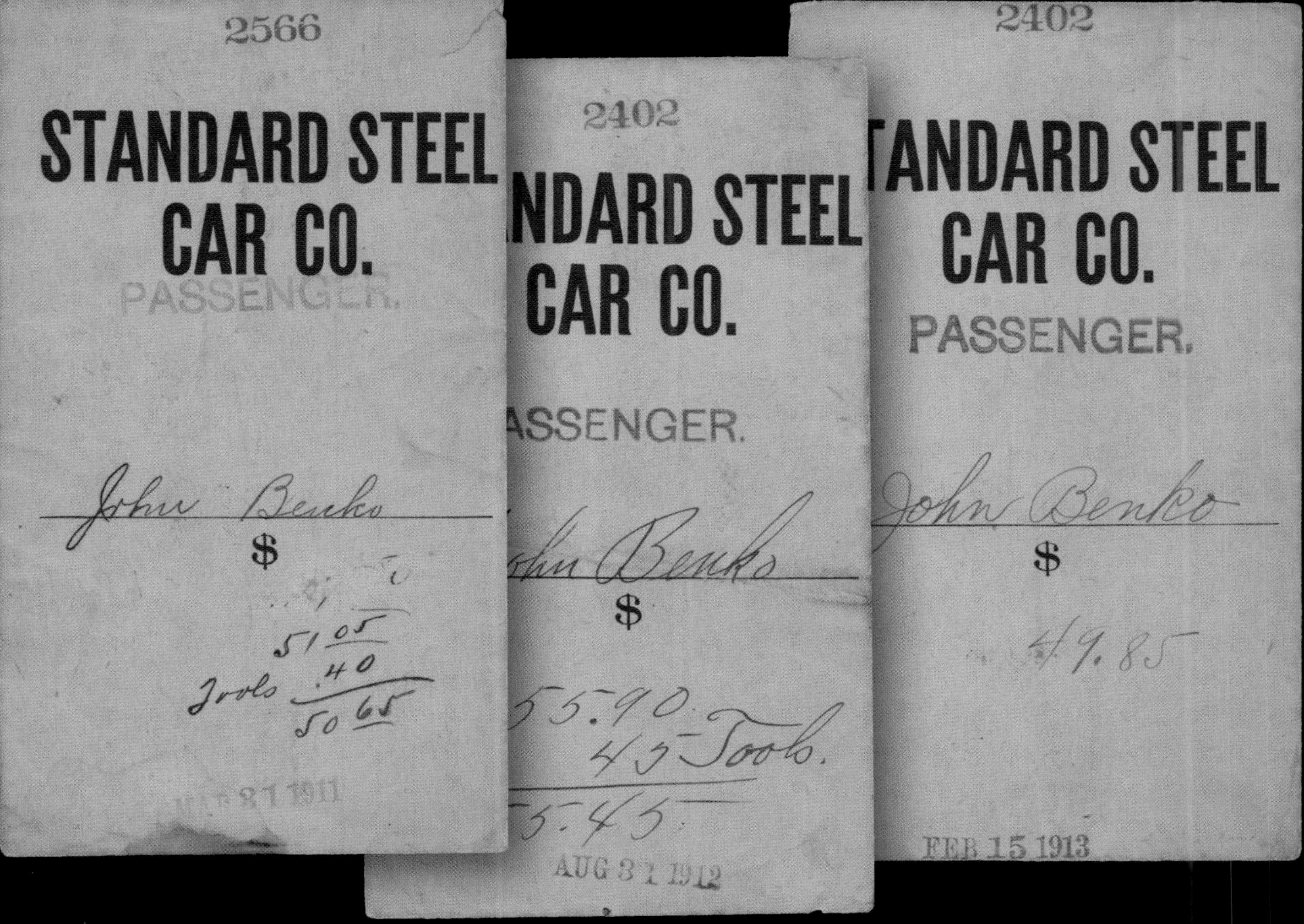

2566

STANDARD STEEL
CAR CO.

PASSENGER.

John Benko

$

51.05
Tools .40
50.65

[illegible] 21 1911

2402

[ST]ANDARD STEEL
CAR CO.

[P]ASSENGER.

John Benko

$

55.90
.45 Tools.
55.45

AUG 31 1912

2402

[S]TANDARD STEEL
CAR CO.

PASSENGER.

John Benko

$

49.85

FEB 15 1913

"Just a few pay envelopes of my John's that he got when employed at this place the Standard Steel Car Co., from Oct 31–1909 to Feb 15–1913 — he was only 20-yrs old when started there & in the U.S., only 2-yrs, as came to U.S., 6/22 – 1907 — this was some pay for that time, how young he was too & of course was a first class machinist — got paid weekly. This place was in Gary, Indiana — John's sister lived in Chicago."

Quoted from letter from Anna Benko to Clyde Davis

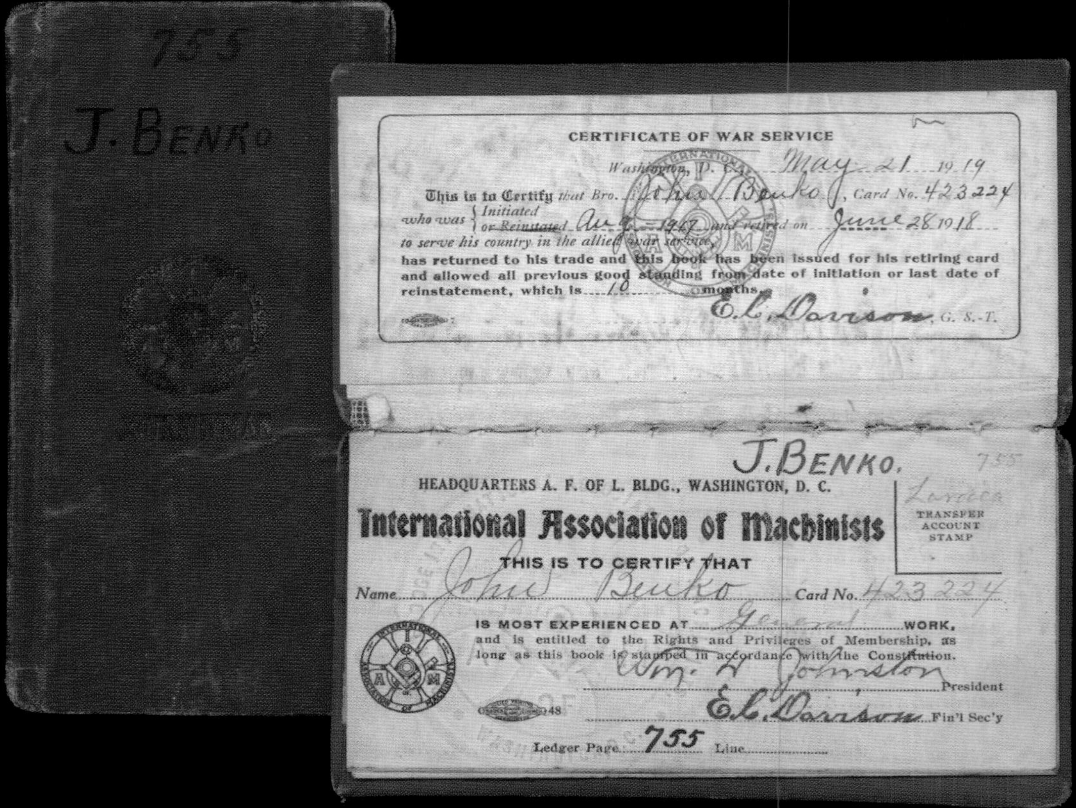

János "John" Benkó Employment

John Benko's work record is reflected in the pay envelopes from Standard Steel Car Co. on the preceding pages, and his union membership books. Above: His reinstatement to active union membership following his service in World War I. Below: A record showing his union dues payments.

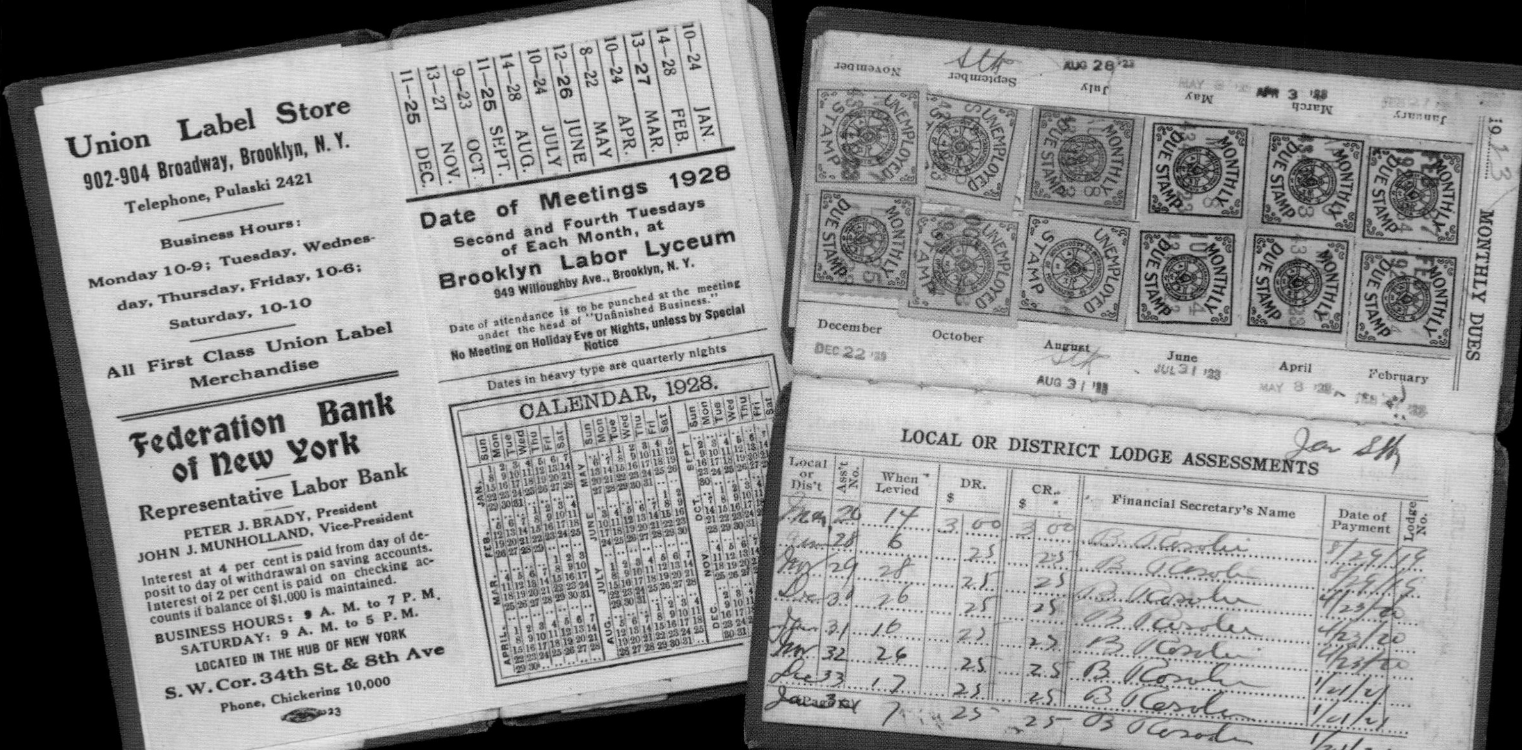

Left: Plaque honoring John Benko's retirement in 1957 from the New York Naval Shipyard. Below: A Certificate of Service dated July 31, 1957, for the 24 years John worked at the shipyard.

1957

UNITED STATES NAVY

GOOD LUCK AND A HAPPY RETIREMENT
TO
JOHN BENKO
FROM FRIENDS AND ASSOCIATES
OF THE
NEW YORK NAVAL SHIPYARD

JOHN BENKO

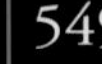

NEW YORK NAVAL SHIPYARD

BROOKLYN, NEW YORK

Certificate of Service

John Benko

having worked for a total period of Twenty-Two years in the Government Service including Nineteen years at

New York Naval Shipyard

The Commander *desires to honor his allegiance and devotion to* The Navy *and in recognition thereof presents this certificate with appreciation for his long and faithful service.*

Dated 31 July 1957

L. A. Knisken

Retirement Date 31 July 1957 *Rear Admiral U.S.N.*

3ND-P&PO-(472) 3ND-NYNS-GEN-157

...nos "John" Benkó Employment

THE GRAND LODGE
OF THE

International Association of Machinists and Aerospace Workers

FOUNDED  MAY 5, 1888

Washington, D.C., May 1, 1968

Fifty Year Veteran

This is to certify that Brother John Benko *Card No.* 423224 *Lodge No.* 556, *has been awarded a Jewelled Veteran's Badge as an honor conferred by the Grand Lodge of the International Association of Machinists and Aerospace Workers, due to his loyalty and service to his fellow men for a period of fifty years, he having, during this period of time, exemplified his true value to his fellow men, and therefore, is entitled to the lasting respect and esteem of all members of this Association.*

50

Given under our hand and seal by authority of the Executive Council of the International Association of Machinists and Aerospace Workers, this 1st *day of* May, 1968.

P. L. Siemiller
International President

Matthew DeMore
General Secretary-Treasurer

7

John Benko standing on the lawn in front of his home in Mt. Sinai, Long Island, New York. This is probably one of the last photographs taken of John prior to his passing on February 21, 1971.

Following his retirement in 1957 from the New York Naval Shipyard at the age of 68, he continued his union membership, and received a certificate marking 50 years as a member of the International Association of Machinists and Aerospace Workers on May 1, 1968.

The Statue of Liberty-Ellis Island Foundation, Inc.

proudly presents this

Official Certificate of Registration

in

THE AMERICAN IMMIGRANT WALL OF HONOR

to officially certify that

Janos F. Benko

came to the United States of America from

Hungary

joining those courageous men and women who came to this country in search of personal freedom, economic opportunity and a future hope for their families.

Lee Iacocca

Lee A. Iacocca
The Statue of Liberty-Ellis Island Foundation, Inc.

V.S. 60 (1/70)

NEW YORK STATE DEPARTMENT OF HEALTH
BUREAU OF VITAL RECORDS
CERTIFICATE OF DEATH
TYPE ALL ENTRIES OR PRINT IN PERMANENT BLACK INK.

RECORDED DISTRICT: 5198
REGISTER NUMBER: 11
STATE FILE NUMBER:

1. Name: First / Middle / Last	John / F. / BENKO
2. Sex	Male [X] Female [ ]
3A. Date of Death (Month / Day / Year)	2 / 21 / 71
3B. Hour	8:35 p.
4. Race (White, Negro, American Indian, etc.)	White
5. Age	81 yrs.
6A. Veteran of U.S. Armed Forces?	Yes [X] No [ ] Unknown [ ]
6B. If yes – specify war, or dates of service	WW I
7A. County (N.Y.S.)	Suffolk
7B. Town	Huntington
7C. City or Village	Northport
7D. Length of stay in town, city or village	2 days
7E. Hospital or other institution (if neither, give street & no.)	VA Hospital, Northport, N.Y.
8. State of Birth (Country, if not USA)	Hungary
9. Decedent Born (Month / Day / Year)	5 / 27 / 89
10. Citizen of what country?	U.S.A.
11. Marital Status	Married
12. Surviving Spouse (if wife, maiden name)	Anna Arendas
13A. Usual Occupation (even if retired)	Machinist (Retired)
13B. Kind of Business or Industry	Unknown
13C. Social Security No.	055-01-6844
14A. State	New York
14B. County	Suffolk
14C. Town	Brookhaven
14D. City or Village	Mt. Sinai
14E. Within the corporate limits?	Yes [X] No [ ]
14F. Street and Number	Hayward Ave.
15A. Father's Name: First / Middle / Last	Michael / / Benko
15B. Mother's Maiden Name: First / Middle / Last	Julia / / Toth
16A. Informant's Name	VA Hospital Records
16B. Mailing Address (include zip code)	Middleville Rd., Northport, N.Y. 11768

Usual residence where deceased lived. If death occurred in institution, give residence before admission.

ATTENTION

If an error is noted in a certificate before acceptance by registrar a corrected certificate may be substituted.

If an incorrect certificate has been accepted by the registrar, file form V.S. 64.

PART I. DEATH WAS CAUSED BY — ENTER ONLY ONE CAUSE PER LINE FOR (A), (B), AND (C).

17.	Cause	Approximate interval between onset & death
(A) Immediate cause	Uremia	
(B) Due to or as a consequence of	Acute & Chronic Pyelocystitis	2 years
(C) Due to or as a consequence of	Diabetes Mellitus	over 5 years

PART II. Other significant conditions: conditions contributing to death but not related to cause given in Part I (A)

18A. Autopsy? Yes [ ] No [X]
18B. If yes, were findings considered in determining the cause of death? Yes [ ] No [ ]

19A. Accident, homicide, suicide, undetermined — 19B. Month Day Year — 19C. Hour — 19D. How did injury occur? (Enter nature of injuries in #17 I, or II.)
19E. Injury at work? Yes [ ] No [ ] — 19F. Place of injury: home, factory, office bldg., etc. — 19G. Location (street & no., city or village, town, county, state)

TO BE COMPLETED BY CERTIFYING PHYSICIAN ONLY — OR — TO BE COMPLETED BY CORONER OR MEDICAL EXAMINER ONLY

20. PART I
A. To the best of my knowledge, death occurred at the time, date and place and due to the causes stated.
Signed: Paul T. Egidio — 2 / 22 / 71
B. The physician attended the deceased from 2 / 19 / 71 to 2 / 21 / 71 — C. Last seen alive
D. Attending physician, if other than certifier:

20. PART II
A. On the basis of examination and/or investigation, in my opinion death occurred at the time, date and place and due to the causes stated.
Signed — Title
B. Pronounced dead — C. Hour — On — At — M.
D. Date signed
E. Coroner's physician, if other than certifier:

21. Name and address of certifier (physician, coroner, medical examiner, coroner's physician, medical director): P.T. Egidio, M.D. VA Hospital, Middleville Rd., Northport, N.Y. 11768

22A. Burial / Cremation / Removal	Burial [X] Cremation [ ] Removal [ ] — 2 / 26 / 71
22B. Place of burial, cremation or removal	Washington Memorial Park
22C. Location (city or town, state)	Coram, N.Y.
23A. Name and address of funeral home	O.B.Davis Inc. Funeral Home, Port Jefferson, N.Y.
23B. Registration No.	00596
24A. Name of funeral director	George E. Robinson
24B. Signature of funeral director	George E. Robinson
24C. Registration No.	04733
25A. Signature of registrar	Caroline Dija
25B. Date filed	2 / 22 / 71
26A. Burial or removal permit issued by	Caroline Dija, Sub-registrar
26B. Month / Day / Year	2 / 22 / 71

I used the above Ellis Island Certif[…] Benkó as an introduction to the B[…] at our first meeting to establish ou[…]

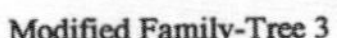

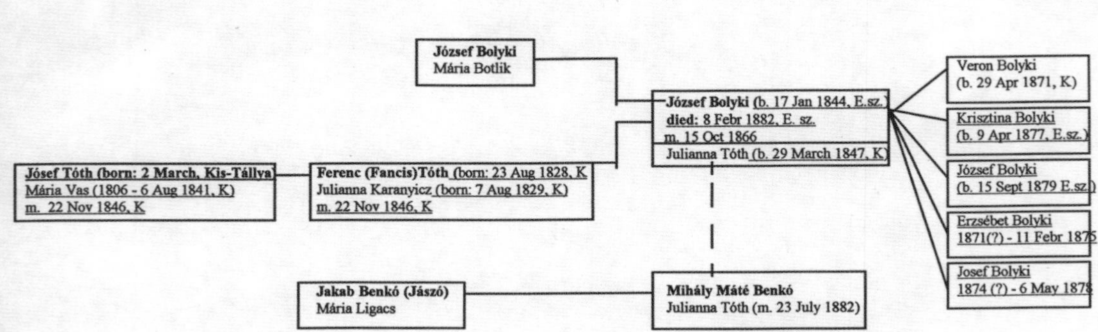
1
Modified Family-Tree 3
József Bolyki
Mária Botlik
József Bolyki (b. 17 Jan 1844, E.sz.)
died: 8 Febr 1882, E. sz.
m. 15 Oct 1866
Julianna Tóth (b. 29 March 1847, K)
Jósef Tóth (born: 2 March, Kis-Tállya)
Mária Vas (1806 - 6 Aug 1841, K)
m. 22 Nov 1846, K
Ferenc (Fancis)Tóth (born: 23 Aug 1828, K
Julianna Karanyicz (born: 7 Aug 1829, K)
m. 22 Nov 1846, K
Veron Bolyki
(b. 29 Apr 1871, K)
Krisztina Bolyki
(b. 9 Apr 1877, E.sz.)
József Bolyki
(b. 15 Sept 1879 E.sz.)
Erzsébet Bolyki
1871(?) - 11 Febr 1875
Josef Bolyki
1874 (?) - 6 May 1878
Jakab Benkó (Jászó)
Mária Ligacs
Mihály Máté Benkó
Julianna Tóth (m. 23 July 1882)

552

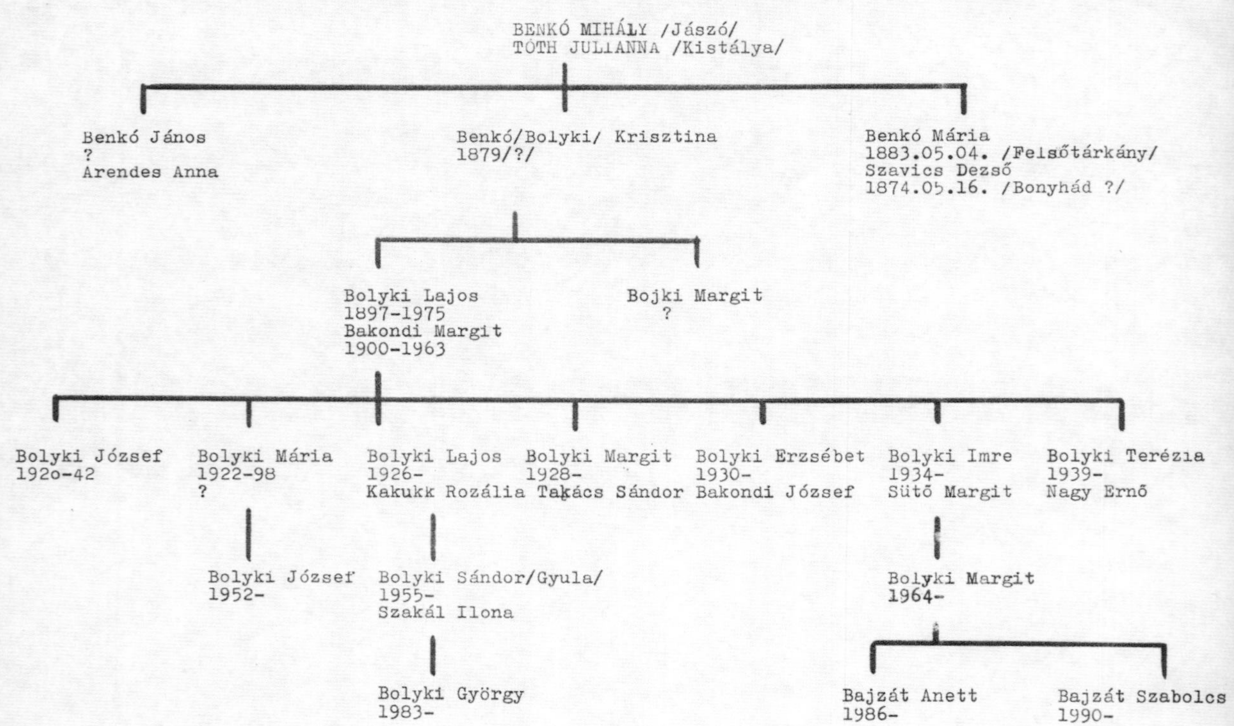
BENKÓ MIHÁLY /Jászó/
TÓTH JULIANNA /Kistálya/
Benkó János
?
Arendes Anna
Benkó/Bolyki/ Krisztina
1879/?/
Benkó Mária
1883.05.04. /Felsőtárkány/
Szavics Dezső
1874.05.16. /Bonyhád ?/
Bolyki Lajos
1897-1975
Bakondi Margit
1900-1963
Bojki Margit
?
Bolyki József
192o-42
Bolyki Mária
1922-98
?
Bolyki Lajos
1926-
Kakukk Rozália
Bolyki Margit
1928-
Takács Sándor
Bolyki Erzsébet
1930-
Bakondi József
Bolyki Imre
1934-
Sütő Margit
Bolyki Terézia
1939-
Nagy Ernő
Bolyki József
1952-
Bolyki Sándor/Gyula/
1955-
Szakál Ilona
Bolyki Margit
1964-
Bolyki György
1983-
Bajzát Anett
1986-
Bajzát Szabolcs
1990-
Rec'd 6/26/98

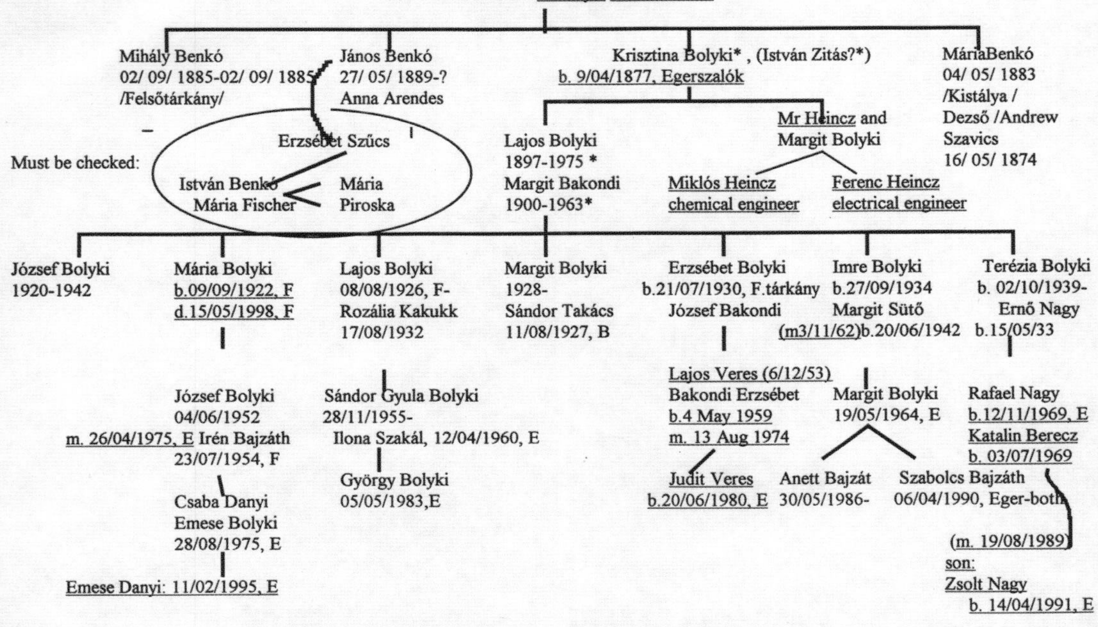

Gyula "Julius" Fülep, of Eger, Hungary, a researcher employed by Clyde Davis, wrote in a letter received December 22, 1998: "As for the encircled information [See attached] on the 'Modified Family - Tree 2,' Mr. Lajos Bolyki said that János Benkó had had a love affair before he married Anna Arendes. A girl was born called Erzsébet Szűcs. Her son, István Benkó got married to Mária Fischer and their children are Mária Benkó and Piroska Benkó."

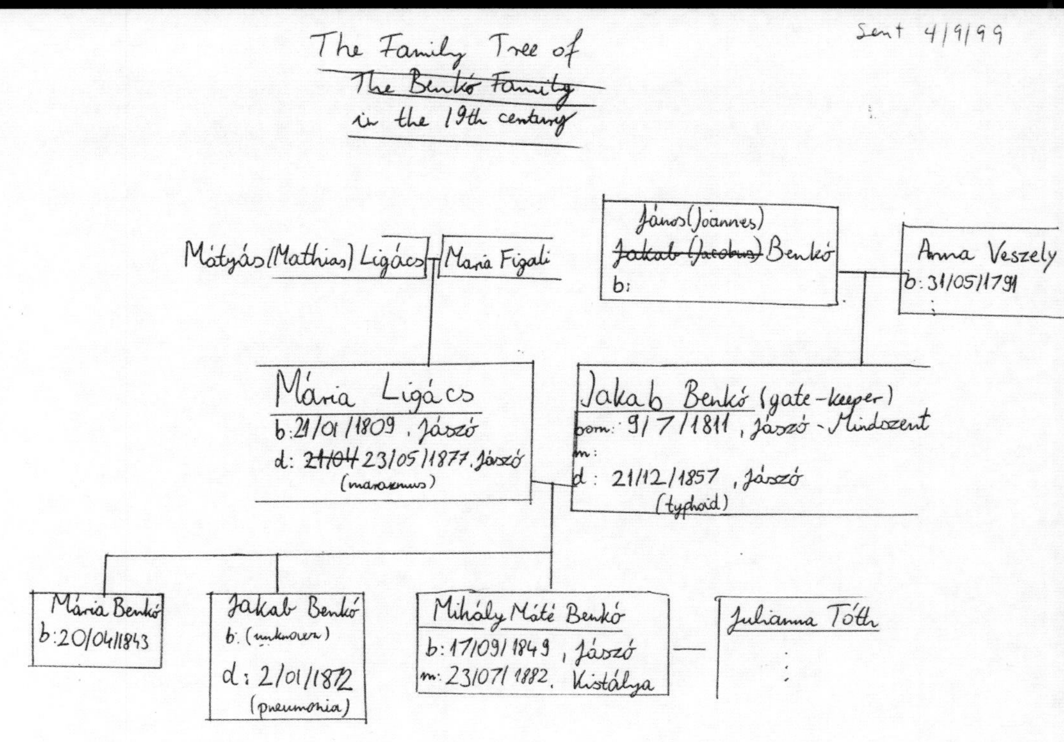

ee of the Benkó fa

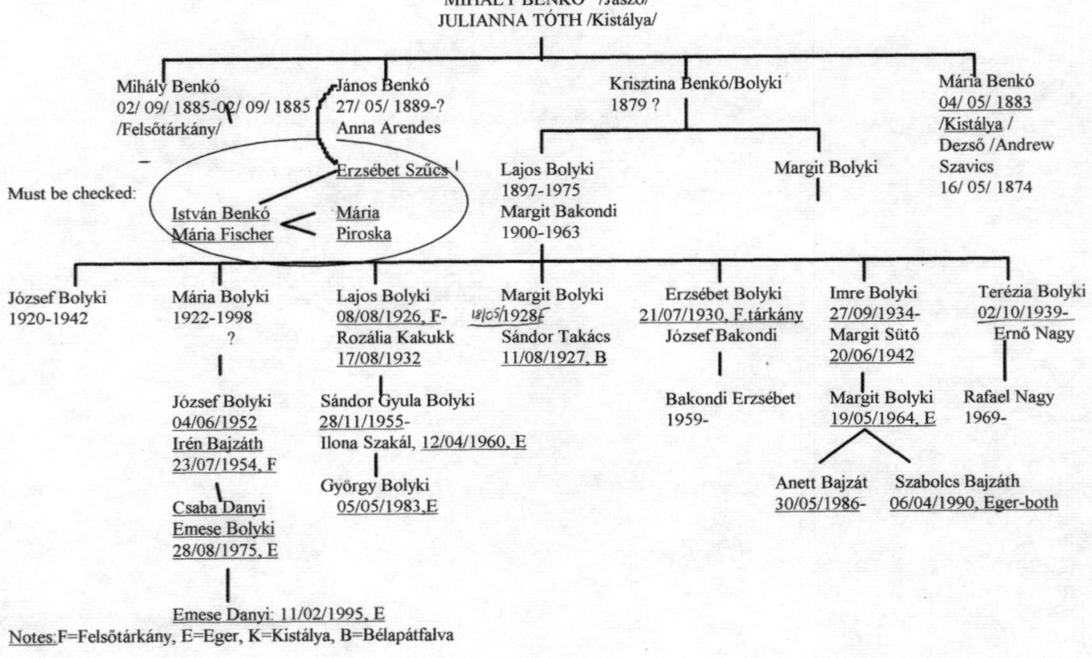

n a letter received from Gyula (Julius) Fülep, Eger, Hungary, dated September 29, 1998,
e writes:

> *I found several of your relatives' dates and places of births and marriages. They are indicated on the photocopies of registers and certificates and on the "Modified Family Tree 2," underlined. All of them were baptized Roman Catholics like everyone else in Felsötárkány and in Kistálya. It has turned out that Julianna Tóth must have got married twice. Her first husband's name was József Bolkyi. However, her mother's family name is not the same as at the time of her wedding with Mihály Benkó (see Family Tree, registers). The first name is Julianna in both cases. One solution may be the idea that she had her surname "hungarianized." The other one is obvious: there may have been two women called Julianna Tóth. In any case, I have found that a girl called "Veron" was born from the marriage and I did not find Krisztina in either the register of births of Felsötárkány or in that of Kistálya. It is said to be possible that her name was not registered. I think I must check whether József Bolyki died before Julianna's wedding with Mihály Benkó. By the way Julianna Tóth used to work as a craftsman.*

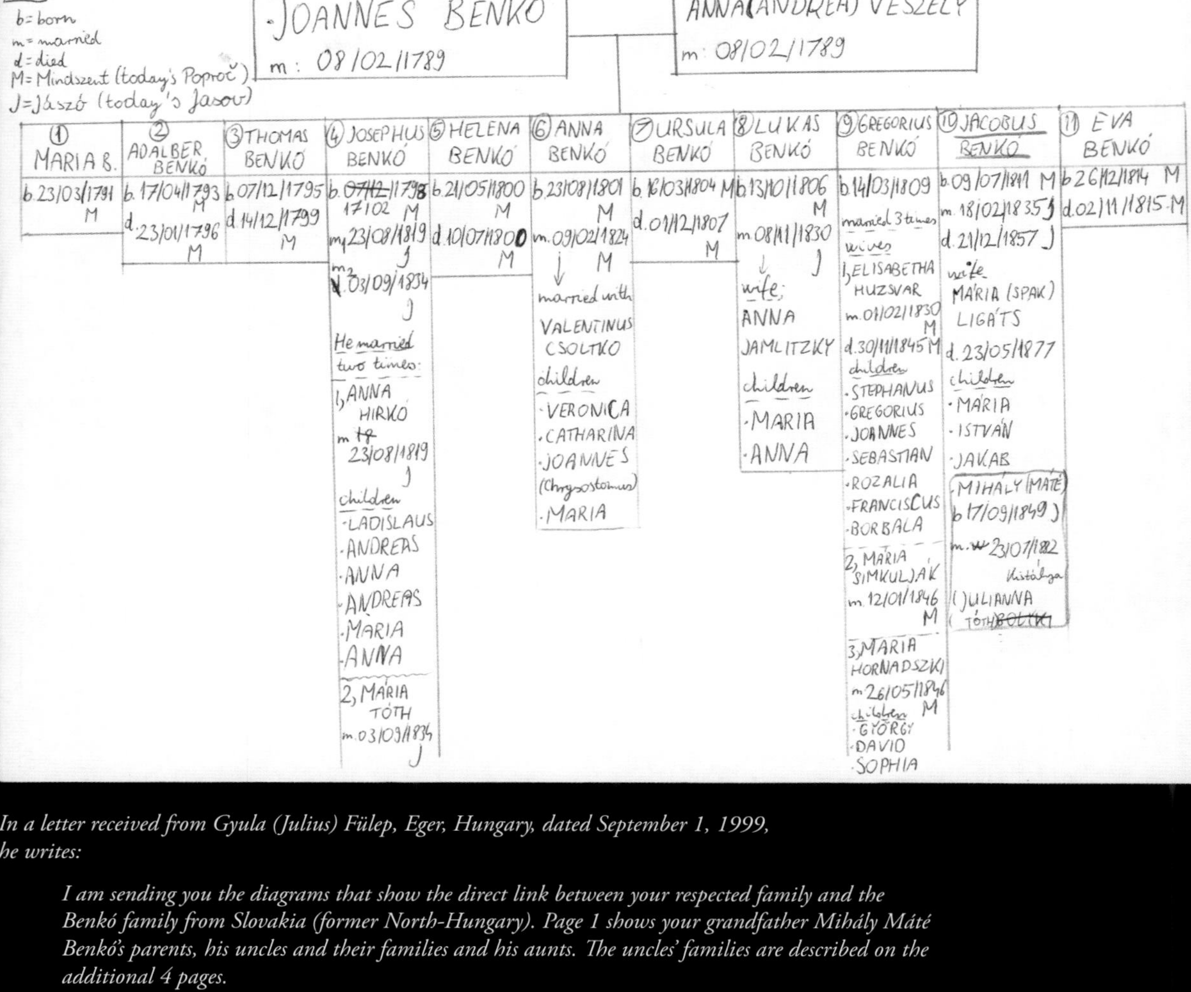

In a letter received from Gyula (Julius) Fülep, Eger, Hungary, dated September 1, 1999, he writes:

> *I am sending you the diagrams that show the direct link between your respected family and the Benkó family from Slovakia (former North-Hungary). Page 1 shows your grandfather Mihály Máté Benkő's parents, his uncles and their families and his aunts. The uncles' families are described on the additional 4 pages.*

⑩

JACOBUS BENKÓ
b. 09/07/1811 Mindszenth
m. 18/02/1835 Jászó
d. 21/12/1857 J

MÁRIA SPAK
(born MÁRIA LIGÁTS)
b. 21/01/1809 J
m. 18/02/1835 J
d. 23/05/1877 J

→ Her first husband was
JOANNES SPAK
m: 17/10/1831, Jászó

MÁRIA BENKÓ
b. 20/04/1843 J

ISTVÁN BENKÓ
b. 15/06/1845 J
d. 03/02/1846 J

JAKAB BENKÓ
b. 12/01/1847 J
m. 02/01/1872 J

MIHÁLY - MÁTÉ BENKÓ
b. 17/09/1849 J
m. 23/07/1882 Kistálya
wife: JULIANNA TÓTH

your family...

In a letter received from Gyula (Julius) Fülep, Hungary, dated September 1, 1999, he writes:

> *I am sending you the diagrams of Joannes Benkó, Anna Andrea Veszely and their descendants. Their tenth child was Jacobus Benkó (in Hungarian 'Jakab') who married Mária Spak whose former husband Joannes Spak had died. The woman's maiden name was Mária Ligáts. Their son was Mihály (Michael) Máté Benkó, your great-grandfather.*

Benkó Family

Two documents follow, which arrived with a letter from Julius Fülep dated June 15, 1999. In his letter, Julius reports that he had Peter Balázs carry out research in Slovakia. This included research into the history of the towns of Jászó Mindszent / Poproč and Jászó / Jasov. Members of the Benkó family lived in these towns, and some of their descendants still live in the area. Jakobus (or Joannes) Benkó married Anna Veszely in Jászó Mindszent / Poproč on February 8, 1789. Their son, Jakobus (Jakab) Benkó was born July 9, 1811, in Jászó Mindszent / Poproč and died in Jászó. Their son, Mihály Máté Benkó was born September 17, 1849, in Jászó. Mihály's daughter Mária (Mary) Dersöné Benkó was born in Kistálya and on May 5, 1903, she married Dusán Dezsó Szávics born June 2, 1874, and subsequently emigrated to the United States. Mihály's son János "John" Benkó was born in Felsötárkány.

The histories of the towns are transcribed from the documents Julius sent.

Jászó Mindszent / Poproč

The village was first mentioned as a royal mining village called "Olchuan" in a gift-deed of King of Hungary Béla IV in 1255. Consequently, the local residents used to deal with mining before the Tartar invasion. They had a monastery at that time according to that document.

The village of Olchuan was located west of today's Poproč. Later the residents moved to a newly formed village because of the mine. This fact is mentioned in documents from 1383. At that time the settlement was called Mendzenth (an ancient version of the Hungarian word 'Mindszent' that means 'All Saints'). It belonged to the district under the provost of Jászó.

The name of the village changed during the centuries several times:

- 1407 Mendszent
- 1427 Menthzenth
- 1481 Myndzenth
- 1590 Podprocz aliter Myndzenth
- 1630 Jaszó-Mindszent
- 1808 Podproč
- 1903 Poproč

In the area of today's Slovakia (one-time Northern-Hungary) there were four villages called Poproč in the Middle Ages. All of them were in the mountains and the population was Slav.

According to Slovakian historians and linguists, the name comes from the Slavic word 'paprad' that means fern.

In the Middle Ages noblemen such as kings, landlords, and the church gave prospecting rights to certain experts who had to

Copy of an engraving of the Premonstratensian Monastery in Jászó, Slovakia. In a handwritten letter to Clyde Davis dated April 3, 1999, along with the engraving above, Julius Fülep, wrote:

> *Jászó was part of Hungary until 1920. Now it belongs to Slovakia. You can see the Premonstrean* [sic] *monastery of Jászó in one of he enclosed copies. The small town is about 700 years old. It's the center of a medieval provostship as well. Mihály Benkó's father, Jakab [Clyde Davis's great-great grandfather], was probably one of the provost's gatekeepers. He was from the nearest village, Jászó-Mindszent that is called Poproč in Slovakian today. Both Hungarians and Slovaks live in the settlements that can be found in a beautiful valley of the Carpathian Mountains (drawing).*

search for ores in their estates. After some ore was found, mining villages or towns were founded near mines. They actually found iron and gold near the settlement. Probably Polish miners settled down here.

In 1407 the village became the landlords' property.

In 1408 the Perényi family owned it.

In 1427 it was the provost's property again with twenty serfs' farms.

In addition to mining, the inhabitants used to deal with agriculture and forest clearing. There are no documents left about their nationality. Its parsonage was mentioned in a manuscript in 1506. Its Gothic altar was built in 1518.

In 1564, during the war against the Ottoman Empire, only six landowners and their families lived in Myndzenth. However, fifty-eight mostly Slovak families had cottages in 1596. It is proved by a letter written by Lord Chief of Justice István Báthory. At that time it belonged to the Hungarian Kingdom that was part of the Hapsburg Empire. In 1603 Prince of Transylvania István Bocskai's soldiers occupied the village.

In peace the abbots of Jászó used to pay attention to their serfs' economic and cultural development, and that is why they used to establish church schools in their estates. It is unknown when the first school of Mindszent was established, but there are written documents proving that András Lindvay was a headmaster there in 1646. He was also the local cantor and notary, as he did not know how to keep his head above the water as a teacher.

In 1709, during the war of independence led by Prince Ferenc Rákóczi II against the Austrian Empire ruling Hungary, most local residents died of plague.

After the war that unfortunately failed, the epidemic was over and Roman Catholic Slovak families moved to the village. It was mentioned as Poproč in a lexicon of 1773.

The Gothic church dates back to the 16th century. It was erected to the honor of All Saints and transformed in Baroque — neoclassical style in 1766. That was the time when the first organ was made.

The parsonage burnt down in 1823, but it was rebuilt two years later. It has had registers of birth, marriages, and deaths since 1739.

They took a census of the population in 1828, and according to that, 1,147 residents lived in 153 cottages. Peasants and miners lived there. They used to carry iron and brass to the nearby foundries of Aranyida and Jászó. They also used to transport charcoal and wheat.

At the beginning of the 20th century, a lot of people emigrated to America to find a job.

The village had 1,464 residents in 1900.

In 1902, 1,652 Roman Catholics, four Greek Catholics, two Protestants and thirty-five Israelites lived there. Three hundred twenty-four children went to school where two teachers and a schoolmistress worked.

In 1910 the number of population was only 1,263.

Twenty-five men died in World War I.

The village was part of the Czechoslovakian Republic from 1918 to 1938. The local residents were happy about it though their lives did not change. They still used to work in the mines, in the quarries, or in the forest. The settlement belonged to the district of Szepsi (Moldava nad Bodvou in Slovakian). In the 1930s more and more people sympathized with the Social Democratic Party and with the Communist Party for the hard conditions of life. Only events of minor significance happened:

- The first local bicycle owner was Jan Majcher in 1921.
- The first motorbike-owner was Imrich Sopko in 1936.

From 1939 to 1945 Poproč belonged to Hungary again. That was the time when Hungary regained her lost territories in the southern part and in the eastern part of Slovakia on the basis of the First Viennese Decision made by British Prime Minister Chamberlain, the Italian dictator Mussolini, and Hitler. Most of the population consisted of Hungarians in those areas.

Hungarian teachers appeared in the Slovakian village in 1939, although there was a Slovakian school, too. Nevertheless, only a few pupils attended that school.

The local men as citizens of Hungary had to take part in World War II, so several young men escaped to Slovakia, the border of which was a distance of some miles. Twenty-two soldiers of Poproč died in the war. Hitler's army occupied Hungary in March 1944 as the country was "not faithful enough," looking for a way to make peace with the Allied Powers. Many people participated in the fights against the Nazis as members of the Czechoslovakian Army set up in the Soviet Union.

Finally the village was occupied by the Soviet Army on January 21, 1945. From then to 1991 Poproč belonged to Czechoslovakia, which was under Communist oppression. Since then it has been part of Slovakia, where there is democracy again.

Jászó / Jasov

The oldest written memory dates from 1234. It says that Jászó was a village with a monastery: "Filia S. Stephani — Vallis S. Joannis Baptiste que alio nomime dictus Turna." According to this, Saint John the Baptist's Monastery of Jászó was the affiliated church of Saint Stephen's Monastery of Nagyvárad. Its area and village of that time were parts of the Castle of Torna and its estate.

The following names of the village occur in charters:

1243 Jazow　　1251 Jazou
1280 Jasov　　1440 Jassw (in German)
1487 Josza (in German)　　1527 Jossa (in German)
1773 Jászó (in Hungarian) 1808 Jásow (in Slovakian), Jászó (in Hungarian), Joss (in German)
1851 Jászó (in Hungarian), Joss (in German)
1903 Jászó (in Hungarian), Jasov (in Slovakian)

The name derives from the Old Slav word 'Jasa,' which means 'mountaintop without a forest' or 'plateau.' There is a real plateau on the hill opposite the village and the monastery.

Jászó was a mining settlement and it got the right of holding markets at the beginning of the 12th century. During the reign of King András II, German settlers and members of the Premonstratensian Monastic Order arrived in Jászó. The provostship was probably established at the end of the 12th century although the documents of the foundation burned away.

The Tartars destroyed the still unfinished monastery, the convent, and the archives, just like most of Hungary in 1241. The residents of the village escaped.

When King Béla IV returned from Dalmatia after the invasion was over, he ordered the people to build new stone fortresses all over Hungary. The nearby Castle of Torna was erected at that time. In 1255 he was carousing in the castle with local lords and Provost Albert begged him for help. As a result, he issued a new deed of foundation, in which you can read about the Tartar destruction and about the fact that the King confirmed the provost's rights. He determined the boundaries of the estate, most of which consisted of pine forests and beech forests. In its agricultural area, these settlements were located in the 13th century: Jászó, Olchoun, Rudnok, and Debrőd. In the second half of the century further villages were mentioned such as Stosz, Also-Mecenzéf, Felső Mecenzéf and Jászóujfalu. The name of the village of Jászómindszent appeared in the last decades of the 14th century and that of Olchuan disappeared. It probably means that the residents of Olchuan founded a new settlement. However, it is only the central part of the provostship because ten other settlements belonged to it outside that area.

Benkó Family Documents

Also a faraway mill and a huge fish pond located in the Great Hungarian Plain belonged to the estate as the kings' grants in the 14th century.

The document of 1255 also regulated the manorial legal relationship between the monastery and the residents. It confirmed the people's obligations to the provostship and their privileges. Jászó became the place within the central estate where there used to be fairs, especially because the local industry developed well. That is why the whole settlement developed and became stronger. As a result, the residents were given privileges as advantageous as those living in free royal towns. For instance, they had rights to elect a priest and a judge, to hold markets, and to search for ores freely. Everyone who had a cottage or a mill had to pay three silvers to the monastery for these rights.

The mining rights of the provostship date back to the year 1290. King András III allowed the provosts and the convent of the monastery to search for any kinds of ores except silver within the boundaries of the estate and to pay duties on them to the treasury.

However, the size of the mining area was reduced in the 14th century as King Károly Robert donated its northern part to the territory of another mining town called Szomolnokbánya. He promised to give other areas instead, but it was postponed. That was the reason the lords of the monastery were given the right to mine any kinds of ores, including silver by King Nagy Lajos (Lewis The Great). This was the privilege that enabled the settlement to develop into a real mining town. In the 15th century it was the fourth one of the seven richest North-Hungarian mining towns that formed an alliance.

Saint Michael's Church was mentioned in documents in 1243 and in 1255. This parish-church had been built as the first one in the surroundings before the provostship was established.

There was a watch-tower or 'castrum' on a rock near Jászó built in the 14th century according to the king's order in order to defend the locals from robber barons' attacks. From 1390 on, it was owned by the provost. You can still see its ruins. Its story after 1402 is unknown. In 1436 the monastery itself was fortified and became a castle. King Zsigmond ordered the people to participate in the construction of the castle and the fish pond in 1421.

Sources for both pieces:

A Jászói Premontrei Apátság évkönyve, 1944 (*The Almanac of The Premonstratensian Abbey of Jászó, 1944*) — published by the Abbey

Dr. Takács Menyhért: *A Jászói Prépostsag története* (*The History of The Provostship of Jászó* by Dr. Menyhért Takács) — published in 1902 in Budapest

Dr. Spilka A.: *A Jászói Prépostság kivonatos története* (*The Abridged History of The Provostship of Jászó* by Dr. A. Spilka) — published in 1944 in Gödöllő

Abaúj vármegye közügyi iratai, 1489 – 1850 (The Documents of Public Affairs of County Abaúj, 1489 – 1850)

Photo by **Julius Fülep**

...NYAKÖNYVE.

...s a k				A tanúk neve és állapotja.	Az eskető neve és hivatala.	Voltak-e hirdetve, vagy fölmentve a hirdetéstől, vagy valamely akadálytól?	Jegyzetek.
Vallás.	Életkor.	Nőtlen, hajadon.	Özvegy.				
R.k.	33	nőtl		Kovács Gábor telkes			
R.k.	.	.	özv.	Kovács Imre telkes	"	"	
							Borsodmegye Kis-Tálya Andornaki ... s. k. Házasultak anyakönyve 1882-ről.

HÁZAS...

Folyó szám.	A házasságkötés éve, hava, napja.	A házas... Neve és állapotja.	Szülőik.	Származ...
17	Julius 23.	Benkó Mihály Máté ... / Tóth Julianna zsellér	Jakab ... Mária ... / Juhász Julianna	Kis Tállya

559

Register of marriage between Julianna Tóth and Mihály Máté Benkó on July 23, 1882.

Video grabs by **Clyde Davis**

Far left: Andornak church in Andornaktálya [Kistálya], Hungary, as it appears today. It is also known as the Church of the Virgin Lady, or as the "Virgin Mary with sickle." She is the patron saint, "Sarlós Bóldogasszony." "Bóldogasszony" is a special word in Hungarian, which translates as "our lady" or "happy woman." Center left: Cemetery behind the church as it appears today. Center right: Kay following Julius Fülep and the local priest to the cemetery during our visit in June 1998. Far right: A caretaker carrying a sickle in 1998. Much of the cemetery was overgrown with weeds and wildflowers at the time. Photos at left by Julius Fülep. Pictures at right are from my video camcorder.

App. 1

1885.

KERESZTELTEK

Folyó szám	A születés	A keresztelés	A kereszteltnek Neve	Neme fi.	Neme nő.	törvényes	törvénytelen	elsőszülött	A szülök neve, vallása, állapotja és származás helye.
	éve, hava, napja.								
50.	Augustus 22.	23.	József	1	—	1	—	1	Kolló Mihály Bakondi Rozália r.kat. zsellér
51.	17.	20.	Veronika Piroska Ilonka	—	1	1	—	—	Hangay Antal Csató Erzsébet r.kat. uras. vadász.
52.	September 2.	2.	Mihály	1	—	1	—	—	Benkó Mihály Tóth Juliana r.kat. kovácsmester.
53.	2.	5.	Rozália	—	1	1	—	—	Bakondi Máté ... Mária ...

App. 2

1885.

HALOTTAK

Folyó szám.	(death) A meghalás éve, hava, napja.	A halottnak s az ő hitvestársának vagy szülőinek neve és állapotja. (parents)	Származása és lakhelye, ház-szám.	Neme fi.	Neme nő.	Életkora. (age)	Vallása. (relig)
46	Julius ...	Terézia, Vásárhelyi ... Karuk...	Tarkány ...	—	1	7.	r.
47.	25.	Dávid, és Karuk Katalin fia, zsellér	168.sz.	1	—	3 év 4 hó	r.k.
48.	Septemb. 2.	Benkó Mihály és Tóth Juliánna fia Mihály, kovács	8.sz.	1	—	3 óra (hours)	r.k.
49.	5.	Ilona, Tóke András és Karuk Teréz leánya. zsellér	75.sz.	—	1	7 hó	r.k.

Top: Record of Mihály Benkő's birth on September 2, 1885, in Felsötárkány, Hungary. Bottom: Record of Mihály Benkő's death on September 2, 1885. Mihály lived for only three hours, as noted in pencil in the second column from the right.

App. 3

KERESZTELTEK

Folyó szám	A születés (birth)	A keresztelés (baptism)	A kereszteltnek Neve. (Name)	Neme fi.	Neme nő.	törvényes.	törvénytelen.	elsőszülött.	A szülők neve, vallása, állapotja, és származás helye. (Parents)
	éve, hava, napja.								
29.	1889. Május 26	28.	Borbála	–	1	1	–	–	Sitke József, Varus Ilona, rk. [illegible]
30.	27	28.	János	1	–	1	–	–	Benkó Mihály (Párád) Tóth Julianna (Kisfalva) rk. kovácsmester
31.	28.	29.	Lajos	1	–	–	1	–	Vass Rozália [illegible]

Record of Janós (John) Benkő's birth on May 27, 1889, in Felsötárkány, Hungary

Above: Looking south on Széchenyi Street in Eger, Hungary. The red building is a youth center. Below: Kethüda minaret, the northern-most minaret of the Ottoman Empire in Europe. It was built shortly after the Turks' victory in 1596 during their 91-year occupation of the town.

Former secondary Jesuit grammar school in Eger, Hungary. Today, it is a state school. The school was originally named after Dobó István.

Photos by **Julius Fülep**, Eger, Hungary, October 2009.

Benkó Family Documents

4/9/99 (4) of (14)

ŠTÁTNY OBLASTNÝ ARCHÍV V KOŠICIACH
041 56 KOŠICE, BAČÍKOVA 1

STATE REGIONAL ARCHIVES IN KOŠICE
041 56 KOŠICE, BAČÍKOVA 1
Slovakia

Číslo: ŠA- 98/989-VS2
Reference/file number

VÝPIS PRE RODNÝ LIST
EXTRACT FOR CERTIFICATE OF BIRTH

V matrike narodených farského úradu cirkvi / In Birth Registers of the church parochial office: rímskokatolíckej

v / in: Jasove vo zväzku / volume: III. na strane / page: 48

pod poradovým číslom / number: 8 z roku / from the year: 1809 je zapísané: / is registered:

Deň, mesiac a rok narodenia / Day, month and the year of birth: 21.1.1809 (dvadsiaty prvý január jedentisíc osemstodeväť)

Miesto narodenia / Birth place: Jászó (Jasov)

Meno a priezvisko dieťaťa / Children's first name and surname: Maria LIGÁCS

Pohlavie / Sex: ženské Legitimnosť: legitímne

Meno a priezvisko (zamestnanie) otca / Father's first name and surname (occupation): Mathias LIGÁCS

Meno a priezvisko matky / First name and Surname of mother: Maria FIGALI

Krstní rodičia / Christian's parents: Franciscus NAGY, Catharina BUJDOSO

Poznámky / Notes: ---

V Košiciach dňa / In Košice: 21.1.1999

Tento výpis obsahuje všetky údaje zapísané v horeuvedenej matrike, ktorá je uložená v tunajšom archíve; meno a priezvisko a miesto matričnej udalosti sú uvedené v jazyku matriky; všetky ďalšie údaje sú doslovným prekladom z latinského jazyka do štátneho jazyka.

Riaditeľ / Director

Copy of Extract for Certificate of Birth of Maria Ligács b. January 21, 1809, d. May 23, 1877. Maria was the wife of Jacobus Benko b. July 9, 1811.

4/9/99 (6) of (14)

ŠTÁTNY OBLASTNÝ ARCHÍV V KOŠICIACH
041 56 KOŠICE, BAČÍKOVA 1

STATE REGIONAL ARCHIVES IN KOŠICE
041 56 KOŠICE, BAČÍKOVA 1
Slovakia

Číslo: ŠA- 98/989-VS2
Reference/file number

VÝPIS PRE RODNÝ LIST
EXTRACT FOR CERTIFICATE OF BIRTH

V matrike narodených farského úradu cirkvi / In Birth Registers of the church parochial office: rímskokatolíckej

v / in: Poproči vo zväzku / volume: II. na strane / page: 43

pod poradovým číslom / number: --- z roku / from the year: 1811 je zapísané: / is registered:

Deň, mesiac a rok narodenia / Day, month and the year of birth: 9.7.1811 (deviaty júl jedentisíc osemsto-jedenásť)

Miesto narodenia / Birth place: Jászó Mindszent (Poproč)

Meno a priezvisko dieťaťa / Children's first name and surname: Jacobus BENKO

Pohlavie / Sex: mužské male MUŽSKÉ Legitimnosť: legitímne

Meno a priezvisko (zamestnanie) otca / Father's first name and surname (occupation): Joannes BENKO

Meno a priezvisko matky / First name and Surname of mother: Anna WESZELY Joannes' wife

Krstní rodičia / Christian's parents: Michael TOMCSICSKO, Veronica PETRÁS, manželka Joannesa Hilyovszkého

Poznámky / Notes: ---

V Košiciach dňa / In Košice: 21.1.1999

Tento výpis obsahuje všetky údaje zapísané v horeuvedenej matrike, ktorá je uložená v tunajšom archíve; meno a priezvisko a miesto matričnej udalosti sú uvedené v jazyku matriky; všetky ďalšie údaje sú doslovným prekladom z latinského jazyka do štátneho jazyka.

Riaditeľ / Director

Copy of Extract for Certificate of Birth of Jacobus Benkó b. July 9, 1811

4/9/99 (3) of (14)

ŠTÁTNY OBLASTNÝ ARCHÍV V KOŠICIACH
041 56 KOŠICE, BAČÍKOVA 1

STATE REGIONAL ARCHIVES IN KOŠICE
041 56 KOŠICE, BAČÍKOVA 1
Slovakia

Číslo: 98/989-VS2
Reference/file number

VÝPIS PRE ÚMRTNÝ LIST
EXTRACT FOR CERTIFICATE OF DEATH

V matrike zomrelých farského úradu cirkvi / In Death Registers of the church parochial office: rímskokatolíckej Roman Cath.

v / in: Jasove vo zväzku / volume: V. na strane / page: 74

pod poradovým číslom / number: 30 z roku / from the year: 1877 je zapísané: / is registered:

Deň, mesiac a rok úmrtia / Day, month and the year of death: 23.5.1877 (dvadsiaty tretí máj jedentisíc osemsto sedemdesiatsedem)

Miesto úmrtia / Place of death: Jászó (Jasov) č.d. 208

Meno a priezvisko (vek, stav) zomrelého / First name and Surname (age, status) of person died: Maria LIGÁCS (70 r., vdova)

Rodičia (manžel, manželka) zomrelého / Parents (husband, wife) of person died: nebohý Jacobus BENKO

Príčina smrti / Reason of death: marazmus

Poznámky / Notes: ---

Tento výpis obsahuje všetky údaje zapísané v horeuvedenej matrike, ktorá je uložená v tunajšom archíve; meno a priezvisko a miesto matričnej udalosti sú uvedené v jazyku matriky; všetky ďalšie údaje sú doslovným prekladom z latinského jazyka do štátneho jazyka.

V Košiciach dňa / In Košice: 21.1.1999

Riaditeľ / Director

Copy of Extract for Certificate of Death of Maria Ligács b. January 21, 1809, d. May 23, 1877

4/9/99 (2) of (14)

ŠTÁTNY OBLASTNÝ ARCHÍV V KOŠICIACH
041 56 KOŠICE, BAČÍKOVA 1

STATE REGIONAL ARCHIVES IN KOŠICE
041 56 KOŠICE, BAČÍKOVA 1
Slovakia

Číslo: 98/989-VS2
Reference/file number

VÝPIS PRE ÚMRTNÝ LIST
EXTRACT FOR CERTIFICATE OF DEATH

V matrike zomrelých farského úradu cirkvi / In Death Registers of the church parochial office: rímskokatolíckej

v / in: Jasove vo zväzku / volume: IV. na strane / page: 30

pod poradovým číslom / number: 42 z roku / from the year: 1857 je zapísané: / is registered:

Deň, mesiac a rok úmrtia / Day, month and the year of death: 21.12.1857 (dvadsiaty prvý december jedentisíc osemsto päťdesiatsedem)

Miesto úmrtia / Place of death: Jászó (Jasov) č.d. 110

Meno a priezvisko (vek, stav) zomrelého / First name and Surname (age, status) of person died: Jacobus BENKO (46 r., ženatý) married

Rodičia (manžel, manželka) zomrelého / Parents (husband, wife) of person died: Maria LIGÁCS

Príčina smrti / Reason of death: brušný týfus typhoid

Poznámky / Notes: ---

Tento výpis obsahuje všetky údaje zapísané v horeuvedenej matrike, ktorá je uložená v tunajšom archíve; meno a priezvisko a miesto matričnej udalosti sú uvedené v jazyku matriky; všetky ďalšie údaje sú doslovným prekladom z latinského jazyka do štátneho jazyka.

V Košiciach dňa / In Košice: 21.1.1999

Riaditeľ / Director

Copy of Extract for Certificate of Death of Jacobus Benkó b. July 9, 1811 d. December 21, 1857

4/9/99 ⑤ of ⑭

ŠTÁTNY OBLASTNÝ ARCHÍV V KOŠICIACH
041 56 KOŠICE, BAČÍKOVA 1

STATE REGIONAL ARCHIVES IN KOŠICE
041 56 KOŠICE, BAČÍKOVA 1
Slovakia

Číslo: ~~SA-~~ 98/989-VS2
Reference/file number

VÝPIS PRE RODNÝ LIST
EXTRACT FOR CERTIFICATE OF BIRTH

V matrike narodených farského úradu cirkvi rímskokatolíckej = Roman Catholic
In Birth Registers of the church parochial office
v Poproči vo zväzku II. na strane 10
in volume page
pod poradovým číslom --- z roku 1791 je zapísané:
number from the year is registered:
Deň, mesiac a rok narodenia 31.5.1791 (tridsiaty prvý máj jedentisíc sedemsto deväťdesiatjeden) the year in Slovakian
Day, month and the year of birth
Miesto narodenia Jászó Mindszent (Poproč)
Birth place
Meno a priezvisko dieťaťa Anna VESZELY
Children's first name and surname
Pohlavie ženské female Legitimnosť: legitimné
Sex
Meno a priezvisko (zamestnanie) otca Mathias VESZELY
Father's first name and surname (occupation)
Meno a priezvisko matky Maria BANÍK
First name and Surname of mother
Krstní rodičia Michael KOMTSIK, Maria, dcéra Mathiasa MELCZENA
Christian's parents
Poznámky ---
Notes
V Košiciach dňa 21.1.1999
In Košice
Tento výpis obsahuje všetky údaje zapísané v horeuvedenej matrike, ktorá je uložená v tunajšom archíve; meno a priezvisko a miesto matričnej udalosti sú uvedené v jazyku matriky; všetky ďalšie údaje sú doslovným prekladom z latinského jazyka do štátneho jazyka.

Riaditeľ
Director

Copy of Extract for Certificate of Birth of Anna Veszely b. May 31, 1791. Anna was the wife of Jakobus (or Joannes) Benkó.

Rec'd from Julius (GYULA) FÜLEP 4/9/99 ① of ⑭

ŠTÁTNY OBLASTNÝ ARCHÍV V KOŠICIACH
041 56 KOŠICE, BAČÍKOVA 1

STATE REGIONAL ARCHIVES IN KOŠICE
041 56 KOŠICE, BAČÍKOVA 1
Slovakia

Číslo: 98/989-VS2
Reference/file number

VÝPIS PRE ÚMRTNÝ LIST
EXTRACT FOR CERTIFICATE OF DEATH

V matrike zomrelých farského úradu cirkvi rímskokatolíckej
In Death Registers of the church parochial office
v Jasove vo zväzku V. na strane 37
in volume page
pod poradovým číslom 1 z roku 1872 je zapísané:
number from the year is registered:
Deň, mesiac a rok úmrtia 2.1.1872 (druhý január jedentisíc osemsto sedemdesiatdva)
Day, month and the year of death
Miesto úmrtia Jászó (Jasov) č.d. 120
Place of death
Meno a priezvisko (vek, stav) zomrelého Jacobus BENKO (24 r., slobodný) single
First name and Surname (age, status) of person died
Rodičia (manžel, manželka) zomrelého matka - vdova Maria LIGÁCS mother widow
Parents (husband, wife) of person died
Príčina smrti zápal pľúc pneumonia
Reason of death
Poznámky ---
Notes

Tento výpis obsahuje všetky údaje zapísané v horeuvedenej matrike, ktorá je uložená v tunajšom archíve; meno a priezvisko a miesto matričnej udalosti sú uvedené v jazyku matriky; všetky ďalšie údaje sú doslovným prekladom z latinského jazyka do štátneho jazyka.

V Košiciach dňa 21.1.1999
In Košice

Riaditeľ
Director

Copy of Extract for Certificate of Death of Jacobus Benkó b. 1848

4/9/99 ⑧ of ⑭

ŠTÁTNY OBLASTNÝ ARCHÍV V KOŠICIACH
041 56 KOŠICE, BAČÍKOVA 1

STATE REGIONAL ARCHIVES IN KOŠICE
041 56 KOŠICE, BAČÍKOVA 1
Slovakia

Číslo: ~~SA-~~ 98/989-VS2
Reference/file number

VÝPIS PRE RODNÝ LIST
EXTRACT FOR CERTIFICATE OF BIRTH

V matrike narodených farského úradu cirkvi rímskokatolíckej
In Birth Registers of the church parochial office
v Jasove vo zväzku III. na strane 172
in volume page
pod poradovým číslom 31 z roku 1843 je zapísané:
number from the year is registered:
Deň, mesiac a rok narodenia 20.4.1843 (dvadsiaty apríl jedentisíc osemsto štyridsaťtri)
Day, month and the year of birth
Miesto narodenia Jászó (Jasov)
Birth place
Meno a priezvisko dieťaťa Mária BENKO
Children's first name and surname
Pohlavie ženské Legitimnosť: legitimné
Sex
Meno a priezvisko (zamestnanie) otca Jakab BENKO
Father's first name and surname (occupation)
Meno a priezvisko matky Mária LIGÁTS
First name and Surname of mother
Krstní rodičia Ferenc HORVÁTH, Anna SÁRKÖZI
Christian's parents
Poznámky ---
Notes
V Košiciach dňa 21.1.1999
In Košice
Tento výpis obsahuje všetky údaje zapísané v horeuvedenej matrike, ktorá je uložená v tunajšom archíve; meno a priezvisko a miesto matričnej udalosti sú uvedené v jazyku matriky; všetky ďalšie údaje sú doslovným prekladom z maďarského jazyka do štátneho jazyka.

Riaditeľ
Director

Copy of Extract for Certificate of Birth of Mária Benkó b. April 20, 1843

4/9/99 ⑦ of ⑭

ŠTÁTNY OBLASTNÝ ARCHÍV V KOŠICIACH
041 56 KOŠICE, BAČÍKOVA 1

STATE REGIONAL ARCHIVES IN KOŠICE
041 56 KOŠICE, BAČÍKOVA 1
Slovakia

Číslo: ~~SA-~~ 98/989-VS2
Reference/file number

VÝPIS PRE RODNÝ LIST
EXTRACT FOR CERTIFICATE OF BIRTH

V matrike narodených farského úradu cirkvi rímskokatolíckej
In Birth Registers of the church parochial office
v Jasove vo zväzku III. na strane 190
in volume page
pod poradovým číslom 75 z roku 1849 je zapísané:
number from the year is registered:
Deň, mesiac a rok narodenia 17.9.1849 (sedemnásty september jedentisíc osemsto štyridsaťdeväť)
Day, month and the year of birth
Miesto narodenia Jászó (Jasov)
Birth place
Meno a priezvisko dieťaťa Mihály Máté BENKŐ
Children's first name and surname
Pohlavie mužské Legitimnosť: legitimné
Sex
Meno a priezvisko (zamestnanie) otca Jakab BENKŐ (vrátnik) (gate-keeper)
Father's first name and surname (occupation)
Meno a priezvisko matky Mária LIGÁCS
First name and Surname of mother
Krstní rodičia Ferenc HORVÁTH, Anna SÁRKÖZI
Christian's parents
Poznámky ---
Notes
V Košiciach dňa 21.1.1999
In Košice
Tento výpis obsahuje všetky údaje zapísané v horeuvedenej matrike, ktorá je uložená v tunajšom archíve; meno a priezvisko a miesto matričnej udalosti sú uvedené v jazyku matriky; všetky ďalšie údaje sú doslovným prekladom z maďarského jazyka do štátneho jazyka.

Riaditeľ
Director

Copy of Extract for Certificate of Birth of Mihály Máté Benkó b. September 17, 1849. These documents received from Gyula Fülep on April 4, 1999.

From Julius Fülep's letter to Clyde Davis received December 22, 1998:
"13. Birth of Ferenc Tóth, Julianna Tóth's father (<u>23</u> August though it can't be seen well, the year <u>1828</u> is encircled in line 4 (register)." Ferenc Tóth is the great-great-grandfather of Clyde P. Davis.

From Julius Fülep's letter to Clyde Davis received December 22, 1998:
"14. (Theresia) Julianna Tóth's birth (register)." Julianna Tóth is the great-grandmother of Clyde P. Davis.

1877 évi A.B.C.
ANYAKÖNYVE.

Lakhely, ház-szám.	A keresztatyák és anyák neve és állapotja.	A keresztelő neve és állapotja.	Jegyzetek.

From Julius Fülep's letter to Clyde Davis received December 22, 1998:
"12. Krisztina Bolyki's date of birth (register)." Krisztina was Julianna Tóth's daughter by her first marriage.

M. DCCC. XLIV.

From Julius Fülep's letter to Clyde Davis received December 22, 1998: "15. Jósef Bolyki's birth (register)." (See the last complete line in the above document.) Jósef was Julianna Tóth's son by her first marriage.

ANYAKÖNYVE.

Lakhely, ház-szám.	A keresztatyák és anyák neve és állapotja.	A keresztelő neve és állapotja.	Jegyzetek.

From Julius Fülep's letter to Clyde Davis received December 22, 1998: "11. Krisztina Bolyki's brother's, Jószef Bolyki's birth (register 1979 [sic])." József was Julianna Tóth's son by her first marriage.

4/9/99 (9) of (14)

Street No. Haus-Nr. Ház szám 210 — Owner's name Name des Hausbesitzers A házbirtokos neve Jakob Benko

Place Ortschaft Saszó -helység — Village Gemeinde Saszó község

Regist[...] **Aufnahmsbogen** **Fölvételi ív**

Nummer der Wohnung / A lakszám	Familien- und Tauf- oder Vorname, sammt Bezeichnung des Adelsgrades und des Prädicates / Család és kereszt-vagy melléknév, a nemességi fok, s az előnév (praedicatum) meg jelölésével (First name, surname)	Jahr, Monat und Tag der Geburt / A születés éve, holnapja, és napja (Day month and year of birth)	I. Nach der Religion / I. Vallásukra nézve — katholisch / katholikusok: lateinisch — deákszertartású (Roman Catholic)	griechisch — görögszertartású	armenisch — örményszertartású	nicht unirt / nem-egyesültek: griechisch — görögök	armenisch — örmények	evangelisch / evángel.: lutherisch — lutheránusok	reformirt — reformatusok	unitarisch — unitariusok	Juden — Zsidók	Sonstige Glaubensgenossen egyéb hitvallásuak	II. Nach dem Berufe, Erwerbe oder der Unterhaltsquelle / II. Hivatásukra, keresetökre vagy élelmi forrásukra nézve (II. Job, salary): Geistliche — Papok	Beamte — hivatalnokok	Militär — katonák	Literaten, Künstler — tudósok és művészek	Rechtsanwälte, Notäre — ügyvédek, jegyzők	Sanitätspersonen — egészségügyi személyek	Grundbesitzer — Földbirtokosok	Haus- und Rentenbesitzer — ház és járadék birtokosok	Fabrikanten und Gewerbsleute — gyárosok, és iparűzők	Handelsleute — kereskedők	Schiffer und Fischer — hajósok és halászok	Hilfsarbeiter der Landwirthschaft — mezőgazdászati segédmunkások	Hilfsarbeiter für Gewerbe — iparüzleti segédmunkások	Hilfsarbeiter beim Handel — kereskedelmi segédmunkások	Andere Diener — másféle szolgák (other servants)	Taglöhner — napszámosok	sonstige / egyébféle: Mannspersonen über 14 Jahre — Férfi személyek 14. éven felül	Frauen u. Kinder — nők és gyermekek
			1	2	3	4	5	6	7	8	9	10	11	12	13	14	15	16	17	18	19	20	21	22	23	24	25	26	27	28
	Jakob Benkó	5/7 1811	/																						unskilled worker in a shop		/			Women and children
	[Wife] Gyatton Maria	10/1 1809	/																											/
	Sohn = son Johann Benkó	13/2 1837	/																						/					
	Sohn = son Jakob	23/1 1847	/																											/
	Sohn = son Mihael	29/9 1849	/																											/
	Tochter = daughter Maria	14/1 1843	/																											/
	Summe.		6																						1		1			4
			1	2	3	4	5	6	7	8	9	10	11	12	13	14	15	16	17	18	19	20	21	22	23	24	25	26	27	28

Mathik [...] Commissär

Tóth [...]

(Deutsch-Ungarisch.)

Form. F.

On the document below, which is the Register of the Census of 1857, there are a number of penciled annotations in English, e.g., "Registration form of 1857," "Wife," "Illegible German script," etc.

[...]ration form of 1857

vom Jahre 1857.

y 1857. évről

County **Bezirk** Szepsi **járás**

Area **Kreis** Kaschau **kerület**

Hungary

Country **Land** Ungarn **Ország**

4/9/99 (10) of (14)

IV. Sex

III. Nach dem Alter / III. Korukra nézve Age

männlich / férfiak — men: 29 Von der Geburt bis zum 6. Jahre / A születéstől 6 évig; 30 über 6 bis 12 Jahre — 6en felül 12 évig; 31 über 12 bis 14 Jahre — 12en felül 14 évig; 32–39 14, 15, 16, 17, 18, 19, 20, 21 jährige / évesek (years old); 40 über 21 bis 24 Jahre — 21en felül 24 évig; 41 über 24 bis 26 Jahre — 24en felül 26 évig; 42 über 26 bis 40 Jahre — 26en felül 40 évig; 43 über 40 bis 60 Jahre — 40en felül 60 évig; 44 über 60 Jahre — 60 éven felül

weiblich / nők — women: 45 Von der Geburt bis zum 6. Jahre / A születéstől 6 évig; 46 über 6 bis 12 Jahre — 6en felül 12 évig; 47 über 12 bis 14 Jahre — 12en felül 14 évig; 48 über 14 bis 24 Jahre — 14en felül 24 évig; 49 über 24 bis 40 Jahre — 24en felül 40 évig; 50 über 40 bis 60 Jahre — 40en felül 60 évig; 51 über 60 Jahre — 60 éven felül

IV. Nach dem Stande / IV. Állapotukra nézve

männlich / férfiak — men: 52 ledig — nőtlenek (single); 53 verheirathet — házasok (married); 54 verwitwet — özvegyek

weiblich / nők — women: 55 ledig — hajadonok (single); 56 verheirathet — férjezettek (married); 57 verwitwet — özvegyek

V. Nach d. Aufenthalte / V. Tartózkodásukra nézve

männlich / férfiak — men: 58 anwesend — jelenlevők (present); 59 abwesend — távollevők (not present)

weiblich / nők — women: 60 anwesend — jelenlevők (p); 61 abwesend — távollevők (n. p.)

Anmerkungen. / Jegyzetek. Notes

29	30	31	32	33	34	35	36	37	38	39	40	41	42	43	44	45	46	47	48	49	50	51	52	53	54	55	56	57	58	59	60	61	Notes
	6-12 years old													/									/	/					/				died gestorben
														40-60 years old				12-14			/						/				/		Illegible German
									/												40-60 years old		/							/			[illegible] Szepsi
	/																						/						/				
	/																						/						/				
																		/								/					/		
	2								1					1				1			1		3	1		1	1		3	1	2		
29	30	31	32	33	34	35	36	37	38	39	40	41	42	43	44	45	46	47	48	49	50	51	52	53	54	55	56	57	58	59	60	61	

Mündlich [illegible] Jakob Binder [illegible]

Illegible German script

567

KRISZTINA BOLYKI b. April 9, 1877

Krisztina Bolyki b. April 9, 1877, in Egerszalók, Hungary, was the half-sister of János Benkó. Their mother was Julianna Tóth. János's father was Mihály Benkó, Krisztina's father was Julianna Tóth's first husband, József Bolyki Jr.. Krisztina and her son Lajos were the progenitors of the Bolyki family members featured on the following pages, whom Clyde and Kay Davis met on their trip to Hungary in June 1998.

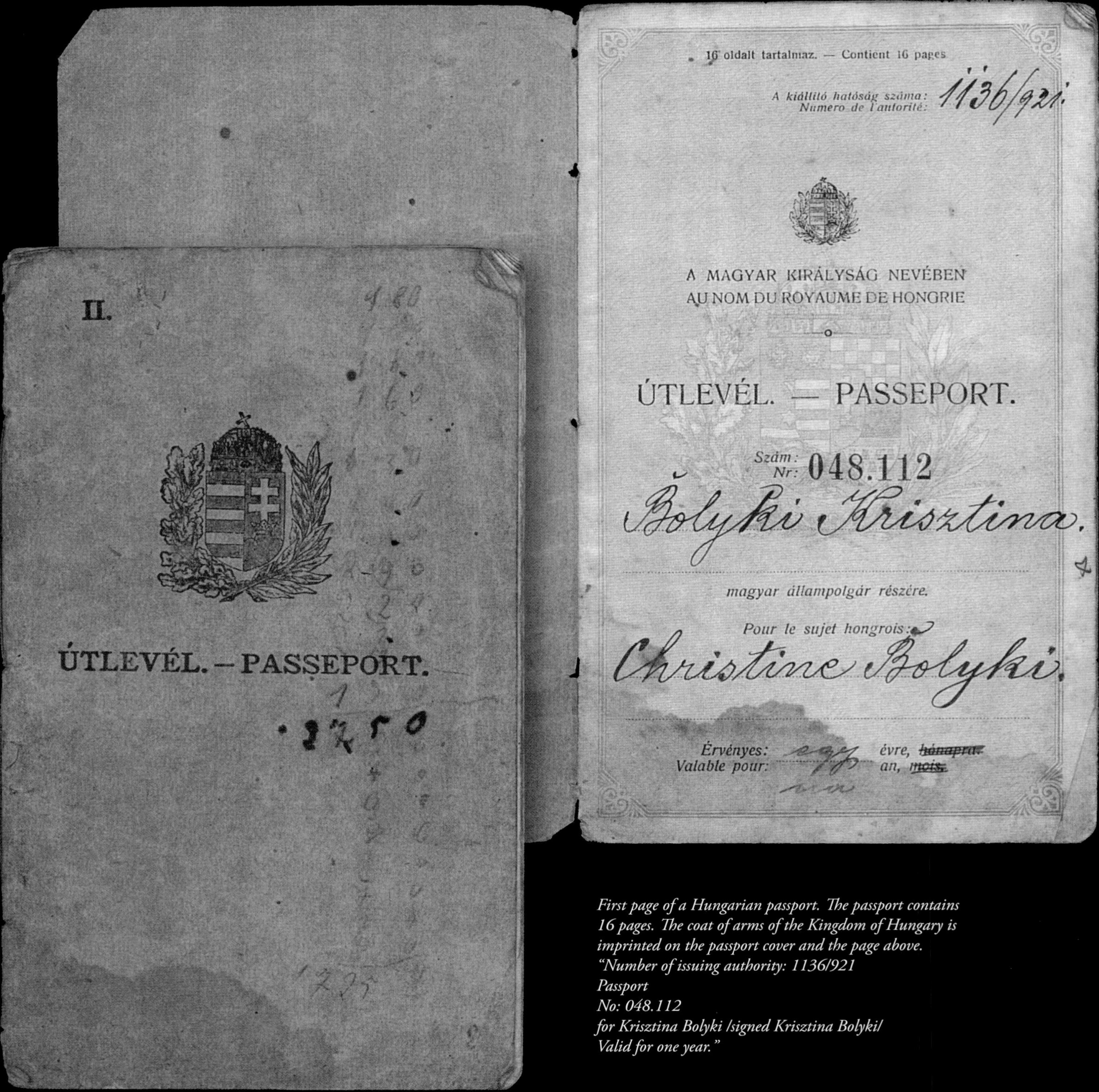

II.

ÚTLEVÉL. – PASSEPORT.

16 oldalt tartalmaz. — Contient 16 pages

A kiállító hatóság száma: 1136/921.
Numero de l'autorité:

A MAGYAR KIRÁLYSÁG NEVÉBEN
AU NOM DU ROYAUME DE HONGRIE

ÚTLEVÉL. — PASSEPORT.

Szám: 048.112
Nr:

Bolyki Krisztina.

magyar állampolgár részére.

Pour le sujet hongrois:

Christine Bolyki.

Érvényes: egy évre, ~~hónapra.~~
Valable pour: 1 an, ~~mois.~~

First page of a Hungarian passport. The passport contains 16 pages. The coat of arms of the Kingdom of Hungary is imprinted on the passport cover and the page above.
"Number of issuing authority: 1136/921
Passport
No: 048.112
for Krisztina Bolyki /signed Krisztina Bolyki/
Valid for one year."

2

Az utazó állása vagy foglalkozása: háztartásbeli

Profession: membre du ménage.

Lakhelye: / Domicile: Felsőtárkány.

Kora: / Âge: 42.

Családi állapot: / État de famille: hajadon, fille.

Vallása: / Religion: róm. kath., cath. rom.

Az állam vagy világrész, ahova utazás terveztetik: Ausztria, Németország, Északamerikai Egyesült Államok.

Délivré pour le voyage et le séjour en: Autriche, Allemagne, États-Unis de l'Amérique du Nord.

Az utazás célja: / But du voyage: kivándorlás. émigration.

3

Az utazó személy leirása. — Signalement.

Termete — Taille: középs, moyenne.

Arcza — Visage: hosszas, long.

Haja — Cheveux: gesztenyeszín, chatains.

Szakálla — Barbe: /.

Bajusza — Moustache: /.

Szeme — Yeux: sárgás, jaunâtres.

Szája — Bouche: rendes, régulière.

Orra — Nez: rendes, régulier.

Különös ismertetőjel: sánta a bal lábára

Signes particuliers: boiteuse sur la jambe gauche

Two pages of Krisztina Bolyki's passport. All lines are stated in French, too.

Occupation or employment of the traveler: Domestic employee
Address: Felsötárkány
Age: 42
Family status: unmarried
Religion: Roman Catholic
The country or continent of intended travel: Austria, Germany U.S.A.
Purpose of travel: Emigration

Description of the traveler:
Build: Medium
Face: Oblong
Hair: Chestnut
Beard:
Mustache:
Eyes: yellowish
Mouth: regular
Nose: regular
Special distinguishing features: left leg lame

KRISZTINA BOLYKI b. April 9, 1877

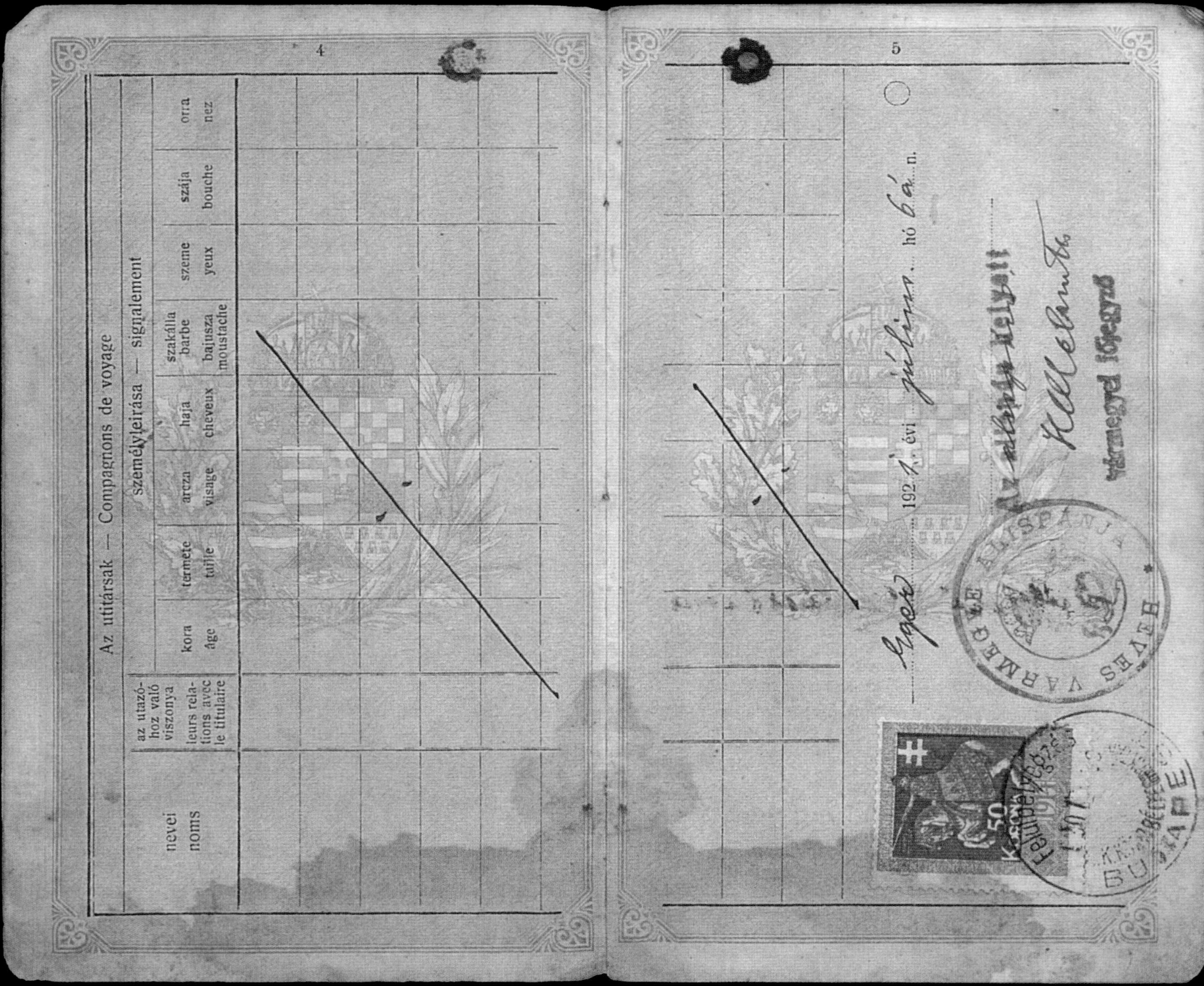

Pages 4–5 of Krisztina Bolyki's passport

Description of traveling companions.
Name, Relation to traveler, Age, Build, Face, Hair, Beard/ Mustache, Eyes, Mouth, Nose
/all crossed out/

Continuation of page 4 (crossed out)
Dated in Eger July 6, 1921
Receipt stamp; stamped by Ministry of Interior Budapest, Sheriff of Heves County

Bolyki Khrisztina

Saját aláirása. — Signature du titulaire.

Bolyki Khrisztina

Igazolom, hogy jelen fénykép az útlevél tulajdonosát ábrázolja, aki az útlevelet és a fényképet e hivatal előtt sajátkezüleg irta alá (látta el kézjegyével).

Soussigné certifie, que la phothographie represente le propriétaire du passeport et que ç'est lui-même, qui a signé (ou y a ajouté son signe) la phothographie et le passeport devant cette autorité.

Kelt, Felsőtárkány 1921 évi július hó 16 án.

HEVES VÁRMEGYE FELSŐTÁRKÁNY KÖZSÉG 1901

7

Page 6 of Krisztina Bolyki's passport

Photo of Krisztina Bolyki stamped by Heves County Sheriff
"I certify that this photo is that of the owner of this passport who signed both the photo and the passport in presence of this authority."
Dated Felsötárkány, July 16 1921
Stamp of the village of Felsötárkány, signed by illegible signature, Notary

16
Bolyki Lajosné
Rakondi Margit
Rakondi Katalin
M. kir. állami nyomda. Budapest, 1920.
HEVES VÁRMEGYE ALISPÁNJA

A Continuing Dilemma

There are a number of inconsistencies in the record regarding Krisztina Bolyki's relationship to John/János Benkó. On page 575, there is a photo with a label pasted on the back written by his wife, Anna Arendas Benko, reading: "John Benko with nephew, brothers son — taken when John was in Europe — May 1932. John was just 43 years old then."

Passport photo of Krisztina Bolyki dated July 16, 1921 and photo in Army ID book of Lajos Bolyki.

John's brother, Mihály, died at birth. However, the records show that John's and Krisztina's mother, Julianna Tóth, was married twice, and it appears that John and Krisztina were half-brother and sister. Julianna had five children, including two boys in her first marriage, so the young man in the picture could be a son of one of John's half-brothers, Josef (born 1874 [?]) or József (born September 15, 1879). The records in my possession do not show that either of them had children, but the researchers did not pursue these lines of the family, so the records are incomplete.

The younger man pictured with John could be Krisztina's son, Lajos, who was born in 1897. That would make him about thirty-five at the time of the photograph. Lajos also had a son named Lajos, born on August 8, 1926 (and clearly too young to be the man in the photograph), and the Lajos born in 1926 is in a number of pictures from our Hungarian Roots Trip. A comparison of the photo on page 443 of the Lajos born in 1926 with the man pictured with John shows a strong resemblance. This suggests that Anna Arendas Benko might have been mistaken in saying the picture was of his brother's son; he could easily be John's nephew, Lajos, the son of his half-sister, Krisztina.

Yet another possibility is suggested by the strong resemblance between John and the young man pictured with him. John was said to have had a love affair before leaving Hungary, discussed further in Julius Fülep's letter below. This photo, taken many years later, could be a portrait of John with an illegitimate son. John could have told his wife, Anna, that the young man was his nephew, when the truth might be that he was John's son. This may explain John's devotion in remitting money to assist his family during difficult times. Also, according to Krisztina's passport, pictured on page 571, she is forty-two years old and unmarried. Yet the genealogical records show that she had two children, a son, Lajos/Louis born in 1897, and a daughter, Margit.

In this context, the notes on two bank remittance reply post cards, pictured on pages 536–537, may take on additional meaning. The note on the first post card to Weiner Bank-Verein reads: "My beloved dear sister/brother I received the money I beg you send me the traveling expenses to go out there. Goodbye." "My beloved dear sister/brother" would refer to Anna and John Benko. On the reverse side at bottom is a receipt for $25 signed by Krisztina Bolyki.

The second post card to Magyar Leszámitoló-És Pénzváltó-Bank is postmarked June 4, 1923. The note reads: "My dear brother Johnny, Mother received the $40 you sent and the emigration permit. She'll write a letter about everything. I've just sent you a letter with all the news, I received the gift, too. I remain your loving younger brother Lajos Bolyki." On the reverse side at the bottom is a receipt for $40 signed by Krisztina Bolyki, Felsötárkány. Lajos, according to the genealogical records, is Krisztina's son, and therefore John's nephew, not his younger brother. This could, of course, simply be a family endearment. But it adds to the confusion!

As if that were not enough, in a letter to Clyde Davis received on December 22, 1998, Julius Fülep writes:

> As for the encircled information on "Modified Family-Tree 2" (see page 554), Mr Lajos Bolyki said that "János Benkó had had a love affair before he married Anna Arendes. A girl was born called Ersébet Szücs. Her son, István Benkó got married to Mária Fischer and their children are Mária Benkó and Piroska Benkó… I'm going to search this information, too."

Lajos Bolyki b. 1897

574

Lajos Bolyki b. 1897 is the son of Krisztina Bolyki and the nephew of John/János Benkó.

Krisztina Bolyki's Son?

Lajos Bolyki and his mother, Krisztina, were the beneficiaries of much of John Benko's generosity, as shown by the records of his remittances on pages 535–539 and the postal package receipt to the right to Lajos weighing 7 kilograms and 700 grams, or 17 pounds. The note on the back of the photo below says John Benko is with his brother's son, but the resemblance to Lajos Bolyki is very strong and suggests otherwise.

A feladó tölti ki.

FELADÓVEVÉNY

P f értékű, U 044.782 ragszámú csomagról.

Cím: Bolyki Lajos
Felsőtarkány

Rendeltetési hely: Heves m.

A csomag súlya: 7 kg 700 g | Bérmentesítési díj: P f

A felvevő postahivatal keletbélyegzője:

A felvevő posta-alkalmazott aláírása:

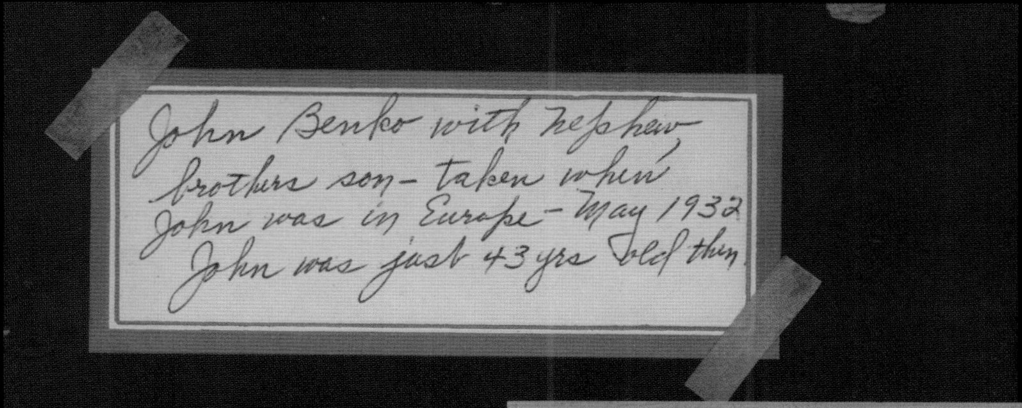

John Benko with nephew
brothers son - taken when
John was in Europe - May 1932
John was just 43 yrs old then

Anna Benko's caption on the back of this photo identifies this as a picture of John Benko with a nephew, his brother's son, while John was in Europe in May 1932. However, there is reason to believe otherwise, as described in "A Continuing Dilemma" on page 573.

Lajos Bolyki b. 1897

Vezeték- és keresztnév	Bolyki Lajos	
Rendfokozat	közv.	Anyakönyvi lapszám:
Csapattest és beosztás	M. kir. egri gyal. ezr. 4 század	Sorozási év: 1915 / Avatási év: 1920
		Szeme: barna
		Haja: g. barna
		Testmagasság méterben: 165
		Lábbeli nagyság-száma: 16
		Különös ismertető jele és fogyatkozása:
Született (év, hely, megye)	Kistálya 1897. Borsod m.	
Illetékes (község, ország)	Felsőtárkány Heves m. Egri járás	

1980. r. sz. (L.) 1

Mily nyelven beszél és ír	magyarul	
Vallása	róm. kath.	
Iskolai képzettség	polgári	VI. elemi oszt. III. ipari isk.
	katonai	telefon
Élelmezési adag váltságra jogosult családtagok neve és kora	Bolyki Lajosné szül. Bakondi Margit Bolyki József	
Mely kitüntetésekre, vitézségi érmekre jogosult	/	
	/	

Leg. illetm.-könyvecske 2

Pages 1–2 of the Army ID book of Lajos Bolyki

Last and First name: Lajos Bolyki
Rank: PFC1 Registry number:
Unit and assignment: Hungarian Royal Infantry Dvision Company 4.
Year of draft: 1915
Year of qualifying: 1920

Eyes: Brown
Hair: c. brown/chestnut/
Height: 5' 6"
Shoe size: 16
Distinguishing marks and defects:
Place and year of birth: Kistálya Borsod County 1897
Town of jurisdiction: Felsötárkány, Heves County, Eger district

Spoken and written language: Hungarian
Religion: Roman Catholic
Civilian education: 6 years grade school, 3 years trade school
Military education: telephone
Names of family members entitled to food coupons:
Lajos Bolykiné née Bakondi Margit, Bolyki József
Decorations, military medals: None

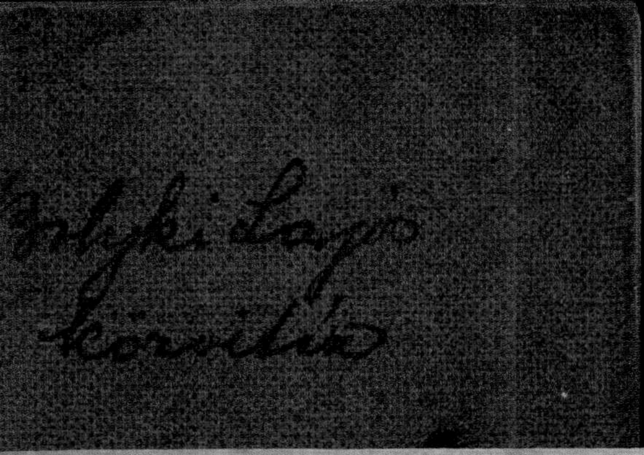

Cover of Army ID book of Lajos Bolyki.

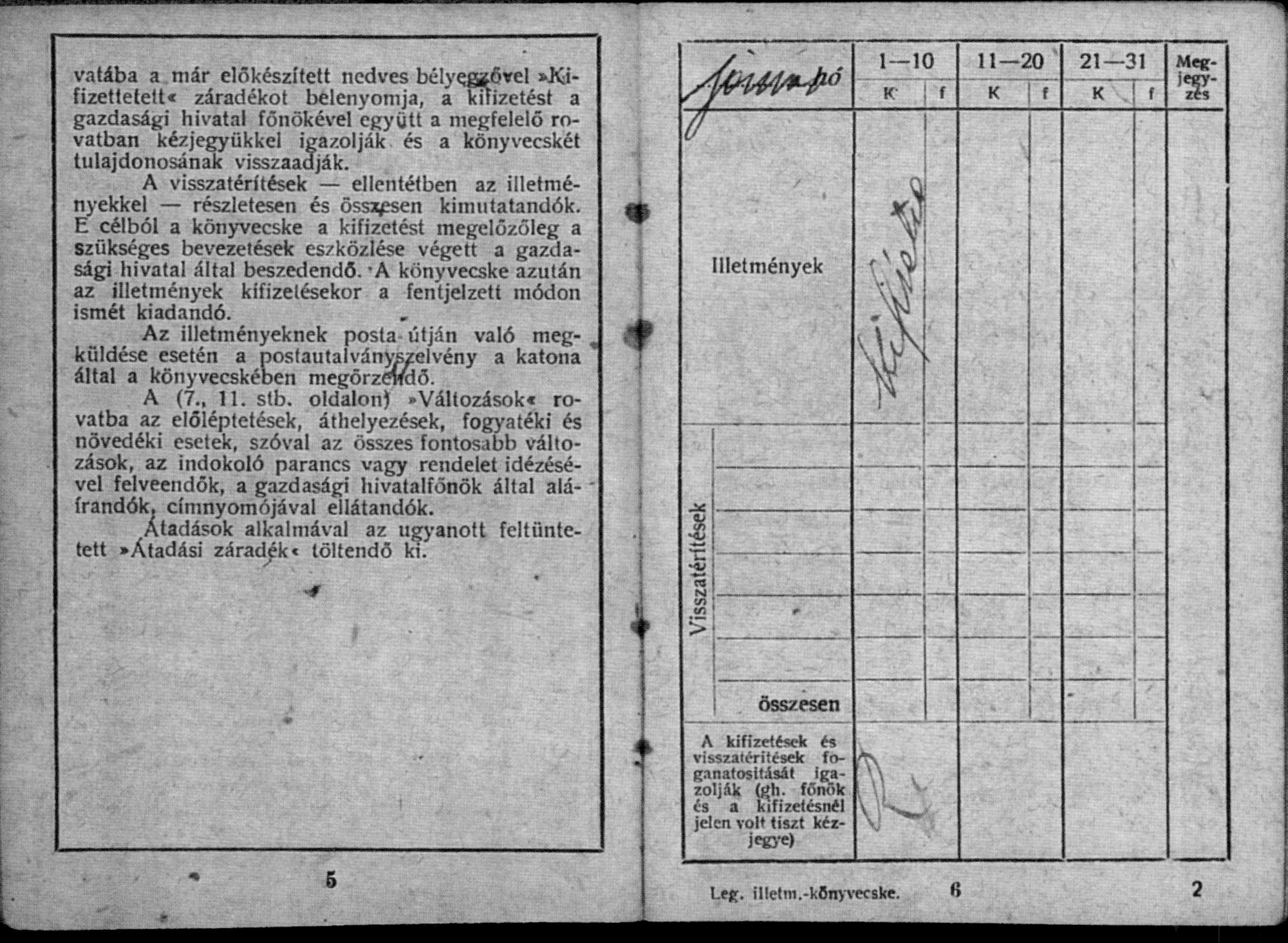

vatába a már előkészített nedves bélyegzővel »Kifizettetett« záradékot belenyomja, a kifizetést a gazdasági hivatal főnökével együtt a megfelelő rovatban kézjegyükkel igazolják és a könyvecskét tulajdonosának visszaadják.

A visszatérítések — ellentétben az illetményekkel — részletesen és összesen kimutatandók. E célból a könyvecske a kifizetést megelőzőleg a szükséges bevezetések eszközlése végett a gazdasági hivatal által beszedendő. A könyvecske azután az illetmények kifizetésekor a fentjelzett módon ismét kiadandó.

Az illetményeknek posta útján való megküldése esetén a postautalványszelvény a katona által a könyvecskében megőrzendő.

A (7., 11. stb. oldalon) »Változások« rovatba az előléptetések, áthelyezések, fogyatéki és növedéki esetek, szóval az összes fontosabb változások, az indokoló parancs vagy rendelet idézésével felveendők, a gazdasági hivatalfőnök által aláírandók, címnyomójával ellátandók.

Átadások alkalmával az ugyanott feltüntetett »Átadási záradék« töltendő ki.

5

Január hó	1—10 K	1—10 f	11—20 K	11—20 f	21—31 K	21—31 f	Megjegyzés
Illetmények	Kifizetve						
Visszatérítések							
összesen							
A kifizetések és visszatérítések foganatosítását igazolják (gh. főnök és a kifizetésnél jelen volt tiszt kézjegye)	[illegible]						

Leg. illetm.-könyvecske. 6 2

f the Army ID book of Lajos Bolyki

nt Period" with the already prepared wet stamp, together with the fice Head verify the payment with initialing the booklet returned owner.

— unlike payments — must be shown in detail and total. To this booklet must be collected by the Finance Office prior to payment ooklet then, after making the payment must be returned the same

ding the payments through mail the postal slip must be retained er in the booklet.

7, 11, Etc.) into the column "Changes" all promotions, transfers r deletions i.e. all important changes must be entered indicating f the order and signed by the Finance Office Chief and his official

transfers the indicated "Transfer Clause" must be filled out.

Payment records:
Month of January 1–10, 11–20, 21–31, Remark
Payments Paid
Refunds
Total
Payments and Refunds verified by the Initials of the paying officer and Head of Finance Office

Kelt	Változások	Gh. főnök aláírása és címnyomat

Átadási záradék.

E könyvecske tulajdonosa ....K ......f napizsolddal ....-ig, készétkezéssel ....-ig, kenyérrel ....-ig, ...K......f élelmezési váltsággal (saját személy és család után) ....-ig, ...K ......f családi lakbérrel ....-ig bezárólag ellátva, a ....-nak átadatott.

Egyéb illetményadatok:

Élelmezési okmányok megküldetnek.

Kelt.................... (Címnyomó) .... gazdasági hivatal főnöke.

7

Egyéb bejegyzések.

8 2*

Pages 7–8 of the Army ID book of Lajos Bolyki

Date Changes Signature and Stamp of Finance Office Chief
Transfer Clause:
The owner of this booklet ...... Korona ...... fillér daily payment until ......, with meals until ......, with bread until ......, ... Korona ... fillér

Invalid due to demobilization
January 9, 1921
Signed by illegible signature Finance Office Chief

Kelt	Változások	Gh. főnök aláírása és címnyomat

Átadási záradék.

E könyvecske tulajdonosa ....K ......f napizsolddal ....-ig, készétkezéssel ....-ig, kenyérrel ....-ig, ...K ......f élelmezési váltsággal (saját személy és család után) ....-ig, ...K ......f családi lakbérrel ....-ig bezárólag ellátva, a ....-nak átadatott.

Egyéb illetményadatok :

Élelmezési okmányok stb. megküldetnek.

Kelt.................... Cím-nyomó .... gazdasági hivatal főnöke.

E könyvecske negyvenkettő számozott lapoldalt tartalmaz és 19 21 évi január .... hó 15 ......n adatott ki.

Előjegyzés folyószáma : ....

Kelt Eger, 1921. január 15.

Cím-nyomó *)

.... alosztályparancsnok.*) .... gazdasági hivatali főnök.*)

*) Aláírások és bélyegző nélkül a könyvecske érvénytelen.

Budapest, Athenaeum r.-t.

Pages 41–42 of the Army ID book of Lajos Bolyki

Date Changes Signature and Stamp of Finance Office Chief
Transfer Clause:
The owner of this booklet …… Korona …… fillér daily payment until …… , with meals until …… , with bread until …… , …… Korona … fillér food redemption (for self and family) until …… , family rent until …… inclusive provided …… transferred to ……
Other remuneration data:
Food provision documents to be sent.
Date …… Stamp ……
Chief of Finance Office

This booklet contains forty-two numbered pages and was issued on January 15, 1921.
Number of memorandum: ……
Date: Eger, January 15, 1921
Stamp
Illegible signature ……… Illegible signature ………
*Subcommand Commander * Chief of Finance Office*
** Booklet invalid without signatures and stamp*

✓ faxed to Zoltan Zorandy 5th dt 3/8/01

Mr. Clyde Davis
10 Tatomuck Circle
Pound Ridge,Ny 10576

2001. március 01.

Kedves Clyde

Remélem levelem minden gondtól mentesen találja, amit
kívánok Mindannyiuknak.
A mellékelt levelet a tavalyi év végén próbáltam eljuttatni
Önnek. Érdeklődésemre Fülep Gyula azt a felvilágosítást adta,
hogy már nincs semmilyen kapcsolat Önök között. Ezek után a
levelet postára adtam, ami sajnos később - a megkötött biztosí-
tásoknak köszönhetően - visszajött hozzám. A postán nem tudtak
felvilágosítást adni arról, hogy a levél miért volt kézbesíthe-
tetlen. A borítékon talált jelzésekből azt a következtetést von-
tam le, hogy nem rossz címzés vagy elköltözés miatt nem ért
célba a küldemény, hanem valószínűleg távollét miatt.Azt gondol-
tam egy kis idővel később megpróbálom újra eljuttatni, de most
a FED-EX borítékon található -
valószínűbb hogy megkapja.Ezért próbáltam Mr. Zorándy Zoltánra
hivatkozva segítséget kérni.
Az Internet világában kicsit
célba jutást, mert a küldeményt
vagy lovasfutárral küldve is
A nyelvi nehézségek miatt nehéz kommunikálnunk, sajnos közvetí-
tőkre vagyunk utalva.Mennyivel egyszerűbb volna a telefonkagy-
lót felvéve megbeszélni a problémákat, de sajnos angol nyelvtudás
hiányában ez nem lehetséges.
Itt szeretném megköszönni Mr. Zorándy
érzem korrekt segítségét. Ugyanezt Fülep Gyuláról elmondani nyu-
godt szívvel nem tudom.
Remélem végre sikerül eljuttatni ezt a küldeményt, mert elég
sok izgalmat okoz, hogy a biztosítások
az eredeti számlák, mert számomra nagyon kellemetlen volna, ha a
rám bízott pénzzel, ennek hiányában

Mr Clyde Davis
10 Tatomuck Circle
Pound Ridge, Ny 10576

March 1, 2001

Dear Clyde

I hope my letter reaches you worry-free which I wish you all.

I attempted to send the enclosed letter at the end of last year. To my inquiries Fülep Gyula informed me that there is no longer any contact between you. After that I mailed the letter which later unfortunately - due to the insurances paid - was returned to me. The Post Office had no information why the letter was undeliverable. Observing the markings on the envelope I reasoned that it was not due to invalid address or moving but probably due to absence. I thought in a little while I'll try again to get it to you but this time to an address shown on a Fedex envelope - I think business - address where you are more likely to get it. That's why I tried to ask for help mentioning Mr Zoltan Zorandy.

In the age of Internet I find it a bit ridiculous this slowness because the letter could get faster there by sending it on CD disk, carrier pigeon or horseback to its destination. Due to language difficulties it is hard for us to communicate we need intermediaries.
How much simpler would it be to pick up the receiver and talk about the problems on the phone but lacking English knowledge this is not possible.

I would like to thank Mr Zoltan Zorandy for his - I feel - correct assistance. To say the same about Fülep Gyula I can't honestly do.

I hope finally this consignment will get there because I'm concerned enough about the loss of the original invoices, it would be very unpleasant for me if lacking those I could not account for the money I was entrusted with.

Finally I would like to wish everybody lots of happiness and good health and I fervently hope that once I can tell these things in person meaning that we'll meet.

With lots of love:

Sandor (signed)

....
Bolyki Sandor
Felsötárkány
Rakoczi utca 92, sz 3324

Végül szeretnék mindenkinek sok boldogságot, erőt és egészséget kívánni és nagyon remélem , egyszer személyesen is sikerül elmondanom ezeket, tehát találkozunk.

Sok szeretettel:

Sándor
....

Bolyki Sándor
Felsőtárkány
Rákóczi utca 92.sz.
3324

Top: "2000. nyarán, alakásunk udvarán. Ilona (Icu) a feleséyem György a finnk (Gyuri) Sándor." *Bottom:* "Szüleim 2000-ben"

Kedves Clyde

Remélem levelem egészségben és probléma mentesen találja az egész családot. Itt sajnos összegyűltek azok az események, amelyekben nagyon aktívan részt kellett vennem, többet megszerveznem vagy végrehajtanom. Munkám mellett (reggel 3-kor kelek és éjfélkor kerülök haza) havonta általában 1 hetem van szabad, ami nagyon kevés arra, hogy a munkaidő alatt összegyűlt rám háruló feladatokat elvégezzem.

Clyde 1999-ben rám bízott 2 feladatot, amiket végrehajtottam. A síremlék tavaly elkészült és az adatokat is összegyűjtöttem. Az erről szóló számlákat most van időm összerendezni és elküldeni.

1999. április 28-i levéllel kaptam egy 500 dolláros csekket. Ezt 1999. május 11-én a bank átvette, de 6 hétre (99. jun. 22-ig) zárolta, amíg New York-bó ... költséget, jutalékot ... vesekkel nem tudt... A junius 29-i, Zorándy Zoltán tolmácsolásával történt beszélgetésünk után, julius 15-i levelével kaptam egy 300 dolláros csekket, amit julius 20-án beváltottam. ... gondolom a számlán lévő 500 dollár ...

A sírkőkészítők k... a síremlék elkészít... értesített, amikor elkezdték az alap... győződjek meg az ... a síremlék elkészül... ranciát vállalt, ami a megrendelőlap ...

A sírkőkészítő ál... rült elérni, hogy az egyik banki alkalmazott tanácsára, 793.06 dollárt átutaltattam a saját forint számlámra ... volt az átváltási ár.

A síremléket Édesapám Keresztapja (John Benko) 1963-as ... szerette volna megvalósítani, de később feledésbe merült a dolog, ahogy későbbi levelében utalt rá.

A közismert mondás szerint: Clyde ... síremléket készítte... tudta, hogy kik nyugszanak abban a sírban, ... bízta annak gondozását. Érdeklődésemre a testvérei csak arra emlékeztek, hogy gyermekkorukban ápolták a sírt ... elődei nyugszanak benne, de hogy milyen mértékű ez a rokonság, ez csak Clyde kutatásai nyomán derült ki.

Dear Clyde,

I hope my letter finds your whole family in good health and problem-free. Here unfortunately there were lot of events I had to organize or participate in very actively. Beside my job (I get up at 3 A.M. and get home near midnight) I have one free week every month which is pretty little to deal with tasks that accumulate while I work.

Clyde, you gave me 2 tasks in 1999 which I fulfilled. The memorial was completed last year and I collected the data, too. Now I have time to organize and send you the relevant bills. On April 28 1999 I received a cheque of $500. On May 11 1999 the bank accepted it but held it for 6 weeks (till June 22 1999) when it was cleared from New York. In the meantime I could not ascertain the cost and fees so I could not talk with the headstone people about exact prices.

After our June 29 conversation - interpreted by Zoltan Zorandy - I received a $300 cheque enclosed in your July 15 letter which I cashed on July 20. This was not held by the bank, I suppose because of the $500 already on the account.

I reached an agreement with the stonecutter offering the best price but unfortunately he didn't keep his promise to notify me when the groundwork commenced so I could not check personally the depth of the groundwork. As a result of the argument about this he gave a 10 year warranty instead of 3 years which be endorsed on the back page of the order sheet.

We were able to reach the HUF 190.000 asked by the stonemason by transferring $793.06 to my forint account at the advice of a bank employee to obtain a more favorable exchange rate (239.64 HUF).

My father's godfather (John Benko) wanted to erect the headstone during his 1963 visit here but as he indicated in a later letter it just got forgotten.

As the saying goes Clyde decided in the 24th hour to have a memorial stone made on the grave of his Great-grand parents. After all only my father knew who were resting in that grave since my grandfather asked him to take care of it. To my inquiries his brothers they only remembered that as children they cared for the grave and that predecessors of relations living in America are resting there but the degree of relationship was revealed only as a result of Clyde's research.

The enclosed photos show that flowers grow only in the flower holder since the flower surface needs care every week. Because of my above described work schedule I'm unable to do that. The rest of my cousins (Jozsef, Erzsebet, Margit. Rafael) are unlikely to contribute neither in the construction nor care of the memorial. So it seems that I alone will have to care for it.

I hope I completed the other task you asked me to do in a comprehendible manner. On the Family Tree portion the number next to the names is the birth date to better

A mellékelt képeken látható, hogy csak virágtartóban nevelkedik virág mivel a teljes virágfelület minden héten igényli a gondozást. Erre Nekem a korábban leírt munkahelyi problémák miatt nagyon kevés szabadidőm van. A többi Unokatestvérem (József, Erzsébet, Margit, Ráfael) ahogy a sírkő elkészítésében, úgy a gondozásában sem valószínű hogy nagy részt vállal. Így elképzelhető, hogy Én fogom a továbbiakban ápolni azt.

A másik rám bízott feladatot remélem értelmezhetően készítettem el. A családfa részleten a nevek melletti évszám a születésiidő, az azonos nevűek könnyebb megkülönböztetése miatt. A kékkel írt nevek a házastársaké. A többi személyes adat szerintemnem mutat semmi újat, mert ezeket F...
könyvi kivonatokba...
újra összegyűjtötte...

Sajnos a rokonsá...
Édesapám egyik nő...
án a másik nővérén...
csak meghalt. Ekkor...
tözött, mert segítsé...
kük. Sajnos a lakás...
kányban egy másik...
még növelte, hogy 2...
küli házat feltörték...
Ekkor az ajtókat és...
tettük, hogy a megn...
kat nem térítette m...
dott elviselni, így fe...
Felsőtárkányban. 2...

Csak azért terhel...
szabadidőm menny...
számlákat. Egyébk...
ezeket átadni.

Az a néhány levél...
ríthat arra, hogy al...
kapcsolaton túl job...
ját.

Tavaly tavasszal Fü...
nagyon foglalkozza...
mondott, hogy fotó...

Nekünk nem rok...
nak Németország n...
német családokkal,...
rokkal. Ezeket azér...

distinguish those with identical names. The names written in blue are those of spouses. The rest of the personal data does not show anything new since these were told to Gyula Fülep or given over in the birth registry extracts but I collected these again anyway as per Clyde's request.

Unfortunately several deaths occurred in the family. On May 18 1998 one of my father's sisters (Bolyki Maria) died. On November 3 1998 his other (Bolyki Margit) sister's husband (Takacs Sandor) also died. At this point my aunt moved from Belapatfalva to Felsötárkány because she was left without help in the apartment since they were childless. Unfortunately we could not sell the apartment at a price which would have afforded us to buy another smaller one for her in Felsötárkány. The trouble was exacerbated by the fact that the now empty house was broken into in January 2000 and burglarized) even the fence was broken. Then we reinforced the doors and windows to save the remaining valuables. The insurance company paid nothing. Not being able to deal with so much pain my aunt gave up the hope to acquire a new apartment and died on February 29th 2000.

The only reason I burden you with these news to illustrate how busy my free time is and that's the reason I'm sending the bank invoices belatedly. By the way I was hoping to hand these over to you personally this summer.

The few pieces of our correspondence and their contents I think may encourage me to hope that beyond our "Employers-Employee" relationship we'll get to know each other and families better.

Last spring Fülep Gyula told me at the receipt of your letter not to invest too much time with this relationship and about Clyde he only said the he does photographing.

We have very warm friendly - not family - relationship with German families living in Germany's western part (between Frankfurt and the Rhine) and in the other direction Hungarian living in Romania. I write about this because we value contacts between people very highly and for this reason I dare to write a few words about ourselves in the hope that it will be reciprocated by Clyde.

I was born on November 28 1955, after completing my schools in 1973 I received my diploma as car mechanic. From then on for 2 years I worked as truck driver later on tourist buses till 1981 when I got married and I was put on the Felsötárkány-Eger route which I do till this day. My wife Szakal Ilona was born on April 12th 1960. She got her college degree as a kindergarten teacher, she prepares children under 7 for school.

Our son Gyuri (Bolyki Gyorgy) was born on May 5 1983. Besides school he studied piano and drums. He plays drums in the village brass band. Piano studies help him in the use of his synthesizer. He is a senior at the Vocational Middle School for car mechanics.

You got to know my parents at your visit so I won't write about them. Our living standards are average by local standards we have no major problems but the winters due

rek közti jó kapcsolat, ezért bátorkodom egy pár szót Magunkról írni, amit remélem Clyde viszonoz majd.

Én 1955. november 28-án születtem, iskoláim elvégzése után autó-szerelői képesítést kaptam 1973-ban. Ettől kezdve gépkocsivezetőként dolgozom a jelenlegi munkahelyemen. Két évig tehergépkocsival, később turista autóbusszal 1981-ig, amikor megnősültem és a Felsőtárkány-Eger útvonalra kerültem, amit a mai napig is végzek.
Feleségem, Szakál Ilona, 196O. április l2-én született. Főiskolán szerzett diplomát óvónőként, 198l-óta Felsőtárkányban végzi a 7 év alatti gyermekek iskolára való felkészítését.
Gyermekünk Gyuri (Bolyki György) 1983. május 5-én született. Az iskolai tanulmányok mellett dobolni és zongorázni tanult. Az előbbinek a falu Fúvószenekarában veszi hasznát. A zongora óráit a szintetizá-

to energy prices are tougher. Major expenditures, appliance purchases, car replacements incur serious installment payments.

Dear Clyde! I would like to ask a copy of the videotapes you made during your visit to Hungary because events devolved so that I have no videos of my Parents. We wanted to purchase a video camera this year but it looks like due to the high taxes and fees we'll just have to forgo that. For this reason if it poses no problem I ask you to send the copy in our VHS format which I thank you in advance.

I'd like to ask you whether you have received the greeting cards sent by us and our parents since we have not received any indication of that. True they were not sent by Fedex but Air Mail.

Finally one more thing. We would like to install heating in our Church in the village. Varga Jozsef came to me to ask me to ask Clyde for a contribution. Varga Jozsef works with the priest handling as a lay president handling all kinds of matters including economic issues. Because of my work I only get to the Church maybe 1–2 times in a year. We made our own contributions for the heating system. I spoke to Clyde twice on the phone and both times I asked for money. The invoices about the money received I was not able to send due to being busy.

I have no right to ask Clyde for money. Weighing this I declined that request, but I gave them your business address so they might write to Clyde who then will decide what he wants to do in this matter. I hope I didn't cause any nuisance in which case I apologize.

With this I close my letter, I nope once we'll be able to meet in person. I don't know when this letter finds its way to New York so I wish lot of happiness and good health to the whole family to the approaching Christmas and New Year holidays.

With sincere love: Sandor

November 27, 2000, Felsötárkány.

után visszautasítottam a kérést, de a vállalati címét megadtam, hogy írjanak Clyde-nak, majd eldönti mit akar az ügyben tenni. Remélem nem okoztam kellemetlenséget a cím átadásával, mert ha igen akkor bocsánatot kérek.

Ezzel zárom soraimat, remélem egyszer sikerül személyesen is találkoznunk. Nem tudom mikorra keveredik ki ez a levél New York-ba, ezért sok boldogságot és jó egészséget kívánunk az egész családnak a közelgő Karácsonyi és Újévi ünnepek alkalmából.

Őszinte szeretettel: Sándor

27.nov.2ooo.Felsőtárkány Sándor

The two photos above are of the memorial and headstone erected in honor of Clyde Patrick Davis's great-grandmother, Julia (Julianna) Tóth. Sándor Bolyki contracted and oversaw the construction and stonecutting work, which was donated by Clyde Davis. Prior to this, there was only a small marker and no headstone.

Douthart Maloney

Henry "Harry" Douthart b. September 8, 1867, in a portrait with his wife Catherine A. Maloney Douthart b. May 4, 1866 and wih their eldest child, Mary Lenore Douthart b. May 30, 1890

September 8, 1867

y Douthart, "Roadmaster" for the EJ&E Railroad

KATE DOUTHART (D)
SISTER OF
HARRY DOUTHART

NEVER MARRIED
LIVED & DIED IN
IRELAND
BURIED IN LOUGHGIEL

ROSE DOUTHART WATSON
SISTER OF
HARRY DOUTHART

HENRY HARRY DOUTHART FAMILY

Harry and Catherine Douthart holding their grandson
Richard James Douthart

Harry Douthart
Catherine Douthart
Mary Cushing

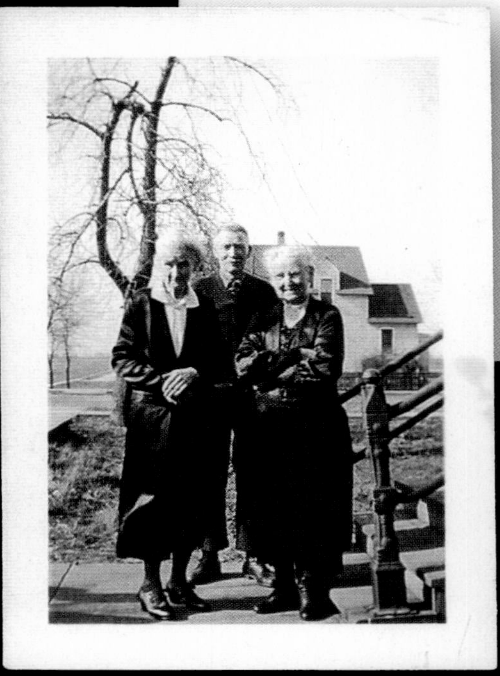

Pictured left to right: Catherine Maloney Douthart, Henry "Harry" Douthart, and Mary Cushing

Douthart / Bauer Families

by Kay Douthart Davis

My parents never seemed to have close relations with their families, and as I grew older, the few relatives I had seen or known as a child seemed to disappear from our lives. My parents never shared many details of our extended families — either Douthart or Bauer — and I, certainly, had few firsthand experiences with any of my grandparents, aunts, uncles, or cousins.

When Clyde embarked on his project of "Finding Fathers," he mentioned that my family tree would be included in his book. This sent a shiver through me, since I knew very little and have since learned very little more. My research has not rendered information of "American pioneers" or exact, well-founded, traceable links to ancestors abroad. The following accounts are retrieved from conversations, letters, road trips, memory, hearsay, and some verifiable research.

In reflecting on my participation in Clyde's book, I have attempted to highlight a few of those ancestors and relatives whom I have been fortunate to know and/or for whom I have briefly summarizing my grandfather (Henry Douthart), my father and mother, my siblings and myself to begin the story of the Dootharts during my lifetime. Further information on the Douthart family has been added to the featured information, documents, and photos, as they are set within the pages of this book. Information of the Bauer Family follows.

Douthart Family

The first "myth" that I must discount is one passed to me by my father (and encouraged by my brother, Dick) that the Douthart family was a "bunch of pirates." Nothing I have found supports their romantic "joke" about the Douthart family.

I have had one important resource for Douthart information — my cousin Mary Lou (Douthart) Ambre, the daughter of my father's sister Mary Lenore — my "Aunt Mame." Many years ago Mary Lou's mother (Mary Lenore) took on the job of documenting and researching the family tree. Mary Lou had numerous historical documents, including a family tree, that she shared with me. In conversations with Mary Lou over many

Ed & Helen Douthart
wedding day

Ed & Helen
Priest
Helen's Sisters
Dick Douthart

Ed Douthart, son of Henry "Harry" Douthart, on his wedding day, pictured with wife Helen, a priest, Helen's sisters and Ed's brother Richard C. Douthart, father of Catherine Douthart Davis

Ed & Helen

Class 20 -
July - 7 - 1935

taken at - 9105 Colfax av. Chi Ill

Send by
N. Douthart -
9205 Clyde av Chi Ill

No Postage

10

Ed and Helen Douthart in photo taken July 7, 1935, at 9105 Colfax Avenue, Chicago, Illinois

Henry "Harry" Douthart Family

Left: My uncle Daniel Douthart with my cousin Lorraine, at Rockaway Beach, New York, July 1930

Below: My uncle Daniel Douthart and his wife Ruth with my cousin Lorraine, June 16, 1935

Lorraine and Ruth Douthart, Ruth's mom, and my uncle Daniel Douthart

with the Douthart family in a much more intimate way than I had ever known. I barely knew the names of relatives, let alone, their place in the family. The following accounting of early family history was essentially the information provided to me by Mary Lou. When my own research served to update this information, I have included it within the text below.

The Doutharts of Ireland and North America

Research for this genealogy began in earnest with Mary Lenore Douthart Carlson, the eldest daughter of Harry Douthart. Her father told her that he knew of three branches of Doutharts in the United States. They are descendants of the following three branches from Ireland: John of Belfast, whose descendents settled in Iowa; Robert, who emigrated from Ireland to Boston, and Henry, whose sons Harry and Tom came to Illinois around 1885.

I received a copy of a large family tree from Tim Douthart of Auburn, Kansas, the son of William Douthart, whose research on his family began in 1968. Along with that family tree were some handwritten notes. One note said that Ruth, the daughter of Robert Douthart, who was born in Galway, Ireland, in 1807, is the first generation in the United States of Tim's family tree and "recalled her grandfather's name as John." Further, Tim told me in a telephone conversation that his great-great grandfather Robert emigrated from Belfast.

Mary Lou also indicated in her notes that her mother, Mary Lenore Douthart, conducted her family research in the late 1940s. Her mother wrote at that time that Harry had two cousins in the Midwest. They were Simon P. Douthart, an attorney in Chicago, and John Douthart: "We have no information today about the direct lineage of either Simon P. or John Douthart."

The above-mentioned family tree shared with me by Tim Douthart, includes a Simon P. Douthart who was an attorney in Chicago. This certainly ties the two families together; however, a more formal, hard link must be solidified in Ireland to trace exactly the lineage of both families to prove the existence of "cousins." Nonetheless, Robert and Emerline (Wright) Douthart — she was from Hillsboro, Iowa — were responsible for the "Iowa" branch of Doutharts. Robert appears to be the descendent of John Douthart of Belfast.

One thing is certain in reviewing the various lines in both family trees, the Douthart families were well educated and often found their careers in the academic world and/or professional positions that require higher education. This is evidenced by the two sisters Lela and Ava Douthart (married name Chronister — husband, Bert Chronister) found on the "Ohio" branch of the Douthart family. They were teachers and heavy contributors to the construction fund for a residence hall at the University of Kansas. The residence hall still exists today and is named Douthart Scholarship Hall.

As Mary Lenore Douthart Carlson wrote: "There was communication between the Harry Douthart family and their cousins in Ireland. Mary Douthart Carlson wrote to cousin Mary Douthart McLernon in Armoy. Several times fresh shamrocks arrived in time to celebrate St. Patrick's Day in Indiana and Chicago — courtesy of the Irish cousins." But efforts to trace and chart the family tree waned until the 1960s.

It was then that Mary Carlson heard from Agnes Douthart Harvey of Rockville, Indiana. Agnes indicated that a grandson of Robert Douthart (the Boston Branch) was trying to compile a family history. Also, in 1962, Mary Carlson's cousin Frank Douthart contacted her from Los Angeles.

In 1969, Mary Carlson's grandson, John Ambre, son of Mary Lou (Ambre) Douthart, was studying for the priesthood in Austria, and during summer vacation, traveled to County Antrim to visit the cousins there. He was warmly welcomed and learned more facts about the Doutharts in Northern Ireland. Additionally, Mary Lou's daughter, Sister Jeanne, a Catholic nun, traveled to Ireland in June 1995 to make contact with known, proven family relatives. These trips, as well as the previous family tree research conducted by Mary Lenore, have verified the Douthart heritage to a small village in Ireland, Armoy, in the county of Antrim.

Two Douthart brothers, Henry and William, married two sisters in Breene, near Armoy, County Antrim, Ireland probably in the early 1840s. Henry's wife was Catholic and his Protestant family disowned him. Before his death, Henry converted to Catholicism. Henry, wife Mary Cain (Gillian) Douthart and one daughter, Kathryn, were buried in St. Olcan's Church Cemetery in Armoy. The family farm was sold in 1915 and the rest of

Henry "Harry" Douthart Family

Front of a Butler's Post Card. "Photographed and published by S.R. Butler & Sons, Cardonagh, Phone 25". It is believed that Henry "Harry" Douthart emigrated from Armoy, Ireland.

Henry's family moved to other areas of County Antrim. The International Genealogical Index® — Main File — Version 4.01 for the British Isles indicates Henry Douthart and Mary Cain as parents to Henry (Harry) Douthart (b. November 1, 1866). This is my grandfather.

Family stories say that two of Henry's sons, Harry and Tom, left Ireland for America around 1885. They went straight to Wilmington, Illinois, and stayed with the Morgan family, friends who preceded them to America. Harry and Tom went to work for the railroad. Harry rose to become Roadmaster at Joliet for the Elgin, Joliet, and Eastern railway, part of the U.S. Steel Corporation. Both men met and married their wives in the Wilmington/Joliet area.

The State of Illinois, Will County, Petition for Naturalization, dated October 26, 1896, and signed by Harry Douthart verifies Harry's presence in the United States.

Harry Douthart settled in the Chicago area and married my grandmother Catherine Maloney. I don't recall meeting either one of my grandparents, though I recall the day we moved from their house on Clyde Avenue to our own home just one block away at 9137 Merrill Avenue. This is the only family home I ever knew, and I lived there until my marriage to Clyde on September 19, 1959.

Mary Lou and her sisters created a letter — found separately in this book — about their times and recalled the Harry and Catherine Douthart family house on Clyde Avenue on Chicago's South Side (rather coincidental that I would marry someone by the name of "Clyde").

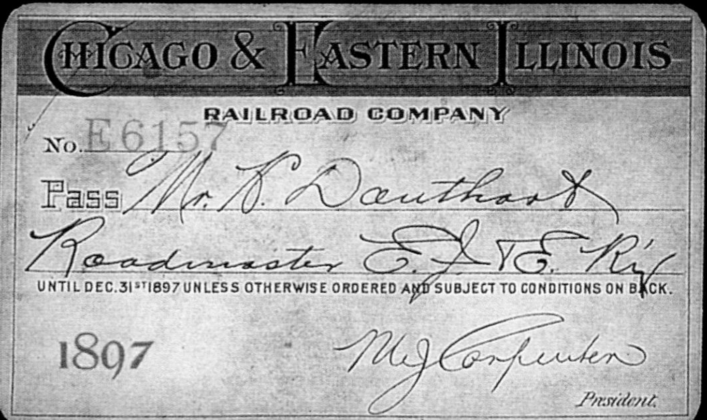

CHICAGO & EASTERN ILLINOIS

RAILROAD COMPANY

No. E6157

Pass Mr. H. Douthart

Roadmaster E. J. & E. Ry

UNTIL DEC. 31ST 1897 UNLESS OTHERWISE ORDERED AND SUBJECT TO CONDITIONS ON BACK.

1897

M J Carpenter

President.

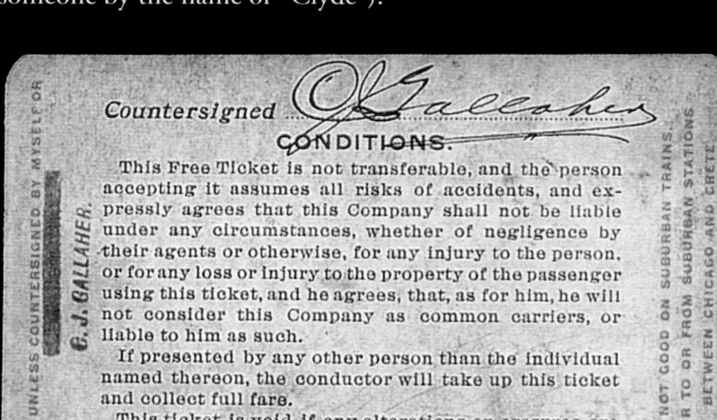

VOID UNLESS COUNTERSIGNED BY MYSELF OR

G. J. GALLAHER.

Countersigned G J Gallaher

CONDITIONS.

This Free Ticket is not transferable, and the person accepting it assumes all risks of accidents, and expressly agrees that this Company shall not be liable under any circumstances, whether of negligence by their agents or otherwise, for any injury to the person, or for any loss or injury to the property of the passenger using this ticket, and he agrees, that, as for him, he will not consider this Company as common carriers, or liable to him as such.

If presented by any other person than the individual named thereon, the conductor will take up this ticket and collect full fare.

This ticket is void if any alterations or erasures are made and may be revoked by the Company at any time.

NOT GOOD ON SUBURBAN TRAINS, NOR TO OR FROM SUBURBAN STATIONS BETWEEN CHICAGO AND CRETE.

Front and back of railroad "Free Travel" passes issued to Harry Douthart for the Chicago & Eastern Illinois

STATE OF ILLINOIS, Will COUNTY, } Sct.

At a Regular Term of the County Court of said County of Will begun and holden in the Court House in Joliet in said County of Will Monday the fifth day of October year of our Lord one thousand eight hundred and ninety-six

Present—Honorable Albert O. Marshall John Granger Wm. F. Hutchinson

PETITION.

In the Matter of the Naturalization of Harry Douthart an Alien

To the Honorable Albert O. Marshall Judge of the County Court of Will

Your petitioner Harry Douthart an alien, free person, a native of Ireland respectfully represents unto your Honor that he arrived in the United S[tates] under the age of twenty-one; that he resided in the United States three years preceding his arrival at the age of twenty-one years; that he has conti[nued] therein to the time of his making this, his application to be admitted a citizen thereof; that he has arrived at the age of twenty-one years; that h[e] in the United States five years and upwards, to wit: for the term of eleven years, including the three years of his minorit[y] State of Illinois for ten years; that it is *bona fide* his intention to become a citizen of the United States, and to renoun[ce] allegiance and fidelity to every foreign Prince, Potentate, State or Sovereignty whatever, and particularly the allegiance and fidelity which he in to the Queen of Great Britain & Ireland whereof he was heretofore a citizen or su[bject] two years next preceding, it has been *bona fide* his intention to become a citizen of the United States.

Harry Douthart

STATE OF ILLINOIS, Will COUNTY, } Sct. Harry Douthart being duly [sworn on] his oath says that the above petition is true.

Subscribed and sworn to before me, this 26th day of Oct. A. D. 1896 Wm. F. Hutchinson CLERK.

Harry Douthart

STATE OF ILLINOIS, Will COUNTY, } ss. We Frank Maloney of Grundy Wm. Mooney of the County of Will and State of Illinois, having b[een] sworn, do depose and say that we have been personally acquainted with Harry Douthart an a[lien] applied to be admitted as a Naturalized Citizen of the United States, for the space of five years last past and upwards; that during the whole of sai[d] continued to reside within the limits and under the jurisdiction of the United States, and one year, at least, in the said State of Illinois, preceding t[he] date hereof; and that, as far as our knowledge and observation has extended, he has behaved himself as a man of good moral character, and appears to the principles contained in the Constitution of the United States, and well disposed to the good order, well-being and happiness of the same; two years next preceding it has been *bona fide* his intention to become a citizen of the United States.

Subscribed and sworn to in open Court, this 26th day of Oct. A. D. 1896 Attest: Wm. F. Hutchinson CLERK.

Frank Maloney
William Mooney

STATE OF ILLINOIS, Will COUNTY, } ss I, Harry Douthart do solemnly sw[ear] in the presence of Almighty God, that I will support the Constitution of the United States, and that I do absolutely and entirely renounce allegiance and fidelity to every foreign Prince, Potentate, State or Sovereignty whatever, and more particularly the allegiance and fidelity I in a[ny wise owe to] the Queen of Great Britain & Ireland whereof I was heretofore a citizen or subje[ct].

Subscribed and sworn to in open Court, this 28th day of Oct. A. D. 1896 Attest: Wm. F. Hutchinson CLERK.

Harry Douthart

UNITED STATES OF AMERICA.

STATE OF ILLINOIS, County of Will } ss.

Be It Remembered, That on the 26th day of October in the year of our Lord One Thousand Eight Hundred and ninety-s[ix] appeared before the Honorable Albert O. Marshall Presiding Judge of the County Cou[rt of] Will and State aforesaid (the same being a court of Record, having and exercising common law jurisdiction, a Seal and a Clerk), and sitting judicially for the disp[atch of business at] the Court House in Joliet in the County aforesaid Harry Douthart an alien born, free, male pers[on] twenty-one years, and applied to the said Court to be admitted to become a naturalized citizen of the United States of America, pursuant to the several Acts of Congress heretofore passed on that subject, Revised Statutes of the United States, approved June 22d, 1874,

Harry Douthart having thereupon produced to the Court, Record testimony showing that he has himself and filed his declaration of his intention to become a citizen of the United States, according to the provisions of the said several Acts of Congress and the Court being satisfied, as well from Harry Douthart as from the testimony of Frank Maloney and Wm. Mooney who are known to be competent witnesses, that the said applicant arrived in the United States a min[or] twenty-one years, has resided within the limits and under the jurisdiction of the United States, for and during the full term of five years, including the three years previous to his arrival at the age of twenty-one within the State of Illinois; and having declared on oath, and proven to the satisfaction of the Court that for two years next preceding his application it has been *bona fide* his intention to become a citizen of and that during said term of five years, he has sustained a good moral character, and appeared to be attached to the principles contained in the Constitution of the United States and well disposed to the go[od order] and happiness of the same; and the said applicant having now here filed his declaration of intention to become a Citizen of the United States, according to the provisions of the several Acts of Congress h[eretofore passed on] that subject; and he having now here in open Court taken and subscribed the oath required by those laws, to support the Constitution of the United States, and to renounce and abjure all allegiance and fidel[ity to every foreign] Prince, Potentate, State or Sovereignty whatever, and more particularly all allegiance which he may in anywise owe to the Queen of Great Britain and Ireland whereof he was heretofore a subject.

It is thereupon Considered, Ordered and Adjudged by the Court, That the said Harry Douthart [be admitted] to all and singular the rights, privileges and immunities of a naturalized citizen of the United States, and that the same be certified by the Clerk of this Court under the Seal of said Court, accordingly.

Harry Douthart's petition to become a naturalized citizen of the United States, executed on October 28, 1896, in Joliet, Illinois. Frank Maloney, the brother of Catherine Maloney, Harry's spouse, and William Mooney attested to his residency in the U.S. for at least a year and to his "good character."

THE WABASH Railroad Company

No. T

TIME PASS.

Pass H. Douthart
Between Chicago Brisbane
And Crocker
Over Middle & Detroit Div.
Account R. Master EJ & E Ry
Until Dec 31st 1901, unless otherwise ordered.

NOT GOOD UNLESS COUNTERSIGNED ON BACK BY EDW. T. CLAPP.

J. Ramsey Jr. VICE-PRESIDENT AND GENERAL MANAGER.

NOT GOOD IN BOUDOIR CARS.

This Pass is Not Transferable,

And will be forfeited if presented for passage by a person not named thereon.

In consideration of this pass, the holder assumes all risk of injury to his person or property, and hereby releases the Wabash Railroad Company from liability for any personal injury or loss or damage to baggage, which may occur to him while using this pass.

The above conditions are understood and accepted by me as the consideration upon which this pass is issued to me.

H. Douthart

To be signed in ink before presentation.

COUNTERSIGNED:

Though Harry Douthart was employed by the EJ&E Railroad, he had free passage in 1901 granted by the Wabash Railroad Company. Harry's signature appears on the reverse side of the pass.

State Illinois

County Cook

Township or other division of county X

(Insert proper name and also name of class, as township, town, precinct, district, etc. See instructions.)

Incorporated place Chicago City

(Insert proper name and also name of class, as city, village, town, or borough. See instructions.)

Ward of city Tenth Com Area (Part of) Block No. 141

Unincorporated place

(Enter name of any unincorporated place having approximately 500 inhabitants or more. See instructions.)

	PLACE OF ABODE				NAME	RELATION	HOME DATA				PERSONAL DESCRIPTION					EDUCATION		
	Street, avenue, road, etc.	House number (in cities or towns)	Number of dwelling house in order of visitation	Number of family in order of visitation	of each person whose *place of abode* on April 1, 1930, was in this family. Enter surname first, then the given name and middle initial, if any. Include every person living on April 1, 1930. Omit children born since April 1, 1930	Relationship of this person to the head of the family	Home owned or rented	Value of home, if owned, or monthly rental, if rented	Radio set	Does this family live on a farm?	Sex	Color or race	Age at last birthday	Marital condition	Age at first marriage	Attended school or college any time since Sept. 1, 1929	Whether able to read and write	Place of birth of each person … the United States, … which birthplace is … French from Canada … PERSON
	1	2	3	4	5	6	7	8	9	10	11	12	13	14	15	16	17	18
51					Burke, John	Son					M	W	27	S		no		Illinois
…					…	Son					M	W	18	S		no	yes	Illinois
86					———, Geraldine	Daughter					F	W	17	S		no	yes	Illinois
87		9205	93	94	Douthart, Harry	Head	O	4500	R		M	W	45	M	21	no	yes	Northern Ireland
88					———, Catherine	Wife-H					F	W	45	M	21	no	yes	Illinois
89					———, Nora	Daughter					F	W	32	S		no	yes	Illinois
90					———, Harry	Son					M	W	30	S		no	yes	Illinois
91					———, Richard	Son					M	W	21	S		no	yes	Illinois
92					Maloney, Dennis	Relative					M	W	70	S		no	yes	New York

Herewith Ends the Enumeration of Block 141.

Fifteenth Census of the United States of 1930 showing the family of Harry Douthart living at 9205 Clyde Avenue, Chicago, Illinois. The census enumerates Harry as head of household at age 65 (b. September 8, 1865); Catherine, his wife, listed as being 65, though she was born in 1863 and was probably actually 67; their daughter Nora, age 32; his son Harry, age 30; his son Richard, age 21; and Dennis Maloney, listed as a "Relative," age 70. Kay Davis believes that Dennis was Catherine Maloney Douthart's older brother. Richard Douthart later moved to 9137 Merrill Avenue, just one street west and about a block south. His daughter, Catherine "Kay" was to later marry a young man named "Clyde" Patrick Davis.

Form 15-6

DEPARTMENT OF COMMERCE—BUREAU OF THE CENSUS

FIFTEENTH CENSUS OF THE UNITED STATES: 1930

POPULATION SCHEDULE

Enumeration District No. 16-415

Supervisor's District No. 29

Sheet No. 17 B

0352

Enumerated by me on April 22, 23, 1930, Maria B. Sonnenschein, Enumerator.

...tion, if any, and indicate the lines on which the entries are made. See instructions.)

...IRTH (...d of his or her parents. If born in ... If of foreign birth, give country in ...nstructions.) Distinguish Canada-...ee State from Northern Ireland) Mother (20)	Mother tongue (or native language) of foreign born: Language spoken in home before coming to the United States (21)	Code (For office use only. Do not write in these columns): State or M.T. (A)	Country (B)	Nativity (C)	Citizenship, etc.: Year of immigration to the United States (22)	Naturalization (23)	Whether able to speak English (24)	Occupation and Industry: Occupation — Trade, profession, or particular kind of work, as spinner, salesman, riveter, teacher, etc. (25)	Industry — Industry or business, as cotton mill, dry-goods store, shipyard, public school, etc. (26)	Code (For office use only. Do not write in this column) (D)	Class of worker (27)	Employment: Whether actually at work yesterday (or the last regular working day) — Yes or No (28)	If not, line number on Unemployment Schedule (29)	Veterans: Whether a veteran of U.S. military or naval forces — Yes or No (30)	What war or expedition? (31)	Number of farm schedule (32)	
Illinois		61						None									51
Illinois		61					[illegible]	[illegible]						No			52
[illegible]		61	03	1				[illegible]									53
Pennsylvania		61	03	1			yes	None									86
Northern Ireland	English	60	03	V	1886	Na	yes	Yard Foreman	Steel Mill	[illegible]	W	yes		No			87
Irish Free State		61	04	0			yes	None									88
Illinois		61	03	1			yes	Clerk-demonstrator	Cosmetics	[illegible]	W	No	18				89
Illinois		61					yes	Switchman	Railroad	[illegible]	W	yes		yes	WW		90
Illinois		61					yes	Timekeeper	Railroad	[illegible]	W	yes	[illegible]	No			91
Irish Free State		56	04	0			yes	None						No			92
																	93

Harry Douthart residence at 9205 Clyde Avenue

My Father, a Study in Contrasts

by Kay Douthart Davis

It seemed my father's life revolved around work, drinking beer with his friends at the neighborhood "tavern," and driving my mother to and from work. I don't recall that he had any leisure time activities or hobbies — save fiddling around with old radios and TVs — always trying to "fix" them. Friends at his job would give him their broken radios, and he would bring them home to tinker with. He was always messing with our TV. (We were the first on our block to own one.) He would set a chair in front of the TV, prop a large mirror on it, and go to the rear of the TV to make things happen, like creating bad picture quality with "snow" or vertical lines through the images. All good things if you are a fiddler.

He did not like the out-of-doors. He never went on picnics or to the beach. He liked cars and always had a pretty nice one. He was not a man who expressed his love — but you knew he loved you. He was stern but generous and he had a really unique sense of humor — a dry wit, quick and funny, and he loved to "doubletalk." He would say strange things that seemed to make sense, but never really did. He had sayings and words that fascinated us all, like calling my cat "Throckmorton" or saying we were going to "Saskatchewan" or "Timbuktoo" — places we didn't even know existed. He always shopped for our Christmas trees — late, when pickin's were slim — but cheap! We had the strangest-looking, $2 Christmas trees you could imagine. He brought a miniature tree home for me once that he made while at work. It was constructed of wood, stood about twelve inches high and had rubber bands and paper clips hanging from it. He placed it on my bedside table one morning and woke me by pulling my toe. He loved to wake me up that way. He bought me a white, mother-of-pearl accordion (that I sold when Clyde and I were broke at college) and had me play it for his friends. He always wore a hat, was rail thin, and hated doctors. As he got older and his health slipped, some of my most tense moments were when I wanted him to schedule an appointment with a doctor. He could become angry and intimidating. It took some time before I learned to take him on.

He was a man of predictable habits and routines, including the "nightly ritual" of beer drinking at the local, neighborhood tavern. My father was a regular customer there and could be found in the darkened bar side of an establishment that dedicated one half to its packaged goods business and the other side (or half) to the bar.

I would often enter the packaged goods side to purchase a large bag of barbequed potato chips and a large bottle of Coca-Cola. I could usually peek through to the other side and see my father's back as he sat on a barstool. Often he would shout out "Hi, Kay-Kay."

Richard C. Douthart with Mary Lou Carlson in 1919.

My girlfriend and I would ride our bikes to the store and then return to the stoop at the front entrance of my home and eat the entire bag of chips as well as drink all the Coke. Our routine was *almost* as regular as my dad's.

Although my father drank a lot of beer — very often — he never drank or kept any alcohol or beer in our home. As a matter of fact, other than seeing a beer on the counter beside him at the neighborhood bar, I never saw my father drinking beer or alcohol.

Nonetheless, he did become mean toward my mother when he drank, creating arguments when he would sometimes hit her, hurting her badly. My brothers and I became fearful of our father as we were lying in our beds while our parents fought. However, again, I have to say that I can't recall my father ever striking my brothers or me. Maybe this drinking and brawling was an "Irish thing."

He was a proud man and could be heard saying that he never missed a day of work because of his drinking habit. He would place his weekly earnings in the bedroom dresser, top drawer, for my mother to retrieve — another of his routines.

As I have mentioned before, my father was a man of regular behavior. This behavior, however, never included the regular jobs required to maintain a home. My mother assumed all these. She cut the lawn, watered it, planted all the flowers, and essentially tended to every outdoor task. As well, she painted the interior walls, applied wallpaper borders to various rooms, selected and purchased all the furnishings and interior decorations, and did

Richard C. Douthart Family

Richard "Skinny" James Douthart b. June 11, 1935, Robert "Butch" Henry Douthart b. July 26, 1938, and Catherine "Kay Kay" Ann Douthart Davis b. January 2, 1940

August 1964 family gathering. Left to right: Richard C. Douthart, Ann Bauer Douthart, Edward Douthart, Howard Carlson, Mame Douthart Carlson, and Harry Douthart

all the household cleaning. I often thought some of this unequal sharing of the workload was because of a hand injury my father suffered due to an accident while working on the railroad.

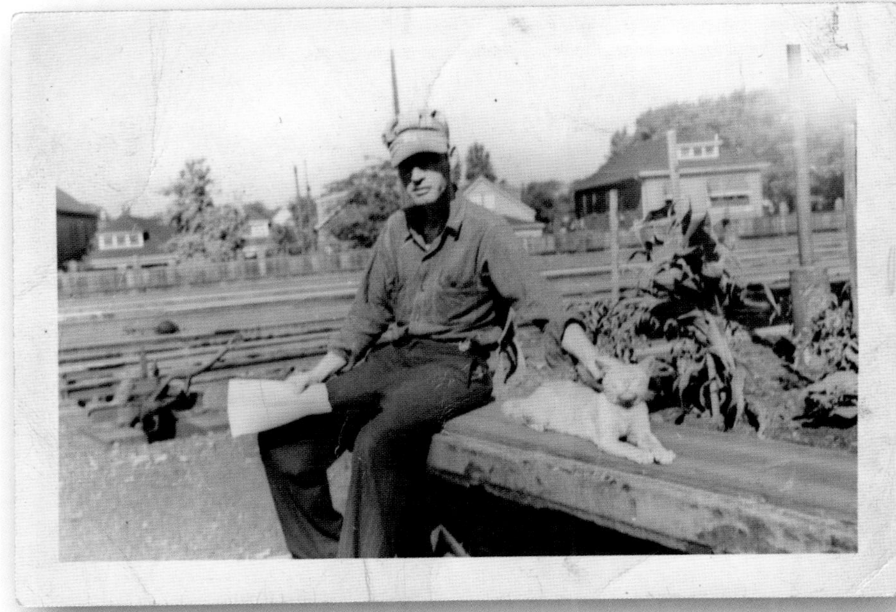

Richard C. Douthart in railroad hat with cat

A severe accident almost caused him to lose a hand. He was uncoupling and recoupling various cars on a train — a job known as switchman. He got his hand caught between two cars as they were coming together. The doctors wanted to remove several fingers because they were so badly damaged, but my father refused. That decision left his hand intact, but it was filled with wires to help it operate. He never could bend his last two fingers well after that, so gripping things (like paint brushes, lawn mowers, etc.) became a problem. I'm not sure, to this day, the sequence of these events — no help around the house, injured hand — or, injured hand and no help around the house. He did manage, though, to always tinker with the TVs and radios, and that required some delicate handwork to be sure.

I have bittersweet memories of my father. His Irish temper and drinking habits made him a difficult personality. However, his hard work, generosity, deep love of his children, and his wit and funny bone combined to make him truly a good and kind person.

Richard C. Douthart Family

Richard C. Douthart in center with his son Robert (far right) and his brother Edward between them. At far left is Edmund Carlson, Richard's sister Mame's son, and Edmund's father, Howard Carlson.

My Family

Because both my father and mother held full-time jobs and my mother never learned to drive a car, many of the usual household chores, such as getting groceries and paying bills, became my responsibility.

On any given morning my mother would phone the grocery store to place her order. It would be ready at the noon hour for my pick-up. On weekdays I would run out of school at the sound of the lunch bell and race to the grocery store several blocks away and pick up the groceries that often consisted of two bags, potatoes and soda — quite a heavy load for me. Then I would loop back to go home, meeting the other children on my way, who were still casually walking to their homes for lunch.

My mom, who worked six-hour shifts as a telephone operator in the evenings, would prepare a grilled cheese or peanut butter sandwich with Campbell's chicken noodle soup (one of my son Cole's favorites to this day) for me to eat while I watched *The Gary Moore Show* on TV. We were the first on our block to own one. I would eat a five-minute lunch before racing back to school in time for the afternoon session.

As for bill paying, the procedure was more complex. My parents never had a checking account. The only reason they ever went into a bank was to purchase U.S. Savings Bonds, and they purchased them whenever they could. Perhaps they also held a savings account in the South Chicago Savings Bank.

South Chicago was a retail area where most of our family's needs were satisfied. It included a department store, Goldblatt's; a furniture store, L. Fish & Co.; and many small shops, including a 5 & 10 cent store. There was also a Currency Exchange located just steps away from the streetcar stop where I was deposited after about a twenty-minute ride from my home. The Currency Exchange offered check cashing as well as services for people who did not use banks, allowing them to pay utility bills directly at the Exchange.

Each week my mother would give me a packet of bills that required payment. The packet usually included the telephone bill, water bill, electric bill, which were directly paid at the Currency Exchange, and/or a few requests for money orders for bills she intended to pay by mail. Also there might be a payment for the furniture store, L. Fish, and a payment to Goldblatt's. Each of these two bills was paid at a special counter within the stores.

My mother was rather anxious each time she sent me out the door loaded with cash for bills to be paid and instructions for each item. Until she received my phone call after I had accomplished her goals and rid myself of virtually all the cash, I'm sure she sat holding her breath that all would go well. I must have been ten or eleven years old at the time.

With the bills paid, I could now proceed to the fun part of my weekly trip — buying all the things the family might need or want including a special "something" for myself for being such a good girl.

I would purchase candy and bakery goods for the family — I could make my own selections — necessary clothing for my father at work such as pants, shirts, underwear, socks, and handkerchiefs. Or socks and underwear for my brothers and usually a "surprise" for my mother — sometimes a blouse for work or a new nightgown. I enjoyed doing the rounds and always felt satisfied on my way home. I never had returns, and everyone got what they needed or wanted. A job well done. Unfortunately, this little exercise each week most likely set me up for a life of trying to please everyone through the things that I get for them. My mother is probably smiling down on me. I have gotten very good over the years.

My mother had one day off from her job each week. It usually occurred on a weekday. Because she would be home alone and also because she loved to do things in which my father had no interest, she often recruited me to join her in pursuing those

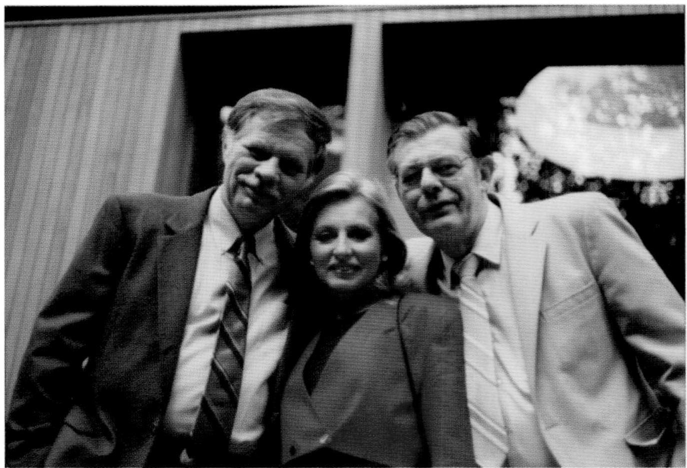

Children of Richard C. Douthart — Robert "Bob," Catherine Ann "Kay," and Richard James "Dick"

interests. Usually she liked to go shopping and have lunch out followed by a movie. Sometimes when I would arrive home for lunch on her day off she would ask me not to return to school for the afternoon. Instead, after all the kids had gone back to school, we would take the streetcar to South Chicago and spend time together. Her promise to take me to the 5 & 10 cent store for either a sloppy joe or my favorite lunch — chop suey — and then take in a movie — was an irresistible draw even though I loved school. In hindsight, I recall feeling sorry for my mother and wanting to please her.

On occasion, in the summer months when all the kids were on vacation from school, my mother would pack a huge lunch and take us to Wolf Lake (my brother drove by then) or Riverview Amusement Park. She loved the outdoors and her sister, my aunt Ruth, told me that my mom was quite a good athlete, especially a good swimmer. My father hated the sand, the sun, and the bugs.

Cut this off and give to Parties married

This Certifies that

Mr. Richard Douthart AND Miss Ann Bauer
of Chicago — of Chicago
State of Illinois — State of Illinois

WERE UNITED IN
Holy Matrimony

According to the ORDINANCE OF GOD and the Laws of the State of Illinois at Waukegan on the 27th day of October in the year of OUR LORD One Thousand Nine Hundred and Thirty-two

MATTHEW. For this cause shall a man leave father and mother, and shall cleave to his wife: and they twain

MATTHEW. shall be one flesh. What therefore God hath joined together, let not man put asunder.

Witnesses: Mrs. Ann Hunt
John F Hunt

Harry Hoyt
Justice of the Peace

Though it was believed by family members that Richard Douthart and Ann Bauer were married in a civil ceremony in Chicago, Illinois, the above marriage certificate states otherwise, giving the place of their marriage as Waukegan, Illinois. The marriage was performed by a Justice of the Peace. Later, Richard, a lifelong Catholic, and his spouse were remarried in St. Albee's Catholic Church in Chicago after Ann converted to Catholicism.

The location of Waukegan, Illinois, for this marriage has been confusing. However, according to The Newberry Library Genealogy News, *January 29, 2008, "Chicago couples flocked to Milwaukee, Wisconsin to tie the knot in the 1890's. The tide turned in 1899 when a new Wisconsin marriage law imposed a delay of five days between issuance of the license and the performance of the ceremony. Waukegan, Illinois then became a popular spot for a quick wedding."*

Richard C. Douthart Family

Harry Douthart b. February 21, 1897, older brother of Richard C. Douthart, lived at the South Chicago Hotel and Restaurant located near 92nd and Commercial Avenues in 1916 depicted above in a photo from Images of America Chicago's Southeast Side *by Rod Sellers and Dominic A. Pacyga (Arcadia Publishing, 1998, p. 35). Courtesy of the Southeast Chicago Historical Society.*

Uncle Harry

by Kay Douthart Davis

My uncle Harry (my father's brother) never married and usually lived alone. For some years he lived in a room at the South Chicago Hotel and Restaurant, located at 92nd Commercial Avenue. He also lived, from time to time, at the YMCA in South Chicago.

Living alone as he did, I recall he would often join us for Sunday dinner. When he did, it became a special meal because we ate in the formal dining room, the kitchen being too small for all of us to be seated at the table.

We always gave Uncle Harry a carton of Tarrington cigarettes and half dozen white handkerchiefs for Christmas. Again, he would join us for the holiday meal.

Later in his life, he rented an apartment at 9328 South Marquette Avenue, Chicago, and took his sister, my aunt Nora, in with him. She had been institutionalized for some years (for reasons I don't know), and he felt guilty about that situation. I remember she was not able, even then, to do the most routine of tasks. I am certain it caused my Uncle Harry much difficulty because she "passed" out money to strangers and did not pay the electric bills, causing the service to be disconnected. I believe he was living with her at the time of his death on January 13, 1966.

My father was a younger brother to Harry. They both worked on the EJ&E (Elgin, Joliet and Eastern) railroad within the U.S. Steel Mill. Because my father was Harry's supervisor, it could become an uncomfortable situation for a younger brother. I recall my father making mention of this.

Though both my father and Uncle Harry were heavy drinkers — my father beer and Uncle Harry whiskey — neither man ever drank in our home or in front of my brothers and me.

Uncle Harry was the only relative whom we saw (or knew) on a regular basis.

Dave "Butchie" Davis at age 13 and Kay's uncle Harry Douthart on September 19, 1959, on Clyde's and Kay's wedding day in Kay's family's living room. This is one of the few pictures we have of Kay's uncle Harry.

Harry Douthart Residence
9205 Clyde Av.
Chicago, IL.

This house was on the "Hill" in an area known as South Chicago. Transportation was convenient - the streetcar stopped at the corner just a block away, headed North to downtown Chicago, or South toward another streetcar which crossed the Indiana State line into Whiting. A NYC train depot was less than a mile away and provided local and long distance rides to the East.

There were five bedrooms, and a large living room and dining room, some victorian style furnishings and a rosewood piano which had been purchased at the close of the Columbian exposition in the 1890s. The large front hall boasted a telephone corner with a 5¢ coin-operated phone, to keep up with family communication.

Harry Douthart was a railroad man, but he loved farming. He had a terrific vegetable garden on the vacant lot next door, and there was a chicken coop in the back yard for many years. 9205 Clyde was a vacation place and overnight stop for three Carlson grandaughters, enjoying visits with all the relatives while growing up. Holidays and all visits were feasting and sharing times - memories to hold on to.

Margaret Douthart died suddenly just before Christmas in 1927. She had gone to Detroit by train just before the holiday to visit friends. She became ill and returned to Chicago, went right to the hospital -- her appendix had ruptured but the operation was too late to save her life. The two day wake and

9205 Clyde (con'd)

the funeral on the day after Christmas made for a very sad time for her family and friends, especially for Jim Johnson, her fiance.

Grandmother Catherine Douthart died of pneumonia in 1937, with her children at her bedside. Her husband Harry died a year later.

It was late in May, 1938. Alice and Rita Jane were getting ready for the Prom at Catholic Central High. Alice was to be the date of Emmet Kolb, an alumnus; Mom and Dad were to be Dance Chaperones; Rita Jane was to be the date of Edward Hannon of Gary, Freshman brother Edmund was on punch detail. At 6:30 p.m. we received a call from South Chicago that Grandpa Douthart had suffered a heart attack. Emmet took us all there in his car (seats all covered with white sheets to protect delicate prom dresses), but Grandpa had expired by the time we arrived. A prospective merry evening turned into one of great sadness.

Harry Douthart was a legendary man--he had survived a fall while walking home from the mill one wintry evening; a fall from the high porch roof at home; and what could have been a disastrous tragedy: One day he and his crew (he was a supervisor in the railroad division of the South Chicago Steel Mill) were standing near a huge cauldron of molten steel, when the crane operator mistakenly began pouring the steel too soon. Harry shouted to his men as the first drops began to fall in front of them: "Let's walk through it!" They did, but Grandpa suffered burns over much of his upper body. We remember him recovering in the South Chicago Community Hospital, all bandaged except for his eyes, nose, and mouth. His teeth were particularly amazing to the doctors ...badly stained (from his corn cob pipe smoking) but not a single filling, crown, or cavity.

After the family no longer needed the big old house, Aunt Nora distributed the keepsakes to the family members desiring them, and Harry Douthart Jr. found a buyer for the house.

In 1985, we drove past the old address and found the house gone. A one story apartment building now fills the place of the old Douthart house and garden.

Rita Jane Glazebrook
Alice M. Dauro
Mary Lou Ambre

Kay Davis received this story from her first cousins, Rita Jane Carlson Glazebrook, Alice M. Carlson Dauro, and Mary Lou Carlson Ambre, the three daughters of Kay's aunt "Mayme," who was the sister to Kay's father, Richard C. Douthart. Kay also remembers the day she and her family moved from this house to their own home at 9137 Merrill Avenue, just one street west and about a block south of the house on Clyde Avenue. She recalls her father standing her on a chair near the telephone corner to dress her for the departure to their new home. It was an exciting day.

Photo at left is of Catherine "Kay" Douthart at age 7 in front of the house on Clyde Avenue.

Richard C. Douthart Family

Thursday

Dear Anne,

I will try to explain the cemetary name puzzle as short as I can. It is kind of complicated. The Wilmington cemetery and the original owners are older than the Civil War -- much older.

The lots were originally bought by Daniel Maloney and John Heslin -- who did not know each other.

Daniel was married to a Catherine Maloney. They had 7 children before she died. Uncle Denny (Dennis) was one of them. Aunt Mary was one of the younger ones. Uncle Frank Maloney in Joliet was <u>not</u> one of them. Our Grandmother (who is buried in the Heslin lot) was Daniel Maloney's <u>second</u> wife.

The owner of the second lot, John Heslin, was first married to Mary O'Rourke Heslin. They had three children. Uncle John Heslin (who lived out West), Aunt Bridget of Clinton, Ill. (She was the Ducy family's grandmother), and an infant son who died at birth. The Maloney and Heslin lots are only a short distance apart.

After the death of their partners, Daniel Maloney and Mary Heslin married. They decided that they would each be buried alongside their first mates. They had two children from their marriage - Uncle Frank (Joliet) and our Mother (Catherine), plus one infant son who died soon after birth. After Grandmother Maloney's death, our Dad (her son-in-law) took over the maintance of the Heslin Lot, and two small Douthart children and Margaret are buried there in addition to Dad and Mother. Dad put the Heslin/Douthart headstone on the lot after Margaret's death.

Aunt Mary Cushing paid the upkeep on the Maloney lot; after Denny was buried there Mary gave the lot to our Brother Harry for himself, on condition that he pay the upkeep from then on.

Aunt Mary and her Husband Pat XXX Cushing have their own lot separate from this Maloney lot -- there is also a Garret Cushing lot (Pat Cushing's brother) and an Edmund Cushing (the Famous Mun) is also buried in the Wilmington Cemetery. The Frank Maloneys of Joliet have their lot in a Joliet cemetery, but it is not the Maloney lot that brother Harry is buried in, and not the one that Harry paid upkeep on.

There is one grave left in the Heslin-Douthart lot which is being saved for Nora. Our Dad never bought it, but did pay the upkeep and improvements on it for years after he married Mother. That is why the lot is still registered in the name Heslin. Our Brother, Harry, being the grandson of Daniel Maloney has every right to be buried in the Maloney lot. The name Douthart is not in the cemetery records of ownership, but it is on the mailing list for the upkeep charges of these two lots.

Hope this information helps a little.

Love Mayme

PS by Mary Lou - From Mother's remarks I figured out a few extra pages of information which I enclose - Hope they don't confuse you. I'm working on a family tree too. Maybe I'll get a correct one that I can eventually send you for your own records. Love,

Mary Lou

CATHOLIC CEMETERY.

Certificate No. 40. May 17 1868

Wilmington, Ill.,

This Certifies that John Heslen of Town Wilmington having this day paid $5.00

proprietor ½ of Lot numbered 216, on the plat of the same, in the Catholic Cemetery, in the city of Wilmington, being a subdivision of OUT LOT 19, in H. O. Alden's Addition to Wilmington; and that he is entitled to the exclusive occupation of said subdivided Lot, only as a family burying-ground, so long as he shall conform to such rules and regulations for burial as may from time to time be established by a majority of the proprietors of said lots.

By Order of the Bishop.

A. Krause, Sexton.

Printed on back of photo: "St. Rose Church, 603 S. Main Street, Wilmington, Ill. 60481"

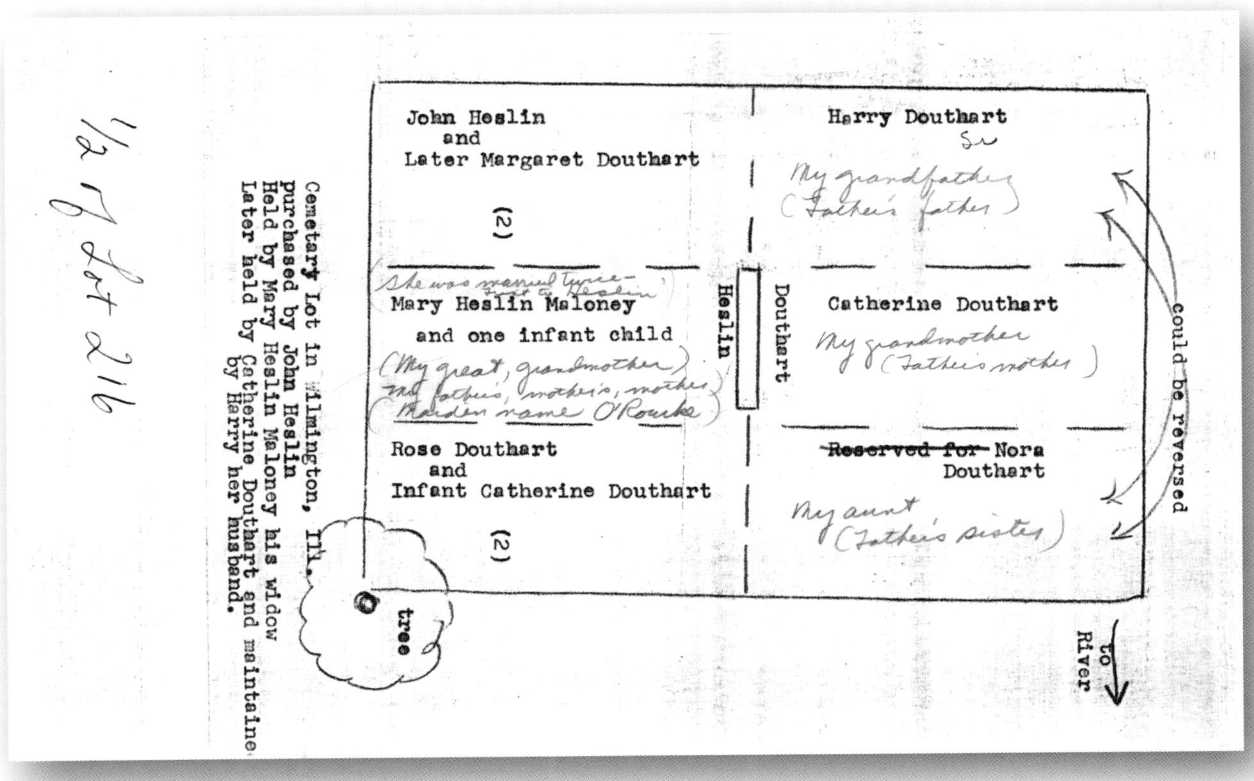

Wilmington Cemetery, Illinois, Plat Plan — Original Cemetery lot in Wilmington. Owned by Daniel Maloney — later held by Mary Cushing who gave the last lot to Harry Douthart, grandson of original owner

Buried in this lot: *Daniel Maloney*
Catherine Maloney and infant child
Edward Maloney
Dennis Maloney
Kate Glenny — related to Catherine
Harry Douthart Jr.

Lot nearby — owned by John Heslin — later maintained by Harry Douthart
Buried in this lot: *John Heslin and Margaret Douthart*
Mary Heslin Maloney & infant child
Rose Douthart and an infant sister (Catherine died 8 months)
Harry Douthart
Catherine Douthart
One empty space reserved for Nora

Mary Lou Carlson Ambre, my first cousin, is the daughter of my father's older sister, Mary Lenore Douthart Carlson, who was my godmother — my "Aunt Mayme." Mary Lou recalls that my father, who was the youngest child in his family, would often babysit her. This book shows a photo of my father and Mary Lou sitting on the front stairs of the house on Clyde Avenue in Chicago.

Thomas Ambre, October 1985, husband of my cousin, Mary Lou

My cousin, Mary Lou Carlson Ambre, October 1985

Not having strong ties to the extended families of my parents, I found it extremely difficult to uncover background information about those families. However, Mary Lou became a critical link for me to the past history of the Douthart family. On numerous visits she shared documents, family trees, research, and letters from her mother's pursuit of Douthart genealogy, and interesting stories about the evolution of the family.

We would often sit and chat in her home or at the home of Clyde's mother. These latter visits would be followed by ice cream at Gayety's Ice Cream Shop — an old favorite that had become an institution in South Chicago. The shop, along with others and entire neighborhoods, migrated further south to Lansing, Illinois. This is the location that we would go to with Mary Lou and Clyde's mother. Actually, we still make a stop there whenever we are in the Chicago area.

On one afternoon we even took a trip to the Mt. Olivet Cemetery in Wilmington, Illinois, to visit the gravesite that I recalled visiting as a child with my father, mother, Uncle Harry, and my brothers. These were harrowing trips, usually in an old car that seemed to get a flat tire every time. Add to that, my father had to drive along a narrow, high dirt road at the edge of a river (far below), which passed along the cemetery to reach our particular place to visit. I recognized the scene as soon as we arrived with Mary Lou. She explained the layout of multiple graves and the significance of those people at rest there. My father's parents and several other relatives were buried at Mt. Olivert Cemetery.

Mary Lou has been a vital resource and a dear friend as I struggled to find my way back in time.

#69

ORIGINAL

FILL IN WITH TYPEWRITER OR LEGIBLE PRINTING

STATE OF ILLINOIS

STATE FILE NUMBER 1413

CORONER'S CERTIFICATE OF DEATH

REGISTRATION DISTRICT NO. 1610

REGISTERED NUMBER

1. PLACE OF DEATH a. STATE ILLINOIS b. COUNTY COOK

c. INSIDE corporate limits and in City, Village, or Incorporated Town: Chicago

e. LENGTH OF STAY IN Ic or Id: 68 Yrs

f. NAME OF HOSPITAL OR INSTITUTION: South Chgo Hospital

g. LENGTH OF STAY IN 1f: D.O.A.

2. USUAL RESIDENCE a. STATE Illinois b. COUNTY Cook

c. INSIDE corporate limits and in City, Village, or Incorporated Town: Chicago

e. LENGTH OF RESIDENCE AT 2c or 2d: 68 Yrs

f. RESIDENCE ADDRESS: 9328 S. Marquette Avenue

g. Did decedent reside ON A FARM? YES ☐ NO ☒

3. NAME OF DECEASED a. (FIRST) Harry b. (MIDDLE) G. c. (LAST) Douthart

4. DATE OF DEATH: January 13, 1966

5. SEX: Male 6. RACE: White 7. MARRIED, NEVER MARRIED, WIDOWED, DIVORCED: Never Married

8. DATE OF BIRTH: Feb. 21, 1897 9. AGE: 68

10a. USUAL OCCUPATION: Ret. Switchman 10b. KIND OF BUSINESS OR INDUSTRY: Railroad

11. BIRTHPLACE: Chicago, Illinois 12. Citizen of what country: USA

13. FATHER'S FULL NAME: Harry Douthart

14. MOTHER'S FULL MAIDEN NAME: Catherine Maloney

15. Was deceased ever in U. S. Armed Forces? Yes — World War I

16. SOCIAL SECURITY NUMBER: Unknown

17. INFORMANT a. SIGNATURE: Nora Douthart

b. ADDRESS: 9328 S. Marquette Ave. c. RELATIONSHIP TO DECEASED: Sister

18. MEDICAL CAUSE OF DEATH

PART I. IMMEDIATE CAUSE (A): Arteriosclerotic Heart Disease

INTERVAL BETWEEN ONSET AND DEATH: Unknown

20. AUTOPSY? YES ☐ NO ☒

22a. Upon medical investigation I find this death was caused as stated above. DATE: 1-13-66 SIGNED: [signature] M.D. CORONER'S PHYSICIAN

22b. Upon official investigation I find the person described died as stated above. SIGNED: [signature] COUNTY CORONER

23. DISPOSITION: BURIAL Date 1-15-66

CEMETERY: Mt Olivet Cemetery

LOCATION: Wilmington, Illinois

24. FUNERAL DIRECTOR: Tews Funeral Home, Inc

SIGNATURE: Gustave E. Tews

ADDRESS: 2434 E. 79th St. Chicago, Illinois License Number 291

25. Received for filing on: JAN 14 1966 (Signed) Samuel L. Andelman, M.D. LOCAL REGISTRAR

JAN. 18, 1966

STATE OF ILLINOIS
COUNTY OF COOK } SS
CITY OF CHICAGO

I, Samuel L. Andelman, M.D., Local Registrar of Vital Statistics of the City of Chicago, do hereby certify that I am the keeper of the records of births, stillbirths and deaths of the City of Chicago by virtue of the laws of the State of Illinois and the ordinances of the City of Chicago; that the accompanying certificate or this sheet is a true copy of a record kept by me in pursuance of said laws and ordinances.

This Certified Copy VALID Only When Original BLUE SEAL And BLUE SIGNATURE Are Affixed.

Samuel L. Andelman, M.D.
LOCAL REGISTRAR

BOARD OF HEALTH — CITY OF CHICAGO

Certificate of Death for Harry G. Douthart, brother of Richard Douthart, b. Febrary 21, 1897, d. at age 68 on January 13, 1966. Harry was living with his sister, Nora, at the time of his death.

DEATH NOTICES

DOUTHART, RICHARD CHARLES

Age 78, passed away July 6, 1986. Late of Burlington, N.C., formerly of Southeast Chicago. Husband of the late Ann Bauer Douthart; dear father of Robert H. Douthart, of Burlington, N.C., Richard James Douthart, of Richland, Wash. and Catherine Anne Davis, of Pond Ridge, N.Y.; grandfather of ten. Retired Yard Master of E.J. & E. Railroad, former member of St. Kevin Church and K. of C. Committal 1 p.m., Thursday at St. Mary's Cemetery, Evergreen Park. 798-5300.

Death notice of Richard Charles Douthart published in the Daily Calumet, *July 9, 1986*

V. S. 4
REVISION
3M Bks.

STATE OF ILLINOIS
HENRY HORNER, Governor
Department of Public Health—Division of Vital Statistics
ORIGINAL

1. PLACE OF DEATH. County of Cook. Registration Dist. No. 3104. Chicago. Primary Dist. No. 3104. 48-678

CERTIFICATE OF DEATH. Registered No. 5037

Street and Number, No. 9205 Clyde Ave

LENGTH OF RESIDENCE WHERE DEATH OCCURRED 34 yrs.

1a. PLACE OF RESIDENCE: STATE Illinois County Cook. City or Village Chicago. Street and Number 9205 Clyde Ave

2. FULL NAME Catherine A Douthart

PERSONAL AND STATISTICAL PARTICULARS

3. SEX Female 4. COLOR OR RACE White 5. Single, Married, Widowed, or Divorced married

5a. If married, widowed, or divorced HUSBAND of (or) WIFE of Harry Douthart

6. DATE OF BIRTH May 4 1866

7. AGE 70 Years 9 Months 8 Days

8. Trade, profession, or particular kind of work done House Wife

9. Industry or business in which work was done Own Home

10. Date deceased last worked at this occupation June 10 1937. 11. Total time (years) spent in this occupation 40

12. BIRTHPLACE (city or town) Wilmington (State or country) Illinois

13. NAME (Father) Daniel Maloney

14. BIRTHPLACE (city or town) Don't Know (State or country) Ireland

15. MAIDEN NAME (Mother) Mary O'Rourke

16. BIRTHPLACE (city or town) Dont Know (State or country) Ireland

17. INFORMANT Harry Douthart. P. O. Address 9205 Clyde Ave

18. PLACE OF BURIAL, Cremation or Removal. Cemetery Wilmington. 19. DATE Mar 15 1937. Location Illinois. County Will. State Ill

20. UNDERTAKER Thomas J Murphy. ADDRESS 302 E 91st St

MEDICAL CERTIFICATE OF DEATH

21. DATE OF DEATH March 12th 1937

22. I HEREBY CERTIFY, That I attended deceased from Mch 8th 1937 to Mch 12th 1937. I last saw her alive on Mch 12th 1937; death is said to have occurred on the date stated above, at 9 P m.

The principal cause of death and related causes of importance were as follows: Chronic Myocarditis. Date of onset Jan 1937

Other contributory causes of importance: none

23. Was an operation performed? no

Was there an autopsy? no

What test confirmed diagnosis? Clinical findings

Was disease in any way related to occupation of deceased? no

(Signed) Don S Harvey M.D. Address 4152 Commercial Av. Date Mch 13th 1937. Telephone So Chicago 1077

25. Filed 1937 MAR 14 AM 9 20. Registrar

Copy of Death Certificate of Catherine A. Douthart, b. May 4, 1866, d. March 12, 1937

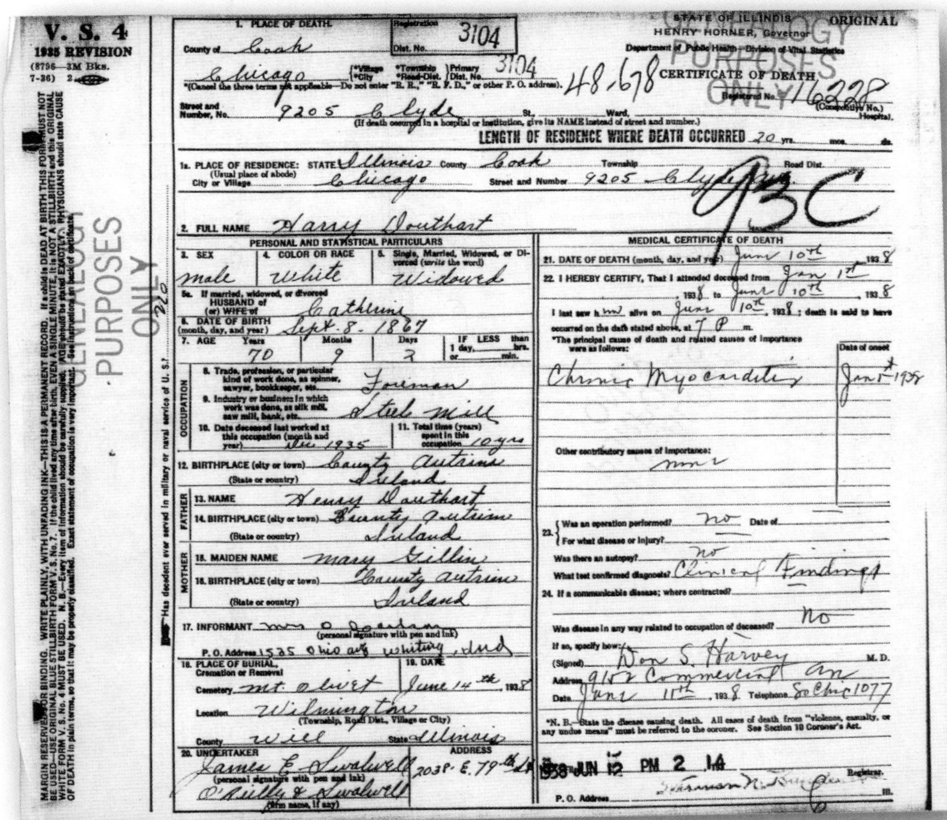

V. S. 4
1935 REVISION
(8796—3M Bks. 7-36)

STATE OF ILLINOIS
HENRY HORNER, Governor
Department of Public Health—Division of Vital Statistics
ORIGINAL

1. PLACE OF DEATH. County of Cook. Registration Dist. No. 3104. Chicago. Primary Dist. No. 3104. 48-678

CERTIFICATE OF DEATH. Registered No. 16228

Street and Number, No. 9205 Clyde

LENGTH OF RESIDENCE WHERE DEATH OCCURRED 20 yrs.

1a. PLACE OF RESIDENCE: STATE Illinois County Cook. City or Village Chicago. Street and Number 9205 Clyde Ave

2. FULL NAME Harry Douthart

PERSONAL AND STATISTICAL PARTICULARS

3. SEX male 4. COLOR OR RACE white 5. Single, Married, Widowed, or Divorced Widowed

5a. If married, widowed, or divorced HUSBAND of (or) WIFE of Catherine

6. DATE OF BIRTH Sept. 8. 1867

7. AGE 70 Years 9 Months 2 Days

8. Trade, profession, or particular kind of work done Foreman

9. Industry or business in which work was done Steel mill

10. Date deceased last worked at this occupation 1935. 11. Total time (years) spent in this occupation 10 yrs

12. BIRTHPLACE (city or town) County Antrim (State or country) Ireland

13. NAME (Father) Henry Douthart

14. BIRTHPLACE (city or town) County Antrim (State or country) Ireland

15. MAIDEN NAME (Mother) Mary Gillin

16. BIRTHPLACE (city or town) County Antrim (State or country) Ireland

17. INFORMANT Mrs O Jordan. P. O. Address 1535 Ohio Ave Whiting, Ind

18. PLACE OF BURIAL, Cremation or Removal. Cemetery Mt Olivet. 19. DATE June 14th 1938. Location Wilmington. County Will. State Illinois

20. UNDERTAKER James E Swalwell. ADDRESS 2038 E. 79th St. O'Reilly & Swalwell

MEDICAL CERTIFICATE OF DEATH

21. DATE OF DEATH June 10th 1938

22. I HEREBY CERTIFY, That I attended deceased from Jan 1st 1938 to June 10th 1938. I last saw him alive on June 10th 1938; death is said to have occurred on the date stated above, at 7 P m.

The principal cause of death and related causes of importance were as follows: Chronic Myocarditis. Date of onset Jan 1st 1938

Other contributory causes of importance: none

23. Was an operation performed? no

Was there an autopsy? no

What test confirmed diagnosis? Clinical Findings

Was disease in any way related to occupation of deceased? no

(Signed) Don S. Harvey M.D. Address 9152 Commercial Av. Date June 11th 1938. Telephone So Chic 1077

1938 JUN 12 PM 2 14. Registrar

Copy of Death Certificate of Harry Douthart, b. September 8, 1867, d. June 10, 1938

Ann May Bauer Douthart

Ann May Bauer Douthart pictured with her oldest son, Richard James Douthart

My Mother, "Annie Pinky Pie"
by Kay Douthart Davis

My mother loved the color pink. When she was a youngster she would buy a small pink sugar candy that came in a tiny tin for a penny. The kids called her "Annie Pinky Pie."

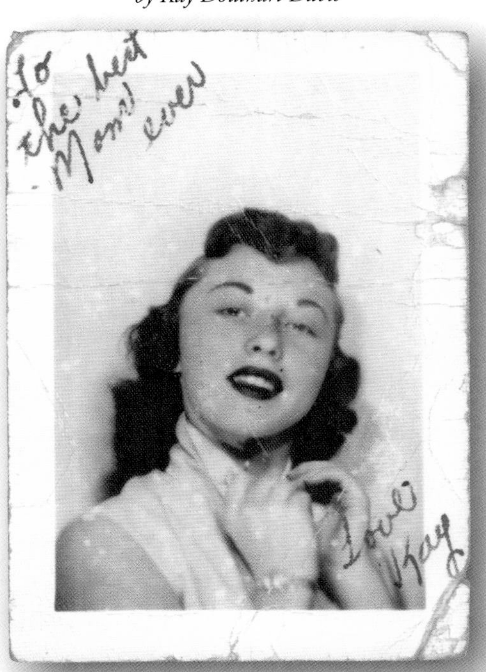

She recalled not having much as a child and having a father who drank and beat her mother until one day when her mother was so badly beaten, the older girls in the family called the police. Necessary complaints were filed by my mother's sister Florence, and John William Bauer was placed in an institution. All the sisters "considered him dead" and had nothing to do with him again until some years later when Ginger, the oldest sister, came upon him in Goldblatt's department store, where they both happened to work. Ginger again began a relationship with her father, but the other sisters were not interested in reconnecting with him. My mother did not speak of her father, except to say that he was an alcoholic who beat her mother. I never met him.

When my mother married and created a life and home of her own, material things were quite important. Having a full refrigerator and shelves lined with food were essentials that comforted her, a trait passed down to me, and from me to my daughter, Cynthia, and, perhaps, even to my son Cole. Christine seems to be the only child to have escaped the need.

The third-born of eight girls, my mother was hardworking and smart. Singlehandedly, she maintained our home, inside and out. My father rarely did work at home. Perhaps this was because of his hand injury (explained elsewhere), but I think he really didn't like household work at all. My mother painted, cleaned, gardened (she loved taking care of her flowers), mowed the lawn, cooked, and held a full-time job as a telephone operator. Actually, she was the only woman in our neighborhood who held a full-time, professional job. Most women stayed at home, and tended to the house and family. One female neighbor had a part-time factory job, but no one worked in an office environment. I was very proud of my mother, and loved listening to her as she fielded calls in her trained, staccato voice, saying, "Numba, please."

My mother was a woman who kept to herself, and never seemed to spend time with friends, sisters, or extended family. When she had free days, she would try to spend them with her children at a movie, the beach, or Riverview (a huge amusement park) — whatever she could persuade us to do with her. She loved the outdoors and wished to spend time outside whenever she could. My father hated the beach, sun, grass, and all the bugs that came with outdoor activities. He never joined us when we had our days together. Likewise, when my mother was at home for an evening, she liked to watch TV in the company of her three children. My father would never be home for these evenings. He would be at the neighborhood tavern, drinking beer with all of his friends from the railroad. So my mom, my brothers, and I would order our favorite pizza, which was always delivered to our home; this was an expected service when you lived in Chicago, nothing special. We would watch our favorite programs while my mother took over the chair usually occupied by my father. She loved to have me comb her hair and put makeup on her while she relaxed for the evening. I have often thought about these habits of my mother. When I was very young, she would also take an afternoon nap with me (because she worked in the evenings after my father returned home from work), saying that I was like a "little heater." We would snuggle and fall asleep for a short while. I never really saw my mother and father express tender or loving behavior toward each other. I believe my mother was simply looking for tenderness and loving treatment when she sought my care and company.

Dying on December 13, 1968, at the age of fifty-five, my mother never really got to see my children grow up or witness the successes of her own three children. We believe a blood clot passed through her heart or her brain. She suffered from phlebitis, but never received proper medical treatment for it.

She was a generous woman, who never denied someone in need. Her ways were quite different from those of my father. She was approachable, while he was distant; yet he was quite funny and entertaining at times. She enjoyed laughing, but never told stories or jokes, while my father was a double-talking jokester. But they were a team, a team that did the best they could with the tools they had. They really wanted to provide a good home for their family and, even with their limited resources, did all they could to see that their three children got a university education.

I would have loved to share more of my life with my mother. I lost her way too soon.

Ann May Bauer Douthart

DAVID ORR, COUNTY CLERK

SEAL OF COOK COUNTY ILLINOIS

COOK COUNTY

CERTIFICATION THAT RECORD WAS NOT FOUND

RECORD REQUESTED WAS: XXX BIRTH ☐ MARRIAGE ☐ DEATH

UNDER THE NAME(S) ANN MAY BUAER

DATE SEPTEMBER 14,1914 PLACE Chicago and Cook County, Illinois

OTHER DATA FATHER JOHN W. BAUER MOTHER ANNA M. LAUFF SEARCHED 1913 TO 1915

I HEREBY CERTIFY THAT I AM THE OFFICIAL CUSTODIAN OF THE VITAL STATISTICS FILES WHICH SHOULD CONTAIN THE RECORD REQUESTED AS DESCRIBED ABOVE, BUT THAT UPON DILIGENT SEARCH NO RECORD COULD BE FOUND.

DATED SEPTEMBER 18,2000 AT CHICAGO, COOK COUNTY, ILLINOIS

SIGNED David Orr OFFICIAL TITLE COUNTY CLERK OF COOK COUNTY

SEAL OF COOK COUNTY

JS/DAWN-EXPRESS

FORM C21

Ann Douthart holding Christine, her first grandchild, the daughter of Kay and Clyde Davis. Photo taken 1960 or 1961?

Ann and Richard Douthart. Photo believed to have been taken at the wedding of their son Robert and Shelley Miller, October 22, 1966.

b. March 14, 1914

The physician or midwife (when in attendance), or the parent or householder should immediately send this certificate accurately filled out to the County Clerk of the County in which the birth takes place. Penalty for not making report within 30 days, fine of $10 to $100, or imprisonment in jail for 30 days, or both.

WRITE PLAINLY, WITH UNFADING INK—THIS IS A PERMANENT RECORD.

STATE OF ILLINOIS, Cook County. — 1452

REPORT OF BIRTH.*

VITAL STATISTICS DEPARTMENT—COUNTY CLERK'S OFFICE.

1. † Full Name of Child: Anna Bauer
2. Sex: Female. Race or Color (if not of the white race): White
3. Number of Child of this Mother: 3. How many now living (in all): 3
4. Date of this Birth: September 14/13 5.30 p.m.
5. Place of Birth, No. 1949 Street Evergreen Av. (City/Village/Town)
6. Residence of Mother, No. 1949 Street Evergreen Av.
7. Place of Birth — TOWN — STATE OR COUNTRY — AGE OF
   a. Father: Radalen — Hungary — 27 years
   b. Mother: Radalen — Hungary — 27 "
8. Full Name of Mother: Annya Bauer
9. Maiden Name of Mother: Kavalcik
10. Full name of Father: John William Bauer
11. Occupation of Father: Cutter of Clothing
12. Name and Address of Nurse or Attendant (if any)

Reported by: Philip H. Reiger (M. D. or Midwife)

Date: Sept 21/13. 1913. Residence: 1301 N. Western Av. Telephone: 2776

* Still-births should be reported on a separate blank form.
† The baptismal or christian name of child should be certified, if possible, when this certificate is made, and should, in any case, be reported to the County Clerk within a year.
‡ In case of more than one child at birth, a SEPARATE RETURN must be made for each, and the number of each, in order of birth, stated.

Opposite page, top: Though an attempt was made on August 24, 2000, by Kay Davis to secure the Birth Certificate of her mother, Ann May Bauer, from the Office of the County Clerk, Cook County, Illinois, Kay received a "Certification That Record Was Not Found" from the County Clerk's office. She was advised by David Orr, Cook County Clerk, that "birth or death records were not mandatory until the year 1916 in the State of Illinois. It is possible that no original record was ever recorded with the County Clerk's Office."

Above: A subsequent search in 2008 by Alice Henson, professional genealogist, located the Report of Birth above of Anna Bauer in the Office of the County Clerk, Cook County, Illinois. Perhaps the initial search was unsuccessful because of a discrepancy in the maiden name of the mother, which is shown as "Kavalcik," not "Lauff," in the above Report of Birth. This discrepancy has not been resolved as of this date, March 26, 2008.

Below, right: In her final resting place, St. Mary's Cemetery, Ann Douthart rests beneath a "pink" memorial stone. She loved the color pink.

Douthart

Mrs. Ann Douthart, Dec. 13, 1968; beloved wife of Richard; dear mother of Catherine [Clyde] Davis of New York, Dr. Richard J. of Indianapolis, Ind., and Robert of Streamwood, Ill.; grandmother of six; sister of Lorraine Martin, Helen, Nann, Mary Swede, Ethel, Florence Martin, and Ruth Bamard. Member of Telephone Pioneers of America. Funeral 8:45 a. m. Tuesday, from the Tews Funeral Home, 79th and Phillips avenue, to St. Kevin's church. Mass 9:30 a. m. Interment St. Mary's cemetery. SO 8-6959.

Death notice of Ann May Bauer Douthart published in the Chicago Tribune, *December 16, 1968*

Richard James Douthart

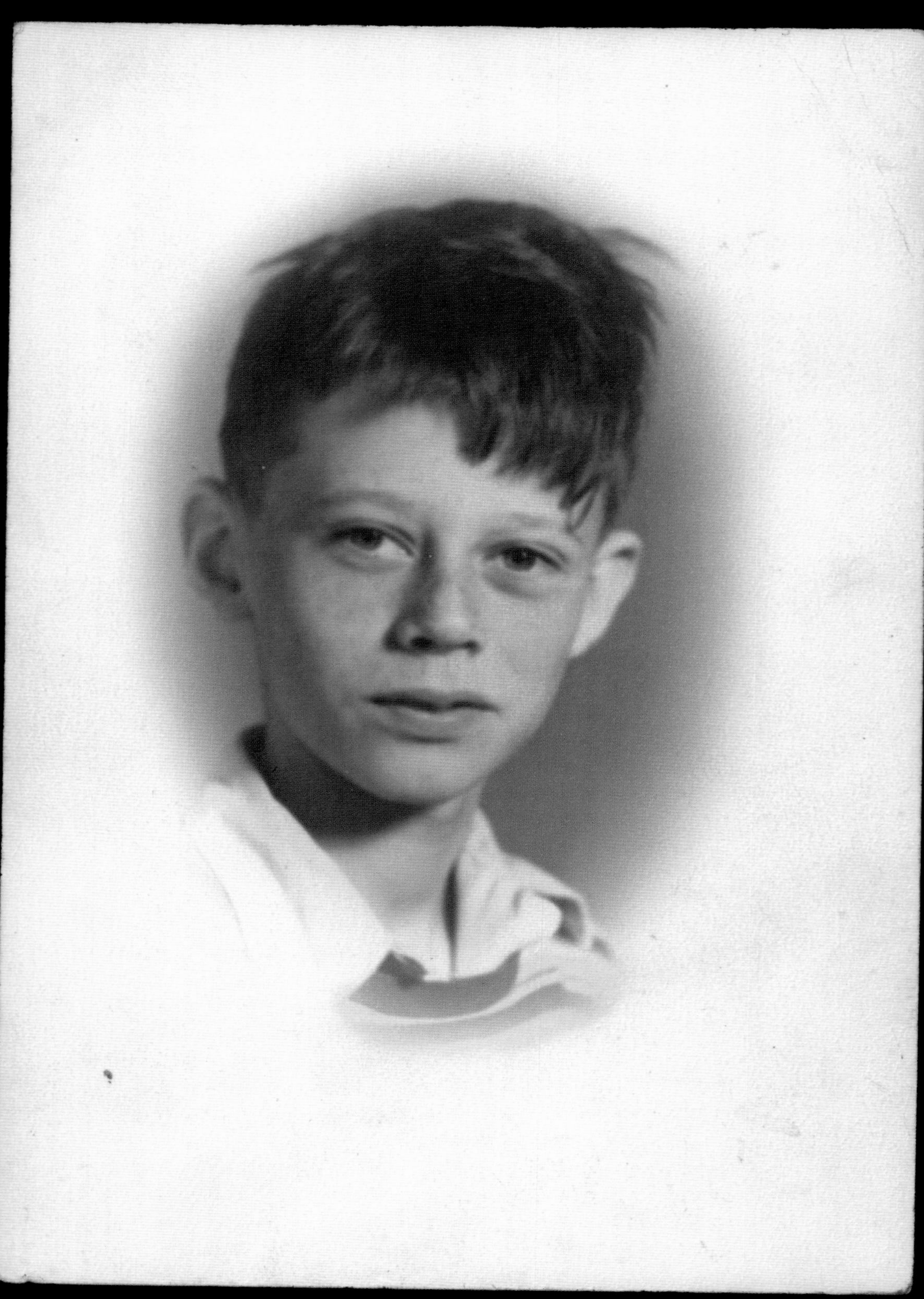

Richard "Dick," "Skinny" Douthart

b. June 11, 1935

"The Genius"
by Kay Douthart Davis

Dick was always very smart. He loved chemistry. When he was thirteen years old he received his first chemistry set for Christmas. After that introduction, his love of chemistry never stopped. He built a laboratory in our basement (skull and crossbones on the door), and only a few special people could enter the room. He created quite unique things in that room. I recall two in particular — an electric stove that blew every light in the house and a stink bomb that emitted the worst smelling, putrid, green smoke through every heat/air ventilation outlet in the house. That brainstorm caused me some emotional discomfort because my father thought the smell was from my cat.

Dick, the first-born child of Richard and Ann (Bauer) Douthart recalled (in a conversation with me at my home in Pound Ridge on November 16, 2007) living on Burley Avenue (before I was born). He said that the house was located across from a commercial laundry. Dick went to the Thorpe Elementary School before transferring to the Warren Elementary School (when the family moved to 9137 Merrill Avenue). While at Warren School, Dick decided that he wanted to be class president when he was in the eighth grade. All I can recall of that effort was Dick, raised high on the shoulders of other boys, throwing free bubble gum to those around so they would vote for him. Of course, he became the class president. Two other events stand out in my memory. One was when Dick ran away from home. He couldn't be found anywhere. Being so smart, he decided to hide in the family garage for a day or so, knowing no one ever would look there. He eventually got hungry and came into the house. But, by far, the smartest thing he ever did was to go to the roof of a nearby apartment building (at least four stories high) with a towel cape tied around his neck saying he was going to jump off, because with the towel he could fly like Superman. In the end, he came down by the stairs, rather than by towel. Yes, Dick was very, very smart.

Dick graduated Bowen High School in 1953 and went on to college. He first attended the University of Illinois when its Chicago location was Navy Pier in downtown Chicago — long before the construction of its current U of I Chicago Campus. He commuted from our home on the south side of town (about one hour) every day to attend classes. After a short time, Dick entered the Air Force. For most of his time he was stationed at the Little Rock Air Force Base in Arkansas. He did travel to the Bikini and Eniwetok atolls in the Pacific for a period of about eight months.

Richard James Douthart on his May 1945 Communion Day. Left to right: Dick's cousin, Sharon Douthart; sister Kay; Dick; and brother Robert.

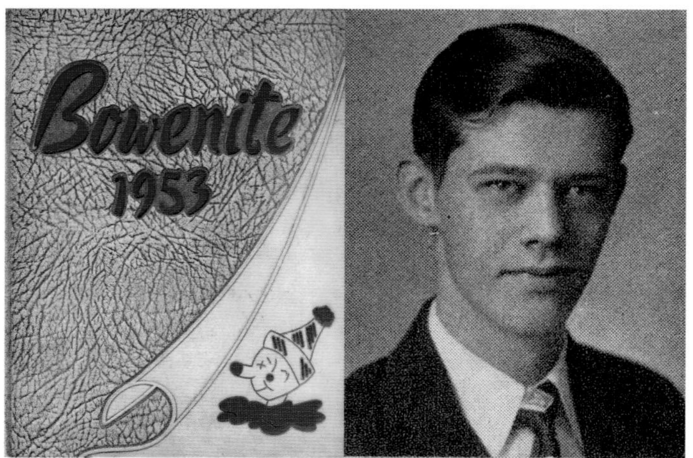

Richard Douthart's graduation picture and the cover of the 1953 Bowenite, the yearbook of Bowen High School, Chicago, Illinois. His activities were listed as: "Wrestling '59, '50 [sic], Chess, Catalyzers, Teachers Aide."

Dick Douthart standing at the rear of his parents' home at 9137 Merrill Avenue, Chicago, Illinois

Dick, probably at the Little Rock U.S. Air Force Base — date of photo unknown. Upon discharge his military rank was Airman First Class.

However, for the majority of his time he was in Little Rock where he obtained about three and one-half years of college at the University of Arkansas while still in the service. After discharge from the Air Force, he stayed in Arkansas to complete his studies and graduated with a degree in mathematics and chemistry in the year 1962. He met Roz at a Unitarian church in Little Rock, and they were married before he finished his term in the Air Force. His rank then was Airman First Class.

Richard James Douthart with his wife, Irene Rosalind McKelvey Douthart

With his undergraduate studies complete and military service finished, they returned to Chicago where Dick attended the Illinois Institute of Technology. He and Roz eventually moved to downstate Illinois and to the University of Illinois in Champaign-Urbana. Because Dick wanted to receive his doctorate degree in some area of chemistry, and also because I worked in the Chemistry Department for the Dean of Organic Chemistry, I was able to secure Dick a position as a teaching assistant in that department. For a short while, Dick, Roz, Clyde, and I were all living in Urbana, Illinois, where both Dick and Clyde were attending the university. Dick earned his Ph.D. in Biophysical Chemistry at the University of Illinois in 1968. There was a brief time when Dick and Roz had to leave the campus and return to Chicago because of financial needs. While in Chicago, Dick worked at IIT (Illinois Institute of Technology) and finally, with enough money in hand, returned to Champaign-Urbana to complete the requirements for his Ph.D.

After graduation Dick and Roz moved to Indiana with a two-fold purpose. Dick got a job as a scientist at Eli Lilly, and Roz went back to school. She attended Indiana University in a new program for nurse practitioners. It was the first program in the U.S. with only four universities participating, each with four teachers and ten students. Roz was also interested in the area of mental health and becoming a therapist. During their marriage, Roz achieved multiple degrees. Her focus was nursing and social work. She spent many years in the field working in clinics that often treated the most poor and abused individuals in our society.

Dick and Roz stayed in Martinsville, Indiana, for approximately fifteen years. While Dick was at Eli Lilly, he was involved in setting up a computer system for genetic engineering. At that time, genetic engineering was becoming big business. Dick was also part of a team that developed the drug Humulin for diabetes treatment. While working on their careers, Dick and Roz were also able to construct a house in Martinsville in a beautiful, wooded community of suburban homes with a clubhouse, where the community could meet and dine, and the children could swim at the enormous pool. Dick and Roz built their home with

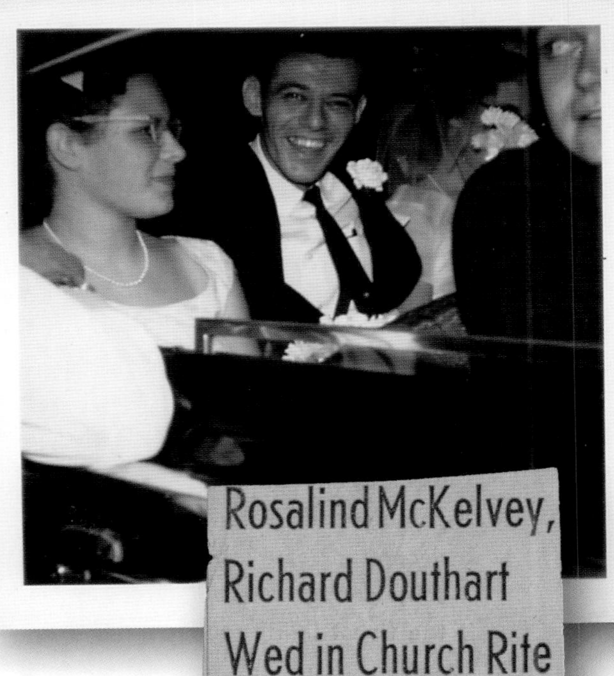

Rosalind McKelvey, Richard Douthart Wed in Church Rite

The marriage of Miss Irene Rosalind Alexandra McKelvey, daughter of Dr. and Mrs. Morley A. McKelvey, 6306 Ridgecrest Drive, to Richard James Douthart, son of Mr. and Mrs. Richard C. Douthart of Chicago, Illinois, was solemnized at 4 p. m. Thursday in the Unitarian Church. The reception was held in the home of the bride's parents after the ceremony.

Rev. Richard Kelley officiated at the ceremony. The bride, given in marriage by her father, wore a ballerina dress of white nylon taffeta and matching veil and carried an arrangement of white carnations and orchids.

Miss Cecily McKelvey was her sister's maid of honor. Francis A. Threlkeld served as best man. Ushers were Dexter McKelvey, brother of the bride, and Jim Pat Gunn.

The bridegroom is a student at the University of Arkansas School of Medicine.

a special eye toward accommodating our father, who by this time was alone — my mother having abruptly died at the early age of fifty-five years. My father had an apartment within their home with his own entrance, bedroom/living area, containing a Murphy bed (which folded up against the wall to save space), and a small kitchen, though he ate dinner with the family each evening. He kept a watchful eye on Bill and Julia, the children of Dick and Roz. My father often told me of his adventures with those kids and how he was able to keep them under the radar of their parents while they were growing up. My father was quite mischievous himself throughout his childhood, and I am sure he relished the role of bailing Bill and Julia out of trouble without their parents even knowing — especially Julia who, by the way, became quite a stellar swimmer in that community pool. Being tall and lanky, she also became quite good at basketball as she advanced in school. Bill, though, was the one who drew extremely close to his grandfather and to this day has the fondest memories of him.

Eventually a friend from graduate school, who was the head of chemistry at Battelle Memorial Institute running the northwest laboratory at Battelle wooed Dick away from Eli Lilly. At Batelle, Dick became the head of the biotechnology division for five years.

December 1985

EDITOR Oliver S. Moore III

MANAGING EDITOR Margo Crabtree

ART DIRECTOR Michael Valenti

SENIOR EDITORS James Kotsilibas-Davis, Josh Eppinger, Signe Hammer, Michael D. Lemonick

EDITOR/WRITERS Susan Gilbert, Amy Wilbur

SENIOR COPY EDITOR Eliza Woodward

CHIEF OF RESEARCH Joan Shaw

ASSOCIATE PICTURE EDITOR Johanna V. Boublik

ASSISTANT TO THE EDITOR Sonia Waites

ASSISTANT EDITOR Cynthia A. Adame

EDITORIAL ASSISTANTS Frances Bishop,

Software • Protein St

THE TOP 100

INNOVATION: CAD System for Genetic Engineering
INNOVATORS: RICHARD DOUTHART/JAMES J. THOMAS/S. DANIEL ROSIER/RICHARD J. LITTLEFIELD/JEFFREY E. SCHMALTZ *(Battelle Pacific Northwest Labs)*

DOUTHART

Graphics software with a novel color-coding scheme and continuous links between different levels of magnification gives bioengineers a new computer-aided design (CAD) system. Created for use on a VAX, including the MicroVAX and the Hewlett-Packard 9000, the Computer-Aided Genetic Engineering System uses genetic information and DNA sequence information to produce mock designs of genetic structures. Working dynamically and interactively with bull's-eye-style colored graphs, a user can visualize complex structural relationships. Unlike analytically oriented systems, "this one is closer to the way people think," says Douthart, 50, manager of biotechnology development for Battelle Northwest.

209 Enterprise Drive
Richland, Wa 99352
December 20, 1982

Dear Kay, Clyde, and Cynthia,

This has really been a year of transition for all of us.
And I hope 1983 bodes well for all of us. I do hope that
making this move to Richland was a sound one for Dick's
career. Here he has had an opportunity to break into
management at a high level. If we find that Battelle can't
afford to start biotechnology then I feel fairly sure we
would move to the east coast. In the mean time, we have
decided not to buy a house. Although I know Dick is absolutely
right to be careful, I find living in a state of uncertainty
difficult. I like roots and permanence and I would like
to get back to work again. This, however, may not happen
for a while. Dick gives his total energy to his job and
I take care of everything else. After Julia finishes high
school, my life will be a lot easier.

I was so happy to hear Dad's voice several days ago. He
had just had the chest tubes removed and was doing well.
In fact he was looking forward to going home so I know
he was feeling better. I am so glad life is working out
for him in Burlington.

Bill is home now for a month from NTSU. He has decided to
change his major to photojournalism and only minor in music.
Hopefully, this will give him broader job options after
graduation. But he knows that no degree will guarantee
employment. Of course there is always the option of the
military service after college.

Congratulations on Clyde's promotion. Yesterday Dick just
learned that there was a major reorganization here. Up to
now there has been a dual directorship of Battelle. Now Dick's
boss has been made clear heir apparent of the Presidencyof
Battelle. This will mean that his boss will now be able to
put his hands on more discretionary funds which Dick needs
to start up Biotechnology. I am happy but cautious. I hope
there are not too many thorns along with this rose.

Have a really happy New Year.

Love,

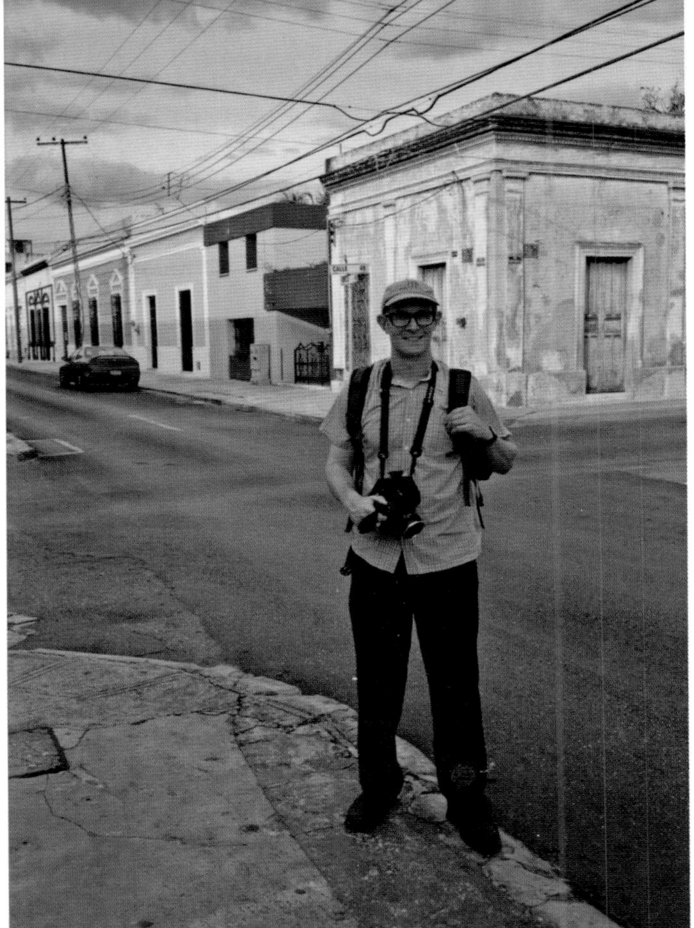

William "Billy" Douthart b. August 8, 1962, on location in Merida, Mexico, the capital of the Yucatan. Photo was taken by Megan Cogswell in January 2008.

Following that he became manager of Northwest Biotechnology Operation, Batelle, Pacific Northwest Laboratories, and finally he served as a Scientific Advisor before his retirement. During his years at Battelle Laboratories, Dick developed a program called CAGE (Computer Aided Genetic Engineering), working on the Human Genome Program. He won a few prizes for his work, but ultimately found it impossible to secure continued government funding for his projects. He made numerous trips to the Department of Energy outside of Washington D.C., attempting to get money, a task that he never enjoyed with the ever-changing bureaucrats on the other side of the negotiating table. He always worked with DNA and invented a Genome Sequencing Device that could have made him world famous but for the lack of funding. And even though that part of his career eluded him, in the end we all know him as a genius. As a young researcher, he was featured in the magazine *Science Digest* in its December 1985 issue, highlighting "The Year's Top 100 Innovations and the Men and Women Behind Them." Dick is probably the most intelligent person I know, and I only make fun of him when he relies on his "people" and "street" smarts. This is when he forgets where he parked the car, where the salt and dirty dishes should go, and the "political" smarts of existing in this world. It is then that Dick shoots himself in the foot.

Now retired, Dick enjoys a more peaceful life pursuing his interests wherever they take him. He always enjoys playing chess and has found many games on the Internet as well as playing with opponents nearby in his community. Together he and Roz enjoy cruises and have found their way to the world's best destinations as they travel the waters far and wide. More recently, they have been available as a support system for their daughter Julia whenever (and wherever) they can care for Julia's young daughter Alexandria while Julia focuses on her job.

Bill and Julia: New York-bound

Both their son Bill and daughter Julia have received college degrees. Bill had desired to be a musician, a percussionist. He developed a deep knowledge of music, but decided that his talent as a musician would not offer him enough career opportunities to succeed in a most competitive industry, so he switched to a degree in photojournalism. He moved to New York soon after graduating from the North Texas State University in Denton, Texas. With his strong interest in the music field and his skills as a photographer, he found New York to be an ideal environment to focus on photographing musicians. He has done just that for many years and has had numerous photos in the pages of *Downbeat Jazz Magazine*, as well as taking portrait photos of musicians. Though his passion is for photography, the bills have to be paid, so Bill has always had a day job in retail. This allows him the luxury of following his passion in free time, but still being able to pay the bills. Some years ago he took up residence with his companion Megan Cogswell (who is a producer for numerous TV programs and documentaries) in New York City. Both Bill and Megan have a love of travel and have been able to travel the world. Often they are in the company of each other, but when Bill has free time and the desire to go somewhere, he will venture out alone. He has surpassed anyone I know in number of trips to destinations around the world. He is the envy of everyone, having seen some of the most fantastic places while doing it on a shoestring, since he is naturally a frugal individual. As of late 2009, Bill has traveled to at least thirty-one countries in Asia, Europe, and the Americas, including such exotic places as Beijing, China; Hiroshima, Japan; Salzburg, Austria; Brno in the Czech Republic; Heraklion, Greece; Sligo, Ireland; Pureto Varas, Chile; and Coeur d'Alene, Idaho.

Julia graduated from Washington State University in 1993 with a BS in physical science and a minor in mathematics. She has one year of graduate study in both biochemistry and computer science.

She remained in Washington for several years as an entrepreneur working out of the family home in Richland. She developed web sites for businesses and government entities, but found that this endeavor was not enough to keep her interest or earn a good enough income. She made a decision to move to New York City in October 2001, shortly after 9/11, when jobs were scarce in that city. Nonetheless, she found work immediately, moved into an apartment (on the fringe of Harlem) and proved all of us wrong for discouraging her from the move. She has been able to utilize her science background in the business world, marketing and organizing marketing events and seminars for doctors and scholars. Always the spirited one, she decided to have a child. Having no boyfriend or significant other, she did it on her own. *In vitro* fertilization produced a most wonderful daughter, Alexandria, who is now three years old. Needless to say, she is the apple of a few eyes in the family. Julia is pictured on these pages with her beautiful daughter. Desiring to have a home of her own where she and Alexandria could reside, Julia bought a house in

Stratford, Connecticut. She is fortunate to have a job where she can spend some time working at home while she commutes to New York City when necessary. Also, this home provides a place where Dick and Roz can stay for extended times and visit them.

1985: A Good Year

Throughout 1985, my brother Dick, his wife Roz, and their two children, Bill and Julia, were involved in many personal, career, and school activities that Roz communicated to us in a number of letters. The following thoughts are from those letters:

On February 17, 1985, Roz wrote that Bill had traveled home from school in Texas to spend the Christmas holiday. He was searching for an internship in photojournalism for the coming summer prior to graduation, indicating that he also had been working on the college newspaper. She also mentioned that Julia was continuing to play basketball and was having a good year playing in the regional basketball tournament.

Roz had just been hired to start a hospital-based home care service at Kennewick General Hospital. Meanwhile, Dick was looking for another position as a director somewhere in

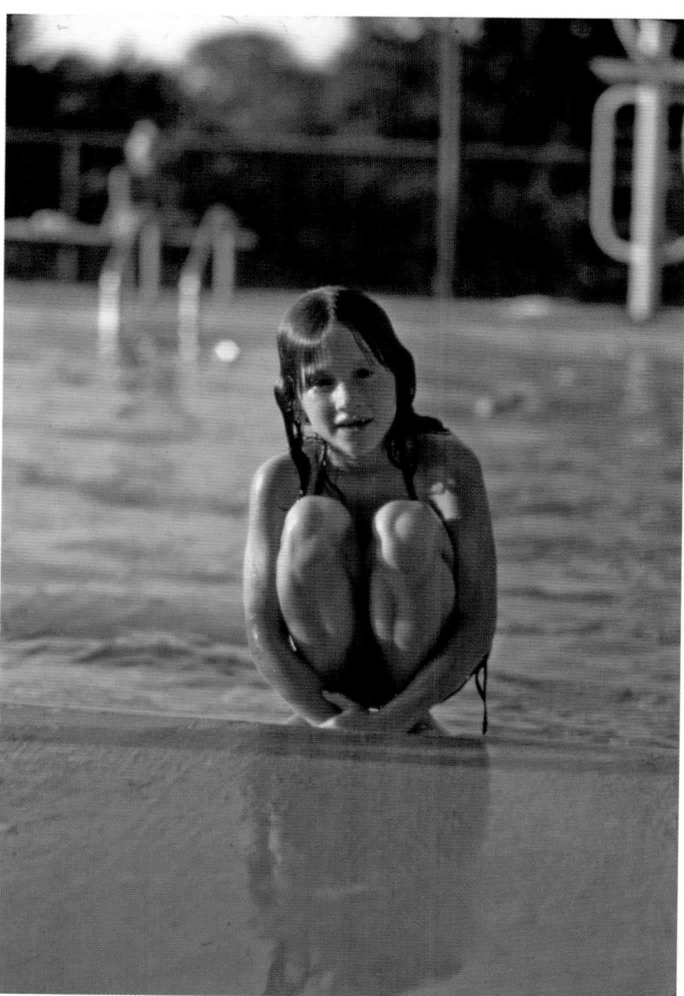

Julia, poolside at the community clubhouse, October 1973, in Martinsville, Indiana

biotechnology research.

By April 21, 1985, Dick (according to a letter from Roz on that date) was traveling to California for meetings, but still searching for another position that would have more security.

At this time, Roz had already established the hospital-based home care service, having completed the state and federal certification process. Julia was searching for a college where she could study her desired curriculum while playing with a good basketball team. Bill had done well at North Texas State University, being named Outstanding Photojournalism student that year. Roz mentioned that Bill would be traveling to Rochester, New York, to attend classes at Rochester Institute of Technology during the week of August 11–17 and that he might come to visit us if we were home at that time. Bill was due to graduate that coming December from his school in Texas.

On October 27, 1985, Roz sent her last letter of the year. It was by far the most interesting of them all. Julia was attending school at Spokane Falls Community College, taking classes in a general scientific curriculum. Bill had recently spent some time with us in Pound Ridge, New York. This was Bill's first ever trip to New York. Obviously, he liked what he saw because he later moved to New Jersey and finally settled in New York City where he has lived ever since.

Roz also talked about her busy work schedule, having started the Kennewick Hospital home care program almost a year earlier. However, the most entertaining part of her letter was about Dick. She mentioned that Dick had spent a few days with us in Pound Ridge (he often did this after he had traveled to Washington, D.C., to "beg" for money from the National Institutes of Health — a task he detested). He was probably tired when he came, and she mentioned that a few days with us were really a good rest for him. She also said that he brought back a gown for her that was "absolutely splendid. One could not find anything as classy looking around here." However, she also stated that "I am sending you back the slippers that Dick brought me in hopes that you could go to Bloomingdales and get me a slipper for the right foot. Dick brought back slippers for two left feet." Need I say more? He must have been quite exhausted (or just being Dick) while shopping for Roz, but nonetheless, he shopped for her. Just like when he tried to put things away at home in Chicago after eating a sandwich. The salt would be in the frig, the dirty plate in the cabinet and who knows where the glass would be placed after he finished his drink. For all that he is — we love him so much.

As an additional footnote to the nature of Dick he recently told us, "Don't tell Roz, but Julia calls me and tells me when my anniversary is."

It should be noted that Roz has an extended and expansive education in nursing. Among her educational credentials, she has a masters degree in Nursing (MSN), Indiana University, with a Clinical Specialty in Primary Care. She also has a masters degree in Social Work (MSW), and she is a Family Nurse Practitioner (ARNP), Board Certified Nurse Practitioner.

In addition to the work she described in her letters from 1985, she worked at Community Health Care, a clinic in Tacoma,

Julia Celeste Douthart b. December 10, 1966, with daugther Alexandria Irene b. November 25, 2007, in a photo taken July 20, 2008

Julia Douthart's fixer-upper house in Stratford, Connecticut, where she and her daughter, Alexandria, reside. Julia moved there in 2006.

Washington, from 1994 to 2006. This is a non-profit clinic for people with little health/medical coverage or none at all. The costs for patients are determined on a sliding scale of affordability.

Now fully retired, Roz still volunteers her services at two clinics near her home. She works at the Neighborhood Clinic, a United Way Agency. She also volunteers at the RotaCare Free Clinic, which is a nonprofit corporation to bring free medical care to those who have the most need and the least access to medical care. Ever the good soldier, she has always found heart, energy, and skill to help where it is needed most.

Below: Richard James "Dick" Douthart, second from left, with his wife, Irene Rosalind McKelvey Douthart on far left and their daughter Julia Celeste and son William "Billy" Douthart

Robert Henry Douthart

Robert "Bob" Douthart

b. July 26, 1938

"The Inventor"
by Kay Douthart Davis

Bob was never really a great student; he was left-handed (this is not meant as negative, except that Bob's writing was barely legible), he couldn't spell very well and, in hindsight, perhaps, he was dyslexic. But he, too, was inventive and ingenious. Bob's bent was toward electrical engineering. In the second grade he constructed a bird identification machine for his class. It had electrical contacts that hooked up to pictures of birds and correct answers about the birds. Lights went on when the correct answer was selected. Like his brother, bright and clever. Bob received an associate degree from Purdue University in electrical engineering and used his creativity in all of his various jobs to improve products and/or the process by which they were produced.

Bob was stuck in the middle. He wasn't the oldest, smartest brother like Dick, and he wasn't the youngest, baby, only girl, like me. We should have noticed the signs of stress and difficulty when he, as a young adult, fell out of bed, was rushed to an emergency room, and diagnosed with a stomach ulcer. He was late to start dating and married the only girl I can remember he ever dated — Shelly, the niece of a neighbor who lived next to our family home in Chicago. Bob and Shelly had five children and eventually settled in Burlington, North Carolina. As I mentioned before, he was always inventive, but lacking a full four-year degree, he never really achieved the "engineering" or "design" level or title at the various companies where he was employed. However, his talent was always surfacing and being used to improve products and procedures. Some lawsuits arose because his employer had implemented some of his suggestions to improve manufacture of their products, but he received no compensation or reward because he hadn't been hired as an engineer. Unfortunately, Bob never really profited from his many inventions. Further, he suffered greatly when his marriage dissolved under extreme, public discord between himself and his wife. He lost his job, sold his home, and became depressed and severely ill. In his late fifties it was discovered that he had multiple myeloma (bone cancer). He died when he was sixty years old.

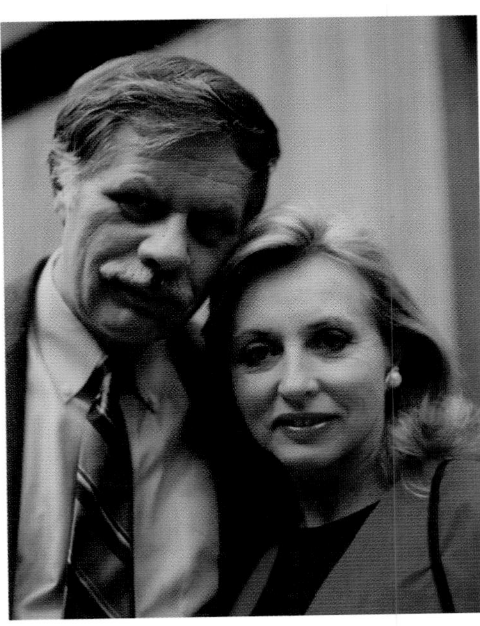

Bob Douthart and Kay Davis in front of Kay's home in Pound Ridge, New York, when both Dick and Bob visited to celebrate Dick's 50th birthday. The photo was taken as everyone departed for New York City and the Broadway production of Into the Woods.

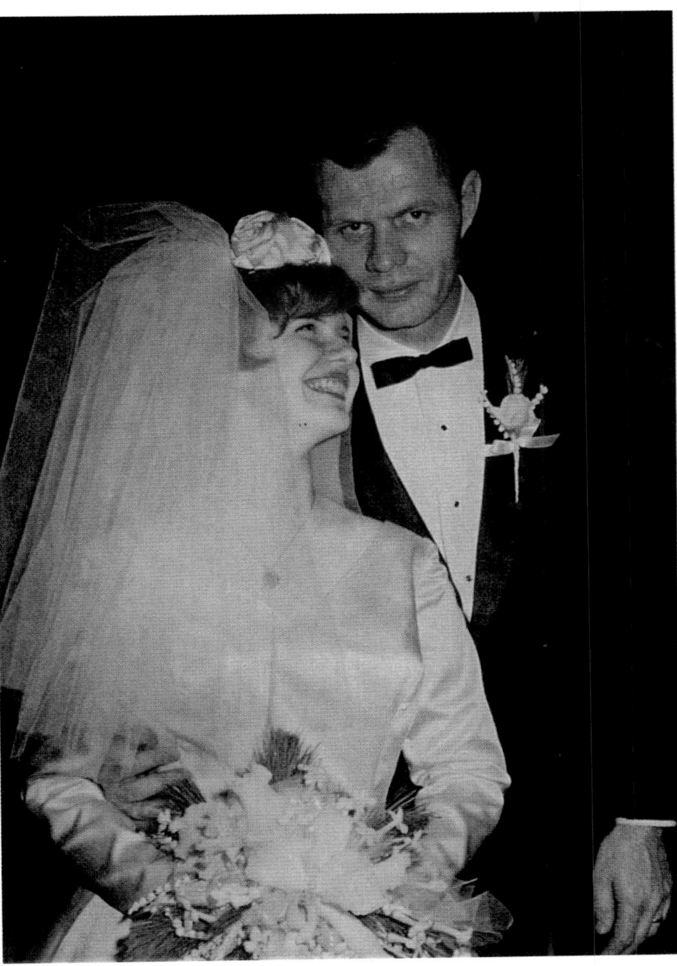

Marriage of Shelley Kenyon Miller to Robert H. Douthart on October 22, 1966, at University Church, 5655 University Avenue, Chicago, Illinois

His last year of life was most disastrous with it ending, prematurely, in a hospital bed with a morphine drip to ease his last moments. He never got to fully enjoy his wonderful children as adults and their growing families. He would have loved tremendously the role of grandfather, for he was probably the single most generous person I ever knew. I choose to linger on the lighter moments of his life such as the one that follows:

When we were kids Bob had a crazy idea. He would create a new and totally unique piece of machinery. It would literally sail down the street at a very high speed. He had all the pieces he needed right from our home to make this unique thing. He took the pink shower curtain from our only bathroom. Did I mention that my mother loved the color pink? That shower curtain was covered with pink flamingoes. He created a base to sit on from old wood he found laying around the basement. He took the wheels

Robert Henry Douthart Family

Douthart family photo taken in Martinsville, Indiana, September 1977. Left to right, rear row: Robert Douthart; Rosalind Douthart, wife of Richard James Douthart; Richard James Douthart; Julia Douthart, daughter of Richard and Rosalind Douthart; Richard C. Douthart, father of Robert and Richard James Douthart and Kay Davis; Cynthia Davis, daughter of Clyde and Kay Davis; Shelly Douthart, wife of Robert Douthart; Nathan Douthart, son of Robert and Shelly Douthart; Cole Davis, son of Clyde and Kay Davis; and Kay Davis. Front row: cut off on the far left, Christine Davis, daughter of Clyde and Kay Davis; and Karen, Charles, Jennifer, and Kathie Douthart, children of Robert and Shelly Douthart

off my skates. Come to think of it, he probably made the first skate board, had he only stopped there. But, no, he continued. He constructed a tall pole to attach to this skateboard — of course to hold the sail (shower curtain). It was a masterpiece. Really tall. Really impressive. When it rolled out of our garage the entire neighborhood was excited. But who would ride such a thing? Certainly not Dick — he was too smart. Not Bob — he was the inventor. They convinced "Rauncho" to do it. You can figure out that a kid with the name "Rauncho" was the perfect candidate for such a job. Needless to say the maiden voyage was the only voyage. It really went fast but also it really crashed! In the end, Bob was the smartest of all — he had all the fun and none of the pain — at least at that point in his life.

His five children have all grown to marry and have families of their own. Karen, the oldest child, married first to Mickey Horner and a few years later they divorced. One child, Taylor (a son), was born from that marriage. Karen has a two-year degree, and over the years has been employed in the fields of childcare and public welfare. She married again to Brian McClung and had a second son, Greyson. Karen has always loved horses and her rural location allows her to have a few. Her husband, Brian, teaches criminal law. He has also held positions in law enforcement as a member of the Sheriff's Department and as a prison guard.

Chuck, the second-born child, obtained his bachelor's degree in computer science at North Carolina State University, and is currently employed as a software architect at Teradata Corporation. He married Joye Hodges. Joye received her bachelor's degree *cum laude* in English and communications from Meredith College in Raleigh, North Carolina, and a Master of Arts in English and Creative Writing at North Carolina State. She works in North Carolina's non-profit sector in event planning, public relations, and fundraising. She has also worked as a teacher and children's ministry director. Chuck and Joye have two children, Rebecca and Ryan. The family lives in Raleigh, North Carolina.

Jennifer is in the middle. She attended North Carolina State University for two years (1989–1991) and graduated from the University of North Carolina at Greensboro in 1993 with a B.S. in Education. She married Scott Bean who was in banking at the time, but switched career paths and became employed by the FBI. He graduated from North Carolina State University (1986–1990) with a degree in business. He graduated from the FBI Academy in 1997 and is currently a Supervisory Special Agent.

Scott and Jennifer have moved several times (as required by his job) and presently live in Woodbridge, Virginia, with Scott commuting to Washington, D.C., for his work.

They have two children. Their older child, Kylie, was diagnosed early in her life with a cancerous brain tumor and has required extensive treatment for it. Thankfully, she has responded well and is currently trouble free, though she receives regular MRIs and still goes to physical and occupational therapy. She is in middle school, and loves and rides horses. Kylie has a younger

Left to right: Jennifer Douthart Bean, Shelly Douthart (Robert Douthart's widow and the mother of everyone else pictured), Kathie Douthart Townson, Karen Douthart Horner, Nathan and Charles "Chuck" Douthart. The photo was taken on the beach at Myrtle Beach, South Carolina, on June 14, 2008, at Kathie's wedding to Ray Townson, her second marriage.

brother, Conor, who leads a happy, healthy existence. Conor is in fourth grade, plays touch football and takes Hap ki do. Both children are doing well in school.

Throughout her marriage, Jennifer has attempted to return to her career in teaching (usually parttime). She recently returned to work fulltime and is currently teaching fifth grade.

Kathy, the next of Bob's children, has bright red hair and freckles. She certainly looks like a descendent of her grandfather, (Bob's father) Richard. As a child she endured a long bout with Lyme disease long before it became commonly known. She has been employed in the field of special education. She is a signing instructor for deaf children. Kathy recently married Ray Townson and they live in Greensboro, North Carolina. All of Bob's children are shown in a picture from that wedding day (see above).

The youngest child, Nathan, is the only one of Bob's children who has not attained a college education. Nathan was quite young when the discord between Bob and Shelly began to disrupt family life. The dissolution of his parents' marriage as well as Bob's early death, I am sure, were the main reasons for Nathan not going on to additional schooling. Bob was always proud of Nathan's artistic talents and at one time thought that Nathan might attend school for computer animation. Instead, life passed from Bob, and life moved on for Nathan. He had a son, Ashton, and married Ashton's mother, Terri. Both Nathan and Terri found work with her family at their produce stands. Nathan has since gone on to open a store of his own and remains a hard-working, industrious entrepreneur.

As life takes members of a family in different directions, it becomes quite difficult to maintain relationships. Even before Bob died, he and his family were not in close communication with my brother Dick or me. Perhaps we were all too busy growing our own families and careers. However, Dick often traveled to our home in New York when he was on his way to or from Washington, D.C., to secure money from the National Institutes of Health for one of his great ideas that he wanted them to fund. And, eventually, both of his children ended up in the New York City area, so we see them with regularity. And, of course, Dick and Roz travel to see all of us. Somehow, Bob and his clan in North Carolina fell off the page. Then Bob died; I am saddened by it all.

DOUTHART
Robert H. Douthart, 60, of Hawfields Presbyterian
Home, Mebane, NC, and a onetime resident of
Chicago, IL, passed away on Monday, Sept. 7,
1998, at 3:30 p.m., at the University of North
Carolina Hospitals, Chapel Hill, NC. A native of
Chicago, IL, Mr. Douthart was the beloved son of
the late Richard C. Douthart and Anne M. Bauer
Douthart. He was the dear brother of Richard
Douthart and his wife Rosalind of Richland, WA,
and also the loving brother of Mrs. Kay Davis and
her husband Clyde of Pount Ridge, NY. Mr. Douthart was the loving father of five surviving children including his daughters Ms. Karen Horner of
Mebane, NC, Mrs. Jennifer Bean of Jordan, UT
and Mrs. Kathie Kupsick of Albemarle, NY; sons
Charles Douthart of Garner, NC and Nathan Douthart of Yanceyville, NC. Mr. Douthart was most
proud of his six grahdchildren. A Mass of the
Resurrection will be held at the Blessed Sacrament Catholic Church, Burlington, NC, where he
was a member, at 12:30 p.m. Thursday, Sept. 10,
1998. The service will be conducted by Fr. Terr-
ence Pescatore, O.F.M. Conv. Interment will be in
Alamance Memorial Park, Burlington, NC. The
family will receive friends at the **Rich and Thompson Mortuary,** 306 Glenwood Ave., Burlington, NC
27215, from 6 until 8 p.m. Wednesday, Sept. 9,.
1998. Memorials may be made to the Blessed
Sacrament Catholic Church, 328 W. Davis St.,
Burlington, NC 27215.

Top: Death notice of Robert H. Douthart, b. July 26, 1938, d. September 7, 1998, published in the Chicago Tribune, *September 9, 1998. Bottom: Robert's headstone in Alamance Memorial Park, Burlington, North Carolina.*

Kay Douthart 1957 high school portrait

b. January 2, 1940

My Story
by Kay Douthart Davis

Our family home was always comfortable, clean, and well furnished. Both my parents worked (it was unusual for women to hold full-time jobs during those years), and my mother was something of a professional, wearing nice clothes to go to her "office" location near the University of Chicago, where she worked as a telephone operator. My father was a yard master at the Elgin, Joliet, and Eastern Railroad (EJ&E). He was situated within the steel mill on the South Side of Chicago. I remember touring the mill once and seeing my father's office, a little house, located in the center of a massive open area where the railroad cars were loaded with steel to be transported to all destinations within the United States. My father's job was to oversee those activities. I felt very proud of him.

Kay Davis in photo taken October 18, 2005, in front of house she lived in most of her life prior to marrying and leaving home

Though our home was physically comfortable, it was also a place of much discord and stress. My father was a drinker — only beer — nonetheless, he drank so much and so regularly that the impact on our family was substantial. He abused our mother, resulting in an atmosphere of fear in the household. He never hurt any of his children and never missed a day of work because of his drinking (he was quite proud of this). Even with all the strife, he and my mother were hard-working, responsible people who wanted a good life for their good family in a really good home. Between the lines of that dream was the reality of a difficult home environment. I grew up within that environment with my two older brothers, Richard (Dick) and Robert (Bob).

Clyde and I met at a young age, while still students in high school. He was seventeen years old and I was fifteen. He was already a talented art student, who was being recognized. As a matter of fact, his art talent led to our meeting. My best friend, Jeanette Rock (now Arvia), knew Clyde's best friend, Conrad Fiakowski. Jan and I were given an assignment by our biology teacher to create a science project to be entered in a city-wide competition and exhibited at the Museum of Science and Industry in Chicago. Jan decided we needed artistic help with our project — the life cycle of a frog. We enlisted Conrad and Clyde to assist us. Though Clyde won a full scholarship to the Art Institute to study, he decided to decline that scholarship and instead attend the University of Illinois in Champaign-Urbana (no scholarship there) to be with his friends, who swam on the high school swimming team with him.

I always *loved* school. Achieving excellent grades came easily. I always seemed to be on the Honor Roll. I don't recall ever having homework in elementary school and, save for an occasional project, I don't recall homework assignments in high school.

I adored sports — couldn't wait to go to gym. While a student at Warren Elementary School, I would wear my green gym suit on gym days with a skirt over it and wait all day for the afternoon class. When we entered the huge gymnasium with its highly polished blonde wood floors, I thought of nothing but the fun ahead. I excelled at all the required calisthenics, was really good at high jump and broad jump. After school I would go to the outdoor playground to engage in softball or simply play on the swings, slides, or to check out various athletic equipment and balls for any number of games. I competed in many track meets held all over the city and recall receiving ribbons for my running and broad jump efforts.

Ready to leave from Kay's house for Clyde's Junior Prom, May 14, 1955

I attended Chicago Vocational High School (CVS), a wonderful facility within walking distance from my home at 9137 Merrill Avenue in a neighborhood known as The Hill. Not planning on a college education at that time, I was delighted to attend

Back of picture reads: "1945 Ruth Bauer (in uniform) & Kay Douthart"

CVS, the "Palace," a beautiful, enormous, stone school that was dedicated to preparing students for graduation and entry into numerous careers with advanced skill sets that they developed at CVS. Clyde and Conrad were in their senior year at CVS when we met, so soon they would be off to college.

I still had another year until I would graduate from high school, since I was only in my junior year when I met Clyde. Throughout my high school years (as in my primary school years), I excelled as a student (and athlete). I became a cheerleader and had the honor of cheering at Soldiers Field when CVS played for (and won) the Citywide Football Championship. I was a member of an assortment of clubs at school, including the Honor Society. I graduated in the Top 10 of a graduating class of more than 500 students. I enjoyed membership in the Girls Chorus and then the Mixed Chorus, and we performed all over the city. As an upper classman, I decided I should attend college, so I quickly gave up free time and music classes to complete the required math classes for college entrance.

I considered attending Northwestern University, especially since I thought I might one day be a journalist and travel to either Washington D.C. (or Paris!) to work. Northwestern was a superb school with an outstanding School of Journalism. Further, they indicated interest in me on a recruitment visit to our high school, and I was invited to live in the home of a family that resided just off campus. I had worked at a summer camp for children with cerebral palsy. During two summers there, I met and cared for a child named Jeffrey Kulwin who suffered from the disease. I became close to him and his family. They invited me to live with them while attending Northwestern University. This arrangement would have been mutually beneficial in that I could care for Jeffrey and a normal, healthy, younger brother in the evenings, allowing their parents peace of mind and freedom to leave the house, knowing the boys were in good hands, and I could attend the university without the cost of housing or meals. But, instead, I decided to follow my heart and Clyde and go to the University of Illinois in Champaign-Urbana.

New Beginnings

I attended classes there for a year. Thereafter, we were married, stayed on campus, so Clyde could graduate, but had two of our three children while Clyde tried to complete his studies. Broke and frustrated, we departed for New York with our young family when Clyde was just four credit hours short of his degree.

Clyde always worked in Manhattan. But because we already had two children when we arrived in New York (and no money for city rents), we decided to live outside the city. Our family home was then in the suburbs and has always remained in the wooded, bedroom communities of Westchester County.

We always struggled in those early years, but we found many ways to grow up along with our children and enjoy inexpensive, family time together, taking picnic lunches to New York City to enjoy Central Park and the carousel or tour the newly opened Lincoln Center. Jones Beach was quite a car ride, but it was a cheap way to have a wonderful day — always making sure we had enough money for the tolls on the way home. We took family bike rides to a local bakery or ice-cream stand, and once we moved to Pound Ridge, we would spend the entire weekend at the town park swimming in the pool where the kids swam on the town team. Clyde and I would play tennis — a game we never knew in Chicago — on the park courts.

We had purchased a three-acre parcel of land in Pound Ridge with the dream of designing and constructing our own home on that land. It took six years of rentals and assistance from a host of family and friends before we would realize that dream.

My friend Angela Heizman found us a six-month rental at Caramoor in Katonah, New York, when our previous lease had terminated and our new home was not finished. These were the most stressful of times but spent on one of the most beautiful and serene of properties imaginable. The property, for years, has been

b. January 2, 1940

Catherine "Kay" Douthart in two pictures from the Warren School in Chicago, Illinois. At top in Grade 2 in the bib overalls second from right in the second row, and at the bottom, fourth from the right in the front row in June 1953.

Kay's high school yearbook portrait

the home of Caramoor Summer Music Festivals.

My friend Lesley (Jaffe) Gehr took our family into her home (cats and all) when the Caramoor rental had to be vacated in the month of June for the music conductor to return and take residence for the summer music events.

Our friends George and Celia Euringer allowed Clyde to stay with them during the week while both George and Clyde went to work. This allowed our family to join Clyde on the weekends in the city, when George joined Celia and their two sons in Remsenburg, New York, their summer home in the Hamptons.

My father gave us $10,000 when construction all but stopped on our house, because we ran out of money and couldn't get it anywhere.

Finally, Lesley's mother Evelyn gave us a $10,000 loan when work stopped again. I'll never forget the day I phoned Evelyn, saying, "Evelyn, I have something I would like to talk to you about." Her reply was, "How much do you need, Kay?" Without further conversation, she immediately marched down to the bank and drew a check for the full amount I requested.

We have known some kind and generous people over the years, but I don't think any other group we have known at any other time have combined to be of so much help to us. Each gesture was an individual act but all together they moved us and our dream forward.

Leaving The Nest

Once settled in our new home we realized we would have to mobilize again to keep it. With foreclosure facing us, I returned to work full time. Cole was twelve years old, and Christine and Cynthia were in their early years of high school. I was fortunate to secure a job at Omega Engineering, a rather small company in the Springdale area of Stamford, Connecticut, about fifteen minutes from our home in Pound Ridge, New York.

I started as an administrative assistant to the company's president and quickly moved up the ranks in this thriving engineering company, which was headed by a smart, strong, savvy business woman, Betty Ruth Hollander. She recognized a quality in me that was akin to her own disposition and heart. Essentially, she made me her spokesperson within the company and the person in charge of bringing in new employees. I started the first Department of Human Resources and stayed within that discipline for all my ten years there. Though I left Omega when Clyde was fully established in his own advertising agency, I never forgot the life lessons I learned from my time working for Mrs. Hollander. Both she and Clyde are tough, smart people who have stretched me to my limits of capability and personal growth. I will always view the world from my own perspective, but I will always understand the larger world they introduced to me. I believe I am better for that.

After leaving Omega, I became a residential realtor in Stamford, Connecticut. I remained active in that career for ten years and still retain my Realtor's license. I truly enjoyed this period in my life. It provided another channel for my professional assets to develop, while giving me a chance to assist our family

Clyde and Kay at Busey Hall, University of Illinois, Champaign-Urbana

Kay on September 18, 1988

with the purchase of a few homes along the way. In retrospect, I view my adult life as having evolved in stages of personal growth that were given to me by my choices and my circumstances. All along the way I have been most fortunate to engage in efforts that allowed me the best opportunities to assist my husband, my children, and my extended family from the knowledge I have gained. While at Omega I learned how to counsel my children regarding their entry into business, as they were preparing to begin work. When I became a Realtor, I was able to guide and assist our children and other family members as they were preparing to purchase their own homes. Finally, as I have advanced into the role of the go-to person for advice when anyone in the family has questions about his or her own life situations or choices, I have been able to make use of all that I brought into this world in the form of my own character and all that I learned along the way from my personal and professional experiences. I feel privileged to be able to make a difference in someone's life and that I am regarded with enough trust and comfort that people seek my involvement.

The Golden Years

Now fully retired, I have several areas of interest. As mentioned above, I often participate in resolving the needs of our extended family. Some years ago, I was fortunate to receive a generous bequest in the will of Clyde's uncle Dave. I had many conversations with him before he died about how he might use his money to help his family. He declined to respond positively regarding any of my suggestions, so I decided when he gave me some money that I would use it for the education of children in the family, especially since this was the direction that I urged most strongly to him. I have been pleased to see several of June's (Clyde's sister) granddaughters take advantage of my plan to assist them with their educational pursuits. Since Clyde has committed to fully underwriting the educational/financial needs of our five grandsons, I am liberated to use this bequeathed money chiefly for other children in the family.

As Clyde and I have always enjoyed time together engaged in athletic endeavors, biking for us seemed a natural activity. Add to that our desire to see countries around the world and *voilà*! we have spent the last fifteen years touring the world on our bikes. We often assemble our children and, on occasion, our grandchildren, to join us on these trips. This has been a wonderful way to stay active and enjoy special, beautiful destinations.

The world of art and specifically our interest in art deco furnishings and decorative arts has contributed another layer of activity that is completely satisfying to me. As time has allowed, I have become a self-taught, highly interested victim of the arts and art collecting. Though we are clearly novices in this world, both Clyde and I take great pleasure in the chase to view, appreciate and, on occasion, purchase the beautiful objects of our desire. It is a lot of fun, but passion of this sort can mete out great heartache when the pursuit of an object is unsuccessful, as well as great happiness. It's all in the game.

Our home in Pound Ridge has always been a source of pleasure and pride. Of course, when we are at all successful in our pursuit of beautiful art and decorations, they find their way to this home. We are surrounded by the best of what nature can create outdoors and what we view as the best that man can create indoors. We are in the midst of beauty every day we spend here. My participation in the creation of this envelope of beauty, though minimal in the early years, has grown through time. I am more sensitive to all that it offers and more included in the making of it. Not at all artistic, I am amazed that I can now create a somewhat good-looking flower arrangement. Our home in Pound Ridge continues to be our anchor residence and hopefully we will be here for many years to come.

I still dream of a year in Paris — maybe I'll settle for a month in Provence. I still have my own "bucket list" — and like a fool keep adding to it. I still want my children (and grandchildren) to enjoy happy and successful lives. Only time will tell which of these things I will actually get. I've got my fingers crossed. After all, the best description of me is that I am, forever, the optimist.

Catherine Ann Douthart Davis

The Love of My Life… Kay

Recently, my daughter Christine asked, "Dad, do you and Mom do everything together?" This, during an otherwise normal Sunday morning phone conversation. I paused a moment, was a little taken aback, hesitating, not to respond too quickly, since I detected a bit of innocent wonderment mixed with a note of disapproval. It was as if her mother and I were spending far too much time together, insinuating that we didn't have separate lives of our own. As if we should step out of our life and meet other people, socialize more, like "normal" people.

"Well," I finally responded, "we don't do everything together, but your mom is my best friend." Our conversation went on to review the various aspects of Christine's parents' fixation on one another. I was after all, never a guy who wanted to simply hang out with his buddies. Actually, I discovered early in life that I preferred spending most of my time in the company of the opposite sex. I do get along with women better than with men. I'm more comfortable inducing my female counterparts than I am in the challenging male rivalry one so often confronts, attempting to best one another at every turn. Simply put, I compete with men, and women comfort me.

So, yes, I do almost everything with Kay. She is the love of my life, its centerpiece. There is no one I'd rather be with more. No one. She knows how I like it. This state of proximity is not something that occurred recently. It has evolved over time from the first day of our relationship in 1955 and continues in our 50th year of marriage. Kay has been more than simply a best friend, of course. She's been my lifelong companion, serving as lover, financial supporter, advocate, health advisor, confidant, partner, sounding board, surrogate mother, social counselor, and fitness exercise partner. Most importantly, Kay has become as knowledgeable about the things I most care about as I am. She's a good wife and mother — giving and forgiving. A good sport, she is adventurous, up for anything. In today's vernacular, "she's got game."

Kay stepped into my life and from that moment on, step by step, became integral to its existence. We're very different, and as I've often said, "come from opposite corners of the room," but somehow, we have remained in the same room all these years, contributing together to our common cause, a better life together and for all those who depend on us. Kay was there in the early years before marriage, feeding me, waiting for me after high school swim team practice, attending meets, traveling with me on the CTA from the far South Side of Chicago downtown, accompanying me to my place of work during summer employment between school years. When I went off to college, she sent me her car-hop tip money to augment my meager financial status as a student. When I left the University of Illinois in my junior year for New York City seeking a career in advertising, she stayed behind, for once no longer at my side. Failing to convince her to marry and join me in New York, she instead convinced me to return to her and school and wired me the $69 in airfare to seal the deal.

When we finally returned to New York, she was there at my side staining the milled lumber that would serve as the siding and ceiling boards of our house then under construction, contributing along with me "sweat equity" to a project we could ill afford. It was winter and the structure was open to the elements.

Often I found myself working late in those early years in New York City, well past the last departing train from Grand Central to the suburbs. This was *(continued on page 636)*

Galerie Félix Marcilhac, Paris, 1987
Oliver Gardens, CT, Sep. 2, 1989
1992
Paris, Sep. 23, 1993
Galerie Duo, Paris, Nov. 15, 19
ABC Carpet, NYC, Sep., 1994
Paris, Nov. 15, 1994
Paris, Nov. 15, 1994
L'Hôtel Drouot, Paris, May 9, 1995
Warehouse, Paris, Nov. 14, 199
Valois Gallery, Paris, Nov. 15, 1996
Galerie Vallois, Paris, Nov. 15, 19
Louvre des Antiquaires, Paris, May 31, 2000
Paris, Nov. 21, 1996
Louvre des Antiquaires Paris, May 30, 2000
Galerie Vallois, Paris, Jul. 30, 2000
Macassar Gallery, Paris, Jun. 27, 2000
Dutko Gallery, Paris, Sep. 20, 2002
Paris, July 2000
P. Kovacs Gallery, Vienna, Aug. 9,
GALERIE
PATRICK
FOURTIN
Friedman & Vallois, NYC, May 17, 2001
Dutko Gallery, Paris, Sep. 20, 2002
Paris, Jun. 1, 2000
Delorenzo Gallery, NYC, Feb. 9, 2001
Delorenzo Gallery, NYC, Feb. 9, 2001
Paris, Sep. 21, 2002

If one looks closely at most of these photos of Kay, a certain theme begins to present itself — objets d'art of interest to us which required a reference as to type and scale. They also serve as a decades long fashion review of sorts, mixed in with an occasional personal event or place we visited. Note her various hair styles.

Marguiles Gallery, Wynwood t District, Miami, Mar. 18, 2005

Met. Mus. of Art, NYC, Jun. 21, 2004

Paris, Sep. 14, 2004

Cotton field, Virginia, Oct. 9, 2004

Marguiles Gallery, Wynwood Art District, Miami, Mar. 18, 2005

Hawaii in Dec. 28, 2005

Princeton University, Apr. 6, 2005

Fairchild Gardens, Miami, Jan. 13, 2006

Joan Miro Mus., Barcelona, Sep. 25, 2005

Bahia, Brazil, Sep. 27, 2005

Design Miami, Dec. 1, 2005

Kisco Medical Group, Sep. 4 2007

Paris Biennale, Sep. 14, 2006

Paris, Sep. 9, 2008

W. Isle, Aventura, Florida, Dec. 25, 2006

Gormley Sculptures, Nov. 14, 2007

Paris Biennale, Sep. 10, 2008

Valois Gallery, Paris, Sep. 11, 2008

"Revolver Girl," Dec. 8, 2007

Rome, May 31, 2008

Sornay cabinet, Paris, Sep. 10, 2008

Chris's birthday cake, Jan. 19, 2009

Garage sale, Lansing, IL, Nov. 14, 2009

Christie's, NYC, Oct. 16, 2008

Getty Art Mus., LA, Sep. 30, 2009

Art Basel, Miami, Dec. 6, 2008

long before the limos that are so commonly available to hard-working employees today. She would bundle up the children and drive from Briarcliff Manor, our first home, and pick me up curbside, so we could have something of an evening together. On other occasions, when I'd commute from work on a more timely basis, after dinner and putting the kids to bed and leaving them in the care of a sitter, she would return with me, making the hundred-mile round trip to New York City to see a movie. We like movies.

One of Kay's most amazing characteristics is her ability to readily adapt, to co-opt almost any interest of mine. She's become an Art Deco expert. She's been at my side during our gallery crawls, exhibitions, fairs, and the Paris Biennale des Antiquaires. We collect Art Deco furniture and she is the one, despite my artistic proclivity, who is most able to identify the designer of a specific piece or period.

Side-By-Side

A few weeks back I was on my way home from work coming up on Tatomuck Road when I noticed in the distance two people walking. As I got closer, I realized it was Mom and Dad, or should I say Dad and Mom. As always, Dad was walking a few steps ahead of Mom. As I went by them I honked the horn and caught a glimpse of Mom's face. The expression was priceless. She had that look as if to say, "Clyde, why are you making me do this?!!" But, as always, Mom was by Dad's side, even when she probably would have preferred to be doing anything other than exercise!"

One of the memories written by our son-in-law John Parrino, Christine's spouse. Each of our children composed a fond recollection of us and presented it as a gift to us at our 50th Wedding Anniversary celebration in Encinitas, California, September 19, 2009. Kay and I were asked, as we selected an unsigned memory from an antique crystal bowl, "which member of our family was the author." There were lots of surprises, tears, laughs, and, of course, wonderful memories shared by all.

She's far more adept at managing our physical exercise regimen. She is moderate, yet consistent in applying her considerable physical abilities to the task at hand, all the while producing better numbers, heart rate, blood pressure, cholesterol, etc., than my own with all my extreme effort notwithstanding. As she says, "He's always so concerned about my physical well-being, and his efforts are legendary for getting me out and yet, it is I who have all the trophies for being athletic and he hasn't a one."

She's guided and counseled me. She's encouraged me to take the risks I was prone to take, job hopping or giving up certain financial security to found my own company. She was beside me when I chose to research my family history. Traveling about the countryside, she avidly joined me in seeking the information held in innumerable state archives, libraries, and courthouses as well as those abroad in Hungary and Slovakia. She was at my side during those long research trips by car through the states of Illinois, Indiana, Kentucky, Missouri, Virginia, and Maryland. She's also been at my side during those long car trips between our homes in New York and Florida and on trips to Chicago to visit my aging mother and to the West Coast to be with our three grandsons and their parents.

She was there, with me, in the Atlas Mountains of Morocco, in the teeming streets of Ho Chi Minh City and on the beaches of Bahia, Brazil, as well as the islands of Capri, Corsica, and Sardinia. And she was by my side aboard the *Auntie Kay* when we were caught at sea in a vicious thunderstorm trying to make safe harbor in the Bahamas. The seas were so bad that day that I informed her, between bolts of lightning as wide as a house, that in addition to her life vest, she should hang onto the cooler chest for flotation when, not if, we went down.

So yes, Christine, your mother and I do everything together, and so much more.

Her experience at sea did not, however, deter her from "escorting" me on my *Queen Mary 2* first class cruise from New York to Southampton, England, a surprise 70th birthday gift from her to me. That is typical Kay. Always willing to do for others, no matter the cost. Always at my side.

And, we like it that way.

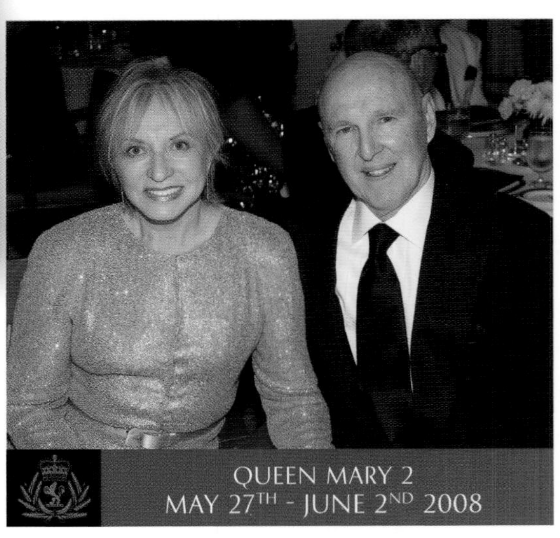

Lauff

Bauer

Form 2203
DEPARTMENT OF LABOR
NATURALIZATION SERVICE

No. 46783

TRIPLICATE
[To be given to the person making the Declaration]

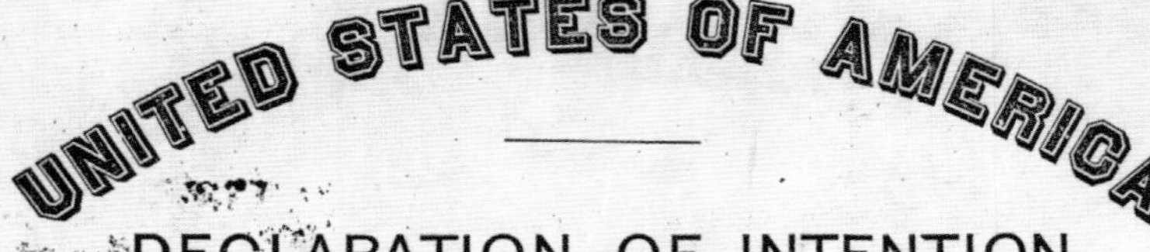

DECLARATION OF INTENTION

(Invalid for all purposes seven years after the date hereof)

State of Illinois, } ss:
County of Cook, }

In the Superior Court of Cook County.

I, John William Bauer, aged 29 years, occupation Tailor, do declare on oath that my personal description is: Color white, complexion dark, height 5 feet 6 inches, weight 145 pounds, color of hair brown, color of eyes brown other visible distinctive marks none

I was born in Podolin Hungary on the 12 day of March, anno Domini 1886; I now reside at 1756 N. Hoyne Ave (Give number and street), Chicago, Ill.

I emigrated to the United States of America from Bremen Germany on the vessel Dont remember (If the alien arrived otherwise than by vessel, the character of conveyance or name of transportation company should be given.); my last foreign residence was Podolin Hungary

It is my bona fide intention to renounce forever all allegiance and fidelity to any foreign prince, potentate, state, or sovereignty, and particularly to Francis Joseph EMPEROR OF AUSTRIA AND APOSTOLIC KING of HUNGARY, of whom I am now a subject; I arrived at the port of Baltimore, in the State of Maryland, on or about the 1st day of September, anno Domini 1905; I am not an anarchist; I am not a polygamist nor a believer in the practice of polygamy; and it is my intention in good faith to become a citizen of the United States of America and to permanently reside therein: SO HELP ME GOD.

x John William Bauer
(Original signature of declarant.)

Subscribed and sworn to before me at Chicago, Ill., this 6th

[SEAL] day of July anno Domini 1915

Richard J McGrath
Clerk of the Superior Court.

By Walter Heath, Deputy Clerk.

11—3784

John William Bauer, age 29, who was a tailor by trade, entered the United States "on or about" September 1, 1905, from Bremen, Germany. His place of birth was given as Podelin, Hungary.

No. 42933

U. S. DEPARTMENT OF LABOR
NATURALIZATION SERVICE

ORIGINAL

UNITED STATES OF AMERICA

PETITION FOR NATURALIZATION

To the Honorable the Superior Court of Cook County, Illinois:

The petition of John William Bauer *hereby filed, respectfully showeth:*

First. My place of residence is 10550 Torrence Ave (Give number and street.), *Chicago, Ill.*

Second. My occupation is Tailor

Third. I was born on the 12 *day of* March *anno Domini* 1886 *at* Todolis Hungary

Fourth. I emigrated to the United States from Bremen, Germany *on or about the* 18 *day of* Aug *anno Domini* 1905 *and arrived in the United States, at the port of* Baltimore Maryland *on the* 1 *day of* Sept *anno Domini* 1905 *on the vessel* Unknown (If the alien arrived otherwise than by vessel, the character of conveyance or name of transportation company should be given.)

Fifth. I declared my intention to become a citizen of the United States on the 6 *day of* July *anno Domini* 1915 *at* Chicago, Illinois *in the* Superior *Court of* Cook County, Illinois

Sixth. I am — *married. My wife's name is* Anna *she was born on the* 27 *day of* Nov *anno Domini* 1885 *at* Todolis Hungary *and now resides at* 10550 Torrence Ave. (Give number and street.) *Chicago, Ill.*

I have 5 *children, and the name, date and place of birth, and place of residence of each of said children is as follows:*

Stella - Born - Aug - 27 - 1911 at Detroit Michigan
Hellen - " - Sept - 4 - 1912 " " "
Annie - " - Sept 14 - 1915 " Chicago, Illinois
Florence - " - March - 29 - 1917 " " "
Ethel - " - July - 4 - 1919 " " "
} All Resides at Chicago, Illinois

Seventh. I am not a disbeliever in or opposed to organized government or a member of or affiliated with any organization or body of persons teaching disbelief in or opposed to organized government. I am not a polygamist nor a believer in the practice of polygamy. I am attached to the principles of the Constitution of the United States, and it is my intention to become a citizen of the United States and to renounce absolutely and forever all allegiance and fidelity to any foreign prince, potentate, state, or sovereignty, and particularly to Hungary or any Independent State within former Austria-Hungary Empire *of whom at this time I am a subject, and it is my intention to reside permanently in the United States.*

Eighth. I am able to speak the English language.

Ninth. I have resided continuously in the United States of America for the term of five years at least, immediately preceding the date of this petition, to wit, since the 1 *day of* Sept *anno Domini* 1905 *and in the State of Illinois, continuously next preceding the date of this petition, since the* 16 *day of* Jany *anno Domini* 1912 *being a residence within this State of at least one year next preceding the date of this petition.*

Tenth. I have not heretofore made petition for citizenship to any court. (I made petition for citizenship to the ______ Court of ______ at ______, on the ______ day of ______, anno Domini 1____, and the said petition was denied by the said Court for the following reasons and causes, to wit, ______, and the cause of such denial has since been cured or removed.)

Attached hereto and made a part of this petition are my declaration of intention to become a citizen of the United States and the certificate from the Department of Labor, together with my affidavit and the affidavits of the two verifying witnesses thereto, required by law. Wherefore your petitioner prays that he may be admitted a citizen of the United States of America.

X John William Bauer
(Complete and true signature of petitioner.)

Declaration of Intention No. 46783 *and Certificate of Arrival No.* ______ *from Department of Labor filed this* 22 *day of* Sept *1920*

NOTE TO CLERK OF COURT.—If petitioner arrived in the United States ON OR BEFORE JUNE 29, 1906, strike out the words reading "and Certificate of Arrival No. ______ from Department of Labor."

AFFIDAVITS OF PETITIONER AND WITNESSES

STATE OF ILLINOIS, }
County of Cook, } *ss:*

The aforesaid petitioner being duly sworn, deposes and says that he is the petitioner in the above-entitled proceedings; that he has read the foregoing petition and knows the contents thereof; that the said petition is signed with his full, true name; that the same is true of his own knowledge except as to matters therein stated to be alleged upon information and belief, and that as to those matters he believes it to be true.

X John William Bauer
(Complete and true signature of petitioner.)

Sam Morris, *occupation* Tailor, *residing at* 2132 Evergreen Ave, *Chicago, Ill.,*
and William Perman, *occupation* ", *residing at* 3133 E. 92nd St, *Chicago, Ill.,*
each being severally, duly, and respectively sworn, deposes and says that he is a citizen of the United States of America; that he has personally known John William Bauer, *the petitioner above mentioned, to have resided in the United States continuously immediately preceding the date of filing his petition, since the* 1 *day of* Jany *anno Domini* 1915 *and in the State in which the above-entitled petition is made continuously since the* 1 *day of* Jany *anno Domini* 1915; *and that he has personal knowledge that the said petitioner is a person of good moral character, attached to the principles of the Constitution of the United States, and that the petitioner is in every way qualified, in his opinion, to be admitted a citizen of the United States.*

Sam Morris
(Signature of witness.)

William Perman
(Signature of witness.)

[SEAL.]

Subscribed and sworn to before me by the above-named petitioner and witnesses in the office of the Clerk of said Court at Chicago, Ill., this 22 *day of* Sept *anno Domini* 1920

JOHN KJELLANDER, *Clerk.*
LH By L. H. Hatley, *Deputy Clerk.*

[OVER.]

On July 6, 1915, at age 29, John William Bauer declared his intention to become a citizen of the United States and submitted his Petition for Naturalization in Cook County, Illinois, Superior Court, September 2[illegible] 1920. His residence was given as 10550 Torrence Ave., Chicago, Illinois. Occupation: Tailor.

IN THE MATTER OF THE PETITION OF

John William Bauer

TO BE ADMITTED A CITIZEN OF THE UNITED STATES OF AMERICA.

Filed Sept. 22, 1920

OATH OF ALLEGIANCE

I hereby declare, on oath, that I absolutely and entirely renounce and abjure all allegiance and fidelity to any foreign prince, potentate, state, or sovereignty, and particularly to Independent State within Hungary or any Independent State within former Austria-Hungary Empire *of whom I have heretofore been a subject; that I will support and defend the Constitution and laws of the United States of America against all enemies, foreign and domestic; and that I will bear true faith and allegiance to the same.*

John William Bauer

Subscribed and sworn to before me, in open Court, this 7 *day of* Jany *A. D. 19*21

S. E. Erickson, *Clerk.*

NOTE.—In renunciation of title of nobility, add the following to the oath of allegiance before it is executed: "I further renounce the title of (give title), an order of nobility, which I have heretofore held."

ORDER OF COURT ADMITTING PETITIONER

Upon consideration of the petition of John William Bauer*, and affidavits in support thereof, and further testimony taken in open Court, it is ordered that the said petitioner, who has taken the oath required by law, be, and hereby is, admitted to become a citizen of the United States of America, this* 7 *day of* Jany*, A. D. 19*21.

(It is further ordered, upon consideration of the petition of the said ______*, that his name be, and hereby is, changed to* ______*, under authority of the provisions of section 6 of the act approved June 29, 1906 (34 Stat. L., pt. 1, p. 596), as amended by the act approved March 4, 1913, entitled "An act to create a Department of Labor.")*

By the Court:

Henry [illegible] Sullivan, Judge.

ORDER OF COURT DENYING PETITION

Upon consideration of the petition of ______ *and the motion of* ______ *for the United States in open Court this* ______ *day of* ______*, 19*___*, it appearing that* ______

THE SAID PETITION IS HEREBY DENIED.

______, J.

MEMORANDUM OF CONTINUANCES

REASONS FOR CONTINUANCE

Continued from ______, *19*___

to ______, *19*___

Continued from ______, *19*___

to ______, *19*___

NAMES OF SUBSTITUTED WITNESSES

______, *occupation* ______, *residing at* ______

______, *occupation* ______, *residing at* ______

Certificate of Naturalization, No. 1350555*, issued on the* 7 *day of* Jany *A. D. 19*21

[INSERT ON FOLLOWING LINES MARRIAGES AND BIRTHS OCCURRING AFTER PETITIONING AND BEFORE NATURALIZATION.]

On January 7, 1921, John William Bauer took the Oath of Allegiance and became a citizen of the United States.

Source Citation: Registration Location: Cook County, Illinois; Roll 1493514; Draft Board: 20.

Source Information: Ancestry.com. World War I Draft Registration Cards, 1917-1918 [database online]. Original data: United States, Selective Service System. World War I Selective Service System Draft Registration Cards, 1917-1918. Washington, D.C.: National Archives and Records Administration. M1509, 4,582 rolls. Imaged from Family History Library microfilm.

REGISTRATION CARD—(Men born on or after April 28, 1877 and on or before February 16, 1897)

SERIAL NUMBER U 1197 — 1. NAME (Print) JOHN WILLIAM BAUER — ORDER NUMBER

2. PLACE OF RESIDENCE (Print) 530 S. MILLARD AVE CHICAGO - COOK - ILL.

[THE PLACE OF RESIDENCE GIVEN ON THE LINE ABOVE WILL DETERMINE LOCAL BOARD JURISDICTION; LINE 2 OF REGISTRATION CERTIFICATE WILL BE IDENTICAL]

3. MAILING ADDRESS SAME

4. TELEPHONE KED 308 — 5. AGE IN YEARS 56, DATE OF BIRTH MAR - 12 - 1886 — 6. PLACE OF BIRTH PODOLIN HUNGARY

7. NAME AND ADDRESS OF PERSON WHO WILL ALWAYS KNOW YOUR ADDRESS

8. EMPLOYER'S NAME AND ADDRESS GOLD BLATT BROS. STATE + JACKSON CHICAGO - ILL.

9. PLACE OF EMPLOYMENT OR BUSINESS GOLD BLATT BROS. STATE + JACKSON - CHICAGO - ILL.

I AFFIRM THAT I HAVE VERIFIED ABOVE ANSWERS AND THAT THEY ARE TRUE.

D. S. S. Form 1 (Revised 4-1-42) (over) John William Bauer (Registrant's signature)

John William Bauer's World War II registration card and registration report. Source Citation: Roll 30955_164599; Local board: Chicago , Illinois.

Source Information: Ancestry.com. U.S. World War II Draft Registration Cards, 1942 [database online]. Original data: United States, Selective Service System. Selective Service Registration Cards, World War II: Fourth Registration. National Archives and Records Administration Branch locations: National Archives and Records Administration Region Branches

Top left: Monastery in Podolínec. Top right: Podolínec from the west. Bottom: Two photos of Podolínec and surroundings. Photos reproduced from <http://www.podolinec.eu/klastor-piaristov-s-kostolom/> by permission of Marian Beno of the municipality of Podolínec.

Our Sojourn in Slovakia
by Kay Douthart Davis

Similar to the feelings I experienced when researching the Doutharts, I felt greatly disadvantaged by the lack of contact with family members through the years. However, I have succeeded in finding a number of people who have helped me, through their conversations and contributions, in developing the story of this family. The results of my findings on the Bauer Family are highlighted below.

When I began my search for family members (either Doutharts or Bauers), my first resource was an address book that I found after my father died. It was his personal book of family contacts. My attempts to phone numerous listings in the book were met with many failures. However, I made two key contacts: Ruth Broholm (Ruth Bauer — my mother's sister) and Joe Martin, the husband of Lee Martin (Bauer), my mother's sister. I remember the first time I spoke to Aunt Ruth on the phone. As soon as she answered my call to her, I knew who she was! I remembered her unique voice from my childhood days. It made me so comfortable, I couldn't help but smile.

After more research, I was eventually lucky enough to find my cousin Don Marten (twin with Dan Marten and son to my mother's sister Florence — no relation to Joe Martin.) These several contacts eventually opened many doors to the Bauer/Lauff family history.

In a phone conversation on August 25, 1997, Joe Martin told me that Anna Lauff, born November 27, 1885, traveled to New York with her sister when they were young girls just having graduated from high school. Their trip was a gift from their father, who was mayor of their small town of Podelin, which at that time was a German-speaking town in Hungary. (*German Towns in Slovakia & Upper Hungary, A Genealogical Gazetteer* by Duncan B. Gardiner). Anna's sister returned to Podelin after the planned vacation, but Anna decided to stay in New York and took work in

This map, a portion of which is shown below, was found in the Library of Congress — Genealogy Room — Washington, D.C. on June 12, 1999. It was within the following book: German Towns in Slovakia & Upper Hungary, a Genealogical Gazetteer *by Duncan B. Gardiner, Lakewood, Ohio, 1988.*

Gazetteer: *The gazetteer includes the names of towns and villages in Slovakia, which had some German population in 1921.*

Map: *Page & quadrant in map appendix of this guide:*
Sl: *The Slovak name (used on post-1945 maps)*
Hu: *The Hungarian name (administrative name until 1918)*

Pop: *The first population figure is total population of the town; the second figure is the German population. The percentage is that of Germans to total population. The population statistics are from the 1921 Czechoslovak census.*

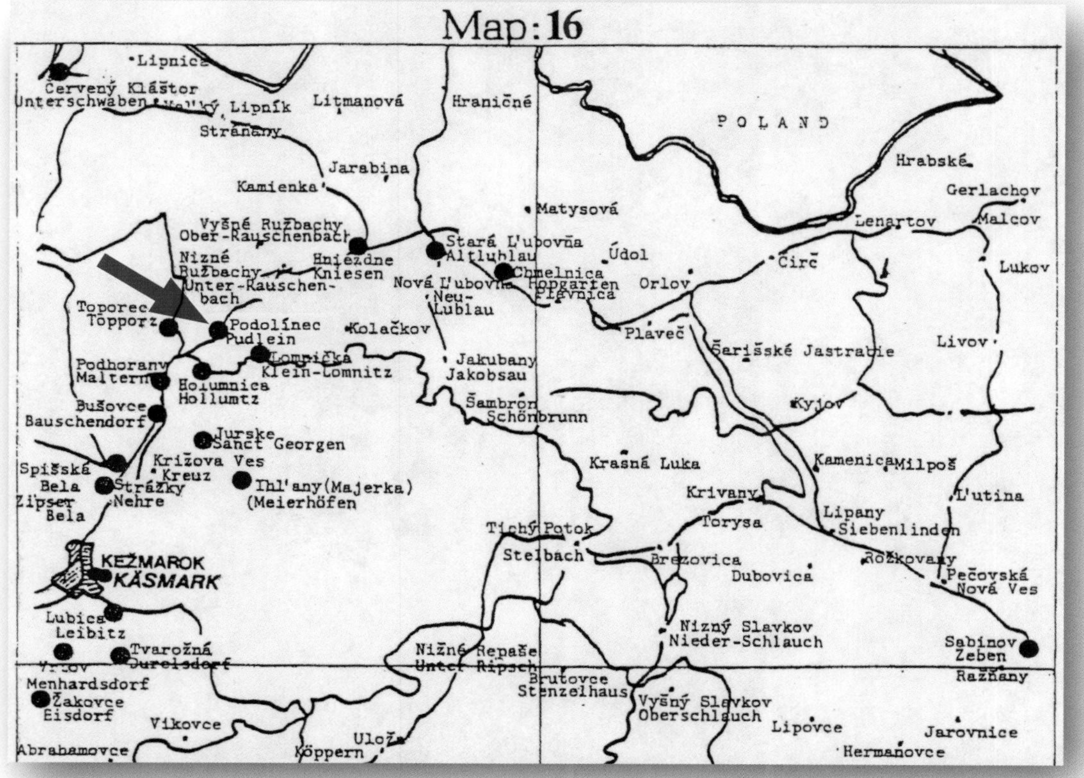

Pudlin Map: 16A
Sl: *Podolinec*
HU: *Podalin*
Pop: *1707, 905 Ge (53%)*

First mentioned in 1244. Traditional trades.

the home of a school teacher, who taught her English. Soon after, John Bauer (Anna's boyfriend from Podelin) immigrated to the United States to be with Anna. I have secured documents on John Bauer to substantiate his arrival in the United States. The United States of America, Declaration of Intention, dated July 6, 1915, signed by John William Bauer, age twenty-nine, stated he was born in Podelin, Hungary, and traveled to the United States on or about September 1, 1905. Anna Lauff (though listed as Anna *Loftis* Bauer on the American Immigrant Wall of Honor at Ellis Island) has no actual documents secured as of yet to verify her date of arrival.

Clyde and I traveled to the ancient city of Podelin on August 4, 2002, in an effort to verify family stories of my grandmother (Anna Lauff), her sister, their father (the mayor) and of course, John Bauer (my grandfather). It was a rather disappointing trip, since the town was quite poor with gypsies living in totally depressed areas, no real town records, and little verifiable information even after diligent efforts by us, and a translator and researcher who went to the region's archival center in search of birth, death, and any other possible family records. We were able to visit a few cemeteries and found both the Lauff and Bauer names on headstones, so I believe this town is the place of birth for both my grandmother and grandfather. The above-mentioned immigration papers for John Bauer verify this belief and a certificate of birth issued in Cook County, Illinois, for the birth of Lorraine Eileen Bauer on July 21, 1924, indicates that both her father John William Bauer and mother Anna (Lauff) Bauer were born in "Podalein [*sic*]," Germany. Regretfully, I do not recall ever meeting my grandfather, John Bauer, and I do not have a single photo of him. He abused my grandmother and according to my aunt Ruth, he was sent away for it. Many years passed before any family members had contact with him.

JOHN WILLIAM BAUER b. March 12, 1887

STATE: Illinois
COUNTY: Cook
TOWNSHIP OR OTHER DIVISION OF COUNTY
NAME OF INSTITUTION

DEPARTMENT OF COMMER
FOURTEENTH CENSUS OF THE U

				Name	Relation													Place of birth
1	1653	27	42	Solecka				M	W	5	S				no			Illinois
				Demiak Clemens	boarder			M	W	27	S	1911	Na	1914	yes	yes		Italy
	1655	31	47	Bauer John	head	R		M	W	33	M	1905	Pa		yes	yes		Hungary
				Anna	wife			F	W	34	M	1908	Al		yes	no		Hungary
				Stella	daughter			F	W	9	S			yes	yes	yes		Michigan
				Helen	daughter			F	W	8	S			yes	yes	yes		Michigan
				Anna	daughter			F	W	6	S			yes	yes	yes		Illinois
				Florence	daughter			F	W	3 3/12	S			no				Illinois
				Ethel	daughter			F	W	1 1/2	S			no				Illinois
	1654	32	48	Brita Eli...	head	R		F	W	47								

Finally, Estelle (Ginger) found him, and he had lived out his old age in and around her household. In the end, he died in a rented apartment nearby Ginger's house in Bristol, Indiana. This accounting was given to me by "Skeets" Wilcox, my cousin, son of Estelle "Ginger" Bauer.

Sisters Galore

I had one lengthy conversation with Joe Martin before he suddenly died. His wife Lee had already passed when I contacted Joe. He filled me in on all my mother's sisters, both dead and alive. At that time only two of my mother's sisters were still alive — my aunt Ruth (in Texas) and my aunt "Bunny" (my mother's sister, Ethel). I have been able to visit with both these wonderful ladies, but, sadly, Aunt "Bunny" has since passed. Aunt Ruth gave me the names of two living cousins — Clare (Sred) Martin and Jim "Skeets" Wilcox. I have met and had numerous conversations with them.

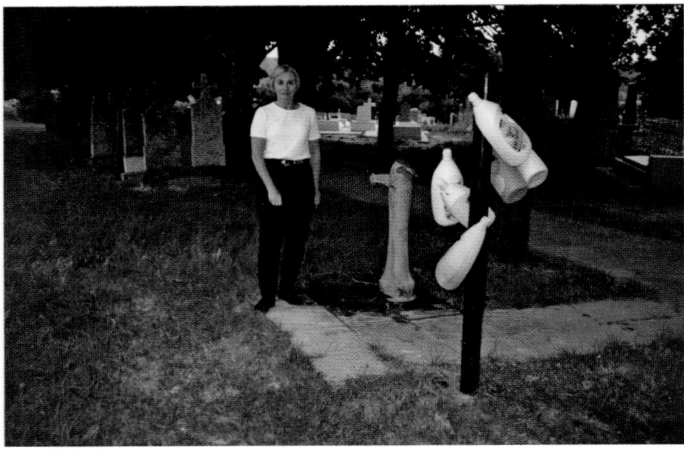

Kay at the well water pump with various plastic containers used mostly by women who water the flowers on their loved ones' gravesites. Unlike the U.S., this seems to be a tradition that still prevails throughout eastern Europe, at least in the spring, summer, and fall seasons.

I spoke to my cousin Don Marten (twin son of Florence) by phone on one occasion before he died. His wife, Dorothy, has supplied me with much detail about Don's mother Florence, as well as several others of my mother's sisters. I have tried to describe the family, especially the eight sisters, as they appear in the book to the best of my knowledge based on personal research or from conversations with the above-mentioned individuals.

John and Anna Bauer took up residence chiefly in Chicago and had eight daughters:

1. Esther "Ginger," born August 27, 1910, died May, 1997.
2. Helen "Mag," born September 4, 1911, died October 1974.
3. Ann May (Kay Davis's mother), born September 14, 1913, died December 13, 1968.
4. Florence Alice "Daisy," born March 29, 1916, died May 25, 1970.
5. Ethel Irene "Bunny," born July 4, 1918, died September 23, 2002.
6. Ruth "Gooney," born February 2, 1921.

Above: The Bauer family as listed in the 1920 U.S. Census at 10550 Torrence Avenue, Chicago, Illinois. Left: The Marriage License of John W. Bauer and Anna Kavolcik.

7. Lorraine "Lee," born July 21, 1924, died October 17, 1995.
8. Rose Marie Margaret "Mushy," born November 7, 1926, died September 18, 1972.

My mother, Ann, was the third-born child. All the girls were successful in their lives; some entered the military, and others took jobs in clerical or professional positions. None attended college. My grandfather John was a tailor. The 1930 U.S. census shows the family living at 10550 Torrence Avenue, where my aunt Ruth said my grandfather also had a tailor's shop. There is suspicion raised by the birth certificate of my aunt Florence that she was born to another woman with my grandfather John as the father. Therefore, if this is true, Florence is a half-sister to the other girls in the family. However, at this time there is also great confusion by the various maiden names (Kowalski, Kavalcik, Kfolik, Lauff, Lauf, Louff, Louf, and Loftis) used by my grandmother Anna Bauer throughout the years on various documents. This matter has yet to be clarified.

In discussions with Aunt Ruth and Aunt Bunny, it was evident that my mother and father had little contact with the Bauer sisters and other family members after the early years, when my brothers and I were young children. I have attempted to gather as much information on the family as possible from the few living relatives I was able to contact.

ARI

Pictured left to right are Lorraine "Lee" Bauer Martin, Anna Marie/Mary Lauff Bauer, and Ethel "Bunny" Weis. On the back of the photo is written, "Lee, Grandma Bauer, Ethel (Bunny)."

Grandma Anna Bauer

Five Minutes with Grandma
by Kay Douthart Davis

It seems like five minutes when you consider the lifespan of an individual. My single memory was when my father dropped me off to spend a night with Grandma and one of my aunts (I can't recall which of my mother's sisters was there that night) at their apartment in the South Shore neighborhood of Chicago. And the reason it was a five-minute memory is because I can only remember that the next morning they sat me on some phone books (so I could reach the table) and allowed me to have a cup of coffee (very milked down version) with a piece of buttered toast that I dipped into the coffee. It remained my favorite breakfast item for years to come.

Over the years I made a number of attempts to reach my cousin Clare Martin, Rose Marie's daughter. Eventually, Clare visited me in Pound Ridge on September 11, 1999, and delivered a treasure-trove of Bauer history in all manner of things — photos, letters, newspaper clippings, obituaries, Ellis Island Wall of Honor certificates, as well as endless stories of the family in Texas, which included Clare and her mother Rose Marie, Lorraine, and Joe Martin, Ruth Bauer, her husband Al and their son Kenneth, as well as our grandmother, Anna Bauer. Clare shared many details of the Bauer sisters, especially those who migrated to Texas. Some of these facts, along with information I received from my aunt Ruth, are responsible for the accounting that follows:

Lee was the seventh born of eight daughters, spent several years in the Armed Services (she was a WAVE [Women Accepted for Volunteer Emergency Service]), and met Joe Martin, her husband-to-be, while in the service. She settled in Texas and became the matriarch of the family. She and her husband moved to Richland Hills, Texas, in 1958, where Joe took a job in banking, having graduated from St. Louis University. They lived in Richland Hills until 1972, when they purchased a large parcel of land in Ft. Worth, developed a ranch on the property, consisting of several dwellings, numerous farm animals, and their home on "the hill" as it was called. Over the years many of Lee's sisters and extended family lived with and/or visited them at the ranch for long periods of time.

Clare Ann Sredzinsky/Sred Martin b. 1955, daughter of Rose Marie Bauer and her first husband, Clark Sredzinsky/Sred. Above is from a video taken during Clare's visit to Pound Ridge in September 1999, when Clare was going over Bauer family memorabilia with Kay Davis.

The first to arrive was my grandmother Anna Bauer, who arrived in Texas in the 1950s and lived with Lee and Joe until her death on November 15, 1969.

Rose Marie (Bauer) Sred(zinski) moved to Texas with Clare, her daughter, to live with Lee and Joe. In January 1960, Rose Marie's husband, who was a firefighter in Chicago, died in an accident at the scene of a fire. Clare was only six years old at the time. Rose Marie and Clare moved into Lee's home and remained there for many years.

Since Clare spent most of her childhood and early adult life in Texas, she had many firsthand experiences with those family members who resided in Texas.

Clare shared the following information regarding the causes of death for the various Bauer sisters. Because of the high number of deaths caused by cancer among the eight sisters, this fact certainly should be noted for future generations. At this writing, seven of the eight sisters are deceased. Ruth is the only living sister. She resides in Texas with her son Kenneth and her granddaughter Nicole. Though Ruth had breast cancer late in her life, she is cancer-free now.

The statistics:

Stella "Ginger" — Though she had colon cancer, she survived it and ultimately died of unrelated causes.

Helen "Mag" — She died of lung cancer.

Ann — My mother died at an early age (fifty-five years), most likely from a blood clot in her heart or brain.

Florence "Daisy" — She died of skin cancer — melanoma.

Ethel "Bunny" —

Lorraine "Lee" — She died of cancer of the adrenal gland.

Rose Marie "Mushy" — Suicide

Ruth (Bauer) Broholm also moved to Texas with her husband Allan. They had one son, Kenneth. Ruth and Al never lived at the ranch, but had a home nearby in North Richland. When she was young, Ruth also served in the Armed Services along with Lee. They seemed quite close as sisters, so it is not surprising that they lived near one another once married and settled down. Ruth still lives in her home in Texas along with her son Ken (Al has passed). Ken, who is a single parent, has one daughter, Nicole.

Some years ago another of the eight sisters, Florence (Bauer) Marten (mother of twins — Don and Dan), who lived in Utah, was experiencing a severe decline in her health due to skin cancer, which had been diagnosed a number of years earlier. Rose Marie traveled from Texas to Utah to care for Florence, leaving Clare (her daughter) behind in the care of Lee (Rose Marie's sister). After some time, Florence died, and within one month Rose Marie married Fred Marten (Florence's husband). Her full name became Rose Marie (Bauer) Sred Marten.

My cousin Clare Sred Martin

Eventually Lee and Joe Martin adopted Clare and raised her as their own. Clare's full name became Clare Sred Martin. I note all of the above for clarity, because records can appear to be incorrect unless the facts are known regarding the last names of Fred Marten (Florence and Rose Marie) and Joe Martin (Lee and Clare).

This union between Rose Marie and Fred Marten caused stress among the remaining sisters, since it was highly discouraged. Most unfortunate of the news shared with me was that my aunt Rose Marie committed suicide by asphyxiation in the garage of her home in Utah.

In March 1998, Clyde and I visited with Aunt Ruth, her son Ken, and her granddaughter Nicole. We traveled to the Greenwood Memorial Park in Ft. Worth, Texas, together to visit the Bauer family mausoleum. Aunt Ruth conducted a tour and explained all about the family members therein. Several of the Bauer sisters — Lee, Rose Marie, Florence, Esther, and Ethel already rest there along, with Anna Bauer (their mother). Space is provided for Ruth (the only remaining living sister). My mother, Ann (Bauer) Douthart, rests along with my father in St. Mary's

Ruth Bauer Broholm with me at the Bauer family mausoleum in Greenwood Memorial Park, Ft. Worth, Texas, in March 1998.

Cemetery in Evergreen, Illinois, and Helen "Mag" (Bauer) Mann was buried in Bristol, Michigan. Although Esther has a marked space in the mausoleum, none of her remains are located there. Esther "Ginger" (Bauer) Wilcox's ashes were scattered in the water at the Seven Mile Bridge in the Florida Keys by her son Jim "Skeets" Wilcox. Ginger spent much of her adult life in the Keys and this was her wish. Joe Martin and Allan Broholm are also at rest in the mausoleum along with the Bauer sisters. Jack Weis (Ethel's husband) is at rest in the cemetery at the memorial park but not in the mausoleum.

On that same trip when Clyde and I spent time with Ruth, Kenneth, and Nicole, I spent one long afternoon and evening in Ruth's home. At that time Al, her husband, was still alive. It was my first meeting with them since I had been a child. We shared a meal, enjoyed one another's company, and filled in the details of lives spent separately and quite apart but within the framework of the same family. It was a delight to see them at that time and once again when both Clyde and I toured the mausoleum with Aunt Ruth, Ken, and Nicole, followed by a great Texas barbeque lunch at Gilley's, a renowned eating and entertainment emporium in the Dallas/Ft. Worth area.

Clare and I have met several times since that first encounter and have resolved to continue our search for information on family history so that our story can be more complete.

Though my work on family roots has not rendered the breakthrough links I had hoped for in respect to generations past, I have enjoyed the journey and hope that the presence of our families in this book will shed some light for future generations..

Photographs below: Kay Davis at Podelin Cemetery in Slovakia at the headstone of Anna Lauf, believed to be a family member, and a closeup of the headstone.
The commemorative Certificate of Registration (bottom) issued by The Statue of Liberty, Ellis Island Foundation, Inc., was secured by Lorraine "Lee" Bauer to acknowledge her mother's entry into the United States from Austria. There appears to be a discrepancy regarding her mother's maiden name, Loftis vs. Lauff. Kay Davis received the certificate from Clare Martin.

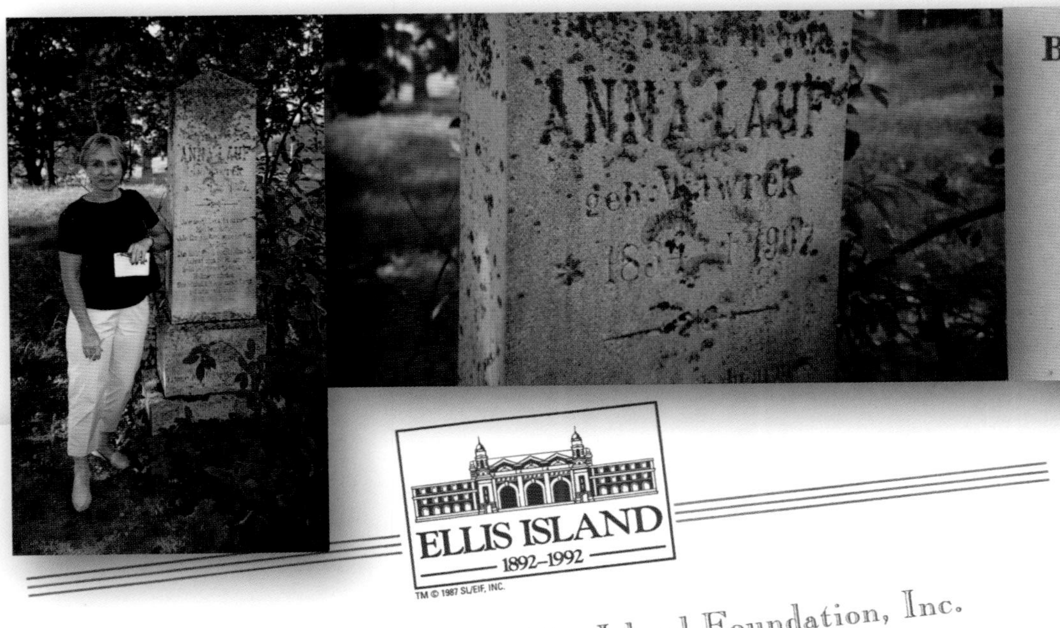

BAUER
ANNA BAUER, 4705 Holidan Lane East, passed away Saturday, 86 years old. Survivors: Daughters, Mrs. Loraine B Martin, Mrs. Rose Marie Sred Ruth Brohelm, Estelle Bauer, Key West, Fla., Helen Mann Key West, Florence Martin, Roy, Utah, Ethel Weis, Fort Lauderdale; 8 grandchildren; 10 great-grandchildren. Services 4 p.m. Monday Greenwood Chapel, Rev. James F. Garwin. Entombment Greenwood Mausoleum. Arrangements Greenwood, 3100 White Settlement at University.

649

Obituary for Anna Bauer, died November 15, 1969, at age 86 (source unknown).

ELLIS ISLAND
1892–1992
TM © 1987 SL/EIF, INC.

The Statue of Liberty-Ellis Island Foundation, Inc.
proudly presents this
Official Certificate of Registration
in
THE AMERICAN IMMIGRANT WALL OF HONOR
to officially certify that
Anna Loftis Bauer
came to the United States of America from
Austria
joining those courageous men and women who came to this country in search of personal freedom, economic opportunity and a future hope for their families.

Lee Iacocca
Lee A. Iacocca
The Statue of Liberty-Ellis Island Foundation, Inc.

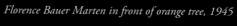

Florence Bauer Marten in front of orange tree, 1945

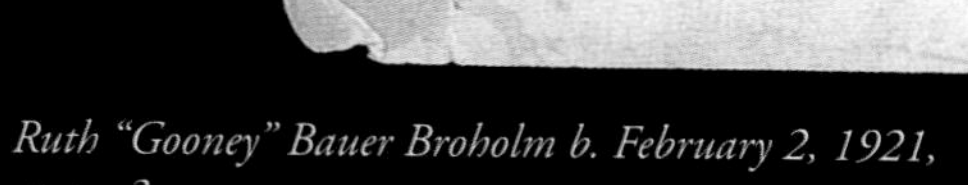

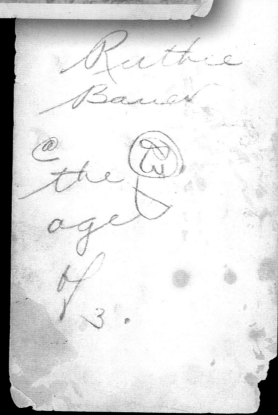

Ruth "Gooney" Bauer Broholm b. February 2, 1921, at age 3

Ethel "Bunny" Bauer Weis

On the back of this photo dated 1945 is "Grandma (Anna) Bauer, Ann Bauer Douthart, Mary Lenore Douthart (Aunt Mame) Carlson"

Lorraine "Lee" Bauer Martin, Florence Alice "Daisy" Bauer Marten, and Ruth "Gooney" Bauer Broholm

Rose Marie Margaret "Mushy" Bauer Marten and Ethel "Bunny" Bauer Weis in 1945

Lorraine "Lee" Bauer Martin holding dog in 1945

Written on back of photo is "Rose Marie, Ruth, Bunny. May, 1945 Dick's Communion."

Rose Marie Margaret "Mushy" Bauer Sred Marten b. November 7, 1926

Florence Alice "Daisy" Baueer Marten

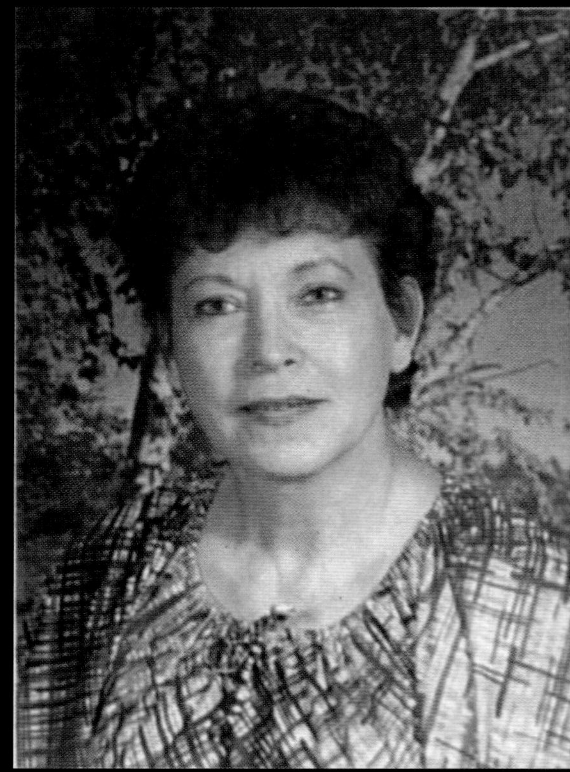

Ethel "Bunny" Bauer Weis b. July 4, 1918

" Bauer Martin b. July 21, 1924
-d uniform

Ruth "Gooney" Bauer Broholm b. February 2, 1921
in Coast Guard uniform

Ethel Irene "Bunny" Bauer Weis:

born of the Bauer girls, Ethel came into this world
n of July 1918. I can barely recall any contact with
vas growing up, except for the day of my brother
Communion and photographs taken to celebrate the
t prompted that memory. However, in recent years,
n Aunt Bunny at her home in Tamarac, Florida, on
occasions. Bunny's home in Tamarac is located about
es from our Florida residence in Aventura.
rst visit was a highlight o f my research. In January
eled to her house with Clyde, our daughter Cynthia,
Phil, and their two sons Ross and Dylan. In the photo below, the family resemblance is so clear to see in the three generations of women, with my Aunt Bunny bearing such a strong look of my mother, and Cynthia bearing such a strong resemblance to Aunt Bunny. That trip was a real treat for me.

The second and last visit on December 3, 1999, involved a small family reunion attended by James "Skeets" Wilcox (the son of Ethel's sister Stella and, therefore, my first cousin), and his wife Sylvia "Boe," my brother Dick and his wife Roz, Aunt Bunny, and, finally, Clyde and me. Many memories were shared during the visit and facts revealed that were previously unknown to me. I will recount a summary of those salient facts.

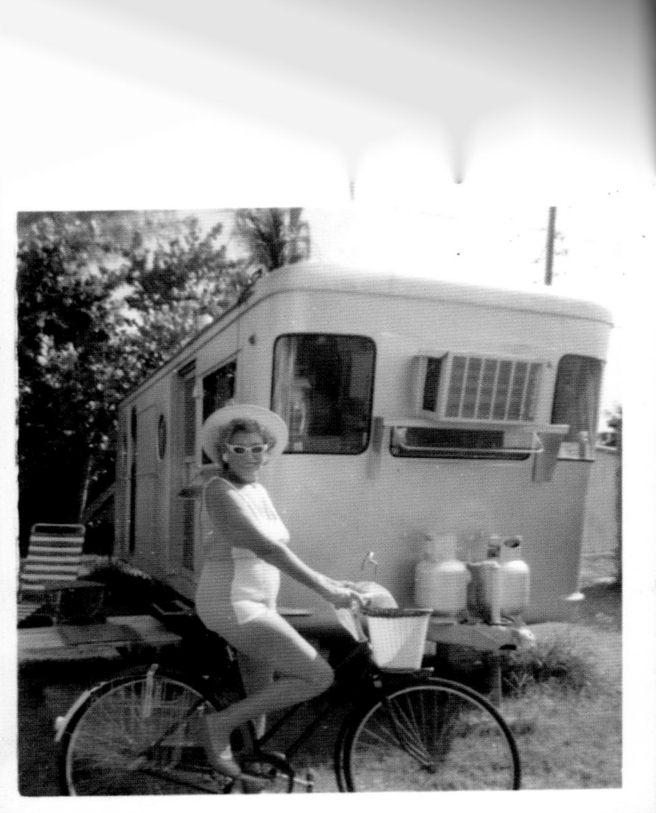

Esther "Ginger" Bauer Wilcox in Marathon, Florida

James Henry "Skeets" Wilcox

My Cousin "Skeets"

James Wilcox was originally nicknamed "Skeezix grandmother, Anna Bauer. It was picked up from a co but was eventually shortened to just "Skeets" — a nam carries with family and close friends.

Skeets said he learned about our grandmother's, Bauer's, entry into the United States from Anna Bauer that she told it to him many times over the years, but changed from time to time. However, essentially she sa (Anna) came on a boat with her sister. Skeets believes Bauer's family had some money. John Bauer was a stov the same boat. He may have worked as a gardener at t home in Europe. Anna and John were in love but not that time. They traveled to Detroit, Michigan. Skeets's Stella was born in Detroit. She was the first born of ei

Skeets said that his mother was always changing (she didn't like her given name of Stella). It changed to then Estelle, Esther, and finally Ginger. Most of the B had nicknames. Ruth was "Gooney." She said my fath that name. Rose Marie was "Mushy." Ethel was "Bunn was "Peanuts," and Ginger was "Skinny." And all the s calling my brother Dick "Dickie Boy."

When Skeets was young, he recalls living in the on the South Side of Chicago for about four years — same housing project where Clyde spent his youth. In notes, they determined that, most likely, Skeets lived a and Bensley Avenue not far from Clyde. Skeets recalle

"Skeets" tells all as Dick listens intently, along with Aunt "Bunny" in her home in Tamarac, Florida, on December 3, 1999

Later, as a teenager, Skeets recalls that his mother was working in the office at Goldblatt's Department Store in Hammond, Indiana. While going to lunch in the store's cafeteria one day, she saw a man who looked familiar. It was her father, John Bauer, who had been sent away by his family years before, and who was also working at Goldblatt's as a tailor.

Skeets explained that they started having him over for dinner once in a while, and then John moved in with them for a time. John and Skeets shared a room and played pinochle. However, John was an alcoholic and was difficult to control. Finally, John went off on his own, renting an apartment in Bristol, Indiana. Skeets added that none of the other Bauer sisters wanted anything to do with John, but Ginger, his mother, had strong feelings for her father. When John's health was failing, he stayed with them again but was not with them when he died. John Bauer was cremated, and his ashes were left at the only funeral home in Bristol, Indiana.

After a tour in the Navy, Skeets attended Purdue University on the GI Bill. He got his degree in electrical engineering from Purdue, then went to Honeywell Controls in California working on Commercial Guidance Systems. For a time he was an associate lecturer at UCLA. Graduate work was done at American University, where Skeets earned a masters degree in mathematic statistics. He joined IBM and, in his own words, he had a career there that was "made in heaven." He spent three years in Tokyo as a project control manager, working on large computer systems. He then moved to Boca Raton, Florida, where he worked on small computer systems, saying it was there that the PC was developed. Later, Skeets spent three years in Munich and finally was back in Boca Raton, where he retired from IBM. He and his wife, Boe, still live in Florida.

The two met while Skeets was at Purdue University. Boe had a career as a teacher of second grade until their first child was born. They have three children, Michelle, Debbie, and James, who are all grown. Michelle has two children.

Skeets had much to share that day, and it was fun to see him and my brother Dick compare notes. Ultimately, Skeets called himself an engineer, and Dick explained that he was a scientist…pretty heavy company for Clyde and me who have great difficulty with very basic math formulas. Then, again, I was pretty good as a human resources director and Realtor, and Clyde was pretty good at running his own company.

Aunt "Bunny" in her usual sea of pink,
a color I was always fond of, as was my mother, Ann Douthart

Florence Alice "Daisy" Bauer Marten with Fred Marten

Helen Bauer with husband Lawrence in December 1954

Fred Daniel Marten and Florence Alice "Daisy" Marten in photos with twin sons Daniel Wayne "Danny" and Donald Alan "Donny," b. March 19, 1947

Back of photo reads: "Fred Marten and Rose Marie Bauer Sredzinski Marten after Marriage 1970"

Ruth "Gooney" Bauer Broholm and Al Broholm

Pictured left to right: Rose Marie Bauer Sredzinski/Sred with her husband Clark, and Ruth Bauer Broholm with her husband Al

WM. HALE THOMPSON
MAYOR

HERMAN N. BUNDESEN, M.D., Sc.D.
COMMISSIONER OF HEALTH

CITY OF CHICAGO
DEPARTMENT OF HEALTH

Notification of Birth Registration

This is to advise you that there is preserved under File No. 9116
in the Department of Health of Chicago, Illinois, a Record of Birth
of Florence Bauer Sex Female
Born on March 29, 1916 at 1752 North Hoyne Avenue
Name of father John Bauer
Name of mother Mary Kowalski 10550 Torrence Avenue
MAIDEN NAME ADDRESS
Birth attended by Rose Glombieski

Herman N. Bundesen M.D.
COMMISSIONER OF HEALTH

9116

STATE OF ILLINOIS
State Board of Health - Bureau of Vital Statistics
CERTIFICATE OF BIRTH
HEALTH DEPARTMENT'S RECORD CITY OF CHICAGO

GENEALOGY PURPOSES ONLY

1. PLACE OF BIRTH
County of COOK
City of CHICAGO No. 1752 N. Hoyne Ave
Registered No. 9116
2. FULL NAME OF CHILD Florence Bauer
3. Sex of Child F 5. Date of birth Mch 29 1916

FATHER	MOTHER
6. FULL NAME John Bauer	12. FULL MAIDEN NAME Mary Kowalski
7. RESIDENCE	13. RESIDENCE 1752 N. Hoyne Ave
8. COLOR	14. COLOR
9. AGE AT LAST BIRTHDAY 30 Years	15. AGE AT LAST BIRTHDAY 29 Years
10. BIRTHPLACE (State or Country) Austria	16. BIRTHPLACE (State or Country) Austria
11. OCCUPATION Laborer	17. OCCUPATION

18. Number of children born to this mother, including present birth 4
19. Number of children of this mother now living 4

20. CERTIFICATE OF ATTENDING PHYSICIAN OR MIDWIFE.*
I hereby certify that I attended the birth of this child, who was born alive at ....M., on the date above stated.
21. (Signature) Rose Golombiewski Midwife
Address 2034 Coblenz St
22. Give name added from a supplemental report
23. Filed Apr 21 1916 Registrar

GENEALOGY PURPOSES ONLY

lorence “Daisy” Bauer b. March 29, 1916, is the fourth of eight auer sisters. The question is: Is she a half-sister because these documents ndicate that John Bauer is the father, and the mother's name is Mary Kowalski, not Anna Lauff Bauer. The two documents relating to lorence's birth show two different addresses for Mary Kowalski.

GENEALOGY PURPOSES ONLY

STATE OF ILLINOIS
DEPARTMENT OF PUBLIC HEALTH
Division of Vital Statistics
Certificate of Birth
HEALTH DEPARTMENT'S RECORD CITY OF CHICAGO

1. PLACE OF BIRTH
Registration Dist. No. 3104
County of COOK
Registered No. 6793
City of CHICAGO No. 8055 Torrence Ave
2. FULL NAME OF CHILD Ruth Bauer
3. Sex of Child Fe 5. Date of birth Feb 2 1921

FATHER	MOTHER
6. FULL NAME John Bauer	12. FULL MAIDEN NAME Anna Kfolik
7. RESIDENCE 8055 Torrence Av	13. RESIDENCE 8055 Torrence Ave
8. COLOR Wh	14. COLOR Wh
9. AGE AT LAST BIRTHDAY 34 Years	15. AGE AT LAST BIRTHDAY 34 Years
10. BIRTHPLACE (State or Country) Austria	16. BIRTHPLACE (State or Country) Austria
11. OCCUPATION Tailor	17. OCCUPATION H.W.

18. Number of children born to this mother, including present birth 6
19. Number of children of this mother now living 6

20. CERTIFICATE OF ATTENDING PHYSICIAN OR MIDWIFE.*
I hereby certify that I attended the birth of this child, who was born alive at 7 am, on the date above stated.
21. (Signature) Marie Kosinska Midwife
Address 8348 Brandon Av
22. Give name added from a supplemental report
23. Filed MAR 04 1921 Registrar

STATE OF ILLINOIS COOK COUNTY } ss.

Certification of Birth

No. 6793

I, MICHAEL J. FLYNN, County Clerk of the County of Cook, in the State of Illinois, do hereby certify that Ruth Bauer of the Female sex, was born on February 2, 1921 at Chicago in the County of Cook and State of Illinois, all of which appears from the records and files in my office.

GIVEN under my hand and the seal of Cook County, at my office in the City of Chicago, this 10th day of January A. D. 19 46.

RECORDED February 9, 1921

lb-mp

Michael J. Flynn
COUNTY CLERK

(Void if the seal of Cook County is not impressed hereon.)

(Void unless the impressed signature of Michael J. Flynn appears above.)

[OVER]

Copy of Certificate of Birth, and Certification of Birth for Ruth “Gooney” Bauer b. February 2, 1921, the sixth of the eight Bauer sisters

---

Baptismal Certificate

Church of St.Kevins

The Records of this Church Certify, under date of Jan.2nd. 1931

to the Baptism of Ruth I , born Feb.2nd. 1921

of John Bauer and Anna Louff

Said Record is signed by Rev. F.T.Byrnes

with sponsors, Leonard Schoenfielt and Eileen McQuade

ST. KEVINS CHURCH SO. DEERING CHICAGO

Rev. E.B. McNally

Date, Sept 25-1935

Baptismal Certificate for Ruth “Gooney” Bauer b. February 2, 1921,

CERTIFICATE OF BIRTH

CERTIFICATE OF BIRTH

STATE OF ILLINOIS
DWIGHT H. GREEN, Governor
Department of Public Health
Division of Vital Statistics
ORIGINAL

1. PLACE OF BIRTH — County of Cook — Registration Dist. No. 3104 — 65997
Chicago — Primary Dist. No. 3104 — Street and Number 10550 Torrence Ave.

2. FULL NAME AT BIRTH: Lorraine Eileen Bauer

3. Sex: Female — 4. Twin, Triplet, or other? — 5. Number in order of birth — 6. Legitimate? Yes — 7. Date of birth: July 21 1924

FATHER
8. Full Name: John William Bauer
9. Residence at time of this birth: 10550 Torrence Ave.
10. Color: White — 11. Age at time of this birth: 37 yrs.
12. Birthplace (City or Place): Podalein — GERMANY
13. Occupation: Tailor

MOTHER
14. Full Maiden Name: Anna Lauff
15. Residence at time of this birth: 10550 Torrence Ave.
16. Color: White — 17. Age at time of this birth: 37 yrs.
18. Birthplace (City or Place): Podalein — GERMANY
19. Occupation: Housewife

20. (a) Number of children born to this mother at the time of and including this birth: 7 — (b) Number of children living at the time of and including this birth: 7

21. I HEREBY CERTIFY that I was the Attendant at this Birth.
Signed ... Address ... Date ...

IF SIGNATURE OF BIRTH ATTENDANT IS OBTAINABLE, AN AFFIDAVIT IS NOT REQUIRED.

STATE OF Illinois, County of Cook } ss.
I HEREBY CERTIFY that I have knowledge of the facts as stated in this RECORD OF BIRTH and believe them to be true; and that I am related to this person as Mother
Signature: Anna Bauer
Present Address: 3023 South Shore Drive–Chicago Illinois
Subscribed to, and sworn before me this 22 day of July 1942
Fred Whitcomb, Notary Public
SEAL — My commission expires November 27 1942

22. Filed AUG 5 194_ — Registrar
Post Office Address

Certificate of Birth for Lorraine Eileen "Lee" Bauer b. July 21, 1924, the seventh of the eight Bauer sisters

STATE OF ILLINOIS
DEPARTMENT OF PUBLIC HEALTH

DELAYED RECORD OF BIRTH
(REGISTERED AFTER SEVENTH BIRTHDAY)

County File No. 1527 — State File No. 201404 — ORIGINAL

1. PLACE OF BIRTH: City: Chicago — County: Cook — ILLINOIS
2. FULL NAME AT BIRTH: Ethel Irene Bauer — 3. DATE OF BIRTH: July 4 1918
4. If your name has been changed (except by marriage) enter the name you are now known by in this space: No change — 5. COLOR OR RACE: Caucasian — 6. SEX: Female
7. FATHER'S FULL NAME: John Bauer — 8. FATHER'S BIRTHPLACE: Austria
9. MOTHER'S MAIDEN NAME: Anna Louff — 10. MOTHER'S BIRTHPLACE: Austria
11. AFFIDAVIT: I hereby declare upon oath that the above statements are true to the best of my knowledge and belief.
a. Signed: Ethel Irene Bauer Weis — Address: 1139 N.E. 12 Ave. Fort Lauderdale, Florida
(SEAL) c. Subscribed and sworn to before me this 8th day of April 1968 at Ft. Lauderdale, Fla — Thelma H. Lanier, Notary Public, State of Florida at Large. My Commission Expires Jan. 13, 1971

APPLICANT! DO NOT WRITE BELOW THIS LINE

ABSTRACT OF SUPPORTING EVIDENCE

Document	Kind of document and date made	Information given in document
No. 1	Baptismal Record, St Kevin's Catholic Church, Chicago, Illinois. Baptized January 2, 1931	Age or birth date: July 4, 1918; Father: John Bauer; Mother: Anna Louff
No. 2	Insurance Record, Metropolitan Life Insurance Co. Policy #15 322 154A. Dated December 9, 1944	Age or birth date: July 4, 1918; Birthplace: Chicago, Illinois
No. 3	School Record, Board of Education Chicago, Illinois. Bright School - School Year 1923-1924	Age or birth date: July 4, 1918; Birthplace: Chicago, Illinois; Father: John Bauer; Mother: Anna ----
No. 4	Affidavit of Mother, Anna Bauer, 4705 Holiday Lane E. Fort Worth, Texas. Dated April 8, 1968	Age or birth date: July 4, 1918; Birthplace: Chicago, Illinois; Father: John Bauer; Mother: Anna Louff

ACCEPTED AND FILED AT SPRINGFIELD FOR THE STATE REGISTRAR OF VITAL STATISTICS
by Leo A. Ozier — Deputy State Registrar, on May 27, 1968
This record is valid only if it has been accepted by and filed with the State Registrar of Vital Statistics at Springfield, Illinois.
BUREAU OF STATISTICS — ILLINOIS DEPARTMENT OF PUBLIC HEALTH — SPRINGFIELD

Certificate of Delayed Record of Birth for Ethel Irene "Bunny" Bauer Weis b. July 4, 1918, the fifth of the eight Bauer sisters

Florence A. Marten

ROY — Mrs. Florence Alice Marten, 54, of 5211 S. 2375 W., died Monday at St. Benedict's Hospital after an extended illness.

Mrs. Marten was born March 29, 1916, in Chicago, Ill., a daughter of John and Anna Louff Bauer.

On May 23, 1943, she was married to Fred D. Marten in Chicago.

She had lived in Roy since 1965, and formerly resided in San Bernardino, Calif., and Chicago. She was educated in Chicago.

She was a member of the Lutheran Church.

Surviving are her husband, two sons, Daniel Wayne Marten, Ogden; Donald Alan Marten, Riverdale; one grandchild, six sisters, Miss Esther Bauer, Mrs. Helen Mann, both of Bristol, Ind.; Mrs. Ethel Weiss, Fort Lauderdale, Fla.; Mrs. Alan (Ruth) Broholm, Mrs. Joseph (Lorraine) Martin, Mrs. Clarke (Rose Marie) Sred, all of Fort Worth, Tex.

Funeral services will be held Wednesday at 8:30 a.m. at Lindquist and Sons Colonial Chapel with Rev. Dale B. Johnson of Our Savior's Lutheran Church officiating. There will be no public viewing.

Entombment will be in the Greenwood Memorial Park Mausoleum in Fort Worth, Tex. Donations may be made to the Cancer Society.

STATE OF UTAH
COUNTY OF WEBER
This is to Certify that the above Death Certificate is a true and correct copy of the record on file in this office.
20th day of Sept 1972
BY: Shirley Hinder, M.D.

857-HH — UTAH STATE DIVISION OF HEALTH — 143
CERTIFICATE OF DEATH

Deceased: Rose Marie MARTEN — Sex: Female — Date of death: September 18, 1972
Race: White — Age: 45 — Date of birth: Nov. 7, 1926 — County of death: Weber
City, town, or location of death: Roy — Inside city limits: yes — 5211 So. 2375 West, Roy, Utah
State of birth: Illinois — Citizen of what country: U.S.A. — Married — Surviving spouse: Fred D. Marten
Social Security Number: 359-16-4655 — Usual occupation: Bookkeeper — Kind of business or industry: Bookkeeping
Residence — State: Utah — County: Weber — City, town or location: Roy — Inside city limits: yes — Street and number: 5211 So. 2375 West
Father: John Bauer — Mother: Anna Lauff
Informant: Fred D. Marten — Mailing address: 5211 So. 2375 West, Roy, Utah
Death was caused by: Immediate cause: Carbon monoxide poisoning
Autopsy: Yes — If yes were findings considered in determining cause of death: Yes
Accident, suicide, homicide or undetermined: Suicide — Date of injury: 9-18-72 — Hour: found 4:00p — How injury occurred: Hose from exhaust into car.
Injury at work: No — Place of injury: Garage — Location: 5211 So. 2375 W., Roy, Utah
Certification — Medical Examiner: 9-18-72 — 4:45 p.m.
James T. Weston, M.D. — M.D. — Date signed: 9-18-72
Office of Medical Examiner, 44 Medical Drive, Salt Lake City, Utah 84113
Burial–Removal — Greenwood Cemetery — Fort Worth, Texas
Sept. 21, 1972 — Lindquist & Sons Mortuary, 3408 Washington Blvd. Ogden, Utah
Shirley Hinder, M.D. — September 20, 1972

Utah State Division of Health, Certificate of Death for Rose Marie Marten, died September 18, 1972. Cause of death was "Carbon Monoxide Poisoning — hose from exhaust into car." The death was officially

futur

Where we go from here…

…is anyone's guess.

Throughout this book I've been addressing the subject of finding fathers. Having little contact with my father during childhood, I often found myself in the company of other men, sometimes relatives, sometimes not, who served as what I call father figures. As an adult of seventy-two years, I have reflected on the lives of men I have admired and who have to some greater or lesser degree influenced the formation of my character and behavior as a father. My uncles David Savage and Victor Lucas, and my great uncle John Benko (see page 491) were supportive of youngsters such as myself when they had no children of their own. Hugh Purkey (see page 275) was a man of quiet dignity. His son, Glenn Purkey, my cousin, was a handsome, down-to-earth man who served his country as a pilot with distinction during World War II. My grandfather Charlie Davis never really amounted

fa

Beau Davis Dylan Malara Taylor Davis

Ross Malara, Clyde Davis and Codie Davis at Greenview Cemetery, Fairmount, Illinois, *May 15, 2004*

e

thers

to much in respect to worldly achievements or possessions; however, I credit him with remaining in a marital relationship for some fifty-eight years.

Even after all I have learned about my own father, in no way have I any rancor or bitterness toward him. I know little of the circumstances of his childhood or the forces that shaped him as a man. I do know from the many photographs I have what he looked like at varying times in his life. Those photographs also reveal his association with others, friends, and many family members. I have been able to establish, somewhat, a timeline from his birth on June 3, 1907, to his death on November 13, 1974. I am familiar with his employment record, the places he's worked and when he's worked. I know of his female companions. I've learned of his physical ailments and what eventually led to his passing.

Most importantly though, I've learned that he was a pleasant man who liked to be among people, and yet his greatest failing was not being able to sustain a relationship with those who should have been closest to him — his children.

As I stated earlier in this book (see page 138), there is "a strain of recklessness, a spirit of adventure," that the Davises have "always been willing to test the limits of social mores." Each of us — my father, my brother, my son, myself — embodies those traits. We are all risk takers, courting the chance of getting hurt, or losing it all.

Each of us had to first survive or avoid being consumed by our misadventures and risk taking. My father went to prison, deserted his family, and never managed to overcome his drinking. My son broke free of drug addiction. For my part, I overreached time and again. Mostly aggressive, at times lucky, frequently called reckless, ever seeking a better life, I paid the price of the accompanying years of stress. Then I retired. Each of us as fathers had to give up, to some degree, an aspect of his personal freedom for the welfare of his offspring. Some come to accept this responsibility, others do not. Why not, I don't think I shall ever really know.

The father I found and defined in the pages of this book was not the ideal father, but *he was my father*. A comforting thought, one affording me an inner peace. In my search for my father I've also been deeply enriched by the family that has evolved around him, past and present.

It's September 2011, and summer is quickly coming to a close, as is the completion of this book. Within its pages I'm attempting to gather my thoughts, to summarize, in some meaningful way what I have managed to contribute and record of the family I've shaped.

Scott

Scott Ryan Davis, 2004

Scott, my brother's only son, seemed to be the least likely to become a father. He had established himself as a teacher of biology and was living alone. In December of 2002, at age thirty, he wrote, "By the way, I still haven't found Mrs. Right yet, but I'm looking and I'll let you know when I do." Eight years later we find him married. He and his wife Michelle had a daughter, Belle Marie, born June 4, 2008. Surprise. Surprise. Most notable about this turn of events is how prepared Scott was to move into the role of father. They have since had a second child, a son, Grant Ryan, born April 27, 2010.

Scott and Michelle count their blessings as "abundant." Scott is in his sixteenth year of teaching high school science in Oregon, "… and is blessed to know he is right where the Lord wants him." Michelle, is a stay-at-home mom and a pastor in their church. And, even with a growing family they manage to do a great deal of traveling both here and abroad.

As he says on his Facebook page, "It's the Davis version of 'The Amazing Race.'" In one short year, he managed to spend New Year's Eve at Disneyland in Anaheim, California, followed by numerous trips up and down the West Coast as well as to the heartland. He visited Glacier National Park; Dollywood in Tennessee; Sitka National Historic Park in Alaska; Lima, Peru; concerts in Chicago; and fish dinners in Seattle.

When questioned about his ability to keep his job by one of his friends on Facebook, he replied that it was Saturday, and that is a good day to do mileage runs to California and back.

Top: Ross and Dylan with their father, Phil, at Turnberry Country Club, Aventura, Florida

My two oldest grandchildren, Ross and Codie, have entered adulthood. Their lives have taken quite divergent paths with differing outcomes today. And there is no certainty in predicting that their past performance will be an indicator of future success.

Ross

Ross completed his first year, 2006, at Florida Atlantic University in Boca Raton, Florida. Common to many freshmen students, he struggled academically. He returned his third semester determined to do better. In October 2007, Ross received the shocking news that his lifetime best friend, attending another university, had fatally overdosed on heroin. This event was emotionally overwhelming and coupled with a lackluster return to academics, eventually resulted in Ross leaving school mid-semester. Ross became deeply engaged in the passing of his friend and the circumstances surrounding his death. While reaching out to the young man's grief-stricken family and friends, he provided all support and solace.

Of all my grandchildren, none has a stronger sense of family than Ross. I'd like to be the one to take credit for this admirable trait; however, I believe its existence is attributable to Ross's father, Philip Malara. Perhaps being Italian has something to do with it. Whatever its origin, no one is more genuinely interested in or affectionately involved with and caring for those closest to him than Ross. Ross loves his parents, is a true big brother to Dylan, enjoys hanging with Duke and his grandmother Kay, helping his Nana, and being with as many of his aunts, uncles, cousins, and dog "Shocky" as often as possible.

As I mentioned, if Ross is about anything, it's family and friends. Unfortunately, over the past several years his mother and father have grown apart and now live separated from one another and are drifting into divorce. These years have been economically challenging for us all, including the Malaras. Against this backdrop of a disintegrating family, Ross has seen his continuing education as a series of starts and stops. In the fall of 2009, after a few classes at Manchester Community College in Connecticut, Ross enrolled at the Culinary Institute of America, in Hyde Park, New York,

Ross, Viet Nam, January 4, 2008

believing, that he had finally found his calling as a future chef. He managed to complete six months of study while getting really good grades. However, like a moth drawn to a flame, and despite my advising him to concentrate on his studies and remain in school, Ross could not resist the draw of a conflicted family and the every day strife associated with unwinding its affairs. It was too much for Ross to handle, family and school, and he withdrew from school in July of 2010. He is now planning to work in a kitchen at a local restaurant with hopes of returning to CIA in the near future.

Codie

In the spring of 2006, Codie asked his grandparents if they would accompany him on a tour of several eastern colleges and universities, namely Yale, MIT, Princeton, Cambridge, Brown, and Boston University. He had applied to Stanford, UCLA, and the University of California at Berkeley as well. Of course, he fell in love with Princeton and it became his number one choice, but ultimately he was wait-listed and ended up selecting the University of California, Berkeley.

Codie spent the last four years at Cal Berkeley and graduated in May 2010 with a Bachelor of Science degree in civil engineering, with academic honors. He was a member of the Sigma Chi fraternity while on campus. During the summer of 2008, he worked in San Francisco as an intern for the Turner Construction Company. Given the economic climate in the summer of 2009, Codie took advantage of the opportunity to study abroad and attended Cambridge University in Great Britain. He traveled extensively throughout

Cole with his son, Codie, discussing a house foundation concrete pour in June 2008.

Europe during that summer. Not surprisingly, his grades have been all As and Bs both at Berkeley and Cambridge. After graduation from Berkeley, Codie secured a return position with Turner Construction Company for the summer of 2010 (see his letter of June 17, 2010, on page 675).

Codie, seeking a Master of Science in construction engineering and management, has been accepted at Stanford University, California and begins his program of study in September 2010. With his eyes always on the prize, Codie can amaze one with his perseverance and tenacity.

He, like the other children, was given the opportunity to play a musical instrument. Codie chose the piano at an early age,

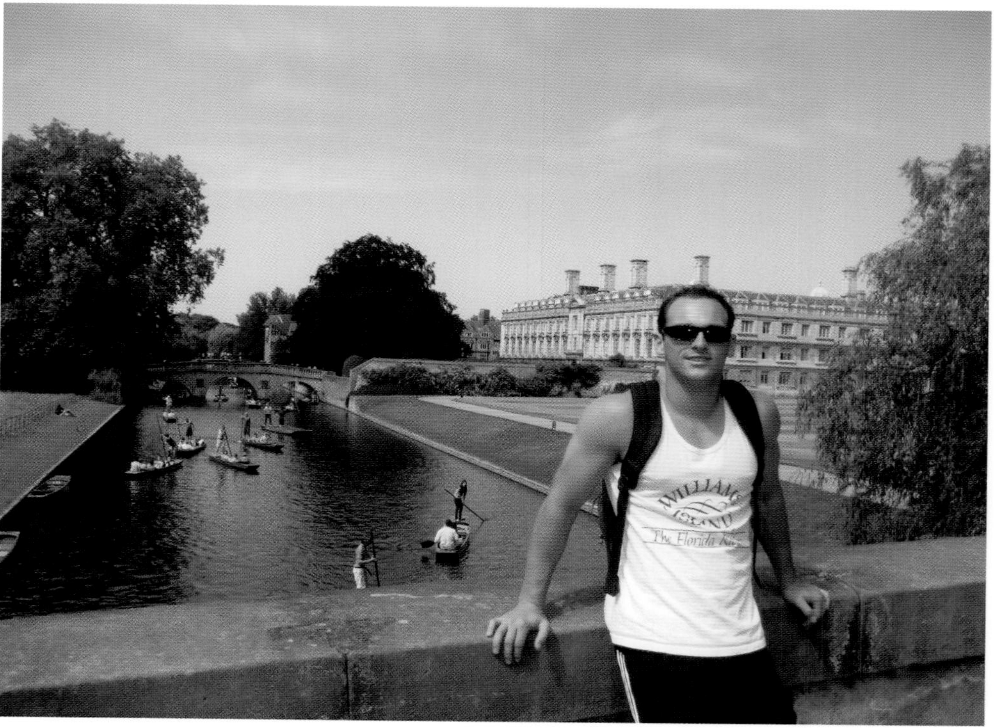

Codie Davis on July 1, 2009, with boats punting on the River Cam at Cambridge, England. The building on the right is King's College. This area is known as The Backs. Codie took advantage of the economic downturn to enroll in three courses at Cambridge for the summer.

practicing religiously and became quite accomplished by the time he went off to college. However, his musical interest turned to rock concerts, fraternity parties, and football games. He loves a good time and is happy to share his pleasure with all 774 friends who visit his Facebook page.

Taylor

Taylor Davis with his mother Tammi in Palo Alto, California, November 6, 2010, on the occasion of the Arizona State vs. Stanford football game. The front of Taylor's highly prized 2007 Ford Mustang GT Premium, a 380-horsepower beast, can be seen to the left.

Between the two oldest and the two youngest grandsons is Taylor. This fall Taylor returns as a junior at Sonoma State University. Being the middle child among my grandsons, Taylor moves freely among his brothers and cousins as easily as he does among his peers. As a youngster, he was something of a thrill-seeker, and, like his father, had managed to do some physical harm to himself as a result of his misadventures. Also, like his father he has a love of transport. His 2007 Ford Mustang is kept in immaculate condition. He's obsessive about its care. It is not unusual for Taylor, when leaving the vehicle in a parking lot, to ask the attendant, "Where do you want it parked?" and then promptly parking the vehicle himself in the designated area, thus insuring there will be no damage.

Surprisingly, Taylor also joined a fraternity at Sonoma State though he lives off campus with his roommate, whom he met the first day of school at orientation. Academically, he's a steady and solid middle of the road performer. He's talked of going on for a masters degree after his four years at SSU and is interested in the field of psychology. He benefits from the nearness of his older brother Codie in San Francisco. They spend frequent weekends together and often drive from northern California to their home in San Diego and back again on school holidays. Like his brother Codie, Taylor is athletic but not an athlete. He did play lacrosse in high school. Both work out with weights, as does their dad to this day, and Taylor still skateboards to his classes at SSU.

Since I have elected to financially support each of my grandsons in their continuing education, a fair amount of contact and dialogue about fiscal management ensues between us. As one might suspect, some are more buttoned up than others in managing their funds. Taylor, though not the best performer at this task initially, is always willing to learn how to do better and eagerly seeks my advice and counsel. We enjoy a wonderful personal and working relationship. It's been a pleasure to watch him grow on so many different levels.

When staying at his home in Encinitas, I enjoy our early morning doughnut runs together to VG's Bakery, on Aberdeen Drive in nearby Cardiff By Sea, while the rest of the family sleeps in. Thankfully, I don't spend much time with him at school sharing his penchant for frequenting every Taqueria in town. Or so it seems when reviewing his spending habits and budget.

Dylan

Dylan Malara with his Dad in Glastonbury, Connecticut, on October 3, 2004

Dylan, Ross's younger brother, at age nine, wrote a story in school about himself. His nickname was "monster Malara," and, after a short description of his pets and some details about his physical appearance, he stated, "My talent is football," and, "My hero is my dad and my football coach and his name is coach Hans." He continued with, "My hobby is football." "My favorite channel on TV is ESPN." And, should we not get the message this young man was imparting, he added, "I want to be a pro football player when I grow up. I love football a lot and that's why I want to be a pro football player when I grow up. I would live in New York because I love the New York Giants."

Dylan played recreational football for the town of Glastonbury, Connecticut, youth football Association (GYFA) age seven through fourteen. He honed his skills at summer training camps and went on to play football in high school for the Glastonbury Blue Devils. He also spent a fair amount of time on basketball and lacrosse teams.

Dylan graduated high school in May 2010. As indicated above, Dylan was more interested and engaged in sports than his studies, and did not choose to seek college entry in the fall of 2010.

At an early age, nine or ten years, I observed Dylan playing with his utensils at the dinner table while waiting to be served. He was tapping out a very rapid and musically pleasant rhythm. I remarked to his grandmother that Dylan seemed to have talent, and, with his birthday approaching, we rushed out to buy him a set of drums. Little did we realize that long after his drums began to gather dust in the basement, he would pick up the musical beat in his last year in high school. In his art class he demonstrated a talent for drawing.

Life That I'm Livin'

Yeah!
This is Dee Mal
Here to tell you my story
Bout the life that I'm livin'

Chorus: 2x

Everybody listen this is Dee Mal spitting
Here to rap you a song about the life that I'm livin'
Here to tell you a thing or two about who I am
Because when times get tough I put a mic in my hand

Started writing my lyrics in June 2009
Helped me get stuff off my chest, helped me free my mind
From all these problems at home, my whole family was crying
Till the day that I die I will be writing my rhymes
Yeah uh I am surrounded by depression
My mother, father, brother, say they're not but they're pretending
Yeah that's why my mom had to leave
She couldn't take all the fighting that's why she drank heavily
Uh now we're selling our house so finally I see
I gotta move on and follow my dreams
Go and swallow my pride and then I will realize
That all this pain I feel has changed me inside
Has made me a better man that stands strong
'Cuz with these hands I will create some great songs
Produce my own beats, take over the industry
My name is Dee Mal, I'm the best MC

Chorus: 2x

Everybody listen this is Dee Mal spitting
Here to rap you a song about the life that I'm livin'
Here to tell you a thing or two about who I am
Because when times get tough I put a mic in my hand

I'm from the suburbs with rhymes that are superb
Just waiting for the day when I will finally be heard
Then I will rise to the top and I will never be stopped
'Cuz at the end of the day, you'll say I'm better then Pac
But I will not get shot, I ain't got hate in my heart
And Yeah I'm ready to start recording music that will fly to the top of the charts
I paint a picture like art
That's why all you haters say that I'm the light when it's dark
'Cuz I be guiding the way, so they can see better days
No matter how hard I work I will remember to pray
Just an ordinary kid make mistakes take risks
But I've been blessed by the Lord with this gift to spit
Separating from my grade everybody judgmental
So all I need now is a page and a pencil
Writing down these verses Yeah I'm memorizing every word
Doing what I gotta do my flow is so absurd

Chorus: 2x

Everybody listen this is Dee Mal spitting
Here to rap you a song about the life that I'm livin'
Here to tell you a thing or two about who I am
Because when times get tough I put a mic in my hand

I need to start thinking about what's right and what's wrong
Trying to figure out my life and what I need to stay strong
Because all of these lies, they got me feelin paralyzed
With this feelin inside, see the tears that I cry
See the pain fall from my eyes, full of shame I'm full of pride
So I hold my head high, till the day that I will die
Seventeen years old story untold of a white boy with flow
That will show all of you who probably didn't know
So listen up silence be quiet unless you want some violence
Then rewind it so all of you haters can start to recognize it
'Cuz I know that I am tough but these times are just so rough
And in my mind I'm not enough, I take my time I never rush
Keep on writing my lyrics and I will be free
I just want a chance to prove exactly what I can be
'Cuz I got motivation and no longer am I waiting
I'm just proving to myself and all of you that I'm the greatest

Chorus: 2x

Dear Duke,
I finished my first solo song recently and I thought you'd like to see the lyrics and hear how it came out. The song is called "Life that I'm Livin'." I hope you enjoy it.
Love,
Dee Mal (my rapper name)

The above, along with a CD, on which Dee Mal (Dylan) performs the song, was received by me May 331, 2010

Dylan Davis Malara celebrating his graduation from Glastonbury High School, Glastonbury, CT, June 18, 2010

But it was to be a poetry class that brought the creative in Dylan to the surface. Today, he keeps a journal and writes musical verse, which he performs to the beat of rap. His music has been played over the radio (see page 669) and has been recognized as artistically worthy. His rapper name is Dee Mal. There is now even talk about auditioning for study at the Berklee College of Music in Boston, Massachusetts. The school does not have a football team.

I don't know much about football, and I'm not musically inclined. As Dylan's grandfather, I do know he is a sweet young man who favors sweets. He loves fresh fruit — sliced mango with lemon prepared by his grandmother is a favorite treat of his — candy, ice cream, and vanilla cake with strawberries for special occasions. He doesn't have a mean bone in his body. Not necessarily the best of traits for a football player.

Both Dylan and Ross have set school aside for the moment. They are in Glastonbury, Connecticut, gravitating between parents, each working and each spending time with their father on his field of dreams, volunteer coaching Glastonbury's town football teams. The two boys, who have played for him in the past and assisted him in his coaching duties, still show up for weekly practices and games on Sunday. They play golf with their father and go to New York Yankee games together. Sports have been a constant bond among them over the years.

As Dylan turns eighteen, he is busy selecting the car that I give each of my grandsons on this special birthday. This begins a period (eighteen-to-twenty-nine-year-olds) described in the *New York Times Magazine*, August 22, 2010, as "The Post-Adolescent, Pre-Adult, Not-Quite-Decided Life Stage," when they, each in his own way, will try "to bring their identities into focus."

My challenge, at age seventy-two, is to be patient during this time and allow them the freedom to seek their futures, ever ready to assist in any way I can.

Beau

Many times I have been asked if, during my genealogical search, I have ever found the source of my talent. By that, I think others believe there is some sort of genetic link. I have, over the years, gone to and fro in my mind between my artistic ability being God-given or a product of environment, culture, and social circumstance, coupled with interest and application of one's effort.

Whatever the source, I'm happy to see artistic expression rise in my two youngest grandsons.

Beau with his electric bass guitar playing a few chords to Duke's iPod tunes, September 23, 2009, in Encinitas, California.

Beau, now sixteen years of age, always seemed to love critters — a nature boy at heart, fascinated with the complexities, the intricacies, the oddities and simple beauty he discovers daily. Beau, for most of his young life, has marched pretty much to his own drummer. He is independent and very confident, yet loving and sensitive.

Sports have not been a primary interest of Beau's; however, he did play lacrosse from kindergarten through junior high. When his grades suffered in school, his mother withdrew him from lacrosse. He has taken golf lessons and has become quite good at it. Like his brothers, he has spent summers at horse camp and is an accomplished rider. He skateboards to this day (mostly the long board), plays online video games, enjoys swimming in his pool with friends, fishing, and hiking.

Over the years I've enjoyed watching Beau's character be defined. Quirky may not be the appropriate word, but it's close enough in describing the interests of this grandson of mine over the years. He loved to dress up, especially for occasions like Halloween (capes were a favorite of his), or family events, wearing a sport coat and tie. In the fifth grade, he was invited by a girl to join the "San Bieguito Cotillion," a club involving dancing and the teaching of good manners. You had to dress up, which appealed to Beau. He

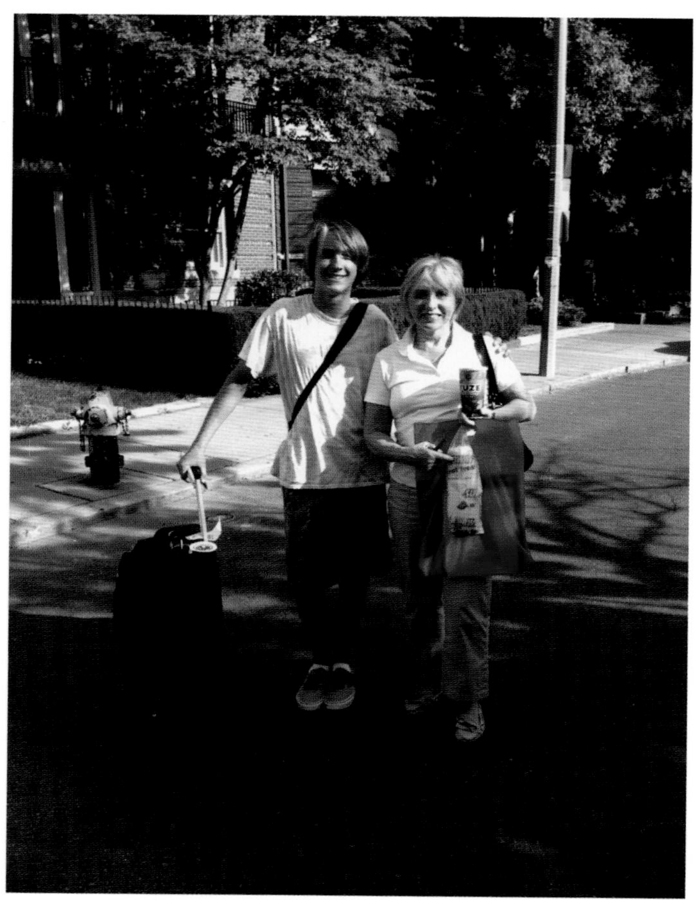

Beau Davis with his grandmother Kay in front of Berklee School of Boston, August 28, 2011, following a five-day summer course in music production

liked it so much that he considered becoming a paid chaperone associated with the Cotillion, much like his brother Codie, who became a counselor in training at horseback-riding camp.

He has, over the years, developed a "mature palate," and likes pepperchinies, guacamole, Mexican food, and coffee. He also likes to cook.

At age eight, while attending the Montessori Mission Bay School in La Jolla, Beau began playing the piano and has continued to play all these years. He wanted to switch instruments a few years ago and play the bass guitar; however, his mother insisted that he continue with the piano. He now plays both, still taking lessons, and has performed on the bass guitar in a band.

For the longest time, he wanted to be a marine biologist. Since then, he has sort of morphed from nature into the creative arts of music and cinematography. A year ago, rather than accept a car at age sixteen from his parents, Beau requested a video camcorder. He has already scripted, directed, and shot a short film that he submitted in a school competition. Out of sixteen films, his won first prize for best picture, "Subtropic Thunder." Through a serendipitous meeting with a film director and producer from Los Angeles, he has been given the chance to intern on the set of film and TV productions just prior to the start of the fall 2010 school year.

Beau continues to surprise by signing up for yoga as a physical education requirement (rather than weightlifting), claiming there are more girls in a yoga class than weightlifting. He now "dresses down," doesn't take his cell phone to school, wants his parents to buy a smaller house, and is generally offended by ostentatious displays of wealth. He likes old, beat-up cars and wants one day to own a used Mercedes. His father has told him that they don't come with airbags and are unsafe. Beau's reply is that you can put them in an old car, even though the installation could easily cost more than the old Mercedes. His trips from San Diego to Los Angeles and back regarding his film interning have caused him to reconsider getting a driver's license.

He has just returned from a three-week trip abroad as a student international ambassador, visiting Greece, France, Italy, Austria, and Germany.

He still wears his hair long.

Fathers Found

When Codie was applying to Princeton, my business partner and longtime friend and former Princeton graduate, Fred Mann, wrote him a letter of recommendation. In anticipation of writing the letter, Fred suggested that it would be helpful if Codie provided him some background on his high school history, extracurricular activities, and other aspects of his life with which Fred was not entirely familiar. Codie responded to Fred's request. The letter was written and within it, Fred wrote, "Once having seen his remarkable record of achievement, I was, to use contemporary vernacular, 'blown away.' I told Codie that from my standpoint, his admission to Princeton was all but assured — measuring his credentials against my own relatively meager ones more than a half-century earlier. But Codie would hear none of that." "Fred," he said, "I am competing against thousands of other students with equal or superior records. Yes, my grades are good and I've worked hard. But so have many others. Perhaps where I may be a little different is that I take nothing for granted, and I know that success in life requires more than high marks and a long list of accomplishments. It takes the setting of ambitious goals and doing everything in your power to reach them. I've tried to do this throughout my high school years. I intend to do it when I'm in college — hopefully, at Princeton. And, I plan to do it when I'm through with my academic training and am out in the real world."

These words spoken by this young man, my grandson, may be the genesis of all I've been searching for in trying to distill the meaning of fatherhood. Is it about "the setting of ambitious goals and doing everything in your power to reach them?" Realizing the responsibility that comes with fatherhood certainly requires the setting of lofty goals that ensure your offspring will have a better life than you. The danger is that, over the years, we may have created a culture of dependency and entitlement, a too-loved-to-fail environment that often allows irresponsible behavior to be excused away and even, at times, seemingly rewarded.

I grew up in an age when the father was supposedly the "rock" of a family. He was called the "breadwinner." Now, some are called "stay-at-home dads," or surrogate fathers. There are still too many absentee fathers. For my part, I've done the best I can to do some good and better the lives of others who will follow me, while wearing the mantle of fatherhood.

At some point the marriages in our family stopped happening — we've had four with our children. Of course, they will start once again with our grandchildren after two decades or so of growth and schooling. We are fast closing in on that time. I am blessed to know these fine young men, and look forward to a growing family built on their shoulders, around their goals and aspirations.

It's been a wonderful life and if it ended tomorrow, I would thank my maker for all that has been given to me. Perhaps, during that time, as I mentioned in the beginning of this book, I've managed to leave a few footprints in the sands of time. Now, the future fathers I so love will carry on, surrounded by a family that I had a small, but hopefully, important role in shaping and sustaining.

6/17/2010

Dearest Duke and Grandma,

No words could describe what I have experienced throughout my four years at UC Berkeley. However, I was able to translate some thoughts and memories into words, which follow.

As a result of my collegiate experience, I feel forever indebted to you both. It took years of forethought and investment to be able to send me to one of the world's top institutions. You have always had the best intentions for me, as well as the heart to provide your family with a better quality of life than would otherwise be possible. There could be no better gift. I am eager to show you both what I am capable of now that I possess a respectable degree and a sense of what I hope to achieve in my lifetime.

The opportunity to attend college has placed me in an advantageous position and I feel so privileged to have the support that I have received from you both my entire life. Our relationship has developed into one of example. I can proudly say that your influences have made me a better man and I could only hope to bestow such a positive presence in my own children's and grandchildren's lives.

The environment I integrated myself into produced relationships that I will undoubtedly possess for the remainder of my life. The ambitions and habits of those that surrounded me matched my own, which resulted in the marriage of our purpose and method. This fostered a healthy atmosphere in which I found myself a second home. I never thought Berkeley would be such a tremendous fit for me, but I'm overjoyed that it proved otherwise. Inside and outside of the classroom, there was always some form of maturing and personal growth going on. The fast-paced life teaches you how to milk every opportunity you have, whether it be to try and win over that girl that keeps studying you from the across the party, or to win over the recruiter standing at the Turner booth at the career fair.

Berkeley will always be a part of me, and I left a bit of myself there the day I graduated. I made it without submitting to the hippy cults, but rather was initiated as a fraternity brother. Who knew? Joining a fraternity was the best decision I made while at Berkeley. When I think of Berkeley, I think of Sigma Chi. It gave me the opportunity to sharpen my social skills and push my comfort zone. It taught me how to hold leadership positions and balance a healthy lifestyle. It forged networks that run as deep as the Grand Canyon. The sum was greater than the parts, and that's hard to come by.

College is a time for a transformation from dependent to independent. This transition would not have been as smooth if it weren't for your generosity and support. I thank you until the end of days and aim to make you as proud as proud can be. I have only begun, but have already done so much. 15,000 pictures from my time at Berkeley will forever remind me of the troubles and the triumphs. I have laughed countless times and made some incredible stories. I have no regrets looking back over my time at Cal. It is impossible to do everything, but what I did do has set me up for a fulfilling life full of good people and success. Thank you, thank you, thank you, and thank you. Here's to the best grandparents and friends a grandson could ask for.

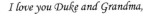

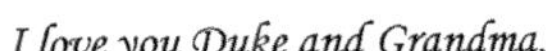
I love you Duke and Grandma,

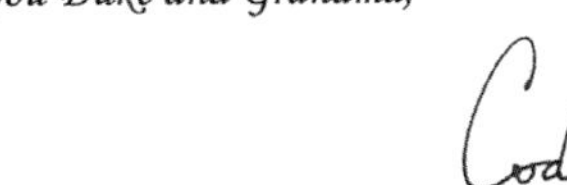

Kay, Codie and Clyde Davis on June 12, 2011, at Codie's graduation from Stanford with a Master of Science in Civil and Environmental Engineering degree

Epilogue

Lessons Learned

Nearing the end of this venture I reflect on the many rich and meaningful experiences I've enjoyed, and concurrently, on the unexpected, asking myself, "Would I do it again?" Probably not!

People die on you.

People aren't as enamored with their shared family history as you are. Many are private persons who don't wish to share with others, especially, with those whom they don't know, haven't met, or don't care about. Some bear long-seated family grudges and simply don't like one another.

Many are suspicious of your motives, suspecting you may have a hidden agenda, that you are seeking information for ulterior purposes, and perhaps are out to steal their identity in order to defraud them. Such is our world today. There are, of course, much more sophisticated, high-tech ways to steal one's identity than my low-tech efforts to establish their place in the family tree.

I'm struck by the number of people who have said, "I'm a very private person," who chose not to share personal information, with a "not that I have anything to hide," often added to their comment. In this era of Facebook, YouTube and Twitter, privacy is becoming less so, certainly among the younger generations. A trend too late for me to benefit from.

In an exchange of correspondence with my editor Sharon Carmack, I raised the issue of privacy, permissions, and copyright. She, it turns out, is a writing coach for nonfiction books, as well as family histories, and also advises on issues of privacy and permissions. She responded in a letter dated March 24, 2010 (a copy of which follows), expressing deep concerns that I should get permissions to write about living people in my book. I found this very troubling — not that I hadn't felt concern far earlier — and wrote back to her. In my reply to her, which follows, I felt the need to explain how this book, and my thoughts and feelings about the process, have evolved.

Often I've been faulted for not remaining in touch, running afoul of relatives long neglected by me. A cousin, quite ill and fearing his passing was imminent, who I was attempting to comfort on the phone, abruptly mentioned that I had allowed "my money to get in the way" of our relationship. My wife assures me that we are very comfortable with our financial well-being, and it is they who find our wealth an issue, especially when it's not shared more freely with them, or when their requests for financial aid are not always met, or are not at the levels they expected (or hoped for). Money, and having it, has its problems.

Then there are the promises not kept. I realize folks have busy lives. I'm certainly not, nor is the publication of my book, at the top of their list of priorities. I can have the most wonderful conversation with somone on the phone. I can fill them in on my project and promise them a copy of the book (at no expense to them). They often agree, at my request, to forward additional material, documents, photographs, etc. Despite my follow-up letter of confirmation, including FedEx return envelope with my account number to cover any expense, they fail to comply — I hate when that happens.

Speaking of promises not kept, it is I who have, time and again, failed to complete this book as promised (see page 153).

People die. Have I mentioned that before?

They divorce.

Relatives whom you may not have contact with for decades want to keep it that way.

Folks don't always want to be sociable.

Attempting to write about one's children in a balanced way while omitting their faults was a task I was not prepared for as a father, particularly with their mother looking over my shoulder.

Attempting to be inclusive of those living an aberrant, dysfunctional lifestyle was, also, particularly challenging. Condoning such behavior was to be avoided, but always with compassion and understanding, realizing we are all not "cut from the same cloth."

Not all one's relatives are necessarily folks you would enjoy hanging out with.

Clyde Davis
10 Tatomuck Circle
Pound Ridge, NY 10576

25 March 2010
Sharon DeBartolo Carmack
Warren, Carmack & Associates
358 South 700 East, #603
Salt Lake City, UT 84102

Dear Sharon,

Your letter of 24 March 2010 was quite disturbing. It's a letter that I have been dreading receiving for some time. I was just never sure who the person and/or authority would be sending it to me. The issue you raise of privacy for the living and their lives I've profiled in my book, to some lesser or greater degree, has been a matter of great concern to me.

When I first began this book, I simply wanted to find the father I had barely known. As I proceeded, his story began to evolve, mostly articulated by those who knew him and from what few artifacts I could find. I began to understand that I was searching for more than simply the raw facts of my father's existence. His birth, childhood, employment history, date of death, and place in the family tree, as it developed, seemed not to be enough for me. I struggled to know the man and, of course, my mother, and others in our family. Along the way, a strictly genealogical effort became something more than a "tree." It became a family history, past, present and future. It was to include the deceased and the living.

To a very large extent, the book became autobiographical. Painfully shy most of my life, I have never been one to seek the limelight or appear center stage, so it was quite atypical of me to speak so much of myself in the book. But, as time passed, I began to use the book not only as a repository for my genealogical findings, but as something of a vessel that I could pour my heart and soul into. The book was to become an expression of my artistic capabilities, as well as the sentiments and experiences of my life and the family I had managed to create. I suppose there has been a need to tell my story, as you put it "warts and all" — some, anyway, but not all. My intention was to do a book that was true to the grit and grain of the family I was a part of.

Privacy and copyright issues first became a consideration of mine when I began receiving photographs from family members of those deceased. Within those photographs there were living members of the family and even individuals who were not family. I wondered how I would ever be able to use these photographs, because seeking permission from all who were pictured was almost an impossible task for this project, which I envisioned as more graphics than text. There are over 950 photos, and over 1,500 graphics altogether in the book (photos, charts, diagrams, and documents). Having spent a long career in advertising and having taken thousands of photographs of individuals, I know only too well the permissions one must have to reproduce an individual's image, especially if it's being used for financial gain. I, and corporations I have represented, have had to defend ourselves against legal claims for mistakenly not having secured proper releases.

In addition to the issue of photography, several years ago I began to realize that there were those in the genealogy field who frowned heavily upon giving detailed information about individuals in family trees, such as full name, birth or date of death, and the address of any living person. And though I've secured much of this sort of information from living relatives, informing them that I was doing a book and would include them in the book, I never specifically asked that they sign a release or verify what could or could not be said about them.

With considerable thought, I decided to put my head down and plow forward with my project of building a family tree while telling my story, hoping I could stay within legal boundaries. My principal position was that the book was primarily a work of research, reflecting my personal opinions and data I freely compiled. I never planned, once the book was published, to sell copies of it. My intent, expressed to all I contacted, was to give each of them a free copy — totally at my expense. Another desire of mine was to contribute a copy of the book to each and every library and archival center that I visited in states where members of my family lived, as well as the Library of Congress. I have even entertained the idea of publishing the book on the Internet. Because the book was a work of research and was not being produced for financial gain, I felt that I did not have to be paranoid about privacy issues. In this age of information being so freely exchanged through media such as Google, Twitter, Facebook, and YouTube on the Internet, it does seem a little ridiculous to keep people from gaining information from my book when it's so easily found elsewhere.

Sharon, you should know that though my immediate family has long been aware of my working on a book, I have not shown any part of it to any of them, nor have I sought their permission. The one exception is my wife Kay. As a matter of fact, it was she who insisted I include my two daughters, despite my desire to only address the male component of my theme of "Finding Fathers." There are those — a cousin, and my sister June — who have frankly asked me not to include certain facts about them in my book, and their requests have been honored.

The biggest question for me is not the "tell-all" nature of the book, but rather the inclusion of folks within its pages who had no way of knowing what I would be writing at the time of their contribution. Given the opportunity to preview the entire book, they might choose instead to opt out. They may simply not want to be associated with any of the intimate details as expressed by me. Many of them may have envisioned a more typically rendered genealogical work with diagrams, a few photographs, perhaps a family tree, but certainly not a soulful rendition including controversial subject matter concerning one family's progression through life. I was never going to write a typical genealogical book.

Going forward I would like to suggest that you, Sharon, given your knowledge regarding privacy issues, highlight or otherwise indicate subject matter that you feel would be troublesome and should be deleted. We can always seek permission from those who are subjects of the book by allowing them to review its content prior to publication. I'm concerned that if someone reads the section about him or herself, he or she will want to read sections about other family members to see how they were treated. I could find myself having to delete much of the material in the book and rewriting the rest as a cascade effect ripples throughout, destroying the vision that has infused my efforts over many years: of what "family" means, of what it takes to create a family, of the successes and failures that sometimes can't be explained, but can only be observed and recorded.

I would very much like you to finish editing the book before I make any final decision as to what content I will or will not allow to remain within its covers in the final redactions. Even I have not managed this feat — to read the book, quietly, from cover to cover. I've been too busy putting the thing together through a myriad number of changes, inclusions and exclusions. I consider myself very fortunate to have your services and appreciate your concern for me and my project. Perhaps I will end up printing only one copy of the book, placing it in my safe and allowing it to be released after I have passed. As Alice Henson said in an e-mail to me recently "I'm sure that your children will cherish this book, and, if they don't, your grandchildren will (sometimes it takes a generation's spacing to appreciate the previous generation)."

My hope is that we will, however, manage to publish the book without intentionally offending anyone. With your help my dream might just come true.

Your troubled client,

Clyde

Acknowledgments

Art direction and cover design by Clyde P. Davis

Production artist Richard Mendes

Editing, Proofreading and Indexing Sharon DeBartolo Carmack, CG and James W. Warren of Warren, Carmack & Associates, Salt Lake City, Utah

Copy editors Sharon DeBartolo Carmack, Richard Mendes

Additional text written by Alice Henson and Kay Davis

Legal Services F. Robert Stein Of Counsel / Pryor Cashman LLP, New York, New York

Photograph Credits

There are close to sixteen-hundred images — photographs, document scans, and maps — within the pages of this book. Every effort has been made to credit and/or indicate the source within proximity of the material depicted, including the identity of copyright holders. In case of oversight, upon notification to the publisher, corrections will be made, and an errata sheet will be distributed to all original recipients of the book.

Other Permissions and Credits

Pages 72-77

June Rogers, photographs and interviews used with permission.

Page 55

Life Magazine, November 9, 1953, cover, logo, and text of article entitled "Night Watch" reproduced by permission from The Picture Collection, Inc., a wholly owned subsidiary of Time, Inc..

Color photograph of police on night watch by Art Shay, reproduced by permission from Getty Images, Inc..

Black and white photographs captioned "Night Shift" and "Cluster of Cops" by Art Shay, reproduced by permission from Getty Images, Inc..

Black and white photograph captioned "Angry Women."

Page 148

Reproduction of book cover, map, and autographed title page by permission of William B. Claycomb

Pages 236–237

Eula Davis House family tree reproduced wtih permission of Carol Sue Feemster, on behalf of Bernetta Fae Triplett Stump, deceased.

Page 272

Contents of "Growing up Sundays" letter to Clyde Davis reprinted with permission of Michelle Schmal.

Pages 279–281

Page 316

Portions of letter from Ollie Davis to Elizabeth and Hugh Purkey reproduced with permission of Eugene L. Davis.

Pages 447–449

Research report by Gábor Aradi and Tamásné Gréczy reproduced with permission.

Pages 580–585

Letters from Sándor Bolyki to Clyde Davis, with translations, reproduced with permission.

Page 605

Letter from Rita Jane Carlson Glazebrook to Kay Davis reproduced with permission.

Pages 606–607

Letter and diagram forwarded from Mary Lou Carlson Ambre to Kay Davis reproduced with permission.

Page 618

Portions of pages, including article and photograph, *Science Digest,* December, 1985. Permission granted October 26, 2010, by Hearst Communications, Inc. ("Hearst"). Article and image for non-exclusive, one-time use with the name of the magazine and any credits and bylines intact.

Letter from Rosalind Douthart to Kay, Clyde and Cynthia Davis reproduced with permission.

Index

ABC Carpet, New York City, N.Y., 634
Abrams, Solomon, 368
Accra, Gold Coast, 279
Ada S. McKinley Community Services Center, Chicago, Ill., 481
Ada S. McKinley South Chicago Neighborhood House, 482
Adams
G.C., 329
John, 205
Adriatic Sea, 483
Africa, 23
Agárd (currently said "Sióagárd"), Hungary, 451–453
Agee, Roy, 205
Alamance Memorial Park, Burlington, N.C., 625
Albemarle Co., Va., 145, 176, 336
Albers, Joseph, 109
Albertson, William, 337
Alexandria, La., 70
Allen
Henry Red, 85
John, 329
Allen County Public Library, Fort Wayne, Ind, 364
Allerton Village, Sidell Township, Vermilion Co., Ill., 391
Alliance, Nebraska, 279
Also-Mecenzef, Hungary, 557
Alsónána, Hungary, 442, 450–451, 454
Altgeld Hall, University of Illinois, Champaign-Urbana, Ill., 87
Ambre
John, 593
Mary Lou (Carlson) [daughter of Mary Lenore (Douthart) and cousin of Kay Davis], 11, 590, 593–594, 605, 607
Thomas [husband of Mary Lou (Carlson)], 607
American University, Washington, D.C., 655
Anaheim, Calif., 663
Anders
Maxine (Davis), 272
Mike, 272
Richard Gene "Dick" [husband of Maxine (Davis)], 272
Anderson, Garland, 346
Andornak church, Andornaktalya [Kistalya], Hungary, 559
Andornaktálya (previously named Kistálya), Hungary, 441, 483
Andras II, King, 557
Andras III, King, 558
Annapolis, Md., 14, 142
Anthony, Elizabeth, 346
Apel
Emma, 487
Florence, 487
Robert, 487
Appalachian Mountains, 275
Aradi, Gábor, 13, 446, 450–451, 453–455, 463
Aranyida, Hungary, 557
Arendas/Arendes, Anna. See Benko, Anna (Arendas/Arendes) [wife of John Benko, the granduncle of Clyde P. Davis]
Arizona, 70, 76
Blue Mesa, Petrified Forest National Park, 113
Hardy, 12
Tucson, 10
Arizona State University, 667
Arkansas, 175
Armoy, County Antrim, Ireland, 593–594
Armstrong, Shannon Eilber, 327
Arna Bontemps African-American Museum, Alexandria, La., 70
Arndt, Roger, 306
Arnold
Irene. See Davis, Irene (Arnold)
Minnie Irene, 221
Art Basel, Miami, Fla., 635
Arvia, Jeanette. See Rock, Jeanette (Arvia)
Asbury College, Willmore, Ky., 69
Ascension Island, 279
Asia, 619
Astoria, Queens, New York, 511
Aszman, Al, [husband of Donna Ann Davis, daugther of Everett and Vondell Davis], 276
Atlas Mountains of Morocco, 279, 636
Auburn, Kansas, 593
Auffenberg. See Sanders, Glenna [wife of Jack Shelby Sanders]
Aulville, Lafayette Co., Mo., 302-303, 305
Australia, 105, 134
Austria, 467, 520, 569, 593, 649, 673
Vienna, 110
Aventura, Fla., 108, 635, 653
Back Barn Farm, Bedford, N.Y., 124
Bagels and... to Go, Annapolis, Md., 142
Bahamas, 141, 636
Bahia, Brazil, 635
Bajzat
Annet, 444
Bolyki, 444
Baker, Romelia, 175
Bakondi
Juliska, 445
Margit, 445, 576
Balazs, Peter, 556
Balboa Naval Hospital, San Diego, Calif., 135
Balsam, Martin, 85
Baltimore and Reisterstown Turnpike, Md., 155
Baltimore Co., Md., 154–173
Baltimore, Md., 154–155, 170–171, 174–176
Bangkok, 122
Bangladesh, 122
Banks, Mrs. A.J., 80, 81
Barcelona, Spain, 94
Barkley
Ernest, 321
Maxine, 321
Barnett, Katherine L., 154, 171
Barrow, Alaska, 69
Bass, Fred, 497
Bátaszék, Hungary, 442, 450–451, 458, 460–461
Bates, Daniel, 363, 365
Bath Co., Ky., 174, 175
Bathory, Istvan, 557
Battelle Memorial Institute, Pacific Northwest Laboratory, Richland, Wash., 618
Bauer, 18
Ann May [Douthart] (1913–1968). See Douthart, Ann May (Bauer) [daughter of John and Anna Bauer, wife of Richard Charles Douthart, and mother of Kay Davis].
Anna Marie (Lauff) (1884–1969) [wife of John William Bauer and grandmother of Kay Davis], 643–649, 651, 654, 658
Barbara, 489
Bunny. See Bauer, Ethel Irene "Bunny" (Weis)
Daisy. See Bauer, Florence Alice "Daisy" (Marten)
Estelle. See Bauer, Stella/Estelle/Esther/Ginger
Esther. See Bauer, Stella/Estelle/Esther/Ginger
Ethel Irene "Bunny" [Weis] (1918–2002) [daughter of John and Anna Bauer, and aunt of Kay Davis], 644–645, 647–655, 659
Florence Alice "Daisy" [Marten] (1916–1970) [daughter of John and Anna Bauer, and aunt of Kay Davis], 611, 644, 648, 650–652, 656–659
Ginger. See Bauer, Stella/Estelle/Esther/Ginger
Gooney. See Bauer, Ruth "Gooney" (Broholm)
Helen "Mag" [Mann] (1911–1974) [daughter of John and Anna Bauer, and aunt of Kay Davis], 644, 648–649, 651, 656
John William (1887–) [father of Ann Bauer (Douthart) and Kay Davis's grandfather, 611, 638–645, 654–655, 658
Lee. See Bauer, Lorraine "Lee" "Peanuts" (Martin)
Lorraine Eileen "Lee" "Peanuts" [Martin] (1924–1995) [daughter of John and Anna Bauer, and aunt of Kay Davis], 643–645, 647–649, 651, 653–654, 659
Mag. See Bauer, Helen "Mag" (Mann)
Mushy. See Bauer, Rose Marie Margaret "Mushy" (Sred) (Marten)
Peanuts. See Bauer, Lorraine "Lee" "Peanuts" (Martin)
Rose Marie Margaret "Mushy" (Sred) (Marten) (1926–1972) [daughter of John and Anna Bauer, and aunt of Kay Davis], 647–648,

651–653, 654, 657–659
Ruth "Gooney" (Broholm) [daughter of John and Anna Bauer, and aunt of Kay Davis], 628, 643–645, 648–654, 657–658
Skinny. See Bauer, Stella/Estelle/Esther/Ginger
Stella/Estelle/Esther/Ginger (Wilcox) (1910–1997) [daughter of John and Anna Bauer, and aunt of Kay Davis], 611, 644, 648–649, 651, 653–655
Bauer family, 11, 13, 590, 637, 644–645, 648
Baxter
Edmund, 201, 318
Elizabeth [wife of Richard Davis], 201, 318
Milo, 363, 365, 389
Baxter Cemetery, Madison Co., Ky., 319
Baxter family, 319
Beaman, Pettis Co., Mo., 403
Bean
Connor [son of Jennifer (Douthart) and Scott Bean], 625
Jennifer (Douthart) [wife of Scott Bean], 624–625
Kylie [daughter of Jennifer (Douthart) and Scott Bean], 624
Scott, 624
Bedford, N.Y., 129, 143
Beijing, China, 619
Bela IV, King of Hungary, 556–557
Belem, Brazil, 277
Belfast, Ireland, 593
Belton, Mo., 253, 316
Ben Lomond, Calif.
St. Andrews Episcopal Church, 116
Benko/Benkó
Anna Andrea. See Veszely, Anna Andrea (Benko) (1783–) [wife of Jacobus Benko and mother of Jacobus Benko]
Anna (Arendas/Arendes) [wife of John Benko, the ganduncle of Clyde P. Davis], 11, 86, 442, 506, 511–513, 518, 526, 534, 547, 553, 573, 575
Istvan [son of Erzsebet Szűcs and possibly son of John/Janos Benko], 553, 573
Jacobus/Jakab (1811–1857) [father of Mihály Máté Benko], 554, 556, 562–563
Janos F. See Benko, John/Janos F.
Joannes/Jacobus (1789–) [father of Jacobus Benko], 554, 556
John/Janos F. [son of Mihály Máté Benko, brother of Maria (Benko) Savage and granduncle of Clyde P. Davis], 86, 442, 475, 485, 491, 506, 510–526, 528, 530–532, 534–538, 540–544, 546–551, 556, 561, 568, 573–575, 660
Julianna (Tóth), [wife of Mihály Máté Benko, mother of Mary (Benko) Savage, and maternal great–grandmother of Clyde P. Davis],], 477, 479, 483, 515–516, 554, 559, 564– 565, 568, 573, 585
Maria [daughter of Istvan and Maria Benko], 553, 573
Maria. See Ligacs/Ligats, Maria (Ligacs/Ligats) (Spak) (Benko) (1809– 1877) [wife of Joannes Spak and wife of Jacobus Benko]
Maria Angyela (Mary Benko Savage) (1843–) [daughter of Mihály Máté Benko, wife of John Savage Sr., and maternal grandmother of Clyde P. Davis], 465, 467, 475, 476, 478–479, 481–485, 487, 502, 512, 520, 563
Maria (Fischer) [wife of Istvan and Maria Benko], 553, 573
Mihály Máté (1849–)[father of Mary (Benko) Savage and maternal great-grandfather of Clyde P. Davis], 479, 483, 512, 515–516, 534, 554–556, 559, 563, 568
Mihaly (1885–1885) [son of Mihály Máté Benko], 560, 573
Piroska [daughter of Istvan and Maria Benko], 553, 573
Benkó family, 12, 13, 18, 439, 446, 552, 553–556, 558, 560, 562, 566
Beno, Marian, 644
Bennett, LaVonne (Davis), 315
Benton College,St. Louis, Mo., 305
Berea Co., Ky., 143
Bergal, Dr., 270
Berguent, Morocco, 279, 280
Berkeley, Calif., 140-141, 665-668
Berklee College of Music, Boston, Mass., 672, 674
Bethlehem Christian Church, Longwood, Mo., 150
Bibb
Henry, 346
Thomas, 358–359
Bicknell, Ada (Davis), 318
Biennale des Antiquaires, Paris, France, 636
Big Ten Restaurant, Champaign-Urbana, Ill., 84
Bikini Atoll, 615
Bindrim, Brittany, 105, 260
Bjorklund-Wolny, Niki, 104
Blackburn, Barbara Jean. *See Davis, Barbara Jean (Mehl)*
Black Jack [land plat], Baltimore Co., Md., 169
Blackwater Creek, Valley City, Mo., 151
Blackwell, 18
Sarah. See Davis, Sarah (Blackwell) [wife of Solomon Davis and 3rd great-grandmother of Clyde P. Davis]
William, 176
Blakemore, Charles , Rev., 205
Bledsoe, I [or J], 177
Bloomingdales, New York City, 620
Bluegrass region of Kentucky, 144
Bob Roberts Hospital at the University of Chicago Clinic, Chicago, Ill., 33, 80, 498
Boca Raton, Fla., 655, 663
Bogert, Pen, 11, 147, 152–153, 157, 178–179
Bokelia, Fla., 318
Bolyki
Imre (Benkó), 443, 444
Josef (1879–) [son of Julianna Toth] [half–brother of John/János Benko], 445, 565, 573, 576
Jozsef [husband of Julianna Toth], 554
Jozsef Jr. [father of Krisztina Bolyki], 568
Krisztina [half–sister of John/János Benko], 535, 536–539, 554, 564–565, 568–575
Lajos, 12
Lajos (1897–) [nephew of John/János Benko], 537, 568, 573–580, 582, 584
Lajos (1926–) [son of Lajos b. 1897], 553, 573
Lajos (Benkó), 442–445
Margit (Sütó), 444
Maria, 445
Sandor, 585
Veron (1871–) [daughter of Jozsef Bolyki and Julianna Toth], 555
Bolyki family, 441, 444, 551, 552, 552
Bolykine
Lajos. See Lajos Bolyki
Bomar, Captain, 280
Bonghard/Bonnhard, Hungary. See Bonyhád, Hungary
Bontemps
Arna [husband of Shelley René (Davis) Bontemps], 70, 71
Arna [writer and librarian], 70
Arna Alexander [son of Shelley (Davis) Bontemps], 71
Pasia Dawn [daughter of Shelley (Davis) Bontemps], 71
Shelley. See Davis, Shelley René (Davis) (Bontemps), [daughter of David O. Davis]
Tyler [son of Shelley (Davis) Bontemps], 71
Zachery [son of Shelley (Davis) Bontemps], 71
Zebadiah Alexander [son of Shelley (Davis) Bontemps], 71
Bonyhád, Hungary, 440–443, 450, 459–460, 467, 470, 474
Boone, Daniel, 20
Boone Co., Mo., 174, 204–205, 217
Boonesborough, Ky., 144
Boren, John, 154, 170
Borsod County, Hungary, 576
Bosnyák
Daniel, 456–457, 460
Epjoan, 457
Sándor, 459
Boston University, Boston, Mass., 123, 665
Boston, Mass., 92, 110, 123, 134, 271, 593, 665, 670, 672
Botero, Fernando, 109
Boulder City, Nev., 67
Bourbon Co., Ky., 174, 175
Bowen High School, Chicago, Ill., 81, 615, 616
Bowers, Eugene W., 175
Bowman
Viola. See Davis, Viola (Bowman)
W.I., 335
Box Kite House, Westhampton, N.Y., 120
Boxankle Road, Madison Co., Ky., 201
Brandkamp, Nellie, 291
Brant
Florence, 283
Phillip, 283
Brazil, 110, 112, 145
São Paulo, 94
Breene, near Armoy, County Antrim, Ireland, 593
Bremen, Germany, 638
Brezany Dolni, Czech Republic, 13
Briarcliff Manor, Westchester Co, N.Y., 88, 90, 106, 119, 636
Bridgeport, Conn., 481
Bright Elementary School, Chicago, Ill., 654
Bristol Sheraton, Vienna, Austria, 440
Bristol, Ind., 644, 655
Bristol, Mich., 649
Britain, 145
Brno, Czech Republic, 619
Brockton, Mass., 205
Broholm
Allan "Al" [husband of Ruth "Gooney" (Bauer) Broholm], 647–649, 657
Kenneth [son of Al and Ruth "Gooney" (Bauer) Broholm], 647–649

Nicole [daughter of Kenneth Broholm], 648–649
Ruth. See Bauer, Ruth "Gooney"(Broholm)
Bronx, N. Y., 131
Brookfield Zoo, Brookfield, Ill., 272
Brookfield, Wisc., 489
Brooklyn, N. Y., 511
Brooks
Archibald "Arch," 204–205, 214
Henry, 176
John, 200, 202, 204–205, 214
Levisa, 176
Lucy, 204
Mary Jane (Davis), 204–205, 214, 217
Mary/Mollie, 204
Mattie, 204
Pattie, 201, 204
Pauline, 204
Peggy (Davis). See Davis, Peggy (Brooks)
Polly (Davis). See Davis, Polly (Brooks)
Robert, 176, 194
Sallie, 201, 204
Brookstown Christian Church, Richmond Co., Ky., 318
Brookstown farm on Otter Creek, Madison Co., Ky., 201
Brookstown, Madison Co., Ky., 318
Brown
Elizabeth Bell "Betty" (Gooch). See Gooch, Elizabeth Bell "Betty" (Brown)
Everett E. [husband of Elizabeth Bell Gooch], 391, 438
John, 176
Vicki K., 313

Brown Avenue Baptist Church, Springfield, Mo., 239
Brown Mackie College, 271
Brown Univ., Providence, R.I., 665
Budapest, Hungary, 440-441, 487, 558, 570, 644
Bugatti, Rembrandt, 109
Bukk Hills, Hungary, 441
Burger King, Harvey, Ill., 22
Burgundy, France, 110, 112
Burlington, N.C., 623
Burns, John, 329
Burtville, Mo., 151
Busey Hall, University of Illinois, Champaign-Urbana, 630
Buthaud, René, 109
Butler, S.R., 594
Butternut, Vt., 130
Cabell, Cathleen, 142
Cade, Charles, 183, 193
Cagliari-Elmas Airfield, Sardinia, 281
Caldwell, James, 198
California, 36–37, 64, 67, 76, 140, 271, 503, 620, 655, 665, 667
Ben Lomond, St. Andrews Episcopal Church, 116
Berkeley, University of California, 140–141
Del Mar, 138, 140
Del Mar, The Meadows/The Grand, 140
Encincitas, 58, 81, 135, 136, 138–139, 141
Encincitas, Olivenhein, 140
Encincitas, Wildflower Estates, 138–139
La Costa, Rancho Bernardo, 140
La Mesa, 134, 136, 138
Laguna Beach, 140
Lakeside, 136, 138–139
Los Angeles, 94
Rancho Bernardo, 140
Rancho Santa Fe, 140
Rancho Santa Fe, Cielo Estates, 140
Rancho Santa Fe, the Covenant, 140
Rancho Santa Fe, Santa Luz
San Diego, 57, 135–136, 140
San Diego Bay, 111
San Diego Co., 141
San Diego, Balboa Naval Hospital, 135
San Diego, Mission Bay Park, 111
San Francisco, 92, 134
Santa Cruz, 136
Seal Beach, 134
Southern, 141
Calumet Bakery, Chicago, Ill., 80
Calumet City, Ill., 56, 77
Calumet Park, Chicago, Ill., 56
Cambridge, England, 665, 666
Cambridge, University, Cambridge, England, 665, 666
Cambridge, Mass., 110
Camden, S.C., 337
Cameron, Stuart, 468
Camp Douglas, Chicago, Ill., 145, 206, 217
Camp Lejeune, S.C., 411
Camp Shanks, N.Y., 279
Camp Upton, Yaphank, Long Island, N.Y., 531
Canada, 15, 147
Montreal, 94
Capital Region Medical Center, Jefferson City, Mo., 306
Capri, Italy, 636
Caramoor Summer Music Festival, Katonah, N.Y., 630
Cardiff-by-the-Sea, Calif., 65, **66-67,** 668
Cardonagh, Ireland, 594
Caribbean, 145
Carlson
Edmund [son of Mary Louise Douthart], 602
Howard [husband of Mary Louise Douthart], 601–602
Mary Lenore (Douthart) [wife of Howard Carlson, aunt of Kay Davis]. See Douthart, Mary Lenore (Carlson)
Mary Louise "Mary Lou." See Ambre, Mary Louise "Mary Lou" (Carlson) [daughter of Mary Lenore (Douthart) Carlson and cousin of Kay Davis]
Sister Jeanne, 593
Carmack, Sharon DeBartolo, 676, 678–679
Carman, Vincent, Rev., 198
Carnegie Steel Corporation, Chicago, Ill., 32, 39, 467, 483
Carnegie, Ill., 39
Carpathian Mountains, 556
Carrington Funeral Home, Fairmount, Ill., 434
Carter, J.R. Mrs., 239
Casablanca, Morocco, 279–280
Cassatta, Bernie, 488
Cassidy, Hopalong, 33
Castelvetrano, Sicily, 281
Castle of Torna, Hungary, 557
Catalonia, Italy, 110
Cate, Unknown, 280
Catlin, Vermilion Co., Ill., 38, 147, 329, 332
Catlin Township, Vermillion Co., Ill., 253, 328, 391–392, 412
Centerview, Mo., 236
Centerville, Iowa, 79, 100
Central Christian Church, Moberly, Mo., 209
Central Park, New York City, N.Y., 85, 628
Chamberlain, Neville, 557
Champaign, Ill., 328
Champaign-Urbana, Ill., 23, 104, 105, 484, 491
Altgeld Hall, University of Illinois, 87
Big Ten Restaurant, 84
Newman Ford Service, 83
Newman Hall, University of Illinois, 87
University of Illinois, 83, 84, 86–87, 93, 100, 102–103
University Press, 84
Chapman, Nathan, 170
Charles Kaiser Funeral Home, Fairmount, Ill., 22
Charleston, S.C., 337
Charlie's Tavern, Lafayette, Ind., 27
Charnock
Brent [husband of Kathy Davis], 327
Brittany, 327
Justin, 327
Kathryn "Kathy" Davis (1956–). See Davis, Kathryn "Kathy" (Charnock)
Chase, Andy, 329
Cheshire, Ohio, 206, 217
Chicago, Ill., 16–17, 21–23, 25, 27, 31–34, 39, 41, 45, 49, 53–61, 64, 77, 80–83, 85–87, 105, 133, 145, 147, 207, 217, 260, 325, 328–329, 333, 335, 400, 466–467, 477, 481, 483, 487–491, 495, 497–499, 503, 511, 541, 545, 547, 591, 593, 597, 603–604, 607, 613, 617, 620, 623, 636, 644–645, 648, 663
Bob Roberts Hospital, 80
Bowen Public High School, 81
Calumet Bakery, 80
Calumet Park, 56
Camp Douglas, 145
Chicago Vocational High School, 81–83
Conrad Hilton Hotel, 84
Crest Recreation's Bowling Alley, 83
The Drake Hotel, 142
East Side, 56
Federation of Musicians, 84
Irondale, 81
Jeffrey Manor, 56
Merrionette Manor, 55
Mt. Carmel Catholic High School, 81
Olympia Fields Country Club, 83
Oriental Movie Theater, 83
Orville T. Bright Grammar School, 80
Rainbow Beach, 56
Rumpus Room Tavern, 83
Rush Presbyterian Hospital, 59
Saks Fifth Avenue, 87
South Deering neighborhood, 56, 80–81
South Side, 81, 83, 100, 102
St. Luke's Presbyterian Hosptial, 58
The Bush, 56
Trumball Park, 56

Trumball Park Homes, 49, 55, 56
Universal Music Corp., 83
University Club, 102
University of Chicago Hospital Clinics, 49
Vogue Wright Studios, 83
Whitaker Guernsey Studio, 83
Wisconsin Steel Mill, 56
Chicago & Eastern Illinois Railroad, 594
Chicago Teachers Center, Northeastern Illinois University, 55
Chicago Transit Authority (CTA), 83
Chicago Vocational High School Chicago, Ill., 81, 82, 83, 627
Chickahominy River, a tributary of the James River, 336
Chilbolton Airfield, 281
Children's Habilitation Center, Harvey, Ill., 22
Children's Haven, Inc., Harvey, Ill. See Children's Habilitation Center
Childs, David M., 98
Chilhowee, Mo., 10, 235
Chrisman, Ill., 419
Christie's, New York City, 635
Chronister
Ava. See Dowthart, Ava (Chronister)
Bert, 593
Churchill, Neldean (Davis), 239
Cielo estates, Rancho Santa Fe, Calif., 140
Cincinnati, Ohio, 214
Clark Co., Ky., 176–178, 198, 200–201, 204, 218, 221
Clarke, Rev., 345
Clay
Green, 192
Green, General, 198
H., 183
Paulina, 198
Claycomb
Dorothy, 147, 151
William "Bill" B., 10, 146–152, 397, 302, 403
Clayton, Young, 348, 358
Clear Creek, Madison Co., Ky., 214, 364
Cleaver, June, 73, 140
Cleveland, Ginger Lee. See Davis, Ginger Lee
Clifton, James, 201
Cline, Morgan, 25, 32, 79, 92, 94, 98, 100, 101, 108
Cline, Davis & Mann, New York, N.Y., 89, 92, 94, 98, 100, 101, 108, 126, 131
Clyde Davis Scholarship, School of Art and Design, University of Illinois, 104, 105
Clyde's Tavern, Lafayette, Ind., 26–27, 40
Cobb
J. Tevis, 385–386
Jesse, 361
Coconut Grove, Fla., 108
Coeur d'Alene, Idaho, 619
Coggin, Nan, 105
Cogswell, Megan, 619
Cole, Polly C., 346
Collier, Beulah M., 302
Collins, 18
Albert G., 198, 200
Amelia "Milly" (Oldham) [wife of Josiah Collins], 198–200, 204
Ann, 198
Arthusa, 200
Catherine (McHendree), 198
Clifton, 200
Elizabeth "Betsy," 198
James, 200
Jeremiah V., 198
Jerry, 207
Joel, 198
John P., 214
Josiah, 201–202, 206, 217, 363
Josiah "Si," Rev., 198–200
Louisa, 198
Martha, 214
Mary Jane, 200
Millie, 198
Milly. See Collins, Amelia "Milly" (Oldham)
Milton P., 202
Paulina/Pauline See Davis, Paulina/Pauline (Collins) (1808–1864), [wife of Richard Davis and 2nd great-grandmother of Clyde P. Davis]
Sally, 200
Sophia [wife of Josiah Jr.], 200
Stephen, 198
William C., 198
Colorado, 503
Columbia Presbyterian Medical Center , New York City, N.Y., 135
Columbia, Mo., 236, 313
Commercial Theatre, Chicago, Ill., 33, 35
Community Health Care, Tacoma, Wash., 621
Concordia, Mo., 304
Connecticut, 664
Glastonbury, 668, 670
Manchester, 664
New Haven, 110
Norwalk, 110
South Kent, 107
Stamford, 110, 127
Uncasville, Mohegan Sun, 141
Connery, Sean, 54
Conowangoe Wagon Road, Baltimore Co., Md., 170
Conques, France, 110, 112
Conrad Hilton Hotel, Chicago, Ill., 84
Cook, Guy., Mrs., 411
Cook Co., Ill., 443, 467, 487, 489, 497–498, 613, 643
Cornelison, Eli, 201
Cornelius, George, 329
Cornwallis, General, 336–337
Corpus Christi, Tex, 175
Corsica, Italy, 110, 440, 636
Cotton, Mike, 119
Coulter, Sarah, 209
Country Wood Burner, Pound Ridge, N.Y., 132
County Abauj, Hungary, 558
County Antrim, Ireland, 593–594
Cowherd, Colby/Coleby, 358
Cox, Myrtle "Eileen" [wife of Ollie L. Davis], 315
Coyle
R.J., 383
T.J., 372
T.Y., 373
Crabb, Anne, 387
Crabbe, Anne, 12
Craven, Unknown, 280
Crest Recreation's Bowling Alley, Chicago, Ill., 83
Croatia, 467, 520
Crooke, Kiah, 363
Cross Plains, Fayette Co., Ky., 188
Croton Falls, N.Y., 88
Cuba, 145, 396
Culinary Institute of America, Hyde Park, N.Y., 664, 665
Cumberland Plateau, 144
Currency Exchange, Chicago, Ill., 602
Cushing, Mary, 590, 607
Cveics, Makavia, 456
Czech Republic, 513
Brezany Dolni, 13
Prague, 110
Czechoslovakia, 557
D. M. Bright Building, Richmond, Ky., 143
D'Amato, Alfonse "Gus," Senator, 21, **23**
Dabney, Corneilus, 346
Dakar, French West Africa, 279
Daley, Richard J., Mayor, 80
Dallas, Ore., 175
Dalmatia, 557
Danville, Ky., 367
Danville, Vermilion Co., Ill., 22, 32, 36, 39, 147, 247, 328–329, 332–335, 390, 397–398, 400, 411, 424
Darien, Conn., 124
Dark, Maxine Ball, 12, 348
Dauro, Alice M. Douthart [daughter of Mary Lenore (Douthart) Carlson], 605
Davis
Ada (Bicknell), 318
Agnes, 283
Albert Lloyd "Bert" "Brother Albert," [brother of James Davis] 17, 18, 145, 201, 205, 208–213
Alice (Toombs), 218, 282–286, 305
Amanda [daughter of Edward Davis Jr.], 327
Amelia "Milly" (Johnston), 204–205
Andrew, 321
Andrew/Anderson, 318
Ann [wife of Lester], 11
Anna, 291
Anne, 291
Archibald, 214
Aron, 186
Art, 321
Arthur, 318
Arthusa (Tevis) [, 201, 204–206
Arthusa D., 205
Barbara Jean (Mehl) (Davis) Blackburn [2nd wife of David O. Davis], 64–65, 69–71
Beau Chase [son of Cole and Tammi Davis, grandson of Clyde P. and Kay Davis], 56, 58, 89, 100, 109–111, 117, 136, 140, 144, 475, 660, 671–673
Belle Marie [daughter of Scott Ryan and Michelle Davis], 68–70, 663
Bessie/Bess. See Honey, Bessie/Bess (Davis)
Betty, 292
Betty Jean (Tucker), 243
Blanch, 291, 292
Carl, 146, 282, 286

Carl Cecil, 292
Carl W., 283–284
Carrie, 283
Catharine (Hopkins), 174–175
Catherine Ann "Kay." See Davis, Kay (Catherine Ann "Kay" Douthart) [daughter of Richard C. and Ann (Bauer) Douthart, and wife of Clyde P. Davis]
Cecil Wilburn, 239–240, 244–245 286
Chantel, 327
Charles "Charlie" [son of James Davis and Nancy "Nannie" Gooch, grandfather of Clyde P. Davis], 10, 12, 17, 20, 22– 23, 31–32, 38, 69, 79, 83, 217–218, 246–281, 285, 293, 297, 301, 305, 307, 313, 316, 329, 332–334, 336, 362, 373, 377, 390, 398, 483, 660
Christine Rene (Davis) (Ledingham) (Parrino) [daughter of Clyde P. and Kay Davis, wife of John Parrino], 25, 66, 76, 87–89, 106, 110–111, 114–124, 126, 130, 133, 247, 477, 611–612, 624, 630, 633, 636
Cindy. See Davis, Cynthia
Clara. See Latimer, Clara Lou (Davis)
Claude, 11, 151–152
Claude Beverly, 221
Clayton, 214
Clifton, 201–202, 204–205, 214–215
Clyde [son of Joseph S. Davis], 283, 285
Clyde Otis "Cotton" (1907–1974) [son of Charles Davis, husband of Mary M. "Spare Ribs" (Savage), father of Clyde P. Davis], 17, 21–22, 24–32, 34, 36–39, 41, 43–44, 46, 53, 60, 63, 67, 69, 79, 86, 138, 247, 253, 257, 259, 261–262, 264–265, 270–272, 275–276, 285, 329, 332–334, 336, 400, 481, 660, 662, 678
Clyde Patrick "Duke," [son of Clyde Otis Davis and Mary Savage, husband of Catherine Ann "Kay"Douthart Davis], 9–23, 31–39, 41, 43–47, 49, 53–61 , 63–117, 119–124, 126, 129–141, 142–145, 147–153, 217–218, 247, 253, 254, 257, 260, 262, 264, 275–276, 280, 285, 315, 328–329, 331–336, 348, 400, 412, 440–444, 446–449, 451, 453–455, 463, 465–467, 475, 481, 483–484, 487–489, 491, 495, 497–499, 503, 505, 511, 522–523, 526, 547, 553, 556, 559, 564, 565, 568, 573, 580, 582, 584, 585, 590, 594, 596, 599, 604, 607, 612, 617, 624, 627–628, 630–631, 633, 636, 643, 648–649, 653–655, 660–679
Clyde, Scholarship at University of Illinois, 104, 105
Codie Brian [son of Cole and Tammi Davis, grandson of Clyde P. and Kay Davis], 56, 89, 100, 109–111, 130, 134, 136, 138, 140–141, 475, 483, 661, 664–667, 672–673, 675
Cole Matthew [son of Clyde P. and Kay Davis], 25, 57–58, 65–66, 76, 81, 89, 100, 106, 109–112, 114–118, 128–141, 475, 602, 611, 625, 630, 662, 666
Cotton. See Davis, Clyde Otis "Cotton"
Cynthia "Cindy" (Eilber) (1954–) [daughter of Edward W. Davis], 10, 320, 325, 326
Cynthia Leigh (Malara) [daughter of Clyde P. and Kay Davis, wife of Philip Malara], 25, 64–65, 67, 76, 88–89, 100, 110–111, 114–115–124, 126, 130, 475, 611, 624, 630, 652–653
Daniel, 174–176
Daniel "Dan" (1958–), 326–327
Darlene Ann (Pool) [daughter of Everett Davis], 10, 262, 264, 276
David Otis "Butchie" [son of Clyde Otis Davis and Mary Savage, brother of Clyde P. Davis], 21–22, 34, 36–37, 39, 49, 53, 57, 62–71, 79, 114–115, 119, 133, 270, 486–487, 604
Deborah "Debbie." See Lane, Debra "Debbie" Lenore (Davis) [daughter of Larry Joe Davis]
Derek Mitchell (1992–), 327
Diane [wife of Richard William Davis], 326
Donna, 273
Dora May (Hogue), 209–213
Duke. See Davis, Clyde Patrick "Duke"
Earl, 151, 218
Earl (1901–1918), 303
Earl N., 302
Earlene, 151, 224, 235
Eddie. See Davis, Everett
Edmund, 201, 202, 217
Edmund Edward (1868–1917) [son of Richard Davis and Elizabeth Baxter], 318, 319
Edward, 181–193, 318
Edward (1957–), 326
Edward (Jr.) (1987–) [son of Edward Davis Jr.], 327
Edward W. (1923–), 321, 323–325
Eliza "Liza." See Gooch Eliza "Liza" (Gooch) (Pettis) (Davis) (Goodwin) (1875–1951) [wife of William Davis and wife of Thomas C. Goodwin]
Elizabeth, 176, 217, 264–265, 269, 274–275
Elizabeth "Lizzie." See Purkey, Elizabeth "Lizzie" (1892–1982) [wife of Hugh Purkey]
Elizabeth A. [daughter of Levi Davis (1798–ca.1837) and Catharine Hopkins), 175
Elizabeth (Baxter) [wife of Richard Davis], 201, 318
Elizabeth "Betsy" (McClain) [daughter of Nathaniel and Margaret Davis, and wife of Thomas McClain], 174
Elizabeth Etta "Lizzie." See Wells, Elizabeth Etta "Lizzie" (Davis) [daughter of Edmund Davis (1868–1909), husband of J. Richa [sic] Wells]
Ernest, 283
Ethel, 149, 150, 221–222, 226–228, 230, 236, 268, 270, 272, 286
Ethel (Singleton), 334
Ethel "Eddie," 268, 334
Ethel Earlene (Scott), 315
Ethel S. Reid, 284
Eugene, 11, 152
Eugene L. [son of Ollie L. Davis], 314–317
Eula. See House, Eula Davis
Everett, 22, 32, 149–151, 221, 223–224, 226–231, 233, 252, 254, 262, 273, 305
Everett "Eddie," 264, 272, 276
Everett (1905 –1983) [son of Edmund Edward Davis], 318–319, 323–334
Everett [nephew of Clyde O. Davis], 10
Finis "Boss" Arnold, 238, 239, 241–242, 244-245
Florence (Brant), 283
Florentine (Verkennis) [wife of Everett Davis], 318
Fred, 239, 286, 300, 410
Fred (1895–) [son of Eliza "Liza" Gooch], 291, 438
Fred "Freddie" "Dick" Morgan, 239, 241, 243–244
Fred Cornell, 12, 243, 286
Ginger Lee (Cleveland) (Davis) Hart, 36, 63–65, 70
Glennvel "Glenn" Lewis, 151, 221–222, 224, 305
Glennice Irene, 221
Grant Ryan [son of Scott Ryan and Michelle Davis], 69, 663
Hannah [Nathaniel's 2nd wife], 158, 175, 154
Hattie, 214
Hazel Irene (Mullins) [daughter of Joseph S. Davis and Alice Toombs), 283
Irene (Arnold), 234
Irene Hazel, 289
Isaac, 154
J. Ernest, 302
J.C., 151, 224
J.M., 283
James, 239, 247, 283, 291, 305, 315, 362, 364, 365, 373, 377
James (1841–1902) [son of Solomon, husband of Nannie Gooch, and great–grandfather of Clyde P. Davis] , 17–18, 145, 150–152, 204–205, 208–210, 216–219, 221, 270, 302–303, 336, 340
James (1875–) [son of James and Nannie Gooch], 217, 302–303
James C., 292
James Nathaniel, 175
Jefferson C. "JC" "Jeffrey" [son of James Davis and Nancy "Nannie" Gooch], 10–11, 149, 150–151, 217–218, 220–235, 302, 315, 373, 377
Jeremiah, 186–187
Jessie Pettis (1891–), [son of Eliza "Liza" Gooch], 291
Joe, 151, 222, 283, 334, 373, 377
Joe (–1932), 151
Joe [brother of Charles Davis], 10
Joe Larry. See Davis, Joseph "Joe Larry
Joe Marshall, 151, 292
John, 154, 176, 194, 373, 377
John [son of Edmund Edward Davis], 318
John Morgan "Morg" (1863–), 12, 149–151, 217, 238–239, 241–245, 283, 286, 315
John Richard, 209–212. See also Davis, Richard
John W., 318
Joseph, 217, 305
Joseph "Joe Larry," [father of Larry Joe Davis], 31, 270–273
Joseph S., 218, 282–293
Joseph S. "Dump," 150
Josiah (1830–), 202, 204, 206–207, 217
Julia, 151
June "Tootsie" (Davis) Mora Rogers [daughter of Clyde Otis Davis and Mary Savage, sister of Clyde P. Davis], 10, 20, 22–23, 31–37, 39, 44–45, 47, 49–50, 53–54, 56–57, 59–60, 63–70, 72–77, 114–115, 117, 132, 257, 260, 262, 264, 270, 280, 334, 481, 483–484, 494, 498, 631, 679
Kathryn "Kathy" (Charnock) (1956–), 32, 327
Kay (Catherine Ann "Kay" Douthart) [daughter of Richard C. and Ann (Bauer) Douthart, and wife of Clyde P. Davis], 10–11, 14–15, 20–23, 25, 37, 49, 54, 56, 59–60, 63–66, 73, 76–77, 79, 83–89, 100, 106–117, 119–122, 124, 126–127, 129, 130–133, 136, 138–139, 141–142, 144–146, 149, 260, 270, 329, 332, 334, 444–447, 475, 484, 487, 491, 503, 512–513, 559, 568, 590–594, 598–607,

611–621, 623–636, 642–645, 647–649, 652–655, 664, 672, 675, 679
Kenneth, 292
Larry, 262, 270, 273
Larry Joe [son of Joe Larry and Violet Davis], 41, 262, 271–273
Laura, 302
LaVonne (Bennett), 315
Leoma, 291, 292
Leona [wife of H.P. Dykes], 318
Lester, 11, 153, 155
Letha A. (Massters) [wife of Edmund Davis], 318–319
Levi (1798–ca1837), 174–176
Levice, 194
Lillie Marie, 242
Linnie J., 292
Lizzie, 247
Lois, 233
Lois Frances. See Murphy, Lois Frances (Davis)
Lola Frances, 221
Loma, 300
Loren, 315
Loyola M. (Remnant) [wife of Woodson Masters Davis], 318, 320–321, 323
Lula "Lu." See Sanders, Lula "Lu" (Davis) (1877–) [wife of Thomas Luther Sanders]
Mabel, 152
Mabel M. (Garner), 314–316
Mable (Pulley), 315
Mae (Renfro) [wife of Roy Lee "Jack Dog" Davis], 247, 267– 270
Marelyn [wife of Edward Davis], 326
Margaret (Stocksdale) [wife of Richard Davis and 4th great-grandmother of Clyde P. Davis], 153–154, 174, 176, 209
Margaret A."Peggy" (Lucas) [daughter of Nathaniel and Margaret Davis, wife of Fieldling Lucas], 174–175
Margie, 221–222, 224
Margie (Turner). See Turner, Margie (Davis)
Marie (wife of Daniel Davis), 327
Marie Freeman (Kilgore) [daughter of John Morgan Davis], 239, 242
Mary M. "Spare Ribs" (Savage) (1917–2011) [daughter of Mary Benko and David Andrew Savage Sr., wife of Clyde Otis Davis, and mother of Clyde P. Davis] 20–23, 25, 32–36, 44–61, 63–64, 69, 78–83, 86–87, 115, 117, 141, 247, 257, 260, 270–271, 334, 465, 467, 477, 481–485, 487, 490, 494–495, 503
Mary [1st wife of Nathaniel], 158–174, 154
Mary Jane. See Brooks, Mary Jane (Davis)
Mary S. (Jenkins), 318
Mattie, 146
Mattie Melvina (Toombs) [wife of John Morgan Davis]. 218, 238–240, 283, 286, 315
Mattie (Odell), 151, 292, 301
Maud R., 218, 302
Maude, 151
Maude (1903–1923), 303
Maude [wife of Everett Davis], 318
Maxine, 11, 268, 270
May, 334
Melissa, 209–210
Michael [son of Debbie (Davis) Lane], 271
Michelle, 273
Michelle [wife of Joe Larry Davis], 271
Michelle "Micki." See Schmal, Michelle "Micki" (Davis) " [daughter of Larry Joe Davis]
Michelle (Dingnan) [wife of Scott Ryan Davis], 68–70, 663
Mildred [Webster], 315
Miriam "Mimi" "Mima" (Dodd) (Marquess) (Sprinkle) "Grandma Sprinkles" [widow of James Davis], 152, 216–218.
Morgan, 146, 217
Morgan [brother of Charles Davis], 10
Myrtle, 218
Myrtle "Eileen" (Cox), [wife of Ollie L. Davis], 315
Nancy "Nannie" (Gooch) (1838–1882) [daughter of Chiswell D. Gooch and Eliza White, wife of James Davis and great-grandmother of Clyde P. Davis], 20, 150–153, 217–218, 221, 239, 247, 283, 291, 302, 305–306, 314–315, 319, 336, 362
Nathaniel, 11
Nathaniel (Sr.) (ca 1700–1785) [father of Richard and 5th great-grandfather of Clyde P. Davis], 153, 154–169
Nathaniel (1750/60 –) [son of Richard Davis and Margaret Stockdale], 171, 174–176, 178–179, 187
Nellia, 292
Nellie, 286
Nellie M. (Thomas), 243, 244, 291
Noah H., 205
Norma Ruth (Gardner), 327
Nowland [son of Edmund Edward Davis], 318
Olalee, 292
Ollie Lester (1882–) [son of James and Nannie Gooch Davis], 149, 151–152, 217–218, 253, 283, 305, 314–317, 377
Opal, 209, 211–212, 292
Ora Mae (Kennedy) (1898–) [daughter of John Morgan Davis, wife of Charles Kennedy], 238–240
Pamelia (Elliott), 214
Paul, 292
Paulina/Pauline (Collins) (1808–1864), [wife of Richard Davis and 2nd great-grandmother of Clyde P. Davis], 198–200, 204–206, 208–209, 214
Pearl, 283
Peggy (Brooks), 174, 176, 194
Polly (Brooks), 176
Polly (Igo). See Igo, Polly (Davis)
Rebecca "Becca" (Gooch) (1867–1957) [wife of Charles Davis, mother of Clyde O. Davis, and paternal grandmother of Clyde P. Davis], 12, 17, 20, 22–23, 31–32, 38, 69, 79, 247–249, 252–254, 257, 259–262, 264–265, 268–269, 272, 280, 292, 301, 316, 329, 332–334, 362, 389–392, 394–396, 398, 400, 411–412, 438, 483
Richard, 181, 183, 184, 186, 189, 193, 194, 198, 318, 363
Richard H., 175
Richard [son of Edward W. Davis, brother of Cindy (Davis) Eilber], 10
Richard William (1964–), 326, 327
Richard (1734–1796) [son of Nathaniel (1700–1785) and 4th great-grandfather of Clyde P. Davis], 18, 153–155, 170–173, 174
Richard (1799–1874) [son of Solomon and 2nd great-grandfather of Clyde P. Davis], 11, 198–199, 200–203, 204–205, 206, 214–215, 217, 362
Richard (–1840) [son of Nathaniel (ca.1750/60–), 174–176
Rickie Dean "Rick" [son of Larry Joe Davis], 41, 271, 273
Robert, 153
Rory Cornell, 243
Rosa Nannie (Tatum) [wife of Jefferson C. Davis], 11, 149, 151, 218, 221–222, 224–227
Roy, 25, 31, 33, 37, 247, 253, 257, 262, 265, 271–272, 276, 334
Roy [son of Charles Davis & Rebecca Gooch Davis], 329, 332
Roy Lee "Jack Dog," 23, 43, 247, 252–253, 264, 266–270
S. Gertrude (Murphy). See Davis, Sarah Gertrude
Sally/Sarah (Dunbar), 185, 204–205
Sarah [daughter of Robert (1738–1829) and Margaret Davis], 154
Sarah (Blackwell) (Davis) (Suddeth) [wife of Solomon Davis and 3rd great-grandmother of Clyde P. Davis, later wife of James Suddeth], 175–176, 181, 194, 200, 204
Sarah Gertrude (Murphy), 151, 218, 302
Scott Ryan [son of David Otis Davis and nephew of Clyde P. Davis], 64–70, 114–115, 663
Shelley René (Davis) (Bontemps) [daughter of David O. Davis, wife of Arna Bontemps], 64–65, 69–71
Solomon (ca.1760/70–1801) [3rd great-grandfather of Clyde P. Davis], 18, 145, 147, 170, 174–197, 200–201
Sophia, 202, 207
Spice/Spicy. See Lanter, Spice/Spicy (Davis)
Susannah, 153
Tammi Ann (Taylor) [wife of Cole Davis and daughter-in-law of Clyde P. and Kay Davis], 57–58, 81, 89, 100, 109–112, 114–117, 126, 134–136, 138–141, 477, 669
Taylor [son of Cole and Tammi Davis, grandson of Clyde P. and Kay Davis], 56, 89, 100, 109–111, 117, 136, 138, 140, 475, 660, 667–668
Thomas, 153
Tonya Renee, 243
Tootsie. See Davis, June "Tootsie"
Unknown, 292
Viola, 151, 291–292, 299
Viola (Bowman), 218, 291–292, 300
Violet, 11, 31, 37, 41, 252, 272–273, 276
Violet May (Gillow) [wife of Larry Joe Davis], 270–272
Vondell, 22, 32, 41, 252, 254, 260, 264, 272, 276
William, 151, 217–218, 290–292, 300, 373, 377, 410
William "Will," 20, 151, 217, 247, 290–301
William [husband of Eliza (Gooch) [Pettis], 390
Woodson Masters (1899–1978), 318–323
Yvonne [wife of Everett], 10
Ziporah, 153
Davis Cemetery, Fairmount, Ill., 335
Davis Cemetery, Saline Co., Mo., 151
Davis family, 10–11, 14, 18–20, 67, 76, 126, 145, 148–149, 153–154, 157, 210, 218, 239, 243, 247, 249, 253, 271, 291–292, 303, 305–307, 315, 318, 328, 335, 376, 400, 411, 446
Davis Peach Farm, Wading River, Long Island, N.Y.,

512
Davis's Hope [land tract], Baltimore Co., Md., 168, 170, 164
de Lafayette, Marquis, 336
Dearborn Heights, Mich., 318
Dearborn, Mich, 38, 332
Debrod, Hungary, 557
Debrot, Jacques, 73
Decatur, Ill., 329
Décorchemont, François- Emile, 109
Dee Mal, 669-670. See also Malara, Dylan Davis
Deel
Grace, 259–260
Robert "Bob," 259–260
Del Mar, Calif., 140
Delaney
Dale, 398, 402, 411
Dale Wilbur (1900–1967), 390, 438
Dorsa J., 390
Doyle, 390
Edna "Edney." See Gooch, Edna "Edney" (Delaney) [wife of William Harry Delaney]
Hallie M., 390
Mildred, 390
Thomas E. (1866–), 333, 438
Tom, 398, 402
Unknown [son of Edna Gooch Delaney], 438
William, 333
William H., 405
William Harry, 390
William Harvey, 389
Willie, 390
Delaney family, 335
Delaware, 145
Delmar, Calif., 138
Delphi, Ill., 22
Delphi, Ind., 247, 260
Delton
Edith, 315
Percival, 315
Denney, John, 363
Design Miami, Miami, Fla., 635
Designers 3, **New York City, N.Y.,** 90
Detroit, Mich., 10, 318, 324, 654
Dietz Lake Beach Club, Inc., Center Point, Ind., 36, 41
Dingnan, Michelle. *See Davis, Michelle (Dingnan) [wife of Scott Ryan Davis]*
Dinuba, Calif., 66, 69
Disneyland, Anaheim, Calif., 663
Disney World, Orlando, Fla., 141
District of Columbia,, Washington, 110, 134
Dole, Bob, Senator, 93
Dollywood, Pigeon Forge, Tenn., 663
Donnellan Funeral Home, Chicago, Ill., 484
Dordogne Valley, France, 110
Dougherty, Francis, 329
Douglas
A.T., 205
Bernice (Tevis) [wife of A.T. Douglas], 205
Robin, 104, 105
William, Rev., 346, 348
Douthart, 18
Agnes (Harvey), 593
Alexandria Irene [daughter of Julia Douthart], 619–621
Ann May (Bauer) (1913–1968) [daughter of John and Ann Bauer, wife of Richard Charles Douthart, mother of Kay Davis], 86–87, 601, 603, 610–613, 615, 618, 644, 645, 648, 653, 655
Ashton [son of Nathan and Terri Douthart], 625
Ava (Chronister), 593
Bill [son of Richard James Douthart], 618
Catherine A. (Maloney) (1866–) [wife of Henry "Harry" Douthart, mother of Richard C. Douthart and grandmother of Kay Davis], 588, 590, 594–596, 607
Catherine Ann "Kay" See Davis, Kay (Catherine Ann "Kay" Douthart) [daughter of Richard C. and Ann (Bauer) Douthart, and wife of Clyde P. Davis]
Charles "Chuck" [son of Robert H. and Shelley Douthart], 624–625
Daniel [son of Henry "Harry" Douthart and Kay Davis's uncle], 592
Dickie Boy. See Douthart, James Richard "Dick"
Edward "Ed"[son of Henry "Harry" Douthart and brother of Richard C. Douthart], 591, 601–602
Frank [cousin of Mary Lou Douthart Carlson], 593
Harry. See Douthart, Henry "Harry"
Henry [Of Breene, County Antrim, Ireland; father of Henry "Harry" Douthart, and great-grandfather of Kay Davis], 593–595
Henry "Harry" (1867–) [father of Richard C. Douthart and grandfather of Kay Davis], 588–597, 607, 609
Harry G.(1897–1966) [son of Henry "Harry," brother of Richard C. Douthart, and uncle of Kay Davis], 596, 601, 604, 607–608
Helen [wife of Ed Douthart], 591
Irene Rosalind "Roz" (McKelvey) [wife of Richard James Douthart], 616–621, 624, 653
Jennifer (Bean) [daughter of Robert H. and Shelley Douthart, wife of Scott Bean], 624–625
John (of Belfast, Ireland), 593
Joye (Hodges) [wife of Charles "Chuck" Douthart], 624
Julia Celeste [daughter of Richard James Douthart], 618–621, 624
Karen (Horner) (McClung) [daughter of Robert H. and Shelley Douthart], 624–625
Kathie (Townson) [daughter of Robert H. and Shelley Douthart], 624–625
Kathryn [daughter of Henry Douthart of Armoy, Ireland], 593
Lela, 593
Kay. See Davis, Catherine Ann (Douthart) (Davis) [daughter of Richard C. and Ann (Bauer) Douthart, and wife of Clyde P. Davis]
Lorraine [daughter of Daniel Douthart], 592
Margaret, 607
Mary (McLernon) [Armoy, Ireland], 593
Mary Cain (Gillian) [wife of Henry Douthart of Armoy, Ireland, and mother of Henry "Harry" Douthart], 593
Mary Lenore (Carlson) (1890–) [daughter of Henry "Harry" Douthart, sister of Richard C. Douthart, mother of Mary Lou (Carlson) Ambre, and aunt of Kay (Douthart) Davis], 588, 590, 593, 599, 602, 607
Nathan [son of Robert H. and Shelley Douthart]," 624, 625
Nora [daughter of Henry "Harry" Douthart and sister of Richard C. Douthart], 596, 604, 607–608
Rebecca [daughter of Charles "Chuck" and Joye Douthart], 624
Richard Charles [son of Henry "Harry" and father of Kay Davis], 86–87, 114, 133, 591, 596, 598–600, 600–606, 608, 612, 615, 618, 624–625, 627, 644
Richard James "Dick" "Skinny" (1935–) [son of Richard Charles and brother of Kay Davis], 590, 600, 602, 610, 614–621, 623–625, 627, 652–655
Robert [b. Galway, Ireland, then to Boston], 593
Robert Henry "Bob" "Butch" (1938–1998) [son of Richard Charles and brother of Kay Davis], 600, 602, 612, 616, 622–625, 627
Rose, 607
Ruth [wife of Daniel Douthart, aunt of Kay Davis], 592, 603
Ruth [dau. of Robert, b. Galway], 593
Ryan [son of Charles "Chuck" and Joye Douthart], 624
Sharon, 616
Shelley Kenyon (Miller) [wife of Robert Henry "Butch" Douthart], 612, 623–625
Simon P., 593
Terri [wife of Nathan Douthart], 625
Tim, 593
Tom [brother of Henry "Harry" Douthart], 594
William, 593, 619–620
William [of Breene, County Antrim, Ireland], 593
Douthart family, 11, 587, 590, 644
Douthart Scholarship Hall, University of Kansas, Lawrence, Kans., 593
Downey, Calif., 63
Doylesville, Madison Co., Ky., 201, 214
Drake, Francis, 189, 191
Draper
Elizabeth (Gooch), 348
John, 346–348
Duckinghole Creek, Orange Co., Va., 358
Ducky Sloan's, Chicago, Ill., 34
Dudley, Sophia, 204
Duffy's Saloon [Tavern], Torrance Ave. at East 106th St., Chicago, Ill., 34
Dunbar
Dudley, 200, 204, 206
Sally/Sarah. See Davis, Sally/Sarah
Dutko Gallery, Paris, France, 634
Dyer Hospital, Chicago, Ill., 34
Dyer, Ind., 34
Dykes
H.P., 318
Leona (Davis), 318
East Side, Chicago, Ill., 56
Eastern Kentucky University Library, Richmond, Ky., 363, 387
Eastern Kentucky University, Richmond, Ky., 205
Eddyville, Ky., 176
Edwards
Coleman, 205
Elizabeth (Gooch). See Gooch, Elizabeth [daughter of Thomas]
Henry, 346
John, 346–347
Eger district, Hungary, 578

Eger, Hungary, 12–13, 440–441, 454, 457, 460, 477, 553–555, 561, 570, 579
Eichinger
Gertrude, 310
Marsh, 310
Eilber
Cynthia "Cindy." See Davis, Cynthia "Cindy") (1954–) [daughter of Edward W. Davis]
Michael, 326
Michelle. See Pomorski, Michelle (Eilber)
Eitel's Old Heidelberg Rathskeller, Chicago, Ill., 31
EJ&E Railroad. See Elgin, Joliet and Eastern Railroad
Eleuthera, 141
Elgin, Joliet and Eastern Railroad [EJ&E], 594–595, 604, 627
Eli Lilly, Indianapolis, Ind., 618
Elkin, E.S, 204
Ellington Field, Tex., 256, 279
Elliott
Pamelia. See Davis, Pamelia (Elliott)
Pliney C. (Rev.), 305
Thomas, 214
Ellis Island, New York, 521, 551, 647
Empire State College, State University of New York, 126
Encinitas, Calif., 58, 66, 81, 89, 135–136, 138–139, 141, 636, 668, 671
England, 105, 143
London, 94, 109
Eniwetok Atoll, 615
Entwistle, Michael Brian Sr., 9, 278
Epple
David "Dave," 224, 283
Mollie. See Tatum, Mollie
Estill Co., Ky., 199, 214
Euringer
Celia, 100, 630
George, 88, 93–94, 100, 113, 630
Europe, 23, 442, 561, 619, 654, 665
Evans, Bessie. See Gooch, Bessie (Evans) [wife of Darrel Ira "Hoopie" Gooch]
Evansville, Ind., 333
Evergreen, Ill., 649
Ezell, J.W., 283
Fairchild Gardens, Miami, Fla., 635
Fairmount Jamaica Historical Society and Building, Fairmont, Ill., 331–332
Fairmount Nazarene Church, Fairmount, Ill., 411
Fairmount United Methodist Church, Fairmount, Ill., 333
Fairmount Village, Vance Twp., Vermillion Co., Ill., 20–23, 25, 36, 38, 43, 147, 247, 252–254, **270**– 271, 275, 328–330, 332–335, 362, 390–392, 398, 400, 411–412, 415, 422, 434,
Faith Evangelical Methodist Church, Fairmount, Ill., 333
Falahi
Emron [husband of Wendy Johnson Savage], 507
Wendy. See Johnson, Wendy Savage (Falahi)
Far Rockaway, N.Y., 85
Fayette Co., Ky., 170, 174–175, 178–179, 181–183
FBI Academy, Quantico, Va., 624
Federation of Musicians, Chicago, Ill., 84
Federico, Gene, 106
Feldman, Marie, 147
Felso, Hungary, 557
Felsötárkány, Hungary, 12, 441, 443–445, 483, 487, 512, 534, 537, 551, 554, 556, 560–561, 569, 571, 573, 576
Fiakowski, Conrad, 627, 628
Fiji, 134
Filson Historical Society Library, Louisville, Ky., 11, 147, 179
First Baptist Church, Fairmount, Ill., 332–333
First Baptist Church, Nevada, Mo., 309
First National Bank of Fairmount, Fairmount, Ill., 332
Fischer, Maria. See Benko, Maria (Fischer) [wife of Istvan Benko]
Fisher
E. Paul, 309
Russell, 130
Fiume, Italy, 478, 483, 520
Flatwood Christian Church, 205
Floral Hills Cemetery, Kansas City, Mo., 317
Florence, Italy, 110
Florida, 49, 76, 108, 141, 438, 636
Aventura, 108
Boca Raton, 655, 664
Coconut Grove, 108
Key West, 108
Miami, 81
Miami Beach, 109
Orlando, Disney World, 141
Florida Atlantic University, Boca Raton, Fla., 664
Flour Seasons Restaurant, New York City, N.Y., 85
Flutz, Donna, 332
Ford, Mary, 283
Fort Benning, Ga., 279
Fort Boonesboro, Ky., 20
Fosella, Vito, 107
Foster
Ann, 11
Melvin B., 221
Fourmile Road, Madison Co., Ky., 201
Fourth District, Baltimore Co., Md., 155
Fox Lane High School, Bedford, N.Y., 122, 130
France, 281, 673
Boulogne-Billlancourt, 109
Burgundy, 110, 112
Conques, 110, 112
Dordogne Valley, 110
Lot Valley, 110, 112
Paris, 109, 141
Provence, 110
Frank, Michael, 107
Frankfort, Ky., 11–12, 142–143, 178
Franktown, Colo., 306
Freedom Twp., Lafayette Co., Mo., 306
Freeman, Marie. See Davis, Marie (Freeman)
French, Dr., 201
Friedman & Vallois, New York City, 634
Fritsch, Tim, 136
Ft. Worth, Tx., 647
Fulara, William, 105
Fülep, Gyula "Julius," 13, 440–441, 454, 456–458, 460, 479, 553–556, 559, 563–565, 573
Gabes, Tunisia, 281
Gage, Bob, 106
Galen White Cemetery, Madison Co., Ky., 337, 360
Galerie Duo, Paris, 634
Galerie Félix Marcilhac, Paris, France, 634
Galerie Vallois, Paris, France, 634
Galloway, Peggy, 12, 367
Galway, Ireland, 593
Gamo, Paul C., 105
Garage sale, Lansing, Ill., 633
Gardiner, Duncan B., 643–644
Gardner, Norma Ruth. *See Davis, Norma Ruth (Gardner)*
Garner, Mabel M. See Davis, Mabel M. (Garner)
Garrett, William C., 385
Garrison, 260
Andrew, 260
Charles, 260
Lena "Linnie," 218, 291
Ray, 259
Garrison family, 259
Garrison Forest, Baltimore Co., Md., 170
Garrison Forest Protestant Episcopal Church, Baltimore Co., Md., 154
Gary, Shawn, 306
Gary, Ind., 270, 512, 521, 547–548
Gatehouse Furniture Studios,Holyoke, Mass., 108
Gates
Cynthia (Maupin), 336
General, 337
Thomas, 336
Gayety's Candies and Ice Cream, Chicago, Ill., 33, 607
Gayety's movie theater, Chicago, Ill., 33
Gehr, Lesley. See Jaffe, Lesley (Gehr)
Gela, 280
Geller, Andrew Michael, 120
Gentry
Betsy, 336
Martin, 336
Germany, 324, 528, 569, 673
Munich, 94
Gess, John, 185, 189
Getty Art Museum, Los Angeles, Calif., 635
Gibby's, Frankfort, Ky., 142
Gibson, Michael, 142
Gibson Co., Ind., 174–176
Gilley's, Dallas/Ft. Worth, Tex., 649
Gillian Mary. *See Douthart, Mary Cain (Gillian) [wife of Henry Douthart of Armoy, Ireland, and mother of Henry "Harry" Douthart]*
Gillow, Violet May. See David, Violet May (Gillow)
Gilman, Jeanne, 488–489
Glacier National Park, Montana, 663
Glastonbury, Conn., 123, 668, **670**
Glastonbury High School Blue Devils, 668
Glastonbury Youth Football Association, 668
Glazebrook
Rita Jane Douthart [daughter of Mary Lenore (Douthart) Carlson], 605
Glenn, David, 335
Glenny, Kate, 607
Glover , John H., 363, 365
Goldblatt's department store, Chicago, Ill., 602, 611
Golden
Mahala Jane. See Gooch, Mahala Jane [wife of Cornelius Gooch (1831–)]
William J., 364

Gooch, 18–19, 20, 292
Ada, 390
Addie, 390, 436
Alexander, 389–390
Ann, 362
Any, 362
Arzelia, 362, 368
Audrey "Bug" Lee (Smith) (Waggoner (1916–) [daughter of Thos. Emanuel "Moody" Gooch, wife of Erville Jesse "Smitty" Smith and wife of H.M. Waggoner], 391, 411–412, 425, 438
Bertha "Bertie" (1909–) [daughter of William Tearle Gooch], 391–394, 438
Bessie (Evans)) [wife of Darrel Ira "Hoopie" Gooch], 412, 418–419, 421, 424, 429, 434, 437–438
Bettie, 362
Bill, 395
Byler, 362
C.D. See Gooch, Chiswell D.
Catharine, 346
Charles/Charley/Charlie 260, 362, 373, 395
Charles W. "Charley" (1904–1973) [son of William Tearle Gooch], 390, 395, 436, 438
Chisel. See Gooch, Chiswell D.
Chiswell D. (1809–1877) [son of Cornelius Gooch, husband of Eliza Ann (Maupin)], 217, 336, 358, 360–370, 372, 374, 376, 378–380, 382, 384, 386, 389
Cornelison. See Gooch, Cornelius
Cornelius, 336, 359
Cornelius "Neill" [son of Chiswell D.], 363, 364, 365, 373
Cornelius (1780–1810) [husband of Eliza (White) (Gooch) (Hill), father of Chiswell D. Gooch], 358–362
Cornelius (1831–), 362
Cornelius [son of Thomas, (–1803)], 346–348
Cynthia Ann (Hill), 362
Dale "Jessie" (1936–2007) [son of Darrel Ira "Hoopie" Gooch" (1942–2007), 333, 411–412, 418, 421–424, 434, 438
Darrel Ira "Hoopie" (1913–1969) [son of Thos. Emanuel "Moody" Gooch], 22, 391, 411–412, 418–419, 421–424, 426–427, 429, 432, 434, 437–438
Dean, 333, 425
Edna M. "Edney" (Delaney) (1862–1918) [wife of William Harry Delaney], 389–390, 398, 402, 405, 438.
Eliza "Liza" (Gooch) (Pettis) (Davis) (Goodwin) (1875–1951) [wife of William Davis and wife of Thomas C. Goodwin], 218, 242, 247, 262, 267, 290–292, 300, 389–390, 402–403, 410–411, 438
Eliza Ann (Maupin) (–1892) [wife of Chiswell D. Gooch], 217, 364, 366–369, 379
Eliza B. (White) (Hill) (1788–1859) [wife of Cornelius Gooch and wife of John Hill, mother of Nancy "Nannie" Gooch Davis], 336–337, 346, 358, 360–365, 372–373, 375–377, 381, 383, 385–387, 389
Elizabeth, 361
Elizabeth Bell "Bettie" (Brown) [daughter of Wm. Tearle Gooch, wife of Everett Brown], 390–393, 407, 438
Elizabeth (Draper), 348
Elizabeth (Edwards) [daughter of Thomas], 346
Emanuel. See Gooch, Thomas Emanuel "Moody" "Mann"
Frances Mae, 407
Gary, 11, 20–22, 434
Gary "Boone" (1955–) [son of Darrel Ira "Hoopie" Gooch], 423, 438
George, 362
Gideon (poss 1773–) [son of Thomas], 346, 348–349
Gideon [also listed as Gideon Gouge], 358
Gideon [of Louisa Co., Va.], 358
Harold, 390, 397
Harold (1913–1955), 438
Hazel E. (Lane) [wife of Roy Dean Gooch], 411–412
Henry, 362, 373, 383
James, 291, 358–359, 362, 369, 373
James [of King William Co., Va.], 346
James [son of Thomas, –1803], 346–347
Jeffrey, 425
Jesper, 362
Jessie Doney "Doll/Dollie" Gooch (Reeves) (1888–1969) [daughter of Thomas E. Gooch (1836–1918)], 262, 389–391, 398–400, 438
Jo Ann (Maupin), 362, 373, 387
Joel (1871–), 390
Joel M., 389
John, 362, 389–390, 406
Judy [wife of Dale Gooch], 434
Judy L. (Olinger) [wife of Dale "Jessie" Gooch], 424, 438
Karen [wife of Gary Gooch], 434
Laurel, 362
Lillie, 362
Lucy, 358, 359, 362
Lucy (possibily Higgins) [wife of Thomas, –1803], 346–348
Lucy (Graves) (1859–) [daughter of Chiswell D. Gooch, wife of Milton Graves), 362, 373, 378–379
Lucy [wife of William B. Gooch], 370
Mahala Jane (Golden) [wife of Cornelius Gooch (1831–)], 362, 364–365
Manuel, 390
Margie, 436
Marlene (1934–1999) [daughter of Darrel Ira "Hoopie" Gooch], 412, 421, 424, 438
Martha. See Woolery, Martha (Gooch)
Mary, 348, 362
Mary (Turner), 362
Mary E., 373
Mary Mildred (Smith) (1905–1992) [daughter of Thomas E. "Moody" Gooch, wife of Cornice Hobert Smith], 11, 22–23, 333–334, 391, 411–412, 414–416, 419–422, 426, 429, 432, 436, 438
Maude, 410
Maude E., See Higgins, Maude Ethel [wife of William Tearle Gooch]
Melvin [son of Wm. Tearle Gooch], 395, 438
Mildred, 20, 412, 436
Mildred Elizabeth (Oldham) (Williams) (1838–1917), [wife of Thos. E. Gooch Sr.], 20, 147, 198, 247, 290, 361–363, 388–391, 410–412, 435–436, 438
Myrtle (Woodward), 268
Nancy "Nannie." See Davis, Nancy "Nannie" (Gooch) (1838–1882) [daughter of Chiswell D. Gooch and Eliza White, wife of James Davis, great-grandmother of Clyde P. Davis]
Neill S., 364
Oakley, 390
Overton [son of Thomas, –1803], 346, 358
Paul, 20–23, 25, 32, 36, 412, 421
Paul Duayne "Frank" (1942–) [son of Darrel Ira "Hoopie" Gooch, 434, 438
Polly [daughter of Thomas, –1803], 346, 347
Rebecca "Becca." See Davis, Rebecca "Becca" (Gooch) (1867–1957) [wife of Charles Davis, mother of Clyde O. Davis, and paternal grandmother of Clyde P. Davis
Remus [husband of Nancy Gooch], 201, 362, 368
Robert, 390, 405
Robert E., 436
Robert Otis (1895–), 333, 406, 438
Robert T. Jr., 390
Robert T. Sr. (1865–1930) [son of Thomas E. Gooch Sr.], 389–390, 396, 438
Robert Tearle, 397
Roger [son of Charles W. Gooch], 395, 438
Rosa Lee (1880–1939) [daughter of Thomas Emanuel "Moody" Gooch], 268, 390–391, 398, 436, 438
Rosa M. (1883–), 389
Roy, 21, 22, 435
Roy Dean (1908–1984) [son of Thomas. Emanuel "Moody" Gooch], 391, 411–412, 417, 419, 422, 438
Roy Dean (Jr.), 412
S.B. [May be the same man as William Gooch, 1849–1929], 364, 370, 373 383
Sallie, 362
Sarshel/Sashel B., 362
Sharon. See Viano, Sharon (Gooch) [wife of Dale "Jessie" Gooch]
Stanley, 395
Stanley [son of Wm. Tearle Gooch], 438
Susan, 346
Tammy, 425
Thomas, 20, 247, 359–361, 363, 373, 385
Thomas (–1803) (of Louisa Co., Va.), 346–361, 412
Thomas (1907–) [son of John and Minnie Reffett Gooch], 390
Thomas E. (1836–1918), 247, 290, 336, 362, 388–409, 410–411, 415, 417, 419–420, 422, 426, 429, 432, 435, 438
Thomas Emanuel "Moody" "Mann" (1877–1955), 334, 389–391, 394, 399–402, 410–438
Thomas M., 411. See also Gooch, Thomas Emanuel "Moody" "Mann"
Thomas Washington [son of Thomas, –1803], 346–348, 358
Verlea, 362
Viney, 362
Viola May (Goodwin) [wife of Thomas E. "Moody" Gooch, 390–391, 410–412, 414–415, 422–423, 435–436, 438
Vivian, 395
Vivian [daughter of Melvin Gooch], 438
Walter, 390
William, 355, 365, 390
William (–1656), 346
William [Gov. of Va.], 346

William [son of Thomas], 346–348
William B. (1849–1929), 370. See also Gooch, S.B.
William Tearle "Will" [brother of Rebecca Gooch Davis (1870–1945), 389–392, 394–395, 410, 435, 438
William [Royal Lt. Gov. of Va.], 143, 346
Gooch Co., Va., 20
Gooch family, 12, 14, 142–145, 147, 153, 157, 218, 247, 249, 271, 291–292, 306, 328, 332, 335, 358, 360, 400, 411, 446
Gooch Place, Madison Co., Ky., 371
Goochland Co., Va., 145
Goochland Historical Society, Goochland, Va., 142, 143
Good, Chiswell D., 365. See also Gooch, Chiswell D.
Gooden, Mary, 154
Goodwin, 236
Allen [father of Glona Howe], 334
Eliza "Liza." See Gooch Eliza "Liza" (Gooch) (Pettis) (Davis) (Goodwin) (1875–1951) [wife of William Davis and wife of Thomas C. Goodwin] (1875–1951)
Hugh, 346
John B. [father of Viola (Goodwin) Gooch, 411
Thomas "Tom," 262, 291, 292, 398, 402, 403, 411
Thomas C. [husband of Eliza "Liza" (Gooch)], 390, 398, 438
Viola May. See Gooch, Viola May (Goodwin) [wife of Thomas E. "Moody" Gooch
Goodwin family, 335, 411
Gormley Sculptures, 635
Gouge
Giddeon, 358. See also Gooch, Gideon
Nancy, 239. See also Gooch, Nancy
Thomas, 346. See also Gooch, Thomas, (–1803).
Gough, Edna. See Gooch, Edney M. "Edna" (Delaney)
Grábóc, Hungary, 442, 456–457, 459–461
Grand Central neighborhood, New York City, N.Y., 98
Grand Central Post Office, New York City, N.Y., 98
Grand Central Station, New York City, 633
Grand Rapids, Mich., 306
Graul's shopping center, Annapolis, Md., 142
Graval Lick, Madison Co., Ky., 371
Gravel Lick Fork of Red Lick Creek, Madison Co., Ky., 376, 379, 383, 385
Graves
Lucy (Gooch). See Gooch, Lucy [daughter of Chiswell D. Gooch, wife of Milton Graves]
Mary Addie, 362, 369
Milton, 362, 373
Milton Jr., 378
Gray, Daniel M., 147
Great Falls of the Patapsco [River], Md., 170
Great Hungarian Plain, Hungary, 558
Great Lakes National Cemetery, Holly, Mich., 324
Gréczy, Tamásné, 450–451, 453–455, 463–464
Greece, 673
Green
Karen Mauer, 178
Nancy Jane. See Purkey, Nancy Jane [mother of Hugh Purkey]
Green Ridge, Mo., 149, 239
Green Spring Punch, Baltimore Co., Md., 154
Greenbay Street Tavern, Chicago, Ill., 49
Greensboro, N.C., 625
Greenview Cemetery, Fairmount, Ill., 22–23, 32, 41, 43, 271, 329, 332–335, 392, 398, 411, 437, 661
Greenwood Memorial Park, Ft. Worth, Tex., 648
Greer
J. W., 283
Jack, 147, 149
Jack R., 10
John (1800–), 147
Grey Advertising, New York, N.Y., 124
Grove Isle, Fla., 76
Grover Twp., Johnson Co., Mo., 303
Grundy Co., Mo., 315
Guam, 396
Gyula, Dobos, 449
Hahn, Morgan, Rev., 198
Haley, Alex, 142
Halifax Co., Va., 198
Hamburg, Germany, 468
Hammond, Ind., 521
Phil Smidt's Restaurant, 86–87
Hancock Co., Tenn., 275
Hapsburg Empire, 557
Harbor Grill Restaurant, Mich. City, Ind., 271
Harding, Kans., 239
Hardy, Ariz., 12
Harlem, New York, 619
Harmon, Richard, Chancellor of the University of Illinois, 102–103, 106–107, 110,
Harrison Co., Ky., 174
Harrisonville, Mo., 151, 152
Harsel, Anthony, 189
Harvard Medical School, Cambridge, Mass., 306
Harvey, Agnes. See Douthart, Agnes (Harvey)
Hart, Ginger Lee. *See Davis, Ginger Lee (Cleveland)*
Hawaii, 49, 134
Maui, 141
Maui, Mt. Haleakala, 111
Hays Fork Baptist Church, Richmond, Ky., 198
Hayse
Hallie (Tevis) (wife of Morbin Hayse), 205
Morbin, 205
Hayward, Wisc., 488
Heizman, Angela, 628
Heline, Berton, Rev., 32
Henrico Co, Va., 143
Henry Co., Ky., 176
Henson
Alice S., 12–14, 18, 20, 32, 153, 218, 290, 303, 306, 308, 313, 337, 360, 613, 679
Don, 14
Heraklion, Greece, 619
Heritage Hills, Somers, N.Y., 120
Hermosa Beach, Calif., 64
Heslin
John, 607
Mary. See Maloney, Mary (Heslin)
Hess, John, 90
Heves County, Hungary, 570–571, 576
Hickman, Wilfred, 328, 329
Hickman Creek, Fayette Co., Ky., 171
Hieronymus, Sam, 283
Higgins/Higgs
Bertha "Bertie" (Meyer), 334
Edith "Aunt Edith" [possibly a sister of Maude Ethel Higgins], 395
Lucy. See Gooch, Lucy (possibly Higgins) [wife of Thomas Gooch/Gouge of Louisa Co., Va.]
Maude Ethel, [wife of William Tearle Gooch], 390–395, 435, 438
Higginsville, Lafayette Co., Mo., 305
Higgs, Lucy. See Higgins, Lucy
Hill
Cynthia Ann. See Gooch, Cynthia Ann.
Dora Alice, 390, 405
Eliza B. See Gooch, Eliza (White) (Gooch) (Hill)
Emily Noland, 360–361
Henry, 361
Henry L., 360, 362
Jane (Oldham), [daughter of John Hill and Eliza B. (White) (Gooch) (Hill), and wife of Edmond Oldham], 360, 362, 389
Jefferson, 361, 363
Jefferson A., 360, 362
Jefferson D., 361
John, 337, 360, 362, 389 [husband of Eliza (White) (Gooch) (Hill)]
Nancy (Gooch) [wife of Remus Gooch], 368
Hill family, 360
Hillsboro, Iowa, 593
Hillsboro, Ky, 411
Hiroshima, Japan, 619
Historical Cemetery, Boone Co., Ky., 198
Hitler, Adoph, 557
Ho Chi Minh City, Viet Nam, 111, 636
Hobart, Ind., 11, 37
Hockney, David, 109
Hodges, Joye. See Douthart, Joye (Hodges) [wife of Charles "Chuck" Douthart]
Hodgkins, Howard, 109
Hogue
Dora. See Davis, Dora (Hogue)
John, 209
Holden, Mo., 152
Holland, 644
Holland, Mich., 281
Hollander, Betty Ruth, 630
Hollins, Benjamin, 346
Holly, Mich., 324
Holmes, Archie, 12
Holy Cross Catholic Cemetery, Calumet City, Ill., 77
Holyoke, Mass., 108
Homer, Ill., 411
Honey
Bessie "Bess" D. (Davis), 149, 151, 221, 224, 230
Emory Dale, 221, 224
Joe Marvin, 149, 221, 224
Mrs. Joseph, 151
Honeywell Controls in California, 655
Hong Kong, China, 122, 134
Hopkins
Catharine (Davis). See Davis, Catharine (Hopkins)
G.M., 154
Horner
Karen. See Douthart, Karen (Horner) (McClung) [daughter of Robert H. and Shelley

Douthart]
Mickey [husband of Karen Douthart], 624
Taylor [son of Karen Douthart], 624
Hotel Eger Park, Eger, Hungary, 440
Hotel Romantik, Egar, Hungary, 441
House, 221, 302, 315
Eula (Davis), 149, 151, 221, 223–225, 235–236, 283, 292, 302, 305, 315
Fred Byron, 221, 236
Houston, Tex., 205
Howard, Donald, 55
Howe
George, 335
Glona (Kirby), 23, 271, 332–335
Howell
Minnie (Tevis) [wife of W.C. Howell], 205
W.C. [husband of Minnie (Tevis)], 205
Hughes
Barbara Jean, 411
Patty Dean, 411
Hughesville, Mo., 147
Humphreys, Allan Sparrow, 319
Hungary, 13, 49, 440–443, 448, 452, 467, 513, 520, 535, 556, 557, 643
Eger, 12–13
Felsötárkány, 12
Szekszárd, 13
Hunt
Bryan, 109
Joseph/Josiah, 329
Huntsville Cemetery, Huntsville, Mo., 209
Huntsville, Randolph Co., Mo.., 149
Hurd, Unknown, 276
Hutson, Margaret, 174, 176
Hyde, Sherry Lynn, 424
Hyde Park Bank and Trust, Chicago, Ill., 488
Hyde Park Telephone Company, Chicago, Ill., 36
Hyde Park, N.Y., 664
Igo
Daniel, 174
Diana, 13
Jack, 174
Levi, 174
Nathaniel, 174
Polly (Davis), 174
Thomas, 174
William, 170, 174, 191
Igo family, 170
Illinois, 17, 20, 147, 247, 276, 283, 291, 329, 332, 389, 391, 403, 467, 503, 595, 617, 636
Calumet City, 56
Catlin, 147
Chicago, 49, 53–54, 56–61, 80–83, 85–87, 133, 145, 147, 207, 217
Chicago, Camp Douglas, 145
Chicago, Federation of Musicians, 84
Chicago, South Side, 100, 102
Chicago, The Drake Hotel, 142
Chicago, University Club, 102
Chicago Vocational High School, 81
Danville, Vermilion County Courthouse, 147
Fairmount, 147
Great Lakes, Naval Training Center, 132
Lansing, 56, 132
Orland Park, 49, 56, 58
Palos Park, 59, 60
Tinley Park, 56
Illinois Institute of Technology, Chicago, Ill., 617
Indiana, 20, 53, 79, 147, 175, 283, 332, 438, 593, 636
Hobart, 12
Lake Station, 11
Merriville, 12, 56
Munster, 56, 60
Indiana University, Indianapolis, Ind., 617, 620
Indianapolis, Ind., 279
Inland Steel, Chicago, Ill., 34
Iowa, 593
Centerville, 79, 100
Ireland, 15, 593
Irondale, Chicago, Ill., 81
Irvine, David, 367
Istvan, Dobo, 561
Istvánji, Kornelia, 442
Italy, 105, 110, 520, 673
Catalonia, 110
Corsica, 110
Florence, 110
Ostuni, Puglia, 111
Puglia, 110, 141
Sardinia, 110
Sicily, 110, 112
Sienna, 110
Tuscany, 110
Umbria, 110
Veneto, 110
Ivco, Ms., 21
J.C. Davis Store, Valley City, Mo., 151
J.N. Thorpe Elementary School, Chicago, Ill., 53
Jackson Co., Mo., 283, 285, 305
Jackson Co., Ky., 363, 364
Jackson Prison, Wayne Co., Mich., 38, 49
Jackson Township, Randolph Co., Mo., 212
Jackson, Mich., 325
Jacksonville, Fla., 318
Jacksonville, Ill., 264
Jaffe
Evelyn [mother of Lesley], 630
Lesley (Gehr), 630
Jamaican School District, Ill., 332
Jamestown, Va., 336
Janelunas
Johanna, 496, 498
Julius, 496, 498
Olga, 496, 498
Japan, 112
Sasbo, 134
Tokyo, 134
Jaszo/Jasov/Jazou/Jazow, Hungary/Slovakia, 556–558
Jaszó-Mindszent, Hungary/Slovakia, 556-557
Jaszoujfalu, Hungary, 557
Jefferson, Thomas, 143, 145
Jefferson City, Mo., 14, 68, 142, 152, 209, 218, 306, 313
Jeffrey Manor, Chicago, Ill., 56
Jenkins, Mary S. See Davis, Mary S. (Jenkins)
Jett, Hiram, 318
Jimmy Doolittle Air and Space Museum Foundation, Travis AFB, Ca., 280
Joan Miro Museum., Barcelona, Spain, 635
John Fox Jr. Memorial Library, at Duncan's Tavern, Paris, Bourbon Co., Ky., 153, 171
Johnson
George, 204, 214, 277
James Arthur, 509
James John "Jimmy John," 509
Jess, 277
Mary Lou. See Savage, Mary Lou (Johnson)
Milly, 205
Mr., 276
Unknown, 276
Wendy Louise "Wendy Lou" Savage (Johnson) (Falahi) [daughter of Mary Lou Savage and James Johnson], 507, 509
Johnson Co., Mo., 17, 151, 209, 214, 217–218, 236, 247, 255, 283, 291–292, 302, 306, 315
Johnson County Missouri Historical Society, 153, 219, 255
Johnston
Amelia/Milly. See Davis, Amelia "Milly"
George, 204
Johnstone, Hallie Tipton, 199
Joliet, Ill., 594
Jones Beach, Long Island, N.Y., 88, 628
Jordan, Robert, 199, 201, 364, 365
Joss, Hungary, 557
Josza, Hungary, 557
Jouve, Georges, 109
Judy
Maralyn Laier, 488–490
Robert V. "Bob," 489
June, 257
Kaerntner Ring, Vienna, Austria, 440
Kairouan, Tunisia, 280
Kaiser
Charles, 22
Mrs., 22
Kansas, 174, 283
Topeka, 12
Kansas City, Mo., 27, 152, 210, 218, 234, 283, 314–315
Kappel, Katelyn, 105
Karoly Robert, King, 558
Karr, Joel, 389
Katonah, N.Y., 628
Kavalcik, Anna, 613
Kavolcik, Anna, 613. See also Lauff, Anna Marie [Bauer]
Kearney, Sam, 283
Kelley, Samuel, 177
Kelly
Ellsworth, 109
William, 154, 160, 162
Kennedy
Charles, 239
Nancy, 361
Ora. See Davis, Ora Mae (Kennedy) (1898–) [daughter of John Morgan Davis, wife of Charles Kennedy]
Kennewick General Hospital, Kennewick, Wash., 620
Kenney, Arthur, 409
Kentucky, 12, 17, 20, 143–145, 147–149, 152,

170–171, 176, 179, 198, 204–205, 207, 210, 214, 217–218, 221, 247, 291, 305, 319, 336, 345, 348, 391, 438, 636
Berea Co., 143
Bluegrass region, 144
Boonesborough, 144
Frankfort, 11–14, 142, 143
Frankfort, Gibby's, 142
Frankfort, Kentucky History Center, 142
Lexington, Marriott's Griffin Gate Resort, 143
Louisville, 11
Louisville, Filson Historical Society Library, 147
Madison Co., 147, 149, 151, 143
Richmond, 150
Richmond Co., 143
Richmond, D. M. Bright Building, 143
Richmond, Madison Co., , 143, 147, 148, 143
Richmond, Madison County Courthouse, 144, 148–149, 144
Richmond, Nicholas Donuts & Pastries, 144
Richmond, Old Tyme Toys antique shop,, 144
Richmond, Richmond Tourism and Visitor Center, 152
Richmond, Stouffer Building, 143
Kentucky History Center, Frankfort, Ky., 142
Kentucky River, 198, 200
Kentucky State Archives, Frankfort, Ky, 11, 153, 171, 175, 181–182, 194, 199, 201–202, 205, 207, 214, 364, 366, 372, 376
Keswick Hall, Keswick, Va., 142
Kethuda Minaret, Hungary, 563
Key West, Fla., 65, 108
Kfolik, Anna. See Lauff, Anna Marie [Bauer]
Kilgore, Marie. See Davis, Marie Freeman (Kilgore)
Killington, Vt., 130
Kimbrough
Opal (Davis), 209–210, 213
Roscoe, 210
King William Co., Va., 346
King's College, Cambridge, England, 668
Kirby
Edith Allen [mother of Glona Howe], 11, 334–335
George, 283
Hazel Irene, 283
Kistálya (present-day Andornaktálya), Borsod County, Hungary, 441, 483, 554, 556, 559, 576
Knob Noster, Mo., 151, 217–219, 221, 236, **315**
Knob Noster Cemetery, Knob Noster, Mo., 149, 234
Knox, William, 174–175
Kodonsky, Alexis, 105
Kokomo, Ind
Kokomo, Lafayette, Ind., 17, 22, 32, 41, 398
Kolalski, Anna. See Lauff, Anna Marie (Bauer)
Kovacs, Anna, 35
Kowalsk, Mary [possibly the mother of Florence "Daisy" (Bauer) Marten], 658
Krecsut, Figmilijan, 461
Krupa, Gene, 85
Kruszewski, Katrina, 104
Kulwin, Jeffrey, 628
L. Fish & Co. furniture, Chicago, Ill., 602
L.W. Frohlich, Intercon International New York City, N.Y., 91
L'Hôtel Drouot, Paris, France, 634
La Mesa, Calif., 134, 136, 138
La Monte, Mo., 242
Lafayette Co., Mo., 218, 236, 303, 306
Lafayette Country Club, Lafayette, Ind., 27, 32
Lafayette, Tippecanoe Co., Ind Ind., 17, 26–27, 32–33, 252–253, 275, 305, 411
Lago Di Bivarre, 280
Laguna Beach, Calif., 140
Laier, Gottlieb, 491
Lake George, N.Y., 58
Lake Michigan, 145, 488–489
Lake Station, Ind., 11, 270
Lakeside, Calif., 65, 136, 138–139
Lalique, Ferdinand, 109
Lamar, Rae, 497
Lancaster Co., Penn., 154
Lane
Debra "Debbie" Lenore (Davis) [daughter of Larry Joe Davis], 31, 270–273, 276
Hazel E. See Gooch, Hazel E. (Lane) [wife of Roy Dean Gooch]
Langan, John, 105
Lansing, Ill., 20, 22, 33, 35–56, 132, 270, 489, 607
Lanter
John, 217
Spice/Spicy (Davis), 176, 194
Thomas, 176, 194
William, 364–365
Laramee, Roger, 105
LaRue, Lash, 33
Las Animas Cemetery, Las Animas, Colo., 218
Las Animas, Colo., 217
Las Vegas, Nev., 65, 67, 76–77, 141, 506, 507
Latimer, Clara Lou (Davis), 239
Lauf
Anna. See Lauff, Anna Marie (Bauer)
Anna [relative buried in Podelin, Slovakia], 649
Lauff
Anna, 613
Anna Marie. See Bauer, Anna Marie (1884–1969) [wife of John William Bauer and grandmother of Kay Davis]
Lauff family, 13, 637, 644
Lawson Field, Fort Benning, Ga., 279
Le Château Restaurant, South Salem, N.Y., 117
Le Musée des Années 30, **Boulogne-Billlancourt, France,** 109
Ledingham
Christine Rene (Davis) (Parrino). See Davis, Christine Rene
Sean "Scott," 25, 66, 114–116
Lenz
Bob, 93, 100, 107
Carol, 100, 107
Leperd, Hungary, 451
Lewis, Richard, 162
Lewinski, Col. Thomas, 144
Lexington, Ky., 143, 176, 198, 204, 205
Liberace, 35
Library of Congress, Washington, D.C., 643
Lichtenstein, Roy, 109
Ligacs/Ligats, Maria (Ligacs/Ligats) (Spak) (Benko) (1809– 1877) [wife of Joannes Spak and wife of Jacobus Benko], 555, 562
Ligon
Glennice, 11
Harold E., 221
Lima, Peru, 663
Lincoln Center, New York City, N.Y., 628
Lindberg, Anne, 104
Lindvay, Anddras, 557
Littell, William, 176, 179
Little Mountain [land tract], Baltimore Co., Md., 168
Little Rock Air Force Base, Ark., 615–616
Little Rock, Ark., 616
Liverpool, England, 468
Livingston Co., Ky., 178
Loew, Dick, 106, 107
Loftis, Anna. See Lauff, Anna Marie (Bauer)
Logansport, Ill., 260
London, England, 94, 109, 123
Lone Jack Cemetery, Lone Jack, Saline Co., Mo., 151–152
Lone Jack, Mo., 152, 305
Lone Tree, Cass Co., Mo., 151
Long Island, N.Y., 515, 552
Jones Beach, 88
Longwood Cemetery, Longwood, Pettis Co., Mo., 149, 239, 283
Longwood Cemetery, Warrensburg, Mo., 239
Longwood Presbyterian Church, Longwood, Pettis Co., Mo., 146, 148
Longwood Twp., Pettis Co., Mo., 10, 146–152, 217–218, 221, 239, 247, 283, 332, 335, 403
Los Angeles, Calif., 21, 94, 593, 672
Lot Valley, France, 110, 112
Louf/Louff, Anna. See Lauff, Anna (Bauer)

Louisa Co., Va., 145, 346–348, 352, 358–359
Louisiana Territory, 175
Louisville, Ky., 11, 180, 279
Lovett-Lorski, Boris, 109
Lower Mississippi Valley, 178
Loyola University, Chicago, Ill., 503
Lubalin, Herb, 91
Lucas
America, 175
Fielding, 174–175
Frances, 175
Francis, 175
Julia "June" (Savage) (1911–) [daughter of Mary Benko Savage, wife of Victor Lucas], 47, 49, 64, 79, 477, 484, 491–500, 505
Levi, 175
Louisa, 175
Margaret A."Peggy." See Davis, Margaret A."Peggy" [daughter of Nathaniel and Margaret Davis, wife of Fieldling Lucas]
Minerva, 175
Peggy. See Davis, Margaret A."Peggy" (Lucas) [daughter of Nathaniel and Margaret Davis, wife of Fieldling Lucas]
Thomas, 175
Victor J. (1910–1978) [husband of June Julia (Savage) and uncle of Clyde P. Davis], 467, 483–485, 491, 493, 496–500, 660
Luce, Jean, 109
Ludeke, Maria, 105
Lukes, Fieldan, 175
Lunch Counter, Toledo, Lucas Co., Ohio, 254
Luth

Carl, 318
Elizabeth (Wells) [daughter of Elizabeth Etta "Lizzie" Davis Wells, 318
Lux, Loretta, 109
Lying-In Hospital, University of Chicago, Chicago, Ill., 33
Lyon, Merrill, Miss, 81, 83, 86
Macassar Gallery, Paris, France, 636
Macon, Macon Co., Mo., 239
Macon, Mo., 239
Maddison
John, 346
Sally, 346
Madison, Ambrose, Commander, 337
Madison Avenue, New York City, N.Y., 93
Madison County Courthouse, Richmond, Ky., 148,**149**, 144
Madison Co., Ky., 17, 143, 147, 149, 151, 170–171, 176, 178, 190, 192, 194, 198–200, 202, 204–207, 209–210, 214, 217–218, 221, 239, 247, 291, 302, 305, 318–319, 336–337, 344–346, 358–364, 367–368, 370, 372, 376, 379, 381, 387, 389, 391, 396, 398, 411
Madison's Café, Jefferson City, Mo., 142
Madrid, Spain, 94
Magyar Leszamitolo-Es Penzvalto-Bank, 537, 573
Mahar, Daniel, 348, 359
Maine, Sugar Loaf, 130
Maison Lafitte, Westchester Co., N.Y., 88
Majcher, Jan, 557
Malara
Cynthia Leigh (Davis) [daughter of Clyde P. and Kay Davis, wife of Philip Malara], 25, 64, 65, 67, 76, 88–89, 100, 110–111, 114–124, 126, 130, 475, 611, 624, 630, 652–653, 664
Dylan Davis [son of Philip and Cynthia (Davis) Malara, grandson of Clyde P. and Kay Davis], 56, 89, 100, 109–111, 117, 121, 123–124, 475, 653, 660, 664, 668–670
Philip [husband of Cynthia (Davis), son-in-law of Clyde P. and Kay Davis], 89, 100, 109–111, 115–117, 120, 124, 475, 653, 664, 667, 668
Ross Philip [son of Philip and Cynthia (Davis) Malara, grandson of Clyde P. and Kay Davis], 56, 81, 89, 100, 109–111, 117, 121, 123–124, 475, 653, 661, 664–665, 668, 670
Malara family, 67
Malawista, Lawrence, 106
Maloney
Catherine A. See Douthart, Catherine A. (1866–) [wife of Henry Douthart]
Daniel, 607
Dennis [brother of Catherine Maloney Douthart], 596, 607
Edward, 607
Frank [brother of Catherine Maloney Douthart], 595
Mary (Heslin), 607
Maloney family, 587
Malta, 280
Manchester Community College, Manchester, Conn., 664
Manchester, Conn., 664
Manhattan, New York, 628
Mann
Frederic "Fred," 25, 94, 98, 100, 101, 108, 673
Helen. See Bauer, Helen "Mag" (Mann)
Lawrence [husband of Helen "Mag" Bauer], 656
Manship, Paul, 109
Marguiles Gallery, Wynwood Art District, Miami, Fla., 634–635
Marina del Rey, Calif., 64
Marks, Lillian Bayly, 154
Marquess, L.W., 217
Marriott Hotel, White Plains, N.Y., 115
Marriott's Griffin Gate Resort, Lexington, Ky., 143
Marshall, Saline Co., Mo., 151, 289, 291–293, 296–297, 299
Marten
Daniel Wayne "Dan" [twin son of Florence "Daisy" (Bauer)], 644, 648, 656–657
Donald Alan "Don" [twin son of Florence "Daisy" (Bauer)], 644, 648, 656–657
Dorothy [wife of Don Marten], 644
Florence. See Bauer, Florence Alice "Daisy" (Marten)
Fred [husband of Florence "Daisy" Bauer and husband of Rose Marie Margaret "Mushy"(Bauer) (Sred) (Marten)], 648, 656–657
Rose Marie. See Bauer, Rose Marie Margaret "Mushy" (Sred) (Marten)]
Martin
Clare Ann (Sred) (Martin)] [daughter of Rose Marie (Bauer) Sred and adopted daughter of of Lorriane Bauer Martin], 11, 647, 649
Joe [husband of Lorraine "Lee" Bauer], 644, 647–649
Lorraine. See Bauer, Lorraine Eileen "Lee" "Peanuts" (Martin)
Martinsville, Ind., 617, 620, 624
Mary Miller Smiser Heritage Library, Warrensburg, Mo., 219
Maryland, 11, 20, 145, 153–154, 170–171, 176, 319, 636
Annapolis, 14, 142
Annapolis, Bagels and… to Go, 142
Annapolis, Graul's shopping center, 142
Annapolis, Maryland State Archives, 142, 154–155, 157, 158, 164, 166, 168–169, 171–172
Baltimore Co., Garrison Forest Protestant Episcopal Church, 154
Baltimore Co., Green Spring Punch, 154, 160–162
Baltimore Co., Spring Garden [land tract], 154
Baltimore, 154–155, 170
Reistertown, 11, 154–155, 170, 173
St. Thomas, 154
Sykesville, 155
Maryland Hotel, Chicago, Ill., 40
Maryland State Archives, Annapolis, Md., 142, 153–155, 157–158, 164, 166, 168–169, 171–172
Massachusetts, 108
Boston, 92, 110, 134
Cambridge, 110
Holyoke, 108
Holyoke, Gatehouse Furniture Studios, 108
Massachusetts Institute of Technology (MIT), Cambridge, Mass., 665
Masters
Letha A.. See Davis, Letha A. (Masters) [wife of Edmund Davis]
Woodson, 318
Maui, Hawii, 141
Maupin
Cynthia. See Gates, Cynthia (Maupin)
Daniel (1754–1832), 336–349, 362, 366, 373, 387
Eliza Ann. See Gooch, Eliza Ann (Maupin) [wife of Chiswell Gooch]
Elizabeth, 362
Gabriel, 337
George W., 336
James, 368
Jo Ann. See Gooch, Jo Ann (Maupin)
L.D., 336, 367
Leland, 336
Lola, 362
Margaret "Peggy" (McWilliams) [3rd wife of Daniel Maupin], 336, 337, 341, 344–345, 362, 364
Marie, 337
Washington, 336
Maupin family, 18, 145, 387
Maxfield, Goodwin, 332
Mayodan, Jean-Claude, 109
McAllister, James, 346
McAugham
Bertha (Tevis) [wife of S.J. McAugham], 205
S.J., 205
McCarthy
Daniel L., 489
Lynn C., 12
McCarty, George, 204
McClain
Elizabeth "Betsy." See (Davis), Elizabeth "Betsy [daughter of Nathaniel and Margaret Davis]
John Thompson, 174
Levi D., 174
Louisa "Eliza," 174
Lucinda, 174
Malinda, 174
Rachel, 174
Thomas, 174
McClung
Brian [son of Karen Douthart], 624
Greyson [son of Karen McClung], 624
Karen. See Douthart, Karen (Horner) (McClung) [daughter of Robert H. and Shelley Douthart]
McCormick Place Convention Center, Chicago, Ill., 73
McDougal, E.C., 387
McGehee, 346
McGruder, Mark A., 152
McGuire, Mrs. Unknown [2nd wife of Edmund Edward Davis], 318
McHendree, Catherine (Collins), 198
McKay, Amanda, 487
McKees Rocks, Penn., 483
McKelvey, Irene Rosalind "Roz." See Douthart Irene Rosalind "Roz" (McKelvey) [wife of Richard James Douthart]
McLain, Fran, 175
McLernon, Mary. See Douthart, Mary (McLernon) [Armoy, Ireland]
McMahon, Franklin, 84
McMurtry, John, 84
McWilliams
James, 364
John C., 364
Margaret "Peggy." See Maupin, Margaret "Peggy" (McWilliams) [3rd wife of Daniel Maupin]

Mecenzef, Hungary, 557
Medical Advertising Hall of Fame, 98–101, 120
Mehl, Barbara Jean. *See Davis, Barbara Jean (Mehl)*
Meinecke
Ludwell, 305–306
Mary M. (Sanders) [wife of Ludwell Meinecke], 305–306, 309
Mendes
Rica, 15
Richard, 15
Ruth, 15
Mendszent/Mendzenth, Hungary, 556
Mequon, Wisc., 503
Meredith College, Raleigh, N.C., 624
Merida, Mexico, 619
Merrick, John, 176
Merrillville, Ill., 271
Merrionette Manor, Chicago, Ill., 55
Merriville, Ind., 12, 56
Metropole, New York City, N.Y., 85
Metropolitan Museum of Art, New York City, 635
Mette, Alan, 105
Mexico
Tijuana, 135
Meyer
Bertie. See Higgins, Bertha "Bertie" (Meyer)
Freddy, 334
Miami Beach, Fla., 32, 109
Miami River, Ky., 198
Miami, Fla., 81
Michigan, 17, 324, 332, 488
Detroit, 10
Pinckney, 10
Wayne Co., 49
Michigan City, Ind., 270–271
Milan, Italy, 440
Milford, Ky,. 143
Miller
John, 143
Shelley Kenyon. See Douthart, Shelley Kenyon (Miller) [wife of Robert Henry "Butch" Douthart],
Milwaukee, Wisc., 603
Mindszent, Hungary, 557
Minnesota, 14, 271
Miro, Joan, 109
Mission Bay Park, San Diego, Calif., 111
Missouri, 10–11, 14, 20, 27, 145, 147, 149, 151–152, 174–175, 204–205, 211, 214, 217–218, 221, 234, 243, 247, 255, 275, 283, 291–292, 300, 315, 329, 332, 362, 364, 411, 438, 636
Boone Co., 205
Burtville, 151
Cass Co., Pleasant Ridge Cemetery, 151–152
Chilhowee, 10
Davis Cemetery, Saline Co., 151
Green Ridge, 149
Harrisonville, 151–152
Holden, 152
Hughesville, 147
Huntsville, Randolph Co., 149, 209
Jefferson City, 14, 142, 152
Jefferson City, Madison's Café, 142
Kansas City, 152
Knob Noster, 151
Knob Noster Cemetery, Knob Noster, 149
Lone Jack, 152
Lone Jack Cemetery, Saline Co., 151–152
Lone Tree, Cass Co., 151
Longwood, 10
Longwood, Bethlehem Christian Church, 150
Longwood, Pettis Co., 146–152
Longwood, Pettis Co., Longwood Cemetery, 149
Longwood, Pettis Co., Longwood Presbyterian Church, 146, 148
Marshall, 151
Nelson, Salt Fork Cemetery, 151
Peculiar, 152
Pettis Co., 146–147, 152
Randolph Co., 145
Saline Co., 150–151, 217
Sedalia, 10, 147
Sedalia Sedalia Public Library, 150
Sedlaia, Pettis County Courthouse, 142
Smith Chapel, Saline Co., 151
Valley City, 151
Valley City, Blackwater Creek, 151
Valley City, J.C. Davis Store, 151
Valley City, Johnson Co., 149
Valley City, Smith Shop, 151
Valley City, Zion Hill Church and Cemetery, 151
Warrensburg, 151
Missouri State Archives, Jefferson City, Mo., 14, 218, 296–297
Moberly, Harold, 205
Moberly High School, Moberly, Mo., 209
Moberly, Randolph Co., Mo., 17, 205, 209–210, 213, 239
Moffatt, Tracy, 109
Mohegan Sun, Uncasville, Conn., 141
Moldava nad Bodvou. Slovakia, 557
Monastery of Grábóc, Grábóc, Hungary, 456–457
Monroe, Phillip, 193
Montabon, France, 122
Montessori Mission Bay School, La Jolla, Calif., 672
Montgomery Co., Ky., 174–176, 189
Monticello, Va., 143
Montoya, Juan, 107, 109
Montreal Museum of Fine Arts, Montreal, Canada, 109
Montreal, Canada, 94
Montreal Museum of Fine Arts, 109
Mooney, William, 597
Moore
Chauncey, 81
Gary, 602
William, 329
Mora
Alfonse (Jr.) "Chubby" [son of June "Tootsie" (Davis) (Mora) Rogers, nephew of Clyde P. Davis], 60, 66, 76, 114–115
Alfonse Andre, [husband of June Davis] 35, 36, 114–115
April Lynn (Mora) (Morain) [daughter of June "Tootsie" (Davis) Mora Rogers, niece of Clyde P. Davis], 58–61, 76, 114–115
David Andrew "Bubs" [son of June "Tootsie" (Davis) (Mora) Rogers, nephew of Clyde P. Davis], 66, 76, 114–115
Erin (Mora) (Quenzler) [daughter of June "Tootsie" (Davis) (Mora) Rogers, niece of Clyde P. Davis], 36, 54, 64, 76, 114–115
Julie, 76
June "Tootsie." See (Davis, June "Tootsie" (Davis) Mora Rogers [daughter of Clyde Otis Davis and Mary Savage, sister of Clyde P. Davis]
Karen, 76
Mora family, 76
Morain, April Lynn. See Mora, April Lynn (Morain) [daughter of June "Tootsie" (Davis) (Mora) Rogers, niece of Clyde P. Davis]
Morgan Co., Ill., 218, 291, 292
Morgan family, 594
Morocco, 110
Zagora, 111
Morris
Joshua, 358–359
Naomi (Mrs.), 411
Sheldon, 497
Morris, Ill., 332, 411, 424
Morrison Field, West Palm Beach, Fla., 279
Mount Zion Christian Church and Cemetery, Taylor Twp., Sullivan Co., Mo., 151
Mountsterling, Montgomery Co., Ky., 186
Mt. Carmel Catholic High School, Chicago, Ill., 81, 503
Mt. Carmel Cemetery, Clever, Mo., 239
Mt. Carmel Prep Seminary, Niagara Falls, Ontario, 503
Mt. Haleakala, Maui, Hawaii, 111
Mt. Kisco Medical Group, 635
Mt. Olivet Cemetery, Wilmington, Ill., 607
Mt. Sinai, Long Island, N.Y., 512, 550
Mt. Stowe, Vt., 130
Muddy Creek, Madison Co., Ky., 200, 364
Mullins
Hazel Irene. See Davis, Hazel Irene (Mullins) [daughter of Joseph S. Davis and Alice Toombs)
Helen, 283
J.R., 283
Martha Jean, 283
Matthew, 336–337
Ruby, 283
William Edward D., 283, 289
Munich, Germany, 94, 655
Municipality of Tolna CountyArchives, Szekszárd, Hungary, 446, 449
Munster, Ind., 56, 60, 76
Murphy, 302
Columbus, 302
Fannie, 302
Lois Frances (Davis), 10, 11, 151, 233, 235
Newt, 302
Robert, 221
Sarah Gertrude. See Davis, Sarah Gertrude (Murphy)
Murphy family, 10, 302
Museum of Science and Industry, Chicago, Ill., 627
Mussolini, Benito, 557
Myndzenth, Hungary, 556
Nagy Lajos, King (King Lewis The Great), 558
Napton, Mo., 283
Nassau, 141
Natal, Brazil, 279

National Archives, Washington, D.C., 154, 207
National Institutes of Health, Bethesda, Md., 620, 625
Naval Hospital, Balboa Park, Calif., 134
Naval Training Center, Great Lakes, Ill., 132
Naval Yard, Brooklyn, N.Y., 511–512
Navy Pier, downtown Chicago, Ill., 615
Neighborhood Clinic, Tacoma, Wash., 621
Neil Duffy's Tavern, Chicago, Ill., 34
Nelson
Harriet, 271
Ozzie, 271
Nelson, Mo., 151, 291, 297
Netherlands, Maastricht, 109
Nevada
Las Vegas, 141
Virginia City, 12
Nevada, Mo.,
Nevada, Vernon Co., Mo., 218, 305–306, 309, 312
New Canaan, Conn., 77
New Hope Community Church, Fairmount, Ill., 333
New Jersey, 620
Princeton, 12, 94
New Mexico Highlands University, Las Vegas, N.M., 70
New Orleans, La., 174
New York [state], 13, 14, 54, 58, 65, 76, 79, 81, 86, 88, 90, 100, 106–110, 132, 134, 141–142, 149, 152, 440, 442, 449, 487, 491, 503, 526, 530, 628, 636
Bedford, 129, 143
Bedford, Fox Lane High School, 130
Briarcliff Manor, Westchester Co., 90, 106
Croton Falls, 88
Far Rockaway, 85
Lake George, 58
Long Island, Jones Beach, 88
Pound Ridge, 14–15, 54, 92, 106–111, 114, 129, 130, 132, 140, 143, 152–153, 677
Pound Ridge, Pound Ridge Community Church, 114
Pound Ridge, Pound Ridge Park, 113
South Salem, Le Château Restaurant, 117
Tappan Zee Bridge, 88
Westchester Co., 88
White Plains, Marriott Hotel, 115
New York City, 21, 76–77, 79, 81, 85–86, 88, 90, 93–94, 98, 100, 108–110, 121, 123–124, 134, 141–142, 511, 513, 619–620, 623, 625, 628, 633, 636, 644, 667
34th Street Bus Terminal, 85
Bronx, 131
Central Park, 85
Columbia Presbyterian Medical Center, 135
Designers 3, 90
Four Seasons Restaurant, 85
Grand Central neighborhood, 98
Grand Central Post Office, 98
L.W. Frohlich, Intercon International, 91
Madison Avenue, 93
Metropole, 85
Metropolitan Museum of Modern Art, 109
Plaza Hotel, 100
Rockaway Beach, Queens, 85
Seagram's Building, 85
Sudler & Hennessey, 91
Ted Bates Ad Agency, 85
Times Square, 85
Upper Manhattsn, 86
Upper West Side, 85
William Douglas McAdams Agency, 90
World Trade Center, 110
YMCA Sloan House, 85
New York Naval Shipyard, New York, 532, **549–550**
New York Yankees, 670
Newcastle, England, 478
Newman Food Service, Champaign-Urbana, Ill., 83
Newman Hall, University of Ill., Champaign-Urbana, Ill., 87
Niagara Falls, Ontario, 503
Nicholas Donuts & Pastries, Richmond, Ky., 144
Nobel Fool Theater, Chicago, Ill., 31
Normile, Frances, 488
North Africa, 279
North Carolina, 358, 625
North Carolina State University, Raleigh, N.C., 624
North Richland, Tex., 648
North Texas State University, 620
Northern Ireland, 593
North-Hungary, 555
Norwalk, Conn., 110
Notre Dame, South Bend, Ind., 503
O'Brien, Patrick K, 152
O'Hare International Airport, Chicago, 21
O'Neil, William, 329
Oakland Cemetery, Moberly, Mo., 209
Oakwood Township, Vermillion Co., Ill., 328
Oakwood., Vermillion Co., Ill., 392
Obama, Barack, President, 147
Odell, Mattie. *See Davis, Mattie (Odell)*
Oder/Ody, Thomas, 361
Ogden, Carlos C., 1st Lt., 333
Oglesby
Earlene, 233
Frances Earlene, 221
Ohio, 179, 328, 593
Ohio River, 174–176, 178
Ohio Valley, 176
Okinawa, 134
Olchoun, Hungary, 557
Olchuan, Hungary, 556
Old Tyme Toys antique shop, Richmond, Ky., 144
Oldham
Amelia "Milly" [wife of Josiah Collins]. See Collins, Amelia "Milly"
Ann (Pepper), 198
Ed, 389
Edmond [husband of Jane (Hill) Oldham], 360, 361
Jane. See Hill, Jane (Oldham) [daughter of John Hill and Eliza B. (White) (Gooch) (Hill), and wife of Edmond Oldham]
Mildred Elizabeth (Williams) (Oldham) (Gooch) [wife of Thomas E. Gooch Sr.]. See Gooch, Mildred Elizabeth (Oldham) (Williams) Gooch
Richard, 198
Oldham family, 18, 145
Olinger, Judy L. See Gooch, Judy L. (Olinger) [wife of Dale "Jessie" Gooch]
Olivenhein, Encinitas, Calif., 140
Oliver Gardens, Conn., 634
Olympia Fields Country Club, Chicago, Ill., 65, 83
Omega Engineering, Stamford, Connn., 630–631
Orange Co., Va., 336–337
Oregon, 153, 663
Portland, 134
Oriental Movie Theater.Chicago, Ill., 31, 83
Orland Park, Ill., 49, 56, 58, 489
Orr, David, 613
Ortega, Olivia, 105
Orville T. Bright Grammar School, Chicago, Ill., 32, 64, 80
Osborne, Robert, 329
Ostuni, Puglia, Italy, 111
Otter Creek, Madison Co., Ky., 176, 201
Ottoman Empire, 561
Ouidja, 279
Owings, Samuel, 154, 160, 162
Ox Ridge Hunt Club, Darien, Conn, 124
P. Kovacs Gallery, Vienna, Austria, 634
Pacific Ocean, 134
Pacyga, Dominic A., 481, 604
Page, 174
Paint Lick Creek, Madison Co., Ky., 358
Paint Lick, Ky., 205
Palkovics
Jakov, [husband of Matrona, father of Julianna Szávics) 457–458
Julianna (Szávics) [wife of Joann Szávics, mother of David Andrew Savage, Sr.],, 457–458
Matrona, [wife of Jakov Palkovics, mother of Julianna (Szávics) David Andrew Savage, Sr.], 457–458
Palo Alto, Calif., 667
Palos Park, Ill., 59–60, 270
Pantello, Ron, 101
Papageorge, James, 33
Paré, Dave, 136
Paris Biennale 2008 in Paris, France, 635
Paris, France, 76, 109, 123, 141, 628, 631, 634–636
Paris, Ky., 170
Parke, Horace, 200
Parker
Alexander, Captain, 337
Richard, Colonel, 337
Parrino
Christine Rene (Davis) (Ledingham) [daughter of Clyde P. and Kay Davis, wife of John Parrino], 25, 66, 76, 87–89, 106, 110–111, 114–124, 126, 130, 133, 247, 475, 611–613, 624, 630, 633, 636
John [husband of Christine (Davis) and son-in-law of Clyde P. and Kay Davis], 89, 106, 110, 117–118, 120–122, 126, 636
Parrish's Folly [land tract], Baltimore Co., Md., 170–172
Patapsco River, Md., 155
Patton, General, 280
Paxton, W.M., 175
Pecs, Hungary, 440–441, 443
Peculiar, Mo., 152, 317
Peden, Henry C. Jr., 171
Pennington, Ill., 362
Pennsylvania, 154, 176
Lancaster Co., 154

Pepper, Ann. *See Oldham, Ann (Pepper)*
Petrified Forest National Park, Blue Mesa, Ariz., 113
Pettis
Daniel "Eddie" [son of Eliza "Liza" Gooch], 291, 403
Eliza "Liza" (1875–1951) [wife of William Davis and wife of Thomas C. Goodwin]. See Gooch Eliza "Liza" (1875–1951)
Fred/Freddie, [son of Eliza "Liza" Gooch], 291, 300
Jess/Jessie, [son of Eliza "Liza" Gooch], 291, 300
Mr., 390
Victoria, 291
Pettis County Courthouse, Sedalia, Mo., 142
Pettis Co., Mo., 146–147, 152, 217–218, 221, 239, 247, 315, 403
Phil Smidt's Restaurant, Hammond, Ind., 86–87
Philadelphia, Penn., 534
Philippines, 133, 134, **396**
Manilla, Playboy Club, 133
Philips, Beverly [companion of David O. Davis], 65–67, 69
Phillips
Joseph, 400, 409
Leoria. See Reeves, Leoria "Peggy" (Phillips) (1909–1972) [daughter of Jessie Doney "Doll/Dollie" Gooch and Ernest W. Reeves]
Mary, 209
Picasso, Pablo, 109
Piggly Wiggly, Urbana, Ill., 63
Pilot Township, Vermillion Co., Ill., 38, 253
Pinckney, Mich., 10
Pipe Creek Road, Baltimore Co., Md., 170
Pittsburgh, Penn., 483
Platte Co., Mo., 174, 175
Playboy Club, Manila, Phillipines, 133
Plaza Hotel, New York City, N.Y., 100
Pleasant Ridge Cemetery, Cass Co., Mo., 151, 152
Podalein, Germany, 643. See also Podelin, Hungary
Podalin, Hungary, 643. See also Podelin, Hungary
Podelin Cemetery, Podelin, Slovakia, 649
Podelin, Hungary, 638, **644. See also Podolinic, Slovakia**
Podolínec, Slovakia, 642. 643**. See also Podelin, Hungary**
Podproč,Hungary, 556
Podprocz aliter Myndzenth, Hungary, 556
Poillerat, Gilbert, 109
Pomorski, Michelle Eilber, 327
Ponte Oliva Airfield, Gela, 280
Pool, Jon [husband of Darlene Ann Davis Pool], 276
Pool, Darlene Ann. See Davis, Darlene Ann (Pool)
Poproč, Hungary, 556–557
Poproč, Slovakia, 556–557
Porteneuve, Alfred, 109
Portland, Ore., 134
Pound Ridge, N.Y., 14–15, 54, 64–65, 77, 92, 106–111, 121, 123–124, 126, 129–130, 132, 140, 143, 152–153, 615, 620, 623, 628, 630–631, 647–648, 677
Pound Ridge Community Church, Pound Ridge, N.Y., 114
Pound Ridge Elementary School, Pound Ridge, N.Y., 120
Pound Ridge Park Swim Team, Pound Ridge, N.Y., 119–120, 122
Pound Ridge Park, Pound Ridge, N.Y., 113
Prague, Czech Republic, 110
Premonstrean [sic] monastery of Jaszo, Hungary, 556
Prewitt, Richard A., 199
Primrose Farms, Katonah, N.Y., 124
Princeton University, Princeton, N.J., 635, 665, 673
Princeton, N.J., 94
Printz, Eugene, 109
Provence, France, 110, 631
Providence, R.I., 110
Provost Albert, 557
Prowell, Bill, 149
Puerto Rico, 279, 396
Puglia, Italy, 110, 141
Pulley, Mable (Davis), 315
Pully, Sophia, 206
Purdue University, West Lafayette, Ind., 623, 655
Pureto Varas, Chile, 619
Purkey
Adam [son of Daniel A. and Terri (Whitlock) Purkey], 278
Becky, 278
Beverly, 257, 262, 280
Daniel Alan [husband of Terri (Whitlock) Purkey], 277–278
Elizabeth "Lizzie" (Davis)) [sister of Clyde Otis "Cotton" Davis], 11–12, 17, 32, 53, 249, 251–253, 256–257, 269, 275–277, 293, 307, 316, 332–333, 402, 438
Eric [son of Daniel A. and Terri (Whitlock) Purkey], 278
Everett Lee [husband of Elizabeth Davis, sister of Clyde Otis Cotton], 12, 257, 262, 276–277, 280
Glenn Edward (1922–1986) [son of Elizabeth (Davis) Purkey, husband of LaVerne, and cousin of Clyde P. Davis], 12, 22–23, 151, 256–257, 259–260, 262, 275–277, 280–281, 333, 402, 438, 660
Hugh [husband of Elizabeth (Davis) Purkey], 247, 252, 256–257, 262, 274–276, 316, 333, 660
LaVerne [wife of Glenn Purkey, cousin of Clyde P. Davis], 12, 23, 32, 37, 69, 147, 151, 246–248, 251, 256–257, 259–260, 264–265, 274–278, 280, 293, 297, 315, 333, 390, 410, 412
Nancy Jane (Green) [mother of Hugh Purkey], 276
Patricia Ann Entwistle [grandniece of Clyde Otis Cotton], 9
R.J., 275, 277, 278
Terri (Whitlock) [wife of Daniel A. Purkey], 278
Thomas "Tom" Edward, 27, 278
Queens, New York City, N.Y., 512
Quenzler, Erin (Mora). See Mora, Erin (Mora) (Quenzler) [daughter of June "Tootsie" (Davis) (Mora) Rogers, niece of Clyde P. Davis]
Rackoczy,Maria, 53, 57–59, 61
Rahm, Rosamond. See Sanders, Rosamond (Rahm) [wife of Shelby Otis Sanders]
Rainbow Beach, Chicago, Ill., 56
Rainey
Mary, 219
J. Woodson "Woody" Jr., 107—109
Rains, Dr., 361
Rajkovics,Geranim, 457
Rakoczi, Priince Ferenc II, 557
Raleigh, N.C., 624
Rancho Bernardo, Calif., 140
Rancho Santa Fe, Calif., 140
Randolph Co., Mo., 145, 204, 209–210, 212, 214, 217–218, 239, 247, 253, 291, 302, 305, 315
Raven, Judith, 13, 175
Red River, Ky., 198
Red Lick, Madison Co., Ky., 371
Red River Co., Tex., 174
Redhouse, Madison Co., Ky., 318–319
Redondo Beach, Calif., 64
Reed, Ethel, 283
Reese family, 275
Reeves
Alice, 391, 399
Bill, 414
Dollie, 262
Ernest W., 391, 398, 400
Grace (1919–) [daughter of Jessie Doney "Doll/Dollie" Gooch], 438
Jessie Doney "Doll." See Gooch, Jessie Doney "Doll."
Leoria "Peggy" [Phillips] (1909–1972) [daughter of Jessie Doney "Doll/Dollie" Gooch and Ernest W. Reeves], 25, 41, 391, 399–400, 409, 437–438
Margaret, 206, 209–210
Mary, 399
Mary L., 391
Norman, 391, 399
Ruby (1915–) [daughter of Jessie Doney "Doll/Dollie" Gooch], 391, 399, 438
Ruth, 391, 399
Reeves family, 335
Reffett, Minnie, 390
Reister family, 154
Reisterstown, Md., Public Library, 11
Reisterstown, Md. 154–155, 170, 173
Remmant, Loyola. See Davis, Loyola (Remnant) [wife of Woodson Davis]
Remsenburg, N.Y., 630
Renfro, Mae. See Davis, Mae (Renfro) [wife of Roy Lee "Jack Dog" Davis]
Reno, Nev., 37, 260
Rhein, Corrie, 390
Rhode Island
Providence, 110
Rice, Fountain, 198
Richard's Drive-in Cafeteria, Chicago, Ill., 83
Richardson family, 275
Richland Hills, Tex., 647
Richland, Wash., 619
Richmond Cemetery, Richmond, Ky., 205, 319
Richmond Co., Ky., 143
Richmond Tourism and Visitor Center, Richmond, Ky., 152
Richmond, Madison Co., Ky., 143, 147–148, 150, 188, 199, 202, 205–206, 283, 319, 335–336, 361, 365, 387
Richmond, Va, 336, 348, 359
Ridge Road, Lansing, Ill., 33
Rijeka/Fiume, Croatia, 520. See also Fiume, Italy
River Cam, Cambridge, England, 666
Riverview Amusement Park, Chicago, Ill., 603
Riviera Hotel, Las Vegas, Nev., 65
Roanoke City Library, Roanoke, Va., 143
Roanoke, Va., 143

Robb, W.L., Rev., 283

Roberts

Elisha, 204

Mike, Pastor, 434

Rochester Institute of Technology, Rochester, N.Y., 620

Rochester, N.Y., 620

Rock, Jeanette (Arvia), 86, 627

Rock Lick branch (of Otter Creek), Madison Co., Ky., 217, 371

Rockaway Beach, Queens, N.Y., 85

Rockcastle Co., Ky., 336, 364, 367

Rockfield, Ind., 17, 22–23, 31, 247, 259–261, 333

Rockville, Ind., 593

Rodes, William, Col., 198

Rogers

Adrian Lee. See Rogers, Lee

June (Davis) Mora. See Davis, June "Tootsie" (Mora) (Rogers)

Lee, 36, 77

Sylvia, 77

Romania, 467

Rome, Italy, 635

Rosencrantz, David, Lt., 280

RotaCare Free Clinic, Tacoma, Wash., 621

Rudnok, Hungary, 557

Ruhlmann, Emile-Jacques, 109

Rumpus Room Tavern, Chicago, Ill., 83, **488**

Rush Medical Center, Chicago, Ill., 61

Rush Presbyterian St. Lukes Hospital, Chicago, Ill., 59, 490

Russell, Mary Ann, 152

Ruzsa, Éva, 13, 446

Sackler, Arthur, Dr., 90

Sagamore Inn in Bolton Landing, Lake George, N.Y., 58

Saint John the Baptist's Monastery, Jaszo, Hungary, 557

Saks Fifth Avenue, Chicago, Ill., 87

Salina, Ill., 329

Saline Co., Mo., 150–151, 217–218, 283, 291–292, 296–297, 315

Saline, Ill., 329

Salsig, Gwen, 11

Salt Fork Cemetery, Nelson, Mo., 151, 297, 299

Salt Fork River, Vermillion Co., Ill., 328–329

Salt Lake City, Utah, 678

Salt Spring Twp., Ramdolph Co., Mo., 210

Saltby, England, 281

Salzburg, Austria, 619

San Bieguito Cotillion, 671-672

San Diego Bay, Calif., 111

San Diego Co., Calif., 141

San Diego, Calif., 25, 57, 121, 135–136, 140, 667, 672

San Francisco, Calif., 92, 134, 497, 500, 507, 665, 667

Sandberg, Carolyn, 131

Sanders, 305

Andrew Jackson, 308

Dr. Jack Shelby, 11, 68

Emeline, 308

Glenna (Aufferberg) [wife of Jack Shelby Sanders], 306

Jack Shelby (1929–), 305–308, 313

James Arnold, 305

Jeffrey Stewart, 306

Jimmy Kay (Trenkle) [wife of Jack Shelby Sanders] 308, 313

Laura, 306

Linda (Thomure), 306, 308

Linda Ellen, 306

Lou, 302

Lula "Lu" (Davis) (1877–) [wife of Thomas Luther Sanders], 151, 218, 283, 286, 304–314, 373, 377

Luther. See Sanders, Thomas Luther

Mary Mae. See Meinecke, Mary M. (Sanders) [wife of Ludwell Meinecke]

Matilda [wife of John B. Sanders], 411

Mrs. T.L. See Lula (Davis) Sanders

Patricia (Smashey), 306, 308

Rosamond (Rahm) [wife of Shelby Otis Sanders], 305, 306, 313

Shelby Otis, 306, 313

Thomas Luther, 302, 305–310, 313

Tomas Luther, 218

Winifred. See Travernicht, Winifred (Sanders) [wife of james Arnold Sanders]

Sanders family, 10, 306

Santa Cruz, Calif., 136

Santa Luz, Rancho Santa Fe, Calif., 140

São Paulo, Brazil, 94

Sarasota, Fla., 499–500

Sardinia, Italy, 110, 440, 636

Sasbo, Japan, 134

Saskatchewan, Canada, 599

Saunders, Mrs. Luther. See Sanders, Lula "Lu (Davis)

Savage, 18

Andy. See David Andrew Savage Sr.

Andrew. See David Andrew Savage Sr.

David Andrew Jr. (Szávics, Dusán/Dezsó Andrew Jr.) [son of of Mary Benko and David Andrew Savage Sr., brother of Mary M. "Spare Ribs" Savage, uncle of Clyde P. Davis], 34, 57, 83, 467, 476–478, 483–484, 486–490, 491, 493–494, 496–501, 509, 512, 520, 523, 631, 660

David Andrew Sr. "Andy" (1874–1949) (Szávics, Dusán/Dezsó Sr., [husband of Mary Benko, father of Mary M. Savage Davis, maternal grandfather of Clyde P. Davis], 49, 443, 450, 453, 460, 465, 467–468, 472–474, 477, 481, 483–484, 486–487, 490, 491, 500, 512, 523, 556

Dorothy [wife of John Raymond Savage], 11, 65, 505, 506, 507, 515–517

Dusán. See Savage, David Andrew

Ellen "Ella" (Scrip) [wife of Michael D. Savage Sr.], 47, 502, 503, 512–513

Jesse [son of Paul Savage], 507, 517

John [father of David Andrew Sr. (Dusán/Dezsó Szávics, Sr.), 467

John Raymond (1919–)[son of David Andrew Savage Sr and Mary Benkó, brother of Mary M. "Spare Ribs (Savage) (Davis), uncle of Clyde P. Davis], 11, 46, 483–484, 504–509, 541

Joseph "Joe" (originally József Szávics/Szavics) (1906–) [son of David Andrew Savage Sr. and Mary Benko, brother of Mary Savage Davis, uncle of Clyde P. Davis], 476, 478, 483, 487, 493, 497, 512, 523

Julia (Tornovich) [mother of David Andrew Savage Sr. and great-grandmother of Clyde P. Davis], 467

June Juliet (Savage) (Lucas) (1911–) See Lucas, June (Savage) [sister of Mary (Savage) Davis and aunt of Clyde P. Davis]

Mary (Maria Angyela Benkó) (1843–) [wife of David Andrew Savage Sr., mother of Mary M. (Savage) Davis, and maternal grandmother of Clyde P. Davis], 34, 39, 49, 79, 86–87, 465, 467, 475–479, 481–495, 497–498, 500–502, 504–509, 511–513, 520, 522, 543, 545, 556, 563.

Mary Lou [daughter of John Raymond and Dorothy Savage], 64, 505, 509, 519

Mary M. See Davis, Mary M. "Spare Ribs" (Savage) (Davis) (1917–2011) [daughter of Mary Benko and David Andrew Savage Sr., wife of Clyde Otis Davis, and mother of Clyde P. Davis]

Michael [father of David Andrew Savage, Sr.], 477

Michael David Jr.[cousin of Clyde P. Davis], 11, 467, 477, 481, 486, 488, 491, 493, 495–498, 500–503, 505–507, 511–513

Michael David Sr. [brother of Mary Savage Davis, uncle of Clyde P. Davis], 47, 49, 475, 483, 485, 490, 493, 500–503, 510–513, 541, 543–544

Nancy (McGiveron) [wife of Michael D. Savage Jr.], 503, 513

Nicky [wife of Paul Savage], 507

Paul [son of John Raymond and Dorothy Savage], 497–498, 507–508, 517

Patti Sue [daughter of John Raymond and Dorothy Savage], 497, 507–518, 517

Savage family, 12, 13, **439. See also Szávics**

Savannah, Ga., 337, 411

Savich

Andrew, 477, 481. See also Savage, David Andrew Sr.

Juliet, 481

Mary, 543. See also Mary (Benko) Savage

Saylor, Durston, 107

Schlomer, Dan, 283

Schmal, Michelle "Micki" (Davis) [daughter of Larry Joe Davis], 37, 271–273, 276

School of Art and Design, University of Illinois, Champaign-Urbana, Ill., 104, 105

Schreiner-Yantis, Netti, 348

Sciota River, Ky., 198

Scotland, 105

Scott

Ethel Earlene (Davis). See Davis, Ethel Earlene (Scott)

George C., 337

Henry, 292

Lucille, 292

Randolph, 54

William, 193

Seagram's Building, New York City, N.Y., 85

Seal Beach, Calif., 134

Sears, J.H., 530

Seattle, Washington, 25, 134, 663

Sebestyén, Dobries, 459

Sedalia, Johnson Co., Mo., 10, 147, 239, 244, 247, 255, 279, 288, 333, 402, 403, 411

Sedalia Public Library, Sedalia, Mo., 150

Selig, Gwen, 153

Sellers, Rod, 481, 604
Serbia, 467
Serb-Orthodox Church and Cemetery, Grábóc, Hungary, 456–457
Seress, Józseph, 13, 441
Seven Mile Bridge, Florida Keys, 649
Sevier Co., Ark., 174–175
Shaffett, Dorothy, 337
Shearer
Mr., 361
Reavis, 217
Sheer, William, 329
Shelby, Joe, Col., 305
Sheldon
Drusilla, 13
Drusilla Cochran, 175
Sheldon Business School, St. Louis, Mo., 209
Shoop
Isaac, 362, 373
Lucy (Williams), 362, 373
Short, Wilbur, 329
Shuman, Mae Lane Gooch, 390
Shute, Nancy, 152
Sicily, Italy, 110, 112, 280
Sienna, Italy, 110
Sigma Chi fraternity, Univ. of California, Berkeley, 665
Sinels, Nancy, 283
Singleton
Bobby, 273
Ethel "Eddie" (Davis), 268, 334
Onus [husband of Ethel Davis], 268, 273, 334
Sióagárd (formerly said "Agárd"), Hungary, 450–453
Sitka National Historic Park, Alaska, 663
Skorge, Ralph, 89
Slaves
Ann, 174
Becky, 174
Black John, 179
Bob, 176–178
Capius, 361
Charles, 348, 385
David, 174
Eliza, 204, 361
Fillis, 174
Harriott, 176
Ibsan, 361
Jack, 346, 361, 389
Jane, 363
John, 177
John Brown, 176–177
John Merrick, 176
Kate, 170
Kitty, 361
Nancy, 177
Phillis, 174, 176
Raney, 174
Scott, 174
Phillis, 176
Schuyler, 361
Silas, 200, 214
Simon, 176
Sopha, 174
Stephen, 176
Tom, 346
Vilett, 190
York, 348, 358
Sligo, Ireland, 619
Slovakia, 13, 467, 555–557, 643
Slovenia, 467
Smashey, Patricia. See Sanders, Patricia (Smashey)
Smiser, Mary Miller, 219
Smith
Audrey Lee [wife of H.M. Waggoner]. See Gooch, Audrey Lee "Bug" (Gooch) [Smith] [Waggoner]
Byron Dean (1929–1973), 412, 438
Cindy Lou, 411
Cornice Hobert, [husband of Mary Mildred (Gooch)], 23, 25, 412, 416–419, 421, 426, 429, 432, 436, 438
Dawn, 421
Dean, 421
Deanie, 421
Debra "Debbie" Lynn (1955–) [daughter of Marlene Gooch], 424, 438
Della, 373
Erville Jesse "Smitty" [husband of Audrey "Bug" Lee Gooch], 412, 438
Hobert. See Smith, Cornice Hobert
James "Jim" [husband of Marlene Gooch], 418, 424, 438
James Robert, 420–421
Marlene (Gooch) [daughter of Darrel Ira "Hoopie" Gooch] [wife of James "Jim" Smith], 418, 424
Mary Mildred. See Gooch, Mary Mildred (Smith) (1905–1992) [daughter of Thomas E. "Moody" Gooch, wife of Cornice Hobert Smith]
Michael, 411
Mildred. See Gooch, Mary Mildred (Smith) (1905–1992) [daughter of Thomas E. "Moody" Gooch, wife of Cornice Hobert Smith]
Nathan, 358
Robert Emanuel "Bobby" (1924–1970), 411–412, 419, 421, 426, 438
Sarah, 420
Tina Marie Lynn (1962–) [daughter of Marlene Gooch], 424, 438
William, 373
Smith Chapel, Saline Co., Mo., 151
Smith family, 335
Smith Shop, Valley City, Mo., 151
Smithland, Ky., 176
Smithville, Ky., 174
Sneedville, Hancock Co., Tenn., 275
Snider, Anne, 291, 300
Soldier's Delight Hundred [land tract], Baltimore Co., Md., 170
Soldiers Field, Chicago, Ill., 628
Solomon, Peter, 130
Sonoma State University. Rohnert Park, Calif., 667
Sony (movie theater), Chicago, Illinlois, 33
Sopko, Imrich, 557
Souder, Mary Fern, 13
South Korea, 134
South America, 411
South Chicago Neighborhood House, Chicago, Ill., 481, 483
South Chicago Savings Bank, Chicago, Ill., 602
South Chicago, Ill., 49, 607
St. Peter and Paul's Roman Catholic Church, 87
South Deering ("Irondale"), Ill., 56, 81
South Deering neighborhood, Chicago, Ill., 80
South Kent, Conn., 107
South Shore Country Club, Chicago, Illiinois, 481, 483
South Shore neighborhood of Chicago, 647
South Side of Chicago, Ill., 25, 81, 83, 100, 102, 627, 633, 654
South Suburban Genealogical & Historical Society, Hazel Crest, Ill., 39
Southampton, England, 636
Southeast Chicago Historical Society, Chicago, Ill., 604
Southeast Historical Society, Chicago, Ill., 33–34
Southern California, 141
Southfield, Mich., 318
Southmoor Hotel, Chicago, Ill., 483
Southtown (movie theater), Chicago, Ill., 33
Spain, 396
Barcelona, 94
Madrid, 94
Spak
Joannes [1st husband of Maria Spak], 555
Maria (Ligats) (1809–) [wife of Jacobus Benko, mother of Mihály Máté Benko], 555
Spalding ,Vergie M., 303
Spanish Louisiana, 176
Spasoff, Tom, 86, 484
Spokane Falls Community College, Spokane, Wash., 620
Spring Garden (land tract) , Baltimore Co., Md., 154
Springdale (neighboorhood), Stamford, Conn., 630
Springfield, Mo., 239, 244
Springfield, Va, 348
Sprinkle, 218
Grandma. See Sprinkle, Miriam
Jacob S., 217, 218
Miriam "Mimi" "Mima" "Grandma Sprinkles" See Davis, Miriam "Mimi" Dodd) (Marquess) (Davis) (Sprinkle) [widow of James Davis].
Sprinkles, Mimi/Mima. See Sprinkle, Miriam
Sred/Sredzinsky
Clare Ann. See Martin, Clare Ann (Sred)
Clark [husband of Rose Marie (Bauer) and father of Clare Ann (Sred) (Martin), 648, 657
Rose
Sredzinsky. See Sred
St. Albee's Catholic Church, Chicago, Ill., 603
St. Andrews Episcopal Church, Ben Lomond, Calif., 116
St. Joseph's Hospital, Kokomo, Howard Co., Ind., 22, 41
St. Kevin's Roman Catholic Church, Chicago, Ill., 45, 658
St. Louis University, St. Louis, Mo., 647
St. Louis, Mo., 305
St. Luke's Presbyterian Hospital, Chicago, Ill., 58
St. Mary's Cemetery, Chicago, Ill., 613
St. Mary's Cemetery, Evergreen Park, Cook Co., Ill., 467, 475, 490
St. Olcan's Church Cemetery, Armoy, Co. Antrim,

Ireland, 593
St. Paul's Episcopal Church, Baltimore, Md., 154
St. Peter and Paul's Roman Catholic Church, South Chicago, Ill., 87, 484
St. Rose Church, Wilmington, Ill, 606
St. Stephen of Hungary Church, New York, N.Y., 512–513
St. Thomas Church, Baltimore Co., Md., 170
St. Thomas, Md., 154
Stamford, Conn., 64, 110, 127, 630
Standard Steel Car Company, Gary, Ind., 512, 521, 547–548
Stanford University, Palo Alto, Calif., 665–667
Stapp, Katherine, 335
State Street, Chicago, Ill., 31, 83
Staten Island, New York, 279
Steele
Bob, 33
Virginia, 12
Stewart, Gavin, 468
Stinson ,A.R., 151
Stocksdale
Catherine, 155
Edward, 155
John, 154
Margaret. See Davis, Margaret (Stocksdale) [wife of Richard Davis and 4th great-grandmother of Clyde P. Davis]
Stocksdale family, 170
Stosz, Hungary, 557
Stouffer Building, Richmond, Ky., 143
Stout Field, Indianapolis, Ind., 279
Stratford, Conn., 620, 621
Strathdee, Paul, 468
Stratton, William, Governor, 411
Stump
Bernetta Fae (Triplett), 10, 151, 224, 226, 230, 236, 302, 305
Carol Sue, 305
George Willam, 305
Sturdevant, Katherine Scott, 76
Subes, Raymond, 109
Suddeth/Suddith/Sudduth/Suthard
James, 175–176, 181–182, 184, 186, 188–194, 200
Sally, 182, 184
Sarah. See Davis, Sarah (Blackwell) (Davis) (Suddeth) [wife of Solomon Davis and 3rd great-grandmother of Clyde P. Davis, later wife of James Suddeth]
Sudler & Hennessey, New York City, N.Y., 91
Sugar Creek Twp., Randolph Co., Mo., 210
Sugar Loaf, Maine, 130
Sunrise of Palos Park, Ill., 59–60
Suthard. See Suddeth
Sütó, Margit. See Bolyki, Margit (Sütó)
Swartz TV Home Improvement, Lafayette, Ind., 40
Swifton Company, Chicago, Ill., 54
Sykesville, Md., 155
Syracuse University, Syracuse, N.Y., 122
Szálka, Hungary, 442, 450–451, 454–456, 458, 461
Szavich. See Szávics and Savage
Szávics/Szavics – See also Savage
Andrew. See Savage, David Andrew Savage Sr. (1874–1949) [maternal grandfather of Clyde P. Davis]
Dersöné Maria. See Savage, Mary Benko (Maria Angyela Benkó) (1843–) [wife of David Andrew Savage Sr., mother of Mary M. (Savage) Davis, and maternal grandmother of Clyde P. Davis]
Dezsó/ Dusán/David Sr.. See Savage, David Andrew Sr. (1874–1949) [father of Mary M. "Spare Ribs" Savage, maternal grandfather of Clyde P. Davis]
Deszó/David Jr. [son of Mary (Benko) Savage], 478
Dusán/Dezsó. See Savage, David Andrew Sr. (1874–1949) [father of Mary M. "Spare Ribs" Savage, maternal grandfather of Clyde P. Davis]
György, 458, 459
Ignácz, 455
Janos, 446
Joann. [husband of Julianna (Palkovics) Szávics, father of David Andrew Savage, Sr.], 458, 460–461
Joannes, 454
József/Joe. See Savage, Joseph "Joe" (originally József Szávics/Szavics) (1906–) [son of David Andrew Savage Sr. and Mary Benko, brother of Mary Savage Davis, uncle of Clyde P. Davis]
Julianna (Palkovics) [daughter of Jakov and Matrona Palkovics, wife of Joann Szavics, mother of David Andrew Savage, Sr.], 60, 459–461
Maria. See Savage, Mary Benko (Maria Angyela Benkó) (1843–) [wife of David Andrew Savage Sr., mother of Mary M. (Savage) Davis, and maternal grandmother of Clyde P. Davis]
Mary. See Savage, Mary Benko (Maria Angyela Benkó)
See also Davis, Mary M. "Spare Ribs" (Savage)
Stefan, 451
Szávics family, 442. 446, 448, 450–452, 454, 456, 458, 460, **462. See also Savage**
Szávicz. See Szávics and Savage
Szecsuác
Joann, 456
Matrona, 456
Szekszárd, Hungary, 13, 444, 446, 449, 451, 460, 464
Szepsi, Hungary, 557
Szlavics family. See Szávics and Savage
Szűcs, Erzsebet [possible daughter of John/Janos Benko], 553, 573
Takacs, Menyhert, Dr., 548
Tamarac, Fla., 653, 653
Tamásné, Gréczy, 13
Tappan Arms, Briarcliff Manor, Westchester Co., N.Y., 88
Tappan Zee Bridge, N.Y., 88
Tatum
John Tomas, 221
Mollie. See Epply, Mollie (Tatum)
Rosa Nannie. See Davis, Rosa Nannie (Tatum) [wife of Jefferson C. Davis]
Taylor
Tammi Ann. See Davis, Tammi Ann (Taylor) [wife of Cole Davis and daughter-in-law of Clyde P. and Kay Davis]
Taylor-English Coal Company, Vermillion Co., Ill., 411
Ted Bates Ad Zgency, New York City, N.Y., 85
Tempe, Ariz., 205
Tennessee, 275–276, 329
Teodorovics, Gedeon, 460
Teradata Corp., Raleigh, N.C., 624
Terry, Elizabeth, 346
Tevis
Ann Eliza, 205
Arthusa. See Davis, Arthusa (Tevis)
Ben F., 205
Bernice. See Douglas, Bernice (Tevis) [wife of A. T. Douglas]
Bertha. See McAugham, Bertha [wife of S.J. McAugham]
Charles R., 205
Cleopatra, 205
Clifton, 205
Hallie. See Hayse, Hallie (Tevis)
Ida, 205
J.C., 205
John R., 205
Marion, 205
Mary M., 205
Minnie. See Howell, Minnie (Tevis) [wife of W.C. Howell]
Neal E., 205
Noah H., 205, 214
Richard Davis, 205
Robert, 170, 174–175, 190–191, 193
Robert Evan, 205
William, 205
William Edward, 205
Texas, 175, 620, 644, **647–648**
The Barks, Cambridge, England, 666
The Bush, Chicago, Ill., 56
The Cornell Arms, Hyde Park, Ill., 488
The Covenant, Rancho Santa Fe, Calif., 140
The Drake Hotel, Chicago, Ill., 142
The Filson Club, Louisville, Ky., 176
The Hamptons, N.Y., 630
The Hill neighborhood of Chicago, Ill., 627
The Meadows/The Grand, Del Mar, Calif., 140
The Newport, Chicago, Ill., 488
The Premonstratensian Abbey, Jaszo, Hungary, 558
Thomas
Albert, 283
Lucy, 362
Nellie M. See Davis, Nellie M. (Thomas)
Thomson
Ann [wife of Thomas Thomson], 346
Richard, 346
Thomas, 346
William, 346
Thomure, Linda. See Sanders, Linda (Thomure)
Thorpe Elementary School, Chicago, Ill., 615
Thorton, Ill., 38
Tichánek, Richard, 13
Tijuana, Mexico, 135
Tilsley, Margaret W., 198
Tilton, Charles V., 328–329
Timbuktoo, 599
Times Square, New York City, N.Y., 85
Tindouf, 279
Tinley Park, Ill., 56

Tippecanoe County Historical Assoc., Lafayette, Ind., 40
Tippecanoe County Public Library, Lafayette, Ind., 40
Tippecanoe Co., Ind., 40
Toberman, Walther H., 236
Tokepa, Kans., 243
Tokyo, Japan, 134, 655
Toledo, Lucas Co., Ohio, 254, 333
Tolna County, Hungary, 446, 449–450, 456, 458, 460, 462
Toombs
Alice (Davis). See Davis, Alice (Toombs)
Finis "Boss" Arnold Davis, 149
Fred "Freddy," "Dick," Morgan, 149
Jefferson, 239
Mattie Melvina See Davis, Mattie Melvina (Toombs) [wife of John Morgan Davis]
Topeka, Kans., 12
Tornovich, Julia [mother of David Andrew Savage Sr. and great-grandmother of Clyde P. Davis], 467
Toscano, Wallace J., 106
Tóth/Toth
Ferenc [father of Julianna Toth and 2nd great-grandfather of Clyde P. Davis], 564
Julianna [wife of Mihály Máté Benko, mother of Mary Benko Savage and John/Janos Benko, and great-grandmother of Clyde P. Davis]. See Benko, Julianna (Toth).
Townson
Kathie. See Douthart, Kathie (Towson)
Ray [husband of Kathie Douthart], 625
Transylvania, 557
Travernicht, Winifred [wife of James Arnold Sanders], 305
Travis Air Museum, Travis AFB, Ca., 280
Trebisov (?), Czechoslovakia, 442
Trenkle, Jimmy Kay. See Sanders, Jimmy Kay (Trenkle) [wife of Jack Shelby Sanders]
Treybal, Carol, 13, 283
Trickum, Mo., 150
Trinidad, 279
Triplett, 221
Bernetta Fae, 236
Elmo Dean, 221, 224
Ethel (Davis) [daughter of J.C. Davis], 151, 224, 227, 230, 236, 305
James Elmo, 149, 221
Mrs. Elmo, 151
Trumball Park Homes, Chicago, Ill., 16, 34, 47, 49, 55, 56
Trumball Park, Chicago, Ill., 35, 56, **654**
Tucker, Betty Jean. See Davis, Betty Jean (Tucker)
Tucson, Ariz., 10
Tukwilles, Carol, 143
Tunisia, 280
Turnberry Country Club, Aventura, Fla., 664
Turner
Bob, 373
Della, 362
Donald C., 221
Earl Clifton, 221
Emmett, 204
Everett Bulger, 396
Gary Earl, 221
Ida, 362, 373, 385
James, 362
James Edward, 221
Joe, 373
John, 193
Joseph, 362
Maggie, 362, 373, 385
Margie, 305
Margie Ann, 221
Margie. See Davis, Margie (Turner)
Mollie, 362, 373, 385
Neal E., 362, 373, 385
Robert, 362
Turner Construction Company, San Francisco, Calif., 665, 666
Turpin Funeral Home, Richmond, Ky., 205
Tuscany, Italy, 110
Twin Lakes, Wisc., 484, 498–500
U.S. Department of Energy, Washington D.C, 619
U.S. Marine Corps, 62, 63, 64
U.S. Steel Corporation, 481, 594
U.S. Steel Mill, Chicago, Ill., 604
UCLA (Univ. of California at Los Angeles), 665
Ukraine, 445, 467
Ultonia (ship), 520
Umbria, Italy, 110
Union City, Madison Co. Ky., 319
Union Precinct, Richmond, Madison Co., Il., 391
Union Township, Vermillion Co., Ill., 328
Universal Music, Chicago, Ill., 54
Universal Music Corp., Chicago, Ill., 83
University Church, Chicago, Ill., 623
University Club, Chicago, Ill., 102
University of California at Berkeley, 140–141, 665–666
University of California at Los Angeles, 655
University of Cambridge, Cambridge, England, 665
University of Chicago, Chicago, Ill., 33, 627
University of Chicago Hospital Clinics, Chicago, Ill., 49
University of Illinois, Champaign/Urbana, Ill., 63, 83–84, 86–87, 93, 100, 102–104, 332, 511, 617, 627–628, 633
University of Illinois, Chicago, Ill., 615
University of North Carolina at Greensboro, N.C., 624
University Press, Champaign-Urbana, Ill., 84
Unknown Surname
Brittany, 77
Chuck, 417
Erica, 271
Erle, 420
Erzike, 442
Flora, 420
Gorgeous George, 35
Juliska, 442
Larry, 41
Liberace, 35
Margaret "Maggie," 34
Marie, 33
Mat, 400
Mervin, 54
Sam, 276
Upper Manhattan, New York City, N.Y., 86
Upper West Side, New York City, N.Y., 85
Urbana, Ill., 63, 391, 398, 617
Utah, 648
Salt Lake City, 678
Valley City, Johnson Co., Mo., 149, 151, 217–218, 221, 302–303, 315
Valois Gallery, Paris, France, 634–635
Van Duzan, Miss, 329
Vance
John, Major, 328
Joseph, Governor, 328
Vance Township, Vermilion Co., Ill., 38, 328, 332, 335, 392, 398, 412
Vance Township Building, Fairmount, Ill., 333
Vance Township Library, Fairmount, Vermillion Co., Ill., 331, 333
Vance Township War Veterans Memorial, Fairmount, Ill., 333
Varbel, Philip, 183
Varnon, Lewis A., 204
Vaughn, Mary Ann, 221
Veneto, Italy, 110
Verkennis, Florentine [wife of Everett Davis], 318
Vermilion Co., Ill., 218, 247, 253, 267, 291, 300, 332, 335, 362, 370, 389–390, 405–407, 409, 411–412, 434
Vermilion County Courthouse, Danville, Ill., 147
Vermilion Nursing Home, Fairmount, Ill., 398, 411
Vermont
Butternut, 130
Killington, 130
Mt. Stowe, 130
Vernon Co., Mo., 214
Veszely, Anna Andrea (1783–) [wife of Jacobus Benko and [mother of Jacobus Benko], 555–556, 563
VG's Bakery, Cardiff By Sea, Calif., 668
Viano, Sharon [wife of Dale "Jessie" Gooch], 422, 438
Vienna Marriott Hotel, Vienna, Austria, 446
Vienna, Austria, 110, 440, 444, 446, 644
Vietnam, 63, 110, 133, 141
Dalat, Xuan Huong Park, 111
Ho Chi Min City, 111
Virginia, 12, 20, 143, 170, 176, 283, 336, 339, 346, 348, 358, 636
Albemarle Co., 145
Goochland Co., 145
Goochland, Goochland Historical Society, 142–143
Henrico Co., 143
Keswick, Keswick Hall, 142
Louisa Co., 412
Louisa Co., 145
Monticello, 143
Richmond, Virginia State Library, 142
Roanoke, Roanoke City Library, 143
Virginia Beach, 134
Virginia 147, 149, 145
Virginia Beach, Va., 134
Virginia City, Nev., 12, 278
Virginia State Library, Richmond, Va., 142
Vista, N.Y., 120
Vockery
Kathy, 171, 178, 201, 205, 207, 210, 319, 337, 359, 364–365
William L. "Bill," 178, 201, 205, 207, 210, 319,

359, 364–365
Vogue Wright Studios, Chicago, Ill., 83
Volk, Albert, 151
W. Isle, Aventura, Fla., 635
Wabash Railroad, 594, 595
Wagers, Charles, 205
Waggoner
Audrey Lee (Gooch) [wife of H.M. Waggoner]. See Gooch, Audrey "Bug" Lee (Gooch) (Smith) (Waggoner (1916–)
H.M., 412
Walker
Barbara, 152
James G., 199
Warehouse, Paris, France, 634
Warford, James, 283
Warren Elementary School, Chicago, Ill., 615, 627, 629
Warrensburg, Johnson Co., Mo., 151, 217, 218, 221, 235–236, 239, 279, 305, 315
Washington, 174, 260
George, General, 336
Seattle, 134
Washington State University, Richland, Washington, 619
Washington University, St. Louis, 306
Washington, D.C., 110, 134, 154–155, 171, 217, 619–620, 624–625, 628, 643
Waukegan, Ill., 603
Wayne Co., Mich., 49
Weant, K.E., 204
Weiner Bank-Verein, 536, 573
Weis
Ethel. See Bauer, Ethel Irene "Bunny" (Bauer)
Jack [husband of Ethel Irene "Bunny" (Bauer)], 649
Wells
Altha, 318
Baxter, 204, 214
Elizabeth (Luth). See Luth, Elizabeth (Wells)
Elizabeth Etta "Lizzie" (Davis) [daughter of Edmund Davis (1868–1909)], 318
J. Richard, 318
Richard Jr., 318
West Palm Beach, Fla., 279
Westchester Co., N.Y., 88, 119, 630
Briarcliff Manor, 88
Tappan Arms, 88
Western Union Telegraph Co., 63
Westhampton Beach, N.Y., 120
Wheeler, Richard S., 154
Whitaker Guernsey Studio
Chicago, Ill., 83
White, 18
Ambrose, 337
Eliza B. See Gooch, Eliza (White) (Gooch) (Hill) (1788–1859) [daughter of Galen White, wife of Cornelius Gooch and wife of John Hill, mother of Nancy "Nannie" Gooch Davis]
Galen [father of Eliza (White) (Gooch) (Hill) (1759–1833)], 336–349, 358, 360
Henry, 337
Mildred [wife of Galen White], 337
Virgil D., 178
White Plains, N.Y., 115
Whitlock, Terri. See Davis, Terri (Whitlock) [wife of Daniel A. Purkey],
Whitman, Charles S., Gov., 530
Wickam, Chris, 135
Wilcox
Debbie, 655
James Henry "Jim" "Skeets" [son of Stella/Estelle/Esther/ Ginger (Bauer) Wilcox], 644, 649, 653–655
Michelle, 655
Skeezix. See Wilcox, James Henry "Jim"
Slyvia "Boe" [wife of James "Skeets Wilcox], 653, 655
Stella. See Bauer, Stella/Estelle/Esther/Ginger (Wilcox)
Wildflower Estates, Encinitas, Calif., 138, 139
Will Co., Ill., 594
William Douglas McAdams Agnecy, New York, N.Y., 90
Williams
Kathleen Booth, 348
Mildred Elizabeth. See Gooch, Mildred Elizabeth (Oldham) (Williams) (1838–1917), [wife of Thos. E. Gooch Sr.]
Nathan, 360–361, 389
Nathan Jr., 389
Samuel, 361–362, 368
Thomas, 362
William, 364
Williamsburg, Va., 337
Willmore, Ky., 69
Wilmington Cemetery, Wilmington, Ill., 607
Wilmington, Ill., 594, **607**
Wise, Ed, 100–101
Wilson, Andrew, 205
Winslow, Ind., 411, 426, 429, 432
Wisconsin, 493, 498
Wisconsin Steel Mill, Chicago, Ill., 34, 56
Wolf Lake, Chicago, Ill., 603
Wollenberg, Lou, Rev., 148
Woodard
Carl, 391
Eddie, 391
Freddie, 391
Jessie, 391
John, 411
John R., 391
Lester, 391, 420
Myrtle, 391, 400–401, 420
Myrtle (1908–) [daughter of Rosa Lee Gooch], 268, 438
Rosa Lee (Gooch), 390, 400
Wilford R. "Woody," 437
Woodard family, 335
Woodbridge, Va., 624
Woodlawn Cemetery, Macon, Mo., 239
Woodlawn Neighborhood, Chicago, Ill., 503
Woodridge, Ill., 22
Woods, Archibald Jr., 336
Woodward, John, 262, 398
Woolery, Martha (Gooch), 362
Workman, Bob, 133
World Trade Center, New York City, N.Y., 110
Worthington's Mill, Baltimore Co., Md., 170
Wyoming, 174
Xuan Huong Park, Dalat, Viet Nam, 111
Yale University, New Haven, Conn., 665
Yaphank, Long Island, N.Y., 531
YMCA Sloan House, New York City, N.Y., 85
YMCA, South Chicago, Ill., 604
York Co., Va., 346
Yorktown, Va., 336, 337
Young
Jesse, 269
Laura, 373
Mr., 362
O.J., Rev., 318
Yucatan, Mexico, 619
Yugoslavia, 520
Zagora, Morocco, 111
Zion Hill Cemetery, Lafayette Co., Mo., 218–219
Zion Hill Methodist Church and Cemetery, Valley City, Johnson Co., Mo., 151, 302–303
Zlotogora, Alain, 109
Zorandy, Zoltan, 13
Zsigmond, King, 558
Zucal, Karen L., 13

A Note on the Typography

At a fairly young age, around my second year in high school, I became quite good at lettering, signage, and posters. This led to an early appreciation of letter forms and their distinct graphic qualities. Type was and is today an integral part of my craft. I usually find a way to use it creatively, often dramatically, in any layout I do — the resulting composition of **bold** typography with striking illustration or photography was referred to by my partner Morgan Cline as "Buckeye class." I, like many artists, had my favorite faces or typographical styles. Among them was Garamond Bold.

The text in this book is set primarily in Adobe Garamond® Pro Regular, a version based on the classic old-style face by Claude Garamond (ca. 1480–1561). Garamond is considered to be among the most legible and readable serif typefaces for use in print application.[1] "An Adobe Originals design, and Adobe's first historical revival, Adobe Garamond® is a digital interpretation of the roman types of Claude Garamond and the italic types of Robert Granjon. Since its release in 1989, Adobe Garamond® has become a typographic staple throughout the world of desktop typography and design. Adobe type designer Robert Slimbach has captured the beauty and balance of the original Garamond typefaces while creating a typeface family that offers all the advantages of a contemporary digital type family."[2]

As one can see, I have repeated myself creatively (see the "Cholecystitis" Vibramycin ad on page 95), using an exaggerated initial capital letter for the stories of my brother ***D****avid (butchie,)* my sister ***J****une (tootsie,)* and myself, ***C****lyde (duke.)* I'm particularly fond of the ligature fonts in Garamond, though they were not employed as major design elements.

There is one exception to my use of Garamond typography in this book, and that is on the cover "*finding fathers*." I used Times New Roman lower case italic for the title, preferring the rather cursive nature of the Times New Roman "*ffs*" over a stiffer Garamond style. I used a combination of Times New Roman and

Garamond for the remainder of the cover.

Page layout throughout the book was created with Adobe InDesign® on an Apple iMac.

Interestingly, a version of the Garamond typeface was adopted by Apple in 1984, when the Macintosh computer was introduced. Apple used the ITC Garamond® Light and Book weights, condensed by twenty percent, and provided these as Apple Garamond.[3] This was the same year my advertising agency was founded, and that we purchased our first Macintosh computer.

Notes

1. Wikipedia article on Garamond, http://en.wikipedia.org/wiki/Garamond.
2. <http://www.adobe.com/type/browser/html/readmes/AdobeGaramondProReadMe.html>.
3. Wikipedia article on Garamond, <http://en.wikipedia.org/wiki/Garamond>.

A Final Observation

At the beginning of this project, actually in my very first paragraph, I stated that although I possessed the skills as an art director and creative director and was knowledgeable regarding print production, I admitted that I wasn't much of a writer, and planned to seek the help of others. In the end, far too much has been written by me and for this I fully apologize. My idea at the inception of this project was to let the graphics "do the talking." After all, isn't a picture worth a thousand words?